CONTACT 11
TORONTO 12

Directory of Executive Decision
Makers in the Toronto Region

Table of Contents

List of abbreviations

Acct	Accountant
Acctng	Accounting
Admin	Administration/Administrative
Admr	Administrator
Asst	Assistant
Bldg	Building
Cdn	Canadian
Chmn	Chairman
CAO	Chief Admin. Officer
CEO	Chief Executive Officer
CFO	Chief Financial Officer
CIO	Chief Information Officer
COO	Chief Operating Officer
CTO	Chief Technology Officer
Commr	Commissioner
Commun	Communication(s)
Comptr	Comptroller
Cont	Controller
Coord	Coordinator
Corp	Corporate
Dept	Department
Dev	Development
Dir	Director
Dist	Distributor/Distribution
Exec	Executive
Fin	Finance
Gen	General
GM	General Manager
HR	Human Resources
Info	Information
IS	Information Services/Systems
IT	Information Technology
Mgr	Manager
Mng	Managing
Manuf	Manufacturing
Mktg	Marketing
Nat'l	National
Ops	Operations
Pres	President
Pub Affairs	Public Affairs
PR	Public Relations
Purch	Purchasing
Reg	Regional
Relns	Relations
Rep	Representative
Secy	Secretary
Supr	Supervisor
Tech	Technical/Technology
Treas	Treasurer
VP	Vice President

User's Guide

Who's Here, Who's Not – The Data Collection Process

The majority of the information contained in *Contact Toronto* was provided to us by the employers herein either by mail, e-mail or telephone between November 2010 and July 2011.

While we have compiled the data to the best of our ability, we do not accept responsibility for omissions, errors or inaccuracies as we relied on each organization to provide correct information. There is no fee for inclusion in *Contact Toronto* and inclusion does not imply endorsement.

While every attempt has been made to make this a comprehensive list of Toronto's largest employers, not all employers are listed here. Those excluded may include:

- Non-respondents
- Those who declined to participate
- Federal and Provincial government agencies, boards and commissions
- Selected industries: holding companies, drinking establishments
- Individual retail outlets (chain stores)

Part 1 – Employer Profiles

Arranged alphabetically (letter-by-letter), each employer profile contains a full description of the organization, including head/regional office location, telephone/fax, website, line of business, North American Industry Classification code, employee range and number of locations in the Toronto Region, president/key personnel, affiliated names and parent/ownership company information.

Name: Refers to the proper name of the organization. For related names, see "AKA" below.

Head/Regional Office Address: Refers to the organization's head office or the Toronto regional/executive office if the head office is not within the Toronto Region.

Also Known As (AKA): Refers to names commonly used by the organization, other than the legal name. Includes affiliated names, chain or sign names, and acronyms.

Line: A general description of the organization's line of business.

North American Industry Classification System (NAICS): Codes that are used to define the type(s) of business in which the organization is engaged. The employer profile contains numeric NAICS codes. Part 3 includes a NAICS summary table, keyword index and main index that provides activity descriptions for the numeric codes.

Employee Size Range (#Emp): Includes the total number of full-time and part-time employees in the Toronto Region. Includes employees on short-term/long term disability and on leave of absence; also includes full-time contract employees. Excludes employees of subsidiaries, parent and sister companies.

Total Locations in the Toronto Region (#TorLoc): Refers to the number of locations in the Toronto Region only. See map.

Own: Refers to the ownership of the organization listed. Includes public and private companies, partnerships, government, municipal, provincial, and federal crown corporations, not-for-profits, associations and religious institutions.

Parent Company/Country (Par): Refers to the name and country of the immediate parent company.

Key Personnel (Key): This section contains the full name and title for the president or person responsible for Toronto-based operations. Also listed, when available, are those persons responsible for the following areas: chief executive officer, operations, human resources, finance, purchasing, information technology, sales, marketing and communications.

Part 2 – Affiliated Names Index

This section unravels the corporate infrastructure of Toronto by directing readers from names commonly affiliated with an organization, such as acronyms and other AKAs, to the proper name under which all the employer information is listed.

Part 3 – North American Industry Classification System (NAICS) Index

This section provides quick access to employers by industry using North American Industry Classification System codes. The NAICS numbering system is comprised of a 6-digit code: the first two digits represent the sector, the third the sub-sector, the fourth the industry group, the fifth the industry, and the sixth designates national industries.

A summary table and keyword index is provided at the beginning of this section for readers not familiar with this classification scheme.

Part 4 – Postal Code Index

This section lists organizations by six-character Postal Codes. In most instances, postal codes outside of the L and M postal district represent major Toronto employers whose head office is not located in the Toronto area and who do not have a Toronto regional office.

CONTACT 11
TORONTO 12

Part 1

Employer Profiles
(Alphabetical)

1149318 Ontario Inc.

6900 Tranmere Dr.
Mississauga, ON L5S 1L9
Tel 905-362-9198
Fax 905-364-0150
www.cctlogistics.ca
AKA: CCT Logistics
Line: Provides logistics services.
NAICS: 488990
#Emp: 75-99 (Tor)
Own: Public Company
Key: Tom Hillier, Pres
Dave Campbell, GM
Ian Brooks, VP Sales & Mktg

1561716 Ontario Ltd.

101-472 Morden Rd.
Oakville, ON L6K 3W4
Tel 905-845-5852
Fax 905-845-7091
www.lonestartexasgrill.com
AKA: Lonestar Cafe; Lonestar
Texas Grill; Big Daddy's Crab
Shack & Oyster Bar
Line: Operates themed restaurants.
NAICS: 722110
#Emp: 500-999 (Tor)
#TorLoc: 6
Own: Private Company
Key: Nils Kravis, Pres & CEO

1st Choice Staffing Ltd.

15-6660 Kennedy Rd.
Mississauga, ON L5T 2M9
Tel 905-795-9050
Fax 905-795-9098
www.1stchoicestaffing.com
Line: Recruits temporary and
permanent staffing for industrial
needs.
NAICS: 561310
#Emp: 75-99 (Tor)
#TorLoc: 1
Own: Private Company
Key: Lisa Ingram, GM
Marianne Bowen, Pres
Christopher Winter, Branch Mgr

3M Canada Co.

300 Tartan Dr.
London, ON N5V 4M9
Tel 519-451-2500
Fax 519-452-6262
www.3m.ca
Line: Manufactures abrasives,
adhesives, fluorochemicals, pressure-
sensitive and health care tapes,
sealants and coatings, stain repellants,
glass bubbles, decorative striping
and graphics, epoxy resins, medical
electrodes and surgical, occupational
health masks and micro encapsulated
products.
NAICS: 327910 325520
#Emp: 100-249 (Tor)
#TorLoc: 3
Own: Public Company
Par: Minnesota Mining &
Manufacturing Company Inc. (US)
Key: Brian Young, Pres

407 ETR

6300 Steeles Ave. West
Woodbridge, ON L4H 1J1
Tel 905-265-4070
Fax 905-264-5315
www.407etr.com
Line: Provides administration and
maintenance for Highway 407.
NAICS: 488490
#Emp: 500-999 (Tor)
#TorLoc: 1
Own: Private Company
Key: Jose Tamariz, Pres & CEO
Greg Mackenzie, Gen Counsel
Wayne Anthony, VP HR
Louis M. St Maurice, CFO
Robert Ives, VP IT
Michael Miller,
    Chief Customer Ops Officer
Kevin Sack, VP Commun &
    Government Relns

4 Office Automation Ltd.

1-425 Superior Blvd.
Mississauga, ON L5T 2W5
Tel 905-564-0522
Fax 905-564-2865
www.4office.com
Line: Provides office equipment
and supplies.
NAICS: 419170
#Emp: 100-249 (Tor)
#TorLoc: 2
Own: Private Company
Key: Bill Norgate, Pres
Mary Aduckiewicz, CFO
Clive Lee, Sales Mgr

4 Star Drywall Ltd.

4-6 2900 Langstaff Rd.
Concord, ON L4K 4R9
Tel 905-660-9676
Fax 905-660-5194
www.4stardrywall.ca
Line: Specializes in metal framing
insulation, drywall and acoustics
for the residential, industrial and
commercial sectors.
NAICS: 232410
#Emp: 250-499 (Tor)
#TorLoc: 1
Own: Private Company
Key: Bob Pirocchi, Pres
Rob Devito, Payroll
Bruna Trelle, Cont

88.5 FM The Jewel

5312 Dundas St. West
Toronto, ON M9B 1B3
Tel 416-233-5530
Fax 416-233-8617
www.jewelradio.com
Line: Operates a radio station.
NAICS: 513110
#Emp: 75-99 (Tor)
#TorLoc: 1
Own: Private Company
Key: Bill Evanov, Pres
Paul Evanov, VP Ops & Program Dir
Carmela Laurignano, VP Mktg

A & B Courier

31 Alexander Rd.
Newmarket, ON L3Y 3J2
Tel 905-853-4444
Fax 905-853-5565
www.abcourier.com
Line: Provides courier service.
NAICS: 492110
#Emp: 75-99 (Tor)
#TorLoc: 1
Own: Private Company
Key: Dewane Smalley, Pres

A Towing Service Ltd.

185 Bartley Dr.
Toronto, ON M4A 1E6
Tel 416-656-4000
Fax 416-656-3065
www.atowing.ca
Line: Provides automotive towing
services.
NAICS: 488410
#Emp: 75-99 (Tor)
#TorLoc: 2
Own: Private Company
Key: Alex Anissimoff, CEO
Richard Wendt, Ops Mgr
Michelle Moffatt, Office Mgr

A1 Label

32 Cranfield Rd.
Toronto, ON M4B 3H3
Tel 416-701-9800
Fax 416-701-9836
www.a1label.com
Line: Manufactures labels.
NAICS: 561910 322220
#Emp: 75-99 (Tor)
#TorLoc: 1
Own: Private Company
Key: Rhys Seymour, Dir of Manuf
Brock Seymour, Pres
Ling Wong, VP Ops
Nancy Maher, HR Admin
Luc Barbara, Materials Mgr
Raymond Normandeau, Sales Mgr

Aastra Technologies Limited

155 Snow Blvd.
Concord, ON L4K 4N9
Tel 905-760-4200
Fax 905-760-4233
www.aastra.com
AKA: Aastra Telecom Inc.
Line: Develops and markets
products and systems for accessing
communication networks.
NAICS: 334512 513340
#Emp: 100-249 (Tor)
#TorLoc: 1
Own: Public Company
Key: Yves Laliberte, Exec VP
Tony Shen, Pres
Rosalyn May, Mgr of HR
Allan Brett, CFO
Bruce Cook, VP Sales
Steve Hawkins, Dir of Mktg

ABB Inc.

201 West Creek Blvd.
Brampton, ON L6T 5S6
Tel 905-460-3000
Fax 905-460-3001
www.abb.ca
Line: Designs and builds automated
assembly lines for the automotive
industry.
NAICS: 333990
#Emp: 250-499 (Tor)
#TorLoc: 2
Own: Private Company
Par: ABB Group Zurich (SWITZ)
Key: Roger Costa, VP Ops
Mahmud Khamis, Planning &
Procurement Mgr

Abbott Laboratories Ltd./ Diagnostic Division

7115 Millcreek Dr.
Mississauga, ON L5N 3R3
Tel 905-858-2450
Fax 905-858-2462
www.abbott.ca
Line: Distributes hospital diagnostic
products and instrumentation.
NAICS: 417930
#Emp: 100-249 (Tor)
#TorLoc: 1
Own: Private Company
Par: Abbott Laboratories (US)
Key: Dan Harma, GM
Liz Onwudiwe, Cont

ABC Group

2 Norelco Dr.
Toronto, ON M9L 2X6
Tel 416-246-1782
Fax 416-246-1997
www.abcgroupinc.com
Line: Manufactures automotive parts,
consumer packaging and industrial
products.
NAICS: 336390
#Emp: 1000-4999 (Tor)
#TorLoc: 15
Own: Private Company
Key: Helga Schmidt, Chmn
Mark Poynton, Co-Mng Dir
Robert Kunihiro, Co-Mng Dir

ABC Group Exterior Systems

220 Brockport Dr.
Toronto, ON M9W 5S1
Tel 416-675-7480
Fax 416-675-3667
www.abcgroupinc.com
Line: Manufactures plastic products.
NAICS: 326198 326193
#Emp: 250-499 (Tor)
#TorLoc: 28
Own: Private Company
Key: Adel Dao, GM

Abell Pest Control Inc.

246 Attwell Dr.
Toronto, ON M9W 5B4
Tel 416-675-1635
Fax 416-675-6727
www.abellpestcontrol.com
Line: Provides pest control and related
services to the commercial, industrial
and residential market.
NAICS: 561710
#Emp: 100-249 (Tor)
#TorLoc: 2
Own: Private Company
Key: John R. Abell, Pres
Dennis Walsh, Sr VP
Anna-Maria Iaboni, Payroll & Benefits
Jetmere Vicente, VP Fin
Mike Masterson, VP Sales & Mktg

A. Berger Precision Ltd.

28 Regan Rd.
Brampton, ON L7A 1A7
Tel 905-840-4207
Fax 905-840-8022
www.aberger.com
Line: Manufactures screw machine
components for the automotive
industry.
NAICS: 336390 333519
#Emp: 100-249 (Tor)
#TorLoc: 1
Own: Private Company
Key: Alexander Berger, Pres & CEO
Michael May, Plant & Production Mgr

ABlackCab

6-966 Pantera Dr.
Mississauga, ON L4W 2S1
Tel 905-822-4000
Fax 905-625-4943
www.ablackcab.com
Line: Provides taxi services.
NAICS: 485310
#Emp: 100-249 (Tor)
#TorLoc: 1
Own: Private Company
Key: Shokat Ali, Mgr

ABM Tool & Die Co. Ltd.

80 Walker Dr.
Brampton, ON L6T 4H6
Tel 905-458-2203
Fax 905-458-2235
www.abmtool.com
Line: Manufactures dies and
metal stampings.
NAICS: 332118 336370
#Emp: 100-249 (Tor)
#TorLoc: 1
Own: Private Company
Key: Terry Blagonic, Pres
Doriana Blagonic, HR Dir
Russell Hayes, Cont
Roger Hudson, Account Mgr
Sales & Quoting

Abram's Towing Services Ltd.

124 Lepage Crt.
Toronto, ON M3J 1Z9
Tel 416-398-2500
Fax 416-398-6189
www.abrams.ca
Line: Provides automotive towing services.
NAICS: 488410
#Emp: 100-249 (Tor)
#TorLoc: 8
Own: Private Company
Par: 1512081 Ontario Ltd. (CDA)
Key: Richard Ratcliffe, Pres
Daryl Shock, GM
Shirley Freud, HR Mgr

AB SCIEX

71 Four Valley Dr.
Vaughan, ON L4K 4V8
Tel 905-660-9005
Fax 905-660-2600
www.mdssciex.com
Line: Researches, designs and produces mass spectrometers and scientific instruments for life sciences and high technology markets.
NAICS: 339110
#Emp: 250-499 (Tor)
#TorLoc: 1
Own: Public Company
Par: Donaher (US)
Key: Andrew Boorn, Pres
Suzanne Wolfe, VP Organizational Dev

ABS Machining Inc.

1495 Sedlescomb Dr.
Mississauga, ON L4X 1M4
Tel 905-625-5941
Fax 905-238-9155
www.absmachining.com
AKA: ABS Production Inc.
Line: Operates a fabrication, precision machining and assembly of medium to large parts for original equipment manufacturers.
NAICS: 332999 333990
#Emp: 100-249 (Tor)
#TorLoc: 5
Own: Private Company
Key: Antonio Bosco, Pres
Angelo Venturin, VP Manuf
Paul Marcotte, Cont
Amrit Singh, Purch Agent
Trevor Fulop, Sales Mgr

Academy of Design

1835 Yonge St.
Toronto, ON M5S 1X8
Tel 647-288-8496
www.rccit.ca
Line: Provides private vocational training in design and digital disciplines.
NAICS: 611210
#Emp: 250-499 (Tor)
#TorLoc: 1
Own: Private Company
Key: Michael Markovitz, Pres

Acan Windows Systems Inc.

383 Orenda Rd.
Brampton, ON L6T 1G4
Tel 905-595-0580
Fax 905-595-0590
www.acanwindow.com
Line: Manufactures, sells and services vinyl windows and patio doors.
NAICS: 444190
#Emp: 100-249 (Tor)
#TorLoc: 1
Own: Private Company
Key: Ted Kwon, Pres
Charles Lee, VP
Paul Garg, Cont
Kathy Brown, Mgr of Procurement

Accellos Canada Inc.

700-120 Commerce Valley Dr. West
Markham, ON L3T 7W4
Tel 905-695-9999
Fax 905-695-0607
www.accellos.com
AKA: Freightlogix; Delfour; Headwater Technology Solutions Inc.
Line: Develops software solutions for the supply chain industry.
NAICS: 541510
#Emp: 75-99 (Tor)
#TorLoc: 2
Own: Private Company
Par: Accellos Inc. (US)
Key: Joe Couto, Sr VP
Donna Hawkins, HR Mgr

Accenture Inc.

1401-145 King St. West
Toronto, ON M5H 1J8
Tel 416-641-5220
Fax 416-641-5651
www.accenture.ca
Line: Provides global management, consulting, outsourcing and technology services.
NAICS: 541611
#Emp: 1000-4999 (Tor)
#TorLoc: 2
Own: Public Company
Par: Accenture (BER)
Key: William F. Morris, Cdn Mng Dir
Meg Sintzel, VP Mktg & Commun
Charmaine D'Silva, Media Relns Mgr

Access Care Inc.

1630 O'Connor Dr.
Toronto, ON M4B 3P4
Tel 416-755-4074
Fax 416-285-5581
www.accesscare.ca
AKA: Access Personnel
NAICS: 621390
#Emp: 100-249 (Tor)
#TorLoc: 1
Own: Private Company
Key: Aurora Caballero, Pres
Roger Caballero, Fin & Mktg

ACCO Brands Canada Inc.

5 Precidio Crt.
Brampton, ON L6S 6B7
Tel 905-595-3100
Fax 905-595-3130
www.acco.com
Line: Manufactures and distributes office products.
NAICS: 323119
#Emp: 100-249 (Tor)
#TorLoc: 1
Own: Private Company
Par: ACCO Brands (US)
Key: Ed Lovekin, Mng Dir
Catherine Reid, Dir of HR
Jane Gleadall, VP Sales
Jeff Schoo, VP Mktg & Business Dev

Accolade Group Inc.

202-388 Carlaw Ave.
Toronto, ON M4M 2T4
Tel 416-465-7211
Fax 416-465-4571
www.accolade-group.com
AKA: Levelwear; Kewl Sports
Line: Provides sportswear to the colleges, golf resorts and corporate markets.
NAICS: 323113 313310
#Emp: 100-249 (Tor)
#TorLoc: 1
Own: Private Company
Key: Hilton Ngo, Pres
Herbert Ngo, Exec VP
Harvey Ngo, VP Fin & IT

Accucut Profile & Grinding Ltd.

300 Connie Cres.
Concord, ON L4K 5W6
Tel 416-798-7716
Fax 905-738-9609
www.accucut.ca
Line: Manufactures brake pads.
NAICS: 336340
#Emp: 75-99 (Tor)
#TorLoc: 1
Own: Private Company
Key: Luigi Corso, Pres

Accuristix

2844 Bristol Circ.
Oakville, ON L6H 6G4
Tel 905-829-9927
Fax 905-491-3000
www.accuristix.com
Line: Provides warehousing and
distribution services.
NAICS: 493110
#Emp: 100-249 (Tor)
#TorLoc: 4
Own: Private Company
Key: Cameron Joyce, Pres
Brian MacAskill, VP Strategic Ops
David Ortiz, Dir of Fin
Joe Futino, Dir of IT
Lauren Fox, Mktg Coord

Ace Bakery Ltd.

1 Hafis Rd.
Toronto, ON M6M 2V6
Tel 416-241-3600
Fax 416-241-1330
www.acebakery.com
Line: Operates wholesale artisan
bakery.
NAICS: 311814 413190
#Emp: 250-499 (Tor)
Own: Private Company
Key: Philip Shaw, Pres & CEO
Brian Sisson, VP Ops
Fiona Mitchell, VP HR
Jonathan Roiter, COO
Joe Pengelly, Procurement Mgr
John Nailor, Dir of Cdn Sales
Phil Gaudet, Nat'l Account Mgr

ACE INA Insurance

1400-25 York St., Telus Bldg.
Toronto, ON M5J 2V5
Tel 416-368-2911
Fax 416-368-9825
www.ace-ina-canada.com
AKA: ACE INA Life Insurance
Line: Provides commercial and
specialty niche insurance.
NAICS: 524132

#Emp: 100-249 (Tor)
#TorLoc: 1
Own: Private Company
Par: ACE INA (US)
Key: David Brosnan, CEO
Dale Hawking, VP HR
Ajay Pahwa, Sr VP Fin & CFO
Betty Bingler, VP Strategic Mktg
Lynn Woodburn,
    Dir of Commun & Admin

Ace Painting & Decorating Co. Inc.

A Div. of Evagelou Enterprises
39 Cranfield Rd.
Toronto, ON M4B 3H6
Tel 416-285-5388
Fax 416-285-7088
www.acepainting.ca
NAICS: 232450
#Emp: 100-249 (Tor)
#TorLoc: 1
Own: Private Company
Key: Frank Evagelou, Pres
Jackie Prattis, Ops Mgr
Donna Carfew, Acctng Mgr
Robert Ghaeli, Cont

A.C.I. Accessory Concepts Inc.

2616 Sheridan Garden Dr.
Oakville, ON L6J 7Z2
Tel 905-829-1566
Fax 905-829-1766
www.acibrands.com
AKA: Star Case Canada Inc.; A.C.I
Brands
Line: Distributes fashion, travel
and gift accessory items.
NAICS: 418990
#Emp: 100-249 (Tor)
#TorLoc: 1
Own: Private Company
Par: A.C.I. Starcase Group Inc. (CDA)
Key: Jeff Goraieb, Pres
Bruce Campbell, VP Ops
John Vlacich, Dir of Ops
Saturena Pow, Cont
Annabel Garber, Purch Mgr
Helder Valentim,
    Dir of IT & Supply Chain

ACI Worldwide (Canada) Inc.

200 Wellington St. West, 7th Fl.
Toronto, ON M5V 3C7
Tel 416-813-3000
Fax 416-813-0653
www.aciworldwide.com
Line: Develops computer software for
electronic payment systems, consumer
and corporate banking, and merchant
retail and health care benefits.

NAICS: 541510
#Emp: 75-99 (Tor)
#TorLoc: 1
Own: Private Company
Par: ACI Worldwide (US)
Key: Geoff Parker, Dir of Business Ops
Dorothy Arvisais, Sr Mgr of HR
Ross England, VP Software & Services
David Grindal, Dir of Sales
    Support & Mktg

Acklands-Grainger Inc.

90 West Beaver Creek Rd.
Richmond Hill, ON L4B 1E7
Tel 905-731-5516
Fax 905-731-9263
www.acklandsgrainger.com
AKA: CISCO Industrial Supply;
Westward
Line: Wholesales and distributes
industrial supplies, equipment and
MRO products.
NAICS: 417230
#Emp: 250-499 (Tor)
#TorLoc: 7
Own: Public Company
Par: W.W. Grainger Inc. (US)
Key: Sean O'Brien, Pres
Henry Buckley, VP & GM
Laurie A. Wright, VP HR
Yolanda Daniel, VP Fin
Kevin Weadick, VP Supply Chain
Jarnail Lail, VP IT
Sandro Verrelli, VP Sales & Mktg
George McClean, VP & Gen Counsel

Acorn Packaging

563 Queensway East
Mississauga, ON L5A 3X6
Tel 905-279-5256
Fax 905-279-3234
www.acornpkg.com
Line: Manufactures flexible packaging.
NAICS: 322220
#Emp: 100-249 (Tor)
#TorLoc: 1
Own: Private Company
Key: Moez Chateur, Pres
Liz Grigonis, Pres
Danielle Bursey, Payroll Admr
Carol Peters, Purch

Acosta Canada

250 Rowntree Dairy Rd.
Woodbridge, ON L4L 9J7
Tel 905-264-0466
Fax 905-851-2243
www.acosta.com
Line: Provides sales and marketing solutions.
NAICS: 541619
#Emp: 100-249 (Tor)
#TorLoc: 1
Own: Private Company
Par: Acosta Sales & Marketing (US)
Key: Bill Dunne, Pres
Daniel Armeni, VP Fin

Acrobat Research Ltd.

201-170 Robert Speck Pkwy.
Mississauga, ON L4Z 3G1
Tel 416-503-4343
Fax 416-503-8707
www.acrobat-research.com
NAICS: 541619
#Emp: 100-249 (Tor)
#TorLoc: 1
Own: Private Company
Key: Tim Sinke, Pres
Roland Klassen, CEO
Beth Depatie, VP Field Ops
Michael Churcher, VP IT

ActionPak

1-125 Nashdene Rd.
Toronto, ON M1V 2W3
Tel 416-321-2222
Fax 416-321-5286
www.actionpak.ca
AKA: Q-Ponz Inc.
NAICS: 541860 541870
#Emp: 75-99 (Tor)
#TorLoc: 1
Own: Private Company
Key: Terry Shaw, Pres

Active Exhaust Corporation

1865 Birchmount Rd.
Toronto, ON M1P 2J5
Tel 416-445-9610
Fax 416-445-9765
www.activexhaust.com
Line: Manufactures mufflers for automobiles.
NAICS: 336390
#Emp: 100-249 (Tor)
#TorLoc: 1
Own: Private Company
Key: Peter Hampton, Pres
Lee Hayward, HR Admr

Active Transport Inc.

245 Bronte St. North
Milton, ON L9T 3N7
Tel 905-878-8167
Fax 905-878-7137
www.activetransport.ca
Line: Provides trucking services.
NAICS: 484110 484121
#Emp: 75-99 (Tor)
#TorLoc: 1
Own: Private Company
Key: Bradley Grant, Pres
Robert Mushlian, VP
Marc Tilley, VP Fin

Acura of North Toronto

7064 Yonge St.
Thornhill, ON L4J 1V7
Tel 905-882-9660
Fax 905-882-9661
www.acuraofnorthtoronto.com
Line: Operates a car dealership.
NAICS: 441110 441120
#Emp: 75-99 (Tor)
#TorLoc: 1
Own: Private Company
Key: Phil Martiniello, GM

Acuren Group Inc.

2190 Speers Rd.
Oakville, ON L6L 2X8
Tel 905-825-8595
Fax 905-825-8598
www.acuren.com
Line: Specializes in materials engineering, inspection, and non-destructive testing.
NAICS: 541330
#Emp: 100-249 (Tor)
#TorLoc: 3
Own: Private Company
Par: Rockwood Service Corporation (US)
Key: Kevin Woit, Mng Dir
Guillermo Solano, Ops Mgr
Starre Hussey, Cont
Barry Woit, Business Dev Mgr

Adamson Associates Architects

401 Wellington St. West, 3rd Fl.
Toronto, ON M5V 1E7
Tel 416-967-1500
Fax 416-967-7150
www.adamson-associates.com
Line: Provides architectural services.
NAICS: 541310
#Emp: 100-249 (Tor)
#TorLoc: 1
Own: Private Company

Key: William Bradley, Partner
David Jansen, Partner
Gregory Dunn, Partner
Richard Edwards, Cont

Adastra Corporation

600-8500 Leslie St.
Markham, ON L3T 7M8
Tel 905-881-7946
Fax 905-881-4782
www.adastragrp.com
Line: Provides data warehousing, business intelligence and data integration consultancy services.
NAICS: 541510
#Emp: 100-249 (Tor)
#TorLoc: 1
Own: Private Company
Key: Darren Edery,
  CEO, Adastra Canada
Jan Mrazek, Pres & Chmn
Eva Wong, Mktg Mgr

Add Ink

A Div. of Atlantic Packaging Products Ltd.
36 Overlea Blvd.
Toronto, ON M4H 1B6
Tel 416-421-3636
Fax 416-421-1996
www.addink.ca
Line: Designs graphic packaging and displays.
NAICS: 541899
#Emp: 75-99 (Tor)
#TorLoc: 1
Own: Private Company
Key: Bill Whyte, GM

Addison Chevrolet

1220 Eglinton Ave. East
Mississauga, ON L4W 2M7
Tel 905-238-2886
Fax 905-238-3598
www.addisonchevrolet.com
Line: Operates a car dealership.
NAICS: 441110 441120
#Emp: 75-99 (Tor)
#TorLoc: 1
Own: Private Company
Key: Clarke Addison, Dealer Principal
Ray Sultana, GM
Lynda Forbes, Secy-Treas

Addison Chevrolet Buick GMC

6600 Turner Valley Rd.
Mississauga, ON L5N 5Z1
Tel 866-980-6928
Fax 888-649-5680
www.addisonbuickgmc.com
Line: Operates a car dealership.
NAICS: 441110 441120
#Emp: 75-99 (Tor)
#TorLoc: 3
Own: Private Company
Key: Clark Addison, Owner & Operator
Steve Vieira, Secy-Treas

Adecco Employment Services Limited

10 Bay St., 7th Fl.
Toronto, ON M5J 2R8
Tel 416-364-2020
Fax 416-366-8035
www.adecco.ca
Line: Provides temporary and
permanent placement services.
NAICS: 561310
#Emp: 250-499 (Tor)
#TorLoc: 20
Own: Public Company
Par: Adecco SA (SWITZ)
Key: Sandra Hokansson,
    Pres & Country Mgr
Nicolette Muller,
    VP HR & Legal Counsel
Doug Hamlyn, VP Fin
Angela Payne, VP Sales

Adelt Mechanical Works Ltd.

2640 Argentia Rd.
Mississauga, ON L5N 6C5
Tel 905-812-7900
Fax 905-812-7907
www.adeltmechanical.com
Line: Provides contracting services.
NAICS: 232520
#Emp: 100-249 (Tor)
#TorLoc: 2
Own: Private Company
Key: Scott Munro, CEO
Don Evans, COO
Kim Green, Cont
Carmine Mancini, Purch Agent

Adeptron Technologies Corp.

96 Steelcase Rd. West
Markham, ON L3R 3J9
Tel 905-470-0109
Fax 905-470-0621
www.adeptron.com
Line: Provides assembly and testing of
printed circuit board full turnkey or
consigned material.

NAICS: 334410
#Emp: 100-249 (Tor)
#TorLoc: 3
Own: Private Company
Key: Trent Carruthers, Pres & CEO
Debbie Lau, HR Mgr
Jon Szczur, CFO
Michael Davis, VP Sales & Mktg
Drake MacDonald, VP Supply Chain

ADESA Canada

800-50 Burnhamthorpe Rd. West
Mississauga, ON L5B 3C2
Tel 905-896-4400
Fax 905-896-3244
www.adesa.ca
Line: Offers automotive remarketing
services.
NAICS: 415110
#Emp: 250-499 (Tor)
#TorLoc: 3
Own: Private Company
Key: Stephane St-Hilaire, Pres & COO
Trevor Henderson, VP,
    e-Business & Business Dev
Lisa Scott, VP Sales & Mktg

adidas Canada Limited

3210 Langstaff Rd.
Concord, ON L4K 5B2
Tel 905-761-9900
Fax 905-761-9911
www.adidas.ca
Line: Wholesales sporting goods.
NAICS: 414470
#Emp: 100-249 (Tor)
#TorLoc: 1
Own: Public Company
Par: adidas AG (GER)
Key: Steve Ralph, Pres

Aditya Birla Minacs

180 Duncan Mill Rd.
Toronto, ON M3B 1Z6
Tel 416-380-3800
Fax 416-380-3830
www.minacs.adityabirla.com
AKA: Minacs Worldwide Inc.
Line: Provides customer management
services.
NAICS: 541619
#Emp: 100-249 (Tor)
#TorLoc: 1
Own: Private Company
Par: Aditya Birla (INDIA)
Key: Kailas Agrawal, Reg CFO

The Administrative Assistants Ltd.

1-1425 Norjohn Crt.
Burlington, ON L7L 0E6
Tel 905-632-0864
Fax 905-632-2605
www.aalsolutions.com
AKA: AAL
Line: Develops software for the K to 12
education marketplace.
NAICS: 417310
#Emp: 100-249 (Tor)
#TorLoc: 1
Own: Private Company
Key: Brian Currie, Pres & CEO
Andrea Currie, VP & COO
Robert Lederer, Dir of Product Dev
Linda Malcolm, Dir of Client Services

ADP Canada Co.

3250 Bloor St. West, 16th Fl.
Toronto, ON M8X 2X9
Tel 416-207-2900
Fax 416-207-2880
www.adp.ca
Line: Provides outsourced payroll,
human resources management,
time and attendance and benefits
administration solutions.
NAICS: 514210
#Emp: 1000-4999 (Tor)
#TorLoc: 2
Own: Private Company
Par: Automatic Data Processing Inc.
(US)
Key: Greg Secord, Pres
Rodney A. Dobson, Sr VP
Brad Surminsky, CFO
Sean Harris, Area VP Sales
Heather Nairn-Rand, VP Mktg
Lisa McAvoy, Mktg & Commun Mgr

ADP Dealer Services Ontario

A Div. of ADP Canada Co.
1210 Sheppard Ave. East, 6th Fl.
Toronto, ON M2K 1E3
Tel 416-498-3700
Fax 416-498-3663
www.adp.com
Line: Provides computer services to
automobile dealerships.
NAICS: 541510
#Emp: 100-249 (Tor)
#TorLoc: 1
Own: Private Company
Key: Dean Anton, VP & GM

ADT Security Services Canada Inc.

2815 Matheson Blvd. East
Mississauga, ON L4W 5J8
Tel 905-212-2555
Fax 905-212-2599
www.adt.ca
Line: Provides security systems for commercial and residential establishments.
NAICS: 561621
#Emp: 250-499 (Tor)
#TorLoc: 2
Own: Public Company
Par: Tyco International Ltd. (US)
Key: Kurt Wittkopp, Area Ops Mgr, Central Canada

Advanced Metal Stamping Corp.

2160 South Service Rd. West
Oakville, ON L6L 5N1
Tel 905-847-1700
Fax 905-847-8711
Line: Manufactures metal stampings and assemblies.
NAICS: 336370
#Emp: 75-99 (Tor)
#TorLoc: 1
Own: Private Company
Key: Carson Kramer, Owner

Advanced Product Technologies

A Div. of Magna Powertrain
800 Tesma Way
Concord, ON L4K 5C2
Tel 905-303-1689
Fax 905-303-1694
www.magna.com
Line: Manufactures alternator and water pump pulleys.
NAICS: 336320
#Emp: 100-249 (Tor)
#TorLoc: 1
Own: Private Company
Par: Magna International Inc. (CDA)
Key: Guy Davies, GM
Roy Jocic, Asst GM
Ross Hamilton, Cont

Advantage Personnel Ltd.

225-7025 Tomken Rd.
Mississauga, ON L5S 1R6
Tel 905-564-3616
Fax 905-564-8638
www.onyourteam.com
AKA: Advantage Services Personnel; Advantage Labour Resources; Advantage Group
Line: Provides employment services for industrial supply, office supply, driver leasing and payroll services.
NAICS: 561310
#Emp: 250-499 (Tor)
#TorLoc: 4
Own: Private Company
Key: Stewart W. Sebben, Pres

Advantage Sales & Marketing

4-151 Esna Park Dr.
Markham, ON L3R 3B1
Tel 905-475-9623
Fax 905-475-8361
www.asmnet.com
Line: Provides national sales and marketing services.
NAICS: 541619
#Emp: 250-499 (Tor)
Own: Private Company
Par: Advantage Sales & Marketing (US)
Key: Henry Gerstel, Pres
Donald Crombie, Chmn
Milt Dobson, Exec VP, Grocery Division
Dawn Stewart, HR Mgr
Rick Moore, Exec VP, Pharmacy Division

Aecom

220 Advance Blvd.
Brampton, ON L6T 4J5
Tel 905-459-4780
Fax 905-459-7869
www.aecom.com
Line: Provides water and wastewater engineering services.
NAICS: 541330
#Emp: 1000-4999 (Tor)
#TorLoc: 6
Own: Private Company
Par: Aecom (US)
Key: Robert Fleeton, Reg VP, Central Ontario Region
Deborah E. Ross, Reg Mgr, Waste Water
Helene Bastille, Fin Mgr

AECOM Canada Ltd.

105 Commerce Valley Dr. West, 7th Fl.
Markham, ON L3T 7W3
Tel 905-886-7022
Fax 905-886-9494
www.aecom.com
Line: Provides consulting, engineering and construction services for the transportation, wastewater, facilities, community infrastructure and environmental markets.
NAICS: 541330 541310
#Emp: 1000-4999 (Tor)
#TorLoc: 6
Own: Public Company
Par: AECOM Technology Corporation (US)
Key: John Kinley, Group CEO
John M. Dionisio, CEO
Jim Stewart, COO
Ian R. MacLeod, VP HR
Wayne Gingrich, VP Fin
Sedrick Smith, Nat'l Procurement & Facilities Mgr
Karen Lucas, IT Mgr
Joanne Garcia, Mktg Mgr

Aecon Group Inc.

800-20 Carlson Crt.
Toronto, ON M9W 7K6
Tel 416-293-7004
Fax 416-293-0271
www.aecon.com
Line: Provides construction and development services to private and public sector clients.
NAICS: 231310 231320 231390
#Emp: 1000-4999 (Tor)
#TorLoc: 3
Own: Public Company
Key: Terrance A. McKibbon, COO
John M. Beck, CEO
Dave Brennan, VP HR
David Smales, Exec VP & CFO
Bruce Fleming, VP IT & CIO
Mitch Patten, Sr VP Corp Affairs

AEP Canada Inc.

595 Coronation Dr.
Toronto, ON M1E 2K4
Tel 416-281-6000
Fax 416-281-1212
www.aepinc.com
Line: Manufactures and distributes PVC and polyethylene plastic wrap.
NAICS: 326114
#Emp: 75-99 (Tor)
#TorLoc: 1
Own: Private Company
Par: AEP Industries Inc. (US)
Key: David Laithom, Cont
Jeff Jones, Dir of Sales & Mktg

Aerotek Canada

A Div. of Allegis Group
Canada Corporation
700-350 Burnhamthorpe Rd. West
Mississauga, ON L5B 3J1
Tel 905-283-1400
Fax 905-283-1390
www.aerotekcanada.com
AKA: TEKsystems Canada Inc.; Aerotek ULC
Line: Provides contract services and business solutions.
NAICS: 561320
#Emp: 500-999 (Tor)
#TorLoc: 2
Own: Private Company
Par: Allegis Group Inc. (US)
Key: Bryan Toffey, VP,
   TEKsystems Canada Inc.
Timothy Cerny, Exec VP, Aerotek ULC
Shelly Spence, HR Mgr
Dawn Cavasin, Commun Mgr

A. Farber & Partners Inc.

1200 Sheppard Ave. East
Toronto, ON M2K 2R8
Tel 416-496-1200
Fax 416-496-9651
www.afarber.com
AKA: Farber Financial Group; Klein Farber Corporate Finance; Farber CFO Resources
Line: Specializes in corporate insolvency, restructuring, mergers and acquisitions, finance, fraud, forensic accounting, turnarounds and CFO resources.
NAICS: 541990
#Emp: 75-99 (Tor)
#TorLoc: 1
Own: Private Company
Key: Alan Farber, Joint Mng Partner
Natasha Mills, Dir of HR
Alex Fiore, CFO

Afcan Interlink Ltd.

120 Midair Crt.
Brampton, ON L6T 5V1
Tel 905-458-6086
Fax 905-458-6087
www.afcaninterlink.ca
Line: Distributes used clothing.
NAICS: 453310
#Emp: 100-249 (Tor)
#TorLoc: 1
Own: Private Company
Key: Inder Chopra, Pres

Affordable Personnel Services Inc.

219-1750 Steeles Ave. West
Concord, ON L4K 2L7
Tel 905-761-0415
Fax 905-761-0413
www.affordablepersonnel.com
Line: Provides temporary, permanent and contract placements.
NAICS: 561310
#Emp: 75-99 (Tor)
#TorLoc: 1
Own: Private Company
Key: Glenda Wainer, GM

AFL Display Group

4-89A Connie Cres.
Concord, ON L4K 1L3
Tel 905-660-6666
Fax 905-660-7442
www.afldisplay.com
AKA: Acrylic Fabricators Ltd.
Line: Manufactures store fixtures, decor and point of purchase displays.
NAICS: 541850
#Emp: 75-99 (Tor)
#TorLoc: 1
Own: Private Company
Key: Brian Mandelker, Pres
Pam Mahadeo, Cont

AGAT Laboratories Ltd.

5835 Coopers Ave.
Mississauga, ON L4Z 1N9
Tel 905-712-8100
Fax 905-712-5120
www.agatlabs.com
Line: Operates a full service, diversified laboratory network.
NAICS: 541380
#Emp: 100-249 (Tor)
#TorLoc: 1
Own: Private Company
Key: Marcus Maguire,
VP, Western Canada

AGC Flat Glass North America Ltd.

P.O. Box 628
Mt. Albert, ON L0G 1M0
Tel 905-738-9400
Fax 905-738-1177
www.agc-flatglass.com
AKA: AFGD Glass
Line: Manufactures primary and secondary flat glass for construction and automotive industries.
NAICS: 327214
#Emp: 100-249 (Tor)
#TorLoc: 3
Own: Private Company
Par: AFG Industries Inc. (US)
Key: Tom Holloran, Exec VP
Marilyn Moore, Mktg Asst

Agfa Canada

77 Belfield Rd.
Toronto, ON M9W 1G8
Tel 416-241-1110
Fax 416-241-5409
www.agfa.com
Line: Designs custom software solutions for radiology, cardiology, image and information systems.
NAICS: 541510
#Emp: 250-499 (Tor)
#TorLoc: 1
Own: Private Company
Par: Agfa (BELG)
Key: Michael Green, Pres

AGF Management Ltd.

66 Wellington St. West
TD Bank Tower, 31st Fl.
Toronto, ON M5K 1E9
Tel 416-367-1900
Fax 416-865-4309
www.agf.com
Line: Provides investment management services.
NAICS: 526910 523920
#Emp: 500-999 (Tor)
#TorLoc: 2
Own: Public Company
Key: Blake C. Goldring, Chmn & CEO
Judy Goldring, Sr VP & Gen Counsel
Robert J. Bogart, Sr VP & CFO
Jenny Quinn, VP Fin & Cont

Agilent Technologies Canada Inc.

5-6705 Mill Creek Dr.
Mississauga, ON L5N 5M4
Tel 877-424-4536
Fax 905-282-6300
www.agilent.ca
Line: Services and sells high technology equipment.
NAICS: 811210
#Emp: 75-99 (Tor)
#TorLoc: 1
Own: Public Company
Par: Agilent Technologies (US)
Key: Denis Jacques, Pres & CEO
Ron Podio, Cont

Agility

410 Admiral Blvd.
Mississauga, ON L5T 2N6
Tel 905-612-7500
Fax 905-612-7520
www.agilitylogistics.com
Line: Provides freight forwarding,
customs brokerage and logistics
services.
NAICS: 488519
#Emp: 75-99 (Tor)
#TorLoc: 1
Own: Private Company
Par: Agility Americas (US)
Key: Charles Savva, VP Fin

Agincourt Autohaus Inc.

3450 Sheppard Ave. East
Toronto, ON M1T 3K4
Tel 416-291-6456
Fax 416-291-7699
www.agincourtautohaus.com
Line: Retails new and used
automobiles.
NAICS: 441110 441120
#Emp: 75-99 (Tor)
Own: Private Company
Key: Ken Laird, Pres

Agincourt Chrysler Inc.

20 Cowdray Crt.
Toronto, ON M1S 1A1
Tel 416-321-2201
Fax 416-321-2244
www.agincourtchrysler.net
Line: Retails new and used
automobiles.
NAICS: 441110 441120
#Emp: 75-99 (Tor)
#TorLoc: 1
Own: Private Company
Key: Robbie Stern, Body Shop Mgr
Leigh Gadsden, Sales Mgr

Agincourt Infiniti Nissan Ltd.

1871 McCowan Rd.
Toronto, ON M1S 4L4
Tel 416-291-1188
Fax 416-291-3388
www.agincourt.nissan.ca
Line: Retails new and used
automobiles.
NAICS: 441110 441120
#Emp: 75-99 (Tor)
#TorLoc: 1
Own: Private Company
Key: Bob Stephen, Pres
David Stephen, GM

AGI Traffic Technology

A Div. of Aecon Group Inc.
2960 Markham Rd.
Toronto, ON M1X 1E6
Tel 416-742-8900
Fax 416-746-1920
www.aecon.com
AKA: AGITT
Line: Offers various construction
services.
NAICS: 232990
#Emp: 100-249 (Tor)
#TorLoc: 2
Own: Private Company
Key: Kent Boyce, GM
John Beck, Chmn & CEO

A.G. Simpson Automotive Inc.

675 Progress Ave.
Toronto, ON M1H 2W9
Tel 416-438-6650
Fax 416-431-8775
www.agsautomotive.com
Line: Manufactures auto parts.
NAICS: 336370
#Emp: 100-249 (Tor)
#TorLoc: 2
Own: Private Company
Par: J2 Investments (CDA)
Key: Joseph Leon, Co-Pres
Joe Loparco, Co-Pres
George Dendias, Dir of HR
Michelle Sund, Dir of Fin
Dave Chen, Dir of Procurement
Dan Reid, Dir of IT & Ops
Rob Dinatele, Dir of Sales

Ahearn and Soper Inc.

100 Woodbine Downs Blvd.
Toronto, ON M9W 5S6
Tel 416-675-3999
Fax 416-675-3457
www.ahearn.com
Line: Distributes computer products.
NAICS: 417310
#Emp: 100-249 (Tor)
#TorLoc: 1
Own: Private Company
Key: Paul Pope, VP & GM
Danny DiMarco, Mgr of MIS
Vicki Sylvester, Mktg Mgr

Aim Health Group

9-6400 Millcreek Dr.
Mississauga, ON L5N 3E7
Tel 905-858-1368
Fax 905-858-1399
www.aimhealthgroup.com
Line: Provides medical staffing
services.

NAICS: 541690
#Emp: 100-249 (Tor)
#TorLoc: 1
Own: Private Company
Key: Lu Barbuto, Pres & CEO
Karen Little, HR Mgr
Bill Danis, CFO

Ainsworth Inc.

131 Bermondsey Rd.
Toronto, ON M4A 1X4
Tel 416-751-4420
Fax 416-751-9031
www.ainsworth.com
Line: Contracts and specializes
in electrical, mechanical,
communications, and control systems
for industrial, commercial, and
institutional applications.
NAICS: 232510 232520
#Emp: 250-499 (Tor)
#TorLoc: 5
Own: Private Company
Key: Albert Renaud, Pres & CEO
Dan Mezgec, VP Projects
Jim Thomson, VP HR
Alysia D. Carter, VP & CFO
Glenn Hunt,
    Supply Chain & Quality Mgr
David Lush, Dir of IT

Air Canada

1235 Air Canada Centre
P.O. Box 14000, Stn. Airport
Dorval, PQ H4Y 1H4
Tel 514-422-5500
Fax 514-422-5909
www.aircanada.ca
Line: Provides scheduled and chartered
international air transportation for
passengers and cargo.
NAICS: 481110
#Emp: 5000-9999 (Tor)
#TorLoc: 2
Own: Public Company
Par: ACE Aviation Holdings (CDA)
Key: Calin Rovinescu, CEO
Duncan Dee, Exec VP & COO
Kevin Howlett, Sr VP Employee Relns
Michael Rousseau, Exec VP & CFO
Lise Fournel, Sr VP E-Commerce & CIO
Ben Smith, Exec VP & Chief
    Commercial Officer
Priscille Leblanc, VP Corp Commun

Air Canada Jazz

318-5955 Airport Rd.
Mississauga, ON L4N 1R9
Tel 888-247-2262
Fax 866-222-6686
www.flyjazz.ca
Line: Operates an airline.
NAICS: 481110
#Emp: 250-499 (Tor)
#TorLoc: 1
Own: Private Company
Par: Air Canada (CDA)
Key: Joseph D. Randell, Pres & CEO
Terri Green, Mgr of HR &
    Compensation

Air Canada Vacations Inc.

2700 Matheson Blvd. East
East Tower, 6th Fl.
Mississauga, ON L4W 4V9
Tel 905-615-8020
Fax 905-615-7028
www.aircanadavacations.com
Line: Sells vacation packages.
NAICS: 561510
#Emp: 100-249 (Tor)
#TorLoc: 1
Own: Private Company
Par: Air Canada (CDA)
Key: Zeina Gedeon, Pres & CEO
Hugo Coulombe, VP Fin
Nino Montagnese, Sr Dir
    of Sales & Mktg
Manon LeBlanc, Dir of Mktg

Aird & Berlis LLP

1800-181 Bay St., BCE Pl.
P.O. Box 754
Toronto, ON M5J 2T9
Tel 416-863-1500
Fax 416-863-1515
www.airdberlis.com
Line: Provides legal services.
NAICS: 541110
#Emp: 250-499 (Tor)
#TorLoc: 1
Own: Private Company
Key: Gary Torgis, Exec Dir
Eldon Bennett, Mng Partner
Georgia Rennick, Dir of HR & Facilities
Andrew Morvai, Dir of Fin
Anthony Samuels, Dir of IT
Marla McAlpine, Dir of Mktg

Air Georgian Ltd.

A Div. of Air Canada Alliance
2450 Derry Rd. East
Shell Aerocentre
Mississauga, ON L5S 1B2
Tel 905-676-1221
Fax 905-676-1151
www.airgeorgian.ca
Line: Provides passenger
transportation, air cargo and executive
services.
NAICS: 481110
#Emp: 100-249 (Tor)
#TorLoc: 1
Own: Private Company
Par: Georgian Aircraft Corp. (CDA)
Key: Eric Edmondson, Pres
Daniel J. Revell, CEO
D. Scott Monsen, VP, CFO
Dan Bockner, VP Flight Ops

Air King Ltd.

8-8 Edvac Dr.
Brampton, ON L6S 5P2
Tel 905-456-2033
Fax 905-456-1015
www.airkinglimited.com
NAICS: 335210
#Emp: 75-99 (Tor)
#TorLoc: 1
Own: Private Company
Par: Lasko Products (US)
Key: Chris Galea, Pres & GM
Elizabeth Barnesco, HR Mgr
Les Swain, Nat'l Sales Mgr

Air Liquide Canada Inc.

1700 Steeles Ave. East
Brampton, ON L6T 1A6
Tel 905-793-2000
Fax 905-793-9257
www.airliquide.com
Line: Distributes gases and welding
products.
NAICS: 417230
#Emp: 250-499 (Tor)
#TorLoc: 5
Own: Public Company
Par: Air Liquide Group (FRA)
Key: Michael Tierney, GM
Katherine Calder, HR Mgr

Air Transat A.T. Inc.

5959 Blvd. Cote Vertu
Montreal, PQ H4S 2E6
Tel 514-906-0330
Fax 514-906-5131
www.airtransat.com
Line: Provides air carrier services.
NAICS: 481214
#Emp: 500-999 (Tor)
#TorLoc: 1
Own: Public Company
Par: Transat A.T. Inc. (CDA)
Key: Allen B. Graham, Pres & CEO
Simon Lavoie, VP Flight Ops
Suzanne Viens, VP HR
Johanne Lavoie, Dir of Fin
Gordon Greene,
    VP Strategic Procurement
Desmond Ryan,
    VP In-Flight & Commissary
Jon Turner, VP Tech Ops

Aisling Discoveries Child and Family Centre

110-325 Milner Ave.
Toronto, ON M1B 5N1
Tel 416-321-5464
Fax 416-321-1510
www.aislingdiscoveries.on.ca
Line: Provides special services to
children and their families.
NAICS: 624410
#Emp: 100-249 (Tor)
#TorLoc: 1
Own: Not-for-profit
Key: Betty Kashima, Exec Dir
Valerie Dunham, Dir of Fin & Admin
Joanne Gaston, HR Mgr
Mary-Ann Lyew, Fin Mgr

Ajax Textile Processing Company Ltd.

170 Commercial Ave.
Ajax, ON L1S 2H5
Tel 905-683-6800
Fax 905-683-6783
www.ajaxtextile.com
Line: Performs commissioned dyeing
and finishing of knitted fabric for the
apparel industry.
NAICS: 313310
#Emp: 100-249 (Tor)
#TorLoc: 1
Own: Private Company
Key: Terry Serra, Pres, CEO & COO
John Chiusolo, Plant Mgr
Joe Schmidinger, CFO

AJD Data Services Inc.

1-300 Town Centre Blvd.
Markham, ON L3R 5Z6
Tel 905-475-0200
Fax 905-475-2227
www.ajddataservices.com
Line: Provides telemarketing,
teledata services, cheque and charge
processing, document imaging, storage
and retrieval, data entry, OCR, and
mail processing services.
NAICS: 514210
#Emp: 75-99 (Tor)
#TorLoc: 1
Own: Private Company
Key: Andrew Darbyson, Pres

A.J. Lanzarotta Wholesale Fruit & Vegetables Ltd.

1-1000 Lakeshore Rd. East
Mississauga, ON L5E 1E4
Tel 905-891-0510
Fax 905-891-5527
www.ajlanzarotta.com
Line: Wholesales produce.
NAICS: 413150
#Emp: 75-99 (Tor)
#TorLoc: 1
Own: Private Company
Key: Augustus Lanzarotta, Pres
Sergio Tenuta, Ops Mgr

AkzoNobel

8200 Keele St.
Concord, ON L4K 2A5
Tel 905-669-1020
Fax 905-669-3433
www.akzonobel.com/ca
AKA: Colour Your World; Glidden Paint
Line: Manufactures, wholesales and
retails paint and paint products.
NAICS: 416340 442298
#Emp: 500-999 (Tor)
#TorLoc: 70
Own: Private Company
Key: Vince Rea, VP, Trade & Sales Ops

AlarmForce Industries Inc.

675 Garyray Dr.
Toronto, ON M9L 1R2
Tel 416-445-2001
Fax 416-445-9381
www.alarmforce.com
Line: Provides home security products
and services.
NAICS: 561621
#Emp: 100-249 (Tor)
#TorLoc: 1
Own: Private Company
Key: Joel Matlin, Pres & CEO
Anthony Pizzonia, CFO
Alan Goodley, Sales Mgr

Albany Medical Clinic

807 Broadview Ave.
Toronto, ON M4K 2P8
Tel 416-461-9471
Fax 416-461-2710
www.albanyclinic.ca
NAICS: 621494
#Emp: 100-249 (Tor)
#TorLoc: 1
Own: Private Company
Key: James Higginson-Rollins, Mng Dir
Ruth Ennis, Ops & HR Mgr
Spencer Kopra, Acctng & IT Mgr

Alcoa Howmet Georgetown Casting

93 Mountainview Rd. North
Georgetown, ON L7G 4J6
Tel 905-877-6936
Fax 905-877-6938
www.alcoa.com
Line: Manufactures aluminum
and copper-based castings for the
aerospace and commercial industries.
NAICS: 331529
#Emp: 100-249 (Tor)
Own: Private Company
Par: Alcoa Inc. (CDA)
Key: Ted Laing, Plant Mgr
Larry Hand, Dir of Ops
Sandy Miller, Dir of HR
Bryan Clare, Purch Mgr

Alcohol Countermeasure Systems

60 International Blvd.
Toronto, ON M9W 6J2
Tel 416-619-3500
Fax 416-619-3501
www.acs-corp.com
Line: Manufactures breath alcohol
testing products.
NAICS: 334512

#Emp: 100-249 (Tor)
#TorLoc: 1
Own: Private Company
Key: Felix Comeau, CEO
June Bassant, HR Mgr
Chris Wilson, Dir of Sales

Alcohol & Gaming Commission of Ontario

200-90 Sheppard Ave. East
Toronto, ON M5G 2N6
Tel 416-326-8700
Fax 416-326-5555
www.agco.on.ca
Line: Regulates alcohol and gaming
industry.
NAICS: 912910
#Emp: 250-499 (Tor)
#TorLoc: 1
Own: Provincial Crown Corp.
Key: Jean Major, CEO
George Sweny, Exec Dir, Gaming
    Excellence Center
Carol Cosman, Sr Mgr of Fin & Admin

Alcon Canada Inc.

2665 Meadowpine Blvd.
Mississauga, ON L5N 8C7
Tel 905-826-6700
Fax 905-567-0592
www.alcon.ca
Line: Distributes eye care products
and markets and sells surgical,
pharmaceutical and consumer
products.
NAICS: 417930 414510
#Emp: 100-249 (Tor)
#TorLoc: 1
Own: Public Company
Par: Novartis (SWITZ)
Key: Alex Long, GM
Roy James, VP Ops
Lisa O'Connell, Dir of HR
Pam Mulhall, Cont
Kevin Shearer,
    VP Sales & Mktg, Surgical
Michelle Ummels, VP Sales & Mktg,
    Pharmaceutical
Larry McGirr,
    VP Sales & Mktg, Vision Care

Aldershot Greenhouses

1135 Gallagher Rd.
Burlington, ON L7T 2M7
Tel 905-632-9272
Fax 905-632-4022
www.aldershotgreenhouses.com
Line: Sells potted roses.
NAICS: 453110
#Emp: 100-249 (Tor)
#TorLoc: 2
Own: Private Company
Key: Len Vanderlugt, Pres
Earl Schouten, Plant Mgr
Roman Golovchenko, CFO

Aldershot Landscape Contractors Ltd.

166 Flatt Rd.
Burlington, ON L7R 3X5
Tel 905-825-1802
Fax 905-689-3433
www.aldershotlandscape.com
Line: Provides landscape-contracting services including site development, commercial and residential landscaping and maintenance.
NAICS: 541320
#Emp: 100-249 (Tor)
#TorLoc: 1
Own: Private Company
Key: William DeLuca, Pres
Justin DeLuca, Ops Mgr
Michelle Marshall, Payroll Mgr
Jason Spence, Cont

Aleris Specifications Alloy Products Canada Company

7496 Torbram Rd.
Mississauga, ON L4T 1G9
Tel 905-672-5569
Fax 905-672-5570
www.aleris.com
Line: Manufactures and recycles aluminum.
NAICS: 331317
#Emp: 75-99 (Tor)
#TorLoc: 1
Own: Private Company
Par: Aleris International (US)
Key: Joseph Giorgio, Plant Mgr
Francis Sacarey, Plant Supt
Ellen Coulter, HR & Office Mgr

Algonquin Power Corporation Inc.

2845 Bristol Circ.
Oakville, ON L6H 7H7
Tel 905-465-4500
Fax 905-465-4514
www.algonquinpower.com
Line: Operates and manages hydroelectric generating facilities.
NAICS: 221111
#Emp: 100-249 (Tor)
#TorLoc: 1
Own: Private Company
Par: Algonquin Power Income Fund (CDA)
Key: Ian E. Robertson, CEO
Michel Boudreault, HR Mgr
David Bronicheski, Mng Dir, Admin & CFO

Algorithmics Inc.

185 Spadina Ave.
Toronto, ON M5T 2C6
Tel 416-217-1500
Fax 416-971-6100
www.algorithmics.com
Line: Develops financial risk management software.
NAICS: 511210
#Emp: 250-499 (Tor)
#TorLoc: 1
Own: Private Company
Par: Fimalac (FR)
Key: Michael Zerbs, Pres & COO
Stephen Joynt, CEO
Mina Wallace, Exec VP, Global Services & Support
Katherine Faichnie, Sr VP Ops & Admin
Cynthia Schyff, CFO
Neil Bartlett, CTO
John Macdonald, Exec VP

Allanson International Inc.

33 Cranfield Rd.
Toronto, ON M4B 3H2
Tel 416-755-1191
Fax 416-752-6718
www.allanson.com
Line: Manufactures transformers, ballasts, and igniters.
NAICS: 335311
#Emp: 100-249 (Tor)
#TorLoc: 1
Own: Private Company
Key: Richard E. Woodgate, CEO
Jeannette Flynn, Payroll & Office Admr
Errol Lanns, VP

Allan Windows Technologies

1-131 Caldari Rd.
Concord, ON L4K 3Z9
Tel 905-738-8600
Fax 905-738-1988
www.allanwindows.com
Line: Manufactures windows and doors.
NAICS: 332321
#Emp: 100-249 (Tor)
#TorLoc: 1
Own: Private Company
Key: Brian Cohen, Reg Pres
Stephen Miller, Pres & CEO
Sheila Solomon, HR

All Canada Crane Rental Corp.

7215 Torbram Rd.
Mississauga, ON L4T 1G7
Tel 905-795-1090
Fax 905-795-1121
www.allcanadacrane.com
Line: Rents mobile cranes, crawler cranes, fork trucks and aerial lift equipment.
NAICS: 532410
#Emp: 75-99 (Tor)
#TorLoc: 1
Own: Private Company
Par: All Erection & Crane Rental Corp. (US)
Key: Robert Hanna, GM
Jason Hanna, Ops Mgr
Peter Wraight, Cont

All-Connect Logistical Services Inc.

2139 Wyecroft Rd.
Oakville, ON L6L 5L7
Tel 905-847-6555
Fax 905-847-3339
www.allconnect.ca
Line: Provides logistical services.
NAICS: 488519
#Emp: 75-99 (Tor)
#TorLoc: 1
Own: Private Company
Key: Ian Smith, Pres
Norm Rego, VP Ops
Heather Durnford, Office Admin
Georgine Smith, VP Fin
Sam Hotton, Ops Mgr
John Laub, IT Mgr

Allendale

A Div. of Regional Municipality of Halton
185 Ontario St. South
Milton, ON L9T 2M4
Tel 905-878-4141
Fax 905-878-8797
www.halton.ca
Line: Operates long-term care facility.
NAICS: 623310
#Emp: 250-499 (Tor)
#TorLoc: 1
Own: Government
Key: Cheryl Raycraft, Admr

The Alliance Group Inc.

20 Tomas St.
Mississauga, ON L5M 1Y1
Tel 905-567-3691
Fax 905-567-3069
www.alliancestaffing.ca
AKA: 1733379 Ontario Ltd.
Line: Provides employees to the
logistics industry.
NAICS: 541612 561310
#Emp: 100-249 (Tor)
#TorLoc: 2
Own: Private Company
Key: Jon Cooper, Pres
Cheryl Davis, HR Mgr
William Miranda, Acct

Alliance of Canadian Cinema, Television & Radio Artists

300-625 Church St.
Toronto, ON M4Y 2G1
Tel 416-489-1311
Fax 416-489-8076
www.actra.ca
AKA: ACTRA
Line: Operates arts and culture labour
association.
NAICS: 813930
#Emp: 75-99 (Tor)
#TorLoc: 2
Own: Association
Key: Ferne Downey, Nat'l Pres

Alliance One Ltd.

300-1220 Sheppard Ave. East
Toronto, ON M2K 2S3
Tel 416-447-8899
Fax 416-447-5972
www.tch.com
AKA: TCH International
Line: Operates a collection agency.
NAICS: 561440
#Emp: 250-499 (Tor)
#TorLoc: 4
Own: Private Company
Par: Alliance One Inc. (US)
Key: Scott McIlroy, Sr VP

Allied International Credit Corp.

26-16635 Yonge St.
Newmarket, ON L3X 1V6
Tel 905-470-8181
Fax 905-470-8155
www.aiccorp.com
Line: Offers debt collection and
accounts receivables services.
NAICS: 561440
#Emp: 500-999 (Tor)
#TorLoc: 1
Own: Private Company
Par: Allied Global Holdings Inc. (CDA)
Key: David Rae, Pres & CEO
David Gallagher, Exec VP
Tom McCausland, Sr VP Ops

Allied Systems (Canada) Company

2 North Park Dr.
Brampton, ON L6T 4Y6
Tel 905-458-0900
Fax 905-458-0522
www.alliedsystems.com
Line: Manufactures specialized
material handling equipment.
NAICS: 333310
#Emp: 100-249 (Tor)
#TorLoc: 3
Own: Private Company
Par: Allied Systems Company (US)
Key: Harry Porquet, Mgr

Allseas Fisheries Inc.

55 Vansco Rd.
Toronto, ON M8Z 5Z8
Tel 416-255-3474
Fax 416-255-6760
www.allseasfisheries.com
Line: Imports and exports fresh and
frozen seafood.
NAICS: 413140 413190
#Emp: 75-99 (Tor)
#TorLoc: 1
Own: Private Company
Key: Danny Soberano, Ops Mgr

Allseating Corporation

3-5800 Avebury Rd.
Mississauga, ON L4Z 4B8
Tel 905-502-7200
Fax 905-502-7299
www.allseating.com
Line: Manufactures ergonomic office
chairs.
NAICS: 337214
#Emp: 100-249 (Tor)
#TorLoc: 1
Own: Private Company
Key: Gary Neil, Pres

Allstate Insurance Company of Canada

100-27 Allstate Pkwy.
Markham, ON L3R 5P8
Tel 905-477-6900
Fax 905-513-4018
www.allstate.ca
AKA: Pembridge Insurance Co.; Pafco
Insurance
Line: Provides personal property and
automobile insurance.
NAICS: 524121 524123
#Emp: 500-999 (Tor)
#TorLoc: 1
Own: Public Company
Par: Allstate Corporation (US)
Key: Chris Kiah, Pres & CEO
Eric Pickering, VP HR
Karyn Toon, Dir of Corp Relns

All Stick Label Ltd.

1 Royal Gate Blvd., Unit A
Vaughan, ON L4L 8Z7
Tel 416-798-7310
Fax 905-264-1529
www.allsticklabel.com
AKA: ASL Group Ltd.
Line: Manufactures pressure sensitive
labels and packaging.
NAICS: 323119 322230
#Emp: 75-99 (Tor)
#TorLoc: 1
Own: Private Company
Key: Charlie MacLean, Pres & CEO
Stacy Daly, VP Ops
Nancy Coulter, Acctng Mgr
Yvonne Baker, VP Fin & CFO

All Trade Computer Forms Inc.

60 Admiral Blvd.
Mississauga, ON L5T 2W1
Tel 905-795-1986
Fax 800-366-4017
www.alltrade.com
AKA: Nebs Deluxe Co.
Line: Manufactures business
and computer forms, snap sets,
laser cheques, bar coding, jumbo
numbering, and direct mail up to ten
colours.
NAICS: 323116
#Emp: 75-99 (Tor)
#TorLoc: 1
Own: Private Company
Par: Nebs Deluxe Co. (CDA)
Key: Roger Reid, Plant Mgr

All-Weld Company Ltd.

49 Passmore Ave.
Toronto, ON M1V 4T1
Tel 416-299-3311
Fax 416-299-3387
www.allweld.ca
AKA: Continental Penn Services;
Aurora Filters; Canada Millwrights Ltd.
Line: Provides custom metal fabrication
services in specialty alloys, pressure
vessels, bus bars, pharmaceutical
tanks, conveyors, mixing tanks,
process equipment, reactors and
custom machining.
NAICS: 332420
#Emp: 75-99 (Tor)
#TorLoc: 2
Own: Private Company
Key: William Dunsmoor, Pres & CEO
Scott Dunsmoor, VP Ops
Paul Harris, VP Fin & HR
James Holder, Plant Mgr

Allwood Products Limited

5-115 Drumlin Circ.
Concord, ON L4K 3E6
Tel 905-738-1772
Fax 905-738-4026
AKA: Global Group
Line: Manufactures wooden chairs and
table frames.
NAICS: 337123
#Emp: 100-249 (Tor)
#TorLoc: 1
Own: Private Company
Par: Global Group (CDA)
Key: Frank Trichilo, GM
Bob Ritter, Corp HR Mgr

Almag Aluminum Inc.

22 Finley Rd.
Brampton, ON L6T 1A9
Tel 905-457-9000
Fax 905-457-9006
www.almag.com
Line: Manufactures aluminum
extrusions.
NAICS: 331317
#Emp: 100-249 (Tor)
#TorLoc: 1
Own: Private Company
Key: Robert Peacock, Pres
Herb Matis, VP Fin & Admin
Joe Jackman, VP Sales & Mktg

Alpa Lumber Inc.

7630 Airport Rd.
Mississauga, ON L4T 4G6
Tel 905-612-1222
Fax 905-612-1231
Line: Manufactures wood products.
NAICS: 416320
#Emp: 100-249 (Tor)
Own: Private Company
Key: John DiPoce, Pres
Patty Buckley, Office Mgr
Orest Metkowsky, CFO

Alpa Roof Trusses Inc.

10311 Keele St.
Maple, ON L6A 3Y9
Tel 905-832-2250
Fax 905-832-0286
www.alpart.com
Line: Manufactures roof and floor
trusses.
NAICS: 321215
#Emp: 100-249 (Tor)
#TorLoc: 2
Own: Private Company
Par: Alpa Lumber Inc. (CDA)
Key: Ernie Harris, GM
Keith Summers, HR & Fin Mgr

Alpha Laboratories Inc.

1262 Don Mills Rd.
Toronto, ON M3B 2W7
Tel 416-449-2166
Fax 416-449-2543
www.alphainc.org
Line: Operates a medical laboratory.
NAICS: 621510
#Emp: 250-499 (Tor)
#TorLoc: 8
Own: Private Company
Key: Joseph Kurian, Pres
Idelta Coelho, VP
Kuttimol Kurian, Cont
Babak Poorgholam, Materials Mgr

Alros Products Ltd.

11 Lepage Crt.
Toronto, ON M3J 2A3
Tel 416-633-2231
Fax 416-661-1757
www.polytarp.com
AKA: Polytarp Products
Line: Manufactures and supplies
polyethylene film flexible products.
NAICS: 326114
#Emp: 100-249 (Tor)
#TorLoc: 2
Own: Private Company

Key: Steve Ghantous, Pres
Janet Spencer, HR Mgr
Chris Sullivan, Dir of IT & Plant Logistics

Alte-Rego Corp.

36 Tidemore Ave.
Toronto, ON M9W 5H4
Tel 416-740-3397
Fax 416-741-9991
www.alte-rego.com
Line: Manufactures polyethylene bags.
NAICS: 326114 326111
#Emp: 100-249 (Tor)
#TorLoc: 2
Own: Private Company
Key: Devin Sidhu, Pres & CEO

Alterna Savings & Credit Union Ltd.

165 Attwell Dr.
Toronto, ON M9W 5Y5
Tel 416-252-5625
Fax 416-679-0339
www.alterna.ca
AKA: Alterna Bank
Line: Provides financial services.
NAICS: 522130 522111
#Emp: 100-249 (Tor)
#TorLoc: 11
Own: Private Company
Par: Alterna Savings & Credit Union
Ltd. (CDA)
Key: John Lahey, Pres & CEO
Carl Ramkerrysingh, Sr VP,
    Personal & Business Services
Josette Gauthier, Sr VP HR
Jose Gallant, Sr VP Fin & CFO
Rebecca Robinson, VP IS & Tech
Kimberley Ney, Sr VP, Mktg,
    Commun & Social Responsibility

Altus Group Ltd.

500-33 Yonge St.
Toronto, ON M5E 1G4
Tel 416-641-9500
Fax 416-641-9501
www.altusgroup.com
AKA: Helyar & Associates
Line: Provides commercial real estate
and development industry consulting
services covering cost consulting
and project management, valuation,
research, and realty tax management.
NAICS: 541611
#Emp: 1000-4999 (Tor)
#TorLoc: 7
Own: Public Company
Key: Gary Yeoman, CEO
Paul Morassutti, COO
Angelo Bartolini, CAO
Sayla Nordin, VP
    Corp Commun & Investor Relns

Aluma Systems Canada Inc.

A Div. of Brand Energy
& Infrastructure Services
55 Costa Rd.
Concord, ON L4K 1M8
Tel 905-669-5282
Fax 905-660-8062
www.beis.com
NAICS: 532490
#Emp: 100-249 (Tor)
#TorLoc: 2
Own: Private Company
Key: David J. Witsken,
  Pres, North Region
Paul Wood, Pres & CEO
John A, Durkee, Sr VP
  Business Dev, North Region

Alumicor Ltd.

33 Racine Rd.
Toronto, ON M9W 2Z4
Tel 416-745-4222
Fax 416-745-7759
www.alumicor.com
Line: Manufactures architectural
aluminum products including
windows, skylights, doors, storefronts,
ribbon and curtain walls.
NAICS: 232340 416210
#Emp: 100-249 (Tor)
#TorLoc: 1
Own: Private Company
Par: Alumicor International Inc. (CDA)
Key: Barry Wood, Pres & CEO
Tony Kerwin, COO
Grace Meade, HR Mgr
Pierre Seegmuller, VP Fin
John Castelhano, VP Supply Chain
Sorin Gluck, VP International Sales
Steve Gusterson, Mktg Mgr

Aluminart Products Ltd.

1 Summerlea Rd.
Brampton, ON L6T 4V2
Tel 905-791-7521
Fax 905-791-9928
www.aluminart.com
Line: Manufactures aluminum doors.
NAICS: 332321
#Emp: 100-249 (Tor)
#TorLoc: 1
Own: Private Company
Key: Frank Raponi, Pres & CEO
Maria Lanteigne, VP HR
Anu Agrawal, Cont
Ray Bryer, Dir of Sales

AMD

1 Commerce Valley Dr. East
Markham, ON L3T 7X6
Tel 905-882-2600
Fax 905-882-2620
www.ati.amd.com
AKA: Advanced Micro Devices
Line: Manufactures graphics
accelerators, multimedia video
enhancement products, fax-modems
and PC components.
NAICS: 334110 541510
#Emp: 1000-4999 (Tor)
#TorLoc: 2
Own: Public Company
Par: AMD (US)
Key: Rick Bergman, Sr VP & GM
Nigel Dessau, Chief Mktg Officer

Amdocs Canada

400-2 Bloor St. East
Toronto, ON M4W 3Y7
Tel 416-355-4000
Fax 416-355-4085
www.amdocs.com
Line: Offers computer program
development services.
NAICS: 541510
#Emp: 250-499 (Tor)
Own: Private Company
Key: Michael Couture, VP Mktg

AMEC Americas Ltd.

700-2020 Winston Park Dr.
Oakville, ON L6H 6X7
Tel 905-829-5400
Fax 905-829-5401
www.amec.com
Line: Operates an engineering
consulting company.
NAICS: 541330
#Emp: 500-999 (Tor)
#TorLoc: 3
Own: Private Company
Par: AMEC plc (UK)
Key: Robert Walton, VP Project
Management

AMEC Earth
& Environmental Ltd.

110-160 Traders Blvd. East
Mississauga, ON L4Z 3K7
Tel 905-568-2929
Fax 905-568-1686
www.amec.com
Line: Provides environmental and
engineering consulting services.
NAICS: 541620 541330
#Emp: 250-499 (Tor)
#TorLoc: 4
Own: Public Company
Par: AMEC Americas Limited (CDA)
Key: Laurie Davidson, Exec VP
John Allen, IT Mgr

Ameresco Canada Inc.

90 Sheppard Ave. East
Toronto, ON M2N 6X3
Tel 416-512-7700
Fax 416-218-2288
www.ameresco.ca
Line: Provides energy management
consulting services.
NAICS: 541690
#Emp: 75-99 (Tor)
#TorLoc: 1
Own: Private Company
Par: Ameresco Inc. (US)
Key: Mario Iusi, Pres

American Airlines, Inc.

Lester B. Pearson Airport
P.O. Box 6005
Toronto AMF, ON L5P 1B6
Tel 905-612-7266
Fax 905-612-0144
www.aa.com
Line: Operates an airline business.
NAICS: 481110
#Emp: 100-249 (Tor)
Own: Private Company
Key: Pierre Cote, GM

American-Standard

A Div. of AS Canada, ULC
5900 Avery Rd.
Mississauga, ON L5R 3M3
Tel 905-949-4800
Fax 905-276-9128
www.americanstandard.ca
Line: Manufactures and sells bath and
kitchen products.
NAICS: 332999
#Emp: 100-249 (Tor)
#TorLoc: 1
Own: Private Company
Par: American-Standard Inc. (US)
Key: Harry Kandilas, Pres & GM
Lisa Rei, VP Fin & Cont
Kevin Reeves, IT Dir
Joe Anile, Reg Sales Mgr
Simone Abele, VP Mktg
Graeme Lennox,
  Advertising & Commun Mgr

Amer Sports Canada Inc.

1-2700 14th Ave.
Markham, ON L3R 0J1
Tel 905-470-9966
Fax 905-470-7315
www.amercanada.com
Line: Supplies and distributes sports equipment.
NAICS: 414470
#Emp: 100-249 (Tor)
#TorLoc: 1
Own: Private Company
Par: Amer Sports (US)
Key: David Deasley, Pres

Amex Canada Inc.

101 McNabb St.
Markham, ON L3R 4H8
Tel 905-474-8000
Fax 905-474-1035
www.americanexpress.ca
AKA: American Express Canada
Line: Provides financial services.
NAICS: 522210
#Emp: 1000-4999 (Tor)
Own: Private Company
Par: American Express (US)
Key: Howard Grosfield, Pres & GM
Denise Pickett, Pres & CEO

Amhil Enterprises Ltd.

400 Traders Blvd. East
Mississauga, ON L4Z 1W7
Tel 905-890-5261
Fax 905-890-2078
www.wentworthtechnologies.com
Line: Manufactures disposable plastic lids and cups.
NAICS: 326198
#Emp: 250-499 (Tor)
#TorLoc: 2
Own: Private Company
Par: Wentworth Technologies Company Ltd. (CDA)
Key: Walter T. Kuskowski, Pres & CEO
Bruce H. McNichol, VP & COO
Linda Tanner, Dir of HR
Jeffery D. Barclay, VP Fin

Amico Corp.

85 Fulton Way
Richmond Hill, ON L4B 2N4
Tel 905-764-0800
Fax 905-764-0862
www.amico.com
Line: Manufactures medical gas pipeline equipment.
NAICS: 339110
#Emp: 250-499 (Tor)

#TorLoc: 2
Own: Private Company
Key: Albert Sinyor, Pres
David Chan, Dir of Ops
Wayne Benson, Pres, Amico Source
Paul Phagoo, Dir
of International & OEM Sales

AMJ Campbell Van Lines

830-100 Milverton Dr.
Mississauga, ON L5R 4H1
Tel 905-795-3785
Fax 905-670-3787
www.amjcampbell.com
Line: Moves and stores household goods, stores and installs offices, warehouses and heavy machinery.
NAICS: 484229 484239
#Emp: 250-499 (Tor)
#TorLoc: 6
Own: Private Company
Par: AMJ Campbell Inc. (CDA)
Key: Bruce Bowser, Pres & CEO
Allen Kidd, VP Fin
Denis Frappier, Pres,
Self Storage & Business Dev
Denis Cordick, VP Mktg

Ampere Limited

127 Brisbane Rd.
Toronto, ON M3J 2K3
Tel 416-661-3330
Fax 416-661-4508
www.ampere.ca
Line: Provides electrical, voice data, communications and technical services.
NAICS: 232510
#Emp: 100-249 (Tor)
#TorLoc: 1
Own: Private Company
Key: Mario Bernardini, Pres & CEO
Kelly Burke, VP Division
Renata Strazzeri, HR Mgr
Abdul Ashoor, Cont
Rick Stokes, VP Estimating

Amphenol Canada Corp.

605 Milner Ave.
Toronto, ON M1B 5X6
Tel 416-291-4401
Fax 416-292-0647
www.amphenolcanada.com
Line: Designs and manufactures EMI/RFI/EMP/RJHS connectors for special requirements in communications and computer systems for military and aerospace applications.
NAICS: 334110
#Emp: 100-249 (Tor)

#TorLoc: 1
Own: Private Company
Par: Amphenol Corp. (US)
Key: Andy Toffelmire, Dir of Aerospace
Tony Davidson, Cont
Mary Luk, Asst Cont

Amphora Maintenance Systems

707A Danforth Ave.
Toronto, ON M4J 1L2
Tel 416-461-0401
Fax 416-461-6081
www.amphoracleaners.com
Line: Provides industrial and commercial cleaning services.
NAICS: 561722
#Emp: 100-249 (Tor)
#TorLoc: 1
Own: Private Company
Key: Savvas Krotiris, Mgr

Anderson Merchandisers-Canada Inc.

60 Leek Cres.
Richmond Hill, ON L4B 1H1
Tel 905-763-1999
Fax 905-763-6785
www.amerch.com
Line: Distributes pre-recorded music to leading retailers.
NAICS: 414440
#Emp: 75-99 (Tor)
#TorLoc: 1
Own: Private Company
Par: Anderson Merchandisers (US)
Key: J.E. (Ned) Talmey, VP & GM
Mike Barker, GM
Marianne Harper, HR Mgr
Ken Kozey, Asst VP Product
Management & Logistics
Cindy Liske, Dir of Field
Merchandising & Service

Andorra Building Maintenance Ltd.

46 Chauncey Ave.
Toronto, ON M8Z 2Z4
Tel 416-537-7772
Fax 416-538-1731
www.andorramaintenance.com
Line: Provides janitorial services.
NAICS: 561722
#Emp: 100-249 (Tor)
#TorLoc: 1
Own: Private Company
Key: Anthony P. Vella, Pres
Frida de Paz, HR

Andrews' Scenic Acres

9365 10th Sideroad
R.R. 5
Milton, ON L9T 2X9
Tel 905-878-5807
Fax 905-878-4997
www.andrewsscenicacres.com
Line: Operates a fruit farm and winery.
NAICS: 312130 111330
#Emp: 75-99 (Tor)
#TorLoc: 1
Own: Private Company
Key: Bert Andrews, Pres

Anewtex Inc.

462 Front St. West
Toronto, ON M5V 1B6
Tel 416-586-0757
Fax 416-586-0737
Line: Manufactures women's dresses.
NAICS: 315233
#Emp: 100-249 (Tor)
#TorLoc: 1
Own: Private Company
Key: Huo Zhang, Pres

Angus Consulting Management Ltd.

1129 Leslie St.
Toronto, ON M3C 2J6
Tel 416-443-8300
Fax 416-443-8323
www.angus-group.com
Line: Develops service and
maintenance management software
for commercial real estate.
NAICS: 541510
#Emp: 100-249 (Tor)
#TorLoc: 2
Own: Private Company
Key: Garry Gale, VP
H.G. Angus, Pres

Angus Glen Golf Club

10080 Kennedy Rd.
Markham, ON L6C 1N9
Tel 905-887-0090
Fax 905-887-9424
www.angusglen.com
NAICS: 713910
#Emp: 250-499 (Tor)
#TorLoc: 1
Own: Private Company
Key: Cailey Stollery, Pres
Nigel Hollidge, GM
Helen Plumis, Dir of HR
Allan McDonnell, Dir of Golf
Brian Mason, Golf Shop Mgr

Anixter Canada Inc.

200 Foster Cres.
Mississauga, ON L5R 3Y5
Tel 905-568-8999
Fax 905-568-4921
www.anixter.ca
Line: Specializes in wiring systems
for transmission of voice, video, data
and power.
NAICS: 416110 417320
#Emp: 250-499 (Tor)
#TorLoc: 2
Own: Public Company
Par: Anixter Inc. (US)
Key: Steve Dengate, Pres
Glenn Gammage, VP Ops
Brian Zolper, Dir of HR
Ron Ramjitsingh, Inventory
   Management Mgr
Andy Ali, IT Mgr
Bruce Dowie, VP Area Sales

Annan & Bird Lithographers

1060 Tristar Dr.
Mississauga, ON L5T 1H9
Tel 905-670-0604
Fax 905-670-1069
www.annan-bird.com
NAICS: 323120
#Emp: 100-249 (Tor)
#TorLoc: 2
Own: Private Company
Key: John Bird, Pres of Ops
Allen Kelly, Plant Mgr
Steve Doorey, CFO
Dave Bird, Pres of Sales & Mktg
Mike Pillo, VP Sales

Answer Plus Inc.

10 Canmotor Ave.
Toronto, ON M8Z 4E5
Tel 416-503-8888
Fax 416-503-4499
www.answerplus.ca
Line: Operates a call handling centre.
NAICS: 561420
#Emp: 100-249 (Tor)
#TorLoc: 1
Own: Private Company
Key: Paul Lloyd, Pres

Antalex Inc.

1-170 Sharer Rd.
Woodbridge, ON L4L 8P4
Tel 905-264-5560
Fax 905-264-5521
www.antalex.ca
Line: Operates a custom metal
fabrication facility servicing the store
fixture, office furniture, hospitality and
building supply industries.

NAICS: 416210
#Emp: 75-99 (Tor)
Own: Private Company
Key: Luisa Loffreda, Pres

Antamex International Inc.

210 Great Gulf Dr.
Concord, ON L4K 5W1
Tel 905-660-4520
Fax 905-669-4402
www.antamex.com
Line: Designs, manufactures and
installs curtain wall and cladding
systems.
NAICS: 337920
#Emp: 250-499 (Tor)
#TorLoc: 1
Own: Private Company
Par: Old Castle Glass (US)
Key: Mary Carol Witry, Pres & CEO
Dan Cummings, Cont
Gus Vaswani, Purch Mgr
Walter Iacucci, IT Mgr
James Mitchell, VP Sales

Antex Design Inc.

330 Britannia Rd. East
Mississauga, ON L4Z 1X9
Tel 905-507-8778
Fax 905-507-9810
www.antexdesigns.com
Line: Specializes in fabric design.
NAICS: 314120
#Emp: 100-249 (Tor)
#TorLoc: 1
Own: Private Company
Key: John Sturino, Cont
Ana Markovic,
   Exec Asst of Admin & Fin
Rick Wyse, VP Sales

Anton Manufacturing

300 Basaltic Rd.
Concord, ON L4K 4Y9
Tel 905-879-0500
Fax 905-879-0501
www.multimatic.com
Line: Manufactures automotive door
hinges and checkers.
NAICS: 336390
#Emp: 1000-4999 (Tor)
#TorLoc: 1
Own: Private Company
Key: Peter Czapka, Pres
Hamil Moredelly, Plant Cont
Dave Armstrong, HR Mgr

AOL Canada Inc.

55 St. Clair Ave. West, 7th Fl.
Toronto, ON M4V 2Y7
Tel 416-960-6500
Fax 416-960-6502
www.aol.ca
Line: Provides internet services.
NAICS: 514191
#Emp: 100-249 (Tor)
#TorLoc: 1
Own: Private Company
Key: Graham Moysey, GM
Marieta Mendoza, Dir of HR

AON Benfield Canada ULC

1900-150 King St. West
Toronto, ON M5H 1J9
Tel 416-979-3300
Fax 416-979-7724
www.aonbenfield.com
AKA: Aon Benfield
Line: Provides solutions in insurance
and risk management, human capital
consulting, and reinsurance.
NAICS: 524139
#Emp: 100-249 (Tor)
#TorLoc: 1
Own: Private Company
Par: Aon Corp. (US)
Key: Robert McLean, Pres & CEO
Desmond DosRamos, CAO

Aon Hewitt

1600-225 King St. West
Toronto, ON M5V 3M2
Tel 416-225-5001
Fax 416-542-5504
www.aon.ca
AKA: Aon Hewitt Consulting Inc.
Line: Offers human resources
consulting services in the areas
of health strategies, retirement,
outsourcing and human capital.
NAICS: 541612
#Emp: 1000-4999 (Tor)
#TorLoc: 3
Own: Public Company
Par: Aon Corp. (US)
Key: Ashim Khemani, CEO
Paul Rangcroft, COO
Edgar Aranha, VP Talent
Robert Lynch, CFO

Aon Reed Stenhouse Inc.

2400-20 Bay St.
Toronto, ON M5J 2N9
Tel 416-868-5500
Fax 416-868-5580
www.aon.ca
AKA: Aon Risk Services
Line: Provides international insurance
brokerage and risk management
services.
NAICS: 524210
#Emp: 250-499 (Tor)
#TorLoc: 1
Own: Public Company
Par: Aon Corp. (US)
Key: Chris Fawcus, Pres & CEO
John W. King, COO
James Millard, Sr VP HR
Andrew Wood, CIO

apetito Canada Ltd.

12 Indell Lane
Brampton, ON L6T 3Y3
Tel 905-799-1022
Fax 905-799-2666
www.apetito.ca
AKA: apetito
Line: Produces frozen foods and meals.
NAICS: 311410
#Emp: 75-99 (Tor)
#TorLoc: 1
Own: Private Company
Par: apetito Ltd. (UK)
Key: Jack Book, Exec VP Ops
Troy Brett, Cont
Brian McCafferty,
    Exec VP Sales & Mktg
Nigel Richards, Mktg Mgr

Apex Motor Express Ltd.

60 Ward Rd.
Brampton, ON L6S 4L5
Tel 905 789-5000
Fax 905 789-5050
www.apexltl.com
Line: Provides inter-provincial and
international cross-border carrier
services.
NAICS: 488519
#Emp: 250-499 (Tor)
#TorLoc: 1
Own: Private Company
Par: Reimer World Corporation (CDA)
Key: Elmer Schwarz, Pres
Tom Santaguida, VP Ops
Tony Mistry, Dir of IT
David Heath, VP Sales

Apollo 8 Maintenance Services Inc.

200-1502 Danforth Ave.
Toronto, ON M4J 1N4
Tel 416-461-8748
Fax 416-461-1294
www.apolloeight.com
Line: Provides commercial office
cleaning services.
NAICS: 561722
#Emp: 500-999 (Tor)
#TorLoc: 1
Own: Private Company
Key: Dennis Kaplan, Pres
Kimberly Burns, Exec VP
Shelley Hamilton, Payroll Mgr
Ron Campbell, Sr VP

Apollo Health & Beauty Care

20 Graniteridge Rd.
Vaughan, ON L4K 5M8
Tel 905-695-3700
Fax 905-695-3701
www.apollocorp.com
Line: Manufactures and distributes
health and beauty care products.
NAICS: 414520
#Emp: 100-249 (Tor)
#TorLoc: 2
Own: Private Company
Key: Charles Wachsberg, Pres

Apotex Inc.

150 Signet Dr.
Toronto, ON M9L 1T9
Tel 416-749-9300
Fax 416-401-3835
www.apotex.com
Line: Researches, develops,
manufactures and exports prescription
medicines.
NAICS: 325410
#Emp: 1000-4999 (Tor)
#TorLoc: 13
Own: Private Company
Key: Jack Kay, Pres & COO
Bernard Sherman, Chmn & CEO
Ron Davidson, VP HR
Alex Glassenberg, CFO
Michael Davidson, CIO
Jeff Watson, Chief Commercial Officer
Elie Betito,
    Dir of Public & Government Affairs

Apparel Resource Group Inc.

8 Milner Ave.
Toronto, ON M1S 3P8
Tel 416-298-8800
Fax 416-298-0708
NAICS: 315229 315239
#Emp: 75-99 (Tor)
#TorLoc: 1
Own: Private Company
Key: Michael Friedmann, Pres

Apparel Trimmings Inc.

20 Commander Blvd.
Toronto, ON M1S 3L9
Tel 416-298-6998
Fax 416-298-8802
Line: Specializes in manufacturing
woven edge label, elastic, webbing and
passementeries.
NAICS: 313210
#Emp: 100-249 (Tor)
#TorLoc: 1
Own: Private Company
Key: Francis Liu, Pres

Applanix Corp.

85 Leek Cres.
Richmond Hill, ON L4B 3B3
Tel 905-709-4600
Fax 905-709-6027
www.applanix.com
Line: Manufactures surveying
instruments.
NAICS: 334512 334511
#Emp: 100-249 (Tor)
Own: Public Company
Par: Trimble Navigation Ltd. (US)
Key: Steve Woolven, Pres
Blake Reid, Exec VP
Peter Teixera, Dir of Fin

Appleby College

540 Lakeshore Rd. West
Oakville, ON L6K 3P1
Tel 905-845-4681
Fax 905-845-9828
www.appleby.on.ca
Line: Operates private independent
school.
NAICS: 611110
#Emp: 100-249 (Tor)
#TorLoc: 1
Own: Not-for-profit
Key: Guy S. McLean, Principal
Katrina Samson, Head of School
Val Cambre, Vice Principal
　& Exec Dir HR
Kevin Pashuk, CIO
Michael O'Connor, Chief Mktg &
　Enrollment Officer

Apple Canada Inc.

7495 Birchmount Rd.
Markham, ON L3R 5G2
Tel 905-513-5800
Fax 905-513-6305
www.apple.ca
Line: Markets and sells
microcomputers.
NAICS: 334110 417310
#Emp: 75-99 (Tor)
#TorLoc: 1
Own: Public Company
Par: Apple Computer Inc. (US)
Key: John Hagias, Dir of Fin & Ops
Bethany Kopstick, HR Specialist

Apple Express Courier Ltd.

5300 Satellite Dr.
Mississauga, ON L4W 5J2
Tel 905-602-1225
Fax 905-602-9335
www.appleexpress.com
Line: Provides local and long distance
courier services.
NAICS: 492110
#Emp: 100-249 (Tor)
#TorLoc: 1
Own: Private Company
Key: Nasser Syed, Pres
Paul Campbell, GM

AppleOne Employment Services Ltd.

50 Paxman Rd.
Toronto, ON M9C 1B7
Tel 416-622-0100
Fax 416-622-6327
www.appleone.ca
AKA: BilingualOne; Accounting
Advantage
Line: Provides temporary and full-time
staffing services.
NAICS: 561320
#Emp: 100-249 (Tor)
#TorLoc: 33
Own: Private Company
Par: AppleOne, Inc. (US)
Key: Steven Gregg, Co-Pres
Gary Gregg, Co-Pres
Denise Gregg-Meneray, Dir of Ops
Louise Bom, Mgr of HR
Bimal Maraj, Cont
John Le, Network Admr

Applewood Air Conditioning Ltd.

3525 Hawkestone Rd.
Mississauga, ON L5C 2V1
Tel 905-275-4500
Fax 905-275-7756
www.applewoodair.com
Line: Specializes in residential,
industrial, and commercial heating
and air-conditioning contracting.
NAICS: 232520 232510
#Emp: 75-99 (Tor)
#TorLoc: 1
Own: Private Company
Key: George Gronwall, Pres
John Elinskey, VP Fin
Andy Giamos, VP Sales

Applewood Chevrolet Cadillac

A Div. of Applewood Holdings Inc.
3000 Woodchester Dr.
Mississauga, ON L5L 2R4
Tel 905-828-2221
Fax 905-828-2218
www.applewoodauto.com
Line: Sells, services and leases
automobiles.
NAICS: 441110 441120
#Emp: 100-249 (Tor)
#TorLoc: 1
Own: Private Company
Key: Lee Wittick, GM
Danny Blough, CFO
Brian Kalte, Mktg Mgr

APPS Transport Group

275 Orenda Rd.
Brampton, ON L6T 3T7
Tel 905-451-2720
Fax 905-451-2778
www.appsexpress.com
AKA: Apps Express Cartage Inc.; Apps
Cartage Inc.; Apps International; Apps
West Express
Line: Provides local and long distance
cartage services.
NAICS: 484229 484239
#Emp: 100-249 (Tor)
#TorLoc: 1
Own: Private Company
Par: APPS Cartage (CDA)
Key: Robert M. McDonald, Pres
Brent Byers, VP Ops
Ann Marie Papp, HR Mgr
Andrew Diu, Financial Cont
Paul Cloutier, IS Mgr
James Mitton, VP Sales
Lance Norman, VP
　Mktg & Business Dev

Aquicon Construction Co. Ltd.

131 Delta Park Blvd.
Brampton, ON L6T 5M8
Tel 905-458-1313
Fax 905-458-6020
www.aquicon.com
Line: Provides general contracting
services.
NAICS: 232990
#Emp: 75-99 (Tor)
#TorLoc: 1
Own: Private Company
Key: Frank Aquino, Principal
Mario Aquino, Principal
Rosa Zanuzzi, Cont

ARAMARK Canada Ltd.

811 Islington Ave.
Toronto, ON M8Z 5W8
Tel 416-255-1331
Fax 416-255-4706
www.aramark.ca
Line: Provides outsourced management
services including facility, office,
refreshment, and food services.
NAICS: 722310 561722 722210
#Emp: 1000-4999 (Tor)
#TorLoc: 220
Own: Private Company
Par: ARAMARK Corp. (US)
Key: Karen Wetselaar, VP Fin & CFO
Lynn Ervin, VP HR
Tom Forestall, VP Purch
Myra Vanderwoude, Corp VP Mktg

Arbor Memorial Services Inc.

2 Jane St.
Toronto, ON M6S 4W8
Tel 416-763-4531
Fax 416-763-8714
www.arbormemorial.com
Line: Provides interment rites,
cremations, funerals, and associated
merchandise and services across
Canada.
NAICS: 812220 812210
#Emp: 250-499 (Tor)
#TorLoc: 24
Own: Public Company
Key: Brian Snowdon, Pres & CEO
Michael J. Scanlan, VP Mktg & Ops
Maureen Carey, VP HR
Laurel Ancheta, VP Fin & CFO
David Scanlan, VP Sales & Chmn
Gary Carmichael, VP Gov't, Corp
    Affairs & Chief Privacy Officer

ArcelorMittal Tubular Products Canada Inc.

14 Holtby Ave.
Brampton, ON L6X 2M3
Tel 905-451-2400
Fax 905-874-5608
www.arcelormittal.com
NAICS: 336320
#Emp: 100-249 (Tor)
#TorLoc: 1
Own: Private Company
Key: Glenn Dumoulin, GM

Archdiocese of Toronto

1155 Yonge St.
Toronto, ON M4T 1W2
Tel 416-934-0606
Fax 416-934-3432
www.archtoronto.org
NAICS: 813110
#Emp: 500-999 (Tor)
#TorLoc: 1
Own: Religious
Par: The Roman Catholic Episcopal
Corp. for the Diocese of Toronto in
Canada
Key: Thomas Collins,
    Archbishop of Toronto
Marcel Goulet, Mgr of HR
William C. Dunlop, Comptr
David Finnegan, MIS Admr
Neil MacCarthy, Dir of Commun

Architectural Precast Systems Inc.

121 Bales Dr. East
P.O. Box 207
Newmarket, ON L3Y 4X1
Tel 905-853-7153
Fax 905-853-1139
www.architecturalprecast.com
Line: Manufactures and distributes pre-
cast concrete.
NAICS: 416390
#Emp: 100-249 (Tor)
#TorLoc: 1
Own: Private Company
Key: Antonio Santoro, Pres

Arc Productions Animation & Visual Effects

230 Richmond St. East, 2nd Fl.
Toronto, ON M5A 1P4
Tel 416-682-5200
Fax 416-682-5209
www.starzanimation.com
Line: Produces and develops CG
animation for feature films, TV and
short films.
NAICS: 512190
#Emp: 100-249 (Tor)
Own: Private Company
Par: Starz Entertainment (US)
Key: David Steinberg, Head of Studio
Terry Dale, Head of Ops
Sari Schwartz, Head of HR
Jeff Young, Head of Fin & Business Dev
Rob Burton, Head of Tech
Heather Kenyon, Head of Sales &
    Project Dev
Matthew Teevan, Head of Production

Arctic Glacier Inc.

200 Statesman Dr.
Mississauga, ON L5S 1X7
Tel 905-795-0100
Fax 905-795-0955
www.arcticglacierinc.com
Line: Produces, markets and distributes
packaged ice.
NAICS: 312110
#Emp: 100-249 (Tor)
#TorLoc: 1
Own: Private Company
Key: Keith McMahon, Pres & CEO
Roland Doiron, Reg Mgr, Ontario

ARI Financial Services Inc.

600-1270 Central Pkwy. West
Mississauga, ON L5C 4P4
Tel 905-803-8000
Fax 905-803-8644
www.arifleet.com
AKA: ARI Canada
Line: Operates an automotive fleet
leasing company.
NAICS: 532111 532112
#Emp: 100-249 (Tor)
#TorLoc: 1
Own: Private Company
Par: Holman Enterprises (US)
Key: Fred Booth, Pres
Chris Conroy, Sr VP Ops
Ben Clozza, HR & Facilities Mgr
John McMullin, Division Cont
Monique Powers, Purch Dept Head
Roy Gaysek, Exec VP Sales & Services

Arla Foods, Inc.

675 Rivermede Rd.
Concord, ON L4K 2G9
Tel 905-669-9676
Fax 905-669-5614
www.arlafoods.com
AKA: Tre Stelle; Rosenborg; Dofino &
Buko
Line: Manufactures and imports
specialty cheese products.
NAICS: 311515
#Emp: 100-249 (Tor)
#TorLoc: 1
Own: Private Company
Par: Arla Foods amba (DEN)
Key: Douglas Smith, Pres & CEO
Mette Norgaard, Supply Chain Dir
Laura Fineberg, Dir of HR
Jan N. Poulsen, CFO
Dennis Hingsberg, IT Mgr
Eric Elmhurst, Nat'l Sales Dir
Jens Kauffman,
    Chief Recruitment Officer

Armbro Transport Inc.

6050 Dixie Rd.
Mississauga, ON L5T 1A6
Tel 416-213-7298
Fax 905-670-9483
www.armbrotransport.com
Line: Provides general freight carrier
services.
NAICS: 484110 484121 484229
#Emp: 100-249 (Tor)
#TorLoc: 1
Own: Private Company
Key: Peter Di Tecco, Pres
Hugh Tharby, Dir of Ops
Clifford Burko, Cont
John King, Mgr of IT
Steve McGowan, VP Sales & Mktg

ARMTEC

35 Rutherford Rd. South
Brampton, ON L6W 3J4
Tel 905-457-4140
Fax 905-457-9991
www.armtec.com
Line: Manufactures pre-cast and pre-
stressed concrete products.
NAICS: 327390
#Emp: 100-249 (Tor)
#TorLoc: 1
Own: Public Company
Par: ARMTEC (CAN)
Key: Chuck Phillips, Pres & CEO
Paul Slosarcik, Ops Dir
Angelo Guglielmo, Dir of Fin & Reg Dir
Doug McChesney, Purch Mgr
Shane Sherar, Sales & Mktg Mgr

Arnold Worldwide

300-473 Adelaide St. West
Toronto, ON M5V 1T1
Tel 416-487-9393
Fax 416-920-5043
www.arnoldworldwide.ca
Line: Operates an advertising agency.
NAICS: 541810
#Emp: 100-249 (Tor)
#TorLoc: 1
Own: Private Company
Par: Havas Advertising (FR)
Key: Tom Blackmore, Pres
Bill Sharpe, Chmn
Thomas Olesinski, CFO
Rose Palombi, HR
Jeff Plowman, VP Mktg & Business Dev

Array Canada Inc.

45 Progress Ave.
Toronto, ON M1P 2Y6
Tel 416-299-4865
Fax 416-292-9759
www.arraymarketing.com
Line: Manufactures displays, wood
fixtures, merchandising solutions, and
retail environments.
NAICS: 337215
#Emp: 250-499 (Tor)
#TorLoc: 2
Own: Private Company
Par: Array Marketing Inc. (US)
Key: Tom Hendren, Pres & CEO
Kevin Pattrick, VP Fin & CFO
James Della Rossa, VP Creative

Arrow North American Electronics Components

171 Superior Blvd.
Mississauga, ON L5T 2L6
Tel 905-670-7790
Fax 905-565-4410
www.arrownac.com
Line: Sells electronic parts.
NAICS: 443110
#Emp: 100-249 (Tor)
#TorLoc: 1
Own: Private Company
Par: Arrow Electronics, Inc. (US)
Key: John MacCharles, GM,
Components

Art Gallery of Ontario

317 Dundas St. West
Toronto, ON M5T 1G4
Tel 416-977-0414
Fax 416-979-6646
www.ago.net
AKA: AGO
Line: Maintains an art gallery offering
educational and entertainment
services.
NAICS: 712111
#Emp: 500-999 (Tor)
#TorLoc: 1
Own: Not-for-profit
Key: Matthew Teitelbaum, Dir & CEO
Mike Mahoney, Exec Dir, Corp Special
    Projects & Dir of Ops
Deborah O'Leary, Dir of Staff &
    Volunteer Resources
Rocco Saverino, CFO
Sue Bloch-Nevitte,
    Exec Dir of Pub Affairs

Art Shoppe Limited

2131 Yonge St.
Toronto, ON M4S 2A7
Tel 416-487-3211
Fax 416-487-3221
www.theartshoppe.com
Line: Retails household furniture.
NAICS: 442110
#Emp: 75-99 (Tor)
#TorLoc: 1
Own: Private Company
Key: Martin Offman, Pres

ASA Alloys

*A Div. of Canadian Specialty
Metals U.L.C.*
81 Steinway Blvd.
Toronto, ON M9W 6H6
Tel 416-213-0000
Fax 416-213-9507
www.asaalloys.com
Line: Distributors of stainless steel and
aluminum.
NAICS: 416210
#Emp: 100-249 (Tor)
#TorLoc: 1
Own: Private Company
Key: Ward Seymour, Pres
Tom Campbell, Exec VP
Josie Lee, VP HR
Aqeel Siddiqui, Dir of Fin
Dennis Bishop, Branch Mgr

Asbury Building Services Inc.

323 Evans Ave.
Toronto, ON M8Z 1K2
Tel 416-620-5513
Fax 416-620-4420
www.asbury.ca
Line: Provides janitorial services.
NAICS: 531310
#Emp: 100-249 (Tor)
#TorLoc: 8
Own: Private Company
Key: Kevin Daley, Pres
Henry Picon, Dir of Ops
Arnie Gibbard, Dir of Sales & Mktg

ASC Signal Corp.

606 Beech St. West
P.O. Box 177
Whitby, ON L1N 5S2
Tel 905-668-3348
Fax 905-668-8590
www.ascsignal.com
Line: Manufactures air traffic and
weather radar antennas and pedestals,
high frequency communication and
direction finding antennas; distributes
microwave, wireless and ESA antenna
systems.
NAICS: 334220
#Emp: 75-99 (Tor)
#TorLoc: 1
Own: Private Company
Key: Keith Buckley, CEO
Tracy Brown, HR Mgr
Gordon Smith, Product Line Mgr

ASECO Integrated Systems Ltd.

16 635 Fourth Line
Oakville, ON L6L 5B3
Tel 905-339-0059
Fax 905-339-3857
www.aseco.net
Line: Specializes in engineering and
system integration consulting.
NAICS: 541330
#Emp: 75-99 (Tor)
#TorLoc: 1
Own: Private Company
Key: Brad Walker, Pres
Robert Peters, CEO
Jeff Peters, Exec Dir & CTO

Ash City

A Div. of G.H. Imported
Sales & Merchandise Ltd.
35 Orlando Ave.
Richmond Hill, ON L4B 0B4
Tel 905-787-2650
Fax 905-787-8701
www.ashcity.com
Line: Manufactures men's and ladies'
active wear for specialty advertising
and promotions.
NAICS: 315222
#Emp: 250-499 (Tor)
#TorLoc: 1
Own: Private Company
Key: Gary Hurvitz, Pres & CEO
David Woods, Mng Dir
Maria Ellis, HR Mgr
Michael Suen, CIO

Ashland Canada Corp.

525 Finley Ave.
Ajax, ON L1S 2E3
Tel 905-823-1800
Fax 905-823-5293
www.ashland.com
Line: Manufactures and distributes
organic and inorganic chemicals.
NAICS: 418410
#Emp: 100-249 (Tor)
#TorLoc: 3
Own: Private Company
Par: Ashland, Inc. (US)
Key: Sohail Khan, Plant Mgr

ASL Distribution Services Ltd.

2160 Buckingham Rd.
Oakville, ON L6H 6M7
Tel 905-829-5141
Fax 905-829-8988
www.asldistribution.com
Line: Provides international logistics
services including warehousing,
transportation and consulting.
NAICS: 493110 484229 484239
#Emp: 100-249 (Tor)
#TorLoc: 1
Own: Private Company
Key: Cole Dolny, Pres
Clem D' Alessandro, GM
Simone Stevenson, HR Supr
Sharon Kameka, MIS Mgr
Steve Mackenzie, Business Dev Mgr
Karen Hammel, VP Sales & Mktg

Aspen Ridge Homes Ltd.

29 Floral Pkwy.
Concord, ON L4K 5C5
Tel 905-669-9292
Fax 905-669-9297
www.aspenridgehomes.com
Line: Operates a home building
company.
NAICS: 231210
#Emp: 100-249 (Tor)
#TorLoc: 10
Own: Private Company
Key: Andrew DeGasperis, Pres

Assante Wealth Management

2 Queen St. East, 19th Fl.
Toronto, ON M5C 3G7
Tel 416-348-9994
Fax 416-681-7069
www.assante.com
Line: Provides financial advisory and
money management services.
NAICS: 541611
#Emp: 500-999 (Tor)
#TorLoc: 50
Own: Private Company
Par: Assante Corp. (CDA)
Key: Steven J. Donald, CEO
Robert Dorrell, Sr VP Ops
James E. Ross, Sr VP
    Wealth & Estate Planning
Tony Issa, Exec VP Tech

Associated Tube Industries

A Div. of Samuel Manu-Tech Inc.
7455 Woodbine Ave.
Markham, ON L3R 1A7
Tel 905-475-6464
Fax 905-475-5202
www.associatedtube.com
Line: Manufactures welded stainless
steel, nickel alloy and titanium pipes
and tubes.
NAICS: 331210
#Emp: 250-499 (Tor)
#TorLoc: 1
Own: Public Company
Key: Mark L. Winkler, Pres
Mike Hawkins, Dir of Ops
Jan Arsenault, Payroll & HR Mgr
Peter Neilas, VP Group Fin
John Sullivan, Dir of Materials
    Management
Paul Evers, Dir of Tech
Mark Kowall, Dir of Sales

Associated Youth Services of Peel

201-120 Matheson Blvd. East
Mississauga, ON L4Z 1X1
Tel 905-890-5222
Fax 905-890-5230
www.aysp.ca
Line: Provides assistance to adults, children, youth and their families who are, or are at risk of, experiencing serious social, emotional or behavioural difficulties.
NAICS: 624190
#Emp: 100-249 (Tor)
#TorLoc: 1
Own: Not-for-profit
Key: Kelly Henderson, Exec Dir
Anne Graham, HR
Nancy Russell,
    Systems & Evaluation Admr

Assurant Solutions

500-5160 Yonge St.
Toronto, ON M2N 7C7
Tel 416-733-3360
Fax 416-733-7826
www.assurant.com
Line: Develops, underwrites and markets specialty insurance, extended service contracts and other risk management solutions.
NAICS: 524299
#Emp: 75-99 (Tor)
#TorLoc: 1
Own: Public Company
Par: Assurant Solutions (US)
Key: Keith Demmings, Mng Dir
Shannon DeLenardo,
    Compliance Officer

Assured Packaging Inc.

6080 Vipond Dr.
Mississauga, ON L5T 2V4
Tel 905-565-1410
Fax 905-565-1420
www.assuredpackaging.com
Line: Manufactures aerosol and post-foaming gel products for personal care and cosmetics companies.
NAICS: 325999
#Emp: 100-249 (Tor)
#TorLoc: 1
Own: Private Company
Key: Ralph Webster, Pres
Brian Webster, CEO
Walter Drozdowsky, VP Fin & Admin
Dan Schnurr, VP Sales & Mktg

Astley Gilbert Limited

42 Carnforth Rd.
Toronto, ON M4A 2K7
Tel 416-288-8666
Fax 416-288-1706
www.astleygilbert.com
Line: Provides print solutions, Internet services, online collaboration tools and file transfer solutions.
NAICS: 323119 323115
#Emp: 100-249 (Tor)
#TorLoc: 7
Own: Private Company
Key: Wayne Wilbur, Pres & CEO
John Rozinger, HR Mgr

Astral Media Outdoor

2000-2 St. Clair Ave. West
Toronto, ON M4V 1L5
Tel 416-924-6664
Fax 416-924-9031
www.astralmediaoutdoor.com
Line: Operates an outdoor advertising company.
NAICS: 541850
#Emp: 75-99 (Tor)
#TorLoc: 1
Own: Public Company
Par: Astral Media Inc. (CDA)
Key: Sydney Greenberg, VP

Astral Media Radio

2 St. Clair Ave. West, 2nd Fl.
Toronto, ON M4V 1L6
Tel 416-922-9999
www.astralmedia.com
NAICS: 513110
#Emp: 100-249 (Tor)
#TorLoc: 1
Own: Private Company
Par: Astral Media Inc. (CDA)
Key: Ian Lurie, CFO
Isabell Mayrand, HR Mgr
Wally Lennox, Dir of Engineering
Bill Herz, VP Sales

Astral Television Networks

100-181 Bay St.
P.O. Box 787
Toronto, ON M5J 2T3
Tel 416-956-2010
Fax 416-956-2018
www.astral.com
AKA: The Movie Network
Line: Operates a network available in eastern Canada with access to movies, HBO and Showtime series, and Canadian programming.
NAICS: 513210 513220
#Emp: 100-249 (Tor)

#TorLoc: 1
Own: Private Company
Key: John Riley, Pres
Ian Greenberg, Pres & CEO, Astral
Kim Carter, VP HR
Robert Fortier, VP Fin
Domenic Vivolo, Sr VP Sales & Mktg
Deborah Wilson, VP Commun

AstraZeneca Canada Inc.

1004 Middlegate Rd.
Mississauga, ON L4Y 1M4
Tel 905-277-7111
Fax 905-270-3248
www.astrazeneca.ca
Line: Offers pharmaceutical product portfolio spanning six therapeutic areas.
NAICS: 325410
#Emp: 500-999 (Tor)
#TorLoc: 1
Own: Private Company
Par: AstraZeneca plc (UK)
Key: Marion McCourt, Pres & CEO
Karen Feltmate, VP Regulatory Affairs
Vince Rizzi, VP Fin & CFO
Mario Tremblay, VP Sales
William Charnetski,
    VP Corp Affairs & Gen Counsel

Athletes World

250-145 Renfrew Dr.
Markham, ON L3R 9R6
Tel 905-946-5500
Fax 905-946-5504
www.athletesworld.ca
Line: Sells athletic and non-athletic footwear as well as athletic apparel.
NAICS: 448210
#Emp: 100-249 (Tor)
#TorLoc: 12
Own: Private Company
Par: The Forzani Group Ltd. (CDA)
Key: Steve Bonyhadi, Dir of Store Ops
Nina Bhatt, HR Advisor

Atlantic Collision Group

6121 Atlantic Dr.
Mississauga, ON L5T 1N7
Tel 905-564-7072
Fax 905-564-7321
www.atlanticautobody.ca
Line: Operates an automobile repair shop.
NAICS: 811121
#Emp: 75-99 (Tor)
#TorLoc: 15
Own: Private Company
Key: Argante Tolfa, Shop Mgr

Atlantic Packaging Products Ltd.

111 Progress Ave.
Toronto, ON M1P 2Y9
Tel 416-298-8101
Fax 416-297-2218
www.atlantic.ca
Line: Manufactures paper and plastic bags, corrugated cartons, liner-board, tissues, and newsprint.
NAICS: 322121 322122 322220
#Emp: 1000-4999 (Tor)
#TorLoc: 9
Own: Private Company
Key: John Cherry, Pres
Irving Granovsky, CEO
Fred Marcon, VP HR
Paul Doyle, VP Fin & Admin

Atlantis Pavilions

955 Lake Shore Blvd. West
Toronto, ON M6K 3B9
Tel 416-260-8000
Fax 416-260-0552
www.atlantispavilions.com
NAICS: 711311
#Emp: 100-249 (Tor)
#TorLoc: 1
Own: Private Company
Par: Dynamic Hospitality & Entertainment Group (CDA)
Key: Sam D'Uva, Pres
Fred Ng, Sr Acct
Sheron Darling, Sr Acct

Atlantis Systems International Inc.

1 Kenview Blvd.
Brampton, ON L6T 5E6
Tel 905-792-1981
Fax 905-792-7251
www.atlantissi.com
Line: Provides integrated training solutions and manufactures flight simulators, maintenance trainers and crew trainers for military and commercial applications.
NAICS: 333310 336410
#Emp: 75-99 (Tor)
#TorLoc: 1
Own: Public Company
Par: Atlantis System Corp. (CDA)
Key: Henrik Noesgaard, Pres
Zelia Morton, HR Mgr
Chris Lewis, Corp Cont

Atlas-Apex Roofing Inc.

65 Disco Rd.
Toronto, ON M9W 1M2
Tel 416-421-6244
Fax 416-421-1661
www.atlas-apex.com
Line: Operates a roofing and sheet metal contracting business.
NAICS: 232330
#Emp: 100-249 (Tor)
#TorLoc: 1
Own: Private Company
Key: John Petrachek, Pres & GM
Steve Murray, VP Ops
Brenda Dickson, Cont
Mark Bevington, Business Dev Mgr

Atlas Bearings Inc.

8045 Dixie Rd.
Brampton, ON L6T 3V1
Tel 905-790-0283
Fax 905-790-1996
www.truth.com
AKA: Truth Hardware
Line: Manufactures hardware for the window and door industry.
NAICS: 332510
#Emp: 75-99 (Tor)
#TorLoc: 1
Own: Public Company
Par: Truth Hardware (US)
Key: Valentino Scorcia, GM
Angela Tantone, HR Generalist
Arthur Bray, Cont
Scott McNair, Outside Sales

The Atlas Corp.

111 Ortona Crt.
Concord, ON L4K 3M3
Tel 905-669-6825
Fax 905-669-8288
www.atlascorp.com
Line: Operates a construction company.
NAICS: 231220
#Emp: 100-249 (Tor)
#TorLoc: 1
Own: Private Company
Key: Andrew Famiglietti, Pres & CEO
Lee Curto, VP Ops
Frank Montesanti, VP Fin

Atlas Paper Bag Co. Ltd.

90 Dynamic Dr.
Toronto, ON M1V 2V1
Tel 416-293-2125
Fax 416-293-2369
www.atlaspaperbag.com
Line: Manufactures paper bags.
NAICS: 322220
#Emp: 100-249 (Tor)
#TorLoc: 1
Own: Private Company
Key: Charles Provvidenza, Pres
Joanne Santacroce, Office Mgr

Atlas Van Lines (Canada) Ltd.

485 North Service Rd. East
Oakville, ON L6J 5M7
Tel 905-844-0701
Fax 905-844-7236
www.atlasvanlines.ca
AKA: Atlas Canada
Line: Provides household, commercial and logistic transportation services.
NAICS: 484210
#Emp: 100-249 (Tor)
Own: Private Company
Par: Atlas World Group (US)
Key: Robert J. Clark, Pres & COO
Dave Coughlin, VP Ops
Shirley Sveda, Sr VP Fin & CFO
Tom Marquis, Mgr of IS
Carol Davis, VP Mktg & Commun

Atomic Energy of Canada Ltd.

2251 Speakman Dr.
Mississauga, ON L5K 1B2
Tel 905-823-9040
Fax 905-823-1290
www.aecl.ca
AKA: AECL; CANDU
Line: Provides research and development support, design, engineering, construction management, specialized technology, refurbishment, waste management and decommissioning in support of CANDU reactor products and nuclear utilities.
NAICS: 335311 332410
#Emp: 1000-4999 (Tor)
#TorLoc: 1
Own: Federal Crown Corp.
Key: Hugh MacDiarmid, Pres & CEO
Beth M. Medhurst, Sr VP HR
Kent Harris, Sr VP & CFO
Anthony De Vuono, CTO
George Bothwell, Sr VP
   External Relns & Commun

Atripco Delivery Service

34 Canmotor Ave.
Toronto, ON M8Z 4E5
Tel 416-252-7721
Fax 416-252-1039
www.atripco.net
AKA: Gopher Express Delivery Ltd.;
Kendrew Distribution Services; Kimit
Transportation Logistics; Kirlin
Leasing
Line: Provides courier services.
NAICS: 492110 488990
#Emp: 250-499 (Tor)
#TorLoc: 3
Own: Private Company
Par: Trailmaster Freight Carriers Ltd.
(CDA)
Key: J. Ivan Service, Pres
Lloyd Service, VP Ops
Lindsay Service, Corp HR Mgr
Greg Service, VP Fin
Keith Carter, IT Mgr
Terry Buchkowsky, Business Dev Mgr

ATS Andlauer Transportation Services LP

96 Disco Rd.
Toronto, ON M9W 0A3
Tel 416-679-7979
Fax 416-679-7845
www.atsretailsolutions.ca
AKA: ATS Toronto
Line: Provides transportation and
express package delivery services.
NAICS: 488990 492110
#Emp: 100-249 (Tor)
#TorLoc: 3
Own: Private Company
Par: AMG Inc. (CDA)
Key: Bob Brogan, Sr Exec VP
Michael Andlauer, Pres
Michel Lunardi, Exec VP Ops
Kim Rizzo, Mgr of HR
Brian Mascarenhas, CFO
Jamie Doyle, Dir of Admin

Attridge Transportation Inc.

5439 Harvester Rd.
Burlington, ON L7L 5J7
Tel 905-333-4047
Fax 905-333-3866
www.attridge.com
Line: Provides transportation services
to private and public school boards.
NAICS: 485410
#Emp: 75-99 (Tor)
#TorLoc: 3
Own: Private Company
Key: Jim Attridge, Owner
Glenn Attridge, VP

Aurora Resthaven

*A Div. of Chartwell Seniors
Housing REIT*
32 Mill St.
Aurora, ON L4G 2R9
Tel 905-727-1939
Fax 905-727-6299
www.chartwellreit.ca
Line: Operates a nursing and
retirement home.
NAICS: 623110
#Emp: 250-499 (Tor)
#TorLoc: 1
Own: Private Company
Key: Brent Binions,
    Vice Chair & Pres, Chartwell
Steve Keery, Admr

Autodesk Canada

210 King St. East
Toronto, ON M5A 1J7
Tel 416-362-9181
Fax 416-369-6140
www.autodesk.com
AKA: ADSK Canada Inc.
Line: Develops software for digital
media creation and provides strategic
technology for the entertainment,
product design and graphic design
markets.
NAICS: 541430 541490 541510
#Emp: 100-249 (Tor)
#TorLoc: 1
Own: Private Company
Par: Autodesk (US)
Key: Al Steel, Pres

Autoliv Electronics Canada Inc.

7455 Birchmount Rd.
Markham, ON L3R 5C2
Tel 905-475-8510
Fax 905-474-4511
www.autoliv.com
Line: Manufactures automotive
electronics.
NAICS: 334110
#Emp: 250-499 (Tor)
#TorLoc: 1
Own: Private Company
Par: Autoliv (SWE)
Key: Steve Brohm, GM
Fabio Zoia, New Product & Process
    Introduction Mgr
Paul Tucker, HR Mgr
Lori Valentini, Dir of Fin

Automodular Corporation

6-235 Salem Rd.
Ajax, ON L1Z 0B1
Tel 905-619-4200
Fax 905-619-9466
www.automodular.com
Line: Manufactures automotive parts.
NAICS: 336390
#Emp: 500-999 (Tor)
#TorLoc: 3
Own: Public Company
Par: Automodular Assemblier Corp.
(CDA)
Key: Michael Blair, Pres & CEO
Jim Gazo, VP Ops
John L. DeSouza, Dir of HR
Chris Nutt, VP Fin

Auto Warehousing Co. Canada

1150 Stevenson Rd. South
P.O. Box 860
Oshawa, ON L1H 7N1
Tel 905-725-6549
Fax 905-725-0120
www.autowc.com
Line: Provides new automobile
transportation and short-term storage
services.
NAICS: 484239 493190
#Emp: 250-499 (Tor)
#TorLoc: 1
Own: Private Company
Key: Steve Seher, Pres & CEO
Brian Taylor, VP, Oshawa
Mike Novosedlik, Reg HR Mgr
Belinda Woodford, Division Cont

Avalon Retirement Centre

355 Broadway
Orangeville, ON L9W 3Y3
Tel 519-941-5161
Fax 519-941-9532
www.jarlettehealthservices.com
AKA: 488491 Ontario Inc.; Avalon
Retirement Lodge; Avalon Care Centre
Line: Operates a nursing home and
retirement lodge.
NAICS: 623110 623310
#Emp: 100-249 (Tor)
#TorLoc: 1
Own: Private Company
Par: Jarlette Health Services (CDA)
Key: Chan Sooklal, Admr
Debbie Rydall, GM, Avalon Lodge
Julie Bottomley, Office Mgr

Avanade Canada Inc.

400-5450 Explorer Dr.
Mississauga, ON L4W 5M1
Tel 416-647-2800
Fax 416-641-5671
www.avanade.com/ca
Line: Provides consulting services for technology integration.
NAICS: 541510
#Emp: 75-99 (Tor)
Own: Public Company
Key: Howard Kilman,
Exec VP & Pres of Americas

Avant Imaging & Information Management Inc.

205 Industrial Pkwy. North
Aurora, ON L4G 4C4
Tel 905-841-6444
Fax 905-841-2177
www.aiim.com
AKA: AIIM Inc.
Line: Provides offset and digital printing, lettershop and direct mail inserting, and mailing fulfillment.
NAICS: 323115
#Emp: 100-249 (Tor)
#TorLoc: 1
Own: Private Company
Key: Frank Giorgio, Pres
Mario Giorgio, Chmn & CEO
Anil Sadekar, Exec VP
Tony Vario, VP
Emilio Ciampini, VP Sales & Mktg

Avis Budget Group Inc.

1 Convair Dr. East
Toronto, ON M9W 6Z9
Tel 416-213-8400
Fax 416-213-8505
www.avis.com
AKA: AvisBudget
Line: Provides automobile and truck rental services.
NAICS: 532111
#Emp: 1000-4999 (Tor)
#TorLoc: 22
Own: Private Company
Key: William Boxberger, VP & GM
Russell Evans, Toronto City Mgr

Aviva

1330 Courtneypark Dr.
Mississauga, ON L5T 1K5
Tel 905-670-1351
Fax 905-670-6097
www.avivanow.com
Line: Distributes and wholesales fine paper products.
NAICS: 418210

#Emp: 100-249 (Tor)
#TorLoc: 1
Own: Public Company
Par: Domtar Inc. (CDA)
Key: Gerry Gray, VP Cdn Region
Paul Berdusco, Reg Dist Mgr
Shiraz Hassanali, Dir of Fin
Mary Mitar, Purch Mng Business
    Optimizing Mgr
Diane Yuhasz, Mgr of IT
Michael Morten, Mktg Mgr

Aviva Canada Inc.

160-2206 Eglinton Ave. East
Toronto, ON M1L 4S8
Tel 416-288-1800
Fax 416-288-9756
www.avivacanada.com
Line: Provides property and casualty insurance.
NAICS: 524121
#Emp: 1000-4999 (Tor)
Own: Public Company
Par: Aviva plc (UK)
Key: Maurice Tulloch, Pres & CEO
James Russell, Exec VP Chief
    Underwriting Officer
Esther Winter, Sr VP HR
Jim Falle, Exec VP & CFO
Robert Merizzi, Exec VP Tech & COO
Jim Haskins, Exec VP Claims

A-Way Express Courier Service

2168 Danforth Ave.
Toronto, ON M4C 1K3
Tel 416-424-2266
Fax 416-424-4528
www.awaycourier.ca
Line: Operates a non-profit courier service.
NAICS: 492210
#Emp: 75-99 (Tor)
#TorLoc: 1
Own: Not-for-profit
Key: Laurie Hall, Exec Dir
Graeme Cushing, Office Mgr
Mary Sharp, Personnel Mgr
George Karrandjas, Bookkeeper
Tim Maxwell, Mktg Mgr

AXA Insurance (Canada)

1400-5700 Yonge St.
Toronto, ON M2M 4K2
Tel 416-250-1992
Fax 416-250-5833
www.axa.ca
Line: Provides property and casualty insurance.
NAICS: 524121
#Emp: 250-499 (Tor)

#TorLoc: 1
Own: Private Company
Par: AXA Group (FR)
Key: Mathieu Lamy, Exec VP
Scott Campbell, VP Personal Lines
Andrea Chan, HR Mgr
Joseph Fung, Sr VP Fin & Admin
Bill Davis, VP Sales & Mktg

Axiom Group Inc.

115 Mary St.
Aurora, ON L4G 1G3
Tel 905-727-2878
Fax 905-727-2235
www.axiomgroup.ca
NAICS: 326198
#Emp: 75-99 (Tor)
#TorLoc: 1
Own: Private Company
Key: Perry Rizzo, Pres
Brenda Zimmerman,
    Payroll & Benefits Admr
Majid Sharifi, Cont

AxiSource Inc.

45 Commander Blvd.
Toronto, ON M1S 3Y3
Tel 416-291-7151
Fax 416-291-6410
www.officedepot.ca
Line: Sells computer technology products and computer supplies.
NAICS: 417310 334110
#Emp: 75-99 (Tor)
#TorLoc: 1
Own: Private Company
Key: John Arnott, Dir of Global Sales
Betty Saunders, Dir of HR
Jose Lima, IT Mgr

AXYZ Automation Inc.

5330 South Service Rd.
Burlington, ON L7L 5L1
Tel 905-634-4940
Fax 905-634-4966
www.axyz.com
Line: Manufactures, sells and services CNC router solutions.
NAICS: 541510
#Emp: 75-99 (Tor)
#TorLoc: 1
Own: Private Company
Par: Camtec International (CDA)
Key: Gary Harvey, Reg Mgr
Ellen Hutchings, HR Mgr
Ismar Spanja, Purch Mgr
Greg Jenkins, Mktg & Commun Mgr

AYA Kitchens and Baths, Ltd.

1551 Caterpillar Rd.
Mississauga, ON L4X 2Z6
Tel 905-848-1999
Fax 905-848-5127
www.ayakitchens.com
Line: Manufactures cabinetry for kitchens and bathrooms.
NAICS: 232460
#Emp: 100-249 (Tor)
#TorLoc: 3
Own: Private Company
Key: Dave Marcus, Pres & Owner
Noel Santos, Dir of Manuf & Ops
Nancy Branco, HR Mgr
Warren Hsu, CFO
Hugh Wahab, Dir of Sales

AZ3 Enterprises Inc.

127 Delta Park Blvd.
Brampton, ON L6T 5M8
Tel 905-793-7793
Fax 905 793-0780
www.az3.com
AKA: Azimuth 3 Enterprises
Line: Manufactures steel.
NAICS: 231390
#Emp: 75-99 (Tor)
#TorLoc: 1
Own: Private Company
Key: Pino Tarabelli, Pres
Jean Diab, VP Ops
George Achkar, Financial Cont

B2B Trust

130 Adelaide St. West
Toronto, ON M5H 3P5
Tel 416-947-5100
Fax 416-865-5667
www.b2b-trust.com
Line: Offers services to non-bank partners who offer private label banking products and other financial services.
NAICS: 522112
#Emp: 250-499 (Tor)
#TorLoc: 1
Own: Public Company
Par: Laurentian Bank of Canada (CDA)
Key: Francois Desjardins, Pres & CEO
Doris Tourkoyiannis, VP Ops
Eva Stamadianos, VP HR
Diane Lafresnaye, VP Fin
Louise Bergeron,
   VP Business Solutions
Al Spadaro, VP Business Dev
Susi McCord, VP Mktg

Bacardi Canada Inc.

1000 Steeles Ave. East
Brampton, ON L6T 1A1
Tel 905-451-6100
Fax 905-451-6753
www.bacardi.ca
Line: Manufactures beverage alcohol.
NAICS: 312140
#Emp: 100-249 (Tor)
#TorLoc: 1
Own: Private Company
Par: Bacardi Holdings Ltd. (NETH)
Key: Rich Andrews, VP
Paul Beggan, Pres
Gary LeBlanc, VP Ops
Craig Bradshaw, VP HR
Lisa Smith, VP Fin
Rob McPherson, VP Mktg

Backerhaus Veit Ltd.

70 Whitmore Rd.
Woodbridge, ON L4L 7Z4
Tel 905-850-9229
Fax 905-850-9292
www.backerhausveit.com
Line: Manufactures frozen Artisan European bread and buns.
NAICS: 311814
#Emp: 100-249 (Tor)
#TorLoc: 1
Own: Private Company
Key: Sabine Veit, Pres
Siegfried Heilemann, Ops Mgr
Teresa Rosa, HR Mgr
Farhad Pochkhanawala, CFO
Rahul Mishra, IT Mgr
Michael Hall, Dir of Cdn Sales
Tobias Donath, VP Sales, USA

The Badminton & Racquet Club of Toronto

25 St. Clair Ave. West
Toronto, ON M4V 1K6
Tel 416-921-2159
Fax 416-921-4368
www.thebandr.com
Line: Provides sports, recreation and dining services.
NAICS: 713940
#Emp: 100-249 (Tor)
#TorLoc: 1
Own: Not-for-profit
Key: Cathy Bolla, GM
Wade Sit, Dir of Ops
Connie Bolarinho,
   Exec Office Mgr & HR
Nabih Youssef, Dir of Fin
Maria Dos Santos, Dir of Membership

Bailey Metal Products Ltd.

1 Caldari Rd.
Concord, ON L4K 3Z9
Tel 905-738-6738
Fax 905-738-5712
www.bmp-group.com
Line: Manufactures metal products.
NAICS: 332999 416210
#Emp: 100-249 (Tor)
#TorLoc: 2
Own: Private Company
Par: Bailey-Hunt Ltd. (CDA)
Key: Angelo Sarracini, Pres
David Hunt, Chmn
Maria Cavarretta, HR Mgr

Baird MacGregor Insurance Brokers LP

825 Queen St. East
Toronto, ON M4M 1H8
Tel 416-778-8000
Fax 416-778-4492
www.bairdmacgregor.com
Line: Operates an insurance company.
NAICS: 524210
#Emp: 75-99 (Tor)
#TorLoc: 1
Own: Private Company
Key: Philomena Comerford, Pres & CEO
Cindy Duncan, VP HR

Baka Communications Inc.

630 The East Mall
Toronto, ON M9B 4B1
Tel 416-641-2800
Fax 416-640-2700
www.baka.ca
AKA: Baka Wireless
Line: Offers wireless communication products and services.
NAICS: 417320
#Emp: 75-99 (Tor)
#TorLoc: 12
Own: Private Company
Key: John Marion, Pres
Anne Camastra, Mgr of HR, Ops & Mktg
Susan Subject, Cont
Ronald Lefebvre, Inventory Mgr
Derek Mullin, IT Mgr
Charlene Killbeck, Mktg Mgr

Baker & McKenzie LLP

2100-181 Bay St.
Brookfield Pl., P.O. Box 874
Toronto, ON M5J 2T3
Tel 416-863-1221
Fax 416-863-6275
www.bakernet.com
Line: Operates a law firm that provides legal advice and services to global organizations.
NAICS: 541110
#Emp: 100-249 (Tor)
#TorLoc: 1
Own: Partnership
Key: Jim Holloway, Mng Partner
Brian D. Segal, Financial Partner
Harriet Giannoukos, Mktg Dir

Ballycliffe Lodge

70 Station St.
Ajax, ON L1S 1R9
Tel 905-683-7321
Fax 905-427-5846
www.chartwellreit.ca
Line: Provides nursing and retirement home services.
NAICS: 623110
#Emp: 100-249 (Tor)
#TorLoc: 1
Own: Public Company
Par: Chartwell Seniors Housing REIT (CDA)
Key: W. Brent Binions, Pres & CEO
Richard Noonan, COO
Karen Sullivan, Exec VP People
Vlad Volodarski, CFO
Phil McKenzie, Mktg & PR

Bank of America National Association/Canada Branch

2700-200 Front St. West
Toronto, ON M5V 3L2
Tel 416-349-4100
Fax 416-349-4294
www.bankofamerica.com
Line: Provides corporate banking services.
NAICS: 522112
#Emp: 100-249 (Tor)
#TorLoc: 4
Own: Private Company
Par: Bank of America N.A. (US)
Key: Sophia Ngai, VP
Louise DeCaire, Sr VP & CFO

Bank of Canada

2000-150 King St. West
Toronto, ON M5H 1J9
Tel 416-542-1334
Fax 416-542-1350
www.bankofcanada.ca
Line: Operates Canada's central bank.
NAICS: 521110
#Emp: 100-249 (Tor)
#TorLoc: 1
Own: Government
Key: Marc Carney, Governor

Bank of Nova Scotia

44 King St. West
Toronto, ON M5H 1H1
Tel 416-866-6161
Fax 416-866-3750
www.scotiabank.com
AKA: Scotiabank
Line: Provides financial products and services to individuals, small and medium-size businesses, corporations and governments.
NAICS: 522111 522112
#Emp: 10000+ (Tor)
#TorLoc: 210
Own: Public Company
Key: Richard E. Waugh, Pres & CEO
Sarabjit S. Marwah, Vice Chmn & COO
Sylvia D. Chrominska, Group Head, Global HR & Commun
Luc Vanneste, Exec VP & CFO
Kimberlee McKenzie, Exec VP IT and Solutions
Anatol Von Hahn, Group Head, Cdn Banking

Bard Canada Inc.

1-2715 Bristol Circ.
Oakville, ON L6H 6X5
Tel 289-291-8000
Fax 800-631-2109
www.crbard.com
NAICS: 339110
#Emp: 100-249 (Tor)
#TorLoc: 1
Own: Private Company
Par: C.R. Bard Inc. (US)
Key: John Kondrosky, VP & GM

The Bargain! Shop Holdings Inc.

3-6877 Goreway Dr.
Mississauga, ON L4V 1L9
Tel 905-293-9700
Fax 905-293-7676
www.tbsstores.com
Line: Operates a discount retail store.
NAICS: 452999
#Emp: 100-249 (Tor)

#TorLoc: 9
Own: Private Company
Key: Michael Roellinghoff, Pres & CEO
Kim Vogel, VP Ops
Tracey Mikita, VP HR
Clinton Wolff, VP & CFO

Baron Metal Industries Inc.

101 Ashbridge Circ.
Woodbridge, ON L4L 3R5
Tel 416-749-2111
Fax 905-851-8346
www.baronmetal.com
AKA: Assa Abloy Door Group Inc.
Line: Manufactures steel doors and frames.
NAICS: 332321
#Emp: 100-249 (Tor)
#TorLoc: 1
Own: Public Company
Par: Assa Abloy (SWE)
Key: Steve Everitt, Dir of Ops

Barrick Gold Corp.

3700-161 Bay St., P.O. Box 212
BCE Pl., Canada Trust Tower
Toronto, ON M5J 2S1
Tel 416-861-9911
Fax 416-861-2492
www.barrick.com
Line: Operates a mining company.
NAICS: 212220
#Emp: 250-499 (Tor)
#TorLoc: 2
Own: Public Company
Key: Aaron Regent, Pres & CEO
Peter Kinver, Exec VP & COO
Chad Hiley, VP HR
Jamie Sokalsky, Exec VP & CFO
David Jamieson, VP Info Management & Tech
Vincent Borg, Exec VP, Corp Commun

Barrymore Furniture Co.

1168 Caledonia Rd.
Toronto, ON M6A 2W5
Tel 416-532-2891
Fax 416-533-6650
www.barrymorefurniture.com
NAICS: 337121
#Emp: 100-249 (Tor)
#TorLoc: 1
Own: Private Company
Key: Tom Callahan, Pres
Linda DaSilva, VP Ops
Brian Callahan, Sr VP

BASF Canada

100 Milverton Dr., 5th Fl.
Mississauga, ON L5R 4H1
Tel 289-360-1300
Fax 289-360-6000
www.basf.ca
Line: Manufactures and distributes chemicals, colourants, nylon fibres, polymers, urethane chemicals and systems, plastics, automotive and industrial refinish coatings, construction chemicals and agricultural and nutritional products.
NAICS: 325510 325999 325220
#Emp: 100-249 (Tor)
#TorLoc: 2
Own: Private Company
Par: BASF SE (GER)
Key: Laurent Tianturier, Pres
Francois Paroyan,
    Dir of HR & Gen Counsel
Marc Muff,
    Dir of Fin & Business Services
Darrin Robinson, IS Mgr
Kerry Bowman, Sales & Mktg Mgr
Martine G. Despatie, Commun Mgr

Bass Building Maintenance Ltd.

1233 Aerowood Dr.
Mississauga, ON L4W 1B9
Tel 905-629-2277
Fax 905-629-8237
Line: Provides carpet cleaning and janitorial services.
NAICS: 561722
#Emp: 100-249 (Tor)
#TorLoc: 1
Own: Private Company
Key: Hans Kuehlein, Pres
Michael Hagner, Ops Mgr

Bauer Hockey Corp.

6660A Millcreek Dr.
Mississauga, ON L5N 8B3
Tel 905-363-3200
Fax 905-363-3201
www.bauer.com
Line: Develops, markets and sells hockey skates, sticks, off-ice skates, protective goalie equipment and apparel.
NAICS: 414470
#Emp: 100-249 (Tor)
#TorLoc: 1
Own: Private Company
Key: Bryan McDermott,
    Cdn Business Dir
Lorraine Banton, Dir of HR, Canada
Fred Ciufo, Dir of Sales
Darryl Hughes, Dir of Mktg

Baxter Corp.

700-4 Robert Speck Pkwy.
Mississauga, ON L4Z 3Y4
Tel 905-270-1125
Fax 905-281-6560
www.baxter.ca
Line: Operates a global medical products and services company that provides critical therapies for people with life-threatening conditions.
NAICS: 325410
#Emp: 250-499 (Tor)
#TorLoc: 3
Own: Private Company
Par: Baxter International Inc. (US)
Key: Barbara Leavitt, Pres
Paul De Swef, VP Business Ops
Ann Marie Mercer, Dir of HR

Baycrest Geriatric Health System

3560 Bathurst St.
Toronto, ON M6A 2E1
Tel 416-785-2500
Fax 416-785-2378
www.baycrest.org
Line: Provides in-home, community-based and institutional services for the elderly.
NAICS: 623310
#Emp: 1000-4999 (Tor)
#TorLoc: 1
Own: Not-for-profit
Key: William Reichman, Pres & CEO
David Conn, VP Medical Services
Joni Kent, VP HR & Organizational
    Effectiveness
Laurie A. Harrison, VP Fin & Admin
Mark Gryse, Pres, Baycrest Foundation
Nancy Webb, VP Pub Affairs &
    Stakeholder Relns

Bayer Inc.

77 Belfield Rd.
Toronto, ON M9W 1G6
Tel 416-248-0771
Fax 416-248-6762
www.bayer.ca
Line: Manufactures and markets pharmaceuticals, medical diagnostics, industrial chemicals, and agricultural products.
NAICS: 325410
#Emp: 500-999 (Tor)
#TorLoc: 1
Own: Private Company
Par: Bayer AG (GER)
Key: Phillip Blake, Pres & CEO
Gord Johnson, VP & Head of HR
Ute Bockstegers, CFO & Head of
    Business Admin

Baylis Medical Company Inc.

2645 Matheson Blvd. East
Mississauga, ON L4W 5S4
Tel 905-602-4875
Fax 905-602-5671
www.baylismedical.com
Line: Supplies high-technology cardiology, pain management, and radiology products.
NAICS: 417930
#Emp: 75-99 (Tor)
#TorLoc: 1
Own: Private Company
Key: Frank Baylis, Pres
Kris Shah, VP
Leo Pasia, HR Mgr
Malcolm Bullock, Cont

Bayshore Home Health

10-2155 Dunwin Dr.
Mississauga, ON L5L 4M1
Tel 905-822-8075
Fax 905-822-8397
www.bayshore.ca
Line: Provides health care services including nursing, home support, dialysis and pain therapy.
NAICS: 624120 621390
#Emp: 250-499 (Tor)
#TorLoc: 4
Own: Private Company
Key: Stuart Cottrelle, Pres
Kevin Webster, Mng Dir of Home Care
Barbara Ulakovic, HR Generalist
Michael Deadman, CFO
Leigh Popov, Dir of IT
Mike Krunic, Nat'l Mktg Mgr

Bayview Glen

275 Duncan Mill Rd.
Toronto, ON M3B 3H9
Tel 416-443-1030
Fax 416-443-1032
www.bayviewglen.ca
Line: Operates a private co-educational school.
NAICS: 611110
#Emp: 100-249 (Tor)
#TorLoc: 3
Own: Not-for-profit
Par: Moatfield Foundation (CDA)
Key: Eileen Daunt, Head of School
Nneka MacGregor, Chair
Judy Maxwell, Dir of Admissions
Amy Fernandez, Asst to Head of School
Vince Haines, Dir of Fin

Bayview Golf & Country Club

25 Fairway Heights Dr.
Thornhill, ON L3T 3X1
Tel 905-889-4833
www.bayviewclub.com
Line: Operates a private family club
offering year-round golf, tennis,
curling, swimming, fitness and banquet
facilities for weddings, business
meetings and special occasions.
NAICS: 713910
#Emp: 100-249 (Tor)
#TorLoc: 1
Own: Private Company
Key: Joseph Coleman, GM
Sondi Lance, Cont & Office Mgr

BBDO Canada Inc.

2 Bloor St. West, 29th Fl.
Toronto, ON M4W 3R6
Tel 416-972-1505
Fax 416-972-5656
www.bbdo.ca
Line: Provides advertising services
specializing in business-to-business,
public relations, sales promotion,
direct response, interactive, event
marketing, account planning, and
research.
NAICS: 541810
#Emp: 250-499 (Tor)
#TorLoc: 1
Own: Private Company
Par: Omnicom Services (CDA)
Key: Gerry Frascione, Pres & CEO
Philip Filippopoulos, Exec VP & CFO
Siobhan McCarthy, SR VP,
    Dir of Organizational Dev

BBM Canada

305-1500 Don Mills Rd.
Toronto, ON M3B 3L7
Tel 416-445-9800
Fax 416-445-8644
www.bbm.ca
Line: Specializes in radio and television
audience research.
NAICS: 541910
#Emp: 100-249 (Tor)
#TorLoc: 1
Own: Not-for-profit
Key: Jim MacLeod, Pres & CEO
Dorena Noce, VP Corp Services
Vita DiSerio, Dir of HR
Glen Shipp, Exec VP & CFO
Tom Saint, CIO

B.C. Instruments

A Div. of B.C. Precision Machining Inc.
41 Proctor Rd.
Schomberg, ON L0G 1T0
Tel 905-939-7323
Fax 905-939-8206
www.bc-instruments.com
Line: Manufactures precision machined
components and assemblies.
NAICS: 333990
#Emp: 100-249 (Tor)
#TorLoc: 1
Own: Private Company
Key: Roger Conzelmann, Pres
Marilyn McCormack, HR & Safety Mgr
Bob Goss, Contoller

BDI World Class World Wide

6235 Tomken Rd.
Mississauga, ON L5T 1K2
Tel 905-238-3392
Fax 905-238-1395
www.bdi-canada.com
AKA: Kenscott; PBN; PMC; Norcan;
Industrial Motion; HPPDL
Line: Distributes bearings, power
transmission and fluid power products,
lubricants and adhesives, and
industrial supplies.
NAICS: 417230
#Emp: 100-249 (Tor)
#TorLoc: 7
Own: Private Company
Par: Bearing Distributors, Inc. (US)
Key: Cameron Lawrence, Pres
Paula Cowie, HR Mgr
Ted Chisholm, VP Fin
Christine Ellstrom, Mktg Mgr

BDO Canada LLP

600-36 Toronto St.
P.O. Box 32
Toronto, ON M5C 2C5
Tel 416-865-0111
Fax 416-367-3912
www.bdo.ca
Line: Provides accounting, auditing,
taxation, bookkeeping, insolvency,
bankruptcy, forensic accounting,
mergers and acquisitions, corporate
finance, business valuations, transfer
pricing, and litigation support services.
NAICS: 541212 541611
#Emp: 250-499 (Tor)
#TorLoc: 5
Own: Private Company
Key: J. Keith Farlinger, CEO
Russ Weir, COO
Emree Siaroff, Mng Dir, Human Capital
Ron Watts, CFO
Kim Watt, Dir of IT

Beacon Transit Lines Inc.

11 Blair Dr.
Brampton, ON L6T 2H4
Tel 416-674-7676
Fax 416-674-5733
www.beacontransit.com
Line: Provides refrigerated trucking
services.
NAICS: 484110 484121
#Emp: 100-249 (Tor)
#TorLoc: 1
Own: Private Company
Key: Allan Hume, CEO
Tom Linton, GM
Cindy Murray, HR & Office Mgr
Laura Gusler, Acct

Beard Winter LLP

701-130 Adelaide St. West
Toronto, ON M5H 2K4
Tel 416-593-5555
Fax 416-593-7760
www.beardwinter.com
AKA: B.W. Law Limited Partnership;
Ducartor Holdings Ltd.
Line: Provides legal and consulting
services.
NAICS: 541110
#Emp: 100-249 (Tor)
#TorLoc: 1
Own: Private Company
Key: Mark L. J. Edwards, Mng Partner
Debbie Cymbron, HR Mgr
Julie Holmes, Dir of Fin & Admin
Hasanain Jagani, IT Mgr

Beasley Amusements

84 Advance Rd.
Toronto, ON M8Z 2T7
Tel 416-203-0405
Fax 416-234-2857
www.centreisland.ca
AKA: Centreville Amusement Park
Line: Operates an amusement park and
provides food services and catering.
NAICS: 713110
#Emp: 250-499 (Tor)
#TorLoc: 1
Own: Private Company
Key: Shane Beasley, GM
William Beasley, Owner
Adam Coleman, Rides Supr
Jeff Snow, HR Mgr
Marilyn Hems, Acct
Jennifer King, IT Mgr
Shawnda Walker, Dir of Mktg

Beatty Foods Ltd.

160 Sandalwood Pkwy.
Brampton, ON L6Z 1Y5
Tel 905-840-0700
Fax 905-840-0727
Line: Operates a chain of McDonald's restaurants.
NAICS: 722210
#Emp: 500-999 (Tor)
#TorLoc: 5
Own: Private Company
Key: David Beatty, Owner
Paula McLean, Personnel Mgr

Beauty Systems Group (Canada) Inc.

102-2345 Argentia Rd.
Mississauga, ON L5N 8K4
Tel 905-817-2200
Fax 905-817-2210
www.sallybeauty.com
AKA: Jaguar Beauty Supplies Ltd.;
CosmoProf; Beauticians Beauty Supply
Line: Sells beauty supplies, hair care products, esthetic equipment and beauty shop equipment.
NAICS: 414520
#Emp: 250-499 (Tor)
#TorLoc: 20
Own: Public Company
Par: Sally Beauty Holdings (US)
Key: John Costanza, Group VP
Jasmina Neiser, Dir of HR
Shelly Greene, Cont
Jim Cotton, VP Merchandising
Cathy Witt, CIO
Peter Heines, Dir of Sales

Beck Taxi Ltd.

1 Credit Union Dr.
Toronto, ON M4A 2S6
Tel 416-751-5555
Fax 416-750-0970
www.becktaxi.com
Line: Operates a taxi service.
NAICS: 485310
#Emp: 100-249 (Tor)
#TorLoc: 1
Own: Private Company
Key: Gail Souter, Pres & GM
Julia Norris, HR Mgr

Becton Dickinson Canada Inc.

100-2100 Derry Rd. West
Mississauga, ON L5N 0B3
Tel 905-288-6000
Fax 905-288-6001
www.bd.com/ca
AKA: BD Canada
Line: Distributes and sells medical devices and equipment.
NAICS: 417930
#Emp: 100-249 (Tor)
#TorLoc: 2
Own: Public Company
Par: Becton Dickinson & Co. (US)
Key: Claas Dewitte, VP Ops

Bee-Clean

22-2 Thorncliffe Park Dr.
Toronto, ON M4H 1H2
Tel 416-410-6181
Fax 416-421-2688
www.bee-clean.com
Line: Provides commercial contract cleaning.
NAICS: 561722
#Emp: 1000-4999 (Tor)
#TorLoc: 1
Own: Private Company
Key: Peter Dobrowolski, VP & GM
Manny Rebelo, Ops Mgr
Suzanne Gates, Office Mgr

Behind the Wheel Transportation Services Inc.

4-1330 Midway Blvd.
Mississauga, ON L5T 2K4
Tel 905-670-4243
Fax 905-670-4254
www.behindthewheel.net
AKA: BTW Services Inc.; BTW Trucking Inc.
Line: Provides truck transportation services.
NAICS: 488519
#Emp: 100-249 (Tor)
#TorLoc: 1
Own: Private Company
Key: Dennis Bacon, Pres & Owner
Robert Frost, Mgr of Safety & Compliance

Belair Insurance Company Inc.

1100-700 University Ave.
Toronto, ON M5G 0A2
Tel 416-250-7720
Fax 416-250-0999
www.belairdirect.com
AKA: Belair Direct
Line: Manages call centre for selling home and auto insurance.
NAICS: 524210
#Emp: 250-499 (Tor)
#TorLoc: 1
Own: Private Company
Par: Nordic Insurance (CDA)
Key: Carla Smith, VP, Personal Lines Ontario & Atlantic Region

Bell Canada

401-1000 La Gauchetiere West
Montreal, PQ H3B 4Y7
Tel 514-870-8777
Fax 514-870-2881
www.bell.ca
Line: Provides voice, data and image telecommunications services.
NAICS: 513310 513320
#Emp: 10000+ (Tor)
#TorLoc: 10
Own: Public Company
Par: BCE Inc. (CDA)
Key: George Cope, Pres & CEO
David Wells, Exec VP Corp Services
Siim Vanaselja, CFO
Michael Cole, Exec VP & CIO

Bell Conferencing Inc.

B4-5099 Creekbank Rd.
Mississauga, ON L4W 5N2
Tel 905-614-7505
Fax 905-602-3962
www.conferencing.bell.ca
Line: Offers conferencing services.
NAICS: 513390
#Emp: 75-99 (Tor)
#TorLoc: 2
Own: Private Company
Par: Bell Canada (CDA)
Key: Marilyn McAuslan, COO

Belle-Pak Packaging Inc.

7465 Birchmount Rd.
Markham, ON L3R 5X9
Tel 905-475-5151
Fax 905-475-9295
www.belle-pak.com
Line: Manufactures polyethylene film bags.
NAICS: 326111
#Emp: 100-249 (Tor)
#TorLoc: 1
Own: Private Company
Key: Peter Nanji, Pres
Rob Ramsundar, Plant Mgr
Sona Parekh, Cont
Yves Nahmias, VP Mktg & Sales

Bell Mobility

5099 Creekbank Rd.
Mississauga, ON L4W 5N2
Tel 905-282-2000
Fax 800-818-7449
www.bell.ca/wireless
Line: Provides wireless communication services including paging, cellular, PCS, radio and air-to-ground.
NAICS: 334220 513340
#Emp: 5000-9999 (Tor)
#TorLoc: 1
Own: Private Company
Par: Bell Canada (CDA)
Key: Wade Oosterman, Pres & CEO
Larry Healey, VP Fin
Adel Bazerghi, VP Product & Pricing
Mike Redding, VP Enterprise System
    Billing & Infrastructure
Blaik Kirby, Sr VP Sales & Mktg

Bell Sympatico

600-207 Queens Quay West
Toronto, ON M5J 1A7
Tel 416-353-0123
Fax 416-703-8040
www.sympatico.msn.ca
Line: Provides multi-media development and production services.
NAICS: 514191 513390
#Emp: 500-999 (Tor)
Own: Private Company
Par: Bell Canada (CDA)
Key: Kevin Crull, Pres & CEO
Jennifer Salkild, Facilities Mgr

Bellwood Health Services Inc.

1020 McNicoll Ave.
Toronto, ON M1W 2J6
Tel 416-495-0926
Fax 416-495-7943
www.bellwood.ca
Line: Operates a private hospital for addictions.
NAICS: 622210
#Emp: 75-99 (Tor)
#TorLoc: 1
Own: Private Company
Key: Laura Bhoi, Pres
Linda Bell, CEO
Janice Hambley, VP Health & Clinical
    Services
Noreedah Dean, HR Coord
Janet Lansche, VP Fin & Admin
David Buchberger, Systems Admr
Julie Bowles, Mktg Mgr

Bellwyck Packaging Solutions

100 Carnforth Rd.
Toronto, ON M4A 2K7
Tel 416-752-1210
Fax 416-752-9677
www.bellwyck.com
Line: Manufactures folding cartons.
NAICS: 322130 322212
#Emp: 100-249 (Tor)
#TorLoc: 1
Own: Private Company
Key: John Vella, CEO

Belmont Meat Products Ltd.

230 Signet Dr.
Toronto, ON M9L 1V2
Tel 416-749-7250
Fax 416-749-0604
www.belmontmeats.com
NAICS: 311611 311615
#Emp: 100-249 (Tor)
#TorLoc: 1
Own: Private Company
Key: David Walderman, Pres
Ben Walderman, VP
Marie Slaney, HR Mgr
Greg Palmer, VP Sales

Belrock Construction Ltd.

185 Adesso Dr.
Concord, ON L4K 3C4
Tel 905-669-9481
Fax 416-665-7646
www.belrock.com
Line: Operates a general construction company.
NAICS: 231410
#Emp: 75-99 (Tor)
#TorLoc: 1
Own: Private Company
Key: Gabriel Grossi, Pres

Beltone Electronics of Canada Ltd.

301 Supertest Rd.
Toronto, ON M3J 2M4
Tel 416-736-4444
Fax 416-736-6640
www.beltone.com
Line: Manufactures hearing aids.
NAICS: 334512
#Emp: 75-99 (Tor)
#TorLoc: 1
Own: Private Company
Par: Great Nordic (DEN)
Key: Frank Skubski, GM

Belvedere International Inc.

5675 Keaton Cres.
Mississauga, ON L5R 3G3
Tel 905-568-0700
Fax 905-568-0711
www.belvint.com
Line: Manufactures and distributes toiletries, and health and beauty products.
NAICS: 325620 414520
#Emp: 100-249 (Tor)
#TorLoc: 2
Own: Private Company
Key: Larry Romagnuolo, CEO
Joanne Hancott, VP Ops
Norman Holesh, COO
Sue Irwin, Purch
Parvin Hussain, Sales Admin Mgr
Michelle Sparrock, Exec VP

Bemis Flexible Packaging

130 Arrow Rd.
Toronto, ON M9M 2M1
Tel 416-742-8910
Fax 416-742-6749
www.bemis.com
Line: Prints packaging on paper and film for use in packaging foods.
NAICS: 561910 323119
#Emp: 100-249 (Tor)
#TorLoc: 1
Own: Public Company
Key: Steve Dwyer, Site Mgr
George Bankuti, HR Mgr
Stephane Bois, Cont

Bendale Acres

A Div. of The City of Toronto
2920 Lawrence Ave. East
Toronto, ON M1P 2T8
Tel 416-397-7000
Fax 416-397-7067
www.toronto.ca/ltc/bendaleacres.htm
Line: Provides long-term care facilities and respite care programs.
NAICS: 623310
#Emp: 250-499 (Tor)
#TorLoc: 1
Own: Government
Par: The City of Toronto
Key: Margaret Aerola, Admr

Benevito Foods Inc.

17 Vickers Rd.
Toronto, ON M9B 1C1
Tel 416-233-0040
Fax 416-233-9270
www.benevitofoods.com
Line: Manufactures and distributes bakery, confectionery and snack food products.
NAICS: 311822
#Emp: 250-499 (Tor)
#TorLoc: 2
Own: Private Company
Key: Franco Carrion, VP Ops

Benjamin Moore & Co.

100-7070 Mississauga Rd.
Mississauga, ON L5N 5M8
Tel 905-813-3700
Fax 905-813-3704
www.benjaminmoore.ca
Line: Manufactures paint and coatings for all surfaces including wood, metal, paper and plastics.
NAICS: 325510
#Emp: 75-99 (Tor)
#TorLoc: 2
Own: Private Company
Par: Berkshire Hathaway Inc. (US)
Key: Michael Kolind,
   GM, Central Region
Helen Mullett, Mgr, Brand Mktg

Benlan Inc.

2760 Brighton Rd.
Oakville, ON L6H 5T4
Tel 905-829-5004
Fax 905-829-5006
www.benlan.com
Line: Manufactures and supplies medical grade tubing and molded components to the healthcare market.
NAICS: 334512
#Emp: 100-249 (Tor)
#TorLoc: 1
Own: Private Company
Key: Tom Enns, Pres
Caroline Pick, HR Mgr

Bennett Jones LLP

3400-1 First Canadian Pl.
P.O. Box 130
Toronto, ON M5X 1A4
Tel 416-863-1200
Fax 416-863-1716
www.bennettjones.com
Line: Operates a leading Canadian business law firm.
NAICS: 541110

#Emp: 250-499 (Tor)
#TorLoc: 1
Own: Private Company
Key: Stephen Bowman,
   Toronto Mng Partner
Hugh MacKinnon, Chmn & CEO
Siobhan Walsh, CAO
Barbara Sheperd, Chief Mktg Officer

Bensimon Byrne

420 Wellington St. West
Toronto, ON M5V 1E3
Tel 416-922-2211
Fax 416-922-8590
www.bensimonbyrne.com
AKA: DMB & B; Mighty Digital Direct & Design
Line: Operates a full service advertising agency.
NAICS: 541810
#Emp: 100-249 (Tor)
#TorLoc: 1
Own: Private Company
Par: Publicis Groupe (FR)
Key: Jack Bensimon, Pres
Carol Fox, COO
Michelle Faultless, HR Mgr
Colleen Peddie, CFO

Bentall Kennedy LP

300-55 University Ave.
Toronto, ON M5J 2H7
Tel 416-681-3400
Fax 416-681-3405
www.bentall.com
Line: Manages commercial and industrial real estate.
NAICS: 531310
#Emp: 1000-4999 (Tor)
Own: Private Company
Par: Bentall Kennedy LP (US)
Key: Katherine Weiss, Property Mgr

Benteler Automotive Canada Corp.

9195A Torbram Rd.
Brampton, ON L6S 6H3
Tel 905-494-7600
Fax 905-494-7601
www.benteler.com
Line: Manufactures automotive parts and components.
NAICS: 336390
#Emp: 100-249 (Tor)
#TorLoc: 1
Own: Private Company
Key: Sergio Cavalheiro, Plant Mgr

Bento Nouveau Ltd.

19 Skagway Ave.
Toronto, ON M1M 3T9
Tel 416-778-7469
Fax 416-265-4439
www.bentonouveau.com
Line: Manufactures, distributes and retails prepared foods.
NAICS: 413190 722210
#Emp: 500-999 (Tor)
#TorLoc: 2
Own: Private Company
Key: Frank Hennessey, CEO
Glen Brown, VP
Hugh Johnston, Sr VP Fin

Bereskin & Parr

40 King St. West
P.O. Box 401
Toronto, ON M5H 3Y2
Tel 416-364-7311
Fax 416-361-1398
www.bereskinparr.com
Line: Provides intellectual and industrial property law services.
NAICS: 541110
#Emp: 250-499 (Tor)
Own: Private Company
Key: Daniel Bereskin, Sr Partner
Stephanie Crann, Dir of HR & Admin
Robert Beneteau, Dir of Fin & Admin
Mike Couto, Facilities Mgr
Falon Leach, Mktg Mgr

Bericap North America Inc.

835 Syscon Crt.
Burlington, ON L7L 6C5
Tel 905-634-2248
Fax 905-634-7780
www.bericap.com
Line: Manufactures plastic closures for the beverage, food, chemical, pharmaceutical and automotive industries.
NAICS: 326198
#Emp: 100-249 (Tor)
#TorLoc: 1
Own: Private Company
Par: Amcor Twinpak - North America Inc./Bericap Group (CDA/GER)
Key: David Andison, Pres & COO
Gord Shelley, Dir of Ops
Mary-Lou Bednarski, HR Mgr
David Read, Dir of Sales & Mktg

Bernard Athletic Knit

2 Scarlett Rd.
Toronto, ON M6N 4J6
Tel 416-766-6151
Fax 416-766-0647
www.athleticknit.com
AKA: Athletic Knit
Line: Manufactures team wear
uniforms for hockey, baseball,
basketball and rugby.
NAICS: 315229 315299
#Emp: 100-249 (Tor)
#TorLoc: 1
Own: Private Company
Key: Bernard Sliwin, Pres & Owner
John Larin, Sales & Mktg Mgr

Bernstein Health & Diet Clinics

21 Kern Rd.
Toronto, ON M3B 1S9
Tel 416-447-3438
Fax 416-447-0702
www.drbdiet.com
Line: Operates diet clinics.
NAICS: 812190
#Emp: 100-249 (Tor)
#TorLoc: 20
Own: Private Company
Key: Stanley Bernstein, Owner
Warren Bernstein, COO

Berry Plastics

225 Birmingham St.
Toronto, ON M8V 2C7
Tel 416-252-4455
Fax 416-252-8571
Line: Manufactures plastic film.
NAICS: 326114
#Emp: 75-99 (Tor)
#TorLoc: 1
Own: Private Company
Par: Pliant Corporation (US)
Key: Michael Chartrand, Plant Mgr

Best Buy Canada

65 Dundas St. West
Toronto, ON M5G 2C3
Tel 416-642-8321
Fax 416-642-8322
www.bestbuy.ca
NAICS: 443110
#Emp: 75-99 (Tor)
Own: Public Company
Par: Best Buy Co., Inc. (US)
Key: Zee Soofi, GM

Bestway Cartage Ltd.

6505 Vipond Dr.
Mississauga, ON L5T 1J9
Tel 905-565-8877
Fax 905-565-8878
www.shipviabestway.com
Line: Provides cartage, express and
transportation services.
NAICS: 488519
#Emp: 75-99 (Tor)
#TorLoc: 1
Own: Private Company
Key: Peter Dalessandro, VP
Clemente Dalessandro, Pres
Larry Franch, Ops Mgr
Debbie Kosmalski,
    Safety & Compliance
Doug Bradley, IT Mgr

Best Western Primrose Hotel

A Div. of Arsandco Investments Ltd.
111 Carlton St.
Toronto, ON M5B 2G3
Tel 416-977-8000
Fax 416-977-6323
www.torontoprimrosehotel.com
NAICS: 721111
#Emp: 100-249 (Tor)
#TorLoc: 1
Own: Private Company
Key: Joe Rubin, Pres

Beta-Calco Inc.

88 Saint Regis Cres. South
Toronto, ON M3J 1Y8
Tel 416-531-9942
Fax 416-531-6199
www.betacalco.com
Line: Manufactures architectural
lighting fixtures.
NAICS: 335120
#Emp: 75-99 (Tor)
#TorLoc: 1
Own: Private Company
Key: Remy Silver, CEO
David Black, COO
Brian Onody, VP Sales
Brenda Robinson, VP Mktg

Bethany Lodge

23 Second St.
Markham, ON L3R 2C2
Tel 905-477-3838
Fax 905-477-2888
www.bethanylodge.org
AKA: Bethany West
Line: Operates a long-term care facility.
NAICS: 623310
#Emp: 100-249 (Tor)

#TorLoc: 1
Own: Not-for-profit
Key: Basil Tambakis, Admr
Heather Kelly, Dir of Care
Louise deRoo, Dir of Fin

Beth Tzedec Congregation Inc.

1700 Bathurst St.
Toronto, ON M5P 3K3
Tel 416-781-3511
Fax 416-781-0150
www.beth-tzedec.org
Line: Operates a synagogue.
NAICS: 813110
#Emp: 100-249 (Tor)
#TorLoc: 1
Own: Religious
Key: Randy Spiegel, Exec Dir
Rabbi Baruch Frydman-Kohl,
    Senior Rabbi
Tom Laufer, Comptr

Bevertec CST Inc.

400-5935 Airport Rd.
Mississauga, ON L4V 1W5
Tel 416-695-7525
Fax 416-695-7526
www.bevertec.com
Line: Develops and implements
consulting and recruitment solutions.
NAICS: 541510
#Emp: 75-99 (Tor)
#TorLoc: 1
Own: Public Company
Key: Barry Walsh, Pres
Michael Walsh, VP Ops
Mirjana Tesanovic,
    Recruitment & Account Mgr

BFI Canada Inc.

400 Applewood Cres., 2nd Fl.
Vaughan, ON L4K 0C3
Tel 905-532-7510
Fax 905-532-7580
www.bficanada.com
Line: Operates a non-hazardous solid
waste and recycling collection and
disposal company.
NAICS: 562210
#Emp: 250-499 (Tor)
#TorLoc: 2
Own: Private Company
Key: Keith Carrigan, Pres & CEO
Charles F. Flood, Vice Chmn
Joseph Quarin, Exec VP & COO
Thomas J. Cowee, VP & CFO

B + H Architects

300-481 University Ave.
Toronto, ON M5G 2H4
Tel 416-596-2299
Fax 416-586-0599
www.bharchitects.com
Line: Provides architectural design, interior design, and master planning services for a wide range of commercial and institutional projects.
NAICS: 541310 541410
#Emp: 100-249 (Tor)
#TorLoc: 1
Own: Private Company
Key: Bill Nankivell, CEO
Dan McAlister, Chmn
Jenny Mercer, Dir of Fin
Keyvan Akhavan, Mgr of Data Systems
Greg Heal, Commun Mgr

BIC Inc.

155 Oakdale Rd.
Toronto, ON M3N 1W2
Tel 416-742-9173
Fax 416-741-4965
www.bicworld.com
Line: Wholesales and distributes consumer-packaged products.
NAICS: 339990 339940
#Emp: 75-99 (Tor)
#TorLoc: 1
Own: Private Company
Par: BIC Corp. (US)
Key: Mario Guevara, CEO
Bruno Bich, Chmn
John Yannetta, Plant Mgr
Angelo diPlacido, Cont
Kevin Murphy, VP Sales, Mktg & Ops

Big Carrot Natural Food Market

348 Danforth Ave.
Toronto, ON M4K 1N8
Tel 416-466-2129
Fax 416-466-2366
www.thebigcarrot.ca
Line: Operates a natural health food market.
NAICS: 446191 445110
#Emp: 100-249 (Tor)
#TorLoc: 1
Own: Private Company
Key: Heather Barkley, Pres
Daiva Kryzanauskas, VP
Evis Lasku, Scanning Mgr

Biggs & Narciso Construction Service Inc.

14-181 Bentley St.
Markham, ON L3R 3Y1
Tel 905-470-8788
Fax 905-470-9102
www.biggsandnarciso.com
Line: Provides demolition and fireproofing, asbestos abatement and mould removal services.
NAICS: 232110
#Emp: 100-249 (Tor)
#TorLoc: 1
Own: Private Company
Key: Luis Narciso, Pres
Sue Vernon, Ops
Margaret Biggs, Cont
G. Timothy Biggs, VP

Bigtech Inc.

5990 14th Ave.
Markham, ON L3S 4M4
Tel 905-695-0100
Fax 905-695-0910
www.bigtech.ca
AKA: Computer Logistics
Line: Provides computer, peripherals, electronic and equipment repair and refurbishment services.
NAICS: 541510
#Emp: 100-249 (Tor)
#TorLoc: 1
Own: Private Company
Key: Aldo Cozza, Pres & CEO
Claudio Cozza, VP Ops
Derek Li, Acctng & HR Mgr

bioMérieux

915 Meyerside Dr.
Mississauga, ON L5T 1R8
Tel 905-564-1032
Fax 905-564-8532
www.pmlmicro.com
AKA: PML Microbiologicals, Inc.
Line: Produces cultured media for clinical and pharmaceutical customers.
NAICS: 325410
#Emp: 75-99 (Tor)
Own: Private Company
Par: bioMérieux SA (FRA)
Key: Randy Ferster, Plant Mgr

Bird Construction Company

5403 Eglinton Ave. West
Toronto, ON M9C 5K6
Tel 416-620-7122
Fax 416-620-7121
www.bird.ca
Line: Provides construction management services.

NAICS: 231410 231210 231220
#Emp: 100-249 (Tor)
#TorLoc: 1
Own: Private Company
Key: Tim Talbott, Pres & CEO
Paul A. Charette, Chmn
Richard Ellis-Smith,
    Branch Mgr, Toronto
Lance Livingston, Dir of HR
Stephen R. Entwistle, CFO
Mark McLaren, Business Dev Mgr

Birks & Mayors Inc.

First Canadian Pl.
100 King St. West
Toronto, ON M5X 1K7
Tel 416-363-5663
Fax 416-363-5666
www.birks.com
AKA: Birks Jewellers
Line: Retails jewellery and gift products.
NAICS: 448310
#Emp: 100-249 (Tor)
#TorLoc: 8
Own: Private Company
Par: Borgosesia SpA (ITALY)
Key: Poonam Rajput, Store Mgr
Michael Rabinovitch, Sr VP & CFO
Marco Pasteris, VP Fin

The Bishop Strachan School

298 Lonsdale Rd.
Toronto, ON M4V 1X2
Tel 416-483-4325
Fax 416-481-5632
www.bss.on.ca
Line: Operates independent day and boarding school.
NAICS: 611110
#Emp: 100-249 (Tor)
#TorLoc: 1
Own: Not-for-profit
Key: Deryn Lavell, Head
Angela Terpstra,
    Asst Head, Senior School
Barbara McLean, Asst Head,
    HR & Professional Growth
Janet Ainslie,
    Asst Head, Fin & Facilities
Mary Anne Ballantyne,
    Asst Head, Tech & Innovation
Rachel Yeager, Dir of Mktg & Commun

Bison Transport Inc.

5850 Shawson Dr.
Mississauga, ON L4W 3W5
Tel 905-564-5614
Fax 905-564-9865
www.bisontransport.com
Line: Provides trucking of general
freight throughout North America.
NAICS: 484121
#Emp: 250-499 (Tor)
#TorLoc: 1
Own: Private Company
Key: Mark Irwin, Terminal Mgr

Black Creek Pioneer Village

1000 Murray Ross Pkwy.
Toronto, ON M3J 2P3
Tel 416-736-1733
Fax 416-661-6610
www.blackcreek.ca
AKA: BCPV
Line: Operates conservation authority,
living history attraction and event
venue.
NAICS: 712119
#Emp: 100-249 (Tor)
#TorLoc: 1
Own: Not-for-profit
Par: Toronto Region Conservation
Authority (CDA)
Key: Brian Denney, CAO, TRCA
Derek Edwards, Dir
Catherine MacEwen,
    Sr Mgr of HR & Safety
Rick Sikorski, Mktg Mgr

Black & McDonald Ltd.

2100-2 Bloor St. East
Toronto, ON M4W 1A8
Tel 416-920-5100
Fax 416-922-8768
www.blackandmcdonald.com
Line: Provides electrical, mechanical,
utilities, nuclear and facility
management and service work.
NAICS: 232520 232510
#Emp: 1000-4999 (Tor)
#TorLoc: 3
Own: Private Company
Par: Black & McDonald Limited (CDA)
Key: Ian McDonald, Co-Pres & CEO
Bruce McDonald, Co-Pres & CEO
April Jackson, Reg HR Mgr

Black Photo Corporation

371 Gough Rd.
Markham, ON L3R 4B6
Tel 905-475-2777
Fax 905-475-8814
www.blacks.ca
AKA: Black's Cameras
Line: Provides photofinishing services
and retails photographic equipment
and supplies.
NAICS: 443130 812921
#Emp: 500-999 (Tor)
#TorLoc: 50
Own: Private Company
Par: Reichmann Hauer Capital Partners
(CDA)
Key: Peter Scully, Sr VP Sales & Ops
Angela Delzotto, Dir of HR
Debra Baker,
    Dir of Merchandise Services

Blake, Cassels & Graydon LLP

4000-199 Bay St.
Commerce Crt. West
Toronto, ON M5L 1A9
Tel 416-863-2400
Fax 416-863-2653
www.blakes.com
Line: Operates a private legal practice.
NAICS: 541110
#Emp: 500-999 (Tor)
#TorLoc: 1
Own: Private Company
Key: Robert M. Granatstein,
    Nat'l Mng Partner
Richard Prupas, CFO
Amar Gill, Dir of IT
Alison Jeffrey, Chief Client Relns &
    Mktg Officer

Blaney McMurtry LLP

1500-2 Queen St. East
Toronto, ON M5C 3G5
Tel 416-593-1221
Fax 416-593-5437
www.blaney.com
Line: Provides legal services.
NAICS: 541110
#Emp: 100-249 (Tor)
#TorLoc: 1
Own: Private Company
Key: Michael J. Bennett, Mng Partner
Susan Carr, HR & Facilities Mgr
Angela Palmieri, GM
Grace Oledan, Purch Clerk
Wendy Wiltshire, IS Mgr
Patricia Abbott, Mktg Mgr

Blizzard Courier Service Ltd.

1937 Leslie St.
Toronto, ON M3B 2M3
Tel 416-444-0596
Fax 416-444-0057
NAICS: 492110
#Emp: 75-99 (Tor)
#TorLoc: 1
Own: Private Company
Key: Paul Bresge, Pres
Behzad Khaze, GM

Blockbuster Canada Co.

1100-401 The West Mall
Toronto, ON M9C 5J5
Tel 416-621-7774
Fax 416-621-6191
www.blockbuster.ca
Line: Operates rental and retail stores
featuring DVDs and video game
software.
NAICS: 532230
#Emp: 500-999 (Tor)
Own: Private Company
Key: Ian Paterson, Sr Dir of Ops

Bloomington Cove

13621 Ninth Line
Stouffville, ON L4A 7X3
Tel 905-640-1310
Fax 905-640-0995
www.specialty-care.com
Line: Operates a general long-term care
facility.
NAICS: 623110
#Emp: 100-249 (Tor)
#TorLoc: 1
Own: Private Company
Par: Specialty Care (CDA)
Key: John Sproxton, Mgr
Paula Jourdain, CEO, Specialty Care

Blue Giant Equipment Corp.

85 Heart Lake Rd. South
Brampton, ON L6W 3K2
Tel 905-457-3900
Fax 905-457-2313
www.bluegiant.com
Line: Manufactures materials handling
machinery.
NAICS: 333310
#Emp: 100-249 (Tor)
#TorLoc: 1
Own: Private Company
Par: Blue Giant Holdings (US)
Key: Bill Kostenko, Pres
Trevor Oake, GM, Toronto
Kimberly Griffin, HR Mgr
Jeff Miller, VP Sales & Mktg

Blue Mountain Wallcovering Inc.

15 Akron Rd.
Toronto, ON M8W 1T3
Tel 416-251-1678
Fax 416-251-8968
www.blmtn.com
AKA: Beauport Wallcoverings; Olney
Wallcoverings
Line: Manufactures wall coverings.
NAICS: 326198
#Emp: 75-99 (Tor)
#TorLoc: 1
Own: Private Company
Key: Christopher Wood, Pres & CEO
Michael Skea, COO
Chris De Rochie, Exec Asst
Danielle Beaudoin, VP Fin

Blue Springs Golf Club

RR#1, 13448 Dublin Line
Acton, ON L7J 2L7
Tel 519-853-0904
Fax 519-853-1404
www.clublink.ca
NAICS: 713910
#Emp: 100-249 (Tor)
#TorLoc: 1
Own: Private Company
Par: ClubLink Corp. (CDA)
Key: Greg Pacenti, Head Pro

Blue Star Investigations & Security Inc.

205-61 Alness St.
Toronto, ON M3J 2H2
Tel 416-665-9500
Fax 416-665-9300
www.bluestarpi.com
Line: Provides private investigation
and security services.
NAICS: 561612
#Emp: 100-249 (Tor)
#TorLoc: 1
Own: Private Company
Key: Allen Brik, Pres

BMO Financial Group

1 First Canadian Pl., 68th Fl.
P.O. Box 1
Toronto, ON M5X 1A1
Tel 416-927-6000
Fax 416-927-5543
www.bmo.com
AKA: Bank of Montreal
Line: Provides a full range of
banking services to individuals,
small businesses, corporations and
governments.
NAICS: 522111 522112
#Emp: 10000+ (Tor)

#TorLoc: 170
Own: Public Company
Key: Bill Downe, Pres & CEO
Jean Michel Ares,
    Group Head Tech & Ops
Richard Rudderham,
    Sr Exec VP, Head of HR
Thomas E. Flynn, CFO
Cameron Fowler, Pres & CEO, Personal
    & Commercial Client Group
Douglas B. Stotz,
    Sr VP & Chief Mktg Officer

BMO Guardian Group of Funds Ltd.

250 Yonge St., 9th Fl.
Toronto, ON M5B 2M8
Tel 416-947-4099
Fax 416-364-2889
www.bmoguardianfunds.com
Line: Operates a mutual fund company.
NAICS: 523120
#Emp: 75-99 (Tor)
#TorLoc: 1
Own: Private Company
Par: BMO Group (CDA)
Key: Ross Kappele, Pres

BMO Harris Private Banking

1 First Canadian Pl.
100 King St. West, 10th Fl., P.O. Box 150
Toronto, ON M5X 1H3
Tel 416-359-5001
Fax 416-359-5902
www.bmoharrisprivatebanking.com
NAICS: 523110
#Emp: 100-249 (Tor)
#TorLoc: 2
Own: Private Company
Par: BMO Harris Investment
Management Inc. (CDA)
Key: Graham Parsons,
    Exec VP, Global Private Banking
Andrew Auerbach, Sr VP & COO, BMO
    Harris Private Banking
Michael Cooksey, Reg Dir of Sales, GTA

BMO Nesbitt Burns Inc.

5000-1 First Canadian Pl.
P.O. Box 150
Toronto, ON M5X 1H3
Tel 416-359-4000
Fax 416-359-4311
www.bmonesbittburns.com
Line: Operates a full service investment
banking and securities firm.
NAICS: 523110
#Emp: 1000-4999 (Tor)
#TorLoc: 19
Own: Public Company

Par: Bank of Montreal Securities
Canada Ltd. (CDA)
Key: Gilles Ouellette,
    Pres & CEO, Deputy Chmn,
    BMO Nesbitt Burns & CEO
    BMO Private Client Group
William Downe, Pres & CEO,
    BMO Financial Group
Richard Rudderham, Exec VP & Head
    of Human Resource, BMO
Thomas E. Flynn, Exec VP & CFO
Douglas E. Stotz,
    Chief Mktg Officer, BMO

BMP Metals Inc.

18 Chelsea Lane
Brampton, ON L6T 3Y4
Tel 905-799-2002
Fax 905-799-2003
www.bmpmetals.com
AKA: CableTalk Systems Inc.
Line: Fabricates sheet metal with
additional services in CNC machining
and turning, electronic assembly,
paint coatings and plastic injection-
moulding.
NAICS: 332999
#Emp: 100-249 (Tor)
#TorLoc: 2
Own: Private Company
Par: Bempro Global Holdings (CDA)
Key: Robert Bedard, Pres
Margaret Watson, HR Mgr
Lorraine Bedard, Secy-Treas
Vince DiCerbo,
    Process Compliance Mgr
Jeff Estrela, IT Mgr
Vince Rosa, Sales Mgr

BMW Autohaus

480 Steeles Ave. West
Thornhill, ON L4J 6X6
Tel 905-886-3380
Fax 905-886-3381
www.bmwautohaus.ca
Line: Operates a car dealership.
NAICS: 441110
#Emp: 75-99 (Tor)
#TorLoc: 1
Own: Private Company
Par: Auto World Imports (CDA)
Key: Pauline Chuang, Dealer Principal
Danny Tran, Gen Sales Mgr

BMW Canada Inc.

920 Champlain Crt.
Whitby, ON L1N 6K9
Tel 905-683-1200
Fax 905-428-5033
www.bmwgroup.ca
Line: Distributes automobiles,
motorcycles, and parts.
NAICS: 415110
#Emp: 250-499 (Tor)
#TorLoc: 2
Own: Private Company
Par: BMW (GER)
Key: Franz Jung, Pres
Michelle Lettner, Dir of HR

BNN - Business News Network

299 Queen St. West
Toronto, ON M5V 2Z5
Tel 416-384-8000
Fax 416-957-8189
www.bnn.ca
Line: Operates a television production
company.
NAICS: 513120
#Emp: 100-249 (Tor)
#TorLoc: 1
Own: Private Company
Par: Bell Media (CDA)
Key: Jack Fleischman, GM
Marty Cej, Mng Editor
Lesley Harmer, Exec Producer
Michelle De Cruz, Sr Web Producer

The Board of Governors of Exhibition Place

200 Princes' Blvd.
Queen Elizabeth Bldg.
Toronto, ON M6K 3C3
Tel 416-263-3600
Fax 416-263-3690
www.explace.on.ca
AKA: Exhibition Place; Canadian
National Exhibition; National Trade
Centre
Line: Provides opportunity for
business stimulation and economic
development; provides a focus for
public celebrations and events;
preserves the architecturally and
historically significant structures on
the grounds.
NAICS: 531120 713110
#Emp: 250-499 (Tor)
#TorLoc: 1
Own: Municipal Crown Corp.

Key: Dianne Young, CEO
Mark Goss, GM
Sandy Douglas, Dir of HR, Security,
    Occupational Health & Safety
Hardat Persaud, CFO
Gerd Rose, Purch Mgr
John Koperwas, IT & Telecom Mgr
Laura Purdy, Dir of Mktg & Sales
Jeff Gay, Dir of Event Services

Board of Management of the Toronto Zoo

361A Old Finch Ave.
Toronto, ON M1B 5K7
Tel 416-392-5900
Fax 416-392-5934
www.torontozoo.com
AKA: Toronto Zoo
Line: Operates one of the largest zoo's
in the world with 5,000 animals over
710 acres.
NAICS: 712130
#Emp: 250-499 (Tor)
#TorLoc: 1
Own: Government
Par: The City of Toronto
Key: John Tracogna, CEO
Robin Hale, COO
Curt Shalapata, HR Mgr
Paul Whittam, Fin Mgr
Peter Vasilopoulos,
    Purch & Supply Supr
Charles Duncan,
    Computer & Telecom Services Mgr
Shanna Young,
    Exec Dir of Mktg & Commun

Boart Longyear Canada

2442 South Sheridan Way
Mississauga, ON L5J 2M7
Tel 905-822-7922
Fax 905-822-7232
www.boartlongyear.com
Line: Operates a drilling company.
NAICS: 232110
#Emp: 75-99 (Tor)
#TorLoc: 1
Own: Private Company
Par: Boart Longyear Inc. (US)
Key: Craig Kipp, Pres & CEO

Bob Rumball Centre for the Deaf

2395 Bayview Ave.
Toronto, ON M2L 1A2
Tel 416-449-9651
Fax 416-449-8881
www.bobrumball.org
AKA: The Ontario Community Centre
for the Deaf

Line: Provides residential, educational,
vocational and recreational programs
for the deaf community and sign
language training for the hearing
community.
NAICS: 621499
#Emp: 100-249 (Tor)
#TorLoc: 1
Own: Not-for-profit
Key: Derek Rumball, Exec Dir
Shirley Cassel, Dir of Senior Services
Rhonda Waters, Dir of HR
Peter Visconti, Dir of Fin

Body Blue 2006 Inc.

2300 Drew Rd.
Mississauga, ON L5S 1B8
Tel 905-677-8333
Fax 905-677-0311
www.bodyblue.com
Line: Manufactures personal care
products.
NAICS: 325620
#Emp: 250-499 (Tor)
#TorLoc: 3
Own: Private Company
Par: KDC (CDA)
Key: Phillip Crookshank, VP & GM

Boehringer Ingelheim (Canada) Ltd.

5180 South Service Rd.
Burlington, ON L7L 5H4
Tel 905-639-0333
Fax 905-639-3769
www.boehringer-ingelheim.ca
Line: Sells human and animal health
pharmaceuticals.
NAICS: 325410
#Emp: 250-499 (Tor)
#TorLoc: 1
Own: Private Company
Par: Boehringer Ingelheim (GER)
Key: Theodore Witek, Pres & CEO
Hussein Ladhani, Dir of Ops
Ruta Stauskas, VP HR
Ludwig Reuter, VP Fin & Admin
Gary Roberts, Dir of Purch
Ross Scarrow, Dir of IT
Derek O'Toole, Dir,
    Market Access & Commun

The Boiler Inspection & Insurance Company of Canada

3000-250 Yonge St.
Toronto, ON M5B 2L7
Tel 416-363-5491
Fax 416-363-0920
www.biico.com
Line: Operates an insurance company.
NAICS: 524129
#Emp: 100-249 (Tor)
#TorLoc: 1
Own: Private Company
Par: HSB Group Inc. (US)
Key: John Mulvihoill, Pres & CEO
Shelli Schwartz, HR Mgr
Brenda Crookshanks, Sr VP & CFO

Bombardier Aerospace

123 Garratt Blvd.
Toronto, ON M3K 1Y5
Tel 416-633-7310
Fax 416-375-4546
www.aerospace.bombardier.com
Line: Designs, manufactures, sells and supports regional and business aircraft.
NAICS: 336410
#Emp: 1000-4999 (Tor)
#TorLoc: 1
Own: Public Company
Par: Bombardier Inc. (CDA)
Key: Gaer C. Hachey, Pres & COO
Pierre Beaudoin, CEO
John Paul MacDonald,
    Sr VP HR & Pub Affairs

Bombardier Transportation

125 Judson St.
Toronto, ON M8Z 1A4
Tel 416-253-3700
Fax 416-253-3729
www.bombardier.com
NAICS: 336510
#Emp: 250-499 (Tor)
#TorLoc: 2
Own: Private Company
Par: Bombardier Inc. (CDA)
Key: Pierre Beaudoin, Pres & CEO
Rob Fuller, GM
April Brown, HR Mgr
Yvonne Vanriel, Fin Mgr

Bondfield Construction Company Ltd.

407 Basaltic Rd.
Concord, ON L4K 4W8
Tel 416-667-8422
Fax 416-667-8462
www.bondfield.com
Line: Designs, builds and offers construction management services.
NAICS: 231410
#Emp: 250-499 (Tor)
#TorLoc: 1
Own: Private Company
Key: Ralph Aquino, Pres & Dir
John Aquino, VP & GM
Mike Solano,
    IT & Computer Support Mgr
Steve Aquino, VP Business Dev

Booth Centennial Healthcare Linen Services Inc.

6580 Northwest Dr.
Mississauga, ON L4V 1L5
Tel 905-678-6565
Fax 905-678-4908
www.bchls.ca
Line: Provides laundry services for hospitals and health care facilities.
NAICS: 812320
#Emp: 250-499 (Tor)
#TorLoc: 1
Own: Not-for-profit
Key: Joe Grummel, GM
Maria Ash, VP Corp Services
Carol Baran, CFO
Julie Sarginson, Dir of IS

Borden Ladner Gervais LLP

Scotia Plaza, 40 King St. West, 44th Fl.
Toronto, ON M5H 3Y4
Tel 416-367-6000
Fax 416-367-6749
www.blgcanada.com
Line: Operates a national full service law firm.
NAICS: 541110
#Emp: 500-999 (Tor)
#TorLoc: 1
Own: Partnership
Key: Frank Callaghan,
  Reg Mng Partner, Toronto
Sean Weir, Nat'l Mng Partner
Cheryl O'Donnell, CAO
Sylvia Swiekatun, CFO
Sandra Haynes, CIO

Bosch Rexroth Canada Corp.

3426 Mainway Dr.
Burlington, ON L7M 1A8
Tel 905-335-5511
Fax 905-335-4184
www.boschrexroth.ca
Line: Provides drive and control solutions.
NAICS: 335315 333990
#Emp: 75-99 (Tor)
Own: Private Company
Par: Bosch Rexroth (GER)
Key: Ed Cloutier, GM

Bosley Real Estate Ltd., Brokerage

276 Merton St.
Toronto, ON M4S 1A9
Tel 416-481-6137
Fax 416-480-2548
www.bosleyrealestate.com
NAICS: 531210
#Emp: 100-249 (Tor)
#TorLoc: 3
Own: Private Company
Key: Ann Bosley, VP
Thomas W. Bosley, Pres & CEO
William Statten, VP Fin

The Boston Consulting Group of Canada Ltd.

2400-181 Bay St.
P.O. Box 783
Toronto, ON M5J 2T3
Tel 416-955-4200
Fax 416-955-4201
www.bcg.com
Line: Provides management consulting services.
NAICS: 541611
#Emp: 75-99 (Tor)
#TorLoc: 1
Own: Private Company
Par: BCG Holding Corp. (US)
Key: Joe Manget, Sr VP
Heather McCarten, Office Coord
Dan Leaman, Cont

Boston Pizza International Inc.

708-1 City Centre Dr.
Mississauga, ON L5B 1M2
Tel 905-848-2700
Fax 905-848-1440
www.bostonpizza.com
Line: Operates a restaurant chain.
NAICS: 722110
#Emp: 75-99 (Tor)
Own: Private Company
Key: Mark Pacinda, Pres
Caroline Schein, VP, People Dev

Bot Construction Ltd.

1224 Speers Rd.
Oakville, ON L6L 2X4
Tel 905-827-4167
Fax 905-827-0458
www.botconstruction.ca
Line: Provides road and bridge
constructing services.
NAICS: 231310
#Emp: 75-99 (Tor)
#TorLoc: 1
Own: Private Company
Par: S Bot & Sons Enterprises Ltd.
(CDA)
Key: Roy M. Bot, Pres
Steve Bot, VP & GM
Nancy Mercanti, Exec Admr
Scott Riddell, VP Fin
Marlene Yakabuski, VP Corp Affairs

Bothwell-Accurate Co. (2006) Limited

160 Symes Rd.
Toronto, ON M6N 3T4
Tel 416-762-8243
Fax 416-762-1070
www.baroof.com
AKA: BA Roofing Co.
Line: Provides roofing, waterproofing
and sheet metal contracting services.
NAICS: 232330 332329
#Emp: 100-249 (Tor)
#TorLoc: 1
Own: Private Company
Key: George Vassallo, Pres & CEO
Brian Jamieson, VP Production
Rosemary Vassallo, VP
Keith Boyes, Purch Mgr
Bruce Merstof, VP Sales & Estimating

The Boulevard Club

1491-1553 Lake Shore Blvd. West
Toronto, ON M6K 3C2
Tel 416-532-3341
Fax 416-538-9411
www.boulevardclub.com
Line: Operates private membership
sports and recreation club.
NAICS: 713910
#Emp: 100-249 (Tor)
#TorLoc: 1
Own: Private Company
Key: Ann Geddes, GM
Raffel Francis, Cont
Deborah Carlisle,
    Dir of Membership & Sales

Boutique La Vie en Rose Inc.

4320 Pierre de Coubertin
Montreal, PQ H1V 1A6
Tel 514-256-9446
Fax 514-256-9339
www.lavieenrose.com
AKA: Lingerie & Company
Line: Retails women's lingerie.
NAICS: 448120
#Emp: 100-249 (Tor)
#TorLoc: 31
Own: Private Company
Key: Francois Roberge, Pres & CEO
Lyne Raymond, VP HR
Luc Poirier, CFO
Madeleine Doucet, VP Business Tech

BPO Properties Ltd.

Brookfield Pl., 181 Bay St., Suite 330
Toronto, ON M5J 2T3
Tel 416-369-2300
Fax 416-369-2301
www.brookfieldproperties.com
AKA: Brookfield Properties
Line: Owns and manages commercial
real estate.
NAICS: 531310
#Emp: 250-499 (Tor)
#TorLoc: 1
Own: Public Company
Par: Brookfield Asset Management
(CDA)
Key: Jan Sucharda, Pres & COO

Bradgate Arms Retirement Residence

54 Foxbar Rd.
Toronto, ON M4V 2G6
Tel 416-968-1331
Fax 416-968-3743
www.reveraliving.com
Line: Operates a retirement residence.
NAICS: 721111
#Emp: 75-99 (Tor)
#TorLoc: 1
Own: Private Company
Par: Revera Inc. (CDA)
Key: Shiran Refai, Mgr

Bramalea Medical Centre X-Ray & Ultrasound

206-18 Kensington Rd.
Brampton, ON L6T 4S5
Tel 905-793-5858
Fax 905-793-5428
Line: Operates a medical centre.
NAICS: 621510
#Emp: 75-99 (Tor)
Own: Private Company
Key: Gamal W. Haroun, Owner

Brampton Brick Limited

225 Wanless Dr.
Brampton, ON L7A 1E9
Tel 905-840-1011
Fax 905-840-1535
www.bramptonbrick.com
Line: Manufactures and distributes clay
brick.
NAICS: 327330
#Emp: 100-249 (Tor)
#TorLoc: 1
Own: Public Company
Key: Jeffrey Kerbel, Pres & CEO
Brad Duke, VP Manuf
Ken Mondor, VP Fin
Judy Pryma, VP Sales & Mktg

Brampton Caledon Community Living

34 Church St. West
Brampton, ON L6X 1H3
Tel 905-453-8841
Fax 905-453-8853
www.bcclnet.com
Line: Provides services and support for
people with developmental disabilities.
NAICS: 624120 624310
#Emp: 250-499 (Tor)
#TorLoc: 1
Own: Not-for-profit
Key: Jim Triantafilou, Exec Dir
Wendy Firkins,
    Admin & Resource Support
Joan McGovern, HR Mgr

Brampton Engineering Inc.

8031 Dixie Rd.
Brampton, ON L6T 3V1
Tel 905-793-3000
Fax 905-793-1753
www.be-ca.com
Line: Manufactures plastics extrusion
equipment for the flexible packaging
industry.
NAICS: 333310
#Emp: 100-249 (Tor)
#TorLoc: 1
Own: Private Company
Key: R.L. Bud Smith, Pres & CEO
Bob Smith, VP Ops
Teri Nicolais, HR Mgr
Dean Mastantuono, Exec VP & CFO
Philip Kwok, VP Sales
Bill Mitchell, Mktg Mgr

Brampton Public Library

65 Queen St. East
Brampton, ON L6W 3L6
Tel 905-793-4636
Fax 905-453-0810
www.bramlib.on.ca
NAICS: 514121
#Emp: 100-249 (Tor)
#TorLoc: 6
Own: Government
Par: The City of Brampton
Key: Cathy Natyas, CEO
Lesley Bates, HR

Brampton Transit

A Div. of The City of Brampton
185 Clark Blvd.
Brampton, ON L6T 4G6
Tel 905-874-2750
Fax 905-874-2799
www.brampton.ca/transit
NAICS: 485110
#Emp: 500-999 (Tor)
#TorLoc: 2
Own: Government
Par: The City of Brampton
Key: Suzanne Connor, Dir of Transit
Meva Sellars, Admin Services Mgr

Brand Felt of Canada

2559 Wharton Glen Ave.
Mississauga, ON L4X 2A8
Tel 905-279-6680
Fax 905-279-3099
www.brandfelt.com
Line: Manufactures felts and wool
products.
NAICS: 313230
#Emp: 75-99 (Tor)
#TorLoc: 1
Own: Private Company
Key: Wolfgang Kirsten, Pres
Darren Hanson, Cont

Branksome Hall

10 Elm Ave.
Toronto, ON M4W 1N4
Tel 416-920-9741
Fax 416-920-9079
www.branksome.on.ca
Line: Operates independent school
for girls with both day and boarding
students.
NAICS: 611110
#Emp: 100-249 (Tor)
#TorLoc: 1
Own: Not-for-profit

Key: Karen Murton, Principal
Leslie Morgan, Dir of HR
Judy Gordon, Dir of Fin & Admin
Terence Carty, Dir of IT
Julia Drake, Dir of Commun & Mktg

Bratty & Partners Barristers and Solicitors

200-7501 Keele St.
Vaughan, ON L4K 1Y2
Tel 905-760-2600
Fax 905-760-2900
www.bratty.com
Line: Operates a law firm.
NAICS: 541110
#Emp: 100-249 (Tor)
#TorLoc: 1
Own: Private Company
Key: Michael N. Durisin, Mng Partner

Brenlo Ltd.

41 Racine Rd.
Toronto, ON M9W 2Z4
Tel 416-749-6857
Fax 416-749-8969
www.brenlo.ca
AKA: Brenlo Custom Wood Mouldings
Line: Manufactures custom wood
mouldings for industrial, commercial
and residential use.
NAICS: 321919
#Emp: 75-99 (Tor)
#TorLoc: 2
Own: Private Company
Key: John W. F. Kitchen, Pres
Paul Santin, Cont

Brenmar Heating & Air Conditioning Ltd.

1-3135 Unity Dr.
Mississauga, ON L5L 4L4
Tel 905-608-9330
Fax 905-608-0197
www.brenmar.ca
Line: Installs heating and air
conditioning.
NAICS: 232520
#Emp: 75-99 (Tor)
#TorLoc: 1
Own: Private Company
Key: Louie Martellaci, Pres
Phil Machado, Cont

Brennan Paving & Construction Ltd.

505 Miller Ave.
Markham, ON L6G 1B2
Tel 905-475-1440
Fax 905-475-4805
www.millergroup.ca
Line: Provides concrete, aggregate, and
asphalt products and services.
NAICS: 232220
#Emp: 250-499 (Tor)
#TorLoc: 1
Own: Private Company
Key: Leo McArthur, Pres

Brenntag Canada Inc.

43 Jutland Rd.
Toronto, ON M8Z 2G6
Tel 416-259-8231
Fax 416-259-5333
www.brenntag.ca
Line: Distributes industrial and
specialty chemicals, plastic resins and
colour concentrates.
NAICS: 418410
#Emp: 100-249 (Tor)
#TorLoc: 4
Own: Private Company
Par: Brenntag AG (GER)
Key: Mike Staley, Pres
Bonnie Miller, Dir of HR & Commun
Peter Stinson, CFO
Eric Haaijer, VP Eastern Region

Brewers' Retail Inc.

5900 Explorer Dr.
Mississauga, ON L4W 5L2
Tel 905-361-1005
Fax 905-361-4289
www.thebeerstore.ca
AKA: The Beer Store
Line: Wholesales, distributes and
retails beer in Ontario.
NAICS: 445310
#Emp: 1000-4999 (Tor)
Own: Private Company
Key: Ted Moroz, Pres
Bruce Farrer, VP Retail
Foster Brown, VP HR
Bill Hanchar, VP Fin
John Melodysta, Dir of IT
Don Chamberland, VP Logistics

Briars Estates Ltd.

55 Hedge Rd.
R.R. 1
Jackson's Point, ON L0E 1L0
Tel 905-722-3271
Fax 905-722-9698
www.briars.ca
AKA: The Briars Resort
Line: Offers meals, golf, tennis, and other recreational services at a family owned spa, resort, and conference centre.
NAICS: 721113
#Emp: 100-249 (Tor)
#TorLoc: 1
Own: Private Company
Par: 625631 Ontario Inc. (CDA)
Key: Barbara Sibbald, Pres
Bob Law, Resort Mgr
Janet Sibbald, HR Mgr
Cheryl McMurter, Purch Mgr
Andrew Sibbald, MIS, Asst Corp Secy
Hugh Sibbald, GM, VP Sales & Mktg

The Brick Warehouse Corp.

6765 Kennedy Rd.
Mississauga, ON L5T 0A6
Tel 905-696-3400
Fax 905-696-3402
www.thebrick.com
AKA: The Brick Distribution Centre
Line: Operates a furniture, appliance and electronics chain.
NAICS: 443110
#Emp: 250-499 (Tor)
Own: Private Company
Key: Don Parans, Reg Mgr

Bridgepoint Health

14 St. Matthews Rd.
Toronto, ON M4M 2B5
Tel 416-461-8252
Fax 416-461-5696
www.bridgepointhealth.ca
Line: Operates a chronic and rehabilitation hospital.
NAICS: 622310
#Emp: 1000-4999 (Tor)
#TorLoc: 1
Own: Not-for-profit
Key: Marian T. Walsh, Pres & CEO
Stav D'Andrea, Dir of HR
Nancy Macken, VP Fin & CAO
Anne Trafford, VP IT & CIO

Bridgestone/Firestone (Canada) Inc.

400-5770 Hurontario St.
Mississauga, ON L5R 3G5
Tel 905-890-1990
Fax 905-890-1991
www.bridgestone-firestone.ca
NAICS: 415210
#Emp: 100-249 (Tor)
#TorLoc: 2
Own: Private Company
Par: Bridgestone/Firestone Inc. (US)
Key: Gary Garfield, Pres & CEO

Brink's Canada Ltd.

1000-1 Robert Speck Pkwy.
Mississauga, ON L4Z 3M3
Tel 905-306-9600
Fax 905-306-0850
www.brinks.ca
Line: Provides armoured car, cash management and cash logistics services.
NAICS: 561613
#Emp: 500-999 (Tor)
#TorLoc: 3
Own: Private Company
Par: Brink's Inc. (US)
Key: Peter Panaritis, Pres
Jerry Brown, Sr VP Ops
Larry Locken, Sr VP HR

Brita Canada Corp.

102 Parkshore Dr.
Brampton, ON L6T 5M1
Tel 905-793-5555
Fax 905-793-4008
www.brita.ca
AKA: Brita Water Filter Systems
Line: Sells water filter systems.
NAICS: 453999
#Emp: 75-99 (Tor)
#TorLoc: 1
Own: Private Company
Par: The Clorox Co. (US)
Key: Mark Charlton, Plant Mgr
Anna Burak, HR Mgr
Doina Fogarasi, Plant Acct

Broadleaf Logistics Company

1 Spar Dr.
Brampton, ON L6S 6E1
Tel 905-792-9903
Fax 905-792-4348
www.broadleaflogistics.com
Line: Produces lumber and building materials.
NAICS: 416310
#Emp: 100-249 (Tor)
#TorLoc: 1
Own: Public Company
Par: Platinum Equity LLC (US)
Key: Peter Lawson, Area GM
Bob Simko, CEO
Lynda Pallensen, Dir of HR
Roland Mitchell, CFO
Ron Fuller, Dir of IT
Brian Martin, Dir of Nat'l Accounts
Mike Gibson, Dir of Product
    Management & Mktg

Broadview Foundation

3555 Danforth Ave.
Toronto, ON M1L 1E3
Tel 416-466-2173
Fax 416-466-6781
www.chestervillage.ca
AKA: Chester Village
Line: Operates a non-profit charitable home for the aged.
NAICS: 623310
#Emp: 100-249 (Tor)
#TorLoc: 1
Own: Not-for-profit
Key: Cynthia Diotte, Admr
Bernice Adona,
    Financial Services Coord

Broan-Nutone Canada Inc.

1140 Tristar Dr.
Mississauga, ON L5T 1H9
Tel 905-670-2500
Fax 905-795-9783
www.broan-nutone.com
Line: Manufactures home ventilation products including range hoods, bath fans, energy recovery ventilators, electric furnaces, central vacuum systems, chimes and doorbells.
NAICS: 232590
#Emp: 100-249 (Tor)
#TorLoc: 1
Own: Private Company
Par: Nortek, Inc. (US)
Key: Pascal Ialenti, Pres
Rodier Grondin, VP & GM
Scott Stevens, VP Wholesale & Export

Brookdale Treeland Nurseries Ltd.

6050 17th Sideroad
Schomberg, ON L0G 1T0
Tel 905-859-4571
Fax 905-859-4172
www.btn.on.ca
Line: Grows and distributes trees, shrubs, vines, evergreens, and related horticultural products.
NAICS: 111421
#Emp: 100-249 (Tor)
#TorLoc: 1
Own: Private Company
Key: Jeff Olsen, Pres
Sherri Robertson, Payroll & HR
Ken Omms, CFO
Greg Lightle, Sales Mgr

Brookfield LePage Johnson Controls

7400 Birchmount Rd.
Markham, ON L3R 4E6
Tel 905-943-4100
Fax 905-415-3299
www.bljc.com
AKA: BLJC
Line: Offers clients real estate management services.
NAICS: 531210
#Emp: 500-999 (Tor)
#TorLoc: 9
Own: Private Company
Key: Gord Hicks, Pres
Brian Fellows, Exec VP
Jim Neal, VP Fin

Brookfield Power

300-181 Bay St.
P.O. Box 762
Toronto, ON M5J 2T3
Tel 416-363-9491
Fax 416-363-2856
www.brookfieldpower.com
AKA: Brookfield Renewable Power
Line: Provides electric power distribution.
NAICS: 221122
#Emp: 75-99 (Tor)
#TorLoc: 1
Own: Private Company
Par: Brookfield Asset Management (CDA)
Key: Ben Vaughan, Pres & COO
Richard Legault, CEO
Donald Tremblay, Exec VP & CFO
Colin Clark, Exec VP & CTO

Brooklin Concrete Products

A Div. of Con-Force Division
of Armtec Limited Partnership
6760 Baldwin St., Hwy. 12
P.O. Box 370
Brooklin, ON L1M 1B5
Tel 905-655-3311
Fax 905-655-3847
www.brooklin.com
Line: Manufactures patio and sidewalk slabs, interlocking paving stones, retaining walls, septic tanks, hydro vaults, storage sheds, curbing, and custom precasting.
NAICS: 327390
#Emp: 75-99 (Tor)
#TorLoc: 2
Own: Private Company
Key: Tom Cannon, CEO

Brown Community Centre

454 Avenue Rd.
Toronto, ON M4V 2J1
Tel 416-392-6826
Fax 416-392-6671
Line: Operates a community centre.
NAICS: 624190
#Emp: 75-99 (Tor)
#TorLoc: 1
Own: Private Company
Par: The City of Toronto
Key: Jonah Weslak, Coord

Browne & Co. Ltd.

100 Esna Park Dr.
Markham, ON L3R 1E3
Tel 905-475-6104
Fax 905-475-5843
www.browneco.com
Line: Imports and distributes houseware and tableware.
NAICS: 414310
#Emp: 75-99 (Tor)
#TorLoc: 1
Own: Private Company
Key: Michael Browne, Pres
Peter Browne, CEO
Brian Wood, VP Food Service Division
Anthony Carter, CFO
Michael Farrell, Purch Mgr

Brown Window Corp.

185 Snow Blvd.
Concord, ON L4K 4N9
Tel 905-738-6045
Fax 905-738-1342
www.brownwindow.com
Line: Manufactures vinyl and wood windows and doors.
NAICS: 321911

#Emp: 75-99 (Tor)
#TorLoc: 1
Own: Private Company
Key: Eros Gerardi, Pres
Pino Marinelli, Cont

Bruce R. Smith Ltd.

6550 Danville Rd.
Mississauga, ON L5T 2S6
Tel 905-565-0026
Fax 905-565-1688
www.brsmith.com
Line: Operates a transportation and logistics company.
NAICS: 488519
#Emp: 75-99 (Tor)
#TorLoc: 1
Own: Private Company
Key: John Smith, CEO

Brunico Communication Ltd.

500-366 Adelaide St. West
Toronto, ON M5V 1R9
Tel 416-408-2300
Fax 416-408-0870
www.brunico.com
Line: Publishes trade magazines and produces conferences.
NAICS: 511120
#Emp: 75-99 (Tor)
#TorLoc: 1
Own: Private Company
Key: Russell Goldstein, Pres & CEO
Omri Tintpulver, VP & CIO

Brydson Group Ltd.

18 Elm St.
Toronto, ON M5G 1G7
Tel 416-964-4525
Fax 416-977-8611
www.elmwoodspa.com
AKA: Elmwood Spa; elmspa; Bangkok Garden Restaurant; Elmcrest College
Line: Provides health and beauty services for men and women, authentic Thai cuisine and customized health wellness training and curriculum.
NAICS: 812190
#Emp: 100-249 (Tor)
#TorLoc: 3
Own: Private Company
Key: Marie Picton,
  Exec Mgr, Spa Services
Sherry Brydson, Pres
Brian Gallinger, Cont
Joel Santos, IT Mgr

Buck Consultants Limited

3000-155 Wellington St. West
Toronto, ON M5V 3H1
Tel 416-865-0060
Fax 416-865-1301
www.acsbuckcanada.com
AKA: Affiliated Computer Services,
Inc.
Line: Provides employee benefits and
actuarial consulting, administration
and outsourcing.
NAICS: 541611
#Emp: 100-249 (Tor)
#TorLoc: 1
Own: Public Company
Par: Xerox Corporation (US)
Key: Peter Arnold, Nat'l Practice
  Leader & Global Investment Advisor
Cameron McNeill, Mng Dir, Canada
Michele Bossi, Health &
  Productivity Practice Leader
Michael Davidson,
  Chief of Corp Services
Frederic Brosseau, Sr VP Business Dev
Marina Scassa,
  Dir of Commun & Sales Support

Buckley Cartage Ltd.

1905 Shawson Dr.
Mississauga, ON L4W 1T9
Tel 905-564-3211
Fax 905-564-1231
www.buckleycartage.com
Line: Provides transportation and
cartage services.
NAICS: 484110
#Emp: 100-249 (Tor)
#TorLoc: 1
Own: Private Company
Key: J. Bart Buckley, Pres
Cheryl Foster, HR Mgr
Kirk Doherty, Acctng Mgr

Buduchnist Credit Union Ltd.

2280 Bloor St. West
Toronto, ON M6S 1N9
Tel 416-763-6883
Fax 416-763-4512
www.buduchnist.com
Line: Operates a credit union.
NAICS: 522130
#Emp: 75-99 (Tor)
#TorLoc: 2
Own: Private Company
Key: Roman Medyk, Pres

Bulk Barn Foods Limited

55 Leek Cres.
Richmond Hill, ON L4B 3Y2
Tel 905-886-6756
Fax 905-886-3717
www.bulkbarn.ca
Line: Operates bulk food retail stores.
NAICS: 445299
#Emp: 100-249 (Tor)
#TorLoc: 32
Own: Private Company
Par: Craig Ofield Ltd. (CDA)
Key: Craig Ofield, Pres & CEO
Laura Boland, Exec VP Fin & Systems

Bulk Transfer Systems Inc.

11339 Albion Vaughan Line
Kleinburg, ON L0J 1C0
Tel 905-893-2626
Fax 905-893-2699
www.bulktransfer.com
Line: Operates trucking service.
NAICS: 484110
#Emp: 100-249 (Tor)
#TorLoc: 1
Own: Private Company
Key: Dario Muscillo, Pres
Angelo Muscillo, GM

Bunge Canada

2190 South Service Rd. West
Oakville, ON L6L 5N1
Tel 905-825-7900
Fax 905-847-1336
www.bungecanada.com
AKA: Bunge Canada Holdings Inc.
NAICS: 311225
#Emp: 100-249 (Tor)
#TorLoc: 3
Own: Public Company
Par: Bunge North America (US)
Key: Rick Watson, Country Mgr
Mark Roe, Ops Mgr
Dianna Lusby, Dir of Fin
Andrea Strother, Purch Mgr

Bunn-O-Matic Corporation of Canada Ltd.

280 Industrial Pkwy. South
Aurora, ON L4G 3T9
Tel 905-841-2866
Fax 905-841-2775
www.bunnomatic.com
Line: Manufactures beverage
equipment.
NAICS: 333310
#Emp: 100-249 (Tor)
#TorLoc: 1
Own: Private Company
Par: Bunn-O-Matic Corp. (US)
Key: Peter Neva, VP Manuf
Stephane Lauzon, VP Fin
Cyril Cooper, Materials Mgr
Ken Cox, VP Sales & Mktg

Burger King Restaurants of Canada Inc.

700-401 The West Mall
Toronto, ON M9C 5J4
Tel 416-626-6464
Fax 416-626-6891
www.burgerking.ca
Line: Operates fast food restaurants.
NAICS: 722210
#Emp: 1000-4999 (Tor)
#TorLoc: 55
Own: Private Company
Par: Burger King Corp. (US)
Key: Minirva Villa, HR Specialist

Burke's Restoration Inc.

21-17817 Leslie St.
Newmarket, ON L3Y 8C6
Tel 905-895-2456
Fax 905-895-2460
www.burkesrestoration.com
Line: Provides fire and water
restoration services including carpet
and duct cleaning.
NAICS: 561791
#Emp: 75-99 (Tor)
#TorLoc: 2
Own: Private Company
Key: Gary Burke, Owner

Burlington Fire Department

A Div. of The Corporation of the
City of Burlington
1255 Fairview St.
Burlington, ON L7S 1Y3
Tel 905-637-9536
Fax 905-333-8727
www.burlington.ca/fire
Line: Provides vital emergency
response, prevention and education
services.
NAICS: 913140
#Emp: 100-249 (Tor)
#TorLoc: 7
Own: Government
Key: Shayne Mintz, Fire Chief
Dave Beatty, Deputy Fire Chief
Tony Bavota, Deputy Fire Chief
Jeff Weber, Deputy Fire Chief

Burlington Golf & Country Club

422 North Shore Blvd. East
Burlington, ON L7T 1W9
Tel 905-634-7726
Fax 905-634-4843
www.burlingtongolfclub.com
Line: Operates a private golf and
curling club.
NAICS: 713910
#Emp: 100-249 (Tor)
#TorLoc: 1
Own: Private Company
Key: David Griffith, Pres
David DeSaverio, COO
Trisha Scalero, Cont

Burlington Hydro Inc.

1340 Brant St.
Burlington, ON L7R 3Z7
Tel 905-332-1851
Fax 905-332-8384
www.burlingtonhydro.com
Line: Manages electrical distribution.
NAICS: 221111
#Emp: 75-99 (Tor)
#TorLoc: 1
Own: Private Company
Key: Gerry Smallegange, Pres & CEO
Jennifer Smith, Dir of HR

Burlington Public Library

2331 New St.
Burlington, ON L7R 1J4
Tel 905-639-3611
Fax 905-681-7277
www.bpl.on.ca
NAICS: 514121
#Emp: 100-249 (Tor)
#TorLoc: 6
Own: Private Company
Key: Maureen Barry, CEO
Linda Dobson, Dir of HR
Rick Craig, Dir of Fin

Burlington Taxi Inc.

3472 Landmark Rd.
Burlington, ON L7M 1S8
Tel 905-333-3333
Fax 905-333-1688
www.burlingtontaxi.com
Line: Provides taxi, airport
transportation and courier services.
NAICS: 485310
#Emp: 100-249 (Tor)
#TorLoc: 1
Own: Private Company
Key: Scott Wallace, Pres
Chris Belec, Ops Mgr
Terri Masters, Admin Mgr

Burlington Technologies Inc.

3267 Mainway Dr.
Burlington, ON L7M 1A6
Tel 905-335-2742
Fax 905-335-4679
www.burltech.com
Line: Manufactures automotive
components.
NAICS: 336390
#Emp: 250-499 (Tor)
#TorLoc: 5
Own: Private Company
Par: Castings International Inc. (CDA)
Key: Curtis French, Pres & CEO
Joe Bianco, Plant Mgr
Susan Stevens, CFO
Edward Dam, IT Mgr
Harry Cowan, VP Sales & Mktg

Burman & Fellows Group Inc.

8-700 Progress Ave.
Toronto, ON M1H 2Z7
Tel 416-431-1322
Fax 416-431-4466
www.bfg.ca
Line: Provides electrical and data-voice
communication connectivity solutions.
NAICS: 514210
#Emp: 75-99 (Tor)
#TorLoc: 1
Own: Private Company
Key: Jon Burman, Pres

Burnbrae Farms Mississauga

A Div. of Burnbrae Farms Limited
5434 Tomken Rd.
Mississauga, ON L4W 1P2
Tel 905-624-3600
Fax 905-624-5298
www.burnbraefarms.com
Line: Manufactures and wholesales
eggs.
NAICS: 413130 311990
#Emp: 100-249 (Tor)
#TorLoc: 1
Own: Private Company
Par: Burnbrae Holdings Ltd. (CDA)
Key: Margaret Hudson, Pres
Joe Hudson, Chmn & CEO
Pierre Boileau, VP HR
Harris Cooper, Sr VP Fin
Errol Roulstone, Sr Sales Dir

Business Development Bank of Canada

1200-121 King St. West
Toronto, ON M5H 3T9
Tel 416-973-0341
Fax 416-954-5009
www.bdc.ca
AKA: BDC
Line: Operates bank for small
businesses.
NAICS: 522112
#Emp: 250-499 (Tor)
#TorLoc: 5
Own: Federal Crown Corp.
Key: Peter Lawler, Sr VP Ops, Ontario
Ellen Austin, Dir of HR

Business Information Group

800-12 Concorde Pl.
Toronto, ON M3C 4J2
Tel 416-442-5600
Fax 416-442-2191
www.businessinformationgroup.ca
Line: Publishes business magazines,
construction information and
subscription-based print and electronic
products serving a broad range of
industries and professional groups.
NAICS: 511120
#Emp: 250-499 (Tor)
#TorLoc: 1
Own: Public Company
Par: Glacier Ventures (CDA)
Key: Bruce Creighton, Pres
Suzanne White, HR Mgr
Debbie Wan, Fin Mgr
Jennifer Hunter, Mktg & Sales Mgr

Butcher Engineering Enterprises Ltd.

120 Orenda Rd.
Brampton, ON L6W 1W2
Tel 905-459-3030
Fax 905-459-0689
www.butcherent.com
Line: Operates an automotive body,
industrial parts painter and interior
repair shop.
NAICS: 811121
#Emp: 100-249 (Tor)
#TorLoc: 2
Own: Private Company
Key: Colin McKillop, CEO

The Butcher Shoppe

A Div. of 573349 Ontario Ltd.
121 Shorncliffe Rd.
Toronto, ON M8Z 5K7
Tel 416-234-2290
Fax 416-234-1038
www.butchershoppe.com
Line: Wholesales meat products.
NAICS: 413160
#Emp: 100-249 (Tor)
#TorLoc: 1
Own: Private Company
Key: Allan Weisberg, Pres
Tom Dimitriadis, CFO

byPeterandPauls.com

6-8601 Jane St.
Concord, ON L4K 5N9
Tel 905-326-2000
Fax 905-326-2500
www.bypeterandpauls.com
Line: Provides special food services.
NAICS: 722320
#Emp: 100-249 (Tor)
#TorLoc: 1
Own: Private Company
Key: Kostas Marmaras,
   Mng Dir, Paramount
Peter Eliopoulos, Creative Dir
Peniel Cherian, Cont

CAA South Central Ontario

60 Commerce Valley Dr. East
Thornhill, ON L3T 7P9
Tel 905-771-3000
Fax 905-771-3101
www.caasco.com
AKA: Canadian Automobile
Association
Line: Provides roadside assistance,
insurance, travel services and
automotive repair facilities.
NAICS: 561590 524210
#Emp: 1000-4999 (Tor)
#TorLoc: 10
Own: Association
Key: Nick Parks, Pres & CEO
Hank P. Keyzers, Sr VP Club Services
Cynthia Hillaby, VP HR
Teddy Chien, VP & CFO
Sav Chalwa, VP IT
Lynda Breakey, VP Travel & Retail
Rhonda English, VP Corp Mktg
Mary Duncan, VP Change
   Management & Corp Commun

Cable Control Systems Inc.

2800 Coventry Rd.
Oakville, ON L6H 6R1
Tel 905-829-9910
Fax 905-829-9590
www.cablecontrol.ca
Line: Offers communication cable
repairs and installation.
NAICS: 232510
#Emp: 100-249 (Tor)
#TorLoc: 3
Own: Private Company
Key: Mike Rauseo, Pres

CA Canada

5935 Airport Rd., 11th Fl.
Mississauga, ON L4V 1W5
Tel 905-676-6700
Fax 905-676-6734
www.ca.com/ca
AKA: CA Technologies; Computer
Associates Canada Co.
NAICS: 541510 511210
#Emp: 100-249 (Tor)
#TorLoc: 1
Own: Private Company
Par: Computer Associates International
Inc. (US)
Key: David Ridout,
   Country Mgr & VP Sales

The Cadillac Fairview Corp. Limited

20 Queen St. West, 5th Fl.
Toronto, ON M5H 3R4
Tel 416-598-8200
Fax 416-598-8607
www.cadillacfairview.com
Line: Invests, owns and manages
commercial real estate.
NAICS: 531120
#Emp: 1000-4999 (Tor)
#TorLoc: 17
Own: Private Company
Par: Cadillac Fairview Corporation
(CDA)
Key: Peter Sharpe, Pres & CEO
Ron Wratschko, Exec VP Ops
Cheryl Clark, Sr VP HR
Cathal O'Connor, Exec VP & CFO
Scot Adams, Sr VP & CIO
John Sullivan, Exec VP Dev

Calea Ltd.

2-2785 Skymark Ave.
Mississauga, ON L4W 4Y3
Tel 905-624-1234
Fax 905-629-0123
www.calea.ca
AKA: Calea's Pharmacy
Line: Operates a health-care
solutions provider that supplies
home I.V., medical equipment and
pharmaceutical sales of drugs and
devices.
NAICS: 417930 339110
#Emp: 250-499 (Tor)
#TorLoc: 1
Own: Private Company
Par: Fresenius AG (GER)
Key: Matthew Rotenberg, CEO
Daryl Austin, Dir of Ops
Lisa Beck, Dir of HR
Patricia Mueller, CFO
Albert Rizzo, CIO
Adrian Kirby, Dir of Sales
Bette Krasnoff, VP Pharmacy Services

Caledon Community Services

18 King St. East
Royal Courtyards, Upper Level
Bolton, ON L7E 1E8
Tel 905-584-2300
Fax 905-951-2303
www.ccs4u.org
NAICS: 813410
#Emp: 100-249 (Tor)
Own: Not-for-profit
Key: Monty Laskin, Exec Dir
Beth Speers,
   Dir of Fin & Operational Support
Kari Simpson, Dir of Health Services
Cathy Perennec McLean, Dir of
   Employment & Dev
Fiona Ott,
   Dir of Fundraising & Commun

Caledon Ski Club Limited

17431 Mississauga Rd.
Caledon, ON L7K 0E9
Tel 519-927-5221
Fax 519-927-3592
www.caledonskiclub.on.ca
NAICS: 713920 721113
#Emp: 100-249 (Tor)
#TorLoc: 1
Own: Private Company
Key: Mike Porter, GM
Jamie Sievwright, Ops Mgr

Caledon Woods Golf Club

15608 Regional Rd., Hwy. 50
Bolton, ON L7E 3E5
Tel 905-880-1400
Fax 905-880-2498
www.clublink.ca
NAICS: 713910
#Emp: 100-249 (Tor)
#TorLoc: 1
Own: Private Company
Par: ClubLink Corp. (CDA)
Key: David Belletrutti, Dir of Ops

Cambridge Group of Clubs

444-100 Richmond St. West
Toronto, ON M5H 3K6
Tel 416-363-9454
Fax 416-363-4123
www.cambridgegroupofclubs.com
AKA: Cambridge Club; Adelaide Club;
Toronto Athletic Club
Line: Operates a chain of fitness
centres.
NAICS: 713940
#Emp: 250-499 (Tor)
#TorLoc: 3
Own: Private Company
Key: Clive Caldwell, Pres
Andrea Larsen, HR Generalist
Azard Kallan, Corp Group Cont
Donald Blair, IT Mgr
Bill MacDonell, Membership Dir
Nancy Sawler, Corp Mktg Dir

Cambridge Suites Hotel Toronto

15 Richmond St. East
Toronto, ON M5C 1N2
Tel 416-368-1990
Fax 416-601-3751
www.cambridgesuitestoronto.com
Line: Operates an all suite hotel located
in downtown Toronto.
NAICS: 721111
#Emp: 100-249 (Tor)
#TorLoc: 1
Own: Private Company
Par: Centennial Hotels Ltd. (CDA)
Key: Tim Ostrem, GM
Van Nguyen, Cont
Elizabeth Tanaskovic, Dir of Revenue
Kimberly Whitnell, Dir of Sales & Mktg

Camilion Solutions Inc.

123 Commerce Valley Dr. East, 6th Fl.
Markham, ON L3T 7W8
Tel 905-482-3450
Fax 905-482-2805
www.camilion.com
Line: Provides insurance product
development solutions.
NAICS: 541510
#Emp: 100-249 (Tor)
Own: Private Company
Key: Ross Orrett, Pres & CEO

Campbell Company of Canada

60 Birmingham St.
Toronto, ON M8V 2B8
Tel 416-251-1131
Fax 416-253-8623
www.campbellsoup.ca
Line: Manufactures and markets quality
branded food and beverage products in
the grocery and food service areas.
NAICS: 311420
#Emp: 500-999 (Tor)
#TorLoc: 2
Own: Private Company
Par: Campbell Investment Company
(US)
Key: Phillip E. Donne, Pres
Kevin Matier, VP & GM
Greg Smith, VP HR
Earl Ellis, VP Fin
John Grange, Dir of IT
Mark Rutledge, VP Sales
Mark Childs, VP Mktg

Camp Forming Ltd.

105 Rivalda Rd.
Toronto, ON M9M 2M6
Tel 416-745-8680
Fax 416-742-4443
Line: Specializes in residential and
industrial basement foundations.
NAICS: 232220
#Emp: 100-249 (Tor)
#TorLoc: 1
Own: Private Company
Key: Frank Campoli, Pres
Gerry Campoli, GM

Campio Furniture Ltd.

180 New Huntington Rd.
Woodbridge, ON L4H 0P5
Tel 905-850-6636
Fax 905-850-6640
www.campiofurniture.com
Line: Manufactures upholstered
furniture.
NAICS: 337121
#Emp: 100-249 (Tor)
#TorLoc: 1
Own: Private Company
Key: Vito Servello, Owner
Madaline Servello, Office Mgr
Yvonne Ciliberti, Accounts Receivable
Vince Servello, VP Mktg

Canaccord Capital Corp.

161 Bay St., 29th Fl.
P.O. Box 519
Toronto, ON M5J 2S1
Tel 416-869-7368
Fax 416-869-7356
www.canaccord.com
Line: Provides independent investment
globally.
NAICS: 523110
#Emp: 1000-4999 (Tor)
#TorLoc: 1
Own: Public Company
Key: Mark Maybank, Pres & COO
Mike Reynolds,
    Sr VP, Dir & Branch Mgr
Lori Seguin, HR Mgr
Brad Kotush, Exec VP & CFO
Matthew Gaasenbeek,
    Exec VP & Mng Dir
Scott Davidson, Mng Dir & Global Head
    of Mktg & Commun

Canada Bonded Attorney & Legal Directory Ltd.

1280 Courtney Park Dr. East
Mississauga, ON L5T 1N6
Tel 905-740-3222
Fax 905-740-3105
www.canadabonded.com
Line: Operates a collection agency.
NAICS: 561440
#Emp: 100-249 (Tor)
Own: Private Company
Key: John L. Smith, Pres & CEO

Canada Bread Company Limited

10 Four Seasons Pl., 12th Fl.
Toronto, ON M9B 6H7
Tel 416-622-2040
Fax 416-622-9332
www.canadabread.com
Line: Manufactures breads, pastas and
sauces.
NAICS: 311814
#Emp: 1000-4999 (Tor)
#TorLoc: 12
Own: Public Company
Par: Maple Leaf Foods (CDA)
Key: Barry McLean, Pres, Fresh Bakery
Richard Lan, Pres & CEO
Walter Miller, Sr VP Ops, Fresh Bakery
Robert I. Busch, Sr., VP HR & Corp
  Affairs, Bakery Group
Eric Martin, IT Business Partner
Tania Goecke, Dir of Mktg

Canada Cartage System Ltd.

1115 Cardiff Blvd.
Mississauga, ON L5S 1L8
Tel 905-564-2115
Fax 905-795-4253
www.canadacartage.com
Line: Provides local cartage and long
distance transportation in North
America.
NAICS: 484110 484121
#Emp: 1000-4999 (Tor)
#TorLoc: 3
Own: Private Company
Key: Sandro Caccaro,
  VP Ops & GM, Ontario
Jeffrey Lindsay, Pres & CEO
Mike Knorr, Sr VP Ops & Tech
Dave Kennedy, Dir of HR,
  Safety & Compliance
David Bacon, Sr VP Finace & CFO
Brian Martin, Sr VP Sales & Mktg

Canada Catering Company Ltd.

5 Southvale Dr.
Toronto, ON M4G 1G2
Tel 416-421-7474
Fax 416-421-5694
www.canadacatering.ca
Line: Provides food services.
NAICS: 722320 722210 454210
#Emp: 250-499 (Tor)
#TorLoc: 48
Own: Private Company
Key: William Mark Hatch, Pres
Mary Kuschnir, VP
Ron Hornsby, Exec VP
Bradley Hatch, Reg Dev Dir

Canada Centre for Inland Waters

A Div. of Environment Canada
867 Lakeshore Rd.
P.O. Box 5050
Burlington, ON L7R 4A6
Tel 905-336-4999
Fax 905-336-6444
www.ec.gc.ca
NAICS: 911910
#Emp: 1000-4999 (Tor)
#TorLoc: 2
Own: Government
Key: John Lawrence, Dir
Carol Mackay-Gordon, HR Mgr
Ann Vize, Fin Mgr

Canada Colors & Chemicals Ltd.

130-175 Bloor St. East, North Tower
Toronto, ON M4W 3R8
Tel 416-443-5500
Fax 416-449-9039
www.canadacolors.com
Line: Manufactures and distributes
industrial chemicals, solvents, plastics,
resins and compounds.
NAICS: 418410
#Emp: 100-249 (Tor)
#TorLoc: 4
Own: Private Company
Key: Dave Emerson,
  Pres & COO, Chemicals
Guy S. Carr-Harris, Chmn & CEO
Rick Rundle, Exec Dir, Logistics
Margo E. Vanderland, Dir of HR
Brian Fisher, CIO

Canada Fibers Ltd.

3-322 Horner Ave.
Toronto, ON M8W 1Z3
Tel 416-253-0400
Fax 416-253-1230
www.canadafibersltd.com
Line: Wholesales recycled paper.
NAICS: 418220
#Emp: 75-99 (Tor)
#TorLoc: 1
Own: Private Company
Key: Paul Clarfield, Pres
David Long, Cont

Canada Goose

1381 Castlefield Ave.
Toronto, ON M6B 1G7
Tel 416-780-9850
Fax 416-780-9854
www.canada-goose.com
Line: Manufactures down-filled
outerwear.
NAICS: 315229 315239

#Emp: 100-249 (Tor)
#TorLoc: 1
Own: Private Company
Key: Dani Reiss, Pres & CEO
Paul Riddlestone, VP
  Manuf & Supply Chain
Rhonda Misener, VP HR
Ron Price, VP Fin
Paul Silvertown, VP Sales,
  North America
Kevin Spreekmeester, VP Mktg

Canada Lands Company Ltd.

301 Front St. West
Toronto, ON M5V 2T6
Tel 416-868-6937
Fax 416-601-4722
www.cntower.ca
AKA: CN Tower Ltd.
Line: Operates a communications
tower with entertainment, hospitality
and retail facilities.
NAICS: 713990 722110
#Emp: 500-999 (Tor)
#TorLoc: 1
Own: Federal Crown Corp.
Key: Jack Robinson, COO
Mark Laroche, Pres & CEO
Neil Jones, Dir of Ops
Annamaria Di Cesare, Dir of HR
Sarfaraz Haq, Dir of Fin & CFO
Andre Saker,
  Dir of Facilities & Engineering
Carrie Jackson, Dir of Sales
Lisa Tompkins, Dir of Mktg & Commun
Peter George, Dir & Exec Chef

Canada Law Book Inc.

A Div. of Thompson Reuters
One Corporate Plaza,
2025 Kennedy Rd.
Toronto, ON M1T 3V4
Tel 905-841-6472
Fax 905-841-5085
www.canadalawbook.ca
Line: Publishes legal and business-to-
business magazines.
NAICS: 511130 511120
#Emp: 100-249 (Tor)
#TorLoc: 1
Own: Private Company
Par: The Cartwright Group (CDA)
Key: Mark Davidson,
  Mng Dir, Thompson Reuters
Scott Walters, HR
David Overall, VP IT
Debbie Hogan, Dir of Sales & Mktg

The Canada Life Assurance Co.

330 University Ave.
Toronto, ON M5G 1R8
Tel 416-597-1456
Fax 416-597-6520
www.canadalife.com
Line: Provides financial services including life, medical, dental, and disability; accumulates assets in the form of annuity, pension and investment products; and provides financial and investment management.
NAICS: 524112
#Emp: 1000-4999 (Tor)
#TorLoc: 8
Own: Public Company
Par: Great West Life Assurance Company (CDA)
Key: Paul Mahon, Pres & COO, Canada
D. Allen Lowney, Pres & CEO
Bill Lovatt, Exec VP & CFO

Canada Loyal Financial

2866 Portland Dr.
Oakville, ON L6H 5W8
Tel 905-829-5514
Fax 905-829-5516
www.canadaloyal.com
Line: Operates an insurance brokerage office.
NAICS: 524210
#Emp: 1000-4999 (Tor)
#TorLoc: 3
Own: Private Company
Key: Lawrence Fuller, Pres & Owner
Jackie Fuller, Office Mgr
Ward Fuller, VP Fin & Sales

Canada Mortgage and Housing Corp.

300-100 Sheppard Ave. East
Toronto, ON M2N 6Z1
Tel 416-221-2642
Fax 416-218-3310
www.cmhc-schl.gc.ca
AKA: CMHC
Line: Provides housing quality research, mortgage underwriting services and assistance to low-income persons.
NAICS: 911910 522310
#Emp: 250-499 (Tor)
#TorLoc: 2
Own: Federal Crown Corp.
Par: Government of Canada
Key: Peter Friedmann, GM
Mark Salerno, Corp Rep

Canada Post Corp./ Central Region

4567 Dixie Rd.
Mississauga, ON L4W 1S2
Tel 905-214-9539
Fax 905-214-9283
www.canadapost.ca
Line: Provides postal services.
NAICS: 491110
#Emp: 10000+ (Tor)
#TorLoc: 68
Own: Federal Crown Corp.
Par: Government of Canada
Key: Arlene Yam, Dir of Human Performance Management

Canada's Wonderland Company

9580 Jane St.
Vaughan, ON L6A 1S6
Tel 905-832-7000
Fax 905-832-7419
www.canadaswonderland.com
Line: Operates a theme park.
NAICS: 713110
#Emp: 1000-4999 (Tor)
#TorLoc: 1
Own: Private Company
Par: Cedar Fair Entertainment Company (US)
Key: Raffi Kaprelyan, GM
Heather Hill, Dir of Ops
Susan Edwards, Dir of HR
Ganesh Prasad, Dir of Fin
Dave Phillips, VP Mktg

Cana-Datum Moulds Ltd.

55 Goldthorne Ave.
Toronto, ON M8Z 5S7
Tel 416-252-1212
Fax 416-252-3539
www.cana-datum.com
Line: Manufactures die-casting tooling for aluminum and magnesium automotive industry including product development, prototyping permanent mould castings.
NAICS: 333519
#Emp: 100-249 (Tor)
#TorLoc: 2
Own: Private Company
Key: Ignacio Musalem, GM
Rodrigom Merino, Manuf Mgr
Randy Barton, HR Mgr

Canadian Apartment Properties Real Estate Investment Trust

401-11 Church St.
Toronto, ON M5E 1W1
Tel 416-861-9404
Fax 416-861-9209
www.capreit.net
AKA: CAPREIT
Line: Owns and manages multi-residential real estate.
NAICS: 526920
#Emp: 250-499 (Tor)
#TorLoc: 75
Own: Public Company
Key: Thomas Schwartz, Pres & CEO
Mark Kenney, COO
Jodi Lieberman, Asst VP & Dir of HR
Richard Smith, CFO
Perry Rose, VP Procurement
Robert Sestito, VP IT & Chief IS Officer
Patricia MacPherson, VP Sales & Mktg

Canadian Auto Workers Union

205 Placer Crt.
Toronto, ON M2H 3H9
Tel 416-497-4110
Fax 416-495-6552
www.caw.ca
AKA: CAW Canada; Canadian Auto Workers; CAW-TCA Canada
Line: Represents the rights of workers in the workplace on a variety of issues in a variety of industries.
NAICS: 813930
#Emp: 100-249 (Tor)
#TorLoc: 1
Own: Association
Key: Ken Lewenza, Pres
Karen Davis, Dir of Office Admin
Peter Kennedy, Secy-Treas

Canadian Bearings Ltd.

1600 Drew Rd.
Mississauga, ON L5S 1S5
Tel 905-670-6700
Fax 905-670-0795
www.canadianbearings.com
Line: Distributes bearings and power transmission products.
NAICS: 417230
#Emp: 100-249 (Tor)
#TorLoc: 3
Own: Private Company
Par: Lilco Holdings (CDA)
Key: Dane McElroy, VP
Farrokh Khalili, CEO
Marion Younan, Dir of HR
Roland Bissoon, VP Fin
Farhang Manucheran, Dir of IT

Canadian Blood Services

67 College St.
Toronto, ON M5G 2M1
Tel 416-974-9900
www.bloodservices.ca
Line: Operates a voluntary blood donor program for the provision of blood transfusion needs for patients.
NAICS: 813310 621990
#Emp: 500-999 (Tor)
#TorLoc: 5
Own: Not-for-profit
Key: Judy Compton,
   Dir of Donor & Clinic Services,
   Central Ontario Region
Gina Dimanis, HR Mgr
Kwei Chu, Fin Mgr

Canadian Broadcasting Corp.

250 Front St. West
P.O. Box 500, Stn. A
Toronto, ON M5W 1E6
Tel 416-205-3311
Fax 416-205-2841
www.cbc.ca
AKA: CBC
Line: Operates a television and radio broadcasting company.
NAICS: 513110 513120
#Emp: 1000-4999 (Tor)
#TorLoc: 1
Own: Federal Crown Corp.
Par: Government of Canada
Key: Sylvain Lafrance,
   Exec VP, French Services
Hubert P. Lacroix, Pres & CEO
Kristine Stewart, Exec VP,
   English Services
Suzanne Morris, VP & CFO

Canadian Business Machines Ltd.

8750 Holgate Cres.
High Point Business Park
Milton, ON L9T 0K3
Tel 905-878-0648
Fax 905-878-6748
www.cbmmetal.com
Line: Manufactures light steel products.
NAICS: 337214 337215
#Emp: 100-249 (Tor)
#TorLoc: 2
Own: Private Company
Key: John H. Williams, Pres
Cheryl Balch, HR Generalist
Anjita Pateo, Cont
Les Houle, Dir of Sales
Jeff Williams, Business Dev Mgr

Canadian Cancer Society Ontario Division

500-55 St. Clair West
Toronto, ON M4V 2Y7
Tel 416-488-5400
Fax 416-488-2872
www.cancer.ca
Line: Operates a charitable organization whose mission is the eradication of cancer and the enhancement of the quality of life for people living with cancer.
NAICS: 813310
#Emp: 100-249 (Tor)
#TorLoc: 15
Own: Not-for-profit
Par: Canadian Cancer Society (CDA)
Key: Martin Cabat, CEO
Jeffrey Gullberg, VP Ops & CFO
Leslie Raing, VP Dev & Mktg

Canadian Clothing International Inc.

541 Conlins Rd.
Toronto, ON M1B 5S1
Tel 416-335-1300
Fax 416-335-0087
Line: Exports and imports second hand clothing.
NAICS: 414110
#Emp: 100-249 (Tor)
Own: Private Company
Key: Raza Nasser, Pres
Rukhsana Jessa, Ops Mgr
Ash Manji, Sales & Mktg Mgr

The Canadian College of Naturopathic Medicine

1255 Sheppard Ave. East
Toronto, ON M2K 1E2
Tel 416-498-1255
Fax 416-498-3177
www.ccnm.edu
AKA: Institute of Naturopathic Education & Research
Line: Provides education in the field of naturopathic medicine.
NAICS: 611690
#Emp: 100-249 (Tor)
#TorLoc: 1
Own: Not-for-profit
Key: Bob Bernhardt, Pres & CEO
Robert Witkowski,
   Dir of Procurement & Facilities
Barbara Young, Exec Dir of HR
Paul Battistuzzi, CFO
Anna Couto, Procurement Coord
Lawrence Higgins, Dir of IS & Services
Catherine Kenwell,
   Dir of Mktg & Commun

Canadian Custom Packaging Co.

333 Rimrock Rd.
Toronto, ON M3J 3J9
Tel 416-638-1111
Fax 416-638-3800
www.cdncustompackaging.com
Line: Manufactures pharmaceutical, health and beauty products.
NAICS: 325410
#Emp: 75-99 (Tor)
#TorLoc: 1
Own: Private Company
Key: Gord Connelly, Pres

Canadian Depository for Securities Ltd.

85 Richmond St. West
Toronto, ON M5H 2C9
Tel 416-365-8400
Fax 416-365-0842
www.cds.ca
AKA: CDS
Line: Clears and settles security transactions.
NAICS: 523990
#Emp: 250-499 (Tor)
#TorLoc: 2
Own: Private Company
Key: Ian Gilhooley, Pres & CEO
Wendy Nunn, Chief HR Officer
Steve Blake, CFO
Brian Gill, CIO
Janet Comeau, Corp Commun Mgr

Canadian Diabetes Association

1400-522 University Ave.
Toronto, ON M5G 2R5
Tel 416-363-7071
Fax 416-363-7465
www.diabetes.ca
Line: Operates a non-governmental organization supporting diabetes research, education and advocacy.
NAICS: 813310
#Emp: 100-249 (Tor)
#TorLoc: 5
Own: Not-for-profit
Key: Michael Cloutier, Pres & CEO
Angelique Berg, VP Fund Dev

Canadian Food Inspection Agency

2-1124 Finch Ave. West
Toronto, ON M3J 2E2
Tel 416-665-5055
Fax 416-665-5069
www.inspection.gc.ca
Line: Provides inspection services for food.
NAICS: 561990
#Emp: 250-499 (Tor)
Own: Private Company
Key: Josee Rousseau, Reg Dir
Carole Swan, Pres

Canadian Hearing Society

271 Spadina Rd.
Toronto, ON M5R 2V3
Tel 416-928-2500
Fax 416-928-2523
www.chs.ca
AKA: CHS
Line: Advocates prevention of hearing loss and provides services to enhance the independence of deaf, deafened and hard of hearing people.
NAICS: 813310 624190
#Emp: 100-249 (Tor)
#TorLoc: 1
Own: Not-for-profit
Key: Chris Kenopic, Acting Pres & CEO
Stephanie Ozorio, Reg Dir
Donald Prong, Sr Mgr of HR
Susan Main, VP Strategic
    Commun & Fundraising

Canadian Imperial Bank of Commerce

Commerce Crt., Postal Stn.
Toronto, ON M5L 1A2
Tel 416-980-2211
Fax 416-980-4728
www.cibc.com
AKA: CIBC
Line: Operates a leading financial institution with nearly 11 million personal banking and business clients, offering a range of financial products and services.
NAICS: 522111 522112
#Emp: 10000+ (Tor)
#TorLoc: 213
Own: Public Company
Key: Gerald McCaughey, Pres & CEO
Richard Nesbitt,
    Sr Exec VP, Tech & Ops
Jackie Moss, Exec VP HR
Kevin Glass, Sr Exec VP & CFO
Stephen Forbes, Sr Exec VP, Mktg,
    Commun & Pub Affairs

Canadian Industrial Distributors Inc.

2A-175 Sun Pac Blvd.
Brampton, ON L6S 5Z6
Tel 905-595-0411
Fax 905-595-0425
www.cid.ca
Line: Distributes construction related equipment and supplies.
NAICS: 417210
#Emp: 75-99 (Tor)
#TorLoc: 1
Own: Private Company
Key: Larry Johns, Pres

Canadian Institute for Health Information

300-4110 Yonge St.
Toronto, ON M2P 2B7
Tel 416-481-2002
Fax 416-481-2950
www.cihi.ca
AKA: CIHI
Line: Develops and maintains a nationwide health information system.
NAICS: 813310
#Emp: 250-499 (Tor)
#TorLoc: 1
Own: Not-for-profit
Key: John Wright, Pres & CEO
Jean-Marie Berthelot, VP Programs
Elizabeth Blunden, Dir of HR & Admin
Lorraine Cayer, Dir of Fin

Canadian Institute of Chartered Accountants

277 Wellington St. West
Toronto, ON M5V 3H2
Tel 416-977-3222
Fax 416-977-8585
www.cica.ca
AKA: Chartered Accountants of Canada; CICA
Line: Develops accounting and auditing standards for the public and private sectors; researches in the field; publishes studies and articles; liaises with the federal government; issues post-certification education; and, contributes towards worldwide harmonization of accounting and auditing standards through participation in international organizations.
NAICS: 813920
#Emp: 100-249 (Tor)
#TorLoc: 1

Own: Association
Key: Kevin Dancey, Pres & CEO
Nigel Byars, Exec VP
Alan Burger, Dir of HR
Steve Anisman, Cont
George Greer, Dir of IT Services

Canadian Linen and Uniform Service Inc.

24 Atomic Ave.
Toronto, ON M8Z 5L2
Tel 416-251-2251
Fax 416-253-1748
www.canadianuniform.com
Line: Provides uniform, linen, and mat rental services.
NAICS: 812330
#Emp: 100-249 (Tor)
#TorLoc: 3
Own: Private Company
Par: Ameripride Services Inc. (US)
Key: Bob Kupchak, GM
Digna Ramos, Office & Personnel Mgr
John Annibale, Production Mgr
Daniel Ternawski, District IT Support
Kevin Doucet, Sales Mgr

Canadian Memorial Chiropractic College

6100 Leslie St.
Toronto, ON M2H 3J1
Tel 416-482-2340
Fax 416-646-1114
www.cmcc.ca
AKA: CMCC
Line: Provides chiropractic education and research services.
NAICS: 611690
#Emp: 100-249 (Tor)
#TorLoc: 6
Own: Private Company
Key: Jean A. Moss, Pres
Brenda Smith, VP Admin &
    Institutional Planning
George Keller, VP Fin
Fred Rajabi, Dir of IT
Ian Mishkel, VP Institutional
    Advancement

The Canadian Mental Health Association - Toronto Branch

480-700 Lawrence Ave. West
Toronto, ON M6A 3B4
Tel 416-789-7957
Fax 416-789-9079
www.cmha.ca
Line: Provides community support services to people with serious mental illnesses and promotes mental health awareness in the community.
NAICS: 813920

#Emp: 100-249 (Tor)
#TorLoc: 2
Own: Not-for-profit
Key: Steve Lurie, Exec Dir
Michelle Rehder, Program Dir,
   Specialized Services
Norma Mahoney, HR Mgr
Brian Pollock, Asst Exec Dir
Frank Sirotich, Program Dir,
   Community Support

Canadian Mothercraft Society

32 Heath St. West
Toronto, ON M4V 1T3
Tel 416-920-3515
Fax 416-920-5983
www.mothercraft.ca
AKA: Mothercraft; Robertson House
Line: Offers services for children and
families with special needs, training
programs for providers and other
professionals, and child care.
NAICS: 624110
#Emp: 75-99 (Tor)
#TorLoc: 3
Own: Not-for-profit
Key: Beverley Koven, CEO

The Canadian National Institute for the Blind/Ontario Div.

1929 Bayview Ave.
Toronto, ON M4G 3E8
Tel 416-486-2500
Fax 416-480-7000
www.cnib.ca
AKA: CNIB
Line: Operates a not-for-profit
rehabilitation agency to serve blind,
visually impaired and deaf blind
Canadians in their home communities.
NAICS: 624310 813310
#Emp: 250-499 (Tor)
#TorLoc: 1
Own: Not-for-profit
Key: John M. Rafferty, Pres & CEO
Cindy Lee, HR Coord
Ed Oikawa,
   Toronto Dir of Financial Acctng

Canadian Opera Company

227 Front St. East
Toronto, ON M5A 1E8
Tel 416-363-6671
Fax 416-363-5584
www.coc.ca
Line: Produces opera, concerts and
educational programmes.
NAICS: 711112 711130
#Emp: 100-249 (Tor)
#TorLoc: 2
Own: Not-for-profit

Key: Alexander Neef, Gen Dir
Robert Lamb, Mng Dir
Lindy Cowan, Dir of Fin & Admin
Michael Tremblay,
   Mgr of Office & Bldg Ops
Steven Sherwood, Mgr of IT
Jeremy Elbourne, Dir of Mktg
Claudine Dominique, Dir of PR

Canadian Pacific Railway

1290 Central Pkwy. West, 8th Fl.
Mississauga, ON L5C 4R3
Tel 905-803-3200
Fax 905-803-3300
www.cpr.ca
Line: Operates a transportation
company.
NAICS: 482113 482112
#Emp: 500-999 (Tor)
Own: Public Company
Key: Fred Green, Pres & CEO
Maureen Roach, HR Rep
Kathyn McQuade, Exec VP & CFO

Canadian Posters International Inc.

1180 Caledonia Rd.
Toronto, ON M6A 2W5
Tel 416-789-7156
Fax 416-789-7159
www.postersinternational.net
AKA: PI Fine Art
Line: Publishes posters and offers
framing.
NAICS: 511190
#Emp: 75-99 (Tor)
#TorLoc: 1
Own: Private Company
Key: Esther Bartfield, Pres
Andrew Cohen, VP
Richie Cohen, VP

Canadian Premier Life Insurance Co.

80 Tiverton Crt., 5th Fl.
Markham, ON L3R 0G4
Tel 905-479-3122
Fax 905-948-2100
www.canadianpremier.ca
AKA: Heritage General Insurance Co.
Line: Provides life insurance.
NAICS: 524210
#Emp: 75-99 (Tor)
#TorLoc: 1
Own: Private Company
Par: Aegon DMS (US)
Key: Isaac Sananes, Pres & CEO
Lidia Finlayson, Mgr, HR & Admin
Tamesh Paraboo, Asst VP & Asst Cont
Derek Cadden, Systems Mgr

The Canadian Press

36 King St. East, 3rd Fl.
Toronto, ON M5C 2L9
Tel 416-364-0321
Fax 416-364-9283
www.thecanadianpress.com
AKA: Broadcast News Ltd.; La Presse
Canadienne; Nouvelles Télé-Radio;
Press News Ltd.; CP Images
Line: Provides news and information to
daily newspapers, broadcasters, web
sites and corporate and government
clients.
NAICS: 514110
#Emp: 100-249 (Tor)
#TorLoc: 1
Own: Association
Key: Eric Morrison, Pres
Paul Woods, Dir of HR
Sandra Clarke, CFO
Carol Lamonaca, Support Services Mgr
Andrew Glenny, Dir of IT
Charles Messina, Dir of Sales & Mktg
Terry Scott, Dir of Broadcasting

Canadian Real Estate Investment Trust

500-175 Bloor St. East
North Tower
Toronto, ON M4W 3R8
Tel 416-628-7771
Fax 416-628-7777
www.creit.ca
AKA: CREIT Management LP
Line: Operates a real estate investment
trust and property management.
NAICS: 526920
#Emp: 75-99 (Tor)
#TorLoc: 1
Own: Public Company
Key: Stephen Johnson, Pres & CEO
Sylvie Lourenco, HR Mgr
Tim McSorley, VP & CFO

The Canadian Red Cross/ Ontario Zone

5700 Cancross Crt.
Mississauga, ON L5R 3E9
Tel 905-890-1000
Fax 905-890-1008
www.redcross.ca
Line: Provides first aid, water safety,
community health, home support,
disaster relief and emergency services,
and abuse prevention services.
NAICS: 624230
#Emp: 100-249 (Tor)
#TorLoc: 7
Own: Not-for-profit
Key: Ron Kelusky, GM, Field Ops
John Saunders, Dir of Disaster Mgt

Canadian Springs

1200 Britannia Rd. East
Mississauga, ON L4W 4T5
Tel 905-795-6500
Fax 905-670-3628
www.canadiansprings.ca
Line: Manufactures bottled spring and distilled water and supplies water coolers and filtration equipment.
NAICS: 333416
#Emp: 100-249 (Tor)
#TorLoc: 1
Own: Public Company
Par: Aquatera Utilities Inc. (CDA)
Key: Richard Stephens, Pres
Deborah Raine, Dir of HR
Joe Baker, IT Mgr

Canadian Standards Association

A Div. of CSA Group
100-5060 Spectrum Way
Mississauga, ON L4W 5N6
Tel 416-747-4000
Fax 416-747-2473
www.csa.ca
AKA: CSA
Line: Develops standards for businesses, industries, government and consumers in Canada.
NAICS: 813310
#Emp: 100-249 (Tor)
#TorLoc: 2
Own: Not-for-profit
Key: Bonnie Rose, Pres

Canadian Starter Drives Inc.

176 Milvan Dr.
Toronto, ON M9L 1Z9
Tel 416-748-1458
Fax 416-748-2497
www.4csd.net
Line: Provides engine rebuilding services.
NAICS: 336310
#Emp: 250-499 (Tor)
#TorLoc: 2
Own: Private Company
Key: Frank Colosimo, Pres & Owner
Tzvetam Deliyski, Plant Mgr

Canadian Tire Corporation Ltd.

2180 Yonge St.
P.O. Box 770, Stn. K
Toronto, ON M4P 2V8
Tel 416-480-3000
Fax 416-480-3996
www.canadiantire.ca
Line: Retails house wares, sports, leisure, and automotive products.
NAICS: 444130
#Emp: 5000-9999 (Tor)
Own: Public Company
Key: Stephen Wetmore, Pres & CEO
Sharon Patterson, Sr VP HR
Marco Marrone, Exec VP & CFO
Kristine Freudenthaler, Sr VP, IT & CIO

Canam

1739 Drew Rd.
Mississauga, ON L5S 1J5
Tel 905-671-3460
Fax 905-671-3924
www.canamgroup.ws
Line: Fabricates, distributes, and sells open web steel joists, trusses, and steel decks.
NAICS: 332319
#Emp: 100-249 (Tor)
#TorLoc: 1
Own: Public Company
Par: Canam Group Inc. (CDA)
Key: Abdul Hadibhai, GM
Warren Fournier, Ops Mgr
Cathy Hill, HR Mgr
Judy Simpson, Buyer
Coralee Johnson, Sales Mgr

Canamex Trucking System Inc.

30 Lethbridge Dr.
Brampton, ON L6S 6K7
Tel 905-458-5363
Fax 905-458-1240
www.canamexlogistics.com
Line: Operates a trucking company.
NAICS: 484121
#Emp: 100-249 (Tor)
#TorLoc: 1
Own: Private Company
Key: Gord Hundal, Pres
Suzanne McCowan, Cont

Can-Ar Coach Service

A Div. of Tokmakjian Ltd.
221 Caldari Rd.
Concord, ON L4K 3Z9
Tel 905-738-2290
Fax 905-660-0474
www.can-arcoach.com
NAICS: 485210

#Emp: 100-249 (Tor)
#TorLoc: 1
Own: Private Company
Key: Ajay Mehra, VP
Cy Tokmakjian, Pres

Cancable Inc.

2321 Fairview St.
Burlington, ON L7R 2E3
Tel 905-634-7152
Fax 905-634-1156
www.cancable.com
AKA: Dependable IT
NAICS: 541510
#Emp: 250-499 (Tor)
Own: Private Company
Par: Creative Vistas Inc. (CDA)
Key: Ross Jepson, Pres & CEO
Paul Mease, Sr VP Ops
Catherine Lewis, CFO

Can-Care Health Services Inc.

204-45 Sheppard Ave. East
Toronto, ON M2N 5W9
Tel 416-226-6995
Fax 416-226-6930
www.cancarehealth.com
Line: Provides in-home health care.
NAICS: 621610
#Emp: 250-499 (Tor)
#TorLoc: 1
Own: Private Company
Key: Eric Paul, Pres

Cancer Care Ontario

1500-620 University Ave.
Toronto, ON M5G 2L7
Tel 416-971-9800
Fax 416-971-6888
www.cancercare.on.ca
Line: Coordinates and steers Ontario's cancer services and prevention efforts so that fewer people get cancer and patients receive the highest quality of care.
NAICS: 813310 912910
#Emp: 500-999 (Tor)
#TorLoc: 1
Own: Government
Key: Michael Sherar, Pres & CEO
Helen Angus, VP Renal Network
Elham Roushani, CFO & HR
Rick Skinner, VP & CIO
Mitchell Toker, VP Pub Affairs

Canerector Inc.

930-100 Sheppard Ave. East
Toronto, ON M2N 6N5
Tel 416-225-6240
Fax 416-225-1232
www.marshallbarwick.ca
AKA: Canadian Erectors Ltd.
NAICS: 232230
#Emp: 250-499 (Tor)
#TorLoc: 2
Own: Private Company
Key: Cecil S. Hawkins, Pres

Canlan Ice Sports Corp.

989 Murray Ross Pkwy.
Toronto, ON M2H 2N5
Tel 416-661-4423
Fax 416-661-4422
www.icesports.com
Line: Operates recreational ice
facilities.
NAICS: 713940
#Emp: 250-499 (Tor)
#TorLoc: 6
Own: Public Company
Key: Andrew Nobel, GM
Joey St-Aubin, Pres & CEO
Kcn Male, VP Eastern Ops
Michael F. Gellard, Sr VP & CFO

Canoe Inc.

333 King St. East, 3rd Fl.
Toronto, ON M5A 3X5
Tel 416-350-6150
Fax 416-350-6238
www.canoe.ca
Line: Operates an Internet information
service.
NAICS: 514191
#Emp: 100-249 (Tor)
#TorLoc: 1
Own: Private Company
Par: Quebecor Media (CDA)
Key: John Williams, Sr Editor

Canon Canada Inc.

6390 Dixie Rd.
Mississauga, ON L5T 1P7
Tel 905-795-1111
Fax 905-795-2020
www.canon.ca
Line: Provides consumer and business
imaging solutions.
NAICS: 414430 334110
#Emp: 500-999 (Tor)
#TorLoc: 3
Own: Private Company
Par: Canon U.S.A. Inc. (US)

Key: Kevin Ogawa, Pres & CEO
Ian MacFarlane, VP & GM, Consumer
    Imaging Group
D. Mason Olds, Sr VP & GM
Hiroshi Miyazato, Dir of IT
Colleen Ryan, Sr Dir of Commun
    & Gen Environment Affairs

Canopco

1200-48 Yonge St.
Toronto, ON M5E 1G6
Tel 416-204-0247
Fax 416-640-1089
www.canopco.com
AKA: Globalive Communications; One
Connect Services
Line: Provides communication
services.
NAICS: 513330
#Emp: 100-249 (Tor)
#TorLoc: 1
Own: Private Company
Par: Globalive Communications Corp.
(CDA)
Key: Ezio D'Onofrio, Pres & CEO
Tony Lacavera, Chmn
Pierre Methe, Dir of Ops
Maryjane Encina, HR Mgr
Brice Scheschuk, CFO
Rishi Bahall,
    Dir of Network Engineering
Andre Cote, VP Business Dev
Nisha Amin, Dir of Mktg

Canpark Services Ltd.

404-234 Eglinton Ave. East
Toronto, ON M4P 1K5
Tel 416-482-2203
Fax 416-482-2866
www.canparkservices.com
Line: Provides parking operations,
management and consulting.
NAICS: 812930
#Emp: 75-99 (Tor)
#TorLoc: 40
Own: Private Company
Par: Jagramstef Holdings (Canada) Ltd.
(CDA)
Key: Edward G. Pace, Pres & CEO
Graham D. Pace, VP
Jason E. Pace, VP
Ashok Master, Acct

CANPAR Transport Ltd.

500-1290 Central Pkwy. West
Mississauga, ON L5C 4R9
Tel 905-276-3700
Fax 905-897-3630
www.canpar.com
Line: Provides small package delivery
service with terminals across the
country.

NAICS: 492110
#Emp: 500-999 (Tor)
#TorLoc: 5
Own: Private Company
Par: TransForce Inc. (CDA)
Key: James Houston, Pres
Larry Funco, VP Ops
Brent Neill, VP HR
Kent McDonald, VP Fin
Ronald Pogson, Dir of IT
Laurie Stoneburgh,
    VP Sales & Customer Service

Capgemini Canada Inc.

1100-200 University Ave.
Toronto, ON M5H 3C6
Tel 416-365-4400
Fax 416-365-4401
www.ca.capgemini.com
Line: Offers worldwide information
technology and consulting services.
NAICS: 541510
#Emp: 1000-4999 (Tor)
#TorLoc: 1
Own: Public Company
Par: Capgemini (FRA)
Key: Geoffrey B. Cronin, VP

Capital C Communications Inc.

500-340 King St. East
Toronto, ON M5A 1K8
Tel 416-777-1124
Fax 416-777-0060
www.capitalc.net
Line: Provides promotional and
communication services.
NAICS: 513390
#Emp: 100-249 (Tor)
#TorLoc: 1
Own: Private Company
Key: Tony Chapman, CEO

Capital One Services (Canada), Inc.

5140 Yonge St., 19th Fl.
Toronto, ON M2N 6L7
Tel 416-549-2500
Fax 416-549-2769
www.capitalone.ca
Line: Operates a credit lending
institution.
NAICS: 522210
#Emp: 100-249 (Tor)
#TorLoc: 1
Own: Private Company
Par: Capital One (US)
Key: William Cilluffo, Pres, International
Rob Livingston, Pres, Canada
Felix Wu, CFO
Ian Cunningham,
    Chief Mktg & Sales Officer

Capital Safety - Canada

260 Export Blvd.
Mississauga, ON L5S 1Y9
Tel 905-795-9333
Fax 905-795-8777
www.capitalsafety.ca
AKA: Can-Sling/DBI
Line: Manufactures and sells fall
protection safety equipment,
industrial slings, and industrial and
consumer nets.
NAICS: 339110 514191
#Emp: 100-249 (Tor)
#TorLoc: 1
Own: Private Company
Par: Capital Safety Group (UK)
Key: Peter Mammone, GM
Andres Pettersson, CEO
Frank Courtemanche, VP Quality

Cara Operations Limited

199 Four Valley Dr.
Vaughan, ON L4K 0B8
Tel 905-760-2244
www.cara.com
AKA: Cara Airline Solutions; Harvey's;
Kelsey's; Milestone's; Montana's; Swiss
Chalet; Coza
Line: Operates branded restaurants
and provides airline catering and food
distribution services.
NAICS: 722210 722320
#Emp: 5000-9999 (Tor)
#TorLoc: 158
Own: Private Company
Key: Don Robinson, Pres & CEO
Arjen Melis, Pres, Corp Dev
Steve Smith, CFO
Todd Barclay, VP
    Restaurant Dev & Franchising
Stephanie Fry, VP IT

Caravan Logistics Inc.

2284 Wyecroft Rd.
Oakville, ON L6L 6M1
Tel 905-338-5885
Fax 905-338-8450
www.caravanlogistics.ca
Line: Operates a trucking company.
NAICS: 484121
#Emp: 100-249 (Tor)
#TorLoc: 1
Own: Private Company
Key: John Iwaniura, Pres
Bob Workun, VP Ops
Kevin Snobel, GM
Bob Kobelak, Cont
Scott Cull, Corp Accounts Mgr
Steve Merena,
    VP Safety & Maintenance

Carbone of America

A Div. of Mersen Canada
496 Evans Ave.
Toronto, ON M8W 2T7
Tel 416-251-2334
Fax 416-251-7488
www.carbonebrush.com
Line: Manufactures carbon brushes
used in electric motors.
NAICS: 336390
#Emp: 75-99 (Tor)
#TorLoc: 1
Own: Private Company
Par: Mersen (FR)
Key: Marc Charlebois, GM

Cardinal Couriers Ltd.

400 Brunel Rd.
Mississauga, ON L4Z 2C2
Tel 905-507-4111
Fax 905-507-4177
www.cardinalcouriers.com
Line: Provides courier services.
NAICS: 492110
#Emp: 100-249 (Tor)
#TorLoc: 1
Own: Private Company
Key: Ian McLean, Pres
Cindy Webster, HR Mgr
Leanne Dalgleiesh, Purch & Admin Mgr
Adrian Pavone, CIO

Cardinal Golf Club

2740 Davis Dr. West
Kettleby, ON L0G 1J0
Tel 905-841-7378
Fax 905-841-3511
www.cardinalgolfclub.com
NAICS: 713910
#Emp: 100-249 (Tor)
#TorLoc: 1
Own: Private Company
Key: Rob Brandon, Dir of Golf
Bob Kilgour, GM
Susan Sheardown, Payroll
Darlene Atherley, Acctng
Jason McNally,
    Tournament & Mktg Coord

Cardinal Health Canada

1000 Tesma Way
Vaughan, ON L4K 5R8
Tel 905-417-2900
www.cardinalhealth.com
Line: Distributes healthcare products,
medical supplies and equipment.
NAICS: 417930
#Emp: 250-499 (Tor)
#TorLoc: 3
Own: Private Company

Key: David H. Lees, Pres & CEO
Jim Berneche, VP Dist Ops
Michael Rodgers, VP HR
Jay Shoemaker, VP Fin & CFO
John O'Connor, CIO

Cardinal Meat Specialists Ltd.

3160 Caravelle Dr.
Mississauga, ON L4V 1K9
Tel 905-672-1411
Fax 905-672-0450
www.cardinalmeats.com
Line: Manufactures and markets
portion controlled ground meat and
pre-cooked meat products.
NAICS: 413160
#Emp: 100-249 (Tor)
#TorLoc: 2
Own: Private Company
Par: 722140 Ontario Ltd. (CDA)
Key: Brent Cator, Pres
John Vatri,
    Dir of Food Safety & Logistics
Dominic Parravano, CFO
John Edward, VP Sales
Jeff Griffin, Dir of Mktg

Carecor Health Services Ltd.

600-415 Yonge St.
Toronto, ON M5B 2E7
Tel 416-593-5997
Fax 416-593-6362
www.carecor.com
Line: Provides nursing, transportation
and other support services to
healthcare facilities and private clients.
NAICS: 621390 541690
#Emp: 250-499 (Tor)
#TorLoc: 1
Own: Private Company
Key: Robert Yeo, Pres
Michelle Shaw, HR Coord
Hakan Vesterberg, Dir of Fin & Acctng

Carefirst Seniors & Community Services Association

501-3601 Victoria Park Ave.
Toronto, ON M1W 3Y3
Tel 416-502-2323
Fax 416-502-2382
www.carefirstseniors.com
AKA: Carefirst Foundation; Carefirst
Family Health Team
Line: Provides social services.
NAICS: 813410
#Emp: 250-499 (Tor)
#TorLoc: 8
Own: Not-for-profit
Key: Helen Leung, CEO
Edith Lam, Program Dir
Connie Chiu, HR Officer
Edmund Kwan, Dir of Fin

Cargill Foods Toronto

A Div. of Cargill Ltd.
71 Rexdale Blvd.
Toronto, ON M9W 6Y2
Tel 416-748-5000
Fax 416-748-5026
www.cargill.ca
Line: Processes fresh meat.
NAICS: 413130 413160
#Emp: 500-999 (Tor)
#TorLoc: 1
Own: Private Company
Par: Cargill Inc. (US)
Key: Jason Kuan, VP & GM
Jasko Turulja, Plant Mgr
Chris Riecker, HR Mgr

Carillion Canada Inc.

7077 Keele St., 4th Fl.
Concord, ON L4K 0B6
Tel 905-532-5200
www.carillion.ca
Line: Operates a building division
whose work includes major
construction and infrastructure.
NAICS: 231310 231390
#Emp: 1000-4999 (Tor)
#TorLoc: 1
Own: Private Company
Par: Carillion plc (UK)
Key: Graham Brown, Pres & CEO
Elaine Dray, Sr VP HR
Kirsty Vlemmiks, CFO
Jim Guest, Sr VP Supply Chain

Carlson Marketing Group Canada Ltd.

2845 Matheson Blvd. East
Mississauga, ON L4W 5K2
Tel 905-214-8699
Fax 905-214-8692
www.carlsoncanada.com
Line: Assists clients with relationship
marketing strategies designed for
employees, channels and consumers.
NAICS: 541619
#Emp: 500-999 (Tor)
#TorLoc: 3
Own: Private Company
Par: Groupe Aeroplan (US)
Key: Michael Pepin, Pres
Martha Barss, Sr VP Client Services
Gord Duncan, Dir of HR
Brian Patreau, Sr VP IT
Steve Fraser, Sr VP Mktg Strategies

Carlson Wagonlit Travel

800-10 Carlson Crt.
Toronto, ON M9W 6L2
Tel 416-679-6444
Fax 416-798-3803
www.carlsonwagonlit.com
Line: Operates travel management
company.
NAICS: 561510
#Emp: 500-999 (Tor)
#TorLoc: 9
Own: Private Company
Par: Carlson Companies Inc. (US)
Key: Sherry Saunders, Sr VP & GM
Patricia Quance, Sr Dir of HR
Andrea Knappich, CFO
Kathleen Pilgrim,
    Sr Dir of Business Dev
Mike Thompson, VP
    Leisure Travel, North America

Carlton Cards Ltd.

1820 Matheson Blvd.
Mississauga, ON L4W 0B3
Tel 905-219-6410
Fax 905-219-6415
www.carltoncards.ca
Line: Produces greeting cards.
NAICS: 323119
#Emp: 75-99 (Tor)
#TorLoc: 1
Own: Private Company
Par: American Greetings Corp. (US)
Key: Ron Sturtridge, VP
Larry Green, Dir of HR

Carl Zeiss Canada Ltd.

45 Valleybrook Dr.
Toronto, ON M3B 2S6
Tel 416-449-4660
Fax 416-449-3524
www.zeiss.ca
Line: Manufactures and wholesales
ophthalmic equipment, service
microscopes and prescription lenses.
NAICS: 339110
#Emp: 100-249 (Tor)
#TorLoc: 1
Own: Private Company
Par: Carl Zeiss AG (GER)
Key: Lynn Mousmanis, VP Fin & Ops
Vicki Rousakos, Personnel Admr

Carmichael Engineering Ltd.

3146 Lenworth Dr.
Mississauga, ON L4X 2G1
Tel 905-625-4701
Fax 905-625-4349
www.carmichael-eng.ca
Line: Manufactures refrigeration, air
conditioning, heating and laboratory
equipment.
NAICS: 333416
#Emp: 75-99 (Tor)
#TorLoc: 1
Own: Private Company
Key: Ray Carmichael, VP & GM

Car Park Management Services Ltd.

40 Isabella St.
Toronto, ON M4Y 1N1
Tel 416-920-3382
Fax 416-920-0367
www.carpark.ca
Line: Manages, leases, and maintains
parking lots.
NAICS: 812930
#Emp: 100-249 (Tor)
Own: Private Company
Key: Gerard MacLean, Pres
Paul MacLean, VP
Catherine Zwaryck, VP
Carol MacLean, Secy-Treas

Carpenter Canada Co.

500 Hanlan Rd.
Woodbridge, ON L4L 3P6
Tel 905-851-6764
Fax 905-856-0339
www.carpenter.com
Line: Manufactures polyurethane foam.
NAICS: 326150
#Emp: 75-99 (Tor)
#TorLoc: 1
Own: Private Company
Key: Carlo Fazzalari, GM

Carquest Canada Ltd.

35 Worcester Rd.
Toronto, ON M9W 1K9
Tel 416-675-2100
Fax 416-675-1013
www.carquest.ca
Line: Operates auto parts warehouse.
NAICS: 415290
#Emp: 100-249 (Tor)
#TorLoc: 15
Own: Private Company
Par: General Parts Inc. (US)
Key: Steve Gushie, Pres
Normand Delisle, Dir of Ops & IT
Doug Gilbert, VP Fin & Admin
Gordon Sadler, Dir of Nat'l Mktg

Carrier Canada

1515 Drew Rd.
Mississauga, ON L5S 1Y8
Tel 905-672-0606
Fax 905-405-4002
www.carrier.ca
Line: Sells and services heating, ventilation, air conditioning and refrigeration equipment and systems.
NAICS: 416120
#Emp: 100-249 (Tor)
#TorLoc: 8
Own: Private Company
Par: Carrier Corp. (US)
Key: Abas Khan, Pres & GM
Steve Hemphill, Dir of Ops
Barbara Balaban, VP HR
Rob Alidina, Reg Fin Mgr
Steve Alison, VP Commercial Serv Sales
Navia Fharma, Mktg Mgr

Cartier Kitchens Inc.

8 Chelsea Lane
Brampton, ON L6T 3Y4
Tel 905-793-0063
Fax 905-793-6720
www.cartierkitchens.com
Line: Manufactures kitchen products.
NAICS: 337110
#Emp: 100-249 (Tor)
#TorLoc: 1
Own: Private Company
Key: Frank Converso, Owner

Carwell Construction Ltd.

1-85 Ortona Crt.
Concord, ON L4K 3M3
Tel 905-669-6303
Fax 905-738-0233
Line: Provides general construction services.
NAICS: 231220
#Emp: 100-249 (Tor)
#TorLoc: 1
Own: Private Company
Key: Angelo Ricciuto, Mgr

Casa Bella Windows Inc.

A Div. of Alpa Lumber Group
7630 Airport Rd.
Mississauga, ON L4T 4G6
Tel 416-650-1033
Fax 416-650-5580
www.casabellawindows.ca
Line: Manufactures windows.
NAICS: 332321
#Emp: 100-249 (Tor)
#TorLoc: 1
Own: Private Company
Key: Tim Smith, GM

Cascades Boxboard Group Inc.

300-772 Rue Sherbrooke West
Montreal, PQ H3A 1G1
Tel 514-284-9800
Fax 514-289-1773
www.cascades.com
Line: Manufactures coated boxboard for conversion into folding cartons and micro-flute packaging.
NAICS: 322130 322212
#Emp: 500-999 (Tor)
#TorLoc: 5
Own: Private Company
Par: Cascades Inc. (CDA)
Key: Marc Andre Depin, Pres & CEO
Yves Menard, Reg GM, Eastern Canada
Jean Francois Neault, Dir of Admin
Louis Lemaire,
    VP Mktg & Business Dev
Nathalie Theberge, Legal Counsel

Cashcode Company Inc.

A Div. of Crane Payment Solutions
2720 Steeles Ave. West
Concord, ON L4K 4S3
Tel 905-303-8874
Fax 905-303-8875
www.cashcode.com
Line: Manufactures bill validators.
NAICS: 333310
#Emp: 100-249 (Tor)
#TorLoc: 1
Own: Private Company
Key: Brian Sweeney, Pres
Naily Garipova, HR Generalist
Val Levitan, VP Sales

Cash Money Financial Services Inc.

16-5155 Spectrum Way
Mississauga, ON L4W 5A1
Tel 905-602-8820
Fax 905-602-4460
www.cashmoney.ca
Line: Provides financial services.
NAICS: 541611
#Emp: 75-99 (Tor)
Own: Private Company
Key: David Hews, Pres

Cassels Brock & Blackwell LLP

2100-40 King St. West
Scotia Plaza
Toronto, ON M5H 3C2
Tel 416-869-5300
Fax 416-360-8877
www.casselsbrock.com
Line: Provides legal services.
NAICS: 541110
#Emp: 250-499 (Tor)
#TorLoc: 1
Own: Private Company
Key: Mark Young, Mng Partner
John Tsiofas, COO
Kelli Wight, Dir of Business Dev
James Wilson, Business Advisor

Castleview-Wychwood Towers

A Div. of The City of Toronto
351 Christie St.
Toronto, ON M6G 3C3
Tel 416-392-5700
Fax 416-392-4157
www.toronto.ca/ltc/castleview.htm
Line: Operates home for the aged that provides personal care, support, programs and services to adults.
NAICS: 623310
#Emp: 250-499 (Tor)
#TorLoc: 1
Own: Government
Key: Vija Mallia, Admr

Castool Tooling Systems

2 Parratt Rd.
Uxbridge, ON L9P 1R1
Tel 905-852-0121
Fax 905-852-2300
www.castool.com
Line: Manufactures tooling systems for the extrusion and diecast industry.
NAICS: 333299
#Emp: 75-99 (Tor)
#TorLoc: 1
Own: Public Company
Par: Exco Technologies Ltd. (CDA)
Key: Paul Robbins, GM
John Cullum, Production Mgr
Siri Sugirthalingham, Cont

Catech Systems Ltd.

4-201 Whitehall Dr.
Markham, ON L3R 9Y3
Tel 905-944-0000
Fax 905-944-4844
www.catech-systems.com
Line: Provides computer data and voice calling installation.
NAICS: 541510
#Emp: 75-99 (Tor)
#TorLoc: 1
Own: Private Company
Par: Catech (CDA)
Key: Scott Forrestall, Pres & CEO
Scott Ginther, VP

Catelectric Inc.

125 Commander Blvd.
Toronto, ON M1S 3M7
Tel 416-299-4864
Fax 416-299-6919
Line: Provides Electra/Coating service
processes.
NAICS: 332810
#Emp: 75-99 (Tor)
#TorLoc: 2
Own: Private Company
Key: David Lund, Owner
Shaun Reid, VP Fin

The Catholic Children's Aid Society of Toronto

26 Maitland St.
Toronto, ON M4Y 1C6
Tel 416-395-1500
Fax 416-395-1581
www.torontoccas.org
AKA: CCAS
Line: Provides child protection services
and family support programs.
NAICS: 624110 624190
#Emp: 500-999 (Tor)
#TorLoc: 5
Own: Not-for-profit
Key: Mary McConville, Exec Dir
Terry Daly, Dir of HR
Louis To, Dir of Fin,
    Admin Services & IT
Anne Rappe, PR Mgr

Catholic Cross-Cultural Services

401-55 Town Centre Crt.
Toronto, ON M1P 4X4
Tel 416-644-0816
Fax 416-644-0819
www.cathcrosscultural.org
AKA: CCS
Line: Provides counselling services.
NAICS: 624190
#Emp: 100-249 (Tor)
#TorLoc: 7
Own: Not-for-profit
Key: Caroline Davis, Exec Dir
Lisa Loong, Reg Dir

Caulfeild Apparel Group Ltd.

1400 Whitehorse Rd.
Toronto, ON M3J 3A7
Tel 416-636-5900
Fax 416-636-8451
www.caulfeild.com
Line: Distributes clothing.
NAICS: 414110
#Emp: 75-99 (Tor)
#TorLoc: 1
Own: Private Company
Key: Mike Purkis, Pres
Craig Wilson, VP Fin

Cavalier Transportation Services Inc.

14091 Humber Station Rd.
P.O. Box 10
Bolton, ON L7E 5T1
Tel 905-857-6981
Fax 905-857-3701
www.cavalier.ca
Line: Provides warehousing,
transportation and logistics services.
NAICS: 484110 484121 493110
#Emp: 100-249 (Tor)
#TorLoc: 2
Own: Private Company
Par: The Cavalier Group of Companies
(CDA)
Key: George P. Ledson, Pres & CEO
Geordie Ledson, VP Ops
Vicki Stafford, VP Resource Dev
Nancy Hageman, Comptr
Murray Hannah, Dir of Pricing
Scott Stafford, Project Mgr
Brian Ledson, Exec VP Sales & Mktg

Cavalluzzo Hayes Shilton McIntyre & Cornish LLP

300-474 Bathurst St.
Toronto, ON M5T 2S6
Tel 416-964-1115
Fax 416-964-5895
www.cavalluzzo.com
Line: Operates a law firm.
NAICS: 541110
#Emp: 75-99 (Tor)
#TorLoc: 1
Own: Private Company
Key: Jayne Ivall, Office Mgr

Cawthra Gardens Long Term Care Community

590 Lolita Gardens
Mississauga, ON L5A 4N8
Tel 905-306-9984
Fax 905-306-1164
www.delcare.com
Line: Operates a senior's residence.
NAICS: 623310
#Emp: 100-249 (Tor)
#TorLoc: 1
Own: Private Company
Par: Delcare Long Term Care (CDA)
Key: Bob Bowyer, Business Mgr
Mary Jane Glassco, Admr

CBI Home Health

302-5001 Yonge St.
Toronto, ON M2N 6P6
Tel 416-222-6567
Fax 416-222-6949
www.cbi.ca
Line: Provides in-home health care.
NAICS: 621610
#Emp: 250-499 (Tor)
#TorLoc: 1
Own: Private Company
Key: Christine Reno, Dir of Ops
Shirley Parsons, HR Mgr

CB Richard Ellis Limited

600-145 King St. West
Toronto, ON M5H 1J8
Tel 416-362-2244
Fax 416-362-8085
www.cbre.ca
AKA: CBRE
Line: Provides financial, corporate
and commercial real estate services
including office, industrial and
retail leasing and sales; investment
services including commercial and
retail, apartment building and land
sales; and real estate consulting,
property management and facilities
management.
NAICS: 531210
#Emp: 500-999 (Tor)
#TorLoc: 4
Own: Public Company
Par: CB Richard Ellis, Inc. (US)
Key: Stefan Ciotlos, Pres & CEO
John O'Toole, Exec VP & Mng Dir
Bob Macleod, CIO

CBS Outdoor Canada

A Div. of CBS Canada Holdings Co.
377 Horner Ave.
Toronto, ON M8W 1Z6
Tel 416-255-1392
Fax 416-255-2063
www.cbsoutdoor.ca
Line: Sells outdoor advertising space and offers lithographic and digital printing services.
NAICS: 541850 323115
#Emp: 100-249 (Tor)
#TorLoc: 1
Own: Private Company
Par: CBS Inc. (US)
Key: Nick Arakgi, VP & GM
Tim Bouchard, Dir of Ops
Esther Niven, Dir of HR
Nadine Schiratti, Dir of Fin
Tony Martins, Purch Mgr
Milvi Salurand, Dir of IS
Rob Sinasac, Nat'l Sales Mgr
Michele Erskine, Dir of Mktg

CBV Collection Services Ltd.

1200-100 Sheppard Ave. East
Toronto, ON M2N 6N5
Tel 416-482-9323
Fax 416-482-9359
www.cbvcollections.com
Line: Operates a collection agency.
NAICS: 561440
#Emp: 100-249 (Tor)
#TorLoc: 1
Own: Private Company
Key: Bob Richards, Exec VP & COO
K.F Downie, Pres & CEO
Dave Demerchant, VP Ops
Sandra McLaren, Cont

CCH Canadian Ltd.

300-90 Sheppard Ave. East
Toronto, ON M2N 6X1
Tel 416-224-2224
Fax 416-224-2243
www.cch.ca
Line: Provides information on tax, business, and human resources law.
NAICS: 511120
#Emp: 100-249 (Tor)
#TorLoc: 1
Own: Private Company
Par: Wolters Kluwer NV (NETH)
Key: Doug Finley, COO
Marie Croteau, VP Dev
Lisa Fernandes, Dir of HR
Allan Orr, VP Fin & Admin
Steve Monk,
    VP Legal & Business Markets

CCI Thermal Technologies Inc.

2721 Plymouth Dr.
Oakville, ON L6H 5R5
Tel 905-829-4422
Fax 905-829-4430
www.ccithermal.com
Line: Designs and manufactures electrical heating equipment.
NAICS: 333416
#Emp: 100-249 (Tor)
#TorLoc: 1
Own: Private Company
Key: Bernie Moore, Pres & COO
Susan Nagy, HR Mgr
Barry Moore, VP Fin

CCL Label

35 McLachlan Dr.
Toronto, ON M9W 1E4
Tel 416-675-3161
Fax 416-675-8831
www.cclind.com
Line: Manufactures pressure-sensitive labels.
NAICS: 561910
#Emp: 100-249 (Tor)
#TorLoc: 2
Own: Public Company
Par: CCL Industries Inc. (CDA)
Key: Jim Sellors, VP & GM
Pramit Sen, Ops Mgr
Sheila McKimmie, HR Mgr
Doug Codner, Cont

CCSI CompuCom

100-2480 Meadowvale Blvd.
Mississauga, ON L5N 7Y1
Tel 905-816-3000
Fax 905-816-3333
www.compucom.com
Line: Provides information technology and communication network solutions and services to corporations and government.
NAICS: 541510
#Emp: 250-499 (Tor)
#TorLoc: 2
Own: Private Company
Par: Getronics N.V. (NETH)
Key: Phil Sober, GM (Canada)
Mark Middel, Dir of Fin & Admin

CDC Contracting

1-10 Bradwick Dr.
Vaughan, ON L4K 2T3
Tel 905-738-4303
Fax 905-738-2412
Line: Constructs sewer and water mains in new developments.

NAICS: 231320
#Emp: 100-249 (Tor)
#TorLoc: 1
Own: Private Company
Key: Pat Pillitteri, Pres

CDI Computer Dealers Inc.

130 South Town Centre Blvd.
Markham, ON L6G 1B2
Tel 888-226-5727
Fax 888-449-5920
www.cdicomputers.com
Line: Sells refurbished computers.
NAICS: 443120
#Emp: 100-249 (Tor)
#TorLoc: 1
Own: Private Company
Par: Relational LLC (US)
Key: Saar Pikar, GM & Sr VP
Chris Bristow, Mgr of Ops
Naipaul Sheosankar, Dir of Fin
Fred Hastings, Purch Mgr
Gal Pikar, Mktg Mgr

CDS Global Inc.

2930 14th Ave.
Markham, ON L3R 5Z8
Tel 905-946-0400
Fax 905-946-0410
www.indas.ca
Line: Provides customer information and data management solutions.
NAICS: 514210
#Emp: 100-249 (Tor)
#TorLoc: 1
Own: Private Company
Par: CDS Global Inc. (US)
Key: Chris Simpson, VP & GM
Marc Tomei, VP Ops
Giles Boynowski, CFO

CDW

300-20 Carlson Crt.
Toronto, ON M9W 7K6
Tel 647-288-5700
Fax 647-288-5947
www.cdw.ca
Line: Offers a single destination for organizations to research, inquire and purchase technology solutions.
NAICS: 417310
#Emp: 250-499 (Tor)
#TorLoc: 1
Own: Private Company
Par: CDW Corporation (US)
Key: Mary Ann Yule, GM

Cedarbrook Lodge Ltd.

520 Markham Rd.
Toronto, ON M1H 3A1
Tel 416-431-6400
Fax 416-431-3660
www.reveraliving.com
AKA: Revera Inc.
Line: Operates a retirement residence
providing a continuum of care.
NAICS: 623310
#Emp: 100-249 (Tor)
#TorLoc: 1
Own: Private Company
Par: Revera Inc. (CDA)
Key: Ron Mehta, Exec Dir
Jeffrey Lozon, Pres & CEO
Daniel Gagnon, CFO
Janet Ko, Sr VP Commun & Pub Affairs

Cedar Springs Health, Racquet & Sports Club

960 Cumberland Ave.
Burlington, ON L7N 3J6
Tel 905-632-4800
Fax 905-632-4041
www.cedarspringsclub.com
AKA: Cedar Springs Physiotherapy and
Sports Injury Clinic
Line: Operates a multi-sport health and
recreation facility.
NAICS: 713940
#Emp: 100-249 (Tor)
#TorLoc: 1
Own: Private Company
Key: Jack Dennison, Owner
Val Dimitroff, Asst GM
George Schroeder, Membership Dir
Bonnie Tomkins, Fitness Dir

Cedarvale Terrace Nursing Home

429 Walmer Rd.
Toronto, ON M5P 2X9
Tel 416-967-6949
Fax 416-928-1965
www.cedarvaleterrace.com
Line: Operates a nursing home.
NAICS: 623310 623110
#Emp: 100-249 (Tor)
#TorLoc: 1
Own: Private Company
Key: Linda Calabrese, Admr
Christine Douglas, Dir of Ops
Enzo Cuttini, Dir of Fin

Ce De Candy Company Ltd.

150 Harry Walker Pkwy. North
Newmarket, ON L3Y 7B2
Tel 905-853-7171
Fax 905-853-7160
www.smarties.com
Line: Manufactures confections.
NAICS: 311340
#Emp: 100-249 (Tor)
#TorLoc: 1
Own: Private Company
Par: Ce De Candy Inc. (US)
Key: Gloria Henderson, Office Mgr
Danielle Conway,
    Dir of HR & Sales Mgr

CELESTICA Inc.

1150 Eglinton Ave. East
Toronto, ON M3C 1H7
Tel 416-448-5800
Fax 416-448-4810
www.celestica.com
Line: Delivers innovative electronics
manufacturing services.
NAICS: 334410
#Emp: 1000-4999 (Tor)
#TorLoc: 1
Own: Public Company
Key: Craig Muhlhauser, Pres & CEO
Betty Del Bianco, Exec VP,
    Chief Legal & Admin Officer
Paul Nicoletti, Exec VP & CFO
Mary Gendron, Sr VP & CIO

Cello Products Inc.

210 Avenue Rd.
P.O. Box 37
Cambridge, ON N1R 5S9
Tel 519-621-9150
Fax 519-621-4108
www.cello.on.ca
Line: Manufactures copper and brass
solder fittings.
NAICS: 332910
#Emp: 75-99 (Tor)
#TorLoc: 1
Own: Private Company
Key: Terry Aurini, Pres
Hans Ratz, VP New Product Dev
Paul Petrie, VP Fin
Jason Aurini, Exec VP
Peter Howell, VP Mktg & Sales

Centennial College

P.O. Box 631, Stn. A
Toronto, ON M1K 5E9
Tel 416-289-5000
Fax 416-439-7358
www.centennialcollege.ca
Line: Provides post-secondary
education and training.
NAICS: 611210
#Emp: 1000-4999 (Tor)
#TorLoc: 8
Own: Government
Key: Ann Buller, Pres
Marilyn Scott, Chief of Staff
Yves Deschesnes, Asst VP HR
Brad Chapman,
    VP Corp Services & CFO
Rosanna Cavallaro,
    Asst VP Mktg & Commun

Centennial Optical Limited

158 Norfinch Dr.
Toronto, ON M3N 1X6
Tel 416-739-8539
Fax 416-739-6504
www.centennialoptical.com
AKA: L'Optique Centennial Lteé
Line: Distributes optical lenses and
frames.
NAICS: 417930
#Emp: 100-249 (Tor)
#TorLoc: 2
Own: Private Company
Key: Steve DePinto, Pres
Roger DePinto, Chmn
Shraga Bellon, Dir of Ops & Systems
Lina Connor, IIR Mgr
Grahame Freeland, Dir of Fin

Centerplate

100 Princes Blvd.
Toronto, ON M6K 3C3
Tel 416-263-3153
Fax 416-263-3157
www.centerplate.ca
Line: Provides catering and food
services.
NAICS: 722320
#Emp: 100-249 (Tor)
#TorLoc: 1
Own: Public Company
Par: Centerplate (US)
Key: Ashton Seccura, GM

Central 1 Credit Union

2810 Matheson Blvd. East
Mississauga, ON L4W 4X7
Tel 905-238-9400
Fax 905-219-9205
www.central1.com
Line: Provides financial and trade association services to Ontario credit unions.
NAICS: 522130 813910
#Emp: 100-249 (Tor)
#TorLoc: 1
Own: Association
Key: Don Rolfe, Pres & CEO
Rowland Kelly, COO & CFO
Linda Archer, Sr VP Mktg & HR
Oscar Van Der Meer,
    Chief Tech & Payments Officer
Susan Walters, Dir of Commun

Central - Community Care Access Centre

700-45 Sheppard Ave. East
Toronto, ON M2N 5W9
Tel 416-222-2241
www.central.ccac-ont.ca
AKA: Central CCAC
Line: Provides home care services, information and referral community services, and placement services for long term care homes.
NAICS: 621610 624120
#Emp: 500-999 (Tor)
Own: Government
Key: Cathy Szabo, CEO

Central East - Community Care Access Centre

209 Dundas St. East, 5th Fl.
Whitby, ON L1N 7H8
Tel 905-430-3308
Fax 905-430-3297
www.ccac-ont.ca
Line: Operates long-term care homes and provides home and community services.
NAICS: 623310 624120
#Emp: 500-999 (Tor)
#TorLoc: 7
Own: Government
Key: Don Ford, Exec Dir

Central Fairbank Lumber

A Div. of Alpa Lumber Ltd.
1900 Steeles Ave. West
Concord, ON L4K 1A1
Tel 905-738-2111
Fax 905-738-2263
www.centralfairbank.com
Line: Provides lumber, mouldings, doors, plywood, paint, house decor, hardware, drywall and millwork.
NAICS: 416320 321919
#Emp: 100-249 (Tor)
#TorLoc: 2
Own: Private Company
Par: Alpa Lumber Group (CDA)
Key: Mark DiPoce, GM
Arie Dunnik, Ops Mgr
Anna Gullia, Office Admr & Secy
Anthony Lotto, Cont
Adrian Grbic, Purchaser

Central Graphics & Container Group Ltd.

5526 Timberlea Blvd.
Mississauga, ON L4W 2T7
Tel 905-238-8400
Fax 905-238-8127
www.centralgrp.com
AKA: The Central Group
Line: Manufactures corrugated boxes.
NAICS: 322211
#Emp: 100-249 (Tor)
#TorLoc: 2
Own: Private Company
Key: Richard Eastwood, Pres & CEO

Central West Specialized Development Service

53 Bond St.
Oakville, ON L6K 1L8
Tel 905-844-7864
Fax 905-844-3545
www.cwsds.ca
Line: Provides residential and non-residential support and specialized resources for people with developmental disabilities.
NAICS: 624120
#Emp: 100-249 (Tor)
#TorLoc: 1
Own: Not-for-profit
Key: James Duncan, Exec Dir
Terri Britten-Kennedy, Dir of
    Residential & Resources
Kelly Kocken, Fin Mgr

Centrecorp Management Services Ltd.

1-2851 John St.
Markham, ON L3R 5R7
Tel 905-477-9200
Fax 905-477-7390
www.centrecorp.com
Line: Specializes in the management and leasing of shopping centres and retail properties.
NAICS: 531120
#Emp: 100-249 (Tor)
#TorLoc: 1
Own: Private Company
Key: Robert S. Green, Pres
Tracy Butler, Exec VP

Centre for Addiction and Mental Health

1001 Queen St. West
Toronto, ON M6J 1H4
Tel 416-535-8501
Fax 416-595-5017
www.camh.net
AKA: CAMH
Line: Provides inpatient and outpatient care for people with mental health and addiction problems.
NAICS: 621420 622210
#Emp: 1000-4999 (Tor)
#TorLoc: 2
Own: Not-for-profit
Key: Catherine Zahn, Pres & CEO
Bill Manley, Dir of HR
Dev Chopra, Exec VP Corp Services
Mary McKeen, CIO
Gail Czukar, Exec VP Policy & Planning

Centre for Early Learning-West Hill

4010 Lawrence Ave. East
Toronto, ON M1E 2R4
Tel 416-283-4294
Fax 416-283-3659
www.cfel.ca
Line: Operates a day care centre.
NAICS: 624410
#Emp: 100-249 (Tor)
#TorLoc: 9
Own: Private Company
Key: Patricia London, Dir
Antonietta Grosso, Supr

Centre for Education & Training

190 Robert Speck Pkwy.
Mississauga, ON L4Z 3K3
Tel 905-949-0049
Fax 905-949-6004
www.tcet.com
AKA: CET
Line: Provides educational, training
and career resource services.
NAICS: 611690
#Emp: 250-499 (Tor)
#TorLoc: 1
Own: Not-for-profit
Key: Rhys Davies, CEO
David Lew, Chief HR & Privacy Officer
Robert Olson, Dir of Corp Services

Centre for Information and Community Services

2330 Midland Ave.
Toronto, ON M1S 5G5
Tel 416-292-7510
Fax 416-292-9120
www.cicscanada.com
AKA: CICS
Line: Operates charitable social service
organization.
NAICS: 813410
#Emp: 100-249 (Tor)
#TorLoc: 10
Own: Not-for-profit
Key: Moy Wong Tam, Exec Dir
Suba Satgunaraj, Dir of Fin & Ops
Elizabeth Lynn, HR Consultant

Centre for Skills Development & Training

860 Harrington Crt.
Burlington, ON L7N 3N4
Tel 905-333-3499
Fax 905-634-2775
www.thecentre.on.ca
AKA: The Bay Area Learning Centre
Line: Provides career and workforce
development services.
NAICS: 541690
#Emp: 100-249 (Tor)
#TorLoc: 6
Own: Not-for-profit
Par: Halton District School Board
(CDA)
Key: Kathy Mills, CAO
Barb Krukowski,
   Mgr of Newcomer Services
Vivian Healy, Mgr of Office Services
Iqbal Merchant, Mgr of Acctng
Lorna Hart, Mgr of Corp Dev Services
Nancy Moore, Sr Mgr
   of Programs & Services

Centura (Toronto) Ltd.

53 Apex Rd.
Toronto, ON M6A 2V6
Tel 416-785-5165
Fax 416-783-0636
www.centura.ca
Line: Wholesales floor coverings.
NAICS: 416330
#Emp: 75-99 (Tor)
#TorLoc: 1
Own: Private Company
Par: Centura Limited (CDA)
Key: Brian Cowie, Pres
Peter Donath, VP Fin & CFO

Century 21 Heritage Group Ltd.

4-17565 Yonge St.
Newmarket, ON L3Y 5H6
Tel 905-895-1822
Fax 905-895-1990
www.homesbyheritage.ca
Line: Operates a real estate firm.
NAICS: 531210
#Emp: 75-99 (Tor)
#TorLoc: 6
Own: Private Company
Key: Larry Mandlsohn,
Mgr & Broker of Record

Century 21 King's Quay Real Estate Inc., Brokerage

401-7300 Warden Ave.
Markham, ON L3R 9Z6
Tel 905-940-3428
Fax 905-940-0293
www.c21kq.com
Line: Operates a real estate firm.
NAICS: 531210
#Emp: 100-249 (Tor)
#TorLoc: 1
Own: Private Company
Key: Steve Kwan Lum Chow,
   Broker of Record
David Cheung, Owner

Century 21 Landstars Realty Inc.

203-350 Hwy. 7 East
Richmond Hill, ON L4B 3N2
Tel 905-707-1188
Fax 905-707-8080
www.century21landstars.com
Line: Operates a real estate brokerage.
NAICS: 531210
#Emp: 75-99 (Tor)
#TorLoc: 1
Own: Private Company
Key: Jimmy Lee, Pres

Century 21 Leading Edge Realty Inc.

301-1825 Markham Rd.
Toronto, ON M1B 4Z9
Tel 416-298-6000
Fax 416-298-6910
www.century21.ca
Line: Operates a real estate agency.
NAICS: 531210
#Emp: 250-499 (Tor)
#TorLoc: 4
Own: Private Company
Key: Paul R.M. Baron, Pres

Century 21 Percy Fulton Ltd.

2911 Kennedy Rd.
Toronto, ON M1V 1S8
Tel 416-298-8200
Fax 416-298-6602
www.c21fulton.com
NAICS: 531210
#Emp: 100-249 (Tor)
#TorLoc: 5
Own: Private Company
Key: Clare Fulton, Broker & Owner
Linda Sebastian, Sales Mgr

Cenveo, McLaren Morris and Todd

3270 American Dr.
Mississauga, ON L4V 1B5
Tel 905-677-3592
Fax 905-677-3675
www.mmt.ca
Line: Manufactures commercial printed
products.
NAICS: 323114
#Emp: 100-249 (Tor)
#TorLoc: 1
Own: Private Company
Par: Cenveo Inc. (US)
Key: Tony Sgro, Pres
Ken Oswald, VP Ops
Tom Engelhart, Dir of Fin

Cerebral Palsy Parent Council of Toronto

9 Butternut Lane
Markham, ON L3P 3M1
Tel 905-294-0944
Fax 905-294-7834
AKA: Participation House
Line: Provides services for adults with disabilities.
NAICS: 813310
#Emp: 100-249 (Tor)
#TorLoc: 7
Own: Not-for-profit
Key: Frances DiCarlo, Exec Dir

Ceridian Canada Ltd.

675 Cochrane Dr., Ceridian Tower
Markham, ON L3R 0B8
Tel 905-947-7200
Fax 905-947-7004
www.ceridian.ca
Line: Provides managed human resource solutions.
NAICS: 541612
#Emp: 500-999 (Tor)
#TorLoc: 2
Own: Public Company
Par: Ceridian Corp. (US)
Key: Dave MacKay, Pres
Paul Elliot, COO
John Cardella, VP HR
Susie Hester, CFO
Sandy Lovell, Exec VP Business Tech
Cande Dandele,
   Exec VP Mktg & Product Dev

CertainTeed Gypsum Canada Inc.

2424 Lakeshore Rd. West
Mississauga, ON L5J 1K4
Tel 905-823-9881
Fax 905-823-4860
www.certainteed.com
NAICS: 327420
#Emp: 100-249 (Tor)
#TorLoc: 3
Own: Private Company
Par: Saint-Gobain (FR)
Key: John Donaldson, Pres & CEO
Dave Englehardt, Sr VP Ops
Stephen Williams, Dir of HR
Michelle Farrugia,
   Mgr of Business Process Support

Certicom Corp.

5520 Explorer Dr., 4th Fl.
Mississauga, ON L4W 5L1
Tel 905-507-4220
Fax 905-507-4230
www.certicom.com
Line: Develops encryption technology for e-commerce software, wireless messaging and smart card applications.
NAICS: 511210
#Emp: 100-249 (Tor)
#TorLoc: 1
Own: Public Company
Key: Frank Cotter, VP

Certified General Accountants of Ontario

240 Eglinton Ave. East
Toronto, ON M4P 1K8
Tel 416-322-6520
Fax 416-322-6481
www.cga-ontario.org
Line: Provides educational programs in the accounting field and grants exclusive rights to the CGA designation.
NAICS: 813920 813910
#Emp: 75-99 (Tor)
#TorLoc: 1
Own: Private Company
Key: Doug Brooks, CEO
Steve D'Alessandro, VP Fin

Certified Laboratories

239 Orenda Rd.
Brampton, ON L6T 1E6
Tel 905-457-5243
Fax 905-457-2687
www.certifiedlabs.com
Line: Provides maintenance, repair, operating solutions and lubricants to the construction industry.
NAICS: 333310
#Emp: 100-249 (Tor)
#TorLoc: 1
Own: Private Company
Par: NCH Corporation (US)
Key: Robert Putnins, VP
Anne Ignasz, Plant Mgr
Monty Harkies, Cont
Jim Rodgers, Head of Mktg

Cetero Research

4520 Dixie Rd.
Mississauga, ON L4W 1N2
Tel 905-238-0599
Fax 905-238-0682
www.allied-research.com
NAICS: 621510

#Emp: 250-499 (Tor)
#TorLoc: 3
Own: Private Company
Key: Graham Wood, Pres

CEVA Logistics

1880 Matheson Blvd. East
Mississauga, ON L4W 5N4
Tel 905-672-3456
Fax 905-672-3655
www.cevalogistics.com
Line: Provides supply chain solutions and services covering domestic and international freight transportation, integrated logistics management and information technology.
NAICS: 488519
#Emp: 250-499 (Tor)
#TorLoc: 1
Own: Public Company
Par: Eagle Global Logistics Corp. (US)
Key: Wendy Trudeau,
   VP & Country Mgr
John Pattulo, CEO
Jonathon Gardiner, Fin Mgr & Cont

CFA Communications Ltd.

3-1121 Leslie St.
Toronto, ON M3C 2J9
Tel 416-504-5071
Fax 416-504-7390
www.cfacommunications.com
AKA: The Production Partners; The Multi-Media Partners; Partners In Learning
Line: Operates a communications consulting business.
NAICS: 541611
#Emp: 100-249 (Tor)
#TorLoc: 2
Own: Private Company
Key: Andre Desroches, Pres & CEO
Jennifer Desroches, Exec VP

CFN Precision Ltd.

1000 Creditstone Rd.
Concord, ON L4K 4P8
Tel 905-669-8191
Fax 905-669-8684
www.cfn-inc.com
Line: Manufactures parts and assemblies.
NAICS: 332710
#Emp: 75-99 (Tor)
#TorLoc: 1
Own: Private Company
Key: Eli Brigler, CEO
Andrew Morrow, CFO
Tony Karadimas, VP Sales

CFNY FM 102.1

Corus Quay, 25 Dockside Dr.
Toronto, ON M5A 0B5
Tel 416-479-7000
Fax 416-479-7002
www.edge.ca
AKA: 102.1 The Edge
Line: Operates radio and television services.
NAICS: 513110
#Emp: 100-249 (Tor)
#TorLoc: 1
Own: Private Company
Key: Chris Sisam, GM
Cheryl Bechtel, Cont
Victor Giacomelli, Gen Sales Mgr
Pina Crispo, Mktg Mgr

The CG&B Group Inc.

120 South Town Centre Blvd.
Markham, ON L6G 1C3
Tel 905-479-6670
Fax 905-479-9164
www.cgbgroup.com
AKA: CG&B Financial Services Inc.;
CG&B Investment Services Inc.; CG&B
Professional Liability Inc.
Line: Provides insurance, investment and financial services.
NAICS: 524210
#Emp: 100-249 (Tor)
#TorLoc: 2
Own: Private Company
Key: H. Larry Later, Pres & CEO
Kevin A.G. Goranson, Exec VP
Ross H. Sykes, CFO

CGC Inc.

350 Burnhamthorpe Rd. West, 5th Fl.
Mississauga, ON L5B 3J1
Tel 905-803-5600
Fax 905-803-5688
www.cgcinc.com
Line: Manufactures building materials.
NAICS: 232410 232490
#Emp: 100-249 (Tor)
#TorLoc: 2
Own: Private Company
Par: USG Corp. (US)
Key: Chris Macey, VP & GM
Jennifer Scanlon, VP
Angela Hiltz, VP HR & Admin
Rick Lowes, VP & CFO
Ebrahim Gomez, Dir of IS

CGI Adjusters Inc.

200-150 Commerce Valley Dr. West
Markham, ON L3T 7Z3
Tel 905-762-2700
www.cgi.com
Line: Provides insurance adjusting services.
NAICS: 524291
#Emp: 100-249 (Tor)
Own: Private Company
Key: Douglas McCuaig, Pres, Canada
Michael E. Roach, Pres & CEO

CGI Group Inc.

2000-250 Yonge St.
Toronto, ON M5B 2L7
Tel 416-363-7827
Fax 416-363-9766
www.cgi.ca
AKA: CGI IS and Management Consultants Inc.
NAICS: 541510 541611
#Emp: 1000-4999 (Tor)
#TorLoc: 19
Own: Public Company
Key: Michael Roach, Pres & CEO
Serge Godin, Chmn
Douglas McCuaig, Pres, Canada

CH2M HILL Canada Limited

255 Consumers Rd.
Toronto, ON M2J 5B6
Tel 416-499-9000
Fax 416-499-4687
www.ch2mhill.com
Line: Offers engineering, procurement, construction management and operations services for government, civil, industrial and energy clients.
NAICS: 541330
#Emp: 250-499 (Tor)
#TorLoc: 1
Own: Private Company
Par: CH2M HILL Limited (US)
Key: Rene Massinon, Pres

Chair-Man Mills Inc.

184 Railside Rd.
Toronto, ON M3A 3R4
Tel 416-391-0400
Fax 416-391-2960
www.chairmanmills.com
Line: Provides party rental services and tents.
NAICS: 532290
#Emp: 100-249 (Tor)
#TorLoc: 1
Own: Private Company

Key: George W. Crothers, VP
Mary Crothers, Pres
John Upper, VP Warehouse Ops
Gerry McElwain, VP & CFO

Charlie's Meat & Seafood Supply Ltd.

61 Skagway Ave.
Toronto, ON M1M 3T9
Tel 416-261-1312
Fax 416-261-2267
www.charliesmeat.com
Line: Wholesales meat products.
NAICS: 413160 413140
#Emp: 100-249 (Tor)
#TorLoc: 4
Own: Private Company
Key: Jim Cheung, Pres

Chartis Insurance Company of Canada

145 Wellington St. West
Toronto, ON M5J 1H8
Tel 416-596-3000
Fax 416-977-2743
www.chartisinsurance.com
Line: Provides property, casualty, marine and life insurance; and other types of financial services and investments.
NAICS: 524121
#Emp: 250-499 (Tor)
#TorLoc: 1
Own: Private Company
Par: AIG Holdings, Inc. (US)
Key: Lynn Oldfield, Pres
Gary McMillan, CEO
Marjory MacKay, Reg HR Mgr
Omar Rasul, CFO

Chartright Air Group

2450 Derry Rd. East
Mississauga, ON L5S 1B2
Tel 905-671-4674
Fax 905-362-0935
www.chartright.com
Line: Provides business aviation services.
NAICS: 481214
#Emp: 75-99 (Tor)
#TorLoc: 1
Own: Private Company
Key: Adam Keller, Pres
Robert Squires, VP Ops
Brenda Butler, VP Fin
Thomas Kolli, Production Mgr
David Shaver, Business Dev Mgr

Chartwell Seniors Housing REIT

700-100 Milverton Dr.
Mississauga, ON L5R 4H1
Tel 905-501-9219
Fax 905-501-0813
www.chartwellreit.ca
Line: Operates long-term care and residences for seniors.
NAICS: 623110
#Emp: 100-249 (Tor)
#TorLoc: 1
Own: Public Company
Key: Brent Binions, Pres & CEO
Richard J. Noonan, COO
Karen Sullivan, VP HR
Vlad Volodarski, CFO
Phil McKenzie, VP Sales & Mktg

CHATS - Community Home Assistance To Seniors

103-126 Wellington St. West
Aurora, ON L4G 2N9
Tel 905-713-6596
Fax 905-713-1705
www.chats.on.ca
Line: Provides assistance services to seniors.
NAICS: 624120
#Emp: 100-249 (Tor)
#TorLoc: 1
Own: Not-for-profit
Key: Wyn Chivers, CEO
Deborah Compton, Dir of Ops
Janet Williams, HR Mgr
Sheri Fiegehen,
    Mktg & Commun Specialist

Chembond

A Div. of Mapei Inc.
2130 Williams Pkwy. East
Brampton, ON L6S 5X7
Tel 905-799-2663
Fax 905-799-2436
www.chembond.com
Line: Manufactures adhesives and sealants.
NAICS: 325520
#Emp: 75-99 (Tor)
#TorLoc: 1
Own: Private Company
Key: Jim MacNeil, Plant Mgr
Bob Welsh, Unit Mgr
Heather Coates, Purch Mgr

Chemtura Corp.

565 Coronation Dr.
Toronto, ON M1E 2K3
Tel 416-284-1661
Fax 416-284-4316
www.chemtura.com
Line: Manufactures lubricants and specialty chemicals.
NAICS: 325999
#Emp: 100-249 (Tor)
Own: Private Company
Par: Chemtura Corp. (US)
Key: John Clarke, Cont

CHEP Canada Inc.

7400 East Danbro Cres.
Mississauga, ON L5N 8C6
Tel 905-790-2437
Fax 905-790-6545
www.chep.com
Line: Offers pallet and container pooling services.
NAICS: 488519
#Emp: 500-999 (Tor)
#TorLoc: 2
Own: Private Company
Par: Brambles Industries Ltd. (AUS)
Key: Michael F. Dimond, Pres
D.J. Dantas, Dir of HR
Grgo Lauc, Dir of Fin
Chris Young, Dir of IT
Jason Adlam,
    VP Customer Service & Sales

Chester Cartage & Movers Ltd.

1995 Markham Rd.
Toronto, ON M1B 2W3
Tel 416-754-7720
Fax 416-754-4897
www.chestercartage.com
Line: Provides trucking and warehousing services.
NAICS: 484229 484239 493190
#Emp: 75-99 (Tor)
#TorLoc: 1
Own: Private Company
Key: Harry Cummins, Pres
Peter Cummins, Treas

Chestnut Park Real Estate Ltd.

100-1300 Yonge St.
Toronto, ON M4T 1X3
Tel 416-925-9191
Fax 416-925-3935
www.chestnutpark.com
Line: Offers residential, commercial and industrial real estate services.
NAICS: 531210
#Emp: 100-249 (Tor)

#TorLoc: 1
Own: Private Company
Key: Catherine Deluce, Pres & CEO
Justine Deluce, VP Ops

Children's Aid Society of Toronto

30 Isabella St.
Toronto, ON M4Y 1N1
Tel 416-924-4640
Fax 416-324-2485
www.torontocas.ca
AKA: CAST
Line: Provides child welfare services.
NAICS: 624110
#Emp: 500-999 (Tor)
#TorLoc: 6
Own: Government
Par: The City of Toronto
Key: Janet Morrison, Chair
David Rivard, CEO
Nancy Dale, COO
Laurie Hewson, Dir of HR
Tony Quan, CFO
Richard Kwan, Dir of Admin Services
Robert Thompson, Dir of Commun

Children's Aid Society of York Region

16915 Leslie St.
Kennedy Pl.
Newmarket, ON L3Y 9A1
Tel 905-895-2318
Fax 905-895-2113
www.yorkcas.on.ca
Line: Provides social services for children and families.
NAICS: 813310
#Emp: 250-499 (Tor)
#TorLoc: 3
Own: Not-for-profit
Key: Patrick Lake, Exec Dir
Douglas Smith, Dir of HR &
    Organizational Dev
Jennifer Grant,
    Dir of Commun & Fund Dev

Chouinard Bros. Roofing

120 Gibson Dr.
Markham, ON L3R 2Z3
Tel 905-479-8300
Fax 905-479-8305
www.chouinardbros.com
Line: Provides roofing, window and siding contracting services.
NAICS: 232330
#Emp: 75-99 (Tor)
#TorLoc: 1
Own: Private Company
Key: Cathy Chouinard, Owner

Christie Gardens Apartments and Care Inc.

600 Melita Cres.
Toronto, ON M6G 3Z4
Tel 416-530-1330
Fax 416-530-1686
www.christiegardens.org
Line: Operates a continuing care facility for seniors.
NAICS: 623310
#Emp: 100-249 (Tor)
#TorLoc: 1
Own: Not-for-profit
Key: David Alexander, Pres & Chmn
Grace Sweatman, CEO
Catherine Belmore, VP Ops
Charla Patel, Dir of HR
Josefine Santos, Accountants Clerk
Jim Sweatman, IT Mgr
Heather Janes, VP Resident Services

Christie Lites Ltd.

A-100 Carson St.
Toronto, ON M8W 3R9
Tel 416-644-1010
Fax 416-644-0404
www.christielites.com
Line: Sells and rents production and stage lighting equipment.
NAICS: 419190
#Emp: 75-99 (Tor)
#TorLoc: 1
Own: Private Company
Par: 966850 Ontario Inc. (CDA)
Key: Dan Souwand, VP Ops
Paul Dhingra, VP Info Management

Chrysler Canada Inc.

1 Riverside Dr. West
P.O. Box 1621
Windsor, ON N9A 4H6
Tel 519-973-2000
Fax 519-973-2226
www.chrysler.ca
Line: Supports dealer activities and manufactures vehicles and parts.
NAICS: 336110
#Emp: 1000-4999 (Tor)
#TorLoc: 3
Own: Private Company
Par: Chrysler LLC (US)
Key: Reid Bigland, Pres & CEO

Chrysler Financial

300-2425 Matheson Blvd. East
Mississauga, ON L4W 5N7
Tel 905-629-6000
Fax 905-629-7961
www.chryslerfinancialcanada.ca
Line: Provides financing and leasing to wholesale, retail and fleet customers.
NAICS: 532112 532120
#Emp: 100-249 (Tor)
#TorLoc: 1
Own: Private Company
Par: Cerebus Corp. (US)
Key: Gino Cozza, Pres & CEO

Chubb Insurance Company of Canada

1600-1 Adelaide St. East
1 Financial Pl.
Toronto, ON M5C 2V9
Tel 416-863-0550
Fax 416-863-5010
www.chubb.com/international/canada
Line: Provides property and casualty insurance.
NAICS: 524121
#Emp: 250-499 (Tor)
#TorLoc: 1
Own: Private Company
Par: The Chubb Corp. (US)
Key: Ellen Moore, Pres & Chmn
Patricia Ewen, Sr VP HR
Grant McEwen, CFO
Nicole Brouillard, CIO
Giovanni Damiano, Sr VP Mktg

Chudleigh's Ltd.

8501 Chudleigh Way
Milton, ON L9T 0L9
Tel 905-878-8781
Fax 905-878-6979
www.chudleighs.com
Line: Manufactures frozen baked goods and frozen desserts.
NAICS: 311410
#Emp: 100-249 (Tor)
#TorLoc: 1
Own: Private Company
Key: Dean Chudleigh, Pres
Scott Chudleigh, Chmn & CEO
Rob Gonsalves, VP Ops
Brent Winterton,
    VP HR & Quality Assurance
Robert Bona, CFO

Ciba Vision Canada Inc.

2150 Torquay Mews
Mississauga, ON L5N 2M6
Tel 905-821-4774
Fax 905-821-8106
www.cibavision.ca
Line: Manufactures eye care products including contact lenses, lens care solutions and ophthalmic drugs.
NAICS: 339110
#Emp: 100-249 (Tor)
#TorLoc: 1
Own: Private Company
Par: Novartis AG (SWITZ)
Key: Paul Smyth, Site Dir & Head of Customer Service, North America
Andrea Saia, Pres & CEO
Lisa O'Connell, HR Mgr
John McKenna, CFO
Baron Banschewski, IT Mgr

CIBC Global Asset Management

2200-130 King St. West
The Exchange Tower
Toronto, ON M5X 1B1
Tel 416-364-5620
Fax 416-364-4472
www.cibc.com/ca/am
Line: Provides investment services in mutual funds, institutional and private management.
NAICS: 523920
#Emp: 100-249 (Tor)
#TorLoc: 1
Own: Private Company
Par: Canadian Imperial Bank of Commerce (CDA)
Key: Victor Dodig, Pres & CEO
Deborah Lewis, VP
Duncan Webster, Chief Investment Officer & Head of CIBC Global Asset Management
Michael Jalbert, VP Business Dev & Mktg

CIBC Mellon

320 Bay St., P.O. Box 1
Toronto, ON M5H 4A6
Tel 416-643-5000
Fax 416-643-5501
www.cibcmellon.com
Line: Provides custody services and trust services.
NAICS: 523990
#Emp: 1000-4999 (Tor)
Own: Private Company
Key: Thomas S. Monahan, Pres & CEO
Thomas C. MacMillan, Chair
Robert Shier, Sr VP & COO
Brian Naish, Sr VP & CFO
David Linds, Sr VP, Business Dev & Client Relationship Management

CIBC World Markets Inc.

BCE Pl., 161 Bay St., 4th Fl.
P.O. Box 500
Toronto, ON M5J 2S8
Tel 416-594-7000
Fax 416-594-7470
www.cibcwm.com
Line: Operates a full service investment dealing company.
NAICS: 523110
#Emp: 250-499 (Tor)
#TorLoc: 6
Own: Private Company
Par: Canadian Imperial Bank of Commerce (CDA)
Key: Richard Nesbitt, Chmn & CEO
Geoffery Belsher, Mng Dir & Global
    Head, Investment Banking
Gary W. Brown, Mng Dir & Head,
    Risk World Markets
Stephen Forbes, Exec VP Mktg,
    Commun & Pub Affairs

CiF Lab Casework Solutions

56 Edilcan Dr.
Concord, ON L4K 3S6
Tel 905-738-5821
Fax 905-738-6537
www.cifsolutions.com
Line: Manufactures laboratory furniture and fume hoods.
NAICS: 339110
#Emp: 100-249 (Tor)
#TorLoc: 1
Own: Private Company
Key: Larry Bedford, VP Ops
Paul Woodman, Territory Mgr

CI Fund Management Inc.

2 Queen St. East, 20th Fl.
Toronto, ON M5C 3G7
Tel 416-364-1145
Fax 416-364-6299
www.cifunds.com
AKA: CI Funds
Line: Provides investment services.
NAICS: 523120
#Emp: 1000-4999 (Tor)
#TorLoc: 4
Own: Public Company
Key: Derek Green, Pres
Peter Anderson, CEO
David Pauli, VP & COO
Douglas Jamieson, Sr VP & CFO

Cimco Refrigeration

65 Villiers St.
Toronto, ON M5A 3S1
Tel 416-465-7581
Fax 416-465-8815
www.cimcorefrigeration.com
Line: Operates an industrial refrigeration company that provides engineering, construction, equipment and post-installation factory service to the food, beverage, cold storage and recreation industries.
NAICS: 232540 333416
#Emp: 250-499 (Tor)
#TorLoc: 2
Own: Public Company
Par: Toromont Industries Ltd. (CDA)
Key: Steve McLeod, Pres
Jack Hayes, Manuf Mgr
Karen Mihay, Payroll Mgr
Guy Russell, Group Cont
Kevin Hubert, Mgr of Purch

Cineplex Entertainment LP

1303 Yonge St.
Toronto, ON M4T 2Y9
Tel 416-323-6600
Fax 416-323-6612
www.cineplex.com
Line: Exhibits motion pictures through a company-operated theatre circuit.
NAICS: 512130
#Emp: 1000-4999 (Tor)
#TorLoc: 29
Own: Public Company
Key: Ellis Jacob, Pres & CEO
Paul Nonis, Sr VP Ops
Heather Briant, Sr VP HR
Gord Nelson, CFO
Ian Shaw, VP Purch
Jeff Kent, CTO
John Tsirlis, VP Sales
Susan Mandryk,
    Sr VP Customer Strategies
Pat Marshall,
    VP Commun & Investor Relns

Cinram International Inc.

2255 Markham Rd.
Toronto, ON M1B 2W3
Tel 416-298-8190
Fax 416-298-0612
www.cinram.com
Line: Manufactures and distributes pre-recorded DVDs, CDs and CD-ROMs for major motion picture studios and record labels.
NAICS: 334610
#Emp: 1000-4999 (Tor)
#TorLoc: 3
Own: Public Company

Key: Steven G. Brown, Pres & CFO
David Ashton, Exec VP Manuf
John Bell, Exec VP Fin & CFO
Jeffery Fink,
    Exec VP Sales & Studio Relns

Cintas Canada Ltd.

3-6300 Kennedy Rd.
Mississauga, ON L5T 2X5
Tel 905-670-4409
Fax 905-670-4435
www.cintas.com
AKA: The Uniform People
Line: Provides uniform rentals.
NAICS: 812330
#Emp: 1000-4999 (Tor)
Own: Public Company
Par: Cintas Corp. (US)
Key: Joe Melo, GM
Angela Aubry,
    Employment Practices Mgr
Suhayl Muhtaseh, Dir of Sales

C.I.P. Group Ltd.

5 Mansewood Crt.
Acton, ON L7J 0A1
Tel 905-864-1400
Fax 905-864-9094
www.cipgroup.com
AKA: Rapid Forming Inc.
NAICS: 232220
#Emp: 100-249 (Tor)
#TorLoc: 1
Own: Private Company
Key: Milton Croucher, Chief Estimator

Circa Metals

A Div. of Circa Enterprises Inc.
206 Great Gulf Dr.
Vaughan, ON L4K 5W1
Tel 905-669-5511
Fax 905-669-4518
www.circametals.com
Line: Manufactures meter sockets for metal enclosures.
NAICS: 335990
#Emp: 100-249 (Tor)
#TorLoc: 1
Own: Public Company
Key: Ivan Smith, Pres & CEO
Graham Reid, VP Fin
Tom Lepera, Nat'l Sales & Product Mgr

Circle of Home Care Services (Toronto)

530 Wilson Ave., 4th Fl.
Toronto, ON M3H 5Y9
Tel 416-635-2860
Fax 416-635-1692
www.circleofcare.com
NAICS: 621610
#Emp: 250-499 (Tor)
#TorLoc: 1
Own: Not-for-profit
Key: Michael Scheinert, Pres & CEO
Carolyn Acton, VP Client Services
Lisa Levin, VP Commun & Dev

Cisco Systems Canada Co.

3400-181 Bay St.
BCE Pl.
Toronto, ON M5J 2T3
Tel 416-306-7000
Fax 416-306-7099
www.cisco.com/ca
Line: Manufactures hardware and
software for Internet networking.
NAICS: 334410 541330
#Emp: 500-999 (Tor)
#TorLoc: 1
Own: Private Company
Par: Cisco Systems Inc. (US)
Key: Nitin Kawale, Pres
Rick Otway, VP Ops, Central Canada
Angelo Valentini, CFO

Cision Canada Inc.

1100-150 Ferrand Dr.
Toronto, ON M3C 3E5
Tel 416-750-2220
Fax 416-750-2233
www.ca.cision.com
Line: Provides media monitoring,
analysis, mailing, specialized
fulfillment and publishing.
NAICS: 541910
#Emp: 100-249 (Tor)
#TorLoc: 1
Own: Private Company
Par: The Observer Group (SWE)
Key: Phil Crompton, Sr VP & GM
Heather Hoffmann, HR Mgr
Karim Farag, VP & Cont
Ernie de Wal, VP Knowledge
    Management & Sales

Citco (Canada) Inc.

2700-2 Bloor St. East
Toronto, ON M4W 1A8
Tel 416-966-9200
Fax 416-966-9210
www.citco.com
Line: Provides financial planning
services.
NAICS: 523930
#Emp: 250-499 (Tor)
#TorLoc: 2
Own: Private Company
Key: Kieran Conroy, CFO
Deb Mason, Dir of HR

CIT Group Inc.

5035 South Service Rd.
Burlington, ON L7R 4C8
Tel 905-633-2400
Fax 905-632-1332
www.cit.com
Line: Provides corporate financial
services.
NAICS: 522112
#Emp: 250-499 (Tor)
#TorLoc: 2
Own: Private Company
Par: CIT (US)
Key: Ben Wyett, Sr VP

Citi Cards Canada

123 Front St. West
Toronto, ON M5J 2M3
Tel 416-947-5500
Fax 416-947-5387
www.citicards.ca
Line: Provides banking and financial
services.
NAICS: 522112
#Emp: 250-499 (Tor)
#TorLoc: 1
Own: Private Company
Par: Citigroup Inc. (US)
Key: Bruce Clark, Pres & CEO
Lynn Diseri, Sr VP Ops
Christine Di Scola, Dir HR
Steve Stobie, CFO
Ann Grannan, VP Ops

Citigroup Fund Services Inc.

2920 Matheson Blvd. East
Mississauga, ON L4W 5J4
Tel 905-624-9889
Fax 905-214-8100
www.citigroup.com
Line: Provides processing,
administration, fund valuation, and
technology services.
NAICS: 561110

#Emp: 1000-4999 (Tor)
#TorLoc: 2
Own: Private Company
Key: Robert Smuk, Pres & CEO

Citiguard Security Services Inc.

201-1560 Brimley Rd.
Toronto, ON M1P 3G9
Tel 416-431-6888
Fax 416-431-7402
www.citiguard.ca
Line: Provides security patrol and
surveillance services.
NAICS: 334511 561612
#Emp: 100-249 (Tor)
#TorLoc: 1
Own: Private Company
Key: Steve Boseovski, Pres
Stelwart Chagwedera, Ops Mgr
John Li, Acctng Mgr
Tony Boseovski, Sales Mgr

The City of Brampton

2 Wellington St. West
Brampton, ON L6Y 4R2
Tel 905-874-2000
Fax 905-874-2670
www.brampton.ca
Line: Plans and delivers municipal
services to the residents and businesses
of Brampton.
NAICS: 913910
#Emp: 5000-9999 (Tor)
Own: Government
Key: Susan Fennell, Mayor
Deborah Dubenofsky, City Mgr
Mo Lewis, Commr of Fin & Info
Rob Meikle, CIO
Dennis Cutajar, Comr of
    Economic Dev & Commun
T-Jay Upper, Dir of Commun

The City of Burlington

426 Brant St.
P.O. Box 5013
Burlington, ON L7R 3Z6
Tel 905-335-7600
Fax 905-335-7881
www.burlington.ca
AKA: Burlington
NAICS: 913910
#Emp: 1000-4999 (Tor)
#TorLoc: 1
Own: Government
Key: Rick Goldring, Mayor
Roman Martiuk, City Mgr

The City of Oshawa

50 Centre St. South
Oshawa, ON L1H 3Z7
Tel 905-436-3311
Fax 905-436-5623
www.oshawa.ca
AKA: Oshawa
NAICS: 913910
#Emp: 500-999 (Tor)
#TorLoc: 1
Own: Government
Key: John Henry, Mayor
Robert Duignan, City Mgr
Jackie Long, Dir of HR
Dave Lyon, Mgr of Purch Services
Dave Mawby, Dir of ITS
Tracy Adams,
   Dir of Mktg & Corp Commun

The City of Toronto

City Hall, 100 Queen St. West
Toronto, ON M5H 2N2
Tel 416-338-0338
Fax 416-392-1553
www.toronto.ca
AKA: Toronto
NAICS: 913910
#Emp: 10000+ (Tor)
#TorLoc: 85
Own: Government
Key: Rob Ford, Mayor
Joseph P. Pennachetti, City Mgr
Bruce Anderson, Exec Dir of HR
David W. Wallace, CIO

The City of Vaughan

2141 Major MacKenzie Dr.
Vaughan, ON L6A 1T1
Tel 905-832-2281
Fax 905-832-8143
www.vaughan.ca
AKA: Vaughan
NAICS: 913910
#Emp: 1000-4999 (Tor)
#TorLoc: 1
Own: Government
Key: Maurizio Bevilacqua, Mayor
Clayton Harris, City Mgr
Janet Ashfield, Dir of HR
Barbara Cribbett,
   Commr of Fin & City Treas
George Wilson, Dir of Purch
Dimitri Yampolsky, CIO
Madeline Zito, Dir of Corp Commun

City Taxi

219-130 Westmore Dr.
Toronto, ON M9V 5E2
Tel 416-740-2222
Fax 416-241-5634
www.citytaxitoronto.com
NAICS: 485310
#Emp: 250-499 (Tor)
#TorLoc: 1
Own: Private Company
Key: Savi Sekhon, CEO

C.J. Graphics Inc.

134 Park Lawn Rd.
Toronto, ON M8Y 3H9
Tel 416-588-0808
Fax 416-588-5015
www.cjgraphics.com
Line: Operates a printing and
lithography company.
NAICS: 323115
#Emp: 75-99 (Tor)
Own: Private Company
Key: Jay Mandarino, Pres

CKF Inc.

610-10 Carlson Crt.
Toronto, ON M9W 6L2
Tel 416-249-2207
Fax 416-249-7267
www.royalchinet.com
Line: Manufactures moulded pulp and
polystyrene foam products including
egg cartons, meat and produce trays,
hinged-lids and private labels.
NAICS: 322219 322299
#Emp: 100-249 (Tor)
#TorLoc: 1
Own: Private Company
Par: Scotia Investments Ltd. (CDA)
Key: Ian Anderson, Exec VP & COO
Michael Green, VP Fin
Bradley K. Dennis, VP Sales & Mktg

Clariant (Canada) Inc.

2 Lone Oak Crt.
Toronto, ON M9C 5R9
Tel 416-847-7000
Fax 416-847-7001
www.clariant.masterbatches.com
AKA: Clariant Masterbatches
Line: Produces colour and additive
concentrates for the plastics industry.
NAICS: 418410 325999
#Emp: 75-99 (Tor)
#TorLoc: 1
Own: Private Company
Par: Clariant Inc. (SWITZ)
Key: Luke Ng, Site Mgr
Yvon Garneau, Mktg & Sales Mgr

Clarke Inc.

751 Bowes Rd.
P.O. Box 32
Concord, ON L4K 1B2
Tel 416-665-5585
Fax 416-695-9544
www.clarkelink.com
AKA: Clarke Transport Inc.; Clarke
Road Transport Inc.; Clarke Contract
Services; ITC Inc.
Line: Provides transportation services.
NAICS: 484239
#Emp: 250-499 (Tor)
#TorLoc: 3
Own: Public Company
Key: Darell Hornby, Pres
Dean Cull, COO
Ruby Murphy-Collins, Corp Cont
Kelly O'Brien, VP Sales, Ontario & US

Classic Fire Protection Inc.

645 Garyray Dr.
Toronto, ON M9L 1P9
Tel 416-740-3000
Fax 416-740-2039
www.classicfire.com
Line: Provides total fire protection
installation and services.
NAICS: 334512
#Emp: 100-249 (Tor)
#TorLoc: 2
Own: Private Company
Key: Richard Berwick, Pres
Lina Conte, HR
Steve Peckam, Sales

Clearview Industries Ltd.

45 Fenmar Dr.
Toronto, ON M9L 1M1
Tel 416-745-6666
Fax 416-745-3711
www.clearview.on.ca
Line: Manufactures doors.
NAICS: 332321
#Emp: 75-99 (Tor)
#TorLoc: 1
Own: Private Company
Par: ShredEx! Aluminum (CDA)
Key: Tom Marsala, GM

Clearway Construction Inc.

379 Bowes Rd.
Vaughan, ON L4K 1J1
Tel 905-761-6955
Fax 905-761-9770
www.clearwaygroup.com
Line: Provides water and sewer mains
construction services.
NAICS: 231320
#Emp: 100-249 (Tor)

#TorLoc: 6
Own: Private Company
Key: Nick DiBattista, Pres
Anthony DiBattista, Secy-Treas
Alvin Chan, Cont

Cleveland Range Ltd.

8251 Keele St.
Concord, ON L4K 1Z1
Tel 905-660-4747
Fax 905-660-4492
www.clevelandrange.com
Line: Manufactures restaurant and food
service equipment.
NAICS: 333299 333310
#Emp: 100-249 (Tor)
#TorLoc: 1
Own: Private Company
Par: Manitowoc (US)
Key: Wing Yeung, Pres
Tony Cariati, Plant Mgr
Laura Chehadi-Jaja, Mgr of HR
Rick McRobert, Purch Mgr

Clintar - Franchise Support Office

A Div. of Clintar
Groundskeeping Services
1-70 Esna Park Dr.
Markham, ON L3R 1E3
Tel 905-943-9530
Fax 905-943-9529
www.clintar.com
Line: Provides landscape management
services.
NAICS: 561730
#Emp: 250-499 (Tor)
#TorLoc: 12
Own: Private Company
Key: Robert Wilton, Pres
Todd Wilton, Field Ops Mgr
Joanne Nicholson, Comptr

Clover Tool Manufacturing Ltd.

8271 Keele St., Bldg. 3
Vaughan, ON L4K 1Z1
Tel 905-669-1999
Fax 905-669-3565
www.clovertoolmfg.com
Line: Designs and builds tooling for the
automotive industry.
NAICS: 332118 332210
#Emp: 100-249 (Tor)
#TorLoc: 1
Own: Private Company
Key: Frank Zeni, Pres
Bruce Patterson, Ops Mgr
Emilia Rachitan, Office Mgr
Robert Zeni, IT Admr & Privacy Mgr
George Zeni, GM

CLS Catering Services Ltd.

2950 Convair Dr.
P.O. Box 3
Toronto AMF, ON L5P 1A2
Tel 905-676-3218
Fax 905-676-0707
www.clscatering.com
Line: Provides in-flight airline catering
services.
NAICS: 722320
#Emp: 100-249 (Tor)
#TorLoc: 1
Own: Private Company
Key: David Caruana, Ops Mgr

Club Coffee

55 Carrier Dr.
Toronto, ON M9W 5V9
Tel 416-675-1300
Fax 416-675-8902
www.clubcoffee.ca
Line: Roasts, grinds and packages
coffee.
NAICS: 311920
#Emp: 100-249 (Tor)
#TorLoc: 1
Own: Private Company
Par: Morrison Lamothe (CDA)
Key: Merv Edgar, VP Ops
Pilar Torres, HR Mgr
Chesley Gates, Purch Mgr

ClubLink Corp.

15675 Dufferin St.
King City, ON L7B 1K5
Tel 905-841-3730
Fax 905-841-1134
www.clublink.ca
Line: Owns and operates golf courses.
NAICS: 713910
#Emp: 1000-4999 (Tor)
#TorLoc: 14
Own: Public Company
Key: Ray Sahi, Pres & CEO
Edge Caravaggio, VP Golf Operation
Steve Scott, Dir of HR
Robert Visentin, CFO
Neil Osborne, VP Clubhouse Ops

Club Markham

8500 Warden Ave.
Markham, ON L6G 1A5
Tel 905-470-2400
Fax 905-470-2444
www.clubmarkham.ca
Line: Operates a fitness club.
NAICS: 713940
#Emp: 100-249 (Tor)

#TorLoc: 1
Own: Private Company
Key: Tom Jones, GM
Jodi Shoniker, Dir of Admin

Club Monaco Corp.

157 Bloor St. West
Toronto, ON M5S 1P7
Tel 416-591-8837
Fax 416-586-6339
www.clubmonaco.com
NAICS: 448140 448150
#Emp: 1000-4999 (Tor)
#TorLoc: 9
Own: Public Company
Par: Polo Ralph Lauren (US)
Key: Catherine Kelly, Dir of Cdn Stores

Clyde Union

4211 Mainway Dr.
Burlington, ON L7L 5N9
Tel 905-315-3800
Fax 905-336-2693
www.clydeunion.com
AKA: David Brown Union Pumps
Line: Manufactures pumps and
components.
NAICS: 333910
#Emp: 75-99 (Tor)
#TorLoc: 1
Own: Private Company
Par: Clyde Union Pumps Ltd. (US)
Key: Shakil Ahmed, Plant Mgr

CML Healthcare Inc.

60 Courtneypark Dr. West
Mississauga, ON L5W 0B3
Tel 905-565-0043
Fax 905-565-6704
www.cmlhealthcare.com
Line: Provides diagnostic laboratory
and imaging services.
NAICS: 621510
#Emp: 1000-4999 (Tor)
#TorLoc: 95
Own: Public Company
Key: Patrice Merrin,
   Chmn & Interim CEO
Kent Nicholson, COO
Rebecca Waddell, VP HR
Tom Weber, CFO
Don Kerr, GM

CN

935 de la Gauchetiere St. West
Montreal, PQ H3B 2M9
Tel 514-399-5186
Fax 514-399-5832
www.cn.ca
AKA: Canadian National Railway Co.
Line: Provides rail-based freight
transportation services.
NAICS: 482113
#Emp: 1000-4999 (Tor)
#TorLoc: 11
Own: Private Company
Key: Claude Mongeau, Pres & CEO
Keith Creel, Exec VP & COO
Kimberly Madigan, VP HR
Luc Jobin, Exec VP & CFO
James Bright, VP & CIO
Doug MacDonald, VP Corp Mktg
Sean Finn, Exec VP, Corp Services &
    Chief Legal Officer

CNW Group

1500-20 Bay St.
Water Park Place
Toronto, ON M5J 2N8
Tel 416-863-9350
Fax 416-863-4825
www.newswire.ca
Line: Operates a media company.
NAICS: 514110
#Emp: 100-249 (Tor)
#TorLoc: 1
Own: Private Company
Key: Carolyn McGill-Davidson,
    Pres & CEO
Nicole Cuillot, VP
    Project Management & Ops
Dianna Klatt, HR Mgr
Dennis Moir, Sr VP Fin & HR
David Frost, VP Tech
Elisa Schupp, VP Nat'l Sales

Coast Paper

200 Galcat Dr.
Vaughan, ON L4L 0B9
Tel 905-850-1170
www.paperlinx.com
AKA: PaperlinX Canada
Line: Sells, markets and distributes fine
paper, graphic arts consumables and
equipment, and industrial products.
NAICS: 418210
#Emp: 100-249 (Tor)
#TorLoc: 1
Own: Public Company
Par: Paperlinx (AUS)
Key: James Tovell, GM, Ontario Region
Sandra Stewart, Mktg Mgr

Coatings 85 Ltd.

7007 Davand Dr.
Mississauga, ON L5T 1L5
Tel 905-564-1711
Fax 905-564-2819
www.acadiangroup.ca
NAICS: 325510
#Emp: 250-499 (Tor)
#TorLoc: 1
Own: Private Company
Par: The Acadian Group (CDA)
Key: Mike Pitman, Pres
Dan Welsh, Ops Mgr
Phil Pitman, Sr Mgr Sales & Mktg

Cobalt Pharmaceuticals Inc.

6500 Kitimat Rd.
Mississauga, ON L5N 2B8
Tel 905-814-1820
Fax 905-814-8696
www.cobaltpharma.com
Line: Manufactures pharmaceutical
medicine.
NAICS: 325410
#Emp: 250-499 (Tor)
#TorLoc: 2
Own: Private Company
Key: Terry Fretz, Pres
Joe Beyger, Pres, Ops
Linda Stewart, HR Mgr
Henry Koziarski, CFO

Coca-Cola Bottling Company

42 Overlea Blvd.
Toronto, ON M4H 1B8
Tel 416-424-6000
Fax 416-424-6329
www.cocacola.ca
Line: Bottles and sells carbonated and
non-carbonated beverages.
NAICS: 312110
#Emp: 1000-4999 (Tor)
#TorLoc: 6
Own: Public Company
Par: Coca-Cola Enterprises Inc. (US)
Key: Kevin Warren, Pres & COO
Alain Robichaud, VP Ops
Tova White, VP HR
Ed Walker, VP Fin
Scott Lindsay, VP Sales
Sandra Banks, VP PR & Commun

Coco Paving Inc.

949 Wilson Ave.
Toronto, ON M3K 1G2
Tel 416-633-9670
Fax 416-633-4959
www.cocopaving.com
Line: Manufactures asphalt paving
mixtures; recycles asphalt and concrete
materials; builds and paves roads; and
provides comprehensive site services.
NAICS: 231310 324121
#Emp: 250-499 (Tor)
Own: Public Company
Par: Lafarge SA (CDA)
Key: Rock Anthony Coco, Pres
Jenny Coco, CEO
Steve Smith, VP, Construction

Co-Ex-Tec

140 Staffern Dr.
Concord, ON L4K 2X3
Tel 905-738-8710
Fax 905-738-1347
www.magna.com
AKA: Co-Ex-Tec Industries Inc.
Line: Manufactures automotive parts
and accessories.
NAICS: 336390
#Emp: 500-999 (Tor)
#TorLoc: 2
Own: Private Company
Par: Magna International Inc. (CDA)
Key: Chris Bitsakakis, GM
Cathy O'Hara, HR Mgr
Frank Ientile, Cont

Coffee Time Donuts Inc.

77 Progress Ave.
Toronto, ON M1P 2Y7
Tel 416-288-8515
Fax 416-288-8895
www.coffeetime.ca
Line: Operates a chain of coffee and
donut shops.
NAICS: 722210 533110
#Emp: 100-249 (Tor)
#TorLoc: 250
Own: Private Company
Key: Anastasios Michalpoulos, Pres

Coffey Geotechnics Inc.

20 Meteor Dr.
Toronto, ON M9W 1A4
Tel 416-213-1255
Fax 416-213-1260
www.coffey.com
Line: Operates an engineering
consultancy specializing in
geotechnical, environmental,
construction materials, building
sciences, pavement and transportation.
NAICS: 541330
#Emp: 100-249 (Tor)
#TorLoc: 4
Own: Private Company
Par: Coffey International Ltd. Co. (AUS)
Key: Michael Norman, VP
Anna Leone, HR Consultant

Cogeco Cable Canada Inc.

950 Syscon Rd.
P.O. Box 5076
Burlington, ON L7R 4S6
Tel 905-333-5343
Fax 905-332-8426
www.cogeco.ca
Line: Offers cable television, high speed
internet, digital phone and business
services and solutions.
NAICS: 513220 514191
#Emp: 1000-4999 (Tor)
#TorLoc: 3
Own: Public Company
Par: Cogeco Cable Inc. (CDA)
Key: Louis Audet, Pres & CEO
Louise St-Pierre, Sr VP,
  Residential Services
Pierre Gagne, Sr VP & CFO
Maureen Tilson Dyment, Sr Dir of
  Commun & Programming

Cogent Power Inc.

845 Laurentian Dr.
Burlington, ON L7N 3W7
Tel 905-637-3033
Fax 905-637-7968
www.cogentpowerinc.com
Line: Manufactures magnetic cores for
transformers.
NAICS: 335311
#Emp: 100-249 (Tor)
#TorLoc: 1
Own: Private Company
Par: Corus (UK)
Key: Ron Harper, Pres
Chris Brown, Dir of Commercial
Jim Rudnisky, Cont

Coinamatic Canada Inc.

301 Matheson Blvd. West
Mississauga, ON L5R 3G3
Tel 905-755-1946
Fax 905-755-8885
www.coinamatic.com
Line: Leases, sells and services coin
and smart card operated parking
equipment and commercial washers
and dryers.
NAICS: 532210 414220
#Emp: 100-249 (Tor)
#TorLoc: 2
Own: Private Company
Key: Don Watt, COO
Meredith Brown, VP HR

Coldwell Banker Terrequity Realty

105-211 Consumers Rd.
Toronto, ON M2J 4G8
Tel 416-496-9220
Fax 416-496-2144
www.terrequity.com
NAICS: 531210
#Emp: 100-249 (Tor)
#TorLoc: 6
Own: Private Company
Key: Andrew Zsolt,
Broker of Record & Pres

Colgate-Palmolive Canada Inc.

Two Morneau Sobeco Centre, 6th Fl.
895 Don Mills Rd.
Toronto, ON M3C 1W3
Tel 416-421-6000
Fax 416-421-6913
www.colgate.com
Line: Manufactures and sells personal
and household care and laundry
products.
NAICS: 325610 325999
#Emp: 100-249 (Tor)
#TorLoc: 1
Own: Private Company
Par: Colgate-Palmolive Co. (US)
Key: Scott Jeffery, Pres
John Menecola, Plant Mgr
Carolyn Annand, VP HR
Godfrey Nthunzi, VP Fin
Samantha Wan, Purch Mgr
Peter Noble, IT Mgr
Fabrizio Guccione, VP Sales

Colio Estates Wines Inc.

2300 Haines Rd.
Mississauga, ON L4Y 1Y6
Tel 905-896-8512
Fax 905-896-7133
www.coliowinery.com
Line: Operates a winery.
NAICS: 312130
#Emp: 100-249 (Tor)
#TorLoc: 1
Own: Private Company
Key: Jim Clark, Pres
Doug Beatty, VP Mktg

Collectcents Inc.

1450 Meyerside Dr., 7th Fl.
Mississauga, ON L5T 2N5
Tel 905-670-7575
Fax 905-670-7069
www.collectcents.com
AKA: Credit Bureau of Canada
Collections
Line: Operates a full service third party
accounts receivable management
solution services company.
NAICS: 561440
#Emp: 100-249 (Tor)
Own: Private Company
Key: Jonathan Finley, Pres

Collectcorp Inc.

2000-415 Yonge St.
Toronto, On M5B 2E7
Tel 416-961-9622
Fax 416-961-2037
Line: Provides collection services.
NAICS: 561440
#Emp: 1000-4999 (Tor)
#TorLoc: 3
Own: Private Company
Key: John Tilley, Pres
Nicholas Wilson, Chmn & CEO
Tim Collins, Ops Mgr
Suzanne Huether, Mgr of HR
Boris Dybenko, Exec VP & CFO

Collega International Inc.

210 Lesmill Rd.
Toronto, ON M3B 2T5
Tel 416-754-1444
Fax 416-754-2484
www.collega.com
Line: Wholesales beauty parlour
equipment.
NAICS: 417920
#Emp: 100-249 (Tor)
#TorLoc: 1
Own: Private Company
Key: Ray Civello, Pres & CEO
Raffaela Caruso, Sr VP Fin & Ops
Catherine Mok, Exec Asst

The College of Family Physicians of Canada

2630 Skymark Ave.
Mississauga, ON L4W 5A4
Tel 905-629-0900
Fax 905-629-0893
www.cfpc.ca
Line: Operates a continuing medical education college.
NAICS: 813920
#Emp: 75-99 (Tor)
#TorLoc: 1
Own: Association
Key: Calvin Gutkin, Exec Dir & CEO

College of Nurses of Ontario

101 Davenport Rd.
Toronto, ON M5R 3P1
Tel 416-928-0900
Fax 416-928-6507
www.cno.org
Line: Provides official regulatory services for nurses in Ontario in order to protect the public interest.
NAICS: 813920 621390
#Emp: 100-249 (Tor)
#TorLoc: 1
Own: Not-for-profit
Key: Anne L. Coghlan, Exec Dir
Elizabeth Horlock, HR Mgr
Paul Reinhart, Dir of Corp Services

College of Physicians and Surgeons of Ontario

80 College St.
Toronto, ON M5G 2E2
Tel 416-967-2600
Fax 416-961-3330
www.cpso.on.ca
AKA: CPSO
Line: Licenses physicians and regulates the practice of medicine in the province in order to serve and protect the public interest.
NAICS: 813920 621390
#Emp: 250-499 (Tor)
#TorLoc: 1
Own: Not-for-profit
Key: Lynne Thurling, Pres
Rocco Gerace, Registrar
Douglas Anderson, Corp Services
   Officer & Associate Registrar
Clark McIntosh, Dir of Fin & Facilities
Louise Verity, Dir, Associate Registrar,
   Policy & Commun

College Woodwork

A Div. of Seventh Day Adventist Church
145 Clarence Biesenthal Dr.
Oshawa, ON L1K 2H5
Tel 905-725-3566
Fax 905-725-2912
www.collegewoodwork.com
Line: Manufactures solid birch bedroom, home office and accent furniture.
NAICS: 337213 337127
#Emp: 100-249 (Tor)
#TorLoc: 1
Own: Private Company
Key: Sheldon Smith, COO
Wade Van Wart, Plant Mgr
Mac Moreau, HR Generalist
Ann Hau, Cont

Colliers Macaulay Nicolls Inc.

2200-1 Queen St. East
Toronto, ON M5C 2Z2
Tel 416-777-2200
Fax 416-777-2277
www.colliers.com
AKA: Colliers International
Line: Operates full service commercial real estate business.
NAICS: 531390
#Emp: 250-499 (Tor)
#TorLoc: 3
Own: Public Company
Key: Franklin Holtforster, Pres & CEO
David Bowden, CEO, Canada
Scott Addison, VP Ops, Eastern Cda
Ken Bosch, HR Mgr
Lex Perry, Mgr of Mktg & Commun

Colombo Chrysler Dodge Ltd.

1 Auto Park Circ.
Woodbridge, ON L4L 8R1
Tel 905-850-7879
Fax 905-850-8401
www.colombochrysler.com
Line: Operates a car sales and leasing company.
NAICS: 532112
#Emp: 75-99 (Tor)
#TorLoc: 3
Own: Private Company
Key: Griff Jarvis, Dealer Principal
Max Shabazlli, Business Mgr
Teresa DiMarco, Cont

Columbia Building Maintenance Co. Ltd.

1-65 Martin Ross Ave.
Toronto, ON M3J 2L6
Tel 416-663-5020
Fax 416-663-5025
www.cbmontario.com
Line: Provides janitorial services.
NAICS: 561722
#Emp: 100-249 (Tor)
#TorLoc: 1
Own: Private Company
Key: Todd White, Pres

Columbus Centre of Toronto

901 Lawrence Ave. West
Toronto, ON M6A 1C3
Tel 416-789-7011
Fax 416-789-3951
www.villacharities.com
AKA: Villa Charities Inc.
Line: Operates an Italian-Canadian cultural recreation centre which provides services including day care, a fitness centre, a restaurant, catering facilities and the Joseph D. Carrier Art Gallery.
NAICS: 713940
#Emp: 100-249 (Tor)
#TorLoc: 1
Own: Not-for-profit
Par: Villa Charities Inc. (CDA)
Key: Pal Di Iulio, Pres & CEO
Ugo Di Fedirico,
   Admr of Columbus Centre
Paul Pass, Payroll & HR Mgr
Jan Sebek, Dir of Athletics
Paola Marcoccio,
   Catering & Events Sales Mgr
Stefanie Polsinelli,
   Mktg & Commun Coord

Comark Services Inc.

6789 Millcreek Dr.
Mississauga, ON L5N 5M4
Tel 905-567-7375
Fax 905-567-5965
www.comark.ca
AKA: CLEO
Line: Operates a retail store selling ladies' apparel.
NAICS: 448120
#Emp: 100-249 (Tor)
#TorLoc: 1
Own: Private Company
Key: Jerry Bachynski, Pres, CEO & COO
Daniel Saucier, COO
Connie Chryssoulakis, HR Mgr
Bill King, VP & CFO

Combined Insurance Company of America

300-7300 Warden Ave.
Markham, ON L3R 0X3
Tel 905-305-1922
Fax 905-305-8600
www.combined.ca
AKA: Aon Canada Inc.
Line: Provides supplemental accident, health, sickness, long-term care, and life insurance.
NAICS: 524112 524111
#Emp: 100-249 (Tor)
#TorLoc: 2
Own: Public Company
Par: Ace Insurance Inc. (US)
Key: Vince Iozzo,
   VP & Chief Agent, Canada
Guy Sauve, Sr VP & Mng Dir, Cdn Ops
Anna-Marie Di-Cesare,
   Asst VP HR & Admin
Leon Levy, Mgr of IS
James Bishop, Mgr of Mktg Services

Comcare Health Services

120-255 Consumers Rd.
Toronto, ON M2J 1R4
Tel 416-929-3364
Fax 416-929-1738
www.comcarehealthnetwork.ca
Line: Provides home health care services and health care personnel.
NAICS: 561310
#Emp: 250-499 (Tor)
#TorLoc: 3
Own: Private Company
Key: Peter Tanaka, Pres & CEO
Wendy Theis, VP Branch Ops
Katie Hunter, VP HR

Comda Calendar

15 Densley Ave.
Toronto, ON M6M 2P5
Tel 416-243-8766
Fax 416-243-5391
www.comda.com
AKA: Comda Advertising Group; Comda, The Calendar People
Line: Distributes promotional products.
NAICS: 418990
#Emp: 100-249 (Tor)
#TorLoc: 1
Own: Private Company
Par: Stincor Van Smith Marketing (CDA)

Key: Michael Warren, Pres
Peter Warren, CEO
Pat Warren, Ops Mgr
Winnie Sukardi, HR Supr
Errol Verasami, VP Fin
Julie Jack, Purch Sr
Lee Warren, VP IT
Susan Kaschuk, Deputy Exec Officer
Scott Ferguson, VP Mktg
Sandra Lewis, VP Admin

The Comedy Network

299 Queen St. West
Toronto, ON M5V 2Z5
Tel 416-384-5300
Fax 416-384-5301
www.thecomedynetwork.ca
Line: Operates a television broadcasting station.
NAICS: 513120
#Emp: 1000-4999 (Tor)
#TorLoc: 1
Own: Private Company
Par: Bell Media (CDA)
Key: Millan Curry-Sharples, VP

Commercial Bakeries Corp.

45 Torbarrie Rd.
Toronto, ON M3L 1G5
Tel 416-247-5478
Fax 416-242-4129
www.commercialbakeries.com
Line: Manufactures cookies and crackers.
NAICS: 311821
#Emp: 100-249 (Tor)
#TorLoc: 1
Own: Private Company
Key: Anthony J. Fusco, Sr., Pres
Joseph Fusco, VP
Philip Fusco, VP
Anthony Fusco, Jr., VP

Commercial Spring & Tool Company Ltd.

160 Watline Ave.
Mississauga, ON L4Z 1R1
Tel 905-568-3899
Fax 905-568-1929
www.commercialspring.com
Line: Manufactures wire forming and auto assembly parts.
NAICS: 332619 332118
#Emp: 250-499 (Tor)
#TorLoc: 5
Own: Private Company
Key: Frank Martinitz, Pres
Gurmail Gill, VP
Paul White, Cont
Jonathan Mumford, Purch Mgr

Commissionaires Great Lakes

80 Church St.
Toronto, ON M5C 2G1
Tel 416-364-4496
Fax 416-364-3361
www.commissionaires.ca
Line: Provides security, office support, municipal by-law enforcement, security training, and fingerprinting services.
NAICS: 561310
#Emp: 1000-4999 (Tor)
#TorLoc: 1
Own: Private Company
Key: Jim Watts, Pres & CEO
Phillip Day, HR Mgr
Karen Courser, VP Fin & Corp Services
Jonathan Fields, Dir of Sales
Donna D'Arcy, Dir of Mktg & Commun

Communications Repair Logistics Company

2390 Argentia Rd.
Mississauga, ON L5N 5Z7
Tel 905-816-2000
Fax 905-816-1013
www.ctdi.com
Line: Tests and repairs printed circuit boards for telecommunications equipment.
NAICS: 334410
#Emp: 100-249 (Tor)
#TorLoc: 1
Own: Private Company
Par: Communications Test Design Inc. (US)
Key: Greg Search, HR Mgr

Community Care Access Centre - Central West

199 County Crt. Blvd.
Brampton, ON L6W 4P3
Tel 905-796-0040
Fax 905-796-5619
www.ccac-ont.ca
AKA: Peel CCAC
Line: Offers in-home nursing and personal support services.
NAICS: 623310 624120
#Emp: 250-499 (Tor)
#TorLoc: 1
Own: Not-for-profit
Key: Cathy Hecimovich, Exec Dir
Al Madden, Sr Dir
Richlyn Lorimer, HR Mgr
Suzanne Jones,
   Dir of Contracts & Procurement

Community Care - East York

303-840 Coxwell Ave.
Toronto, ON M4C 5T2
Tel 416-422-2026
Fax 416-422-1513
www.ccey.org
Line: Operates a community health and personal support services organization.
NAICS: 623310 624120
#Emp: 100-249 (Tor)
#TorLoc: 1
Own: Not-for-profit
Key: Duane Gonsalves, Dir of HR

Community Living Ajax, Pickering & Whitby

36 Emperor St.
Ajax, ON L1S 1M7
Tel 905-427-3300
Fax 905-427-3310
www.cl-apw.org
AKA: CLAPW
Line: Provides support for the developmentally handicapped.
NAICS: 624120 624310
#Emp: 100-249 (Tor)
Own: Not-for-profit
Key: Chris Cook, Pres
Barbara Andrews, CEO
Marilyn Flanagan, HR
Julian Carver, Dir of Fin

Community Living Association for South Simcoe

125 Dufferin St. South
Alliston, ON L9R 1E9
Tel 705-435-4792
Fax 705-435-2766
www.class.on.ca
Line: Provides support services to children, youth and adults with a developmental handicap.
NAICS: 624120 624310
#Emp: 100-249 (Tor)
#TorLoc: 14
Own: Association
Key: Mary Munnoch, Pres
Vito Facciolo, Exec Dir
Mary Kay Tombu, HR Dir
Carolyn Garton, Dir of Fin

Community Living Burlington

3057 Mainway Dr.
Burlington, ON L7M 1A1
Tel 905-336-2225
Fax 905-335-9919
www.clburlington.ca
Line: Provides services and support to children and adults who have a developmental disability in the Burlington community.
NAICS: 624120 624310
#Emp: 250-499 (Tor)
#TorLoc: 1
Own: Not-for-profit
Key: Judy Pryde, Exec Dir
Judy Shaw, Dir of Program Supports
Donna Clausnitzer,
    HR Coord & Website Mgr
Lisa Morikawa, Dir of Fin
Karen Lade, Dir of Program Supports

Community Living Georgina

26943 Hwy. 48
P.O. Box 68
Sutton, ON L0E 1R0
Tel 905-722-8947
Fax 905-722-9591
www.communitylivinggeorgina.com
Line: Provides individual and family services.
NAICS: 624190
#Emp: 100-249 (Tor)
#TorLoc: 1
Own: Private Company
Key: Susan Rome, Exec Dir
Deborah Guiga, HR Coord

Community Living Mississauga

1-6695 Millcreek Dr.
Mississauga, ON L5N 5R8
Tel 905-542-2694
Fax 905-542-0987
www.clmiss.ca
Line: Provides services and support to people who have an intellectual disability.
NAICS: 624120 624310
#Emp: 250-499 (Tor)
#TorLoc: 1
Own: Not-for-profit
Key: Keith Tansley, Exec Dir
Maria Delfino, Dir of HR & Fin
Susan Hawke, Cont
Brett Paveling, Mgr of Commun

Community Living - Newmarket/Aurora District

757 Bogart Ave.
Newmarket, ON L3Y 2A7
Tel 905-898-3000
Fax 905-898-6441
www.clnad.com
NAICS: 624120 624310
#Emp: 75-99 (Tor)
#TorLoc: 1
Own: Not-for-profit
Par: United Way (CDA)
Key: Janet Lorimer, Exec Dir
Tara Watt, HR Mgr

Community Living Oakville

301 Wyecroft Rd.
Oakville, ON L6K 2H2
Tel 905-844-0146
Fax 905-844-1832
www.oakcl.org
Line: Provides quality services, supports and opportunities, enabling people with developmental disabilities to live active, rewarding and fulfilling lives.
NAICS: 623210
#Emp: 100-249 (Tor)
#TorLoc: 2
Own: Not-for-profit
Key: Tom Crawford, Pres
John Wilson, Exec Dir
Shannon Coles, HR Mgr
Nancy Steptoe, Fin Mgr

Community Living Oshawa / Clarington

39 Wellington Ave. East
Oshawa, ON L1H 3Y1
Tel 905-576-3011
Fax 905-579-9754
www.communitylivingcoc.ca
AKA: CLOC
Line: Provides support to people with intellectual disabilities.
NAICS: 624120 624310
#Emp: 250-499 (Tor)
#TorLoc: 1
Own: Not-for-profit
Key: Steven Finlay, Exec Dir
Terri Gray, Dir of Ops
Kay Corbier, HR Mgr
Barb Feyko, Dir of Fin & Admin

Community Living Toronto

20 Spadina Rd.
Toronto, ON M5R 2S7
Tel 416-968-0650
Fax 416-968-6463
www.communitylivingtoronto.ca
Line: Supports people with intellectual disabilities and their families.
NAICS: 624120 624310
#Emp: 1000-4999 (Tor)
#TorLoc: 80
Own: Association
Key: Bruce Rivers, CEO
Flavian Pinto, CFO
Angela Bradley,
    Dir of PR & Fundraising

Compact Mould Ltd.

120 Haist Ave.
Woodbridge, ON L4L 5V4
Tel 905-851-7724
Fax 905-851-7548
www.compactmould.com
Line: Manufactures extrusion and stretch blow moulds.
NAICS: 326198
#Emp: 75-99 (Tor)
#TorLoc: 1
Own: Private Company
Key: Miguel Petrucci, Pres

Compass Group Canada Ltd.

400-5560 Explorer Dr.
Mississauga, ON L4W 5M3
Tel 905-568-4636
Fax 905-568-8945
www.compass-canada.com
Line: Provides national food services and facilities management.
NAICS: 722210
#Emp: 1000-4999 (Tor)
#TorLoc: 115
Own: Private Company
Par: Compass Group plc (UK)
Key: Saajid Khan, CEO
Jack MacDonald, Chmn
Brenda Brown, Sr VP HR
Stephen Kelly, CFO
Ian Bullock, VP Purch
Cathy Dilworth, VP IT
Paul Finn, VP Sales
Leslie Sawyer, VP Mktg

Compugen Inc.

100 Via Renzo Dr.
Richmond Hill, ON L4S 0B8
Tel 905-707-2000
Fax 905-707-2020
www.compugen.com
Line: Provides IT products and services.

NAICS: 541510 417310
#Emp: 500-999 (Tor)
#TorLoc: 1
Own: Private Company
Key: Harry Zarek, Pres & CEO
Andrew Stewart,
    VP Corp Services & Mktg
David Austin, CFO
Ken Goessaert, VP Logistics
Greg Larnder, VP Sales, Central

Computer Methods International Corp.

4850 Keele St., Main Fl.
Toronto, ON M3J 3K1
Tel 416-736-0123
Fax 416-736-1851
www.cmic.ca
NAICS: 511210 541510
#Emp: 100-249 (Tor)
#TorLoc: 1
Own: Private Company
Par: Computer Facility Services (CDA)
Key: Gord Rawlins, Pres
Allen Berg, Chmn
Pat Shah, CFO
Jeff Weiss, VP Sales & Mktg

Computershare Canada

100 University Ave., 11th Fl.
Toronto, ON M5J 2Y1
Tel 416-263-9200
Fax 888-453-0330
www.computershare.com
AKA: Computer Trust Company of Canada; Computershare Investor Services Inc.; Computershare Governance Services; Georgeson Shareholder Communications Inc.; Computershare Technology Services Inc.
Line: Specializes in corporate trust services, tax voucher solutions, bankruptcy administration and a range of other diversified financial and governance services.
NAICS: 523990
#Emp: 500-999 (Tor)
#TorLoc: 2
Own: Public Company
Key: Wayne Newling, Pres
Roy Shanks, COO
Dennis Massicotte, VP HR
Matthew Cox, CFO
Leah Young, Dir of Mktg

Compuware Corp.

300-30 Leek Cres.
Richmond Hill, ON L4B 4N4
Tel 905-886-7000
Fax 905-886-7023
www.compuware.com
Line: Manufactures computer software and provides training and consulting services.
NAICS: 541510
#Emp: 100-249 (Tor)
#TorLoc: 1
Own: Private Company
Par: Compuware Corp. (US)
Key: Brad Lucas, Dir of Sales
Jeff Jackson, VP Technological Dev

Comstock Canada Ltd.

3455 Landmark Rd.
Burlington, ON L7M 1T4
Tel 905-335-3333
Fax 905-335-0304
www.comstockcanada.com
Line: Provides electrical and mechanical constructing services.
NAICS: 232510 232520
#Emp: 500-999 (Tor)
#TorLoc: 3
Own: Private Company
Par: Emcor Inc. (US)
Key: Pete Semmens, Pres & COO
Geoff Birkbeck, CEO
Robert Kilmartin, VP Shared Services,
    HR & Tools
Aldo Morabito, CFO

Comtek Advanced Structures Ltd.

1360 Artisans Crt.
Burlington, ON L7L 5Y2
Tel 905-331-8121
Fax 905-331-8126
www.comtekadvanced.com
Line: Repairs, engineers and manufactures aircraft structural parts.
NAICS: 336410
#Emp: 75-99 (Tor)
#TorLoc: 1
Own: Private Company
Par: Arcorp Industries (CDA)
Key: Patrick Whyte, Pres
Anna-Marie Damiani, HR Mgr
Brett Richardson, Dir of Fin
Robert Di Giovanni,
    Materials Group Mgr
Craig Verburgh, IT Mgr

ConAgra Foods Canada Inc.

405-5935 Airport Rd.
Mississauga, ON L4V 1W5
Tel 416-679-4200
Fax 416-679-4338
www.conagrafoods.com
AKA: ConAgra Grocery Products Ltd.
Line: Distributes and produces grocery products.
NAICS: 413110
#Emp: 75-99 (Tor)
#TorLoc: 1
Own: Private Company
Par: Con Agra Foods (US)
Key: Tom Gunter, Pres
Mary Parniak, VP Fin
Tom Shurrie, VP Sales
Pina Sciarra, VP Mktg

ConceptWave Software Inc.

1105-5935 Airport Rd.
Mississauga, ON L4V 1W5
Tel 905-405-2188
Fax 905-678-3135
www.conceptwave.com
NAICS: 541510
#Emp: 100-249 (Tor)
Own: Private Company
Key: Zarar Rana, Pres, Co-Founder & CEO
Ivan Chochlekov, Co-Founder & CTO
Stuart Griffith, VP Corp Dev & CFO

Concord Concrete & Drain Ltd.

125 Edilcan Dr.
Concord, ON L4K 3S6
Tel 905-738-7979
Fax 905-738-9369
www.concordconstructiongroup.ca
Line: Provides concrete and drain contracting services.
NAICS: 232220
#Emp: 75-99 (Tor)
#TorLoc: 1
Own: Private Company
Key: Mark Weiner, GM

Concord Confections

A Div. of Tootsie Roll of Canada ULC
345 Courtland Ave.
Concord, ON L4K 5A6
Tel 905-660-8989
Fax 905-660-8979
www.tootsieroll.com
Line: Manufactures confections.
NAICS: 311340
#Emp: 250-499 (Tor)
#TorLoc: 2
Own: Private Company
Key: Paraj Khopkar, Plant Mgr
Tom Gadzovski, HR Coord

Concord Food Centre Ltd.

1438 Centre St.
Thornhill, ON L4J 3N1
Tel 905-886-2180
Fax 905-886-3065
www.concordfoodcentre.com
Line: Operates a supermarket.
NAICS: 445110
#Emp: 100-249 (Tor)
#TorLoc: 1
Own: Private Company
Key: Joe Greco, Pres & Owner
Rina Virgilio, Dir of Ops

Concord Idea Corp.

3993 14th Ave.
Markham, ON L3R 4Z6
Tel 905-513-7686
Fax 905-513-9572
www.concordidea.com
AKA: Digital V6
Line: Manufactures, wholesales and exports computer memory chips and modules.
NAICS: 334110
#Emp: 100-249 (Tor)
#TorLoc: 1
Own: Private Company
Key: Angus Lai, Pres & CEO
Sam Lam, COO

Concord Metal Manufacturing

121 Spinnaker Way
Concord, ON L4K 2T2
Tel 905-738-2127
Fax 905-738-9457
www.concordmetal.com
Line: Manufactures metal store fixtures.
NAICS: 337215
#Emp: 75-99 (Tor)
#TorLoc: 1
Own: Private Company
Key: Ermanno Torelli, Pres
Marie Pagliaroli, Cont

Concord Steel Centre Ltd.

147 Ashbridge Circ.
Vaughan, ON L4L 3R5
Tel 905-856-1717
Fax 905-856-4099
www.concordsteel.com
Line: Operates a metal services centre.
NAICS: 416210
#Emp: 75-99 (Tor)
#TorLoc: 1
Own: Private Company
Key: Bruno Bellisario, Pres
Marco Bellisario,
   Mgr of Support Services

ConCreate USL Ltd.

2 Manchester Crt.
Bolton, ON L7E 2J3
Tel 905-857-6962
Fax 905-857-0175
www.usl-1983.com
Line: Performs structural concrete rehabilitation and protection, strengthening, and geotechnical work.
NAICS: 232290
#Emp: 100-249 (Tor)
Own: Private Company
Key: Gordon Tozer, Pres

Con-Drain Company (1983) Ltd.

30 Floral Pkwy.
Concord, ON L4K 4R1
Tel 905-669-5400
Fax 905-669-2296
www.condrain.com
Line: Provides sewer and water main construction, general contracting with road building and electrical construction.
NAICS: 231320
#Emp: 500-999 (Tor)
#TorLoc: 1
Own: Private Company
Key: Fred DeGasperis, Chmn
Angelo DeGasperis, Co-Chmn
Tony DeGasperis, Secy
Nunzio Bitondo, CFO

Con-Elco Ltd.

200 Bradwick Dr.
Concord, ON L4K 1K8
Tel 905-669-4942
Fax 416-798-7125
www.con-elco.com
Line: Provides utility contracting services.
NAICS: 231320 231390
#Emp: 100-249 (Tor)
#TorLoc: 1
Own: Private Company
Key: Fiore Melatti, Pres
Marisa Stirpe, Payroll & HR
Namby Vithiananthan, Cont

Conestoga Cold Storage

2660 Meadowpine Blvd.
Mississauga, ON L5N 7E6
Tel 905-567-1144
Fax 905-567-1040
www.coldstorage.com
Line: Operates cold storage warehouses.
NAICS: 493120
#Emp: 75-99 (Tor)

#TorLoc: 1
Own: Private Company
Key: Larry Laurin, Pres
Greg Laurin, VP Ops

Confederation Freezers

A Div. of Sterling Packers Ltd.
250 Summerlea Rd.
Brampton, ON L6T 3V6
Tel 905-791-1564
Fax 905-791-0535
www.confederationfreezers.com
Line: Provides refrigerated
warehousing and distribution.
NAICS: 493120
#Emp: 100-249 (Tor)
#TorLoc: 3
Own: Private Company
Key: Harry Greenspan, CEO
David MacLeod, VP Fin
Alan Greenspan, Exec VP
Chad Harper, VP Mktg

Connex See Service

301-7270 Woodbine Ave.
Markham, ON L3R 4B9
Tel 905-944-6500
Fax 905-944-6520
www.connexservice.ca
Line: Designs, integrates and maintains
wired and wireless broadband, data
and telecommunications networks.
NAICS: 513310
#Emp: 100-249 (Tor)
#TorLoc: 1
Own: Public Company
Key: Christopher Pay, COO
George Vareldzis, CFO

Conros Corporation

125 Bermondsey Rd.
Toronto, ON M4A 1X3
Tel 416-757-6700
Fax 416-757-8087
www.conros.com
NAICS: 561910
#Emp: 75-99 (Tor)
#TorLoc: 2
Own: Private Company
Par: Navhein Holdings Ltd. (CDA)
Key: Sunir Chandaria, Pres
Navin Chandaria, CEO
Joe Nunes, Group GM
Ajay Rao, Group Fin
Shernee Chandaria, VP Sales & Mktg

Conseil Scolaire de District du Centre-Sud-Ouest

116 Cornelius Pkwy.
Toronto, ON M6L 2K5
Tel 416-614-0844
Fax 416-397-2012
www.csdcso.on.ca
AKA: CSDCSO
Line: Operates an elementary and
secondary school board.
NAICS: 611110
#Emp: 1000-4999 (Tor)
#TorLoc: 11
Own: Government
Key: Ronald Marion, Pres
Gyslaine Hunter-Perreault,
    Dir of Education
Marie-Eve Blais, Dir of HR
Francoise Fournier, Supt of Business
Claire Francoeur,
    Dir of Mktg & Commun

Consolidated Aviation Fuelling of Toronto ULC

5600 Silver Dart Dr.,
Pearson International Airport
P.O. Box 88
Toronto AMF, ON L5P 1A2
Tel 905-694-2846
Fax 905-694-2820
Line: Fuels commercial airlines at
Pearson International Airport.
NAICS: 412110
#Emp: 250-499 (Tor)
#TorLoc: 1
Own: Private Company
Par: Allied Aviation Services (US)
Key: Jules Molinari, VP
Steve Chamczuk, GM
Eva Lovie, Acctng Mgr

Consolidated Fastfrate Inc.

9701 Hwy. 50
Woodbridge, ON L4H 2G4
Tel 905-893-2600
Fax 905-893-1575
www.fastfrate.com
Line: Provides transportation and
freight forwarding services.
NAICS: 484110 484121 488519
#Emp: 250-499 (Tor)
#TorLoc: 1
Own: Private Company
Key: Peter Marshall, Pres
Ron C. Tepper, Exec Chmn
Don Kennedy, CFO
Patricia Scott, VP HR
Leonard Wyss, VP Fin
Sam Anania, Purch
Ahmet Taran, VP IT
Scott Newby, VP Sales & Mktg

Constellation Software Inc.

1200-20 Adelaide St. East
Toronto, ON M5C 2T6
Tel 416-861-2279
Fax 416-861-2287
www.csisoftware.com
NAICS: 541510
#Emp: 100-249 (Tor)
Own: Private Company
Key: Mark Leonard, Pres & Chmn
Mark Miller, COO
John Billowits, CFO

Construction Control Inc.

70 Haist Ave.
Woodbridge, ON L4L 5V4
Tel 905-856-1438
Fax 905-856-1455
www.constructioncontrol.com
Line: Provides engineering consulting
services.
NAICS: 541330
#Emp: 75-99 (Tor)
#TorLoc: 1
Own: Private Company
Key: Gina Cody, Pres

Consumer Impact Marketing Ltd.

500-191 The West Mall
Toronto, ON M9C 5K8
Tel 416-695-1246
Fax 416-695-0246
www.cimweb.com
AKA: CIM Ltd.
Line: Provides third party sales and
marketing services.
NAICS: 541619
#Emp: 250-499 (Tor)
#TorLoc: 1
Own: Private Company
Key: Michael Smith, CEO

Continental Casualty Company

1500-250 Yonge St.
Toronto, ON M5B 2L7
Tel 416-542-7300
Fax 416-542-7310
www.cnacanada.ca
AKA: CNA Canada
Line: Provides commercial, property
and casualty, and marine insurance.
NAICS: 524210 524129
#Emp: 100-249 (Tor)
Own: Private Company
Par: CNA (US)
Key: Gary J. Owcar, Pres & COO
Stacey Shepherd, VP HR
Gale Lockbaum, Sr VP & CFO
Lynne Vonwistinghausen, VP Ops & IT
Greg Knowles, VP Dist & Mktg

Continental Press Ltd.

81 Buttermill Ave.
Concord, ON L4K 3X2
Tel 905-660-0311
Fax 905-660-0316
www.continentalpress.ca
Line: Operates a printing company.
NAICS: 323119
#Emp: 75-99 (Tor)
#TorLoc: 1
Own: Private Company
Key: Jack Oziel, Pres

Contract Pharmaceuticals Limited Canada

7600 Danbro Cres.
Mississauga, ON L5N 6L6
Tel 905-821-7600
Fax 905-821-7602
www.cplltd.com
AKA: CPL
Line: Manufactures and packages
pharmaceuticals.
NAICS: 325410 561910
#Emp: 100-249 (Tor)
#TorLoc: 2
Own: Private Company
Key: Kenneth Paige, CEO
John Ross, COO
Tony Martin, HR Council Leader
Marcel Vieno, Corp Cont
Eduardo Lopez, Dir of IT
Jan Sahai, Exec Dir of Business Dev

Con-way Freight Canada

202-5425 Dixie Rd.
Mississauga, ON L4W 1E6
Tel 905-602-9477
Fax 905-602-9358
www.con-way.com
AKA: Conway Central Express
Line: Provides freight and logistics
services.
NAICS: 488519
#Emp: 75-99 (Tor)
#TorLoc: 1
Own: Public Company
Par: Con-Way Inc. (US)
Key: Brad Reid, Terminal Mgr

Cooksville Care Centre

A Div. of Royalcrest Lifecare Group Inc.
55 Queensway West
Mississauga, ON L5B 1B5
Tel 905-270-0171
Fax 905-270-8465
Line: Provides nursing care facilities
and services.
NAICS: 623110

#Emp: 100-249 (Tor)
#TorLoc: 1
Own: Private Company
Key: Nicole Fisher, Admr
Jasdeep Grewal, Dir of Care
Nancy Kamler, Social Worker

Co-operators General Insurance Company

Priory Sq., 130 MacDonell St.
Guelph, ON N1H 6P8
Tel 519-824-4400
Fax 519-823-9944
www.cooperators.ca
Line: Provides insurance and financial
services.
NAICS: 524129 524111
#Emp: 1000-4999 (Tor)
#TorLoc: 16
Own: Private Company
Par: The Co-operators Group Ltd.
(CDA)
Key: Kathy Bardswick, Pres & CEO
Martin Eric Tremblay,
   Sr Pres, Quebec Ops
Bernie Mitchell, VP HR
Chuck Ellis, VP IT
Rick McCombie,
   Sr VP Direct Dist & Insurance Ops
Paul Mlodzik, VP Mktg
Barb Stephens, Dir of Commun

The Co-Operators Group Ltd.

110-7300 Warden Ave.
Markham, ON L3R 9Z6
Tel 905-470-7300
Fax 905-474-1303
www.cooperators.ca
Line: Operates an insurance company
offering auto, home and life insurance.
NAICS: 524210
#Emp: 75-99 (Tor)
#TorLoc: 4
Own: Private Company
Key: Maggie Nevin, Sr Reg Claims Mgr

Cooper Industries (Canada) Inc.

5925 McLaughlin Rd.
Mississauga, ON L5R 1B8
Tel 905-507-4000
Fax 905-560-7040
www.cooperindustries.com
AKA: Cooper Lighting; Flexillume;
Halo; Lumark; Lumiere; Metalux;
McGraw-Edison; Neo-Ray; Optiance;
SureLites; Cooper Wiring Devices;
Bussmann; B-Line; Cooper Crouse-
Hinds
Line: Manufactures and distributes
electrical products.

NAICS: 335120
#Emp: 100-249 (Tor)
#TorLoc: 1
Own: Public Company
Par: Cooper Industries, Inc. (US)
Key: Roger Shea,
   VP, Cooper Connections Canada
Marc Tigh, HR Mgr
Ken Munn, Cont

Cooper-Standard Automotive Canada Ltd.

346 Guelph St.
Georgetown, ON L7G 4B5
Tel 905-873-6921
Fax 905-877-2940
www.cooperstandard.com
Line: Produces automotive parts.
NAICS: 336390
#Emp: 100-249 (Tor)
#TorLoc: 1
Own: Private Company
Par: Cooper-Standard Automotive (US)
Key: Collin Stewart, Interim Plant Mgr
Brian Hiempel, Acctng Mgr
Tracy Clifford, IT Coord

Copernicus Lodge

66 Roncesvalles Ave.
Toronto, ON M6R 3A7
Tel 416-536-7122
Fax 416-536-8242
www.copernicuslodge.com
Line: Operates long-term care facility
and seniors' apartments with housing
services.
NAICS: 623310
#Emp: 75-99 (Tor)
#TorLoc: 1
Own: Private Company
Key: Tracy Kamino, Exec Dir
Catherine Kowalenko,
   Dir of Employee Relns
Richard Sredzinski, Dir of Fin

Copper Creek Golf Club

11191 Hwy. 27
Kleinburg, ON L0J 1C0
Tel 905-893-3370
Fax 905-893-0443
www.coppercreek.ca
NAICS: 713910
#Emp: 250-499 (Tor)
#TorLoc: 1
Own: Private Company
Key: Chris Neil, GM
John Young, Dir of Golf

Core Logistics International Inc.

3133 Orlando Dr.
Mississauga, ON L4V 1C5
Tel 905-612-1060
Fax 905-612-1044
www.corelogistics.net
AKA: The Solution People
Line: Specializes in the logistics supply
chain including international and
domestic airfreight, wholesale, ocean
freight, warehousing and distribution.
NAICS: 488519 541619
#Emp: 75-99 (Tor)
#TorLoc: 2
Own: Private Company
Key: Frank Esposito, Pres & CEO
Brian Gomes, CEO

Corma Inc.

10 McCleary Crt.
Concord, ON L4K 2Z3
Tel 905-669-9397
Fax 905-738-4744
www.corma.com
Line: Manufactures corrugated plastic
pipe production systems.
NAICS: 326122
#Emp: 100-249 (Tor)
#TorLoc: 1
Own: Private Company
Key: Manfred Lupke,
   Chmn, Pres & CEO
Stefan Lupke, Exec VP
Frank Ricci, HR Mgr

Cormark Securities Inc.

2800-200 Bay St.
Royal Bank Plaza, South Tower
Toronto, ON M5J 2J2
Tel 416-362-7485
Fax 416-943-6499
www.cormark.com
Line: Operates investment dealer
serving institutional and corporate
clients.
NAICS: 523120
#Emp: 100-249 (Tor)
#TorLoc: 1
Own: Private Company
Key: Peter Charton,
   Mng Dir & Head of Sales
Scott Lamacraft, CEO & Mng Dir,
   Institutional Equities
Lorna Sandejas,
   Payroll & Benefits Admr
Jeff Kennedy, CFO

Cornerstone Group
of Companies Limited

20 Eglinton Ave. West, 4th Fl.
Toronto, ON M4R 1K8
Tel 416-932-9555
Fax 416-932-9566
www.cstonecanada.com
Line: Provides direct marketing
services.
NAICS: 454110 511140
#Emp: 100-249 (Tor)
Own: Private Company
Key: Ossie Hinds, Pres & CEO
Bob Coles, COO
Jim Grant, VP HR
Dan Vickruck, CFO
Don Lange, Sr VP

Cornerstone Insurance
Brokers Inc.

300-8001 Weston Rd.
Woodbridge, ON L4L 9C8
Tel 416-798-8001
Fax 905-856-6129
www.csib.org
Line: Operates multi-line insurance
brokerage firm offering home, auto,
commercial, life, health and travel
insurance.
NAICS: 524210
#Emp: 75-99 (Tor)
#TorLoc: 1
Own: Private Company
Key: Peter DaSilva, Pres & COO
Wendy DaSilva, CEO
Lynne Ray, VP Ops
Cathy Baleck, VP Fin & Admin
Jeff Aube, Dir of Commercial Sales

Cornerstone Landscaping Ltd.

12782 Kennedy Rd. North
Caledon, ON L7C 2E9
Tel 905-843-1106
Fax 905-843-1938
www.cornerstonelandscaping.com
AKA: Kengrove Tree & Topsoil
Line: Provides landscaping services.
NAICS: 561730
#Emp: 75-99 (Tor)
Own: Private Company
Key: Rick Sova, Pres
Dave Skanes, Cont

Corona Jewellery Company

16 Ripley Ave.
Toronto, ON M6S 3N9
Tel 416-762-2222
Fax 416-762-2445
www.coronajewellery.com
Line: Manufactures jewellery.
NAICS: 339910
#Emp: 100-249 (Tor)
#TorLoc: 1
Own: Private Company
Key: Francis Arasaratnam, Cont

Corpap Inc.

102-7400 Woodbine Ave.
Markham, ON L3R 1A5
Tel 905-946-9499
Fax 905-946-7648
www.corpap.com
Line: Operates a paper converter
company.
NAICS: 418120
#Emp: 100-249 (Tor)
#TorLoc: 1
Own: Private Company
Key: Dean McNeil, Pres
Tony Almeida, VP

The Corporation of Massey Hall
and Roy Thomson Hall

60 Simcoe St.
Toronto, ON M5J 2H5
Tel 416-593-4822
Fax 416-593-4224
www.roythomson.com
AKA: Massey Hall; Roy Thomson Hall
Line: Operates entertainment and
hospitality facilities.
NAICS: 531120 711311
#Emp: 250-499 (Tor)
#TorLoc: 2
Own: Not-for-profit
Key: Charles S. Cutts, Pres & CEO
Colleen A. Smith, Dir of Ops & Admin
Jenny Basov, HR Mgr
Leiw Wong, Dir of Fin & HR
Lillian Thalheimer,
   Booking & Event Services Mgr
Mary Landreth, Mktg Mgr

The Corporation of the City of Mississauga

300 City Centre Dr.
Mississauga, ON L5B 3C1
Tel 905-896-5000
Fax 905-615-4081
www.city.mississauga.on.ca
AKA: Mississauga
NAICS: 913910
#Emp: 5000-9999 (Tor)
#TorLoc: 1
Own: Government
Key: Hazel McCallion, Mayor
Janice Baker, City Mgr & CAO
Martin Powell,
    Comr of Transportation & Works
Sharon Willock, Dir of HR
Patti Elliot-Spencer, Dir of Fin
Jack Lawrence, Dir of IT
Larry Petovello, Dir of Economic Dev

The Corporation of The City of Pickering

1 The Esplanade
Pickering, ON L1V 6K7
Tel 905-420-2222
Fax 905-420-6064
www.cityofpickering.com
AKA: Pickering; The City of Pickering
NAICS: 913910
#Emp: 500-999 (Tor)
#TorLoc: 1
Own: Government
Key: David Ryan, CEO & Mayor
Thomas J. Quinn, CAO
Everett Buntsma, Dir of Ops &
    Emergency Services
Jennifer Parent, Division Head of HR
Gil Paterson,
    Dir of Corp Services & Treas
Vera Felgemacher,
    Supply & Services Mgr
Lynn Winterstein, Mktg & Business Dev

The Corporation of the Town of Caledon

6311 Old Church Rd.
Caledon, ON L7C 1J6
Tel 905-584-2272
Fax 905-584-4325
www.caledon.ca
AKA: Caledon
NAICS: 913910
#Emp: 500-999 (Tor)
#TorLoc: 1
Own: Government

Key: Marolyn Morrison, Mayor
Douglas Barnes, CAO
Craig Campbell,
    Dir of Public Works & Engineering
Rebecca Moore-Whitsitt, Dir of HR
Ronald Kaufman, Dir of Corp Services,
    CFO & Deputy CAO
Paul Cerson, IT Mgr
Benjamin Roberts,
    Economic Dev Officer
Mary Hall, Dir of Planning and Dev
Norman Lingard, Mgr of Economic Dev

The Corporation of the Town of Markham

Anthony Roman Centre
101 Town Centre Blvd.
Markham, ON L3R 9W3
Tel 905-477-7000
Fax 905-470-3584
www.markham.ca
AKA: Markham
NAICS: 913910
#Emp: 1000-4999 (Tor)
Own: Government
Key: Frank Scarpetti, Mayor
John Livey, CAO
Sharon Laing, Dir of HR
Andrew Taylor, Cmmr, Corp Services
Nasir Kenea, CIO
Steven Chait, Dir of Economic Dev
Janet Carnegie, Dir of Corp Commun

The Corporation of the Town of New Tecumseth

10 Wellington St. East
P.O. Box 910
Alliston, ON L9R 1A1
Tel 705-435-6219
Fax 705-435-2873
www.town.newtecumseth.on.ca
AKA: New Tecumseth
NAICS: 913910
#Emp: 100-249 (Tor)
#TorLoc: 1
Own: Government
Key: Mike MacEachern, Mayor
Terri Caron, CAO
Hilary McCormack, HR Mgr
Mark Sirr, Treas & Mgr of Fin
Lori Archibald,
    Sr Buyer & Insurance Admr
Trevor Peyton, IS Coord

The Corporation of the Town of Oakville

1225 Trafalgar Rd.
P.O. Box 310
Oakville, ON L6H 0H3
Tel 905-845-6601
Fax 905-815-2001
www.oakville.ca
AKA: Oakville
Line: Provides lower tier municipal
services.
NAICS: 913910
#Emp: 500-999 (Tor)
#TorLoc: 1
Own: Government
Key: Rob Burton, Mayor
Ray Green, CAO
David Bloomer, Comr of Infrastructure
    & Transportation Services
Liz Bourns, Dir of HR
Nancy Sully, Dir of Fin & Deputy Treas
Kim Dooling, Mgr of Fin
Jeff Lanaus, Dir of IS & Solutions
Jane Courtemanche, Dir of Strategy,
    Policy & Commun

The Corporation of the Town of Orangeville

87 Broadway
Orangeville, ON L9W 1K1
Tel 519-941-0440
Fax 519-941-9033
www.town.orangeville.on.ca
AKA: Orangeville
NAICS: 913910
#Emp: 250-499 (Tor)
#TorLoc: 2
Own: Government
Key: Rob Adams, Mayor
Richard Schwarzer, CAO
Jason Hall, IS Mgr
Nancy Huether, Economic Dev Mgr
Sheila Duncan, Commun Officer

The Corporation of the Town of Richmond Hill

225 East Beaver Creek Rd.
P.O. Box 300
Richmond Hill, ON L4B 3P4
Tel 905-771-8800
Fax 905-771-2520
www.richmondhill.ca
AKA: Richmond Hill
NAICS: 913910
#Emp: 500-999 (Tor)
#TorLoc: 1
Own: Government
Key: Dave Barrow, Mayor
Joan Anderton, CAO
Samara Kaplan, Dir of HR

The Corporation of the Township of Brock

1 Cameron St. East
P.O. Box 10
Cannington, ON L0E 1E0
Tel 705-432-2355
Fax 705-432-3487
www.townshipofbrock.ca
AKA: Brock; Township of Brock
NAICS: 913910
#Emp: 100-249 (Tor)
#TorLoc: 1
Own: Government
Key: Larry O'Connor, Mayor
Thomas G. Gettinby,
    Acting CAO & Municipal Clerk
Laura Barta, Treas

Cortina Kitchens Inc.

70 Regina Rd.
Woodbridge, ON L4L 8L6
Tel 905-264-6464
Fax 905-264-0664
www.cortinakitchens.com
Line: Manufactures and installs kitchen
cabinets and accessories.
NAICS: 232460
#Emp: 100-249 (Tor)
#TorLoc: 1
Own: Private Company
Par: Cort Holdings Inc. (CDA)
Key: Peter Tommasino, Pres
Paul Tommasino, VP Ops
Frank Roth, Cont
Tony Tommasino, VP Sales

Corus Entertainment Inc.

25 Dockside Dr.
Toronto, ON M5A 0B5
Tel 416-479-7000
Fax 416-479-7006
www.corusent.com
AKA: YTV Television
Line: Operates a media and
entertainment company.
NAICS: 513120
#Emp: 1000-4999 (Tor)
#TorLoc: 4
Own: Public Company
Key: John Cassaday, Pres & CEO
Tom Peddie, Sr VP & CFO

Corvin Building Maintenance Ltd.

4-2 Thorncliffe Park Dr.
Toronto, ON M4H 1H2
Tel 416-429-7452
Fax 416-429-7779
www.corvin.ca
NAICS: 561722
#Emp: 75-99 (Tor)
#TorLoc: 1
Own: Private Company
Key: Alan Ashton, Pres
James Hewitt, CEO

Cosma International Inc.

2550 Steeles Ave. East
Brampton, ON L6T 5R3
Tel 905-799-7600
Fax 905-799-7648
www.cosma.com
Line: Manufactures stampings, role
forms, weldments and chassis systems.
NAICS: 336370 336211
#Emp: 500-999 (Tor)
#TorLoc: 1
Own: Private Company
Par: Magna International Inc. (CDA)
Key: Horst Prelog, Pres

Cosmetica Laboratories Inc.

1960 Eglinton Ave. East
Toronto, ON M1L 2M5
Tel 416-615-2400
Fax 416-615-2399
www.cosmeticalabs.com
Line: Manufactures cosmetics.
NAICS: 325620
#Emp: 250-499 (Tor)
#TorLoc: 1
Own: Private Company
Key: Marlene Oilgisser, Pres
Michael Kehoe, CEO
Robert Murray, CFO
Anna-Maria Rocco, Dir of HR
Barbara DaFonseca, Cont
Paul Hutchison, Dir of Supply Chain
Gerald Levac, Exec VP

Cossette Communication Group

502 King St. West
Toronto, ON M5V 1L7
Tel 416-922-2727
Fax 416-922-9450
www.cossette.com
Line: Provides full range of
communication and marketing
services.
NAICS: 541810

#Emp: 250-499 (Tor)
#TorLoc: 1
Own: Public Company
Key: Brett Marchand, Pres & CEO
Georges Morin, Sr VP Corp Dev
Shalom Shapurkar, VP Business
    Fin & Admin

Costco Wholesale - Ajax

150 Kingston Rd. East
Ajax, ON L1Z 1E5
Tel 905-619-6677
Fax 905-619-6654
www.costco.ca
Line: Provides wholesale membership
shopping services.
NAICS: 452910
#Emp: 250-499 (Tor)
#TorLoc: 10
Own: Private Company
Par: Costco Wholesale Corp. (US)
Key: Randy Martel, Warehouse Mgr

COSTI

1710 Dufferin St.
Toronto, ON M6E 3P2
Tel 416-658-1600
Fax 416-658-8537
www.costi.org
AKA: COSTI Immigrant Services
Line: Provides educational and
social services not readily available
elsewhere; enables immigrants in the
Toronto area to attain self-sufficiency
in Canadian society; addresses
the needs of the Italian Canadian
community; and offers services to
other immigrants with a focus on those
from communities with a shortage of
self-help.
NAICS: 624310 624190
#Emp: 100-249 (Tor)
#TorLoc: 12
Own: Not-for-profit
Key: Mario J. Calla, Exec Dir
Josie Di Zio, Sr Dr,
    Planning & Programme Dev
Ed Kothiringer,
    Dir of Employment Services
Matthew S. K. Chan, Dir of Fin
Robert Cazzola, Dir of Education & IT

COTA Health

2901 Dufferin St.
Toronto, ON M6B 3S7
Tel 416-785-9230
Fax 416-785-9358
www.cotahealth.ca
Line: Operates a non-profit accredited community health and social services organization that provides rehabilitation, mental health and support services.
NAICS: 624310
#Emp: 100-249 (Tor)
#TorLoc: 1
Own: Not-for-profit
Key: Paul Bruce, Exec Dir

Cott Beverages Canada

6525 Viscount Rd.
Mississauga, ON L4V 1H6
Tel 905-672-1900
Fax 905-672-5229
www.cott.com
Line: Manufactures carbonated beverages including water and soft drinks.
NAICS: 312110
#Emp: 250-499 (Tor)
#TorLoc: 1
Own: Public Company
Par: Cott Corporation (CDA)
Key: Jerry Fowden, CEO
John Wren, VP Ops, Canada
Sandra Sterman, HR Mgr
Neal Cravens, CFO
Mark Hillis, Sr Buyer
Nathalie Spadafora, Sales
Glen Muir, Mktg Dir, Canada
Kimball Chapman,
    Dir of Investor Relns

Cotton Ginny Inc.

2800 Matheson Blvd. East
Mississauga, ON L4W 4X5
Tel 905-625-3334
Fax 905-625-9995
www.cottonginny.ca
Line: Sells women's clothes.
NAICS: 448120
#Emp: 500-999 (Tor)
#TorLoc: 15
Own: Private Company
Key: Tony Chahine, Pres & CEO
Laurie Dubrovac,
    Dir of Mktg & Commun

Counterforce Inc.

2A-2740 Matheson Blvd. East
Mississauga, ON L4W 4X3
Tel 905-282-6200
Fax 905-282-6201
www.counterforce.com
Line: Provides security systems and services.
NAICS: 561621
#Emp: 75-99 (Tor)
#TorLoc: 1
Own: Private Company
Key: Susan Goncalves, Dir of Mktg

The Country Club

20 Lloyd St.
Woodbridge, ON L4L 2B9
Tel 905-856-4317
Fax 905-856-3625
www.clublink.ca
Line: Operates a golf course and country club.
NAICS: 713910
#Emp: 100-249 (Tor)
#TorLoc: 1
Own: Private Company
Par: ClubLink Corp. (CDA)
Key: Dave Garner, Dir of Ops
Justin Shim, Food & Beverage Mgr
Glenn Phillips, Reg Dir of Hospitality
Linda Magliocchi, Catering Coord

The Country Day School

13415 Dufferin St.
King City, ON L7B 1K5
Tel 905-833-1220
Fax 905-833-1350
www.cds.on.ca
Line: Operates independent university preparatory school.
NAICS: 611110
#Emp: 100-249 (Tor)
Own: Not-for-profit
Key: Paul C. Duckett, Head of School
Melanie Sheppard, Cont
Sheldon Rose, Dir of IT
David Huckvale, Dir of Admissions
Brenda Castle, Dir of Commun

Courtesy Chevrolet

1635 The Queensway
Toronto, ON M8Z 1T8
Tel 416-255-9151
Fax 416-255-3641
www.courtesychevrolet.ca
Line: Sells, leases and repairs cars and trucks.
NAICS: 441110 441120
#Emp: 75-99 (Tor)
#TorLoc: 1
Own: Private Company
Key: Don Polyschuk, Pres
Rick Layzell, GM
Joanne Werstroh, Secy-Treas

Courtyard By Marriott Downtown Toronto

475 Yonge St.
Toronto, ON M4Y 1X7
Tel 416-924-0611
Fax 416-924-8692
www.marriott.com
Line: Operates a full service hotel.
NAICS: 721111
#Emp: 250-499 (Tor)
#TorLoc: 1
Own: Private Company
Key: Ronit Keith, GM
Vicki Lonsdale, Dir of HR
John Speller, Cont

Cousins-Currie

A Div. of Silgan Plastic Canada Inc.
400 Rowntree Dairy Rd.
Woodbridge, ON L4C 8H2
Tel 416-746-8300
Fax 905-856-6294
www.cousinscurrie.com
Line: Manufactures custom blow moulded technical components and industrial plastic containers for the industrial, chemical and institutional food markets.
NAICS: 326150
#Emp: 100-249 (Tor)
#TorLoc: 4
Own: Private Company
Par: Silgan Plastics (US)
Key: Emidio Dimeo,
    Sr VP, Silgan Plastics
Jim Tesoriere, HR Mgr
Paolo Rubinia, Purch Agent

Covenant House Toronto

20 Gerrard St. East
Toronto, ON M5B 2P3
Tel 416-598-4898
Fax 416-204-7030
www.convenanthouse.ca
Line: Provides both residential and
non-residential services to street youth,
both male and female, between 16 and
24 years of age.
NAICS: 624110
#Emp: 100-249 (Tor)
#TorLoc: 1
Own: Not-for-profit
Par: Covenant House New York (US)
Key: Kevin M. Ryan, Pres
Ruth daCosta, Exec Dir
John Tarnawsky, Ops Mgr
Brian Donald, Assoc Dir of HR
Josie do Rego, Dir of Dev & Commun
Rose Cino, Commun Mgr

Covertech Fabricating Inc.

279 Humberline Dr.
Toronto, ON M9W 5T6
Tel 416-798-1340
Fax 416-798-1342
www.covertechfab.com
NAICS: 313210
#Emp: 75-99 (Tor)
#TorLoc: 1
Own: Private Company
Key: Furio Orologio, Pres
John Starr, VP
Ida Orologio, HR Mgr

Coyle Corrugated Containers Inc.

5600 Finch Ave. East
Toronto, ON M1B 1T1
Tel 416-291-2963
Fax 416-291-3899
www.coylecor.com
AKA: Coyle Packaging Group
Line: Manufactures corrugated boxes
and point-of-purchase displays.
NAICS: 322211
#Emp: 100-249 (Tor)
#TorLoc: 1
Own: Private Company
Key: William Coyle, Pres & CEO
John Ovsonka, Ops Mgr
Donna Palmer, Corp Cont
Chris Casey, Purch Agent
Jaime Lopes, Network Admr
Bill Lavery, Dir of Corp Sales
Debi Bowins, Sales Mgr

CPAS Systems Inc.

250 Ferrand Dr., 7th Fl.
Toronto, ON M3C 3G8
Tel 416-422-0563
Fax 416-422-5617
www.cpas.com
NAICS: 511210
#Emp: 75-99 (Tor)
#TorLoc: 1
Own: Private Company
Key: David Rive, Pres
Lyn Francis, VP HR & Admin
Liam Robertson, VP & Cont
Lori Walsh, Sr VP Tech
Adrian Praysner, VP Sales & Mktg

CPC Pumps International Inc.

5200 Mainway Dr.
Burlington, ON L7L 5Z1
Tel 289-288-4753
Fax 289-288-4754
www.cpcpumps.com
Line: Manufactures process pumps.
NAICS: 333910
#Emp: 75-99 (Tor)
#TorLoc: 2
Own: Private Company
Key: Hani Fayed, Pres
Paul Gallo, VP Manuf

CPI Canada Inc.

45 River Dr.
Georgetown, ON L7G 2J4
Tel 905-877-0161
Fax 905-877-5327
www.cpii.com/cmp
Line: Manufactures and designs
satellite communication up-link
amplifiers, power supplies and X-ray
generators, and communication
klystrons for the broadcast industry.
NAICS: 334220
#Emp: 250-499 (Tor)
#TorLoc: 1
Own: Public Company
Par: Communications & Power
Industries Inc. (US)
Key: Andrew Tafler, Pres, Sat Com
Joseph Caldarelli, Pres, CMP
Tammy Hilts, Mgr of HR
Tony Russell, VP Ops & Microwaves

Craiglee Nursing Home Ltd.

102 Craiglee Dr.
Toronto, ON M1N 2M7
Tel 416-264-2260
Fax 416-267-8176
www.craiglee.ca
Line: Operates a nursing home.
NAICS: 623110

#Emp: 100-249 (Tor)
#TorLoc: 1
Own: Private Company
Key: Angie Heinz, Admr

Crane Supply

615 Dixon Rd.
Toronto, ON M9W 1H9
Tel 416-244-5351
Fax 416-240-8755
www.cranesupply.com
Line: Distributes pipe, valve, fitting and
plumbing supplies.
NAICS: 416120
#Emp: 100-249 (Tor)
#TorLoc: 1
Own: Private Company
Par: Crane Co. (US)
Key: Tom Frazer, Pres

Crawford & Company (Canada) Inc.

300-123 Front St. West
Toronto, ON M5J 2M2
Tel 416-867-1188
www.crawfordandcompany.ca
Line: Provides a complete range
of claims, risk and healthcare
management services.
NAICS: 524291
#Emp: 250-499 (Tor)
#TorLoc: 8
Own: Public Company
Par: Crawford & Company (US)
Key: John Sharoun, CEO
Gary Gardner, VP Sales
Sandra MacInnis, Mktg Mgr

Creation Technologies LP

6820 Creditview Rd.
Mississauga, ON L5N 0A9
Tel 905-814-6323
Fax 905-814-6324
www.creationtech.com
Line: Manufactures electronics and
circuit board assemblies.
NAICS: 334410
#Emp: 250-499 (Tor)
#TorLoc: 2
Own: Private Company
Key: Mark Krzyczkowski,
  GM, Mississauga
Duncan Reed, GM, Toronto
Jon Barclay, People & Culture Leader
Allan Raven, IT Admr
Jeff Lambkin, Market Dev Mgr

Credit Suisse Securities (Canada), Inc.

3000-1 First Canadian Pl.
Toronto, ON M5X 1C9
Tel 416-352-4500
Fax 416-352-4685
www.credit-suisse.com
Line: Provides financial services
including investment banking and
equity stocks trading and research.
NAICS: 522111 522112
#Emp: 75-99 (Tor)
#TorLoc: 1
Own: Private Company
Par: Credit Suisse (SWITZ)
Key: Ronald S. Lloyd, Chmn & CEO

Credit Valley Conservation

1255 Old Derry Rd.
Mississauga, ON L5N 6R4
Tel 905-670-1615
Fax 905-670-2210
www.creditvalleyca.ca
Line: Operates a conservation
authority.
NAICS: 712190
#Emp: 100-249 (Tor)
Own: Government
Key: Rae Horst, CAO
Marlene Ferrera, HR Supr
Gerry Robin, Dir of Corp Services
Larissa Fenn, Corp Commun Supr

Credit Valley Golf and Country Club

2500 Old Carriage Rd.
Mississauga, ON L5C 1Y7
Tel 905-275-2505
Fax 905-275-6201
www.creditvalleygolf.com
NAICS: 713910
#Emp: 75-99 (Tor)
#TorLoc: 1
Own: Private Company
Key: Ian Webb, GM
Adam Cherry, Dir of Golf
Michael Binns, Food & Beverage Mgr

The Credit Valley Hospital

2200 Eglinton Ave. West
Mississauga, ON L5M 2N1
Tel 905-813-2200
Fax 905-813-4444
www.cvh.on.ca
Line: Provides health care.
NAICS: 622111
#Emp: 1000-4999 (Tor)
#TorLoc: 1
Own: Not-for-profit
Key: Michelle DiEmanuele, Pres & CEO
Cindy Fleming, Chief HR Officer

Crescent School

2365 Bayview Ave.
Toronto, ON M2L 1A2
Tel 416-449-2556
Fax 416-449-0952
www.crescentschool.org
Line: Operates independent boys'
school for Grades 3 to 12.
NAICS: 611110
#Emp: 100-249 (Tor)
#TorLoc: 1
Own: Not-for-profit
Key: Geoff Roberts, Headmaster
Christopher White, Dir of Admissions
Cameron Bourne, Dir of HR
Ken Barnard, CFO
Sue Gillan, Dir of Mktg & Commun

Crest Circuit Inc.

2701 John St.
Markham, ON L3R 2W5
Tel 905-479-9515
Fax 905-479-8304
www.crestcircuit.com
Line: Manufactures circuit boards.
NAICS: 334410
#Emp: 75-99 (Tor)
#TorLoc: 1
Own: Private Company
Key: Dahyabhai Patel, Pres
Jeshbhai Patel, VP
Ramesh Patel, Secy-Treas
Rastimikant Patel, Purch Mgr

Critical Control Solutions

100-2820 14th Ave.
Markham, ON L3R 0S9
Tel 905-940-0190
Fax 905-940-0192
www.criticalcontrol.com
AKA: SDS
Line: Provides document and data
conversion and database management
services.
NAICS: 514210
#Emp: 75-99 (Tor)
Own: Private Company
Key: Nizar Huddani, GM
Andrea South, Dir of HR
Vladimir Radzinski,
    Sr Programmer Analyst

Crosby Canada

145 Heart Lake Rd.
Brampton, ON L6W 3K3
Tel 905-451-9261
Fax 905-457-3331
www.crosby.ca
Line: Manufactures drop forged steel
fittings for use with wire rope and
chain.
NAICS: 332113
#Emp: 100-249 (Tor)
#TorLoc: 1
Own: Private Company
Par: Crosby Canada Inc. (CDA)
Key: Andrew Strudwicke, VP & GM
Teresa Ball, HR
Paul Jones, Cont
Kimberley Tapp, Buyer
Boris Dubov, IT Mgr
Colin Basinger, Sales Mgr

Crossby Dewar Inc.

1935 Silicone Dr.
Pickering, ON L1W 3V7
Tel 905-683-5102
Fax 905-683-1481
www.crossbydewar.com
Line: Provides specialized services to
the nuclear industry.
NAICS: 232440
#Emp: 500-999 (Tor)
#TorLoc: 1
Own: Private Company
Key: Scott Dewar, Co-Pres
John Crossby, Co-Pres
Clayton O'Brien, VP Ops
Dori Hiebert, Mng Dir
Stuart Pasternak, CFO
Ian Morton, Exec VP

Crossey Engineering Ltd.

E-331-2255 Sheppard Ave. East
Toronto, ON M2J 4Y1
Tel 416-497-3111
Fax 416-497-7210
www.cel.ca
AKA: CEL
Line: Provides mechanical and
electrical consulting engineering
services.
NAICS: 541330
#Emp: 100-249 (Tor)
#TorLoc: 1
Own: Private Company
Key: Clive R. Lacey, Pres & Principal
Wallace Eley, CEO & Principal
Adele Argirakis, HR Dir
Helena Szymanski,
    Fin Mgr & Sr Associate
Duane Waite, VP & Principal
Andrew Pratt, VP & Principal

Crossmark Canada Inc.

112-2233 Argentia Rd.
Mississauga, ON L5N 2X7
Tel 905-363-1000
Fax 905-363-0710
www.crossmark.com
Line: Operates a national broker and
retail field force company in consumer
packaged goods.
NAICS: 419130
#Emp: 75-99 (Tor)
#TorLoc: 1
Own: Private Company
Par: Crossmark (US)
Key: Atul Gupta, Pres & CEO
Glen Wilson, Chmn
Kathy Morin, Ops Mgr
Kevin Salmon, Fin Mgr

Crossroads Christian Communications Inc.

1295 North Service Rd.
P.O. Box 5100
Burlington, ON L7R 4M2
Tel 905-335-7100
Fax 905-332-6655
www.crossroads.ca
AKA: 100 Huntley St.
NAICS: 813110
#Emp: 100-249 (Tor)
#TorLoc: 1
Own: Not-for-profit
Key: Ronald Mainse, Pres
Don Simmonds, Chmn & CEO
Shirley Lealess, Dir of HR
Gary Gerard, VP Mktg
George McEachern, VP Media

Cross Toronto Community Development Corp.

207-761 Queen St. West
Toronto, ON M6J 1G1
Tel 416-504-4262
Fax 416-504-3429
www.freshstartclean.com
AKA: Fresh Start
Line: Provides janitorial, lawn care and
snow removal services.
NAICS: 561722
#Emp: 75-99 (Tor)
#TorLoc: 1
Own: Not-for-profit
Key: Richard Worr, Dir
Karen Schwartz, HR Coord
Debra Anderson, Fin Admr
Shawn Lauzon, PR & Mktg Coord

Crowne Plaza - Toronto Airport

33 Carlson Crt.
Toronto, ON M9W 6H5
Tel 416-675-1234
Fax 416-675-3436
www.crownplazatorontoairport.ca
Line: Provides hotel, bedroom,
restaurant and banquet facilities.
NAICS: 721111
#Emp: 100-249 (Tor)
#TorLoc: 1
Own: Private Company
Par: Royal Equator Inc. (CDA)
Key: Julian Bugledich, CEO
Angela Racco, Dir of HR
William Morgan, CFO
Tony Fernandes,
    Dir of Food & Beverage
James Wu, Dir of Sales & Mktg
Karim Giga, Group Dir
    of Revenue Management

Crown Food Service Equipment Ltd.

70 Oakdale Rd.
Toronto, ON M3N 1V9
Tel 416-746-2358
Fax 416-746-8324
Line: Manufactures commercial
kitchen equipment.
NAICS: 333310
#Emp: 75-99 (Tor)
#TorLoc: 2
Own: Private Company
Key: Ed Mueller, Exec VP
Joseph Stritzl, Pres
Dave Sodi, VP Ops
Rudy Daez, Cont

Crown Metal Packaging Canada LP

7900 Keele St.
Vaughan, ON L4K 2A3
Tel 905-669-1401
Fax 905-669-1692
www.crowncork.com
Line: Manufactures metal packaging
materials.
NAICS: 332431 332118
#Emp: 1000-4999 (Tor)
#TorLoc: 4
Own: Private Company
Par: Crown Holdings, Inc. (US)
Key: Mark Ketcheson, VP Sales
Barry Curran, VP Purch & Admin

Cryptologic Inc.

1867 Yonge St.
Toronto, ON M4S 1Y5
Tel 416-545-1455
Fax 416-545-1454
www.cryptologic.com
Line: Designs Internet software for
online gaming applications.
NAICS: 541510
#Emp: 100-249 (Tor)
#TorLoc: 1
Own: Public Company
Key: David Gavagan,
    Chmn & Interim CEO
Donna Husack, VP HR
Huw Spiers, CFO

Crystal Claire Cosmetics Inc.

20 Overlea Blvd.
Toronto, ON M4H 1A4
Tel 416-421-1882
Fax 416-421-5025
www.crystalclaire.com
Line: Manufactures cosmetics and skin
care products.
NAICS: 325620
#Emp: 250-499 (Tor)
#TorLoc: 1
Own: Private Company
Key: Bob Patterson, Pres
Roger Hwang, CEO
Lily Shen, HR Mgr
Yvonne Ou, CFO
Wendy Tung, VP Sales & Mktg

C&S Auto Parts Limited

151 Nugget Ave.
Toronto, ON M1S 3B1
Tel 416-754-8500
Fax 416-754-7128
www.collinsautoparts.com
Line: Sells auto parts and supplies.
NAICS: 415290
#Emp: 75-99 (Tor)
#TorLoc: 1
Own: Private Company
Key: Arthur Collins, Pres

C/S Construction Specialties Company

895 Lakefront Promenade
Mississauga, ON L5E 2C2
Tel 905-274-3611
Fax 905-274-6241
www.c-sgroup.com
Line: Manufactures louvers, grilles, expansion joints, sun controls, wall protection products, entrance mats and grids, explosion and pressure relief vents, and fire and smoke vents.
NAICS: 332910
#Emp: 75-99 (Tor)
#TorLoc: 1
Own: Private Company
Par: C/S Group (US)
Key: Rick Morris, VP & GM
Carol Wanamaker, Payroll & HR Mgr

CSG Security Inc.

5201 Explorer Dr.
Mississauga, ON L4W 4H1
Tel 905-629-2600
Fax 905-206-8469
www.chubbsecurity.com
AKA: Chubb Security
Line: Manufactures, sells, installs and services alarm systems, access control and CCTV.
NAICS: 334290 561621 232510
#Emp: 500-999 (Tor)
#TorLoc: 1
Own: Public Company
Par: UTC Technologies (US)
Key: Mike Pavano, VP Fin
Jack Hayes, VP HR
Daryl MacNeil, Dir of Purch
Randy Krzak, VP Mktg
Bruce Bowlby, Mktg Mgr

CSI Global Education Inc.

200 Wellington St. West, 15th Fl.
Toronto, ON M5V 3C7
Tel 416-364-9130
Fax 416-359-0486
www.csi.ca
Line: Operates an investment learning institution for financial professionals.
NAICS: 611410
#Emp: 100-249 (Tor)
#TorLoc: 1
Own: Private Company
Par: Moody's Corp. (US)
Key: Roberta Wilton, Pres & CEO
Simon Parmer, CFO
Dean Musclow,
    Sr Dir of HR & Client Dev
Jerry Fahrer, VP Fin
Brent Scowen, Sr VP Sales & Mktg

C.S.T. Consultants Inc.

600-2225 Sheppard Ave. East
Toronto, ON M2J 5C2
Tel 416-445-7377
Fax 416-445-3100
www.cst.org
AKA: CSTC Inc.
Line: Advocates, develops, delivers and supports solutions that enable Canadians to have sufficient financial resources to pursue post-secondary education.
NAICS: 541611
#Emp: 100-249 (Tor)
#TorLoc: 1
Own: Not-for-profit
Par: Canadian Scholarship Trust Foundation (CDA)
Key: Sherry MacDonald, Pres & CEO
Peter Lewis,
    VP Regulatory & Corp Affairs
Joe Spagnuolo, CFO
Kevin Netterfield, VP Sales & Mktg

CTG Brands

123 Great Gulf Dr.
Vaughan, ON L4K 5V1
Tel 905-761-3330
Fax 905-761-8028
www.canasia.ca
Line: Imports and exports consumer products.
NAICS: 418990
#Emp: 100-249 (Tor)
#TorLoc: 1
Own: Private Company
Key: Grant Pittam, Pres

CTI Industries

5621 Finch Ave. East
Toronto, ON M1B 2T9
Tel 416-297-8738
Fax 416-297-0421
www.ctiind.com
Line: Manufactures wired cables and harnesses.
NAICS: 335920
#Emp: 100-249 (Tor)
#TorLoc: 1
Own: Private Company
Key: Roman Brenner, Pres
Adam Gabriele, Dir of Fin

C & T Reinforcing Steel Co. (1987) Limited

93 Passmore Ave.
Toronto, ON M1V 4S9
Tel 416-291-7349
Fax 416-291-0698
www.ctsteel.com
Line: Manufactures steel reinforcing products.
NAICS: 331110
#Emp: 75-99 (Tor)
Own: Private Company
Key: Sam Costa, Pres
Peter Costa, VP
Anita Chan, Office Mgr
Ken Leung, Cont

CTS of Canada Company

80 Thomas St.
Streetsville, ON L5M 1Y9
Tel 905-826-1141
Fax 905-858-9058
www.ctscorp.com
Line: Manufactures sensors, actuators, and related sub-systems for automotive, transportation and small engine industries.
NAICS: 334512
#Emp: 100-249 (Tor)
#TorLoc: 1
Own: Public Company
Par: CTS Corp. (US)
Key: Ugo Baldassare, Plant Mgr
Bob Cortese, Cont

CTV Inc.

9 Channel Nine Crt.
Toronto, ON M1S 4B5
Tel 416-332-5000
www.ctv.ca
Line: Provides conventional and specialty broadcasting services that include news, sports, information and entertainment programming.
NAICS: 513120
#Emp: 1000-4999 (Tor)
#TorLoc: 3
Own: Public Company
Par: CTVglobemedia Inc. (CDA)
Key: Susanne Boyce,
    Pres, Creative Content & Channels
Ivan Fecan, CEO
Rick Brace, Pres of Revenue,
    Business Planning & Sports

Culinary Destinations

35 Jutland Rd.
Toronto, ON M8Z 2G6
Tel 416-201-0707
Fax 416-201-3014
www.culinarydestinations.com
Line: Develops and produces private label food products.
NAICS: 311990
#Emp: 75-99 (Tor)
#TorLoc: 1
Own: Private Company
Key: Keith Chen, Pres

The CUMIS Group Ltd.

151 North Service Rd.
P.O. Box 5065
Burlington, ON L7R 4C2
Tel 905-632-1221
Fax 905-632-9412
www.cumis.com
Line: Partners with credit unions to deliver insurance and financial solutions.
NAICS: 524129
#Emp: 250-499 (Tor)
#TorLoc: 1
Own: Private Company
Par: CUNA Mutual Group (US)
Key: Kathy Bardswick, Pres & CEO
Mavis Whiting, VP HR
John Asher, VP Fin
Linda Yeo, VP IT & Facilities
Steve Richard, VP Sales
Paul Mlodzik, VP Mktg & Commun

Cummer Lodge

205 Cummer Ave.
Toronto, ON M2M 2E8
Tel 416-392-9500
Fax 416-392-9499
www.toronto.ca/ltc/cummer.htm
Line: Operates long-term care facility.
NAICS: 623310
#Emp: 250-499 (Tor)
#TorLoc: 1
Own: Government
Par: The City of Toronto
Key: Leah Walters, Admr
Carlos Herrera, Asst Admr

The Cundari Group

26 Duncan St.
Toronto, ON M5V 2B9
Tel 416-510-1771
Fax 416-510-1769
www.cundari.com
Line: Operates a full-service communication agency.
NAICS: 541810
#Emp: 100-249 (Tor)
#TorLoc: 2
Own: Private Company
Key: Garry Lee, Pres
Aldo Cundari, Chmn & CEO
Jennifer Steinmann, Exec VP
Maria Orsini, VP Fin & Admin

Cunningham Lindsey Canada Ltd.

1102-50 Burnhamthorpe Rd.
West Sussex Centre
Mississauga, ON L5B 3C2
Tel 905-896-8181
Fax 905-896-3485
www.cunninghamlindsey.com
Line: Provides independent insurance claims adjusting, appraisal and loss management services.
NAICS: 524291
#Emp: 250-499 (Tor)
#TorLoc: 17
Own: Public Company
Par: Lindsey Morden Group (CDA)
Key: Robert Seal, Pres

Curry's Art Store Ltd.

2485 Tedlo St.
Mississauga, ON L5A 4A8
Tel 416-798-7983
Fax 905-272-0778
www.currys.com
Line: Distributes art supplies.
NAICS: 417930
#Emp: 100-249 (Tor)
#TorLoc: 7
Own: Private Company
Key: Rod Ghent, Pres
J.M. Ghent, Ops Mgr
Jennifer Waye, Payroll
Bill Waters, Store Sales Mgr
David Waye, Mktg Mgr

Cushman & Wakefield Ltd.

1000-33 Yonge St.
Toronto, ON M5E 1S9
Tel 416-862-0611
Fax 416-359-2395
www.cushwake.com
Line: Provides commercial real estate services.

NAICS: 531210
#Emp: 250-499 (Tor)
#TorLoc: 3
Own: Private Company
Par: Cushman & Wakefield (US)
Key: Pierre Bergevin, Pres
Beth Connor, Dir of HR
Rene Gulliver, CFO
Ken Duff, CIO
Brad Dugard, Dir of Commun

Custom Insulation Systems

52-53 70 Pippin Rd.
Vaughan, ON L4K 4M9
Tel 905-669-0002
Fax 905-669-0826
www.custominsultation.ca
Line: Offers industrial and commercial mechanical piping insulation.
NAICS: 232440
#Emp: 75-99 (Tor)
#TorLoc: 1
Own: Private Company
Key: Joe Fabing, Pres
Susan Train, Fin & Office Mgr
Jim Smiley, Mgr, Fire Stopping
Kerry Wallace, Mgr, Fire Proofing

Cutler Forest Products Inc.

1265 Aerowood Dr.
Mississauga, ON L4W 1B9
Tel 905-212 1414
Fax 905-238-5512
www.cutlerforestproducts.com
Line: Wholesales and fabricates wood products.
NAICS: 416320
#Emp: 75-99 (Tor)
#TorLoc: 1
Own: Private Company
Key: Jonathan Glick, Pres

CWH Distribution Services Inc.

1245 Martin Grove Rd.
Toronto, ON M9W 4X2
Tel 416-674-5826
Fax 416-674-5387
www.cwhenderson.ca
AKA: C W Henderson
Line: Offers truck transportation services.
NAICS: 484110 484121
#Emp: 100-249 (Tor)
#TorLoc: 1
Own: Private Company
Key: David Hardy, Pres
Dermot Holwell, VP Fin

CWT Concierge

800-10 Carlson Crt.
Toronto, ON M9W 6L2
Tel 416-679-6444
Fax 416-798-3803
www.cwtconcierge.com
Line: Provides corporate and leisure travel and meeting planning, and incentives services.
NAICS: 561510
#Emp: 100-249 (Tor)
#TorLoc: 1
Own: Private Company
Par: Carlson Wagonlit Travel (US)
Key: Kim Cross, Nat'l Mgr, Canada

Cyberplex Inc.

400-1255 Bay St.
Toronto, ON M5R 2A9
Tel 416-597-8889
Fax 416-597-2345
www.cyberplex.com
Line: Provides web advertising solutions, online customer acquisition strategies and technology development.
NAICS: 541510
#Emp: 75-99 (Tor)
Own: Private Company
Key: Geoffrey Rotstein, CEO
Ted Hastings, Pres
Richard Maisel, CFO
David Benoliel, VP Sales & Mktg

Cyclone Manufacturing Inc.

7300 Rapistan Crt.
Mississauga, ON L5N 5S1
Tel 905-567-5601
Fax 905-567-6911
www.cyclonemfg.com
Line: Manufactures components and assemblies for the aircraft, aerospace, nuclear and defense industries.
NAICS: 336410
#Emp: 100-249 (Tor)
#TorLoc: 1
Own: Private Company
Key: Andrew Sochaj, Pres
Robert Sochaj, VP

D & A Collection Corp.

131 Brunel Rd.
Mississauga, ON L4Z 1X3
Tel 905-507-8889
Fax 905-507-6566
www.dacollections.com
Line: Provides collection agency services.
NAICS: 561440
#Emp: 75-99 (Tor)

#TorLoc: 1
Own: Private Company
Key: Ray Caruana, Ops Mgr
Jason Nazim, HR Operational Coord

Dagmar Construction Ltd.

7350 Markham Rd.
Markham, ON L3S 3K1
Tel 905-294-7480
Fax 905-294-8414
www.dagmarconstruction.com
Line: Provides road, bridge and sewer construction services.
NAICS: 231310 231320
#Emp: 100-249 (Tor)
#TorLoc: 1
Own: Private Company
Key: Denis Bigioni, Pres

Dahl Brothers (Canada) Ltd.

2600 South Sheridan Way
Mississauga, ON L5J 2M4
Tel 905-822-2330
Fax 905-855-1450
www.dahlvalves.com
Line: Manufactures plumbing and heating valves.
NAICS: 332910
#Emp: 100-249 (Tor)
#TorLoc: 1
Own: Private Company
Key: Jannike Godfrey, Pres
Trygve Husebye, Chmn
Stephen Worthy, Plant Mgr
Maria Costa, HR Mgr
Thomas Husebye,
    VP New Business & Product Dev

Daimler Buses North America

350 Hazelhurst Rd.
Mississauga, ON L5J 4T8
Tel 905-403-1111
Fax 905-403-8808
www.dcbusna.ca
Line: Manufactures transit buses.
NAICS: 336211 336120
#Emp: 250-499 (Tor)
#TorLoc: 1
Own: Private Company
Par: Daimler AG (GER)
Key: Rich Ferguson, Pres & CEO
Martin Walz, COO
Mary-Jo Fiorini, Dir of HR
Harry Rendel, CFO
Mark Renton, Dir of Materials
Cheryl Davis, CIO
Patrick Scully,
    Chief Commercial Officer

Daimler Trucks Financial Ltd.

500- 2680 Matheson Blvd. East
Mississauga, ON L4W 0A5
Tel 800-361-4680
Fax 866-246-4435
www.daimler-truckfinancial.ca
AKA: DCFS Canada Corp.
Line: Provides car, light truck, and freightliner/sterling/western star truck financing and leasing.
NAICS: 522220
#Emp: 75-99 (Tor)
#TorLoc: 1
Own: Private Company
Key: Ian Loveless, Mng Dir
Denis Gingras, Sales & Mktg Mgr

Dalton Chemical Laboratories Inc.

349 Wildcat Rd.
Toronto, ON M3J 2S3
Tel 416-661-2102
Fax 416-661-2108
www.dalton.com
Line: Manufactures fine chemicals, peptides and antisense oligos.
NAICS: 325410 325320
#Emp: 75-99 (Tor)
#TorLoc: 1
Own: Private Company
Key: Peter Pekos, Pres
Natalie Lazarowych,
    Dir of Tech Solutions
Mary Kanaris, HR Mgr
Jack Tase, Cont
James Kanaris, Purch Mgr
Kathy Deiuliis, Account Mgr
Lenka Fousek, Mktg Asst

Dana Hospitality Inc.

200-2898 South Sheridan Way
Oakville, ON L6J 7L5
Tel 905-829-0292
Fax 905-829-2898
www.danahospitality.ca
Line: Provides cafeteria management, catering, vending and coffee services.
NAICS: 722210
#Emp: 500-999 (Tor)
#TorLoc: 60
Own: Private Company
Key: Byron Kaczmarek, Pres
Samjiv Seth, VP Ops
Lorenzo Nicodemo, VP Sales & HR

D'Angelo Brands Ltd.

4544 Eastgate Pkwy.
Mississauga, ON L4W 3W6
Tel 905-238-6300
Fax 905-238-1837
www.dangelobrands.ca
Line: Produces food and beverage products.
NAICS: 312110 311930
#Emp: 100-249 (Tor)
Own: Public Company
Key: Frank D'Angelo, Pres

The Daniels Group Inc.

3400-20 Queen St. West
Box #50
Toronto, ON M5H 3R3
Tel 416-598-2129
Fax 416-979-0415
www.danielshomes.ca
NAICS: 231210
#Emp: 250-499 (Tor)
#TorLoc: 2
Own: Private Company
Key: Mitchell Cohen, Pres
John Daniels, CEO
Judy Lem, CFO

Danier Leather Inc.

2650 St. Clair Ave. West
Toronto, ON M6N 1M2
Tel 416-762-8175
Fax 416-762-4570
www.danier.com
Line: Designs, manufactures and retails leather and suede clothing and accessories.
NAICS: 315292 448150 448140
#Emp: 500-999 (Tor)
#TorLoc: 24
Own: Public Company
Key: Jeffrey Wortsman, Pres & CEO
Cris Ruivo, VP Store Ops
Cheryl Sproul, VP HR
Bryan Tatoff, VP & CFO
Philip Cutter, VP IT & CIO
Jennifer Steckel-Elliott, VP Mktg

The DATA Group of Companies

9195 Torbram Rd.
Brampton, ON L6S 6H2
Tel 905-791-3151
Fax 905-791-3277
www.datagroup.ca
Line: Provides preprinted business forms, document management services, electronic forms software, pressure-sensitive labels, digital printing, security printing, business communication services, outsourcing and facilities management services.
NAICS: 323116 323119
#Emp: 500-999 (Tor)
#TorLoc: 4
Own: Public Company
Par: Workflow Management Inc. (US)
Key: Michael Suksi, Pres & CEO
Diane Schwind, VP Ops
Elaine Deramo, VP HR
Paul O'Shea, VP & CFO

Datarush Courier

900-6 Adelaide St. East
Toronto, ON M5C 1H6
Tel 416-598-0440
Fax 416-979-8265
www.datarushcourier.com
NAICS: 492110
#Emp: 100-249 (Tor)
#TorLoc: 1
Own: Private Company
Key: Jason Etheridge, Pres

Dave and Busters

120 Interchange Way
Concord, ON L4K 5C3
Tel 905-760-7601
Fax 905-760-7610
www.daveandbusters.com
Line: Operates restaurant and entertainment facility.
NAICS: 722110
#Emp: 100-249 (Tor)
#TorLoc: 1
Own: Private Company
Par: Dave and Busters (US)
Key: Brian Light, GM
Cam Curran, Asst GM
Tracy Morgan, Business Analyst
Mary Patrick, Special Events Mgr

Davies Ward Phillips & Vineberg LLP

1 First Canadian Pl., 44th Fl.
Toronto, ON M5X 1B1
Tel 416-863-0900
Fax 416-863-0871
www.dwpv.com
AKA: DWPV Services Limited Partnership; DWPV Management Limited
Line: Operates a law firm.
NAICS: 541110
#Emp: 250-499 (Tor)
#TorLoc: 1
Own: Partnership
Key: D. Shaun McReynolds, Mng Part
Mclanie Koszegi, Exec Dir
Lynda Stewart Dame, Dir of HR
Jim Dodsworth, CFO
Ivo Nikolov, Dir of IT
Graham Ross, Dir of Mktg & Bus Dev

Da Vinci Banquet Hall & Restaurant

33-5732 Hwy. 7
Woodbridge, ON L4L 3A2
Tel 905-851-2768
Fax 905-851-8952
www.davincibanquethall.com
Line: Operates a banquet hall.
NAICS: 722320
#Emp: 100-249 (Tor)
#TorLoc: 1
Own: Private Company
Key: Vince Deluca, Pres
Carmelo Messina, Mgr

Davis Group of Companies Corp.

25 Riviera Dr.
Markham, ON L3R 8N4
Tel 905-477-7440
Fax 905-477-0515
www.davisgroup.net
AKA: Fletcher Davis; Focus Promotion Products; MMOD Industries; R&G Office Products
Line: Manufactures vinyl stationary products.
NAICS: 323119
#Emp: 75-99 (Tor)
#TorLoc: 1
Own: Private Company
Key: Larry Morin, VP & GM
Douglas Davis, CEO
Gordon Mitchell, Ops Mgr
Shawn Rastan, Acctng Mgr
Jim Davies, VP Sales & Mktg

Davis + Henderson

201-939 Eglinton Ave. East
Toronto, ON M4G 4H7
Tel 416-696-7702
Fax 416-696-8308
www.dhltd.com
AKA: D+H Ltd.
Line: Provides manufacturing and specialty printing.
NAICS: 323116
#Emp: 1000-4999 (Tor)
#TorLoc: 3
Own: Public Company
Key: Gerrard Schmid, Pres & COO
Robert J. Cronin, CEO
Yves Denomme, VP Ops
Susan Mandrozos, Exec VP HR
Brian Kyle, Exec VP & CFO
Chad Alderson, VP & CTO
Serge Rivest, Exec VP Sales & Mktg

Dawn Food Products Canada Ltd.

75 Vickers Rd.
Toronto, ON M9B 6B6
Tel 416-233-5851
Fax 416-233-1963
www.dawnfoods.ca
Line: Supplies flour, dry mixes, icings, fillings, and glazed fruit to the bakery, food service and dairy industries.
NAICS: 311940 311930
#Emp: 100-249 (Tor)
#TorLoc: 1
Own: Private Company
Par: Dawn Food Products Inc. (US)
Key: David Hawkins, Pres
Julie Clarke, Dir HR
Paul Henrie, Gen Sales Mgr
Lesley Brooks, Dir of Mktg

Day & Ross Inc.

170 Van Kirk Dr.
Brampton, ON L7A 1K9
Tel 905-846-6300
Fax 905-846-6368
www.dayross.ca
Line: Owns and operates freight transportation terminals and facilities across Canada.
NAICS: 484110 484121 492110
#Emp: 250-499 (Tor)
#TorLoc: 1
Own: Private Company
Par: McCain Foods Ltd. (CDA)
Key: Chris Haworth, Terminal Mgr
Bruce Morin, VP Sales
Krista Deering, Mktg Mgr

D & B Canada

A Div. of The D & B Companies of Canada Ltd.
305-6750 Century Ave.
Mississauga, ON L5N 0B7
Tel 905-812-5900
Fax 1-800-668-7800
www.dnb.ca
AKA: Dun & Bradstreet Canada
Line: Provides business-to-business credit, marketing and purchasing information.
NAICS: 511140 541860
#Emp: 75-99 (Tor)
#TorLoc: 1
Own: Private Company
Par: The Dun & Bradstreet Corp. (US)
Key: Heba Enain, HR Business Partner

DBG

110 Ambassador Dr.
Mississauga, ON L5T 2X8
Tel 905-670-1555
Fax 905-362-2315
www.debiasi.com
AKA: The Debiasi Group
Line: Manufactures metal stampings for the automotive, heavy truck and appliance industries.
NAICS: 336370
#Emp: 250-499 (Tor)
#TorLoc: 3
Own: Private Company
Key: Mike DeBiasi, Pres & CEO
Linda Ryall, Corp HR Mgr
Joe Novak, VP Fin
Julian Wainewright, IT Mgr
John Albrecht, VP Mktg & Sales

DBPC Group of Companies

250 Consumers Rd.
Toronto, ON M2J 4V6
Tel 416-755-9198
Fax 416-755-0569
www.dbpc.ca
AKA: Diverse Business & Personnel Corporation
Line: Operates an employment agency.
NAICS: 561310
#Emp: 100-249 (Tor)
#TorLoc: 2
Own: Private Company
Key: Samuel Levinson, Pres

DCL International Inc.

241 Bradwick Dr.
Concord, ON L4K 1K5
Tel 905-660-6450
Fax 905-660-6435
www.dcl-inc.com
Line: Manufactures and wholesales emission control systems.
NAICS: 334512
#Emp: 100-249 (Tor)
#TorLoc: 2
Own: Private Company
Key: George Swiatek, Pres
Laura Simpson, Office Mgr
Nicholas Wai, Cont

D. Crupi & Sons Ltd.

85 Passmore Ave.
P.O. Box 272
Toronto, ON M1V 4S9
Tel 416-291-1986
Fax 416-291-3252
www.crupigroup.com
Line: Provides asphalt and paving services.
NAICS: 231310
#Emp: 250-499 (Tor)
#TorLoc: 7
Own: Private Company
Key: Cosimo Crupi, Pres
Tony Gaglia, Ops Mgr
Sam DiFilippo, HR Mgr
Tim Hand, CFO

D.C. Security Inc.

20-22 Goodmark Pl.
Toronto, ON M9W 6R2
Tel 416-213-1995
Fax 416-213-1328
www.dc-security.com
Line: Provides security guard services.
NAICS: 523120
#Emp: 100-249 (Tor)
#TorLoc: 1
Own: Private Company
Key: Clement G. Dennis, Pres
Farisha Mohammed, Office Mgr

DDB Canada

33 Bloor St. East, 17th Fl.
Toronto, ON M4W 3T4
Tel 416-925-9819
Fax 416-921-4180
www.ddbcanada.com
Line: Operates an advertising agency.
NAICS: 541810
#Emp: 100-249 (Tor)
#TorLoc: 1
Own: Public Company
Key: David Leonard, Pres
Frank Palmer, Chmn & CEO
Michael Davidson, VP Business Unit Dir
Greg Geralde, CFO

DDi

8150 Sheppard Ave. East
Toronto, ON M1B 5K2
Tel 416-208-2100
Fax 416-208-2196
www.ddiglobal.com
Line: Manufactures printed circuit boards.
NAICS: 334410
#Emp: 100-249 (Tor)
#TorLoc: 2
Own: Public Company
Par: DDi (US)
Key: Michael Mathews, Sr VP & COO
Mikel Williams, CEO
Barry Ling, Plant Mgr, Canada
J. Michael Dodson, CFO

Deacro Industries Ltd.

135 Capital Crt.
Mississauga, ON L5T 2R8
Tel 905-564-6566
Fax 905-564-6533
www.deacro.com
Line: Designs and manufactures slitter
rewinders for converting industry.
NAICS: 333990
#Emp: 100-249 (Tor)
#TorLoc: 1
Own: Private Company
Key: Ed DeBoer, Pres
Wilma DeBoer, HR Mgr

DealerTrack Canada Inc.

700-2700 Matheson Blvd. East
Mississauga, ON L4W 4V9
Tel 1-877-288-2191
Fax 1-877-872-2564
www.dealertrack.ca
Line: Provides online financing
solutions.
NAICS: 541611
#Emp: 100-249 (Tor)
Own: Private Company
Key: Rick Van Pusch, Sr VP Sales,
  Mktg & International
Michael Collins, GM,
  DealerTrack Canada
Carroll Thompson, Cont
Debbie Oberender,
  VP Mktg & Corp Commun

Dean Myers Chevrolet Corvette

3180 Dufferin St.
Toronto, ON M6A 2T1
Tel 416-256-1405
Fax 416-789-2789
www.deanmyers.com
Line: Operates a car dealership.
NAICS: 441110
#Emp: 100-249 (Tor)
#TorLoc: 1
Own: Private Company
Key: Richard Chamberlin, Pres
Angelo Capogna, GM

Debco Bag Distributors Ltd.

111 Villarboit Cres.
Concord, ON L4K 4K2
Tel 905-669-2247
Fax 905-881-7783
www.debcobag.com
Line: Distributes bags, chairs, gift sets,
umbrellas and conference items.
NAICS: 414110
#Emp: 75-99 (Tor)
#TorLoc: 1
Own: Private Company
Key: Steven Gallen, Pres

De Boer's Furniture Ltd.

275 Drumlin Circ.
Concord, ON L4K 3E4
Tel 905-669-9455
Fax 905-669-3534
www.deboers.com
AKA: De Boer's
Line: Retails home furnishings.
NAICS: 442110
#Emp: 75-99 (Tor)
#TorLoc: 3
Own: Private Company
Key: John DeBoer, Pres

DecisionOne Corp.

3-25 Kinnear Crt.
Richmond Hill, ON L4B 1H9
Tel 905-882-1551
Fax 905-882-1579
www.decisionone.ca
Line: Provides computer repairs.
NAICS: 811210
#Emp: 75-99 (Tor)
#TorLoc: 1
Own: Private Company
Par: DecisionOne Corp. (US)
Key: Rick Gray, VP & GM
Sylvain Simard, VP Ops
Cathy Lykopoulos, HR Mgr

Deco Labels & Tags

28 Greensboro Dr.
Toronto, ON M9W 1E1
Tel 416-247-7878
Fax 416-247-9030
www.decolabels.com
NAICS: 325520
#Emp: 75-99 (Tor)
#TorLoc: 1
Own: Private Company
Key: Doug Ford, Pres
Steven Chan, Cont

Decora Window & Door Systems

A-B 45 Connie Cres.
Concord, ON L4K 1L3
Tel 905-660-9212
Fax 905-669-1687
www.decora.ca
Line: Manufactures window and door
systems.
NAICS: 321911 332321
#Emp: 100-249 (Tor)
#TorLoc: 1
Own: Private Company
Key: Robert Brunino, Owner
Jack Cascone, Owner
Frank Plasa, VP Sales & Mktg

Decor-Rest Furniture Ltd.

511 Chrislea Rd.
Woodbridge, ON L4L 8N6
Tel 905-856-5956
Fax 905-856-2034
www.decor-rest.com
Line: Manufactures custom upholstery
and distributes tables, lamps and
mirrors.
NAICS: 337121
#Emp: 100-249 (Tor)
#TorLoc: 1
Own: Private Company
Key: Angelo Marzilli, Pres
Roxanna Schonberger, Dir of Manuf
Christina Marzilli, VP & COO
Ron Penney, Sales Mgr

Decoustics Ltd.

61 Royal Group Cres.
Vaughan, ON L4H 1X9
Tel 905-652-5200
Fax 905-652-2505
www.decoustics.com
Line: Manufactures acoustic wall
panels.
NAICS: 232410
#Emp: 100-249 (Tor)
#TorLoc: 3
Own: Private Company
Par: Saint Gobain (FRA)
Key: Eric Bishun, GM
Carlos Ramirez,
  International Sales Mgr

Deeley Harley Davidson Canada

830 Edgeley Blvd.
Concord, ON L4K 4X1
Tel 905-660-3500
Fax 905-660-3372
www.harleycanada.com
AKA: Harley Owners Group of Canada
Line: Distributes Harley-Davidson
motorcycles, parts and accessories, and
general merchandise.
NAICS: 415190
#Emp: 100-249 (Tor)
#TorLoc: 1
Own: Private Company
Key: Malcolm Hunter, Pres & COO
Don James, Chmn & CEO
Buzz Green, VP & GM
Mike Harwood, HR Dir
Rick Hanna, VP & CFO
Rick Ballard, Ops Dir
Stacey Arthur, IT Dir
Lawson Greer,
  Retail Sales & Support Dir
Dom Bovalino, Mktg Dir
Rob Wiens, Fin Dir

Deep Foundations Contractors Inc.

145 Ram Forest Rd.
Gormley, ON L0H 1G0
Tel 905-750-5900
www.deepfoundations.ca
AKA: Deep Foundation Group Management
Line: Contractors specializing in foundation systems for large excavations, including shoring, underpinning, pile driving and caisson work.
NAICS: 232110
#Emp: 75-99 (Tor)
#TorLoc: 1
Own: Private Company
Par: 1015708 Ontario Ltd. (CDA)
Key: Peter McDonald, VP
Mario Cianchetti, Treas & Officer Mgr

Deer Creek Golf & Banquet Facility

2700 Audley Rd. North
Ajax, ON L1Z 1T7
Tel 905-427-7737
Fax 905-427-1574
www.golfdeercreek.com
AKA: Glen Cedars Golf Club; Deer Creek Academy
Line: Operates a full service golf course offering banquet, teaching and practice facilities and a steak and seafood restaurant.
NAICS: 713910
#Emp: 100-249 (Tor)
#TorLoc: 2
Own: Private Company
Par: Cougs Investments Ltd. (CDA)
Key: Scott Collins, Pres
Terry Knox, GM
Gloria Cooper, Mktg & Sales Mgr

Delcan Corp.

500-625 Cochrane Dr.
Markham, ON L3R 9R9
Tel 905-943-0500
Fax 905-943-0400
www.delcan.com
Line: Provides professional consulting services in transportation, environmental and structural engineering, and program and project management.
NAICS: 541619 541330
#Emp: 250-499 (Tor)
#TorLoc: 1
Own: Private Company
Key: Jim Kerr, Chmn & CEO
Bruce Darlington, VP Acctng & Admin
Jack Powers, VP Fin
Jim Corbett, VP Procurement

Del Equipment Limited

139 Laird Dr.
Toronto, ON M4G 3V6
Tel 416-421-5851
Fax 416-421-7663
www.delequipment.com
Line: Manufactures truck bodies and truck equipment.
NAICS: 333920 336211
#Emp: 75-99 (Tor)
#TorLoc: 1
Own: Private Company
Key: Paul H. Martin, Pres
Robert Scott, GM
Dawn Edmonds, Payroll & HR Mgr
Terry Quinn, CFO
Rod Barrowcliffe, VP Sales & Mktg

Delgant Construction Ltd.

7 Marconi Crt.
Bolton, ON L7E 1H3
Tel 905-857-7858
Fax 905-857-7801
Line: Operates a construction company specializing in concrete form work.
NAICS: 232210 232220
#Emp: 100-249 (Tor)
#TorLoc: 1
Own: Private Company
Key: Carlo Delle Doni, Pres

Dell Canada Inc.

501-155 Gordon Baker Rd.
Toronto, ON M2H 3N5
Tel 416-758-2100
Fax 416-758-2305
www.dell.ca
Line: Manufactures, sells and services computers.
NAICS: 417310
#Emp: 500-999 (Tor)
#TorLoc: 1
Own: Private Company
Par: Dell Computer Corp. (US)
Key: Paul Cooper, Dir
Michael Dell, CEO
Larry Baldachin, Dir of Corp Sales

Dell Financial Services Canada Ltd.

501-155 Gordon Baker Rd.
Toronto, ON M2H 3N5
Tel 416-773-5300
Fax 416-758-2314
www.dfsdirect.ca
NAICS: 417310
#Emp: 75-99 (Tor)
#TorLoc: 1
Own: Private Company
Key: Danny Lebovics, Sr VP & GM

Deloitte & Touche LLP

1200-2 Queen St. East, P.O. Box 8
Toronto, ON M5C 3G7
Tel 416-874-3875
Fax 416-874-3888
www.deloitte.ca
AKA: Deloitte.
Line: Provides a full range of assurance and advisory, tax, and management consulting services.
NAICS: 541212 541611
#Emp: 1000-4999 (Tor)
#TorLoc: 9
Own: Partnership
Key: Colin Taylor, Mng Partner & Chmn
Alan MacGibbon, Mng Partner & CEO

Delphax Technologies

5030 Timberlea Blvd.
Mississauga, ON L4W 2S5
Tel 905-238-2961
Fax 905-238-3402
www.delphax.com
Line: Manufactures, designs, and delivers advanced printer-production systems.
NAICS: 334110 417310
#Emp: 100-249 (Tor)
#TorLoc: 1
Own: Public Company
Par: Delphax Technologies Inc. (US)
Key: Michael Wroblewski, VP Manuf
Ray Vella, Cont

Del Property Management Inc.

4800 Dufferin St.
Toronto, ON M3H 5S9
Tel 416-661-3151
Fax 416-661-8653
www.delpropertymanagement.com
Line: Specializes in condominium property management services.
NAICS: 531310
#Emp: 250-499 (Tor)
#TorLoc: 150
Own: Private Company
Par: Tridel Corp. (CDA)
Key: Saul York, Pres & CEO
Allan L. Rosenberg, VP
Lucy Dias, VP Acctng & Admin

Delso Restoration Ltd.

7200 Tranmere Dr.
Mississauga, ON L5S 1L6
Tel 905-671-3985
Fax 905-671-2732
www.delsogroup.com
Line: Provides restoration services.
NAICS: 232290
#Emp: 100-249 (Tor)
#TorLoc: 1
Own: Private Company
Key: Domenic Eramo, Pres

Del's Pastry Ltd.

344 Bering Ave.
Toronto, ON M8Z 3A7
Tel 416-231-4383
Fax 416-231-3254
www.delspastry.com
Line: Manufactures and sells baked
goods.
NAICS: 311814
#Emp: 75-99 (Tor)
#TorLoc: 1
Own: Private Company
Key: Benno Mattes, Pres
Tom Mattes, VP Ops
Sandra Sandra, VP Fin

Delta Hotels Limited

1200-100 Wellington St. West,
  TD Centre
P.O. Box 227
Toronto, ON M5K 1J3
Tel 416-874-2000
Fax 416-874-2001
www.deltahotels.com
AKA: Delta Chelsea; Delta Markham;
Delta Meadowvale Resort & Conference
Centre; Delta Toronto Airport West;
Delta Toronto East
Line: Provides hospitality management
services.
NAICS: 721111
#Emp: 1000-4999 (Tor)
#TorLoc: 4
Own: Private Company
Key: Hank Stackhouse, Pres
William J. Pallett,
  Sr VP People & Quality

Delta Markham

50 East Valhalla Dr.
Markham, ON L3R 0A3
Tel 905-477-2010
Fax 905-477-2026
www.deltahotels.com
Line: Manages hotel operations.
NAICS: 721111 722110
#Emp: 250-499 (Tor)
#TorLoc: 3
Own: Private Company
Par: Nor-Sham Group (CDA)
Key: Tracy Boyd, Ops Mgr
Janet Miller,
  People Resources Exec Admr
Thas Thambapillai, Cont
Laura Boyden, Dir of Sales & Mktg

Delta Meadowvale Hotel and Conference Centre

6750 Mississauga Rd.
Mississauga, ON L5N 2L3
Tel 905-821-1981
Fax 905-542-6757
www.deltahotels.com
Line: Operates a full service hotel with
meeting facilities and fitness centre.
NAICS: 721111
#Emp: 250-499 (Tor)
#TorLoc: 3
Own: Private Company
Par: Delta Hotels & Resorts (CDA)
Key: Rob Housez, GM
Elaine Stover, Dir of Ops
Anita Stafford, Dir of People Resources
Brian Farrugia, Cont
Laura Pallotta, Dir of Sales & Mktg

Delta Toronto Airport West

5444 Dixie Rd.
Mississauga, ON L4W 2L2
Tel 905-624-1144
Fax 905-624-9477
www.deltahotels.com
Line: Operates a hotel.
NAICS: 721111
#Emp: 100-249 (Tor)
#TorLoc: 1
Own: Private Company
Par: Delta Hotels (CDA)
Key: Martin Stitt,
  Reg Dir of Ontario & GM
Trina Goldsworthy,
  People Resources Dir
Colin Jones, Reg Revenue Mgr
Debbie Hastings, Dir of Sales & Mktg

Delta Toronto East

2035 Kennedy Rd.
Toronto, ON M1T 3G2
Tel 416-299-1500
Fax 416-299-8959
www.deltatorontoeast.com
Line: Provides hospitality services.
NAICS: 721111
#Emp: 250-499 (Tor)
#TorLoc: 1
Own: Private Company
Par: Delta Hotels (CDA)
Key: Christopher Lund, Reg VP & GM
Ragnar Pedersen, Hotel Mgr
Anna Salvati, HR Dir
Caroline Tam, Reg Cont, Ontario
Susan Welsby, Dir of Sales & Mktg

Deluxe Laboratories

350 Evans Ave.
Toronto, ON M8Z 1K5
Tel 416-205-8155
Fax 416-591-8782
www.bydeluxe.com
NAICS: 512190
#Emp: 250-499 (Tor)
#TorLoc: 2
Own: Private Company
Key: Cyril Drabinsky, Pres
Catherine McEwan, VP HR
Diane Cuthbert, VP Sales

Dentsply Canada Inc.

161 Vinyl Crt.
Woodbridge, ON L4L 4A3
Tel 905-851-6060
Fax 905-851-5374
www.dentsply.ca
Line: Manufactures products for the
dental industry.
NAICS: 339110
#Emp: 75-99 (Tor)
#TorLoc: 1
Own: Public Company
Par: Dentsply International (US)
Key: Judy Dautovich, Cont
Eva Hajtko, HR Mgr
Andrea Ferencz, Dir of Mktg

Dependable Anodizing Ltd.

268 Don Park Rd.
Markham, ON L3R 1C3
Tel 905-475-1229
Fax 905-475-8056
www.dependableanodizing.com
NAICS: 332810
#Emp: 75-99 (Tor)
#TorLoc: 1
Own: Association
Key: Horst Stoll, Pres
Jochim Schauer, VP
Karl Mueller, Secy-Treas

Dependable Truck & Tank Repairs Ltd.

275 Clarence St.
Brampton, ON L6W 3R3
Tel 905-453-6724
Fax 905-453-7005
www.dependable.ca
Line: Manufactures tank trucks and fire trucks.
NAICS: 336211
#Emp: 75-99 (Tor)
#TorLoc: 1
Own: Private Company
Key: Santo Natale, Pres
Salvatore Natale, VP

Derma Sciences Canada Inc.

104 Shorting Rd.
Toronto, ON M1S 3S4
Tel 416-299-4003
Fax 416-299-4912
www.dermasciences.com
AKA: Wound Care Direct
Line: Manufactures and distributes medical products.
NAICS: 339110
#Emp: 100-249 (Tor)
#TorLoc: 1
Own: Private Company
Key: Ed Quilty, Pres & CEO
Fred Eigner, Exec VP & GM
Geoff Reid, Cont
Peter Crawford, Dir of Cdn Sales

Desco Plumbing and Heating Supply Inc.

65 Worcester Rd.
Toronto, ON M9W 5N7
Tel 416-213-1555
Fax 416-798-1440
www.desco.ca
AKA: Rocamora Triangle
Line: Sells and supplies plumbing and heating products.
NAICS: 416120
#Emp: 100-249 (Tor)

#TorLoc: 14
Own: Private Company
Par: Groupe Deschenes Inc. (CDA)
Key: Jon Leeson, VP & GM
Kevin Rutherford, Ops Mgr
Matt Cloyd, HR Mgr
Tom Bissegger, Cont
Brian Ruetz, Western Sales Mgr

Desjardins Financial Security Life Assurance Company

200 des Commandeurs
Levis, PQ G6V 6R2
Tel 800-463-7870
Fax 416 -366-2444
www.desjardinsfinancialsecurity.com
Line: Provides individual and group life insurance, retirement and investment products, health insurance and financial planning.
NAICS: 524112
#Emp: 500-999 (Tor)
#TorLoc: 1
Own: Private Company
Par: Desjardins Group (CDA)
Key: Richard Fortier, Pres & COO, DFS
Monique F. Leroux, Pres & CEO, Desjardins Group

Desjardins Financial Security Life Assurance Company - Toronto

95 St. Clair Ave. West
Toronto, ON M4V 1N7
Tel 416-926-2700
Fax 416-926-2777
www.desjardinsfinancialsecurity.com
AKA: Imperial Life Financial; Laurentian Financial Services
Line: Provides individual and group life insurance, retirement and investment products, health insurance, and financial planning.
NAICS: 524112 524111
#Emp: 500-999 (Tor)
#TorLoc: 1
Own: Private Company
Par: Desjardins Group (CDA)
Key: Peter Ferland, VP Sales, Savings & Segregated Funds

Desjardins General Insurance Group

400-3 Robert Speck Pkwy.
Mississauga, ON L4Z 3Z9
Tel 905-306-3900
Fax 905-306-5054
www.desjardins.com
Line: Operates general insurance company.

NAICS: 524210
#Emp: 500-999 (Tor)
#TorLoc: 1
Own: Private Company
Par: Desjardins Group (CDA)
Key: Sylvie Paquette, Pres & COO
Dianne Fortune, VP HR
Louis Chantal, Sr Exec VP Fin

Desjardins Securities

2750-145 King St. West
Toronto, ON M5H 1J8
Tel 416-867-6000
Fax 416-867-8009
www.desjardinssecurities.com
Line: Operates a stock brokerage firm.
NAICS: 523120
#Emp: 75-99 (Tor)
#TorLoc: 5
Own: Private Company
Par: Desjardins Group (CDA)
Key: Marc Jobin, Ontario Reg Mgr

Deutsche Bank AG/ Canada Branch

4700-199 Bay St., Commerce Crt. West
P.O. Box 263
Toronto, ON M5L 1E9
Tel 416-682-8000
Fax 416-682-8383
www.db.com
NAICS: 522112
#Emp: 100-249 (Tor)
#TorLoc: 1
Own: Private Company
Par: Deutsche Bank AG (GER)
Key: Paul Jurist, Pres & CEO

Devil's Pulpit Golf Association

3035 Escarpment Sideroad
P.O. Box 68
Caledon, ON L7K 3L3
Tel 519-927-3001
Fax 519-927-3850
www.devilspulpit.com
NAICS: 713910
#Emp: 100-249 (Tor)
#TorLoc: 1
Own: Private Company
Key: Rae Armstrong, GM
Jerry Olijnyk, Cont

Devry Smith & Frank LLP

100-95 Barber Greene Rd.
Toronto, ON M3C 3E9
Tel 416-449-1400
Fax 416-449-7071
www.devrylaw.ca
Line: Operates a law firm.
NAICS: 541110
#Emp: 75-99 (Tor)
Own: Partnership
Key: George Frank, Partner

D & E Wood Industries Ltd.

6399 Netherhart Rd.
Mississauga, ON L5T 1B8
Tel 905-670-6617
Fax 905-670-2899
www.dewood.com
Line: Manufactures office furniture.
NAICS: 337213 337215
#Emp: 75-99 (Tor)
#TorLoc: 1
Own: Private Company
Key: Emil Shamash, Pres
George Guthrie, CFO

DGN Marketing Services Ltd.

1633 Meyerside Dr.
Mississauga, ON L5T 1B9
Tel 905-670-4070
Fax 905-670-5777
www.dgn-marketing.com
Line: Provides warehousing and
distribution services.
NAICS: 493110 488519
#Emp: 100-249 (Tor)
#TorLoc: 1
Own: Private Company
Par: Gerry Marsh Holdings Ltd. (CDA)
Key: Neil Phillips,
 Pres & Dir of Mktg & Sales
Gerry Nudds, CEO
John Nudds, COO
Paul Valtas, Dir of HR
Doug Smith, Dir of Fin
Blair Solonik, Warehouse Mgr
Allen George, IS Mgr

DHL Express (Canada), Ltd.

200-201 Westcreek Blvd.
Brampton, ON L6T 5S6
Tel 905-452-1260
Fax 905-452-8770
www.dhl.ca
Line: Provides courier services.
NAICS: 492110
#Emp: 1000-4999 (Tor)
#TorLoc: 5
Own: Private Company
Par: Deutsche Post AG (GER)

Key: Mathieu Floreani, Pres
Priya Patel, HR Generalist
Jan-Willem de Groot, CFO
Andrew Williams, VP Commercial

DHL Global Forwarding (Canada) Inc.

6200 Edwards Blvd.
Mississauga, ON L5T 2V7
Tel 289-562-6500
Fax 905-405-9301
www.dhl-dgf.com
Line: Provides international freight
forwarding by air, ocean, truck and
rail, and provides customs brokerage.
NAICS: 488519
#Emp: 250-499 (Tor)
#TorLoc: 2
Own: Private Company
Par: Deutsche Post World Net (DPWN)
(SWITZ)
Key: Donna Letterio, Country Mgr
Sara McLellan, Dir of HR
Nick Verrecchia, CFO

Diageo Canada Inc.

800-401 The West Mall
Toronto, ON M9C 5P8
Tel 416-626-2000
Fax 416-626-2688
www.diageo.com
Line: Manufactures, markets, and
distributes whiskies, gins, rums,
vodkas, liqueurs, wines, and beers.
NAICS: 312140 312130
#Emp: 100-249 (Tor)
#TorLoc: 2
Own: Private Company
Par: Diageo (UK)
Key: Debra Kelly-Ennis, Pres & CEO

Diamond and Schmitt Architects Inc.

300-384 Adelaide St. West
Toronto, ON M5V 1R7
Tel 416-862-8800
Fax 416-862-5508
www.dsai.ca
Line: Provides architectural, planning
and interior design services.
NAICS: 541410 541310
#Emp: 100-249 (Tor)
#TorLoc: 1
Own: Private Company
Key: Donald Schmitt, Principal
A.J. Diamond, Principal
Lilia Kiriakou, HR Generalist
Helen Kabriel, Comptr
Sonja Shuffler, IT Mgr
Robert Graham, Mktg Mgr

DiamondBack Golf Club

13300 Leslie St.
Richmond Hill, ON L4E 1A2
Tel 905-888-9612
Fax 905-888-9605
www.clublink.ca
NAICS: 713910
#Emp: 75-99 (Tor)
#TorLoc: 1
Own: Private Company
Par: ClubLink Corp. (CDA)
Key: Brad Dove, Dir of Golf

Dickinson Wright LLP

Ernst & Young Tower, TD Centre
222 Bay St., 18 Fl., P.O. Box 124
Toronto, ON M5K 1H1
Tel 416-777-0101
Fax 416-865-1398
www.dickinsonwright.ca
Line: Operates a law firm.
NAICS: 541110
#Emp: 75-99 (Tor)
#TorLoc: 1
Own: Private Company
Key: Eric Kay, Partner
Janice Feheley, Office Admr
Scott Janssen, Cont

Dicom Express

300 Biscayne Cres.
Brampton, ON L6W 4S1
Tel 905-457-7757
Fax 905-457-0153
www.dicomexpress.com
Line: Provides courier services.
NAICS: 492110
#Emp: 100-249 (Tor)
#TorLoc: 1
Own: Private Company
Key: Rick Barnes, VP
Jason Kirk, Branch Mgr
Lorna Rose, HR Dir

Di Crete Construction Ltd.

71 Creditstone Rd.
Concord, ON L4K 1N3
Tel 905-669-9595
Fax 905-669-9164
Line: Provides curb and sidewalk
contracting services.
NAICS: 231310 231210
#Emp: 100-249 (Tor)
#TorLoc: 1
Own: Private Company
Key: Joe DiGravino, Pres
Angelo DiGravino, GM

Diebold Company of Canada Ltd.

6630 Campobello Rd.
Mississauga, ON L5N 2L8
Tel 905-817-7600
Fax 905-813-7567
www.diebold.com
Line: Provides business sales and support for electronic security products and automatic bank machines.
NAICS: 561621
#Emp: 100-249 (Tor)
#TorLoc: 1
Own: Private Company
Par: Diebold Inc. (US)
Key: Thom Zaugg, Mng Dir
Jan Comin, Dir of HR
Mike Kopoulos, Dir of Fin & Admin
Peter Thomas, Dir of Sales

Digi Canada Inc.

87 Moyal Crt.
Concord, ON L4K 4R8
Tel 905-738-8333
Fax 905-879-4008
www.digicanada.ca
Line: Sells and services digital scales, food processing equipment, smallwares and related products.
NAICS: 811210
#Emp: 75-99 (Tor)
Own: Private Company
Par: Teroaka (JAPAN)
Key: Prashant Parekh, Pres
Deanna Del Col, HR Generalist

Digital Cement Inc.

100 Liberty St.
Toronto, ON M6K 3L7
Tel 416-537-3237
Fax 416-537-9899
www.digitalcement.com
Line: Operates a marketing firm.
NAICS: 541619
#Emp: 100-249 (Tor)
#TorLoc: 1
Own: Private Company
Par: Pitney Bowes Company (US)
Key: Sharad Verma, Pres
Lysian Hoffshmidt, HR Mgr

Digital Security Controls Ltd.

3301 Langstaff Rd.
Concord, ON L4K 4L2
Tel 905-760-3000
Fax 905-760-3004
www.dsc.com
AKA: DSC
Line: Manufactures specialty systems and alarms for commercial and residential use.
NAICS: 561621
#Emp: 1000-4999 (Tor)
#TorLoc: 3
Own: Private Company
Par: Tyco Safety Products (US)
Key: Mark Vandover, Pres, Tyco
Glen Brislan, Dir of Strategic Ops

Dimpflmeier Bakery Ltd.

26 Advance Rd.
Toronto, ON M8Z 2T4
Tel 416-239-3031
Fax 416-239-5370
www.dimpflmeierbakery.com
NAICS: 311814
#Emp: 250-499 (Tor)
#TorLoc: 1
Own: Private Company
Key: Susan Dimpflmeier, Pres
Carol Meissner, HR Mgr

Direct Energy Marketing Ltd.

100-2225 Sheppard Ave. East.
Toronto, ON M2J 5C2
Tel 416-758-8700
www.directenergy.com
AKA: Direct Energy
Line: Provides gas, electricity and related energy services.
NAICS: 221210
#Emp: 1000-4999 (Tor)
#TorLoc: 6
Own: Private Company
Par: Centrica plc (UK)
Key: Chris Weston, Pres & CEO
James Spence, CFO
Kumud Kalia, CIO
Andrew Reaney, Chief Mktg Officer

Direct Plastics Ltd.

20 Stewart Crt.
Orangeville, ON L9W 3Z9
Tel 519-942-8511
Fax 519-942-3979
www.directplasticsgroup.com
Line: Produces plastic bags and film.
NAICS: 326111
#Emp: 75-99 (Tor)
#TorLoc: 1

Own: Private Company
Par: Clondalkin Group (UK)
Key: Michael Vidler, Sr VP & GM
Bernd Klarholz, COO
Susan Zylski, Cont
Kirk Stover, VP Mktg & Sales

Discovery Ford Sales Limited

850 Brant St.
Burlington, ON L7R 2J5
Tel 905-632-8696
Fax 905-632-0914
www.discoveryford.com
NAICS: 441110 441120
#Emp: 100-249 (Tor)
#TorLoc: 2
Own: Private Company
Key: Allan Pearson, Pres
Ian Thomas, Sales Mgr

Distinctive Designs Furniture Inc.

600 Clayson Rd.
Toronto, ON M9M 2H2
Tel 416-740-7773
Fax 416-740-7776
www.distinctivedesignsfurniture.com
AKA: Kroehler Furniture Inc.
Line: Manufactures household leather and fabric furniture.
NAICS: 337121
#Emp: 100-249 (Tor)
#TorLoc: 1
Own: Private Company
Key: Alan Kornblum, Pres & CEO
Jim McAloney, VP Ops
Sue Silvestri, Payroll Admr
Eugene Gorgichuk, VP Sales

Diversey Inc.

2401 Bristol Circ.
Oakville, ON L6H 6P1
Tel 905-829-1200
Fax 905-829-1218
www.diversey.com
Line: Manufactures cleaning and hygiene solutions.
NAICS: 325181 325610
#Emp: 100-249 (Tor)
#TorLoc: 1
Own: Private Company
Key: Domenic Rapini, Reg Pres
Tracey Healey, Dir of HR
Jayne Brown, Dir of Fin

Dixie Electric Ltd.

517 Basaltic Rd.
Concord, ON L4K 4W8
Tel 905-879-0533
Fax 905-879-0532
www.dixie-electric.com
Line: Manufactures automotive
alternators and starters.
NAICS: 336320
#Emp: 100-249 (Tor)
#TorLoc: 1
Own: Private Company
Key: Angelo Bucciol, Pres
Neeraj Gopi, Plant Mgr
Daniela Ringhofer, HR Mgr
Jill Comm, Corp Fin & Acctng Mgr
Robert Sinclair, Cdn Sales Mgr

Dixon Hall

58 Sumach St.
Toronto, ON M5A 3J7
Tel 416-863-0499
Fax 416-863-9981
www.dixonhall.on.ca
NAICS: 813310
#Emp: 250-499 (Tor)
Own: Not-for-profit
Key: Kate Stark, Exec Dir
Tom Lewis, Dir of Fin & Supports
Lynn Cullaton,
    Dir of Strategic Initiatives

D-Link Canada Inc.

2525 Meadowvale Blvd.
Mississauga, ON L5N 5S2
Tel 905-829-5033
Fax 905-829-5223
www.dlink.ca
AKA: D-Link Networks
Line: Designs, manufactures and
markets advanced networking,
broadband, digital, voice and data
communications solutions.
NAICS: 541510
#Emp: 75-99 (Tor)
#TorLoc: 3
Own: Private Company
Par: D-Link Corp (TWN)
Key: Dominic Chan, GM
Shirley Chen, Cont
Junie Wong, SCM Mgr
Lou Reda, Dir of Retail Sales
Pete Marino, Mktg Mgr

DMTI Spatial Inc.

625 Cochrane Dr., 3rd Fl.
Markham, ON L3R 9R9
Tel 905-948-2000
Fax 905-948-9404
www.dmtispatial.com
Line: Delivers content and technology
solutions to help customers derive
measurable business value from
location intelligence.
NAICS: 541510
#Emp: 75-99 (Tor)
Own: Private Company
Key: John Fisher, Chmn & CEO
Glenor Pitters, COO
Christina Kwan, Cont
Eugene Khaitov, IT Mgr
Kristina Cleary, VP Mktg

Doellken-Woodtape Ltd.

230 Orenda Rd.
Brampton, ON L6T 1E9
Tel 905-673-5156
Fax 905-673-9372
www.doellken-woodtape.com
Line: Manufactures and supplies
polymer edge banding, extruded
profiles and related products.
NAICS: 326130
#Emp: 100-249 (Tor)
#TorLoc: 1
Own: Private Company
Par: Surteco (GER)
Key: Peter Schulte, CEO
Jurgen Krupp, COO
Gene Dera, VP Sales
Markus Raves, Dir of Mktg,
    Sales & Support Services

Dollar Thrifty Automotive Group Canada Inc.

6050 Indian Line
Mississauga, ON L4V 1G5
Tel 905-612-1881
Fax 905-612-1893
www.dtag.com
AKA: Thrifty Car Rental; Dollar Rent-
A-Car
Line: Operates a car rental franchisor
and car rental agency.
NAICS: 532111 532112
#Emp: 100-249 (Tor)
#TorLoc: 17
Own: Public Company
Par: Dollar Thrifty Automotive Group,
Inc. (US)
Key: Joseph Adamo, Pres
Ross Lancaster, VP Corp Ops & Fleet
Michelle Rowland, Sr Mgr of HR
Cecille Atienza, Dir of Fin
Susan Wesenhagen, Dir of Sales & Mktg

Dominion Citrus Income Fund

51 Kelfield St.
Toronto, ON M9W 5A3
Tel 416-242-8341
Fax 416-242-4591
www.dominioncitrus.com
AKA: Country Fresh Packaging
Line: Processes, packages, and
wholesales fruit and vegetables.
NAICS: 413150
#Emp: 100-249 (Tor)
#TorLoc: 4
Own: Public Company
Key: Jason Fielden, Pres & CEO
Winston Ash, Chmn
Susan Bricks, VP

Dominion Colour Corp.

515 Consumers Rd., 7th Fl.
Toronto, ON M2J 4Z2
Tel 416-791-4200
Fax 416-497-5198
www.dcc.ca
AKA: DCC
Line: Manufactures organic and
inorganic colour pigments.
NAICS: 325130 325190
#Emp: 100-249 (Tor)
#TorLoc: 3
Own: Private Company
Key: Mike Klein, Pres

The Dominion Group Inc.

580 Secretariat Crt.
Mississauga, ON L5S 2A5
Tel 905-564-2460
Fax 905-564-2470
www.dominiongroupinc.com
AKA: DGI
Line: Provides packaging services and
logistics for the automotive industry.
NAICS: 561910
#Emp: 100-249 (Tor)
#TorLoc: 1
Own: Private Company
Par: The Dominion Group Inc. (CDA)
Key: Dario DiCenso, Pres
Paul Wilkes, VP Ops

The Dominion of Canada General Insurance Co.

165 University Ave.
Toronto, ON M5H 3B9
Tel 416-362-7231
Fax 416-362-9918
www.thedominion.ca
Line: Provides personal and commercial property and casualty insurance.
NAICS: 524121
#Emp: 500-999 (Tor)
#TorLoc: 4
Own: Private Company
Par: E-L Financial Corporation Ltd. (CDA)
Key: George L. Cooke, Pres & CEO
Shelly Rae, VP HR
R. Douglas Hogan, Sr VP & CFO
Janet Babcock, VP & CIO
Alan J. Hanks, VP Field Ops

Dominion Warehousing & Distribution Services Ltd.

1920 Albion Rd.
Toronto, ON M9W 5T2
Tel 416-744-2438
Fax 416-744-0569
www.dominionwarehousing.com
Line: Provides warehousing and distribution services.
NAICS: 493190
#Emp: 75-99 (Tor)
#TorLoc: 4
Own: Private Company
Key: Robert Dineen, Pres
Bill Hall, Dir of IT
Bob Rose, VP Sales & Mktg

Dom-Meridian Construction Ltd.

10-1021 Meyerside Dr.
Mississauga, ON L5T 1J6
Tel 905-564-5594
Fax 905-564-5595
Line: Provides site development services for sewer, water and road construction.
NAICS: 231320
#Emp: 75-99 (Tor)
#TorLoc: 1
Own: Private Company
Key: Archie Iacobucci, Pres
Frank Salituro, Commun Mgr

Domtar Inc.

395 de Maisonneuve Blvd. West
Montreal, PQ H3A 1L6
Tel 514-848-5555
Fax 514-848-5393
www.domtar.com
Line: Manufactures and markets wood, pulp, paper and packaging products.
NAICS: 322121 322211
#Emp: 500-999 (Tor)
#TorLoc: 1
Own: Public Company
Key: John D. Williams, Pres & CEO
Michael Edwards, VP Manuf
Melissa Anderson, Sr VP HR
Daniel Buron, Sr VP & CFO
Michelle Meunier, Sr VP IT
Patrick Loulou, Sr VP, Corp Dev
Richard L. Thomas, Sr VP Sales & Mktg

Donalda Club

12 Bushbury Dr.
Toronto, ON M3A 2Z7
Tel 416-447-5575
Fax 416-447-7805
www.donaldaclub.ca
Line: Operates a private multi-activity golf and country club.
NAICS: 713910
#Emp: 100-249 (Tor)
#TorLoc: 1
Own: Private Company
Key: Glen Stevens, Pres
Charles Powell, GM
Mike Mullen, Cont
Daniel Cameirao, Clubhouse Mgr

Donald Construction Ltd.

333 Humberline Dr.
Toronto, ON M9W 5X3
Tel 416-675-4134
Fax 416-675-9874
Line: Operates a construction company.
NAICS: 232220 232110
#Emp: 100-249 (Tor)
#TorLoc: 1
Own: Private Company
Key: Sergio Manarin, Pres

Don Anderson Haulage Ltd.

36 Gordon Collins Dr.
Gormley, ON L0H 1G0
Tel 416-798-7737
Fax 905-927-2701
www.andersonhaulage.com
Line: Provides haulage services.
NAICS: 484110
#Emp: 75-99 (Tor)
#TorLoc: 1
Own: Private Company
Key: Michael Anderson, Pres

Donato Salon & Spa

100 City Centre Dr.
Mississauga, ON L5B 2C9
Tel 905-566-5900
Fax 905-566-8985
www.donato.ca
Line: Operates a hair salon and spa.
NAICS: 812190 812116
#Emp: 75-99 (Tor)
#TorLoc: 3
Own: Private Company
Key: John Donato, Pres & Owner

Donlee Precision

A Div. of General Donlee Ltd.
9 Fenmar Dr.
Toronto, ON M9L 1L5
Tel 416-743-4417
Fax 416-746-8998
www.donleeprecision.com
Line: Manufactures aircraft shafts.
NAICS: 336410
#Emp: 75-99 (Tor)
#TorLoc: 1
Own: Public Company
Key: Mike Snow, Pres & CEO
Rose Greco, Personnel Admr
Gerry Thain, Cont
Chris Sanvido, Purch Agent
Tony Audia, Sales Mgr

Don Park LP

842 York Mills Rd.
Toronto, ON M3B 3A8
Tel 416-449-7275
Fax 416-449-2614
www.donpark.com
AKA: Don Park Fire Protection Systems
Line: Manufactures sheet metal for residential and commercial air distribution products, gas venting systems and chimney liner components.
NAICS: 416210
#Emp: 250-499 (Tor)
#TorLoc: 13
Own: Partnership
Key: Peter Olierook, Pres & CEO
David Bergeron, VP Ops
Sandra Nakalamich, HR Mgr
Brian Damianidis, VP & CFO

Don Valley North Automotive Inc.

3120 Steeles Ave. East
Markham, ON L3R 1G9
Tel 905-475-0722
Fax 905-475-8044
www.dvnag.com
AKA: Don Valley North Toyota; Don
Valley North Lexus; Markville Toyota;
Lexus of Richmond Hill; Gormley
Automotive Centre; Don Valley North
Automotive Group; Don Valley North
Hyundai
Line: Retails new and used vehicles.
NAICS: 441110 441120
#Emp: 500-999 (Tor)
#TorLoc: 6
Own: Private Company
Par: Yokohama Toyopet (JAPAN)
Key: Dave Lalonde, VP Ops
Chris Betty, HR Mgr
Grant DeMarsh, GM, Lexus
Amin Tejani, GM, Toyota

Donway Ford Sales Ltd.

1975 Eglinton Ave. East
Toronto, ON M1L 2N1
Tel 416-751-2200
Fax 416-751-9301
www.donwayford.com
AKA: Donway Ford Lincoln Sales
Line: Offers sales, leasing, and
servicing of motor vehicles.
NAICS: 441110 441120
#Emp: 75-99 (Tor)
#TorLoc: 1
Own: Private Company
Par: Metropolitan Motors Ltd. (CDA)
Key: Paul Lenneard, Pres
Gail Papadimitriou, Office Mgr
Lynda Kelly, Secy-Treas
Terry Fisher, Gen Sales Mgr

Dorothea Knitting Mills Ltd.

20 Research Rd.
Toronto, ON M4G 2G6
Tel 416-421-3773
Fax 416-421-9084
www.parkhurst.ca
AKA: Cotton Country; Parkhurst;
steven b.
Line: Manufactures knitwear, sweaters,
headwear, and accessories.
NAICS: 315190
#Emp: 100-249 (Tor)
#TorLoc: 2
Own: Private Company
Key: Steven Borsook, Pres
Beryl Borsook, Chmn & CEO
Sedat Ethem, Production Dir
Steve Himmelman, Payroll & HR Mgr
Philippa Madigan, Exec VP.

Dortec Industries

581 Newpark Blvd.
P.O. Box 357
Newmarket, ON L3Y 4X7
Tel 905-853-1800
Fax 905-853-9320
www.dortec.com
Line: Manufactures automotive parts.
NAICS: 336390
#Emp: 1000-4999 (Tor)
#TorLoc: 1
Own: Private Company
Par: Magna International Inc. (CDA)
Key: John O'Hara, GM

Dorvict Resource & Consulting Centre Inc.

380 Chesswood Dr.
Toronto, ON M3J 2W6
Tel 416-661-1740
Fax 416-661-3855
www.dorvict.com
AKA: Dorvict Home & Health Care
Services
Line: Provides training and home care
services.
NAICS: 621610
#Emp: 100-249 (Tor)
#TorLoc: 2
Own: Private Company
Key: Dayo Idowu, Exec Dir
Bukola Farinde, Branch Mgr
Sonia Brown, Service Support Coord
Valerie Duffie, Service Support Coord

Doubletree by Hilton - Toronto Airport

655 Dixon Rd.
Toronto, ON M9W 1J3
Tel 416-244-1711
Fax 416-244-8031
doubletree.hilton.com
Line: Provides hospitality services.
NAICS: 721111
#Emp: 250-499 (Tor)
#TorLoc: 1
Own: Private Company
Key: Daniel Blachut, GM
Raymond Yip, Dir of Fin

Dove Foods Limited

8-110 Pony Dr.
Newmarket, ON L3Y 7B6
Tel 905-953-9434
Fax 905-953-9435
www.dovefoods.com
Line: Operates a restaurant chain.
NAICS: 722210
#Emp: 100-249 (Tor)
Own: Private Company
Key: Evan Gogou, Pres
Margaret Organ, GM

Dover Industries Ltd.

1060 Fountain St. North
Cambridge, ON N3E 0A1
Tel 519-650-6400
Fax 519-650-6429
www.dovergrp.com
AKA: P&H Milling Group
Line: Manufactures food and packaging
products.
NAICS: 311211 311821
#Emp: 250-499 (Tor)
#TorLoc: 7
Own: Public Company
Key: Howard Rowley, Pres & CEO
Peter Downe, VP HR
Jerry Dmetrichuk, IT Mgr

Downsview Chrysler Plymouth (1964) Ltd.

199 Rimrock Rd.
Toronto, ON M3J 3C6
Tel 416-635-1660
Fax 416-635-1797
www.downsviewchryslerdealer.com
Line: Sells new and used automobiles.
NAICS: 441110 441120
#Emp: 100-249 (Tor)
#TorLoc: 1
Own: Private Company
Key: Peter Kepecs, Pres
Carlos Baptista, VP
Dave McKerracher, Cont

Downsview Drywall Contracting

160 Bass Pro Mills Dr.
Concord, ON L4K 0A7
Tel 905-660-0048
Fax 905-738-3864
www.downsviewdrywall.com
Line: Provides drywall and acoustic
installation services.
NAICS: 232410
#Emp: 100-249 (Tor)
#TorLoc: 1
Own: Private Company
Key: Sam Sgotto, Pres
Eugene Conte, GM

Downsview Woodworking Ltd.

2635 Rena Rd.
Mississauga, ON L4T 1G6
Tel 905-677-9354
Fax 905-677-5776
www.downsviewkitchens.com
AKA: Downsview Kitchens
NAICS: 337110
#Emp: 250-499 (Tor)
#TorLoc: 2
Own: Private Company
Key: Mike D'Uva, Pres

Downtown Fine Cars Inc.

265 Front St. East
Toronto, ON M5A 1G1
Tel 416-603-9988
Fax 416-603-8899
www.downtownfinecars.com
AKA: Downtown Porsche; Downtown
Infiniti; Audi Uptown
Line: Sells new and used automobiles
and operates a full service centre.
NAICS: 441110 441120
#Emp: 100-249 (Tor)
#TorLoc: 2
Own: Private Company
Key: Helen Ching-Kircher, Pres & CEO
Peter A. Kircher, Dealer Principal
Constantine Siomos, VP Ops
Karen Cummings, VP Fin & Cont

Draft FCB Canada

300-245 Eglinton Ave. East
Toronto, ON M4P 3C2
Tel 416-483-3600
Fax 416-489-8782
www.draftfcb.com
AKA: Foote, Cone & Belding Canada
Ltd.
Line: Operates advertising agency.
NAICS: 541810
#Emp: 250-499 (Tor)
#TorLoc: 1
Own: Public Company
Par: The Interpublic Group of
Companies (US)
Key: John Boniface, COO
Paul Mead, Pres
Robin Heisey, Chief Creative Officer
Anne-Marie Tseretopoulos, HR Dir
Mike Panov, VP Fin

Drakkar Human Resources Ontario Inc.

1131 Derry Rd. East
Mississauga, ON L5T 1P3
Tel 905-795-1397
Fax 905-795-1391
www.drakkar.ca
Line: Provides human resources
consulting and placement services.
NAICS: 541612 561310
#Emp: 250-499 (Tor)
#TorLoc: 2
Own: Private Company
Par: Drakkar Human Resources Inc.
(CDA)
Key: Michel Blaquiere, Pres & COO
Roger Roy, Mng Dir, Ontario

Dranco Construction Ltd.

1919 Albion Rd.
Toronto, ON M9W 6J9
Tel 416-675-2682
Fax 416-674-5788
www.dranco.com
Line: Operates a construction company
specializing in sewer and drain
installation.
NAICS: 231320
#Emp: 100-249 (Tor)
#TorLoc: 1
Own: Private Company
Key: Realdo Di Donato, Pres
Nino D'Aversa, Chief Estimator
Matthew Di Donato, Estimator

Drive Products

1665 Shawson Dr.
Mississauga, ON L4W 1T7
Tel 905-564-5800
Fax 905-564-5799
www.driveproducts.com
Line: Manufactures and wholesales
drive shafts, hydraulic components,
power take-off and snow removal
equipment.
NAICS: 336350 333416
#Emp: 100-249 (Tor)
#TorLoc: 3
Own: Private Company
Key: Russ Bilyk, Pres
Greg Edmonds, CEO
Brad Fleming, VP Eastern Canada
Riz Premji, Dir of HR & Compliance
Chris Boudreau, CFO

Dr. Oetker Canada Ltd.

2229 Drew Rd.
Mississauga, ON L5S 1E5
Tel 905-678-1311
Fax 905-678-9334
www.oetker.ca
AKA: Dr. Oetker Ltd.
Line: Manufactures and distributes
food products.
NAICS: 311990
#Emp: 100-249 (Tor)
#TorLoc: 1
Own: Private Company
Par: Dr. Oetker International
Beteilgungs GmbH (GER)
Key: Christian von Twickel,
Exec VP Fin & Admin
Cecile Van Zandijcke,
Exec VP Sales & Mktg

The Drs. Paul & John Rekai Centre

345 Sherbourne St.
Toronto, ON M5A 2S3
Tel 416-964-1599
Fax 416-964-3907
www.rekaicentre.com
AKA: Wellesley Central Place
Line: Operates fully accredited nursing
home.
NAICS: 621110 623110
#Emp: 250-499 (Tor)
#TorLoc: 2
Own: Not-for-profit
Key: David Marriott, Exec Dir
Mary Hoare, CEO

Druxy's Inc.

802-1200 Eglinton Ave. East
Toronto, ON M3C 1H9
Tel 416-385-9500
Fax 416-385-9501
www.druxys.com
AKA: Druxy's Famous Deli Sandwiches
Line: Operates and franchises
delicatessen restaurants specializing
in sandwiches, salads, coffees, bagels
and soups.
NAICS: 722210 722110
#Emp: 250-499 (Tor)
#TorLoc: 54
Own: Private Company
Key: Bruce Druxerman, Pres
David Fine, Dir of Ops
Harold Druxerman, VP Fin & Admin
Peter Druxerman, VP Mktg

DST Output Inc.

2637 14th Ave.
Markham, ON L3R 0H9
Tel 905-470-2000
Fax 905-470-9233
www.dstoutput.ca
Line: Provides high-impact printing
of statements and invoices as well as
document scanning, viewing and work
flow technologies.
NAICS: 514210
#Emp: 100-249 (Tor)
#TorLoc: 1
Own: Public Company
Par: DST Output (US)
Key: Steve Towle, Pres
Joseph D. Faria, Exec VP
Wendy Brown, HR
Robert S. Wylie, Cont
L. Andrew Idzior, Exec VP Sales & Mktg

DTZ Barnicke

2500-401 Bay St.
Toronto, ON M5H 2Y4
Tel 416-863-1215
Fax 416-863-9855
www.dtzbarnicke.com
Line: Provides transaction and
investment advice in office, industrial,
retail, hospitality and corporate
services.
NAICS: 531310
#Emp: 100-249 (Tor)
#TorLoc: 4
Own: Private Company
Key: Thomas McCarthy, Chmn & CEO
Laurie McGee, CFO & CAO
Suneet Arora, IT Mgr
Ted Bloom, Sr Mgr

DUCA Financial Services Credit Union Ltd.

5290 Yonge St.
Toronto, ON M2N 5P9
Tel 416-223-8502
Fax 416-223-2575
www.duca.com
Line: Provides financial services to its
members.
NAICS: 522130
#Emp: 100-249 (Tor)
#TorLoc: 12
Own: Private Company
Key: Jack Vanderkooy, Pres & CEO
Rob Cook, VP Ops
Evert Akkerman, HR Mgr
Michael Creasor, VP Fin
Ed Sweet, Sr VP Audit & IT
Arnold Denton, Sr VP Credit
Chris Zegers, Mktg Mgr

Dufferin Construction Co.

A Div. of St. Lawrence Cement Inc.
200-690 Dorval Dr.
Oakville, ON L6K 3W7
Tel 905-842-2741
Fax 905-842-9278
www.dufferinconstruction.com
Line: Provides heavy construction
services.
NAICS: 231310 231410
#Emp: 500-999 (Tor)
#TorLoc: 1
Own: Public Company
Par: Holderbank Financiere Glaris Ltd.
(SWITZ)
Key: Wayne Lazzarato, VP
Eddy Marin, District Mgr, Central Reg
Fred Stremble, Cont
Andrew Jones, IT Mgr

The Dufferin-Peel Catholic District School Board

40 Matheson Blvd. West
Mississauga, ON L5R 1C5
Tel 905-890-1221
Fax 905-890-7595
www.dpcdsb.org
NAICS: 611110
#Emp: 10000+ (Tor)
#TorLoc: 145
Own: Government
Key: John B. Kostoff, Dir of Education
Anna Abbruscato, Chair
Beth Bjarnason, Supt of Planning & Ops
Nick Milanetti, Supt of HR
John Hrajnik,
    Assoc Dir Corp Services & CFO
Donna Reid, Purch Mgr
John Steele, CIO
Bruce Campbell, GM of Commun

Dufflet Pastries

A Div. of Best Baking Inc.
166 Norseman St.
Toronto, ON M8Z 2R4
Tel 416-536-1330
Fax 416-538-2366
www.dufflet.com
Line: Prepares and distributes cakes
and pastries for wholesale and retail
trade.
NAICS: 311814
#Emp: 100-249 (Tor)
#TorLoc: 4
Own: Private Company
Key: Daniele Bertrand, Pres
Dufflet Rosenberg, CEO
Martin Desroches, Production Mgr
Karla Huckvale, Office Mgr
Karin Jensen, Mktg Mgr

Dundas Data Visualization

500-250 Ferrand Dr.
Toronto, ON M3C 3G8
Tel 416-467-5100
Fax 416-422-4801
www.dundas.com
Line: Provides data visualization and
dashboarding solutions.
NAICS: 541510
#Emp: 75-99 (Tor)
Own: Private Company
Key: David Cunningham, CEO

Dundee Corporation

1 Adelaide St. East, 28th Fl.
Toronto, ON M5H 4A9
Tel 416-863-6990
Fax 416-363-4536
www.dundeebancorp.com
Line: Operates a wealth management
company.
NAICS: 523120
#Emp: 500-999 (Tor)
#TorLoc: 1
Own: Private Company
Key: David Goodman,
    Pres & CEO, Dundee Wealth
Ned Goodman, Chmn & CEO
Jean-Francois Thibault, Exec VP
Joanne Ferstman, Vice Chair,
    Head of Capital Markets

Dundee Realty Management Corp.

1600-30 Adelaide St. East
Toronto, ON M5C 3H1
Tel 416-365-3535
Fax 416-365-6565
www.dundeerealty.com
Line: Owns, manages, and develops
commercial real estate.
NAICS: 531120
#Emp: 100-249 (Tor)
#TorLoc: 2
Own: Public Company
Par: Dundee Corporation (CDA)
Key: Michael Cooper, Pres & CEO
Michael Knowlton, COO
Catherine Mammoliti, HR Generalist
Carol Webb, VP Commun

Dundee Wealth

1 Adelaide St. East, 27th Fl.
Toronto, ON M5C 2V9
Tel 416-350-3250
Fax 416-363-5850
www.dundeewealth.com
AKA: Dundee Securities; Dynamic
Mutual Funds
Line: Offers mutual fund investment
services.
NAICS: 523920
#Emp: 1000-4999 (Tor)
#TorLoc: 1
Own: Public Company
Par: Dundee Wealth (CDA)
Key: David Goodman, Pres & CEO
Jean Francois Thibault, Exec VP
John Pereira, Exec VP & CFO
To Anh Tran, Sr VP Business
    Transformation & Tech
Jordy Chilcott, Exec VP
Robert Pattillo,
    Exec VP, Mktg & Commun

Duplium

35 Minthorn Blvd.
Thornhill, ON L3T 7N5
Tel 905-709-9930
Fax 905-709-9439
www.duplium.com
Line: Provides replication of optical
and audio media as well as global
fulfillment services.
NAICS: 334610
#Emp: 100-249 (Tor)
#TorLoc: 1
Own: Private Company
Key: Robert Hashimoto, Pres
Kalman Weber, VP Ops

Durapaint Industries Ltd.

1-2 247 Finchdene Sq.
Toronto, ON M1X 1B9
Tel 416-754-3664
Fax 416-754-4911
www.durapaint.net
Line: Offers architectural paint
finishing.
NAICS: 332810
#Emp: 75-99 (Tor)
#TorLoc: 1
Own: Private Company
Key: Elio Zarlenga, Pres
Domenic Zarlenga, VP
Olga Janecek, Cont

Durham Catholic District School Board

650 Rossland Rd. West
Oshawa, ON L1J 7C4
Tel 905-576-6150
Fax 905-576-0953
www.dcdsb.ca
Line: Manages Catholic schools in the
Durham region.
NAICS: 611110
#Emp: 1000-4999 (Tor)
#TorLoc: 46
Own: Government
Key: Paul Pulla, Dir of Education
Michael Gray,
    Asst Supt HR & Admin Services
Roy Hart, CIO

Durham Children's Aid Society

1320 Airport Blvd.
Oshawa, ON L1H 7K4
Tel 905-433-1551
Fax 905-433-0603
www.durhamcas.ca
Line: Provides child welfare services.
NAICS: 813310
#Emp: 250-499 (Tor)
#TorLoc: 1
Own: Not-for-profit
Key: Wanda Secord, Exec Dir
Brian Prousky, Dir of Services
Marna Shecter, Dir of HR
Martin Smith, Dir of Fin & Admin

Durham College

2000 Simcoe St. North
P.O. Box 385
Oshawa, ON L1H 7K4
Tel 905-721-2000
Fax 905-721-3113
www.durhamcollege.ca
Line: Provides post-secondary
education, adult education and
training, technical trades and skills
training, management, productivity
improvement and technology training,
and training consulting.
NAICS: 611210
#Emp: 500-999 (Tor)
#TorLoc: 7
Own: Government
Key: Don Lovisa, Pres
Judith Robinson, VP Academic
Ken Robb, VP HR
Nevzat Gurmen, VP Fin
Donna McFarlane, VP Commun & Mktg

Durham District School Board

400 Taunton Rd. East
Whitby, ON L1R 2K6
Tel 905-666-5500
Fax 905-666-6010
www.durham.edu.on.ca
NAICS: 611110
#Emp: 5000-9999 (Tor)
#TorLoc: 130
Own: Government
Key: Martyn Beckett, Dir of Education
Mark Joel, Supt of Education Ops
Lou Vavougios, Supt of Education
    Employee Relns
Edward Hodgins, Supt of Education
    Business & Treas
Dennis Homeniuk, Mgr of Purch
Andrea Pidwerbecki, Commun Mgr

Durham Regional Police Service

*A Div. of Regional
Municipality of Durham*
605 Rossland Rd. East
Box 911
Whitby, ON L1N 0B8
Tel 905-579-1520
Fax 905-721-4218
www.drps.ca
NAICS: 913130
#Emp: 1000-4999 (Tor)
#TorLoc: 5
Own: Government
Key: Mike Ewles, Chief of Police
Sherry Whiteway, Deputy Chief Ops

Durham Region Media Group

A Div. of Metroland Media Group Ltd.
865 Farewell St.
P.O. Box 481
Oshawa, ON L1H 7L5
Tel 905-579-4400
Fax 905-579-7809
www.durhamregion.com
AKA: Ajax-Pickering News Advertiser;
Oshawa This Week; Whitby This Week;
Clarington This Week; Port Perry Star;
Uxbridge Times Journal
NAICS: 511110
#Emp: 250-499 (Tor)
#TorLoc: 7
Own: Private Company
Par: Torstar Corp. (CDA)
Key: Tim Whittaker,
    Sr VP & Reg Publisher
Joanne Burghardt, Editor-in-Chief
Lillian Hook, Office Mgr
Fred Eismont, Dir of Advertising

Durham Region Transit

605 Rossland Rd. East
P.O. Box 623
Whitby, ON L1N 6A3
Tel 905-668-7711
www.durhamregiontransit.com
Line: Operates public transit service in Durham Region.
NAICS: 485110 485990
#Emp: 250-499 (Tor)
#TorLoc: 1
Own: Government
Key: Ted Galinis, GM

Duron Ontario Ltd.

1860 Shawson Dr.
Mississauga, ON L4W 1R7
Tel 905-670-1998
Fax 905-670-4662
www.duron.ca
NAICS: 232920 324121
#Emp: 100-249 (Tor)
#TorLoc: 1
Own: Private Company
Key: John Schenk, Sr Partner & GM
George Kouros, Purch Agent

Dutton Brock LLP

1700-438 University Ave.
Toronto, ON M5G 2L9
Tel 416-593-4411
Fax 416-593-5922
www.duttonbrock.com
Line: Operates a law firm specializing in insurance and personal injury matters.
NAICS: 541110
#Emp: 75-99 (Tor)
#TorLoc: 2
Own: Private Company
Key: Paul Tushinski, Mng Partner

Duvet Comfort Inc.

130 Commander Blvd.
Toronto, ON M1S 3H7
Tel 416-754-1455
Fax 416-754-1717
Line: Manufactures clothing.
NAICS: 315229 315239
#Emp: 75-99 (Tor)
#TorLoc: 1
Own: Private Company
Par: Duvet Comfort Inc. (CDA)
Key: Johnny Yiu, Pres
Frankie Chu, VP
Allen Szeto, Cont

D & W Forwarders Inc.

81 Orenda Rd.
Brampton, ON L6W 1V7
Tel 905-459-3560
Fax 905-459-2156
Line: Provides trucking services.
NAICS: 484110 484121
#Emp: 100-249 (Tor)
#TorLoc: 1
Own: Private Company
Par: IKL (CDA)
Key: Bruce Teeter, Pres & Ops Mgr
Indra Sankar, Payroll Admr
Dean Seidel, Cont
Peter Keegstra, Maintenance Dir

Dyadem International Ltd.

401-155 Gordon Baker Rd.
Toronto, ON M2H 3N5
Tel 416-649-9200
Fax 416-649-9250
www.dyadem.com
Line: Provides software and services that manage the risks to people and products in the design and manufacturing processes.
NAICS: 541510
#Emp: 100-249 (Tor)
Own: Private Company
Key: Kevin North, Pres & CEO
Andrew Shannon, COO & CFO

Dynamex Canada Limited

6860 Rexwood Rd.
Mississauga, ON L4V 1L8
Tel 905-672-5555
Fax 905-672-7172
www.dynamex.com
Line: Provides courier services.
NAICS: 492110
#Emp: 500-999 (Tor)
#TorLoc: 6
Own: Public Company
Par: Dynamex Inc. (US)
Key: James Welch, Pres & CEO
Doris Oloton, VP HR
Ray E. Schmitz, CFO

Dynamic Details Canada Inc.

8150 Sheppard Ave. East
Toronto, ON M1B 5K2
Tel 416-283-4888
Fax 416-283-4439
www.ddiglobal.com
Line: Manufactures printed circuit board products.
NAICS: 541510
#Emp: 250-499 (Tor)
#TorLoc: 1
Own: Private Company

Par: Dynamic Details Inc. (US)
Key: John Pereira, VP Ops
Bonnie Fowle, HR Business Partner
Michael Cherrington,
Toronto Divisional Cont
Sahib Arafat, IT Admr

Dynamic Paint Products Inc.

7040 Financial Dr.
Mississauga, ON L5N 7H5
Tel 905-812-9319
Fax 905-812-9322
www.getpainting.com
AKA: Mumby & Associates Ltd.
Line: Distributes decorating products, paintware.
NAICS: 414390
#Emp: 75-99 (Tor)
#TorLoc: 1
Own: Private Company
Key: James Mumby, Pres
Paul Lobb, COO
Alistair McGowan, Purch Mgr
David Moon, IT Mgr
Pat Power, Dir of Mktg

Dynamic Tire Corp.

155 Delta Park Blvd.
Brampton, ON L6T 5M8
Tel 905-595-5558
Fax 905-595-0469
www.dynamictire.com
Line: Manufactures solid tires for the material handling industry.
NAICS: 326210
#Emp: 75-99 (Tor)
#TorLoc: 1
Own: Private Company
Key: Robert Sherkin, Pres & CEO
Radick Costa-Sarnicki, VP Fin
Renzo Castagna, Dir of Mktg

DYN Exports Inc.

40 Carl Hall Rd.
Toronto, ON M3K 2C1
Tel 416-398-3044
Fax 416-398-6927
Line: Exports recycling products.
NAICS: 453310
#Emp: 100-249 (Tor)
#TorLoc: 1
Own: Private Company
Key: Marc Nanthakumar, Pres
Judy Nanthakumar, VP
Bala Suppiramaniam, HR Mgr
Yvonne Thirumaran, GM

E1 Entertainment

1-70 Driver Rd.
Brampton, ON L6T 5V2
Tel 905-624-7337
Fax 905-463-9847
www.entertainmentonegroup.com
Line: Distributes video games.
NAICS: 414210
#Emp: 500-999 (Tor)
#TorLoc: 2
Own: Private Company
Key: Darren Throop, Pres & CEO
Nicole Gervasio, Dir of HR
Jim Hreljac, Sr VP Fin
Taylor Battye, Sr VP IS
Steve Miller, Sr VP Sales
Jody Sadofsky, Dir of Mktg

Eagle Ridge Golf Club

R.R. #4, 11742 Tenth Line
Georgetown, ON L7G 4S7
Tel 905-877-8468
Fax 905-877-0766
www.clublink.ca
NAICS: 713910
#Emp: 100-249 (Tor)
Own: Private Company
Par: ClubLink Corp. (CDA)
Key: Andrew Vento, Dir of Ops

Eastend Bindery Limited

1840 Birchmount Rd.
Toronto, ON M1P 2H7
Tel 416-321-2333
Fax 416-321-0650
www.eastendbindery.com
Line: Provides book binding services.
NAICS: 323119
#Emp: 75-99 (Tor)
#TorLoc: 1
Own: Private Company
Key: Ray Civello, Pres
George Civello, GM
Natalino Civello, Secy-Treas
Sam Civello, Sales Mgr

Eastern Construction Company Ltd.

1100-505 Consumers Rd.
Toronto, ON M2J 5G2
Tel 416-497-7110
Fax 416-497-7241
www.easternconstruction.com
Line: Provides construction services
including general contracting,
construction management and design/
build.
NAICS: 231220
#Emp: 100-249 (Tor)
#TorLoc: 8

Own: Private Company
Key: Frank DeCaria, Pres & CEO
Renato Tacconelli, VP Ops
Terry Doyle, Dir of HR
Ron J. Littlejohns, VP Fin
Dennis Thanasse,
   VP Contracts & Procurement
Lewis Mackay, IT Mgr
Gerry Harding, VP Business Dev

East Penn Power Battery Sales Ltd.

165 Harwood Ave. North
Ajax, ON L1Z 1L9
Tel 905-427-2718
Fax 905-427-0854
www.eastpenncanada.com
AKA: East Penn Canada
Line: Distributes lead acid batteries
for automotive and small engine,
commercial truck and equipment,
industrial motive power and UPS
standby systems.
NAICS: 418990
#Emp: 100-249 (Tor)
#TorLoc: 2
Own: Private Company
Par: East Penn Manufacturing, Inc.
(US)
Key: James Bouchard, Pres
Luc Theriault, Dir of Ops
Lisa Primeau, HR Mgr
Mike Wells, VP Fin
David Chiu, IS Mgr
Shaun Keogn, VP Business Dev
Lisa Dyble, Mktg Mgr

East Side Mario's

17175 Yonge St.
Newmarket, ON L3Y 5L8
Tel 905-830-6800
Fax 905-830-1312
www.eastsidemarios.com
AKA: Newmarco Foods Ltd.
Line: Operates a restaurant.
NAICS: 722110
#Emp: 75-99 (Tor)
#TorLoc: 2
Own: Private Company
Par: Prime Restaurants (CDA)
Key: Jeff Campbell, Owner

Easy Plastic Containers Ltd.

101 Jardin Dr.
Concord, ON L4K 1X6
Tel 905-669-4466
Fax 905-669-5635
www.easyplastics.com
Line: Manufactures plastic bottles.
NAICS: 326160

#Emp: 100-249 (Tor)
#TorLoc: 1
Own: Private Company
Key: Shirley Protopapas, Mgr & Cont

Eaton Electrical Group

5050 Mainway
Burlington, ON L7L 5Z1
Tel 905-333-6442
Fax 905-631-4248
www.eatoncanada.ca
Line: Manufactures electrical
distribution and control components
and assemblies.
NAICS: 335315
#Emp: 250-499 (Tor)
#TorLoc: 4
Own: Private Company
Par: Eaton Corporation (US)
Key: Steve Boccadoro, VP & GM
John Iannuzzi, Divisional HR Mgr

Echelon General Insurance Co.

300-2680 Matheson Blvd. East
Mississauga, ON L4W 0H5
Tel 905-214-7880
Fax 905-214-7881
www.echelon-insurance.ca
Line: Provides specialized insurance
products.
NAICS: 524210
#Emp: 75-99 (Tor)
#TorLoc: 1
Own: Public Company
Key: George Kalopsis, Pres & COO
Douglas McIntyre, Exec Chmn
Hemraj Singh, VP & CFO

Eckler Ltd.

900-110 Sheppard Ave. East
Toronto, ON M2N 7A3
Tel 416-429-3330
Fax 416-429-3794
www.eckler.ca
Line: Provides actuarial services.
NAICS: 541612
#Emp: 100-249 (Tor)
#TorLoc: 1
Own: Private Company
Key: Bill Weiland, Mng Partner
Barbara Larcina, CAO
Vivien Woo, Payroll & Benefits Mgr
Amar Sookram, Dir of IT

Eclipse Colour and Imaging Corp.

875 Laurentian Dr.
Burlington, ON L7N 3W7
Tel 905-634-1900
Fax 905-335-2453
www.eclipseimaging.ca
AKA: Eclipse Imaging
Line: Specializes in large format printing and digital imaging.
NAICS: 323115
#Emp: 75-99 (Tor)
#TorLoc: 1
Own: Private Company
Key: Ralph Misale, COO
Andrea Street, VP HR
Grant Malcolm, CFO
Kelly Caplan, VP Client Services

Ecolab Co.

5105 Tomken Rd.
Mississauga, ON L4W 2X5
Tel 905-238-0171
Fax 905-238-2006
www.ecolab.com
Line: Manufactures and sells specialty cleaning and sanitizing products.
NAICS: 325610
#Emp: 500-999 (Tor)
#TorLoc: 1
Own: Private Company
Par: Ecolab Inc. (US)
Key: Astrid Mitchell, Dir of HR

Economical Mutual Insurance Co.

111 Westmount Rd. South
P.O. Box 2000
Waterloo, ON N2J 4S4
Tel 519-570-8200
Fax 519-570-8389
www.economicalinsurance.com
AKA: The Economical Insurance Group; Federation Insurance; Perth Insurance; Waterloo Insurance; The Missisquoi Insurance Company
Line: Offers property and casualty insurance services.
NAICS: 524121
#Emp: 250-499 (Tor)
#TorLoc: 3
Own: Private Company
Key: Noel G. Walpole, Pres & CEO
Jorge Arruda, Sr VP Ops
Dean Bulloch, VP HR
Sandeep Uppal, Sr VP & CFO

Econ-O-Pac Ltd.

490 Midwest Rd.
Toronto, ON M1P 3A9
Tel 416-750-7200
Fax 416-750-7201
www.econopac.com
Line: Provides contract packaging and co-packing for food and consumer goods industries.
NAICS: 561910
#Emp: 100-249 (Tor)
#TorLoc: 1
Own: Private Company
Key: Howie Nisenbaum, Mng Partner
Kaye Powell, HR

Econo-Rack Storage Equipment Ltd.

3-1303 North Service Rd. East
Oakville, ON L4H 1A7
Tel 905-337-5700
Fax 905-337-5721
www.econorack.com
Line: Designs, supplies, and installs steel shelving and pallet racks.
NAICS: 337215
#Emp: 100-249 (Tor)
#TorLoc: 1
Own: Private Company
Par: Konstant Group of Companies (CDA)
Key: Paul Hagget, GM

Eco-Tec Inc.

1145 Squires Beach Rd.
Pickering, ON L1W 3T9
Tel 905-427-0077
Fax 905-427-4477
www.eco-tec.com
Line: Manufactures chemical recovery equipment and water treatment systems.
NAICS: 333310 333299
#Emp: 75-99 (Tor)
#TorLoc: 1
Own: Private Company
Key: Phillip Simmones, Pres & CEO
Christine Anderson, HR Mgr
Jeffrey Potter, VP Fin
Ambro Fitzpatrick, Materials
   Management Mgr
Mike Dejak, VP Sales & Mktg
Bonnie Goodspeed,
   Mktg Commun Specialist

ECS Engineering & Construction Ltd.

1-51 Ritin Lane
Vaughan, ON L4K 4E1
Tel 905-761-7009
Fax 905-791-7110
www.ecsengineering.com
Line: Performs general construction including commercial, specialty and industrial petroleum facilities.
NAICS: 231330 541330
#Emp: 75-99 (Tor)
#TorLoc: 1
Own: Private Company
Key: Jason Chidiac, Pres
Amel Zaag, Office & Acctng Mgr

Eddie Bauer Inc.

201 Aviva Park Dr.
Vaughan, ON L4L 9C1
Tel 905-851-6700
Fax 905-351-6437
www.eddiebauer.com
Line: Retails men's and women casual clothing, accessories, footwear and miscellaneous items.
NAICS: 448150 448140
#Emp: 250-499 (Tor)
#TorLoc: 10
Own: Private Company
Par: Eddie Bauer Inc. (US)
Key: Jocelyn Miller, District Dir

Edward Jones

902-90 Burnhamthorpe Rd. West
Mississauga, ON L5B 3C3
Tel 905-306-8600
Fax 905-306-8624
www.edwardjones.com
Line: Provides investment-consulting services to individual investors.
NAICS: 523120
#Emp: 250-499 (Tor)
Own: Private Company
Par: Edward Jones (US)
Key: Gary Reamey, Principal
Doug Bennett, Dir of Ops
Veronica Ding, Dir of HR

Egan LLP

222 Bay St., 24th Fl.
P.O. Box 251
Toronto, ON M5K 1H6
Tel 416-943-2400
Fax 416-943-3445
www.ey.com
Line: Helps organizations to process the movement of expatriates across and into the United States and Canada.
NAICS: 541110
#Emp: 100-249 (Tor)
#TorLoc: 1
Own: Private Company
Par: Ernst & Young (CDA)
Key: James Egan, Partner
George Reis, Partner

Egan & Teamboard

300 Hanlan Rd.
Woodbridge, ON L4L 3P6
Tel 905-851-2826
Fax 905-851-3426
www.egan.com
AKA: Teamboard; Egan Visuals
Line: Manufactures visual aid products used for training facilities, conference rooms, offices and related locations.
NAICS: 337213 337214
#Emp: 100-249 (Tor)
#TorLoc: 2
Own: Private Company
Key: James E. Egan, Pres
Rosa Sinopoli, HR Mgr
Victor Skakun, Cont

EHC Global Inc.

1287 Boundary Rd.
Oshawa, ON L1J 6Z7
Tel 905-432-3200
Fax 905-432-1735
www.ehc-global.com
Line: Manufactures products for the lift industry.
NAICS: 232550
#Emp: 75-99 (Tor)
#TorLoc: 1
Own: Private Company
Key: Jeno Eppel, Pres
John McIntyre, CEO
Greg Hanoski, Corp Sr Mgr, Ops
Patricia Cole, Corp Sr Mgr, HR

E. Hofmann Plastics Canada Inc.

51 Centennial Rd.
Orangeville, ON L9W 3R1
Tel 905-457-6776
Fax 905-457-7332
www.hofmannplastics.com
Line: Produces plastic products.

NAICS: 326198
#Emp: 75-99 (Tor)
#TorLoc: 1
Own: Private Company
Key: Paul Kalia, Pres
Lynda Semec, Cont

E.I duPont Canada Company

P.O. Box 2200, Stn. Streetsville
Mississauga, ON L5M 2H3
Tel 905-821-3300
Fax 905-821-5519
www.dupont.ca
Line: Manufactures and sells industrial products.
NAICS: 325999
#Emp: 250-499 (Tor)
#TorLoc: 3
Own: Public Company
Par: E.I. du Pont de Nemours & Co. (US)
Key: Michael J. Oxley, Pres & CFO
Al Forsyth, Dir of Ops
Linda Gillespie, Dir of HR
Ann-Marie Sullivan, IT Mgr
Kevin Derbyshire, Gen Counsel & Dir
    of Gov't & Pub Affairs

Electrical Safety Authority

202-155A Matheson Blvd. West
Mississauga, ON L5R 3L5
Tel 905-712-5657
Fax 905-712-7845
www.esasafe.com
Line: Provides public electrical safety information and services in Ontario.
NAICS: 813310
#Emp: 100-249 (Tor)
#TorLoc: 2
Own: Not-for-profit
Key: David Collie, Pres & CEO
Scott Saint, VP & COO
Dave Kirkconnell, VP HR
Michael Heilbronn, VP Fin & CFO

Electrolux Home Products

5855 Terry Fox Way
Mississauga, ON L5V 3E4
Tel 905-813-7700
Fax 905-813-7737
www.electroluxappliances.ca
AKA: Frigidaire; Poulan Pro; Weedeater
Line: Distributes fridges, stoves, and lawn and garden products.
NAICS: 414220 417110
#Emp: 100-249 (Tor)
#TorLoc: 1
Own: Private Company
Par: AB Electrolux (SWE)
Key: Sue Stevenson, GM

Electronic Imaging Systems Corp.

8-1361 Huntingwood Dr.
Toronto, ON M1S 3J1
Tel 416-292-0900
Fax 416-292-0641
www.eisca.com
Line: Provides cheque fraud detection and cheque reconciliation services, image based workflow solutions and wholesale lockbox services.
NAICS: 561490
#Emp: 100-249 (Tor)
#TorLoc: 1
Own: Private Company
Key: Rose Kramer, Pres

Electro Sonic Inc.

100-55 Renfrew Dr.
Markham, ON L3R 8H3
Tel 416-494-1666
Fax 905-946-1900
www.e-sonic.com
Line: Distributes and wholesales electronics.
NAICS: 417320
#Emp: 75-99 (Tor)
#TorLoc: 1
Own: Private Company
Key: Eric Taylor, Pres

Elementary Teachers' Federation of Ontario

1000-480 University Ave.
Toronto, ON M5G 1V2
Tel 416-962-3836
Fax 416-642-2424
www.etfo.ca
Line: Provides collective bargaining, counselling, and professional development for teachers in public elementary schools in Ontario.
NAICS: 813920 813930
#Emp: 100-249 (Tor)
#TorLoc: 1
Own: Association
Key: Gene Lewis, Gen Secy
Jo Anne Alzner,
    Operation Services Mgr
Ruth Alam, HR Mgr
Massimo Ascenzi, Cont
Tania Bogachova, IT Mgr

El-En Packaging Company Ltd.

200 Great Golf Dr.
Vaughan, ON L4K 5W1
Tel 905-761-5975
Fax 905-761-2145
NAICS: 326198
#Emp: 75-99 (Tor)
#TorLoc: 1
Own: Private Company
Key: Cheryl Babcock, VP Ops
Dahlia Levitan, HR & Services Mgr

The Elgin & Winter Garden Theatre Centre

189 Yonge St.
Toronto, ON M5B 1M4
Tel 416-314-2901
Fax 416-314-3583
www.heritagetrust.on.ca
Line: Operates a theatre.
NAICS: 711311
#Emp: 75-99 (Tor)
#TorLoc: 1
Own: Private Company
Par: Ontario Heritage Trust (CDA)
Key: Brett Randall, GM

Eli Lilly Canada Inc.

3650 Danforth Ave.
Toronto, ON M1N 2E8
Tel 416-694-3221
Fax 416-699-7241
www.lilly.ca
Line: Discovers and develops
medicines.
NAICS: 325410
#Emp: 250-499 (Tor)
#TorLoc: 1
Own: Public Company
Par: Eli Lilly & Co. (US)
Key: Marcel Lechanteur, Pres & GM
Karen McKay, VP HR
Anuj Bhatnagar, VP Fin
Andre Cote, VP Nat'l Sales
Laurel Swartz,
    Associate Dir of Commun

Elite Window Fashions

1-1 Applewood Cres.
Concord, ON L4K 4K1
Tel 905-660-0049
Fax 905-738-5759
www.elitewf.com
Line: Offers custom window fashions,
blinds, shutters and drapes.
NAICS: 337920
#Emp: 75-99 (Tor)
#TorLoc: 1
Own: Private Company

Key: Josef Zimner, Pres
Ron Merza, Plant Mgr
Diane Murphy, HR & Office Mgr
Eswar Perunkulam, Purch Admr
Noah Zimner, Systems Admr
Danny Zukier, Sales Mgr
Paula DaSilva, Mktg Coord

Ellas Restaurant (Scarborough) Ltd.

35 Danforth Rd.
Toronto, ON M1L 3W5
Tel 416-694-1194
Fax 416-694-1286
www.ellas.com
AKA: Ellas Banquet Hall
NAICS: 722110
#Emp: 100-249 (Tor)
#TorLoc: 1
Own: Private Company
Key: Anastasios Dimacopoulos, Pres
Elizabeth Dimacopoulos, Mgr

Elliott Family Care Limited

33 Osborne Ave.
Toronto, ON M4E 3A8
Tel 416-698-9298
Fax 416-698-6015
Line: Operates a health-care centre.
NAICS: 621494
#Emp: 75-99 (Tor)
#TorLoc: 1
Own: Private Company
Key: Ernie Philip, Dir

EllisDon Corporation

800-89 Queensway Ave. West
Mississauga, ON L5B 2V2
Tel 905-896-8900
Fax 905-896-8911
www.ellisdon.com
Line: Operates a construction company
and provides project management,
construction management, design-
build and general contracting for
the industrial, commercial and
institutional sector.
NAICS: 231210 231220
#Emp: 250-499 (Tor)
#TorLoc: 1
Own: Private Company
Par: Ellis-Don Inc. (CDA)
Key: Rick Maggiacomo, Exec VP
Geoff Smith, Pres & CEO
Bruno Antidormi, Exec VP
Janine Szczepanowski, VP Leadership
    & Entrepreneurial Dev
John Bernhardt, CFO
Joe Jagodich, CIO
Michael Smith, VP Mktg

Ellis Packaging Ltd.

1830 Sandstone Manor
Pickering, ON L1W 3Y1
Tel 416-798-7715
Fax 905-831-7571
www.ellispkg.com
AKA: Elvidge Paper Box Inc.
Line: Manufactures folding cartons,
blister cards and paperboard printing.
NAICS: 561910 322299
#Emp: 100-249 (Tor)
#TorLoc: 2
Own: Private Company
Key: Peter William Ellis, Pres & CEO
Cathie Ellis, VP
Faith Neilson, Payroll
Bruce Paterson, VP Fin
Paul Colicchio, Exec VP

Ell-Rod Holdings Inc.

19 Tamblyn Rd.
Orono, ON L0B 1M0
Tel 905-683-8444
Fax 905-428-1463
www.ellrod.ca
Line: Manufactures custom millwork.
NAICS: 321919
#Emp: 100-249 (Tor)
#TorLoc: 1
Own: Private Company
Key: Rod Finney, Pres
Barry McIntosh, Payroll
Sandy Smith, Secy Treas

Elm Grove Living Centre Inc.

35 Elm Grove Ave.
Toronto, ON M6K 2J2
Tel 416-537-2465
Fax 416-537-9435
www.elmgrovelivingcentre.com
Line: Operates a nursing home.
NAICS: 623110
#Emp: 100-249 (Tor)
#TorLoc: 1
Own: Private Company
Key: Sandro Perciamontani, Admr
Vivek Nayak, Financial Officer

Elte

80 Ronald Ave.
Toronto, ON M6E 5A2
Tel 416-785-7885
Fax 416-785-9157
www.elte.com
Line: Retails home furnishings and accessories.
NAICS: 314110 313210
#Emp: 100-249 (Tor)
#TorLoc: 1
Own: Private Company
Key: Allan Goldberg, Pres
Kenneth Metrick, CEO
Jamie Metrick, VP Ops

EMC Corporation of Canada

1400-120 Adelaide St. West
Toronto, ON M5H 1T1
Tel 416-628-5973
Fax 416-628-5990
www.canada.emc.com
Line: Provides information storage, software and professional services.
NAICS: 541510
#Emp: 500-999 (Tor)
#TorLoc: 3
Own: Public Company
Par: EMC Corp. (US)
Key: Michael Sharun, Mng Dir
Adam Wellwood, Dir of HR

EMCO Corporation

1108 Dundas St.
London, ON N5W 3A7
Tel 519-453-9600
Fax 519-645-2465
www.emcoltd.com
Line: Distributes and manufactures building materials for the home improvement and building construction markets.
NAICS: 416120
#Emp: 100-249 (Tor)
#TorLoc: 10
Own: Private Company
Key: Rick Fantham, Pres & CEO

EMD Serono Canada Inc.

200-2695 North Sheridan Way
Mississauga, ON L5K 2N6
Tel 905-919-0200
Fax 905-919-0299
www.emdserono.ca
Line: Registers and markets pharmaceutical and biotech industry products.
NAICS: 325410 414510
#Emp: 100-249 (Tor)
#TorLoc: 1
Own: Public Company
Par: Merk Serono International (GER)
Key: Deborah Brown, Pres & Mng Dir

Emerald Hills Golf Club

14001 Concession #5
Stouffville, ON L4A 7X5
Tel 905-888-1100
Fax 905-888-1674
en.clublink.ca
Line: Operates private country club.
NAICS: 713910
#Emp: 100-249 (Tor)
#TorLoc: 1
Own: Private Company
Par: ClubLink Corp. (CDA)
Key: Andrew Crichton, Dir of Ops

Emerson Electric Canada Ltd.

306 Town Centre Blvd.
Markham, ON L3R 0Y6
Tel 905-948-3400
Fax 905-948-3414
www.emersoncanada.ca
Line: Manufactures and distributes electrical and mechanical equipment for industrial and commercial applications.
NAICS: 417230 335312
#Emp: 100-249 (Tor)
#TorLoc: 3
Own: Private Company
Par: Emerson Electric Co. (US)
Key: Cary Eagleson, Pres

EMI Music Canada

301-109 Atlantic Ave.
Toronto, ON M6K 1X4
Tel 416-583-5000
Fax 416-583-5478
www.emimusic.ca
Line: Manufactures, promotes and distributes DVDs and compact discs.
NAICS: 512220 512210 334610
#Emp: 100-249 (Tor)
#TorLoc: 1
Own: Private Company
Par: EMI Group plc (UK)
Key: Deane Cameron, Pres
Sharon MacDonald, VP HR
Mark Ditmar, VP Corp Partnerships
Rob Brooks, VP Mktg

The Employment Solution

705-1 City Centre Dr.
Mississauga, ON L5B 1M2
Tel 905-272-4296
Fax 905-272-1068
www.tes.net
Line: Provides staffing solutions.
NAICS: 561310
#Emp: 75-99 (Tor)
#TorLoc: 3
Own: Private Company
Key: Joe Zeki, Reg Branch Mgr

Enbridge Gas Distribution Inc.

500 Consumers Rd.
P.O. Box 650
Toronto, ON M1K 5E3
Tel 416-492-5000
www.enbridge.com
Line: Distributes natural gas and provides energy services.
NAICS: 221210
#Emp: 1000-4999 (Tor)
#TorLoc: 5
Own: Private Company
Par: Enbridge Inc. (CDA)
Key: Janet Holder, Pres
Glenn Beaumont, VP Ops
Bill Ross, VP Fin & IT
Jim Grant, VP Energy Supply, Storage
    Dev & Regulatory
Jamie Milner, VP Engineering
Arunas Pleckaitis, VP Business
    Dev & Customer Strategy
Debbie Boukydis, Dir of Public,
    Government & Aboriginal Affairs

Encore Sales Ltd.

333 North Rivermede Rd.
Concord, ON L4K 3N7
Tel 905-738-8888
Fax 905-738-5435
www.encoresales.com
Line: Operates an importing company.
NAICS: 414390 416330
#Emp: 100-249 (Tor)
#TorLoc: 2
Own: Private Company
Key: Howard Bloomberg, Pres
Stephen Bloomberg, CEO
Cintra Hospedales, HR Mgr
Karen Wilson, Cont

Enersource Corp.

3240 Mavis Rd.
Mississauga, ON L5C 3K1
Tel 905-273-9050
Fax 905-566-2737
www.enersource.com
Line: Provides electrical distribution.
NAICS: 221122
#Emp: 250-499 (Tor)
#TorLoc: 1
Own: Government
Par: The City of Mississauga
Key: Craig Fleming, Pres & CEO
Dan Pastoric, Exec VP & COO
Jo Ann Morello, VP HR
Norm Wolff, VP & CFO
Sonya Potocnik,
    VP Customer Care & Billing Ops

Enesco Canada Corp.

7550 Tranmere Dr.
Mississauga, ON L5S 1S6
Tel 905-673-9200
Fax 905-673-7385
www.enescocanada.com
Line: Imports and wholesales giftware
and collectables.
NAICS: 418990
#Emp: 100-249 (Tor)
#TorLoc: 1
Own: Private Company
Par: Enesco Corp. (US)
Key: Craig D. Cameron, Pres & CEO
Grace Kiss, VP Ops
Pierre Lanctot, Exec VP
Michael Sanscartier, VP Sales

Engineered Air

1175 Twinney Dr.
Newmarket, ON L3Y 9C8
Tel 905-898-1114
Fax 905-898-7244
www.engineeredair.com
Line: Manufactures heating and air
conditioning equipment.
NAICS: 333416
#Emp: 100-249 (Tor)
#TorLoc: 4
Own: Private Company
Key: David Kukkonen,
   GM, Newmarket Division
Greg Garland, Purch Supr

English Bay Batter (Toronto) Inc.

1307 Midway Blvd.
Mississauga, ON L5T 2G8
Tel 905-670-1110
Fax 905-670-9417
www.englishbaycookies.com
Line: Manufactures cookie dough.
NAICS: 311822
#Emp: 100-249 (Tor)
#TorLoc: 1
Own: Private Company
Key: Constantin Trusca, Plant Mgr
Keith O'Neil, Sales Mgr, Toronto

Enterprise Holdings

280 Attwell Dr.
Toronto, ON M9W 5B2
Tel 416-798-8802
Fax 416-798-4363
www.enterpriseholdings.com
Line: Provides car and truck rental
services.
NAICS: 532112
#Emp: 100-249 (Tor)
Own: Public Company
Par: Enterprise Rent-A-Car Company
(US)
Key: Matthew G. Darrah, Exec VP,
North American Ops

Entire Imaging Solutions Inc.

31 Constellation Crt.
Toronto, ON M9W 1K4
Tel 905-673-2000
Fax 905-673-0668
www.entireimaging.com
Line: Specializes in print
communications.
NAICS: 541430
#Emp: 75-99 (Tor)
#TorLoc: 2
Own: Private Company
Key: Andy Chiodo, Pres

Environics Research Group Ltd.

900-33 Bloor St. East
Toronto, ON M4W 3H1
Tel 416-920-9010
Fax 416-920-3299
www.environics.net
Line: Provides market research, public
affairs research and consulting.
NAICS: 541910 541619
#Emp: 100-249 (Tor)
#TorLoc: 1
Own: Private Company
Key: Barry Watson, Pres & CEO
Stanley Ramdath, Dir of Fin

Enwave Energy Corporation

181 University Ave.
17th Fl., P.O. Box 105
Toronto, ON M5H 3M7
Tel 416-392-6838
Fax 416-363-6052
www.enwave.com
Line: Provides heating and cooling
services to institutional and
commercial buildings.
NAICS: 221330
#Emp: 75-99 (Tor)
#TorLoc: 4
Own: Private Company
Key: Dennis Fotinos, Pres & CEO
Krishnan Iyer, CFO

EPM Global Services Inc.

195 Royal Crest Crt.
Markham, ON L3R 9X6
Tel 905-479-6203
Fax 905-479-6990
www.epmglobal.com
Line: Provides electronic
manufacturing services.
NAICS: 334410
#Emp: 100-249 (Tor)
#TorLoc: 1
Own: Private Company
Key: James McColl, Pres & CEO
Karen Meir, HR Mgr
Lianne Bastien, CFO
Ron Singh, Dir of Materials
Mike Ruse, VP Sales
Cyril Fernandes,
    Sr VP Mktg & Corp Dev

Epson Canada Ltd.

185 Renfrew Dr.
Markham, ON L3R 6G3
Tel 905-944-3254
Fax 905-944-3762
www.epson.ca
Line: Manufactures and distributes
printer products and point of sale
printers.
NAICS: 334110
#Emp: 75-99 (Tor)
#TorLoc: 1
Own: Private Company
Par: Epson America Inc. (US)
Key: Jim Innes, Nat'l Service Mgr
Lynne Lyon, HR Mgr
James de Pinho, IT Admr
Tamara Walsh, Mktg Mgr

Equifax Canada Inc.

5650 Yonge St.
Toronto, ON M2M 4G3
Tel 416-227-8800
Fax 416-227-5417
www.equifax.ca
AKA: Equifax Inc.
Line: Operates direct to consumer, commercial, and authentication businesses.
NAICS: 561450
#Emp: 100-249 (Tor)
#TorLoc: 1
Own: Public Company
Par: Equifax Inc. (US)
Key: Carol Gray, Pres
Odette Auger, VP Ops
Donna Taylor, VP HR
Robert Brabers, CFO
Rosella Venanzi, VP IT

Erb Transport Ltd.

1889 Britannia Rd. East
Mississauga, ON L4W 3C3
Tel 905-670-8490
Fax 905-670-8467
www.erbgroup.com
NAICS: 484110 484121
#Emp: 100-249 (Tor)
#TorLoc: 1
Own: Private Company
Par: Erb Group of Companies (CDA)
Key: Vernon Erb, CEO
Wendell Erb, GM

ERCO Worldwide LP

A Div. of Superior Plus Inc.
200-302 The East Mall
Toronto, ON M9B 6C7
Tel 416-239-7111
Fax 416-239-0235
www.ercoworldwide.com
Line: Manufactures sodium chlorate, sodium chlorite and chlorine dioxide generators.
NAICS: 325189
#Emp: 75-99 (Tor)
#TorLoc: 1
Own: Private Company
Par: Superior Plus LP (CDA)
Key: Paul Timmons, Pres

Ericsson Canada Inc.

5255 Satellite Dr.
Mississauga, ON L4W 5E3
Tel 905-629-6700
Fax 905-629-6701
www.ericsson.com/en
Line: Provides end-to-end communication solutions including advanced mobile Internet and wireless solutions, IP and data systems solutions, and consulting services.
NAICS: 417320
#Emp: 100-249 (Tor)
#TorLoc: 1
Own: Private Company
Par: LM Ericsson (SWE)
Key: Mark Henderson, Pres & CEO
Patricia MacLean, Dir of Commun

Erie Meat Products Ltd.

3180 Wharton Way
Mississauga, ON L4X 2C1
Tel 905-624-3811
Fax 905-625-8815
Line: Processes beef and poultry.
NAICS: 311615
#Emp: 100-249 (Tor)
#TorLoc: 1
Own: Private Company
Key: Simon Rosen, Pres

Erin Dodge Chrysler Ltd.

2365 Motorway Blvd.
Mississauga, ON L5L 2M4
Tel 905-828-2004
Fax 905-828-6172
www.erindodge.com
Line: Operates an automobile dealership.
NAICS: 441110 441120
#Emp: 100-249 (Tor)
#TorLoc: 1
Own: Private Company
Key: Paul Kaye, Dealer Principal
Mark Keenan, GM
Debra Jones, Secy-Treas
Steve Kaye, IT Mgr
Lynne Barry, Leasing Mgr

Erin Mills Retirement Nursing Home

2132 Dundas St. West
Mississauga, ON L5K 2K7
Tel 905-823-6700
Fax 905-823-2410
www.erinmillscare.com
AKA: Erin Mills Lodge & Nursing Home
Line: Operates a nursing and retirement home.
NAICS: 623110

#Emp: 100-249 (Tor)
#TorLoc: 1
Own: Private Company
Par: Sifton Properties (CDA)
Key: Maudy Duncan, GM

Erinoak Kids

2277 South Millway
Mississauga, ON L5L 2M5
Tel 905-820-7111
Fax 905-820-1333
www.erinoakkids.ca
Line: Operates treatment centre providing support to children and youth with physical developmental and communicational disabilities.
NAICS: 623210
#Emp: 500-999 (Tor)
#TorLoc: 7
Own: Not-for-profit
Key: Bridget Fewtrell, CEO

Erin Park Automotive Partnership

2411 Motorway Blvd.
Mississauga, ON L5L 3R2
Tel 905-828-7711
Fax 905-820-9128
www.erinparkonline.ca
AKA: Erin Park Lexus Toyota
Line: Operates an automobile dealership.
NAICS: 441110 441120
#Emp: 100-249 (Tor)
#TorLoc: 2
Own: Private Company
Key: Gino Caletti, Owner
Joel Cohen, Owner
Joe Anthony, Cont

Erinwood Ford Sales Ltd.

2395 Motorway Blvd.
Mississauga, ON L5L 1V4
Tel 905-828-1600
Fax 905-828-6966
www.erinwoodford.com
Line: Sells cars, automotive parts and provides servicing and repairs.
NAICS: 441110 441120
#Emp: 75-99 (Tor)
#TorLoc: 1
Own: Private Company
Key: Sean Hallett, Pres
Al Porretta, Gen Sales Mgr
Avery Abbott-Hill, HR Mgr
Dan Letual, Parts Mgr

Ernest Green & Son Ltd.

2395 Skymark Ave.
Mississauga, ON L4W 4Y6
Tel 905-629-8999
Fax 905-629-3970
www.ernestgreen.com
Line: Distributes graphic arts products
and services.
NAICS: 323115
#Emp: 75-99 (Tor)
#TorLoc: 1
Own: Private Company
Key: Doug Green, Pres

Ernst & Young LLP

Ernst & Young Tower, TD Centre
P.O. Box 251
Toronto, ON M5K 1J7
Tel 416-864-1234
Fax 416-864-1174
www.ey.com
Line: Provides assurance, advisory, tax
and transaction services.
NAICS: 541611 541212
#Emp: 1000-4999 (Tor)
#TorLoc: 2
Own: Private Company
Key: Trent Henry, Chmn & CEO
Tom Kornya, Mng Partner, GTA
Stephen Shea, Mng Partner, People
Alan Smith, CFO
Lori Benson, Mgr of Strategic Sourcing
Jeff Charriere, Mng Partner, Markets

Escar Entertainment Ltd.

308-1210 Sheppard Ave. East
Toronto, ON M2K 1E3
Tel 416-260-7103
Fax 416-260-7121
www.escarentertainment.com
Line: Provides food services and
operates games.
NAICS: 454210 713120
#Emp: 250-499 (Tor)
#TorLoc: 1
Own: Private Company
Key: Larry Regan, Pres

Escort Manufacturing Corporation

3730 Laird Rd.
Mississauga, ON L5L 5Z7
Tel 905-828-1002
Fax 905-828-2951
www.escortradar.com
Line: Designs, develops and
manufactures radar detectors.
NAICS: 334511
#Emp: 100-249 (Tor)
#TorLoc: 1

Own: Private Company
Key: John Larson, Pres & CEO
Hani Abdelgalil, VP Ops
Les Boyles, HR Mgr
Jackie Randall, IT Mgr

ESI Canada

5770 Hurontario St., 10th Fl.
Mississauga, ON L5R 3G5
Tel 905-712-8615
Fax 905-712-4341
www.express-scripts.com
Line: Adjudicates health claims for the
insurance industry.
NAICS: 524291
#Emp: 100-249 (Tor)
#TorLoc: 1
Own: Private Company
Key: Michael Biskey, Pres
Anthea Gomez, Dir of HR
Mark Murphy, VP Fin
Mary Johanneson, Dir of Sales & Mktg

Esmond Manufacturing

A Div. of TK Canada Ltd.
195 Nantucket Blvd.
Toronto, ON M1P 2P2
Tel 416-759-3573
Fax 416-759-0488
www.teknion.com
Line: Manufactures harnesses, cable
assemblies, lamps and lighting fixtures.
NAICS: 335120
#Emp: 75-99 (Tor)
#TorLoc: 1
Own: Private Company
Par: Teknion Corporation (CDA)
Key: Hanna Shaheen, Pres & GM
Dave Bartrem, HR Mgr

Esplanade Restaurants Ltd.

201-56 The Esplanade
Toronto, ON M5E 1A6
Tel 416-864-9775
Fax 416-864-0956
www.oldspaghettifactory.net
AKA: The Old Spaghetti Factory;
Scotland Yard; Tony Roma's (Famous
for Ribs)
Line: Operates holding company that
manages full-service restaurants.
NAICS: 722110 722210
#Emp: 100-249 (Tor)
#TorLoc: 1
Own: Private Company
Key: Peter Hnatiw, Pres
Graham Hnatiw, GM
Lesley Scott, Cont

ESRI Canada Limited

900-12 Concorde Pl.
Toronto, ON M3C 3R8
Tel 416-441-6035
Fax 416-441-6838
www.esricanada.com
Line: Develops GIS software and
provides consulting services for
needs assessment, database design,
application design and development,
project and technical management, and
product orientation seminars.
NAICS: 541510
#Emp: 100-249 (Tor)
#TorLoc: 1
Own: Private Company
Key: Alex Miller, Pres
John Kitchen, VP & GM
Robert Alldritt, Dir of HR
Doug Bayley, CFO

Esselte Canada Inc.

2-333 Foster Cres.
Mississauga, ON L5R 3Z9
Tel 905-890-1080
Fax 905-890-8946
www.esselte.com
NAICS: 322230 322220
#Emp: 100-249 (Tor)
#TorLoc: 1
Own: Private Company
Par: Esselte Corp. (US)
Key: Jeff Good, VP Fin
Gord Shillington, MIS Mgr
Ron McCormack, VP Sales

The Estates of Sunnybrook

2075 Bayview Ave.
Toronto, ON M4N 3M5
Tel 416-487-3841
Fax 416-487-5708
www.estatesofsunnybrook.com
Line: Operates a banquet hall.
NAICS: 722320
#Emp: 75-99 (Tor)
#TorLoc: 1
Own: Private Company
Par: Sunnybrook Hospital (CDA)
Key: Elizabeth Hollyer, Mng Dir

Estee Lauder Cosmetics Ltd.

801-130 Bloor St. West
Toronto, ON M5S 1N5
Tel 416-413-5250
Fax 416-413-5254
www.elcompanies.com
AKA: Aramis; Clinique; M·A·C
Line: Manufactures and sells perfumes
and cosmetics.
NAICS: 325620
#Emp: 500-999 (Tor)
#TorLoc: 3
Own: Public Company
Par: Estee Lauder Companies Inc. (US)
Key: Bob Jugovic,
   Exec Dir of HR & Supply Chain
Michelle Spencer, Dir of HR
Teri Deering, VP Sales
Tim Pickles, VP Sales, Estee Lauder
Kelly Amsterdam,
   Commun Officer, Clinique

Etobicoke Ironworks Ltd.

141 Rivalda Rd.
Toronto, ON M9M 2M6
Tel 416-742-7111
Fax 416-742-2737
www.eiw-ca.com
Line: Manufactures scaffolding and
provides structural engineering
services.
NAICS: 232230 332329
#Emp: 75-99 (Tor)
Own: Private Company
Key: John Brasil, Pres & COO
Raj Gupta, Cont
Sanjay Kulkarni, CFO
Ron Chafee, Purch Mgr
Benson Chong, IT Mgr
Luc Leveille, Structural Sales Mgr
Lyn Hardy, Miscellaneous
   Metals Sales Mgr
Elizabeth Oliveira, Mktg & Commun
   Coord

The Etobicoke Medical Centre

400 The East Mall
Toronto, ON M9B 3Z9
Tel 416-621-2220
Fax 416-621-2203
www.medicocentre.sites.toronto.com
NAICS: 621110
#Emp: 100-249 (Tor)
#TorLoc: 1
Own: Private Company
Key: Howard Stevens, Physician

Etobicoke Olympium

590 Rathburn Rd.
Toronto, ON M9C 3T3
Tel 416-394-8111
Fax 416-394-8808
www.etobicokeolympium.com
Line: Operates a multi-purpose fitness
and recreational sports centre.
NAICS: 713940
#Emp: 100-249 (Tor)
#TorLoc: 1
Own: Government
Par: The City of Toronto
Key: Peter Sanderson, Supr of
Recreation & Facilities

Etratech Inc.

1047 Cooke Blvd.
Burlington, ON L7T 4A8
Tel 905-681-7544
Fax 905-681-7601
www.etratech.com
Line: Designs and manufactures
electronic controls.
NAICS: 335315
#Emp: 100-249 (Tor)
#TorLoc: 1
Own: Private Company
Key: Michael Desnoyers, Pres & CEO
Carol Wright-Desnoyers, Dir of HR
Richard Loh, CFO

Eurofase Inc.

33 West Beaver Creek Rd.
Richmond Hill, ON L4B 1L8
Tel 905-695-2055
Fax 905-695-2056
www.eurofase.com
Line: Manufactures and distributes
lighting fixtures.
NAICS: 416110
#Emp: 100-249 (Tor)
Own: Private Company
Key: Joseph Bitton, Pres
Frank Di Matteo, COO
Jack Bitton, Sr VP
Peter Sears, Cont
Antonio Zitoli, VP Sales
Maurice Amzallag, VP

European Quality Meats

14 Westwyn Crt.
Brampton, ON L6T 4T5
Tel 905-453-6060
Fax 905-453-9733
www.europeanmeats.com
AKA: 733907 Ontario Ltd.
Line: Manufactures, processes and
wholesales meats.
NAICS: 413160

#Emp: 100-249 (Tor)
#TorLoc: 3
Own: Private Company
Key: Larry Leider, VP
Larry McCabe, Dir of Ops
Frank LaVerdi, Cont
Ross Bamford, Purch Mgr
Adeo Calcagni, Dir of Food Service
Sandy Leider, Gen Counsel

Eurospec Tooling Inc.

1-130 Harry Walker Pkwy. North
Newmarket, ON L3Y 7B2
Tel 905-898-2291
Fax 905-898-0851
www.eurospectooling.com
Line: Manufactures motor vehicle
parts.
NAICS: 336390
#Emp: 100-249 (Tor)
#TorLoc: 1
Own: Private Company
Key: Chris Potter, Owner
Steve Potter, Owner
Angela Anderson, HR Mgr
Nancy Kirkpatrick, Financial Cont

Eva's Initiatives

370-215 Spadina Ave.
Toronto, ON M5T 2C7
Tel 416-977-4497
Fax 416-977-6210
www.evasinitiatives.com
AKA: Eva's Place; Eva's Satellite; Eva's
Phoenix
Line: Operates a shelter for youth.
NAICS: 624110
#Emp: 100-249 (Tor)
#TorLoc: 4
Own: Not-for-profit
Par: Eva's Initiatives (CDA)
Key: Maria Crawford, Exec Dir
Suzanne Marion, HR Mgr
Althea Whyte, Fin Mgr

Everest College

117 Eglinton Ave. East, 2nd Fl.
Toronto, ON M4P 1A4
Tel 416-733-4452
Fax 416-480-2250
www.everest.ca
Line: Provides job focused diploma
courses in information technology,
business and health care.
NAICS: 611410
#Emp: 100-249 (Tor)
#TorLoc: 11
Own: Public Company
Par: Corinthian College, Inc. (US)
Key: Nasir Ishmael, Pres

Evertz Microsystems Ltd.

5292 John Lucas Dr.
Burlington, ON L7L 5Z9
Tel 905-335-3700
Fax 905-335-3573
www.evertz.com
Line: Designs and manufactures
professional equipment for the
television broadcast, film and HDTV
production, post-production, cable and
telco industries.
NAICS: 334110
#Emp: 250-499 (Tor)
#TorLoc: 1
Own: Private Company
Key: Romolo Magarelli, CEO
Doug DeBruin,
    Chairman & Exec VP Admin
Anthony Gridley,
    VP Corp Security & CFO

Exacta Precision Products Ltd.

3115 Kennedy Rd.
Toronto, ON M1V 4Y1
Tel 416-291-1942
Fax 416-291-8387
www.exactapunch.com
Line: Manufactures catalogue standard
punches and dies for piercing systems.
NAICS: 332210
#Emp: 75-99 (Tor)
#TorLoc: 1
Own: Private Company
Key: Dave Rawlings, VP
Nubar Kokorian, VP Ops
Judy White, MIS Mgr
Grace Takenaka, Cont
Ken Caverly, Purch Mgr
Brad White, VP Sales

Excel Employment Tempro Inc.

218-130 Westmore Dr.
Toronto, ON M9V 5E2
Tel 416-740-1542
Fax 416-745-3001
www.excelemployment.net
NAICS: 561310
#Emp: 250-499 (Tor)
Own: Private Company
Key: Vijay Prashad, Pres

Excel Tech Ltd.

A Div. of Natus Inc.
2568 Bristol Circ.
Oakville, ON L6H 5S1
Tel 905-829-5300
Fax 905-829-5304
www.natus.com
Line: Manufactures medical equipment
for intensive care, operating and
outpatient units.
NAICS: 339110
#Emp: 100-249 (Tor)
#TorLoc: 1
Own: Private Company
Key: Steve Plymale, VP & GM
Maureen Belza, Dir of HR &
    Organizational Dev

Exchange Solutions Inc.

1200-36 Toronto St.
Toronto, ON M5C 2C5
Tel 416-646-7000
Fax 416-646-7050
www.exchangesolutions.com
Line: Provides business consulting
services.
NAICS: 541619
#Emp: 75-99 (Tor)
#TorLoc: 1
Own: Private Company
Key: Alan Grant, CEO

Exco Technologies Ltd.

130 Spy Crt., 2nd Fl.
Markham, ON L3R 5H6
Tel 905-477-3065
Fax 905-477-2449
www.excocorp.com
Line: Supplies technologies servicing
the die-cast, extrusion and automotive
industries.
NAICS: 333519
#Emp: 250-499 (Tor)
#TorLoc: 6
Own: Public Company
Key: Brian A. Robbins, Pres & CEO
Paul Riganelli, VP Fin, CFO & Secy

Executive Woodwork Ltd.

330 Spinnaker Way
Concord, ON L4K 4W1
Tel 905-669-6429
Fax 905-669-3613
www.executivewoodwork.com
Line: Manufactures veneer laminates.
NAICS: 321211
#Emp: 75-99 ('Tor)
#TorLoc: 3
Own: Private Company
Key: Tina Siniscalco, Pres
Domenic Richichi, HR Mgr

Exel Logistics Canada Inc.

100 Sandalwood Pkwy.
Brampton, ON L7A 1A8
Tel 905-840-7540
Fax 905-840-2539
www.exel.com
NAICS: 493110
#Emp: 100-249 (Tor)
Own: Private Company
Key: Terry O'Neil, GM, Cdn Ops
Ross Ferreira, Dir of Ops
Roxanne VanBerkel, Sr HR Mgr

Exopack Concord

300 Spinaker Way
Concord, ON L4K 4W1
Tel 905 761-7040
Fax 905-761-0617
www.exopack.com
Line: Manufactures flexible packaging
materials.
NAICS: 326198
#Emp: 100-249 (Tor)
#TorLoc: 1
Own: Private Company
Par: Exopack LLC (US)
Key: Dale Edwards, Facilities Mgr
Andrea Chui, Dir of HR

Exopack Performance Films Inc.

201 South Blair St.
Whitby, ON L1N 5S6
Tel 905-668-5811
Fax 905-666-7005
www.exopack.com
Line: Manufactures film and packaging
systems.
NAICS: 326114
#Emp: 100-249 (Tor)
#TorLoc: 3
Own: Private Company
Par: Exopack (US)
Key: Ron Tutak, GM, Cdn Ops
Andrea Chiu, Dir of HR

Exova

2395 Speakman Dr.
Mississauga, ON L5K 1B3
Tel 905-822-4111
Fax 905-823-1446
www.exova.ca
Line: Specializes in metals and material
testing as well as technical consulting.
NAICS: 541380
#Emp: 250-499 (Tor)
#TorLoc: 2
Own: Private Company
Key: Grant Rumbles, CEO
Frank McQuade, Dir of Business Dev

EXP.

301-56 Queen St. East
Brampton, ON L6V 4M8
Tel 905-796-3200
Fax 905-793-5533
www.exp.com
Line: Operates engineering and
consulting company that specializes
in buildings, earth, environment,
infrastructure, and materials and
quality management.
NAICS: 541330
#Emp: 500-999 (Tor)
#TorLoc: 4
Own: Private Company
Key: Vladimir Stritesky, Pres
Wilfred Marin, COO
Ben Schwartz, Chief HR Officer
Greg Henderson, CFO
Anthony Brown,
    Chief Business Dev Officer

Expeditors Canada Inc.

55 Standish Crt, 11th Fl.
Mississauga, ON L5R 4A1
Tel 905-290-6000
Fax 905-290-7167
www.expeditors.com
Line: Provides logistics services
including air, ocean and trucking.
NAICS: 488519
#Emp: 100-249 (Tor)
#TorLoc: 1
Own: Private Company
Par: Expeditors International of
Washington Inc. (US)
Key: Ross Hurst, Reg VP
Mike Robbins, District Mgr
Julie Rossall, Cont
Jeff Wallis, Sales Mgr

Export Packers Company Limited

107 Walker Dr.
Brampton, ON L6T 5K5
Tel 905-792-9700
Fax 905-792-9547
www.exportpackers.com
Line: Exports and imports wholesale
food products.
NAICS: 413190 413140
#Emp: 100-249 (Tor)
#TorLoc: 1
Own: Private Company
Par: Export Packers Company Inc. (CDA)
Key: Dan LeBlanc, Pres & CFO
Jeffrey Rubenstein, CEO
Lisa Tracey, HR Mgr
Brian Lampert, VP Fin
Scott Maynard, Dir of Business Systems
Werter Mior, Exec VP

Extendicare (Canada) Inc.

700-3000 Steeles Ave. East
Markham, ON L3R 9W2
Tel 905-470-4000
Fax 905-470-5588
www.extendicare.com
Line: Operates long-term care facilities
and offers home health care services.
NAICS: 623110
#Emp: 1000-4999 (Tor)
#TorLoc: 16
Own: Public Company
Par: Extendicare Inc. (CDA)
Key: Paul Tuttle, Pres
Timothy L. Lukenda, CEO
Douglas Harris, Sr VP & CFO

Extreme Fitness, Inc.

8281 Yonge St.
Thornhill, ON L3T 2C7
Tel 905-709-1248
Fax 905-709-2960
www.extremefitness.info
Line: Provides fitness and recreational
services.
NAICS: 713940
#Emp: 1000-4999 (Tor)
#TorLoc: 13
Own: Private Company
Key: Taso Pappas, Pres
Jim Soloman, CEO
Gene Mina, Financial Cont

Extrudex Aluminum

411 Chrislea Rd.
Woodbridge, ON L4L 8N4
Tel 416-745-4444
Fax 416-745-0925
www.extrudex.com
Line: Extrudes aluminum rod, bar,
angles, channel and custom shapes.
NAICS: 331317
#Emp: 100-249 (Tor)
#TorLoc: 1
Own: Private Company
Par: 740768 Ontario Ltd. (CDA)
Key: Andrew Gucciardi, Pres
Lorie Sloan, HR Mgr
Michael Buffa, Cont
John Albanese, GM

Fabricated Plastics Ltd.

2175 Teston Rd.
Maple, ON L6A 1T3
Tel 905-832-8161
Fax 905-832-2111
www.fabricatedplastics.com
Line: Designs, engineers and custom
fabricates chemical processing and
pollution control equipment using
plastic materials.
NAICS: 326198
#Emp: 75-99 (Tor)
#TorLoc: 1
Own: Private Company
Par: Denali Group (US)
Key: Peter Young, Pres
Lam Y. Woo, VP Engineering
Rose De Palma, HR Mgr
Daimon Jacobs, Cont
Joe Penariol, Purch Mgr
Randal Hansen, MIS Mgr
Greg Landry, VP Sales

Fabricland Distributors Inc.

1450 Castlefield Ave.
Toronto, ON M6M 1Y6
Tel 416-658-2200
Fax 416-658-2201
www.fabricland.ca
Line: Distributes textiles.
NAICS: 414130 451130
#Emp: 500-999 (Tor)
#TorLoc: 15
Own: Private Company
Key: Warren Kimel, Pres
Susan Barber, HR Mgr
Irene Stepkowski, Cont

FactoryDirect.ca

501 Applewood Cres.
Concord, ON L4K 4J3
Tel 905-660-5030
Fax 905-660-9793
www.factorydirect.ca
AKA: 1313256 Ontario Inc.
Line: Retails new, used and
refurbished end of line, surplus
and closeout computer hardware
from major manufacturers, OEMs,
leasing companies, bankruptcies and
distributors.
NAICS: 443120
#Emp: 75-99 (Tor)
#TorLoc: 7
Own: Private Company
Par: R-Logistics (CDA)
Key: Riaz Mavani, VP

Fairchild Television Ltd.

8-35 East Beaver Creek Rd.
Richmond Hill, ON L4B 1B3
Tel 905-889-8090
Fax 905-882-7120
www.fairchildtv.com
Line: Operates national Chinese language TV production and broadcasting company.
NAICS: 513220
#Emp: 100-249 (Tor)
#TorLoc: 1
Own: Private Company
Key: Joseph Chan, Pres

Fairmont Hotels & Resorts Inc.

1600-100 Wellington St. West
TD Centre, P.O. Box 40
Toronto, ON M5K 1B7
Tel 416-874-2600
Fax 416-874-2601
www.fairmont.com
AKA: Raffles Hotels; Swissotel Hotels & Resorts
Line: Operates luxury hotels.
NAICS: 721111 721113
#Emp: 250-499 (Tor)
#TorLoc: 2
Own: Private Company
Par: British Columbia Investment Management Corporation (CDA)
Key: Chris J. Cahill, Pres & COO
William R. Fatt, CEO
Kevin Frid, Sr VP Ops
Carolyn J. Clark, Sr VP HR
John Carnella, Exec VP & CFO
Fred Lawlor, VP Procurement
Vineet Gupta, Sr VP Tech
Jeff Doane, VP Hotel Sales, NA
Jeff Senior, Exec VP Mktg & Sales
Brian A. Richardson,
    VP Brand Mktg & Commun

The Fairmont Royal York

100 Front St. West
Toronto, ON M5J 1E3
Tel 416-368-2511
Fax 416-368-9040
www.fairmont.com
Line: Operates a hotel.
NAICS: 721111
#Emp: 1000-4999 (Tor)
#TorLoc: 1
Own: Private Company
Par: Cadbridge Investors LP (CDA)
Key: Heather McCrory, Reg VP & GM
Craig Reaume, Hotel Mgr
Anna Chartres, Reg Dir of HR
Serge Laroche, Reg Cont
Kerry Ann Kotani,
    Reg Dir of Sales & Mktg
Melanie Coates, Reg Dir of PR

Fairview Fittings & Manufacturing Limited

449 Attwell Dr.
Toronto, ON M9W 5C4
Tel 416-675-4233
Fax 416-675-9416
www.fairviewfittings.com
Line: Distributes brass and steel fittings, hose, tubing and valves.
NAICS: 416120
#Emp: 100-249 (Tor)
#TorLoc: 1
Own: Private Company
Key: Leslie Woodward, Pres
D. McQuade, Admin Mgr
Robin Pittaway, VP Fin & HR
Chris Kilpin, Purch Mgr
Raymond Singh, IT Mgr
Jim Forbes, VP Sales
Jeff Woodward, VP Mktg

Fairview Nursing Home Ltd.

14 Cross St.
Toronto, ON M6J 1S8
Tel 416-534-8829
Fax 416-538-1658
www.fairviewnursinghome.com
Line: Operates a nursing home.
NAICS: 623110
#Emp: 75-99 (Tor)
#TorLoc: 1
Own: Private Company
Key: Herbert Chambers, Pres

Falcon Fasteners Registered

251 Nantucket Blvd.
Toronto, ON M1P 2P2
Tel 416-751-8284
Fax 416-751-5590
Line: Manufactures nails for pneumatic equipment.
NAICS: 331222
#Emp: 100-249 (Tor)
#TorLoc: 1
Own: Private Company
Key: Martin Leistner, Owner
Roger Moteelall, Plant Mgr
Iona Pereira, Payroll Admr
Mark Pearl, Cont
Lisa Campbell, IT Mgr
Fernanda Poole, Ops Mgr

Family Day Care Services

400-155 Gordon Baker Rd.
Toronto, ON M2H 3M5
Tel 416-922-9556
Fax 416-922-5335
www.familydaycare.com
Line: Operates a non-profit, charitable organization that provides early learning and care services to families in the Greater Toronto Area.
NAICS: 624410
#Emp: 250-499 (Tor)
#TorLoc: 34
Own: Not-for-profit
Key: Diane Daley,
    Dir of Dev & Programs
Joan Arruda, CEO
Joan White, Dir of HR
Mark Woodhouse, Dir of Fin

Farco Enterprises Ltd.

B10-136 800 Steeles Ave. West
Thornhill, ON L4J 7L2
Tel 905-761-0010
Fax 905-761-9948
www.farcoentertainment.com
AKA: Farco Entertainment
Line: Provides children's entertainment services.
NAICS: 711190
#Emp: 75-99 (Tor)
#TorLoc: 1
Own: Private Company
Par: Farco Enterprises Ltd. (CDA)
Key: Shane Farberman, Owner
Aaron Farberman, VP Sales
Kaitlyn Farberman, Admr
Serena Malkin, VP Mktg

Fasken Martineau DuMoulin LLP

2400-333 Bay St.
Bay Adelaide Centre, P.O. Box 20
Toronto, ON M5H 2T6
Tel 416-366-8381
Fax 416-364-7813
www.fasken.com
Line: Provides legal services.
NAICS: 541110
#Emp: 500-999 (Tor)
#TorLoc: 1
Own: Partnership
Key: Walter Palmer, Mng Partner
David Corbett, Mng Partner
Tony Pierro, GM
Daria Juchimenko, Dir of HR
Martin Denyes, Mng Partner
Clint Marcham, Dir of Mktg & Bus Dev

Faster Linen Service Ltd.

89 Torlake Cres.
Toronto, ON M8Z 1B4
Tel 416-252-2030
Fax 416-252-9515
www.fasterlinen.com
NAICS: 812330
#Emp: 100-249 (Tor)
#TorLoc: 1
Own: Private Company
Key: Mark Halberstadt, Pres
Hyla Shabsove, Office Mgr
Barbara Isenberg, Account Receivables

Federal Express Canada Ltd.

5985 Explorer Dr.
Mississauga, ON L4W 5K6
Tel 905-212-5405
Fax 905-212-5668
www.fedex.ca
AKA: FEDEX
Line: Operates air express courier
company.
NAICS: 492110
#Emp: 1000-4999 (Tor)
#TorLoc: 8
Own: Private Company
Par: FedEx Corp. (US)
Key: Lisa Lisson, Pres
Pina Starnino, VP Cdn Ops
Sean McNamee, VP Legal,
    Regulatory Affairs & HR
Peter McQuillan, VP Fin, P&E Canada
Scot Struminger, VP IT

Federal Mogul Canada Ltd.

59 Administration Rd.
Concord, ON L4K 2R8
Tel 905-761-5400
Fax 905-761-2709
www.federal-mogul.com
Line: Sells and distributes automotive
aftermarket parts.
NAICS: 415290
#Emp: 100-249 (Tor)
#TorLoc: 1
Own: Public Company
Par: Federal-Mogul Corp. (US)
Key: Brad Shaddick, Dir of Sales
Linda Simone, HR Mgr

FedEx Freight Canada

1011 Wilson Ave.
Toronto, ON M3K 1G4
Tel 416-638-0104
Fax 416-638-8224
www.fedex.com
Line: Provides trucking services across
Canada, US, and Mexico.
NAICS: 484110 484121
#Emp: 100-249 (Tor)
#TorLoc: 1
Own: Private Company
Key: Grant Crawford, VP
Anne Tennenbaum, HR Generalist

FedEx Ground Package System Ltd.

10A-2785 Skymark Ave.
Mississauga, ON L4W 4Y3
Tel 905-602-4445
Fax 905-602-9917
www.fedex.ca
Line: Provides courier services.
NAICS: 492110
#Emp: 250-499 (Tor)
#TorLoc: 3
Own: Private Company
Par: FedEx Corp. (US)
Key: Bob Wilson, VP & GM
Tara Darby, HR Mgr

FedEx Trade Networks Transport & Brokerage (Canada) Inc.

7075 Ordan Dr.
Mississauga, ON L5T 1K6
Tel 905-677-7371
Fax 905-677-2026
www.ftn.fedex.com
Line: Provides customs brokerage,
freight forwarding and logistics
provider services.
NAICS: 488519
#Emp: 100-249 (Tor)
#TorLoc: 1
Own: Private Company
Par: FedEx Corp. (US)
Key: Lynn Wark,
    Mng Dir & GM, Central
Glenna Stewart, HR Mgr

Fenwick Automotive Products Ltd.

1100 Caledonia Rd.
Toronto, ON M6A 2W5
Tel 416-787-1723
Fax 416-787-7621
www.fencoparts.com
AKA: Fenco

Line: Remanufactures motor vehicle
clutches, CV Drive shafts, water
pumps, brake calipers, brake master
cylinders, rack and pinion steering,
and power steering pumps and gears.
NAICS: 336340 336330
#Emp: 500-999 (Tor)
#TorLoc: 1
Own: Private Company
Key: Gordon E. Fenwick, Pres & CEO
Paul Fenwick, VP Ops

Ferma Construction Company Inc.

2666 Rena Rd.
Mississauga, ON L4T 3C8
Tel 416-677-9241
Fax 416-677-9817
NAICS: 231310
#Emp: 100-249 (Tor)
#TorLoc: 1
Own: Private Company
Key: Antonio Ferragine, Pres

Fermar Paving Ltd.

1921 Albion Rd.
Toronto, ON M9W 5S8
Tel 416-675-3550
Fax 416-675-3556
www.fermarltd.com
AKA: Fermar Asphalt Ltd.; Fermar
Crushing Ltd.
Line: Provides road paving contract and
asphalt manufacturing services.
NAICS: 324121
#Emp: 100-249 (Tor)
#TorLoc: 1
Own: Private Company
Key: Ashton Martin, VP
Mary Accardi, HR Mgr

Fernie House

2 Island Rd.
Toronto, ON M1C 2P5
Tel 416-284-3711
Fax 416-284-7286
www.ferniehouse.org
AKA: Fernie House Child and Youth
Services; Cedar Brook; Tidefall; Island
Road Rosebank; Donbarton; Twyn
Rivers
Line: Operates group homes for
children with mental health and
behavioural impairments.
NAICS: 623992
#Emp: 100-249 (Tor)
#TorLoc: 2
Own: Not-for-profit
Key: Patrick Reber, CEO
Jim Clumpus, Dir of Ops
Karen Haw, CFO

Fer-Pal Construction Ltd.

169 Fenmar Dr.
Toronto, ON M9L 1M6
Tel 416-742-3713
Fax 416-742-3889
www.ferpalconstruction.com
Line: Operates a construction company.
NAICS: 231320
#Emp: 75-99 (Tor)
#TorLoc: 1
Own: Private Company
Key: Paul Ferretti, Pres

Ferraz Shawmut Canada Inc.

A Div. of Mersen Canada
88 Horner Ave.
Toronto, ON M8Z 5Y3
Tel 416-252-9371
Fax 416-252-9245
www.circuitprotection.ca
Line: Manufactures electrical fuses.
NAICS: 335315
#Emp: 75-99 (Tor)
#TorLoc: 1
Own: Private Company
Par: Mersen (FR)
Key: Bruce Brown, GM
Tom Brown, Dir of Ops
Rita O'Brien, HR Mgr
Allan Schwager, Cont
Tom Arbanas, Nat'l Sales Mgr

Festo Inc.

5300 Explorer Dr.
Mississauga, ON L4W 5G4
Tel 905-624-9000
Fax 905-624-9001
www.festo.com
NAICS: 333990
#Emp: 100-249 (Tor)
#TorLoc: 1
Own: Private Company
Key: Thomas Lichtenberger, Pres
Perry Jameson, Cont

F G Lister & Company Ltd.

475 Horner Ave.
Toronto, ON M8W 4X7
Tel 416-259-7621
Fax 416-259-9990
www.fglister.com
Line: Wholesales fruits and vegetables.
NAICS: 413150
#Emp: 100-249 (Tor)
#TorLoc: 3
Own: Private Company

Key: Anthony Arrigo, Pres
Mike Arrigo, VP
Ian MacClennan, Cont
Tony Fallico, VP Fin
Frank Fallico, Warehouse Mgr
Brad MacEachern, IT Mgr

Fidelity Investments Canada ULC

300-483 Bay St.
Toronto, ON M5G 2N7
Tel 416-307-5300
www.fidelity.ca
AKA: Pyramis Canada ULC; Fidelity Clearing Corp.
Line: Provides retirement and investment solutions.
NAICS: 526910 526989
#Emp: 500-999 (Tor)
#TorLoc: 1
Own: Private Company
Par: FMR Corp. (US)
Key: Rob Strickland, Pres
Nancy Lupi, VP HR
Phil McDowell, Sr VP Fin & CFO
Jaime Harper, Sr VP Advisor Dist
Cameron Murray,
   Sr VP & CIO, Client Services
Michael Barnett,
   Exec VP Retirement Services
Mark Wettlaufer,
   Exec VP Products & Mktg

Field Aviation Company Inc.

2450 Derry Rd. East
Mississauga, ON L5S 1B2
Tel 905-676-1540
www.fieldav.com
Line: Specializes in aircraft modifications and special mission integrations.
NAICS: 336410
#Emp: 100-249 (Tor)
#TorLoc: 3
Own: Private Company
Par: Hunting Canadian Holdings Ltd. (CDA)
Key: John Mactaggart, Pres & CEO
Brian Love, VP Ops
Cheryl Burklen, HR Mgr
Christina Friesen, VP Fin
Dave Jensen, VP Business Dev
Chris Cooper-Slipper, VP Mktg

Fiera Foods Inc.

50 Marmora St.
Toronto, ON M9M 2X5
Tel 416-746-1010
Fax 416-744-8250
www.fierafoods.com
AKA: Bakery Deluxe Company
Line: Manufactures bakery products.
NAICS: 311814
#Emp: 500-999 (Tor)
#TorLoc: 2
Own: Private Company
Key: Boris Serebryany, Pres & CEO
Alex Garber, COO
David Gelbloom, Dir of HR
Mahendra Bungaroo, CFO
Shawn O'Shaughnessy,
   VP Sales & Mktg

Fileco Inc.

A Div. of TK Canada Limited
177 Snidercroft Rd.
Vaughan, ON L4K 2J8
Tel 905-660-9718
Fax 905-660-5070
www.teknion.com
Line: Designs and manufactures metal filing and storage systems for offices.
NAICS: 337214
#Emp: 100-249 (Tor)
#TorLoc: 1
Own: Private Company
Par: Teknion Corporation (CDA)
Key: Jeff Stal, VP & GM
Gene Varaschin, Dir of Ops
Tasha Fung, HR Mgr

Financial Services Commission of Ontario

5160 Yonge St., P.O. Box 85
Toronto, ON M2N 6L9
Tel 416-250-7250
Fax 416-590-7070
www.fsco.gov.on.ca
Line: Offers provincial regulatory services.
NAICS: 912150
#Emp: 250-499 (Tor)
Own: Private Company
Key: Phil Howell, CEO

Firan Technology Group - Aerospace Division

A Div. of FTG Circuits
250 Finchdene Sq.
Toronto, ON M1X IA5
Tel 416-299-4000
Fax 416-299-4308
www.ftgcorp.com
AKA: FTG Aerospace Division
Line: Manufactures circuit boards, aircraft panels and keyboards, and electro-luminescent displays.
NAICS: 334410 335315
#Emp: 100-249 (Tor)
#TorLoc: 2
Own: Private Company
Key: Brad Bourne, Pres & CEO
Collin Latchman, GM
Delphine Keeping, Dir of HR
Joseph Ricci, VP Fin & CFO
Gary Ferrari, Dir of Tech Support

Firefly Books Ltd.

66 Leek Cres.
Richmond Hill, ON L4B 1H1
Tel 416-499-8412
Fax 416-499-8313
www.fireflybooks.com
Line: Publishes and distributes non-fiction and children's books.
NAICS: 511130
#Emp: 100-249 (Tor)
#TorLoc: 1
Own: Private Company
Key: Lionel Koffler, Pres
Nancy Marquis, HR Mgr & Payroll
Louie Plastina, Cont
Leon Gouzoules, IT Mgr
Mark Veldhuizen, Mktg Dir

FireFox Marketing Services

29-90 Nolan Crt.
Markham, ON L3R 0H8
Tel 905-946-0570
Fax 905-946-0206
www.firefoxmarketing.com
Line: Provides marketing services.
NAICS: 541619
#Emp: 75-99 (Tor)
#TorLoc: 1
Own: Private Company
Key: Jeff Burrell, Pres

First Canada/Greyhound

700-1111 International Blvd.
Burlington, ON L7L 6W1
Tel 800-563-6072
Fax 905-332-9736
www.firststudentcanada.com
AKA: Laidlaw Education Services
Line: Provides school and public charter transportation, routing, and planning services.
NAICS: 485410
#Emp: 10000+ (Tor)
#TorLoc: 120
Own: Public Company
Par: FirstGroup PLC (SCOT)
Key: Rob Proctor, Sr VP
Brian Hayman, Mgr of Business Dev
Rich Bagdonas, Dir of Human Capital & Organizational Design
John Hollick, Recruitment & Retension Mgr

First Canadian Title

2235 Sheridan Garden Dr.
Oakville, ON L6J 7Y5
Tel 905-287-1000
Fax 905-287-2400
www.firstcanadiantitle.com
Line: Provides title insurance and other real estate related products and services.
NAICS: 524129
#Emp: 500-999 (Tor)
#TorLoc: 1
Own: Private Company
Par: First American Title (US)
Key: Patrick Chetcuti, Pres & COO
Thomas Grifferty, CEO
Renzo Farronato, VP Ops
Faith Tull, Asst VP HR
David Coulthard, VP Fin
Sam Dotson, CIO

First Capital Realty Inc.

400-85 Hanna Ave.
Toronto, ON M6K 3S3
Tel 416-504-4114
Fax 416-941-1655
www.firstcapitalrealty.ca
Line: Owns, develops and operates supermarket anchored neighbourhood and community shopping centres.
NAICS: 531120
#Emp: 75-99 (Tor)
Own: Public Company
Key: Dori J. Segal, Pres & CEO
Ann-Marie Williams, HR Mgr

First Data

500-2630 Skymark Ave.
Mississauga, ON L4W 5A4
Tel 905-625-3113
Fax 1-888-507-2822
www.firstdata.com
Line: Provides card issuing and merchant acquiring processing solutions.
NAICS: 541510
#Emp: 100-249 (Tor)
#TorLoc: 2
Own: Private Company
Par: First Data Corporation (US)
Key: Brian Green, Pres
Guy Lauren, VP Payment Solutions
Elliott Brown, VP TASQ Technologies
Umesh Vatsraj, VP Fin
Robert McGarry, VP Sales

First Gulf Corp.

3751 Victoria Park Ave.
Toronto, ON M1W 3Z4
Tel 416-491-7778
Fax 416-491-1351
www.firstgulf.com
Line: Operates a commercial real estate development and construction services company.
NAICS: 531390
#Emp: 75-99 (Tor)
#TorLoc: 1
Own: Private Company
Key: John MacNeil, Pres & COO
David Gerofsky, CEO
Dave Carveiro, Exec VP

First Health Care Services Inc.

102-7030 Woodbine Ave.
Markham, ON L3R 6G2
Tel 905-305-9551
Fax 905-477-1956
www.firsthealthcare.ca
Line: Provides nursing and personal health care services within hospitals, long-term care facilities, and private homes.
NAICS: 621390
#Emp: 500-999 (Tor)
#TorLoc: 1
Own: Private Company
Key: Gail Giordani, VP Health Care Services
Leanna Matthews, Office Mgr

First Lady Coiffures

2180 Matheson Blvd. East
Mississauga, ON L4W 5E1
Tel 905-206-5500
Fax 905-625-3441
www.firstladyproducts.com
AKA: New Image
Line: Wholesales wigs and beauty
supplies and retails ladies' accessories.
NAICS: 418990 414520
#Emp: 75-99 (Tor)
#TorLoc: 1
Own: Private Company
Key: Les Martin, Pres & CEO
Doug Sauder, Ops Mgr
Peter Mattiuzzo, CFO
Lillian Sciara, VP Sales & Mktg

First National Financial Corp.

700-100 University Ave., North Tower
Toronto, ON M5J 1V6
Tel 416-593-1100
Fax 416-593-1900
www.firstnational.ca
Line: Specializes in mortgage
investment trusts.
NAICS: 526920
#Emp: 100-249 (Tor)
#TorLoc: 1
Own: Private Company
Key: Stephen Smith, Pres
Moray Tawse, VP Mortgage Investment
Robert Inglis, CFO

FirstService Corp.

4000-1140 Bay St.
Toronto, ON M5S 2B4
Tel 416-960-9500
Fax 416-960-5333
www.firstservice.com
Line: Provides commercial real estate,
residential property management and
property services.
NAICS: 531310 531390
#Emp: 250-499 (Tor)
#TorLoc: 1
Own: Public Company
Key: Scott Patterson, Pres & COO
Jay S. Hennick, CEO
Douglas G. Cooke,
   VP Corp Cont & Corp Secy
John B. Friedrichsen, Sr VP & CFO

Fisher & Ludlow

750 Appleby Line
P.O. Box 5025
Burlington, ON L7R 3Y8
Tel 905-632-2121
Fax 905-632-6295
www.fisherludlow.com
Line: Manufactures steel and
aluminum grating.
NAICS: 332329
#Emp: 100-249 (Tor)
#TorLoc: 1
Own: Private Company
Par: Newcor (CDA)
Key: Brian Rutter, Pres
Mike Fernie, VP Ops
Cheryl Turner, Payroll Admr
Jim Kowalchuk, Fin Mgr
Wayne Anderson, Purch Mgr
Mark Gilbey, Computer Systems Admr
Murray Antram, Ontario Sales Mgr

The Fish House

7501 Woodbine Ave.
Markham, ON L3R 2W1
Tel 905-948-1982
Fax 905-948-0161
www.thefishhouse.ca
NAICS: 722110
#Emp: 100-249 (Tor)
#TorLoc: 1
Own: Private Company
Key: Ken Baxter, Owner
Richard Ulster, Owner
Sharon O'Hearn, HR & Payroll Admr
Rudy Moretto, Cont

Fitness Institute

2235 Sheppard Ave. East
Toronto, ON M2J 5B5
Tel 416-491-5830
Fax 416-491-3463
www.fitnessinstitute.com
AKA: The Willowdale Club Fitness
Institute; Fitness Institute-North York
NAICS: 713940
#Emp: 75-99 (Tor)
#TorLoc: 2
Own: Private Company
Key: Steve Roest, Pres

Five Star Rags Inc.

7500 Kimbel St.
Mississauga, ON L5S 1A7
Tel 905-405-8365
Fax 905-405-1409
www.fivestarrags.com
Line: Exports used clothing.
NAICS: 453310
#Emp: 75-99 (Tor)

#TorLoc: 1
Own: Private Company
Key: Salim Karmali, Pres

F & K Manufacturing Company Ltd.

155 Turbine Dr.
Toronto, ON M9L 2S7
Tel 416-749-3980
Fax 416-749-1814
www.fnkmfg.com
Line: Manufactures metal stampings,
tools and dies.
NAICS: 332118
#Emp: 75-99 (Tor)
#TorLoc: 2
Own: Private Company
Par: 976336 Ontario Inc. (CDA)
Key: Jurgen Walch, Pres
George Spinola, Production Mgr
Sanja Bandula, HR Mgr
Steven Rappaport, CFO
Corinne Salt, Purch Mgr
Glenn Cane, Systems Mgr

Fleetwood Fine Furniture LP

80 North Queen St.
Toronto, ON M8Z 2C9
Tel 416-255-1004
Fax 416-255-8975
www.fleetwoodfinefurniture.com
Line: Manufactures custom case goods
for the hospitality industry.
NAICS: 337127
#Emp: 75-99 (Tor)
#TorLoc: 1
Own: Partnership
Par: Counsel Corp. (CDA)
Key: Reg Tiessen, Pres
Inderjeet Khartal, Cont

Fleming Door Products

101 Ashbridge Circ.
Woodbridge, ON L4L 3R5
Tel 416-749-2111
Fax 905-851-8346
www.flemingdoor.com
Line: Manufactures steel doors and
frames for the non-residential building
construction market.
NAICS: 332321
#Emp: 100-249 (Tor)
#TorLoc: 1
Own: Private Company
Par: Assa Abloy (SWE)
Key: Shane McGee, Pres
Steve Everitt, Dir of Ops
Betsy Rampersad, Materials Mgr
David Mezic, IS Mgr
Craig Allan, Sr Mktg Mgr

FlexITy Solutions Inc.

45 Vogell Rd., 8th Fl.
Richmond Hill, ON L4B 3P6
Tel 905-787-3500
Fax 905-787-3599
www.flexity.ca
Line: Offers technology consulting
services.
NAICS: 541510
#Emp: 75-99 (Tor)
Own: Private Company
Key: Peter Stavropoulos, CEO

Flexmaster Canada Limited

1-20 East Pearce St.
Richmond Hill, ON L4B 1B7
Tel 905-731-9411
Fax 905-731-7086
www.flexmaster.com
AKA: Z-Flex; U-Nova Hose; U-Nova
Plastics; Novaflex Group
Line: Manufactures flexible hose and
ducting for construction, boiler and
furnace vent systems.
NAICS: 326220 332999
#Emp: 100-249 (Tor)
#TorLoc: 4
Own: Private Company
Par: Don Flex Holdings Inc. (CDA)
Key: Ian Donnelly, Pres & CEO
Paul Goldfarb, Cont
Melinda Donnelly, Mktg Mgr

Flex-N-Gate Seeburn

65 Industrial Rd.
Tottenham, ON L0G 1W0
Tel 905-936-4245
Fax 905-936-3329
www.flex-n-gate.com
NAICS: 332999 332720 332510
#Emp: 250-499 (Tor)
#TorLoc: 2
Own: Private Company
Par: Flex-N-Gate Seeburn (US)
Key: Elgin Dewar, GM

Flextronics

213 Harry Walker Pkwy. South
Newmarket, ON L3Y 8T3
Tel 905-952-1000
Fax 905-952-1041
www.flextronics.com
Line: Manufactures and services
electronic components.
NAICS: 334410
#Emp: 500-999 (Tor)
#TorLoc: 3
Own: Private Company
Par: Solectron (US)
Key: Tony Shamata, GM
Ettore Bissola, Cont & Corp Services

FlightSafety Canada Ltd.

95 Garratt Blvd.
Toronto, ON M3K 2A5
Tel 416-638-9313
Fax 416-638-3348
www.flightsafety.com
Line: Provides flying instruction
services.
NAICS: 611510
#Emp: 75-99 (Tor)
#TorLoc: 1
Own: Private Company
Par: Flight Safety International (US)
Key: Patrick Coulter, Centre Mgr

Flite Hockey Inc.

2-3400 Ridgeway Dr.
Mississauga, ON L5L 0A2
Tel 905-828-6030
Fax 905-828-1840
www.flitehockey.com
Line: Manufactures and retails ice
hockey equipment.
NAICS: 339920 451110
#Emp: 100-249 (Tor)
#TorLoc: 1
Own: Private Company
Key: Gerry McSorley, Founder & Pres

Flying Colours International

128 Sterling Rd.
Toronto, ON M6R 2B7
Tel 416-535-1151
Fax 416-535-0971
www.flyingcoloursintl.com
AKA: FCI Custom Manufacturing
Line: Manufactures flags and banners,
commission textile furnishing and
custom medical and sports supports.
NAICS: 314910 314990
#Emp: 75-99 (Tor)
#TorLoc: 1
Own: Private Company
Par: Dafina Holdings Ltd. (CDA)
Key: Azam Dawood, Pres & CEO

Flynn Canada Ltd.

6435 Northwest Dr.
Mississauga, ON L4V 1K2
Tel 905-671-3971
Fax 905-740-2048
www.flynn.ca
Line: Provides roofing contracting and
sheet metal work for sidings and decks.
NAICS: 232330 232340
#Emp: 100-249 (Tor)
#TorLoc: 1
Own: Private Company

Key: Doug Flynn, Pres & CEO
John McManus, VP & COO
Sharon Sorak, VP Fin
Jeff Aviss, VP Service

FM Windows & Doors

31 Pennsylvania Ave.
Concord, ON L4K 5V5
Tel 905-738-1870
Fax 905-738-0586
www.fmwindows.com
Line: Manufactures and distributes
vinyl windows.
NAICS: 416390
#Emp: 100-249 (Tor)
#TorLoc: 1
Own: Private Company
Key: Raj Kain, VP Sales & Mktg
Vito Mastorillo, Cont

FNF Canada

A Div. of Fidelity National Financial
55 Supieror Blvd.
Mississauga, ON L5T 2X9
Tel 289-562-0088
Fax 289-562-2494
www.fnf.ca
Line: Provides business solutions
services.
NAICS: 541611
#Emp: 100-249 (Tor)
#TorLoc: 1
Own: Private Company
Key: Peter Coburn, Pres
Paul Zappala, VP Ops, Central Canada
Gillian Shull, Dir of HR
Varun Kumar Singh, VP Fin & Admin
Dustin Allen, VP Sales & Business Dev

Fogler, Rubinoff LLP

1200-95 Wellington St. West
TD Centre
Toronto, ON M5J 2Z9
Tel 416-864-9700
Fax 416-941-8852
www.foglers.com
Line: Operates a legal practice.
NAICS: 541110
#Emp: 100-249 (Tor)
#TorLoc: 2
Own: Private Company
Key: Michael H. Appleton, Mng Partner
Karen Schrempf, Admr
Jennifer Norman, HR Mgr
Marilynn Goodman, Cont

Forbes Hewlett Transport Inc.

156 Glidden Rd.
Brampton, ON L6W 3L2
Tel 905-455-2211
Fax 905-455-9213
www.forbeshewlett.com
Line: Specializes in transborder
shipping and offers contract trucking
and logistics management services.
NAICS: 484121
#Emp: 75-99 (Tor)
#TorLoc: 1
Own: Private Company
Key: George Stott, Pres
Nick Moschella, VP Ops
Vince Valeri, Cont

Ford Motor Company of Canada, Limited

The Canadian Rd.
P.O. Box 2000
Oakville, ON L6J 5E4
Tel 905-845-2511
Fax 905-844-8085
www.ford.ca
NAICS: 336110 415290
#Emp: 1000-4999 (Tor)
#TorLoc: 4
Own: Private Company
Par: Ford Motor Co. (US)
Key: David Mondragon, Pres & CEO

Foresters

789 Don Mills Rd.
Toronto, ON M3C 1T9
Tel 416-429-3000
Fax 416-467-2573
www.foresters.com
AKA: The Independent Order of
Foresters
Line: Offers life insurance products and
services.
NAICS: 524111
#Emp: 500-999 (Tor)
#TorLoc: 2
Own: Private Company
Key: George Mohacsi, Pres & CEO
Peter Sweers, Chief Info & Ops Officer
Suanne Nielsen,
   Sr VP & Chief Talent Officer
Sharon Giffen, CFO
Kasia Czarski, Sr VP
   Chief Membership & Mktg Officer
Irene Shimoda, Dir of PR

Forest Hill Place

A Div. of Lifestyle
Retirement Communities Ltd.
645 Castlefield Ave.
Toronto, ON M5N 3A5
Tel 416-785-1511
Fax 416-785-6228
www.lrc.ca
Line: Operates a for profit retirement
residence.
NAICS: 623110
#Emp: 75-99 (Tor)
#TorLoc: 1
Own: Private Company
Par: Revera Inc. (CDA)
Key: Hartini Kumar, Exec Dir
Tenzin Yanki, Dir of Care
Adrian Antoche, Service Mgr

Forest Hill Real Estate Inc. Brokerage

441 Spadina Rd.
Toronto, ON M5P 2W3
Tel 416-488-2875
Fax 416-488-6024
www.foresthill.com
Line: Operates a real estate brokerage.
NAICS: 531210
#Emp: 250-499 (Tor)
#TorLoc: 3
Own: Private Company
Key: David Wagman, Mng Partner
Ronni Fingold, Mng Partner
Wilma Freedman, Exec Admr
Arnold Bobkin, Mng Partner
Ed Wolf, Mng Partner
Jeffrey Wagman, Broker of Record

Forest Hill Tutoring

303-439 Spadina Rd.
Toronto, ON M5P 3M6
Tel 416-483-6023
Fax 416-483-6107
www.foresthilltutoring.com
Line: Operates a tutoring school.
NAICS: 611690
#Emp: 75-99 (Tor)
#TorLoc: 1
Own: Private Company
Key: Susan Feindel, Dir

Formglas Inc.

2 Champagne Dr.
Toronto, ON M3J 2C5
Tel 416-635-8030
Fax 416-635-6588
www.formglas.com
Line: Manufactures gypsum based
architectural products, fireplace, FG
residential and CNC machining of
patterns for a variety of composite
applications.
NAICS: 327420
#Emp: 75-99 (Tor)
#TorLoc: 1
Own: Private Company
Key: John Chettleburgh, CEO
Richard Samson, VP International
David Williams, VP Fin & Admin

Forrec Ltd.

100C-219 Dufferin St.
Toronto, ON M6K 3J1
Tel 416-696-8686
Fax 416-696-8866
www.forrec.com
Line: Specializes in the design
and planning of themed attraction
entertainment facilities and
environments.
NAICS: 541490
#Emp: 75-99 (Tor)
#TorLoc: 1
Own: Private Company
Key: Gordon Dorrett, Pres
Steve Rhys, Sr VP

Four Points By Sheraton Mississauga - Meadowvale

2501 Argentia Rd.
Mississauga, ON L5N 4G8
Tel 905-858-2424
Fax 905-821-1592
www.fourpoints.com/meadowvale
Line: Operates a hotel.
NAICS: 721111
#Emp: 75-99 (Tor)
#TorLoc: 1
Own: Private Company
Par: Silver Hotel Group (US)
Key: Denzil Miranda, GM
Reggie Bello, Acctng Mgr
Glenna Mitchell, Dir of Sales & Mktg

Four Points by Sheraton Toronto Airport

6257 Airport Rd.
Mississauga, ON L4V 1E4
Tel 905-678-1400
Fax 905-678-9130
www.fourpoints.com/torontoairport
Line: Operates full service hotel.
NAICS: 721111
#Emp: 100-249 (Tor)
#TorLoc: 3
Own: Private Company
Par: Royal Equator Inc. (US)
Key: Ferdinando Miranda, GM
Julian Bugledich, CEO
Caitlin Alwyn, HR Mgr
William Morgan, CFO
Wendy Turner, Dir of Sales & Mktg

Four Seasons Drywall Ltd.

200 Konrad Cres.
Markham, ON L3R 8T9
Tel 905-474-9960
Fax 905-477-6696
Line: Provides drywall and acoustic
ceiling services.
NAICS: 232410
#Emp: 100-249 (Tor)
#TorLoc: 1
Own: Private Company
Key: Werner Zapfe, Owner
Martin Zapfe, Ops Mgr
Ann Downie, Cont

Four Seasons Hotels Limited

1165 Leslie St.
Toronto, ON M3C 2K8
Tel 416-449-1750
Fax 416-441-4319
www.fourseasons.com
AKA: Four Seasons Hotels & Resorts
Line: Operates luxury hotels.
NAICS: 721111
#Emp: 500-999 (Tor)
#TorLoc: 2
Own: Private Company
Par: Four Seasons Hotels Inc. (CDA)
Key: Kathleen Taylor, Pres & COO
Isadore Sharp, Chmn & CEO
James FitzGibbon, Pres,
    Worldwide Hotel Ops
Nicholas Mutton, Exec VP HR & Admin
John Davidson, Exec VP & CFO
Michele Sweeting,
    Sr VP Design & Procurement
Yu Jin, VP IS
Susan Helstab, Exec VP Mktg
Elizabeth Pizzinato,
    VP Brand Commun

Four Star Plating Industries Ltd.

1162 Barmac Dr.
Toronto, ON M9L 1X5
Tel 416-745-1742
Fax 416-745-2960
www.fourstarmetal.com
AKA: Four Star Group
Line: Manufactures plating metal.
NAICS: 332810
#Emp: 100-249 (Tor)
#TorLoc: 1
Own: Private Company
Key: Bronco Lebar, Pres
Christine Lebar, Office Mgr

FPC Flexible Packaging Corp.

1891 Eglinton Ave. East
Toronto, ON M1L 2L7
Tel 416-288-3060
Fax 416-288-0808
www.fpcflexible.com
Line: Manufactures plastic, paper
and foil packaging materials for the
pharmaceutical, tobacco, food and
dairy industries.
NAICS: 326140 322220
#Emp: 100-249 (Tor)
#TorLoc: 1
Own: Private Company
Par: Jacobsen Partners (US)
Key: Don Iwacha, Chmn & CEO
Raj Premsukh, Payroll & HR Mgr
Raj Thangavelu, VP Fin & CFO
Brian Bailey, VP IT

F & P Manufacturing Inc.

1 Nolan Rd.
P.O. Box 4000
Tottenham, ON L0G 1W0
Tel 905-936-3435
Fax 905-936-4809
www.fandpmfg.com
Line: Performs automotive metal
stamping, welding, hydroforming and
assembly.
NAICS: 332118
#Emp: 500-999 (Tor)
#TorLoc: 1
Own: Private Company
Par: F-Tech Inc. (JAPAN)
Key: Andrew Kochanek, Plant Mgr
Kenichi Ando, Pres
Paul Gill, Personnel Mgr

Frankie Tomatto's Ltd.

7225 Woodbine Ave.
Markham, ON L3R 1A3
Tel 905-940-1900
Fax 905-940-1990
www.frankietomatto.com
Line: Operates a family restaurant.
NAICS: 722110
#Emp: 100-249 (Tor)
#TorLoc: 1
Own: Private Company
Key: Hal Roback, Pres
Vicente Sy, VP

Franklin Templeton Investments Corp.

900-5000 Yonge St.
Toronto, ON M2N 0A7
Tel 416-957-6000
Fax 416-364-1163
www.franklintempleton.ca
Line: Operates an investment
management company.
NAICS: 523920
#Emp: 500-999 (Tor)
#TorLoc: 2
Own: Private Company
Par: Franklin Resources, Inc. (US)
Key: Donald Reed, Pres & CEO
Sherry M. Dondo, VP HR
Chen Winston, VP & Cont
Pierre McLean, Sr VP Nat'l Sales
Jennifer Ball, Sr VP Mktg
Keith Damsell, Dir of Commun

Frank's Food Basics

530 Kerr St.
Oakville, ON L6K 3C7
Tel 905-842-1363
Fax 905-842-1453
www.foodbasics.com
Line: Operates a supermarket.
NAICS: 445110
#Emp: 75-99 (Tor)
Own: Private Company
Par: Food Basics (US)
Key: Bob Gillis, Mgr

Fraser Milner Casgrain LLP

Toronto-Dominion Centre,
400-77 King St. West
Toronto, ON M5K 0A1
Tel 416-863-4511
Fax 416-863-4592
www.fmc-law.com
Line: Provides business-to-business
legal services.
NAICS: 541110
#Emp: 250-499 (Tor)
#TorLoc: 1
Own: Private Company
Key: Chris Pinnington, CEO
Mike Kaplan, Mng Partner, Toronto
Chantal Desmarais, CFO

Fraser Papers Inc.

200-181 Bay St.
Brookfield Pl.
Toronto, ON M5J 2T3
Tel 416-359-8605
Fax 416-365-9642
www.fraserpapers.com
Line: Focuses on niche segments in the paper markets.
NAICS: 322299
#Emp: 1000-4999 (Tor)
Own: Public Company
Key: Peter Gordon, Pres & CEO

Fred Victor Centre

145 Queen St. East
Toronto, ON M5A 1S1
Tel 416-364-8228
Fax 416-364-8526
www.fredvictor.org
Line: Operates a not-for-profit multi-service community based organization that assists people living on low income or on the streets of Toronto.
NAICS: 531112
#Emp: 100-249 (Tor)
#TorLoc: 9
Own: Not-for-profit
Key: Mark Aston, Exec Dir
Bernard Granka, Dir of Ops
Debbie Dos Ramos, Dir of HR
Keith Madley, Dir of Fin
Jane Truemner, Dir of Capital
   Fundraising & Commun

Freeman Formalwear Limited

111 Bermondsey Rd.
Toronto, ON M4A 2T7
Tel 416-288-1919
Fax 416-755-9548
www.freemanformal.com
Line: Rents and distributes men's formal wear.
NAICS: 532220
#Emp: 250-499 (Tor)
#TorLoc: 20
Own: Private Company
Key: Sam Freeman, Pres
Leonard Goldstein, VP

Frendel Kitchens Limited

1350 Shawson Dr.
Mississauga, ON L4W 1C5
Tel 905-670-7898
Fax 905-670-1986
www.frendel.com
Line: Manufactures kitchen cabinets and vanities.
NAICS: 337110
#Emp: 100-249 (Tor)
#TorLoc: 1
Own: Private Company
Key: Tony Deltin, Pres
Mike Draganjac, HR Mgr
Marika Zigon, Accounts Payable
Sam Pantusa, Purch Mgr

Freshline Foods Ltd.

A-2501 Stanfield Rd.
Mississauga, ON L4Y 1R6
Tel 905-848-6040
Fax 905-848-6048
www.freshlinefoods.com
NAICS: 413150
#Emp: 100-249 (Tor)
#TorLoc: 1
Own: Private Company
Key: Jim Bamford, Pres
Sanjeev Thakore, VP Fin
Noel Brigido, VP Sales

Fresh Taste Produce Ltd.

343-165 The Queensway
Toronto, ON M8Y 1H8
Tel 416-255-2361
Fax 416-255-9079
www.freshtaste.ca
Line: Wholesales fresh fruit and vegetables.
NAICS: 413150
#Emp: 75-99 (Tor)
#TorLoc: 1
Own: Private Company
Key: Ron Doucet, Pres
Sal Sarraino, CEO
Nelson D'Costa, Cont

Fripes Export Ltd.

310 Midwest Rd.
Toronto, ON M1P 3A9
Tel 416-752-5046
Fax 416-752-8695
Line: Exports second hand clothing.
NAICS: 453310
#Emp: 100-249 (Tor)
#TorLoc: 1
Own: Private Company
Key: Rustam Dharsi, Pres
Sukaina Dharsi, Acctng, Payroll & HR
Chandrika Patel, Export & Import Mgr

Frischkorn Associates Inc.

2440 Tedlo St.
Mississauga, ON L5A 3V3
Tel 905-281-9000
Fax 905-281-8685
www.frischkornav.com
AKA: Frischkorn Audio Visual Rentals Inc.; Audience Response Systems
Line: Provides audio visual staging services and equipment.
NAICS: 532490
#Emp: 75-99 (Tor)
#TorLoc: 9
Own: Private Company
Key: Norbert Frischkorn, Pres
Brad Beach, Ops Mgr
Nancy Bugbee, Cont
Heidi Finnigan, VP Mktg

Frost Pontiac Buick Cadillac Ltd.

320 Queen St. East
Brampton, ON L6V 1C2
Tel 905-459-0126
Fax 905-459-8442
www.frostpontiac.gm.ca
Line: Operates a car dealership.
NAICS: 441110 441120
#Emp: 75-99 (Tor)
#TorLoc: 1
Own: Private Company
Key: Bob Johnston, Pres
John Douglas, CFO

The FSA Group

1351 Rodick Rd.
Markham, ON L3R 5K4
Tel 905-513-6000
Fax 905-513-6001
www.thefsagroup.com
Line: Provides full service lettershop fulfillment, international mailing service and logistics, colour digital variable printing and call centre services.
NAICS: 561430
#Emp: 100-249 (Tor)
#TorLoc: 1
Own: Private Company
Key: Rob Van Velzen, Pres
Christine Custodio,
   Dir of Client Services
Ling Ma, Cont
Rod MacMillan, Dir of IS & Tech
Esme Hurst, Sales Dir

Fudger House

A Div. of The City of Toronto
439 Sherbourne St.
Toronto, ON M4X 1K6
Tel 416-392-5252
Fax 416-392-4174
www.toronto.ca/ltc/fudger.htm
Line: Provides long-term care facility for the aged.
NAICS: 623310
#Emp: 250-499 (Tor)
#TorLoc: 1
Own: Government
Par: The City of Toronto
Key: Lorraine Siu, Admr
Alice Marak, Asst Admr

Fuel Advertising Inc.

308C-219 Dufferin St.
Toronto, ON M6K 3J1
Tel 416-484-6565
Fax 416-484-1046
www.fueladvertising.com
AKA: Draftworldwide Canada Inc.
Line: Operates an advertising agency.
NAICS: 541810
#Emp: 100-249 (Tor)
#TorLoc: 1
Own: Private Company
Key: Tim Hammond, GM
Leslie Kellow-Hall, VP Production
Erica Henry, Office Admr

Fugro Airborne Surveys Corp.

A Div. of C.G.G. Canada Ltd.
2505 Meadowvale Blvd.
Mississauga, ON L5N 5S2
Tel 905-812-0212
Fax 905-812-1504
www.fugroairborne.com
Line: Compiles helicopter geographical surveys.
NAICS: 541360
#Emp: 75-99 (Tor)
#TorLoc: 1
Own: Private Company
Par: Fugro (NETH)
Key: Greg Paleolog, GM
Tina Sabido, HR Mgr

Fujifilm Canada Inc.

600 Suffolk Crt.
Mississauga, ON L5R 4G4
Tel 905-890-6611
Fax 905-890-6446
www.fujifilm.ca
Line: Sells and distributes photo imaging, computer media, video, motion picture and photofinishing products as well as graphic art equipment and consumables.
NAICS: 414430 417930
#Emp: 250-499 (Tor)
#TorLoc: 1
Own: Private Company
Par: Fuji Photo Film Company Ltd. (JAPAN)
Key: Shunji Saito, Pres
Brian Boulanger,
   Group VP & GM, Corp Services
Carol Unruh, VP HR
Harry Weening, Sr Dir of IT

Fujitec Canada Inc.

15 East Wilmot St.
Richmond Hill, ON L4B 1A3
Tel 905-731-8681
Fax 905-731-4608
www.fujiteccanada.com
Line: Manufactures, installs, and services elevators.
NAICS: 232550
#Emp: 75-99 (Tor)
#TorLoc: 1
Own: Private Company
Par: Fijitec Co Ltd. (JAPAN)
Key: Ralph Wischnewski, Pres
Michelle McWhirter, Cont

Fujitsu Consulting (Canada) Inc.

1600-155 University Ave.
Toronto, ON M5H 3B7
Tel 416-363-8661
Fax 416-363-4739
www.fujitsu.com/ca
Line: Provides information technology consulting and delivery services.
NAICS: 541510
#Emp: 100-249 (Tor)
#TorLoc: 1
Own: Private Company
Par: Fujitsu Ltd. (JAPAN)
Key: Andre Pouliot, Pres
Linda Aquino, Dir of HR

Fundserv Inc.

1700-130 King St. West,
The Exchange Tower
P.O. Box 485
Toronto, ON M5X 1E5
Tel 416-362-2400
Fax 416-362-8772
www.fundserv.com
Line: Provides network and application services for the Canadian investment fund industry.
NAICS: 526989
#Emp: 75-99 (Tor)
#TorLoc: 1
Own: Private Company
Key: Brian Gore, Pres & CEO
Harry Gundy, Dir of Product
   Management
Julie Loyola, HR Mgr
Ian Cook, VP Corp Services & CFO
Amir Jafri, VP Tech

Furlani's Food Corp.

1730 Aimco Blvd.
Mississauga, ON L4W 1V1
Tel 905-602-6102
Fax 905-602-9415
www.furlanis.com
Line: Produces bakery products.
NAICS: 311814
#Emp: 100-249 (Tor)
#TorLoc: 1
Own: Private Company
Key: Paul Kawaja, Owner
James Kawaja, Dir of Ops
Greg Cleary, Cont

Future Bakery Ltd.

106 North Queen St.
Toronto, ON M8Z 2E2
Tel 416-231-1491
Fax 416-231-1879
AKA: Aunt Irene's Outlet Store; M-C Dairy Ltd.
Line: Manufactures and sells baked products.
NAICS: 311814 722210
#Emp: 75-99 (Tor)
#TorLoc: 1
Own: Private Company
Key: Boris Wrzesnewskyj,
   Pres & Owner
Edward Pakula, Dir of Fin
Alan Shikitani, Purch Mgr
Ron Galinas, Dir of Sales

Fybon Industries Ltd.

202 Fairbank Ave.
Toronto, ON M6B 4C5
Tel 416-787-0191
Fax 416-787-2077
www.fybon.com
Line: Manufactures non woven textiles.
NAICS: 313230 314990
#Emp: 75-99 (Tor)
#TorLoc: 1
Own: Private Company
Key: Steve Knapp, VP

G4S Cash Solutions (Canada) Ltd.

600-1500 Ferrand Dr.
Toronto, ON M3C 3E5
Tel 416-597-2777
Fax 416-645-5402
www.g4s.com/ca
AKA: Group 4 Securicor (Canada) Ltd.
Line: Provides cash management services to financial institutions, and retail and commercial clients.
NAICS: 561110
#Emp: 500-999 (Tor)
#TorLoc: 2
Own: Private Company
Key: Ed Jamieson, CEO
Han Koren, COO
Mary Bayne, VP HR
Alain Roy, CFO
Glen Wood, Dir of IT
Bill Oliver, VP Sales
Robin Steimberg, Mktg & Commun Mgr

G4S Security Services (Canada) Ltd.

252-50 McIntosh Dr.
Markham, ON L3R 9T3
Tel 905-946-1884
Fax 905-946-1925
www.g4s.com
AKA: G4S Secure Solutions
Line: Provides security officers for industrial, commercial, retail and mall condominiums, airport passenger screening, alarm response and patrol work.
NAICS: 561612
#Emp: 1000-4999 (Tor)
#TorLoc: 5
Own: Public Company
Par: Group 4 Securicor PLC (UK)
Key: Jean P. Taillon, Pres & CEO
Angela Moncada, Corp HR Mgr
Brian Hinton, VP & CFO
Piero Romani, CTO

G.A. Foss Transport Ltd.

220 Doney Cres.
Concord, ON L4K 3A8
Tel 905-761-6601
Fax 905-738-7143
www.fosstransport.ca
Line: Provides transportation services.
NAICS: 488519
#Emp: 75-99 (Tor)
#TorLoc: 1
Own: Private Company
Key: Gordon Foss, VP

Galmar Electrical Contracting Inc.

6-11 Steinway Blvd.
Toronto, ON M9W 6S9
Tel 416-675-6305
Fax 416-675-3991
www.galmarelectric.com
Line: Provides electrical services.
NAICS: 232510
#Emp: 75-99 (Tor)
#TorLoc: 1
Own: Private Company
Key: Giulio Martellacci, Pres
Luigi Martellacci, Ops Mgr
Marie Colella, Fin Mgr
John Martellacci, Estimator

Galvcast Manufacturing Inc.

49 Commerce Cres.
Acton, ON L7J 2X2
Tel 519-853-3540
Fax 519-853-3381
www.galvcast.net
Line: Operates a steel treatment enterprise.
NAICS: 416210
#Emp: 100-249 (Tor)
#TorLoc: 1
Own: Private Company
Key: Steve Christopher, Pres
Ken Christopher, VP

Gambles Ontario Produce Inc.

240-165 The Queensway
Toronto, ON M8Y 1H8
Tel 416-259-6391
Fax 416-259-4302
www.goproduce.com
Line: Wholesales produce.
NAICS: 413150
#Emp: 250-499 (Tor)
#TorLoc: 2
Own: Private Company
Key: Jeff Hughes, Pres & GM
Terry Galati, Cont
Rick Ashford, VP Produce Procurement
Rob Giles, VP Retail Accounts
Angelo Vento, Sales Mgr
Richard Rose, VP Chain Accounts

Gamma-Dynacare Medical Laboratories

115 Midair Crt.
Brampton, ON L6T 5M3
Tel 905-790-3000
Fax 905-790-2990
www.gamma-dynacare.com
Line: Operates a medical diagnostic laboratory.
NAICS: 621510
#Emp: 500-999 (Tor)
#TorLoc: 77
Own: Private Company
Par: Laboratory Corporation of America (US)
Key: Naseem Somani, CEO
Vito Ciciretto, VP Laboratory
    Ops & Customer Service
Pierre Belanger,
    VP HR & Talent Management
Walt Stothers, VP Fin & CFO
Craig Ivany,
    VP Patient Services & Logistics
Chuck Quigley, VP IS
Scott Hickey, VP Strategic
    Planning & Corp Commun

Ganz

1 Pearce Rd.
Woodbridge, ON L4L 3T2
Tel 905-851-6661
Fax 905-851-6669
www.ganz.com
Line: Manufactures stuffed toys and giftware.
NAICS: 339930
#Emp: 500-999 (Tor)
#TorLoc: 1
Own: Private Company
Key: Howard Ganz, Pres
Michael Palumbo, Exec Dir
Marilyn Redfern, Dir of HR
Owen Rogers, Exec VP

G.A.P Adventures Inc.

19 Charlotte St.
Toronto, ON M5V 2H5
Tel 416-260-0999
Fax 416-260-1888
www.gapadventures.com
Line: Offers organized adventure tours.
NAICS: 561510
#Emp: 75-99 (Tor)
#TorLoc: 1
Own: Private Company
Key: Bruce Poon Tip, Pres
Sue Silk, Dir of HR

Gap Inc. Canada

1501-60 Bloor St. West
Toronto, ON M4W 3B8
Tel 416-921-2711
Fax 416-921-2966
www.gapcanada.com
AKA: Old Navy Canada; Banana
Republic Canada; Baby Gap; Gap Kids
Line: Retails casual apparel brand
names.
NAICS: 448140
#Emp: 1000-4999 (Tor)
#TorLoc: 40
Own: Public Company
Par: Gap Inc. (US)
Key: Glenn Murphy, Pres & CEO
Jeff Gomez, Sr Dir of Stores
Paul Kezin, Reg Dir, Banana Republic
Tara Wickwire, Sr Mgr, PR

Garda World Security

36 Scarsdale Rd.
Toronto, ON M3B 2R7
Tel 416-915-9500
Fax 416-915-9700
www.gardaglobal.com
Line: Supplies, installs and services
alarm systems, CCTV card access
and RVM (remote video monitoring)
security; supplies security officers for
malls, high rise buildings, condo's and
special events.
NAICS: 561621 232510
#Emp: 500-999 (Tor)
#TorLoc: 1
Own: Private Company
Key: Warren Greig, GM
Anand Maharaj, HR Mgr

The Garden Basket Food Markets Inc.

1-7676 Woodbine Ave.
Markham, ON L3R 2N2
Tel 905-305-8220
Fax 905-305-8221
www.thegardenbasket.ca
Line: Operates food markets.
NAICS: 445110
#Emp: 100-249 (Tor)
#TorLoc: 1
Own: Private Company
Key: Jack Comella, Pres
Sandy Di Nardo, Store Mgr
Gregory Smith, Cont
Joseph Comella, Produce Buyer

Gardiner Roberts LLP

3100-40 King St. West, Scotia Plaza
Toronto, ON M5H 3Y2
Tel 416-865-6600
Fax 416-865-6636
www.gardiner-roberts.com
Line: Operates law firm.
NAICS: 541110
#Emp: 100-249 (Tor)
#TorLoc: 1
Own: Private Company
Key: David Fine, Mng Partner
Paul Stoyan, Chmn
Mary Fraizinger, CFO
Tracy Ross, Dir of HR

Garland Commercial Ranges Ltd.

1177 Kamato Rd.
Mississauga, ON L4W 1X4
Tel 905-624-0260
Fax 905-624-5669
www.garland.group.com
AKA: The Garland Group
Line: Manufactures commercial
cooking equipment.
NAICS: 333413 333310
#Emp: 250-499 (Tor)
#TorLoc: 1
Own: Public Company
Par: Enodis plc (UK)
Key: Jacques Seguin, Pres
John Beck, VP & GM
Jane Frost, HR Mgr
Victor Gray, Dir of IS
Mary Chiarot, Dir of Mktg

Garnet A. Williams Community Centre

501 Clark Ave. West
Thornhill, ON L4J 4E5
Tel 905-832-8552
Fax 905-881-0692
www.vaughan.ca
NAICS: 624190
#Emp: 100-249 (Tor)
#TorLoc: 1
Own: Private Company
Par: City of Vaughan
Key: Lorne Hilts,
Recreation Services Supr

Gary Jonas Computing Ltd.

500-45 Vogell Rd.
Richmond Hill, ON L4B 3P6
Tel 905-886-0544
Fax 905-763-8324
www.jonassoftware.com
Line: Provides fully integrated
software solutions for private club,
golf, construction and food service
industries.
NAICS: 511210
#Emp: 100-249 (Tor)
#TorLoc: 1
Own: Private Company
Par: Constellation Software Inc. (CDA)
Key: Barry Symons, CEO
Jim Fedigan, COO, Club Division
Gail Dennison, Dir of HR
Trace Keats, CFO
Bill Buck, VP Tech, Club Division
Paul Gillard, VP Sales, Club Division
Vache Hagopian, Dir of Mktg

Gates Canada Inc.

1325 Cormorant Rd.
Ancaster, ON L9G 4V5
Tel 905-304-9455
Fax 905-304-8972
www.gates.com
Line: Manufactures and designs power
metal parts and components for
automotive engines and transmissions.
NAICS: 336390 336350
#Emp: 500-999 (Tor)
#TorLoc: 5
Own: Public Company
Par: Tomkins plc (UK)
Key: Ron Duke, VP Sales & Mktg
Jennifer Foster, VP HR
Wendy Young, Dir of IT

Gateway Chevrolet Inc.

2 Gateway Blvd.
Brampton, ON L6T 4A7
Tel 905-791-7111
Fax 905-791-0651
www.gatewaychev.gmcanada.com
Line: Operates a car dealership.
NAICS: 441110 441120
#Emp: 75-99 (Tor)
#TorLoc: 1
Own: Private Company
Key: William Wallace, Dealer Principal
Ron Motz, Secy-Treas

Gatsteel Industries Inc.

361 Attwell Dr.
Toronto, ON M9W 5C2
Tel 416-675-2370
Fax 416-675-6785
www.gatsteel.com
Line: Wholesales steel.
NAICS: 416210
#Emp: 75-99 (Tor)
#TorLoc: 1
Own: Private Company
Key: Toros Assadourian, Pres

Gay Lea Foods

5200 Orbitor Dr.
Mississauga, ON L4W 5B4
Tel 905-283-5300
Fax 800-268-0509
www.gaylea.com
NAICS: 311990
#Emp: 100-249 (Tor)
#TorLoc: 2
Own: Private Company
Key: Andrew MacGillivray, Pres
Michael Barrett, COO
John Rebry, CFO
Larry Hook, VP Sales & Mktg

Gazzola Paving Ltd.

529 Carlingview Dr.
Toronto, ON M9W 5H2
Tel 416-675-7007
Fax 416-675-4370
www.gazzolapaving.com
Line: Operates a construction company.
NAICS: 231310
#Emp: 100-249 (Tor)
#TorLoc: 1
Own: Private Company
Key: Mark Gazzola, Pres
Vern Gazzola, VP
Virgil Gazzola, Ops Mgr
Vickie Piscione, Office Mgr
Russel Brenmer, Cont

GBC Canada

5 Precidio Crt.
Brampton, ON L6S 6B7
Tel 416-447-4951
Fax 800-422-7135
www.gbccanada.com
Line: Manufactures and markets
binding, laminating, shredding and
security identification systems and
related supplies.
NAICS: 323120
#Emp: 100-249 (Tor)
#TorLoc: 1
Own: Private Company
Par: Acco Brands Inc. (CDA)
Key: Blair Seward, VP & GM
Francis Ko, Production Supr
Vince Fanizza, Cont
Martin Cox, VP Sales & Mktg

G. Brandt Meat Packers Ltd.

1878 Mattawa Ave.
Mississauga, ON L4X 1K1
Tel 905-279-4460
Fax 905-279-9155
www.brandtmeats.com
Line: Produces European style cold
cuts, hams and salamis.
NAICS: 311614
#Emp: 100-249 (Tor)
#TorLoc: 1
Own: Private Company
Key: Ida Brandt-Kuehn, Pres
Peter D'uva, Ops Mgr
Irene O'Hara, Payroll & HR Admin
Tom Martens, Cont
Brigitte Brandt-Welzel,
    VP Sales & Mktg

GCAN Insurance Co.

181 University Ave., 10th Fl.
Toronto, ON M5H 3M7
Tel 416-682-5300
Fax 416-682-9213
www.gcan.ca
Line: Provides property and casualty
insurance.
NAICS: 524129 524124
#Emp: 75-99 (Tor)
#TorLoc: 1
Own: Private Company
Par: Glenstone Capital (CDA)
Key: Daniel Courtemanche,
    Pres, CEO & Dir
Sandra Henkel, VP HR,
    Admin & Compliance
Tom P. MacDowall, Sr VP & Treas

GE Capital

100-2300 Meadowvale Blvd.
Mississauga, ON L5N 5P9
Tel 905-858-4900
Fax 905-858-4910
www.gecapitalsolutions.ca
Line: Operates a commercial finance
institution.
NAICS: 522299
#Emp: 100-249 (Tor)
#TorLoc: 1
Own: Public Company
Par: GE Capital (US)
Key: Brady Dunlop, VP

GE Capital Fleet Services

2300 Meadowvale Blvd.
Mississauga, ON L5N 5P9
Tel 905-858-4900
Fax 905-288-3717
www.gecapital.ca
Line: Offers vehicle leasing and fleet
management services and access to GE
Capital's extensive financial expertise,
cross-industry specialization and a
network of 21 offices across Canada.
NAICS: 532111
#Emp: 100-249 (Tor)
#TorLoc: 1
Own: Private Company
Par: General Electric Co. (US)
Key: Prithviraj Dasgupta, Sr VP &
    Business Leader, Fleet Services
Rob Dalicandro, IT Mgr
Chris Gittens, VP Sales

GE Commercial Distribution Finance Canada

1000-1290 Central Pkwy. West
Mississauga, ON L5C 4R3
Tel 905-273-7500
Fax 905-273-7598
www.gecdf.com
Line: Offers commercial lending.
NAICS: 522190
#Emp: 100-249 (Tor)
#TorLoc: 1
Own: Private Company
Par: General Electric Company (US)
Key: Peter Ringler, Pres
Sonia Boyle, Sr HR Leader

Gemma Communications LP

375-700 Lawrence Ave. West
Toronto, ON M6A 3B4
Tel 416-256-1800
Fax 416-256-6499
www.gemmacom.com
Line: Provides a full range of call centre services including inbound and outbound sales and services.
NAICS: 541611
#Emp: 1000-4999 (Tor)
#TorLoc: 3
Own: Private Company
Key: Stephen Gross, Pres & CEO
Allan Jurgens, VP
Michael Cravit, VP Sales

General Electric Canada

2300 Meadowvale Blvd.
Mississauga, ON L5N 5P9
Tel 905-858-5100
www.ge.com/canada
AKA: GE Canada
Line: Provides financial services and manufactures and distributes a variety of industrial and consumer products.
NAICS: 335312 333611 336410
#Emp: 1000-4999 (Tor)
Own: Private Company
Par: General Electric Co. (US)
Key: Elyse Allan, Pres & CEO
Anna Cvecich, VP HR
Manjit Sharma, VP Fin
Hani Ayoub, VP GE Trading
Kim Warburton, VP PR

General Kinetics Engineering Corp.

110 East Dr.
Brampton, ON L6T 1C1
Tel 905-458-0888
Fax 905-458-7566
www.kinetics.ca
Line: Produces shock absorbers.
NAICS: 336330
#Emp: 75-99 (Tor)
#TorLoc: 1
Own: Private Company
Key: Charles Williamson, Pres
Nigel Sizmur, Manuf Mgr
Janey Obad, Cont & HR
Melissa Morris, Customer Service Mgr

General Mills Canada Corp.

5825 Explorer Dr.
Mississauga, ON L4W 5P6
Tel 905-212-4000
Fax 905-212-4122
www.generalmills.com
Line: Manufactures, markets, and distributes packaged foods.
NAICS: 311230 311990 413110
#Emp: 250-499 (Tor)
#TorLoc: 1
Own: Private Company
Par: General Mills, Inc. (US)
Key: Dave Homer, Pres
Erin Lien, VP Supply Chain
Brad Taylor, VP HR
Brett White, VP Fin
Mark Ostlie, Dir of IT
Doug McGillivray, VP Sales

General Motors Acceptance Corporation of Canada Ltd.

2800-3300 Bloor St. West
Toronto, ON M8X 2X5
Tel 416-234-6600
Fax 416-234-6614
www.gmcanada.com
AKA: Allied Credit
Line: Provides automotive finance services.
NAICS: 522220
#Emp: 250-499 (Tor)
#TorLoc: 3
Own: Private Company
Par: General Motors Acceptance Corp. (US)
Key: Tom E. Dickerson, Pres
Peter A. Andrew,
    Reg Dir, Consumer Lending
Paul Jeffrey, Commun Supr

General Motors Financial of Canada Ltd.

600-2001 Sheppard Ave. East
Toronto, ON M2J 4Z8
Tel 416-753-4000
Fax 416-753-4101
www.financialinx.com
Line: Provides car and auto leasing services.
NAICS: 532112 532120
#Emp: 100-249 (Tor)
#TorLoc: 1
Own: Private Company
Key: Howard Cobham,
  Sr VP Dealer Services
Cheryl Wallace, Dir of HR
Robert Coulman, VP Fin
John Moreira, Dir of IT

General Motors of Canada Ltd.

1908 Colonel Sam Dr.
Oshawa, ON L1H 8P7
Tel 905-644-5000
Fax 905-644-3830
www.gmcanada.com
Line: Manufactures, assembles and distributes passenger cars and trucks as well as parts and accessories.
NAICS: 336110 336390
#Emp: 5000-9999 (Tor)
#TorLoc: 5
Own: Private Company
Par: General Motors Corp. (US)
Key: Kevin Williams, Pres
Elise Grenier,
    Gen Dir of HR Management
Rick Westenberg, VP Fin
Timothy Fenton, CIO
Marc Comeau,
    VP Sales, Service & Mktg

General Sprinklers Inc.

4-315 Deerhide Cres.
Toronto, ON M9M 2Z2
Tel 416-748-1175
Fax 416-748-1548
Line: Installs sprinkler systems.
NAICS: 232530
#Emp: 75-99 (Tor)
#TorLoc: 1
Own: Private Company
Key: Danny Palumbo, Pres & GM

General Switchgear & Controls Ltd./Markham Electric Division

380 Markland St.
Markham, ON L6C 1T6
Tel 905-888-0557
Fax 905-888-0551
www.gs.on.ca
Line: Manufactures and sells electrical switchgears, control panels, disconnect switches and related electrical products.
NAICS: 335315 332319
#Emp: 75-99 (Tor)
#TorLoc: 1
Own: Private Company
Par: GS Management Group Inc. (CDA)
Key: Joy Sarkar, Pres
Mike O'Brien, Mgr of Ops
Rini Robertson, Accounts & Payroll Mgr
Rakesh Dewan, Cont
John Bender, Mgr of Mktg & Sales

The General Synod of the Anglican Church of Canada

80 Hayden St.
Toronto, ON M4Y 3G2
Tel 416-924-9192
Fax 416-924-0211
www.anglican.ca
AKA: Anglican Church of Canada
NAICS: 813110
#Emp: 100-249 (Tor)
#TorLoc: 1
Own: Not-for-profit
Key: Fred Hiltz,
  Primate, Anglican Church of Canada
Sandra Kitson, HR Mgr,
  Gen Secy's Office
Michelle George, Acting Treas,
  Financial Management
Nancy Hurn, Archivist
Henriette Thompson, Coord for
  Ecuminial Interface Advocacy
Vianney (Sam) Carriere, Dir of
  Commun & Info Resources

Genesis Worldwide Inc.

2-125 Traders Blvd. East
Vaughan, ON L6A 0K6
Tel 647-295-2284
Fax 905-858-2273
www.genesisworldwide.com
Line: Provides structural light steel
framing technologies.
NAICS: 541510
#Emp: 75-99 (Tor)
Own: Public Company
Key: Richard Pope, Pres & CEO
Brett Hutington, VP Ops
Wil Lindgren, VP Fin

Genivar Ontario Inc.

600 Cochrane Dr., 5th Fl.
Markham, ON L3R 5K3
Tel 905-475-7270
Fax 905-475-5994
www.genivar.com
Line: Provides engineering and project
management services.
NAICS: 541619
#Emp: 250-499 (Tor)
#TorLoc: 4
Own: Public Company
Par: Genivar Inc. (CDA)
Key: Brian Barber, Sr VP, GTA
Andrea Mackenzie, HR Mgr

Gennum Corp.

4281 Harvester Rd.
Burlington, ON L7L 5M4
Tel 905-632-2996
Fax 905-632-2055
www.gennum.com
Line: Designs and manufactures
integrated circuits for the hearing
instrument, professional video
broadcast, and data communications
market.
NAICS: 334220
#Emp: 500-999 (Tor)
#TorLoc: 1
Own: Public Company
Key: Frank Fink, Pres & CEO
Hari Subramaniam, Dir of Ops
Bruce W. Hannah, HR
Gregory Miller, VP Fin & Admin
Ken Martin, CTO
Robin Vaitonis, Dir of Corp Commun

Genpak LP

285 Industrial Pkwy. South
Aurora, ON L4G 3V8
Tel 905-727-0121
Fax 905-727-6953
www.progressivepac.com
AKA: Progressive Pac
Line: Manufactures flexible packaging
and plastic bags.
NAICS: 326198
#Emp: 100-249 (Tor)
#TorLoc: 2
Own: Private Company
Par: Jim Pattison Group (CDA)
Key: Andy Pattenden, Plant Mgr
Kristine Arthurs, Dir of Fin

Gensys Telecommunications Laboratories Inc.

1380 Rodick Rd.
Markham, ON L3R 4G5
Tel 905-968-3300
www.genesys.com
Line: Develops computer software.
NAICS: 541510
#Emp: 75-99 (Tor)
Own: Private Company
Par: Alcatel (FR)
Key: Adrian Lee-Kwen, VP Engineering
Gloria Karauskas, Mgr of HR

Gentec International Ltd.

90 Royal Crest Crt.
Markham, ON L3R 9X6
Tel 905-513-7733
Fax 905-513-7740
www.gentec-intl.com
Line: Distributes photographic,
optical, cellular phone and electronic
accessories.
NAICS: 417320
#Emp: 75-99 (Tor)
#TorLoc: 1
Own: Private Company
Key: Joel Seigel, Pres & CEO
Garry Toon, VP Ops
Margaret Adat, Exec VP & CFO
Brad Lloyd,
  Mng Dir for Imaging Division
Aimee Houston,
  Sr Mktg & Commun Mgr

Gentek Building Products Ltd.

1001 Corporate Dr.
Burlington, ON L7L 5V5
Tel 905-319-5561
Fax 905-319-5620
www.gentek.ca
Line: Manufactures and markets
building products materials for
renovation and new construction
in the residential housing and
light commercial markets through
authorized dealers, contractors,
distributors and DIY service centres.
NAICS: 416390
#Emp: 100-249 (Tor)
#TorLoc: 1
Own: Private Company
Par: Associated Materials Inc. (US)
Key: Thomas Chieffe, CEO
Carol Matthewson, HR Mgr
Christine Van Egmond, Mktg Supr

Genworth Financial Mortgage Insurance Company Canada

300-2060 Winston Park Dr.
Oakville, ON L6H 5R7
Tel 800-511-8888
Fax 800-927-6323
www.gemortgage.ca
AKA: Genworth Financial
Line: Offers default mortgage insurance.
NAICS: 561420
#Emp: 100-249 (Tor)
#TorLoc: 1
Own: Public Company
Par: General Electric Co. (US)
Key: Peter Vukanovich,
    Exec VP Corp Dev
Brian Hurley, Chmn & CEO
Susan Noonan, VP Ops
Gordon McDonald, Dir of HR
Philip Mayers, Sr VP & CFO
Cecilia Carbonelli, VP IT
Debbie McPherson, Sr VP Sales & Mktg

GenX Inc.

510-1075 Bay St.
Toronto, ON M5S 2B1
Tel 416-920-3000
Fax 416-920-0368
www.genx.ca
AKA: GenX Solutions
Line: Provides information technology services.
NAICS: 541510 541611
#Emp: 75-99 (Tor)
#TorLoc: 1
Own: Public Company
Key: Eric Lo, Pres
Ted Kernaghan, Sales Mgr

Geo. A. Kelson Company Limited

1135 Stellar Dr.
Newmarket, ON L3Y 7B8
Tel 905-898-3400
Fax 905-898-5491
www.kelson.on.ca
Line: Supplies, installs and maintains mechanical services in the ICI sector of the construction industry.
NAICS: 232520
#Emp: 100-249 (Tor)
#TorLoc: 1
Own: Private Company
Key: Rod Kelson, Pres
Michelle Kelson, CFO

George Brown College of Applied Arts and Technology

P.O. Box 1015, Stn. B
Toronto, ON M5T 2T9
Tel 416-415-5000
Fax 416-415-4384
www.georgebrown.ca
Line: Operates post-secondary educational facilities offering diplomas, degrees, continuous education courses and programs, apprenticeship training and certificates.
NAICS: 611210
#Emp: 1000-4999 (Tor)
#TorLoc: 3
Own: Government
Key: Anne Sado, Pres
Eugene Harrigan, VP Corp Services & External Relns
Nancy Hood, Exec Dir of HR
Ric Ho, Cont
Karic Au,
    Mgr of Financial Planning & Purch
Yves Hebert, CIO
Michael Cooke, VP Academic
Karen Thomson, VP Mktg & Strategic Enrolment Management
Brian Stock, Commun Mgr

George Kelk Corp.

48 Lesmill Rd.
Toronto, ON M3B 2T5
Tel 416-445-5850
Fax 416-445-5972
www.kelk.com
Line: Manufactures and designs electronic measurement equipment used in steel and aluminum rolling mills, paper mills and mining applications.
NAICS: 334512
#Emp: 100-249 (Tor)
#TorLoc: 1
Own: Private Company
Par: Endevor Inc. (CDA)
Key: Peter Kelk, Pres
Keith Thompson, VP Production
Sabrina Ramprashad, HR Mgr
Rob Ricciatti, VP Sales & Mktg

Georgetown Terminal Warehouses Ltd.

34 Armstrong Ave.
Georgetown, ON L7G 4R9
Tel 905-873-2750
Fax 905-873-6170
www.gtwcanada.com
Line: Provides warehousing and distribution for the book industry.
NAICS: 493110

#Emp: 75-99 (Tor)
#TorLoc: 1
Own: Private Company
Key: Brenda Sisnett, Pres
Christine Castello, COO
Hank Visser, Dir of Business Dev

Georgia-Pacific Canada/ Consumer Products, Inc.

228 Queen St. West
Brampton, ON L6X 1A9
Tel 905-451-0620
Fax 905-451-8466
www.gp.com
Line: Manufactures and distributes paper and plastic single service food and beverage containers, cutlery, towel and tissue products.
NAICS: 418220
#Emp: 250-499 (Tor)
#TorLoc: 2
Own: Public Company
Par: Georgia-Pacific Corp. (US)
Key: Greg Clement,
    Dir of Dixie Cdn Ops
Joyce Compton, HR Mgr, Canada

Georgia-Pacific Canada, Inc.

350 Argyle St. North
Caledonia, ON N3W 1M2
Tel 905-765-1570
Fax 905-765-1512
www.gp.com
Line: Sells gypsum wallboard, drywall finishing products, industrial and building plasters, and related products.
NAICS: 416390
#Emp: 100-249 (Tor)
#TorLoc: 2
Own: Public Company
Par: Georgia-Pacific Corp. (US)
Key: Ed Koopman, Plant Mgr
Connie Stubbs, HR Mgr
Scott Overbaugh, Cont, Eastern Canada

GeoSoft Inc.

810-207 Queens Quay West
P.O. Box 131
Toronto, ON M5J 1A7
Tel 416-369-0111
Fax 416-369-9599
www.geosoft.com
NAICS: 541510
#Emp: 75-99 (Tor)
#TorLoc: 1
Own: Private Company
Key: Tim Dobush, CEO

Gerber Canada Inc.

A Div. of Novartis Consumer
Health Canada Inc.
205-2233 Argentia Rd.
Mississauga, ON L5N 2X7
Tel 905-812-4190
Fax 905-821-4936
www.novartis.ca
Line: Manufactures baby products.
NAICS: 311420 339930
#Emp: 75-99 (Tor)
#TorLoc: 3
Own: Private Company
Key: Rick Lloyd,
Pres & CEO, Animal Health

Gerdau Ameristeel

1801 Hopkins St. South
Whitby, ON L1N 5T1
Tel 905-668-3535
Fax 905-668-1512
www.gerdauameristeel.com
Line: Produces hot rolled rebar, angles,
channels, rounds, beams and flats
for construction and light structural
fabrication throughout North America.
NAICS: 416210
#Emp: 500-999 (Tor)
#TorLoc: 2
Own: Public Company
Par: Gerdau (BRZ)
Key: Mike Garcia, Reg Mgr
Roger Paiva, VP & GM, Whitby Mill
Al Lamb, Bar Mill Mgr
Natasha Cotter, Mgr of HR
Wayne Thiessen, Cont, Whitby Mill

Gerrard-Oval Strapping

735 Oval Crt.
Burlington, ON L7L 6A9
Tel 905-632-3662
Fax 905-639-2290
www.goval.com
AKA: GO Packaging
Line: Manufactures equipment for the
reinforcing of all products.
NAICS: 322220
#Emp: 100-249 (Tor)
#TorLoc: 1
Own: Private Company
Par: Samuel & Son Ltd. (CDA)
Key: Doug Lakusta, VP
Yvonne McCurbin, HR Mgr
Lisa Schneider, Cont

Gerrie Electric Wholesale Ltd.

4104 South Service Rd.
Burlington, ON L7L 4X5
Tel 905-681-3656
Fax 905-681-3221
www.gerrie.com
NAICS: 416110
#Emp: 100-249 (Tor)
#TorLoc: 15
Own: Private Company
Key: Heather Gerrie, Co-Pres & CEO
Kenneth Gerrie, Chmn
Elaine Gerrie, Co-Pres & CEO
Richard Solonenko,
    Exec VP Ops & CFO
Carmen Stewart, Exec VP Sales & CMO

Gerrity Corrugated Paper Products Ltd.

75 Doney Cres.
Concord, ON L4K 1P6
Tel 416-798-7758
Fax 416-798-1130
www.gerrity.com
AKA: Gerrity Corrugated & Computer
Line: Manufactures corrugated
packaging products.
NAICS: 322130
#Emp: 100-249 (Tor)
#TorLoc: 2
Own: Private Company
Key: Blaine Gerrity, Pres
Tom Gerrity, CEO
Scott Gerrity, VP
Tammi Chalk, Acctng

Gertex Hosiery Inc.

9 Densley Ave.
Toronto, ON M6M 2P5
Tel 416-241-2345
Fax 416-241-6904
www.gertex.com
Line: Manufactures hosiery.
NAICS: 315110
#Emp: 75-99 (Tor)
#TorLoc: 1
Own: Private Company
Key: Aaron Mendelbaum, Pres
Morley Goldman, CFO

GES Canada Exposition Services Ltd.

5675 McLaughlin Rd.
Mississauga, ON L5R 3K5
Tel 905-283-0500
Fax 905-283-0501
www.gesexpo.ca
AKA: Showtech Power & Lighting
Line: Provides decorative and electrical
contracting services for tradeshows.
NAICS: 561920
#Emp: 75-99 (Tor)
#TorLoc: 1
Own: Public Company
Par: GES Exposition Services (US)
Key: Michael Lecour, Exec VP
Brian Eaton, Reg Dir of HR
Brian Blenkarn, Reg Dir of Fin
Rena Menzies, Reg Sales Mgr

Gesco Industries Inc.

50 Kenview Blvd.
Brampton, ON L6T 5S8
Tel 905-789-3755
Fax 905-789-3757
www.geshnier.com
AKA: G.E. Shnier Co.
Line: Markets, sells, and distributes
floor covering products, programs and
services.
NAICS: 414320 442210
#Emp: 75-99 (Tor)
#TorLoc: 1
Own: Private Company
Key: Edward duDomaine, Pres & CEO
Doug Wilcox, Dir of Ops
Elaine Peace, Dir of HR
John Deotto, Dir of Fin
Paul Green, Dir of Sales
Carmen Chilelli, Dir of Merchandising

Gib-San Pools Ltd.

59 Milvan Dr.
Toronto, ON M9L 1Y8
Tel 416-749-4361
Fax 416-749-4348
www.gibsanpools.com
AKA: Gib-San Pool & Hot Tub Centre
Line: Retails, constructs and maintains
swimming pools.
NAICS: 232990
#Emp: 100-249 (Tor)
#TorLoc: 2
Own: Private Company
Key: Edward Gibbs, Pres & CEO
Peter Friis, COO
Cathy Barrett, HR Mgr
Chris Tanaka, Cont

Giesecke & Devrient Systems Canada, Inc.

316 Markland St.
Markham, ON L6C 0C1
Tel 905-475-1333
Fax 905-475-0300
www.gi-de.com
Line: Manufactures plastic cards.
NAICS: 326198 541510
#Emp: 250-499 (Tor)
#TorLoc: 1
Own: Private Company
Par: Gieseke & Devrient GmbH (GER)
Key: Edgar Salib, Pres
Paul Winkelstein, VP Ops
Susan Bishop, VP HR
Mark Wright, CFO
Mark Keating, VP IT
Willis Morettin, Sr VP Sales & Mktg
Cheryl Hutton,
    Sr Mgr Mktg & Commun

Giftcraft Ltd.

8550 Airport Rd.
Brampton, ON L6T 5A3
Tel 905-790-2000
Fax 905-790-0738
www.giftcraft.com
Line: Distributes wholesale giftware,
home decor and collectibles.
NAICS: 418990
#Emp: 250-499 (Tor)
#TorLoc: 1
Own: Private Company
Key: Trevor Cohen, Pres & CEO
Ron Tomiuck, COO
Ivona Kluza Shymko, HR Mgr
Leslie LePage, VP Fin
John Brooks, VP Sales, North America
Christine Lagerwij, VP Merchandising

Gilbert Steel Ltd.

1650 Britannia Rd. East
Mississauga, ON L4W 1J2
Tel 905-670-5771
Fax 905-670-5668
www.gilbertsteel.com
Line: Fabricates reinforcing steel
products.
NAICS: 331110
#Emp: 100-249 (Tor)
#TorLoc: 1
Own: Private Company
Key: Gary Gilbert, Pres
Tony Plobner, GM
Al Farmer, HR
Ken Jones, Cont
Ahmad Ghanavatian,
    Chief Estimating & Project Mgr

Give & Go Prepared Foods Ltd.

6650 Finch Ave. West
Toronto, ON M9W 5Y6
Tel 416-675-0114
Fax 416-675-0155
www.giveandgo.com
Line: Wholesales bakery products.
NAICS: 413190
#Emp: 500-999 (Tor)
#TorLoc: 2
Own: Private Company
Key: Joel Flatt, Pres
Todd Parsons, COO & CFO
Christine Packham, Dir of HR

G & K Services Canada Inc.

101-6299 Airport Rd.
Mississauga, ON L4V 1N3
Tel 905-677-6161
Fax 905-677-6301
www.gkservices.com
Line: Rents uniform apparel.
NAICS: 812330
#Emp: 250-499 (Tor)
#TorLoc: 3
Own: Public Company
Par: G&K Services Inc. (US)
Key: Robert Wood, Pres
Giuseppe Brumale, Reg VP
Deen Maharaj, Dir of HR
George Guthrie, Cont
Michael Fox, Dir of Sales
Keshia Khan, Sr Mktg Mgr

Glasvan Trailers Inc.

1201 Aimco Blvd.
Mississauga, ON L4W 1B3
Tel 905-625-8441
Fax 905-625-9787
www.glasvangreatdane.com
Line: Distributes transport trailers and
parts.
NAICS: 417230
#Emp: 100-249 (Tor)
#TorLoc: 4
Own: Private Company
Key: Paul Cobham, Pres
George Cobham Sr., Chmn & CEO
Joe Bradica, Service Mgr
Rod McGillivray, VP Fin

GlaxoSmithKline Inc.

7333 Mississauga Rd. North
Mississauga, ON L5N 6L4
Tel 905-819-3000
Fax 905-819-3099
www.gsk.ca
Line: Operates a pharmaceutical
company.
NAICS: 325410 325999
#Emp: 1000-4999 (Tor)
#TorLoc: 3
Own: Private Company
Par: Glaxo Holdings plc (UK)
Key: Paul N. Lucas, Pres & CEO
Kenn Lendrum, VP, GMS Canada
Herman Van Barneveld, VP Fin
Ravinder Kumar,
    VP Regulatory Affairs & Dev Ops
Savino DiPasquale, VP IT Business Dev
Cheryl MacDiarmid, VP Sales
Ed Dybka, VP Mktg
Patrick McGrade,
    Legal Gen Counsel Commun

Glen Abbey Golf Club

1333 Dorval Dr.
Oakville, ON L6J 4Z3
Tel 905-844-1800
Fax 905-844-2035
www.clublink.ca
NAICS: 713910
#Emp: 250-499 (Tor)
#TorLoc: 1
Own: Private Company
Par: ClubLink Corp. (CDA)
Key: John Finlayson, Dir of Ops

Glencairn Golf Club

9807 Regional Rd. 25
Halton Hills, ON L9T 2X7
Tel 905-876-3666
Fax 905-876-0496
www.clublink.ca
NAICS: 713910
#Emp: 100-249 (Tor)
#TorLoc: 1
Own: Private Company
Par: ClubLink Corp. (CDA)
Key: Craig Cupido, Dir of Ops

Glenn A. Davis & Associates Ltd.

301-755 Queensway East
Mississauga, ON L4Y 4C5
Tel 905-270-2501
Fax 905-270-3969
www.davisdesign.ca
AKA: Davis Bridgemark; B2 Retail Solutions
Line: Provides branding and graphic design services with specialty in consumer packaging.
NAICS: 541430
#Emp: 100-249 (Tor)
#TorLoc: 3
Own: Private Company
Key: Aubrey Ferguson, Pres, Bridgemark
Ron Davis, CEO
Steve Davis, COO
Celeste Mendonca, HR Mgr
Warren Clayton, VP Fin
Jeff Ridpath, Tech Developer

Glenway Country Club (1994) Ltd.

470 Crossland Gate
Newmarket, ON L3X 1B8
Tel 905-853-5590
Fax 905-853-7954
www.glenwaycountryclub.com
Line: Operates membership sports and fitness facility.
NAICS: 713910 713940
#Emp: 100-249 (Tor)
#TorLoc: 1
Own: Private Company
Par: Glenway Country Club (CDA)
Key: Gary Lester, Pres
Peter Williams, Cont
Lisa Brooks, Dir of Sales & Mktg
Christine Wong, Mktg Coord

Global Contract Inc.

565 Petrolia Rd.
Toronto, ON M3J 2X8
Tel 416-739-5000
Fax 416-739-7848
www.globalcontract.com
Line: Manufactures office furniture.
NAICS: 337214
#Emp: 250-499 (Tor)
#TorLoc: 3
Own: Private Company
Key: Chanoch Friedel, Pres
Tony Davis, HR Mgr
Tony Sacco, Cont

Global Driver Services Inc.

16&17-1415 Bonhill Dr.
Mississauga, ON L5T 1R2
Tel 416-249-2373
Fax 905-564-6058
www.fordrivers.com
Line: Operates truck driver leasing, placement and recruiting company.
NAICS: 561310
#Emp: 500-999 (Tor)
#TorLoc: 1
Own: Private Company
Par: CPC Logistics (CDA)
Key: John Harrison, GM

Global File Inc.

1350 Flint Rd.
Toronto, ON M3J 2J7
Tel 905-761-3284
Fax 905-761-3282
AKA: Global Upholstery
Line: Manufactures filing cabinets.
NAICS: 337214
#Emp: 100-249 (Tor)
#TorLoc: 1
Own: Private Company
Key: Saul Feldberg, Pres
Joel Feldberg, COO
Helen Bennett, Office Mgr

Global Human Resource Centre

217-777 Warden Ave.
Toronto, ON M1L 4C3
Tel 416-285-6858
Fax 416-285-9193
www.ghrc.ca
Line: Provides temporary help and personnel services.
NAICS: 561320
#Emp: 100-249 (Tor)
#TorLoc: 2
Own: Private Company
Key: Fred Wood, Owner

Global Knowledge

1200-2 Bloor St. West
Toronto, ON M4W 3E2
Tel 416-964-8688
Fax 416-920-2180
www.globalknowledge.ca
Line: Provides information technology training services to individuals and corporate clients.
NAICS: 611420 611430
#Emp: 100-249 (Tor)
#TorLoc: 3
Own: Public Company
Par: Global Knowledge LLC (US)
Key: Scott Williams, Pres, Canada
Brian K. Branson, Pres & CEO

Global Precast Inc.

2101 Teston Rd.
Maple, ON L6A 1R3
Tel 905-832-4307
Fax 905-832-4388
www.globalprecast.com
Line: Manufactures architectural precast panels.
NAICS: 232230
#Emp: 100-249 (Tor)
#TorLoc: 1
Own: Private Company
Key: Vito Cannone, Pres
Amy DiVincentiis, HR Mgr
Maryanne Ostella, Cont
Lui DiVincentiis, Purch Mgr
Donny DiVincentiis, Chief Estimator

Global Upholstery Company Inc.

560 Supertest Rd.
Toronto, ON M3J 2M6
Tel 416-661-3660
Fax 416-661-4300
www.globaltotaloffice.com
Line: Manufactures metal office furniture.
NAICS: 337121 337127
#Emp: 1000-4999 (Tor)
Own: Private Company
Key: Joel Feldberg, Pres
Saul Feldberg, Chmn
Tony Davis, Dir of HR
Ron Flam, CFO
Ron Berman, Dir of Purch
Mervyn Melamed, VP Admin

The Globe & Mail Newspaper

A Div. of CTVglobemedia Publishing Inc.
444 Front St. West
Toronto, ON M5V 2S9
Tel 416-585-5000
Fax 416-585-5085
www.globeandmail.com
Line: Publishes a national newspaper.
NAICS: 511110
#Emp: 500-999 (Tor)
#TorLoc: 1
Own: Private Company
Key: John Stackhouse, Editor in Chief
Phillip Crawley, Publisher & CEO
Perry Nixdorf, VP Ops
Sandra Mason, CFO
Angus Frame, VP Digital Media
Jim Zoras, VP IT
Andrew Saunders, VP Advertising
Roger Dunbar, VP Mktg & Business Dev
Sue Gaudi, VP & Gen Counsel

Globe Spring

A Div. of Leggat Platt Canada Corp.
4040 Chesswood Dr.
Toronto, ON M3J 2B9
Tel 416-630-1833
Fax 416-630-1824
NAICS: 332619
#Emp: 100-249 (Tor)
#TorLoc: 3
Own: Private Company
Key: Malcolm Marcus, Pres
Ida Rende, GM
Todd Dubreuil, HR Mgr
Charlie Bayani, Cont

GMP Securities LP

300-145 King St. West
Toronto, ON M5H 1J8
Tel 416-367-8600
Fax 416-367-8164
www.gmponline.com
AKA: Griffiths McBurney & Partners
NAICS: 523120
#Emp: 100-249 (Tor)
#TorLoc: 1
Own: Private Company
Key: Harris A. Fricker, Pres & CEO
Kevin Sullivan, Deputy Chmn
Cynthia Bruce, HR Mgr

G.N. Johnston Equipment Company Ltd.

5990 Avebury Rd.
Mississauga, ON L5R 3R2
Tel 905-712-6000
Fax 905-712-6002
www.johnstonequipment.com
AKA: Johnston Equipment
Line: Distributes storage products, and narrow aisle lift trucks and pedestrian vehicles.
NAICS: 417230
#Emp: 250-499 (Tor)
#TorLoc: 2
Own: Private Company
Par: Raymond Corp. (US)
Key: Michael Marcotte, Pres

Golden Cut Poultry Ltd.

42 Taber Rd.
Toronto, ON M9W 3A8
Tel 416-746-6367
Fax 416-746-7793
Line: Processes poultry products.
NAICS: 311615
#Emp: 75-99 (Tor)
#TorLoc: 1
Own: Private Company
Key: Aderito Marques, GM
Allan Notonen, Plant Mgr
Leslie Thompson, HR & Office Mgr
Sherene Singh, Sr Acct
Laurie Marland, Purch & Order Desk
Mike Haworth,
    Sales & Procurement Mgr

Golder Associates Ltd.

2390 Argentia Rd.
Mississauga, ON L5N 5Z7
Tel 905-567-4444
Fax 905-567-6561
www.golder.com
Line: Provides engineering and earth sciences consulting services.
NAICS: 541330 541690
#Emp: 500-999 (Tor)
#TorLoc: 3
Own: Private Company
Par: Golder Associates Corp. (CDA)
Key: Mark Brightman, Pres & CEO
Louise Menard, COO
Alan Reed, Cont
Brent Doell, IT Mgr

Golf Town Canada Inc.

800-90 Allstate Pkwy.
Markham, ON L3R 6H3
Tel 905-479-0343
Fax 905-479-7108
www.golftown.com
AKA: Golf Town Income Fund
Line: Retails golf goods and equipment.
NAICS: 451110
#Emp: 250-499 (Tor)
#TorLoc: 10
Own: Public Company
Key: Stephen Bebis, Pres & CEO

Goodfellow Inc.

9184 Twiss Rd.
Campbellville, ON L0P 1B0
Tel 905-854-5800
Fax 905-854-6104
www.goodfellowinc.com
Line: Manufactures and distributes lumber and flooring.
NAICS: 416320

#Emp: 75-99 (Tor)
#TorLoc: 1
Own: Public Company
Key: Mary Lohmus, VP

Goodlaw Services Limited Partnership

Bay Adelaide Centre
3400-300 Bay St.
Toronto, ON M5H 2S7
Tel 416-979-2211
Fax 416-979-1234
www.goodmans.ca
AKA: Goodmans LLP
Line: Provides administrative support for legal services.
NAICS: 541110
#Emp: 250-499 (Tor)
#TorLoc: 1
Own: Private Company
Key: Byron Sonberg, Mng Dir
Leanne Anderson, Dir of HR
Andrea Engels, Dir of Fin
Dick Jensen, Dir of Tech
Lindsay Everitt, Dir of Commun

Goodlife Fitness

201 King St.
London, ON N6A 1C9
Tel 519-661-0190
Fax 519-434-6701
www.goodlifefitness.com
AKA: Alliance Fitness Corp.; Family Fitness; Exclusively Women's
Line: Operates fitness centres.
NAICS: 713940
#Emp: 500-999 (Tor)
#TorLoc: 15
Own: Private Company
Par: Goodlife Fitness (CDA)
Key: David Patchell-Evans, CEO

Goodrich Aerospace Canada Ltd.

A Div. of Goodrich Corp.
1400 South Service Rd. West
Oakville, ON L6L 5Y7
Tel 905-827-7777
Fax 905-825-1583
www.lgd.goodrich.com
Line: Designs and manufactures landing gear and flight control systems.
NAICS: 336410
#Emp: 500-999 (Tor)
#TorLoc: 2
Own: Private Company
Key: Mike Brand, Pres
Mary Moody, Dir of HR
Bob Cortese, Cont

Goodwill Toronto

365 Bloor St. East, 14th Fl.
Toronto, ON M4W 3L4
Tel 416-362-4711
Fax 416-362-0720
www.goodwill.on.ca
Line: Provides work opportunities and
skill development for people who face
employment barriers.
NAICS: 624190 453310
#Emp: 100-249 (Tor)
#TorLoc: 23
Own: Not-for-profit
Par: Goodwill Industries International
(US)
Key: Ken Connelly, Pres & CEO
Vijay Goutam, COO
Sheree McClelland, HR Mgr
Chris Panagiotopoulos, IS

Goodyear Canada Inc.

450 Kipling Ave.
Toronto, ON M8Z 5E1
Tel 416-201-4300
Fax 416-201-4242
www.goodyear.com
AKA: Goodyear Certified Auto Service
Centres
Line: Manufactures tires and inner
tubes, rubber and plastic hose
and belting, and vehicle parts and
accessories.
NAICS: 326210 336390
#Emp: 100-249 (Tor)
Own: Private Company
Par: The Goodyear Tire & Rubber Co
Ltd. (US)
Key: Doug Hamilton, Pres
Bryan DeMarchi, Dir of Corp HR
Carol Pajot, Cont
Haresh Hingorani, Dir of IT
Gus Liotta,
    Dir of Consumer Tire Sales & Mktg
Mark Pillow,
    Dir of Commercial Tire Systems

Gordon Food Service

2999 James Snow Pkwy.
Milton, ON L9T 5G4
Tel 905-864-3700
Fax 905-864-3845
www.gfscanada.com
Line: Provides products and services to
the food service industry.
NAICS: 484229
#Emp: 500-999 (Tor)
#TorLoc: 1
Own: Private Company
Par: Gordon Food Service (US)

Key: Steve Kampstra, GM
Cliff Baker, VP Ops
Janice Tonna, HR Mgr
Rick Dainard, Cont
Steve Taylor, Dir of Street Sales
Lisa MacNeil, Dir of Multi Unit Sales

Gottardo Construction

277 Pennsylvania Ave.
Concord, ON L4K 5R9
Tel 905-761-7707
Fax 905-761-6588
www.gottardogroup.com
Line: Operates a site development
company.
NAICS: 231110
#Emp: 100-249 (Tor)
#TorLoc: 1
Own: Private Company
Key: Aldo Gottardo, Pres & CEO
Erminia Aquino,
    Dir of Financial Planning
Frank Sanita, Cont

The Governing Council of the Salvation Army in Canada

2 Overlea Blvd.
Toronto, ON M4H 1P4
Tel 416-425-2111
Fax 416-422-6201
www.salvationarmy.ca
AKA: The Salvation Army
Line: Preaches the Gospel, supplies
basic human needs, provides personal
counselling and undertakes the
spiritual and moral regeneration and
physical rehabilitations of all persons.
NAICS: 813110
#Emp: 1000-4999 (Tor)
#TorLoc: 59
Own: Religious
Par: The Salvation Army (UK)
Key: Brian Peddle, Territorial
Commander

Goway Travel Ltd.

500-3284 Yonge St.
Toronto, ON M4N 3M7
Tel 416-322-1034
Fax 416-322-9656
www.goway.com
Line: Assembles travel packages.
NAICS: 561510
#Emp: 100-249 (Tor)
#TorLoc: 1
Own: Private Company
Key: Bruce Hodge, Pres
Claire Hodge, VP Admin
Melanie Leelook, HR Advisor
Peter Lacy, VP Fin

Gowling Lafleur Henderson LLP

1600-100 King St. West, 1 First
    Canadian Pl.
Toronto, ON M5X 1G5
Tel 416-862-7525
Fax 416-862-7661
www.gowlings.com
NAICS: 541110
#Emp: 500-999 (Tor)
#TorLoc: 1
Own: Private Company
Key: Scott Jolliffe, Chair & CEO
Peter J. Lukasiewicz, Mng Partner
Sharon Mitchell, COO
Pierre Nadeau, HR Mgr
Heather Caldwell, GM, Toronto
Richard McConnell, Nat'l Dir of IT
Evelyn Dempsey, Dir of Mktg

Gracious Living Corporation

7200 Martin Grove Rd.
Woodbridge, ON L4L 9J3
Tel 905-850-6400
Fax 905-264-3720
www.graciousliving.com
Line: Provides custom injection-
moulding services.
NAICS: 333220
#Emp: 100-249 (Tor)
#TorLoc: 1
Own: Private Company
Key: Enzo Macri, Pres
Vito Galloro, VP
Angela Moak, HR Mgr

Graff Concrete

25 Hale Rd.
Brampton, ON L6W 3J9
Tel 905-457-8120
Fax 905-457-8944
www.graffconcrete.com
Line: Manufactures diamond and CBN
tooling.
NAICS: 333519
#Emp: 75-99 (Tor)
#TorLoc: 1
Own: Private Company
Key: Dave Neal, VP

Grafton-Fraser Inc.

44 Apex Rd.
Toronto, ON M6A 2V2
Tel 416-780-9922
Fax 416-780-2159
AKA: Britches; George Richards;
Grafton & Co.; Jack Fraser; Mr. Big &
Tall; The Suit Exchange; Timberland;
Tip Top Tailors
Line: Retails men's clothing.
NAICS: 448150 448110
#Emp: 500-999 (Tor)
#TorLoc: 60
Own: Private Company
Key: Glenn A. Stonehouse,
    Chmn & CEO
Brian Reel, Sr VP & CFO
Bob Christie, Sr VP Real Estate &
    Business Dev

Graham Bros. Construction Limited

290 Clarence St.
Brampton, ON L6W 1T4
Tel 905-453-1200
Fax 905-453-2217
www.grahambros.com
Line: Constructs roads, sewers, water
mains, bridges and asphalt.
NAICS: 231320 231310
#Emp: 250-499 (Tor)
#TorLoc: 1
Own: Private Company
Key: Alfredo Maggio, Pres
William Graham, Owner
Carl Graham, VP Ops
Janice Campbell, Cont & CFO

Graham Packaging Canada Ltd.

3174 Mavis Rd.
Mississauga, ON L5C 1T8
Tel 905-277-1486
Fax 905-277-0995
www.grahampackaging.com
Line: Manufactures blow moulded
plastic bottles.
NAICS: 326160
#Emp: 75-99 (Tor)
#TorLoc: 1
Own: Private Company
Par: Graham Packaging Co. (US)
Key: John Alves, Plant Mgr
Kathy Beyette, Plant Admr

Grande Cheese Company Ltd.

468 Jevlan Dr.
Woodbridge, ON L4L 8L4
Tel 905-856-6880
Fax 905-856-6884
Line: Manufactures cheese.
NAICS: 311515
#Emp: 75-99 (Tor)
#TorLoc: 5
Own: Private Company
Key: Albert Contardi, Pres

Grand & Toy Ltd.

33 Green Belt Dr.
Toronto, ON M3C 1M1
Tel 416-391-8100
Fax 416-445-4855
www.grandandtoy.com
Line: Retails and provides business-to-
business distribution of office supplies,
computer supplies, technology
solutions and custom business
interiors.
NAICS: 453210
#Emp: 1000-4999 (Tor)
#TorLoc: 34
Own: Private Company
Par: Office Max Inc. (US)
Key: Gary D'Andrea, COO
David Hodd, VP HR
Ralph Berzins, VP Fin
Steve Johnston, VP Sales
Kevin Edwards, VP Mktg
Maria Borges, VP Business Dev

Grandview Sales & Distribution Ltd.

4630 Sheppard Ave. East
Toronto, ON M1V 3V5
Tel 416-298-0000
Fax 416-431-0035
www.canadiantire.ca
AKA: Canadian Tire
Line: Operates a retail store and an
automotive service garage.
NAICS: 444130
#Emp: 100-249 (Tor)
Own: Private Company
Key: Stephen Grand, Store Dealer
Joy Brown, Payroll Admin

Granite Club

2350 Bayview Ave.
Toronto, ON M2L 1E4
Tel 416-449-8713
Fax 416-445-0838
www.graniteclub.com
Line: Operates a private social and
athletic club.
NAICS: 713910 713940
#Emp: 250-499 (Tor)
#TorLoc: 1
Own: Not-for-profit
Key: Peter Fyvie, GM
Joanne Hogg, Dir of HR
Lori Tymchyk, CFO
Shawn Huggins, IT Mgr
Susanne Willans, Membership Dir
Mary Elizabeth Sullivan, Asst GM
Leila Harwood, Creative Dir

Grant Thornton LLP

Royal Bank Plaza, South Tower
200 Bay St., 19th Fl., P.O. Box 55
Toronto, ON M5J 2P9
Tel 416-366-0100
Fax 416-360-4949
www.grantthornton.ca
Line: Provides a full range of
audit, taxation, accounting,
management consulting and
financial re-organization services to
entrepreneurial enterprises, financial
institutions, governments, health-care
organization and others.
NAICS: 541212 541611
#Emp: 250-499 (Tor)
#TorLoc: 3
Own: Private Company
Key: Anita Ferrari,
    Reg Mng Partner, Central Canada
Deborah Orzel, Sr Mgr of
    Organizational Dev & HR
Carlo Torti, Cont
Marnie Housley, IT Mgr

Graphic Transportation Services

5780 Hwy. 7
Woodbridge, ON L4L 1T8
Tel 905-264-0441
Fax 905-264-1926
www.graphictransportation.ca
Line: Provides warehousing,
distribution and transportation
services.
NAICS: 493190
#Emp: 75-99 (Tor)
#TorLoc: 1
Own: Private Company
Key: Ken Dunphy, Owner

Greater Toronto Airports Authority

Toronto Pearson International Airport
3111 Convair Dr., P.O. Box 6031
Toronto AMF, ON L5P 1B2
Tel 416-776-3000
Fax 416-776-7593
www.gtaa.com
AKA: GTAA; Toronto Pearson
Line: Specializes in airport management and operation.
NAICS: 488119
#Emp: 1000-4999 (Tor)
#TorLoc: 1
Own: Private Company
Key: Brian Lackey,
   VP Strategic Planning & Airport Dev
Lloyd McCoomb, Pres & CEO, Strategic
   Planning & Airport Dev
Howard Bohan,
   VP Ops & Customer Experience
Nicole Desloges, VP People & Culture
Brian Gabel, VP & CFO
Doug Love, VP Gen Counsel & Secy
Gary Long, VP & CIO
Pat Neville, VP Facilities
Toby Lennox,
   VP Corp Affairs & Commun

Great West Life Assurance Co.

600-2005 Sheppard Ave. East
Toronto, ON M2J 5B4
Tel 416-492-4300
Fax 416-492-1406
www.greatwestlife.com
Line: Provides financial services.
NAICS: 524210
#Emp: 75-99 (Tor)
#TorLoc: 1
Own: Public Company
Par: Great West Life (CDA)
Key: Mark Foris, Dir
Catherine Perry, Ops Mgr
Chad Shea, Reg Mgr

Greeley Containment & Rework Inc.

200 Baseline Rd. East
Bowmanville, ON L1C 1A4
Tel 905-623-5678
Fax 905-623-3557
www.greeley.ca
Line: Provides container and rework services.
NAICS: 336390
#Emp: 100-249 (Tor)
#TorLoc: 1
Own: Private Company
Key: Neil Clark, Pres
Dan Ruddock, Ops Mgr
Brenda Kelly, VP

Green Grove Foods Corp.

6880 Columbus Rd.
Mississauga, ON L5T 2G1
Tel 905-565-3600
Fax 905-565-0603
www.greengrovefoods.com
Line: Provides packaging services and also manufactures juices, drinks, isotonics, ice teas, and enhanced waters.
NAICS: 561910
#Emp: 100-249 (Tor)
#TorLoc: 1
Own: Private Company
Key: Makesh Lakhani, GM

Greenlawn Ltd.

2385 Matheson Blvd. East
Mississauga, ON L4W 5B3
Tel 905-290-1884
Fax 905-290-1835
www.greenlawncare.com
Line: Provides commercial and residential landscaping services.
NAICS: 561730
#Emp: 500-999 (Tor)
#TorLoc: 6
Own: Public Company
Par: Service Master Canada (CDA)
Key: Jim Mercer, Pres
Sheila Casey, HR Mgr
Gavin Dawson, Tech Mgr
Jeff Ankemann, Dir of Mktg & Sales

Greenpark Homes

8700 Dufferin St.
Concord, ON L4K 4S6
Tel 416-661-5329
Fax 905-738-0342
www.greenparkhomes.com
Line: Operates a construction company.
NAICS: 231210
#Emp: 100-249 (Tor)
#TorLoc: 1
Own: Private Company
Key: Carlo Baldassarra, Pres

Greenspoon Specialty Contracting Ltd.

42 Stafford Dr.
Brampton, ON L6W 1L4
Tel 905-458-1005
Fax 905-458-4149
www.greenspoon.net
Line: Provides demolition and asbestos abatement services.
NAICS: 232110
#Emp: 100-249 (Tor)
#TorLoc: 1
Own: Private Company

Key: Kevin Mitchell, Pres
Jon Williams, Chmn
Tony Pirone, HR Mgr
Jim Williams, VP Fin

Greenwin Property Management Inc.

200-1 Valleybrook Dr.
Toronto, ON M3B 2S7
Tel 416-322-4080
Fax 416-544-4882
www.greenwinpm.com
Line: Provides property management, development and construction.
NAICS: 531310
#Emp: 500-999 (Tor)
#TorLoc: 1
Own: Private Company
Key: Kevin Green, Pres
Haya Zilberboim, CEO
Ana Bellamy, HR Mgr
Craig Harwood, Dir of Fin
Jessica Green, Dir of Mktg

The Grenadier Retirement Residence

2100 Bloor St. West
Toronto, ON M6S 1M7
Tel 416-769-2885
Fax 416-769-7238
www.thegrenadier.com
AKA: 582958 Ontario Ltd.
Line: Operates a retirement residence.
NAICS: 531111
#Emp: 75-99 (Tor)
#TorLoc: 1
Own: Private Company
Key: Dwight Mountney, GM
Gina Aquino, Admin Office Mgr & Bookeeper
Julie Gavin, Mktg Mgr

Grey Group Canada

500-48 Spadina Ave.
Toronto, ON M5V 2H8
Tel 416-486-0700
Fax 416-486-8907
www.grey.com/canada
Line: Operates a full service advertising agency.
NAICS: 541810
#Emp: 100-249 (Tor)
#TorLoc: 1
Own: Private Company
Par: Grey Advertising Inc. (US)
Key: Stephanie Nerlich, Pres & CEO
Jocelyn Renaud, VP & Mng Dir
Karen Barootes, Dir of HR & Admin
Tony Fernandes, VP & CFO
Gary Stothers, Dir of IT

Greyhound Canada Transportation Corp.

700-1111 International Blvd.
Burlington, ON L7L 6W1
Tel 289-288-0123
Fax 905-336-5987
www.greyhound.ca
AKA: Greyhound Canada
Line: Provides commuter service throughout the GTA, and charter, tour and sightseeing services throughout North America.
NAICS: 485210 485510
#Emp: 250-499 (Tor)
#TorLoc: 5
Own: Private Company
Par: First Group PLC (UK)
Key: Stuart Kendrick, Sr VP, Canada
Anne Cunningham, Charter Sales Rep

Grey Power Insurance Brokers Inc.

600-105 Gordon Baker Rd.
Toronto, ON M2H 3P8
Tel 1-866-473-9650
Fax 1-866-415-9795
www.greypower.com
Line: Provides auto and home insurance.
NAICS: 524210
#Emp: 100-249 (Tor)
#TorLoc: 1
Own: Private Company
Par: ING Canada (CDA)
Key: Catherine Smoula, Pres

Greystone Golf Club

9689 Dublin Line
Milton, ON L9T 2X7
Tel 905-875-3808
Fax 905-875-3435
www.clublink.ca
NAICS: 713910
#Emp: 75-99 (Tor)
#TorLoc: 1
Own: Private Company
Par: ClubLink Corp. (CDA)
Key: Rob Hickson, Dir of Ops

Griffen Manimpex Ltd.

2-945 Wilson Ave.
Toronto, ON M3K 1E8
Tel 416-630-7007
Fax 416-630-2034
Line: Wholesales and exports used clothing.
NAICS: 414110 453310
#Emp: 75-99 (Tor)
#TorLoc: 1
Own: Private Company
Key: Firoz Nasser, Pres
Shenaz Jaffer, HR Secy
Firoz Jessa, Cont

Griffith Laboratories Ltd.

757 Pharmacy Ave.
Toronto, ON M1L 3J8
Tel 416-288-3050
Fax 416-288-8910
www.griffithlaboratories.com
Line: Manufactures food ingredients.
NAICS: 311990 311940
#Emp: 250-499 (Tor)
#TorLoc: 1
Own: Private Company
Par: Griffith Laboratories Inc. (US)
Key: Christopher Savage, Pres
David Jagdeo, VP Ops
Tony Caprio, VP Fin
David C. Smith, VP, Research
& Dev & Quality Assurance

Grohe Canada Inc.

1230 Lakeshore Rd. East
Mississauga, ON L5E 1E9
Tel 905-274-3323
Fax 905-274-2737
www.grohe.ca
Line: Manufactures safety-mixers, valves and faucets.
NAICS: 332910
#Emp: 100-249 (Tor)
#TorLoc: 1
Own: Private Company
Par: Grohe AG & Co. KG (GER)
Key: Frank Profiti, GM
Pat Hurley, VP Manuf
Marta Ziarno, HR Specialist
Frank Hunnisett, Cont
Liam Douglas, Dir of Supply Chain
Maria Bosco,
Mktg, Commun & Training Mgr

Grosnor Industries Inc.

375 Rexdale Blvd.
Toronto, ON M9W 1R9
Tel 416-744-2011
Fax 416-744-2374
www.grosnorind.com
AKA: ECWalkers; ProDesign; Medi-inn; SampleWorks
Line: Manufactures custom vinyl products.
NAICS: 326198
#Emp: 100-249 (Tor)
#TorLoc: 1
Own: Private Company
Key: George Schnarr, Pres & CEO

Grote Industries

230 Travail Rd.
Markham, ON L3S 3J1
Tel 905-209-9744
Fax 905-209-9757
www.grote.com
AKA: Grote Manufacturing; Grote Electronics
Line: Wholesales automotive parts.
NAICS: 415290
#Emp: 75-99 (Tor)
#TorLoc: 1
Own: Private Company
Par: Grote LLC (US)
Key: Brad Morris, GM
Eric Morris, Pres
Gill Leblanc, Ops Mgr
Regina Chou, Acctng Mgr
Kirk Batten, Cont
Sharron Williams, IT Coord
Mark Paul, Mktg & Dev Mgr

Group of Goldline

180 West Beaver Creek Rd.
Richmond Hill, ON L4B 1B4
Tel 905-709-3570
Fax 905-709-3796
www.goldline.net
Line: Provides long distance calling cards.
NAICS: 418990
#Emp: 100-249 (Tor)
#TorLoc: 1
Own: Private Company
Key: Ata Moeini, Pres
Shala Yazdani, CFO
Reza Divani, IT Mgr
Fred Missaghi, VP Sales

Gruven International Inc.

19 Newgale Gate
Toronto, ON M1X 1B6
Tel 416-292-7331
Fax 416-754-8675
www.gruven.com
NAICS: 315299
#Emp: 100-249 (Tor)
#TorLoc: 1
Own: Private Company
Key: Jimmy Yiu, Pres
Cindy Yiu, Secy-Treas
David Rushton, Sales Mgr

GS1 Canada

800-1500 Don Mills Rd.
Toronto, ON M3B 3L1
Tel 416-510-8039
Fax 416-510-1916
www.gs1ca.org
Line: Provides business services.
NAICS: 813910
#Emp: 100-249 (Tor)
#TorLoc: 1
Own: Not-for-profit
Key: Arthur Smith, Pres & CEO
Eileen MacDonald, COO
Susan Orenbach, Dir of HR
Daisy Kaur, Dir of Fin

Guardall

A Div. of UTC Fire & Security Company
5201 Explorer Dr.
Mississauga, ON L4W 4H1
Tel 905-206-8434
Fax 905-629-4970
www.guardall.com
Line: Engineers web-based software
solutions.
NAICS: 541510
#Emp: 75-99 (Tor)
#TorLoc: 1
Own: Private Company
Key: Phil Eldridge, GM

Guardian Capital Group Ltd.

3100-199 Bay St., P.O. Box 201
Commerce Crt. West
Toronto, ON M5L 1E8
Tel 416-364-8341
Fax 416-947-0601
www.guardiancapital.com
Line: Provides investment counselling,
mutual fund management and
marketing.
NAICS: 523920 526910
#Emp: 100-249 (Tor)
#TorLoc: 1

Own: Public Company
Key: George Mavroudis, Pres
John M. Christodoulou, Chmn & CEO
C. Verner Christensen, VP Fin & Secy

Guild Electric Ltd.

470 Midwest Rd.
Toronto, ON M1P 4Y5
Tel 416-288-8222
Fax 416-288-1939
www.guildelectric.com
Line: Provides electrical and
communications contracting services.
NAICS: 232510
#Emp: 500-999 (Tor)
#TorLoc: 1
Own: Private Company
Par: Lengyel Investments Ltd. (CDA)
Key: Gary Lengyel, CEO
George Docherty, Exec VP
Atri Ray, Cont

The Guvernment

132 Queens Quay East
Toronto, ON M5A 3Y5
Tel 416-869-1462
Fax 416-869-0387
www.theguvernment.com
AKA: 1263528 Ontario Ltd.
Line: Operates an entertainment
complex.
NAICS: 722110
#Emp: 100-249 (Tor)
#TorLoc: 1
Own: Private Company
Key: Charles Khabouth, Pres & Owner
Orin Bristol, Dir of Ops
Johnny Abou Jaoude, Club Mgr
Wallace Chow, Acct
Jeff Wojcik,
    Bookings & Special Events Mgr
Jerrod Florence, Dir of Mktg

Hachette Distribution Services Retail North America

370 King St. West, 6th Fl.
Toronto, ON M5V 1J9
Tel 416-863-6400
Fax 416-863-6552
www.hdsrna.com
AKA: Bienvenue; Canadian Scene;
Front Page; The Great Canadian
Newsstand Co.; Impulse; Inclination;
Lamplighter; Mag Monde; Maison de
la Presse; Relay; Piccadilly Place; La
Tabagie; Transit Shop; UCS; The Great
Canadian Book Co.; Xpress; HDS Retail
North America

Line: Retails press, confectionary and
gifts.
NAICS: 451210 445292 453999
#Emp: 250-499 (Tor)
#TorLoc: 55
Own: Private Company
Par: Matra-Hachette SA (FR)
Key: Gerald Savaria, Pres & CEO
Craig Liden, Exec VP Ops
Ann Barna, Dir of HR
Vadim Motlik, Exec VP & CFO
Mario Bartolozzi, VP IT
Jonathan Albert,
    Exec VP Merchandising

Hadrian Manufacturing Inc.

965 Syscon Rd.
Burlington, ON L7L 5S3
Tel 905-333-0300
Fax 905-333-1841
www.hadrian-inc.com
Line: Manufactures metal toilet
partitions and lockers.
NAICS: 337215
#Emp: 100-249 (Tor)
#TorLoc: 1
Own: Private Company
Key: James Peters, Pres
Gary Greenway, VP Ops
Jennifer Coleman, HR Supr
Robert Snyder, VP Fin
Mike Razem, VP Sales
Jeff Bell, VP Mktg

H.A. Kidd and Company Limited

5 Northline Rd.
Toronto, ON M4B 3P2
Tel 416-364-6451
Fax 416-364-4860
www.hakidd.com
Line: Distributes and manufactures
sewing notions for craft and hobby
industry.
NAICS: 451130
#Emp: 100-249 (Tor)
#TorLoc: 1
Own: Private Company
Key: Barton J. Earle, Pres
Douglas Earle, CEO
Sue Flanagan, Ops Mgr
Amir Mirza, Cont & HR Mgr
Timothy Earle, Dir of Mktg

Hakim Optical Laboratory Ltd.

128 Hazelton Ave., 3rd Fl.
Toronto, ON M5R 2E5
Tel 416-924-8866
Fax 416-924-7678
www.hakimoptical.ca
NAICS: 446130
#Emp: 250-499 (Tor)
#TorLoc: 44
Own: Private Company
Key: Karim Hakim, Pres
Ricu Haras, VP
Marilyn Dale, HR Mgr
John Warden,
    Dir of Advertising & Mktg

Halcrow Yolles

550-207 Queen's Quay West
Toronto, ON M5J 1A7
Tel 416-363-8123
Fax 416-363-0341
www.halcrowyolles.com
Line: Delivers planning, design and
management services for developing
infrastructure and buildings
worldwide.
NAICS: 541330
#Emp: 100-249 (Tor)
#TorLoc: 1
Own: Private Company
Key: Chris Andrews, Mng Dir, Canada
Pejman Saifi, Reg IT Mgr

Hallmark Canada

501 Consumers Rd.
Toronto, ON M2J 5E2
Tel 416-492-1300
Fax 416-494-0027
www.hallmark.ca
AKA: Hallmark Card Shops
Line: Manufactures and distributes
greeting cards.
NAICS: 323119
#Emp: 500-999 (Tor)
#TorLoc: 29
Own: Private Company
Par: Hallmark Cards Inc. (US)
Key: Patrick Carr, Pres
Roger King, VP HR
Kevin Hennessy, CFO
Liz Orton, Purch & Admin Services Dir
Michael Gibbons, VP Sales

Hallmark Housekeeping Services Inc.

34 Racine Rd.
Toronto, ON M9W 2Z3
Tel 416-748-0330
Fax 416-748-0333
www.hallmarkhousekeeping.ca
NAICS: 561722
#Emp: 1000-4999 (Tor)
#TorLoc: 12
Own: Private Company
Key: Philip M. Calementino, Exec VP
Manuel J. Clementino, CEO

Halsall Associates Ltd.

2300-2300 Yonge St.
P.O. Box 2385
Toronto, ON M4P 1E4
Tel 416-487-5256
Fax 416-487-9766
www.halsall.com
Line: Provides engineering consulting
services.
NAICS: 541330
#Emp: 100-249 (Tor)
#TorLoc: 2
Own: Private Company
Key: Peter Halsall, Pres
Michael Buckley, VP

Halton Catholic District School Board

802 Drury Lane
P.O. Box 5308
Burlington, ON L7R 2Y2
Tel 905-632-6300
Fax 905-333-4661
www.hcdsb.org
Line: Operates Catholic education
schools at the elementary, secondary
and adult learning level.
NAICS: 611110
#Emp: 1000-4999 (Tor)
#TorLoc: 49
Own: Government
Key: Michael W. Paulter,
  Dir of Education & Secy
Alice Anne LeMay, Chair
Giacomo Corbacio,
    Supt of Facility Management
Joseph O'Hara,
    Exec Officer, HR Services
Paul McMahon,
    Supt of Business Services & Treas

Halton District School Board

2050 Guelph Line
P.O. Box 5005
Burlington, ON L7R 3Z2
Tel 905-335-3663
Fax 905-335-9802
www.hdsb.ca
AKA: Halton Public School Board
NAICS: 611110
#Emp: 5000-9999 (Tor)
#TorLoc: 95
Own: Government
Key: David Euale, Dir of Education
Don Vrooman, Chair
Gerry Cullen, Supt of Facility Services
Dawn Beckett-Morton,
    Exec Officer of HR
Steven Parfeniuk,
    Supt of Business Services
Kathy Wyatt, Mgr of Purch & Admin
Bruce Smith, CIO
Marnie Denton,
    Mgr of Commun Services

Halton Forming Ltd.

593 Main St. East
Milton, ON L9T 3J2
Tel 905-693-4889
Fax 905-693-8091
Line: Operates a concrete forming
company.
NAICS: 232210
#Emp: 75-99 (Tor)
#TorLoc: 1
Own: Private Company
Key: Lou Rocca, Pres

Halton Healthcare Services - Oakville Site

327 Reynolds St.
Oakville, ON L6J 3L7
Tel 905-845-2571
Fax 905-338-4636
www.haltonhealthcare.com
NAICS: 622111
#Emp: 1000-4999 (Tor)
#TorLoc: 3
Own: Not-for-profit
Key: Lorne Martin, Chief of Staff
John Oliver, Pres & CEO

Halton Indoor Climate Systems, Ltd.

1021 Brevik Pl.
Mississauga, ON L4W 3R7
Tel 905-624-0301
Fax 905-624-5547
www.haltoncompany.com
NAICS: 232520
#Emp: 75-99 (Tor)
#TorLoc: 1
Own: Private Company
Key: Nick Kakarelis, Mng Dir
Matylda Jach, HR Mgr
Michael Ianniello, Cont
Janet Kellesis, Purch Agent
Mike Nicholls, Reg Sales Mgr

Halton Regional Police Service

1151 Bronte Rd.
Oakville, ON L6M 3L1
Tel 905-825-4777
Fax 905-825-9416
www.hrps.on.ca
NAICS: 913130
#Emp: 500-999 (Tor)
#TorLoc: 5
Own: Government
Key: Gary Crowell, Chief of Police
Bob Percy, Deputy Chief, Ops
Andrew Fletcher, Deputy Chief, Admin
Janice Coffin, Dir of Corp Services,
    Commun & Mktg

Halton Region Media Group

A Div. of Metroland Media Group Ltd.
467 Speers Rd.
Oakville, ON L6K 3S4
Tel 905-845-3824
Fax 905-337-5567
www.haltonsearch.com
AKA: Burlington Post; Oakville Beaver;
Milton Canadian Champion; Niagara
This Week; Flamborough Review
Line: Publishes tri-weekly community
newspaper.
NAICS: 511110
#Emp: 250-499 (Tor)
#TorLoc: 4
Own: Private Company
Par: Torstar Corp. (CDA)
Key: Jill Davis, Editor in Chief
Mark Dills, Dir of Production

Hamilton Kent Inc.

77 Carlingview Dr.
Toronto, ON M9W 5E6
Tel 416-675-7822
Fax 416-674-6960
www.hamiltonkent.com
Line: Manufactures rubber products
for concrete and plastic pipe
manufacturers and for the construction
industry.
NAICS: 326290
#Emp: 100-249 (Tor)
#TorLoc: 1
Own: Private Company
Par: IPEX Inc. (CDA)
Key: Bernard Gregoire, Pres & GM
Patrick van den Berg, Plant Mgr
Henry Flattery, Dir of Mktg Dev
Pardeep Sharma,
    Dir of Quality & Manuf Services
Randy Reimer, Dir of Sales

Hamsar Diversco Inc.

5320 Downey St.
Burlington, ON L7L 6M2
Tel 905-332-4094
Fax 905-332-9020
www.hamsar.com
Line: Supplies, designs and produces
lighting and electronic products to
original equipment manufacturers and
automotive aftermarket markets.
NAICS: 417320 334410
#Emp: 75-99 (Tor)
#TorLoc: 1
Own: Private Company
Key: Fred Kelly, Pres
Garri Eloriaga, Plant Mgr
Vida Kelly, Secy-Treas
Laura Smith, Nat'l Account Mgr

Hanson Brick Ltd.

5155 Dundas St. West
Burlington, ON L7R 3Y2
Tel 905-335-3401
Fax 905-335-3013
www.hansonbrick.com
Line: Manufactures clay, brick, and
concrete pavers.
NAICS: 327120
#Emp: 250-499 (Tor)
#TorLoc: 3
Own: Private Company
Par: Heidelberg Cement Group (GER)
Key: Leo Steffler, VP & GM

Hanson Pressure Pipes (Stouffville Pressure Facility)

5387 Bethesda Rd.
Stouffville, ON L4A 7X3
Tel 905-640-5151
Fax 905-640-5154
www.hansonpressurepipes.com
Line: Manufactures concrete pressure
pipes, reinforced concrete pipes, pre-
cast concrete girders, hyspan and box
culverts.
NAICS: 327330
#Emp: 100-249 (Tor)
#TorLoc: 2
Own: Private Company
Par: Heidelberg Cement Group (GER)
Key: Mike Leathers, Pres
Chris Saurenmann, VP Ops
Brad Orders, Dir of Fin
Tim Kennedy, VP Sales

Harbourfront Centre

235 Queen's Quay West
Toronto, ON M5J 2G8
Tel 416-973-4600
Fax 416-973-6055
www.harbourfrontcentre.com
Line: Presents arts, cultural events and
activities for public enjoyment.
NAICS: 711311
#Emp: 250-499 (Tor)
#TorLoc: 1
Own: Not-for-profit
Key: William Boyle, CEO
Helder Melo, Dir of Site Ops & Services
Susan Latremouille, Dir of HR
Ed Kremblewski, Dir of Fin
George Rodaro, Dir of IT
Bruce Hutchinson,
    Dir of Mktg & Media Relns

Hard-Co Construction Ltd.

625 Conlin Rd.
Whitby, ON L1R 2W8
Tel 905-655-2001
Fax 905-620-0323
www.hard-co.com
Line: Operates a construction
contracting company.
NAICS: 231390
#Emp: 75-99 (Tor)
#TorLoc: 1
Own: Private Company
Key: Barry Harding, Pres

Harding Display Corp.

150 Dynamic Dr.
Toronto, ON M1V 5A5
Tel 416-754-3215
Fax 416-754-3289
www.hardingdisplay.com
Line: Manufactures advertisement
displays.
NAICS: 339950
#Emp: 75-99 (Tor)
#TorLoc: 1
Own: Private Company
Key: Bob Harding, Pres
Al Stobbart, Ops Mgr

Hardrock Forming Co.

17-30 Pennsylvania Ave.
Concord, ON L4K 4A5
Tel 905-760-1166
Fax 905-760-1053
AKA: Hardwall Construction
Line: Provides high-rise and
commercial concrete forming services.
NAICS: 232220
#Emp: 250-499 (Tor)
#TorLoc: 1
Own: Private Company
Key: Dan Cesana, Pres
Alice Znava, Office Admr
Mirka Sulipka, Cont
Michael Naccarato, Chief Estimator

Haremar Plastic Manufacturing Ltd.

200 Great Gulf Dr.
Vaughan, ON L4K 5W1
Tel 905-761-7552
Fax 905-761-2808
www.haremar.com
Line: Manufactures plastic products.
NAICS: 417230 332510
#Emp: 100-249 (Tor)
#TorLoc: 1
Own: Private Company
Key: Mark Lichtblau, VP
Cheryl Babcock, VP Ops
Dahlia Levitin, HR Mgr

Harlequin Enterprises Ltd.

225 Duncan Mill Rd.
Toronto, ON M3B 3K9
Tel 416-445-5860
Fax 416-445-8655
www.eHarlequin.com
Line: Publishes books.
NAICS: 511130
#Emp: 250-499 (Tor)
#TorLoc: 1
Own: Public Company
Par: Torstar Corp. (CDA)

Key: Donna Hayes, Publisher & CEO
James Robinson, VP Ops & Admin
Christine Johnson, HR Coord
Andrew Wright, Sr VP Fin & CFO
Darrell Cowan,
    Dir of Procurement Services
Alex Osuszek, VP Retail Sales
Christina Clifford,
    Exec VP, Direct To Consumer
Katherine Orr, VP PR

Harold & Grace Baker Centre

1 Northwestern Ave.
Toronto, ON M6M 2J7
Tel 416-654-2889
Fax 416-654-0217
www.bakercentre.com
Line: Operates a nursing home and
retirement residence.
NAICS: 623110
#Emp: 100-249 (Tor)
#TorLoc: 1
Own: Not-for-profit
Par: Revera Inc. (CDA)
Key: Milena Sujer, Exec Dir
Flordeliza Galang,
    Dir of Nursing & Resident Care
Sue Nemanic, Dir of Placement & Mktg

HarperCollins Canada Ltd.

1995 Markham Rd.
Toronto, ON M1B 5M8
Tel 416-321-2241
Fax 416-321-3033
www.harpercollins.ca
Line: Publishes and distributes print
materials.
NAICS: 511130
#Emp: 100-249 (Tor)
#TorLoc: 2
Own: Private Company
Par: HarperCollins Publishers Ltd. (US)
Key: David Kent, Pres
Olive Khan, VP Ops
Dianne Aquilina, VP, Dir of HR
Wayne Playter, VP Fin

Harper Ontario Truck Centres

7035 Pacific Circ.
Mississauga, ON L5T 2A8
Tel 905-564-8270
Fax 905-564-8292
www.harperotc.com
Line: Specializes in selling heavy
trucks.
NAICS: 336120
#Emp: 75-99 (Tor)
#TorLoc: 5
Own: Private Company
Key: Paul Harper, Dealer Principal

Harper Power Products

10 Diesel Dr.
Toronto, ON M8W 2T8
Tel 416-259-3281
Fax 416-259-1863
www.harperpowerproducts.com
Line: Distributes diesel engines
and transmissions and provides
major repair and rebuilding service
operations.
NAICS: 417990 333619
#Emp: 100-249 (Tor)
#TorLoc: 2
Own: Private Company
Par: The Harper Group (CDA)
Key: John Cosgrove, Pres & COO
Donald Mitchell, VP Fin

Harris Corporation

25 Dyas Rd.
Toronto, ON M3B 1V7
Tel 416-445-9640
Fax 416-443-3088
www.harris.com
Line: Designs, manufactures and
markets electronic equipment to
distribute, process and switch high-
quality video and audio signals
required by television broadcast
facilities and independent production
or post-production studios.
NAICS: 334220 417320
#Emp: 250-499 (Tor)
#TorLoc: 2
Own: Public Company
Par: Harris Corporation (US)
Key: Howard Lance, Chmn, Pres & CEO
David Cunningham, VP HR

Harry Rosen Inc.

1600-77 Bloor St. West
Toronto, ON M5S 1M2
Tel 416-935-9200
Fax 416-515-7067
www.harryrosen.com
Line: Sells men's specialty clothing.
NAICS: 448110
#Emp: 250-499 (Tor)
#TorLoc: 8
Own: Private Company
Key: Peter Stansfield, Pres & COO
Laurance Rosen, Chmn & CEO
Manuel Maciel, VP & Dir of Stores
Carolyn Tyrie, Dir of HR
Conrad Frejlich, Sr VP & CFO
Steve Jackson, Dir of MIS
Sandra Kennedy, Dir of Mktg

Harry Winston Diamond Corporation

P.O. Box 4569 Stn. A
Toronto, ON M5W 4T9
Tel 416-362-2237
Fax 416-360-7789
www.harrywinston.ca
NAICS: 414410
#Emp: 75-99 (Tor)
Own: Public Company
Key: Robert Gannicott, CEO

Harvey Kalles, Real Estate Ltd.

2145 Avenue Rd.
Toronto, ON M5M 4B2
Tel 416-441-2888
Fax 416-441-9926
www.harveykalles.com
Line: Operates a real estate agency.
NAICS: 531210
#Emp: 250-499 (Tor)
#TorLoc: 2
Own: Private Company
Key: Michael Kalles, Pres
Harvey Kalles, Chmn & CEO
Leslie Richman, VP Ops
Lee Heatherington, Sales Mgr

H.A. Sheldon Canada Ltd.

2220 Midland Ave., Unit 68AP
Toronto, ON M1P 3E6
Tel 416-299-1222
Fax 416-299-1710
www.hasheldon.com
Line: Manufactures, wholesales and imports leather goods for the retail market.
NAICS: 315990
#Emp: 75-99 (Tor)
#TorLoc: 1
Own: Private Company
Par: Tandy Brands Accessories (US)
Key: Sean Aherne, Pres
Lloyd Vanderkooy, VP Ops
Warren Brazier, VP Fin
Amanda Moore, Purchaser
Samantha Dennett, IT Mgr
Kim Stack, VP Sales
Christine Heslop, Product Mgr

Hatch Ltd.

2800 Speakman Dr.
Mississauga, ON L5K 2R7
Tel 905-855-7600
Fax 905-855-8270
www.hatch.ca
AKA: Hatch Mott MacDonald
Line: Provides business-consulting, information technology, engineering, and project and construction management to the mining, metallurgical, manufacturing, energy, and infrastructure industries.
NAICS: 231410 541330
#Emp: 1000-4999 (Tor)
#TorLoc: 7
Own: Private Company
Key: Kurt Strobele, Chmn & CEO
Robert Francki, Global Mng Dir
Pierre Olivier, Global Dir, HR
Doug Stirling, Global Dir, Fin & Acctng
J.D. Fentie, Global Practice Dir, IT
John Bianchini, Global Mng Dir, Mining & Metals
Tom Reid, Global Dir, Mktg & Commun

Havergal College

1451 Avenue Rd.
Toronto, ON M5N 2H9
Tel 416-483-3843
Fax 416-483-6796
www.havergal.on.ca
Line: Operates a Junior, Elementary and Secondary school for girls.
NAICS: 611110
#Emp: 75-99 (Tor)
#TorLoc: 1
Own: Not-for-profit
Key: Susan R. Groesbeck, Principal
Christine Shain, Vice Principal
Catherine Cavan-Ortved, Dir of HR
Kate Balsara-Pardoe, Dir of Fin & Ops
Pietro Caira, IT Mgr

Hay Group Ltd.

700-121 King St. West
Toronto, ON M5H 3X7
Tel 416-868-1371
Fax 416-868-6871
www.haygroup.com/ca
Line: Provides human resources and organizational effectiveness consulting services.
NAICS: 541612
#Emp: 100-249 (Tor)
#TorLoc: 1
Own: Private Company
Key: Chris Mathews, Chmn
Teresa Ahuja, Cont

HB Group Insurance Management Ltd.

5600 Cancross Crt.
Mississauga, ON L5R 3E9
Tel 905-507-6156
Fax 905-507-8661
www.directprotect.com
AKA: Direct Protect;
Coseco Insurance Co.
Line: Sells home and auto insurance.
NAICS: 524129
#Emp: 250-499 (Tor)
#TorLoc: 1
Own: Private Company
Par: The Co-operators Group Ltd. (CDA)
Key: Kathy Bardswick, Pres & CEO

HD Supply Canada

100 Galcat Dr.
Vaughan, ON L4L 0B9
Tel 905-669-0525
Fax 905-669-2603
www.hdsupply.com
AKA: Brafasco
Line: Sells construction tools and fasteners.
NAICS: 416330 417210
#Emp: 75-99 (Tor)
#TorLoc: 4
Own: Private Company
Key: Vasken Altounian, Pres
Roger Skyers, GM

Healthcare of Ontario Pension Plan

1400-1 Toronto St.
Toronto, ON M5C 3B2
Tel 416-369-9212
Fax 416-369-0225
www.hoopp.com
Line: Provides pension fund services.
NAICS: 523920
#Emp: 250-499 (Tor)
#TorLoc: 1
Own: Private Company
Key: John Crocker, Pres
Jim Keohane, Sr VP Investment Management & CIO
Barbara Thomson, Sr VP, Plan Ops
Claudia Veloza, Dir of HR
John Riviere, Sr VP Fin & CFO
David Miller, Sr VP, Governance & Gen Counsel
Reno Bugiardini, Sr VP IT & Facilities Services
Victoria Hubbell, Sr VP, Strategy & Stakeholder Relns

Heart and Stroke Foundation of Ontario

1300-2300 Yonge St.
Toronto, ON M4P 1E4
Tel 416-489-7100
Fax 416-489-9796
www.heartandstroke.ca
AKA: HSFO
Line: Raises funds for research and health promotion in order to reduce the risk of heart diseases and stroke.
NAICS: 813310 813410
#Emp: 100-249 (Tor)
#TorLoc: 12
Own: Not-for-profit
Par: Heart and Stroke Foundation of Canada
Key: David Sculthorpe, CEO
Nickey Alexiou, VP People Resources
Chris Snell, Networking & Infrastructure Mgr

Heenan Blaikie LLP

2900-333 Bay St., Bay Adelaide Centre
P.O. Box 2900
Toronto, ON M5H 2T4
Tel 416-360-6336
Fax 416-360-8425
www.heenanblaikie.com
NAICS: 541110
#Emp: 250-499 (Tor)
#TorLoc: 1
Own: Private Company
Key: Norman Bacal,
    Nat'l Co-Mng Partner
Guy Tremblay, Nat'l Co-Mng Partner
Jessica Mcdonald, Exec VP Western & International Dev

Heidelberg Canada Graphic Equipment Limited

6265 Kenway Dr.
Mississauga, ON L5T 2L3
Tel 905-362-4400
Fax 905-362-0390
www.heidelberg.com
Line: Sells and services printing equipment.
NAICS: 417230
#Emp: 100-249 (Tor)
#TorLoc: 1
Own: Private Company
Par: Heidelberger Druckmaschinen AG (GER)
Key: Richard M. Armstrong, Pres
Robert C. Primeau, Sr VP Fin & Ops
Marie Gasteiger, Dir of HR
Harold Hoff, VP Customer Support
Don Robinson, VP Sales

Hellenic Care for Seniors (Toronto) Inc.

33 Winona Dr.
Toronto, ON M6G 3Z7
Tel 416-654-7700
Fax 416-654-1080
www.hellenichome.org
Line: Operates a general long-term care facility.
NAICS: 623110
#Emp: 100-249 (Tor)
Own: Private Company
Key: Peter Xenias, Pres & Chaiman
Kostas Kostouros, CEO

Henkel Canada Corporation

2225 Meadowpine Blvd.
Mississauga, ON L5N 7P2
Tel 905-814-6511
Fax 905-814-5391
www.henkel.com
Line: Manufactures sealants, adhesives and coatings.
NAICS: 325520
#Emp: 100-249 (Tor)
#TorLoc: 3
Own: Private Company
Key: Paul McLean, Dir of Ops
Darrell Connor, Mktg Mgr

Henry's

A Div. of Cranbrook Glen Enterprises Ltd.
119 Church St.
Toronto, ON M5C 2G5
Tel 416-868-0874
Fax 416-868-0243
www.henrys.com
AKA: Head Shots
Line: Retails photo, video and digital cameras as well as accessories.
NAICS: 443130
#Emp: 250-499 (Tor)
#TorLoc: 9
Own: Private Company
Key: Ian Landy, Pres & COO
Andrew Stein, CEO
David McPherson, VP Ops
Susan Chisholm, Dir of HR
Brian Gardiner, VP Fin
James Fralick, VP Merchandising
Mark Wolfson, VP Retail Sales
Max Payne, Dir of Mktg

Heritage Education Funds Inc.

700-2005 Sheppard Ave. East
Toronto, ON M2J 5B4
Tel 416-502-2500
Fax 416-502-2555
www.heritagefunds.ca
Line: Manages educational trusts and scholarships.
NAICS: 523990
#Emp: 75-99 (Tor)
#TorLoc: 1
Own: Private Company
Key: Jason Maguire, Pres
Onofrio Loduca, CEO
Roberto Nardi,
    VP Client Services & Ops
Salman Syed, CFO
Douglas Topalovic, VP IT
Dilan Frost, VP Sales
Marjorie Cullen,
    Dir of Mktg & Commun

Heritage Nursing Homes Inc.

1195 Queen St. East
Toronto, ON M4M 1L6
Tel 416-461-8185
Fax 416-461-6972
www.heritagenursinghome.com
Line: Provides long-term care facility services.
NAICS: 623310
#Emp: 100-249 (Tor)
#TorLoc: 1
Own: Private Company
Key: Jordan Glick, Pres
Albert Mak, Business Office Mgr
Hui-Jing Chen, Dir of Social Services

Herman Miller Canada Inc.

200-462 Wellington St. West
Toronto, ON M5V 1E3
Tel 416-366-3300
Fax 416-366-2100
www.hermanmiller.com/canada
Line: Specializes in furniture products and workplace management services.
NAICS: 337213 337214
#Emp: 75-99 (Tor)
Own: Private Company
Par: Herman Miller Inc. (US)
Key: Janet Richards,
    Dir of Business Dev
Corrado Fermo, VP Ops & Fin
Christine Henderson, Dir of HR

Hershey Canada Inc.

500-5750 Explorer Dr.
Mississauga, ON L4W 0B1
Tel 905-602-9200
Fax 905-602-8766
www.hersheycanada.com
Line: Manufactures and markets candy,
chocolate, and chocolate-based grocery
products.
NAICS: 311330 311340
#Emp: 250-499 (Tor)
#TorLoc: 1
Own: Private Company
Par: Hershey Foods Corp. (US)
Key: Matt Lindsay, VP & GM
Shari Ellis, Dir of HR
Mario Carbone, Sr Dir of Sales
Lynn Baumgartner, VP Consumer Mktg

Hershey Centre

5500 Rose Cherry Pl.
Mississauga, ON L4Z 4B6
Tel 905-502-9100
Fax 905-615-3299
www.hersheycentre.com
Line: Operates a recreational complex.
NAICS: 711319
#Emp: 250-499 (Tor)
#TorLoc: 1
Own: Private Company
Par: SMG Canada (CDA)
Key: Mike Hamilton, GM
Craig Codlin, Dir of Ops
Jill Topping, Payroll & Human
    Rersources Coord
Connie Ede,
    Asst GM & Dir of Business Ops
Natalie McBoyle, Box Office Mgr
Clara Grassia, Mktg Mgr

Hertz Canada Ltd.

35 Claireville Dr.
Toronto, ON M9W 5Z7
Tel 416-674-5000
Fax 416-620-0651
www.hertz.ca
AKA: Matthews Equipment Limited
Line: Provides auto rental services.
NAICS: 532111
#Emp: 250-499 (Tor)
#TorLoc: 1
Own: Private Company
Key: Steve Conliffe, GM
Abdi Hagar, Nat'l Systems Mgr

Hewitt Material Handling, Inc.

425 Millway Ave.
Concord, ON L4K 3V8
Tel 905-669-6590
Fax 416-661-1513
www.hewittmaterialhandling.ca
Line: Rents, sells and services CAT
forklift trucks.
NAICS: 532490
#Emp: 100-249 (Tor)
#TorLoc: 1
Own: Private Company
Par: Hewitt Equipment Ltd. (CDA)
Key: Bill Botshka, Ops Mgr
Oscar Saavedra,
    Rental Fleet & Asset Mgr
Frank Jurca, Sales Mgr

Hewlett-Packard (Canada) Co.

5150 Spectrum Way
Mississauga, ON L4W 5G1
Tel 905-206-4725
Fax 905-206-4739
www.hp.ca
Line: Performs computing and imaging
services for business and home and
provides business infrastructure
components including servers, storage,
management software, imaging and
printing, personal computers and
access devices.
NAICS: 334110 417310
#Emp: 1000-4999 (Tor)
#TorLoc: 4
Own: Private Company
Par: Hewlett Packard Company (US)
Key: Paul Galanis, Pres & CEO
Jennifer Eby, Ops Mgr
Laura Desjardins, VP HR
Laura Benassi, CFO

H.H. Angus & Associates Ltd.

1127 Leslie St.
Toronto, ON M3C 2J6
Tel 416-443-8200
Fax 416-443-8290
www.hhangus.com
Line: Provides engineering, operation,
and maintenance services.
NAICS: 541330
#Emp: 100-249 (Tor)
#TorLoc: 1
Own: Private Company
Key: Harry G. Angus, Pres
Tom Halpenny, VP Ops
Glen Collins, Cont
Nick Stark,
    VP Knowledge Management

Hibar Systems Ltd.

35 Pollard St.
Richmond Hill, ON L4B 1A8
Tel 905-731-2400
Fax 905-731-3165
www.hibar.com
Line: Manufactures industrial
equipment.
NAICS: 333990
#Emp: 100-249 (Tor)
#TorLoc: 1
Own: Private Company
Key: Iain McColl, Pres & CEO
Robert Flack, VP Manuf
Florence Valenzano, Office Mgr
Stephen Mark, VP Sales

Hicks Morley Hamilton Stewart Storie LLP

TD Centre, TD Bank Tower, 30th Fl.
P.O. Box 371
Toronto, ON M5K 1K8
Tel 416-362-1011
Fax 416-362-9680
www.hicksmorley.com
Line: Provides legal services.
NAICS: 541110
#Emp: 100-249 (Tor)
#TorLoc: 1
Own: Private Company
Key: Stephen J. Shamie, Mng Partner
Arlene E. Dunford, Office Admr
Claudia Martin, CFO
Mark Richards, Dir of IT

Hidi Rae Consulting Engineers Inc.

2100-1 Yonge St.
Toronto, ON M5E 1E5
Tel 416-364-2100
Fax 416-364-2276
www.hidi.com
Line: Provides engineering consulting
services.
NAICS: 541330
#Emp: 100-249 (Tor)
#TorLoc: 1
Own: Private Company
Key: James Hidi, Pres
Shelly Roebuck-Joseph, Dir of Acctng

Highland Chevrolet Cadillac Ltd.

15783 Yonge St.
P.O. Box 275
Aurora, ON L4G 1P4
Tel 905-727-9444
Fax 905-727-6099
www.highlandgm.com
Line: Operates an automobile
dealership.
NAICS: 441110 441120
#Emp: 75-99 ('Tor)
#TorLoc: 1
Own: Private Company
Key: Cliff Sifton, Pres
Gloria Prosser, Cont

Highland Farms Inc.

4750 Dufferin St.
Toronto, ON M3H 5S7
Tel 416-736-6606
Fax 416-736-4795
www.freshathighlandfarms.com
NAICS: 445110
#Emp: 500-999 (Tor)
#TorLoc: 5
Own: Private Company
Key: Charles Coppa, Pres
Louis Coppa, VP
Frances Gabriele, HR Mgr
Frank Romani, Cont
John Louie Coppa, Meat, Seafood &
    Prepared Meals Buyer
Ono Kwan, Logistics Mgr
Michael Coppa, Mktg Mgr

Highland Transport

2815 14th Ave.
Markham, ON L3R 0H9
Tel 1-800-263-3356
Fax 905-477-0940
www.highlandtransport.com
Line: Provides transportation services.
NAICS: 484229 484239
#Emp: 500-999 (Tor)
#TorLoc: 1
Own: Public Company
Par: TransForce Logistics (CDA)
Key: Terry Gardiner, VP Ops
Scott Owens, VP Fin
Donald Maynard, Dir of IS
John Hutton, GM, Containers
Gord Boyd, Dir of Risk Management

Hill & Knowlton Canada Inc.

700-160 Bloor St. East
Toronto, ON M4W 3P7
Tel 416-413-1218
Fax 416-413-1550
www.hillandknowlton.ca
Line: Provides public relations and
public affairs services.
NAICS: 541820
#Emp: 75-99 (Tor)
#TorLoc: 1
Own: Private Company
Par: WPP Group plc (UK)
Key: Michael Coates, Pres & CEO
Jeff Smith, Sr VP & GM
Ruth Clark, Global Chief Talent Dir
Greg Yaroff, CFO
Ilyse Smith, Sr VP Commun

Hill-Rom Canada

3-1705 Tech Ave.
Mississauga, ON L4W 0A2
Tel 905-206-1355
Fax 905-206-0561
www.hill-rom.com
Line: Operates healthcare facilities.
NAICS: 339110
#Emp: 75-99 (Tor)
#TorLoc: 1
Own: Private Company
Key: Wayne Flynn, Mgr

Hillsdale Estates

590 Oshawa Blvd. North
Oshawa, ON L1G 5T9
Tel 905-579-1777
Fax 905-579-3911
www.durham.ca
Line: Operates a general long-term care
home.
NAICS: 623310
#Emp: 500-999 (Tor)
#TorLoc: 2
Own: Government
Par: Region of Durham
Key: Marcey Wilson, Admr

Hilroy

A Div. of MeadWestvaco Canada LP
7381 Bramelea Rd.
Mississauga, ON L5S 1C4
Tel 905-364-2600
Fax 905-364-2651
www.hilroy.ca
Line: Manufactures and distributes
paper converters, supplying office and
school products.
NAICS: 418210 453210
#Emp: 100-249 (Tor)
#TorLoc: 2
Own: Public Company
Par: MeadWestvaco Corp. (US)
Key: Bob Hodan, Pres & GM
Paul West, VP Ops
Sylvia Basso, Dir of HR
Jeff Maple, Acting VP Fin & Cont
Peter Duquette, MIS Mgr
Samantha Hindmarch, Dir of Mktg

Hilti (Canada) Corp.

A Div. of Hilti Group
2360 Meadowpine Blvd.
Mississauga, ON L5N 6S2
Tel 905-813-9200
Fax 905-813-9009
www.hilti.ca
Line: Provides leading-edge technology
to the global construction industry.
NAICS: 333120
#Emp: 100-249 (Tor)
#TorLoc: 4
Own: Private Company
Par: Hilti (LICH)
Key: Rich Knapp, Pres
Umer Qamar, Dir of HR
Larry Selby, Mktg Mgr, Canada

Hilton Garden Inn
Toronto City Centre

200 Dundas St. East
Toronto, ON M5A 4R6
Tel 416-362-7700
Fax 416-362-7706
www.hilton.com
Line: Operates a hotel.
NAICS: 721111
#Emp: 75-99 (Tor)
#TorLoc: 1
Own: Private Company
Key: Karen Hardcastle, GM

The Hilton Suites Toronto/ Markham Conference Centre & Spa

8500 Warden Ave.
Markham, ON L6G 1A5
Tel 905-470-8500
Fax 905-415-7624
www.torontomarkham.hilton.com
Line: Provides hotel accommodations and conference facilities.
NAICS: 721111
#Emp: 250-499 (Tor)
#TorLoc: 1
Own: Private Company
Par: Markham Suites Hotel Limited (CDA)
Key: Patrick Regina, GM
Herman Grad, Pres & Owner
Jeff Handelsman, COO
Penny Benson, Dir of HR
Manicks Rasiah, Cont
Genson Navaprajah, Purchaser
Jennifer Chiappetta,
    Dir of Mktg & Sales
Judy Reicker, Dir of Ops

Hilton Toronto

145 Richmond St. West
Toronto, ON M5H 2L2
Tel 416-869-3456
Fax 416-869-3187
www.hilton.com
NAICS: 721111
#Emp: 250-499 (Tor)
Own: Private Company
Par: Hilton Group plc (UK)
Key: Edwin Frizzel, GM
Jill Miller, Dir of HR
Jenny So, Dir of Fin

Hilton Toronto Airport Hotel & Suites

5875 Airport Rd.
Mississauga, ON L4V 1N1
Tel 905-677-9900
Fax 905-677-5073
www.hilton.com
Line: Provides hospitality services.
NAICS: 721111
#Emp: 100-249 (Tor)
#TorLoc: 1
Own: Public Company
Key: Andy Loges, GM

The Hincks-Dellcrest Centre

440 Jarvis St.
Toronto, ON M4Y 2H4
Tel 416-924-1164
Fax 416-924-8208
www.hincksdellcrest.org
Line: Promotes mental health in infants, children, youth and their families, and contributes to the achievement of healthy communities.
NAICS: 621420
#Emp: 250-499 (Tor)
#TorLoc: 9
Own: Not-for-profit
Par: The Hincks-Dellcrest Centre (CDA)
Key: Donna Duncan,
    Interim Pres & CEO
Marshall Korenblum,
    Psychiatrist in Chief
Mary Pomanti, Program Dir, HR
Annabelle Rocha, CFO

H.J. Heinz Company of Canada Ltd.

400-90 Sheppard Ave. East
Toronto, ON M2N 7K5
Tel 416-226-5757
Fax 416-226-5064
www.heinz.com
AKA: Heinz
Line: Manufactures ketchup, condiments, baby food and sauces.
NAICS: 311420 311940
#Emp: 100-249 (Tor)
#TorLoc: 1
Own: Private Company
Par: H.J. Heinz Company Inc. (US)
Key: Peter Luik, Pres & CEO
Elitra Ducreay, HR Coord
Bruna Gambino, VP Fin & CFO
Barbara Bell, GM IS
Steve Oakes, VP Retail Mktg

H.L. Blachford Ltd.

2323 Royal Windsor Dr.
Mississauga, ON L5J 1K5
Tel 905-823-3200
Fax 905-823-9290
www.blachford.ca
Line: Manufactures products for the automotive and steel industries such as metal-working lubricants, wire-drying compounds, and noise control materials for buses and trucks.
NAICS: 336390
#Emp: 75-99 (Tor)
#TorLoc: 1
Own: Private Company
Key: John Blachford, Pres & CEO
Joe Borean, VP Fin

H & M Hennes & Mauritz Inc.

1808-1 Dundas St. West
P.O. Box 47
Toronto, ON M5G 1Z3
Tel 416-623-4300
Fax 416-260-0420
www.hm.com
Line: Retails casual apparel.
NAICS: 448140
#Emp: 1000-4999 (Tor)
#TorLoc: 20
Own: Private Company
Par: Hennes & Mauritz Inc. (SWE)
Key: Lucy van der Wal, Country Mgr
Vanessa Gray, HR Mgr, Canada
Vincent Truong, Country Cont

HMSHost

306-45 Sheppard Ave. East
Toronto, ON M2N 5W9
Tel 416-221-4900
Fax 416-221-8603
www.hmshost.com
Line: Operates quick service restaurants to travel service centres and the Toronto Airport.
NAICS: 722310 722210
#Emp: 250-499 (Tor)
#TorLoc: 11
Own: Public Company
Par: HMSHost North America (US)
Key: Elie W. Maalouf, Pres & CEO
Bruce Carbone, VP Ops
Richard Carson, HR Mgr
Vijay Francis, VP Fin
Kerry McLeod,
    Construction Maintenance

HMV Canada Inc.

110-5401 Eglinton Ave. West
Toronto, ON M9C 5K6
Tel 416-620-4470
Fax 416-620-5064
www.hmv.ca
Line: Retails prerecorded music and associated products.
NAICS: 451220
#Emp: 500-999 (Tor)
#TorLoc: 20
Own: Private Company
Par: HMV Group plc (UK)
Key: Humphrey Kadaner, Pres
Dan Kuczkowski, VP Product & Ops
Harvey Berkley, VP Fin

Hobart Food Equipment Group Canada Inc.

206-207 716 Gordon Baker Rd.
Toronto, ON M2H 3B4
Tel 416-447-6432
Fax 416-447-8112
www.hobart.ca
AKA: Hobart Canada
Line: Manufactures, sells and services food processing and washing equipment.
NAICS: 335210 417230
#Emp: 100-249 (Tor)
#TorLoc: 2
Own: Public Company
Par: Hobart Food Equipment Group (US)
Key: David Sherman, Pres
Orkhan Musayev, Cont
Paul Stethem, Dir of HR
Ken Booker, Mgr of IT
Doug McKinnon, VP Sales
Robert Murray, GM, Service

Hockey Hall of Fame

30 Yonge St., Brookfield Pl.
Toronto, ON M5E 1X8
Tel 416-360-7735
Fax 416-360-1501
www.hhof.com
NAICS: 712111
#Emp: 100-249 (Tor)
#TorLoc: 1
Own: Not-for-profit
Key: Jeff Denomme, Pres, Treas & COO
Bill Hay, Chmn & CEO
Craig Baines, VP, Ops
Sandra Walters, Office Mgr & Cont
Anthony Fusco, Mgr of IS

Hockley Valley Resort Ltd.

793522 Mono 3rd Line, R.R. #1
Orangeville, ON L9W 2Y8
Tel 519-942-0754
Fax 519-942-8033
www.hockley.com
NAICS: 721113
#Emp: 100-249 (Tor)
#TorLoc: 1
Own: Private Company
Key: Nancy Adamo, Owner & Pres
John Polidamo, GM

Hoffmann-LaRoche Ltd.

2455 Meadowpine Blvd.
Mississauga, ON L5N 6L7
Tel 905-542-5555
Fax 905-542-7130
www.rochecanada.com
AKA: Roche Canada
Line: Sells pharmaceuticals and diagnostic testing equipment.
NAICS: 414510 325410
#Emp: 250-499 (Tor)
#TorLoc: 1
Own: Private Company
Par: F. Hoffmann-LaRoche & Co. AG (SWITZ)
Key: Chris Parker, Pres & GM, Canada
Ronnie Miller, Pres & CEO

Hogan Chevrolet Limited

5000 Sheppard Ave. East
Toronto, ON M1S 4L9
Tel 416-291-5054
Fax 416-291-4234
www.hoganchev.com
AKA: Hogan Chevrolet Oldsmobile Corvette
Line: Provides automotive sales and service.
NAICS: 441110 441120
#Emp: 100-249 (Tor)
#TorLoc: 1
Own: Private Company
Key: Drew Foss, GM
Suzanne Tadeson, Office Mgr
Ron Norman, Secy-Treas & Cont
Jorge Desousa, Gen Sales Mgr

Hok Canada, Inc.

505-720 King St. West
Toronto, ON M5V 2T3
Tel 416-203-9993
Fax 416-203-9992
www.hok.com
AKA: Hok Architects Corporation
Line: Operates an architecture and design firm.
NAICS: 541310
#Emp: 100-249 (Tor)
#TorLoc: 1
Own: Private Company
Key: Gordon Stratford, Sr VP
Lui Mancinelli, Sr VP
Terri Robinson, Sr VP Dev & Mktg

Holcim (Canada) Inc.

2300 Steeles Ave. West, 4th Fl.
Concord, ON L4K 5X6
Tel 905-761-7100
Fax 905-761-7200
www.stlawrencecement.com
Line: Produces and supplies cement, concrete, aggregate products and services for the construction industry.
NAICS: 327310
#Emp: 1000-4999 (Tor)
#TorLoc: 5
Own: Private Company
Par: Holcim Ltd. (SWITZ)
Key: Paul Ostrander, Pres & CEO
Badreddine Filali-Baba, Sr VP HR
Kent Carson, CFO

Holiday Inn Burlington

3063 South Service Rd.
Burlington, ON L7N 3E9
Tel 905-639-4443
Fax 905-333-4033
www.ichotelsgroup.com
NAICS: 721111
#Emp: 100-249 (Tor)
#TorLoc: 1
Own: Private Company
Par: InterContinental Hotels Group (US)
Key: Gordon R. Langford, GM
Anita Gerrard, Dir of HR
James Amores, Cont
Janice Edworthy, Dir of Sales & Mktg

Holiday Inn Hotel & Suites Toronto - Markham

7095 Woodbine Ave.
Markham, ON L3R 1A3
Tel 905-474-0444
Fax 905-474-1877
www.markham.holiday-inn.com
AKA: Markham Woodbine Management Ltd.
NAICS: 721111
#Emp: 100-249 (Tor)
#TorLoc: 1
Own: Private Company
Par: InterContinental Hotels Group (US)
Key: Rawi Zayadi, GM
Camilla Castaneda, Guest Services Mgr
Lori Winokur, HR Mgr
Murray Lathem, Dir of Sales

Holiday Inn Oakville @ Bronte

2525 Wyecroft Rd.
Oakville, ON L6L 6P8
Tel 905-847-1000
Fax 905-847-0032
www.hioakvillebronte.ca
NAICS: 721111
#Emp: 75-99 (Tor)
#TorLoc: 1
Own: Private Company
Par: Intercontinental Hotels Group
(US)
Key: Marcelo Tomazo, GM
Lalita Kumar, Acct
Johanna Redmond, Dir of Sales & Mktg

Holiday Inn Oshawa

1011 Bloor St. East
Oshawa, ON L1H 7K6
Tel 905-576-5101
Fax 905-576-3296
www.hioshawa.ca
NAICS: 721111
#Emp: 100-249 (Tor)
#TorLoc: 1
Own: Private Company
Par: InnVest Real Estate Investment
Trust (CDA)
Key: Anton Ganesh, Cont
Tiffany Gilmore, Dir of Sales & Mktg

Holiday Inn Toronto Airport East

600 Dixon Rd.
Toronto, ON M9W 1J1
Tel 416-240-7511
Fax 416-240-7519
www.hitorontoairport.ca
NAICS: 721111
#Emp: 100-249 (Tor)
#TorLoc: 1
Own: Private Company
Par: Westmont Hospitality Group
(CDA)
Key: Sohail Saeed, GM
Nina Simons, HR Mgr
Nash Foud, Cont
Nadia Gelmo, Dir of Sales

Holiday Inn Toronto Airport West

100 Britannia Rd. East
Mississauga, ON L4Z 2G1
Tel 905-890-5700
Fax 905-568-0868
www.holidayinn.com/yyz-west
NAICS: 721111
#Emp: 75-99 (Tor)
#TorLoc: 1
Own: Private Company

Par: Westmont Hospitality Group
(CDA)
Key: Saleem Jaka, GM
Danielle Parker, Guest Services Mgr
Raymond Rajendra, Cont
Miranda Phillips, Dir of Sales

Holiday Inn Toronto Downtown Centre

30 Carlton St.
Toronto, ON M5B 2E9
Tel 416-977-6655
Fax 416-977-0502
www.holidayinn.com/torontocenter
NAICS: 721111
#Emp: 100-249 (Tor)
#TorLoc: 1
Own: Private Company
Par: 541907 Ontario Ltd. (CDA)
Key: Steve Yates, GM
Jeff Lovenehal, Cont

Holiday Inn Toronto International Airport

970 Dixon Rd.
Toronto, ON M9W 1J9
Tel 416-675-7611
Fax 416-674-4364
www.holidayinn.com
AKA: IHG Intercontinental Hotels
Group
Line: Offers full service hotel.
NAICS: 721111
#Emp: 100-249 (Tor)
#TorLoc: 1
Own: Private Company
Par: IHG (US)
Key: Scott de Savoye, GM
Edwina Mesiano, Dir of HR
Kevin Reeve, Dir of Fin
Hughena Walsh, Dir of Sales

Holiday Inn - Toronto Yorkdale

3450 Dufferin St.
Toronto, ON M6A 2V1
Tel 416-789-5161
Fax 416-785-6845
www.hiyorkdale.com
NAICS: 721111
#Emp: 100-249 (Tor)
#TorLoc: 1
Own: Private Company
Par: InterContinental Hotels Group
(US)
Key: Armand Abitbol, GM
Sassan Shams, Ops Mgr
Franca Ricci McNeill, Dir of HR
Ramesh Thiru, Cont
Stephanie Snowball, Dir of Sales

Holland Bloorview Kids Rehab

150 Kilgour Rd.
Toronto, ON M4G 1R8
Tel 416-425-6220
Fax 416-425-6591
www.bloorview.ca
Line: Serves children and young adults
with disabilities and complex long-
term needs.
NAICS: 622112 622310
#Emp: 500-999 (Tor)
#TorLoc: 1
Own: Not-for-profit
Key: Sheila Jarvis, Pres & CEO
Jackie Schleifer Taylor,
    VP Programs & Services
Judy Hunter,
    VP HR & Organization Dev
Ben Sybring, VP Corp Services
Linda Hatton, Sr Dir of IS
Christa Haanstra,
    Sr Dir of Commun & Pub Affairs

Holland Christian Homes Inc.

7900 McLaughlin Rd. South
Brampton, ON L6Y 5A7
Tel 905-459-3333
Fax 905-459-8667
www.hch.ca
Line: Provides housing and long-term
care for senior citizens.
NAICS: 623310
#Emp: 250-499 (Tor)
#TorLoc: 1
Own: Private Company
Key: John Kalverda, Exec Dir
Peter Dykstra, Admr

Hollander Canada Home Fashions Limited

724 Caledonia Rd.
Toronto, ON M6B 3X7
Tel 416-780-0168
Fax 416-780-0169
www.hollander.com
Line: Manufactures blankets.
NAICS: 314120
#Emp: 100-249 (Tor)
#TorLoc: 1
Own: Private Company
Key: Jeff Hollander, Pres & CEO

Holt Renfrew & Company Ltd.

60 Bloor St. West
Toronto, ON M4W 3B8
Tel 416-922-2333
Fax 416-922-7284
www.holtrenfrew.com
Line: Retails specialty fashion and
lifestyle items.
NAICS: 448140
#Emp: 500-999 (Tor)
#TorLoc: 5
Own: Private Company
Par: Wittington Fashion Retail Group
(CDA)
Key: Mark Derbyshire, Pres & CEO
Kyoko Kobayashi, Dir of IT
Alix Box, Sr VP Sales & Mktg
Moira Wright, Dir of Commun

Holy Blossom Temple

1950 Bathurst St.
Toronto, ON M5P 3K9
Tel 416-789-3291
Fax 416-789-9697
www.holyblossom.org
NAICS: 813110
#Emp: 75-99 (Tor)
#TorLoc: 1
Own: Religious
Key: Mark S. Anshan, Pres
Benjamin Applebaum, Exec Dir
Shelly Berenbaum, Sr Admr
Chello Sittambalam,
    Acctng Mgr & Cont

Holy Trinity School

11300 Bayview Ave.
Richmond Hill, ON L4S 1L4
Tel 905-737-1114
Fax 905-737-5187
www.hts.on.ca
Line: Operates university preparatory
school.
NAICS: 611110
#Emp: 75-99 (Tor)
#TorLoc: 1
Own: Not-for-profit
Key: Barry Hughes, Head of School
Rocki Guzzo, Dir of Admin
Chris Stafeau, Dir of Fin
Carol Ann Horvat,
    Dir of Mktg & Commun

Home Depot Canada

900-1 Concorde Gate
Toronto, ON M3C 4H9
Tel 416-609-0852
Fax 416-412-6791
www.homedepot.ca
Line: Retails merchandise for home
improvement.
NAICS: 444130 444190
#Emp: 5000-9999 (Tor)
#TorLoc: 33
Own: Public Company
Par: Home Depot Inc. (US)
Key: Bill Lennie, Pres
Kim Forgues, VP HR
Mike Rowe, VP Fin
Gino Digioacchino, VP Merchandising
Peg Hunter, VP Mktg & Commun
Paul Berto, Sr Mgr of Corp
    Commun & External Affairs

HomeLife Bayview Realty Inc.

201-505 Hwy. 7 East
Thornhill, ON L3T 7T1
Tel 905-889-2200
Fax 905-889-3322
www.homelifebayview.com
Line: Offers real estate services.
NAICS: 531210
#Emp: 500-999 (Tor)
#TorLoc: 1
Own: Private Company
Key: Tom Tauro, Broker of Record
Steven Schmeiser, Broker & Owner
Olga Pais, HR

HomeLife Cholkan Realty Corp.

109 Judge Rd.
Toronto, ON M8Z 5B5
Tel 416-236-7711
Fax 416-234-5934
www.hlcholkanrealty.com
Line: Specializes in residential,
industrial, and commercial investment
real estate properties.
NAICS: 531210
#Emp: 100-249 (Tor)
#TorLoc: 1
Own: Private Company
Key: Ernst Grenke, Pres
Al Grenke, CEO
Richard A. Korol, GM

HomeLife Cimerman Real Estate Ltd.

2201 Danforth Ave.
Toronto, ON M4C 1K4
Tel 416-690-6363
Fax 416-690-8259
www.homelifecimerman.ca
Line: Provides real estate services.
NAICS: 531210
#Emp: 100-249 (Tor)
#TorLoc: 5
Own: Private Company
Key: Louis Eliopulos, Broker of Record
Doug Wong, Broker

HomeLife Gold Pacific Realty Inc.

401-3601 Victoria Park Ave.
Toronto, ON M1W 3Y3
Tel 416-490-1068
Fax 416-490-8938
www.homelifegoldpacific.com
NAICS: 531210
#Emp: 100-249 (Tor)
#TorLoc: 1
Own: Private Company
Key: Bernard Wong, Pres
Dorris Hung, HR Mgr

HomeLife Gold Trade Realty Ltd.

605-608 3950 14th Ave.
Markham, ON L3R 0A9
Tel 905-415-3800
Fax 905-415-1398
www.goldtradereality.com
Line: Provides real estate brokerage
services.
NAICS: 531210
#Emp: 100-249 (Tor)
#TorLoc: 2
Own: Private Company
Key: Jimmy Wong, Broker of Record
Viola Wong, Admr

HomeLife Metro Realty Inc.

206-5200 Finch Ave. East
Toronto, ON M1S 4Z4
Tel 416-293-5093
Fax 416-293-5237
www.athomes.ca
Line: Operates a real estate agency.
NAICS: 531210
#Emp: 100-249 (Tor)
Own: Private Company
Key: Shan Naz, Broker

HomeLife Miracle Realty Ltd.

11A-5010 Steeles Ave. West
Toronto, ON M9V 5C6
Tel 416-747-9777
Fax 416-747-7135
www.homelifemiracle.com
Line: Operates a real estate company.
NAICS: 531210
#Emp: 75-99 (Tor)
#TorLoc: 3
Own: Private Company
Key: Ajay Shah, Broker & Owner

HomeLife New World Realty Inc.

205-201 Consumers Rd.
Toronto, ON M2J 4G8
Tel 416-490-1177
Fax 416-490-1928
www.newworldcanada.com
Line: Operates real estate company.
NAICS: 531210
#Emp: 250-499 (Tor)
#TorLoc: 1
Own: Private Company
Key: Simon Yeung, Pres

HomeLife Response Realty Inc.

4312 Village Centre Crt.
Mississauga, ON L4Z 1S2
Tel 905-949-0070
Fax 905-949-9814
www.homeliferesponse.com
Line: Provides real estate services.
NAICS: 531210
#Emp: 100-249 (Tor)
#TorLoc: 1
Own: Private Company
Key: Anthony D'Ambrosio,
Broker & Owner

HomeLife United Realty Inc.

215-2980 Drew Rd.
Mississauga, ON L4T 0A7
Tel 905-672-1234
Fax 905-672-0672
Line: Sells residential, investment and
commercial real estate.
NAICS: 531210
#Emp: 250-499 (Tor)
#TorLoc: 4
Own: Private Company
Key: Parvinder Singh, Broker of Record

HomeLife Vision Realty Inc.

1945 Leslie St.
Toronto, ON M3B 2M3
Tel 416-383-1828
Fax 416-383-1821
www.homelifevision.com
Line: Operates a real estate company.
NAICS: 531210
#Emp: 100-249 (Tor)
#TorLoc: 1
Own: Private Company
Key: Ken Kakoullis, Pres & Broker

HomEquity Bank

600-45 St. Clair Ave. West
Toronto, ON M4V 1K9
Tel 416-925-4757
Fax 416-925-9938
www.chip.ca
AKA: Canadian Home Income Plan
Corp.; CHIP
Line: Specializes in reverse mortgages.
NAICS: 523910
#Emp: 75-99 (Tor)
#TorLoc: 1
Own: Public Company
Par: Home Equity Income Trust (CDA)
Key: Steven K. Ranson, Pres & CEO
Scott Cameron, VP Fin
Lori Sone-Cooper, Sr HR Consultant
Gary Krikler, Sr VP & CFO
Wendy Dryden, VP Business Dev
Neil Sider, VP IT
Greg Bandler, Sr VP Sales & Mktg
Arthur Krzycki,
    Dir of Channel Mktg & PR

Homes First Society

90 Shutter St., 2nd Fl.
Toronto, ON M5B 2K6
Tel 416-214-1870
Fax 416-214-1873
www.homesfirst.on.ca
Line: Provides private housing
programs.
NAICS: 531112
#Emp: 75-99 (Tor)
#TorLoc: 1
Own: Not-for-profit
Key: Patricia Mueller, Exec Dir
Caroline Ferris, HR Mgr
Yushan Chio, Mgr of Fin

Homestarts Inc.

C-6537 Mississauga Rd.
Mississauga, ON L5N 1A6
Tel 905-858-1110
Fax 905-858-5040
www.homestarts.org
Line: Provides staffing, property
and management services to owner
controlled housing developments and
community sponsored cooperative and
nonprofit housing projects for families
and seniors.
NAICS: 541611
#Emp: 75-99 (Tor)
#TorLoc: 1
Own: Not-for-profit
Key: Paul Hastie, Exec Dir
Nicola Malony, HR & Admin Mgr

Home Trust Co.

2300-145 King St. West
Toronto, ON M5H 1J8
Tel 416-360-4663
Fax 416-363-7611
www.hometrust.ca
NAICS: 522299
#Emp: 100-249 (Tor)
#TorLoc: 1
Own: Public Company
Par: Home Capital Group Inc. (CDA)
Key: Martin Reid, Pres
Gerald Soloway, CEO
Brian R. Mosko, Exec VP & COO
Cathy Sutherland, Sr. VP Fin

Honda Canada Finance Inc.

400-3650 Victoria Park Ave.
Toronto, ON M2H 3P7
Tel 416-754-2323
Fax 416-754-5100
www.honda.ca
Line: Provides wholesale financing
to Honda dealers as well as retail and
lease financing to consumers of Honda
products.
NAICS: 522291
#Emp: 100-249 (Tor)
#TorLoc: 2
Own: Private Company
Par: American Honda Finance (US)
Key: Hideo Tanaka, Pres
David A. Sudbury, VP Chief
    Compliance Officer & Secy
Harald Ladewig, VP & Treas

Honda Canada Inc.

180 Honda Blvd.
Markham, ON L6C 0H9
Tel 905-888-8110
www.honda.ca
Line: Manufactures and distributes
automobiles, motorcycles and power
equipment.
NAICS: 336110 415190
#Emp: 1000-4999 (Tor)
#TorLoc: 4
Own: Private Company
Par: Honda Motor Company Ltd.
(JAPAN)
Key: Masahiro Takedagawa,
    Pres & CEO
Joan Andersen, Asst VP HR
Katsuyuki Matsui, VP Fin

Honeywell

3333 Unity Dr.
Mississauga, ON L5L 3S6
Tel 905-608-6000
Fax 905-608-6001
www.honeywell.com
Line: Designs and manufactures aircraft equipment and services; control technologies for buildings, homes and industry; automotive products, power generation systems, specialty chemicals, fibres and plastics; and electronic and advanced materials.
NAICS: 336410
#Emp: 1000-4999 (Tor)
#TorLoc: 6
Own: Private Company
Par: Honeywell International Inc. (US)
Key: Deborah Van Damme, Dir of Fin
David M. Cote, Chmn & CEO
Rick Mueller, Dir of Sales & Mktg

Hoodex Industries Ltd.

4-5650 Tomken Rd.
Mississauga, ON L4W 4P1
Tel 905-624-8668
Fax 905-624-3900
www.hoodex.ca
AKA: H.W. & Associates
Line: Provides janitorial services.
NAICS: 561722
#Emp: 75-99 (Tor)
#TorLoc: 1
Own: Private Company
Key: Morley Hood, Pres
Raymond Hood, VP

Hood Packaging Corporation

2380 McDowell Rd.
Burlington, ON L7R 4A1
Tel 905-637-5611
Fax 905-637-9954
www.hoodpkg.com
AKA: Glopak
Line: Manufactures packaging materials, multi-wall industrial paper bags, and multi-layer polyethylene film and bags.
NAICS: 322220
#Emp: 100-249 (Tor)
#TorLoc: 3
Own: Private Company
Par: Hood Co. (US)
Key: Robert Morris, Pres
Warren A. Jr. Hood, Chmn & CEO
Mark Drury, VP Ops, Plastics Division
Ronald J. More, VP HR
Todd Eby, VP Fin & CFO
Gary W. Cameron, VP Purch
Peter Spencer, Dir of IT

Hooper-Holmes Canada Limited

1059 McNicoll Ave.
Toronto, ON M1W 3W6
Tel 416-493-2800
Fax 416-493-7881
www.hooperholmes.ca
Line: Provides insurance advisory services.
NAICS: 524299
#Emp: 100-249 (Tor)
#TorLoc: 2
Own: Private Company
Key: Daniel Gauvin, Pres
Mike Woodroffe, Exec VP

The Hospital for Sick Children

555 University Ave.
Toronto, ON M5G 1X8
Tel 416-813-1500
Fax 416-813-5393
www.sickkids.ca
AKA: SickKids
Line: Operates teaching hospital and paediatric academic health science centre.
NAICS: 622112
#Emp: 5000-9999 (Tor)
#TorLoc: 1
Own: Not-for-profit
Key: Mary Jo Haddad, Pres & CEO
Cheryl Craven, VP HR
Angela Holtham, VP Fin & CFO
Wayne Coros, Dir of Purch
Daniela Crivianu-Gaita, VP & CIO
Judith John,
    VP Strategic Comm & Pub Affairs

Hostmann-Steinberg Ltd.

12 Shaftsbury Lane
Brampton, ON L6T 3X7
Tel 905-793-9970
Fax 905-793-5368
www.hostmann-steinberg.net
Line: Manufactures printing inks and pressroom supplies.
NAICS: 325910
#Emp: 75-99 (Tor)
#TorLoc: 2
Own: Private Company
Par: Farbenfabriken M Huber Munchen GmbH (GER)
Key: Vivy DaCosta, VP Fin & Admin
Peter Simpson, Purch Mgr
John Griffin, Sales Mgr

Hostopia.com Inc.

5915 Airport Rd., 11th Fl.
Mississauga, ON L4V 1T1
Tel 905-673-7575
Fax 905-673-1331
www.hostopia.com
Line: Provides wholesale private label hosting, managed email and application services.
NAICS: 541510
#Emp: 100-249 (Tor)
#TorLoc: 1
Own: Public Company
Par: Hostopia Inc. (US)
Key: Colin Campbell, CEO
Peter Kostandenou, COO
Wendy Oliver, Mgr of HR
Dirk Bhagat, CTO
Dave Murphy, VP Mktg

Hot House Cafe

35 Church St.
Toronto, ON M5E 1T3
Tel 416-366-7800
Fax 416-366-7804
www.hothousecafe.com
Line: Operates a restaurant.
NAICS: 722110
#Emp: 75-99 (Tor)
#TorLoc: 1
Own: Private Company
Key: Andrew Laffey, Owner
Peter Crabbe, Sr Mgr

House & Home Media

A Div. of Canadian Home Publishers
120-511 King St. West
Toronto, ON M5V 2Z4
Tel 416-593-0204
Fax 416-591-1630
www.canadianhouseandhome.com
Line: Provides magazine publication, television production and merchandise design services.
NAICS: 511120
#Emp: 75-99 (Tor)
#TorLoc: 1
Own: Private Company
Key: Lynda Reeves, Pres
Kirby Miller, VP Sales & Ops
Eleanor Codner, Cont
Mark Challen, VP Commun

Howard Marten Company Ltd.

875 Dillingham Rd.
Pickering, ON L1W 2Y5
Tel 905-831-2901
Fax 905-831-5807
www.howardmarten.com
Line: Manufactures oil lubrication
consoles, fluid systems, and
mechanical auxiliary packages.
NAICS: 333990
#Emp: 100-249 (Tor)
#TorLoc: 2
Own: Private Company
Key: Brian Whitehead, VP
Bill McKay, Pres
Jan Ploszaj, Engineering Mgr
Jeff Russell, Reg Sales Mgr

H. Paulin & Company Ltd.

55 Milne Ave.
Toronto, ON M1L 4N3
Tel 416-694-3351
Fax 416-694-1869
www.hpaulin.com
Line: Manufactures fasteners and
fittings for the automotive hardware,
industrial and construction markets.
NAICS: 332720
#Emp: 250-499 (Tor)
#TorLoc: 6
Own: Public Company
Key: Richard Paulin, Pres
Jeff Jonsohn, VP Ops
Lorie Whitcombe, HR Mgr
Carl Krause, Cont
John Timms, Mktg Mgr

H & R Block Canada Inc.

200-340 Midpark Way S.E.
Calgary, AB T2X 1P1
Tel 403-254-8689
Fax 403-254-9949
www.hrblock.ca
Line: Provides tax preparation and
financial services.
NAICS: 541213
#Emp: 1000-4999 (Tor)
#TorLoc: 80
Own: Private Company
Par: H & R Block Inc. (US)
Key: Bob Lougen, Sr Exec VP
Nicky Anderson, Office Mgr

HRC Canada Inc.

279 Yonge St.
Toronto, ON M5B 1N8
Tel 416-362-3636
Fax 416-362-9010
www.hardrock.com
AKA: Hard Rock Cafe Toronto
Line: Operates an eating, drinking and
live music establishment.
NAICS: 722110
#Emp: 100-249 (Tor)
#TorLoc: 2
Own: Private Company
Par: Hard Rock International Inc. (US)
Key: Robert Telewiak, GM
Marcelo D'Oliveira, Sr Sales Mgr

H & R Developments

500-3625 Dufferin St.
Toronto, ON M3K 1N4
Tel 416-635-7520
Fax 416-635-9921
www.hr-newhomes.com
AKA: Batise Investments Ltd.
Line: Develops real estate property.
NAICS: 531310
#Emp: 100-249 (Tor)
#TorLoc: 1
Own: Private Company
Key: Sandor Hofstader, Pres

HRG North America

700-370 King St. West
Toronto, ON M5V 1J9
Tel 416-593-8866
Fax 416-593-7158
www.hrgworldwide.com
AKA: Hogg Robinson Group
Line: Provides travel services for
companies.
NAICS: 561510
#Emp: 100-249 (Tor)
#TorLoc: 2
Own: Private Company
Par: Hogg Robinson plc (UK)
Key: Tom Gleason, Pres & CEO
Jim Pagano, Corp COO
Randy Nanek, Reg CFO
Debra Smith, Dir of IT
Ted Brooks, Exec VP Tech

H & R Property Management Ltd.

409-3625 Dufferin St.
Toronto, ON M3K 1N4
Tel 416-635-0163
Fax 416-635-5997
www.hrpm.ca
NAICS: 531111 531310
#Emp: 75-99 (Tor)
#TorLoc: 11
Own: Private Company
Key: Robert Rubinstein, Pres
Larry Froom, CEO

HSBC Bank Canada

70 York St.
Toronto, ON M5J 1S9
Tel 416-868-8000
Fax 416-868-3800
www.hsbc.ca
Line: Provides full range of domestic
and international banking services to
individuals, corporations, financial
institutions and governments across
Canada.
NAICS: 522111
#Emp: 1000-4999 (Tor)
#TorLoc: 44
Own: Private Company
Par: HSBC Holdings plc (UK)
Key: Lindsay Gordon, Pres & CEO
Matthew Bosrock,
    Exec VP & Deputy CEO
Michael Webb, Sr VP HR
Graham McIsaac, CFO
Ernest Yee, VP Corp Affairs

HSBC Securities (Canada) Inc.

70 York St., 9th Fl.
Toronto, ON M5J 1S9
Tel 416-868-7800
Fax 416-868-3394
www.hsbc.ca/securities
Line: Provides stock brokerage
services.
NAICS: 523120
#Emp: 250-499 (Tor)
#TorLoc: 3
Own: Public Company
Par: HSBC Bank Canada (CDA)
Key: Loren Harper, Pres & CEO
Jacque Fleurant, Sr VP & CFO,
    Global Banking & Markets

H.S.T. Synthetics Ltd.

6630 Edwards Blvd.
Mississauga, ON L5T 2V6
Tel 905-670-3432
Fax 905-670-3485
www.hstsynthetics.com
Line: Manufactures products to protect
pools, spas and patios.
NAICS: 339920
#Emp: 75-99 (Tor)
#TorLoc: 1
Own: Private Company
Key: Julia Tiler, Owner
Gurjinder Bhogal, Office Mgr

HTS Engineering Ltd.

115 Norfinch Dr.
Toronto, ON M3N 1W8
Tel 416-661-3400
Fax 416-661-0100
www.htseng.com
Line: Distributes heating and air
conditioning products.
NAICS: 416120
#Emp: 75-99 (Tor)
#TorLoc: 1
Own: Private Company
Key: Derek Gordon, Pres
Jennifer Estacio, Payroll Mgr
David Kviring, CFO
Roland Boucher, IT Mgr

Hubbell Canada LP

870 Brock Rd. South
Pickering, ON L1W 1Z8
Tel 905-839-1138
Fax 905-839-9108
www.hubbell-canada.com
Line: Sells, markets and distributes
wiring devices and enclosures,
voice and data connectors and jacks,
lighting fixtures, hazardous location
and explosion proof equipment, and
electrical service poles and power bars.
NAICS: 335930 335990
#Emp: 100-249 (Tor)
#TorLoc: 1
Own: Private Company
Par: Hubbell Incorporated (US)
Key: Kevin Mallory, VP & GM
Brenda Carter-Jennings, HR Mgr
Paul Ashworth, Dir of Fin
Debbie Drozda, Dir of Sales & Mktg,
   Lighting Products
David Syer, Dir of Sales & Mktg,
   Wiring Products

Hubbert Processing & Sales Ltd.

109 East Dr.
Brampton, ON L6T 1B6
Tel 905-791-0101
Fax 905-791-9304
Line: Provides edible oils, shortenings,
and meat by-products.
NAICS: 311225
#Emp: 75-99 (Tor)
#TorLoc: 1
Own: Private Company
Key: Bruce Hubbert, Pres
Ken Hubbert, CEO
Carmen Lugo, Cont
Craig Simpkins, Purch Mgr

HUB International Ontario Limited

700-2265 Upper Middle Rd.
Oakville, ON L6H 0G5
Tel 905-847-5500
Fax 905-459-7905
www.hubontario.com
Line: Provides personal and
commercial insurance brokerage and
wealth management services.
NAICS: 524210
#Emp: 250-499 (Tor)
#TorLoc: 3
Own: Private Company
Par: HUB International Limited (US)
Key: Neil Morrisson, Pres & CEO
Erin O'Donoghue, Chief People Officer

Hudbay Minerals Inc.

2501-1 Adelaide St. East
Toronto, ON M5C 2V9
Tel 416-362-8181
Fax 416-362-7844
www.hudbayminerals.com
Line: Operates an integrated mining
company with assets in North and
Central America focused on the
discovery, production and marketing of
base metals.
NAICS: 213119
#Emp: 100-249 (Tor)
Own: Public Company
Key: David Garofalo, Pres & CEO
Tom A. Goodman, Sr VP & COO
Sharon Sanzo, VP HR
David S. Bryson, Sr VP & CFO

Hudson's Bay Company

500-401 Bay St.
Toronto, ON M5H 2Y4
Tel 416-861-6112
Fax 416-861-4720
www.hbc.com
AKA: The Bay; HBC; Fields; Zellers;
Home Outfitters; L&T

Line: Retails general merchandise.
NAICS: 452110 442298
#Emp: 10000+ (Tor)
#TorLoc: 68
Own: Private Company
Par: NRDC Equity Partners LLC (US)
Key: Bonnie Brooks, Pres
Richard Baker, Chmn & CEO
Donald Watros, COO
Bob Kolida, Exec VP HR
Mike Culhane, CFO
William Tracey,
   Sr VP Supply Chain & Logistics

The Hughes Group

100 Dolomite Dr.
Toronto, ON M3J 2N2
Tel 416-665-8200
Fax 416-665-0947
www.hughes-group.com
AKA: Design Plastics Int.; Nova Pack;
Hughes Containers; Decorr Display &
Design
Line: Designs and manufactures point
of sale displays and packaging.
NAICS: 322211
#Emp: 75-99 (Tor)
#TorLoc: 3
Own: Private Company
Key: John Hughes, Pres
Mike Johnston, GM
David Tew, Cont
Colin Charles, CFO
Dennis Nichol, VP Mktg

Humber Institute of Technology & Advanced Learning

205 Humber College Blvd.
Toronto, ON M9W 5L7
Tel 416-675-5000
Fax 416-675-3154
www.humber.ca
Line: Provides post-secondary and
post-graduate diplomas, certificates,
and integrated degree-diploma
programs in education and training
courses on a full and part-time basis in
a wide variety of education programs.
NAICS: 611210
#Emp: 1000-4999 (Tor)
#TorLoc: 6
Own: Government
Key: John Davies, Pres
Deb McCarthy, Dir of HR
Rani Dhaliwal, VP Fin & Admin
Emily Eyre, Dir of Purch
Scott Briggs, CIO

Humber Nurseries Limited

8386 Hwy. 50
Brampton, ON L6T 0A5
Tel 905-794-0555
Fax 905-794-1311
www.humbernurseries.com
Line: Operates a retail and wholesale garden centre.
NAICS: 444220
#Emp: 100-249 (Tor)
#TorLoc: 1
Own: Private Company
Par: 567386 Ontario Ltd. (CDA)
Key: Frans Peters, Co-Owner
Guy Peters, Co-Owner
Frans Peters Jr, Ops Mgr
Vita Peters, Office Mgr

Humber River Regional Hospital

200 Church St.
Toronto, ON M9N 1N8
Tel 416-249-8111
Fax 416-243-4511
www.hrrh.on.ca
Line: Provides health care, hospital and acute care services.
NAICS: 622111
#Emp: 1000-4999 (Tor)
#TorLoc: 3
Own: Not-for-profit
Key: Rueben Devlin, Pres & CEO
Barb Collins, COO
Peter Wegener, VP Fin, CIO & Chief
    Privacy Officer
Bozena Blaszczyk, Dir of Purch &
    Logistics
Gerard Power, Dir of Public &
    Community Relns

Humber Valley Terrace

95 Humber College Blvd.
Toronto, ON M9V 5B5
Tel 416-746-7466
Fax 416-740-5812
www.reveraliving.com
NAICS: 623110
#Emp: 100-249 (Tor)
#TorLoc: 1
Own: Private Company
Par: Revera Inc. (CDA)
Key: Andrew Shinder, Exec Dir
Marie McKenzie, Program Mgr

Hunter Amenities International Ltd.

1205 Corporate Dr.
Burlington, ON L7L 5V5
Tel 905-331-2855
Fax 905-331-2832
www.hunteramenities.com
Line: Supplies hotel and airline amenity products, retail products, bath and beauty products.
NAICS: 325610
#Emp: 100-249 (Tor)
#TorLoc: 1
Own: Private Company
Key: John Hunter, Pres
Berny Amiel, CEO
Tobias Schmalz, Dir of Ops, Burlington
Mary Tagarelli, HR Exec Asst
David Robinson, VP Fin & Admin
Rick Belford, Dir of MIS

Hunter Douglas Canada Limited Partnership

132 First Gulf Blvd.
Brampton, ON L6W 4T7
Tel 905-796-7883
Fax 905-796-7376
www.hunterdouglas.ca
Line: Manufactures custom window blinds and shades.
NAICS: 337920
#Emp: 100-249 (Tor)
#TorLoc: 1
Own: Private Company
Par: Hunter Douglas N.V. (NETH)
Key: John Sager, GM
Frances Snow, HR Mgr
Christine Mikler, Cont
Sue Rainville, Dir of Mktg

Hunter Keilty Muntz & Beatty Ltd.

900-595 Bay St.
Toronto, ON M5G 2E3
Tel 416-597-0008
Fax 416-597-2313
www.hkmb.com
Line: Offers services in risk management, risk optimization and insurance.
NAICS: 524210
#Emp: 100-249 (Tor)
#TorLoc: 1
Own: Private Company
Par: Hub International (CDA)

Key: Neil Morrison,
    Mng Partner & CEO
Greg Belton, Chmn
Robert Keilty, COO
Erin O'Donohue, Chief People Officer
Dana Williams, CFO
John Hawkrigg, Chief Sales Officer
Heather Masterson, Exec VP & Chief
    Mktg Officer

Hurley Group

5560 Explorer Dr.
Mississauga, ON L4W 5M3
Tel 905-568-4636
Fax 905-568-9392
www.hurleycorp.com
AKA: Martin Building Maintenance;
Hunt Brothers; Martin Services
Line: Provides building maintenance services.
NAICS: 561722
#Emp: 1000-4999 (Tor)
#TorLoc: 83
Own: Private Company
Par: Compass Group Canada (CDA)
Key: J. Michael Horgan,
    Chmn of the Board
Philippe D. Mack, CEO
Paul Barfoot, VP
Diane MacLeod,
    Dir of HR & Gen Counsel
Manny Silva, VP Industrial Relns
Paul Welsman, VP Sales

Huron Services Group Ltd.

3C-418 North Service Rd. East
Oakville, ON L6H 5R2
Tel 905-845-4075
Fax 905-845-4802
www.hurongroup.ca
AKA: The Huron Group of Companies
Line: Provides facility management, personnel and management services.
NAICS: 541611
#Emp: 100-249 (Tor)
#TorLoc: 3
Own: Private Company
Key: John Thomson, Pres
Joan Ramsay,
    Fin, Benefits & Admin Mgr

Husky Injection Molding Systems Ltd.

500 Queen St. South
Bolton, ON L7E 5S5
Tel 905-951-5000
Fax 905-951-5323
www.husky.ca
Line: Provides complete manufacturing solutions and supplies integrated systems to the plastics injection-moulding industry.
NAICS: 333220 333511
#Emp: 1000-4999 (Tor)
#TorLoc: 1
Own: Public Company
Par: Onex Corp. (CDA)
Key: John Galt, Pres & CEO
Keith Carlton, COO
James Reid, VP Organizational Dev
George Halatsis, VP Fin & CFO
Jeff MacDonald, VP Mktg

Husky Truck Stop

6625 Kennedy Rd.
Mississauga, ON L5T 2W4
Tel 905-565-9548
Fax 905-565-6022
Line: Operates a highway truck stop.
NAICS: 447190 722110
#Emp: 75-99 (Tor)
#TorLoc: 3
Own: Private Company
Par: Unipetro (CDA)
Key: Mohammed Asrar, Mgr

Hyatt Regency Toronto

370 King St. West
Toronto, ON M5V 1J9
Tel 416-343-1234
Fax 416-599-7394
www.hiok.com
NAICS: 721111
#Emp: 250-499 (Tor)
#TorLoc: 1
Own: Private Company
Par: Westmont Hospitality Group (CDA)
Key: Bruce Flyer, GM

Hydrogenics Corp.

220 Admiral Blvd.
Mississauga, ON L5T 2N6
Tel 905-361-3660
Fax 905-361-3626
www.hydrogenics.com
Line: Manufactures hydrogen generation, fuel cell and renewable energy storage equipment.
NAICS: 325120
#Emp: 100-249 (Tor)
#TorLoc: 1
Own: Public Company
Key: Daryl Wilson, Pres & CEO
Jennifer Barber, VP Fin & Cont
Lawrence Davis, CFO
Joseph Cargnelli, CTO

Hydro One Brampton Networks Inc.

175 Sandalwood Pkwy. West
Brampton, ON L7A 1E8
Tel 905-840-6300
Fax 905-840-1915
www.hydroonebrampton.com
Line: Provides electric utilities.
NAICS: 221122
#Emp: 100-249 (Tor)
#TorLoc: 1
Own: Provincial Crown Corp.
Par: Hydro One Inc. (CDA)
Key: Remy Fernandes, Pres & CEO
Aldo Mastro-Francesco, VP Engineering & Ops
Laurie Kavanaugh, HR
Jamie Gribbon, VP Fin & Admin
Lee Dapp, Commun Rep

Hydro One Networks Inc.

483 Bay St., North Tower, 15th Fl.
Toronto, ON M5G 2P5
Tel 416-345-5000
Fax 416-345-5866
www.hydroonenetworks.com
Line: Operates a utilities company.
NAICS: 541330
#Emp: 250-499 (Tor)
#TorLoc: 4
Own: Provincial Crown Corp.
Par: Hydro One Inc. (CDA)
Key: Laura Formusa, Pres & CEO
Peter Gregg, Exec VP Ops
Sandy Struthers, CFO

Hydropool Industries

335 Superior Blvd.
Mississauga, ON L5T 2L6
Tel 905-565-6810
Fax 905-565-6820
www.hydropoolhottubs.com
Line: Manufactures hot tubs and swim spas.
NAICS: 332999 326191
#Emp: 100-249 (Tor)
#TorLoc: 1
Own: Private Company
Key: David Jackson, Pres & CEO

Hymopack Ltd.

41 Medulla Ave.
Toronto, ON M8Z 5L6
Tel 416-232-1733
Fax 416-232-2194
www.hymopack.com
Line: Manufactures various merchandise and polyethylene bags.
NAICS: 325210
#Emp: 100-249 (Tor)
#TorLoc: 1
Own: Private Company
Key: Gerry Moldoff, Pres
Blair Fraser, VP Manuf
Judy Wickham, Payroll & HR
Henry Wojciechowicz, Cont

Hyundai Auto Canada Corp.

75 Frontenac Dr.
Markham, ON L3R 6H2
Tel 905-477-0202
Fax 905-477-0187
www.hyundaicanada.com
Line: Imports and distributes automobiles.
NAICS: 415110 415290
#Emp: 100-249 (Tor)
#TorLoc: 1
Own: Private Company
Par: Hyundai Motor Co. (KOREA)
Key: Steve Kelleher, Pres & CEO
Peter Kim, Exec VP & Chief Exec Coord
Paul Farkas, Nat'l Mgr, HR
Milena Ernjakovic, Nat'l Mgr, Fin & Admin
Danielle Minckler, Acting Nat'l Mgr, IT
John Vernile, VP Sales & Mktg
Chad Heard, PR Mgr

i365

2315 Bristol Circ., Bldg. A, 2nd Fl.
Oakville, ON L6H 6P8
Tel 905-287-2600
Fax 905-829-3840
www.i365.com
AKA: EVault Canada Inc.
Line: Provides online data backup and
restore services.
NAICS: 541510
#Emp: 75-99 (Tor)
#TorLoc: 1
Own: Private Company
Par: Seagate Company (US)
Key: Diana Tearle, Office Mgr
Christine Klassen, HR Mgr

i3 Canada

1016A Sutton Dr.
Burlington, ON L7L 6B8
Tel 905-331-9911
Fax 905-331-9912
www.i3innovus.com
AKA: i3 Innovus; i3 Research; i3
Statprobe
Line: Provides contract research
and consulting services to the
pharmaceutical and biotechnology
industries.
NAICS: 541619 541710
#Emp: 100-249 (Tor)
#TorLoc: 1
Own: Private Company
Par: Ingenix (US)
Key: Lauren Cuddy, Exec VP
William H. Crown, Pres
Ben Faunza, VP Cdn Ops
Beth Feyerer, Human Capital Partner

IAC Automotive Components Alberta Ltd.

375 Basaltic Rd.
Concord, ON L4K 4W8
Tel 905-879-0292
Fax 905-879-0295
www.iacna.com
Line: Manufactures and supplies
automotive seating and interior
components.
NAICS: 336360
#Emp: 100-249 (Tor)
#TorLoc: 2
Own: Private Company
Par: IAC Automotive Components
Alberta Ltd. (US)
Key: Robert Cook, GM
Raju Patel, Materials Mgr
Nunzio Martone, Mgr of HR
Bill Wallace, Cont

Iamgold Corp.

3200-401 Bay St.
Toronto, ON M5H 2Y4
Tel 416-360-4710
Fax 416-360-4750
www.iamgold.com
Line: Manages exploration and
development projects.
NAICS: 213119
#Emp: 100-249 (Tor)
Own: Private Company
Key: Stephen J.J. Letwin, Pres & CEO
Gordon Stothart, Exec VP & COO
Lisa Zangari, Sr VP HR
Carol Banducci, Exec VP & CFO

Ian Martin Group

465 Morden Rd., 2nd Fl.
Oakville, ON L6K 3W6
Tel 905-815-1600
Fax 905-845-2100
www.ianmartin.com
Line: Provides contract engineering,
outsource services and temporary
staffing.
NAICS: 561310
#Emp: 1000-4999 (Tor)
#TorLoc: 3
Own: Private Company
Key: B. William Masson, Pres
Loree Gamble, Dir of Corp Affairs
R. Singaratnam, CFO

IBI Group

230 Richmond St. West, 5th Fl.
Toronto, ON M5V 1V6
Tel 416-596-1930
Fax 416-596-0644
www.ibigroup.com
AKA: Interbase Consultants Ltd.
Line: Provides consulting and
design services in the fields of urban
development, transportation, IT
systems, and engineering/architectural
services.
NAICS: 541330
#Emp: 500-999 (Tor)
#TorLoc: 7
Own: Public Company
Key: Philip Beinhaker, Chmn & CEO
Scott Stewart, Mng Dir
Jane Sillberg, VP HR
Allan Kamerman, Assoc Dir & CFO

IBM Canada Ltd.

3600 Steeles Ave. East
Markham, ON L3R 9Z7
Tel 905-316-5000
Fax 905-316-2535
www.ibm.com/ca
Line: Sells information technology
products and services.
NAICS: 334110 541510
#Emp: 10000+ (Tor)
#TorLoc: 14
Own: Private Company
Par: IBM Corp. (US)
Key: Dan Fortin, GM
Patrick Horgan, VP Ops
John Ostrander, VP Central Business
Jennifer Ballantyne,
    Dir, Commun Sector

ICICI Bank Canada

700-150 Ferrand Dr.
Don Valley Business Park
Toronto, ON M3C 3E5
Tel 416-360-0909
Fax 416-422-5896
www.icicibank.ca
NAICS: 522112 522111
#Emp: 100-249 (Tor)
#TorLoc: 7
Own: Private Company
Par: ICICI Bank Limited (INDIA)
Key: Sriram H. Iyer, Pres & CEO
Atul Chandra, Sr VP & CFO

ICOM Information & Communications Inc.

41 Metropolitan Rd.
Toronto, ON M1R 2T5
Tel 416-297-7887
Fax 416-297-6638
www.epsilon.com
Line: Provides database marketing and
market research.
NAICS: 541910 511140
#Emp: 100-249 (Tor)
#TorLoc: 2
Own: Private Company
Par: Epsilon (US)
Key: Brian Rainey, Pres
Jennifer Vaninbilog, HR Mgr

ICS Courier

1290 Central Pkwy. West, 2nd. Fl.
Mississauga, ON L5C 4R9
Tel 905-897-3771
Fax 905-276-6723
www.ics-canada.net
Line: Provides document and package pick up and delivery services.
NAICS: 492110
#Emp: 250-499 (Tor)
#TorLoc: 3
Own: Private Company
Par: Transforce Inc. (CDA)
Key: Ping Yan, VP Ops

Icynene Inc.

6747 Campobello Rd.
Mississauga, ON L5N 2L7
Tel 905-363-4040
Fax 905-363-0102
www.icynene.com
Line: Develops and markets foam insulations.
NAICS: 232440 326140
#Emp: 75-99 (Tor)
Own: Private Company
Key: Howard Deck, Pres & CEO
Peter Andrianopoulos, VP Ops
Dorothy Lange, VP HR
Susan Brioux, CFO

Ideaca Knowledge Services Inc.

502-36 York Mills Rd.
Toronto, ON M2P 2E9
Tel 416-961-4332
Fax 416-673-5165
www.ideaca.com
Line: Operates a consulting firm that advises, implements and supports business applications.
NAICS: 541611
#Emp: 100-249 (Tor)
Own: Private Company
Key: Muneer Hirji, CEO

Ideal Honda

5500 Dixie Rd.
Mississauga, ON L4W 4N3
Tel 905-238-3480
Fax 905-238-0502
www.idealhonda.com
Line: Operates an automotive dealership.
NAICS: 441110
#Emp: 75-99 (Tor)
#TorLoc: 1
Own: Private Company
Key: Dean Tsicolas, Gen Sales Mgr
Don Blacker, Fleet Mgr

Idexx Reference Laboratories Ltd.

1345 Denison St.
Markham, ON L3R 5V2
Tel 1-800-667-3411
Fax 905-475-7309
www.idexx.ca
Line: Provides veterinary diagnostic testing services for small and large animal healthcare.
NAICS: 541710
#Emp: 250-499 (Tor)
#TorLoc: 2
Own: Public Company
Par: Idexx Laboratories (US)
Key: Peter Mosney, GM & Dir
Sylvie LeBouthillier, Sr HR Mgr
Anton Minderhoud, Cont
Diane Reilly, VP IT
Veena Chong, Sales Coord

IDX Toronto

280 Basaltic Rd.
Concord, ON L4K 2N6
Tel 905-695-3000
Fax 905-695-3010
www.idxcorporation.com
AKA: Universal Showcase Ltd.
Line: Manufactures metal and wood store fixtures.
NAICS: 337215
#Emp: 250-499 (Tor)
#TorLoc: 1
Own: Private Company
Par: IDX Corp. (US)
Key: Brian Bylykbashi, GM

IG Machine & Fibres Ltd.

87 Orenda Rd.
Brampton, ON L6W 1V7
Tel 905-457-2880
Fax 905-457-9923
www.iko.com
AKA: IKO
Line: Produces shingles and roofing products.
NAICS: 324122 327120
#Emp: 75-99 (Tor)
#TorLoc: 1
Own: Private Company
Par: IKO (CDA)
Key: Tony Querques, Plant Mgr

IKEA Canada Ltd.

1065 Plains Rd. East
Burlington, ON L7T 4K1
Tel 905-637-9440
Fax 905-637-6505
www.ikea.com
Line: Retails home furnishings.
NAICS: 442110 442298
#Emp: 1000-4999 (Tor)
#TorLoc: 4
Own: Private Company
Par: Ingka Holdings Overseas BV (SWE)
Key: Kerri Molinaro, Country Mgr
Cory Randles, HR Mgr, IKEA Canada
Doug Pass, Fin & Admin Mgr
Paul Ekelschot, Sales Mgr
Thom Kyle, Mktg Mgr

IKO Industries Ltd.

602-1 Yorkdale Rd.
Toronto, ON M6A 3A1
Tel 416-781-5545
Fax 416-781-8411
www.iko.com
Line: Manufactures building papers, asphalt roofing, felt, and shingles.
NAICS: 324122
#Emp: 100-249 (Tor)
#TorLoc: 2
Own: Private Company
Key: Henry Koschitzky, Pres
May Chu, Treasury Mgr
Eudora LeBlanc, Dir of Admin
Martin Vaughan, VP Fin

Il Fornello Restaurants Ltd.

112 Isabella St.
Toronto, ON M4Y 1P1
Tel 416-920-9410
Fax 416-920-0474
www.ilfornello.com
NAICS: 722110
#Emp: 250-499 (Tor)
#TorLoc: 11
Own: Private Company
Key: Ian Sorbie, Chmn & Pres
Sean Fleming, HR Mgr
Joven Talampas, Cont

Ilsco of Canada Company

1050 Lakeshore Rd. East
Mississauga, ON L5E 1E4
Tel 905-274-2341
Fax 905-274-2689
www.ilsco.com
Line: Manufactures electrical connectors for housing and construction applications.
NAICS: 334410

#Emp: 100-249 (Tor)
#TorLoc: 1
Own: Private Company
Par: Ilsco Corp. (US)
Key: Jim Smith, VP & GM
Cheryl Corbin, HR
Ken Warren, Purch Agent
Vaseil Konstantin, Office Admr
Al Legare, Sales Mgr, Ontario

Images 2000 Inc.

33 Drummond St.
Toronto, ON M8V 1Y7
Tel 416-252-9693
Fax 416-252-0984
www.images2000inc.com
Line: Manufactures picture frames.
NAICS: 442292
#Emp: 100-249 (Tor)
#TorLoc: 2
Own: Private Company
Key: Sam Oskooei, Pres

IMAX Corporation

2525 Speakman Dr.
Mississauga, ON L5K 1B1
Tel 905-403-6500
Fax 905-403-6450
www.imax.com
Line: Researches, develops and
manufactures large format motion
picture projection systems and 3D
animation systems.
NAICS: 512130
#Emp: 100-249 (Tor)
#TorLoc: 1
Own: Public Company
Key: Greg Foster, Pres
Richard Gelfond, CEO
Gary Moss, COO
Joseph Sparacio, Exec VP & CFO

Impact Cleaning Services Ltd.

8-21 Goodrich Rd.
Toronto, ON M8Z 6A3
Tel 416-253-1234
Fax 416-253-6179
www.impactcsl.com
Line: Provides emergency response
on call personnel, exterior grounds
maintenance, construction clean-up,
general maintenance, and carpet,
window and escalator cleaning.
NAICS: 561722
#Emp: 250-499 (Tor)
#TorLoc: 1
Own: Private Company
Key: Chris Boutsalis, Pres
Paul Raftis, VP Ops
Clark Gilbert, VP HR
Peter Konstantos, CFO

Imperial Coffee Services Inc.

12 Kodiak Cres.
Toronto, ON M3J 3G5
Tel 416-638-7404
Fax 416-638-7947
www.imperialcoffee.com
Line: Provides food service including
vending machines, coffee and water.
NAICS: 454210 532490
#Emp: 100-249 (Tor)
#TorLoc: 1
Own: Private Company
Key: Mark Steiner, Pres
Frederick Steiner, CEO
Nick Kammer, VP Ops
Kevin Newton, HR Mgr

Imperial Flavours Inc.

7550 Torbram Rd.
Mississauga, ON L4T 3L8
Tel 905-678-6680
Fax 905-678-6684
www.imperialflavours.com
Line: Produces products for the dairy,
bakery and food industries.
NAICS: 311814 311330
#Emp: 75-99 (Tor)
#TorLoc: 1
Own: Private Company
Key: Val Miller, CEO

Imperial Oil Limited

237-4 Ave. S.W.
P.O. Box 2480, Station M
Calgary, AB T2P 3M9
Tel 1-800-668-3776
Fax 403-237-4017
www.imperialoil.ca
Line: Produces crude oil and natural
gas, refines and markets petroleum
products, and manufactures and
markets chemicals.
NAICS: 324110 325999 447190
#Emp: 500-999 (Tor)
#TorLoc: 3
Own: Public Company
Par: Exxon Mobil Corp. (US)
Key: Bruce March, CEO

Imperial Parking Canada Corp.

178 Queens Quay East
Toronto, ON M5A 1B4
Tel 416-369-1801
Fax 416-369-1802
www.impark.com
Line: Specializes in commercial pay
parking management.
NAICS: 812930
#Emp: 75-99 (Tor)
#TorLoc: 120

Own: Private Company
Key: Gordon Craig, VP Eastern Canada
Allan Copping, CEO
Tom Iannacchino, Reg Mgr
Susan Chow-Dhukan, Cont

Ina Grafton Gage Home

40 Bell Estate Rd.
Toronto, ON M1L 0E2
Tel 416-422-4890
Fax 416-422-1613
Line: Offers residence to senior
citizens.
NAICS: 623310
#Emp: 100-249 (Tor)
#TorLoc: 1
Own: Private Company
Key: Sara Rooney, Admr

Incorporated Synod of the Diocese of Toronto

135 Adelaide St. East
Toronto, ON M5C 1L8
Tel 416-363-6021
Fax 416-363-7678
www.toronto.anglican.ca
AKA: Anglican Diocese of Toronto
NAICS: 813110
#Emp: 250-499 (Tor)
#TorLoc: 211
Own: Not-for-profit
Key: Elizabeth Hardy,
    CAO & Secy of Synod
Colin Johnson, Archbishop of Toronto
Richard Detinger, HR Mgr
Michael Joshua, Treas & Dir of Fin
Stuart Mann, Dir of Commun

Indalco Alloys

*A Div. of Lincoln Electric
Company of Canada LP*
939 Gana Crt.
Mississauga, ON L5S 1N9
Tel 905-564-1151
Fax 905-564-1405
www.indalco.com
Line: Manufactures aluminum weld
wire products and aluminum rod.
NAICS: 331317
#Emp: 100-249 (Tor)
#TorLoc: 2
Own: Private Company
Par: The Lincoln Electric Co. (US)
Key: Joe Doria, Pres
Les Thoms, Production & HR Mgr
Belinda Carino, Cont
Mark Burke, Sales & Mktg Mgr

Indal Technologies Inc.

3570 Hawkestone Rd.
Mississauga, ON L5C 2V8
Tel 905-275-5300
Fax 905-273-7004
www.indaltech.com
AKA: Curtiss-Wright Flow Control
Company
Line: Designs, develops, manufactures
and supports marine aircraft handling
systems, specialized structures and
cable handling systems.
NAICS: 336410
#Emp: 100-249 (Tor)
#TorLoc: 1
Own: Private Company
Par: Curtiss-Wright Corp. (US)
Key: Colleen Williams, VP & GM
Diego Fiorino, Dir of Ops
Chuck Gordon,
    Dir of Personnel & Admin
Trish Haslegrave, Dir of Fin
David Stone, Dir of Materials
Don McKay, Dir of Sales & Mktg

Indeka Imports Ltd.

2120 Bristol Circ.
Oakville, ON L6H 5R3
Tel 905-829-3000
Fax 905-829-4800
www.indeka.com
AKA: Greatway Imports Ltd.
Line: Imports and distributes footwear.
NAICS: 414120
#Emp: 75-99 (Tor)
#TorLoc: 1
Own: Private Company
Key: Paul Papadopoulos, Pres
Inder Sharma, Chmn & CEO
Kamal Sharma, COO
Mariusz Wiercioch, IT Mgr

Independent Electricity System Operator

Station A, P.O. Box 4474
Toronto, ON M5W 4E5
Tel 905-403-6900
Fax 905-403-6921
www.ieso.ca
Line: Manages Ontario's electricity
system and operates the wholesale
electricity market by forecasting
demand for electricity and ensuring
available supplies.
NAICS: 221121
#Emp: 250-499 (Tor)
#TorLoc: 2
Own: Provincial Crown Corp.

Key: Paul Murphy, Pres & CEO
Ken Kozlik, COO
Ted Leonard, CFO
Bill Limbrick,
    VP Organizational Dev & CIO
Bruce Campbell,
    VP Corp Relns & Market Dev
Terry Young, VP Corp Relns

Indigo Books & Music, Inc.

500-468 King St. West
Toronto, ON M5V 1L8
Tel 416-364-4499
Fax 416-364-0355
www.chapters.ca
AKA: Coles, The Book People;
World's Biggest Bookstore; The Book
Company; SmithBooks; Classic Books;
LibrairieSmith
Line: Retails books and related items.
NAICS: 451210
#Emp: 1000-4999 (Tor)
#TorLoc: 67
Own: Public Company
Key: Joel Silver, Pres
Heather Reisman, CEO
Sue Croft, VP HR
Jim McGill, CFO & COO
Sumit Oberai, CTO
Dierdra Horgan, Chief Mktg Officer

Industrial Alliance Insurance & Financial Services Inc.

522 University Ave.
Toronto, ON M5G 1Y7
Tel 416-598-2122
Fax 416-598-4574
www.inalco.com
Line: Provides life and health insurance
products and retirement income plans.
NAICS: 524112 524111
#Emp: 250-499 (Tor)
#TorLoc: 1
Own: Private Company
Par: Industrial-Alliance Life Insurance
Co. (CDA)
Key: Gary Coles, Sr VP Admin
Karen Dell'Anno, Dir, HR

Industrial Electrical Contractors Ltd.

93 Penn Dr.
Toronto, ON M9L 2B1
Tel 416-749-9782
Fax 416-749-8720
Line: Provides electrical services.
NAICS: 232510
#Emp: 75-99 (Tor)
#TorLoc: 1
Own: Private Company
Key: Keith Rundle, Pres
Bruce Maltby, Cont

Industrial Thermo Polymers Ltd.

153 Van Kirk Dr.
Brampton, ON L7A 1A4
Tel 905-846-3666
Fax 905-846-0363
www.tundrafoam.com
Line: Manufactures foam products.
NAICS: 326140
#Emp: 100-249 (Tor)
Own: Private Company
Key: Steve Hartman, Pres
Art Cyr, Exec VP
Annette Kelly, HR Mgr
Mesfin Hagos, Cont
Shelly Pucci, Purch Agent

Industry Canada-Ontario Region

151 Yonge St., 4th Fl.
Toronto, ON M5C 2W7
Tel 416-973-5001
Fax 416-954-6656
www.ic.gc.ca
NAICS: 911390
#Emp: 100-249 (Tor)
#TorLoc: 1
Own: Government
Key: Sam Boonstra, Acting Exec Dir
Bill James, Dir of HR
Kelly Gillis, CFO

Infinium Capital Corp.

200-106 Front St. East
Toronto, ON M5A 1E1
Tel 416-360-7000
Fax 416-360-7703
www.infiniumcapital.ca
Line: Operates an independent
electronic trading firm specializing in
alternative quantitative and arbitrage
strategies.
NAICS: 523130
#Emp: 75-99 (Tor)
Own: Private Company
Key: Predrag Risticevic, Head of Ops

Infor Global Solutions

1200-250 Ferrand Dr.
Toronto, ON M3C 3G8
Tel 416-421-6700
Fax 416-421-8440
www.infor.com
Line: Develops, implements and
supports workplace management
applications.
NAICS: 541510
#Emp: 250-499 (Tor)
#TorLoc: 1
Own: Public Company
Par: Infor Global Solutions (US)
Key: Charles Phillips, CEO

Inforica Inc.

405-5255 Orbitor Dr.
Mississauga, ON L4W 5M6
Tel 905-602-0686
Fax 905-602-0668
www.inforica.com
Line: Provides business and technical consulting services.
NAICS: 541611
#Emp: 75-99 (Tor)
#TorLoc: 1
Own: Private Company
Key: Mario Correira, Mng Partner, Ops & Delivery
Rohan D'Souza, Mng Partner, Tech Solutions

Information Builders (Canada) Inc.

1000-150 York St.
Toronto, ON M5H 3S5
Tel 416-364-2760
Fax 416-364-6552
www.informationbuilders.com
Line: Provides web based reporting and enterprise integration software including consulting and education.
NAICS: 541510
#Emp: 75-99 (Tor)
#TorLoc: 1
Own: Private Company
Par: Information Builders Inc. (US)
Key: Brian Joynt, VP & GM
Daniela Remondi, Cont
Joe Walsh, Branch Tech Mgr

Infrastructure Health & Safety Association of Ontario

400-5110 Creekbank Rd.
Mississauga, ON L4W 0A1
Tel 905-625-0100
Fax 905-625-8998
www.ihsa.ca
AKA: CHSI
Line: Provides health and safety consultation, instruction, information, research and related support services to Ontario construction industry workers and employers.
NAICS: 813910
#Emp: 100-249 (Tor)
#TorLoc: 2
Own: Association
Key: Al Beattie, Pres & CEO
Fatima Luis, VP Corp Services
Janice Wheeler, HR Mgr

Infusion Development Corp.

1101-119 Spadina Ave.
Toronto, ON M5V 2L1
Tel 416-593-6595
Fax 416-593-8540
www.infusion.com
AKA: Infusion Toronto
Line: Provides computer consulting services.
NAICS: 541510
#Emp: 100-249 (Tor)
#TorLoc: 1
Own: Private Company
Key: Alim Somani, Pres
Greg Brill, CEO

ING Bank of Canada

900-111 Gordon Baker Rd.
Toronto, ON M2H 3R1
Tel 416-497-5157
Fax 416-758-5215
www.ingdirect.ca
AKA: ING Direct
Line: Provides a wide range of banking services via Internet and telephone.
NAICS: 522111
#Emp: 500-999 (Tor)
#TorLoc: 1
Own: Private Company
Par: ING Bank (NETH)
Key: Peter Aceto, Pres & CEO
Mimi Wong, Dir of Ops
Natasha Mascarenhas, VP HR
Stephen Stewart, CFO
Charaka Kithulegoda, CIO
Brenda Rideout, Head of Mktg, Quality & Process Engineering

Ingenia Polymers Corp.

900-200 Yorkland Blvd.
Toronto, ON M2J 5C1
Tel 416-920-8100
Fax 416-920-1479
www.ingeniapolymers.com
Line: Manufactures polymers.
NAICS: 325210
#Emp: 100-249 (Tor)
#TorLoc: 1
Own: Private Company
Key: John Lefas, Pres

Ingenico Canada Ltd.

79 Torbarrie Rd.
Toronto, ON M3L 1G5
Tel 416-245-6700
Fax 416-245-9896
www.ingenico.ca
Line: Designs, develops and markets hardware and software solutions for the financial retail, travel, entertainment, healthcare and transportation industries.
NAICS: 541510
#Emp: 75-99 (Tor)
#TorLoc: 1
Own: Private Company
Par: Ingenico Corp. (US)
Key: Christopher Justice, Pres, North America
Philippe Piovesan, Dir of Ops
Victor Young, Cont

Ingram Micro

55 Standish Crt.
Mississauga, ON L5R 4A1
Tel 905-755-5000
Fax 905-755-1300
www.ingrammicro.ca
Line: Distributes computer technology and services.
NAICS: 417310
#Emp: 500-999 (Tor)
#TorLoc: 2
Own: Public Company
Par: Ingram Micro (US)
Key: Mark Snider, GM & VP Sales
Denisa Leiba, Dir of HR
David Mason, VP Cdn Sales

Inline Fiberglass Ltd.

30 Constellation Crt.
Toronto, ON M9W 1K1
Tel 416-679-1171
Fax 416-679-1150
www.inlinefiberglass.com
Line: Manufactures fiberglass windows, doors and pultrusions.
NAICS: 327990
#Emp: 100-249 (Tor)
#TorLoc: 1
Own: Private Company
Key: Stanley M. Rockicki, Owner
Pauline James, Office Mgr
Liza Rokicki, Purch Mgr
Larry Bidner, Sales Mgr

Innocon Inc.

50 Newkirk Rd.
Richmond Hill, ON L4C 3G3
Tel 905-508-7676
Fax 905-508-7647
www.innocon.on.ca
Line: Produces and distributes ready mix concrete.
NAICS: 327320 327310 327390
#Emp: 250-499 (Tor)
Own: Private Company
Key: John McCabe, Pres
Nigel Fenty, Cont
Wayne London, GM of Sales

Innova Medical Ophthalmics Inc.

1430 Birchmount Rd.
Toronto, ON M1P 2E8
Tel 416-615-0185
Fax 416-631-8272
www.innovamed.com
Line: Supplies ophthalmic products.
NAICS: 339110
#Emp: 100-249 (Tor)
#TorLoc: 1
Own: Private Company
Key: Stephen Hale, Pres

Innovapost

5280 Solar Dr.
Mississauga, ON L4W 5M8
Tel 905-214-8800
Fax 905-214-8801
www.innovapost.com
Line: Offers information technology consulting services.
NAICS: 541510
#Emp: 100-249 (Tor)
#TorLoc: 1
Own: Private Company
Par: Canada Post Corp./CGI Group Inc. (CDA)
Key: David Rea,
   VP Purolator Client Services
Brendan Timmins, CEO
David Clark, Sr VP Admin & CFO
Catherine Leja, HR Specialist

Innovation Institute of Ontario

HL20-101 College St.
Mars Centre, Heritage Bldg.
Toronto, ON M5G 1L7
Tel 416-977-3355
Fax 416-977-9460
www.iio.on.ca
Line: Provides financial services.
NAICS: 522299
#Emp: 75-99 (Tor)
#TorLoc: 1

Own: Private Company
Key: Kenneth Knox, Pres & CEO
Janet Faas, COO
Patti Minialoff, Dir of Fin
Michael Radu, Sr IT Mgr

Innovative Cooling Dynamics

6400 Ordan Dr.
Mississauga, ON L5T 2H6
Tel 905-564-9522
Fax 905-564-9523
www.magnapowertrain.com
AKA: ICD
Line: Manufactures water pumps.
NAICS: 333910
#Emp: 100-249 (Tor)
#TorLoc: 1
Own: Private Company
Par: Magna International Inc. (CDA)
Key: Guy Davis, GM
Ross Hamilton, Cont

Innovative Vision Marketing Inc.

204-55 Nugget Ave.
Toronto, ON M1S 3L1
Tel 416-321-8189
Fax 416-321-0487
www.innovativevision.ca
Line: Operates a customer management firm specializing in contact centre sourcing.
NAICS: 561420
#Emp: 100-249 (Tor)
Own: Private Company
Key: Sajan Choksi, Mng Dir

Inquiry Management Systems Ltd.

1-55 Horner Ave.
Toronto, ON M8Z 4X6
Tel 416-620-1965
Fax 416-620-9790
www.ims.ca
AKA: IMS
Line: Manages, collects, cleans, stores, processes, distributes and exploits data on behalf of clients.
NAICS: 514210
#Emp: 100-249 (Tor)
#TorLoc: 1
Own: Private Company
Key: Jim Panousis, Sr VP
Martin Hochstein, Pres & Owner
Gina Palmer, VP Ops
Tracey Cameron, HR Mgr
Sandra Conflitti, VP & Cont
Norm Borg, Dir of IT

Inscape Corp.

67 Toll Rd.
Holland Landing, ON L9N 1H2
Tel 905-836-7676
Fax 905-836-6000
www.inscapesolutions.com
Line: Manufactures metal office furniture.
NAICS: 337214
#Emp: 250-499 (Tor)
#TorLoc: 2
Own: Public Company
Key: Madan M. Bhayana,
   Chmn & Interim CEO
Dennis Dyke, VP HR
Kent Smallwood, CFO
Sharad Mathur, VP Mktg

Institute for Clinical Evaluative Sciences

G106-2075 Bayview Ave.
Toronto, ON M4N 3M5
Tel 416-480-4055
Fax 416-480-6048
www.ices.on.ca
AKA: ICES
Line: Operates a medical research centre.
NAICS: 541710
#Emp: 100-249 (Tor)
#TorLoc: 1
Own: Not-for-profit
Key: David Henry, Pres & CEO
Janet Hux, COO
Margaret Foulds, Dir of Fin & Admin

Institute for Work & Health

800-481 University Ave.
Toronto, ON M5G 2E9
Tel 416-927-2027
Fax 416-927-4167
www.iwh.on.ca
Line: Conducts applied research.
NAICS: 541710
#Emp: 75-99 (Tor)
#TorLoc: 1
Own: Not-for-profit
Key: Cameron Mustard,
   Pres & Senior Scientist
Emma Irvin, Dir, Research Ops
Mary Cicinelli, Dir, HR & Corp Services

Institute of Chartered Accountants of Ontario

69 Bloor St. East
Toronto, ON M4W 1B3
Tel 416-962-1841
Fax 416-962-8900
www.icao.on.ca
AKA: CA Ontario; ICAO
Line: Provides educational, professional, technical, and ethical advisory services; practice inspection and standards enforcement; and helps chartered accountants serve the public interest and the needs of their clients and employers.
NAICS: 813920
#Emp: 100-249 (Tor)
#TorLoc: 1
Own: Association
Key: Rod N. Barr, Pres & CEO
Nora Murrant, Exec VP & COO
Janet Blais, Dir of IT

Insurance Bureau of Canada

2400-777 Bay St.
P.O. Box 121
Toronto, ON M5G 2C8
Tel 416-362-2031
Fax 416-361-5952
www.ibc.ca
AKA: IBC
Line: Acts as the spokesperson for the property and casualty insurance industry in Canada and a statistical agent for the provincial insurance commissions.
NAICS: 813910 524299
#Emp: 250-499 (Tor)
#TorLoc: 3
Own: Association
Key: Don Forgeron, Pres & CEO
Randy Bundus, VP Ops & Gen Counsel
Gilles Calmels, VP HR & Admin
Fred Wolfe, VP Fin
Maria Dalcin, CIO
Mary Lou O'Reilly, VP Issues Management & Commun

The Insurers Financial Group

201-30 Leek Cres.
Richmond Hill, ON L4B 4N4
Tel 905-707-8007
Fax 905-707-9963
www.ifgcanada.com
Line: Operates an insurance brokerage firm.
NAICS: 524210
#Emp: 100-249 (Tor)
#TorLoc: 1
Own: Private Company
Key: Stephen W. Kearley, Pres & CEO
Michael McQuaid, Partner & Exec VP
Kelly Shillington, Cont
Scott Logan, Personal Lines Sales Mgr

Intact Financial Corporation

700 University Ave.
Toronto, ON M5G 0A1
Tel 416-341-1464
Fax 416-941-5320
www.intactfc.com
Line: Provides home, auto and business insurance.
NAICS: 524210
#Emp: 1000-4999 (Tor)
#TorLoc: 3
Own: Public Company
Key: Charles Brindamour, Pres & CEO
Debbie Coull-Ciechini, Sr VP Ontario
Susan Black, Chief HR Officer
Mark Tullis, CFO
Jack Ott, Sr VP & CIO

Intec Billing Canada Ltd.

2-730 Cochrane Dr.
Markham, ON L3R 8E1
Tel 905-944-6900
Fax 905-949-9430
www.intecbilling.com
Line: Develops convergent billing and customer care software solutions for local, data, long distance, wireless, cable, and energy telecommunications markets.
NAICS: 541510
#Emp: 75-99 (Tor)
#TorLoc: 1
Own: Public Company
Par: Intec Telecom Systems plc (UK)
Key: Deborah Hartley, Exec Dir of HR
Joe Spencer, Consulting Mgr

Integracare Inc.

396 Moore Ave.
Toronto, ON M4G 1C7
Tel 416-421-4243
Fax 416-421-4617
www.integracare.on.ca
Line: Provides private health care and nursing services.
NAICS: 621390
#Emp: 250-499 (Tor)
#TorLoc: 1
Own: Private Company
Key: Philip Russel, Mng Dir
Martha Russel, Mng Dir

Integrated Asset Management Corp.

1200-70 University Ave.
Toronto, ON M5J 2M4
Tel 416-360-7667
Fax 416-360-7446
www.iamgroup.ca
AKA: Integrated Partners; Blumont Capital; Integrated Managed Futures
Line: Operates an asset management company.
NAICS: 523990
#Emp: 100-249 (Tor)
#TorLoc: 4
Own: Public Company
Key: Victor Koloshuk, Chmn, Pres & CEO
David Mather, Exec VP
Stephen Johnson, CFO

Integrated Plastics Inc.

170 Commander Blvd.
Toronto, ON M1S 3C8
Tel 416-291-7196
Fax 416-291-0045
NAICS: 326198
#Emp: 100-249 (Tor)
#TorLoc: 1
Own: Private Company
Key: Lydia Shaw, Pres
Cynthia Dicare, HR Mgr

Integrated Technology Ltd.

90 Don Park Rd.
Markham, ON L3R 1C4
Tel 905-475-6658
Fax 905-475-5097
www.itlcircuits.com
AKA: ITL Circuits
Line: Manufactures bare printed circuit boards.
NAICS: 334410
#Emp: 100-249 (Tor)
#TorLoc: 1
Own: Private Company
Key: Adolf Czudnochowsky, VP Ops
Barry Witcher, Ops Mgr
Bernie Hann, HR Mgr
Michael Campbell, VP Fin
Scott Bullock, Purch Mgr
Paul Czudnochowsky, IT Mgr

Intelligarde International Inc.

55 Unwin Ave.
Toronto, ON M5A 1A2
Tel 416-760-0000
Fax 416-469-4255
www.intelligarde.org
Line: Provides security and
investigation services.
NAICS: 561611
#Emp: 250-499 (Tor)
#TorLoc: 1
Own: Private Company
Key: Ross McLeod, Pres
Ryan Leeson, Ops Mgr
Eric Hovland, HR Mgr
David Singh, Cont
Joohyun Kwon, IT Mgr
Michael Gavendo, Nat'l Accounts Mgr
Valerie Kates, Dir of Staff Dev

Intelliware Development Inc.

200-1709 Bloor St. West
Toronto, ON M6P 4E5
Tel 416-762-0032
Fax 416-762-9001
www.intelliware.ca
Line: Provides custom software and
business solutions.
NAICS: 541510
#Emp: 75-99 (Tor)
#TorLoc: 2
Own: Private Company
Key: Greg Betty, Founder & Pres
Greg McKenzie, GM & COO
Caren DesBrisay, VP HR
Don Harkness, CFO
Glen Johnson, VP Business Dev

Intercity Realty Inc. Brokerage

14-3600 Langstaff Rd.
Woodbridge, ON L4L 9E7
Tel 416-798-7070
Fax 905-851-8794
www.intercityrealty.com
Line: Operates a real estate firm.
NAICS: 531210
#Emp: 75-99 (Tor)
#TorLoc: 2
Own: Private Company
Key: Luciano Grossi, Broker
Alda Neves, Dir of Mktg

Intercon Security Ltd.

40 Sheppard Ave. West
Toronto, ON M2N 6K9
Tel 416-229-6811
Fax 416-229-1207
www.interconsecurity.com
AKA: ADT Advanced Integration
Line: Provides security personnel and
systems.
NAICS: 561621
#Emp: 1000-4999 (Tor)
#TorLoc: 1
Own: Public Company
Par: ADT Security Services (CDA)
Key: Ian Morton, VP, Canada
Max Warmuth, Reg VP Ops
Scott Karsen, Dir Fin & Admin

InterContinental Toronto Centre

225 Front St. West
Toronto, ON M5V 2X3
Tel 416-597-1400
Fax 416-597-8128
www.torontocentre.
   intercontinental.com
Line: Operates a hotel.
NAICS: 721111
#Emp: 250-499 (Tor)
#TorLoc: 1
Own: Private Company
Par: InterContinental Hotels Group
(US)
Key: Renaud Payette, GM
Dallas Hopko, Dir of HR
Jorge Navarro Benitez, IT Mgr
Yola Marshall, Dir of Sales & Mktg

InterContinental Toronto-Yorkville

220 Bloor St. West
Toronto, ON M5S 1T8
Tel 416-960-5200
Fax 416-324-5881
www.toronto.intercontinental.com
Line: Provides hospitality services.
NAICS: 721111
#Emp: 100-249 (Tor)
#TorLoc: 1
Own: Private Company
Par: InterContinental Hotels Group
(US)
Key: Andrew Gajary, GM
Erin Elkin, Dir of HR
Rick Mak, Cont
Judy Mahony, Dir of Sales & Mktg

Interfast Inc.

22 Worcester Rd.
Toronto, ON M9W 1L1
Tel 416-674-0770
Fax 416-674-5804
www.interfast.ca
AKA: International Fasteners Ltd.
Line: Distributes fasteners, hardware,
aerospace components, rivets, nuts,
bolts, fittings, clamps, wire and cables.
NAICS: 416330
#Emp: 75-99 (Tor)
Own: Private Company
Key: S. Woollings, Pres
Donna Matys, HR Mgr
Pauline Mainville, Cont
Conrad Lennert, VP Sales & Mktg

Interior Manufacturing Group Inc.

974 Lakeshore Rd. East
Mississauga, ON L5E 1E4
Tel 905-278-9510
Fax 905-278-9234
www.imgmfg.com
AKA: IMG Inc.
Line: Manufactures custom commercial
furniture and retail store fixtures.
NAICS: 337214 337215
#Emp: 100-249 (Tor)
#TorLoc: 3
Own: Private Company
Key: Marcus Pachul, Pres
Michael Scafetta, VP Ops, Wood Plant
Fritz Winkels, VP & CFO

International Centre

120-6900 Airport Rd.
Mississauga, ON L4V 1E8
Tel 905-677-6131
Fax 905-677-3089
www.internationalcentre.com
AKA: T.I.C.C. Ltd.
Line: Operates multipurpose facility.
NAICS: 561920
#Emp: 100-249 (Tor)
#TorLoc: 1
Own: Private Company
Key: Michael Prescott, CEO
Gerry Rego, Engineering Mgr
Dany Lester, CFO
Leslie Bruce, Dir of Sales
Serena Quaglia, Dir of Mktg

International Clothiers Inc.

111 Orfus Rd.
Toronto, ON M6A 1M4
Tel 416-785-1771
Fax 416-785-9156
www.internationalclothiers.com
NAICS: 448150 448110
#Emp: 100-249 (Tor)
#TorLoc: 1
Own: Private Company
Key: Isaac Benitah, Pres
Otilia Araujo, HR Mgr

International Custom Products Inc.

49 Howden Rd.
Toronto, ON M1R 3C7
Tel 416-285-4311
Fax 416-285-7329
www.icpinc.com
AKA: ICP
Line: Manufactures custom carrying cases, stitched products, unmanned parachutes, business cases and accessories, mailroom sorting units and tamper evident courier bags.
NAICS: 314910 314990
#Emp: 100-249 (Tor)
#TorLoc: 1
Own: Private Company
Key: Robert A. Harper, Pres
John C. Newton, Exec VP
Lyle Nadon, VP Sales

International Financial Data Services (Canada) Ltd.

30 Adelaide St. East
Toronto, ON M5C 3G9
Tel 416-506-8000
Fax 416-506-8487
www.ifdsgroup.com
AKA: IFDS Canada
Line: Operates as a transfer agency and business process solutions provider for the investment fund agency.
NAICS: 522329
#Emp: 500-999 (Tor)
#TorLoc: 1
Own: Private Company
Par: Joint Venture (US)
Key: Debralee Goldberg, Pres & CEO
Marilyn Flanagan, Sr VP Ops
Noelle Sargeant, VP HR
Joe De Sario, CAO
Bruce Pinn, CIO
Brian Jerry, Sr VP,
    Head of Sales & Business Dev
Toby McGrory,
    VP Maketing & Commun

The International Group, Inc.

50 Salome Dr.
Toronto, ON M1S 2A8
Tel 416-293-4151
Fax 416-293-5858
www.igiwax.com
AKA: IGI; International Waxes
Line: Refines petroleum waxes, white oil, petrolatum waxes for coatings, cups, candles and tires.
NAICS: 325210
#Emp: 100-249 (Tor)
#TorLoc: 1
Own: Private Company
Key: Kenneth W. Reucassel,
    Pres & COO
Heather Meikle, Dir of HR
David Imrie, CFO
Jesse Anagnostopoulos, Purch Mgr
William Sandblom, Dir of MIS
Reg Barrett, Dir of Sales

International Landscaping Inc.

1114 Lower Base Line
Milton, ON L0P 1E0
Tel 905-876-3000
Fax 905-876-0400
www.internationallandscaping.com
Line: Provides landscaping, construction and maintenance services.
NAICS: 561730
#Emp: 75-99 (Tor)
#TorLoc: 1
Own: Private Company
Key: Baldo Gucciardi, GM

In Transit Personnel Inc.

112-114 6200 Dixie Rd.
Mississauga, ON L5T 2E1
Tel 905-564-9424
Fax 905-564-8970
www.in-transit.com
Line: Provides staffing services for the transportation industry.
NAICS: 561320
#Emp: 100-249 (Tor)
#TorLoc: 1
Own: Private Company
Key: Adam Clayson, Mng Partner & GM
Tracy Clayson,
    Mng Partner & VP Business Dev
Bob Allwood, Ops Mgr
Sherril Freund, Cont

Intria Items Inc.

5705 Cancross Crt.
Mississauga, ON L5R 3E9
Tel 905-755-2400
Fax 905-755-4799
www.intriaitemsinc.com
Line: Provides commercial printing, outsourcing and remote computing services.
NAICS: 323119
#Emp: 1000-4999 (Tor)
Own: Private Company
Key: Bob Bouey, Pres

Invensys Systems Canada Inc.

200-550 South Service Rd.
Burlington, ON L7O 5Y7
Tel 905-632-6015
Fax 905-333-2600
www.invensys.com
Line: Develops, sells, implements and supports software; and provides custom programming.
NAICS: 541510
#Emp: 100-249 (Tor)
#TorLoc: 1
Own: Private Company
Par: Invensys Systems Inc. (US)
Key: Mark Levell, Cont
Ann Perrault, HR Mgr
Kim Custeau, Dir of Mktg

Invesco Trimark

900-5140 Yonge St.
Toronto, ON M2N 6X7
Tel 416-228-5500
Fax 416-590-9868
www.invescotrimark.com
Line: Manages mutual funds.
NAICS: 523920 526910
#Emp: 500-999 (Tor)
#TorLoc: 2
Own: Private Company
Par: Invesco (US)
Key: Peter Intraligi, Pres & CEO
Phil Taylor, Sr Mng Dir & Head of
    North American Retail
Graham Anderson,
    Chief Investment Officer

Investigation Services Ltd.

300-180 Dundas St. West
Toronto, ON M5G 1Z8
Tel 416-599-5454
Fax 416-599-5656
www.investigation-services.ca
Line: Provides security guard services
and investigation services.
NAICS: 561611
#Emp: 75-99 (Tor)
#TorLoc: 2
Own: Private Company
Key: Clark Court, Pres & CEO

The Investigators Group Inc.

2-2061 McCowan Rd.
Toronto, ON M1S 3Y6
Tel 416-955-9450
Fax 416-955-0334
www.investigators-group.com
Line: Offers private investigation
services.
NAICS: 561611
#Emp: 100-249 (Tor)
#TorLoc: 2
Own: Private Company
Key: Bill Joynt, Pres

Investment Industry Regulatory Organization of Canada

1600-121 King St. West
Toronto, ON M5H 3T9
Tel 416-364-6133
Fax 416-364-0753
www.iiroc.ca
AKA: IIROC
Line: Protects investors and enhances
the efficiency and competitiveness of
Canadian capital markets.
NAICS: 813910
#Emp: 250-499 (Tor)
#TorLoc: 1
Own: Association
Key: Susan Wolburgh Jenah,
   Pres & CEO
Rob Martin, Dir of HR
Keith Persaud, Sr VP Fin & Admin
Wes J. Henry, VP Fin
Connie Craddock, VP Pub Affairs

Investment Planning Counsel Inc.

700-2680 Skymark Ave.
Mississauga, ON L4W 5L6
Tel 905-212-9799
Fax 905-212-9798
www.ipcc.ca
NAICS: 523930
#Emp: 100-249 (Tor)

#TorLoc: 1
Own: Private Company
Key: Christopher Reynolds, Pres
Stephen Meehan, CEO
Colin Gladwish, Nat'l Dir of Project
   Management & Advisor Support
Marianne Pelletier, Dir of HR
Scott Franklin, CFO
Meredith Malloch, Dir of Mktg

Investors Group Inc.

One Canada Centre
447 Portage Ave.
Winnipeg, MB R3C 3B6
Tel 204-943-0361
Fax 204-949-1340
www.investorsgroup.com
AKA: Investors Syndicate
Line: Provides financial services.
NAICS: 523120 523110
#Emp: 1000-4999 (Tor)
#TorLoc: 18
Own: Public Company
Par: Power Financial Corp. (CDA)
Key: Murray Taylor, Pres & CEO
Greg Tretiak, Exec VP Fin & CFO

IOF Business Furniture Manufacturing Inc.

1710 Bonhill Rd.
Mississauga, ON L5T 1C8
Tel 905-672-0942
Fax 905-672-5806
www.iofonline.com
Line: Manufactures business furniture.
NAICS: 337213
#Emp: 75-99 (Tor)
#TorLoc: 1
Own: Private Company
Key: Joel Klerer, Pres

IPEX Management Inc.

2441 Royal Windsor Dr.
Mississauga, ON L5J 4C7
Tel 905-403-0264
Fax 905-403-9195
www.ipexna.com
Line: Manufactures plastic pipes and
fittings.
NAICS: 326122
#Emp: 500-999 (Tor)
#TorLoc: 7
Own: Private Company
Par: Aliaxis Group (BELG)
Key: Paul Leonard, Pres & COO
Paul Graddon, Chmn & CEO
Frank Yorio, Sr VP Ops
Joanne Rivard, VP HR
Jean Paiva, VP Fin

iPro Realty Inc.

123 West Dr.
Brampton, ON L6T 2J6
Tel 905-454-1100
Fax 905-454-7335
www.iprorealty.com
NAICS: 531210
#Emp: 100-249 (Tor)
#TorLoc: 2
Own: Private Company
Key: Fedele Colucci, Broker Mgr

Ipsos Reid Corp.

300-160 Bloor St. East
Toronto, ON M4W 1B9
Tel 416-324-2900
Fax 416-324-2865
www.ipsos.ca
Line: Conducts market research.
NAICS: 541910
#Emp: 250-499 (Tor)
#TorLoc: 3
Own: Public Company
Par: AFI (FR)
Key: Gary Bennewies, Country Mgr
Steve Levy, Pres, MRC East
Andrew Cochrane, CFO & CPO

iQor Canada Inc.

130-225 Consumers Rd.
Toronto, ON M2J 1R4
Tel 519-620-6365
Fax 519-620-6397
www.iqor.com
AKA: IRMC - Intellirisk
Line: Provides collection services,
receivables management, customer
care and contact business process
outsourcing.
NAICS: 561440
#Emp: 500-999 (Tor)
Own: Private Company
Par: iQor (US)
Key: Vikas Kapoor, Pres & CEO
James Shaw, Exec VP, Canada
Danielle Parker, VP HR
Norm Merritt, Chief Acctng Officer
Steve Koch, VP IT
Victor Sawision, VP Sales

Iris Power LP

3110 American Dr.
Mississauga, ON L4T 1T2
Tel 905-677-4824
Fax 905-677-8498
www.irispower.com
AKA: Iris Power Engineering
Line: Manufactures measuring
instruments and meters.
NAICS: 334515

#Emp: 75-99 (Tor)
#TorLoc: 1
Own: Private Company
Par: Koch Chemical Technology
Finance Co. (US)
Key: Joseph Mbuyi, Pres
Blake Lloyd, Ops Mgr
Nancy Covassin, HR Mgr
Mushan Zhou, Cont
Rajiv Sharma, Sales Mgr

Iron Mountain Canada Corp.

195 Summerlea Rd.
Brampton, ON L6T 4P6
Tel 905-792-7099
Fax 905-792-2617
www.ironmountain.com
Line: Provides storage and information
management services for records
including secure shredding, magnetic
tapes and open file records.
NAICS: 541510 334610
#Emp: 250-499 (Tor)
#TorLoc: 8
Own: Public Company
Par: Iron Mountain Inc. (US)
Key: Pierre Matteau, Exec VP
Richard Reese, Chair & CEO
Daryl Westman, Reg VP

Irpinia Kitchens

A Div. of 1118741 Ontario Ltd.
278 Newkirk Rd.
Richmond Hill, ON L4C 3G7
Tel 905-780-7722
Fax 905-780-0554
www.irpinia.com
Line: Manufactures and distributes
cabinetry.
NAICS: 337110
#Emp: 75-99 (Tor)
#TorLoc: 2
Own: Private Company
Key: Joseph Marcantonio, Pres
Felice Marcantonio, GM
Marcello Marcantonio, VP

Irving Tissue

A Div. of Irving Group of Companies
1551 Weston Rd.
Toronto, ON M6M 4Y4
Tel 416-246-6666
Fax 416-246-6667
www.majesta.com
Line: Produces paper products.
NAICS: 322121 322291
#Emp: 250-499 (Tor)
#TorLoc: 1
Own: Private Company
Key: Ed Lamoureux, Dir of Bus Relns
Phil Viger, VP Ops

Islington Golf Club Ltd.

45 Riverbank Dr.
Toronto, ON M9A 5B8
Tel 416-231-1114
Fax 416-231-1304
www.islingtongolfclub.com
NAICS: 713910
#Emp: 100-249 (Tor)
#TorLoc: 1
Own: Not-for-profit
Key: Dave Fox, GM
Marilena Pasqualitto, Cont

Italian Home Bakery Ltd.

271 Attwell Dr.
Toronto, ON M9W 5B9
Tel 416-674-4555
Fax 416-674-0558
www.ihbakery.com
Line: Manufactures and sells baked
goods.
NAICS: 311814
#Emp: 100-249 (Tor)
#TorLoc: 1
Own: Private Company
Key: Dennis Rossetti, Pres
John Rossetti, VP & CFO
Sherry Harribersad, Cont
Rick Mazza, Purch

Italpasta Ltd.

116 Nugget Crt.
Brampton, ON L6T 5A9
Tel 905-792-9928
Fax 905-792-2381
www.italpasta.com
Line: Manufactures and sells pasta and
related products.
NAICS: 311823
#Emp: 250-499 (Tor)
#TorLoc: 2
Own: Private Company
Key: Joseph Vitale, Pres
Riccardo Bordignon, Plant Mgr
Robert Ivancic, HR Mgr
Frank DeMichino, Corp VP

itravel 2000

2350 Matheson Blvd. East
Mississauga, ON L4W 5G9
Tel 905-238-3399
Fax 905-238-6177
www.itravel2000.com
Line: Operates a travel agency.
NAICS: 561510
#Emp: 100-249 (Tor)
#TorLoc: 1
Own: Public Company
Key: Jonathan Carroll, CEO
Jack Fraser, CFO

Itwal Ltd.

440 Railside Dr.
Brampton, ON L7A 1L1
Tel 905-840-9400
Fax 905-840-9404
www.itwal.com
Line: Provides suppliers with
measurable distribution, marketing,
selling and information solutions.
NAICS: 484239
#Emp: 75-99 (Tor)
#TorLoc: 1
Own: Private Company
Key: Ross Robertson, Pres
Glenn Stevens, CEO
Suzanne Walker, Dir of Fin & Admin
Ron Williams, Cont

ITW Construction Products

120 Travail Rd.
Markham, ON L3S 3J1
Tel 905-471-7403
Fax 905-471-4407
www.itwconstruction.ca
Line: Manufactures and distributes
construction products.
NAICS: 333990
#Emp: 100-249 (Tor)
#TorLoc: 3
Own: Private Company
Par: Illinois Tool Works, Inc. (US)
Key: Paul Plourde, GM

Ivanhoe Cambridge

300-95 Wellington St. West
Toronto, ON M5J 2R2
Tel 416-369-1200
Fax 416-369-1327
www.ivanhoecambridge.com
Line: Manages and develops shopping
centres, mixed-use properties and
retail related commercial properties.
NAICS: 531310
#Emp: 100-249 (Tor)
#TorLoc: 1
Own: Private Company
Par: Ivanhoe Cambridge (CDA)
Key: Kim D. McInnes, Pres
Paul Gleeson, Sr VP & Chief Dev Officer
David Smith, VP HR
Rene Demchuck, VP IT

Ivers-Lee Inc.

31 Hansen Rd. South
Brampton, ON L6W 3H7
Tel 905-451-5535
Fax 905-451-1255
www.ivers-lee.ca
Line: Offers packaging and labelling
services for pharmaceutical products.
NAICS: 561910
#Emp: 100-249 (Tor)
#TorLoc: 1
Own: Public Company
Par: Jones Packaging Inc. (CDA)
Key: Rob Reddick, GM
Edna Dowell,
    Payroll & Personnel Admr
Bo Ly, Cont
Darrell Coombs, Tech Services

J&A Cleaning Solutions Ltd.

2-80 Kincort St.
Toronto, ON M6M 5G1
Tel 416-242-4151
Fax 416-242-3023
www.jacleaning.ca
Line: Provides integrated facility
maintenance including cleaning,
grounds services, mechanical
maintenance, interior design, supplies
and equipment.
NAICS: 561722
#Emp: 1000-4999 (Tor)
Own: Private Company
Key: Spyros Kourkoutis, CEO
Robert Kowauewski, Ops Mgr

Jacobs & Thompson Inc.

89 Kenhar Dr.
Toronto, ON M9L 2R3
Tel 416-749-0600
Fax 416-749-6618
www.foamparts.ca
Line: Manufactures weather stripping,
automotive foam seals, gaskets and
tapes.
NAICS: 339990
#Emp: 100-249 (Tor)
#TorLoc: 1
Own: Private Company
Key: Chris Brand, Pres
Shawn Greene, VP Sales & Mktg

James Dick Construction Ltd.

14442 Regional Rd. 50
P.O. Box 470
Bolton, ON L7E 5T4
Tel 905-857-3500
Fax 905-857-4833
www.jamesdick.com
AKA: James Dick Ready Mix; James
Dick Aggregates
Line: Supplies concrete, aggregates and
heavy equipment.
NAICS: 327390 416390
#Emp: 250-499 (Tor)
#TorLoc: 18
Own: Private Company
Key: James Dick, Pres
Greg Sweetnam, VP
Anne Dick, HR Mgr
Ken Dick, MIS Mgr
George Hill, VP Mktg & Sales

James Moto Enterprises Inc.

315 Adelaide St. West
Toronto, ON M5V 1P8
Tel 416-977-2603
Fax 416-977-0765
www.jamesmoto.com
AKA: Showflex Inc.
Line: Distributes fur and leather goods.
NAICS: 315292
#Emp: 75-99 (Tor)
Own: Private Company
Key: James Matsumoto, Owner
Hisako Setoyama, Ops Mgr
Takeshi Sugawara, Mgr
Ritsuko Ikushima, Dir of Fin

Janes Family Foods Ltd.

3340 Orlando Dr.
Mississauga, ON L4V 1C7
Tel 905-673-7145
Fax 905-677-0607
www.janesfamilyfoods.com
AKA: Belpak Foods
Line: Manufactures fresh and frozen
food products.
NAICS: 311710 311515
#Emp: 100-249 (Tor)
#TorLoc: 3
Own: Private Company
Key: Steve Malinowski, Pres
Lem Janes, CEO

Janssen Inc.

19 Green Belt Dr.
Toronto, ON M3C 1L9
Tel 416-449-9444
Fax 416-449-2658
www.janssen-ortho.com
Line: Develops, sells and markets
pharmaceutical products.
NAICS: 325410 414520
#Emp: 500-999 (Tor)
#TorLoc: 1
Own: Private Company
Par: Johnson & Johnson Inc. (US)
Key: Chris Halyk, Pres
Sandra Heymann, VP HR
Kelly Martin, VP Fin
Suzanne Frost, Dir of Commun

Jarden Consumer Solutions

B-20 Hereford St.
Brampton, ON L6Y 0M1
Tel 905-501-0090
Fax 905-593-6200
www.jardencs.com
AKA: Sunbeam-Oster; Powermate;
Coleman; First Alert; Mr. Coffee
Line: Distributes household appliances,
camping and leisure products, and
safety equipment.
NAICS: 414220
#Emp: 100-249 (Tor)
#TorLoc: 1
Own: Private Company
Par: Jarden Corporation (US)
Key: David Simmons, VP & GM
Michael Ricci, VP Fin & Ops
Mariann Mackey, Dir of HR

J.A. Wilson Display

1645 Aimco Blvd.
Mississauga, ON L4W 1H8
Tel 905-625-9200
Fax 905-625-3199
www.wilsondisplay.com
AKA: Store Fixtures & Wilson Display
Line: Manufactures metal store fixtures
for retail stores.
NAICS: 337215
#Emp: 100-249 (Tor)
#TorLoc: 1
Own: Private Company
Key: Frank Ruffolo, Chmn & CEO
John Allen, VP Manuf
Barbara Nickel, HR Mgr
Nancy Hansen, Cont
Gordana Romic,
    Purch & Inventory Mgr
Elizabeth Wilson, Sales Mgr

Jay Electric Ltd.

2-21 Kenview Blvd.
Brampton, ON L6T 5G7
Tel 905-793-4000
Fax 905-793-0095
www.jayelectric.com
AKA: Enerscan Controls
Line: Provides electrical services.
NAICS: 232510
#Emp: 100-249 (Tor)
#TorLoc: 1
Own: Private Company
Key: Frank L. Malisani, Pres
Aaron Malisani, Purch
Louis Malisani, Project Management

Jaytex of Canada Ltd.

29 Gurney Cres.
Toronto, ON M6B 1S9
Tel 416-785-1099
Fax 416-787-8563
www.jaytexgroup.com
AKA: The Jaytex Group
Line: Imports and distributes men's
clothing.
NAICS: 414110 315229
#Emp: 100-249 (Tor)
#TorLoc: 1
Own: Private Company
Key: David Meyers, Pres
Dalia Shayo, VP Ops
Jeff Awenus, CFO
Pam Morrisson,
    Head of Mktg & Promotions

J.D. Barnes Ltd.

100-140 Renfrew Dr.
Markham, ON L3R 6B3
Tel 905-477-3600
Fax 905-477-3882
www.jdbarnes.com
Line: Provides surveying, mapping,
and geographic information services
to government, utilities, developers,
homebuilders, engineers, planners and
the public.
NAICS: 541370 541330
#Emp: 100-249 (Tor)
#TorLoc: 4
Own: Private Company
Key: Frank Mauro, Pres & CEO
Catriona Hazen, HR Supr
Ron Terin, VP Fin
Andrew Chan, IT Mgr

J.D. Smith and Sons Limited

180 Basaltic Rd.
Vaughan, ON L4K 1G6
Tel 905-669-8980
Fax 905-669-8981
www.jdsmith.com
Line: Provides third party logistics
including cartage, warehousing,
distribution, and contract trucking.
NAICS: 493110 484110 484121
#Emp: 100-249 (Tor)
#TorLoc: 4
Own: Private Company
Key: Scott Smith, Pres & CEO
Brian Smith, Sr VP
Brian Death, VP HR & Admin
Amo Harnarine, Purch Mgr
Cameron Arntsen,
    Sr IS & Technologies Mgr
Kent Hunter, VP Warehousing
Mike Nichols, VP Sales

Jeld-Wen Windows & Doors

90 Stone Ridge Rd.
Vaughan, ON L4H 3G9
Tel 905-265-5700
Fax 905-265-5701
www.jeld-wen.ca
Line: Manufactures vinyl windows and
steel door entrance systems.
NAICS: 332329
#Emp: 250-499 (Tor)
#TorLoc: 1
Own: Private Company
Par: Jeld-Wen Inc. (US)
Key: Jesse Hawthorne, GM
Marcelo Cuenca, Sales Mgr

Jem Pak GK Inc.

80 Doney Cres.
Concord, ON L4K 3P1
Tel 905-738-5656
Fax 905-738-1462
www.jempakgk.com
Line: Develops, manufactures and
sells non-food consumable products
including fabric softener sheets, dust
cloths, wet wipe products, laundry
detergents and household cleaning
liquids.
NAICS: 314990 325610
#Emp: 100-249 (Tor)
#TorLoc: 3
Own: Private Company
Key: Steve Miller, Pres & CEO
Saquib Khan, VP Supply Chain (Ops)
Akil Karim, VP Fin & Admin
Dave MacQuarrie, VP Sales & Mktg

Jems Coating Ltd.

210 Jacob Keffer Pkwy.
Concord, ON L4K 4W3
Tel 905-303-7433
Fax 905-303-7270
www.jemscoating.com
Line: Manufactures plastic custom
coaters.
NAICS: 416340
#Emp: 100-249 (Tor)
#TorLoc: 1
Own: Private Company
Key: John Lamb, Pres
Irina Lavashova, Cont

Jetco Manufacturing Ltd.

36 Milvan Dr.
Toronto, ON M9L 1Z4
Tel 416-741-1800
Fax 416-741-6918
www.jetcomfg.com
Line: Manufactures metal furniture.
NAICS: 337126
#Emp: 100-249 (Tor)
#TorLoc: 1
Own: Private Company
Key: Keith Alexander, Pres
Sam Gogas, VP

Jevco Insurance Company

100-4 Robert Speck Pkwy.
Mississauga, ON L42 1S1
Tel 905-277-9350
Fax 905-277-5008
www.jevco.ca
AKA: Kingsway Financial Services
Line: Provides non-standard
automobile insurance along with
commercial automobile, property,
motorcycle and other insurance to
specialty markets.
NAICS: 524210
#Emp: 250-499 (Tor)
#TorLoc: 1
Own: Private Company
Key: Scot Hopkins, VP & CEO
Grace Kemp, Nat'l Mktg Mgr

Jewish Vocational Service of Greater Toronto

74 Tycos Dr.
Toronto, ON M6B 1V9
Tel 416-787-1151
Fax 416-785-7529
www.jvstoronto.org
AKA: JVS Toronto
Line: Provides leadership in the
development and delivery of
educational and vocational services of
a non-sectarian nature in order to assist
clients and identify educational and
vocational goals.
NAICS: 624310
#Emp: 250-499 (Tor)
#TorLoc: 14
Own: Not-for-profit
Key: Karen Goldenberg,
    Exec Dir & CEO
Kim Coulter, Ops Mgr
Bob Boulton, HR Mgr

J.F. & L. Restaurants Ltd.

5-110 Denison St.
Markham, ON L3R 1B6
Tel 905-479-2402
Fax 905-479-5059
www.picklebarrel.ca
AKA: The Pickle Barrel
Line: Operates a chain of restaurants and catering.
NAICS: 722110
#Emp: 1000-4999 (Tor)
#TorLoc: 12
Own: Private Company
Key: Peter Higley, Pres
Vincent D'cruz, VP
Cathi Bagshaw, Payroll
Beth Pennington, Cont

J.H. McNairn Ltd.

125 Consumers Dr.
Whitby, ON L1N 1C4
Tel 905-668-7533
Fax 905-668-5038
www.mcnairnpackaging.com
AKA: McNairn Packaging
Line: Manufactures packaging materials for food service, supermarket, bakery and food processing businesses.
NAICS: 322220
#Emp: 100-249 (Tor)
#TorLoc: 1
Own: Private Company
Key: Dennis Czosnek, Pres
Kenneth W.A. Miller, CEO
Stuart Mosher, Dir of Manuf
Doug Campbell, HR Mgr
Jim Parkes, VP IT
Brent Quinn, VP Sales

J.H. Ryder Machinery Ltd.

210 Annagem Blvd.
Mississauga, ON L5T 2V5
Tel 905-565-2100
Fax 905-795-9311
www.jhryder.com
Line: Sells, distributes and services new and used lift trucks and provides operator, health and safety training.
NAICS: 417230
#Emp: 100-249 (Tor)
#TorLoc: 4
Own: Private Company
Key: Thomas M. Ryder, Pres
Ron Greer, COO
Danny Fatigati, CFO
David Green, GM, Corp Services
Kevin Mascinic, GM, Equipment Sales
John Ryder, GM, Corp Services

Jitsu Manufacturing Inc.

6880 Davand Dr.
Mississauga, ON L5T 1J5
Tel 905-795-8563
Fax 905-795-7663
www.jitsuautomotive.com
AKA: Jitsu Automotive
Line: Designs and manufactures automotive components.
NAICS: 336390
#Emp: 75-99 (Tor)
#TorLoc: 1
Own: Private Company
Key: Eddy Mudronja, Owner

J.J. Home Products Inc.

110 Walker Dr.
Brampton, ON L6T 4H6
Tel 416-798-7785
Fax 416-798-7792
www.jj.ca
Line: Manufactures mirrors, closet sliding doors, shower and tub enclosures.
NAICS: 339990
#Emp: 75-99 (Tor)
#TorLoc: 2
Own: Private Company
Key: Michael Semerak, GM

J & L Personnel Inc.

1055 Canadian Pl.
Mississauga, ON L4W 0C2
Tel 416-621-1700
Fax 416-621-1704
www.willhireu.com
NAICS: 561310
#Emp: 100-249 (Tor)
#TorLoc: 1
Own: Private Company
Key: Joe Pinto, Pres
Chantelle Watson, Dir of Admin
Josee Doucet, Corp Accounts Exec

J.M. Die Limited

909 Pantera Dr.
Mississauga, ON L4W 2R9
Tel 905-625-9571
Fax 905-625-2855
www.jmdie.ca
Line: Operates a tool and die manufacturing company.
NAICS: 333519
#Emp: 75-99 (Tor)
#TorLoc: 3
Own: Private Company
Key: Joe Skof, Pres
Irene Rezek, Office Mgr
Gurmit Dhanoya, Purch & Product Mgr

Joe Badali's Piazza On Front Inc.

156 Front St. West
Toronto, ON M5J 2L6
Tel 416-977-3064
Fax 416-599-6296
www.joebadalis.com
Line: Operates a restaurant.
NAICS: 722110
#Emp: 100-249 (Tor)
#TorLoc: 1
Own: Private Company
Key: Mike O'Connor, VP
Jessica Manis, Mgr of Mktg
Lisa Jodhan, Bookkeeper

John Brooks Company Ltd.

2625 Meadowpine Blvd.
Mississauga, ON L5N 7K5
Tel 905-567-9222
Fax 905-567-0312
www.johnbrooks.ca
Line: Distributes pressure wash and industrial fluid handling equipment.
NAICS: 417230
#Emp: 100-249 (Tor)
#TorLoc: 1
Own: Private Company
Key: Roger Minkhorst, VP
Heather Collins, HR Mgr

John Deere Credit Inc.

401-1001 Champlain Ave.
Burlington, ON L7L 5Z4
Tel 905-319-9100
Fax 905-319-6382
www.johndeere.com
Line: Administers financing for retail purchases of new and used agricultural, construction, commercial, and consumer equipment.
NAICS: 522299
#Emp: 100-249 (Tor)
#TorLoc: 1
Own: Private Company
Key: John Grosso, Pres, Cdn Ops
Christine Crowley, Mgr of HR

The John Forsyth Shirt Co. Ltd.

6789 Airport Rd.
Mississauga, ON L4V 1N2
Tel 905-362-1400
Fax 905-362-4030
www.careerapparel.ca
Line: Retails shirts and assorted clothing.
NAICS: 448199
#Emp: 75-99 (Tor)
Own: Private Company
Par: Forsyth Holdings Group (US)
Key: Harris Hester, Pres

John G. Hofland Ltd.

6695 Pacific Circ.
Mississauga, ON L5T 1V6
Tel 905-670-8220
Fax 905-670-8257
www.hofland.com
Line: Imports and distributes giftware and flowers.
NAICS: 411130
#Emp: 100-249 (Tor)
#TorLoc: 1
Own: Private Company
Key: Glenn Hofland, Pres
Ben Jardine, Ops Mgr
Heather Hendricks, HR Mgr
Greg Chiykowski, Dir of Fin & Cont
Rodney Hofland, VP
Darren Russell, Sales & Mktg Mgr

John Grant Haulage Ltd.

2111 Lakeshore Rd. West
Mississauga, ON L5J 1J9
Tel 905-822-1609
Fax 905-822-2142
NAICS: 484229 484239
#Emp: 75-99 (Tor)
#TorLoc: 1
Own: Private Company
Key: Bradley Grant, Pres & Dir
Danielle McClure, Cont

Johnson Controls LP

7400 Birchmount Rd.
Markham, ON L3R 5V4
Tel 905-475-7610
Fax 905-415-3299
www.johnsoncontrols.com
Line: Supplies and installs energy management systems for new and existing buildings; and provides building operation and heating, ventilating, air conditioning, security and fire alarm services.
NAICS: 232520
#Emp: 250-499 (Tor)
#TorLoc: 4
Own: Private Company
Par: Johnson Controls Inc. (US)
Key: Robert McCullough, Reg VP & GM
Cindy Theriault, Reg HR Dir
Steve Sales, Corp Cont

Johnson Inc.

700-1595 16th Ave.
Richmond Hill, ON L4B 3S5
Tel 905-764-4900
Fax 905-882-5118
www.johnson.ca
NAICS: 524210
#Emp: 100-249 (Tor)
#TorLoc: 3

Own: Private Company
Par: Royal & Sun Alliance Insurance Company of Canada (CDA)
Key: Doug Munn, Reg VP
Ken Bennett, Pres
Teresa Van Dyk, Reg Facilities Mgr

Johnson & Johnson Medical Products

200 Whitehall Dr.
Markham, ON L3R 0T5
Tel 905-946-8999
Fax 905-946-2168
www.jnjgateway.com
Line: Distributes medical, surgical, and diagnostic products and supplies.
NAICS: 339110
#Emp: 250-499 (Tor)
#TorLoc: 1
Own: Private Company
Par: Johnson & Johnson, Inc. (US)
Key: Bernard Zovighian, Pres

Johnson Matthey Limited

130 Glidden Rd.
Brampton, ON L6W 3M8
Tel 905-453-6120
Fax 905-454-6849
www.matthey.com
Line: Refines precious metals.
NAICS: 331110
#Emp: 75-99 (Tor)
#TorLoc: 1
Own: Private Company
Par: Johnson Matthey plc (UK)
Key: Andy McCullough, GM
David Murray, Ops Mgr
Linda Szeli, HR Mgr
Greg Delazarri, Cont
Ray Gaudet, Sales & Mktg Mgr

Johnvince Foods

555 Steeprock Dr.
Toronto, ON M3J 2Z6
Tel 416-636-6146
Fax 416-636-6177
www.johnvince.com
AKA: Nicklen Logistics; Distributions Alimentaires Le Marquis
Line: Wholesales and distributes bulk food, nuts and dried fruit.
NAICS: 413110 413190
#Emp: 500-999 (Tor)
#TorLoc: 1
Own: Private Company
Key: Vincent Pulla, Pres
Tom Copping, COO
Rita Pulla, HR
Vincent Cosentino, CFO
Domenic Ursini, Nat'l Sales Mgr
Don Lock, VP Sales & Mktg

John Wiley & Sons Canada Ltd.

6045 Freemont Blvd.
Mississauga, ON L5R 4J3
Tel 416-236-4433
Fax 416-236-8743
www.wileycanada.com
Line: Publishes print and electronic products globally, specializing in scientific, technical, and medical books; professional, consumer books; and educational textbooks and materials.
NAICS: 511130
#Emp: 100-249 (Tor)
#TorLoc: 2
Own: Private Company
Par: John Wiley & Sons Inc. (US)
Key: Bill Zerter, COO
Debbie Barton, VP & Dir of Ops
Berni Galway, VP HR
Jason Riley, VP Fin

Jones Apparel Group Canada Ltd.

388 Applewood Cres.
Vaughan, ON L4K 4B4
Tel 905-760-6000
Fax 905-760-6017
www.jonesapparel.com
AKA: Jones New York
Line: Manufactures, sells and distributes apparel for women.
NAICS: 414110
#Emp: 100-249 (Tor)
#TorLoc: 6
Own: Private Company
Par: Jones Apparel Group (US)
Key: Carrie Kirkmam, Pres & CEO
Julie Oakley, VP Ops
Roger Flores, VP Fin & CFO
Judi Willard, VP Sales & Merchandising

Jones, Gable & Company Limited

600-110 Yonge St.
Toronto, ON M5C 1T6
Tel 416-365-8000
Fax 416-365-8037
www.jonesgable.com
Line: Operates as a full service investment dealer.
NAICS: 523120
#Emp: 75-99 (Tor)
#TorLoc: 1
Own: Private Company
Key: Donald Ross, Pres & CEO
Robb Hindson, CFO

Jonview Canada Inc.

800-1300 Yonge St.
Toronto, ON M4T 1X3
Tel 416-323-9090
Fax 416-323-3980
www.jonview.com
Line: Arranges tours for travelers.
NAICS: 561520
#Emp: 100-249 (Tor)
#TorLoc: 1
Own: Public Company
Par: Transat Holidays (CDA)
Key: Annick Guerard,
    VP & GM, Jonview Canada
Andrew Lind, VP & GM, Toronto
Marco Calabretta-Duval, Dir of Fin
Bill Knowlton, VP Sales & Mktg

Joseph Brant Memorial Hospital

1230 North Shore Blvd.
Burlington, ON L7S 1W7
Tel 905-632-3730
Fax 905-366-6480
www.jbmh.com
NAICS: 622111
#Emp: 1000-4999 (Tor)
#TorLoc: 1
Own: Not-for-profit
Key: Eric Vandewall, Pres & CEO
Dave Tisiot,
    VP People & Clinical Services
Dennis Castellan,
    VP Fin & Support Services
Dennis Burrella, Dir of Commun & IS
Mario Joannette, Integrated VP,
    Pub Affairs & Commun

JP Morgan Chase Bank, N.A.

Royal Bank Plaza, South Tower
1800-200 Bay St.
Toronto, ON M5J 2J2
Tel 416-981-9200
Fax 416-981-9175
www.jpmorganchase.com
Line: Specializes in investment
banking.
NAICS: 523110 522299
#Emp: 100-249 (Tor)
#TorLoc: 1
Own: Public Company
Par: JP Morgan Chase & Co. (US)
Key: Adam Howard, Pres

JTI-Macdonald Corp.

1601-1 Robert Speck Pkwy.
Mississauga, ON L4Z 0A2
Tel 905-804-7300
Fax 905-804-7301
www.jti.com
Line: Manufactures consumer product
goods.
NAICS: 312220
#Emp: 100-249 (Tor)
#TorLoc: 2
Own: Private Company
Par: Japan Tobacco Inc. (JAPAN)
Key: Michel Poirier, Pres & CEO
George Metsis, Cont
Nelson Medeiros, Head of IT
Christian Guay, Head of Mktg

Just Energy

200-6345 Dixie Rd.
Mississauga, ON L5T 2E6
Tel 905-670-4440
Fax 905-670-9160
www.justenergy.com
Line: Operates a natural gas and
electricity energy supplier.
NAICS: 221121
#Emp: 250-499 (Tor)
#TorLoc: 5
Own: Private Company
Key: Ken Hartwick, Pres & CEO

Just Energy Group Inc.

First Canadian Pl.
2630-100 King St. West
Toronto, ON M5X 1E1
Tel 416-367-2998
Fax 416-367-4749
www.esif.ca
Line: Manages income investments for
gas and electricity marketers.
NAICS: 526910
#Emp: 500-999 (Tor)
#TorLoc: 2
Own: Public Company
Key: Ken Hartwick, Pres & Co-CEO
Rebecca MacDonald,
    Exec Chmn & Co-CEO

J. Walter Thompson Company Ltd.

160 Bloor St. East
Toronto, ON M4W 3P7
Tel 416-926-7300
Fax 416-926-7389
www.jwt.com
Line: Provides advertising services.
NAICS: 541810
#Emp: 100-249 (Tor)
#TorLoc: 1

Own: Public Company
Par: WPP Group plc (UK)
Key: Tony Pigott, Pres & CEO
Sue Stephenson, HR Mgr
Anthony Ruta, Exec VP & CFO
Linda Good, Admin Mgr

Kafko Pool Products

1231 Kamato Rd.
Mississauga, ON L4W 2M2
Tel 905-624-3171
Fax 905-624-5234
www.kafko.com
Line: Manufactures inground
swimming pools, vinyl liners and metal
fences.
NAICS: 232990
#Emp: 75-99 (Tor)
#TorLoc: 1
Own: Private Company
Par: Latham Splash (CDA)
Key: Tim Golden, Pres

The Kalen Group

262 Avenue Rd.
Toronto, ON M4V 2G7
Tel 416-929-7781
Fax 416-929-7784
www.mrgreenjeans.ca
AKA: Mr. Greenjeans
Line: Operates full service bars and
restaurants.
NAICS: 722110
#Emp: 100-249 (Tor)
#TorLoc: 1
Own: Private Company
Par: Kalen Corp. (CDA)
Key: Maury Kalen, Pres
Linda Allicock, Office Mgr
Krista Locke, Accounts Payable

Kal Tire Ontario

2403 Stanfield Rd.
Mississauga, ON L4Y 1R6
Tel 905-848-3500
Fax 905-848-4584
www.mtctire.com
Line: Operates an independent tire
dealership.
NAICS: 441320
#Emp: 75-99 (Tor)
#TorLoc: 2
Own: Public Company
Key: Danny Funk, COO

Kaneff Group of Companies

200-8501 Mississauga Rd.
Brampton, ON L6Y 5G8
Tel 905-454-0221
Fax 905-454-0297
www.kaneff.com
AKA: Kaneff Properties
Line: Develops, constructs and manages real estate.
NAICS: 531310 231110
#Emp: 500-999 (Tor)
Own: Private Company
Key: Ignat Kaneff, Pres
Martha McCallum, Dir of Fin & Admin
Daniel Kaneff, VP Construction

Kao Brands Canada Inc.

5-60 Courtney Park Dr. West
Mississauga, ON L5W 0B3
Tel 905-670-7890
Fax 905-670-9379
www.kaobrands.com
Line: Manufactures skin care and hair care products.
NAICS: 325620
#Emp: 75-99 (Tor)
#TorLoc: 1
Own: Public Company
Par: Kao Corporation (JAPAN)
Key: Simon Bureau, GM

Kapsch TrafficCom

6020 Ambler Dr.
Mississauga, ON L4W 2P1
Tel 905-624-3020
Fax 905-625-6197
www.kapsch.net
AKA: Mark IV Industries Ltd.; IVHS
Line: Designs and manufactures DSRC technology for use in intelligent transportation systems such as electronic toll collection.
NAICS: 334410
#Emp: 500-999 (Tor)
#TorLoc: 1
Own: Private Company
Par: Mark IV Industries Inc. (US)
Key: T. Martin Capper, CEO
Joe Bianchini, VP Manuf
Adele Burns, Dir of HR
Jim Newton, Cont
Jim Melchers, Dir of Purch
Steve D'Amario, IS Mgr
Paul Manuel, VP Sales

Karmax Heavy Stamping

A Div. of Cosma International Inc.
333 Market Dr.
Milton, ON L9T 4Z7
Tel 905-878-5571
Fax 905-876-1519
www.karmax.com
Line: Manufactures class 1 automotive sheet metal as well as small, medium and large stampings.
NAICS: 332118
#Emp: 500-999 (Tor)
#TorLoc: 1
Own: Private Company
Par: Magna International Inc. (CDA)
Key: Klaus Niemeyer, GM
Gary Love, HR Mgr
Michael Long, Systems Mgr
Graham Postma, Asst GM

Karrys Bros., Limited

180 Courtneypark Dr. East
Mississauga, ON L5T 2S5
Tel 905-565-1000
Fax 905-565-7575
www.karrys.com
AKA: Karrys Wholesale Distributors
Line: Wholesales and distributes products for gas stations and convenience stores.
NAICS: 413190
#Emp: 100-249 (Tor)
#TorLoc: 1
Own: Private Company
Key: Steven Karrys, Pres & CEO
Kerry Anne Nicholson, Exec Dir of HR
Shawn J. Shultz,
    Exec Dir of Fin & Admin
Peter Kerr, VP Sales

Katz Group Canada Ltd.

5965 Coopers Ave.
Mississauga, ON L9Z 1R9
Tel 905-502-5965
Fax 905-502-5618
www.rexall.ca
AKA: Rexall; Pharma Plus
Line: Retails pharmaceuticals.
NAICS: 446110
#Emp: 1000-4999 (Tor)
Own: Private Company
Par: Katz Enterprises Ltd. (CDA)
Key: Andy Giancamilli, Pres & CEO
Warren Jeffery, COO

Kawneer Company Canada Ltd.

1051 Ellesmere Rd.
Toronto, ON M1P 2X1
Tel 416 755-7751
Fax 416-755-1829
www.kawneer.com
Line: Manufactures architectural aluminum products, windows, entrances, and curtain walls.
NAICS: 332329 232340
#Emp: 75-99 (Tor)
#TorLoc: 2
Own: Private Company
Par: Alcoa Inc. (US)
Key: Mark Howard, Plant Mgr

K-Bro Linen Systems (Ontario) Ltd.

15 Shorncliffe Rd.
Toronto, ON M9B 3S4
Tel 416-233-5555
Fax 416-233-4434
www.k-brolinen.com
NAICS: 812330 812320
#Emp: 100-249 (Tor)
#TorLoc: 1
Own: Private Company
Par: K-Bro Linen Systems Inc. (CDA)
Key: Linda McCurdy, Pres & CEO
Jerry Ostrzyzek, GM & VP Eastern Ops
Andrew Tymko, Cont
Michael Beach, Ops Mgr
Salim S. Khimji, IT Mgr

KCI Medical Canada, Inc.

2-75 Courtneypark Dr. West
Mississauga, ON L5W 0E3
Tel 905-565-7187
Fax 905-565-7270
www.kci-medical.com
Line: Designs, manufactures and markets medical technology.
NAICS: 334512
#Emp: 75-99 (Tor)
#TorLoc: 1
Own: Private Company
Par: KCI (UK)
Key: John Simmons, GM

Keane Canada Inc.

206-30 East Beaver Creek Rd.
Richmond Hill, ON L4B 1JA
Tel 416-499-4411
www.keane.com
Line: Provides business and technology services.
NAICS: 541619
#Emp: 75-99 (Tor)
#TorLoc: 2
Own: Public Company
Par: Keane (US)
Key: Terry Riopele, Sr Mgr

Kee Management Solutions Inc.

9-6760 Davand Dr.
Mississauga, ON L5T 2L9
Tel 905-670-0835
Fax 905-670-5513
www.keetransport.com
Line: Supplies AZ drivers to industry.
NAICS: 561310
#Emp: 250-499 (Tor)
#TorLoc: 1
Own: Private Company
Key: Kieran O'Briain, Pres
Dave Waver, GM

Keg Restaurants Ltd.

420-295 The West Mall
Toronto, ON M9C 4Z4
Tel 416-695-2400
Fax 416-695-2401
www.kegsteakhouse.com
AKA: The Keg
Line: Operates a chain of steakhouse restaurants and bars.
NAICS: 722110
#Emp: 1000-4999 (Tor)
#TorLoc: 16
Own: Private Company
Key: Beth Plumstead, Office Mgr
Dean Sockett, Dir of HR
Mary DiCecco, Dir of Mktg

Keilhauer

1450 Birchmount Rd.
Toronto, ON M1P 2E3
Tel 416-759-5665
Fax 416-759-5723
www.keilhauer.com
Line: Manufactures commercial office seating.
NAICS: 337127
#Emp: 100-249 (Tor)
#TorLoc: 2
Own: Private Company

Key: Michael Keilhauer, Pres
Rick Keilhauer, VP Manuf
Indira Persaud,
    Materials & Scheduling Mgr
Jackie Maze, VP Sales & Mktg
Marilyn Maxim, PR Production Mgr

Keith Bagg Staffing Resources Inc.

700-85 Richmond St. West
Toronto, ON M5H 2C9
Tel 416-863-1800
Fax 416-350-9600
www.bagg.com
Line: Operates an employment agency.
NAICS: 561310
#Emp: 500-999 (Tor)
#TorLoc: 3
Own: Private Company
Key: Geoff Bagg, Pres
Norman Chu, Cont

Kellogg Canada Inc.

5350 Creekbank Rd.
Mississauga, ON L4W 5S1
Tel 905-290-5200
Fax 905-290-5399
www.kelloggs.ca
Line: Manufactures and retails cereals and breakfast foods and other related products.
NAICS: 311230
#Emp: 100-249 (Tor)
#TorLoc: 1
Own: Private Company
Par: Kellogg Co. (US)
Key: Francois Rouilly, Pres & CEO
Jose Tafner, VP Fin & Admin
Andrew Loucks, VP Mktg & Sales
Christine Lowry,
    VP Nutrition & Corp Affairs

Kelly Services (Canada) Ltd.

500-1 University Ave.
Toronto, ON M5J 2P1
Tel 416-368-1058
Fax 416-368-3987
www.kellyservices.com
Line: Provides talent management solutions for office, manufacturing, call centre, financial, technical and scientific environments.
NAICS: 561320 561310
#Emp: 5000-9999 (Tor)
#TorLoc: 11
Own: Public Company
Par: Kelly Services Inc. (US)
Key: Karin French, VP & GM

Kenaidan Contracting Ltd.

1275 Cardiff Blvd.
Mississauga, ON L5S 1R1
Tel 905-670-2660
Fax 905-670-9172
www.kenaidan.com
Line: Provides civil general contracts, including sewage and water treatment plants, tunnels, new buildings and restoration.
NAICS: 231320 231310
#Emp: 100-249 (Tor)
#TorLoc: 1
Own: Private Company
Key: Aidan Flatley, Pres & CEO
Deborah Fillippe, Dir of HR
Peter Sullivan, VP Fin & Admin
Brett Browning, Dir of IT & Treas
Greg Stack,
    VP Business Dev & Design Build

Kendle Early Stage

720 King St. West, 7th Fl.
Toronto, ON M5V 2T3
Tel 416-640-4004
Fax 416-963-9732
www.studies4u.com
AKA: Kendle Toronto Inc.; Studies 4 U
Line: Operates a full-service clinical research organization with specialization in Phase I and CNS drug development.
NAICS: 621510 541380
#Emp: 100-249 (Tor)
#TorLoc: 1
Own: Public Company
Par: Kendle International Inc. (US)
Key: Edward Sellers, VP, Early Stage
Germaine Gross, Head of New
    Business Dev & Business Ops
Erin Westbrook, Dir of HR
Mark Leung, Dir of Fin & Acctng

Kenna

1000-90 Burnhamthorpe Rd. West
Mississauga, ON L5B 3C3
Tel 905-277-2900
Fax 905-277-2299
www.kenna.ca
Line: Provides customer management consulting.
NAICS: 541611
#Emp: 75-99 (Tor)
#TorLoc: 1
Own: Private Company
Key: Glenn Chilton, Pres & CEO

Kennedy Lodge Nursing Home Inc.

A Div. of Central Park Lodges Ltd.
1400 Kennedy Rd.
Toronto, ON M1P 4V6
Tel 416-752-8282
Fax 416-752-0645
www.centralparklodges.com
NAICS: 623310
#Emp: 250-499 (Tor)
#TorLoc: 1
Own: Private Company
Key: Heather Reuber, Admr
Angela Rodriguez, Office Mgr

Ken Shaw Lexus Toyota

2336 St. Clair Ave. West
Toronto, ON M6N 1K8
Tel 416-766-1155
Fax 416-766-6112
www.kenshaw.com
Line: Sells new and used cars.
NAICS: 441110 441120
#Emp: 100-249 (Tor)
#TorLoc: 1
Own: Private Company
Key: Ken Shaw, Pres
Paul Shaw, VP & Gen Sales Mgr
Fariba Bina, Acctng Mgr

Kensington Health Centre

25 Brunswick Ave.
Toronto, ON M5S 2L9
Tel 416-963-9640
Fax 416-964-0234
www.tkhc.org
AKA: Kensington Eye Institute;
Kensington Cancer Screening Clinic
Line: Provides long term care.
NAICS: 621494
#Emp: 250-499 (Tor)
#TorLoc: 2
Own: Private Company
Key: William O'Neil, Exec Dir
Patricia Patraj, Payroll & Benefits Admr
Wendy Beckles, CFO
Jad Rabati, Business Coord

Kenworth Toronto Ltd.

500 Creditstone Rd.
Concord, ON L4K 3Z3
Tel 905-695-0740
Fax 905-695-0756
www.kwtoronto.com
AKA: Kenworth Truck Centre
Line: Operates a heavy truck dealership.
NAICS: 811111
#Emp: 75-99 (Tor)

#TorLoc: 3
Own: Private Company
Key: Vince Tarola, Pres & GM
Larry Burns, VP Parts & Service
David Patten, HR Mgr
Charles Chircop, Cont
Brian Delahunt, Parts Mgr
David Byers, IT Mgr
Gary Crudge, New Truck Sales Mgr

K-G Packaging Inc.

8001 Keele St.
P.O. Box 89
Vaughan, ON L4K 1Y8
Tel 905-669-9855
Fax 905-669-6184
www.kgpackaging.com
AKA: Spray-Pak Industries
Line: Formulates and packages quality aerosol products.
NAICS: 325999
#Emp: 250-499 (Tor)
#TorLoc: 3
Own: Private Company
Key: Lee Paige, Pres & CEO
Stan Capobianco, VP & Plant Mgr
David Porcellato, CFO
Bernie Weitzman, VP Sales & Mktg

Kia Canada Inc.

180 Foster Cres.
Mississauga, ON L5R 4J5
Tel 905-755-6250
Fax 905-755-6251
www.kia.ca
Line: Imports and distributes automobiles.
NAICS: 441110 441120
#Emp: 100-249 (Tor)
Own: Private Company
Par: Kia Motors Corporation (KOREA)
Key: Jay Chung, Pres & CEO

Kids and Company Ltd.

100-50 Minthorn Blvd.
Markham, ON L3T 7X8
Tel 905-771-1153
Fax 905-771-1173
www.kidsandcompany.ca
Line: Provides child care services.
NAICS: 624410
#Emp: 250-499 (Tor)
#TorLoc: 14
Own: Private Company
Key: Victoria Sopik, Pres
Sue Purser, VP Ops
Jennifer Nashmi, CFO
Robin Stockfish, Client Services Mgr

Kids Help Phone

300-439 University Ave.
Toronto, ON M5G 1Y8
Tel 416-586-5437
Fax 416-586-0651
www.kidshelpphone.ca
NAICS: 624190
#Emp: 100-249 (Tor)
#TorLoc: 1
Own: Not-for-profit
Key: Sharon Wood, Pres & CEO
Lisa Smecca, VP HR
Susan Morris, VP Fin & Admin
Ted Kaiser, VP IT
David Gray, VP Mktg, Commun & Strategic Dev

KIK Investment Holdings LP

101 MacIntosh Blvd.
Concord, ON L4K 4R5
Tel 905-660-0444
Fax 905-660-7333
www.kikcorp.com
AKA: KIK Operating Partnership; KIK International; KIK Canada; KIK Custom Products Inc.
Line: Manufactures private label household cleaning, laundry products, and national brand personal care products.
NAICS: 325610 325999
#Emp: 500-999 (Tor)
#TorLoc: 3
Own: Private Company
Par: KIK Holdco Company (CDA)
Key: Jeffery Nodland, Pres & CEO
Stratis Katsiris, Pres, Classic Division
Doug Hedges, VP HR
Ben Kaak, Exec VP Fin & CFO
Sam Porcasi, VP IT

Kimberly-Clark Inc.

1402-50 Burnhamthorpe Rd. West
Mississauga, ON L5B 3Y5
Tel 905-277-6500
Fax 905-277-6594
www.kimberly-clark.com
Line: Markets consumer paper products and pulp.
NAICS: 418220
#Emp: 100-249 (Tor)
#TorLoc: 1
Own: Private Company
Par: Kimberly-Clark Corp. (US)
Key: Henry Glowacki, VP Cdn Customer Dev
Gary Keider, VP & Country Mgr

Kinecor

1 Moyal Crt.
Concord, ON L4K 4R8
Tel 905-879-3600
Fax 905-879-9574
www.kinecor.com
Line: Distributes industrial component parts.
NAICS: 333990 417230
#Emp: 100-249 (Tor)
#TorLoc: 1
Own: Private Company
Key: Adrian Trotman, Pres
Russell Grant, VP Fin
Francois Arbique, VP IT

Kinectrics Inc.

800 Kipling Ave.
Toronto, ON M8Z 6C4
Tel 416-207-6000
Fax 416-207-6532
www.kinectrics.com
Line: Provides consulting and technical services to the energy industry.
NAICS: 541619
#Emp: 250-499 (Tor)
#TorLoc: 1
Own: Private Company
Par: Vision Capital (UK)
Key: David Harris, Pres & CEO
Larry Gibbons, VP HR
Nancy MacDonald Exel, CFO
Shahrokh Zangeneh, VP Mktg & Sales

Kingbridge Centre

12750 Jane St.
King City, ON L7B 1A3
Tel 905-833-3086
Fax 905-833-3075
www.kingbridgecentre.com
Line: Provides employee training and conference centre services.
NAICS: 531120
#Emp: 100-249 (Tor)
#TorLoc: 1
Own: Private Company
Key: Lisa Gilbert, GM
Shashi Krishan, Dir of HR

King Cole Ducks Ltd.

P.O. Box 185
Aurora, ON L4G 3H3
Tel 905-836-9461
Fax 905-836-4440
www.kingcoleducks.com
Line: Operates duck farm and processing plant.
NAICS: 311615
#Emp: 100-249 (Tor)
#TorLoc: 1

Own: Private Company
Key: Mike Moerat, Cont
Patricia Thompson,
   Mktg & Cdn Sales Mgr

King Nursing Home Ltd.

49 Stern St.
P.O. Box 43
Bolton, ON L7E 5T1
Tel 905-857-4117
Fax 905-857-5181
Line: Operates a nursing home.
NAICS: 623110
#Emp: 75-99 (Tor)
#TorLoc: 1
Own: Private Company
Key: Edwena Nolan, Dir of Care
Janice King, Admr

Kingsdown Owen & Co. Ltd.

51 Stone Ridge Rd.
Vaughan, ON L4H 0A5
Tel 905-265-9203
Fax 905-265-8685
www.kingsdown.com
Line: Manufactures mattresses.
NAICS: 337910
#Emp: 75-99 (Tor)
#TorLoc: 1
Own: Private Company
Key: Hugh Owen, Pres
Cindy Anisman, VP Ops

King's Pastry

5880 Falbourne St.
Mississauga, ON L5R 3L8
Tel 905-238-8328
Fax 905-238- 8628
www.kingpastry.com
Line: Operates a bakery.
NAICS: 311814
#Emp: 100-249 (Tor)
#TorLoc: 1
Own: Private Company
Key: Sam Ho, Owner
Cindia Li, GM

Kingstar Products Inc.

3350 Langstaff Rd.
Concord, ON L4K 4Z6
Tel 905-669-9335
Fax 905-669-6922
www.kingstar-inc.com
Line: Manufactures doors.
NAICS: 332321 321911
#Emp: 75-99 (Tor)
#TorLoc: 2
Own: Private Company
Par: Renin Corporation (CDA)
Key: Kevin Campbell, Pres

Kingsway Transport

1100 Haultain Crt.
Mississauga, ON L4W 2T1
Tel 905-624-4050
Fax 905-624-4047
www.kingswaytransport.com
Line: Provides freight transportation.
NAICS: 488519
#Emp: 100-249 (Tor)
Own: Private Company
Par: TransForce Inc. (CDA)
Key: Andrew Stratton, Terminal Mgr

King Valley Golf Club

15675 Dufferin St.
King City, ON L7B 1K5
Tel 905-841-9262
www.clublink.ca
Line: Operates a golf club.
NAICS: 713910
#Emp: 75-99 (Tor)
Own: Private Company
Par: ClubLink Corp. (CDA)
Key: Rob McDannold, Dir of Golf

Kinross Gold Corp.

25 York St., 17th Fl.
Toronto, ON M5J 2V5
Tel 416-365-5123
Fax 416-363-6622
www.kinross.com
NAICS: 212220
#Emp: 100-249 (Tor)
Own: Public Company
Key: Tye Burt, Pres & CEO
Brant E. Hinze, Exec VP & COO
Lisa Colnett, Sr VP, HR & Corp Services
Paul H. Barry, Exec VP & CFO
James Crossland, Sr VP External Relns
   & Corp Responsibility

Kintetsu World Express (Canada) Inc.

6405 Northam Dr.
Mississauga, ON L4V 1J2
Tel 905-677-8830
Fax 905-673-8689
www.kwe.ca
Line: Specializes in air and ocean freight forwarding, warehousing, distribution, customs clearance and total logistics.
NAICS: 488519
#Emp: 75-99 (Tor)
#TorLoc: 3
Own: Private Company
Par: Kintetsu World Express Inc. (JAPAN)
Key: Patrick Yung, VP Ops & Admin
Donato Atoni, VP Sales

The Kitchen Table Inc.

12 Queens Quay West
Toronto, ON M5J 2V7
Tel 416-778-4800
Fax 416-778-1172
www.thekitchentable.ca
AKA: Food Depot; Bacchanalia Foods
NAICS: 445110
#Emp: 100-249 (Tor)
#TorLoc: 7
Own: Private Company
Key: John Rumig, Pres
Tony Burt, Cont

K.J. Beamish Construction Co., Limited

3300 King Vaughan Tower Line
King City, ON L7B 1B2
Tel 905-833-4666
Fax 905-833-1400
www.kjbeamish.ca
Line: Provides road construction, asphalt paving, site servicing, recycling and snow removal services.
NAICS: 231310
#Emp: 250-499 (Tor)
#TorLoc: 5
Own: Private Company
Key: Robin Beamish, Pres
Linda Arthur, Chmn
Robert Graham, Sr VP & GM
Michael Henstock, VP Fin

Klick Communications Inc.

175 Bloor St. East
North Tower, 4th Fl.
Toronto, ON M4W 3R9
Tel 416-214-4977
Fax 416-214-4966
www.klick.com
Line: Operates an interactive communications agency.
NAICS: 541613
#Emp: 100-249 (Tor)
Own: Private Company
Key: Lee Segal, Pres & CEO
Aaron Goldstein, COO
Peter Cordy, Chmn & CFO

K-Line Maintenance & Construction Ltd.

12731 Hwy. 48
Stouffville, ON L4A 7X5
Tel 905-640-2002
Fax 905-640-8887
www.k-line.ca
AKA: K-Line Insulators Ltd.; K-Tek Electro-Services Ltd.
Line: Performs high voltage maintenance and construction.
NAICS: 335930 232510
#Emp: 100-249 (Tor)
#TorLoc: 2
Own: Private Company
Key: Allan G. Kellett, Pres
Mark K. Kellett, CEO
Jim Kellett, Sr VP Ops
Thom Ronaldson, VP Fin & Admin
Sashtri Sooknanan, IT
Charles Mossman, VP Sales & Mktg

KMH Cardiology & Diagnostic Centres

2075 Hadwen Rd.
Mississauga, ON L5K 2L3
Tel 905-855-1860
www.kmhlabs.com
AKA: KMH Labs
Line: Provides health services focused on reducing high incidence of death and disability by facilitating fast and accurate diagnosis.
NAICS: 621510
#Emp: 100-249 (Tor)
#TorLoc: 6
Own: Private Company
Key: Vijay Kanwar, Pres & CFO
Neena Kanwar, Pres & CEO

Knightsbridge Human Capital Management Inc.

2 Bloor St. East, 30th Fl.
Toronto, ON M4W 1A8
Tel 416-923-5555
Fax 416-923-6175
www.knightsbridge.ca
AKA: Knightsbridge GSW; Knightsbridge Executive Search; Knightsbridge Interim Management
Line: Provides human capital management services including business strategy and organizational development, recruitment and selection, leadership capability, career management and career transition.
NAICS: 541612
#Emp: 100-249 (Tor)
#TorLoc: 6
Own: Private Company

Key: David Shaw, Pres & CEO
Ralph Shedletsky, COO
David Thack, VP HR
Victoria Davies, CFO

Knights On Guard Protective Services

101-1048 Toy Ave.
Pickering, ON L1W 3P1
Tel 905-427-7863
Fax 905-420-9957
www.knightsonguard.com
AKA: KOG
Line: Provides security personnel.
NAICS: 561612
#Emp: 500-999 (Tor)
#TorLoc: 1
Own: Private Company
Par: GTA Parking Enforcement (CDA)
Key: Steve Dimkovski, Pres
Paul Smith, Staff Sgt

Knoll North America Corp.

1000 Arrow Rd.
Toronto, ON M9M 2Y7
Tel 416-741-5453
Fax 416-741-4297
www.knoll.com
Line: Manufactures high-end office furniture.
NAICS: 337213
#Emp: 1000-4999 (Tor)
#TorLoc: 3
Own: Public Company
Par: Knoll Inc. (US)
Key: Lee Dimascio, Plant Mgr
Alan Goffenberg, VP Ops
Ellen Blahitka, Mgr of HR
Greg Rapier, Reg Sales Mgr

Kobay Enstel Limited

6-125 Nashdene Rd.
Toronto, ON M1V 2W3
Tel 416-292-7088
Fax 416-292-9174
www.kobaytool.com
NAICS: 332118
#Emp: 100-249 (Tor)
#TorLoc: 1
Own: Private Company
Key: Gavin Galansky, Pres & GM
Brian Wisenberg, Principal
Shazila Bolden, HR Mgr
Suriayani Suriayani, Cont
Jennifer Johnson, Sales Account Mgr

Koch-Glitsch Canada LP

18 Dallas St.
Uxbridge, ON L9P 1C6
Tel 905-852-3381
Fax 905-852-7821
www.koch-glitsch.com
Line: Manufactures distillation equipment.
NAICS: 324110
#Emp: 100-249 (Tor)
#TorLoc: 2
Own: Private Company
Par: Koch-Glitsch (US)
Key: Craig Tranmer, Plant Mgr
Eva Cornel, HR Mgr
Tom Pattinson, Cont
Michael McGuire, Mng Dir

Kodak Canada Inc.

200-6 Monogram Pl.
Toronto, ON M9R 0A1
Tel 416-766-8233
Fax 416-761-4399
www.kodak.ca
Line: Provides sales and service for motion picture, digital imaging and document products.
NAICS: 414430
#Emp: 100-249 (Tor)
#TorLoc: 1
Own: Private Company
Par: Eastman Kodak Co. (US)
Key: Joe Morelly, Site Ops Mgr
Ken McMurtrie, Dir of HR
Kevin Innis, Dir of Fin
Wenda Berry, Purch Mgr
Frank Scodellaro, IT Mgr

KOEI Canada Inc.

500-257 Adelaide St. West
Toronto, ON M5H 1X9
Tel 416-599-5634
Fax 416-599-5631
www.koeicanada.ca
Line: Develops video games.
NAICS: 511210
#Emp: 100-249 (Tor)
#TorLoc: 1
Own: Private Company
Par: KOEI Co., Ltd. (JAPAN)
Key: Toshio Otake, VP

Kohl & Frisch Ltd.

7622 Keele St.
Concord, ON L4K 2R5
Tel 905-660-7622
Fax 905-660-0404
www.kohlandfrisch.com
Line: Distributes wholesale pharmaceuticals, over the counters, and beauty supplies.
NAICS: 414510
#Emp: 500-999 (Tor)
#TorLoc: 1
Own: Private Company
Key: Ron Frisch, Pres & CEO
Maria Castro, Exec VP
Harvey Foote, VP HR
Sharon Breuer, VP Fin
Scott Gillis, VP Purch & Manuf Relns

KONE Inc.

2-6696 Financial Dr.
Mississauga, ON L5N 7J6
Tel 416-252-6151
Fax 905-858-3925
www.kone.com
AKA: KONE Elevators & Escalators
Line: Manufactures, installs and services elevators, escalators and autowalks.
NAICS: 232550
#Emp: 250-499 (Tor)
#TorLoc: 2
Own: Public Company
Par: KONE Corporation (FIN)
Key: Kelly Leitch, Pres & CEO
Michael Tominac, VP HR
Ralf Heitz, VP Fin
Debbie Rhodes, Purch Mgr
Edna Morrison, IT Mgr
Sherif Fayek, Sr VP Sales

Konica Minolta Business Solutions (Canada) Ltd.

369 Britannia Rd. East
Mississauga, ON L4Z 2H5
Tel 905-890-6600
Fax 905-890-8997
www.konicaminolta.ca
Line: Retails and wholesales office equipment including copiers, faxes, computers, printers and office supplies.
NAICS: 417910 453210
#Emp: 250-499 (Tor)
#TorLoc: 4
Own: Private Company
Par: Minolta Corp. (US)

Key: Satoshi Tachioka, Pres
Leeann Hines, Dir of HR
George Tanouye, VP Fin & Admin
Barry Thomasen, Corp MIS Mgr
David Morrow, Nat'l VP Sales
Grant Hume, Exec VP

Korea Exchange Bank of Canada

1101-4950 Yonge St.
Madison Centre
Toronto, ON M2N 6K1
Tel 416-222-5200
Fax 416-222-5822
www.kebcanada.com
AKA: KEBOC
Line: Provides retail and commercial banking financial services.
NAICS: 522111
#Emp: 100-249 (Tor)
#TorLoc: 5
Own: Private Company
Par: Korea Exchange Bank (KOREA)
Key: Tae Jong Kang, Pres & CEO

Korex Canada

78 Titan Rd.
Toronto, ON M8Z 2J8
Tel 416-231-7800
Fax 416-231-9266
www.korex-ca.com
NAICS: 325610
#Emp: 100-249 (Tor)
#TorLoc: 1
Own: Private Company
Par: Pensler Capital Corp. (US)
Key: Sanford Pensler, Owner & Pres
Ed Johnson, GM

Korhani of Canada Inc.

7500 Keele St.
Concord, ON L4K 1Z9
Tel 905-660-0863
Fax 905-660-1433
www.korhani.com
Line: Manufactures and supplies rugs and carpets.
NAICS: 314110
#Emp: 100-249 (Tor)
#TorLoc: 1
Own: Private Company
Key: Hessam Korhani, Pres
Margarida Pettipas, HR Mgr

Koskie Minsky

900-20 Queen St. West
P.O. Box 52
Toronto, ON M5H 3R3
Tel 416-977-8353
Fax 416-977-3316
www.kmlaw.ca
Line: Operates a law firm.
NAICS: 541110
#Emp: 100-249 (Tor)
#TorLoc: 1
Own: Partnership
Key: Mark Zigler, Mng Partner
Mary DaRosa, Mgr of HR
Stephen Firth, Dir of Fin & Admin

KP Building Products

323 Main St. North
Acton, ON L7J 2M4
Tel 519-853-1231
Fax 519-853-4547
www.kpproducts.com
Line: Manufactures and distributes
vinyl siding.
NAICS: 416310
#Emp: 250-499 (Tor)
#TorLoc: 2
Own: Private Company
Par: Kaycan (CDA)
Key: Mike Phelan, Plant Mgr
Brenda MacDonald, HR Mgr

KPMG LLP

Bay Adelaide Centre
4600-333 Bay St.
Toronto, ON M5H 2S5
Tel 416-777-8500
Fax 416-777-8818
www.kpmg.ca
AKA: KPMG Canada; KPMG
Management Services LP
Line: Provides audit, tax, and advisory
services to business, public sector, and
not-for-profit organizations.
NAICS: 541212 541215
#Emp: 1000-4999 (Tor)
#TorLoc: 3
Own: Private Company
Key: Bill Thomas, CEO
Beth Wilson, Mng Partner, GTA
Mario Paron, Chief HR Officer
Mary Lou Maher, CFO
Rob Brouwer, Cdn Mng Partner,
   Clients & Markets

KPM Industries

3385 Harvester Rd.
Burlington, ON L7R 3Y5
Tel 905-639-2993
Fax 905-333-3730
www.kpmindustries.com
Line: Manufactures packaged
cement products and provides road
construction services.
NAICS: 232220
#Emp: 100-249 (Tor)
#TorLoc: 1
Own: Private Company
Key: Hank Hutter, Owner
Hugh MacPherson, Owner
Karen King, HR Mgr
Sheldon Vanderwoude,
   VP Fin & Admin

Kraft Canada Inc.

95 Moatfield Dr.
Toronto, ON M3B 3L6
Tel 416-441-5000
Fax 416-441-5807
www.kraftcanada.com
Line: Manufactures and distributes
packaged food products.
NAICS: 311515
#Emp: 500-999 (Tor)
#TorLoc: 4
Own: Private Company
Par: Kraft Foods Inc. (US)
Key: Dino Bianco, Pres

Kretschmar Inc.

71 Curlew Dr.
Toronto, ON M3A 2P8
Tel 416-441-1100
Fax 416-441-3386
www.kretschmar.com
Line: Processes and packs meat
products.
NAICS: 311611
#Emp: 100-249 (Tor)
#TorLoc: 1
Own: Private Company
Key: Gerhart Huber, Pres
Art George, Plant Mgr
Shameza Mohamed, HR Rep
Tatiana Kabanova, Cont
Kathalena Goffe, Purch Coord
Ellen Yau, Systems Mgr
Sean Moriarty, Dir of Retail Sales
Dave Brandow, Dir Sales & Mktg,
   Corp Food Service & Export

Kristofoam Industries Inc.

160 Planchet Rd.
Concord, ON L4K 2C7
Tel 905-669-6616
Fax 905-669-6235
www.kristofoam.com
Line: Manufactures foam packaging.
NAICS: 326140
#Emp: 75-99 (Tor)
#TorLoc: 3
Own: Private Company
Key: Fred Dalakis, Pres
Chris Mitsiou, Plant Mgr

Kristus Darzs Latvian Home

11290 Pine Valley Dr.
Woodbridge, ON L4L 1A6
Tel 905-832-3300
Fax 905-832-2029
www.kdlatvianhome.com
Line: Operates a long-term care facility.
NAICS: 623110
#Emp: 100-249 (Tor)
#TorLoc: 1
Own: Not-for-profit
Par: Kristus Darzs Foundation (CDA)
Key: Lauma Stikuts, Exec Dir
Jolanda Linde, Dir of Ops
Mary Anne Denney, Business Mgr

KRMC Barristers & Solicitors

700-25 Sheppard Ave. West
Toronto, ON M2N 6S6
Tel 416-225-8750
Fax 416-225-3910
www.krmc-law.com
AKA: Kronis Rotsztain Margles Cappel
Barristers & Solicitors
Line: Operates a law firm.
NAICS: 541110
#Emp: 100-249 (Tor)
#TorLoc: 1
Own: Private Company
Key: Allan Weiss, Partner

Kruger Inc.

3285 chemin Bedford
Montreal, PQ H3S 1G5
Tel 514-737-1131
Fax 514-737-1001
www.kruger.com
Line: Manufactures newsprint and
recycled newsprint, coated paper,
recycled paperboard, corrugated
containers, lumber and tissue products.
NAICS: 322122 322220
#Emp: 250-499 (Tor)
#TorLoc: 4
Own: Private Company
Par: Hicliff Corp. (CDA)
Key: Joseph Kruger II, Chmn & CEO
Donald Cayouette, COO

Kruger Products Limited

200-1900 Minnesota Crt.
Mississauga, ON L5N 5R5
Tel 905-812-6900
Fax 905-812-6908
www.krugerproducts.ca
Line: Manufactures and distributes
towel and tissue products for consumer
and commercial use.
NAICS: 322121 418220
#Emp: 100-249 (Tor)
#TorLoc: 1
Own: Private Company
Par: Kruger Inc. (CDA)
Key: Mario Gosselin, COO
Serge Reynaud, Corp VP HR & Legal

Kubik Inc.

1680 Mattawa Ave.
Mississauga, ON L4X 3A5
Tel 905-272-2818
Fax 905-272-2120
www.thinkubik.com
Line: Designs and manufactures
custom exhibits interiors, museums,
world fair pavillions and special
events.
NAICS: 337215 326198
#Emp: 100-249 (Tor)
#TorLoc: 1
Own: Private Company
Key: Sam Kohn, Pres & CEO
Elliot Kohn, COO & Principal
Larry Yunger, CFO

Kubota Canada Ltd.

5900 14th Ave.
Markham, ON L3S 4K4
Tel 905-294-7477
Fax 905-294-6651
www.kubota.ca
Line: Distributes tractors, heavy
construction equipment, engines and
power products.
NAICS: 417210
#Emp: 100-249 (Tor)
#TorLoc: 1
Own: Private Company
Par: Kubota Corporation (JAPAN)
Key: Ross Wallace, Pres
Robert G. Hickey, Exec Sr Mgr,
  Ops, Fin & Admin
Saeko Sasaki, Admr

Kubra

5050 Tomken Rd.
Mississauga, ON L4W 5B1
Tel 905-624-2220
Fax 905-624-2886
www.kubra.com
Line: Specializes in e-billing content
management within an outsourcing
environment.
NAICS: 514210
#Emp: 100-249 (Tor)
#TorLoc: 1
Own: Private Company
Key: Rick Watkin, Pres & CEO
Laura Iantorno, Dir of HR
Lida Sadrazodi, CFO
Andrew Leslie, CTO
Rick Huff, Sr VP Sales & Mktg

Kuehne & Nagel Ltd.

77 Foster Cres.
Mississauga, ON L5R 0K1
Tel 905-502-7776
Fax 905-502-0775
www.kuehne-nagel.com
AKA: KN Air; KN Sea; KN Logistics; KN
Lead Logistics; KN VIA; KN Customs
Line: Provides a complete range of
supply chain solutions and lead
logistics management services
including sea, land and air forwarding,
customs brokerage and distribution.
NAICS: 493110
#Emp: 500-999 (Tor)
#TorLoc: 5
Own: Public Company
Par: Kuehne & Nagel International AG
(SWITZ)
Key: John A. Levin, Pres & CEO
Ray Getson, Dir of HR
Stefan Kneubuhler, VP Fin
Stefan Viehmann, CIO

Kuwabara Payne McKenna Blumberg Architects

322 King St. West, 3rd Fl.
Toronto, ON M5V 1J2
Tel 416-977-5104
Fax 416-598-9840
www.kpmbarchitects.com
Line: Operates an architectural firm.
NAICS: 541310
#Emp: 75-99 (Tor)
#TorLoc: 1
Own: Private Company
Key: Bruce Kuwabara, Partner
Thomas Payne, Partner
Shirley Blumberg, Partner
Marianne McKenna, Partner
Amanda Sebris, Mktg Mgr

K.W. Mann Inc.

839 Yonge St.
Toronto, ON M4W 2H2
Tel 416-925-9592
Fax 416-923-9206
www.canadiantire.ca
AKA: Canadian Tire
Line: Retails general merchandise and
provides automotive services.
NAICS: 444130
#Emp: 250-499 (Tor)
#TorLoc: 1
Own: Private Company
Key: Nick Dimonti, GM
John Mackay, Office Mgr

L-3 Communications Electronic Systems

25 City View Dr.
Toronto, ON M9W 5A7
Tel 416-249-1231
Fax 416-246-2001
www.l-3com.com/es
Line: Designs and manufactures
advanced electronic systems for
military and civil, airborne, maritime
and land based applications.
NAICS: 334512
#Emp: 500-999 (Tor)
#TorLoc: 1
Own: Public Company
Par: L-3 Communications Corp. (US)
Key: Trevor Ratcliffe, Pres
Richard Ackerman, VP Sales & Mktg

La Senza Inc.

107-5401 Eglinton Ave. West
Toronto, ON M9C 5K6
Tel 416-622-2627
Fax 416-622-7439
www.lasenza.com
AKA: La Senza Girl; Silk and Satin
Line: Retails lingerie and girls'
fashionable apparel.
NAICS: 448120
#Emp: 1000-4999 (Tor)
Own: Private Company
Par: Limited Brands (US)
Key: Joanne Nemeroff, Pres
Vince Montemarano, Sr VP Sales & Ops
Anna Palestini, CFO
Martin Thibodeau, VP Management IS
Karine Abraham, Exec VP Mktg

Labatt Breweries of Canada

299-207 Queen's Quay West
Toronto, ON M5J 1A7
Tel 416-361-5050
Fax 416-361-5200
www.labatt.com
Line: Manufactures and sells beer.
NAICS: 312120
#Emp: 500-999 (Tor)
#TorLoc: 2
Own: Private Company
Par: InBev (BRA)
Key: Jeff Ryan, Dir of Corp Affairs

Labelad

400 Cochrane Dr.
Markham, ON L3R 8E3
Tel 905-475-3738
Fax 905-475-1466
www.labelad.com
Line: Manufactures pressure sensitive
labels and stickers.
NAICS: 322220
#Emp: 75-99 (Tor)
#TorLoc: 1
Own: Private Company
Par: Marnlen Management Ltd. (CDA)
Key: Owen Duckman, Pres
Joseph Campbell, VP Sales & GM
Lea Kozak, Dir of HR
Ziggy Krupa, VP Fin

Labour Ready, Inc.

200-265 Enfield Pl.
Mississauga, ON L5B 3Y7
Tel 905-206-9442
Fax 905-206-1410
www.laborready.com
Line: Provides employment services.
NAICS: 561310
#Emp: 75-99 (Tor)
Own: Private Company
Par: Labor Ready (US)
Key: Steve Cardy, Mng Dir

LaBrash Security Services Ltd.

403-55 Eglinton Ave. East
Toronto, ON M4P 1G8
Tel 416-487-4864
Fax 416-487-5702
www.labrashsecurity.ca
Line: Offers security services.
NAICS: 561621
#Emp: 100-249 (Tor)
#TorLoc: 1
Own: Private Company
Key: Mark LaBrash, GM

Lafarge Canada Inc.

201-7880 Keele St.
Concord, ON L4K 4G7
Tel 905-738-7070
Fax 905-738-9179
www.lafarge.com
AKA: Lafarge Construction Materials;
Pre-Con Inc.; Warren Paving;
Innocon Inc.
Line: Manufactures construction
materials.
NAICS: 327310
#Emp: 100-249 (Tor)
#TorLoc: 3
Own: Public Company
Par: Lafarge SA (FRA)
Key: Russell Hopper, VP Business Dev
Dale Hollingsworth, Dir of Mktg

Lakeridge Health Corp.

1-850 Champlain Ave.
Oshawa, ON L1J 8R2
Tel 905-576-8711
Fax 905-721-4865
www.lakeridgehealth.on.ca
AKA: Lakeridge Health Bowmanville;
Lakeridge Health Oshawa; Lakeridge
Health Port Perry; Lakeridge Health
Whitby
Line: Provides health and long-term
care through a network of four acute
care community hospital sites.
NAICS: 622310
#Emp: 1000-4999 (Tor)

#TorLoc: 4
Own: Not-for-profit
Key: Kevin Empey, CEO
John McKinley, Exec VP
Darrell Sewell, VP HR
Natalie Hovey, VP Fin & IT
Lisa Shiozaki,
   Exec VP & Chief Nursing Officer
Laura Visser,
   Sr Dir, Corp Planning & Commun

Lake Scugog Lumber Company Ltd.

11 Vanedward Dr.
Port Perry, ON L9L 1G3
Tel 905-985-7391
Fax 905-985-0674
www.scugoglumberrooftrusses
   ontario.com
Line: Operates a retail lumber yard
store and manufactures wooden roof
trusses.
NAICS: 321215
#Emp: 100-249 (Tor)
#TorLoc: 1
Own: Private Company
Key: Ian Griffen, Owner
Doug Metcalf, Mgr
Jackie Chinn, HR
Paul Griffen, Fin Mgr & Owner
David Lane, Purch Mgr

Lakeshore Lodge

3197 Lakeshore Blvd. West
Toronto, ON M8V 3X5
Tel 416-392-9400
Fax 416-392-9401
www.toronto.ca/ltc/lakeshore.htm
Line: Operates a general long-term
health care facility.
NAICS: 623310
#Emp: 100-249 (Tor)
Own: Private Company
Key: Marcia Minott, Mgr,
   Programs & Services
Robert Price, Admr

Lakeside Process Controls Ltd.

5250 Orbitor Dr.
Mississauga, ON L4W 5G7
Tel 905-629-9340
Fax 905-629-9360
www.lakesidecontrols.com
Line: Sells and distributes process
control equipment.
NAICS: 334512
#Emp: 100-249 (Tor)
#TorLoc: 1
Own: Private Company
Key: Greg Houston, Pres

Langen Packaging Inc.

6154 Kestrel Rd.
Mississauga, ON L5T 1Z2
Tel 905-670-7200
Fax 905-670-5291
www.langeninc.com
Line: Manufactures carton packaging machines.
NAICS: 333291
#Emp: 75-99 (Tor)
#TorLoc: 1
Own: Private Company
Par: Molins plc (UK)
Key: Paul Tichauer, Pres
Tina Biason, HR Mgr
Alan Makins, VP Fin
Peter Guttinger, VP Sales & Mktg

Larcan Inc.

228 Ambassador Dr.
Mississauga, ON L5T 2J2
Tel 905-564-9222
Fax 905-564-9244
www.larcan.com
Line: Manufactures television transmitters.
NAICS: 334220
#Emp: 75-99 (Tor)
#TorLoc: 1
Own: Private Company
Par: ATX Inc. (CDA)
Key: James Adamson, Sr VP
John Tremblay, VP Engineering
Susan Roger, VP Fin
Srini Murthy, Mgr of Tech Services

Lark Hospitality Inc.

21 Old Mill Rd.
Toronto, ON M8X 1G5
Tel 416-236-2641
Fax 416-236-2749
www.oldmilltoronto.com
AKA: The Old Mill Inn and Spa; The Old Mill Restaurant; The Old Mill Lark Hospitality Inc.
Line: Provides accommodations, hospitality and spa services including dining, banquet, wedding and meeting room facilities.
NAICS: 531120
#Emp: 250-499 (Tor)
#TorLoc: 1
Own: Private Company
Key: Michael Kalmar, Pres
Vincent Cotte, GM
Sandra Oak, HR Mgr
Blain Parsons, VP Fin
Tony Cooper, Dir of Purch

Larson-Juhl Ltd.

5830 Coopers Ave.
Mississauga, ON L4Z 1Y3
Tel 905-890-1234
Fax 905-890-2143
www.larsonjuhl.com
Line: Manufactures and distributes picture frame moulding and supplies.
NAICS: 414390
#Emp: 100-249 (Tor)
#TorLoc: 1
Own: Private Company
Par: Larson-Juhl Inc. (US)
Key: Janice Riches,
Exec Asst, Personnel

LaserNetworks

1-2823 Bristol Circ.
Oakville, ON L6H 6X5
Tel 905-847-5990
Fax 905-847-5991
www.lasernetworks.com
Line: Provides business-to-business sales, supplies and services for laser printers and copiers.
NAICS: 811210
#Emp: 100-249 (Tor)
#TorLoc: 2
Own: Private Company
Key: Chris Stoate, Pres
Chris Pigott, VP Fin & Admin
Tracy Haire, Purch Mgr
Quoc Nguyen, IT Mgr
Brian Stevenson, VP Sales

Lassonde Industries Inc.

95 Vulcan St.
Toronto, ON M9W 1L4
Tel 416-244-4224
Fax 416-244-9421
www.lassonde.com
Line: Manufactures and bottles fruit juice.
NAICS: 311420
#Emp: 100-249 (Tor)
#TorLoc: 7
Own: Private Company
Key: Jean Gattuso, Pres & CEO
Michel Tousignant, Corp Cont
Margherita Scioli, HR Mgr
Guy Blanchette, VP & CFO

The Last Minute Experts Inc.

75 Eglinton Ave. East
Toronto, ON M4P 3A4
Tel 416-449-5400
Fax 416-441-9754
www.lastminuteclub.com
AKA: The Last Minute Club
Line: Arranges wholesale and retail travel packages.
NAICS: 561510
#Emp: 75-99 (Tor)
#TorLoc: 1
Own: Private Company
Par: My Travel (CDA)
Key: John Kirk, VP
Michelle Loveridge, Dir of Call Centre

Latham Splash Canada

A Div. of Latham International
460 Finley Ave.
Ajax, ON L1S 2E3
Tel 905-428-6990
Fax 905-683-0708
www.lathamint.com
Line: Manufactures swimming pool components.
NAICS: 339920
#Emp: 500-999 (Tor)
#TorLoc: 2
Own: Private Company
Key: Mark Laven, Pres & CEO
Tim Golden, Pres,
Latham Splash Canada
Nancy Wong, HR Mgr
Stephen Keane, CFO

Laura Secord

800-2700 Matheson Blvd. East
East Tower
Mississauga, ON L4W 4V9
Tel 905-629-5059
Fax 905-629-0023
www.laurasecord.ca
Line: Retail sales of chocolate, ice cream and gifting.
NAICS: 311330 445299
#Emp: 500-999 (Tor)
#TorLoc: 40
Own: Private Company
Par: Gordon Brothers Group LLC (US)
Key: Raj Sharma, Chief Retail Officer
Samina Kitchlew, Dir of HR

Laurel Steel

A Div. of Harris Steel ULC
5400 Harvester Rd.
Burlington, ON L7R 3Y8
Tel 905-681-6811
Fax 905-634-7888
www.laurelsteel.com
Line: Manufactures cold finished steel
bars, cold drawn wires and welded
wire mesh.
NAICS: 331221
#Emp: 100-249 (Tor)
#TorLoc: 1
Own: Public Company
Par: Harris Steel Group (CAN)
Key: John Supple, GM
Mark Cook, VP Fin
David Tidey, VP Sales & Mktg

Laurentian Bank of Canada

Laurentian Bank Tower
1660-1981 McGill College Ave.
Montreal, PQ H3A 3K3
Tel 514-522-1846
www.laurentianbank.com
Line: Provides banking and financial
services.
NAICS: 522112
#Emp: 250-499 (Tor)
#TorLoc: 5
Own: Public Company
Key: Rejean Robitaille, Pres & CEO

The Law Society of Upper Canada

130 Queen St. West
Osgoode Hall
Toronto, ON M5H 2N6
Tel 416-947-3300
Fax 416-947-5967
www.lsuc.on.ca
Line: Governs legal services providers
in the public interest by ensuring that
the people of Ontario are served by
lawyers and paralegals who meet high
standards of learning, competence and
professional conduct.
NAICS: 813920 541190
#Emp: 250-499 (Tor)
#TorLoc: 1
Own: Association
Key: Malcolm Heins, CEO
Laura Cohen, Dir of HR
Wendy Tysall, CFO
John Matos, Dir of IS
Roy Thomas, Dir of Commun

Lawyers Professional Indemnity Co.

3101-250 Yonge St.
P.O. Box 3
Toronto, ON M5B 2L7
Tel 416-598-5800
Fax 416-599-8341
www.lawpro.ca
AKA: Law Pro
Line: Provides professional liability
insurance for lawyers and title
insurance.
NAICS: 524210
#Emp: 100-249 (Tor)
#TorLoc: 1
Own: Private Company
Par: Law Society of Upper Canada
(CDA)
Key: Kathleen Waters, Pres & CEO
Straughn Inman, Dir of HR
Iveri Boudiville, Cont
David Reid, Dir of IT
Mark Farrish, Dir of Sales & Mktg

Le Chateau Inc.

8300 Decarie Blvd.
Montreal, PQ H4P 2P5
Tel 514-738-7000
Fax 514-738-3670
www.le-chateau.com
Line: Retails moderately priced
apparel, accessories and footwear for
men, women and teens.
NAICS: 448140 448150
#Emp: 500-999 (Tor)
#TorLoc: 49
Own: Public Company
Key: Emilia Di Raddo, Pres
Jane Silverstone-Segal, CEO
Franco Rocchi, Sr VP Sales & Ops
Johnny Del Ciancio, VP Fin
Enza Allegro, VP Manuf

Le Méridien King Edward

37 King St. East
Toronto, ON M5C 1E9
Tel 416-863-9700
Fax 416-367-5515
www.starwoodhotels.com/lemeridien/
    index.html
AKA: King Edward Hotel
Line: Operates historic hotel.
NAICS: 721111 722110
#Emp: 250-499 (Tor)
#TorLoc: 1
Own: Private Company
Par: Le Méridien Hotels & Resorts
(CDA)
Key: Tim Reardon, GM

Le Parc Dining & Banquet Ltd.

20 North Rivermede Rd.
Concord, ON L4K 2H2
Tel 416-798-7215
Fax 416-798-7216
www.leparc.ca
Line: Provides restaurant and banquet
hall services.
NAICS: 722320
#Emp: 100-249 (Tor)
#TorLoc: 2
Own: Private Company
Key: John Verdone, Owner

Leader Plumbing & Heating Inc.

3-91 Haist Ave.
Woodbridge, ON L4L 5V5
Tel 905-264-1162
Fax 905-264-1163
Line: Provides plumbing and heating
services.
NAICS: 232520
#Emp: 75-99 (Tor)
#TorLoc: 1
Own: Private Company
Key: Glenn Bortolus, Pres

The Learning Enrichment Foundation

116 Industry St.
Toronto, ON M6M 4L8
Tel 416-769-0830
Fax 416-769-9912
www.lefca.org
Line: Provides community responsive
programs and services including
settlement and recruitment services
and childcare skills training.
NAICS: 611710
#Emp: 250-499 (Tor)
#TorLoc: 33
Own: Not-for-profit
Key: Ed Lamoureux, Pres
Peter Frampton, Exec Dir
Maria Gonzalez, Asst Exec Dir
Peter Marinelli, HR Mgr
Ben Lam, Cont
Shawn McArthur, IT Mgr
Darri Beaulieu, Dev Mgr

Lee Rocca Forming Ltd.

1-488 Morden Rd.
Oakville, ON L6K 3W4
Tel 905-842-2543
Fax 905-842-2593
Line: Provides concrete forming for
basements.
NAICS: 232210
#Emp: 100-249 (Tor)
#TorLoc: 1
Own: Private Company
Key: Lee Rocca, Pres
Phil Di Meo, Contract Mgr

Legal Aid Ontario

40 Dundas St. West
Toronto, ON M5G 2H1
Tel 416-979-1446
Fax 416-979-8669
www.legalaid.on.ca
Line: Promotes access to justice
throughout Ontario for low-income
individuals by providing legal aid
services.
NAICS: 541110
#Emp: 250-499 (Tor)
#TorLoc: 9
Own: Not-for-profit
Key: Robert Ward, Pres & CEO
Michelle Seguin, VP & CAO
Cory Philipzyk-Sambrano, Dir of HR
Colin Boal, Dir of Fin
Leslie Howard, CIO
Heather Robertson, VP Central
    Programming & Innovation

Leisureworld Caregiving Centre, Cheltenham

5935 Bathurst St.
Toronto, ON M2R 1Y8
Tel 416-223-4050
Fax 416-223-4159
www.leisureworld.ca
Line: Provides long-term care and
retirement residences.
NAICS: 623110
#Emp: 100-249 (Tor)
#TorLoc: 1
Own: Private Company
Par: Leisureworld Senior Care LP
(CDA)
Key: Andrea E. McLister, Dir of Admin
Laura Booth, Acting Dir of Care
Alex Tripkoeic, Maintenance Mgr
Kerri Judge,
    Resident Family Social Worker

Leisureworld Caregiving Centre Rockcliffe

3015 Lawrence Ave. East
Toronto, ON M1P 2V7
Tel 416-264-3201
Fax 416-264-2914
www.leisureworld.ca
Line: Operates long-term care facilities.
NAICS: 623110
#Emp: 100-249 (Tor)
#TorLoc: 1
Own: Private Company
Par: Leisureworld Senior Care LP
(CDA)
Key: Jane Smith, Admr

Leisureworld Caregiving Centre, Streetsville

1742 Bristol Rd. West
Streetsville, ON L5M 1X9
Tel 905-826-3045
Fax 905-826-9978
www.leisureworld.ca
Line: Provides personal care programs
and services.
NAICS: 623110
#Emp: 100-249 (Tor)
#TorLoc: 1
Own: Private Company
Par: Leisureworld Senior Care Corp.
(CDA)
Key: Susan Bock, Dir of Admin
David Cutler, CEO
Barb Ashenhurst, Dir of Care
Josephine DesLauriers, VP HR

Leisureworld Caregiving Centre - Tullamore

133 Kennedy Rd. South
Brampton, ON L6W 3G3
Tel 905-459-2324
Fax 905-459-2329
www.leisureworld.ca
Line: Operates long-term care facility
for seniors.
NAICS: 623310
#Emp: 100-249 (Tor)
#TorLoc: 1
Own: Public Company
Par: Leisureworld Senior Care LP
(CDA)
Key: Astrida Kalnins, Dir of Admin
Robert Campbell,
    Dir of Residential Care
Ellen Zammit, Office Mgr

Leisureworld Chelsey Park Mississauga

2250 Hurontario St.
Mississauga, ON L5B 1M8
Tel 905-270-0411
Fax 905-270-1749
www.leisureworld.ca
Line: Provides long-term care.
NAICS: 623310
#Emp: 250-499 (Tor)
#TorLoc: 1
Own: Private Company
Par: Leisureworld Senior Care LP
(CDA)
Key: Gary Butt, Admr
Rebecca Turner, Dir of Care

Leisureworld Senior Care LP

302 Town Centre Bvld.
Markham, ON L3R 0E8
Tel 905-477-4006
Fax 905-415-7623
www.leisureworld.ca
Line: Operates nursing homes.
NAICS: 623310 623110
#Emp: 1000-4999 (Tor)
#TorLoc: 18
Own: Private Company
Key: David Cutler, CEO
Paul Rushforth, COO
Josephine DesLauriers, VP HR
Martin Liddell, CFO
Daniel Neufeld, Dir of IT
Diane McKenzie, Dir of Mktg
Lisa Egan, VP Commun

Leland Industries Inc.

95 Commander Blvd.
Toronto, ON M1S 3S9
Tel 416-291-5308
Fax 416-291-0305
www.lelandindustries.com
Line: Manufactures bolts, nuts and
screws.
NAICS: 332720
#Emp: 100-249 (Tor)
#TorLoc: 1
Own: Private Company
Key: Byron Nelson, Pres & CEO
Zaklina Jovanovski, Dir of HR
Dennis Ebata, CFO
Michael Fraser, Purch Coord
Duane Nelson, IT Mgr

Lenbrook Industries Ltd.

633 Granite Crt.
Pickering, ON L1W 3K1
Tel 905-831-6333
Fax 905-831-6936
www.lenbrook.com
AKA: The Lenbrook Group
Line: Supplies high quality audio/video and home entertainment, commercial wireless, home security and automation, personal communications, multi-media and mobile office products.
NAICS: 417320
#Emp: 100-249 (Tor)
#TorLoc: 1
Own: Private Company
Par: The Lenbrook Group (CDA)
Key: Patrick McKeever, Pres, Lenbrook Canada
Gordon A. Simmonds, Pres & CEO, The Lenbrook Group
Joan M. Wideman, VP Ops
Heather White, Dir of HR
Dennis H. Hill, VP Fin
Terry McCrae, VP Corp Dev

Lenczner Slaght Royce Smith Griffin LLP

2600-130 Adelaide St. West
Toronto, ON M5H 3P5
Tel 416-865-9500
Fax 416-865-9010
www.litigate.com
Line: Operates law firm.
NAICS: 541110
#Emp: 75-99 (Tor)
#TorLoc: 1
Own: Private Company
Key: Ronald Slaght, Mng Partner
Gerry Tipold, Firm Admr
Barbara Russell, HR Mgr

Leo Burnett Company Ltd.

175 Bloor St. East,
North Tower, 12th Fl.
Toronto, ON M4W 3R9
Tel 416-925-5997
Fax 416-925-3343
www.leoburnett.ca
NAICS: 541810
#Emp: 100-249 (Tor)
#TorLoc: 1
Own: Private Company
Par: Leo Burnett Company, Inc. (US)
Key: Dom Caruso, Pres & COO
Judy John, CEO
Lisa March, VP Knowledge Management
Margaret Arnold, Sr VP HR

Leon's Furniture Ltd.

45 Gordon MacKay Rd.
P.O. Box 1100, Stn. B
Toronto, ON M9L 2R8
Tel 416-243-7880
Fax 416-243-7890
www.leons.ca
Line: Sells furniture, electronics and appliances.
NAICS: 442110
#Emp: 1000-4999 (Tor)
#TorLoc: 12
Own: Public Company
Key: Terry Leon, Pres & CEO
Shelley McKibbon, HR Mgr

Lerners LLP

2400-130 Adelaide St. West
Toronto, ON M5H 3P5
Tel 416-867-3076
Fax 416-867-9192
www.lerners.ca
Line: Provides legal services.
NAICS: 541110
#Emp: 100-249 (Tor)
#TorLoc: 1
Own: Private Company
Key: Brian Grant, Sr Partner
Michelle Medel, Exec Dir of Admin & HR

Levi Strauss & Co. (Canada) Inc.

200-1725 16th Ave.
Richmond Hill, ON L4B 4C6
Tel 905-763-4400
Fax 905-763-4401
www.levistrauss.com
Line: Markets and distributes apparel.
NAICS: 414110
#Emp: 100-249 (Tor)
#TorLoc: 2
Own: Private Company
Par: Levi Strauss & Co. International (US)
Key: Patti Johnson, Country Mgr
Lindsay Whillans, Dir of HR
Donna Keon, Dir of Fin & Ops
Eva Brennan, Dir of Sales

Levitt-Safety Ltd.

2872 Bristol Circ.
Oakville, ON L6H 5T5
Tel 905-829-3663
Fax 905-829-2919
www.levitt-safety.com
AKA: N.L. Technologies
Line: Distributes occupational health, environmental safety and fire protection products; manufactures NiMH-powered miners' lamps and custom NiMH battery chargers.
NAICS: 335110 335990
#Emp: 100-249 (Tor)
#TorLoc: 1
Own: Private Company
Key: Bruce Levitt, Pres & CEO
Fraser Gibson, VP Business Process Improvement
Sheelagh Bowers, Dir of HR, Safety & Quality Systems
Stephen Haley, Dir of Fin
Peter Gibhard, Procurement Mgr
Keith Holt, MIS Mgr
Alan Noble, Mktg Mgr
Tim Dillon, VP Support Services

Levolor Kirsch Window Fashions

586 Argus Rd.
Oakville, ON L6J 3J3
Tel 1-800-850-4555
www.newellco.com
Line: Manufactures blinds.
NAICS: 337920
#Emp: 100-249 (Tor)
#TorLoc: 1
Own: Private Company
Par: Newell Rubbermaid Co. (US)
Key: Jamal Hamid, Plant Mgr
Maureen Persad, HR Mgr
Larry Scarlett, VP Sales & Mktg

LexisNexis Canada Inc.

700-123 Commerce Valley Dr. East
Markham, ON L3T 7W8
Tel 905-479-2665
Fax 905-479-2826
www.lexisnexis.ca
Line: Publishes on-line and print legal reference materials.
NAICS: 511140 511190
#Emp: 250-499 (Tor)
#TorLoc: 2
Own: Public Company
Par: Reed Elsevier plc (UK)
Key: Patrick Collins, Pres & CEO
Sharon Henley, HR Dir
Dev Mahendran, VP Fin & Admin
Alan Dingle, VP Mktg & Business Dev

Lexmark Canada Inc.

50 Leek Cres.
Richmond Hill, ON L4B 4J3
Tel 905-763-0560
Fax 905-763-0290
www.lexmark.com
Line: Manufactures network printers,
advanced inkjet printers, and supplies.
NAICS: 334110
#Emp: 100-249 (Tor)
#TorLoc: 1
Own: Private Company
Par: Lexmark International, Inc. (US)
Key: Tim Emens, Pres
Matthew Barnicoat,
    Dir of Global Service
Catherine Fulton, HR Mgr
Peter Siksna, Dir of Enterprise
    Sales-Key Accounts
Todd Greenwood,
    Dir of Channel Sales & Mktg

LG Electronics Canada Inc.

550 Matheson Blvd. East
Mississauga, ON L4Z 4G3
Tel 905-568-6800
Fax 905-507-9149
www.lg.com
NAICS: 414220 417320
#Emp: 250-499 (Tor)
#TorLoc: 1
Own: Private Company
Par: LG Electronics Inc. (KOREA)
Key: Eric Agius, Pres & CEO

Liberté Natural Foods Inc.

2-91 Delta Park Blvd.
Brampton, ON L6T 5E7
Tel 905-458-8696
Fax 905-458-5643
www.libertenaturalfoods.com
Line: Provides cultured dairy products
including natural yogurts, cream
cheese spreads and sour creams.
NAICS: 311511 413120
#Emp: 100-249 (Tor)
#TorLoc: 2
Own: Private Company
Key: Mustafa Koppa, Cont

Liberty International Underwriters Canada

1000-181 Bay St.
Toronto, ON M5J 2T3
Tel 416-365-7587
Fax 416-307-4372
www.libertyiu.com
Line: Provides commercial, property
and casualty insurance.
NAICS: 524121
#Emp: 100-249 (Tor)
#TorLoc: 1
Own: Private Company
Par: Liberty Mutual (US)
Key: Mike Molony, Pres
Janice Cowburn, Office Mgr
Jan Boase, VP HR
Sunil Motwani, CFO
Richard Koo, Asst VP IT

Libman Manufacturing Ltd.

250 Canarctic Dr.
Toronto, ON M3J 2P4
Tel 416-661-2661
Fax 416-667-8830
AKA: Libman & Company Ltd.
Line: Manufactures jewellery.
NAICS: 339910
#Emp: 75-99 (Tor)
#TorLoc: 1
Own: Private Company
Key: Mark Libman, Pres
Morris Robinson, VP

Lick's Concepts Inc.

200-2034 Queen St. East
Toronto, ON M4L 1J4
Tel 416-362-5425
Fax 416-690-0504
www.lickshomeburgers.com
AKA: Lick's
Line: Retails fast food, hamburgers and
ice cream.
NAICS: 722210
#Emp: 500-999 (Tor)
#TorLoc: 24
Own: Private Company
Key: Denise Meehan, Pres
Frank Peruzzi, Franchise Mgr
Lillian Wilson, Product Mgr
Brenda Perry, Mktg Dir

Lido Wall Systems Inc.

582 Bowes Rd.
Concord, ON L4K 1K2
Tel 905-738-1444
Fax 905-738-1292
www.lidowallsystems.com
Line: Specializes in exterior insulated
finishing systems.
NAICS: 232310 232410
#Emp: 100-249 (Tor)
#TorLoc: 1
Own: Private Company
Key: Victor Nonis, Pres
Oscar Chiarotto, VP
Carmen Calone, Office Mgr
Albino Botter, Treas

Lifecare Operations

A Div. of Royalcrest Lifecare Group Inc.
420 The East Mall
Toronto, ON M9B 3Z9
Tel 416-621-8000
Fax 416-621-8003
www.ourhomeyourhomecanada.ca
AKA: Highbourne Lifecare Center
Line: Operates long-term care facility.
NAICS: 623110
#Emp: 250-499 (Tor)
#TorLoc: 11
Own: Private Company
Key: Evelyn MacDonald, Admr
Alicja Bidzinska, Dir of Care
Nadine Roomes, Business Coord
Donnica Williams, Environmental Mgr

Lifemark Health

202-1 Eglinton Ave. East
Toronto, ON M4P 3A1
Tel 416-485-1344
Fax 416-485-1692
www.lifemark.ca
AKA: Lifemark Health
Management Inc.
Line: Provides medical, rehabilitative,
education and wellness services.
NAICS: 623999 624310
#Emp: 250-499 (Tor)
#TorLoc: 12
Own: Private Company
Key: Peter Stymiest, VP Ops
Angie Zannella,
    Payroll & Personnel Admr

Lifestyle Sunrooms Inc.

239 Station St.
Ajax, ON L1S 1S3
Tel 905-686-2445
Fax 905-686-4798
www.lifestylesunrooms.com
Line: Manufactures and installs
sunrooms, decks, windows, doors,
siding, and provides roofing services.
NAICS: 232330
#Emp: 100-249 (Tor)
#TorLoc: 1
Own: Private Company
Key: Bill Carroll, Owner
Rob West, Accounts Payable
Keith Carroll, Sales Mgr
Jane Russell, Mktg Mgr

Liftow Ltd.

3150 American Dr.
Mississauga, ON L4V 1B4
Tel 905-677-3270
Fax 905-677-1429
www.liftow.com
NAICS: 417230
#Emp: 250-499 (Tor)
#TorLoc: 6
Own: Private Company
Key: Roger Sutton, Pres & CEO
Blane Bowen, Chair
Sheri Brimley, GM
Tracy Robinson, HR Mgr
Matt Bender, GM IS

Lincoln Electric Company of Canada

179 Wicksteed Ave.
Toronto, ON M4G 2B9
Tel 416-421-2600
Fax 416-421-2930
www.lincolnelectric.ca
Line: Manufactures mild steel, low
hydrogen, non-ferrous, stainless and
cast iron welding electrodes and
submerged arc and MIG wires for semi-
automatic and automatic welding.
NAICS: 335990 335930
#Emp: 250-499 (Tor)
#TorLoc: 1
Own: Private Company
Par: The Lincoln Electric Co. (US)
Key: Joseph G. Doria, Pres & CEO
Robert Armour, District Mgr, Ontario
Jason Brisebois, HR Leader, Canada
Jason Sutcliffe, Dir of Fin
Dale Malcom, VP Sales

Linde Canada Ltd.

5860 Chedworth Way
Mississauga, ON L5R 0A2
Tel 905-501-1700
Fax 905-501-1717
www.lindecanada.com
Line: Manufactures and distributes
liquids and compressed gases and
supplies a range of welding equipment
and accessories.
NAICS: 325120
#Emp: 250-499 (Tor)
Own: Private Company
Par: The Linde Group AG (GER)
Key: Doug Bonner, Tech & Ops Dir
Bruce Hart, Head of Fin
Dan Hiltz, IT Mgr
Meghan Gibson, Mktg Services Mgr

The Linkage Group Inc.

200-30 Centurian Dr.
Markham, ON L3R 8B8
Tel 905-415-2300
Fax 905-415-2299
www.linkage-group.com
Line: Offers national merchandising
and retail intelligence services.
NAICS: 541910
#Emp: 100-249 (Tor)
#TorLoc: 1
Own: Private Company
Key: Bob Proctor, Pres
Jennifer Richardson, Sr Ops Mgr
Donna D'Ippolito,
    Dir of Merchandising

Link-Line Group of Companies

E-1 Royal Gate Blvd.
Vaughan, ON L4L 8Z7
Tel 905-265-7400
Fax 905-265-7410
www.linkline.ca
Line: Installs pipes for natural gas
utility.
NAICS: 231330
#Emp: 250-499 (Tor)
#TorLoc: 4
Own: Private Company
Key: Rick Delaney, Pres
David Civiero, CEO
Glen Hansen, VP Ops
Meier Miller, CFO

Linsey Foods Ltd.

4248 14th Ave.
Markham, ON L3R 0J3
Tel 905-940-3850
Fax 905-940-3032
www.linsey.com
Line: Packages and markets salad,
dessert and veggie food kits.
NAICS: 413190
#Emp: 75-99 (Tor)
#TorLoc: 1
Own: Private Company
Key: Doug Woolsey, Pres

Liquid Cargo Lines Ltd.

452 Southdown Rd.
Mississauga, ON L5J 2Y4
Tel 905-823-9700
Fax 905-823-7180
www.liquidcargo.ca
Line: Transports liquid bulk
commodities.
NAICS: 484221
#Emp: 75-99 (Tor)
#TorLoc: 1
Own: Private Company

Par: Beamish Construction Limited Co.
(CDA)
Key: Roy Scott, GM
Lilly Fernandes, HR Mgr

Liquor Control Board of Ontario

55 Lake Shore Blvd. East
Toronto, ON M5E 1A4
Tel 416-365-5900
Fax 416-864-2596
www.lcbo.com
AKA: LCBO; Vintages
Line: Retails beverage alcohol.
NAICS: 445310
#Emp: 1000-4999 (Tor)
#TorLoc: 220
Own: Provincial Crown Corp.
Par: Government of Ontario
Key: Bob Peter, Pres & CEO
Philip Olsson, Chair
Murray Kane, Sr VP HR
Alex Browning, Sr VP Fin
Hugh Kelly, Sr VP IT
Nancy Cardinal, Sr VP Mktg &
    Consumer Insights
Bill Kennedy,
    Exec Dir of Corp Commun

Lisi Mechanical Contractors Ltd.

160 Disco Rd.
Toronto, ON M9W 1M4
Tel 416-674-8333
Fax 416-674-5399
www.lisimechanical.com
Line: Provides mechanical contracting
services.
NAICS: 232250
#Emp: 100-249 (Tor)
#TorLoc: 1
Own: Private Company
Key: Bruno Lisi, Pres
Karen Jannetta, Cont & HR
Robert Lisi, VP & Secy-Treas

Litens Automotive Partnership

730 Rowntree Dairy Rd.
Woodbridge, ON L4L 5T7
Tel 905-856-0200
Fax 905-850-3786
www.litens.com
Line: Designs, develops and
manufactures automotive parts.
NAICS: 336350 333619
#Emp: 500-999 (Tor)
#TorLoc: 2
Own: Private Company
Key: Paul Robinson, Pres

Lite Products Inc.

7-6615 Ordan Dr.
Mississauga, ON L5T 1X2
Tel 905-670-7230
Fax 905-670-4990
www.supplierpipeline.com
Line: Operates an aluminum
fabrication plant specializing in
ladders.
NAICS: 332999
#Emp: 75-99 (Tor)
#TorLoc: 1
Own: Private Company
Key: Dan Evans, Pres
Dave Boulanger, CEO

Living Realty Inc.

300-7030 Woodbine Ave.
Markham, ON L3R 6G2
Tel 905-474-0590
Fax 905-474-9856
www.livingrealty.com
Line: Offers real estate agents and
broker services.
NAICS: 531210
#Emp: 500-999 (Tor)
#TorLoc: 6
Own: Private Company
Par: Living Group of Companies Inc.
(CDA)
Key: Eric Chan, Pres
Stephen Wong, Broker of Record
Emily Toong, Admin Mgr
Selwyn Pais, Acctng Mgr

Livingston International Inc.

400-405 The West Mall
Toronto, ON M9C 5K7
Tel 416-626-2828
Fax 416-622-3890
www.livingstonintl.com
AKA: Mendelssohn Trade Shows;
Adminserv; Osowski Company
Line: Operates customs brokerage and
trade services company engaged in:
import, export and customs clearance
services; professional, electronic and
software solutions; trade advisory
management in regulatory compliance,
valuation, and taxation; and
representation before trade tribunals.
NAICS: 488519
#Emp: 500-999 (Tor)
#TorLoc: 4
Own: Public Company
Key: Peter Luit, Pres & CEO
Mara Volpini, VP HR
Chris McMullen, CFO
Philip MacDonald, VP IT
Roy Coburn, VP Sales & Mktg
Dawneen MacKenzie, VP Pub Affairs

LKM

A Div. of SNC Lavalin Inc.
235 Lesmill Rd.
Toronto, ON M3B 2V1
Tel 416-445-8255
Fax 416-445-7885
www.snclavalin.com/slet
Line: Provides mechanical and
electrical engineering consulting
services.
NAICS: 541330
#Emp: 100-249 (Tor)
#TorLoc: 1
Own: Private Company
Key: Lisa Pinkus, Exec Dir

Loblaw Companies Limited

1 Pres's Choice Circ.
Brampton, ON L6Y 5S5
Tel 905-459-2500
Fax 905-861-2357
www.loblaw.ca
AKA: Fortinos Supermarkets; Zehrs;
No Frills; Loblaws; Cash & Carry;
Valumart; Your Independent Grocer;
Freshmart; President's Choice
Line: Provides food distribution and
general merchandise products and
services.
NAICS: 445110
#Emp: 10000+ (Tor)
Own: Public Company
Key: Allan L. Leighton,
    Pres & Deputy Chmn
Galen G. Weston, Exec Chmn & CEO
Judy A. McCrie, Exec VP HR
Sarah R. Davis, CFO
Peter K. McMahon,
    Exec VP Supply Chain & IT
Craig R. Hutchinson, Sr VP Mktg

Logitech Remote Controls

100-2355 Skymark Ave.
Mississauga, ON L4W 4Y6
Tel 905-273-4571
Fax 905-273-9789
www.logitech.com
AKA: Logitech Canada
NAICS: 334110
#Emp: 100-249 (Tor)
#TorLoc: 2
Own: Public Company
Par: Logitech (SWITZ)
Key: Gerald Quindlen, Pres & CEO
L. Joseph Sullivan,
    Sr VP Worldwide Ops
Martha Tuma, VP HR

The Logit Group Inc.

101-5353 Dundas St. West
Toronto, ON M9B 6H8
Tel 416-236-4770
Fax 416-236-4771
www.logitgroup.com
NAICS: 541611
#Emp: 250-499 (Tor)
#TorLoc: 1
Own: Private Company
Key: Sam Pisani, Pres
Anthony Molinaro, CEO
Claudio Ursitti, VP Fin
John Wulff, VP Sales & Mktg

Lombard Canada Ltd.

105 Adelaide St. West
Toronto, ON M5H 1P9
Tel 416-350-4400
Fax 416-350-4412
www.lombard.ca
AKA: Lombard Insurance Co.; Zenith
Insurance Co.
Line: Provides property and casualty
insurance management services.
NAICS: 524121
#Emp: 250-499 (Tor)
#TorLoc: 1
Own: Private Company
Par: Northbridge Financial Corporation
(CDA)
Key: Fabian Richenberger, Pres
Mark J. Ram, CEO
Jane Garder-Robinson, Exec VP
William Dunlop,
    Sr VP & Chief Gen Counsel
Steve McManus, CFO

London Life Insurance Co.

255 Dufferin Ave.
London, ON N6A 4K1
Tel 519-432-5281
Fax 519-435-4445
www.londonlife.com
Line: Offers personal and group life and
health insurance and pensions, as well
as other financial services.
NAICS: 524112 524111
#Emp: 250-499 (Tor)
Own: Public Company
Par: Great West Life Assurance Co.
(CDA)
Key: Allen Loney, Pres & CEO

Longford International Ltd.

41 Lamont Ave.
Toronto, ON M1S 1A8
Tel 416-298-6622
Fax 416-298-6627
www.longfordint.com
Line: Manufactures paper handling
equipment.
NAICS: 333310
#Emp: 75-99 (Tor)
#TorLoc: 1
Own: Private Company
Key: Edward Paterson, Pres & CEO
Marilyn Goodman, Office Mgr
Ralph A. Viegas, VP Fin
Peter Yap, Purch Mgr
Steve Watkins, Sales Mgr

Long & McQuade Musical Instruments

722 Rosebank Rd.
Pickering, ON L1W 4B2
Tel 905-837-9785
Fax 905-837-9786
www.long-mcquade.com
Line: Retails musical instruments.
NAICS: 451140
#Emp: 250-499 (Tor)
#TorLoc: 9
Own: Private Company
Key: Steven Long, Pres
Fred Theriault, Sr VP
Mike Klue, VP
Jeff Long, VP Mktg & PR

Longo Brothers Fruit Markets Inc.

3767 Nashua Dr.
Mississauga, ON L4V 1R3
Tel 905-673-3099
Fax 905-673-1065
www.longos.com
Line: Operates grocery stores.
NAICS: 413150 445110
#Emp: 5000-9999 (Tor)
#TorLoc: 20
Own: Private Company
Key: Anthony Longo, Pres & CEO
Dave Mastroieni, VP Ops
Liz Volk, Dir of HR
Mary Parkes, CFO

Longview Solutions Inc.

200-65 Allstate Pkwy.
Markham, ON L3R 9X1
Tel 905-940-1510
Fax 905-940-8310
www.longview.com
Line: Publishes integrated application
suite software that supports financial
activities.
NAICS: 511210
#Emp: 100-249 (Tor)
#TorLoc: 1
Own: Private Company
Par: Exact (NETH)
Key: John Power, Pres & CEO
Gerard Chiason, Exec VP
Brad Smith, VP Support Services
Jennifer Bentley,
    VP Mktg & Business Dev

Lotek Wireless Inc.

115 Pony Dr.
Newmarket, ON L3Y 7B5
Tel 905-836-6680
Fax 905-836-6455
www.lotek.com
Line: Manufactures and designs radio
telemetry and electronic equipment.
NAICS: 334220
#Emp: 75-99 (Tor)
#TorLoc: 1
Own: Private Company
Key: Jim Lotimer, Pres

Lovat Inc.

A Div. of Caterpillar Inc.
441 Carlingview Dr.
Toronto, ON M9W 5G7
Tel 416-675-3293
Fax 416-675-6702
www.lovat.com
Line: Manufactures tunnel boring
machines and associated equipment.
NAICS: 333120
#Emp: 250-499 (Tor)
#TorLoc: 1
Own: Private Company
Key: Richard Cooper, Pres
Ciro Baldassarra, Ops Mgr
Elda Almeida-Teixeira, HR Mgr
Brian Knaley, VP Fin
Craig Bournes, Sales Mgr

Lowe's Canada

200-5160 Yonge St.
P.O. Box 25
Toronto, ON M2N 6L9
Tel 416-730-7300
www.lowes.ca
Line: Offers home improvement
products and services.
NAICS: 444110
#Emp: 1000-4999 (Tor)
Own: Public Company
Key: Alan Huggins, Pres
Peter Darcy, Reg Dir of Ops
Wanda Walkden, VP HR

Loxcreen Canada Ltd.

5720 Ambler Dr.
Mississauga, ON L4W 2B1
Tel 905-625-3210
Fax 905-625-4249
www.loxcreenflooring.com
AKA: Drummond Metal Products;
Bengard Manufacturing; Dura-Trim
Products
Line: Manufactures metal, wood and
aluminum mouldings and trim.
NAICS: 332999
#Emp: 75-99 (Tor)
#TorLoc: 1
Own: Private Company
Par: The Loxcreen Company Inc. (US)
Key: Joe Comitale, Pres

Loyalty One Inc.

600-438 University Ave.
Toronto, ON M5G 2L1
Tel 416-228-6500
Fax 416-733-1993
www.loyalty.com
AKA: Air Miles Reward Program
Line: Provides coalition loyalty
marketing and customer relationship
management services.
NAICS: 541611
#Emp: 1000-4999 (Tor)
#TorLoc: 2
Own: Public Company
Par: Alliance Data Systems Inc. (US)
Key: Bryan Pearson, Pres
Dave Burns, COO
Sofia Theodorou-Lock, VP HR
Elizabeth Morgan, VP Fin
Bruce Bergetz, Sr VP & CIO
Neil Everett, Sr VP & Corp Mktg Officer

Luminex Molecular Diagnostics Inc.

900-439 University Ave.
Toronto, ON M5G 1Y8
Tel 416-593-4323
Fax 416-593-1066
www.luminexcorp.com
Line: Operates a diagnostic company.
NAICS: 541710
#Emp: 75-99 (Tor)
#TorLoc: 1
Own: Public Company
Par: Luminex Corporation (US)
Key: Nancy Krunic, VP

Lundin Mining Corp.

1500-150 King St. West
P.O. Box 38
Toronto, ON M5H 1J9
Tel 416-342-5560
Fax 416-348-0303
www.lundinmining.com
NAICS: 212233 212299
#Emp: 1000-4999 (Tor)
Own: Public Company
Key: Phil Wright, Pres & CEO
Joao Carrelo, Exec VP Ops
Josephine McCabe, VP HR
Marie Inkster, CFO
Mikael Schauman, VP Maketing

Lundstrom

255 Wicksteed Ave.
Toronto, ON M4H 1G8
Tel 416-696-2818
Fax 416-423-0921
www.lundstrom.ca
AKA: Eleventh Floor Apparel Ltd.
Line: Manufactures women's clothing.
NAICS: 315233
#Emp: 100-249 (Tor)
#TorLoc: 1
Own: Private Company
Par: Elgner Group Investments Ltd. (CDA)
Key: Andreas Schoppel, Plant Mgr
Shyamala Siva, HR & Acctng Mgr
Vijay Kumar, Cont
Anna Aivalis, Customer Service Mgr

Luxell Technologies Inc.

2145 Meadowpine Blvd.
Mississauga, ON L5N 6R8
Tel 905-363-0325
Fax 905-363-0336
www.luxell.com
Line: Researches and develops flat panel display enhancing technologies.
NAICS: 334110

#Emp: 75-99 (Tor)
#TorLoc: 1
Own: Public Company
Key: Jean-Louis Lamor, CEO
Rick Pepperall,
    Sr VP Engineering & Production
Gerard M. Hartley, VP Business Dev
Simon Dann, Dir of Commun

Luxottica Retail

101-2000 Argentia Rd., Plaza 2
Mississauga, ON L5N 1V8
Tel 905-858-0008
Fax 905-858-9774
www.lenscrafters.com
AKA: LensCrafters; Sunglass Hut; Sears Optical; Pearle Vision; Precision Optical; iLORi
Line: Manufactures and sells eyeglasses.
NAICS: 446130
#Emp: 500-999 (Tor)
#TorLoc: 175
Own: Private Company
Par: LensCrafters (US)
Key: Dominic Guglielmi,
    Reg VP, Lenscrafters
Wayne Hobbs, Reg VP, Sunglass Hut
Susan Napier, Reg Dir of Ops
Rosemary Smedley,
    Dir of Associate Relns
Marco Evangelista,
    Reg VP, Pearle Vision

L.V. Lomas Ltd.

99 Summerlea Rd.
Brampton, ON L6T 4V2
Tel 905-458-1555
Fax 905-458-0722
www.lvlomas.com
Line: Distributes and sells industrial and fine chemicals, food oils and filtration equipment.
NAICS: 418410 417230
#Emp: 100-249 (Tor)
#TorLoc: 1
Own: Private Company
Key: Kevin Russell, Pres
Rand Lomas, CEO
Spence Morris, Sr VP Ops
    & Third Party Logistics
Sheila Kendall, HR Mgr
Ross Clark, CFO
Mike Foxwell, Sr VP Sales & Mktg,
    Industrial Chemicals
Devin Chan, Sr VP Sales & Mktg, Fine
    Chemicals & Food

Lyons Auto Body Ltd.

1020 Burnhamthorpe Rd. West
Mississauga, ON L5C 2S4
Tel 905-277-1456
Fax 905-270-4692
www.lyonsautobody.com
Line: Specializes in auto body repair and towing services.
NAICS: 488410
#Emp: 75-99 (Tor)
#TorLoc: 1
Own: Private Company
Key: Jack Lyons, Pres
Valerie Lyons-Sala, Office Mgr

Lyreco (Canada) Inc.

200-7303 Warden Ave.
Unionville, ON L3R 5Y6
Tel 905-968-1325
Fax 905-968-1320
www.lyreco.ca
Line: Sells office products and furniture on a business-to-business basis.
NAICS: 417910 811420 337214
#Emp: 100-249 (Tor)
#TorLoc: 1
Own: Private Company
Par: Lyreco Group (FRA)
Key: Brent Milburn,
    Mng Dir & VP Sales
Chris Traikos, Dir of Logistics
Kristi Barnes, VP HR
Humberta Taylor, Dir of Fin
Predrag Golich, Dir of MIS
Marc Chochoy, Dir of Mktg
Darren Delany, Dir of Quality

M·A·C Cosmetics

A Div. of Estee Lauder Cosmetics Ltd.
100 Alden Rd.
Markham, ON L3R 4C1
Tel 905-470-7877
Fax 905-470-7659
www.maccosmetics.com
Line: Manufactures and retails cosmetics.
NAICS: 446120 325620
#Emp: 500-999 (Tor)
#TorLoc: 23
Own: Public Company
Par: Estee Lauder Companies Inc. (US)
Key: John Demsey, Pres
Tracy Bolin, VP Sales

MacDonald Dettwiler & Associates Inc.

9445 Airport Rd.
Brampton, ON L6S 4J3
Tel 905-790-2800
Fax 905-790-4400
www.mdacorporation.com
AKA: MDA
Line: Supplies advanced robotic systems for space and terrestrial applications.
NAICS: 336410
#Emp: 250-499 (Tor)
#TorLoc: 1
Own: Public Company
Par: MacDonald Dettwiler and Associates Ltd. (CDA)
Key: Mag Iskander, Pres, IS
Tim Reedman,
    Dir of Terrestial Programs
Dominic Macchia, Dir of HR
Makim Hiten, CFO
Cameron Craig, Dir of IS
Christian Sallaberger, VP Business Dev
Lynne Vanin, Pub Affairs Mgr

Macgregor's Meat & Seafood Ltd.

265 Garyray Dr.
Toronto, ON M9L 1P2
Tel 416-749-5951
Fax 888-584-3663
www.macgregors.com
Line: Processes meat, poultry and seafood.
NAICS: 311614 311615 311710
#Emp: 100-249 (Tor)
#TorLoc: 2
Own: Private Company
Key: Don Macgregor, Co-Pres
Duncan Macgregor, CEO
Duncan Jr. Macgregor, Co-Pres
Ed Devries, Cont

Mackenzie Financial Corp.

180 Queen St. West
Toronto, ON M5V 3K1
Tel 416-922-5322
Fax 416-922-5660
www.mackenziefinancial.com
Line: Operates a financial company offering loans, deposits and other financial products.
NAICS: 523920
#Emp: 1000-4999 (Tor)
Own: Public Company
Par: IGM Financial (CDA)
Key: Charles R. Sims, Pres & CEO
Kathy Allan, Sr VP HR
Ed Merchand, Sr VP & CFO

Mackie Moving Systems Corp.

933 Bloor St. West
Oshawa, ON L1J 5Y7
Tel 905-728-2400
Fax 905-434-4655
www.mackiegroup.com
AKA: Mackie Group
Line: Provides household and corporate moving, general freight, high value products and enclosed auto products and services.
NAICS: 484210 493190
#Emp: 250-499 (Tor)
#TorLoc: 2
Own: Private Company
Key: Gilles Bernier, Pres
Norm Mackie, VP Ops
Ron Mosey, Dir of Admin
John Tsagarakis, VP Fin
Scott Mackie, VP Sales
Dean Mackie, Exec VP,
    Mackie Moving Systems

Mackie Research Capital Corporation

4500-199 Bay St.
Commerce Crt. West, P.O. Box 368
Toronto, ON M5L 1G2
Tel 416-860-7600
Fax 416-860-7671
www.mackieresearch.com
Line: Provides financial advisory services to individuals, sales, trading and research services to institutional investors, and investment banking services to growth companies.
NAICS: 523120
#Emp: 100-249 (Tor)
#TorLoc: 1
Own: Private Company
Key: Geoff Whitlam, Pres
Patrick Walsh, Chmn & CEO
Andrew C. Selbie, CFO

MacLaren McCann

10 Bay St., 16th Fl.
Toronto, ON M5J 2S3
Tel 416-594-6000
Fax 416-643-7030
www.maclaren.com
Line: Offers a full service advertising agency and communication company.
NAICS: 541810
#Emp: 500-999 (Tor)
#TorLoc: 1
Own: Private Company
Par: The Interpublic Group of Companies Inc. (US)

Key: Doug Turney, Pres & CEO
Lindsey Feasby, Sr VP & Dir of HR
Monica Hofmann, Exec VP & CFO
Andy Langs, Sr VP & Dir of IT

Macquarie Capital Markets Canada Ltd.

3100-181 Bay St., Brookfield Pl.
Toronto, ON M5J 2T3
Tel 416-848-3500
Fax 416-861-8484
www.macquarie.com/ca/
Line: Provides investment banking and advisory services.
NAICS: 523110
#Emp: 100-249 (Tor)
#TorLoc: 1
Own: Private Company
Key: Paul Donnelly, Pres & CEO
Chris Salapoutis, COO
Colleen Teed, HR Consultant
Alex Rothwell, Sr Mng Dir

Macquarie Private Wealth

3200-181 Bay St., 9th Fl.
BCE Pl.
Toronto, ON M5J 2T3
Tel 416-864-3600
Fax 416-864-9024
www.macquarieprivatewealth.ca
Line: Provides financial investment services.
NAICS: 523110
#Emp: 500-999 (Tor)
Own: Private Company
Key: Earl Evans, CEO
Stanley H. Hartt, Chmn
James Lexovsky, CFO

Macro Engineering & Technology Inc.

199 Traders Blvd. East
Mississauga, ON L4Z 2E5
Tel 905-507-9000
Fax 905-507-3000
www.macroeng.com
Line: Provides engineering services and manufactures machinery for the plastics industry.
NAICS: 333220
#Emp: 75-99 (Tor)
#TorLoc: 2
Own: Private Company
Par: Macro Technology Inc. (CHN)
Key: Mirek Planeta, Pres
Pinder Singh, MIS Mgr

Mac's Convenience Stores Inc.

400-305 Milner Ave.
Toronto, ON M1B 3V4
Tel 416-291-4441
Fax 416-291-4947
www.macs.ca
AKA: Becker's Milk; Mac's Milk;
Mike's Mart
Line: Operates convenience stores.
NAICS: 445120
#Emp: 500-999 (Tor)
#TorLoc: 122
Own: Private Company
Par: Couche-Tard (CDA)
Key: Kim Trowbridge,
    VP Ops, Central Division
Brian Hannasch, Exec VP & COO
Ziyad Mansoor, Dir of Fin

Maersk Canada Inc.

2576 Matheson Blvd. East
Mississauga, ON L4W 5H1
Tel 905-624-5585
Fax 905-624-3585
www.maerskline.com
AKA: Maersk Sealand Safmarine
Line: Provides international
transportation and logistics services.
NAICS: 488519
#Emp: 100-249 (Tor)
#TorLoc: 1
Own: Private Company
Par: AP Moller (DEN)
Key: David Cardin, Pres
Lorraine Craine, GM of HR
John Crewson, CFO
Todd Creange, Dir of Sales

Magellan Aerospace Corp.

3160 Derry Rd. East
Mississauga, ON L4T 1A9
Tel 905-677-1889
Fax 905-677-5658
www.magellan.aero
AKA: Bristol Aerospace; Chicopee
Manufacturing; Fleet Industries;
Orenda Aerospace Corp.
Line: Manufactures aircraft
components and repairs aircraft
engines and structures.
NAICS: 336410
#Emp: 500-999 (Tor)
#TorLoc: 1
Own: Public Company
Key: James Butyniec, Pres & CEO
Jo-Ann Ball, VP HR
John Dekker, VP Fin
Konrad Hahnelt,
    VP Global Strategic Sourcing
Larry Winegarden, VP Strategy

Magic Maintenance Inc.

3-25 Edilcan Dr.
Vaughan, ON L4K 3S4
Tel 905-660-4124
Fax 905-660-4127
www.magicmaint.ca
Line: Provides janitorial services.
NAICS: 561722
#Emp: 250-499 (Tor)
Own: Private Company
Key: Mike Gianmarco, Pres
Luis Rivas, Ops Mgr
Allan Bernstein, GM

Magna Closures Inc.

521 Newpark Blvd.
Newmarket, ON L3Y 4X7
Tel 905-898-2665
Fax 905-853-0377
www.magnaclosures.com
Line: Supplies interior closure systems
and components to North American
automotive original equipment
manufacturers.
NAICS: 336390
#Emp: 1000-4999 (Tor)
#TorLoc: 6
Own: Private Company
Par: Magna International Inc. (CDA)
Key: Frank Seguin, Pres
Joyce Baxter, Dir of HR

Magna Exteriors & Interiors Corp.

50 Casmir Crt.
Vaughan, ON L4K 4J5
Tel 905-669-2888
Fax 905-669-4992
www.magna.com/xchg/exterior_
    systems
Line: Manufactures automotive
components and systems.
NAICS: 336370 336390
#Emp: 75-99 (Tor)
Own: Public Company
Par: Magna International Inc. (CDA)
Key: Bob Brownlee, Pres
Michael Starcevic, Mgr of HR
Michael McCarthy, Exec VP Fin

Magna International Inc.

337 Magna Dr.
Aurora, ON L4G 7K1
Tel 905-726-2462
Fax 905-726-7164
www.magna.com
Line: Manufactures a wide variety of
automotive components and systems
for automotive manufacturers.
NAICS: 336310 336320 336350

#Emp: 10000+ (Tor)
Own: Public Company
Key: Don Walker, CEO
Frank Stronach, Chmn
Tom Skudutis, COO,
    Exteriors & Interiors
Marc Neeb, Exec VP Global HR
Vincent J. Galifi, Exec VP Fin & CFO
Jim Tobin,
    Exec VP Global Sales & Mktg

Magna Powertrain Inc.

1755 Argentia Rd.
Mississauga, ON L5N 1V2
Tel 905-542-1855
Fax 905-542-9739
www.magna.com
Line: Manufactures high-pressure
aluminum die-castings, machined and
assembled for the automotive industry.
NAICS: 336390
#Emp: 250-499 (Tor)
#TorLoc: 1
Own: Public Company
Par: Tesma International Inc. (CDA)
Key: Cristian Huke, GM
Shelly McGuire, Cont
Mark Thompson, Purch Mgr

Magnotta Winery Corporation

271 Chrislea Rd.
Woodbridge, ON L4L 8N6
Tel 905-738-9463
Fax 905-738-5551
www.magnotta.com
Line: Develops, grows, produces,
imports, exports and retails wine, beer
and spirits.
NAICS: 312130 312120
#Emp: 75-99 (Tor)
#TorLoc: 7
Own: Public Company
Key: Rossana Magnotta, Pres & CEO
Nicole Santos, HR Mgr

Magnum Protective Services Ltd.

203-27 Carlton St.
Toronto, ON M5B 1L2
Tel 416-591-1566
Fax 416-591-1568
www.magnumprotective.com
Line: Provides protective services.
NAICS: 561612
#Emp: 250-499 (Tor)
Own: Private Company
Key: Doug McInroy, Pres
Ben Lee, VP
Robert Ing, Project Mgr

Mailing Innovations

20-3397 American Dr.
Mississauga, ON L4V 1T8
Tel 905-219-3196
Fax 905-677-4480
www.mailinginnovations.com
Line: Delivers commercial and
corporate mailing solutions.
NAICS: 333310
#Emp: 100-249 (Tor)
Own: Public Company
Par: Pitney Bowes (CDA)
Key: Chris Brejak, GM

Mailmarketing Corp.

455 Gordon Baker Rd.
Toronto, ON M2H 4H2
Tel 800-508-3941
Fax 416-490-8455
www.mailmarketing.com
NAICS: 541860
#Emp: 100-249 (Tor)
#TorLoc: 1
Own: Private Company
Key: George Rachkovsky, Pres
William Hawthorne, VP Fin

Main Street Terrace

77 Main St.
Toronto, ON M4E 2V6
Tel 416-690-3001
Fax 416-690-6866
www.reveraliving.com
Line: Provides medical and nursing
care on a long-term basis.
NAICS: 623110
#Emp: 100-249 (Tor)
#TorLoc: 1
Own: Federal Crown Corp.
Par: Revera Long Term Care Inc. (CDA)
Key: Elizabeth Bradshaw, Exec Dir
Astrid Lopez, Associate Dir of Care
Marina Gundareva,
    Business Office Services Mgr
Christie Wood,
    Resident Services Coord

Makita Canada Inc.

1950 Forbes St.
Whitby, ON L1N 7B7
Tel 905-571-2200
Fax 905-433-4779
www.makita.ca
Line: Manufactures and sells power
tools.
NAICS: 333990
#Emp: 75-99 (Tor)
#TorLoc: 2
Own: Private Company

Par: Makita Corp. (JAPAN)
Key: Mak Tokui, Pres
Neil Shibata, GM
Stan Sauer, HR Mgr
Nancy Bell, Purch Mgr
Shawn Ottewell, VP Sales & Service

Maksteel

7615 Torbram Rd.
Mississauga, ON L4T 4A8
Tel 905-671-9000
Fax 905-673-4937
www.maksteel.com
Line: Processes steel.
NAICS: 416210
#Emp: 100-249 (Tor)
#TorLoc: 1
Own: Private Company
Key: Phil Dobbs, Pres
Jerry Chopiany, VP Ops
Maureen Clemens, HR Mgr
Lucian Nicholas, Sr Cont
Albert Smid, IS Mgr
Bob Hunter, VP Sales & Market Dev

Malton Village Long Term Care Centre

7075 Rexwood Rd.
Mississauga, ON L4T 4M1
Tel 905-791-1179
www.peelregion.ca/ltc/malton
Line: Operates a long term care home
for seniors.
NAICS: 623110 623310
#Emp: 100-249 (Tor)
#TorLoc: 1
Own: Government
Par: Region of Peel
Key: Wendy Beattie, Admr

Management Systems Resources Inc.

2 Tippett Rd., 4th Fl.
Toronto, ON M3H 2V2
Tel 416-630-3000
Fax 416-630-3300
www.ecustoms.com
AKA: eCustoms
Line: Operates a customs software,
brokerage, and consulting firm,
focusing on country-specific trade
regulations and compliance, tariff
management and import/export
documentation.
NAICS: 541611 541510
#Emp: 75-99 (Tor)
#TorLoc: 1
Own: Private Company
Key: Rajiv Manucha, Pres
Selina Kwan, Cont

Mancor Canada Inc.

2485 Speers Rd.
Oakville, ON L6L 2X9
Tel 905-827-3737
Fax 905-469-8907
www.mancor.com
AKA: Mancor Industries
Line: Manufactures steel fabricated
truck parts and accessories.
NAICS: 336390
#Emp: 250-499 (Tor)
#TorLoc: 2
Own: Private Company
Key: Art Church, Pres & CEO

Mandarin Restaurant Franchise Corp.

8 Clipper Crt.
Brampton, ON L6W 4T9
Tel 905-451-4100
Fax 905-456-3411
www.mandarinbuffet.com
NAICS: 722110 533110
#Emp: 75-99 (Tor)
Own: Private Company
Key: James Chiu, Pres

Manion Wilkins & Associates Ltd.

500-21 Four Seasons Pl.
Toronto, ON M9B 0A5
Tel 416-234-5044
Fax 416-234-2071
www.manionwilkins.com
Line: Provides third party
administration and benefits consulting
services.
NAICS: 541611
#Emp: 100-249 (Tor)
#TorLoc: 2
Own: Private Company
Key: Mike Neheli, Pres
Howard Cadesky, COO
Sharon Dalton, Mgr of HR
Pat Donnelly, Exec VP
Joan Bonkowski, Mgr of Admin

Manitoulin Transport Inc.

1335 Shawson Dr.
Mississauga, ON L4W 1C4
Tel 905-670-5982
Fax 905-670-5980
www.manitoulintransport.com
Line: Specializes in transport services.
NAICS: 488519
#Emp: 100-249 (Tor)
#TorLoc: 1
Own: Private Company
Key: David O'Conner,
   Dir of Central Region
Terry Olmstead, Dir of HR
Terry Daly, Dir of Sales
Rolando Meo, VP Sales & Mktg

Manpower Services Canada Limited

700-4950 Yonge St.
Toronto, ON M2N 6K1
Tel 416-225-6399
Fax 416-225-4211
www.manpower.ca
Line: Provides temporary and
permanent professional and technical
placement and training; career
transition and redeployment; and call
centre, production line and on-site
management.
NAICS: 561310 561320
#Emp: 1000-4999 (Tor)
#TorLoc: 12
Own: Private Company
Par: Manpower International Inc. (US)
Key: Jeffery A. Jones, Pres & CEO
Lori Procher, VP & GM
Nadia Ciani, VP HR & Commun
Sandra Pickering,
   VP Nat'l Accounts & Sales

Manufacturing and Technology Centre

220 Water St.
Whitby, ON L1N 0T9
Tel 905-666-7669
Fax 905-666-2334
www.mtcservice.com
AKA: MTC
Line: Repairs electronic equipment.
NAICS: 811210
#Emp: 100-249 (Tor)
#TorLoc: 1
Own: Private Company
Key: Howard Humphrey, Pres & Owner
Troy Hanson, VP Ops
Bryan Bowden, IT Mgr

Manulife Financial

200 Bloor St. East, North Tower, 2nd Fl.
Toronto, ON M4W 1E5
Tel 416-926-3000
Fax 416-926-5454
www.manulife.com
AKA: The Manufacturers Life
Insurance Co.
Line: Provides life and health
insurance, group benefits, reinsurance,
annuities, pension and retirement
products, and savings and investment
instruments.
NAICS: 524112
#Emp: 10000+ (Tor)
#TorLoc: 19
Own: Public Company
Key: Donald Guloien, Pres & CEO
Paul Rooney,
   Sr Exec VP & GM, Cdn Ops
Stephani E. Kingsmill, Exec VP HR
Michael Bell, Sr Exec VP & CFO
Edwina Stoate, VP Procurement
Joseph Cooper, Exec VP & CIO
David Paterson, VP Corp Affairs

Maple Downs Golf & Country Club Ltd.

11101 Dufferin St.
P.O. Box 150
Maple, ON L6A 1A2
Tel 905-832-0880
Fax 905-832-4914
www.mapledowns.com
Line: Offers golf and catering services.
NAICS: 713910
#Emp: 100-249 (Tor)
#TorLoc: 1
Own: Private Company
Key: Paul Doucet, GM
Kumar Ramjoo, Cont
Lorne Greenspoon, Treas

Maple Drywall

211 Westcreek Dr.
Woodbridge, ON L4L 9T7
Tel 905-850-3020
Fax 905-850-3023
AKA: 410385 Ontario Ltd.
Line: Installs acoustical drywalls.
NAICS: 232410
#Emp: 250-499 (Tor)
#TorLoc: 1
Own: Private Company
Key: Joe Bucci, Dir
Carmine Bucci, Owner
Rob Bucci, Dir
Domenica DaSilva, Dir

Maple Group

16 Nixon Rd.
Bolton, ON L4E 1K3
Tel 905-857-6006
Fax 905-857-6010
www.mapleterrazzo.com
AKA: Stoneworx Marble & Granite;
International Logistics & Stone
Distribution
Line: Supplies and installs granite,
marble, stone and terrazzo products.
NAICS: 232310
#Emp: 100-249 (Tor)
#TorLoc: 2
Own: Private Company
Key: Fred Rossi, Pres & CEO
Domenic Mariani, VP & CFO

Maple Health Centre

*A Div. of The Regional
Municipality of York*
10424 Keele St.
Maple, ON L6A 2L1
Tel 905-303-0133
Fax 905-303-9314
www.york.ca
Line: Operates a long-term care facility.
NAICS: 623110
#Emp: 100-249 (Tor)
#TorLoc: 1
Own: Not-for-profit
Key: Janice Britton, Admr

Maple Leaf Consumer Foods

6897 Financial Dr.
Mississauga, ON L5N 0A8
Tel 905-285-5000
Fax 905-285-6003
www.mapleleaf.ca
Line: Sells processed meat, pork and
poultry.
NAICS: 413160
#Emp: 1000-4999 (Tor)
#TorLoc: 6
Own: Public Company
Par: Maple Leaf Foods Inc. (CDA)
Key: Gary Maksymetz, Pres
Rocco Cappuccitti,
   Sr VP Admin & Transactions
Les Dakens, Sr VP HR
Debbie Simpson, Sr VP Fin
Jeff Hutchinson, CIO
Stephen Graham, Chief Mktg Officer
Lynda Kuhn, Sr VP Commun

Maple Leaf Foods Inc.

30 St. Clair Ave. West
Toronto, ON M4V 3A2
Tel 416-926-2000
Fax 416-926-2018
www.mapleleaf.ca
Line: Produces meat, bakery
and agri-business products.
NAICS: 311615 311611 311814
#Emp: 5000-9999 (Tor)
#TorLoc: 22
Own: Public Company
Key: Michael H. McCain, Pres & CEO
Les Dakens, Sr VP & Chief HR Officer
Mike Vels, Exec VP & CFO
Bill Kaldis, VP Logistics & Purch
Jeffrey Hutchinson, CIO
Stephen Graham, Chief Mktg Officer
Linda Kuhn, Exec VP Commun

Maple Leaf Frozen Bakery - Canada Bread

144 Viceroy Rd.
Concord, ON L4K 2L8
Tel 905-738-1242
Fax 905-738-5056
www.mapleleaf.ca
Line: Processes and distributes bakery
products.
NAICS: 311814
#Emp: 500-999 (Tor)
Own: Public Company
Par: Maple Leaf Foods Inc. (CDA)
Key: Doug Day, Ops Mgr

Maple Leaf Sports & Entertainment Ltd.

500-50 Bay St.
Toronto, ON M5J 2L2
Tel 416-815-5500
Fax 416-815-6050
www.mlse.com
AKA: Toronto Raptors Basketball Club
Inc.; Air Canada Centre; Toronto Maple
Leafs Hockey Club; Toronto Marlies;
Toronto FC; MLSQ
Line: Provides sports and
entertainment.
NAICS: 711319
#Emp: 500-999 (Tor)
#TorLoc: 1
Own: Private Company
Key: Richard Peddie, Pres & CEO
Tom Anselmi, Exec VP & COO
Mardi Walker, Sr VP People
Ian Clarke, Exec VP,
  CFO & Business Dev
Dave Hopkinson,
  Sr VP Business Partnerships
Beth Robertson,
  Sr VP Ticket Sales & Service

Maple Leaf Taxi-Cab Ltd.

203-1245 Danforth Ave.
Toronto, ON M4J 5B5
Tel 416-465-8022
Fax 416-465-5272
www.mapleleaftaxi.com
Line: Offers taxicab services.
NAICS: 485310
#Emp: 100-249 (Tor)
#TorLoc: 1
Own: Private Company
Key: Andy Leonidis, Pres
Paul Eordanidis, Mgr
Gayle Blair, Office Admin

Maple Lodge Farms Ltd.

8301 Winston Churchill Blvd.
Brampton, ON L6Y 0A2
Tel 905-455-8340
Fax 905-455-8370
www.maplelodgefarms.com
Line: Processes poultry and
manufactures wieners and deli
products.
NAICS: 311615 311614
#Emp: 1000-4999 (Tor)
#TorLoc: 1
Own: Private Company
Key: David May, Pres
Michael Burrows, CEO
Nadia Clements, VP HR
Greg Scott, CFO

Maple Reinders Constructors Ltd.

2660 Argentia Rd.
Mississauga, ON L5N 5V4
Tel 905-821-4844
Fax 905-821-4822
www.maple.ca
AKA: Maple Reinders Group
Line: Provides construction and project
management services for industrial,
commercial and institutional
building projects and environmental
infrastructure projects.
NAICS: 231220
#Emp: 75-99 (Tor)
#TorLoc: 1
Own: Private Company
Key: Michael Reinders, Pres
Frederick Reinders, Chmn & CEO
Harold Reinders, VP
Sue Drake, HR Mgr
Eric van Ginkel, CFO
Kevin Dreyer, IT Mgr
Robert Balamut, Mktg Mgr

Mapleridge Mechanical Contracting Ltd.

939 Dillingham Rd.
Pickering, ON L1W 1Z7
Tel 905-831-0524
Fax 905-831-1628
www.mrmmech.com
Line: Installs air conditioner and
heaters and provides heating, air
conditioning, sheet metal, electrical
and plumbing services.
NAICS: 232520
#Emp: 75-99 (Tor)
#TorLoc: 1
Own: Private Company
Key: Robert Allingham, Pres
Michael Gray, VP
Lori Allingham, Cont

Maple Stamping

401 Caldari Dr.
Concord, ON L4K 5P1
Tel 905-738-8033
Fax 905-738-3667
www.magna.com
Line: Provides automotive stamping
and assembly.
NAICS: 336370
#Emp: 250-499 (Tor)
#TorLoc: 1
Own: Private Company
Par: Magna International Inc. (CDA)
Key: Ray Musson, GM

Marc's No Frills

925 Rathburn Rd. East
Mississauga, ON L4W 4C3
Tel 905-276-6560
Fax 905-276-7174
www.shopnofrills.ca
Line: Operates a supermarket.
NAICS: 445110
#Emp: 75-99 (Tor)
#TorLoc: 1
Own: Private Company
Par: Loblaws Companies (CDA)
Key: Marc Borg, Owner

Marcus Evans

151 Yonge St., 19th Fl.
Toronto, ON M5C 2W7
Tel 416-955-0375
Fax 416-955-0380
www.marcusevans.com
AKA: International Championship
Management Ltd.; The Hospitality
Group
Line: Provides business information
services through global conferences
and summits across various industry
sectors.
NAICS: 541611
#Emp: 100-249 (Tor)
#TorLoc: 1
Own: Private Company
Par: Marcus Evans (US)
Key: Theron Burraway, CEO
Reza Ispahany, Dir
Banti Labrie, HR & Payroll Mgr
Geoffrey Reid, Summit Sales Dir

Mariann Home

9915 Yonge St.
Richmond Hill, ON L4C 1V1
Tel 905-884-9276
Fax 905-884-1800
www.mariannhome.org
Line: Provides catholic nursing home
services.
NAICS: 623110
#Emp: 75-99 (Tor)
#TorLoc: 1
Own: Private Company
Key: Bernard Boreland, Admr

Mariposa Cruise Line Ltd.

425-207 Queen's Quay West
Box 101
Toronto, ON M5J 1A7
Tel 416-203-0178
Fax 416-203-6627
www.mariposacruises.com
AKA: Mariposa Cruises
Line: Operates public and private
charters and harbour tours for
corporations, conventions and public
at large.
NAICS: 487210
#Emp: 75-99 (Tor)
#TorLoc: 1
Own: Private Company
Key: Jim Nicholson, Pres & CEO
Cindi Vanden Heuvel, VP
Harold Rubin, Cont
Joseph Cheung, IT Mgr

Maritime Ontario Freight Lines Ltd.

1 Maritime Ontario Blvd.
Brampton, ON L6S 6G4
Tel 905-792-6100
Fax 905-792-6102
www.m-o.com
Line: Provides long distance trucking
services.
NAICS: 484121
#Emp: 100-249 (Tor)
#TorLoc: 2
Own: Private Company
Key: Doug Munro, Pres
Andre Lafontaine, VP Ops
Mike Morra, VP Admin
Eugene Hook, Corp Cont
John Lepore,
    VP Corp Alliances & Mktg Dev

Maritz Canada Inc.

6900 Maritz Dr.
Mississauga, ON L5W 1L8
Tel 905-696-9400
Fax 905-696-9921
www.maritzcanada.com
Line: Designs and delivers marketing
and performance improvement
solutions that inform, educate,
motivate and reward people.
NAICS: 541611
#Emp: 250-499 (Tor)
#TorLoc: 1
Own: Private Company
Par: Maritz Inc. (US)
Key: Bob Macdonald, Pres & CEO
Alison Simpson,
    Exec VP Client Services
Brian Henry, VP People & Values
Dawn Evers, CFO
Carlo Pirillo, VP Digital & Tech
Gayle Duncan, VP Mktg
Stuart Sugar, VP Planning & Strategy

Markham Fire & Emergency Services

101 Town Centre Blvd.
Markham, ON L3R 9W3
Tel 905-415-7521
Fax 905-479-7770
www.markham.ca
NAICS: 913140
#Emp: 250-499 (Tor)
#TorLoc: 8
Own: Government
Key: Bill Snowball, Fire Chief
Phil Alexander, Deputy Fire Chief
Dave Decker, Deputy Fire Chief

Markham Public Library Board

6031 Hwy. 7
Markham, ON L3P 3A7
Tel 905-513-7977
Fax 905-471-6015
www.markhampubliclibrary.ca
NAICS: 514121
#Emp: 100-249 (Tor)
#TorLoc: 6
Own: Government
Par: The Town of Markham
Key: Catherine Biss, CEO
Larry Pogue,
    Dir of Admin & Ops Support
Sandy Chan, Compensation Specialist

Markham Stouffville Hospital Corporation

381 Church St.
P.O. Box 1800
Markham, ON L3P 7P3
Tel 905-472-7000
Fax 905-472-7086
www.msh.on.ca
AKA: Uxbridge Cottage Hospital
Line: Provides acute medical care.
NAICS: 622111
#Emp: 1000-4999 (Tor)
#TorLoc: 2
Own: Not-for-profit
Key: Janet M. Beed, Pres & CEO
Neil Walker, COO
Anne Kennie, Dir of HR
Rob Bull, CFO
Tim Pemberton, Dir of IT
Lisa Joyce, Dir of PR

Markhaven Inc.

54 Parkway Ave.
Markham, ON L3P 2G4
Tel 905-294-2233
Fax 905-294-6521
www.markhaven.ca
Line: Provides long-term nursing care
services.
NAICS: 623110
#Emp: 100-249 (Tor)
#TorLoc: 1
Own: Not-for-profit
Key: Della White, Dir of Care
Noreen Kallai, Exec Dir
Laura Burns, Dir of Admin

Markland Wood Golf Club

245 Markland Dr.
Toronto, ON M9C 1R1
Tel 416-621-2260
Fax 416-626-7814
www.marklandwood.com
Line: Operates a private golf club.
NAICS: 713910
#Emp: 100-249 (Tor)
#TorLoc: 1
Own: Private Company
Key: Alfredo Colalillo, GM
Filipe De Sousa, Club House Mgr
Wanda Symington, Office Mgr
Doug Eatock, Sales & Mktg Mgr

Marmon/Keystone Canada Inc.

1220 Heritage Rd.
Burlington, ON L7L 4X9
Tel 905-319-4646
Fax 905-319-4248
www.mkcanada.com
Line: Distributes pipe, tubing, bar, flanges and fittings in stainless and carbon.
NAICS: 416210
#Emp: 100-249 (Tor)
#TorLoc: 2
Own: Private Company
Par: Marmon Group of Companies (US)
Key: David Rombough, Pres, Canada
Pierre Chenier, Group VP Ops
Tony Peluso, Reg Mgr
Ron Carlucci, Cont
Lou Germano, VP Purch
Ross Hunt, Group VP

Marsan Foods Ltd.

160 Thermos Rd.
Toronto, ON M1L 4W2
Tel 416-755-9262
Fax 416-755-6790
www.marsanfoods.com
Line: Packages and develops premium soups, sauces and entrees for the retail, foodservice and healthcare industries.
NAICS: 311420 311940 311990
#Emp: 100-249 (Tor)
#TorLoc: 2
Own: Private Company
Key: Jim Thorne, Pres & CEO
Graeme P. Jewett, Chmn
Rayanne Webster, Dir of Fin
John Wismayer, Purch Mgr
Sean Lippay, VP Sales & Mktg
Bruce McCullagh, VP Sales & Mktg

Mars Canada Inc.

37 Holland Dr.
Bolton, ON L7E 5S4
Tel 905-857-5780
Fax 905-857-5585
www.mars.com/canada/en/index
AKA: Bounty; Snickers; Denta Bone; Marrow Bone; Pedigree; Whiskas
Line: Manufactures confectionery, pet food and other food products.
NAICS: 311111 311119
#Emp: 250-499 (Tor)
#TorLoc: 2
Own: Private Company
Par: Mars Inc. (US)
Key: Don Robinson, Pres
Roy Benin, VP Sales

Marsh Canada Limited

BCE Pl., 1400-161 Bay St.
Toronto, ON M5J 2S4
Tel 416-868-2600
Fax 416-868-2526
www.marsh.ca
Line: Provides insurance brokerage and consulting services.
NAICS: 524210
#Emp: 500-999 (Tor)
#TorLoc: 2
Own: Private Company
Par: Marsh McLennan Companies (US)
Key: Alan Garner, Pres & CEO
James W. Abernethy, Exec VP & COO
Gail St. Germain, Mng Dir

Martinrea International Inc.

30 Aviva Park Dr.
Vaughan, ON L4L 9C7
Tel 416-749-0314
www.martinrea.com
AKA: Alfield Industries; MJ Manufacturing
Line: Supplies automotive fluid handling systems, assemblies and components.
NAICS: 336390 336350
#Emp: 1000-4999 (Tor)
#TorLoc: 3
Own: Public Company
Key: Nick Orlando, Pres & CFO
Fred Jaekel, CEO
Armando Pagliari, Exec VP HR
Vinay Kamat, Corp Cont

Marvin Starr Motors Ltd.

3132 Eglinton Ave. East
Toronto, ON M1J 2H1
Tel 416-264-2311
Fax 416-264-4513
www.marvinstarr.com
Line: Provides automobile sales and service.
NAICS: 441110 441120
#Emp: 75-99 (Tor)
#TorLoc: 1
Own: Private Company
Key: Marvin Starr, Pres

Marwick Manufacturing Inc.

6325 Northwest Dr.
Mississauga, ON L4V 1P6
Tel 905-677-0677
Fax 905-677-7355
www.marwick.ca
Line: Manufactures wallpaper sample books.
NAICS: 323119
#Emp: 75-99 (Tor)
#TorLoc: 1
Own: Private Company
Key: Roland Leupolt, Pres

Mary Kay Cosmetics Ltd.

2020 Meadowvale Blvd.
Mississauga, ON L5N 6Y2
Tel 905-858-0020
Fax 905-858-8407
www.marykay.ca
Line: Distributes skin care products, cosmetics and fragrances through direct sales.
NAICS: 414520
#Emp: 100-249 (Tor)
#TorLoc: 1
Own: Private Company
Par: Mary Kay Cosmetics Inc. (US)
Key: Ray Patrick, Pres
Eva Liebermann, VP IS & Ops
Tricia Greco,
    Dir of HR & Sales Force Services
Nathalie Cormack, Dir of Fin
Jeff Grigg, Dir of Supply Chain & Dist
Mike Hammel,
    Dir of Tech & Application
Lynda Rose, VP Mktg & Sales
Debra Joseph,
    Dir of Mktg, e-Business & Commun

Mascot Truck Parts Ltd.

475 Admiral Blvd.
Mississauga, ON L5T 2N1
Tel 905-670-9100
Fax 905-670-5309
www.mtpi.com
Line: Remanufactures truck
transmissions, differentials, drivelines
and steering.
NAICS: 336350
#Emp: 100-249 (Tor)
#TorLoc: 3
Own: Private Company
Par: Arvin Meritor (US)
Key: Glenn Hanthorn, Pres
Greg Polan, Reg HR Mgr
Ravi Menon, Fin Mgr
Kevin Jones, IT Mgr

Masonite International Corporation

B4-1820 Matheson Blvd.
Mississauga, ON L4W 0B3
Tel 905-212-9622
www.masonite.com
Line: Manufactures and wholesales
doors.
NAICS: 321911
#Emp: 500-999 (Tor)
#TorLoc: 2
Own: Public Company
Key: Fred Lynch, Chmn, Pres & CEO

Massiv Die Form

7655 Bramalea Rd.
Brampton, ON L6T 4Y5
Tel 905-458-4041
Fax 905-458-0155
www.massiv.com
Line: Manufactures large automotive
dies.
NAICS: 332118
#Emp: 250-499 (Tor)
#TorLoc: 1
Own: Private Company
Par: Cosma Tooling Group (CDA)
Key: Mick O'Neill, GM, Tooling Ops
Oliver Byrne, Massiv Advanced Tech
Heather McCue, HR Mgr
Dave Hill, Cont
Keith Hannan, Purch Mgr
John Powell, IS Mgr
Geoff Palmer, Dir of Sales & Mktg

Masterfile Corp.

3 Concord Gate, 4th Fl.
Toronto, ON M3C 3N7
Tel 416-929-3000
Fax 416-929-2104
www.masterfile.com
Line: Acquires, organizes, distributes
and licenses images for commercial
use.
NAICS: 561490
#Emp: 100-249 (Tor)
#TorLoc: 1
Own: Private Company
Key: Steve Pigeon, Pres
Geoff Cannon, Exec VP

Match Marketing Group

350 Carlingview Dr.
Toronto, ON M9W 5G6
Tel 416-703-9559
Fax 416-703-9069
www.matchmg.com
Line: Offers marketing services.
NAICS: 541619
#Emp: 100-249 (Tor)
Own: Private Company
Key: Brett Farren, Pres
Antoine Adams, VP
Gus Pinto, Fin Mgr

Matcom Industrial Installations Inc.

1531 Creditstone Rd.
Vaughan, ON L4K 5V6
Tel 905-669-5474
Fax 905-669-5563
www.matcominstallations.com
Line: Provides industrial installation
services including millwrighting,
pipefitting, rigging and hoisting.
NAICS: 232590
#Emp: 75-99 (Tor)
#TorLoc: 1
Own: Private Company
Key: Scott Stobo, Pres
Matthew O'Dwyer, CEO
Robert Low, Dir of HR & Staff Dev
Dean Catherwood, Cont
Gary Moore, Mktg Mgr

Matcor Automotive

1620 Steeles Ave. East
Brampton, ON L6T 1A5
Tel 905-793-4035
Fax 905-793-1609
www.matcor-matsu.com
AKA: Matsu Manufacturing
Line: Manufactures metal stampings.
NAICS: 336370 336390
#Emp: 500-999 (Tor)

#TorLoc: 2
Own: Private Company
Key: Scott Mawhinney,
Pres, Automotive
Art Artuso, Pres & Owner

Matrix Logistics Services Ltd.

6941 Kennedy Rd.
Mississauga, On L5T 2R6
Tel 905-795-2200
Fax 905-795-2228
Line: Distributes personal care
products, general merchandise and
pharmaceuticals.
NAICS: 493110
#Emp: 500-999 (Tor)
#TorLoc: 1
Own: Private Company
Par: Exel (UK)
Key: Derek Jones, Dir of Ops
Blaine Caldwell, VP

Matrix Packaging of Canada ULC

245 Brittania Rd. East
Mississauga, ON L4Z 4J3
Tel 905-624-2337
Fax 905-624-2250
www.matrixpackaging.com
Line: Manufactures plastic bottles.
NAICS: 326160
#Emp: 100-249 (Tor)
#TorLoc: 3
Own: Private Company
Key: Audrey Lalande, Cont
Deep Sahota, HR Mgr

Mattel Canada Inc.

6155 Freemont Blvd.
Mississauga, ON L5R 3W2
Tel 905-501-0404
Fax 905-501-6288
www.mattel.com
Line: Manufactures children's toys.
NAICS: 339930
#Emp: 100-249 (Tor)
#TorLoc: 1
Own: Private Company
Par: Mattel Inc. (US)
Key: Howard Smith,
Sr Dir of Business Dev & VP
Alison Doherty, Sr HR Mgr
Reidin Goode, Dir of Mktg

Maxim Group General Contracting Ltd.

440 Sunset Beach Rd.
Richmond Hill, ON L4E 1A8
Tel 905-303-7711
Fax 416-661-1542
www.maximgroup.on.ca
Line: Performs exterior building repairs and maintenance.
NAICS: 231220
#Emp: 75-99 (Tor)
#TorLoc: 1
Own: Private Company
Key: Charles Keslick, Pres
Andrew Porciello, VP

Maxium Financial Services Inc.

1-30 Vogell Rd.
Richmond Hill, ON L4B 3K6
Tel 905-780-6150
Fax 905-780-6273
www.maxium.net
Line: Provides lease financing and asset management services.
NAICS: 541611
#Emp: 75-99 (Tor)
#TorLoc: 1
Own: Private Company
Key: Rob Mabe, VP Mktg

Maxxam Analytics

6740 Campobello Rd.
Mississauga, ON L5N 2L8
Tel 905-817-5700
Fax 905-817-5777
www.maxxamanalytics.com
AKA: Mann Equitest; Philip Analytical Services
Line: Provides analytical laboratory support services to industry and government that assists in risk mitigation, product quality verification, regulatory compliance, and human health and wellness protection.
NAICS: 541380
#Emp: 500-999 (Tor)
#TorLoc: 2
Own: Private Company
Key: Jon Hantho, Pres & CEO
Margaret Bailey, VP HR
Chris Jeppesen, CFO
Randy Leavitt, VP, DNA & Forensics

Mayfair Racquet & Fitness Clubs

200-50 Steelcase Rd. East
Markham, ON L3R 1E8
Tel 905-475-1150
Fax 905-475-6841
www.mayfairclubs.com
Line: Operates health and fitness clubs which include full service spa and wellness centres, tennis, squash, fitness equipment and programming, full aquatic programs, childcare, yoga and pilates.
NAICS: 713940
#Emp: 250-499 (Tor)
#TorLoc: 4
Own: Private Company
Key: Irwin Tobias, Pres & CEO
Voula Treheles, Dir of HR
Melissa Raghurai, Cont

Mayhew & Associates

135 Commerce Valley Dr. East
Thornhill, ON L3T 7T4
Tel 905-707-4747
Fax 905-707-4748
www.mayhew.ca
Line: Provides work space solutions.
NAICS: 541611
#Emp: 100-249 (Tor)
#TorLoc: 1
Own: Private Company
Key: Marcia Mayhew, Pres
Mark Mayhew, Co-Owner
Andrew Healy, VP Ops
Chris Gordon, HR Mgr
Robert Foran, CFO
Robert Burin, Dir of IT
Andrew Keeting, VP Sales
Maurice Benatar,
    VP Mktg & Business Dev
Steve Cascone, VP Consulting Services

Mazda Canada Inc.

55 Vogell Rd.
Richmond Hill, ON L4B 3K5
Tel 905-787-7000
Fax 905-787-7135
www.mazda.ca
Line: Wholesales and distributes vehicles.
NAICS: 415190
#Emp: 100-249 (Tor)
#TorLoc: 1
Own: Private Company
Par: Mazda Motor Corp./Itohchu Corp. (JAPAN)

Key: Don Romano, Pres
Don MacPhee, Dir of Service & Parts
Brian McDougall, Dir of HR
Andrew Kalra, Dir of Fin & Admin
Mike Collinson,
    Dir of Mktg & Vehicle Planning
Greg Young, Dir of PR

MCAP Commercial Limited Partnership

400-200 King St. West
Toronto, ON M5H 3T4
Tel 416-598-2665
Fax 416-598-7857
www.mcap.com
Line: Provides commercial and residential mortgage services.
NAICS: 522310
#Emp: 250-499 (Tor)
#TorLoc: 2
Own: Private Company
Key: Derek Norton, Pres, CEO & Dir
Lorne Jenkins,
    Exec VP Corp Services & CFO
Kirsten Maddocks, VP HR
Mark Aldridge, Exec VP & CFO
Patti Somers, CIO
Jack Shapiro, VP Mktg

McAsphalt Industries Ltd.

8800 Sheppard Ave. East
Toronto, ON M1B 5R4
Tel 416-281-8181
Fax 416-281-8842
www.mcasphalt.com
Line: Manufactures asphalt, paving mixtures and emulsions.
NAICS: 324121
#Emp: 100-249 (Tor)
Own: Private Company
Key: John Carrick, Jr., Pres
Kelly Carrick, Exec VP
Joe Waller, HR Mgr
Craig Smith, CFO

McCague Borlack LLP

2700-130 King St. West
P.O. Box 136
Toronto, ON M5X 1C7
Tel 416-860-0001
Fax 416-860-0003
www.mccagueborlack.com
AKA: Canadian Litigation Counsel
Line: Operates a law firm.
NAICS: 541110
#Emp: 100-249 (Tor)
#TorLoc: 1
Own: Partnership
Key: Paul McCague, Partner
Cindy Davis, Firm Dir
Kathryn Stroscher, HR Mgr
Marc Gardner, IT Mgr

The McCall Centre for Continuing Care

140 Sherway Dr.
Toronto, ON M9C 1A4
Tel 416-259-2573
Fax 416-521-4088
www.extendicarecanada.com
AKA: Extendicare
Line: Operates a general long-term health care facility.
NAICS: 623110
#Emp: 100-249 (Tor)
Own: Private Company
Par: Extendicare Inc. (CDA)
Key: Dwayne Wyrwas, Exec Dir

McCarthy Tetrault

5300 TD Centre, TD Bank Tower
Toronto, ON M5K 1E6
Tel 416-362-1812
Fax 416-868-0673
www.mccarthy.ca
Line: Operates a full service law firm.
NAICS: 541110
#Emp: 500-999 (Tor)
#TorLoc: 1
Own: Private Company
Key: Marc-Andre Blanchard, CEO
Kenneth Morell, COO
Joyce Mah, Dir of HR, Ontario
Heidi Vesely, CFO
Thomas Oakes, Dir of IT

McCluskey Transportation Services Ltd.

200-514 Carlingview Dr.
Toronto, ON M9W 5R3
Tel 416-246-1422
Fax 416-246-1843
Line: Provides transportation services.
NAICS: 485410
#Emp: 75-99 (Tor)
#TorLoc: 1
Own: Private Company
Key: John McCluskey, Pres

McCormick Rankin Corp.

300-2655 North Sheridan Way
Mississauga, ON L5K 2P8
Tel 905-823-8500
Fax 905-823-8503
www.mrc.ca
Line: Provides consulting engineering services for the transportation, design/build, environment, management, structures, heritage structure rehabilitation, systems engineering, ITS, toll highways, road safety, transit and value engineering industries.

NAICS: 541330
#Emp: 250-499 (Tor)
#TorLoc: 1
Own: Private Company
Par: MMM Group (CDA)
Key: Reno Radolli, Chmn & CEO
Rhonda Wild, HR Mgr
Evelyn Gowan, Cont
Mike Grieco, IT Mgr

McDonald's Restaurants of Canada Limited

1 McDonald's Pl.
Toronto, ON M3C 3L4
Tel 416-443-1000
Fax 416-446-3443
www.mcdonalds.ca
Line: Operates quick service restaurants.
NAICS: 722210
#Emp: 10000+ (Tor)
#TorLoc: 231
Own: Private Company
Par: McDonald's Corp. (US)
Key: John Betts, Pres
Jacques Mignault, COO
Len Jillard,
    Sr VP & Chief People Officer
Dave Hederson, Sr VP & CFO
Dave Simsons, VP Shared Services & IT
Joel Yashinsky, VP Mktg
Richard Ellis,
    Sr VP Commun & Pub Affairs

McGraw-Hill Ryerson Ltd.

300 Water St.
Whitby, ON L1N 9B6
Tel 905-430-5000
Fax 905-430-5227
www.mcgrawhill.ca
Line: Publishes and distributes educational and professional products in both print and non-print media.
NAICS: 511130 511140 511210
#Emp: 100-249 (Tor)
#TorLoc: 1
Own: Public Company
Par: McGraw-Hill Cos. (US)
Key: David Swail, Pres & CEO
Clive Powell, Exec VP Editorial,
    Production & Design
Gord Dyer, CFO
Claudia Hawkins, Mktg Mgr

McGregor Industries Inc.

63 Polson St.
Toronto, ON M5A 1A4
Tel 416-593-5353
Fax 416-979-1688
www.mcgregorsocks.com
AKA: American Essentials; McGregor Socks; McGregor Hosiery Mills
Line: Manufactures men's and ladies' socks.
NAICS: 315110
#Emp: 100-249 (Tor)
#TorLoc: 2
Own: Private Company
Par: Tartan Holdings/Ellipse Holdings/Lipco Investments (CDA)
Key: Earl Lipson, Pres & CEO
Diana Neal, Sr VP Ops
Dolores Marciano, HR Mgr
Carl A. Grilo, CFO
Pat Seaton, Purch Mgr
Robert Stanley, Dir of Sales
Richard Cherinuck,
    VP Mktg & Merchandising

McKesson Canada

7510 Bren Rd.
Mississauga, ON L4T 4H1
Tel 905-671-4586
Fax 905-671-8710
www.mckesson.ca
Line: Distributes pharmaceutical products and provides healthcare supply management solutions.
NAICS: 414510
#Emp: 500-999 (Tor)
#TorLoc: 2
Own: Private Company
Par: McKesson Corp. (US)
Key: Domenic Pilla, Pres
Paula Keays, VP & CFO
Robert Jessup-Ramsay, HR Mgr
Jeff Farria, VP & GM, Ontario
Graham Hardie, Dir of Sales

McKesson Specialty

A Div. of McKesson Canada
400-1 Concorde Gate
Toronto, ON M3C 3N6
Tel 416-429-6172
Fax 416-429-2745
www.mckesson.ca
Line: Provides solutions to the biopharmaceutical industry including consulting, distribution, specialty pharmacy, clinical and patient services.
NAICS: 541690
#Emp: 75-99 (Tor)
#TorLoc: 3

Own: Private Company
Par: McKesson Corp. (US)
Key: Dimitris Polygenis, VP

McKinsey & Company

110 Charles St. West
Toronto, ON M5S 1K9
Tel 416-313-3700
Fax 416-313-2999
www.mckinsey.com
Line: Provides management consulting.
NAICS: 541619
#Emp: 100-249 (Tor)
#TorLoc: 1
Own: Private Company
Par: McKinsey & Company, Inc. (US)
Key: Stephen Bear, Mng Dir
Shawn Sanford, Dir of Ops
Leslie Wood, Dir of Admin
Jennifer Iles, Commun Mgr

McLean Budden Ltd.

2525-145 King St. West
Toronto, ON M5H 1J8
Tel 416-862-9800
Fax 416-862-0167
www.mcleanbudden.com
Line: Provides financial consulting and
mutual fund management services.
NAICS: 523920
#Emp: 75-99 (Tor)
#TorLoc: 1
Own: Private Company
Key: Roger Beauchemin, Pres & CEO

McMichael Canadian Art Collection

10365 Islington Ave.
Kleinburg, ON L0J 1C0
Tel 905-893-1121
Fax 905-893-2588
www.mcmichael.com
Line: Operates an art gallery.
NAICS: 712111
#Emp: 100-249 (Tor)
#TorLoc: 1
Own: Provincial Crown Corp.
Key: Victoria Dickenson,
  Exec Dir & CEO
Alex Meadu, Dir of Ops
Mary Benvenuto, Dir of Fin & HR
Peter Ross,
  Dir of Dev, Mktg & Commun

McMillan

Brookfield Pl., Bay Wellington Tower
4400-181 Bay St.
Toronto, ON M5J 2T3
Tel 416-865-7000
Fax 416-865-7048
www.mcmillan.ca
Line: Provides legal services.
NAICS: 541110
#Emp: 250-499 (Tor)
#TorLoc: 1
Own: Private Company
Key: Michael P. Whitcombe,
  Senior Partner
Andrew J.F. Kent, CEO
Robert R. Cranston,
  Office Managment Partner
Nisha Rider, Dir of HR
Sam Clarke, Dir of Fin
Chris Duncan, Dir of IT

MCW Consultants Ltd.

600-156 Front St. West
Toronto, ON M5J 2L6
Tel 416-598-2920
Fax 416-598-5394
www.mcw.com
Line: Provides mechanical and
electrical consulting engineering
services.
NAICS: 541330
#Emp: 75-99 (Tor)
#TorLoc: 1
Own: Private Company
Key: David Bellamy, Pres
Olga Kivell, Office Mgr

MDC Partners Inc.

45 Hazelton Ave.
Toronto, ON M5R 2E3
Tel 416-960-9000
Fax 416-960-9555
www.mdc-partners.com
Line: Operates holding company for
marketing, communications and
advertising agencies.
NAICS: 541910
#Emp: 500-999 (Tor)
#TorLoc: 12
Own: Public Company
Key: Miles S. Nadal, Chmn & CEO
Maria Pappas, Office Mgr

MDF Mechanical Ltd.

2100 Steeles Ave. East
Brampton, ON L6T 1A7
Tel 905-789-9944
Fax 905-789-9945
www.mdfmechanical.ca
NAICS: 232520
#Emp: 100-249 (Tor)
#TorLoc: 1
Own: Private Company
Key: Pasquale Occhicone, Pres
Vincent Triano, VP
Angelo Triano, VP

MDG Computers Canada Inc.

2940 Bristol Circ.
Oakville, ON L6H 6G4
Tel 905-829-3538
Fax 905-829-0441
www.mdg.ca
Line: Manufactures brand desktops and
notebook computers.
NAICS: 334110 417310
#Emp: 75-99 (Tor)
#TorLoc: 1
Own: Private Company
Key: Goran Varaklic, Pres
Brian Monette, Chief Mktg Officer

Meadowvale Ford Sales and Services Ltd.

2230 Battleford Rd.
Mississauga, ON L5N 3K6
Tel 905-542-3673
Fax 905-542-1787
www.meadowvaleford.com
Line: Operates a car dealership.
NAICS: 441110 441120
#Emp: 75-99 (Tor)
#TorLoc: 1
Own: Private Company
Key: Jay Gandhi, GM

MeadWestvaco Packaging Systems LP

281 Fairall St.
Ajax, ON L1S 1R7
Tel 905-683-2330
Fax 905-683-5032
www.meadwestvaco.com
AKA: MWV Packaging Systems LP
Line: Provides packaging and packaging solutions for the beverage market.
NAICS: 322212
#Emp: 250-499 (Tor)
#TorLoc: 4
Own: Private Company
Par: MeadWestvaco Corp. (US)
Key: Doug McMillan, Plant Mgr
David Riberdy, HR Mgr
Robin Underwood, Head of Fin

Medallion Properties Inc.

304-970 Lawrence Ave. West
Toronto, ON M6A 3B6
Tel 416-256-3900
Fax 416-256-2827
www.medallioncorp.com
Line: Manages and develops real estate.
NAICS: 531210
#Emp: 100-249 (Tor)
#TorLoc: 1
Own: Private Company
Key: Nathan Bleeman, VP
Peter Grater, VP Fin

The Medcan Clinic

1500-150 York St.
Toronto, ON M5H 3S5
Tel 416-350-5900
Fax 416-350-5981
www.medcan.com
Line: Provides integrated health management services to individuals, families, employers, insurance companies and government organizations.
NAICS: 541690
#Emp: 100-249 (Tor)
#TorLoc: 1
Own: Private Company
Key: John Mozas, Pres & COO
Shaun Francis, Chmn & CEO
Dan Pawliw, Sr VP, Corp Dev
Andrew Rinzema, Sr VP Fin

MediaCom Canada

2800-1 Dundas St. West
Toronto, ON M5G 1Z1
Tel 416-961-5555
Fax 416-967-8070
www.mediacom.com
AKA: Le Groupe MediaCommunication
Line: Creates innovative media strategies and delivers cost-effective advertising campaigns.
NAICS: 541810
#Emp: 100-249 (Tor)
#TorLoc: 1
Own: Private Company
Key: Jamie Edwards, Pres & CEO
Ken Lee, CFO
Christopher Thompson, CIO

mediaedge:cia

500-160 Bloor St. East
Toronto, ON M4W 3S7
Tel 416-987-9100
Fax 416-987-9150
www.mecglobal.com
Line: Operates an advertising agency.
NAICS: 541810
#Emp: 75-99 (Tor)
#TorLoc: 1
Own: Private Company
Key: Bruce Neve, Pres

Medical Mart Supplies Ltd.

5875 Chedworth Way
Mississauga, ON L5R 3L9
Tel 905-624-6200
Fax 905-624-2848
www.medimart.com
Line: Distributes wholesale hospital and medical supplies as well as home health care products.
NAICS: 417930
#Emp: 100-249 (Tor)
#TorLoc: 2
Own: Private Company
Key: Robert J. West, Exec VP
Robert G. West, Pres
Ken Kirby, Sr VP
Tim Boddington, Cont
Steve Currie, CFO
Dave Forte, VP Sales & Mktg

Medical Pharmacies Group Inc.

590 Granite Crt.
Pickering, ON L1W 3X6
Tel 905-420-7335
Fax 905-420-7342
www.medicalpharmacies.com
Line: Operates pharmacies.
NAICS: 446110
#Emp: 100-249 (Tor)

#TorLoc: 1
Own: Private Company
Key: Erast Huculak, Pres
Richard Sevazlian, CEO
Sydney Shrott, Sr VP Corp Ops
Roxanne Tang,
    VP Professional Services
Tony Dimito, VP Fin

Medieval Times Dinner & Tournament Toronto Inc.

10 Dufferin St.
Toronto, ON M6K 3C3
Tel 416-260-1170
Fax 416-260-1179
www.medievaltimes.com
Line: Operates dinner theatre.
NAICS: 711111 722110
#Emp: 100-249 (Tor)
#TorLoc: 1
Own: Private Company
Par: Medieval Times Entertainment Inc. (US)
Key: Mory DiMaurizio, GM
Cindy Wilson, Mktg Mgr

Medi Group Masonry Ltd.

56 Brockport Dr.
Toronto, ON M9W 5N1
Tel 416-741-2737
Fax 416-741-1593
NAICS: 232310
#Emp: 100-249 (Tor)
#TorLoc: 1
Own: Private Company
Key: Rosa Panettieri, Office Mgr

Medisys Health Group Inc.

95 St. Clair Ave. West, 12th Fl.
Toronto, ON M4V 1N6
Tel 416-926-6464
Fax 416-324-7905
www.medisys.ca
Line: Provides health services.
NAICS: 541710 541690
#Emp: 500-999 (Tor)
#TorLoc: 2
Own: Private Company
Key: Julie Cloutier, Pres
Sheldon Elman, Chmn
Shari Gottschalk, VP Ops,
    Insurance Medical Services

Medtronic of Canada Ltd.

99 Hereford St.
Brampton, ON L6Y 0R3
Tel 905-826-6020
Fax 905-826-6620
www.medtronic.com
Line: Manufactures and sells medical devices.
NAICS: 339110 334512
#Emp: 250-499 (Tor)
#TorLoc: 1
Own: Private Company
Par: Medtronic, Inc. (US)
Key: Neil Fraser, Pres
Andre Guerin, Dir of HR
Laura Cameron-Brooksbank, Dir of Fin
David Singh, Dir of IT & Projects
Jon Olsen, Dir of Sales & Mktg, Cardiac
    Rhythm Disease Management Div
Bernard Souche, Dir of Health
    Systems Strategies, Ontario
Lynda Pike, Sr Mgr PR & Commun

Melburn/Musket Group

2215 Royal Windsor Dr.
Mississauga, ON L5J 1K5
Tel 905-823-7800
Fax 905-823-3609
www.musket.ca
Line: Provides trucking and transport services.
NAICS: 484110
#Emp: 250-499 (Tor)
#TorLoc: 3
Own: Private Company
Key: Andy Balij, Pres & Owner
Bill Vandevalk, Ops Mgr
Robert Hopper, HR Mgr
Rod Alafriz, VP

Memme Excavation Company Ltd.

1315 Shawson Dr.
Mississauga, ON L4W 1C4
Tel 905-564-7972
Fax 905-670-4946
Line: Specializes in sewage and water main contracting.
NAICS: 231320
#Emp: 75-99 (Tor)
#TorLoc: 1
Own: Private Company
Key: Ciro Caravaggio, VP

Menkes Developments Ltd.

1400-4711 Yonge St.
Toronto, ON M2N 7E4
Tel 416-491-2222
Fax 416-491-2304
www.menkes.com
Line: Operates a real estate development company.
NAICS: 231110
#Emp: 100-249 (Tor)
#TorLoc: 5
Own: Private Company
Key: Alan Menkes, Pres

Menu Foods Ltd.

8 Falconer Dr.
Mississauga, ON L5N 1B1
Tel 905-826-3870
Fax 905-826-4995
www.menufoods.com
NAICS: 311111
#Emp: 250-499 (Tor)
#TorLoc: 1
Own: Public Company
Par: Simmons Pet Food (US)
Key: Todd Simmons, Owner
Steve Lindsay, Exec VP Ops
Steve Gardener, Sr VP People Services
Mike Jones, Exec VP & CFO
Bryan Bennett, VP IT
Douglas Haslam, Exec VP Sales & Mktg

Mercedes-Benz Canada Inc.

98 Vanderhoof Ave.
Toronto, ON M4G 4C9
Tel 416-425-3550
Fax 416-423-5027
www.mercedes-benz.ca
Line: Wholesales and retails motor vehicles, parts and accessories.
NAICS: 415190
#Emp: 500-999 (Tor)
#TorLoc: 10
Own: Private Company
Par: Daimler AG (GER)
Key: Tim A. Reuss, Pres & CEO
Susan French, Dir of HR
Christian Spelter, VP & CFO
John Westcott, CIO
Hannu Ylanko, Dir of Nat'l Sales
Marc Boderke, Dir of Mktg
Jo Anne Caza,
    Dir of Corp Commun & PR

Mercer (Canada) Limited

Brookfield Pl., P.O. Box 501
161 Bay St.-18th Fl.
Toronto, ON M5J 2S5
Tel 416-868-2000
Fax 416-868-7671
www.mercer.com
Line: Provides pension, group benefits, communication, compensation and other human resources consulting services.
NAICS: 541612
#Emp: 500-999 (Tor)
#TorLoc: 3
Own: Private Company
Par: Marsh & McLennan (US)
Key: Jacques Theoret, Pres
Terry Hearn, Nat'l Dir of HR
Denise Mitchell, Cont
Nancy Altilia, Dir of Mktg

Merchandising Consultants Associates

A-200 Harlan Rd.
Woodbridge, ON L4L 3P6
Tel 905-850-5544
Fax 905-850-5543
www.mca.ca
AKA: MCA
Line: Provides retail sales merchandising services.
NAICS: 561490
#Emp: 100-249 (Tor)
#TorLoc: 1
Own: Private Company
Key: Marsha Clark, Pres
Steve Kindree, CEO

Merge Healthcare

500-6303 Airport Rd.
Mississauga, ON L4V 1R8
Tel 905-364-8000
Fax 905-237-6742
www.merge.com
Line: Provides medical imaging software to medical device and healthcare information system companies.
NAICS: 541510
#Emp: 100-249 (Tor)
#TorLoc: 1
Own: Public Company
Par: Merge Healthcare (US)
Key: Justin C. Dearborn, Pres
Jeff Surges, CEO
John T. DeVries, GM, Merge eClinical
Greg Leszczynski, VP HR
Steve Oreskovich, CFO

Meridian Credit Union

777 Bay St., 26th Fl.
Toronto, ON M5G 2C8
Tel 416-597-4400
Fax 416-597-5084
www.meridiancu.ca
Line: Provides financial co-operative services.
NAICS: 522130
#Emp: 250-499 (Tor)
#TorLoc: 13
Own: Private Company
Key: Sean Jackson, CEO
Tom Wise, Chief People Officer
Bill Maurin, CFO
Gary Genik, CIO
Bryan Twohey,
    Chief Member Service Officer

Merit Travel Group Inc.

200-111 Peter St.
Toronto, ON M5V 2H1
Tel 416-364-3775
Fax 416-364-5117
www.merit.ca
AKA: MeritBiz; Merit Ski Vacations; Merit Golf Vacations; Merit Loyalty Group
Line: Operates a specialty travel company.
NAICS: 561510
#Emp: 100-249 (Tor)
#TorLoc: 4
Own: Private Company
Key: Mike Dawson, Pres
Michael Merrithew, CEO
Louise de Grandpre, Sr VP
Lilian Ingram-Watts, Dir of HR

Merriam School of Music

2359 Bristol Circ.
Oakville, ON L6H 6P8
Tel 905-829-2020
Fax 905-829-4489
www.intelligentfun.com
Line: Sells musical instruments and provides music lessons.
NAICS: 611610 451140
#Emp: 75-99 (Tor)
#TorLoc: 2
Own: Private Company
Key: Alan Merriam, Pres

Merrill Lynch Canada Inc.

400-181 Bay St.
Toronto, ON M5J 2V8
Tel 416-369-7400
Fax 416-369-7966
www.ml.com
Line: Operates as an investment dealer engaged in serving Canadian corporate clients.
NAICS: 523110
#Emp: 250-499 (Tor)
#TorLoc: 1
Own: Public Company
Par: Bank of America (US)
Key: Daniel Mida, Mng Dir, Head of Investment Banking
Irene Hozjan, HR Dir
Gordon Weir, CFO

Mersen Canada

6220 Kestrel Rd.
Mississauga, ON L5T 1Y9
Tel 905-795-0077
Fax 905-795-2508
www.mersen.com
Line: Manufactures high performance heatsinks.
NAICS: 333416
#Emp: 75-99 (Tor)
#TorLoc: 1
Own: Private Company
Key: Bruce Brown, Pres & GM
Ahmed Zaghlol, VP Engineering & Business Dev

The Messengers International

529 Richmond St. East
Toronto, ON M5A 1R4
Tel 416-365-0155
Fax 416-365-1614
www.themessengers.ca
Line: Provides local and international package delivery services.
NAICS: 492110
#Emp: 100-249 (Tor)
#TorLoc: 3
Own: Private Company
Key: Frank D'Angelo, Pres
Jason Crown, GM
Brian Vanderburg,
    Customer Services Mgr
Donna Hames, Admin Mgr
David Profit, IT Mgr

Messier-Bugatti-Dowty

574 Monarch Ave.
Ajax, ON L1S 2G8
Tel 905-683-3100
Fax 905-686-2914
www.safranmbd.com
Line: Manufactures aircraft parts and specializes in landing gear.
NAICS: 336410
#Emp: 500-999 (Tor)
#TorLoc: 1
Own: Public Company
Par: SAFRAN (FR)
Key: Hélène Moreau-Leroy,
    Acting Exec VP, North American Programs

Meta Centre for the Developmentally Disabled

401 Champagne Dr.
Toronto, ON M3J 2C6
Tel 416-736-0199
Fax 416-736-9181
www.metacentre.ca
AKA: EOH - Meta Foundation
Line: Provides social services to children and adults with developmental disabilities.
NAICS: 813310
#Emp: 100-249 (Tor)
#TorLoc: 3
Own: Not-for-profit
Key: Steven Harrison, Exec Dir
Tullio Orlando,
    Dir of Social Work & HR
Raymond Thai, Fin Mgr

Metafore Limited Partnership

305-1550 Enterprise Rd.
Mississauga, ON L4W 4P4
Tel 905-362-8300
Fax 905-362-0490
www.metafore.ca
AKA: Metafore IT Solutions
Line: Designs, implements and supports information technology solutions.
NAICS: 541510
#Emp: 100-249 (Tor)
#TorLoc: 2
Own: Private Company
Par: Hartco Administration Inc. (CDA)
Key: David Kelly, Exec VP & GM
Bryant Jackson, CEO
Jackie Chavarie, Dir of HR
Barry Dunbar, Dir of Purch

Metal Koting - Continuous Colour Coat Limited

1430 Martin Grove Rd.
Toronto, ON M9W 4Y1
Tel 416-743-7980
Fax 416-743-7138
www.metalkoting.com
AKA: DBA Metal Koting
NAICS: 332810
#Emp: 100-249 (Tor)
#TorLoc: 1
Own: Private Company
Key: Kevin McCallum, Pres & COO
Mauro LoRusso, Corp Cont
Paul Feldkamp, VP Sales & Mktg

MetCap Living Management Inc.

300-260 Richmond St. East
Toronto, ON M5A 1P4
Tel 416-340-1600
Fax 416-340-1593
www.metcap.com
AKA: Metro Capital Group
Line: Operates a property management company.
NAICS: 531310
#Emp: 250-499 (Tor)
#TorLoc: 300
Own: Private Company
Key: Brent Merrill, Pres & CEO

Metex Heat Treating Ltd.

225 Wilkinson Rd.
Brampton, ON L6T 4M2
Tel 905-453-9700
Fax 905-453-8707
www.metexht.com
AKA: Suntech Heat Treating; Polycote Inc.; Dorasort
Line: Offers heat treating, brazing, induction hardening, plasticol dip, powder paint, sorting and packaging services.
NAICS: 332810
#Emp: 75-99 (Tor)
#TorLoc: 3
Own: Private Company
Par: Metex Heat Treating Ltd. (CDA)
Key: Surjit Bawa, Pres
Baljit Bawa, VP
Reena Bawa, HR Mgr

MetriCan Mfg. Co. Inc.

2100 Wyecroft Rd.
Oakville, ON L6L 5V6
Tel 905-332-3200
Fax 905-825-2087
www.metrican.com
Line: Designs and manufactures dyes, jigs and fixtures.
NAICS: 333519 332118
#Emp: 100-249 (Tor)
#TorLoc: 3
Own: Private Company
Key: Frank Bosco, Pres & CEO
Anna Sanchez, CFO

Metro Canada Logistics Inc.

1401 Creditstone Rd.
Concord, ON L4K 4N7
Tel 905-738-5577
Fax 905-738-5227
www.metrocanlogistics.com
Line: Provides logistical services.
NAICS: 493110
#Emp: 500-999 (Tor)
#TorLoc: 7
Own: Private Company
Key: Chiko Nanji, Pres
Rod Shaw, VP Ops
Tony Delutis, VP HR
Albert Furtado, VP Customer Solutions
Richard Cranwill, VP Sales & Mktg

Metro Label Co. Ltd.

999 Progress Ave.
Toronto, ON M1B 6J1
Tel 416-292-6600
Fax 416-292-6133
www.metrolabel.com
Line: Produces printing pressure sensitive labels.
NAICS: 323119
#Emp: 75-99 (Tor)
#TorLoc: 1
Own: Private Company
Key: Sandeep Lal, Pres
Narinder Lal, Chmn
Nandini Chaudhary, VP
Pramod Gupta, CFO
John Payawal, IT Mgr

Metroland Media Group Ltd.

3125 Wolfedale Rd.
Mississauga, ON L5C 1W1
Tel 905-279-0440
Fax 905-279-7763
www.metroland.com
Line: Prints, publishes and distributes newspapers.
NAICS: 511110 323119
#Emp: 1000-4999 (Tor)

#TorLoc: 30
Own: Private Company
Par: Torstar Corp. (CDA)
Key: Ian Oliver, Pres
Peter Marsh, Sr VP Printing
Brenda Biller, Sr VP HR
Ian McLeod, Sr VP, Fin & Admin
Kathie Braid, VP Mktg & Corp Sales

Metrolinx

600-20 Bay St.
Toronto, ON M5J 2W3
Tel 416-869-3620
Fax 416-869-3525
www.gotransit.com
Line: Operates inter-regional train and bus public transit service.
NAICS: 485110 485210
#Emp: 1000-4999 (Tor)
#TorLoc: 100
Own: Provincial Crown Corp.
Key: Gary McNeil, Exec VP & Mng Dir
Rob MacIssac, Chair
Greg Percy, VP Ops
Helen Ferreira-Walker, Dir of HR
Robert Siddall, CFO
Paul Davidson, Mgr of Procurement, Ops & Admin
Robert Power, Dir of IT
Mary Proc, VP Customer Services
Vasie Papadopoulos, Dir of Strategic Commun

Metro News

120 Sinnott Rd.
Toronto, ON M1L 4N1
Tel 416-752-8720
Fax 416-285-2056
www.metronews.org
AKA: Medialogix; Ontario News Service; Canadian Mass Media Inc.
Line: Publishes sales and marketing books and magazines.
NAICS: 414420
#Emp: 100-249 (Tor)
#TorLoc: 1
Own: Private Company
Key: Daniel Shapiro, Pres & CEO
Barry Weir, VP & GM
Karen Merritt, HR Mgr
Henry Slaczka, VP & CFO
Troy Neill, Dir of Sales

Metro Ontario Inc.

5559 Dundas St. West
P.O. Box 68, Stn. A
Toronto, ON M5W 1A6
Tel 416-239-7171
Fax 416-234-6586
www.metro.ca
AKA: The Barn Markets; Ultra Food &
Drug; Loeb; Food Basics
Line: Retails groceries.
NAICS: 445110
#Emp: 10000+ (Tor)
#TorLoc: 100
Own: Public Company
Par: Metro Inc. (CDA)
Key: Robert Sawyer, Sr VP
Richard Beaubien, VP Store Ops
Louisa Furtado, VP HR
Grant Forrest, VP & Cont
Joe Fusco, Sr VP Merchandising
Johanne Choiniere,
    Sr VP Ontario Division
Andre Gagne, VP Conventional
    Merchandising
Marc Giroux, VP Mktg, Metro Location

Metro Paper Industries Inc.

111 Manville Rd.
Toronto, ON M1L 4J2
Tel 416-757-2737
Fax 416-757-0818
www.metropaperindustries.com
Line: Manufactures recycled paper
products including napkins, towels and
tissue.
NAICS: 418220
#Emp: 75-99 (Tor)
#TorLoc: 1
Own: Private Company
Key: Karim Jadavji, Pres
Amin Jadaviji, Exec VP Ops
Oliver Moraes, VP Fin

Metropolitan Hotel Toronto

108 Chestnut St.
Toronto, ON M5G 1R3
Tel 416-977-5000
Fax 416-977-9513
www.metropolitan.com
AKA: Preferred Hotels & Resorts
Worldwide
Line: Operates a full service hotel.
NAICS: 721111
#Emp: 250-499 (Tor)
#TorLoc: 2
Own: Private Company
Par: Liverton Hotels International Inc.
(HK)
Key: Henry Wu, Pres
Nasir Hasan, CFO
Orson Sharpe, Corp Dir, Rooms & Ops

Metro Protective Services

234-415 Oakdale Rd.
Toronto, ON M3N 1W7
Tel 416-240-0911
Fax 416-240-0944
www.metroprotective.ca
Line: Provides security services.
NAICS: 561621
#Emp: 100-249 (Tor)
#TorLoc: 1
Own: Private Company
Key: Frank DeCurtis, Pres & Owner

Metro Toronto Convention Centre Corporation

255 Front St. West
Toronto, ON M5V 2W6
Tel 416-585-8000
Fax 416-585-8224
www.mtccc.com
AKA: MTCC
Line: Provides hospitality, convention
and show services.
NAICS: 561920 531120
#Emp: 1000-4999 (Tor)
#TorLoc: 1
Own: Provincial Crown Corp.
Par: Government of Ontario
Key: Barry L. Smith, Pres & CEO
Vince Quattrociocchi, VP Ops
Esther Lee, VP HR & Admin
Imtiaz Dhanjee, VP Fin
Bill McDonald, Dir of Tech Services
John B. Houghton, VP Sales & Mktg

Metro Waste Paper Recovery Inc.

66 Shorncliffe Rd.
Toronto, ON M8Z 5K1
Tel 416-231-2525
Fax 416-232-8820
www.metrowaste.com
AKA: Waste Recycling Inc.
Line: Provides corrugate and waste
paper recovery, as well as paper
recycling services.
NAICS: 562920
#Emp: 100-249 (Tor)
#TorLoc: 2
Own: Private Company
Par: Cascades Inc. (CDA)
Key: Albino Metauro, CEO
Gary Sexton, VP Ops

Meyers Norris Penny LLP

1100-2 Bloor St. East
Toronto, ON M4W 1A8
Tel 416-596-1711
Fax 416-596-7894
www.mnp.ca
Line: Operates a chartered accounting
firm.
NAICS: 541212
#Emp: 75-99 (Tor)
#TorLoc: 1
Own: Private Company
Key: Jeremy Cole, Partner

Meyers Transport Ltd.

53 Grills Rd.
Belleville, ON K8N 4Z5
Tel 613-967-8440
Fax 613-966-2824
www.meyers.ca
AKA: Motor Express Terminals (MET)
Line: Provides transportation services.
NAICS: 484229 484239
#Emp: 100-249 (Tor)
#TorLoc: 1
Own: Private Company
Key: Roman Slugocki, VP
Jacquie Meyers, Pres
Gerry MacCormack, Terminal Mgr
David Joyce, VP Fin & HR
David Scott, VP, Mosaic Logistics
Shawn Dearman, VP Sales & Mktg

The Mibro Group

111 Sinnott Rd.
Toronto, ON M1L 4S6
Tel 416-285-9000
Fax 416-285-9500
www.mibro.com
Line: Distributes hardware and home
improvement products.
NAICS: 416330
#Emp: 75-99 (Tor)
#TorLoc: 2
Own: Private Company
Key: Leon Lapidus, Pres
Elaine Cruise Smith, Dir of HR

Michael-Angelo's Market Place Inc.

4099 Erin Mills Pkwy.
Mississauga, ON L5L 3P9
Tel 905-820-3300
Fax 905-820-8090
www.michaelangelos.ca
Line: Operates a grocery store.
NAICS: 445110
#Emp: 100-249 (Tor)
#TorLoc: 2
Own: Private Company
Key: Michael Pugliese, Pres

The Michener Institute for Applied Health Sciences

222 St. Patrick St.
Toronto, ON M5T 1V4
Tel 416-596-3101
Fax 416-596-3156
www.michener.ca
AKA: Michener
Line: Operates a post-secondary educational institution specializing in applied health sciences education at entry and post-diploma levels.
NAICS: 611519
#Emp: 100-249 (Tor)
#TorLoc: 1
Own: Government
Key: Paul Gamble, Pres & CEO
Sylvia Schippke, VP Academic
Brad Niblett, Asst VP Ops
Iliana Arapis, Sr Dir of Advancement

MicroAge

55 Director Crt.
Woodbridge, ON L4L 4S5
Tel 905-264-8520
Fax 905-264-8530
www.microage.ca
AKA: Syspro Proven Systems Ltd.
Line: Distributes computers, and supplies consulting and helpdesk services.
NAICS: 511210
#Emp: 250-499 (Tor)
#TorLoc: 1
Own: Private Company
Par: Hartco Enterprises (CDA)
Key: Allan Daitchman, Pres
Mark Daitchman, CEO
Linda McVicar, Team Leader
    Admin Services & Exec Asst
Scott Glen, VP Fin
Perry Kuhnen, IT Mgr

Microsoft Canada Co.

1950 Meadowvale Blvd.
Mississauga, ON L5N 8L9
Tel 905-568-0434
Fax 905-568-1527
www.microsoft.ca
Line: Provides nationwide sales, marketing, consulting and local support services.
NAICS: 541510 511210
#Emp: 500-999 (Tor)
#TorLoc: 2
Own: Private Company
Par: Microsoft Corp. (US)
Key: Eric Gales, Pres
Greg Barber, VP
Carolyn Buccongello, VP HR
Joel Freedman, CFO
Claudia Ferris, VP Business & Mktg

Middleton Graphics Group Inc.

75 Denison St.
Markham, ON L3R 1B5
Tel 905-475-6556
Fax 905-475-2572
www.middletongroup.ca
Line: Manufactures and distributes point-of-purchase advertising, and provides screen printing and design services.
NAICS: 323113
#Emp: 75-99 (Tor)
#TorLoc: 3
Own: Private Company
Key: Rob Stratton, Pres
Herbert Riethmacher, Chmn & CEO
Gina Jeronimo, Cont

Midland Transport Ltd.

102 Glidden Rd.
Brampton, ON L6T 5N4
Tel 905-456-5555
Fax 905-456-5550
www.midlandtransport.com
Line: Provides freight transportation.
NAICS: 484121
#Emp: 100-249 (Tor)
#TorLoc: 3
Own: Private Company
Key: Robert K. Irving, Pres
Vince White, Terminal Mgr
Pat Harknett, VP HR
Ken Mutter, VP Fin
Tim Holdaway,
    Reg Human Resource Mgr
Scott Spidell, VP Sales & Mktg

Midnight Express & Cartage Ltd.

RPO Courtney Park
P.O. Box 77278
Mississauga, ON L5T 2P4
Tel 905-629-0712
Fax 905-629-0619
www.midnightexpress.ca
Line: Provides local and long distance trucking services.
NAICS: 484121 484110
#Emp: 75-99 (Tor)
#TorLoc: 1
Own: Private Company
Key: Grant Garrard, GM

Mijo Corp.

635 Queen St. East
Toronto, ON M4M 1G4
Tel 416-964-7539
Fax 416-964-5920
www.mijo.ca
Line: Offers film production services.
NAICS: 512110
#Emp: 75-99 (Tor)
#TorLoc: 1
Own: Private Company
Key: Joel Reitman, Pres & CEO
Michael Goldberg, Exec VP & COO
Sam Tenizo, Comptr
Tim Lambertus, VP IS
Cynthia Littler, Sr VP & Mng Dir

Miller Paving Ltd.

505 Miller Ave.
P.O. Box 4080
Markham, ON L3R 9R8
Tel 905-475-6660
Fax 905-475-3852
www.millergroup.ca
AKA: The Miller Group
Line: Provides infrastructure construction, road rehabilitation, waste management and recreational services, engineering construction, materials manufacturing and marketing, and municipal services.
NAICS: 232920 231310
#Emp: 1000-4999 (Tor)
#TorLoc: 1
Own: Private Company
Par: The Miller Group (CDA)
Key: Leo A. McArthur, Pres & CEO
Ryan Essex, VP
Dianne Blasiak, HR Dir
Barrie Brayford, CAO

Miller Thomson LLP

Scotia Plaza, 5800-40 King St. West
P.O. Box 1011
Toronto, ON M5H 3S1
Tel 416-595-8500
Fax 416-595-8695
www.millerthomson.com
Line: Operates national full-service business law firm.
NAICS: 541110
#Emp: 250-499 (Tor)
#TorLoc: 2
Own: Private Company
Key: Gerald Courage, Chmn & CEO
Peter McKelvey, COO
John Nicholson, Nat'l Dir of HR
Chris Issar, CFO
Richard Van Dyk, CIO
Monique Wijgerse,
    Chief Mktg & Business Officer

Miller Waste Systems

8050 Woodbine Ave.
Markham, ON L3R 2N8
Tel 905-475-6356
Fax 905-475-6396
www.millergroup.ca
Line: Provides recycling, garbage
pick-up and waste management and
composting.
NAICS: 562210
#Emp: 250-499 (Tor)
#TorLoc: 6
Own: Private Company
Key: Nigel Guilford, GM
Ron MacKinnon, Corp Ops Mgr
David Freemantle, HR Supr
Mike Buchanan, Cont
Kevin Still, Sales & Mktg Mgr

Mills Pontiac Buick GMC Ltd.

240 Bond St. East
Oshawa, ON L1G 1B5
Tel 905-436-1500
Fax 905-436-0648
www.millspontiacbuick.com
Line: Sells and services GM vehicles.
NAICS: 441110 441120
#Emp: 100-249 (Tor)
#TorLoc: 1
Own: Private Company
Par: Wilsonia Industries Ltd. (CDA)
Key: Glenn Willson, Pres & Owner
Jason Craine, GM
Garth Bell, Secy-Treas
Don Switzer, Sales Mgr

Milplex Circuit (Canada) Inc.

70 Maybrook Dr.
Toronto, ON M1V 4B6
Tel 416-292-8645
Fax 416-292-1417
www.milplexcircuit.com
Line: Manufactures circuit boards.
NAICS: 334410
#Emp: 75-99 (Tor)
#TorLoc: 1
Own: Private Company
Key: Natu Patel, Pres
Charles Hazen, GM
Pravin Patel, Purch Mgr
Greg Smith, Sales & Mktg Mgr

Minden Gross LLP

2200-145 King St. West
Toronto, ON M5H 4G2
Tel 416-362-3711
Fax 416-864-9223
www.mindengross.com
Line: Offers a full range of legal
services.

NAICS: 541110
#Emp: 100-249 (Tor)
#TorLoc: 1
Own: Partnership
Key: Ramond Slattery, Mng Partner
Diane Carty, COO
Dorthy Fitzgerald, HR Mgr
Melissa Lyttleton, Accounts
Edward Asmar, MIS Mgr
Mark Hunter, Mktg & Business Dev

Mindshare Canada

600-160 Bloor St. East
Toronto, ON M4E 0A2
Tel 416-987-5100
Fax 416-987-5246
www.mindshareworld.com
Line: Operates an advertising agency.
NAICS: 541810
#Emp: 100-249 (Tor)
#TorLoc: 1
Own: Private Company
Key: Karen Nayler, Mng Dir
Teresa Pereira, HR Dir
Linda Leon, Cont

Ming Pao Newspapers (Canada) Ltd.

1355 Huntingwood Dr.
Toronto, ON M1S 3J1
Tel 416-321-0088
Fax 416-321-9663
www.mingpaotor.com
Line: Operates a daily Chinese
newspaper and a weekly free
newspaper.
NAICS: 511110
#Emp: 100-249 (Tor)
#TorLoc: 1
Own: Private Company
Key: Cyril Lai, Reg GM
Ka Ming Lui, CEO
Richard Ng, Exec Chief Editor
Eddy Chong, Sr Acctng Mgr
Maureen Tang, Dir of Sales & Mktg

Ministry of Community Safety and Correctional Services

25 Grosvenor St., 18th Fl.
Toronto, ON M7A 1Y6
Tel 416-326-5000
Fax 416-325-6067
www.mcscs.jus.gov.on.ca
AKA: MCSCS
Line: Protects the public interest in
the areas of public security, counter-
terrorism, correctional services, police
and emergency services.
NAICS: 912120
#Emp: 1000-4999 (Tor)

#TorLoc: 181
Own: Government
Par: Government of Ontario
Key: Allan Gunn,
Asst Deputy Minister & CAO
Troy Fernandez, Mgr of Advisory
Services & HR
Michael Burger, Dir of Business &
Financial Planning

Minto Communities Toronto Inc.

2239 Yonge St.
Toronto, ON M4S 2B5
Tel 416-977-0777
Fax 416-596-3428
www.minto.com
AKA: Minto Management; Minto Plaza
Line: Provides real estate and property
management services.
NAICS: 531310
#Emp: 500-999 (Tor)
#TorLoc: 5
Own: Private Company
Key: Michael Waters, Pres & CFO
Roger Greenberg, CEO
Diane Wallace,
Office Mgr & Commun Coord

MIQ Logistics

6580 Millcreek Dr.
Mississauga, ON L5N 8B3
Tel 905-542-7525
Fax 905-542-7023
Line: Operates a truck transportation
company.
NAICS: 484110 484121
#Emp: 75-99 (Tor)
#TorLoc: 2
Own: Private Company
Par: YRC Worldwide (CDA)
Key: John Carr, Pres & COO

Miratel Solutions Inc.

200-2501 Steeles Ave. West
Toronto, ON M3J 2P1
Tel 416-650-7850
Fax 416-650-7851
www.miratelinc.com
Line: Operates an inbound and
outbound call centre, e-commerce
solutions and letter shop mail services.
NAICS: 561420 561430
#Emp: 100-249 (Tor)
#TorLoc: 1
Own: Private Company
Key: Tracy Ritson, Mng Partner
Angela Puzzolanti, Mng Partner
Steve Debreczeni, IT Mgr

Mircom Technologies Ltd.

25 Interchange Way
Vaughan, ON L4K 5W3
Tel 905-660-4655
Fax 905-660-4113
www.mircom.com
Line: Manufactures fire alarm, life safety, telephone access and audio communication systems.
NAICS: 417320
#Emp: 250-499 (Tor)
#TorLoc: 2
Own: Private Company
Key: Tony Falbo, Pres & CEO
Rocco Mastromartino, VP Manuf
Siegfried W. Kinitz, Dir HR
Mark Falbo, Exec VP
Rick Falbo, Sr VP Sales & Mktg

Mirolin Industries Corp.

60 Shorncliffe Rd.
Toronto, ON M8Z 5K1
Tel 416-231-9030
Fax 416-231-0929
www.mirolin.com
Line: Manufactures bathroom fixtures.
NAICS: 326191
#Emp: 250-499 (Tor)
#TorLoc: 2
Own: Public Company
Par: Masco Corp. (US)
Key: Dominic Primucci, Pres
Mauro Coluccio, VP Manuf
Debbie Wolak, HR Mgr
Frank Rosato, VP Fin
Nick Nitsos, Logistics & Purch Mgr
Robert Bartucci, VP Sales & Mktg

Mirvish Productions

400-284 King St. West
Toronto, ON M5V 1J2
Tel 416-593-0351
Fax 416-593-9221
www.mirvish.com
AKA: Honest Ed's; Ed Mirvish Enterprises Ltd.; Princess of Wales Theatre; Royal Alexandra Theatre; Canon Theatre; TicketKing
Line: Operates retail and entertainment facilities.
NAICS: 452110 722110
#Emp: 1000-4999 (Tor)
#TorLoc: 5
Own: Private Company
Key: Brian Sewell, Exec Producer
David Mirvish, Producer
David Mucci, Dir of Ops
Francis Sookradge,
    Payroll & Personnel Mgr
Camillo Casciato, Dir of Fin
Jim Valentine, Dir of Sales
Chris Dorscht, Mktg Mgr

Mississauga Business Times

A Div. of Metroland Media Group Ltd.
3145 Wolfedale Rd.
Mississauga, ON L5C 3A9
Tel 905-273-8285
Fax 905-273-8118
www.businesstimes.on.ca
Line: Publishes a monthly business/financial newspaper.
NAICS: 511110
#Emp: 500-999 (Tor)
#TorLoc: 1
Own: Private Company
Par: Torstar Corp. (CDA)
Key: Ken Nugent, Publisher
Rick Drennen, Mng Editor
Jan Dean, Asst Editor
Ingrid Doherty,
    Advertising & Mktg Mgr

Mississauga Fire and Emergency Services

A Div. of The City of Mississauga
15 Fairview Rd. West
Mississauga, ON L5B 1K7
Tel 905-615-3777
Fax 905-615-3773
www.mississauga.ca
AKA: Mississauga Fire Department
Line: Provides fire and emergency services.
NAICS: 913140
#Emp: 500-999 (Tor)
#TorLoc: 20
Own: Government
Key: John McDougall, Fire Chief

Mississauga Honda

2380 Motorway Blvd.
Mississauga, ON L5L 1X3
Tel 905-828-1650
Fax 905-828-0136
www.mississaugahonda.com
Line: Operates an automotive dealership.
NAICS: 441110
#Emp: 75-99 (Tor)
#TorLoc: 1
Own: Private Company
Key: Pat Patsakos, GM
Kathy Elminshawi, Cont

Mississauga Library System

301 Burnhamthorpe Rd. West
Mississauga, ON L5B 3Y3
Tel 905-615-3500
Fax 905-615-3615
www.mississauga.ca/library
NAICS: 514121
#Emp: 500-999 (Tor)

#TorLoc: 18
Own: Government
Par: The City of Mississauga
Key: Don Mills, Library Dir
Debbie MacDonald,
    Mgr, Shared Services

The Mississauga News

A Div. of Metroland Media Group Ltd.
3145 Wolfedale Rd.
Mississauga, ON L5C 3A9
Tel 905-273-8111
Fax 905-273-9119
www.mississauga.com
NAICS: 511110
#Emp: 250-499 (Tor)
#TorLoc: 1
Own: Private Company
Par: Torstar Corp. (CDA)
Key: Ken Nugent, VP & Reg Publisher
Rob Leuschner, GM
Jan Thompson, Reg HR Mgr
Phil Sheehan, Dir of Admin
Keith Henderson, Retail Sales Mgr

Mississauga Transit

A Div. of The City of Mississauga
975 Central Pkwy. West
Mississauga, ON L5C 3B1
Tel 905-615-4636
Fax 905-615-3833
www.mississauga.ca
Line: Provides public transit service.
NAICS: 485110
#Emp: 100-249 (Tor)
#TorLoc: 1
Own: Municipal Crown Corp.
Key: Martin Powell,
    Cmmr of Transportation & Works
Geoff Marinoff, Dir
Terry Dubois, Mktg Mgr

Mississaugua Golf & Country Club Limited

1725 Mississauga Rd. North
Mississauga, ON L5H 2K4
Tel 905-278-5281
Fax 905-278-8086
www.mississaugagolf.com
NAICS: 713910
#Emp: 100-249 (Tor)
#TorLoc: 1
Own: Private Company
Key: Rick Curtis, Dir of Golf
Ian Scott, GM
Debra O'Neill, CFO

Mister Keys Ltd.

5-161 North Rivermede Rd.
Concord, ON L4K 2V3
Tel 905-738-1811
Fax 905-738-9021
www.keymanengravables.com
Line: Retails giftware and provides metal and glass engraving services.
NAICS: 453220
#Emp: 250-499 (Tor)
Own: Private Company
Key: Don Bellisario, Pres

The Mitchell Partnership Inc.

285 Yorkland Blvd.
Toronto, ON M2J 1S5
Tel 416-499-8000
Fax 416-499-7446
www.tmptoronto.com
Line: Provides mechanical engineering services.
NAICS: 541330
#Emp: 75-99 (Tor)
#TorLoc: 1
Own: Private Company
Key: John Lowden, Pres

MMM Group Limited

100 Commerce Valley Dr. West
Thornhill, ON L3T 0A1
Tel 905-882-1100
Fax 905-882-0055
www.mmm.ca
Line: Provides project management, consulting, engineering, surveying and planning services.
NAICS: 541330 541320
#Emp: 500-999 (Tor)
#TorLoc: 6
Own: Private Company
Par: McCormick Rankin Corporation (CDA)
Key: J. Bruce Bodden, Pres & CEO
Tara McMahon, VP HR
C. William Longden, Vice Chmn
Peter Overton, Dir of Mktg & Commun

Mobile Climate Control Inc.

7540 Jane St.
Vaughan, ON L4K 0A6
Tel 905-482-2750
Fax 905-482-2751
www.mcc-hvac.com
AKA: MCCI; MCC
Line: Designs and manufactures custom, fully integrated heating, ventilating and air conditioning systems for the transportation, off-road, and bus industries.
NAICS: 333416

#Emp: 250-499 (Tor)
#TorLoc: 1
Own: Private Company
Par: MCCII Holdings AB (SWE)
Key: Clas Gunneberg, Pres
Bob Kuzminski, Group VP, North American Ops
Nancy Barrett, HR Mgr
Sally Johnstone, Fin Mgr
Larry Pucci, Purch Mgr
Wasim Syed, Dir of IT
Tim Hested, Dir of Sales

Modern Niagara Toronto Inc.

2-12 Penn Dr.
Toronto, ON M9L 2A9
Tel 416-749-6031
Fax 416-749-4673
www.modernniagara.com
Line: Operates a mechanical contracting company.
NAICS: 232520
#Emp: 100-249 (Tor)
#TorLoc: 1
Own: Private Company
Key: Craig Pickering, Pres
Robert Silberstein, Mng Dir

Modis

10 Bay St., 7th Fl.
Toronto, ON M5J 2R8
Tel 416-367-2020
Fax 416-366-2001
www.modiscanada.com
AKA: Ajilon Consulting; Ajilon Communications
Line: Provides information technology solutions including staffing, professional services, and software testing.
NAICS: 541510
#Emp: 75-99 (Tor)
#TorLoc: 1
Own: Private Company
Par: Adecco SA (SWITZ)
Key: John Rutherford, Sr VP, Central Region
Lynn Bouchard, Sr VP

Moen Inc.

2816 Bristol Circ.
Oakville, ON L6H 5S7
Tel 905-829-3400
Fax 905-829-3387
www.moen.ca
Line: Manufactures faucets, bath accessories and specialty plumbing products.
NAICS: 332910 332999
#Emp: 100-249 (Tor)
#TorLoc: 1
Own: Private Company
Par: Moen Incorporated (US)
Key: Michael J. Dennis, Pres
Bob Drake, Dir of Ops
Brandie Oliver, HR Mgr
Bill Essex, Dir of Fin
John Hammill, VP Wholesale Sales
Peter Fealey, VP Retail Sales & Mktg
Tim McDonough, VP Mktg & Brand Dev

Mold-Masters (2007) Limited

233 Armstrong Ave.
Georgetown, ON L7G 4X5
Tel 905-877-0185
Fax 905-873-2818
www.moldmasters.com
Line: Manufactures hot runner systems for the injection-moulding industry.
NAICS: 333990
#Emp: 500-999 (Tor)
#TorLoc: 2
Own: Private Company
Key: William Barker, Pres & CEO
Michael Cybulski, Pres of Mold Masters, Americas
Connie Bender, VP Global HR
Stephen Farrell, CFO
Dario Vettor, VP IT

Molinaro's Fine Italian Foods Ltd.

50-2345 Stanfield Rd.
Mississauga, ON L4Y 3Y3
Tel 905-275-7400
Fax 905-275-6701
www.molinaros.com
Line: Manufactures fresh and frozen pizza, pizza crust, pasta, entrees, panzerotti and stromboli.
NAICS: 311410 311823
#Emp: 100-249 (Tor)
#TorLoc: 1
Own: Private Company
Key: Vince Molinaro, Pres
Gino Molinaro, Chmn
Frank Molinaro, Plant Mgr
Emma Rechichi, Office Mgr
Martin Girouard, Cont

Moloney Electric Inc.

35 Leading Rd.
Toronto, ON M9V 4B7
Tel 416-534-9226
Fax 416-535-1384
www.moloney-electric.com
Line: Manufactures transformers.
NAICS: 335311
#Emp: 75-99 (Tor)
#TorLoc: 1
Own: Private Company
Key: Robert Thompson, Pres
Robert Andrews, Ops Mgr
Ron Turner, HR Mgr
Satpac Kala, MIS Mgr

Molson Canada

33 Carlingview Dr.
Toronto, ON M9W 5E4
Tel 416-679-1786
Fax 416-798-8391
www.molson.com
Line: Manufactures and sells beer.
NAICS: 312120
#Emp: 500-999 (Tor)
#TorLoc: 3
Own: Public Company
Par: Molson Coors Brewing Company
(US)
Key: Dave Perkins, Pres & CEO
Suzanne Niles, Chief People Officer
Peter Nowlan, Chief Mktg Officer
Ferg Devins,
    Chief Legal & Pub Affairs Officer

Momentum Advanced Solutions

155 Commerce Valley Dr. East
Thornhill, ON L3T 7T2
Tel 905-881-4414
Fax 905-881-6533
www.momentum.com
Line: Offers internet outsourcing
solutions.
NAICS: 541510
#Emp: 75-99 (Tor)
Own: Private Company
Key: Sheldon Pollack, CEO

Monarch Corporation

200-2550 Victoria Park Ave.
Toronto, ON M2J 5A9
Tel 416-491-7440
Fax 416-491-3094
www.monarchgroup.net
AKA: The Monarch Group
Line: Constructs and develops real
estate including sub-dividers and non-
residential and residential buildings.
NAICS: 231210 231220 231110

#Emp: 100-249 (Tor)
#TorLoc: 10
Own: Private Company
Par: Taylor Morrison (UK)
Key: Brian Johnston, Pres
Brad Carr, Sr VP Housing,
    Low-Rise Div
Erika Duval, HR Mgr
Lynn Whelan, VP Fin
Emilio Tesolin, Sr VP, High Rise Div

Monarch Plastics Ltd.

116 Walker Dr.
Brampton, ON L6T 4G9
Tel 905-791-8805
Fax 905-791-8825
www.monarch-plastics.com
NAICS: 326198
#Emp: 100-249 (Tor)
#TorLoc: 1
Own: Private Company
Key: Elroy de Xavier, VP Fin & Admin

Moneris Solutions Corp.

3300 Bloor St. West
10th Fl., West Tower
Toronto, ON M8X 2X2
Tel 416-734-1000
Fax 416-734-1009
www.moneris.com
Line: Provides technological payment
processing solutions.
NAICS: 522329 541510
#Emp: 1000-4999 (Tor)
#TorLoc: 1
Own: Private Company
Par: RBC Financial Group/BMO
Financial Group (CDA)
Key: James Baumgartner, Pres & CEO
Jeff Guthrie, COO
Joan Mitchell, Sr VP HR
Samir Zabaneh, CFO
David Ades, Sr VP Sales & Mktg

Mon Sheong Home for the Aged

36 D'Arcy St.
Toronto, ON M5T 1J7
Tel 416-977-3762
Fax 416-977-3231
www.monsheong.org
Line: Operates a residential home
providing long-term care for seniors.
NAICS: 623110
#Emp: 100-249 (Tor)
#TorLoc: 1
Own: Private Company
Par: Mon Sheong Foundation (CDA)
Key: Bernard Cheung, CEO
Grace Lo, Admr

Montage Support Services

504 Oakwood Ave.
Toronto, ON M6E 2X1
Tel 416-780-9630
Fax 416-780-9382
www.montagesupport.ca
AKA: Montage
Line: Provides residential support to
adults with multiple disabilities.
NAICS: 623999
#Emp: 100-249 (Tor)
#TorLoc: 20
Own: Not-for-profit
Key: Robert Morassutti, CEO
Susan McCart, Dir of Services
Eric Man, Dir of Fin

Montecassino Hospitality Group Inc.

3710 Chesswood Dr.
Toronto, ON M3J 2W4
Tel 416-630-8100
Fax 416-630-1929
www.montecassino.on.ca
AKA: Montecassino Place Suites Hotel;
Montecassino Place Banquet Hall
Line: Operates a hotel and banquet hall.
NAICS: 721111 722320
#Emp: 100-249 (Tor)
#TorLoc: 2
Own: Private Company
Key: Toni Varone, Pres
Sabbir Khushbu, GM
Rudy Grossi, Cont
Ernesto Rossini, Purch Mgr

Moore Canada Corp.

6100 Vipond Dr.
Mississauga, ON L5T 2X1
Tel 905-362-3100
Fax 905-362-1046
www.rrdonnelley.com
AKA: RR Donnelley
Line: Manufactures business forms
and systems and provides information
management services including
database services, direct marketing and
business communication services.
NAICS: 323116
#Emp: 500-999 (Tor)
#TorLoc: 2
Own: Public Company
Par: RR Donnelley (US)
Key: Allen Hallis, Pres
Deborah Pikula, Sr Mgr of HR
Lisa Zorzi, Cont

Moores the Suit People, Inc.

129 Carlingview Dr.
Toronto, ON M9W 5E7
Tel 416-798-8082
Fax 416-798-4662
www.mooresclothing.com
Line: Sells men's clothing and offers tuxedo rentals.
NAICS: 448110 448150 532220
#Emp: 250-499 (Tor)
#TorLoc: 21
Own: Private Company
Par: Men's Wearhouse (US)
Key: Dave Starrett, Pres
Richard Bull, VP Merchandising

Morgan Commercial Babcock Inc.

12 Chelsea Lane
Brampton, ON L6T 3Y4
Tel 905-791-8100
Fax 905-791-8057
www.morgancorp.com
Line: Manufactures custom-built truck bodies.
NAICS: 336211
#Emp: 75-99 (Tor)
#TorLoc: 1
Own: Private Company
Key: Paul Clark, Plant Mgr

Morguard Investments Ltd.

1000-55 City Centre Dr.
Mississauga, ON L5B 1M3
Tel 905-281-3800
Fax 905-281-5890
www.morguard.com
Line: Operates an investment management company specializing in the acquisition, development and management of real estate.
NAICS: 531310 523920
#Emp: 250-499 (Tor)
#TorLoc: 2
Own: Private Company
Par: Morguard Corp. (CDA)
Key: Stephen Taylor, Pres & COO
Rai Sahi, Chmn
Nancy Rusk, Dir of HR
Paul Miatello, CFO
Maria Aiello, CIO
Andrea Tushingham, Dir of Retail Mktg

Morneau Sobeco

One Morneau Sobeco Centre
700-895 Don Mills Rd.
Toronto, ON M3C 1W3
Tel 416-445-2700
Fax 416-445-7989
www.morneausobeco.com
Line: Provides human resource management, employee benefit and actuarial consulting; compensation, asset management and communication consulting; benefits and pension administration services.
NAICS: 541612
#Emp: 500-999 (Tor)
#TorLoc: 1
Own: Private Company
Key: Alan Torrie, Pres & CEO
William Morneau Jr., Exec Chmn
Pierre Chamberland, Exec VP & COO
Scott Milligan, VP Fin & CFO
Rene Beaudoin, Exec VP & CIO

Morningstar Research Inc.

500-1 Toronto St.
Toronto, ON M5C 2W4
Tel 416-489-7074
Fax 416-485-6473
www.morningstar.ca
AKA: Morningstar Canada
Line: Provides independent research on investment funds.
NAICS: 523930
#Emp: 75-99 (Tor)
#TorLoc: 1
Own: Private Company
Par: Morningstar Inc. (US)
Key: Scott Mackenzie, Pres & CEO
Renee Morin, Sr VP
Barb Robertson-Mann, Dir of Fin
Ken Lecuyer, VP Sales & Mktg

Morris Brown & Sons Company Ltd.

80 Zenway Blvd.
Vaughan, ON L4H 3H1
Tel 905-856-9064
Fax 905-856-9772
www.morris-brown.com
AKA: Provincial Fruit
Line: Imports, distributes, and wholesales fresh fruits and vegetables.
NAICS: 413150
#Emp: 100-249 (Tor)
#TorLoc: 2
Own: Private Company
Key: Frank DeFrancesco, Pres
Lorie Goldfarb, VP
Diane Irving, HR Mgr

Morrison Hershfield Ltd.

600-235 Yorkland Blvd.
Toronto, ON M2J 1T1
Tel 416-499-3110
Fax 416-499-9658
www.morrisonhershfield.com
Line: Provides consulting engineering and management services.
NAICS: 541330
#Emp: 250-499 (Tor)
#TorLoc: 2
Own: Private Company
Key: Bruce Miller, Pres
Ronald J. Wilson, CEO
Pelly Shafto,
    VP HR & Organizational Dev
David Pavey, VP Fin & Corp Services
Alec Lorentiu,
    Dir of IT, IS & Corp Admin
Elaine Laprairie,
    Dir of Commun & Sales

Morrison Lamothe Inc.

2-5240 Finch Ave. East
Toronto, ON M1S 5A2
Tel 416-291-6762
Fax 416-291-5046
www.morrisonlamothe.com
Line: Produces frozen food.
NAICS: 311410
#Emp: 250-499 (Tor)
#TorLoc: 4
Own: Private Company
Key: John Pigott, Pres
Wes Douglas, COO

Mosaic Sales Solutions Canada Operating Co.

2700 Matheson Blvd. East,
West Tower, 2nd Fl.
Mississauga, ON L4W 4V9
Tel 905-238-8422
Fax 905-238-1998
www.mosaic.com
Line: Provides outsourced sales, merchandising and field marketing solutions.
NAICS: 561310
#Emp: 100-249 (Tor)
#TorLoc: 1
Own: Private Company
Par: Mosaic Sales Solutions (US)
Key: Aidan Tracey, Pres & CEO
Bob Vasley, CFO

Mother Parker's Tea & Coffee Inc.

2530 Stanfield Rd.
Mississauga, ON L4Y 1S4
Tel 905-279-9100
Fax 905-279-9821
www.mother-parkers.com
Line: Manufactures tea and coffee.
NAICS: 311920
#Emp: 250-499 (Tor)
#TorLoc: 3
Own: Private Company
Key: Michael Higgins,
　　Co-CEO & Co-COO
Denny Paynter, VP Ops
Shannon Greer, Mgr of HR
Tom Prychitka,
　　VP Shared Services & CFO
Lib Trombetta, Dir of Strategic
　　Global Sourcing
Kevin Charbonneau, Dir of Business
　　Improvement & IT
Jerry Gilbert, VP Retail Sales
Sean Bredt,
　　VP Coffee & Allied Products
Rusty James, VP Foodservice Sales

Motorcade Industries Ltd.

90 Kincort St.
Toronto, ON M6M 5G1
Tel 416-614-6118
Fax 416-614-6130
www.motorcade-ind.com
Line: Distributes automotive parts.
NAICS: 415290
#Emp: 100-249 (Tor)
#TorLoc: 6
Own: Private Company
Key: Jerold Winter, Pres
Agi Meszaros, HR Mgr
Jeffrey Zacks, CFO

Motor Express Toronto

1335 Shawson Dr.
Mississauga, ON L4W 1C4
Tel 905-564-0241
Fax 905-564-2387
www.motorexpresstoronto.com
Line: Operates a truck terminal and
cartage.
NAICS: 488490
#Emp: 100-249 (Tor)
#TorLoc: 1
Own: Private Company
Par: Manitoulin Transport (CAN)
Key: Adrian O'Brien, GM
Colin Barson, Ops Mgr
Carlo Tomei, Admin Mgr

Motorola Canada Ltd.

8133 Warden Ave.
Markham, ON L6G 1B3
Tel 905-948-5200
Fax 905-948-5250
www.motorola.ca
Line: Provides integrated
communications and embedded
electronic solutions.
NAICS: 417320 417310
#Emp: 250-499 (Tor)
#TorLoc: 2
Own: Private Company
Par: Motorola Inc. (US)
Key: Sean Miller, Pres
Richard Bawly, VP
Donna McKenzie, Dir of HR

Motor Specialty Manufacturers

A Div. of Magna Power Train
390 Hanlan Rd.
Woodbridge, ON L4L 3P6
Tel 905-851-6791
Fax 905-851-5286
www.magnapowertrain.com
Line: Manufactures automotive parts.
NAICS: 336390
#Emp: 250-499 (Tor)
#TorLoc: 1
Own: Private Company
Par: Magna International Inc. (CDA)
Key: Alan Lindsay, GM
Tanya Morissette, HR Mgr

Mountain Equipment Cooperative

400 King St. West
Toronto, ON M5V 1K2
Tel 416-340-2667
Fax 416-340-7708
www.mec.ca
AKA: MEC
Line: Retails outdoor sporting
equipment.
NAICS: 451110 448140
#Emp: 100-249 (Tor)
#TorLoc: 2
Own: Not-for-profit
Key: Sean McSweany, GM

Mount Pleasant Group of Cemeteries

500-65 Overlea Blvd.
Toronto, ON M4H 1P1
Tel 416-696-7866
Fax 416-696-0227
www.mountpleasant
　　groupofcemeteries.com
Line: Operates a non-profit, non-
sectarian corporation that provides
burial, cremation, entombment,
memorialization, visitation chapel and
reception, and pre-planning services.
NAICS: 812220
#Emp: 250-499 (Tor)
#TorLoc: 10
Own: Not-for-profit
Par: Mount Pleasant Group (CDA)
Key: Glenn McClary, Pres
Dennis Moir, Dir of Cemetery Services
Angie Aquino, Dir of Sales
Glen Timney, Dir of Dev

Mount Sinai Hospital

600 University Ave.
Toronto, ON M5G 1X5
Tel 416-586-4200
Fax 416-586-8555
www.mtsinai.on.ca
Line: Operates an acute care teaching
hospital.
NAICS: 622111
#Emp: 1000-4999 (Tor)
#TorLoc: 3
Own: Not-for-profit
Key: Joseph Mapa, Pres & CEO
Debbie Fischer, Sr VP, Organizational
　　Dev & Strategic Projects
Joan Sproul, Sr VP Fin
Prateek Dwivedi, VP & CIO

M. & P. Tool Products Inc.

43 Regan Rd.
Brampton, ON L7A 1B3
Tel 905-840-5550
Fax 905-840-5560
www.mp-tool.com
AKA: Space Aid
Line: Manufactures metal fixtures,
stampings and vehicles.
NAICS: 332118
#Emp: 75-99 (Tor)
#TorLoc: 1
Own: Private Company
Key: Martin Prufer, Pres & GM
Henry Hutzal, Cont

M.R.S. Company Ltd.

214-5535 Eglinton Ave. West
Toronto, ON M9C 5K5
Tel 416-620-2720
Fax 416-622-1724
www.mrscompany.com
Line: Provides information technology
consulting.
NAICS: 541510
#Emp: 75-99 (Tor)
#TorLoc: 1
Own: Private Company
Key: Alex Perklin, Pres & CEO
Ramesh JackPaul,
    Dir of Consulting Services Group
Gus Manios, Dir of Tech & Solutions
Mario Zaborski, Dir of Sales

MSB Plastics Manufacturing Ltd.

23 Disco Rd.
Toronto, ON M9W 1M2
Tel 416-674-1471
Fax 416-674-9611
www.abcgrp.com
Line: Manufactures motor vehicle
plastic parts.
NAICS: 326193
#Emp: 100-249 (Tor)
#TorLoc: 1
Own: Private Company
Par: ABC Group (CDA)
Key: Mike Schmidt, Mgr

M S Employment Consultants Ltd.

43 Havenview Rd.
Toronto, ON M1S 3A4
Tel 416-299-1070
Fax 416-609-8949
Line: Operates an employment agency.
NAICS: 561310
#Emp: 75-99 (Tor)
#TorLoc: 1
Own: Private Company
Key: Milfred Marcos, VP

MSM Transportation Inc.

124 Commercial Rd.
Bolton, ON L7E 1K4
Tel 905-951-6800
Fax 905-951-6818
www.shipmsm.com
Line: Operates a trucking company.
NAICS: 484110 484121
#Emp: 75-99 (Tor)
#TorLoc: 1
Own: Private Company

Key: Robert Murray, Pres
Mike McCammon, Mng Partner
John Wheeler, Dir of Ops
Joanne Murray, HR Mgr
Michael Drake, Cont
Steven Koyanagi, IT
Elden Sammut, VP Nat'l Accounts

MSO Construction Ltd.

175 Bethridge Rd.
Toronto, ON M9W 1N5
Tel 416-743-3224
Fax 416-743-6664
Line: Provides road maintenance.
NAICS: 231310
#Emp: 75-99 (Tor)
#TorLoc: 1
Own: Private Company
Par: TJ Pounder (Ontario) Ltd. (CDA)
Key: Robert Bray, Treas

MSP

37 Penn Dr.
Toronto, ON M9L 2A6
Tel 416-745-9600
Fax 416-745-9620
www.mspmfg.com
NAICS: 333519
#Emp: 75-99 (Tor)
#TorLoc: 1
Own: Private Company
Key: Dave Puri, Production Mgr

MTB Truck & Bus Collision

8170 Lawson Rd.
Milton, ON L9T 5C4
Tel 905-876-0669
Fax 905-875-2566
www.m-t-b.com
AKA: MTB Collision
Line: Operates an automotive repair
shop.
NAICS: 811121
#Emp: 75-99 (Tor)
#TorLoc: 1
Own: Private Company
Key: Bill Finan, Owner
Merrill Hoffman, GM
Sherry Hadlow, Acctng Mgr

MTD Metro Tool & Die Ltd.

1065 Pantera Dr.
Mississauga, ON L4W 2X4
Tel 905-625-8464
Fax 905-625-3397
www.mtdmetro.com
Line: Manufactures sheet metal
stampings, assemblies, subassemblies,
power coat paint line and tool and die.
NAICS: 332118 333519

#Emp: 75-99 (Tor)
#TorLoc: 2
Own: Private Company
Key: Marcel Pantano, Pres & CEO
Edward Cooray, VP Ops
Jini Fernando, Cont
Rosemary Pellicori, Purch Agent
Scott Kolb, VP Sales & Mktg

MTS Allstream Inc.

200 Wellington St. West
Toronto, ON M5V 3G2
Tel 416-345-2000
Fax 416-345-2840
www.mtsallstream.com
Line: Provides a wide range of
telecommunications products and
services.
NAICS: 513330 513340 513390
#Emp: 1000-4999 (Tor)
Own: Public Company
Par: Manitoba Telecom Services Inc.
(CDA)
Key: Dean Prevost, Pres
Pierre Blovia, CEO
Aliana Rozenek, Chief HR Officer
Wayne S. Demkey, CFO
Paul Frizado, Chief Tech & Info Officer
Janet Thompson, VP Sales
Jim DeMerlis, VP Mktg
Helen Reeves, Chief Commun Officer

Mueller Canada

82 Hopper Rd.
Barrie, ON L4N 8Z9
Tel 705-719-9965
Fax 705-719-4959
www.muellercanada.com
Line: Manufactures ULC-FM approved
fire hydrants, IBBM gate valves, check
valves, corporation brass, resilient
seated gate valves, fire protection
product service boxes, municipal
castings and butterfly valves.
NAICS: 332910
#Emp: 100-249 (Tor)
#TorLoc: 1
Own: Private Company
Par: Mueller Co. (US)
Key: Lonni Royal, VP & GM
Christine McCarthy, HR Mgr
Fred Welsh, Cont
Doug Willey, Nat'l Sales Mgr

Muirs Cartage Ltd.

205 Doney Cres.
Concord, ON L4K 1P6
Tel 905-761-8251
Fax 905-761-2089
www.gomuirs.com
NAICS: 484110 484121
#Emp: 250-499 (Tor)
#TorLoc: 1
Own: Private Company
Key: Ted Brown, VP Ops
Kurt Christadler, VP Admin & Cont
Ray Barrett, Nat'l Account Mgr

MukiBaum Treatment Centres

40 Samor Rd.
Toronto, ON M6A 1J6
Tel 416-630-2222
Fax 416-630-2236
www.mukibaum.com
Line: Provides people with
developmental and emotional
disabilities with the opportunity to
achieve personal growth and become
contributing members of society.
NAICS: 813310
#Emp: 100-249 (Tor)
#TorLoc: 12
Own: Not-for-profit
Key: Nehama Baum,
   Founder & Exec Dir
Cheryl Farrugia,
   Dir, Program & Services
Michelle D'Souza, HR Mgr
Suresh Tharma, Fin Mgr

Multichair Inc.

6900 Davand Dr.
Mississauga, ON L5T 1J5
Tel 905-670-1794
Fax 905-670-1887
www.multitube.com
AKA: Multitube Division
Line: Manufactures welded steel tubing
and tubular chair frames.
NAICS: 331210
#Emp: 100-249 (Tor)
#TorLoc: 3
Own: Private Company
Key: Frank Simmons, Pres
Larry Simmons, GM
Michael Feher, IT, Admin & HR Mgr
Jay Jasinghe, Acctng Mgr
Les Nagy, Purch Mgr

Multi-Health Systems Inc.

3770 Victoria Park Ave.
Toronto, ON M2H 3M6
Tel 416-492-2627
Fax 416-492-3343
www.mhs.com
AKA: MHS
Line: Develops, publishes and markets
scientifically validated assessments
in the educational, safety, clinical,
forensic and human resources areas.
NAICS: 511210 541720
#Emp: 75-99 (Tor)
#TorLoc: 1
Own: Private Company
Key: Hazel Weldon, Publisher & COO
Steven Stein, CEO
Martin Block, VP Fin & Ops

Multimatic Inc.

85 Valleywood Dr.
Markham, ON L3R 5E5
Tel 905-470-9149
Fax 905-470-6292
www.multimatic.com
Line: Supplies components, systems
and services to the automotive
industry.
NAICS: 415290
#Emp: 100-249 (Tor)
#TorLoc: 1
Own: Private Company
Key: Peter Czapka, Pres
Brian Pring, Dir of HR
Paul Topp, Cont

Multimedia Nova Corporation

101 Wingold Ave.
Toronto, ON M6B 1P8
Tel 416-785-4300
Fax 416-785-7350
www.multimedianova.com
Line: Operates a diverse publishing and
printing company that owns sixteen
newspapers and represents over
seventy publishers.
NAICS: 511190
#Emp: 100-249 (Tor)
#TorLoc: 1
Own: Public Company
Key: Lori Abittan, Pres & CEO
Pina Moschetti, HR Mgr
Joe Mastrogiacomo, VP Fin & CFO
Joe March, Mktg Mgr

Multipak Ltd.

6417 Viscount Rd.
Mississauga, ON L4V 1K8
Tel 905-678-2825
Fax 905-678-6133
www.multipak.com
AKA: Multipak McLernon
Line: Manufactures flexible packaging
materials.
NAICS: 322220 561910
#Emp: 100-249 (Tor)
#TorLoc: 1
Own: Private Company
Par: Acer McLernon Canada Inc. (CDA)
Key: David H. McLernon, Pres
Greg Beer, VP Fin
Ken Mitchell, Purch Mgr

Multiple Pakfold Business Forms

A Div. of Data Business Forms Ltd.
7765 Tranmere Dr.
Mississauga, ON L5S 1V5
Tel 905-678-2351
Fax 905-678-9525
www.multiple.com
Line: Manufactures business forms and
labels.
NAICS: 323116 322220
#Emp: 100-249 (Tor)
#TorLoc: 2
Own: Private Company
Par: Workflow Management Inc. (US)
Key: David Odell, Pres & CEO
Mario Raposo, Dir of Ops
Rene McIntosh, HR
Robert Griffen, Dir of Sales & Mktg
Dan Maillet, Product Dev

Multiple Retirement Services Inc.

2100-777 Bay St.
Toronto, ON M5G 2N4
Tel 416-964-0660
Fax 416-413-1723
www.mrs.com
AKA: MRS
Line: Provides mutual funds services.
NAICS: 523920
#Emp: 250-499 (Tor)
#TorLoc: 1
Own: Private Company
Par: Mackenzie Financial Corp. (CDA)
Key: Andrew Dalglish, CEO of MRS

Multiple Sclerosis Society of Canada

700-175 Bloor St. East., North Tower
Toronto, ON M4W 3R8
Tel 416-922-6065
Fax 416-922-7538
www.mssociety.ca
Line: Raises awareness and funds for multiple sclerosis research enabling people affected by MS to enhance their quality of life.
NAICS: 813310
#Emp: 5000-9999 (Tor)
Own: Not-for-profit
Key: Yves Savoie, Pres & CEO
Jamie Hall, VP Fin & CFO

Multivans Inc.

40 Nixon Rd.
Bolton, ON L7E 5T2
Tel 905-857-3171
Fax 905-857-0127
www.multivans.com
Line: Manufactures cube vans and straight trucks.
NAICS: 336211
#Emp: 75-99 (Tor)
#TorLoc: 1
Own: Private Company
Key: Fred Seymour, Pres
Rick Rovito, Ops Mgr
Steven Schafer, VP

Multy Home LP

100 Pippin Rd.
Concord, ON L4K 4X9
Tel 905-760-3737
Fax 905-760-3738
www.multyindustries.com
Line: Manufactures floor coverings.
NAICS: 326198
#Emp: 100-249 (Tor)
#TorLoc: 3
Own: Private Company
Key: Derek Erdman, Pres
Pam White, Payroll Admr

Mulvey & Banani International Inc.

44 Mobile Dr.
Toronto, ON M4A 2P2
Tel 416-751-2520
Fax 416-751-1430
www.mulveyandbanani.com
Line: Designs electrical and communication systems for commercial and institutional buildings.
NAICS: 541330
#Emp: 75-99 (Tor)
#TorLoc: 1
Own: Private Company
Key: Bob Lymer, Pres

Munich Life Management Corp Ltd.

390 Bay St., 26th Fl.
Toronto, ON M5H 2Y2
Tel 416-359-2200
Fax 416-361-0305
www.munichre.ca
Line: Provides management services.
NAICS: 524210 541611
#Emp: 100-249 (Tor)
Own: Private Company
Par: Munich Re Group (GER)
Key: Mary Forrest, Pres
Jackie Puchalski, Sr VP HR
Doug Touzer, Sr VP & Actuary
Helene Michaud, Asst VP Mktg

Munich Reinsurance Company of Canada

390 Bay St., 22nd Fl.
Toronto, ON M5H 2Y2
Tel 416-366-9206
Fax 416-366-4330
www.mroc.com
Line: Provides reinsurance of all classes, except life.
NAICS: 524139
#Emp: 100-249 (Tor)
#TorLoc: 1
Own: Private Company
Par: Munich Re Group (GER)
Key: Kenneth B. Irvin, Pres & CEO
Linda J. Wahrer, Exec VP
Denyse Gauer, Asst VP HR
Gary Gray, VP Fin & CFO
Peter L. Walker, Exec VP & CIO

The Municipality of Clarington

40 Temperance St.
Bowmanville, ON L1C 3A6
Tel 905-623-3379
Fax 905-623-5717
www.clarington.net
AKA: Clarington
NAICS: 913910
#Emp: 500-999 (Tor)
#TorLoc: 1
Own: Government
Key: Adrian Foster, Mayor
Franklin Wu, CAO
Frederick Horvath, Dir of Ops
Marie Marano, Dir of Corp Services
Nancy Taylor, Dir of Fin
Jennifer Cooke, Mktg, Tourism & Commun Mgr

Municipal Property Assessment Corp.

1305 Pickering Pkwy.
Pickering, ON L1V 3P2
Tel 1-877-635-6722
Fax 905-837-6346
www.mpac.ca
Line: Provides property assessment services.
NAICS: 541990
#Emp: 500-999 (Tor)
#TorLoc: 6
Own: Not-for-profit
Key: Carl Isenburg, Pres & CAO
Larry Hummel, VP Property Values & Customer Relns
Gerry Stuart, VP Corp and HR
Nicole McNeil, CFO
Antoni Wisniowski, VP IT
Lee Taylor, Dir of Business Dev
Michael Jacoby, Dir of Commun

Mutual Fund Dealers Association of Canada

1000-121 King St. West
Toronto, ON M5H 3T9
Tel 416-361-6332
Fax 416-943-1218
www.mfda.ca
Line: Operates a mutual fund professional membership association.
NAICS: 813920
#Emp: 100-249 (Tor)
#TorLoc: 1
Own: Private Company
Key: Larry Waite, Pres & CEO
Ken Woodard, Dir of Commun & Membership Services

Muzzo Brothers Group Inc.

50 Confederation Pkwy.
Concord, ON L4K 4T8
Tel 905-326-4000
Fax 905-326-4001
AKA: Marel Contractors
Line: Operates a home construction
company.
NAICS: 232410
#Emp: 250-499 (Tor)
#TorLoc: 1
Own: Private Company
Key: Marco Muzzo, Pres
Cecila Gaggi, HR Mgr

Mylan Inc.

85 Advance Rd.
Toronto, ON M8Z 2S6
Tel 416-236-2631
Fax 416-236-2940
www.mylan.ca
NAICS: 325410
#Emp: 500-999 (Tor)
#TorLoc: 5
Own: Private Company
Key: Dick Guest, Pres
Ray Coates, GM & VP Ops
Vidar Bentsen, Business Dev

Myron

5610 Finch Ave. East
Toronto, ON M1B 6A6
Tel 416-291-9000
Fax 416-291-8786
www.myron.com
AKA: Smarter Business Gifts
Line: Offers imprinted business gifts,
promotional and advertising material.
NAICS: 418990 418210
#Emp: 500-999 (Tor)
#TorLoc: 2
Own: Private Company
Par: Adler International Ltd. (US)
Key: James Adler, CEO
Allan Courneya, GM & Chief of Sales
Beth Walland, HR Mgr
Bruce Kaulter, IT Mgr

Mytox Manufacturing

251 Aviva Park Dr.
Woodbridge, ON L4L 9C1
Tel 905-851-6666
Fax 905-851-7800
www.magna.com
Line: Manufactures automobile parts.
NAICS: 336390
#Emp: 500-999 (Tor)
#TorLoc: 1

Own: Private Company
Par: Magna International Inc. (CDA)
Key: John Harding, GM
Julie Wagner, HR Mgr

Nafta Foods & Packaging Ltd.

725 Intermodal Dr.
Brampton, ON L6T 5W2
Tel 905-791-9978
Fax 905-791-9874
www.naftafoods.com
Line: Manufactures gingerbread and
seasonal cookie kits.
NAICS: 311821
#Emp: 75-99 (Tor)
Own: Private Company
Key: Dragon Markovic, Pres
Goca Markovic, HR Mgr

Nailor Industries Inc.

98 Toryork Dr.
Toronto, ON M9L 1X6
Tel 416-744-3300
Fax 416-744-3360
www.nailor.com
Line: Manufactures air distribution
products including grills, registers,
diffusers, terminal units as well as fire,
smoke and control dampers.
NAICS: 334512 332329
#Emp: 100-249 (Tor)
#TorLoc: 3
Own: Private Company
Key: Michael T. Nailor, Pres
John Dollimore, COO
Mary Lewis, HR Mgr
Christine Rumbolt, Acctng Mgr
Janice Mak, Purch Mgr
Denka Mortella, GM

Nalco Canada Co.

1055 Truman St.
Burlington, ON L7R 3V7
Tel 905-632-8791
Fax 905-632-0849
www.nalco.com
Line: Manufactures and distributes
specialty chemicals.
NAICS: 325999
#Emp: 100-249 (Tor)
#TorLoc: 1
Own: Public Company
Par: Nalco Company (US)
Key: Evy Beraldo, Country Admr
Cynthia Jones, HR Mgr

Nanowave Inc.

425 Horner Ave.
Toronto, ON M8W 4W3
Tel 416-252-5602
Fax 416-252-7077
www.nanowavetech.com
Line: Manufactures components for
use in optical electronics, terrestrial
and satellite communications, military
and commercial radar, electronic
warfare and test equipment systems.
NAICS: 334220
#Emp: 100-249 (Tor)
#TorLoc: 1
Own: Private Company
Key: Justin Miller, Pres

NAPA Auto Parts

525 Boxwood Dr.
Cambridge, ON N3E 1A5
Tel 519-650-4444
Fax 519-650-6830
www.napaonlinecanada.com
Line: Distributes wholesale auto parts.
NAICS: 415290 441310
#Emp: 100-249 (Tor)
#TorLoc: 13
Own: Public Company
Par: Genuine Parts Company (US)
Key: Dave Meagher, Ops Mgr
Robert Duncan, Rcg VP
Kevin Patterson, Sales Mgr

The National Ballet of Canada

470 Queens Quay West
Toronto, ON M5V 3K4
Tel 416-345-9686
Fax 416-345-8323
www.national.ballet.ca
AKA: Walter Carsen Centre for the
National Ballet of Canada
NAICS: 711120 711321
#Emp: 100-249 (Tor)
#TorLoc: 1
Own: Not-for-profit
Key: Kevin Garland,
  Exec Dir & Co-CEO
Lucille Joseph, Chair
Leigh Ann Layno, Dir of HR
Barry Shour, Dir of Fin & Admin
Jeffrie Owen,
  Mgr of Systems & Network
Diana Reitberger, Dir of Dev
Belinda Bale, Sr Associate Dir of Mktg
Julia Drake, Dir of Commun

The National Ballet School

400 Jarvis St.
Toronto, ON M4Y 2G6
Tel 416-964-3780
Fax 416-964-5133
www.nbs-enb.ca
Line: Offers professional dance training.
NAICS: 611610
#Emp: 100-249 (Tor)
#TorLoc: 1
Own: Not-for-profit
Key: Jeff Melanson, Exec Dir & Co-CEO
Mavis Staines, Artistic Dir & Co-CEO
Frank Randall, Head of Property & Ops
Elizabeth Wassenich, Sr HR Mgr

National Bank Financial Inc.

3200-130 King St. West
P.O. Box 21
Toronto, ON M5X 1J9
Tel 416-869-3707
Fax 416-869-7500
www.nbfinancial.com
AKA: NBCN Clearing Inc.; National Bank Financial Services Ltd.
Line: Provides broker, dealer, securities clearing, trust and custodian services.
NAICS: 523120
#Emp: 500-999 (Tor)
#TorLoc: 5
Own: Private Company
Par: National Bank of Canada (CDA)
Key: Ricardo Pascoe, Co-Pres & CEO
Luc Paiement, Co-Pres & CEO

National Carpet Mills Ltd.

5195 Maingate Dr.
Mississauga, ON L4W 1G4
Tel 905-282-1730
Fax 905-282-1725
www.nationalcarpet.ca
Line: Manufactures carpets and rugs.
NAICS: 314110
#Emp: 75-99 (Tor)
#TorLoc: 1
Own: Private Company
Key: Richard White, GM

The National Club

303 Bay St.
Toronto, ON M5H 2R1
Tel 416-364-3247
Fax 416-364-5666
www.thenationalclub.com
Line: Operates a private members club.
NAICS: 813920
#Emp: 75-99 (Tor)
#TorLoc: 1

Own: Private Company
Key: Bill Morari, GM
Laurie Farnum,
    Asst Mgr, Private Functions

National Concrete Accessories

110 Belfield Rd.
Toronto, ON M9W 1G1
Tel 416-245-4720
Fax 416-242-2727
www.nca.ca
AKA: Debro Steel; Debro Chemical; Amalgamet Canada; Wilkinson Steel; Exchanger Industries; Premetalco Inc.
Line: Manufactures and distributes concrete form hardware, accessories and products.
NAICS: 332510
#Emp: 500-999 (Tor)
#TorLoc: 1
Own: Private Company
Par: Premetalco Inc. (UK)
Key: Lawry Simon,
Pres, Eastern Canada

National Fast Freight

A Div. of Calyx Transportation
391 Creditstone Rd.
Concord, ON L4K 1N8
Tel 905-761-0009
Fax 905-761-6683
www.nationalfastfreight.com
Line: Operates a transport company offering multimodal transportation services.
NAICS: 488519
#Emp: 100-249 (Tor)
#TorLoc: 1
Own: Private Company
Key: Patrick Cain, Pres
Rob Donaghey, CEO
David Convery, VP Ops
Ken Smale, HR Mgr
Tatiana Kresling, Cont
Mark Breckenridge, IT Mgr

The National Golf Club of Canada

134 Clubhouse Rd.
Woodbridge, ON L4L 2W2
Tel 416-798-4900
Fax 416-798-7324
www.nationalgolf.ca
NAICS: 713910
#Emp: 100-249 (Tor)
#TorLoc: 1
Own: Private Company
Key: Stephen Dickinson, Exec Dir
Michael Young, Cont
Janet Wessner, Club Sales Admr

National Instore Services Corp.

101-2430 Meadowpine Blvd.
Mississauga, ON L5N 6S2
Tel 905-819-6800
Fax 905-542-2773
www.niscorp.ca
AKA: NIS
Line: Provides consulting services for the sales, service and retail merchandising industries.
NAICS: 541611
#Emp: 75-99 (Tor)
#TorLoc: 1
Own: Private Company
Key: Bill MacGillivray, Pres

National Logistics Services

B-475 Admiral Blvd.
Mississauga, ON L5T 1A1
Tel 905-696-7278
www.nls.ca
AKA: NLS
Line: Provides warehousing, distribution and transportation logistics services.
NAICS: 493110
#Emp: 75-99 (Tor)
#TorLoc: 1
Own: Private Company
Key: Terry Vukosa, VP Ops
Blair Smith, Sales Mgr

National Post

300-1450 Don Mills Rd.
Toronto, ON M3B 2X7
Tel 416-383-2300
Fax 416-442-2305
www.nationalpost.com
NAICS: 511110
#Emp: 250-499 (Tor)
#TorLoc: 1
Own: Private Company
Par: Canwest Global Communications Corp. (CDA)
Key: Gordon Fisher, Pres
Douglas Kelly, Publisher
Santina Zito, VP Ops
Cheryl Callahan, Dir of HR
Rena Brickman, Dir of Fin
Yuri Machado, VP Advertising Sales

NATIONAL Public Relations Inc.

500-310 Front St. West
Toronto, ON M5V 3B5
Tel 416-586-0180
Fax 416-586-9916
www.national.ca
Line: Operates a full service public
relations firm.
NAICS: 541820
#Emp: 75-99 (Tor)
#TorLoc: 1
Own: Private Company
Par: Res Publica Consulting Group Inc.
(CDA)
Key: John Crean, Nat'l Mng Partner
David Weiner, Sr Partner
Lina Ko, Partner
Sam Bornstein, Partner
Chuck Johnston, Partner

National Rubber Technologies Corp.

35 Cawthra Ave.
Toronto, ON M6N 5B3
Tel 416-657-1111
Fax 416-656-1231
www.nrtna.com
Line: Designs, manufactures and
supplies finished products from
engineered rubber products to
industrial and automotive companies.
NAICS: 325210
#Emp: 250-499 (Tor)
#TorLoc: 2
Own: Private Company
Key: Al Power, CEO

National Sports

145 Renfrew Dr.
Markham, ON L3R 9R6
Tel 905-946-5545
Fax 905-852-5810
www.forzani.com
AKA: National Sports Practice
Amusement Centre
Line: Retails sporting goods.
NAICS: 451110 448140
#Emp: 500-999 (Tor)
#TorLoc: 12
Own: Private Company
Par: The Forzani Group Ltd. (CDA)
Key: Thomas G. Quinn, Pres & COO
Michael R. Lambert, CFO

National Wireless

8-2679 Bristol Circ.
Oakville, ON L6H 6Z8
Tel 905-828-5345
Fax 905-829-5488
www.nationalwireless.ca
Line: Provides wireless technology
services, mobile data application,
development and implementation, and
fleet tracking services.
NAICS: 513320
#Emp: 75-99 (Tor)
#TorLoc: 8
Own: Private Company
Key: Dan Baker, VP Sales & Mktg
Dave Porco,
    Nat'l Sales Mgr, Corp Accounts

Navantis Inc.

21 Randolph Ave., 2nd Fl.
Toronto, ON M6P 4G4
Tel 647-258-9031
Fax 416-583-4940
www.navantis.com
Line: Provides computer consulting
services.
NAICS: 541510
#Emp: 75-99 (Tor)
#TorLoc: 1
Own: Private Company
Key: John Kvasnic,
    Chief Architect, CEO & Co-Founder
Jason Martin, Pres & Co-Founder
Mario Perez,
    Sr VP Sales & Client Services

NAV Canada

77 Metcalfe St.
P.O. Box 3411, Stn. D
Ottawa, ON K1P 5L6
Tel 1-800-876-4693
Fax 1-877-663-6656
www.navcanada.ca
Line: Provides air navigation.
NAICS: 488190
#Emp: 500-999 (Tor)
#TorLoc: 5
Own: Not-for-profit
Key: John Crichton, Pres & CEO
Rudy Keller, VP Ops

Naylor Group Inc.

455 North Service Rd. East
Oakville, ON L6H 1A5
Tel 905-338-8000
Fax 905-338-8369
www.naylorgroupinc.com
Line: Electrical, communications and
mechanical contractor for industrial
and commercial facilities.
NAICS: 232510 232520
#Emp: 100-249 (Tor)
#TorLoc: 4
Own: Private Company
Key: Tom Hitchman, Pres

NCR Canada Ltd.

6865 Century Ave.
Mississauga, ON L5N 2E2
Tel 905-826-9000
Fax 905-819-4030
www.ncr.com
Line: Provides privacy-enabled
warehouses and customer relationship
management applications, store
automation and automated teller
machines to the retail, financial,
communications, manufacturing,
travel, transportation, and insurance
markets.
NAICS: 541510
#Emp: 500-999 (Tor)
#TorLoc: 4
Own: Public Company
Par: NCR Corp. (US)
Key: Luc Villeneuve, Pres
Kevin Marshman, VP & GM
Steve Walker, Global Procurement

Nealanders International Inc.

6980 Creditview Rd.
Mississauga, ON L5N 8E2
Tel 905-812-7300
Fax 905-812-7308
www.nealanders.com
Line: Manufactures specialized
ingredients and processing aids to the
bakery, food and allied industries.
NAICS: 311990
#Emp: 75-99 (Tor)
#TorLoc: 1
Own: Private Company
Par: Nealanders (CDA)
Key: Tim Sinclair, Pres & CEO
Daryl Holmes,
    Vice Chmn & Co-Founder
Joe Nealon, Dir & Co-Founder

Nedco Ontario

A Div. of Rexel Canada Electrical Inc.
5600 Keaton Cres.
Mississauga, ON L5R 3G3
Tel 905-568-2425
Fax 905-568-2976
www.nedco.ca
Line: Distributes electrical and datacom equipment.
NAICS: 416110
#Emp: 250-499 (Tor)
#TorLoc: 15
Own: Public Company
Key: Richard Ferguson,
   VP, Nedco Canada
Larry McIntosh, GM, Nedco Ontario
Rob Floyd, Mktg Mgr

Neff Kitchen Manufacturing Ltd.

151 East Dr.
Brampton, ON L6T 1B5
Tel 905-791-7770
Fax 905-791-7788
www.neffkitchens.com
Line: Designs and manufactures kitchens.
NAICS: 337123
#Emp: 100-249 (Tor)
#TorLoc: 1
Own: Private Company
Key: Miro Nowak, Pres
Anthony Folan, Mgr of HR
Scott Massie, Mktg Mgr

Neighbourhood Link Support Services

3036 Danforth Ave.
Toronto, ON M4C 1N2
Tel 416-691-7407
Fax 416-691-8466
www.neighbourhoodlink.org
Line: Provides assistance to seniors, newcomers, unemployed and youth.
NAICS: 624120
#Emp: 100-249 (Tor)
#TorLoc: 1
Own: Not-for-profit
Key: Mary McGowan, Exec Dir
Gerri Badcock, Dir of Ops
Brenda Mahoney, Dir of Fin

Nelson Aggregate Co.

2433 No. 2 Sideroad
P.O. Box 1070
Burlington, ON L7R 4L8
Tel 905-335-5250
Fax 905-325-2265
www.nelsonaggregate.com
NAICS: 212314
#Emp: 75-99 (Tor)
#TorLoc: 1
Own: Public Company
Key: Norm Elmhirst, Pres
Dianne Gesztesi, Payroll Clerk
Doug Gilbert, Secy-Treas

Nelson Education Ltd.

A Div. of Thomson Canada Ltd.
1120 Birchmount Rd.
Toronto, ON M1K 5G4
Tel 416-752-9100
Fax 416-752-8101
www.nelson.com
Line: Publishes educational texts.
NAICS: 511130
#Emp: 250-499 (Tor)
#TorLoc: 1
Own: Private Company
Par: Omers Capital Partners (CDA)
Key: Greg Nordal, Pres & CEO
Susan Cline,
   Sr VP Media Production Services
Marlene Nyilassy,
   Sr VP People & Engagement
Michael Andrews, CFO & VP Fin
Chris Besse,
   VP School Division & Mng Dir
James Reeve,
   VP Higher Education & Mng Dir
Jean Bouchard, VP French
   Language Markets & GM

Nelson Industrial Inc.

1155 Squires Beach Rd.
Pickering, ON L1W 3T9
Tel 905-428-2240
Fax 905-428-2392
www.nelsonindust.com
Line: Manufactures customized products that include contract services, architectural metals, access doors, and storage products.
NAICS: 337215 332999
#Emp: 75-99 (Tor)
#TorLoc: 1
Own: Private Company
Key: Jeff Nelson, Pres
Dorin Radu, Corp Mng Dir
Bernadette Flynn, Office Supr & HR
Graham Cuthbertson, Cont
James Nazareth, Purch Coord

Nemato Corp.

1605 McEwen Dr.
Whitby, ON L1N 7L4
Tel 905-571-5305
Fax 905-571-3935
www.nemato.com
AKA: Nemato Composites Corp.
Line: Manufactures engineered fiberglass reinforced plastic products.
NAICS: 326198
#Emp: 75-99 (Tor)
#TorLoc: 1
Own: Private Company
Key: Steve Andrews, Pres
Luis Pacheco, Plant Mgr
Rob Turley, Cont

Neopost Canada Limited

150 Steelcase Rd.
Markham, ON L3R 3J9
Tel 905-475-3722
Fax 905-475-7699
www.neopost.ca
Line: Distributes and supports mailings and postage meters, strippers, and sorters.
NAICS: 334512
#Emp: 100-249 (Tor)
#TorLoc: 3
Own: Private Company
Par: Neopost SA (FR)
Key: Lou Gizzarelli, Pres
Monique Moreau-Gray, Dir of HR
Grant Gillham, VP Fin
Robert Chan, VP Tech Services & Dist
Terry Stroup, Dir of Dealer Sales
Edward Collins, VP Direct Sales

Nesel Fast Freight Inc.

20 Holland Dr.
Bolton, ON L7E 1G6
Tel 905-951-7770
Fax 905-951-0589
www.nesel.com
Line: Provides transport, specializing in moving furniture, appliances and electronics from manufacturer to retailer.
NAICS: 484229
#Emp: 100-249 (Tor)
#TorLoc: 1
Own: Private Company
Key: Kathy McWilliams, Pres

Nestlé Canada Inc.

25 Sheppard Ave. West
Toronto, ON M2N 6S8
Tel 416-512-9000
Fax 416-218-2654
www.nestle.ca
Line: Processes coffee, beverages, ice
cream, frozen meals, confectioneries,
and pet care products as well as
providing food services for restaurants,
hospitals and other facilities.
NAICS: 311920 311330
#Emp: 1000-4999 (Tor)
#TorLoc: 6
Own: Private Company
Par: Nestlé SA (SWITZ)
Key: Tim Brown, Pres & CEO
William Broughton, Sr VP & CFO

New Balance Toronto

1510 Yonge St.
Toronto, ON M4T 1Z6
Tel 416-848-4797
Fax 416-962-8889
www.newbalancetoronto.ca
Line: Retails specialty footwear and
apparel.
NAICS: 448210
#Emp: 100-249 (Tor)
#TorLoc: 5
Own: Private Company
Key: Sean McGrath, Partner
Karin McLean, Display Mgr

Newell Rubbermaid Canada

400-586 Argus Rd.
Oakville, ON L6J 3J3
Tel 800-387-7882
www.newellrubbermaid.com
Line: Distributes writing instruments
and other office products.
NAICS: 418210
#Emp: 100-249 (Tor)
#TorLoc: 1
Own: Public Company
Par: Newell Rubbermaid (US)
Key: Bob King, VP & GM
Gino Tersigni, Pres
Mark Stephen, Dir of Ops
Fiona Morrison, Dir of HR
Jenny Leach, Dir of Fin
Leo Desautels, Dir of Sales, Retail
Kelly Watson, Dir of Mktg
John Ward, Dir of Sales, Commercial

Newly Weds Foods Co.

450 Superior Blvd.
Mississauga, ON L5T 2R9
Tel 905-670-7776
Fax 905-362-1986
www.newlywedsfoods.ca
NAICS: 311990
#Emp: 100-249 (Tor)
#TorLoc: 1
Own: Private Company
Key: Charles Angell, Pres
Ased Malik, VP Fin

Newmarket Health Centre

194 Eagle St.
Newmarket, ON L3Y 1J6
Tel 905-895-2381
Fax 905-895-5368
www.york.ca
Line: Provides long-term care
retirement services.
NAICS: 623110
#Emp: 250-499 (Tor)
#TorLoc: 2
Own: Private Company
Key: Sylvia Patterson, GM

Newmar Window Manufacturing Inc.

7630 Airport Rd.
Mississauga, ON L4T 4G6
Tel 905-672-1233
Fax 905-672-1076
www.newmar.com
Line: Manufactures residential
windows, door systems, and
accessories.
NAICS: 321911
#Emp: 250-499 (Tor)
#TorLoc: 1
Own: Private Company
Par: Alpa Lumber Inc. (CDA)
Key: Tim Smith, GM

The Newroads Automotive Group

18100 Yonge St.
Newmarket, ON L3Y 8V1
Tel 905-898-2277
Fax 905-881-3322
www.newroads.ca
AKA: Newroads National Leasing
Line: Sells and leases new and used
vehicles; provides parts and repairs;
and performs automobile body shop
services.
NAICS: 441110 441120 811121
#Emp: 100-249 (Tor)
#TorLoc: 6

Own: Private Company
Par: Croxon Holdings Inc. (CDA)
Key: Michael Croxon, Pres & CEO
Kim McLeod, Exec Asst
Mike Foley, CFO
Anthony Gilpin, IT

News Marketing Canada

1 First Canadian Pl.,
7000-100 King St. West
Toronto, ON M5X 1A4
Tel 416-775-3000
Fax 416-775-3055
www.newsmarketing.ca
Line: Provides in-store advertising,
media and merchandising services.
NAICS: 541899 541910
#Emp: 75-99 (Tor)
#TorLoc: 1
Own: Private Company
Key: Adam North, Sr VP, Region Mgr
Jessica Jannarone, VP HR

New York Fries/ South St. Burger Co.

400-1220 Yonge St.
Toronto, ON M4T 1W1
Tel 416-963-5005
Fax 416-963-4920
www.newyorkfries.com
AKA: South St. Burger Co.
Line: Operates and franchises South St.
Burger Co. and New York Fries.
NAICS: 722210 533110
#Emp: 100-249 (Tor)
#TorLoc: 11
Own: Private Company
Par: 122164 Canada Ltd. (CDA)
Key: Jay Gould, Pres
Craig Burt, VP Ops, New York Fries
Michael Perrin, HR Mgr
Paul Santos, Cont
Alyssa Berenstein, Mktg Mgr

New Zealand Lamb Company Ltd.

10 Shorncliffe Rd.
Toronto, ON M9B 3S3
Tel 416-231-5262
Fax 416-231-8934
www.nzlamb.ca
Line: Manufactures and wholesales
fresh and frozen foods.
NAICS: 413190
#Emp: 75-99 (Tor)
#TorLoc: 1
Own: Private Company
Key: Anthony Ruffo, Pres & CEO

Nexans Canada Inc.

140 Allstate Pkwy.
Markham, ON L3R 0Z7
Tel 905-944-4300
Fax 905-944-4333
www.nexans.ca
Line: Designs and manufactures an extensive range of advanced copper and optical fibre, cable solutions to the infrastructure industry and building markets.
NAICS: 331420
#Emp: 75-99 (Tor)
#TorLoc: 3
Own: Private Company
Par: Nexans (FR)
Key: Stephen Hall, Pres
Edward Faultless,
   Dir of Employee & Labour Relns
Rick Vascotto,
   VP Sales & Mktg Energy Networks
Christophe Jollivet,
   VP Sales & Mktg, Gen Markets

NexCycle Plastics Inc.

235 Wilkinson Rd.
Brampton, ON L6T 4M2
Tel 905-454-2666
Fax 905-454-2668
www.npiplastic.com
AKA: NPI NexCycle Plastics
Line: Reprocesses post-industrial plastic waste for sale in pelletized form.
NAICS: 326198
#Emp: 75-99 (Tor)
#TorLoc: 1
Own: Private Company
Par: NexCycle Inc. (CDA)
Key: Mary Frazer, CFO

Nexus Protective Services Ltd.

200-56 The Esplanade
Toronto, ON M5E 1A7
Tel 416-815-7575
Fax 416-815-7171
www.nexusps.com
Line: Provides security patrol services.
NAICS: 561612
#Emp: 100-249 (Tor)
#TorLoc: 1
Own: Private Company
Key: Jonathan Lamb, Pres
Fred Kozlo, VP & CEO
Darren Marshall, Dir of Ops

Nicholson & Cates Ltd.

300-3060 Mainway Dr.
Burlington, ON L7M 1A3
Tel 905-335-3366
Fax 905-335-2328
www.niccates.com
Line: Distributes forest and allied building products.
NAICS: 416320
#Emp: 75-99 (Tor)
#TorLoc: 1
Own: Private Company
Key: James Livermore, Pres

The Nielsen Company

160 McNabb St.
Markham, ON L3R 4B8
Tel 905-475-3344
Fax 905-475-8357
www.ca.nielsen.com
Line: Delivers market research information and analysis to the consumer products and services industries.
NAICS: 541910
#Emp: 500-999 (Tor)
#TorLoc: 1
Own: Private Company
Key: Steve Churchill,
   Mng Dir, Consumer
Carolyn Parkinson,
   VP, HR Business Partner
Joanne Van Der Burgt, Mng Dir,
   Nielsen IMS Canada
Vanessa Thomas, Sr VP Sales & Mng
   Dir, Entertainment

Nienkamper Furniture & Accessories Inc.

257 Finchdene Sq.
Toronto, ON M1X 1B9
Tel 416-298-5700
Fax 416-298-9535
www.nienkamper.com
Line: Manufactures contemporary furniture for corporations and residences.
NAICS: 337213 337214
#Emp: 100-249 (Tor)
#TorLoc: 1
Own: Private Company
Key: Klaus Nienkamper, Pres & CEO
Anne-Marie Snook, VP Ops
Romesh Jayarajah, CFO

Nightingale Corporation

2301 Dixie Rd.
Mississauga, ON L4Y 1Z9
Tel 905-896-3434
Fax 905-896-7011
www.nightingalechairs.com
Line: Manufactures office seating products.
NAICS: 337214
#Emp: 100-249 (Tor)
#TorLoc: 1
Own: Private Company
Key: William Breen, Pres
Edward Breen, VP
Martin Mueller, CFO
Philip Paiva, Purch Mgr

NIH Enterprises Inc.

135 Commander Blvd.
Toronto, ON M1S 3M7
Tel 416-299-3631
Fax 416-299-4207
www.canada-products.com
Line: Wholesales second hand clothing.
NAICS: 414110
#Emp: 100-249 (Tor)
#TorLoc: 1
Own: Private Company
Key: Imtiaz Mawji, Pres
Hussein Mawji, Dir

Nike Canada Corp.

500-175 Commerce Valley Dr. West
Thornhill, ON L3T 7P6
Tel 905-764-0400
Fax 905-764-1266
www.nike.ca
Line: Distributes, markets and sells sports and fitness products.
NAICS: 414470 339920
#Emp: 500-999 (Tor)
#TorLoc: 2
Own: Private Company
Par: Nike Inc. (US)
Key: Maria Montano, GM
Karen Adie-Henderson, Dir of Ops & IT
Laura McDonald, Dir of HR
Tim Dunn, Head of Fin
Kate Armstrong, Dir of Mktg

Nikon Canada Inc.

1366 Aerowood Dr.
Mississauga, ON L4W 1C1
Tel 905-625-9910
Fax 905-625-6446
www.nikon.ca
Line: Distributes photographic goods and optical instruments.
NAICS: 414430
#Emp: 75-99 (Tor)
#TorLoc: 1
Own: Private Company
Key: Ryota Satake, Pres & CEO
Diana Pastore, HR & Payroll Mgr

Nino D'Aversa Bakery Ltd.

1 Toro Rd.
Toronto, ON M3J 2A4
Tel 416-638-3271
Fax 416-638-3208
Line: Wholesales and retails baked goods.
NAICS: 311814 311821
#Emp: 75-99 (Tor)
#TorLoc: 3
Own: Private Company
Key: Mike D'Aversa, Owner

Nippon Express Canada Ltd.

6250 Edwards Blvd.
Mississauga, ON L5T 2X3
Tel 905-565-7525
Fax 905-565-5840
www.nipponexpresscanada.ca
Line: Forwards freight internationally.
NAICS: 488519
#Emp: 75-99 (Tor)
#TorLoc: 1
Own: Private Company
Par: Nippon Express U.S.A. Inc. (US)
Key: Toru Teshigawara, Pres
Noriko Ando, Mgr of Admin

Nisbet Lodge

740 Pape Ave.
Toronto, ON M4K 3S7
Tel 416-469-1105
Fax 416-469-2996
www.nisbetlodge.com
AKA: McClintock Manor; Nisbet Lodge-McClintock; Manor Foundation
Line: Provides residential dwellings for senior's and long-term care patients.
NAICS: 623999
#Emp: 100-249 (Tor)
#TorLoc: 2
Own: Not-for-profit

Key: Glen Moorhouse, Exec Dir
Ama Amoa-Williams, Dir of Care
Roxanne Adams, Dir of HR
Jay Jesudas, Dir of Fin

Nissan Canada Inc.

5290 Orbitor Dr.
Mississauga, ON L4W 4Z5
Tel 905-629-2888
Fax 905-629-6553
www.nissancanada.com
Line: Wholesales new automobiles, parts and financial products.
NAICS: 415110 415290
#Emp: 100-249 (Tor)
#TorLoc: 2
Own: Private Company
Par: Nissan Motor Co. Limited (JAPAN)
Key: Allen Childs, Pres
David Venegas, Sr HR Mgr
James Higgins, Dir of Fin
Keith McKee, Mgr of Purch
Victor Tsui, Mgr of IS
Ian Forsyth, Dir of Corp Planning

Nobleton Lakes Golf Course Ltd.

125 Nobleton Lakes Dr.
P.O. Box 594
Nobleton, ON L0G 1N0
Tel 905-859-4080
Fax 905-859-5832
www.nobletonlakesgolf.com
AKA: Nobleton Lakes Golf Club
NAICS: 713910
#Emp: 75-99 (Tor)
#TorLoc: 1
Own: Private Company
Key: Greg Hickey, Dir of Golf & GM

Noble Trade Inc.

7171 Jane St.
Concord, ON L4K 1A7
Tel 905-760-6800
Fax 905-760-6801
www.noble.ca
Line: Wholesales plumbing equipment.
NAICS: 416120
#Emp: 1000-4999 (Tor)
#TorLoc: 24
Own: Private Company
Par: RONA Inc. (CDA)
Key: Michael Storfer, Pres
Jerry Noble, Dir of Ops
Marlena Charlton, HR Mgr
Bob Farrugia, VP Fin

Norampac Inc.

450 Evans Ave.
Toronto, ON M8W 2T5
Tel 416-255-8541
Fax 416-253-2644
www.norampac.com
Line: Manufactures corrugated containers and operates retail factory outlet.
NAICS: 418220
#Emp: 500-999 (Tor)
#TorLoc: 8
Own: Private Company
Key: Marc-Andre Delphin, Pres & CEO
Toni Lionetti, GM
Melanie Winter, Reg HR Mgr

Norampac/Lithotech

A Div. of Cascades Canada Inc.
5910 Finch Ave. East
Toronto, ON M1B 5P8
Tel 416-412-3500
Fax 416-292-7761
www.norampac.com
Line: Manufactures and sells high graphic, litho laminated, corrugated packaging.
NAICS: 322211
#Emp: 100-249 (Tor)
#TorLoc: 1
Own: Private Company
Par: Cascades Inc. (CDA)
Key: Doug Gayman, Reg GM

Noranco Inc. - Woodbine Division

710 Rowntree Dairy Rd.
Woodbridge, ON L4L 5T7
Tel 905-264-2050
Fax 905-264-1471
www.noranco.com
Line: Manufactures and assembles aerospace components.
NAICS: 336410
#Emp: 100-249 (Tor)
#TorLoc: 1
Own: Private Company
Key: Nick Chicconde, VP
Frank Riviglia, Cont

Noranco Manufacturing Ltd.

1842 Clements Rd.
Pickering, ON L1W 3R8
Tel 905-831-0100
Fax 905-831-0104
www.noranco.com
Line: Manufactures parts and products
for the aerospace industry.
NAICS: 336410
#Emp: 100-249 (Tor)
#TorLoc: 1
Own: Private Company
Key: David Camilleri, Pres
Bernardo Sztabinski, CEO
Ted Bronk, VP
Jeff Meilaeh, CFO

Norbord Inc.

600-1 Toronto St.
Toronto, ON M5C 2W4
Tel 416-365-0705
Fax 416-777-4419
www.norbord.com
Line: Manufactures and markets
panelboard products for construction
and industrial use.
NAICS: 321999
#Emp: 75-99 (Tor)
#TorLoc: 1
Own: Public Company
Par: Norbord Inc. (CDA)
Key: Barrie Shineton, Pres & CEO
Peter Wijnbergen, Sr VP & COO
Robert Kinnear, Sr VP, Corp Services
Robin Lampard, Exec VP & CFO
Bob Jackson, VP IS
Mike Dawson,
    Sr VP Mktg, Sales & Logistics
Anita Veel, Dir, Corp Affairs

Nordion Inc.

447 March Rd.
Ottawa, ON K2K 1X8
Tel 613-592-2790
Fax 613-592-6937
www.mdsinc.com
AKA: MDS Nordion; MDS Pharma
Services; MDS Analytical Technologies
Line: Provides products and services
for drug development and the
diagnosis and treatment of disease
including pharmaceutical contract
research, medical isotopes for
molecular imaging, radiotherapeutics
and analytical instruments.
NAICS: 325410 621510
#Emp: 250-499 (Tor)
#TorLoc: 4
Own: Public Company

Key: Steve M. West, Pres & CEO
Scott McIntosh, VP Ops
Mary Federau, Exec VP Global HR
Peter Dans, Exec VP & CFO
Thomas E. Gernon, CIO
Kevin Brooks, Sr VP Sales & Mktg

Nor-Don Collection Network Inc.

1100-325 Milner Ave.
Toronto, ON M1B 5N1
Tel 416-412-3070
Fax 416-412-3042
www.ncn.ca
AKA: NCN
Line: Provides collection services.
NAICS: 561440
#Emp: 100-249 (Tor)
#TorLoc: 1
Own: Private Company
Key: Jim Burke, Pres & CEO
Clayton Dixon, CFO
John Van Dam, MIS Mgr

Norex Ltd.

290 Ferrier St.
Markham, ON L3R 2Z5
Tel 905-513-8889
Fax 905-513-1153
Line: Manufactures plastic injection
mouldings for office products and
miscellaneous plastic items.
NAICS: 326198
#Emp: 75-99 (Tor)
#TorLoc: 2
Own: Private Company
Par: Norspex Ltd. (CDA)
Key: Albert Matsushita, Pres

Normac Kitchens Ltd.

59 Glen Cameron Rd.
Thornhill, ON L3T 1N8
Tel 905-889-1342
Fax 905-889-7917
www.normackitchens.com
Line: Manufactures and installs kitchen
cabinets, vanities and countertops.
NAICS: 337110
#Emp: 100-249 (Tor)
#TorLoc: 2
Own: Private Company
Key: Hans Marcus, Pres & CEO
Simone French, HR & Benefits Admr
Ben Platt, Financial Cont
Alfonso Mendez, Production Mgr

Norman Hill Realty Inc.

2-20 Cachet Woods Crt.
Markham, ON L6C 3G1
Tel 905-886-5678
Fax 905-886-2079
www.normanhillrealty.com
NAICS: 531210
#Emp: 100-249 (Tor)
#TorLoc: 1
Own: Private Company
Key: Warren Hill, Broker of Record
Norman Hill, Founder

Norpak Custom Packaging

*A Div. of Brampton Caledon
Community Living*
46 West Dr.
Brampton, ON L6T 3T6
Tel 905-453-8833
Fax 905-453-8834
www.norpakpackaging.com
Line: Provides general packaging
services.
NAICS: 561910
#Emp: 100-249 (Tor)
#TorLoc: 1
Own: Private Company
Key: Howie O'Neill, GM
Anne-Marie Hawkins, Dir of Fin

NORR Ltd.

175 Bloor St. East
North Tower, 15th Fl.
Toronto, ON M4W 3R8
Tel 416-929-0200
Fax 416-929-3635
www.norrlimited.com
Line: Provides architectural
engineering, project management, and
interior design consulting services.
NAICS: 541330
#Emp: 100-249 (Tor)
#TorLoc: 1
Own: Private Company
Par: Ingenium Group Inc. (CDA)
Key: Brian Gerstmar, VP
Gus Sarrouh, COO
Maureen Koszegi, Cont
Silvio Baldassarra, Exec VP
Luisa D'Amico, Mktg Coord

Nortel Networks Corp.

5945 Airport Rd.
Mississauga, ON L4V 1R9
Tel 905-863-7000
Fax 905-863-8423
www.nortel.com
Line: Operates a global Internet and
communications company.
NAICS: 334410 334110
#Emp: 1000-4999 (Tor)
#TorLoc: 1
Own: Public Company
Key: John M. Doolittle,
    Sr VP Fin & Corp Services
Chris Ricaurte, Pres, Nortel Business
    Services
George Riedel, Chief Strategy Officer

North America Steel Equipment Company Ltd.

300 Hopkins St.
Whitby, ON L1N 2B9
Tel 905-668-3300
Fax 905-668-5477
www.naseco.ca
Line: Manufactures pallet racking,
shelving, workbenches, lockers, and
extension drawer systems.
NAICS: 337215
#Emp: 75-99 (Tor)
#TorLoc: 1
Own: Private Company
Key: Rolf Fabricius, Pres
Ron Wilson, VP Ops
Rosalie Fabricius, Cont

Northern Digital Inc.

103 Randall Dr.
Waterloo, ON N2V 1C5
Tel 519-884-5142
Fax 519-884-5184
www.ndigital.com
AKA: NDI Inc.
Line: Supplies optical tracking
equipment and provides measurement
solutions.
NAICS: 334512
#Emp: 100-249 (Tor)
#TorLoc: 1
Own: Private Company
Key: Jamie Fraiser, Pres
Sheri Embleton, Ops Mgr

North Park Nursing Home Ltd.

450 Rustic Rd.
Toronto, ON M6L 1W9
Tel 416-247-0531
Fax 416-247-6159
Line: Operates a nursing home.
NAICS: 623310
#Emp: 75-99 (Tor)
#TorLoc: 1
Own: Private Company
Key: Natasha Murray, Admr
Chandanbala Shah, Secy-Treas

North Peel Media Group

A Div. of Metroland Media Group Ltd.
7700 Hurontario St.
Brampton, ON L6Y 4M3
Tel 905-454-4344
Fax 905-454-4385
www.bramptonguardian.com
AKA: Brampton Guardian; Caledon
Enterprise; Independent & Free Press;
Georgetown Independent & Free Press;
Erin Advocate; Orangeville Banner;
South Asian Focus
NAICS: 511110
#Emp: 250-499 (Tor)
#TorLoc: 1
Own: Private Company
Par: Torstar Corp. (CDA)
Key: Ken Nugent, VP & Reg Publisher
Rob Leuscher, GM

Northstar Aerospace (Canada) Inc.

180 Market Dr.
Milton, ON L9T 3H5
Tel 905-875-4000
Fax 905-875-4087
www.nsaero.com
Line: Manufactures aerospace
equipment.
NAICS: 336410
#Emp: 100-249 (Tor)
#TorLoc: 2
Own: Public Company
Par: Northstar Aerospace Inc. (CDA)
Key: Glenn E. Hess, Pres & CEO
Craig Yuen, VP & Chief Strategy Officer
William Corley, Dir of HR
Greg Schindler, CFO
Steven Stell, Dir of IT

Northwest Protection Services Ltd.

201-1951 Eglinton Ave. West
Toronto, ON M6E 2J7
Tel 416-787-1448
Fax 416-256-2062
www.northwestprotection.com
Line: Provides security guard, tagging,
investigation and protective services.
NAICS: 561612 561611
#Emp: 500-999 (Tor)
#TorLoc: 1
Own: Private Company
Key: Bruce McBean, Pres
Jim Miller, Dir of Ops
Joanna Lekka, HR Admr

Northwood Mortgage Ltd.

300-7676 Woodbine Ave.
Markham, ON L3R 2N2
Tel 905-889-7676
Fax 905-889-2832
www.northwoodmortgage.com
Line: Specializes in mortgage broker
and banker services.
NAICS: 522310
#Emp: 75-99 (Tor)
#TorLoc: 1
Own: Private Company
Key: Arthur Appleberg, Pres & Broker

North York General Hospital

4001 Leslie St.
Toronto, ON M2K 1E1
Tel 416-756-6000
Fax 416-756-6958
www.nygh.on.ca
Line: Provides healthcare services.
NAICS: 622111
#Emp: 1000-4999 (Tor)
#TorLoc: 3
Own: Not-for-profit
Key: Tim Rutledge, Pres & CEO
Sandra Smith, Chief HR Office
Dean Martin, VP IT & CFO
Karen Popovich,
    VP & Chief Nursing Exec
Alison Steeves,
    Chief of Corp Commun & Pub Affairs

Nortown Electrical Contractors Ltd.

102-3845 Bathurst St.
Toronto, ON M3H 3N2
Tel 416-638-6700
Fax 416-638-0358
Line: Provides electrical services.
NAICS: 232510
#Emp: 100-249 (Tor)
#TorLoc: 1
Own: Private Company
Key: Harry Marder, Owner

Nortrax

1655 Britannia Rd. East
Mississauga, ON L4W 1S5
Tel 905-670-1655
Fax 905-670-4129
www.nortrax.com
Line: Sells and repairs mobile construction equipment.
NAICS: 811310 417210
#Emp: 75-99 (Tor)
#TorLoc: 1
Own: Private Company
Key: Jim Ficzere, GM
Peter Goodman, Dir of HR

Nottawasaga Inn

6015 Hwy. 89
Alliston, ON L9R 1A4
Tel 705-435-5501
Fax 705-435-5840
www.nottawasagaresort.com
NAICS: 721111 722110
#Emp: 250-499 (Tor)
#TorLoc: 1
Own: Private Company
Key: Luigi Biffis, Pres
Eileen Murray, HR Mgr

Novadaq Technologies Inc.

306-2585 Skymark Ave.
Mississauga, ON L4W 4L5
Tel 905-629-3822
Fax 905-629-0282
www.novadaq.com
Line: Develops and markets real-time fluorescence imaging technologies for use in the operating room.
NAICS: 334512
#Emp: 100-249 (Tor)
Own: Private Company
Key: Arun Menawat, Pres & CEO
Rick Mangat, Sr VP & GM
Stephen Purcell, CFO
Douglas R. Carroll, VP Sales

Novaquest Metal Finishing Inc.

6300 Dixie Rd.
Mississauga, ON L5T 1A7
Tel 905-671-9449
Fax 905-671-8939
Line: Specializes in metal finishing for the automotive industry.
NAICS: 332319
#Emp: 100-249 (Tor)
#TorLoc: 1
Own: Private Company
Key: David Lund, Pres
Shaun Reid, VP Fin & GM
Patrick Stevenson, Fin & IT Mgr
Bernie Anstett, Sales Mgr

Nova Services Group Inc.

1-8191 Jane St.
Concord, ON L4K 5P2
Tel 905-669-6565
Fax 905-669-6724
www.novaservicesinc.com
Line: Provides dietary, environmental and building cleaning services.
NAICS: 561722 561740
#Emp: 500-999 (Tor)
#TorLoc: 1
Own: Private Company
Key: Tony Simas, Pres & CEO
Luis Amaro, VP Ops
Cheryl Sandford, Acctng Mgr
Denise Baltazar, Dir of Labour Relns
Victor Rodrigues,
    VP Commun & Business Dev

Novator Systems Ltd.

300-26 Wellington St. East
Toronto, ON M5E 1S2
Tel 416-260-5131
Fax 416-260-5121
www.novator.com
Line: Provides e-commerce, e-merchandising and e-marketing programming services.
NAICS: 541510
#Emp: 75-99 (Tor)
#TorLoc: 1
Own: Private Company
Key: Donald Macdonald, Pres & CEO
Mark Fox, Chmn & Founder
Judy Fields, Exec VP Ops
Paul Kennedy, VP Tech

Novelis Foil Products

191 Evans Ave.
Toronto, ON M8Z 1J5
Tel 416-503-6700
Fax 416-503-6720
www.novelisfoil.com
Line: Converts aluminum foil.
NAICS: 326198
#Emp: 100-249 (Tor)
#TorLoc: 1
Own: Public Company
Par: Aditya Birla (INDIA)
Key: Jean-Marc Germaine,
    Sr VP & Pres, North America
Cary Wasser, Dir of Fin
Mark Telfer, Dir of Logistics & MIS

Novo Nordisk Canada Inc.

300-2680 Skymark Ave.
Mississauga, ON L4W 5L6
Tel 905-629-4222
Fax 905-629-8662
www.novonordisk.ca
Line: Sells pharmaceutical products.
NAICS: 325410
#Emp: 100-249 (Tor)
#TorLoc: 1
Own: Public Company
Par: Novo Nordisk (DEN)
Key: Vince Lamanna, Pres
Marie Percival,
    Dir of People & Corp Relns
Doug Wyatt,
    Dir of Strategic Business Ops
Ian Tu, Dir of Sales, Diabetes

Novotel Hotel North York

A Div. of Novotel Canada Inc.
3 Park Home Ave.
Toronto, ON M2N 6L3
Tel 416-733-2929
Fax 416-733-3403
www.novotel.com
AKA: Novotel
NAICS: 721111
#Emp: 100-249 (Tor)
#TorLoc: 3
Own: Private Company
Par: Accor SA (FR)
Key: Michael Singer, Hotel Mgr

Novotel Mississauga

A Div. of Novotel Canada Inc.
3670 Hurontario St.
Mississauga, ON L5B 1P3
Tel 905-896-1000
Fax 905-896-2521
www.novotel.com
Line: Operates hotel.
NAICS: 721111
#Emp: 100-249 (Tor)
#TorLoc: 4
Own: Private Company
Par: Accor SA (FR)
Key: Didier Dolivet, GM
Selina Louzado, Dir of HR
Robert Gauthier, Cont
Debbie Stellinga, Dir of Sales & Mktg

Novotel Toronto Centre

A Div. of Novotel Canada Inc.
45 The Esplanade
Toronto, ON M5E 1W2
Tel 416-367-8900
Fax 416-360-8285
www.novotel.com
AKA: Novotel
Line: Operates hotel.
NAICS: 721111
#Emp: 100-249 (Tor)
#TorLoc: 3
Own: Private Company
Par: Accor SA (FR)
Key: Janak Bhawnani, Hotel Mgr

Now Communications Inc.

189 Church St.
Toronto, ON M5B 1Y7
Tel 416-364-1300
Fax 416-364-1433
www.nowtoronto.com
AKA: Now Magazine
Line: Operates a local weekly
alternative news and entertainment
newspaper.
NAICS: 511120 511110
#Emp: 75-99 (Tor)
#TorLoc: 1
Own: Private Company
Key: Michael Hollett,
  Editor & Publisher
Alice Klein, CEO & Exec Editor
David Logan, GM
Beverly Williams, HR Mgr
Pam Stephen, VP Sales & Mktg

NRT Technology Corp.

10 Compass Crt.
Toronto, ON M1S 5R3
Tel 416-646-5232
Fax 416-646-5242
www.nrttech.com
Line: Offers cash handling solutions
and products.
NAICS: 541215
#Emp: 100-249 (Tor)
Own: Private Company
Key: John Dominelli, Pres & CEO
Ray Deffner, Sr Exec VP
James Grundy, CFO

NSK Canada Inc.

5585 McAdam Rd.
Mississauga, ON L4Z 1N4
Tel 905-890-0740
Fax 905-890-0434
www.ca.nsk.com
Line: Manufactures, distributes and
warehouses bearings, linear motion,
and automotive component products.
NAICS: 332991 417230
#Emp: 75-99 (Tor)
#TorLoc: 1
Own: Private Company
Par: NSK Ltd. (JAPAN)
Key: Michael St. Jacques, Pres
Ryan Hunter, Dir of Ops
Elisa Romaniello, HR Generalist
Paul McKenzie, Commun Coord

NS Studios

1160 Bellamy Rd. North
Toronto, ON M1H 1H2
Tel 416-438-3385
Fax 416-438-5598
www.nsstudios.com
AKA: North Screen Studios
Line: Manufactures point-of-purchase
displays and store fixturing.
NAICS: 337215
#Emp: 75-99 (Tor)
#TorLoc: 2
Own: Private Company
Par: Miller Group (US)
Key: Alex Scheibli, VP

NTN Bearing Corporation of Canada Ltd.

305 Courtney Park Dr. West
Mississauga, ON L5W 1Y4
Tel 905-564-2700
Fax 905-564-9023
www.ntn.ca
Line: Imports, manufactures and sells
bearings.

NAICS: 332991
#Emp: 100-249 (Tor)
#TorLoc: 3
Own: Private Company
Par: NTN Corp. (JAPAN)
Key: Jerry Maki, Pres
Sylvia Silveira, Corp HR Mgr
John Westerhof, IT Mgr
Paul Meo, VP
Al Rudaitis, Mktg Mgr

Nuance Global Traders (Canada) Inc.

300-5925 Airport Rd.
Mississauga, ON L4V 1W1
Tel 905-673-7299
Fax 905-673-7307
www.thenuancegroup.com
Line: Manages offices for Duty Free
Shops.
NAICS: 453220
#Emp: 250-499 (Tor)
#TorLoc: 5
Own: Private Company
Key: Richard Rendek,
  CEO, North America
John Menchella, Sr VP Business Dev

Nucap Industries Inc.

3370 Pharmacy Ave.
Toronto, ON M1W 3K4
Tel 416-494-1444
Fax 416-494-4941
www.nucap.com
Line: Manufactures automotive
stampings.
NAICS: 336370
#Emp: 250-499 (Tor)
#TorLoc: 2
Own: Private Company
Key: David Weichenberg, Pres
Vince Butera, CEO

Nuco Jewellery Products Inc.

17-11 Progress Ave.
Toronto, ON M1P 4S7
Tel 416-293-3495
Fax 416-293-1227
AKA: Nuco Charms; Rembrandt
Charms
NAICS: 339910
#Emp: 75-99 (Tor)
#TorLoc: 1
Own: Private Company
Key: Robin Sluce, VP
Marlene McDermott, Office Mgr

Nucro-Technics

16-2000 Ellesmere Rd.
Toronto, ON M1H 2W4
Tel 416-438-6727
Fax 416-438-3463
www.nucro-technics.com
Line: Provides consulting and liaison with government agencies and regulatory, quality assurance and analytical services.
NAICS: 325410
#Emp: 100-249 (Tor)
#TorLoc: 1
Own: Private Company
Key: John C. Fanaras, Pres
Bill Ferguson, Cont
Constantine Fanaras,
    Mktg & Tech Affairs Associate

Nyad Community Inc.

204-3090 Kingston Rd.
Toronto, ON M1M 1P2
Tel 416-269-4545
Fax 416-269-4995
www.nyad.org
Line: Operates a day care centre.
NAICS: 624410
#Emp: 75-99 (Tor)
#TorLoc: 6
Own: Not-for-profit
Key: Mara Holdenried, Exec Dir
Jordan Froese, Chair
Mary Gabriele Skelley,
    Dir of Ops & Program Dev
Dan Marcoux, Dir of HR & Commun

Nycomed Canada Inc.

435 North Service Rd. West, 1st Fl.
Oakville, ON L6M 4X8
Tel 905-469-9333
Fax 905-469-4883
www.nycomed.ca
Line: Specializes in pharmaceuticals.
NAICS: 325410
#Emp: 100-249 (Tor)
#TorLoc: 1
Own: Private Company
Par: Nycomed (SWITZ)
Key: Mike Egli, Pres & CEO
Adele Zita, VP HR
Frank Murphy,
    VP Fin & Info Management
Ron Clark, VP Sales & Mktg

Nygard International Ltd.

1 Niagara St.
Toronto, ON M5V 1C2
Tel 416-598-5000
Fax 204-631-5690
www.nygard.com
Line: Manufactures and sells women's clothing.
NAICS: 414110
#Emp: 1000-4999 (Tor)
#TorLoc: 30
Own: Private Company
Key: Jim Bennett, Pres & CEO
Peter Nygard, Chmn

Oakdale Drywall & Acoustics Ltd.

1-499 Edgeley Blvd.
Concord, ON L4K 4H3
Tel 905-660-7733
Fax 905-660-7690
www.oakdaledrywall.com
Line: Supplies and installs acoustical ceiling and drywall products.
NAICS: 232410
#Emp: 100-249 (Tor)
#TorLoc: 1
Own: Private Company
Key: Sandy D'Angelo, Pres
George Molent, Sr Project Mgr
Farouk Bacchus, Admr

The Oakdale Golf & Country Club Ltd.

2388 Jane St.
Toronto, ON M3M 1A8
Tel 416-245-3500
Fax 416-245-9764
www.oakdalegolf.com
NAICS: 713910
#Emp: 100-249 (Tor)
#TorLoc: 1
Own: Private Company
Key: Herb Pirk, GM & Secy
Christine Dudley, Cont

Oak-Land Ford Lincoln Sales Ltd.

570 Trafalgar Rd.
Oakville, ON L6J 3J2
Tel 905-844-3273
Fax 905-844-4472
www.oaklandfordlincoln.
    dealerconnection.com
Line: Operates an automotive dealership.
NAICS: 441110 441120
#Emp: 100-249 (Tor)

#TorLoc: 1
Own: Private Company
Key: David Sanci,
    Pres & Dealer Principal
Lan Sanci, CEO
Peter Lin, VP Fin
Sean Draper, Gen Sales Mgr

Oak Leaf Confections Co.

440 Comstock Rd.
Toronto, ON M1L 2H6
Tel 416-751-0895
Fax 416-751-3915
www.oakleafconfections.com
Line: Manufactures gum and candy products.
NAICS: 311340
#Emp: 100-249 (Tor)
#TorLoc: 1
Own: Private Company
Key: Philip Terranova, Pres

Oakville Family YMCA

410 Rebecca St.
Oakville, ON L6K 1K7
Tel 905-845-3417
Fax 905-842-6792
www.ymcaofoakville.com
Line: Provides fitness, social programs and childcare.
NAICS: 813410
#Emp: 250-499 (Tor)
Own: Private Company
Key: Darryl McKenzie, CEO

Oakville Fire Department

A Div. of The Town of Oakville
1225 Trafalgar Rd.
Oakville, ON L6J 5A6
Tel 905-845-7114
Fax 905-338-4403
www.oakvillefire.ca
Line: Operates training campus and fire stations.
NAICS: 913140
#Emp: 100-249 (Tor)
#TorLoc: 7
Own: Government
Key: Lee Grant, Deputy Fire Chief
Richard Boyes, Fire Chief
Brian Durdin, Deputy Fire Chief
Andy Glynn, Deputy Fire Chief

Oakville Hydro Corp.

861 Redwood Sq.
P.O. Box 1900
Oakville, ON L6J 5E3
Tel 905-825-9400
Fax 905-825-4447
www.oakvillehydro.com
Line: Operates hydro utility.
NAICS: 231390
#Emp: 100-249 (Tor)
Own: Municipal Crown Corp.
Key: Robert Lister, Pres & CEO
Marcia Best, Mgr of HR
Lesley Gallinger, VP Fin & Admin
Corey Dowie, Purch & Facilities Mgr
Everett Chubbs, Dir of IT

Oakville Place

240 Leighland Ave.
Oakville, ON L6H 3H6
Tel 905-842-2140
Fax 905-842-2969
www.oakvilleplace.com
Line: Manages shopping mall.
NAICS: 531120
#Emp: 250-499 (Tor)
#TorLoc: 1
Own: Private Company
Par: Ivanhoe Cambridge Inc. (CDA)
Key: Megan Johnson, GM
Jenny Jovanovic, Dir of Mktg

Oakville Public Library

120 Navy St.
Oakville, ON L6J 2Z4
Tel 905-815-2042
Fax 905-815-2024
www.opl.on.ca
NAICS: 514121
#Emp: 100-249 (Tor)
#TorLoc: 6
Own: Government
Key: Lori Sims, CEO
Janice Kullas,
    Dir of Service Planning & Dev
Chantal Switzer, Mgr of HR
Charlotte Meissner,
    Dir of Corp Services
Randy Kisch, Dir of Library Systems
Melissa Cameron, Mgr of Mktg & Dev

O.C. Tanner Recognition Company Ltd.

4200 Fairview St.
Burlington, ON L7L 4Y8
Tel 905-632-7255
Fax 905-639-7027
www.octanner.com
Line: Manufactures emblematic
corporate recognition awards and logos
displayed in jewellery and rings.
NAICS: 561490
#Emp: 75-99 (Tor)
#TorLoc: 3
Own: Private Company
Par: O.C. Tanner Company (US)
Key: John McVeigh, Pres

Odyssey Financial Technologies

2425 Matheson Blvd. East, 4th Fl.
Mississauga, ON L4W 5K4
Tel 905-214-7600
Fax 905-214-7699
www.odyssey-group.com
Line: Provides consulting for financial
institutions.
NAICS: 541611
#Emp: 100-249 (Tor)
#TorLoc: 1
Own: Private Company
Par: Odyssey (SWITZ)
Key: Craig O'Neill,
Sr VP Corp & Product Dev

OE Quality Friction Inc.

6015 Kestrel Rd.
Mississauga, ON L5T 1S8
Tel 905-564-9500
Fax 905-564-9520
www.oeqf.com
Line: Manufactures disc brake pads.
NAICS: 336340
#Emp: 100-249 (Tor)
#TorLoc: 1
Own: Private Company
Key: Robert Lee, Pres
George Bairstow, Cont
Jason Hathaway, Sales Mgr, Canada
Bryan Watts, VP Sales & Mktg

Oetiker Ltd.

203 Dufferin St. South
P.O. Box 5500
Alliston, ON L9R 1W7
Tel 705-435-4394
Fax 705-481-1157
www.oetiker.com
Line: Manufactures hose clamps and
accessories.
NAICS: 332910 333990
#Emp: 100-249 (Tor)
#TorLoc: 1
Own: Private Company
Par: Hans Oetiker AG (SWITZ)
Key: Sam Wyss, GM
Hooi Lim, Ops Mgr
Karen Currier, HR Mgr
Grant McLeod, Fin Mgr
Mike Horan, Buyer

Office Depot

114-5800 Ambler Dr.
Mississauga, ON L4W 4J4
Tel 905-615-0980
Fax 905-615-0566
www.officedepot.ca
Line: Retails office products.
NAICS: 453210
#Emp: 250-499 (Tor)
#TorLoc: 8
Own: Private Company
Par: Office Depot Inc. (US)
Key: John Warner, Reg VP
Steve Odland, Chmn & CEO

OfficeTeam

820-181 Bay St.
P.O. Box 824
Toronto, ON M5J 2T3
Tel 416-350-2010
Fax 416-350-3573
www.officeteam.com
Line: Operates an employment agency.
NAICS: 561310
#Emp: 100-249 (Tor)
#TorLoc: 7
Own: Private Company
Par: Robert Half International (US)
Key: Kathryn Bolt, District Pres
Sidiki Dhrani, District Admr

Ogilvy & Mather (Canada) Ltd.

33 Yonge St.
Toronto, ON M5E 1X6
Tel 416-367-3573
Fax 416-363-2088
www.ogilvy-canada.com
AKA: Ogilvy & Mather Advertising
Line: Provides full service advertising
and communications services.
NAICS: 541810
#Emp: 100-249 (Tor)
#TorLoc: 1
Own: Private Company
Par: WPP Group plc (UK)
Key: Laurie Young, Mng Dir
Dennis Stief, CEO
Guy Stevenson, Mng Dir

Ogilvy Renault

3800-200 Bay St.,
Royal Bank Plaza, South Tower
P.O. Box 84
Toronto, ON M5J 2Z4
Tel 416-216-4000
Fax 416-216-3930
www.ogilvyrenault.com
Line: Operates full-service law firm
with services provided by lawyers,
patent agents and trademark agents.
NAICS: 541110
#Emp: 250-499 (Tor)
#TorLoc: 1
Own: Private Company
Key: John B. West, Mng Partner
Peter Lockie, Sr Partner
Janell Walsh, GM
Lise Monette, Chief Mktg Officer
Sameer Dhargalkar,
    Dir of Business Dev

O-I Canada Corp.

100 West Dr.
Brampton, ON L6T 2J5
Tel 905-457-2423
Fax 905-796-4426
www.owens-ill.com
AKA: Owens Illinois Canada Corp.
Line: Manufactures glass food and
beverage containers.
NAICS: 327214
#Emp: 250-499 (Tor)
#TorLoc: 1
Own: Private Company
Par: Owens Illinois Inc. (US)
Key: Tony Lipari, Plant Mgr
Tony Varriano, Asst Plant Mgr
Wendy Purvis, HR Mgr
Skevi Louca, Logistics Mgr

Oldcastle Glass Engineered Products

275 Britannia Rd. East
Mississauga, ON L4Z 2E7
Tel 905-890-6970
Fax 905-890-6973
www.oldcastleglass.com
Line: Manufactures windows, curtain
walls and skylights.
NAICS: 332321
#Emp: 100-249 (Tor)
#TorLoc: 1
Own: Private Company
Par: Old Castle Glass (US)
Key: Jonathan Cooper, Dir of HR

Olde York Potato Chips

230 Deerhurst Dr.
Brampton, ON L6T 5R8
Tel 905-458-4100
Fax 905-458-1780
Line: Produces potato chips and
popcorn.
NAICS: 311919
#Emp: 75-99 (Tor)
#TorLoc: 1
Own: Private Company
Key: Peter Margie, Pres

Old Mill Pontiac Buick Cadillac Ltd.

2595 St. Clair Ave. West
Toronto, ON M6N 4Z5
Tel 416-766-2443
Fax 416-766-6230
www.oldmillpontiac.ca
Line: Sells and services automobiles.
NAICS: 441110 441120
#Emp: 75-99 (Tor)
#TorLoc: 1
Own: Private Company
Key: Lou Vavaroutsos, Pres
Charles Grant, Sr Exec, Dealer Ops
Paul Chong, Secy-Treas

Oliver & Bonacini Restaurants

A Div. of 371487 Ontario Ltd.
2433 Yonge St.
Toronto, ON M4P 2E7
Tel 416-485-8047
Fax 416-485-7674
www.oliverbonacini.com
AKA: Oliver & Bonacini Café Grill;
Auberge du Pommier; Biff's Bistro;
Canoe; Jump Café & Bar
Line: Operates restaurants.
NAICS: 722110
#Emp: 500-999 (Tor)
#TorLoc: 11
Own: Private Company
Key: Michael Bonacini,
    Partner & Owner
Peter Oliver, Partner & Owner
Lee Chung, COO & CFO
Amy Chung, Dir of HR
Cliff Snell, Dir of Business Ops
Theresa Suraci, Dir of Mktg & Commun

Olon Industries Inc.

42 Armstrong Ave.
Georgetown, ON L7G 4R9
Tel 905-877-7300
Fax 905-877-7383
www.olon.com
Line: Manufactures edge banding,
wrapped profiles, drawer components,
and decorative laminates.
NAICS: 337213
#Emp: 100-249 (Tor)
#TorLoc: 1
Own: Private Company
Key: Don Hambly, Pres
Ernie Saveriano, VP & CFO

Olsen Fashion Canada Inc.

5112 Timberlea Blvd.
Mississauga, ON L4W 2S5
Tel 905-290-1919
Fax 905-290-4647
www.olseneurope.com
AKA: Olsen Europe
Line: Distributes ladies' apparel.
NAICS: 448120
#Emp: 250-499 (Tor)
Own: Private Company
Par: Wolff & Olsen GmbH & Co. (GER)
Key: Tim Davison, CEO
Esmail Lakkadghatwala, Cont

Olymel

318 Orenda Rd.
Brampton, ON L6T 1G1
Tel 905-793-5757
Fax 905-793-2513
www.olymel.com
Line: Processes poultry.
NAICS: 311615 311990
#Emp: 250-499 (Tor)
#TorLoc: 1
Own: Private Company
Par: Cooperative Federee de Quebec
(CDA)
Key: Cindy Spiers, Reg Mgr, Ontario
Mark Cerbu, Plant Mgr
Lindsay Mackett, Nat'l Sales Mgr

Olympia Tile International Inc.

1000 Lawrence Ave. West
Toronto, ON M6B 4A8
Tel 416-785-6666
Fax 416-785-9682
www.olympiatile.com
AKA: Olympia Floor & Wall Tile;
Olympia Tile
Line: Manufactures and distributes
ceramic tile, resilient tile, natural
stone, bathroom accessories and
installation products.
NAICS: 327120 416330
#Emp: 250-499 (Tor)
#TorLoc: 1
Own: Private Company
Key: Ralph Reichmann, Pres
Nathan Farkas, VP Branch Ops
Sonja Topolinsky, HR Mgr
Jeff Goldwater, Cont
George Gal, VP Purch
Jacob Schechter, IS Mgr

OMD Canada

67 Richmond St. West
Toronto, ON M5H 1Z5
Tel 416-681-5600
Fax 416-681-5620
www.omd.com
Line: Provides media advertising.
NAICS: 541810
#Emp: 100-249 (Tor)
#TorLoc: 1
Own: Partnership
Par: Omnicom Group Inc. (US)
Key: Lorraine Hughes, Pres
Beverly Balleine, HR Mgr
Michael Pitre, CFO

Omni Facility Services Canada Limited

99 St. Regis Cres. North
Toronto, ON M3J 1Y9
Tel 416-736-1144
Fax 416-665-9511
www.omnifacility.ca
AKA: GDI
Line: Provides commercial cleaning
services.
NAICS: 561722 561721
#Emp: 1000-4999 (Tor)
#TorLoc: 10
Own: Private Company
Par: Group Distinction Inc. (CDA)
Key: Peter Pohland, Sr Reg Dir
Claude Bigras, CEO
Daniel Sklivas, Sr VP & COO
Dennis H. Fielding, Dir of HR
Irina Dounaevskaia, Exec VP & CFO

Omron Canada Inc.

885 Milner Ave.
Toronto, ON M1B 5V8
Tel 416-286-6465
Fax 416-286-6774
www.omron247.com
Line: Sells and services electro-
mechanical and electronic devices.
NAICS: 541510
#Emp: 75-99 (Tor)
#TorLoc: 1
Own: Private Company
Par: Omron Corp. (JAPAN)
Key: Ron Gee, Dir of Fin & Ops
Len Starrett, Mgr of HR
John So, Mgr of IT

The O'Neill Centre

33 Christie St.
Toronto, ON M6G 3B1
Tel 416-536-1116
Fax 416-536-6941
www.oneillcentre.ca
Line: Operates a nursing home.
NAICS: 623110
#Emp: 100-249 (Tor)
#TorLoc: 3
Own: Private Company
Key: William Dillaine, Pres
Christine Dalglish, Dir of Ops

Onex Corp.

161 Bay St.
P.O. Box 700
Toronto, ON M5J 2S1
Tel 416-362-7911
Fax 416-362-5765
www.onex.com
Line: Offers private equity investing.
NAICS: 551113
#Emp: 75-99 (Tor)
#TorLoc: 1
Own: Public Company
Key: Gerald Schwartz,
Chmn, Pres & CEO
Donald Lewtas, CFO

On Premise Laundry Systems Inc.

A Div. of Coinamatic Canada Inc.
301 Matheson Blvd. West
Mississauga, ON L5R 3G3
Tel 905-755-1946
Fax 905-755-8885
www.coinamatic.com
AKA: OPLS
Line: Sells and leases laundry
equipment.
NAICS: 532490 417920
#Emp: 100-249 (Tor)
#TorLoc: 2
Own: Private Company
Key: Don Watt, COO
Meredith Brown, VP HR
Joe Catelano, CFO
Alain Belanger, VP Sales
   & Commercial Laundry Division

ON Semiconductor

970 Fraser Dr.
P.O. Box 278, Station A
Burlington, ON L7L 5P5
Tel 905-635-0804
Fax 905-631-5724
www.sounddesigntechnologies.com
Line: Designs and manufactures
semiconductor solutions for hearing
instruments and provides advanced
high density interconnect technologies.
NAICS: 334410
#Emp: 100-249 (Tor)
Own: Private Company
Par: ON Semiconductor Corp (US)
Key: Ian Roane, Pres & CEO
Scott Haddow, Sr VP Ops

Ontario Chrysler Jeep Dodge Inc.

5280 Dixie Rd.
Mississauga, ON L4W 2A7
Tel 905-625-8801
Fax 905-625-7931
www.ontariochrysler.net
Line: Operates a full service dealership.
NAICS: 441110 441120
#Emp: 100-249 (Tor)
#TorLoc: 1
Own: Private Company
Key: Bary Gray, Pres
Bourk Boyd, VP
Janet Revell, Office Mgr
Linda Hillmer, Secy-Treas
Dave Pozzobon, GM

Ontario Clean Water Agency

1700-1 Yonge St.
Toronto, ON M5E 1E5
Tel 416-314-5600
Fax 416-314-8300
www.ocwa.com
AKA: OCWA
Line: Operates, maintains and manages water and wastewater treatment facilities.
NAICS: 221310
#Emp: 100-249 (Tor)
#TorLoc: 3
Own: Government
Par: Government of Ontario
Key: Jane Pagel, Pres & CEO
David Williams, Acting VP Ops
Tony Araujo, Dir of HR
Dan Atkinson,
    Acting VP Fin & Corp Services

Ontario College of Art & Design

100 McCaul St.
Toronto, ON M5T 1W1
Tel 416-977-6000
Fax 416-977-6006
www.ocad.ca
AKA: OCAD
Line: University specializing in art and design education at the post-secondary and graduate levels.
NAICS: 611310 611210
#Emp: 500-999 (Tor)
Own: Government
Par: Government of Ontario
Key: Sara Diamond, Pres
Nicky Davis, Dir of HR
Peter Fraser, Dir of Fin
Aisa Ljubijankic, Purch Agent
Alastair MacLeod, Dir of IT Services
Susan Sutton,
    Exec Dir of Dev & Alumni Relns
Steve Virtue, Dir of Mktg & Commun

Ontario College of Teachers

101 Bloor St. East
Toronto, ON M5S 0A1
Tel 416-961-8800
Fax 416-961-8822
www.oct.ca
Line: Sets and regulates teaching qualifications and standards of conduct, registers members and investigates and disciplines members charged with professional misconduct.
NAICS: 813920
#Emp: 100-249 (Tor)
#TorLoc: 1
Own: Association

Key: Michael Salvatori,
    Registrar & CEO
Richard Lewko,
    Dir of Corp & Council Services
Frank McIntyre, HR Mgr
Michael Kaptein, Cont & Mgr of Fin
Kathy McLaughlin, Office Coord
Rogelio Salvador, IT Mgr
Philip Carter, Commun Mgr

Ontario Electrical Construction Company Ltd.

7 Compass Crt.
Toronto, ON M1S 5N3
Tel 416-363-5741
Fax 416-363-6901
www.onelec.com
Line: Operates an electrical contracting business.
NAICS: 232510
#Emp: 100-249 (Tor)
Own: Private Company
Key: John D. Wright, Pres
Tom Grenon, VP Chief Estimator
Tim Wright, Purch Dir

Ontario Energy Board

2300 Yonge St., 27th Fl.
P.O. Box 2319
Toronto, ON M4P 1E4
Tel 416-481-1967
Fax 416-440-7656
www.oeb.gov.on.ca
Line: Regulates Ontario's natural gas and electricity industries and provides advice on energy matters referred to it by the Minister of Energy and the Minister of Natural Resources.
NAICS: 912910
#Emp: 100-249 (Tor)
#TorLoc: 1
Own: Government
Key: Rosemarie T. Leclair, Chair & CEO
Aleck Dadson, COO
Julie Mitchell, Mng Dir of HR
Suzanne Cowan, Mng Dir of Commun
    & Consumer Relns

Ontario Federation for Cerebral Palsy

104-1630 Lawrence Ave. West
Toronto, ON M6L 1C5
Tel 416-244-9686
Fax 416-244-6543
www.ofcp.on.ca
NAICS: 813310
#Emp: 75-99 (Tor)
#TorLoc: 1
Own: Not-for-profit
Key: Clarence Meyers, Exec Dir
Pit Chiu, Acct

Ontario Financing Authority

1400-1 Dundas St. West
Toronto, ON M5G 1Z3
Tel 416-325-8000
Fax 416-325-8005
www.ofina.on.ca
Line: Manages the borrowing, investment of funds, and financial risk management activities on behalf of the Province of Ontario.
NAICS: 522190
#Emp: 100-249 (Tor)
#TorLoc: 1
Own: Provincial Crown Corp.
Key: Gadi Mayman, CEO

Ontario Flower Growers Co-op

910 Midway Blvd.
Mississauga, ON L5T 1T9
Tel 905-670-9556
Fax 905-670-9637
www.ontarioflowers.com
Line: Grows and distributes flowers and potted plants.
NAICS: 111422
#Emp: 75-99 (Tor)
#TorLoc: 1
Own: Private Company
Key: Jouke Sypkes, GM
Helen Kall, Ops Mgr
Joyce McCormack, Office Mgr
Elizabeth Morris, Cont

Ontario Hospital Association

2800-200 Front St. West
Toronto, ON M5V 3L1
Tel 416-205-1300
Fax 416-205-1301
www.oha.com
AKA: OHA
Line: Operates a voluntary, non-profit organization dedicated to the continuing improvement of health services in Ontario.
NAICS: 813910 813310
#Emp: 100-249 (Tor)
#TorLoc: 1
Own: Association
Key: Tom Closson, Pres & CEO
Warren DiClemente, COO & VP,
    Educational Services
Julie Giraldi, Chief HR & IT Officer
Douglas Miller, CFO
Anthony Dale, VP Policy & Pub Affairs

Ontario Laser Rentals Ltd.

71 Steinway Blvd.
Toronto, ON M9W 6H6
Tel 416-674-1913
Fax 416-674-8660
www.ontariolaserrentals.ca
Line: Leases and rents laser equipment.
NAICS: 532490
#Emp: 75-99 (Tor)
#TorLoc: 1
Own: Private Company
Key: William O'Malley, Pres
Cheryl Washington, Cont

Ontario Lottery and Gaming Corp.

420-4120 Yonge St.
Toronto, ON M2P 2B8
Tel 416-224-1772
Fax 416-224-7000
www.olgc.ca
NAICS: 713291 713210
#Emp: 1000-4999 (Tor)
#TorLoc: 10
Own: Provincial Crown Corp.
Par: Government of Ontario
Key: Rob Moore, Sr VP

Ontario Lung Association

573 King St. East
Toronto, ON M5A 4L3
Tel 416-864-9911
Fax 416-864-9916
www.on.lung.ca
Line: Operates a medical association.
NAICS: 813410
#Emp: 100-249 (Tor)
#TorLoc: 1
Own: Private Company
Key: George Habib, Pres & CEO
Leslie Olsen, Dir of HR
Shirley Somnath, Asst Mgr, Donor
    Fulfillment Centre
Karen Petcoff, Mktg & Commun Mgr

Ontario March of Dimes

10 Overlea Blvd.
Toronto, ON M4H 1A4
Tel 416-425-3463
Fax 416-425-1920
www.marchofdimes.ca
AKA: Rehabilitation Foundation for the
Disabled
Line: Provides rehabilitation and
employment services to people with
physical disabilities.
NAICS: 813310
#Emp: 1000-4999 (Tor)
#TorLoc: 13
Own: Not-for-profit

Key: Andria Spindel, Pres & CEO
Jerry Lucas, VP Programs
Chris Harrison, Dir of HR
Debashish Chakravorty,
    Dir of Fin & Admin
Jason Vallance, IT Mgr

Ontario Medical Association

900-150 Bloor St. West
Toronto, ON M5S 3C1
Tel 416-599-2580
Fax 416-599-9309
www.oma.org
AKA: OMA
Line: Serves the medical profession and
the people of Ontario in the pursuit of
good health and excellent health care.
NAICS: 813920 621390
#Emp: 100-249 (Tor)
#TorLoc: 1
Own: Association
Key: Mark Macleod, Pres
Jonathan Guss, CEO
Bob Mulcaster, Dir of Office Services
Patrick Nelson,
    Exec Dir of Pub Affairs & Commun

Ontario Motor Sales Ltd.

140 Bond St. West
P.O. Box 488
Oshawa, ON L1H 7L8
Tel 905-725-6501
Fax 905-571-3589
www.ontariomotorsales.com
Line: Sells new and used automobiles
and operates a service, parts and
collision repair centre for General
Motors vehicles.
NAICS: 441110 441120
#Emp: 100-249 (Tor)
#TorLoc: 1
Own: Private Company
Par: Wilsonia Industries Ltd. (CDA)
Key: Glenn S. Willson, Dealer Principal
Tony Willson, GM
Brian Snyder, VP Fin

Ontario Municipal Employees Retirement System

800-1 University Ave.
Toronto, ON M5J 2P1
Tel 416-369-2400
Fax 416-360-0217
www.omers.com
AKA: OMERS
Line: Invests and administers for
Ontario municipal employees' pension
plan.
NAICS: 526112
#Emp: 250-499 (Tor)
#TorLoc: 1

Own: Provincial Crown Corp.
Key: Michael Nobrega, Pres & CEO
John MacDonald, COO
Warren Bell, Exec VP & CHRO
Patrick Crowley, CFO

Ontario Natural Food Co-op

5685 McLaughlin Rd.
Mississauga, ON L5R 3K5
Tel 905-507-2021
Fax 905-507-2848
www.onfc.ca
AKA: Ontario Federation of Food Co-
Operatives and Clubs Inc.
Line: Distributes organic and natural
foods and products.
NAICS: 413110
#Emp: 75-99 (Tor)
Own: Not-for-profit
Key: Randy Whitteker, GM
Sheri Holubec, HR Coord
Larry Sadler, IT Mgr
John Landsborough, Sales & Mktg Mgr

Ontario Nurses' Association

400-85 Grenville St.
Toronto, ON M5S 3A2
Tel 416-964-8833
Fax 416-964-8864
www.ona.org
AKA: ONA
Line: Advances the social, economic
and general welfare of nurses and other
allied personnel.
NAICS: 813920 621390
#Emp: 100-249 (Tor)
#TorLoc: 1
Own: Association
Key: Linda Haslam-Stroud, Pres
Lesley Bell, CEO
Grazyna Dudar,
    Employee Services Mgr
Gayle Thomson, Internal Services Mgr
David Laxdal, IT Mgr
Peter Burt, PR Mgr

Ontario Nursing Services

210-80 Acadia Ave.
Markham, ON L3R 9V1
Tel 905-946-8383
Fax 905-946-8117
www.onsnursingservices.com
Line: Provides home health care
services.
NAICS: 621610
#Emp: 250-499 (Tor)
#TorLoc: 1
Own: Private Company
Key: Kelvin Lam, Mng Dir
Angela Wan, Mgr of Support Services

Ontario Pension Board

2200-200 King St. West
Toronto, ON M5H 3X6
Tel 416-364-8558
Fax 416-366-0199
www.opb.ca
Line: Administers and manages the
Ontario Public Service Pension Plan.
NAICS: 523920
#Emp: 100-249 (Tor)
#TorLoc: 1
Own: Provincial Crown Corp.
Par: Government of Ontario
Key: Mark Fuller, Pres & CEO
Anne Catherall, VP Corp Services
Isabelle Simonata, Purch Officer
Thomas Choi, VP
    Enterprise Solutions & IT Services
Mark Henry, Dir of Regulatory Affairs

Ontario Place Corp.

955 Lake Shore Blvd. West
Toronto, ON M6K 3B9
Tel 416-314-9900
Fax 416-314-9989
www.ontarioplace.com
Line: Operates entertainment, cultural
and leisure complex.
NAICS: 713110 512130 722210
#Emp: 250-499 (Tor)
#TorLoc: 1
Own: Provincial Crown Corp.
Par: Ministry of Tourism & Culture
(CDA)
Key: John Tevlin, GM
Mike Hazelton, Mgr, Guest Experience
Marsha O'Connor, Dir of Fin
Shawn Fulton, Dir of Mktg & Commun

Ontario Power Contracting Ltd.

340 Bowes Rd.
Concord, ON L4K 1K1
Tel 905-660-4448
Fax 905-660-6954
Line: Provides underground hydro
services and street lighting.
NAICS: 232510
#Emp: 75-99 (Tor)
#TorLoc: 1
Own: Private Company
Key: Joseph Alfano, Pres

Ontario Power Generation Inc.

700 University Ave.
Toronto, ON M5G 1X6
Tel 416-592-2555
Fax 416-592-2527
www.opg.com
AKA: OPG
Line: Generates and sells electricity
throughout Ontario.
NAICS: 221122
#Emp: 10000+ (Tor)
#TorLoc: 26
Own: Provincial Crown Corp.
Par: Government of Ontario
Key: Tom Mitchell, Pres & CEO
Donn W. Hanbidge, CFO
Rob Boguski,
    Sr VP Business Services & IT
Bruce Boland, Sr VP Corp Affairs

Ontario Power Generation Inc./
Pickering Nuclear

1675 Montgomery Park Rd.
Pickering, ON L1V 2R5
Tel 905-839-1151
Fax 905-837-7352
www.opg.com
Line: Provides nuclear electric power.
NAICS: 221113
#Emp: 1000-4999 (Tor)
#TorLoc: 2
Own: Provincial Crown Corp.
Par: Government of Ontario
Key: Tom Mitchell, Pres & CEO
Glenn Jager, Sr VP, Pickering A
Barb Keenan, Sr VP HR
Paul Pasquet, Sr VP, Pickering B

Ontario Provincial Police

Lincoln M. Alexander Building
777 Memorial Ave.
Orillia, ON L3V 7V3
Tel 705-329-6111
Fax 705-329-6195
www.opp.ca
AKA: O.P.P.
NAICS: 912130
#Emp: 500-999 (Tor)
#TorLoc: 8
Own: Government
Par: Government of Ontario
Key: Chris D. Lewis, Cmmr
Vince Hawkes, Field Ops Command
Noreen Alleyne,
    Prov Commander Corp Services
Larry Beechey, Field Support Services
Scott Tod, Investigations & Organized
    Crime Command
Angie Howe, Corp Commun Bureau

Ontario Public Service
Employees Union

100 Lesmill Rd.
Toronto, ON M3B 3P8
Tel 416-443-8888
Fax 416-443-9670
www.opseu.org
AKA: OPSEU
Line: Represents and negotiates
for employees of the provincial
government, community colleges,
hospitals and some 350 other publicly-
funded agencies and institutions;
combats the privatization of public
services; and fights for pay equity,
health and safety, and employment
equity.
NAICS: 813930
#Emp: 250-499 (Tor)
#TorLoc: 2
Own: Association
Key: Smokey Thomas, Pres
Patty Rout, First VP & Treas
Jeanne Theriault, Admr of Staff Relns
Peter Hammond, Supr of IS
Tim Little, Commun Admr

Ontario Real Estate Association

99 Duncan Mill Rd.
Toronto, ON M3B 1Z2
Tel 416-445-9910
Fax 416-445-2644
www.orea.com
AKA: OREA Real Estate College
Line: Represents real estate vocational
interests of members and provides
licensing education.
NAICS: 813920
#Emp: 100-249 (Tor)
#TorLoc: 1
Own: Association
Key: Ed Barisa, CEO
Dinaz Garda, Mgr, Exec Office Ops
Nalini Bhargava, Dir of Fin

Ontario Realty Corporation

2000-1 Dundas St. West
Toronto, ON M5G 2L5
Tel 416-327-3937
Fax 416-327-1906
www.ontariorealty.ca
Line: Operates an enterprise agency
responsible for the management of the
Ontario Government's real estate.
NAICS: 531310
#Emp: 100-249 (Tor)
#TorLoc: 1
Own: Provincial Crown Corp.
Key: David Livingston, CEO
Dave Glass, COO
Kathy Bull, Sr VP HR
Dale Lawr, CFO

Ontario Science Centre

770 Don Mills Rd.
Toronto, ON M3C 1T3
Tel 416-696-1000
Fax 416-696-3221
www.ontariosciencecentre.ca
Line: Operates a science centre as a
public educational institution.
NAICS: 712119
#Emp: 250-499 (Tor)
#TorLoc: 1
Own: Provincial Crown Corp.
Par: Government of Ontario
Key: Lesley Lewis, Dir Gen & CEO
Lynn Row, Assoc Dir of Ops
    & Service Management
Tammy Browes-Bugden, HR Mgr
Errol D'Costa, Dir of Fin
Martin Timusk, Assoc Dir of IS
Bern Gorecki,
    VP Mktg & Strategic Commun

Ontario Secondary School Teachers Federation

60 Mobile Dr.
Toronto, ON M4A 2P3
Tel 416-751-8300
Fax 416-751-3394
www.osstf.on.ca
AKA: OSSTF
Line: Protects members, both
individually and collectively; ensures
civil, human and legal rights for
members; and secures and maintains
collective bargaining rights, including
the right to strike.
NAICS: 813930 813920
#Emp: 100-249 (Tor)
#TorLoc: 1
Own: Association
Key: Ken Coran, Pres
Pierre Côté, Gen Secy
Jim Spray, CFO
Jason Westmaas, IT Mgr

Ontario Securities Commission

1903-20 Queen St. West
Toronto, ON M5H 3S8
Tel 416-597-0681
Fax 416-593-8122
www.osc.gov.on.ca
AKA: OSC
Line: Regulates and oversees the
securities industry in Ontario.
NAICS: 523990
#Emp: 250-499 (Tor)
#TorLoc: 1
Own: Provincial Crown Corp.
Par: Government of Ontario
Key: Maureen Jenson, Exec Dir & CAO
Howard Wetson, Chair & CEO
Ken Gibson, Dir of Corp Services
Jennifer Laidlaw, Dir of HR
Leslie Byberg, Dir of Corp Fin

Ontario Shores Centre for Mental Health Sciences

700 Gordon St.
Whitby, ON L1N 5S9
Tel 905-430-4055
Fax 905-430-4032
www.ontarioshores.ca
Line: Provides specialized tertiary care
mental health programs.
NAICS: 622210 621494
#Emp: 1000-4999 (Tor)
#TorLoc: 1
Own: Not-for-profit
Key: Glenna Raymond, Pres & CEO
Karim Mamdani, COO
Bob Blewett, Dir of HR
John Chen, Dir of Fin & IS
Susan Nakhle,
    Dir of Commun and Pub Affairs

Ontario Teachers' Pension Plan Board

5650 Yonge St.
Toronto, ON M2M 4H5
Tel 416-228-5900
Fax 416-730-5349
www.otpp.com
AKA: OTPP
Line: Administers the pension plan,
manages its investment assets and pays
entitled members and their survivors.
NAICS: 523920 813930
#Emp: 500-999 (Tor)
#TorLoc: 1
Own: Association

Key: Jim Leech, Pres & CEO
Neil Petroff, Exec VP Investments &
    Chief Investment Officer
Marcia Mendes-d'Abreu, VP HR
David McGraw, Sr VP & CFO
Patrick Boyd, Facilities Mgr
Russ Bruch, VP & CIO
Rosemarie McClean,
    Sr VP, Member Services
Deborah Allan,
    Dir of Commun & Media Relns

Ontario Trillium Foundation

45 Charles St. East
Toronto, ON M4Y 1S2
Tel 416-963-4927
Fax 416-963-8781
www.trilliumfoundation.org
Line: Operates a charitable foundation.
NAICS: 813210
#Emp: 75-99 (Tor)
#TorLoc: 1
Own: Not-for-profit
Key: Robin Cardozo, CEO
Anne Pashley, VP Fin & Admin

Ontex Clothing Inc.

61 Maybrook Dr.
Toronto, ON M1V 5J7
Tel 416-412-3578
Fax 416-412-3579
www.ontexclothing.com
Line: Wholesales used clothing.
NAICS: 453310
#Emp: 100-249 (Tor)
#TorLoc: 1
Own: Private Company
Key: Asafali Nasser, Pres
Samir Nasser, VP Ops

OnX Enterprise Solutions Inc.

155 Commerce Valley Dr. East
Thornhill, ON L3T 7T2
Tel 905-482-2292
Fax 905-482-2295
www.onx.com
Line: Provides hardware and software
professional services.
NAICS: 541510
#Emp: 100-249 (Tor)
#TorLoc: 1
Own: Public Company
Key: Enza Alexander, Exec VP
Ed W. Vos, Pres & CEO
Tracy Hussain, Dir of Fin
Michael Corby, CTO

Open Solutions Canada

202-700 Dorval Dr.
Oakville, ON L6K 3V3
Tel 905-849-1390
Fax 905-849-1396
www.ca.opensolutions.com
Line: Provides financial services.
NAICS: 511210
#Emp: 75-99 (Tor)
#TorLoc: 1
Own: Private Company
Key: Rob Palin, GM
Lana Parker, HR Specialist

Open Text Communications Solutions Group

38 Leek Cres.
Richmond Hill, ON L4B 4N8
Tel 905-762-6000
Fax 905-762-6151
www.firstclass.com
AKA: Open Text FirstClass
Line: Designs software for enterprise content management.
NAICS: 511210
#Emp: 250-499 (Tor)
#TorLoc: 1
Own: Public Company
Key: John Shackleton, Pres & CEO
Paul McFeeters, CFO

Open Window Health Bread Bakery Limited

1125 Finch Ave. West
Toronto, ON M3J 2E8
Tel 416-665-8241
Fax 416-665-9528
www.owbakery.com
AKA: Health Bread; The Baker's Counter; Best Kosher Haimishe Farfel
Line: Manufactures, wholesales, and retails baked goods.
NAICS: 311814 445291
#Emp: 100-249 (Tor)
#TorLoc: 11
Own: Private Company
Key: Max Feig, Pres
Gail Agasi, VP & CEO
Uzi Agasi, GM & CFO

Opinion Search Inc.

704-2345 Yonge St.
Toronto, ON M4P 2E5
Tel 416-962-9109
Fax 416-962-0505
www.opinionsearch.com
Line: Provides marketing research services.
NAICS: 541910
#Emp: 100-249 (Tor)
#TorLoc: 1
Own: Private Company
Key: Ed Hum, Pres
Phyllis Friedman,
    VP, Qualitative Research

Optech Inc.

300 Interchange Way
Vaughan, ON L4K 5Z8
Tel 905-660-0808
Fax 905-660-0829
www.optech.on.ca
Line: Manufactures laser and electro-optical systems, rangefinders, environmental monitoring systems and surveying equipment.
NAICS: 334512 417930
#Emp: 250-499 (Tor)
#TorLoc: 1
Own: Private Company
Key: Donald Carswell, Pres
Allan Carswell, Chmn of the Board
Douglas Houston, VP Ops
Margie Estepa-Kurin, HR Mgr
Elizabeth Carswell, CFO
Joe Liadsky, VP Tech

Optima Communications International Inc.

200-144 Front St. West
Toronto, ON M5J 2L7
Tel 416-581-1236
Fax 416-581-8878
www.optima.net
Line: Provides call centre services and e-mail contact management services.
NAICS: 561420
#Emp: 500-999 (Tor)
#TorLoc: 2
Own: Private Company
Key: Don MacLeod, Pres
Rizvan Juma, Cont
Elizabeth Sedlacek, Business Dev Dir

Oracle Canada ULC

27 Allstate Pkwy.
Markham, ON L3R 5L7
Tel 905-477-6745
Fax 905-477-9423
www.sun.ca
Line: Delivers enterprise wide client-server computing solutions including high-performance workstations and servers, software development environments and advanced networking products.
NAICS: 334110 541510
#Emp: 500-999 (Tor)
#TorLoc: 2
Own: Public Company
Par: Sun Microsystems, Inc. (US)
Key: Andy Canham, CEO, Canada

Oracle Corporation Canada Inc.

100-110 Matheson Blvd. West
Mississauga, ON L5R 3P4
Tel 905-890-0800
Fax 905-890-1207
www.oracle.com/ca-en
Line: Sells computer software and provides consulting services.
NAICS: 541510
#Emp: 500-999 (Tor)
#TorLoc: 2
Own: Public Company
Par: Oracle Corp. (US)
Key: Lawrence J. Ellison, CEO

Oran Industries Ltd.

60 Vinyl Crt.
Woodbridge, ON L4L 4A3
Tel 905-851-7877
Fax 905-851-7928
www.pvcwindows.com
NAICS: 326198
#Emp: 75-99 (Tor)
#TorLoc: 1
Own: Private Company
Key: Mildred Lev, Pres

Orbis Canada Ltd.

39 Westmore Dr.
Toronto, ON M9V 3Y6
Tel 416-745-6980
Fax 416-745-1874
www.norsemanplastics.com
Line: Manufactures plastic injection mouldings.
NAICS: 326198
#Emp: 250-499 (Tor)
#TorLoc: 1
Own: Private Company
Par: Orbis Corporation (US)
Key: Steve Smith, Plant Mgr

Organic Resource Management Inc.

601-3700 Steeles Ave. West
Woodbridge, ON L4L 8K8
Tel 905-264-7700
Fax 905-264-7273
www.ormi.com
AKA: ORMI
Line: Provides waste management
services.
NAICS: 562210
#Emp: 75-99 (Tor)
#TorLoc: 2
Own: Private Company
Key: Ian Kelland, Pres
Douglas Carruthers, VP Corp Dev

Orlando Corp.

6205 Airport Rd.
Mississauga, ON L4V 1E3
Tel 905-677-5480
Fax 905-677-2824
www.orlandocorp.com
Line: Performs real estate development,
general and road contracting, and
manages shopping centres and office
buildings.
NAICS: 231220 231110
#Emp: 100-249 (Tor)
#TorLoc: 1
Own: Private Company
Key: Phil King, Pres
Doug Kilner, Vice Chmn
Tom Hunter, HR Mgr
William O'Rourke, Sr VP Fin
Jim Turner, Sr VP Engineering & Purch
Pascal Fraser, Sr Mgr of IS

Ortho-Clinical Diagnostics

A Div. of A Johnson & Johnson Company
200 Whitall Dr.
Markham, ON L3R 0T5
Tel 905-946-3991
Fax 905-946-5849
www.orthoclinical.com
Line: Provides diagnostic products and
services.
NAICS: 334512
#Emp: 75-99 (Tor)
Own: Public Company
Key: Charlie Sciortino, GM

The Orthotic Group Inc.

160 Markland St.
Markham, ON L6C 0C6
Tel 905-888-8511
Fax 905-946-8100
www.theorthoticgroup.com
Line: Manufactures custom made foot
orthotics.
NAICS: 316210 339110
#Emp: 100-249 (Tor)
#TorLoc: 1
Own: Private Company
Key: Bruce Marrison, Pres
Rob Lee, VP Ops
Irene Krupp, HR Mgr
Anthony Rzepka, CFO
Chris Patten, CIO
Peter Karolidis, VP Client Services

Osgoode Hall Law School

A Div. of York University
4700 Keele St.
Toronto, ON M3J 1P3
Tel 416-736-5030
Fax 416-736-5736
www.osgoode.yorku.ca
Line: Provides education in the area of
law.
NAICS: 611310
#Emp: 100-249 (Tor)
#TorLoc: 2
Own: Government
Key: Lorne Sossin, Interim Dean
Helen Huang, Exec Officer
Sam Wong, Dir of IT

Oshawa Clinic

117 King St. East
Oshawa, ON L1H 1B9
Tel 905-723-8551
Fax 905-723-6319
www.oshawaclinic.com
Line: Provides health services.
NAICS: 621110
#Emp: 250-499 (Tor)
#TorLoc: 3
Own: Private Company
Key: Harry Horricks, CEO
Marilyn VanEyk, HR Mgr

Oshawa Fire Services

A Div. of The City of Oshawa
199 Adelaide Ave. West
Oshawa, ON L1J 7B1
Tel 905-433-1238
Fax 905-433-0276
www.oshawa.ca
NAICS: 913140
#Emp: 100-249 (Tor)

#TorLoc: 4
Own: Government
Key: Steve Maringer, Fire Chief
John Jeffs, Deputy Fire Chief
Bob Warrington, Deputy Fire Chief

Oshawa Public Library/ McLaughlin Branch

65 Bagot St.
Oshawa, ON L1H 1N2
Tel 905-579-6111
Fax 905-433-8107
www.oshawalibrary.on.ca
NAICS: 514121
#Emp: 75-99 (Tor)
Own: Government
Key: Joseph Sansalone, Mgr of Adult IS
Ian Heckford, CEO
Robert Merry, Mgr of Corp Services

Oshawa PUC Networks Inc.

100 Simcoe St. South
Oshawa, ON L1H 7M7
Tel 905-723-4623
Fax 905-723-7947
www.opuc.on.ca
Line: Operates a local electricity
distribution company and telecom
offering.
NAICS: 221122
#Emp: 75-99 (Tor)
#TorLoc: 1
Own: Private Company
Par: Oshawa Power and Utilities Corp.
(CDA)
Key: Atul Mahajan, Pres & CEO
Denise Flores, VP Engineering & Ops

Osler Hoskin & Harcourt, LLP

1 First Canadian Pl.
P.O. Box 50
Toronto, ON M5X 1B8
Tel 416-362-2111
Fax 416-862-6666
www.osler.com
Line: Provides integrated legal services
with business law specialists.
NAICS: 541110
#Emp: 500-999 (Tor)
#TorLoc: 1
Own: Private Company
Key: Dale Ponder, Mng Partner
Clay Horner, Chair
Ruth Woods, COO
Ellen Hryniowski, Dir of HR
Craig Fields, CFO
Judy Stein-Korte,
    Chief Client Services Officer

Osram Sylvania Ltd.

2001 Drew Rd.
Mississauga, ON L5S 1S4
Tel 905-673-6171
Fax 905-673-6290
www.sylvania.com
Line: Designs, manufactures, sells,
installs, maintains and finances
lighting systems.
NAICS: 335120 335110
#Emp: 100-249 (Tor)
#TorLoc: 1
Own: Private Company
Par: Osram Sylvania Inc. (US)
Key: Abbas Khan, Pres
Patrick Hatzis, Dir of HR & Legal
Carlos Dall'Orso, VP & Cont
JoAnn McKeown,
    VP Sales & Mktg, Retail

Ostaco 2000 Windoors Inc.

248 Bowes Rd.
Concord, ON L4K 1J9
Tel 905-660-5021
Fax 905-660-2419
www.ostaco.com
Line: Manufactures and distributes
windows, patio doors, and entry door
systems.
NAICS: 332321
#Emp: 75-99 (Tor)
#TorLoc: 1
Own: Private Company
Key: Gianni Martini, Pres

Oticon Canada

1-6950 Creditview Rd.
Mississauga, ON L5N 0A6
Tel 905-677-3231
Fax 905-677-7760
www.oticon.ca
Line: Manufactures hearing aids.
NAICS: 334512
#Emp: 100-249 (Tor)
#TorLoc: 1
Own: Private Company
Key: Brock Neuman, Mng Dir

Otis Canada Inc.

4475 North Service Rd.
Burlington, ON L7L 4X7
Tel 905-332-9919
Fax 905-332-9598
www.otis.com
Line: Sells and services elevators and
moving stairways.
NAICS: 232550
#Emp: 100-249 (Tor)

#TorLoc: 3
Own: Private Company
Par: United Technologies (US)
Key: Tony Grilli, Pres & CEO
Gwen Harpur, HR Admr

Outdoor Outfits Ltd.

372 Richmond St. West, 4th Fl.
Toronto, ON M5V 1X6
Tel 416-598-4111
Fax 416-598-4626
www.outdooroutfits.com
Line: Manufactures uniforms, clothing
and rainwear.
NAICS: 315299
#Emp: 75-99 (Tor)
#TorLoc: 1
Own: Private Company
Key: Sheldon Switzer, Pres

Owens Corning Canada Inc.

3450 McNicoll Ave.
Toronto, ON M1V 1Z5
Tel 416-292-4000
Fax 416-412-6719
www.owenscorning.com
Line: Manufactures and supplies
insulation, textile and reinforcement.
NAICS: 327990 325210
#Emp: 100-249 (Tor)
#TorLoc: 1
Own: Public Company
Par: Owens Corning (US)
Key: Anindya Ghosh,
    Plant Mgr, Toronto
Ric McFadden, Cdn Sales Mgr

Oxford Properties Group Inc.

Royal Bank Plaza
900-200 Bay St.
Toronto, ON M5J 2J2
Tel 416-865-8300
Fax 416-868-3799
www.oxfordproperties.com
Line: Owns and manages commercial
and residential real estate properties.
NAICS: 531310
#Emp: 500-999 (Tor)
#TorLoc: 27
Own: Private Company
Par: BPC Properties Ltd. (CDA)
Key: Blake Hutchenson, Pres & CEO
Michael Kitt, Exec VP, Canada
Colin Loudon, Exec VP & CFO

Oxville Homes Ltd.

5-2220 Hwy. 7
Concord, ON L4K 1W7
Tel 416-667-0447
Fax 416-667-8747
www.fernbrookhomes.com
AKA: Fernbrook Homes
NAICS: 231210
#Emp: 75-99 (Tor)
#TorLoc: 1
Own: Private Company
Key: Danny Salvatore, Pres
Nick Cortellucci, Treas

PACE Independent Living

210-970 Lawrence Ave. West
Toronto, ON M6A 3B6
Tel 416-789-7806
Fax 416-789-7807
www.pace-il.ca
Line: Provides physical support
services to adults with physical
disabilities to assist with independent
community living.
NAICS: 624190
#Emp: 100-249 (Tor)
#TorLoc: 6
Own: Not-for-profit
Key: Kim Knox, Dir of Admin Services
Joanne Wilson, Exec Dir
Shirley Rokos,
    Dir of Supportive Housing
Carolyn Ross, HR Mgr
Maunda Williams, Financial Mgr

Pacific Rubiales Energy Corp.

1100-333 Bay St.
Toronto, ON M5H 2R2
Tel 416-362-7735
Fax 416-360-7783
www.pacificrubiales.com
Line: Operates an independent oil
and gas exploration and production
company in Colombia.
NAICS: 211113 541360
#Emp: 500-999 (Tor)
Own: Private Company
Key: Jose Francisco Arata, Pres
Ronald Pantin, CEO & Exec Dir
Leyda Vargas, VP Human Talent
Carlos Perez, CFO

Pacific Western

6999 Ordan Dr.
Mississauga, ON L5T 1K6
Tel 905-564-3232
Fax 905-564-5959
www.pacificwesterntoronto.com
AKA: P.W. Transportation; Pacific
Western Toronto
Line: Provides group charter, FIT
airport service, shuttle and destination
management services.
NAICS: 485990
#Emp: 100-249 (Tor)
#TorLoc: 2
Own: Private Company
Par: Pacific Western Transportation
Ltd. (CDA)
Key: Dean Wright, GM
Ray Cherrey, Ops Mgr
Terry Spark, HR Mgr
Sandy Lombardo,
    Financial Services Mgr
Patty Pattison, Dir of Sales & Mktg

Packaging Technologies Inc.

310A Courtland Ave.
Vaughan, ON L4K 4Y6
Tel 905-738-8226
Fax 905-738-6182
www.ptibox.com
Line: Manufactures corrugated cartons.
NAICS: 322211 561910
#Emp: 75-99 (Tor)
#TorLoc: 1
Own: Private Company
Key: John Franciosa, Pres & CEO
Clarence Brown, Dir of Manuf

Packall Packaging Inc.

2 Shaftsbury Lane
Brampton, ON L6T 3X7
Tel 905-793-0177
Fax 905-793-9099
www.packall.com
Line: Manufactures flexible packaging
materials for the meat, cheese and
seafood industries.
NAICS: 322220
#Emp: 100-249 (Tor)
#TorLoc: 1
Own: Private Company
Key: Henry Ciszewski, Pres & CEO
Stephan Ciszewski, VP & GM

Padulo Integrated Inc.

1 St. Clair Ave. West
10th Fl.
Toronto, ON M4V 1K7
Tel 416-966-4000
Fax 416-966-1773
www.padulo.ca
Line: Provides fully integrated
communications, marketing and
advertising services.
NAICS: 541810
#Emp: 75-99 (Tor)
#TorLoc: 1
Own: Private Company
Key: Richard Padulo, Chmn & CEO

Page + Steele Architects

200-95 St. Clair Ave. West
Toronto, ON M4V 1N6
Tel 416-924-9966
Fax 416-924-9067
www.pagesteele.com
Line: Provides architectural services.
NAICS: 541330 541310
#Emp: 75-99 (Tor)
#TorLoc: 2
Own: Private Company
Key: Sol Wassermuhl, Pres
Tim Gorley,
    VP Specs & Contract Admin
Robin Clarke, Exec VP
Estrella Polley, Cont
Brian Sickle, Exec VP

Paging Network of Canada Inc.

1-1685 Tech Ave.
Mississauga, ON L4W 0A7
Tel 905-614-3161
Fax 905-614-3171
www.pagenet.ca
Line: Provides telecommunication
services.
NAICS: 513330
#Emp: 75-99 (Tor)
#TorLoc: 1
Own: Private Company
Key: Garry Fitzgerald,
Pres, Chmn & CEO

Pallett Valo LLP

1600-90 Burnhamthorpe Rd. West
Mississauga, ON L5B 3C3
Tel 905-273-3300
Fax 905-273-6920
www.pallettvalo.com
Line: Provides a wide range of legal
services.
NAICS: 541110
#Emp: 75-99 (Tor)
Own: Private Company
Key: Anne Kennedy, Mng Partner
Frances Wales, COO
Maureen Ottner, Dir of Fin

Panalpina Inc.

6350 Cantay Rd.
Mississauga, ON L5R 4E2
Tel 905-755-4500
Fax 905-755-4599
www.panalpina.com
Line: Provides national and
international transport services.
NAICS: 488519
#Emp: 100-249 (Tor)
#TorLoc: 2
Own: Public Company
Par: Panalpina World Transport
(Holding) Ltd. (SWITZ)
Key: Volker Sachse, Mng Dir
Bruno Zwiker, VP Ops
Flavia Iuston-Blair, Dir of HR
Fares Otaki, VP Fin
Laurence Adam, IT Mgr

Panasonic Canada Inc.

5770 Ambler Dr.
Mississauga, ON L4W 2T3
Tel 905-624-5010
Fax 905-624-9714
www.panasonic.ca
Line: Sells, markets and distributes
electronics.
NAICS: 414220 414210 334110
#Emp: 500-999 (Tor)
#TorLoc: 1
Own: Private Company
Par: Panasonic Corporation of North
America (US)
Key: Ian Vatcher, Pres
Deborah Scott, Dir of HR
Ken Buschlen, VP & CFO
Doug Wigmore, Dir of MIS
Chuck Ward,
    VP Consumers Products Div
Ian Kilvert, GM, Corp Brand
    Management

PaperlinX Canada Limited

200 Galcat Dr.
Vaughan, ON L4L 0B9
Tel 905-265-6060
Fax 905-265-2037
www.paperlinx.com
AKA: Spicers; Coast Paper; Roll-O-Vert
Line: Wholesales paper, industrial,
janitorial, sanitorial products, graphic
arts supplies and systems, business
imaging products, printing paper and
consumer brands.
NAICS: 418220
#Emp: 250-499 (Tor)
#TorLoc: 1
Own: Public Company
Par: PaperlinX (AUS)
Key: Terry Pitchford, VP Ops
Bill Moore, GM, Roll-O-Vert
Francine Robert, Dir of HR
Carla Pickard, Dir of Commercial
    Business Systems
Paul Tasker, GM, Spicers
Carolyne McDonnell-Daly,
    Nat'l Mktg Mgr
James Tovell, GM, Coast Paper

Paradigm Electronics Inc.

205 Annagem Blvd.
Mississauga, ON L5T 2V1
Tel 905-564-1994
Fax 905-564-4642
www.paradigm.ca
Line: Specializes in manufacturing
woodworking such as cabinets and
speaker boxes.
NAICS: 334410 334310
#Emp: 250-499 (Tor)
#TorLoc: 1
Own: Private Company
Key: John Phillips, Facilities Mgr
Tim Valters, Pres
Tracy Zason, HR Mgr

Paradise Banquet & Convention Centre

7601 Jane St.
Concord, ON L4K 1X2
Tel 905-669-4680
Fax 905-669-3880
www.paradisehalls.com
Line: Operates a banquet and
convention centre.
NAICS: 722320 531120
#Emp: 100-249 (Tor)
#TorLoc: 1
Own: Private Company
Key: Joseph Pandolfo, Pres

Paragon Health Care (Ontario) Inc.

3595 Keele St.
Toronto, ON M3J 1M7
Tel 416-633-3431
Fax 416-633-6736
www.diversicare.ca
AKA: Casa Verde Health Centre
NAICS: 623110
#Emp: 100-249 (Tor)
#TorLoc: 1
Own: Private Company
Par: Diversicare Management Services
Company Inc. (CDA)
Key: Richard Stewart, Admr

Paragon Protection Ltd.

488-1210 Sheppard Ave. East
Toronto, ON M2K 1E3
Tel 416-498-4000
Fax 416-498-1648
www.paragonprotection.com
Line: Provides security services to
commercial and residential properties.
NAICS: 561612 561621
#Emp: 1000-4999 (Tor)
#TorLoc: 1
Own: Private Company
Key: Ronald J. France, Pres
Kevin Sanjari, VP Ops
David Beck, HR Mgr
Bud Ralph, VP Fin
Barbara Burling, IT Mgr

Paramount Pallet Inc.

1330 Martin Grove Rd.
Toronto, ON M9W 4X3
Tel 416-742-6006
Fax 416-742-2390
www.paramountpallet.com
Line: Manufactures pallets.
NAICS: 416390
#Emp: 100-249 (Tor)
Own: Private Company
Key: Jim Mitrakos, Pres & COO
Clint Sharples, CEO
Christopher Muc, VP Fin & Admin
Mark Sura, VP Sales

Pareto Corporation

2225 Sheppard Ave. East, 17th. Fl.
Toronto, ON M2J 5C2
Tel 416-494-7745
Fax 416-494-3932
www.pareto.ca
Line: Executes marketing strategies and
solutions.
NAICS: 541619
#Emp: 100-249 (Tor)
#TorLoc: 3
Own: Public Company
Key: Kerry Shapansky, Pres & CEO
Brian Warner, COO
Mary-Lynn Misener,
    VP People & Projects
Karen Trudell, CFO

Parker Hannifin

160 Chisholm Dr.
Milton, ON L9T 3G9
Tel 905-693-3020
Fax 905-876-1958
www.parker.com
AKA: Parker; Parker Canada
Line: Manufactures and
supplies hydraulic, pneumatic,
electromechanical fluid connector,
filtration and climate control products
and technologies.
NAICS: 333990
#Emp: 100-249 (Tor)
#TorLoc: 1
Own: Private Company
Par: Parker Hannifin Corp. (US)
Key: Tony Wyszkowski, GM
Janet Craig, HR Mgr

Park Hyatt Toronto

4 Avenue Rd.
Toronto, ON M5R 2E8
Tel 416-925-1234
Fax 416-926-2365
www.parktoronto.hyatt.com
AKA: Hyatt Hotels & Resorts; Grand
Toronto Venture Corp.
Line: Operates a hotel.
NAICS: 721111
#Emp: 250-499 (Tor)
#TorLoc: 1
Own: Private Company
Par: Hyatt Hotels Corp. (US)
Key: Paul Verciglio, GM
Bonnie Strome, Dir of Rooms
Paul Trudel, Dir of HR
Kevin Young, Cont
Kristen Lee, Purch Mgr
Christina Ramsay, Dir of Sales
Kevin Ellis, Dir of Food & Beverage
Alexandra Menear, PR Mgr

Parkin Architects Ltd.

500-1 Valleybrook Dr.
Toronto, ON M3B 2S7
Tel 416-467-8000
Fax 416-467-8001
www.parkin.ca
Line: Offers architectural services.
NAICS: 541310
#Emp: 100-249 (Tor)
#TorLoc: 2
Own: Private Company
Key: Harland Lindsay, Dir
David Driscoll, Principal
Josie Doronila, Principal

Park 'N Fly

5815 Airport Rd.
Mississauga, ON L4V 1C8
Tel 905-677-9143
Fax 905-677-6558
www.parknfly.ca
NAICS: 812930
#Emp: 100-249 (Tor)
#TorLoc: 3
Own: Private Company
Par: BML Group of Companies (CDA)
Key: Todd Faver, VP
Ron Bresler, Owner
Brent Ford, GM
Mike Speirs, Cont

Parkview Home Long Term Care

123 Weldon Rd.
Stouffville, ON L4A 0G8
Tel 905-640-1911
Fax 905-640-4051
www.parkviewhome.ca
AKA: Parkview Services for Seniors
Line: Operates a long term care home.
NAICS: 623310
#Emp: 100-249 (Tor)
#TorLoc: 1
Own: Not-for-profit
Par: Mennonite Home Association of
York County (CDA)
Key: Solange Taylor, Exec Dir
Fran Lind, Asst Admr, Resident Care
Karen Mason, Dir of Business Services
Maurice La Montagne,
    Dir of Facility Service

Parkview Transit

90 Reagens Industrial Pkwy.
Bradford, ON L3Z 2A4
Tel 905-775-5331
Fax 905-775-6361
www.parkviewtransit.ca
Line: Provides bus services to schools
in the York Region.
NAICS: 485410
#Emp: 100-249 (Tor)
#TorLoc: 4
Own: Public Company
Par: Student Transportation of Canada
(CDA)
Key: Jon Knowles, Pres
Laura Cochrane, Mgr
Penny Batherson,
    Mgr of Safety & Training

Parkway Automotive Sales Ltd.

1681 Eglinton Ave. East
Toronto, ON M4A 1J6
Tel 416-752-6666
Fax 416-752-2842
www.parkwayhonda.com
Line: Operates a car dealership.
NAICS: 441110 441120
#Emp: 100-249 (Tor)
#TorLoc: 1
Own: Private Company
Par: Mississauga Honda (CDA)
Key: Nick Palalas, GM
Leontina Stefanescu,
    Financial Admr & Cont
Paul Cunha, Sr Fin & Insurance Mgr

Parmalat Canada Inc.

405 The West Mall, 10th Fl.
Toronto, ON M9C 5J1
Tel 416-626-1973
Fax 416-620-3123
www.parmalat.ca
Line: Manufactures, distributes
and markets dairy and dairy-based
products.
NAICS: 311511 311515
#Emp: 500-999 (Tor)
#TorLoc: 4
Own: Private Company
Par: Parmalat Finanziaria SpA (ITALY)
Key: Nash Lakha, Pres & CEO
Angelo Girotto, VP Ops
Scott Goodman, Nat'l VP, HR
Michel Crahey, CFO
Steve Wuthmann,
    Exec VP, Supply Chain
Stephen Peers, Nat'l VP, Retail Sales
Cheryl Smith, Exec VP
    Mktg Consumer & Trade Mktg
Doug Waite, Exec VP,
    Foodservice & Ingredients

Par-Pak Ltd.

26 Victoria Cres.
Brampton, ON L6T 1E5
Tel 905-792-3000
Fax 905-792-3330
www.parpak.com
Line: Designs and manufactures rigid
plastic containers primarily used for
the food industry.
NAICS: 326198
#Emp: 500-999 (Tor)
#TorLoc: 5
Own: Private Company
Key: Sajjad Ebrahim, Pres
Amin Sajun, VP Ops
Priya Annapurni, HR Mgr
Kevin Rosairo, IS Mgr

Party Packagers

67 Alexdon Rd.
Toronto, ON M3J 2B5
Tel 416-631-8455
Fax 416-631-6621
www.partypackagers.com
Line: Offers balloons, hats and assorted
party favours.
NAICS: 453999
#Emp: 100-249 (Tor)
Own: Private Company
Key: Bill Goodwin, Pres

Patheon Inc.

2100 Syntex Crt.
Mississauga, ON L5N 7K9
Tel 905-821-4001
Fax 905-812-2121
www.patheon.com
Line: Provides outsourced
pharmaceutical manufacturing and
development services.
NAICS: 325410
#Emp: 1000-4999 (Tor)
#TorLoc: 3
Own: Public Company
Key: Wesley P. Wheeler, Pres & CEO
Peter Bigelow, Pres, North America Ops

Patrolman Security Services Inc.

680 Rexdale Blvd.
Toronto, ON M9W 0B5
Tel 416-748-3202
Fax 416-748-6780
www.patrolmansecurity.com
Line: Provides security guards for construction sites and properties.
NAICS: 561612
#Emp: 100-249 (Tor)
#TorLoc: 1
Own: Private Company
Key: Joseph Nawaz, Pres
Sumana Ganguly, HR Mgr
Rafiq Sultan,
    Accounts & Office Services Mgr
Ivaylo Boiadjiev, VP Mktg

Patterson Dental Canada Inc.

A-6300 Viscount Rd.
Mississauga, ON L4V 1H3
Tel 905-677-7711
Fax 905-677-2940
www.pattersondental.ca
Line: Provides dental supplies, equipment, planning services and technical support on equipment.
NAICS: 339110
#Emp: 75-99 (Tor)
Own: Public Company
Par: Patterson Companies Ltd. (US)
Key: Michael Kavanagh, Branch Mgr
Dale Gallant, Ops Mgr

Pattison Outdoor Advertising

2285 Wyecroft Rd.
Oakville, ON L6L 5L7
Tel 905-465-0114
Fax 905-465-0633
www.pattisonoutdoor.com
Line: Specializes in outdoor advertising.
NAICS: 541850
#Emp: 100-249 (Tor)
#TorLoc: 1
Own: Private Company
Par: The Jim Pattison Group (CDA)
Key: Randy Otto, Pres
Steve McGregor, VP Ops & Leasing
Joanne Sparrow, Dir of HR
Barry Wilde, CFO
Bob Leroux, VP & GM, Central Region

Pattison Sign Group

A Div. of Jim Pattison Industries Ltd.
555 Ellesmere Rd.
Toronto, ON M1R 4E8
Tel 416-759-1111
Fax 416-759-9560
www.pattisonsign.com
Line: Designs, manufactures and sells electrical signage and visual communications.
NAICS: 339950
#Emp: 100-249 (Tor)
#TorLoc: 1
Own: Private Company
Key: Don Belanger, Pres
Xenia Lyon, HR Mgr
Rick Macina, Dir of Fin
Joe Quercia, Production Mgr
Brian Knight, Network Admr
Anthony Hollyoak,
    GM Sales & Commun

Pauldonlam Investments Inc.

2240 Markham Rd.
Toronto, ON M1B 2W4
Tel 416-754-4555
Fax 416-754-9465
www.formulahonda.com
AKA: Formula Honda
Line: Operates an automobile dealership.
NAICS: 441110 441120
#Emp: 100-249 (Tor)
#TorLoc: 1
Own: Private Company
Key: Nial Boatswain, GM

Paul K. Brennan Holdings Inc.

5363 Dundas St. West
Toronto, ON M9B 1B1
Tel 416-239-2388
Fax 416-239-7853
www.canadiantire.ca
AKA: Six Point Canadian Tire
NAICS: 441310
#Emp: 100-249 (Tor)
Own: Private Company
Key: Paul Brennan, Owner

Paul Wolf Lighting & Electric Supply Ltd.

425 Alliance Ave.
Toronto, ON M6N 2J1
Tel 416-504-8195
Fax 416-504-6891
www.paulwolf.com
AKA: Kester Electric Supply Limited
Line: Sells electrical and lighting supplies.
NAICS: 416110

#Emp: 75-99 (Tor)
#TorLoc: 3
Own: Private Company
Key: Leslie Clarke, Pres
Michael Mohammed, Cont
Dewayne Elliott, Purch Mgr
Bill McCarroll, Sales Mgr

Pave-Tar Construction Ltd.

366 Watline Ave.
Mississauga, ON L4Z 1X2
Tel 905-502-6673
Fax 905-502-6676
www.pavetarconstruction.com
Line: Provides paving and construction services.
NAICS: 232920
#Emp: 75-99 (Tor)
#TorLoc: 1
Own: Private Company
Key: Mario Canpana, Pres & Owner

PCL Constructors Canada Inc.

400-2085 Hurontario St.
Mississauga, ON L5A 4G1
Tel 905-276-7600
Fax 905-276-4324
www.pcl.com
Line: Builds institutional, educational, industrial and residential projects.
NAICS: 231410
#Emp: 250-499 (Tor)
#TorLoc: 1
Own: Private Company
Par: PCL Constructors Inc. (CDA)
Key: Jim Dougan,
    Pres, Central & Eastern
Brad Nelson, Pres & COO,
    PCL Constructors Inc.
Chris Gower, Reg VP, Central & Eastern
Glen Norman, Purch Mgr
Joe Watson, Dir of Corp Dev
Jennifer Nelson, Commun Specialist

PCO Services Corp.

5840 Falbourne St.
Mississauga, ON L5R 4B5
Tel 905-502-9700
Fax 905-502-9510
www.pco.ca
AKA: Orkin Canada
Line: Operates an extermination company.
NAICS: 561710
#Emp: 250-499 (Tor)
#TorLoc: 4
Own: Public Company
Par: Orkin (US)
Key: Gary Muldoon, Pres
Jean Fader, VP

Pearson Canada

195 Harry Walker Pkwy. North
Newmarket, ON L3Y 7B4
Tel 905-853-7888
Fax 905-853-7865
www.pearsoncanada.ca
Line: Distributes books.
NAICS: 414420
#Emp: 500-999 (Tor)
#TorLoc: 3
Own: Private Company
Key: Allan Reynolds, Pres & CEO
Dan Lee, Exec VP & COO

Pearson Education Canada Inc.

26 Prince Andrew Pl.
Toronto, ON M3C 2T8
Tel 416-447-5101
Fax 416-443-0948
www.pearsoned.ca
AKA: Penguin Canada; Addison-Wesley
Longman Publishers Ltd.; Prentice Hall
Canada Inc.
Line: Publishes and distributes
educational material and consumer
trade books.
NAICS: 511130
#Emp: 500-999 (Tor)
#TorLoc: 3
Own: Public Company
Par: Pearson plc (UK)
Key: Allan Reynolds, Pres & CEO
Dan Lee, COO
Ann Wood, VP HR
Helena Hung, VP Fin

Peel Children's Centre

85A Aventura Crt.
Mississauga, ON L5T 2Y6
Tel 905-795-3500
Fax 905-696-0350
www.peelcc.org
Line: Operates a children's mental
health centre.
NAICS: 622210
#Emp: 250-499 (Tor)
#TorLoc: 1
Own: Not-for-profit
Key: Humphrey Mitchell, Exec Dir
Dilys Watanabe, HR Mgr
Amrit Khaper, Fin Mgr
Mora Thompson, Commun Specialist

Peel District School Board

5650 Hurontario St.
Mississauga, ON L5R 1C6
Tel 905-890-1099
Fax 905-890-6698
www.peelschools.org
NAICS: 611110
#Emp: 10000+ (Tor)
#TorLoc: 235
Own: Government
Key: Tony Pontes, Dir of Education
Rhys Davies, CEO, Centre for
    Education & Training
Pam Tomasevic, Assoc Dir,
    Instructional Support Services
Martin Fowler, Dir of HR, Support
    Services
Carla Kisko, Assoc Dir,
    Operational Support Services
Laura Williams, CIO
Brian Woodland, Dir of Commun
    & Strategic Partnerships,
    Support Services

Peel Manor Long Term Care Facility

525 Main St. North
Brampton, ON L6X 1N9
Tel 905-453-4140
Fax 905-861-9140
www.peelregion.ca
Line: Provides long-term healthcare
and community services for adults.
NAICS: 623110
#Emp: 100-249 (Tor)
#TorLoc: 1
Own: Municipal Crown Corp.
Par: Region of Peel
Key: Rani Calay, Acting Admr

Peel Plastic Products Ltd.

49 Rutherford Rd. South
Brampton, ON L6W 3J3
Tel 905-456-3660
Fax 905-456-0870
www.peelplastics.com
Line: Prints and converts flexible
packaging.
NAICS: 322220 561910
#Emp: 100-249 (Tor)
#TorLoc: 1
Own: Private Company
Key: William Troost, Pres
David Troost, GM
Steve Coulson, VP Business Dev

Peel Regional Police

A Div. of Regional Municipality of Peel
7750 Hurontario St.
Brampton, ON L6V 3W6
Tel 905-453-3311
Fax 905-456-6104
www.peelpolice.ca
NAICS: 913130
#Emp: 1000-4999 (Tor)
#TorLoc: 19
Own: Government
Key: Michael Metcalf, Chief of Police
Paul Tetzlaff, Deputy Chief
Doug Bowman, Dir of HR
Bev Mullins, Dir of Business Services
Stuart Moir, Dir of IT Services

Pelmorex Media Inc.

2655 Bristol Circ.
Oakville, ON L6H 7W1
Tel 905-829-1159
Fax 905-829-5800
www.theweathernetwork.com
AKA: The Weather Network
Line: Provides weather information
through the Internet and specialty
television networks in English and
French.
NAICS: 513120
#Emp: 250-499 (Tor)
#TorLoc: 1
Own: Private Company
Key: Gaston Germain, Pres & COO
Pierre Morrissette,
    Chmn of the Board & CEO
Mitch Charron, VP Television Division
Jerry Humes, VP HR
Robert Lombardi, VP Fin
Alex Leslie, Sr VP & CITO
Rick Devost, VP & GM, PBS

Penauille Servisair

908-5915 Airport Rd.
Mississauga, ON L4V 1T1
Tel 416-776-3914
Fax 416-776-3925
www.servisair.com
Line: Provides airline ground
services including aircraft cleaning
and de-icing.
NAICS: 488119
#Emp: 1000-4999 (Tor)
#TorLoc: 3
Own: Private Company
Par: The Penauille Group (FR)
Key: Sanjay Malik, VP Business Dev
Francesco Fera, GM

Penske Truck Leasing

1610 Enterprise Rd.
Mississauga, ON L4W 4L4
Tel 905-564-4914
Fax 905-564-9923
www.gopenske.com
Line: Sells and services rental trucks.
NAICS: 532120
#Emp: 75-99 (Tor)
#TorLoc: 8
Own: Private Company
Par: Penske (US)
Key: Steven Kingswell,
District Ops Mgr

Pentax Canada Inc.

1770 Argentia Rd.
Mississauga, ON L5N 3S7
Tel 905-286-5585
Fax 905-286-5586
www.pentax.ca
Line: Manufactures cameras,
binoculars, GPS and surveying
products.
NAICS: 334110 333310
#Emp: 100-249 (Tor)
#TorLoc: 1
Own: Private Company
Key: Greg Hall, Pres

The People Bank

204-220 Yonge St.
P.O. Box 603
Toronto, ON M5B 2H1
Tel 416-340-1004
Fax 416-340-0447
www.thepeoplebank.com
Line: Provides temporary, permanent
and contract personnel for employment
opportunities.
NAICS: 561310
#Emp: 75-99 (Tor)
#TorLoc: 6
Own: Private Company
Par: Design Group Staffing Inc. (CDA)
Key: Stephen Jones, Pres
Londa Burke, VP

Pepes Mexican Foods

122 Carrier Dr.
Toronto, ON M9W 5R1
Tel 416-674-0882
Fax 416-674-2805
www.weston.ca
Line: Manufactures tortillas.
NAICS: 311830
#Emp: 75-99 (Tor)

#TorLoc: 1
Own: Private Company
Par: Weston Foods (CDA)
Key: Ralph Robinson, Pres
Robert Lee, Plant Mgr

Pepsico Beverages Canada

5205 Satellite Dr.
Mississauga, ON L4W 5J7
Tel 905-212-7377
Fax 905-212-7337
www.pepsi.ca
AKA: Pepsico Canada
Line: Manufactures and distributes
carbonated and non carbonated soft
drinks.
NAICS: 312110 311930
#Emp: 1000-4999 (Tor)
#TorLoc: 2
Own: Private Company
Par: PepsiCo Inc. (US)
Key: Linda Kuga-Pikulin, Pres
Glen Best, VP Ops
Taylor Flake, VP HR
Andy Siklos, VP Sales & Mktg

Perennial Design Inc.

15 Waulron St.
Toronto, ON M9C 1B4
Tel 416-251-2180
Fax 416-251-3560
www.perennialinc.com
Line: Provides graphic art and design
services.
NAICS: 541430
#Emp: 75-99 (Tor)
#TorLoc: 1
Own: Private Company
Key: Christopher Lund, CEO

Performance Equipment Limited

6950 Tomken Rd.
Mississauga, ON L5T 2S3
Tel 905-564-8333
Fax 905-564-8420
www.mack.on.ca
AKA: Volvo Trucks Toronto
NAICS: 441110
#Emp: 250-499 (Tor)
#TorLoc: 6
Own: Private Company
Par: The Slotegraaf Group (CDA)
Key: John Slotegraaf, Pres
Boyd Brenton, Cont
Joe Palermo, Sales Mgr

PERI Performance Systems

45 Nixon Rd.
Bolton, ON L7E 1K1
Tel 905-951-5400
Fax 905-951-5454
www.peri.ca
Line: Manufactures and supplies
formwork, shoring and scaffolding
systems.
NAICS: 417210
#Emp: 100-249 (Tor)
#TorLoc: 1
Own: Private Company
Key: Stephen Jones, CEO
John Grassa, Scaffolding Mgr

Perle Systems Ltd.

60 Renfrew Dr.
Markham, ON L3R 0E1
Tel 905-475-8885
Fax 905-475-2377
www.perle.com
Line: Produces data communication
controllers, connectivity devices and
related software.
NAICS: 541510
#Emp: 100-249 (Tor)
#TorLoc: 1
Own: Private Company
Key: Joseph E. Perle, Pres & CEO
John Feeney, COO
Derrick Barnett, CFO
Valeri Gavriline, Production Mgr
Julie McDaniel, VP Mktg

Personal Attendant Care Inc.

200-1650 Dundas St. East
Whitby, ON L1N 2K8
Tel 905-576-5603
Fax 905-576-8020
www.pacdurham.ca
Line: Provides personal support to
disabled individuals in their own
homes.
NAICS: 621610
#Emp: 100-249 (Tor)
#TorLoc: 1
Own: Not-for-profit
Key: John Eng, CFO

Peterbilt Ontario Truck Centres

1257 Eglinton Ave. East
Mississauga, ON L4W 1K7
Tel 905-268-2000
Fax 905-268-2002
Line: Sells and services Peterbilt trucks.
NAICS: 417230
#Emp: 100-249 (Tor)
Own: Private Company
Key: Dave Climie, Pres & GM

Peter Hodge Transport Ltd.

100 Market Dr.
Milton, ON L9T 3H5
Tel 905-693-8088
Fax 905-693-8087
www.peterhodgetransport.com
Line: Transports bulk commodities.
NAICS: 484222 484232
#Emp: 75-99 (Tor)
#TorLoc: 1
Own: Private Company
Key: Peter Hodge, Pres
Beverley Hodge, Secy-Treas

Pethealth Inc.

400-710 Dorval Dr.
Oakville, ON L6K 3V7
Tel 905-842-2615
Fax 866-368-7387
www.pethealthinc.com
AKA: PetCare Insurance Brokers
Line: Provides pet recovery database
services and offers health insurance for
cats and dogs.
NAICS: 524129
#Emp: 100-249 (Tor)
#TorLoc: 1
Own: Public Company
Key: Mark Warren, Pres & CEO
Richard Renaud, Chmn
John Warden, VP Insurance Ops
Glen Tennison, CFO
Steve Zeidman, CTO

Peto MacCallum Ltd.

165 Cartwright Ave.
Toronto, ON M6A 1V5
Tel 416-785-5110
Fax 416-785-5120
www.petomaccallum.com
Line: Specializes in geotechnical,
geo-environmental and construction
materials engineering; quality control,
testing and inspection; and building
sciences.
NAICS: 541330 541620
#Emp: 75-99 (Tor)
#TorLoc: 1
Own: Private Company
Key: Turney Lee-Bun, Pres
Angela Caleca, Admin Mgr
Andrew Injodey, Treas
Michael McKenzie, Sales Mgr

Petro-Canada

2489 North Sheridan Way
Mississauga, ON L5K 1A8
Tel 905-804-4500
Fax 905-804-4747
www.petro-canada.ca
Line: Refines and markets petroleum
products including lubricants.
NAICS: 324110 447110
#Emp: 1000-4999 (Tor)
#TorLoc: 4
Own: Public Company
Key: Boris Jackman, Exec VP
Garry Tomala, Dir of
  Human Resource Services

Petro-Canada Lubricants Centre

2310 Lakeshore Rd. West
Mississauga, ON L5J 1K2
Tel 905-804-3600
Fax 905-804-3615
www.htlubricants.com
NAICS: 324110
#Emp: 500-999 (Tor)
#TorLoc: 3
Own: Private Company
Key: Randy Koenig, VP, Lubricants

Petroff Partnership Architects

260 Town Centre Blvd.
Markham, ON L3R 8H8
Tel 905-470-7000
Fax 905-470-2500
www.petroff.com
AKA: Architects + Research +
Knowledge Inc.
Line: Provides architectural services.
NAICS: 541310
#Emp: 100-249 (Tor)
#TorLoc: 2
Own: Private Company
Key: Andrzej Lipinski, Mng Partner
Kelly Harrison, Office & HR Mgr
Kim Sommers, Cont

Pet Valu Canada Inc.

121 McPherson St.
Markham, ON L3R 3L3
Tel 905-946-1200
Fax 905-946-0659
www.petvalu.com
AKA: Paulmac's Pet Food; Pet Food
Plus; Pet Valu
Line: Retails pet food and pet products.
NAICS: 453910 311111
#Emp: 250-499 (Tor)
#TorLoc: 10
Own: Public Company
Par: Pet Valu, Inc. (US)

Key: Ed Casey, Pres & COO
Tom McNeely, CEO
Jim Young, VP Store Ops
Christine Martin-Bevilacqua, VP HR
Dale Winkworth, CFO
Jack Handa, VP & CIO

PGC

29-111 Zenway Blvd.
Vaughan, ON L4H 3H9
Tel 416-674-8046
Fax 416-674-3277
www.pgcservice.com
AKA: Powerful Group of Companies
Corp.
Line: Offers a full-service operations
and maintenance service.
NAICS: 561799
#Emp: 75-99 (Tor)
Own: Private Company
Key: Paul Docherty, Pres

Phantom Industries Inc.

207 Weston Rd.
Toronto, ON M6N 4Z3
Tel 416-762-7177
Fax 416-762-2427
www.phantom.ca
Line: Manufactures swimwear and
hosiery.
NAICS: 315110
#Emp: 100-249 (Tor)
#TorLoc: 1
Own: Private Company
Par: 591046 Ontario Ltd. (CDA)
Key: Ronnie Strasser, Pres
Alex Strasser, CEO
Viji Malaiyandi, Dir of HR
Jeffrey Iceton, VP Fin
Joan Attard, Dir of Purch
Svetlana Sturgeon, VP Sales & Mktg

Pharma Medica Research Inc.

6100 Belgrave Rd.
Mississauga, ON L5R 0B7
Tel 905-624-9115
Fax 905-624-4433
www.pharmamedica.com
Line: Offers contracting pharmaceutical
research services.
NAICS: 325410
#Emp: 250-499 (Tor)
#TorLoc: 2
Own: Private Company
Key: Latifa Yamlahi, GM
Meredith Stratton, HR Dir

PHD Canada

A Div. of Omnicon Canada Inc.
600-96 Spadina Ave
Toronto, ON M5V 2J6
Tel 416-922-0217
Fax 416-922-8469
www.phdcanada.com
Line: Operates a media management
company that offers all phases of the
media function from planning and
analysis to buying and administration.
NAICS: 541810
#Emp: 75-99 (Tor)
#TorLoc: 1
Own: Private Company
Par: Omnicom Group Inc. (US)
Key: Fred Forster, Pres & CEO
David Harrison, Chmn
Fred Auchterlonie,
    Sr VP & Dir of Client Services
Cam Reston, VP Business Affairs & CFO

PHH Arval

400-2233 Argentia Rd.
Mississauga, ON L5N 2X7
Tel 905-286-5300
Fax 905-286-5301
www.phharval.com
Line: Provides vehicle management
consulting and related services.
NAICS: 541611
#Emp: 100-249 (Tor)
#TorLoc: 2
Own: Private Company
Par: Cendant Corp. (US)
Key: Jim Halliday, Pres
Sudha Dwivedi, Dir of HR
Bob Sandler, VP Fin & CFO
John Spadafora, Distributed
    Systems & Support Mgr
Troy Campbell, VP Sales

Philips Electronics Ltd.

281 Hillmount Rd.
Markham, ON L6C 2S3
Tel 905-201-4100
Fax 905-887-4241
www.philips.ca
NAICS: 417320 414220
#Emp: 250-499 (Tor)
#TorLoc: 1
Own: Private Company
Key: Ian Burns, Pres

Philips Lifeline

105-95 Barber Greene Rd.
Toronto, ON M3C 3E9
Tel 416-445-1643
Fax 416-445-1208
www.lifeline.ca
Line: Provides security products and
services.
NAICS: 561612
#Emp: 100-249 (Tor)
#TorLoc: 1
Own: Private Company
Par: Philips (NETH)
Key: Erik Sande, VP & GM

Phonak Canada Ltd.

1-80 Courtney Park Dr. West
Mississauga, ON L5W 0B3
Tel 905-677-1167
Fax 905-677-7536
www.phonak-canada.com
Line: Specializes in the design,
development, production and
worldwide distribution of hearing
systems.
NAICS: 334512 417930
#Emp: 75-99 (Tor)
#TorLoc: 1
Own: Public Company
Par: Phonak AG (SWITZ)
Key: Steve Mahon, GM

Phonetime Inc.

81-1775 Valley Farm Rd.
Pickering, ON L1V 1E7
Tel 905-361-8300
www.phonetime.com
Line: Supplies international wholesale
long distance services to large and
small carriers around the world.
NAICS: 513330
#Emp: 100-249 (Tor)
Own: Private Company
Key: Gary Clifford, Chmn & CEO
Mike Vazquez, VP Ops

Picadilly Fashions

945 Wilson Ave.
Toronto, ON M3K 1E8
Tel 416-783-1889
Fax 416-783-5846
www.picadillyfashions.com
Line: Manufactures women's clothing.
NAICS: 315239 315210
#Emp: 100-249 (Tor)
#TorLoc: 1
Own: Private Company
Key: Jack Dombrowsky, Owner

Pickering College

16945 Bayview Ave.
Newmarket, ON L3Y 4X2
Tel 905-895-1700
Fax 905-895-9076
www.pickeringcollege.on.ca
Line: Operates independent school
from Junior Kindergarten to Grade
12 with co-educational university
preparation.
NAICS: 611110
#Emp: 75-99 (Tor)
#TorLoc: 1
Own: Private Company
Key: Peter Sturrup, Headmaster
Ian Proudfoot, Chair of the Board
Nicole Murphy,
    Asst Head of School, Fin & Ops
Michael Doleman, Dir of IT
Kim Bilous, Exec Dir of Dev
Jessie-May Rowntree,
    Dir of Mktg, Commun & PR

Pier 1 Imports

3135 Hwy. 7
Markham, ON L3R 0T9
Tel 905-940-1504
Fax 905-940-5416
www.pier1.com
Line: Retails home furnishings.
NAICS: 442298
#Emp: 250-499 (Tor)
#TorLoc: 19
Own: Public Company
Par: Pier 1 Imports Inc. (US)
Key: Jim Waechter, VP, Canada Ops
Ann Yurek, Sr HR Mgr, Canada

Pilen Construction of Canada Ltd.

22 Cadetta Rd.
Brampton, ON L6P 0X4
Tel 905-794-0752
Fax 905-794-1051
Line: Offers general contracting
services.
NAICS: 231310
#Emp: 75-99 (Tor)
#TorLoc: 1
Own: Private Company
Key: Tony Marchese, Pres
Anna Marchese, Cont

Pi Media / St Joseph's Content

15 Benton Rd.
Toronto, ON M6M 3G2
Tel 416-248-4868
Fax 416-248-5477
www.pimedia.com
AKA: DW+Partners; CMI
Line: Provides website, digital, signage
and package design and operates
creative, pre-press and photography
studios that focus on catalogue and
flyer content development.
NAICS: 541920
#Emp: 500-999 (Tor)
#TorLoc: 4
Own: Private Company
Par: St. Joseph Communications (CDA)
Key: Doug Templeton, Pres
Michael Cowman, VP Ops
Kristin Sampagan, Dir of HR
Eric Lipman, VP Fin
Mark Zwicker, VP Business Dev
Michael Chase, VP Mktg & Creative

Pinchin Environmental Ltd.

2470 Milltower Crt.
Mississauga, ON L5N 7W5
Tel 905-363-0678
Fax 905-363-0681
www.pinchin.com
AKA: Le Groupe Gesfor Poircr Pinchin;
Pinchin Leblanc Environmental Ltd.;
PHH Environmental Ltd.
Line: Provides engineering,
environmental consulting; air quality
testing; mould management and
control; asbestos and environmental
site inspection; hazardous materials,
ventilation and air emission services;
and health and safety services.
NAICS: 541330 541620
#Emp: 100-249 (Tor)
#TorLoc: 1
Own: Private Company
Key: Don Pinchin, Pres
Jeff Grossi, COO
Shelly Tibido, HR Mgr
Robert Ball, Mgr of Fin

Pine Tree Ford Lincoln

100 Auto Park Circ.
Woodbridge, ON L4L 9T5
Tel 416-798-4777
www.pinetreefordlincoln.com
Line: Sells, leases and services
vehicles.
NAICS: 441110 441120
#Emp: 75-99 (Tor)
#TorLoc: 1
Own: Private Company

Par: Remo Ferri Group of Automobiles
(CDA)
Key: Remo Ferri, Pres
Ray Bernardo, GM

Pine Valley Packaging Ltd.

1 Parratt Rd.
Uxbridge, ON L9P 1R1
Tel 905-862-0830
Fax 905-862-0842
www.pinevalleypackaging.com
Line: Manufactures specialty
packaging.
NAICS: 326198
#Emp: 75-99 (Tor)
#TorLoc: 1
Own: Private Company
Key: Steve Richards, Pres

Pine View Hyundai Ltd.

3790 Hwy. 7
Woodbridge, ON L4L 1A6
Tel 905-851-2851
Fax 905-851-2613
www.pineview.com
AKA: Pine View Motors Limited
Line: Provides automotive sales,
leasing, service, collision, and parts
services.
NAICS: 441110
#Emp: 75-99 (Tor)
#TorLoc: 1
Own: Private Company
Par: Pine View Motors Ltd. (CDA)
Key: Frank Romeo, Pres & GM
Anna DeSantis, Secy-Treas
Vince Palumbo, Gen Sales Mgr

Pinnacle Caterers

40 Bay St.
Air Canada Centre
Toronto, ON M5J 2X2
Tel 416-815-5720
Fax 416-815-5453
www.pinnaclecaterers.com
NAICS: 722110
#Emp: 250-499 (Tor)
#TorLoc: 8
Own: Private Company
Key: Ted Nikolaou, Pres

Pinnacle Transport Ltd.

81 Select Ave.
Toronto, ON M1V 4A9
Tel 416-754-8825
Fax 416-754-7588
www.pinnacletransport.ca
Line: Operates a local trucking
company.

NAICS: 484110
#Emp: 100-249 (Tor)
#TorLoc: 1
Own: Private Company
Key: John Fraser, Pres
Steve McClelland, VP

Pinty's Delicious Foods Inc.

5063 North Service Rd.
Burlington, ON L7L 5H6
Tel 905-829-1130
Fax 905-319-5301
www.pintys.com
Line: Produces fully cooked poultry
meat products.
NAICS: 311615
#Emp: 500-999 (Tor)
#TorLoc: 2
Own: Private Company
Key: Randy Cain, Pres & CEO
Jack Vandelaan, Exec Chmn

Piramal Healthcare Torcan (Toronto) Canada Ltd.

110 Industrial Pkwy. North
Aurora, ON L4G 3H4
Tel 905-727-9417
Fax 905-727-7545
www.piramalpharmasolutions.com
Line: Researches, develops and
manufactures active pharmaceutical
ingredients and advanced
intermediates.
NAICS: 541710
#Emp: 100-249 (Tor)
#TorLoc: 1
Own: Private Company
Key: Wen-Lung Yeh, Pres
Mark Cherutti, VP
Christine Carter, HR Mgr

Pitney Bowes Business Insights

500-26 Wellington St. East
Toronto, ON M5E 1S2
Tel 416-594-5200
Fax 416-594-5201
www.mapinfo.ca
Line: Provides location intelligence
solutions that integrate software, data
and services.
NAICS: 541611
#Emp: 100-249 (Tor)
#TorLoc: 1
Own: Public Company
Par: Pitney Bowes (US)
Key: David Ower, Mng Dir of Sales

Pitney Bowes Canada Ltd.

5500 Explorer Dr.
Mississauga, ON L4W 5C7
Tel 905-219-3000
Fax 905-219-3826
www.pitneybowes.ca
Line: Supplies office equipment
systems including mailing systems,
photocopiers, fax systems, shipping
and logistics systems, production mail
and insertion systems.
NAICS: 417910
#Emp: 500-999 (Tor)
#TorLoc: 3
Own: Public Company
Par: Pitney Bowes Inc. (US)
Key: Deepak Chopra, Pres
Karen Bell, VP HR

Pivotal HR Solutions

1355 Meyerside Dr.
Mississauga, ON L5T 1C9
Tel 289-562-0201
Fax 289-562-0212
www.pivotalsolutions.com
Line: Operates a temporary help
agency.
NAICS: 561320
#Emp: 100-249 (Tor)
#TorLoc: 6
Own: Private Company
Par: Pivotal Integrated HR Solutions
(CDA)
Key: Heather Dowell, Reg Mgr

Pizza Nova Restaurants Ltd.

2247 Midland Ave.
Toronto, ON M1P 4R1
Tel 416-439-0051
Fax 416-291-3558
www.pizzanova.com
Line: Operates pizza stores.
NAICS: 722210
#Emp: 250-499 (Tor)
#TorLoc: 90
Own: Private Company
Key: Sam Primucci, CEO
Dominic Primucci, Pres
Marsha Dufty, Office Mgr
George Swift, Cont

Pizza Pizza Ltd.

580 Jarvis St.
Toronto, ON M4Y 2H9
Tel 416-967-1010
Fax 416-967-1116
www.pizzapizza.ca
Line: Provides eat-in, take-out,
and fast-food delivery services.
NAICS: 722110 722210
#Emp: 1000-4999 (Tor)
Own: Private Company
Key: Paul Goddard, Pres & CEO
Curt Feltner, CFO

PJ's Pet Centres Ltd.

12-4161 Sladeview Cres.
Mississauga, ON L5L 5R3
Tel 905-593-3177
Fax 905-593-3179
www.pjspet.com
AKA: 3499481 Canada Inc.
Line: Retails pets and pet supplies and
provides grooming and photography
services.
NAICS: 453910
#Emp: 500-999 (Tor)
#TorLoc: 11
Own: Private Company
Key: John Jules, Pres
Susan Johnson, COO
Andy Bamrah, Dir of HR

The Plan Group

27 Vanley Cres.
Toronto, ON M3J 2B7
Tel 416-635-9040
Fax 416-635-9764
www.plan-group.com
Line: Provides electrical, mechanical
and telecommunication contracting
services.
NAICS: 232510
#Emp: 250-499 (Tor)
#TorLoc: 1
Own: Private Company
Key: Paul Sheridan, Pres
J. William Kurtin, CEO
Jacqueline Thompson, Labour Mgr
Frank Loewen, VP Fin
Roy Metzger, Purch Mgr
Nelson Cortez, MIS Mgr
Dave Anderson, VP Business Dev

Plan International Canada Inc.

1001-95 St. Clair Ave. West
Toronto, ON M4V 3B5
Tel 416-920-1654
Fax 416-920-9942
www.plancanada.ca
AKA: Plan Canada
Line: Operates an international,
humanitarian, child-centred
development organization without
religious, political or governmental
affiliations.
NAICS: 813410
#Emp: 100-249 (Tor)
#TorLoc: 1
Own: Not-for-profit
Key: Rosemary McCarney, Pres & CEO
Deborah Singh, Dir of HR
Paula Butler, VP Fin
Mark Banbury, VP & CIO
Paula Roberts, Exec VP, Mktg & Dev

Plant Products Company Ltd.

314 Orenda Rd.
Brampton, ON L6T 1G1
Tel 905-793-7000
Fax 905-793-9632
www.plantprod.com
Line: Manufactures horticulture,
agriculture and consumer fertilizers
and crop protection chemicals.
NAICS: 325313 325320
#Emp: 75-99 (Tor)
#TorLoc: 1
Own: Private Company
Par: Trans-Resources, Inc. (US)
Key: John Lewandowski, Pres
Gord Jahn, VP Ops
Catherine Byers, Payroll & Personnel
Allen Pettau, CFO
Doreen Andrea, Dir of Purch
Marion Petersen, IS Mgr
Harold Van Gool, VP Business Dev

Plant World Ltd.

4000 Eglinton Ave. West
Toronto, ON M9A 4M2
Tel 416-241-9174
Fax 416-241-3898
www.plantworld.net
Line: Retails garden supplies and tools.
NAICS: 444220
#Emp: 100-249 (Tor)
#TorLoc: 1
Own: Private Company
Key: Frank Reeves Jr., Pres
Kurt Reeves, VP
Paul Reeves, VP

Planway Poultry Inc.

26 Canmotor Ave.
Toronto, ON M8Z 4E5
Tel 416-252-7676
Fax 416-252-0683
Line: Wholesales poultry products.
NAICS: 413130
#Emp: 75-99 (Tor)
#TorLoc: 1
Own: Private Company
Key: King Lam, Pres

Plastic Moulders Limited

6-1631 The Queensway
Toronto, ON M8Z 5Y4
Tel 416-252-2241
Fax 416-252-0766
www.plasticmoulders.com
Line: Manufactures plastic injection-moulding.
NAICS: 333511 333220
#Emp: 100-249 (Tor)
#TorLoc: 3
Own: Private Company
Key: Ian Milne, Pres & CEO
Marc Campbell, Chmn
Vilma Castillo, Admin Mgr
Bill Damery, Sales Mgr

Plastic Packaging & Components Inc.

310 Matheson Blvd.
Mississauga, ON L4Z 1P5
Tel 905-890-1788
Fax 905-890-9642
www.ppcltd.net
AKA: PPC America
Line: Manufactures custom injection moulds.
NAICS: 326198
#Emp: 75-99 (Tor)
#TorLoc: 2
Own: Private Company
Par: Intropac Group (CDA)
Key: Gary Ullman, Pres
Maggie Urgyn, HR Mgr
Peter Gamoff, VP Sales & Mktg

Plastipak Industries Inc.

260 Rexdale Blvd.
Toronto, ON M9W 1R2
Tel 416-744-4220
Fax 416-744-2464
www.plastipak.ca
Line: Manufactures rigid plastic containers for dairy, food and specific industrial products.
NAICS: 326198
#Emp: 100-249 (Tor)

#TorLoc: 1
Own: Private Company
Par: Hamelin Group Inc. (CDA)
Key: Nadine Hamelin, Pres
Eric Jodoin, VP Ops
Debbie Smyth, HR Consultant
Guy Bellemare, VP Fin
Marc Paquet, Dir of MIS
Roger Cole, Dir of Sales

Platform Computing Corp.

3760 14th Ave.
Markham, ON L3R 3T7
Tel 905-948-8448
Fax 905-948-9975
www.platform.com
Line: Develops grid software and services.
NAICS: 541510
#Emp: 250-499 (Tor)
#TorLoc: 1
Own: Private Company
Key: Songnian Zhou, CEO
Peter Nichol, GM
Peter Richardson, VP HR
Mark Millar, CFO
Tripp Purvis, VP Business Dev
Ian Miller, VP Worldwide Sales

Plats du Chef

575 Oster Lane
Concord, ON L4K 2B9
Tel 905-669-0700
Fax 905-669-0699
www.platsduchef.com
NAICS: 311410 311814
#Emp: 250-499 (Tor)
#TorLoc: 1
Own: Private Company
Par: VLR Food Group Corp. (US)
Key: Don McIntyre, Pres
Grant Crandall, VP Fin

Playdium Corp.

99 Rathburn Rd. West
Mississauga, ON L5B 4C1
Tel 905-273-9000
Fax 905-273-4222
www.playdium.com
Line: Operates an interactive, virtual and physical entertainment centre.
NAICS: 713120
#Emp: 100-249 (Tor)
#TorLoc: 1
Own: Private Company
Par: Starburst Coin Machines Inc. (CDA)
Key: Kashif Ahmad, GM

Plaza Pontiac Buick Ltd.

3400 Dufferin St.
Toronto, ON M6A 2V1
Tel 416-781-5271
Fax 416-781-9699
www.plazagm.com
Line: Operates a retail auto dealership.
NAICS: 441110 441120
#Emp: 75-99 (Tor)
#TorLoc: 1
Own: Private Company
Key: Robert Stein, Pres
Shirley Beach, Cont

PL Foods Ltd.

A Div. of Ralcorp Holdings Inc.
120 Armstrong Ave.
Georgetown, ON L7G 4S3
Tel 905-873-8744
Fax 905-873-8746
www.ralcorp.com
AKA: BFG Canada
Line: Manufactures private label kosher crackers.
NAICS: 311821
#Emp: 100-249 (Tor)
#TorLoc: 1
Own: Private Company
Key: Dennis Hughey, CEO
Siobhan Lucic, HR Mgr
Rick Langver, Dir of Sales & Mktg, BFG

PMA Brethour Real Estate Corporation Inc.

8980 Woodbine Ave.
Markham, ON L3R 0J7
Tel 905-415-2720
Fax 905-415-2724
www.pmabrethour.com
Line: Provides sales and marketing services for new homes, condominiums and retirement communities; provides market research, land planning and development consulting services.
NAICS: 531310
#Emp: 100-249 (Tor)
#TorLoc: 1
Own: Private Company
Key: Andrew Brethour, Pres
Sandie Wells, HR Mgr
Howard Kideckel, Cont
Kent Wengler, VP Research

POI Business Interiors Inc.

120 Valleywood Dr.
Markham, ON L3R 6A7
Tel 905-479-1123
Fax 905-479-6941
www.poi.ca
Line: Sells and installs furniture and
provides a variety of office interior
services.
NAICS: 417910 541410
#Emp: 100-249 (Tor)
#TorLoc: 2
Own: Private Company
Key: Julie Anne Smedley, Pres
Gary Scholl, Chmn & CEO
Laura Looije, HR Mgr
Steven D'Amelio, VP Fin
Neil Ishmael, Mgr of Client Services
Nick Dejulio, VP Corp Account Sales
Anne Gowan,
    VP Project Accounts & Sales

PointClickCare

4-6975 Creditview Rd.
Mississauga, ON L5N 8E9
Tel 905-858-8885
Fax 905-858-2248
www.pointclickcare.com
Line: Offers software solutions to long
term care providers.
NAICS: 541510
#Emp: 100-249 (Tor)
Own: Private Company
Key: Mike Wessinger, CEO
Brett Mellon, Sr VP Ops
David Belbeck, CFO
Dave Wessinger, CTO

Pollara Inc.

900-1255 Bay St.
Toronto, ON M5R 2A9
Tel 416-921-0090
Fax 416-921-3903
www.pollara.ca
Line: Provides marketing research
services.
NAICS: 541910
#Emp: 100-249 (Tor)
#TorLoc: 1
Own: Private Company
Key: Robert Hutton, Exec VP
Michael Marzolini, Chmn

Pollard Windows Inc.

1217 King Rd.
P.O. Box 507
Burlington, ON L7R 3Y3
Tel 905-634-2365
Fax 905-333-3521
www.pollardwindows.com
Line: Manufactures vinyl and wood
windows and steel doors for new
construction and renovation markets.
NAICS: 332321 444190
#Emp: 100-249 (Tor)
#TorLoc: 3
Own: Private Company
Key: Michael N. Pollard, Pres
Reginald Pollard, Chmn
Antonio Versace, GM
Sara Cumin, HR Mgr
Douglas Sluys, Cont
Gary Husen, Cdn Sales Mgr
Karen Pollard-Josling, Mktg Mgr

Polyair Canada Ltd.

330 Humberline Dr.
Toronto, ON M9W 1R5
Tel 416-679-6600
Fax 416-740-6027
www.polyair.com
Line: Manufactures protective
packaging, pool products and
accessories.
NAICS: 333310
#Emp: 75-99 (Tor)
#TorLoc: 1
Own: Public Company
Par: Polyair Corp. (US)
Key: Al Miller, Plant Mgr
Martin Gilvarg, Exec VP
Bob Mundy, Dir of HR
Michael Freel, Dir of Fin
Ron Jacobs, VP of IT

Polybrite

A Div. of Magna International Inc.
254 Centre St. East
Richmond Hill, ON L4C 1A8
Tel 905-883-3600
Fax 905-883-9839
www.magna.com
Line: Manufactures automotive
components.
NAICS: 336390
#Emp: 250-499 (Tor)
#TorLoc: 2
Own: Private Company
Key: Peter Schmied, GM
Roy Jimmerskog, Asst GM

Polycultural Immigrant Community Services

3363 Bloor St. West
Toronto, ON M8X 1G2
Tel 416-233-0055
Fax 416-233-5141
www.polycultural.org
Line: Provides community
services to immigrants.
NAICS: 624190
#Emp: 75-99 (Tor)
#TorLoc: 5
Own: Private Company
Key: Carl Cadogan, Exec Dir

Polytainers Inc.

197 Norseman St.
Toronto, ON M8Z 2R5
Tel 416-239-7311
Fax 416-239-0596
www.polytainersinc.com
Line: Manufactures rigid plastic
packaging for the food and dairy
industry.
NAICS: 326114 326198
#Emp: 500-999 (Tor)
#TorLoc: 1
Own: Private Company
Par: Polytainers Enterprises Inc. (CDA)
Key: Robert K. Barrett, Pres
Leslie Ferrari, COO

Pool People Ltd.

135 Matheson Blvd. East
Mississauga, ON L4Z 1R2
Tel 905-501-7210
Fax 905-501-7211
www.poolpeoplelimited.com
Line: Provides commercial swimming
pool, spa and sauna design,
construction, sales service and staffing.
NAICS: 232990
#Emp: 100-249 (Tor)
#TorLoc: 1
Own: Private Company
Key: Paul Denstedt, Pres
Dale Papke, CEO
Martyn Knowles,
    New Construction Mgr
Celine Andrews, Office Mgr

Porter Airlines Inc.

Toronto City Centre Airport
Toronto ON M5V 1A1
Tel 416-203-8100
Fax 416-203-8150
www.flyporter.com
Line: Operates a regional airline.
NAICS: 481110
#Emp: 500-999 (Tor)
#TorLoc: 1
Own: Private Company
Par: Porter Aviation Holdings Inc.
(CDA)
Key: Robert J. Deluce, Pres & CEO
James Morrison, Sr VP & COO
Debby Newman, VP, People
Robert Payne, VP & CFO
Paul Larocque, Dir of IT
Andrew Wilson, VP Sales & Dist
Laurie Laykish, VP Mktg & Commun

Postlinx

1170 Birchmount Rd.
Toronto, ON M1P 5E3
Tel 416-752-8100
Fax 416-752-8239
www.postlinx.com
AKA: Coverall
Line: Provides direct mail advertising
and fulfillment services.
NAICS: 541860 541870 511140
#Emp: 100-249 (Tor)
#TorLoc: 1
Own: Private Company
Par: Pitney Bowes Inc. (US)
Key: Michael Cloverdale, Pres
Martin Coe, VP Ops
Jack LeDrew, VP Fin
Simon Leung, VP IT

Postmedia Network Inc.

1450 Don Mills Rd.
Toronto, ON M3B 3R5
Tel 416-383-2300
Fax 416-442-2077
www.postmedia.com
Line: Publishes and prints newspapers,
broadcasts over-the-air television
stations, and operates an Internet
network.
NAICS: 511110 513120
#Emp: 1000-4999 (Tor)
#TorLoc: 3
Own: Public Company
Par: Postmedia Network Canada Corp.
(CDA)
Key: Paul Godfrey, Pres & CEO
Gordon Fisher,
    Exec VP, Eastern Canada
Doug Lamb, Exec VP & CFO
Edward Brouwer, CIO
Kirk Allen, Exec VP, Advertising Sales

Powerade Centre

7575 Kennedy Rd. South
Brampton, ON L6W 4T2
Tel 905-459-9340
Fax 905-451-2585
www.poweradecentre.com
Line: Operates a sports and
entertainment complex.
NAICS: 711319
#Emp: 100-249 (Tor)
#TorLoc: 1
Own: Private Company
Key: Mike Hardcastle, GM
Brandon Macor,
    Mgr of Bldg Ops & Event Services
Laura Rennie, HR Mgr
Mary Barlow, Cont
Joseph Bye, Mgr of Food & Beverage
Kathy Stafford, Dir of Sales
Jeff Elia, Mgr of Advertising
    & Sales Promotion

Powerlasers Ltd.

55 Confederation Pkwy.
Concord, ON L4K 4Y7
Tel 905-761-1525
Fax 905-761-1527
www.powerlasers.com
Line: Provides laser welding of steel
blanks for automotive and body-in-
white applications.
NAICS: 333990
#Emp: 75-99 (Tor)
#TorLoc: 1

Own: Private Company
Par: Dofasco Inc. - Arcelor Mittal (CDA)
Key: Mike Schmidt, GM

Powerline Plus Ltd.

160 Silver Star Blvd.
Toronto, ON M1V 5P2
Tel 416-609-8272
Fax 416-609-9165
www.powerlineplus.com
Line: Provides electrical and utility
contracting services.
NAICS: 232510
#Emp: 100-249 (Tor)
#TorLoc: 1
Own: Private Company
Key: Ben Matin, Pres & CEO

PowerStream Inc.

161 Cityview Blvd.
Vaughan, ON L4H 0A9
Tel 905-417-6900
Fax 905-532-4505
www.powerstream.ca
Line: Distributes electricity in Aurora,
Markham, Richmond Hill, Vaughan
and Barrie.
NAICS: 221122
#Emp: 250-499 (Tor)
#TorLoc: 4
Own: Government
Key: Brian Bentz, Pres & CEO
Mark Henderson, Exec VP & COO
Barb Gray, Sr VP HR
John Glicksman, Exec VP & CFO
Robert Antenucci,
    Dir of Supply Chain Management
Bill Schmidt, VP IT
Dennis Nolan, Exec VP Corp Services
Eric Fagen, Dir of Corp Commun

PPG Canada Inc.

2450 Bristol Circ.
Oakville, ON L6H 6P6
Tel 905-823-1100
Fax 905-829-9451
www.ppg.com
Line: Supplies flat glass and industrial,
architectural, automotive refinish and
aerospace coatings.
NAICS: 327214 332810
#Emp: 100-249 (Tor)
#TorLoc: 5
Own: Private Company
Par: PPG Industries, Inc. (US)
Key: Ron Nakamura, GM
Monica Frank, Dir of HR
Tim King, Supr of Financial Analysis
Helen Vachon,
    Mgr of Supply & Chain Logistics

Pratt & Whitney Canada Corp.

1801 Courtneypark Dr.
Mississauga, ON L5T 1J3
Tel 905-564-7500
Fax 905-564-3835
www.pwc.ca
Line: Designs, develops, manufactures,
markets and supports small and
medium-sized gas turbine engines for
the aviation industry.
NAICS: 336410
#Emp: 500-999 (Tor)
#TorLoc: 1
Own: Private Company
Par: United Technologies Corp. (US)
Key: John Saabas, Pres
Edward Hoskins, VP Mississauga Ops
Tiina Zeggiel, HR Mgr
John DiBert, VP Fin

Praxair Canada Inc.

1200-1 City Centre Dr.
Mississauga, ON L5B 1M2
Tel 905-803-1600
Fax 905-803-1693
www.praxair.com
Line: Supplies industrial, medical and
specialty gases and related hard goods
and equipment.
NAICS: 418410
#Emp: 100-249 (Tor)
#TorLoc: 5
Own: Private Company
Par: Praxair Inc. (US)
Key: Rob Hossack, Mng Dir
Carma Shaheen, HR Mgr
Nimal Perera, Cont

Preferred Health Care Services

170 Red Maple Rd.
Richmond Hill, ON L4B 4T8
Tel 905-771-2765
Fax 905-771-2763
www.prefhealthcare.com
NAICS: 621610
#Emp: 250-499 (Tor)
#TorLoc: 1
Own: Private Company
Par: Leisureworld Care Giving Centres
(CDA)
Key: Tracy Jones, Pres
Rene Rogers, Dir of Client Services
Barbara van Maris, Dir of Quality &
   Risk Management
Debra Sayewich, Dir of Mktg

Premetalco Inc.

110 Belfield Rd.
Toronto, ON M9W 1G1
Tel 416-245-7386
Fax 416-242-2839
Line: Manufactures and distributes
specialty chemicals, steel and non-
ferrous metals, concrete forming
accessories, heat exchangers and pump
jacks.
NAICS: 416210
#Emp: 100-249 (Tor)
#TorLoc: 4
Own: Private Company
Par: Amalgamated Metal Corp. plc
(UK)
Key: B. Lee Perricone, Secy-Treas
V.H. Sher, CEO
Carol Festa,
   Payroll Benefits & HR Admr
Gunar Zenaitis, Pres of Debro Steel,
   Wilkinson Steel & Metals Div
Bill Heise, Pres of Debro Chemicals Div
Blair Wetmore,
   Pres of Exchanger Industries Div
Lawry Simon, Pres of Nat'l
   Concrete Accessories Div

Premier Candle Corp.

960 Britannia Rd. East
Mississauga, ON L4W 5M7
Tel 905-795-8833
Fax 905-795-0082
www.premiercandle.com
Line: Manufactures candles.
NAICS: 339990
#Emp: 250-499 (Tor)
#TorLoc: 1
Own: Private Company
Key: Jackie Cheng, Pres
William Cheng, CEO
Joanne Lee, GM
Tony Ching, Treas

Premier Contractors Ltd.

9-21 Parr Blvd.
Bolton, ON L7E 4G3
Tel 905-951-8948
Fax 905-951-6044
www.premiercontractorsltd.com
Line: Provides ceramic tile installation
contracting.
NAICS: 232420
#Emp: 75-99 (Tor)
Own: Private Company
Key: Nick Terlizzi, Owner
Sandra Terlizzi, Office Mgr

Premiere Ballroom & Convention Centre

9019 Leslie St.
Richmond Hill, ON L4B 4A3
Tel 905-709-1759
Fax 905-709-3602
www.premiereballroom.com
Line: Operates a banquet hall and
provides dining services.
NAICS: 722320
#Emp: 100-249 (Tor)
#TorLoc: 1
Own: Private Company
Key: Primo Molella, Owner
Anna Molella, Mng Partner

Premier Operating Corp. Ltd.

92-1262 Don Mills Rd.
Toronto, ON M3B 2W7
Tel 416-443-1645
Fax 416-443-1760
www.5drivein.com
Line: Provides real estate services.
NAICS: 531120
#Emp: 100-249 (Tor)
#TorLoc: 2
Own: Private Company
Key: Brian Allen, Pres

Premier Salon Canada Inc.

200-3762 14th Ave.
Markham, ON L3R 0G7
Tel 905-470-2887
Fax 905-470-8027
www.premiersalons.com
Line: Operates hair salons and spas
throughout Canada and the United
States.
NAICS: 812116
#Emp: 500-999 (Tor)
#TorLoc: 45
Own: Private Company
Key: Brian Luborsky, Chmn & CEO

Presidents Choice Financial

439 King St. West, 5th Fl.
Toronto, ON M5V 1K4
Tel 416-204-2600
Fax 416-204-2660
www.pcfinancial.ca
Line: Provides banking and financial
services.
NAICS: 522111
#Emp: 100-249 (Tor)
#TorLoc: 1
Own: Private Company
Par: Loblaws Group of Companies
(CDA)
Key: Barry Columb, Pres

Prestige Telecom Ltd.

2-1093 Meyerside Dr.
Mississauga, ON L5T 1J6
Tel 905-670-0295
Fax 905-670-0297
www.prestige-tel.com
Line: Provides telecommunications
installation and engineering services.
NAICS: 513330
#Emp: 500-999 (Tor)
#TorLoc: 4
Own: Public Company
Key: Stewart Beatty, VP, Ontario
Brian W. McFadden, COO
Chris Boynton, VP HR
Steve Rouleau, Sr VP Sales & Mktg

Presvac Systems (Burlington) Ltd.

4131 Morris Dr.
Burlington, ON L7L 5L5
Tel 905-637-2353
Fax 905-681-0411
www.presvac.com
Line: Operates a vacuum technology
company.
NAICS: 333910
#Emp: 75-99 (Tor)
#TorLoc: 3
Own: Private Company
Key: Louis Sipkema, Pres
Brent Sipkema, Purch Mgr

PRG Schultz Canada Corp.

4-60 Courtney Park Dr. West
Mississauga, ON L5W 0B3
Tel 905-670-7879
Fax 905-670-4626
www.prgx.com
AKA: The Audit Group
Line: Provides recovery auditing and
process improvement services.
NAICS: 541619
#Emp: 100-249 (Tor)
#TorLoc: 1
Own: Private Company
Key: Mike Mahaney, VP & PMO
Romil Bahl, CEO
Katie Lafiandra, Sr VP HR
Robert B. Lee, CFO
Michael Noel, CIO
Alexandra Gobbi, VP Mktg & Commun

PricewaterhouseCoopers LLP

TD Centre, Royal Trust Tower
P.O. Box 82
Toronto, ON M5K 1G8
Tel 416-863-1133
Fax 416-365-8215
www.pwc.com/ca
Line: Operates professional services
firm offering assurance and related
services, tax services and financial
advisory services.
NAICS: 541212 541611
#Emp: 1000-4999 (Tor)
#TorLoc: 5
Own: Private Company
Key: David Forster, Mng Partner, GTA
Christie J.B. Clark,
    Cdn Sr Partner & CEO
Tony Cancelliere, Mng Partner Ops
Hazel Claxton, Partner, Human Capital
George Sheen, Nat'l Leader, Fin
Tracey Jennings, Cdn Tech Info
    Commun & Entertainment Leader

Pride Pak Canada Ltd.

6768 Financial Dr.
Mississauga, ON L5N 7J6
Tel 905-828-8280
Fax 905-828-8201
www.pridepak.com
Line: Processes fresh-cut vegetables for
food services and retail.
NAICS: 413150
#Emp: 100-249 (Tor)
#TorLoc: 1
Own: Private Company
Key: James Karas, Pres
Steven Karr, CEO
Amanda Chronis, HR Admr
Robert Chapman, Dir of Sales & Mktg

Primary Response Inc.

901-250 Consumers Rd.
Toronto, ON M2J 4V6
Tel 416-658-4536
Fax 416-658-3708
www.primaryresponse.ca
Line: Provides physical and mobile
security.
NAICS: 561612
#Emp: 1000-4999 (Tor)
#TorLoc: 1
Own: Private Company
Key: Sherri Macdonald, Pres
Greg Beglarov, Sales Mgr

Prime Restaurants of Canada Inc.

600-10 Kingsbridge Garden Circ.
Mississauga, ON L5R 3K6
Tel 905-568-0000
Fax 905-568-0080
www.primerestaurants.com
AKA: PRC; Esplanade Bier Market;
Casey's; East Side Mario's; Fionn
MacCool's Irish Pub; Paddy Flaherty's;
Pat & Mario's; D'Arcy McGee's; Slainte;
Tir Nan Og; RD's BBQ and Blues
Line: Owns and franchises restaurants.
NAICS: 722110
#Emp: 1000-4999 (Tor)
#TorLoc: 63
Own: Public Company
Par: Prime Restaurant Holdings Inc.
(CDA)
Key: Nick Perpick, Pres & COO
John Rothschild, Chmn & CEO
Robert Carmichael, VP Ops
Nalini Barma, VP HR
Brian Elliot, VP Acctng Services
Bill Grady, VP Purch
Jack Gardner, VP Mktg, Casey's & Pubs
Andrew Berzins, VP Construction & Dev
John Verdon, VP Mktg, East Side Mario's
Grant Cobb, Sr VP, Brand Management

Primerica Financial Services (Canada) Ltd.

300-2000 Argentia Rd., Plaza V
Mississauga, ON L5N 2R7
Tel 905-812-2900
Fax 905-813-5312
www.primerica.com
AKA: PFSL Investments Canada
Ltd.; Primerica Client Services Inc.;
Primerica Life Insurance Company of
Canada
NAICS: 523930
#Emp: 100-249 (Tor)
#TorLoc: 1
Own: Private Company
Key: John Adams, Exec VP & CEO
Nadine Coulson, Dir of HR

Primo Mechanical Inc.

15-253 Jevlan Dr.
Woodbridge, ON L4L 7Z6
Tel 905-851-6718
Fax 905-851-7543
www.primomechanical.com
Line: Operates a plumbing and heating contracting business.
NAICS: 232520
#Emp: 100-249 (Tor)
#TorLoc: 1
Own: Private Company
Key: Leo Agozzino, Pres
Joe Miniaci, Cont

Primus Telecommunications Canada Inc.

400-5343 Dundas St. West
Toronto, ON M9B 6K5
Tel 416-236-3636
Fax 416-236-7391
www.primustel.ca
Line: Provides domestic and international telecommunications in addition to voice, data, private network, managed services, data centres and value added services.
NAICS: 513330 513320
#Emp: 250-499 (Tor)
#TorLoc: 4
Own: Private Company
Par: Primus Telecommunications Group Inc. (US)
Key: Andrew Day, COO
A.J. Byers, Exec VP Ops
Maureen Merkler, VP HR & Admin
Hilton Reading, VP IT
Jeff Lorenz,
    VP Sales & Mktg, Commercial
Robert Warden,
    VP Sales & Mktg, Residential

Prince Spa & Resort Operations Toronto Ltd.

900 York Mills Rd.
Toronto, ON M3B 3H2
Tel 416-444-2511
Fax 416-444-3566
www.westin.com/prince
AKA: Westmont Hopitality Group
Line: Operates hotel.
NAICS: 721111
#Emp: 250-499 (Tor)
#TorLoc: 1
Own: Private Company

Par: Westmont Hospitality (CDA)
Key: Ashock Baghel, GM
Hazel Tan, Dir of HR
Suresh Kumar, Cont
Carol Parrott, Dir of Sales & Mktg

The Princeton Review Canada

550-1255 Bay St.
Toronto, ON M5R 2A9
Tel 416-944-8001
Fax 416-944-3233
www.princetonreview.com
Line: Provides educational and testing services.
NAICS: 611690
#Emp: 75-99 (Tor)
#TorLoc: 1
Own: Private Company
Par: The Princeton Review (US)
Key: Blaise Moritz, Exec Dir

The Printing House Ltd.

1399 Bathurst St.
Toronto, ON M5R 3H8
Tel 416-538-5031
Fax 416-538-6909
www.tph.ca
AKA: TPH
Line: Provides photocopying, business printing, digital printing, thermography services, consulting and facilities management.
NAICS: 323115 323114
#Emp: 250-499 (Tor)
#TorLoc: 49
Own: Private Company
Key: Jamie O'Born, Pres
Earle O'Born, Chmn & CEO
Shawlyn Brown,
    Mgr of Payroll & Benefits
Yvonne Bland, VP Fin

Priszm Income Fund

101 Exchange Ave.
Vaughan, ON L4K 5R6
Tel 416-739-2900
Fax 416-739-3665
www.priszm.com
AKA: KFC; Pizza Hut; Taco Bell; KIT Inc.
Line: Operates quick service restaurants.
NAICS: 722210
#Emp: 1000-4999 (Tor)
#TorLoc: 100
Own: Public Company
Key: John Bitove, Exec Chmn
Jim Robertson, COO
Deborah Papernick, CFO

Pro-Bel Enterprises

65 Sunray St.
Whitby, ON L1N 8Y3
Tel 905-427-0616
Fax 905-427-2545
www.pro-bel.ca
AKA: The Safety Roof Anchor Co.
Line: Manufactures, engineers, designs, installs and inspects window washing equipment and fall arrest systems.
NAICS: 332329
#Emp: 100-249 (Tor)
#TorLoc: 2
Own: Private Company
Key: Marc Lebel, Pres

Proco Machinery Inc.

1111 Brevik Pl.
Mississauga, ON L4W 3R7
Tel 905-602-6066
Fax 905-602-0560
www.procomachinery.com
Line: Supplies automated machinery and auxiliary equipment to the blow molding industry.
NAICS: 333220
#Emp: 75-99 (Tor)
#TorLoc: 1
Own: Private Company
Key: John McCormick, Pres

Procom Consultants Group Ltd.

400-2323 Yonge St.
Toronto, ON M4P 2C9
Tel 416-483-0766
Fax 416-483-8102
www.procom.ca
AKA: PROCOM
Line: Provides information technology personnel on a supplemental and full time basis.
NAICS: 541612
#Emp: 100-249 (Tor)
#TorLoc: 1
Own: Private Company
Key: Frank McCrea, Pres
Kent McCrea, COO
Fadina Previlon, Mgr of HR
Patty Niles, Comptr

Procor Ltd.

2001 Speers Rd.
Oakville, ON L6J 5E1
Tel 905-827-4111
Fax 905-827-0913
www.procor.com
Line: Manufactures and leases rail cars.
NAICS: 336510
#Emp: 250-499 (Tor)
#TorLoc: 1
Own: Private Company
Par: Marmon Group of Companies (US)
Key: Roger Tipple, GM & VP
Mike Parker, VP Ops
Maria Freitas, Dir of HR
David Patterson, Corp Cont
Brad Burrows, Dir of Materials Mgt
Randy Pocrnick, VP Rail Leasing

Procter & Gamble Inc.

P.O. Box 355, Stn. A
Toronto, ON M5W 1C5
Tel 416-730-4711
Fax 416-730-4666
www.pg.ca
Line: Provides products and services
covering health care, beauty care,
fabric and home care, pharmaceuticals
and snacks.
NAICS: 325610
#Emp: 500-999 (Tor)
#TorLoc: 1
Own: Public Company
Par: The Procter & Gamble Co. (US)
Key: Timothy H. Penner,
   Pres, P&G Canada
A.G. Lafley, CEO
Gord Meyer, Dir of Mktg
Lee Bansil, Dir of External Relns

Prodigy Graphics Group Inc.

731 Millway Ave.
Vaughan, ON L4K 3S8
Tel 905-677-7776
Fax 866-858-5381
www.prodigygraphics.com
Line: Provides bookbinding and
printing services.
NAICS: 323120
#Emp: 100-249 (Tor)
#TorLoc: 1
Own: Private Company
Key: Najib Jamal, Pres

Professional Engineers Ontario

101-40 Sheppard Ave. West
Toronto, ON M2N 6K9
Tel 416-224-1100
Fax 416-224-8168
www.peo.on.ca
AKA: PEO
Line: Regulates the engineering
profession while enhancing
engineering culture and practice.
NAICS: 813920
#Emp: 75-99 (Tor)
#TorLoc: 1
Own: Association
Key: Diane Freeman, Pres
Kim Allen, CEO & Registrar
Fern Goncalves, Dir of HR
Scott Clark, Dir of Admin Services
Eric Brown, Dir of IT Services
Connie Mucklestone, Dir of Commun

Profile Industries Ltd.

201 Garyray Dr.
Toronto, ON M9L 2T2
Tel 416-748-2505
Fax 416-748-0926
Line: Manufactures office furniture.
NAICS: 337214
#Emp: 250-499 (Tor)
#TorLoc: 1
Own: Private Company
Key: Amine Elsemine, GM
George Oliver, Plant Mgr

Progress Packaging Ltd.

25 Tangiers Rd.
Toronto, ON M3J 2B1
Tel 416-638-1221
Fax 416-638-1436
www.progressluv2pak.com
Line: Manufactures and imports
specialty bags, folding cartons and
accessories.
NAICS: 418220
#Emp: 75-99 (Tor)
#TorLoc: 2
Own: Private Company
Key: Roberto Lentino, CEO
David Hertzman, Chmn
Yili Feng, Office Mgr
Oswald Barmasch, Cont
Doran Crocker, Dir of Purch

ProHome Health Services

160 Traders Blvd.
Mississauga, ON L4Z 3K7
Tel 905-275-0544
Fax 905-275-1449
www.prohome.ca
AKA: Community Care Services
Line: Provides nursing and personal
support home care services.
NAICS: 621610
#Emp: 250-499 (Tor)
#TorLoc: 1
Own: Private Company
Par: Trudell Medical Limited (CDA)
Key: Michael Pohanka, Pres
Deborah Warren, Dir of Ops
Joanne Lair, Dir of HR
Rob Wotten, Dir of Fin

Promation Engineering Ltd.

2767 Brighton Rd.
Oakville, ON L6H 6J4
Tel 905-625-6093
Fax 905-625-6910
www.promation.com
Line: Designs and manufactures high-
quality tooling, automation and robotic
systems for the automotive and nuclear
industries.
NAICS: 541330
#Emp: 75-99 (Tor)
#TorLoc: 1
Own: Private Company
Key: Mariusz Zimny, Pres &CEO
Darryl Spector, Ops Mgr

Propak Ltd.

5230 Harvester Rd.
Burlington, ON L7L 4X4
Tel 905-681-2345
Fax 905-681-1023
www.propaklimited.yp.ca
Line: Manufactures corrugated boxes
and sheets.
NAICS: 322211
#Emp: 75-99 (Tor)
#TorLoc: 1
Own: Private Company
Key: Keith Munt, Pres & CEO
John Nadon, Sales Mgr

Pro Pharm Ltd.

131 McNabb St.
Markham, ON L3R 5V7
Tel 905-943-9736
Fax 905-943-4518
www.propharm.com
Line: Provides computer software
consulting.
NAICS: 541510
#Emp: 100-249 (Tor)
#TorLoc: 3
Own: Private Company
Par: Katz Group Canada Ltd. (CDA)
Key: George Edwards, VP
Carolyn Beam, Mktg Asst

Prophix Software Inc.

1000-350 Burnhamthorpe Rd. West
Mississauga, ON L5B 3J1
Tel 905-279-8711
Fax 905-279-2232
www.prophix.com
Line: Designs and manufactures
financial software.
NAICS: 541510
#Emp: 75-99 (Tor)
#TorLoc: 1
Own: Private Company
Key: Paul Barber, Pres
Verne Meredith, VP Sales & Mktg

Protagon Display Inc.

719 Tapscott Rd.
Toronto, ON M1X 1A2
Tel 416-293-9500
Fax 416-293-9600
www.protagon.com
Line: Manufactures corrugated
advertising displays.
NAICS: 337215
#Emp: 75-99 (Tor)
#TorLoc: 1
Own: Private Company
Key: Larry Titchner, Pres
Jeff Lynch, VP Ops
Peter Nodwell, VP Sales

Protech Chemicals Ltd.

150 Klondike Dr.
Toronto, ON M9L 1X3
Tel 416-667-9697
Fax 416-667-0460
www.protechpowder.com
AKA: Protech Powder Coatings
Line: Manufactures powder coatings.
NAICS: 325510
#Emp: 100-249 (Tor)
#TorLoc: 1
Own: Private Company
Key: Michael Reinerth, Sales Mgr

Providence Healthcare

3276 St. Clair Ave. East
Toronto, ON M1L 1W1
Tel 416-285-3666
Fax 416-285-3756
www.providence.on.ca
Line: Specializes in the clinical
treatment and care of individuals
experiencing unique health care
conditions and challenges associated
with aging.
NAICS: 623310
#Emp: 1000-4999 (Tor)
#TorLoc: 1
Own: Not-for-profit
Par: Catholic Health Corporation of
Ontario (CDA)
Key: Josie Walsh, Pres & CEO
Peter Nord, VP & Chief Medical Officer
Marc Beaudry, VP & CHRO
Jim Elliot, Interim CFO
Larissa Wisniewski,
    Dir of Info & Commun Tech
Beth Johnson, Dir of Commun

Provincial Sign Systems

A Div. of Provincial Sign Service Ltd.
1655 Feldspar Crt.
Pickering, ON L1W 3R4
Tel 905-837-1791
Fax 905-428-1799
www.provincialsign.com
Line: Manufactures, installs and
services structural illuminated signage.
NAICS: 339950
#Emp: 75-99 (Tor)
#TorLoc: 1
Own: Private Company
Key: Kevin Van Sickle, Pres
Paul Cotton, CEO
Dale Cotton, VP Sales

Provincial Store Fixtures Ltd.

910 Central Pkwy. West
Mississauga, ON L5C 2V5
Tel 905-564-6700
Fax 905-564-6711
www.psfltd.com
Line: Provides integrated solutions for
woodwork, architectural and retailing
needs.
NAICS: 337215
#Emp: 75-99 (Tor)
#TorLoc: 3
Own: Private Company
Key: Edward Joubran, Pres
Sam Joubran, Chmn

Prudential Sadie Moranis Realty Brokerage

35 Lesmill Rd.
Toronto, ON M3B 2T3
Tel 416-449-2020
Fax 416-449-1564
www.sadiemoranis.com
Line: Operates a real estate agency.
NAICS: 531210
#Emp: 250-499 (Tor)
#TorLoc: 3
Own: Private Company
Key: Helene Katz, Broker of Record
George Ziten, VP Fin

Psion Teklogix Inc.

2100 Meadowvale Blvd.
Mississauga, ON L5N 7J9
Tel 905-813-9900
Fax 905-812-6300
www.psionteklogix.com
Line: Designs RF systems through
software and hardware and provides
integration middleware to SAP
systems.
NAICS: 541510
#Emp: 250-499 (Tor)
#TorLoc: 1
Own: Private Company
Par: Psion plc (UK)
Key: John Conoley, CEO
Rob Gayson, VP Ops & Quality
Maija Michell, VP HR
Fraser Park, CFO
Mike Doyle, CTO

Publicis Inc.

200-111 Queen St. East
Toronto, ON M5C 1S2
Tel 416-925-7733
Fax 416-925-7341
www.publicis.ca
NAICS: 541810
#Emp: 100-249 (Tor)
#TorLoc: 1
Own: Private Company
Key: Andrew Bruce, Pres & COO
Yves Gougoux, Chmn & CEO
Duncan Bruce, Mng Partner
Diane McIntyre, HR Asst
Eric Seguin, Cont

Public Works & Government Services Canada

1205- 4900 Yonge St.
Toronto, ON M2N 6A6
Tel 416-512-5509
www.pwgsc.gc.ca
Line: Operates Federal public works
program.
NAICS: 911910
#Emp: 500-999 (Tor)
#TorLoc: 7
Own: Public Company
Key: Kim Croucher,
   Reg Dir Gen of Ontario
Catherine Vick, Dir of HR

Puddy Brothers Ltd.

1039 Midway Blvd.
Mississauga, ON L5T 2C1
Tel 905-696-9081
Fax 905-795-0047
www.puddybros.com
Line: Processes poultry.
NAICS: 311615
#Emp: 100-249 (Tor)
#TorLoc: 1
Own: Private Company
Key: Lou Masters, Owner

Pullmatic Manufacturing

A Div. of Magna Power Train
430 Cochrane Dr.
Unionville, ON L3R 8E3
Tel 905-474-0899
Fax 905-474-9262
www.magnapowertrain.com
Line: Manufactures and supplies
engine pulleys, brackets and
transmissions to the automotive
industry.
NAICS: 333619
#Emp: 100-249 (Tor)
#TorLoc: 1
Own: Private Company
Par: Magna International Inc. (CDA)
Key: Hartmut Halbach, GM

Purdue Pharma

575 Granite Crt.
Pickering, ON L1W 3W8
Tel 905-420-6400
Fax 905-420-0385
www.purdue.ca
Line: Manufactures pharmaceuticals.
NAICS: 325410
#Emp: 250-499 (Tor)
#TorLoc: 1

Own: Private Company
Par: Purdue Pharma (US)
Key: Cornelia Hentzsch, Pres & CEO
David Mayers, VP Manaufacturing Ops
Marguerite O'Neal, VP HR
Brian Lockwood, Exec VP Fin
Shauna Callaghan, Purch Mgr
John Pinard, Dir of IT
Chris Kostka, VP Sales
William B. Jeffrey, Exec VP Mktg
Randy Steffan,
   Dir of Corp Affairs & Commun

Pure Metal Galvanizing

A Div. of PMT Industries Ltd.
369 Attwell Dr.
Toronto, ON M9W 5C2
Tel 416-675-3352
Fax 416-675-7698
www.puremetal.com
Line: Provides custom hot dip
galvanizing.
NAICS: 333519
#Emp: 100-249 (Tor)
#TorLoc: 3
Own: Private Company
Par: 875417 Ontario Inc. (CDA)
Key: Bruce Phillips, Pres
Doug Phillips, Exec VP
Dennis R. Gower, VP Ops
Mellissa Meggs, Payroll & HR
Jeff Howe, VP Fin
Dan Morgan, Acctng Supr
Brenda J. Neczkar, Sales & Mktg Mgr

Purewood Inc.

341 Heart Lake Service Rd. South
Brampton, ON L6W 3K8
Tel 905-874-9797
Fax 905-874-9997
www.purewoodinc.com
Line: Manufactures wood furniture.
NAICS: 337213
#Emp: 100-249 (Tor)
#TorLoc: 1
Own: Private Company
Key: Mark Bozek, Pres
Eva Bozek, Cont

Purity Life Health Products - A Sunopta Company

6 Commerce Cres.
Acton, ON L7J 2X3
Tel 519-853-3511
Fax 519-853-4660
www.puritylife.com
AKA: Sun Opta Inc.
Line: Distributes wholesale natural
products, food, vitamins, herbs, and
health and beauty products.

NAICS: 413190
#Emp: 100-249 (Tor)
#TorLoc: 2
Own: Public Company
Par: SunOpta Inc. (CDA)
Key: David Chapman, Pres
Matthew James, GM & Sr VP
Carla Reale, Dir of HR
Paul Van Weelie, VP Ops
Ben Schmitt, VP Sales &Mktg

Purolator Courier Ltd.

5995 Avebury Rd.
Mississauga, ON L5R 3T8
Tel 905-712-1251
Fax 905-712-6696
www.purolator.com
AKA: Purolator Global Supply Chain
Services; Purolator Freight; Purolator
USA, Inc.; Purolator International
Line: Provides expedited carriage
of freight by air and ground
transportation.
NAICS: 492110 488519
#Emp: 1000-4999 (Tor)
#TorLoc: 28
Own: Private Company
Par: Purolator Courier Holdings Ltd.
(CDA)
Key: Tom Schmitt, Pres & CEO

Pusateri's Ltd.

1539 Avenue Rd.
Toronto, ON M5M 3X4
Tel 416-785-9100
Fax 416-782-9485
www.pusateris.com
Line: Operates a gourmet grocery store.
NAICS: 445110
#Emp: 250-499 (Tor)
#TorLoc: 2
Own: Private Company
Key: Frank Luchetta, Pres
Ida Pusateri, Owner
John Mastroianni, GM

PYA Importer Ltd.

15 Apex Rd.
Toronto, ON M6A 2V6
Tel 416-929-3300
Fax 416-929-3184
www.pyaimporter.com
Line: Wholesales clothing.
NAICS: 414110
#Emp: 75-99 (Tor)
Own: Private Company
Key: Patrick Assaraf, Pres

Q107 FM

25 Dockside Dr.
Toronto, ON M5A 0B5
Tel 416-221-0107
Fax 416-479-7002
www.q107.com
AKA: CILQ-FM; Corus Radio Toronto
Line: Operates a radio station.
NAICS: 513110
#Emp: 100-249 (Tor)
#TorLoc: 1
Own: Private Company
Par: Corus Entertainment (CDA)
Key: Chris Pandoff, GM
Victor Giacomelli,
    Dir of Sales for Corus Radio
Darren Wasylyk,
    Dir of Mktg & Promotions

Q9 Networks Inc.

4400-77 King St. West
P.O. Box 235
Toronto, ON M5K 1J3
Tel 416-362-7000
Fax 416-362-7001
www.q9.com
Line: Provides Internet hosting
services.
NAICS: 514191
#Emp: 100-249 (Tor)
#TorLoc: 2
Own: Private Company
Key: Paul Sharpe, Pres & COO
Osama Arafat, CEO
Chris Long, Dir of HR
Kareem Arafat, Sr VP Tech
Dave Ralston, Sr VP Sales
Dave Chaloner, Sr VP Mktg

QBD Modular Systems Inc.

31 Bramsteele Rd.
Brampton, ON L6W 3K6
Tel 905-459-0709
Fax 905-459-1478
www.qbd.com
Line: Sells refrigerated display cases.
NAICS: 417910
#Emp: 100-249 (Tor)
#TorLoc: 1
Own: Private Company
Key: Zully Jaffer, VP & GM
Sabit Jaffer, HR Mgr
Mohammed Chowdhury,
    Accounts Payable

Q & I Computer Systems Inc.

115 Symons St.
Toronto, ON M8V 1V1
Tel 416-253-5555
Fax 416-252-6991
www.qiem.com
Line: Offers management consulting
and technology services focused on
sales, marketing and customer service.
NAICS: 541510
#Emp: 500-999 (Tor)
Own: Private Company
Key: Jonathan Schloo, Pres

QRC Logistics Ltd.

1 Woodslea Rd.
Brampton, ON L6T 5J4
Tel 905-791-9004
Fax 905-791-9005
www.quikrun.com
AKA: Quik-Run Delivery; Quik-Run
Courier Ltd.
Line: Warehouses pick and pack
operation and provides local and long
distance cartage and rush courier
services.
NAICS: 492110 493110
#Emp: 75-99 (Tor)
#TorLoc: 1
Own: Private Company
Key: Richard Mutiger, Pres
Ian Patterson, Ops Mgr
Guy Iamonaco, VP Sales & Mktg

Quadgraphics Inc.

275 Wellington St. East
Aurora, ON L4G 6J9
Tel 905-841-4400
Fax 905-841-8572
www.quebecorworld.com
Line: Provides commercial printing
services.
NAICS: 323113
#Emp: 500-999 (Tor)
#TorLoc: 4
Own: Public Company
Par: Quebecor World Inc. (CDA)
Key: Regis Rehel, Pres, Canada
Brad Rickard, HR Mgr
Dave Beleskey, IT Mgr
Karl Broderick, Sr VP Sales, Canada

Qualicom Innovations Inc.

401-3389 Steeles Ave. East
Toronto, ON M2H 3S8
Tel 416-492-3833
Fax 416-492-8603
www.qualicom.com
Line: Provides software consulting and
development services for the retail
sector.
NAICS: 541510
#Emp: 75-99 (Tor)
#TorLoc: 1
Own: Private Company
Key: Bill Chan, Pres
Elena Bailey, HR Generalist

Qualified Metal Fabricators Ltd.

55 Steinway Blvd.
Toronto, ON M9W 6H6
Tel 416-675-7777
Fax 416-675-1660
www.qmf.com
Line: Manufactures custom precision
sheet metal products.
NAICS: 332329
#Emp: 100-249 (Tor)
#TorLoc: 1
Own: Private Company
Key: Brian Haryott, Pres & CEO
Anne Snyders, Office Mgr

Quality Meat Packers Ltd.

2 Tecumseth St.
Toronto, ON M5V 2R5
Tel 416-703-7675
Fax 416-504-3756
www.qualitymeats.on.ca
AKA: Legacy Pork
Line: Processes and sells fresh and
frozen pork products to domestic and
international markets.
NAICS: 311611
#Emp: 500-999 (Tor)
#TorLoc: 1
Own: Private Company
Key: David Schwartz, Pres & CEO
Frank Schwartz, Chmn
Sheldon Garfinkle, VP Fin & Admin
Mike Miller, VP International Sales
Jim Gracie, VP Mktg & Business Dev

Quality Suites Toronto Airport

262 Carlingview Dr.
Toronto, ON M9W 5G1
Tel 416-674-8442
Fax 416-674-3088
www.choicehotels.ca
Line: Operates a hotel.
NAICS: 721111
#Emp: 75-99 (Tor)
#TorLoc: 1
Own: Private Company
Key: Tony Sabourin, GM
Keri Walker, Dir of Sales

Quantum Management Services Ltd.

660-33 City Centre Dr.
Mississauga, ON L5B 2N5
Tel 905-276-8611
Fax 905-276-7739
www.quantum.ca
Line: Operates an employment agency.
NAICS: 561310
#Emp: 250-499 (Tor)
#TorLoc: 5
Own: Private Company
Key: Michela Syrie-Paul, Branch Mgr

Quantum Murray LP

300-345 Horner Ave.
Toronto, ON M8W 1Z6
Tel 416-253-6000
Fax 416-253-6699
www.murraydemolition.com
AKA: M.R.A. Abatement Services; BM2 Remediation
Line: Provides automotive plant cleaning services; demolishes and restores buildings; and performs asbestos removal and site remediation.
NAICS: 232110 231220
#Emp: 100-249 (Tor)
#TorLoc: 1
Own: Private Company
Key: Karim El-Khatib, Pres
Lisa Parisotto, Payroll
Peter McLean, Purch Mgr

Queensway Volkswagen Inc.

1306 The Queensway
Toronto, ON M8Z 1S4
Tel 416-259-7656
Fax 416-259-2016
www.queenswayvw.com
AKA: Queensway Audi; Queensway Pre-Owned
Line: Operates a car dealership.

NAICS: 441110 441120
#Emp: 100-249 (Tor)
#TorLoc: 2
Own: Private Company
Par: David H. Green Investments Ltd. (CDA)
Key: David Green, Pres
Doug Ramsay, GM

Quest Courier Services (1996) Ltd.

207-4121 Lawrence Ave. East
Toronto, ON M1E 2S2
Tel 416-298-9455
Fax 416-281-0610
www.quest-courier.com
Line: Offers courier services.
NAICS: 492110
#Emp: 75-99 (Tor)
#TorLoc: 1
Own: Private Company
Key: Ed McGrath, Pres
Jeff McGrath, Dir of Fin

Quick Messenger Services Ontario Ltd.

104-100 Adelaide St. West
Toronto, ON M5H 1S4
Tel 416-368-1623
Fax 416-979-8265
www.qms-tor.com
Line: Provides courier services.
NAICS: 492110
#Emp: 100-249 (Tor)
#TorLoc: 1
Own: Private Company
Key: Paul Etheridge, Pres
Brian Jeffay, GM

Quik X Transportation Inc.

6767 Davand Dr.
Mississauga, ON L5T 2T2
Tel 905-565-8811
Fax 905-565-8643
www.quikx.com
AKA: Roadfast; Quiktrax; Quik X Logistics; TRO Air
Line: Provides expedited transportation services, show services, intermodal services, and air-freight services in North America.
NAICS: 484239
#Emp: 250-499 (Tor)
#TorLoc: 3
Own: Private Company
Key: Edmund J. Powers, Sr VP
Gary Wayne Babcock, Pres & CEO
David Babcock, VP Ops

Anne McKee, HR Mgr
Jeff L. King, Exec VP & CFO
Irene Spearns, Dir of IS
David A. Murray, VP Sales
William H. Kimmel,
    VP Mktg & Revenue Acctng
Al Ward, VP Business Dev

Quinterra Property Maintenance Inc.

53-6535 Millcreek Dr.
Mississauga, ON L5N 2M2
Tel 905-821-7171
www.quinterrapropertymaintenance.com
Line: Offers building cleaning services.
NAICS: 561722
#Emp: 500-999 (Tor)
#TorLoc: 1
Own: Private Company
Key: Ray Quinn, Pres & CEO
Mark Quinn, VP Ops
D.J. Weakly, VP

Raceway Plymouth Chrysler Ltd.

150 Rexdale Blvd.
Toronto, ON M9W 1P6
Tel 416-743-9900
Fax 416-743-0962
www.racewaychryslerdealer.com
Line: Operates an automotive dealership.
NAICS: 441110 441120
#Emp: 100-249 (Tor)
#TorLoc: 1
Own: Private Company
Key: Reg Nimeck, Pres
Gordon Nimeck, VP
Shozo Yoshihara, Secy-Treas

Radisson Admiral Hotel

249 Queen's Quay West
Toronto, ON M5J 2N5
Tel 416-203-3333
Fax 416-203-3100
www.radissonadmiral.com
AKA: 1548383 Ontario Inc.
NAICS: 721111
#Emp: 100-249 (Tor)
#TorLoc: 1
Own: Private Company
Par: Radisson Hotels & Resorts (US)
Key: Dermot McKeown, GM
Safdar Nasser, Financial Cont

Radke Films

125 George St.
Toronto, ON M5A 2N4
Tel 416-366-9036
Fax 416-366-0006
www.radke.tv
Line: Operates a film production
company.
NAICS: 512110
#Emp: 75-99 (Tor)
#TorLoc: 1
Own: Private Company
Key: Edie Weiss, Owner

Randolph Academy for the Performing Arts

736 Bathurst St.
Toronto, ON M5S 2R4
Tel 416-924-2243
Fax 416-924-1535
www.randolphacademy.com
AKA: Randolph School of the Arts
Line: Provides a musical theatre
training program, post-secondary,
children's dance and a musical theatre
program.
NAICS: 611610
#Emp: 75-99 (Tor)
#TorLoc: 1
Own: Not-for-profit
Key: George Randolph, Pres
Grace Delottinville, GM

Random House of Canada Ltd.

2775 Matheson Blvd. East
Mississauga, ON L4W 4P7
Tel 905-624-0672
Fax 905-624-6217
www.randomhouse.ca
NAICS: 511130
#Emp: 100-249 (Tor)
#TorLoc: 2
Own: Private Company
Par: Random House Inc. (US)
Key: Brad Martin, Pres & Chmn
Douglas Foot, Exec VP & CAO
Trish McGill, Sr VP & Dir of HR
Ed Brooks, Dir of IT
Linda Scott, Dir of Mktg

Randstad Technologies

1400-60 Bloor St. West
Toronto, ON M4W 3B8
Tel 416-962-9262
Fax 416-962-4489
www.randstadtechnologies.ca
Line: Provides information technology
staffing services tond offers customized
solutions for payroll administration,
vendor management, recruitment
advertising and human resource
communications.
NAICS: 561310
#Emp: 100-249 (Tor)
#TorLoc: 3
Own: Private Company
Key: Terry Power, Pres
Leandra Harris, Dir of HR
Andrew Dillane, CIO
Tom Turpin, Exec VP Sales, Randstad
Chris Drummond, Sr VP Mktg

Ranka Enterprises Ltd.

7261 Victoria Park Ave.
Markham, ON L3R 2M7
Tel 905-752-1081
Fax 905-752-1088
AKA: Ranka Group
Line: Manufactures clothing apparel
and accessories.
NAICS: 315990
#Emp: 100-249 (Tor)
#TorLoc: 1
Own: Private Company
Par: Ranka Enterprises Inc. (CDA)
Key: Kashmiri Lal Sood, Pres

Rapid Aid Ltd.

1-4 4120A Sladeview Cres.
Mississauga, ON L5L 5Z3
Tel 905-820-4788
Fax 905-820-9226
www.rapidaid.com
Line: Manufactures medical supplies.
NAICS: 339110
#Emp: 100-249 (Tor)
#TorLoc: 1
Own: Private Company
Key: Jeff Whitely, Pres

Raymond James Ltd.

2200-925 West Georgia St.
Vancouver, BC V6C 3L2
Tel 604-659-8000
Fax 604-659-8099
www.raymondjames.ca
Line: Provides investment services.
NAICS: 523110 523120
#Emp: 500-999 (Tor)
#TorLoc: 2
Own: Public Company
Par: Raymond James Financial Inc.
(US)
Key: Paul Allison, Chmn & CEO
June Sangster, Head of HR

Ray Plastics Ltd.

91 Westmore Dr.
Toronto, ON M9V 3Y6
Tel 416-749-2511
Fax 416-744-1507
Line: Produces custom injection-
moulding.
NAICS: 326198
#Emp: 100-249 (Tor)
#TorLoc: 1
Own: Private Company
Key: Larry Fournier, Pres
C. Michael Haird, VP
Rosanna Coluccio, HR Mgr
Nancy Palermo, Office Mgr

Raywal Ltd.

68 Green Lane
Thornhill, ON L3T 6K8
Tel 905-889-6243
Fax 416-733-7629
www.raywal.com
AKA: Raywal Kitchens
Line: Manufactures kitchen and vanity
cabinets.
NAICS: 337110
#Emp: 100-249 (Tor)
#TorLoc: 1
Own: Private Company
Par: TOM Capital (CDA)
Key: Brian Magee, Pres
Vince DeBlasi, Cont
Jeff Ascott, Purch Mgr

RBC Dominion Securities Inc.

200 Bay St., P.O. Box 50
Royal Bank Plaza, South Tower
Toronto, ON M5J 2W7
Tel 416-842-2000
www.rbccm.com
AKA: RBC Capital Markets
Line: Provides international corporate
and investment banking services.
NAICS: 523110 523120
#Emp: 1000-4999 (Tor)
#TorLoc: 1
Own: Public Company
Par: RBC Financial Group (CDA)
Key: Mark Standish, Pres & Co-CEO
Doug McGregor, Chmn & Co-CEO
Mark Hughes,
   Head of Global Credit & COO
Melanie Burns,
   Mng Dir & Global Head, HR
Troy Maxwell, Mng Dir & CFO
Dave Thomas,
   Head of Capital Markets IT & Ops

RBC Financial Group

Royal Bank Plaza
200 Bay St.
Toronto, ON M5J 2J5
Tel 416-974-5151
Fax 416-955-7800
www.rbc.com
AKA: Royal Bank of Canada
Line: Offers financial and insurance investments.
NAICS: 522111 522112
#Emp: 10000+ (Tor)
#TorLoc: 250
Own: Public Company
Key: Gordon M. Nixon, Pres & CEO
Barbara Stymiest, Group Head,
    Strategy, Treasury & Corp Services
Zabeen Hirji, Chief HR Officer
Janice R. Fukakusa, CAO & CFO
Linda Mantia, Sr VP & Head
    Procurement & Corp Real Estate
David McKay,
    Head of Sales, Cdn Banking
James Little,
    Chief Brand & Commun Officer
Katherine Gay,
    VP & Head of Corp Commun

RBC Global Asset Management

P.O. Box 7500, Station A
Toronto, ON M5W 1P9
Tel 416-974-0616
Fax 416-974-8506
www.rbcam.com
Line: Provides investment advisory services.
NAICS: 523920
#Emp: 100-249 (Tor)
#TorLoc: 1
Own: Private Company
Key: Doug Coulter, Pres
John C. Montalbano, CEO
Frank Lippa, CFO & COO
Dan Chornous,
    Chief Investment Officer

RBC Insurance Holdings Inc.

6880 Financial Dr., West Tower
P.O. Box 53, Stn. A
Mississauga, ON L5A 2Y9
Tel 905-286-5099
Fax 905-813-4854
www.rbcinsurance.com
AKA: RBC Insurance
Line: Provides travel, group, life, individual, home, auto and creditor insurance.
NAICS: 524210
#Emp: 1000-4999 (Tor)
#TorLoc: 1

Own: Private Company
Par: RBC Financial Group (CDA)
Key: Neil Skelding, Pres & CEO
Diane Churilla, Sr VP Fin

RB & W Corporation of Canada

5190 Bradco Blvd.
Mississauga, ON L4W 1G7
Tel 905-624-4490
Fax 905-624-6195
www.rbwmfg.com
Line: Manufactures and sells cold formed products to the international auto industry.
NAICS: 332720
#Emp: 75-99 (Tor)
#TorLoc: 1
Own: Private Company
Par: Park-Ohio Industries Inc. (US)
Key: Mike Moini, GM
Mark Rajcsanyi, Production Mgr
Manuel de Sousa, HR Mgr
Dennis Bolden, CFO
Stacey Clarke, Materials Mgr
Tony Durante, Corp IT Mgr

RCM Technologies Canada Corp.

895 Brock Rd. South
Pickering, ON L1W 3C1
Tel 905-837-8333
Fax 905-859-3717
www.rcmt.ca
Line: Provides business and technology solutions.
NAICS: 541510
#Emp: 75-99 (Tor)
#TorLoc: 2
Own: Private Company
Key: Rocco Campanelli, Exec VP

RCP Inc.

2891 Langstaff Rd.
Concord, ON L4K 4Z2
Tel 905-660-7274
Fax 905-660-9093
www.rcpcanada.com
Line: Manufactures and distributes automotive parts.
NAICS: 336320
#Emp: 75-99 (Tor)
#TorLoc: 2
Own: Private Company
Key: Bernard Ceresne, Pres
Paul Ferrie, COO
Margaret Loprete, HR Admr
Dan Woods, Cont
Sharon Peng, IT Mgr

Ready Honda

230-260 Dundas St. East
Mississauga, ON L5A 1W9
Tel 905-896-3500
Fax 905-896-0759
www.readyhonda.com
AKA: Ready Import Limited
Line: Operates an automotive, motorcycle, ATV, marine and power equipment dealership.
NAICS: 441110
#Emp: 75-99 (Tor)
Own: Private Company
Key: Bob Redinger, GM

Ready Staffing Solutions Inc.

201-5170 Dixie Rd.
Mississauga, ON L4W 1E3
Tel 905-625-4009
Fax 905-625-4369
www.readystaffing.ca
Line: Operates an employment agency.
NAICS: 561310
#Emp: 250-499 (Tor)
#TorLoc: 2
Own: Private Company
Key: Yvan Brodeur, Dir

Realstar Management

2000-77 Bloor St. West
Toronto, ON M5S 1M2
Tel 416-923-2950
Fax 416-923-9315
www.realstar.ca
Line: Provides asset and property management for multi-family residential apartments.
NAICS: 531111
#Emp: 100-249 (Tor)
#TorLoc: 39
Own: Private Company
Par: Realstar Management Partnership (CDA)
Key: G. Wayne Squibb, Pres & CEO
Scott Bigford, Sr VP Ops
Cindy Stockdale, Chief HR Officer
Colin Martin, CFO

Recall

A Div. of Brambles Canada Inc.
5286 Timberlea Blvd.
Mississauga, ON L4W 2S6
Tel 905-629-8440
www.recall.com
Line: Provides worldwide off-site data backup and records management services.
NAICS: 514199 514210
#Emp: 75-99 (Tor)
#TorLoc: 8
Own: Public Company
Par: Brambles Industries Ltd. (AUS)
Key: Lawrence Vella, HR Mgr, Canada
Mark Sidhom, Sales Mgr

Reckitt Benckiser (Canada) Inc.

2-1680 Tech Ave.
Mississauga, ON L4W 5S9
Tel 905-283-7000
Fax 905-283-7001
www.reckittbenckiser.com
Line: Distributes and sells consumer packaged goods including food, household, health and personal care products.
NAICS: 325610 311990
#Emp: 100-249 (Tor)
#TorLoc: 1
Own: Public Company
Par: Reckitt Benckiser plc (UK)
Key: Rob de Groot,
   Exec VP, North America
Alan Thompson, GM
Bill Park, Dir of Sales
Shailesh Shukla, VP Mktg

Recochem Inc.

8725 Holgate Cres.
Milton, ON L9T 5G7
Tel 905-878-5544
Fax 905-864-3460
www.recochem.com
Line: Manufactures and packages household and automotive chemical products.
NAICS: 325999
#Emp: 75-99 (Tor)
#TorLoc: 1
Own: Private Company
Key: Mike Wilson, GM, Central Region
George Czerwinski, Cont
Cheryl Ford,
   Nat'l Packaging Purch Mgr
Lisa Gurusinghe,
   Commun & Design Coord

Redcliff Realty Management Inc.

1200-40 University Ave.
Toronto, ON M5J 1T1
Tel 416-362-0045
Fax 416-362-9646
www.redcliffrealty.com
AKA: Redcliff Realty Group
Line: Provides commercial, industrial and retail real estate management services.
NAICS: 531310
#Emp: 250-499 (Tor)
#TorLoc: 3
Own: Private Company
Key: George Schott, Chmn & CEO
Jonathan Fleischer, Exec VP,
   Commercial Properties
Gina Papazian, Sr VP Corp Admin
Sam Schembri, CFO
Massimo Lucivero, IT Mgr
David Wyatt, Nat'l VP, Retail Leasing
Ryan Schott, Dir of Mktg
David Veale, VP, Leasing, Commercial

RedKnee Inc.

500-2560 Matheson Blvd. East
Mississauga, ON L4W 4Y9
Tel 905-625-2622
Fax 905-625-2773
www.redknee.com
Line: Delivers mobile applications and infrastructure solutions for network operators.
NAICS: 511210
#Emp: 250-499 (Tor)
#TorLoc: 1
Own: Private Company
Key: Lucas Skoczkowski, CEO
Michael Bryce, VP Global Ops
David Charron, CFO
Vishal Kothari, VP Sales & Mktg

Redline Communications

302 Town Centre Blvd., 3rd Fl.
Markham, ON L3R 0E8
Tel 905-479-8344
Fax 905-479-5331
www.redlinecommunications.com
Line: Designs and manufactures standard-based broadband wireless access solutions.
NAICS: 541510
#Emp: 100-249 (Tor)
Own: Private Company
Key: Eric Melka, Acting Pres & CEO
Bruce MacInnis, CFO
Mike Moldoveanu,
   Founder & Chief Strategy Officer
Lynda Partner, VP Mktg

Redpath Sugar Ltd.

95 Queen's Quay East
Toronto, ON M5E 1A3
Tel 416-366-3561
Fax 416-366-7550
www.redpathsugar.com
Line: Refines sugar and blends and packs sugar containing products.
NAICS: 311310
#Emp: 250-499 (Tor)
#TorLoc: 1
Own: Private Company
Par: American Sugar Refining (US)
Key: Jonathan Bamberger, Pres
Peter Toppazzini, Dir of Sales

Reed Construction Data

500 Hood Rd., 4th Fl.
Markham, ON L3R 9Z3
Tel 905-752-5408
Fax 905-752-5454
www.reedconstructiondata.com
AKA: Lexis Nexis; Narcourt; Reed Exhibitions
Line: Develops, prints and publishes products for construction, design and manufacturing professionals.
NAICS: 514210
#Emp: 75-99 (Tor)
#TorLoc: 1
Own: Private Company
Par: Reed Business Information (US)
Key: Mark Casaletto, VP & GM
Kiera Brown, HR Mgr

Reefer Sales and Service

425 Gibraltar Dr.
Mississauga, ON L5T 2S9
Tel 905-795-0234
Fax 905-795-0018
www.reefersales.com
Line: Provides refrigerated transport.
NAICS: 484229
#Emp: 75-99 (Tor)
#TorLoc: 1
Own: Private Company
Key: Ken Henwood, Pres
Larry Palko, CFO

Reena

927 Clark Ave. West
Thornhill, ON L4J 8G6
Tel 905-889-6484
Fax 905-889-3827
www.reena.org
Line: Provides support services for persons with disabilities.
NAICS: 624120
#Emp: 250-499 (Tor)
#TorLoc: 2
Own: Not-for-profit
Key: Sandy Keshen, Pres & CEO
Sandy Stemp,
    Asst Exec Dir & Program Dir
Lalji Mohamed, HR Mgr
Sol Flesing, CFO
Minnie Ross, Commun Mgr

Reflections Furniture Industries Ltd.

600 Calyson Rd.
Toronto, ON M9M 2H2
Tel 905-856-2500
Fax 905-856-6130
www.reflectionsfurniture.net
AKA: Casual Concepts
Line: Manufactures metal casual dining suites and furniture.
NAICS: 337126
#Emp: 100-249 (Tor)
#TorLoc: 1
Own: Private Company
Key: Stanley Mintz, Pres
Alan Mintz, VP Sales
Jim Nopper, Dir of Corp Mktg

Regal Confections

2-175 Britannia Rd. East
Mississauga, ON L4Z 4B8
Tel 905-507-6868
Fax 905-507-3260
www.regalcandy.com
AKA: Sweet Expressions Foods Inc.
Line: Produces gift baskets.
NAICS: 445292
#Emp: 75-99 (Tor)
#TorLoc: 1
Own: Private Company
Key: Lenny Melvin, GM

Regency Apparel Company Ltd.

180 Middlefield Rd.
Toronto, ON M1S 4M6
Tel 416-504-6090
Fax 416-504-6920
Line: Manufactures sports clothing.
NAICS: 315190
#Emp: 100-249 (Tor)
#TorLoc: 1
Own: Private Company
Key: Johnny Wong, Pres

Regional Municipality of Durham

605 Rossland Rd. East
Whitby, ON L1N 6A3
Tel 905-668-7711
Fax 905-668-9935
www.durham.ca
AKA: Durham; Region of Durham
Line: Operates as a guide to municipal government services and provides tourist and business information.
NAICS: 913910
#Emp: 1000-4999 (Tor)
#TorLoc: 8
Own: Government
Key: Garry Cubitt, CAO
Roger M. Anderson, Reg Chair & CEO
Garth Johns, Comr of HR
Jim Clapp, Comr of Fin
Ray Briggs, Corp Info Officer
Doug Lindeblom,
    Dir of Economic Dev & Tourism
Sherri Munns-Audet,
    Dir of Corp Commun

Regional Municipality of Halton

1151 Bronte Rd.
Oakville, ON L6M 3L1
Tel 905-825-6000
Fax 905-825-4032
www.halton.ca
AKA: Halton; Region of Halton
NAICS: 913910
#Emp: 1000-4999 (Tor)
#TorLoc: 4
Own: Government
Key: Gary Carr, Reg Chmn
John Phelan, Dir of HR
David Trevisani,
    Dir of Financial & Purch Services
Ralph Blauel, Dir of Tech Services
John Davidson, Dir of Business Dev
Carleen Carroll,
    Dir of Strategic Commun

Regional Municipality of Peel

10 Peel Centre Dr.
Brampton, ON L6T 4B9
Tel 905-791-7800
Fax 905-791-7871
www.region.peel.on.ca
AKA: Peel; Region of Peel
NAICS: 913910
#Emp: 1000-4999 (Tor)
#TorLoc: 50
Own: Government
Key: David Szwarc, CAO
Emil Kolb, Reg Chair
Janet Menard, Commr of HR
Norma Trim,
    Commr of Corp Services & CFO
James Macintyre, Dir of Purch
Adam Hughes, Dir of IT
Karla Hale, Dir of Commun Services

The Regional Municipality of York

17250 Yonge St.
Newmarket, ON L3Y 6Z1
Tel 905-895-1231
Fax 905-895-0847
www.york.ca
AKA: York Region; Region of York
NAICS: 913910
#Emp: 1000-4999 (Tor)
#TorLoc: 67
Own: Government
Key: Bill Fisch, Reg Chair
Bruce Macgregor, CAO
Karen Close, Dir of HR
Bill Hughes, Comr of Fin & Reg Treas
Louis Shallal, Chief IT Officer
Patrick Casey, Dir of Corp Commun

Regional Nursing Services

2-28 Fulton Way
Richmond Hill, ON L4B 1J5
Tel 905-709-0700
Fax 905-709-4147
www.regionalnursingservices.com
Line: Provides nursing services.
NAICS: 621390
#Emp: 250-499 (Tor)
#TorLoc: 1
Own: Private Company
Key: Angela Westheuser, Pres
Lisa Russomano, Ops Mgr
Carolin Cayle, HR Mgr
Kathleen Kennedy, Cont

Rehab Express Inc.

123-6 Lansing Sq.
Toronto, ON M2J 1T5
Tel 416-226-6141
Fax 416-226-2469
www.closingthegap.ca
AKA: Closing the Gap Healthcare
Group
Line: Provides speech pathology,
physiotherapy and social work
services.
NAICS: 621340
#Emp: 100-249 (Tor)
Own: Private Company
Key: Connie Clerici, Pres & CEO
Kathy Underwood, COO
Israel Mendez, CAO

Reilly's Security Services

11-1120 Caledonia Rd.
Toronto, ON M6A 2W5
Tel 416-256-3199
Fax 416-256-9589
www.reillysecurity.com
Line: Provides security services.
NAICS: 561611 561612
#Emp: 250-499 (Tor)
Own: Private Company
Key: Nick Migliore, Pres

Reinhart Foods Ltd.

500-15 Allstate Pkwy.
Markham, ON L3R 5B4
Tel 905-754-3500
Fax 905-754-3504
www.reinhartfoods.com
Line: Specializes in food processing.
NAICS: 311940 311420
#Emp: 75-99 (Tor)
#TorLoc: 1
Own: Private Company
Key: Tom Singer, Pres
Jennie Soong, HR Mgr
Debra Burgess, Business Dev Mgr

Reliable Bookbinders Ltd.

20 Rolark Dr.
Toronto, ON M1R 4G2
Tel 416-291-5571
Fax 416-291-3669
www.reliablegrp.com
Line: Provides binding and mailing
services.
NAICS: 541860 323120
#Emp: 100-249 (Tor)
#TorLoc: 1

Own: Private Company
Key: Roy David Johnson, Pres
Calvin Williams, Ops Mgr
Bernie Fernandez, CFO
Michael Lecointre, Systems Admr
Mary Pender, Sales & Mktg Mgr

Reliance Comfort Limited Partnership

1200-2 Lansing Sq.
Toronto, ON M2J 4P8
Tel 416-499-7600
Fax 416-499-5085
www.reliancehomecomfort.com
Line: Offers installation and service of
heating and cooling equipment.
NAICS: 232520
#Emp: 250-499 (Tor)
#TorLoc: 1
Own: Private Company
Key: Roger Rossi, Pres & CEO
Rick Muzar, VP Ops
Catherine David Nolan, CFO
Celso Mello, CIO

Re/Max 2000 Realty Inc., Brokerage

1885 Wilson Ave.
Toronto, ON M9M 1A2
Tel 416-743-2000
Fax 416-743-2031
www.remax2000.ca
Line: Operates a real estate business.
NAICS: 531210
#Emp: 100-249 (Tor)
#TorLoc: 2
Own: Private Company
Key: Ralph Nardi, Owner/Broker
Mary Di Felice, VP
Diana Laruccia, Asst to Owner

Re/Max Aboutowne Realty Corp.

67 Lakeshore Rd. West
Oakville, ON L6K 1C9
Tel 905-338-9000
Fax 905-338-3411
www.remaxaboutowne.com
Line: Provides residential, commercial
and business brokerage services.
NAICS: 531210
#Emp: 100-249 (Tor)
#TorLoc: 2
Own: Private Company
Key: Augy Carnovale, Broker & Owner

Re/Max Condos Plus Corp., Brokerage

45 Harbour Sq.
Toronto, ON M5J 2G4
Tel 416-203-6636
Fax 416-203-1908
www.remaxcondosplus.com
Line: Operates a real estate agency.
NAICS: 531210
#Emp: 100-249 (Tor)
#TorLoc: 4
Own: Private Company
Key: Jamie Johnston, Broker & Owner

Re/Max Crossroads Realty Inc., Brokerage

1055 McNicoll Ave.
Toronto, ON M1W 3W6
Tel 416-491-4002
Fax 416-756-1267
www.remaxcrossroads.ca
Line: Provides real estate agents,
brokers and managers.
NAICS: 531210
#Emp: 100-249 (Tor)
#TorLoc: 1
Own: Private Company
Key: Barney Johnson, Broker & Owner
Lois Hampton, Admr

Re/Max Excellence Realty Inc.

3700 Steeles Ave. West
Woodbridge, ON L4L 2S6
Tel 905-856-1111
Fax 905-856-2843
Line: Operates a real estate firm.
NAICS: 531210
#Emp: 100-249 (Tor)
#TorLoc: 2
Own: Private Company
Key: Patricia Costanzo,
Broker of Record

Re/Max Executive Realty Inc.

8 Weldrick Rd. West
Richmond Hill, ON L4C 3T8
Tel 905-883-4922
Fax 905-883-1521
www.remax-executive.com
Line: Operates a real estate firm.
NAICS: 531210
#Emp: 75-99 (Tor)
#TorLoc: 3
Own: Private Company
Key: Debra Bain, Broker of Record

Re/Max First Realty Ltd.

1154 Kingston Rd.
Pickering, ON L1V 1B4
Tel 905-831-3300
Fax 905-831-8147
www.remax-first.com
NAICS: 531210
#Emp: 100-249 (Tor)
#TorLoc: 2
Own: Private Company
Key: Ron Gordon, Broker of Record

Re/Max Garden City Realty Inc.

720 Guelph Line
Burlington, ON L7R 4E2
Tel 905-333-3500
Fax 905-333-3616
www.remax-gardencity-on.com
Line: Operates a real estate agency.
NAICS: 531210
#Emp: 75-99 (Tor)
#TorLoc: 1
Own: Private Company
Key: Wayne Quirk, Broker & Owner

Re/Max Hallmark Realty Ltd.

108-245 Fairview Mall Dr.
Toronto, ON M2J 4T1
Tel 416-494-7653
Fax 416-494-0016
www.remaxhallmark.com
NAICS: 531210
#Emp: 250-499 (Tor)
#TorLoc: 4
Own: Private Company
Key: Debra Bain, Broker & Owner
Ken McLachlan, Broker of Record
Steve Tabrizi, Broker

Re/Max Performance Realty Inc., Brokerage

141-1140 Burnhamthorpe Rd. West
Mississauga, ON L5C 4E9
Tel 905-270-2000
Fax 905-270-0047
www.remaxperformance.ca
Line: Provides real estate services.
NAICS: 531210
#Emp: 100-249 (Tor)
#TorLoc: 2
Own: Private Company
Key: John Bradley,
Broker of Record & Owner

Re/Max Professionals Inc.

1 East Mall Cres.
Toronto, ON M9B 6G8
Tel 416-232-9000
Fax 416-232-1281
www.remax-professionals-on.com
Line: Provides real estate services.
NAICS: 531210
#Emp: 250-499 (Tor)
#TorLoc: 3
Own: Private Company
Key: Darryl Mitchell, Broker & Mgr
Christine Mitchell, Broker & Mgr

Re/Max Realtron Realty Inc., Brokerage

88 Konrad Cres.
Markham, ON L3R 8T7
Tel 905-944-8800
Fax 905-944-1980
www.realtronhomes.com
Line: Provides residential and ICI real estate services.
NAICS: 531210
#Emp: 100-249 (Tor)
#TorLoc: 7
Own: Private Company
Key: Richard Pilarski,
Broker & Co-Owner
Alex Pilarski, Broker & Co-Owner
Louis Glaser, Cont & Tech Support

Re/Max Realty Enterprises Inc.

1697 Lakeshore Rd. West
Mississauga, ON L5J 1J4
Tel 905-855-2200
Fax 905-855-2201
www.remaxrealtyenterprises.com
Line: Operates a real estate agency.
NAICS: 531210
#Emp: 100-249 (Tor)
#TorLoc: 2
Own: Private Company
Key: David Ferrari, Broker

Re/Max Realty One Inc., Brokerage

102-50 Burnhamthorpe Rd. West
Mississauga, ON L5B 3C2
Tel 905-277-0771
Fax 905-277-0086
www.remaxrealtyoneinc.com
Line: Operates a real estate firm.
NAICS: 531210
#Emp: 75-99 (Tor)
#TorLoc: 1
Own: Private Company
Key: Mehrdad Hosseini,
Broker of Record & Owner

Re/Max Realty Services Inc.

295 Queen St. East
Brampton, ON L6W 3R1
Tel 905-456-1000
Fax 905-456-1924
www.4561000.com
Line: Operates a real estate brokerage firm.
NAICS: 531210
#Emp: 100-249 (Tor)
#TorLoc: 2
Own: Private Company
Key: Mike Zuccato, Broker of Record
Dorothy Short, Fin Mgr
Robin Clark, Sales Mgr

Re/Max Realty Specialists Inc.

6850 Millcreek Dr.
Mississauga, ON L5N 4J9
Tel 905-858-3434
Fax 905-858-2682
www.remaxspec.on.ca
Line: Provides real estate services.
NAICS: 531210
#Emp: 250-499 (Tor)
#TorLoc: 5
Own: Private Company
Key: Greg Gilmour, Broker & Owner
Paul Fletcher, Mgr
Kathy Munshi, Corp Admr

Re/Max Rouge River Realty Inc.

1-6758 Kingston Rd.
Toronto, ON M1B 1G8
Tel 416-286-3993
Fax 416-286-3348
www.remaxrougeriver.com
Line: Provides air traffic control, flight information, weather briefings, aeronautical information services, airport advisory services and electronic aids to navigation.
NAICS: 531210
#Emp: 500-999 (Tor)
#TorLoc: 5
Own: Private Company
Key: David Pearce, Pres & CEO
Melody Pearce, GM, Whitby
Dolores Pearce, Fin & Acctng
Jennifer Pearce, GM, Pickering

Re/Max Ultimate Realty Inc.

1739 Bayview Ave.
Toronto, ON M4G 3C1
Tel 416-487-5131
Fax 416-487-1750
www.remaxultimate.com
Line: Provides real estate services.
NAICS: 531210
#Emp: 100-249 (Tor)
#TorLoc: 1
Own: Private Company
Key: Tim Syrianos,
   Broker of Record & Pres
Tom Merrick, VP & Mgr

Re/Max West Realty Inc.

96 Rexdale Blvd.
Toronto, ON M9W 1N7
Tel 416-745-2300
Fax 416-745-1952
www.remaxwest.com
Line: Provides real estate services.
NAICS: 531210
#Emp: 250-499 (Tor)
#TorLoc: 6
Own: Private Company
Key: Frank Colatosti, Pres & CEO

Renaissance Toronto Hotel Downtown

1 Blue Jays Way
Toronto, ON M5V 1J4
Tel 416-341-7100
Fax 416-341-5091
www.marriott.com
NAICS: 721111
#Emp: 100-249 (Tor)
#TorLoc: 1
Own: Private Company
Key: Mark Ive, GM
Natalie Whyte, Dir of HR
Roshan Miskin, Cont
Stephanie Saagi, Sales Mgr

Renin Corp.

110 Walker Dr.
Brampton, ON L6T 4H6
Tel 905-791-7930
Fax 905-791-3813
www.renincorp.com
Line: Manufactures mirrored doors, mirrors, and sliding and bi-fold door hardware.
NAICS: 332321 332510
#Emp: 100-249 (Tor)
#TorLoc: 2
Own: Private Company
Par: Renin Corp. (US)
Key: Leroy James, Plant Mgr
Bryan Sonnenberg, Corp Cont
Susan Cuda, HR Generalist
Aziz Hirji, CFO
Robin Ramenenrin, Materials Mgr
Ali Moghadam, IT Mgr

Replex Automotive Corp.

5395 Maingate Dr.
Mississauga, ON L4W 1G6
Tel 905-238-0224
Fax 905-238-8481
Line: Manufactures automotive brake parts.
NAICS: 336340
#Emp: 75-99 (Tor)
Own: Private Company
Par: Fasa Friction Laboratories Inc. (CDA)
Key: Lorne Cherry, Pres

Reprodux Copy Centres Ltd.

130 Willowdale Ave.
Toronto, ON M2N 4Y2
Tel 416-223-6272
Fax 416-223-6989
www.reprodux.com
Line: Provides printing services.
NAICS: 323120 323119
#Emp: 75-99 (Tor)
#TorLoc: 8
Own: Private Company
Key: Jack Long, Pres
Kim Long, GM

ReserveAmerica

120-2480 Meadowvale Blvd.
Mississauga, ON L5N 8M6
Tel 905-286-6600
Fax 905-286-0371
www.reserveamerica.com
Line: Provides camping reservation and campground management solutions.
NAICS: 541510
#Emp: 100-249 (Tor)
#TorLoc: 1
Own: Public Company
Par: Active Network Inc. (US)
Key: David Dutch, GM
Frank Helwig,
   VP Product Management
Christine Soncin, Dir of HR

Respiron Care-Plus Inc.

103-2085 Hurontario St.
Mississauga, ON L5A 4G1
Tel 905-306-0202
Fax 905-306-1709
www.closingthegap.ca
AKA: Closing the Gap Healthcare Group
Line: Provides multi disciplinary home health care services.
NAICS: 621610
#Emp: 100-249 (Tor)
Own: Private Company
Key: Connie Clerici, Pres & CEO
Kathy Underwood,
   VP Ops & Privacy Officer
Israel Mendez, CAO

Revera Inc.

55 Standish Crt., 8th Fl.
Mississauga, ON L5R 4B2
Tel 289-360-1200
Fax 289-360-1164
www.reveraliving.com
Line: Operates nursing care and retirement care facilities.
NAICS: 623110 623310
#Emp: 1000-4999 (Tor)
#TorLoc: 29
Own: Private Company
Key: Jeffrey C. Lozon, Pres & CEO
Daniel Gagnon, CFO
Cathie Brow, Sr VP HR
Nina Thomsen, CIO
Anna-Lisa Montesso,
   Sr VP Sales & Mktg
Janet Ko, VP Commun & Pub Affairs

Revere Industries, LLC

2150 Williams Pkwy. East
Brampton, ON L6S 5X6
Tel 905-793-6466
Fax 905-790-7408
www.revereindustries.com
AKA: Revere Plastics Systems
Line: Produces injection moulded plastic products.
NAICS: 326198
#Emp: 75-99 (Tor)
#TorLoc: 1
Own: Private Company
Par: Revere Plastic Systems (US)
Key: John Harris, GM
Vicky Nalli, HR Mgr

Reversomatic Manufacturing

790 Rowntree Dairy Rd.
Woodbridge, ON L4L 5V3
Tel 905-851-6701
Fax 905-851-8376
www.reversomatic.com
Line: Manufactures blowers, ensilage and cutters.
NAICS: 333110
#Emp: 100-249 (Tor)
#TorLoc: 1
Own: Private Company
Key: Joe Salerno, Pres

Rexel Canada Electrical Inc.

5600 Keaton Cres.
Mississauga, ON L5R 3G3
Tel 905-568-2425
Fax 905-568-2987
www.rexel.ca
Line: Distributes electrical parts and supplies to the industrial, commercial, communications and utilities markets.
NAICS: 417320
#Emp: 500-999 (Tor)
#TorLoc: 32
Own: Private Company
Par: Rexel Inc. (FR)
Key: Jeff Hall, CEO
Damien Barrett, VP Ops & Logistics
Ed Wyzykowski, VP HR
Patrick Foley, VP Fin
Wayne Donaldson, VP Mktg & Purch

Rex Pak Ltd.

85 Thornmount Dr.
Toronto, ON M1B 5V3
Tel 416-755-3324
Fax 416-755-6520
www.rexpak.com
Line: Blends and packages dry food products.
NAICS: 561910
#Emp: 100-249 (Tor)
#TorLoc: 1
Own: Private Company
Key: Louis Sabatini, Pres
Denis Sabatini, VP

RF Porter Plastering Ltd.

75D Konrad Cres.
Markham, ON L3R 8T8
Tel 905-940-4131
Fax 905-474-1611
www.rfporter.com
Line: Offers contract plastering services.
NAICS: 232410
#Emp: 75-99 (Tor)
Own: Private Company
Key: Reginald Porter, Pres
Mark Porter, GM

RHI Canada Inc.

4355 Fairview St.
P.O. Box 910
Burlington, ON L7L 2A4
Tel 905-639-8660
Fax 905-639-5357
www.rhi-ag.com
Line: Manufactures, installs, sells and services refractory products.
NAICS: 327120
#Emp: 100-249 (Tor)
#TorLoc: 2
Own: Private Company
Par: RHI AG (AUS)
Key: Phil Poulin, Dir of Fin
Larry Reimer, HR Mgr
Dan Masson, Dir of Purch & Logistics
Daniel Lemay, Dir of IT

Richards Packaging Inc.

6095 Ordan Dr.
Mississauga, ON L5T 2M7
Tel 905-670-7760
Fax 905-670-1960
www.richardspackaging.com
AKA: Rigo Products
Line: Manufactures and distributes glass and plastic containers, closures, sprayers, pumps, desiccants, vials and related products.
NAICS: 326198 327214
#Emp: 100-249 (Tor)
#TorLoc: 2
Own: Private Company
Key: David Prupas, Pres
Gerry Glen, CEO
Enzil Digennaro, CFO
Colin Hammar, Purch Mgr

Richards-Wilcox Canada

5100 Timberlea Blvd.
Mississauga, ON L4W 2S5
Tel 905-625-0037
Fax 905-625-0057
www.rwdoors.com
AKA: R-W

Line: Manufactures garage doors.
NAICS: 332321
#Emp: 100-249 (Tor)
#TorLoc: 2
Own: Private Company
Par: Raynor (US)
Key: Raymond Friesen, Pres
Ginette Kent, HR Generalist
Ed Chin, VP Fin
Peter Coley, Purch Mgr
Donald Mann, IS Mgr

Richards Wilcox Door Systems Limited

1045 Rangeview Rd.
Mississauga, ON L5E 1H2
Tel 905-274-5850
Fax 905-274-9413
www.rwdoorsystems.com
AKA: Select Overhead Door Service Inc.
Line: Sells and maintains overhead doors.
NAICS: 416320
#Emp: 75-99 (Tor)
Own: Private Company
Key: Tony Wong, GM

Richmond Hill Country Club

8905 Bathurst St.
Richmond Hill, ON L4C 0H4
Tel 905-731-2800
Fax 905-731-7283
www.richmondhillcountryclub.com
NAICS: 713910
#Emp: 100-249 (Tor)
#TorLoc: 1
Own: Private Company
Par: RHCC Holdings Ltd. (CDA)
Key: Phillip Macarz, Owner
Maureen Arluck, Club Admr

Richmond Hill Fire Department

A Div. of The Town of Richmond Hill
1200 Elgin Mills Rd. East
Richmond Hill, ON L4F 1M4
Tel 905-883-5444
Fax 905-883-0866
www.town.richmond-hill.on.ca
NAICS: 913140
#Emp: 100-249 (Tor)
#TorLoc: 6
Own: Government
Key: Shane Baker,
   Cmmr of Community Services
Steve Kraft, Acting Fire Chief

Richmond Hill Public Library

1 Atkinson St.
Richmond Hill, ON L4C 0H5
Tel 905-770-0310
Fax 905-770-0312
www.rhpl.richmondhill.on.ca
NAICS: 514121
#Emp: 100-249 (Tor)
#TorLoc: 4
Own: Government
Key: Jane Horrocks, CEO

Richtree Market Restaurants Inc.

1210-401 Bay St.
Toronto, ON M5M 2Y4
Tel 416-366-8122
Fax 416-366-8635
www.richtree.ca
Line: Operates and offers restaurant,
consumer products, fast food, take-out
and catering services.
NAICS: 722210
#Emp: 500-999 (Tor)
#TorLoc: 6
Own: Private Company
Key: Matt Williams, VP & COO
Patric Laflamme, Reg Mgr
William Jean, VP & CFO
Kevin McCormack,
   Dir of Corp Mktg & Dev

Ricoh Canada Inc.

300-5520 Explorer Dr.
Mississauga, ON L4W 5L1
Tel 905-795-9659
Fax 905-795-6926
www.ricoh.ca
Line: Provides document and imaging
solutions.
NAICS: 561410
#Emp: 250-499 (Tor)
#TorLoc: 5
Own: Private Company
Par: Ricoh Corp. (US)
Key: Glenn Laverty, Pres & CEO
Kevin Braun,
   Dir of People & Excellence
Phyllis Gallagher, VP Fin & CFO
Mike Fast, VP Tech Services
Kevin Fancey, Sr VP Sales
Dan Newman, Sr Commun Mgr

RioCan Real Estate Investment Trust

500-2300 Yonge St.
P.O. Box 2386
Toronto, ON M4P 1E4
Tel 416-866-3033
Fax 416-866-3020
www.riocan.com
AKA: Riocan Property Services Trust
Line: Provides real estate and property
management services.
NAICS: 531310
#Emp: 250-499 (Tor)
#TorLoc: 56
Own: Public Company
Key: Edward Sonshine, Pres & CEO
Frederic Waks, COO
Suzanne Marianeau, VP HR
Raghunath Davloor, Sr VP & CFO

RioCan Yonge Eglinton Centre

20 Eglinton Ave. West
Toronto, ON M4R 1K8
Tel 416-489-2300
Fax 416-489-7184
www.yongeeglintoncentre.com
Line: Operates a commercial property
management and leasing company.
NAICS: 531310
#Emp: 75-99 (Tor)
#TorLoc: 1
Own: Private Company
Key: Domenic Clarino, GM
Nancy Medlock, Mktg Mgr

Rite Pak Produce Co. Ltd.

342-165 The Queensway
Toronto, ON M8Y 1H8
Tel 416-252-3121
Fax 416-252-0562
www.ritepakproduce.com
Line: Imports produce.
NAICS: 413150
#Emp: 100-249 (Tor)
Own: Private Company
Key: Domenic Raso, CEO

Riva Plumbing Ltd.

8-25 Brodie Dr.
Richmond Hill, ON L4B 3K7
Tel 905-764-2900
Fax 905-771-7632
Line: Provides residential, commercial,
and industrial plumbing contracting.
NAICS: 232520
#Emp: 100-249 (Tor)
#TorLoc: 1
Own: Private Company
Key: Tony Ferrari, Pres
Luca Montanaro, VP

Riverglen Haven Nursing Home-Sutton

160 High St.
Sutton, ON L0E 1R0
Tel 905-722-3631
Fax 905-722-8638
www.atkcareinc.ca
Line: Operates long-term care facility
for the elderly.
NAICS: 623310
#Emp: 100-249 (Tor)
Own: Private Company
Par: ATK Care Inc. (CDA)
Key: Thomas P. Kannampuzha, Pres
Karen Ryan, Admr
Pauline Gallie, Acct

Riviera Parque

2800 Hwy. 7 West
Concord, ON L4K 1W8
Tel 416-987-4400
Fax 905-738-6987
www.rivieraparque.com
Line: Operates a convention and
banquet hall.
NAICS: 531120
#Emp: 100-249 (Tor)
#TorLoc: 1
Own: Private Company
Key: Danny Bonni, Exec Dir
Ivan Tolfa, Owner

RJ McCarthy Ltd.

360 Evans Ave.
Toronto, ON M8Z 1K5
Tel 416-593-6900
Fax 416-593-6229
www.rjmccarthy.com
Line: Manufactures and specializes in
school uniforms, corporate apparel and
corporate promotional products.
NAICS: 315234 315226
#Emp: 75-99 (Tor)
#TorLoc: 6
Own: Private Company
Key: John Kelleher, Pres & CEO

RMP Athletic Locker Ltd.

6085 Belgrave Rd.
Mississauga, ON L5R 4E6
Tel 905-361-2390
Fax 905-361-2418
www.brooksrunning.ca
AKA: Brooks Athletic Shoes
NAICS: 414110 414120
#Emp: 100-249 (Tor)
#TorLoc: 1
Own: Private Company
Key: Mike Dyon, Pres & Owner
Karen Barber, Office Mgr
Stephen Wong, Cont

Roadsport Honda

940 Ellesmere Rd.
Toronto, ON M1P 2W8
Tel 416-291-9501
Fax 416-291-0646
www.roadsport.com
AKA: Roadsport Ltd.
Line: Operates a car dealership.
NAICS: 441110 441120
#Emp: 75-99 (Tor)
#TorLoc: 1
Own: Private Company
Key: Aneta Jaczynski, Pres
Chris Gauthier, GM

Roan International Inc.

4-2155 Dunwin Dr.
Mississauga, ON L5L 4M1
Tel 905-820-3511
Fax 905-820-0679
www.roan.ca
Line: Specializes in engineering design
and drafting services.
NAICS: 541340 541330
#Emp: 100-249 (Tor)
#TorLoc: 1
Own: Private Company
Key: Andrew McGee, Pres

Robert Bosch Inc.

6955 Creditview Rd.
Mississauga, ON L5N 1R1
Tel 905-826-6060
Fax 905-826-5120
www.bosch.com
AKA: Bosch; JKIL; Gilmour
Line: Sells automotive parts, portable
electric power tools and accessories,
security systems, and lawn and garden
products.
NAICS: 416330 415290
#Emp: 100-249 (Tor)
#TorLoc: 1
Own: Private Company
Par: Robert Bosch GmbH (GER)
Key: Niall Davidson,
   VP & GM, Automotive
John Scinocca, VP & GM, Power Tools
Michael Capron, HR Mgr
Michael Langstaff, VP Fin & Admin

Robert B. Somerville Company Ltd.

13176 Dufferin St.
King City, ON L7B 1K5
Tel 905-833-3100
Fax 905-833-3111
www.rbsomerville.com
Line: Constructs pipelines, including
gas, oil, and finished products;
maintains utility, hydro and phone
lines.
NAICS: 231330
#Emp: 250-499 (Tor)
#TorLoc: 3
Own: Private Company
Key: Nick de Koning, Pres
Rodger McGee, VP Ops
Tracy Cooke, Payroll Mgr & HR Rep
Ron Sutton, VP Fin

Robert Half Canada Inc.

820-181 Bay St.
P.O. Box 824
Toronto, ON M5J 2T3
Tel 416-350-2330
Fax 416-350-3573
www.roberthalf.com
Line: Provides temporary and
permanent placement of accounting,
finance, information services and
office personnel.
NAICS: 561310
#Emp: 100-249 (Tor)
#TorLoc: 8
Own: Public Company
Par: Robert Half International Inc. (US)
Key: Kathryn C. Bolt, District Dir
Sidika Dhirani, District Admin Coord
Giselle Jones, Reg Mktg Mgr
Kristie Perrotte, District PR Mgr

Robert Kennedy Publishing

400 Matheson Blvd. West
Mississauga, ON L5R 3M1
Tel 905-507-3545
Fax 905-507-2372
www.rkpubs.com
AKA: Muscle Mag International
Line: Publishes fitness magazines.
NAICS: 511120
#Emp: 75-99 (Tor)
#TorLoc: 1
Own: Private Company
Key: Robert Kennedy, Publisher & Pres
Trudy Boetto, Office Mgr
Trevor Ratz, CFO
Lisa Snow, Dir of Production
Gill Daniels, Dir of Subscription Sales
Bev Greene, VP Newsstand,
   Sales & Mktg
Todd Hughes, VP Advertising

Robert Transport

300 Statesman Dr.
Mississauga, ON L5S 2A2
Tel 905-564-9999
Fax 905-790-1130
www.robert.ca
AKA: Groupe Robert
Line: Provides warehousing and
transportation distribution and logistic
services.
NAICS: 493120
#Emp: 250-499 (Tor)
#TorLoc: 1
Own: Private Company
Par: Groupe Robert (CDA)
Key: Eric Elliott,
   VP Integrated Business Solutions
Terri Ouimet, Admin Services

Robson Enterprises Inc.

2969 Sheppard Ave. East
Toronto, ON M1T 3J5
Tel 416-431-7911
Fax 416-431-8088
www.coverall.com
AKA: Coverall of Canada
Line: Franchises commercial cleaning.
NAICS: 561722
#Emp: 250-499 (Tor)
#TorLoc: 1
Own: Private Company
Key: Karl Robson, Pres
Florence Robson, Secy-Treas

Rocca Dickson Andreis Inc.

290 Rowntree Dairy Rd.
Woodbridge, ON L4L 9J7
Tel 905-652-8680
Fax 905-652-8688
www.rdainsurance.com
Line: Provides insurance and financial services.
NAICS: 524210
#Emp: 75-99 (Tor)
#TorLoc: 1
Own: Private Company
Key: Peter Rocca, Pres

Rochester Aluminum Smelting Canada Ltd.

31-35 Freshway Dr.
Vaughan, ON L4K 1R9
Tel 905-669-1222
Fax 905-669-5379
www.rochesteraluminum.com
Line: Operates aluminium smelting plant.
NAICS: 331313
#Emp: 75-99 (Tor)
#TorLoc: 1
Own: Private Company
Key: Gary Golden, Pres

Rockwell Automation Canada Ltd.

135 Dundas St.
Cambridge, ON N1R 5X1
Tel 519-623-1810
Fax 519-623-8930
www.rockwellautomation.ca
Line: Specializes in industrial automation, avionics, communication and electronic commerce.
NAICS: 541510
#Emp: 1000-4999 (Tor)
#TorLoc: 1
Own: Private Company
Key: Michael O'Sullivan, Plant Mgr
Jim Harding, Cont

Roff Logistics Inc.

241 Clarence St.
Brampton, ON L6W 4P2
Tel 905-457-2698
Fax 888-363-8387
Line: Operates a trucking company.
NAICS: 484229
#Emp: 100-249 (Tor)
#TorLoc: 1
Own: Private Company
Key: Clifford Tyrell, Owner

The Rogers Centre

3200-1 Blue Jays Way
Toronto, ON M5V 1J1
Tel 416-341-3663
Fax 416-341-3101
www.rogerscentre.com
Line: Manages sports and entertainment complex.
NAICS: 711319
#Emp: 100-249 (Tor)
#TorLoc: 1
Own: Private Company
Key: Paul Beeston, Pres & CEO
Fiona Nugent, Dir of HR
Stephen Brooks, VP Fin & Admin
Jason Diplock, VP Sales
Jay Stenhouse, VP Commun

Rogers Communications Inc.

333 Bloor St. East, 10th Fl.
Toronto, ON M4W 1G9
Tel 416-935-7777
Fax 416-935-3599
www.rogers.com
Line: Operates a diversified national communications and media company.
NAICS: 513320 513210 513220
#Emp: 1000-4999 (Tor)
#TorLoc: 181
Own: Public Company
Key: Nadir Mohamed, Pres & CEO
Alan Horn, Chmn
Rob Bruce, Pres, Commun
Kevin Pennington,
   Sr VP & Chief HR Officer
William Linton, Exec VP Fin & CFO
Jerry Brace, CIO
Jim Lovie,
   Exec VP Sales, Service & Dist
Terrie Tweddle, VP Commun

Rogers Media Inc.

777 Jarvis St., 6th Fl.
Toronto, ON M4Y 3B7
Tel 416-935-8200
Fax 416-935-8289
www.rogers.com
Line: Operates a media company involved in radio and television broadcasting, tele-shopping, publishing and new media businesses.
NAICS: 513120 513110
#Emp: 1000-4999 (Tor)
#TorLoc: 5
Own: Private Company
Par: Rogers Communications Inc. (CDA)
Key: Keith Pelley, Pres & CEO
Michael W.T. Gass, VP HR
Shannon Valliant, VP Financial Ops
Jim Diederichs, VP & CIO

Rogers Media Television

545 Lake Shore Blvd. West
Toronto, ON M5V 1A3
Tel 416-260-0060
Fax 416-260-3621
www.omnitv.ca
AKA: Omni Television
NAICS: 513120 513220
#Emp: 250-499 (Tor)
#TorLoc: 2
Own: Private Company
Par: Rogers Communications Inc. (CDA)
Key: Leslie Sole, CEO
Wayne Smith, Dir of HR
Navaid Mansuri, VP Fin & Admin

Rogers Publishing

A Div. of Rogers Media Inc.
333 Bloor St. East
Toronto, ON M4W 1G9
Tel 416-764-2000
Fax 416-764-3934
www.rogers.com
Line: Publishes magazines.
NAICS: 511120
#Emp: 1000-4999 (Tor)
#TorLoc: 1
Own: Public Company
Par: Rogers Communications Inc. (CDA)
Key: Brian Segal, Pres & CEO
Janet Stern, Dir of HR
Patrick Renard, VP Fin
Kathyrn Brownlie,
   Sr VP Advertising Sales
Tracy McKinley, VP Consumer Mktg
Suneel Khanna, Dir of Commun

Rogers Shared Operations

A Div. of Rogers Communications Inc.
45 Esna Park Dr.
Markham, ON L3R 1C9
Tel 905-513-8015
Fax 905-513-5330
www.rogers.com
NAICS: 514210
#Emp: 500-999 (Tor)
#TorLoc: 2
Own: Public Company
Key: Jerry Brace, VP IT & CIO
Terrie Tweddle, VP Corp Commun

Rogers Sportsnet Inc.

1 Mount Pleasant Rd.
Toronto, ON M4Y 3A1
Tel 416-764-6008
Fax 416-764-6001
www.sportsnet.ca
Line: Operates a television
broadcasting station.
NAICS: 513120
#Emp: 250-499 (Tor)
Own: Private Company
Key: Doug Beeforth, Pres

Roll Form Group

2304 Dixie Rd.
Mississauga, ON L4Y 1Z6
Tel 416-626-5436
Fax 416-626-0485
www.rollformgroup.com
Line: Manufactures sheet piling,
highway guide rail, metal roof and
floor decks, pre-painted metal siding
and custom roll formed products, and
heavy construction products.
NAICS: 331490
#Emp: 100-249 (Tor)
#TorLoc: 3
Own: Public Company
Par: Samuel, Son & Co Ltd. (CDA)
Key: Richard M. Balaz, Pres
Nick Parry, VP Ops
Gary C. Pang, VP Fin

Rolling Hills Golf Club

12808 Warden Ave.
Stouffville, ON L4A 7X5
Tel 905-888-1955
Fax 905-888-9561
www.clublink.ca
NAICS: 713910
#Emp: 100-249 (Tor)
#TorLoc: 1
Own: Private Company
Par: ClubLink Corp. (CDA)
Key: John Larter, Dir of Golf

Rollstamp Manufacturing

90 Snidercroft Rd.
Concord, ON L4K 2K1
Tel 905-738-3700
Fax 905-738-6214
www.magna.com
Line: Manufactures automotive trim.
NAICS: 336370
#Emp: 250-499 (Tor)
#TorLoc: 3
Own: Private Company
Par: Magna International Inc. (CDA)
Key: Fritz Reichenberger, GM
Sharon Muongchanh, HR Mgr

Roma Fence Ltd.

24 Cadetta Rd.
Brampton, ON L6T 3Z8
Tel 905-794-0416
Fax 905-794-0276
www.romafence.com
Line: Wholesales, retails and installs
commercial and residential fencing.
NAICS: 232910 416320
#Emp: 75-99 (Tor)
#TorLoc: 4
Own: Private Company
Key: Tony Marra, Pres
Kal Sandhu, HR Mgr
Amelia Valentino, Credit Mgr
Christina Marra, Dir of Sales & Purch
Gabe Vallozzi, Industrial Sales Mgr

Roma Moulding Inc.

360 Hanlan Rd.
Vaughan, ON L4L 8P6
Tel 905-850-1500
Fax 905-850-0706
www.romamoulding.com
Line: Distributes picture frame
mouldings.
NAICS: 339990
#Emp: 75-99 (Tor)
#TorLoc: 1
Own: Private Company
Key: John Gareri, Pres
Joseph Talotta, Dir of Ops

Ronald A. Chisholm Ltd.

3300-2 Bloor St. West
Toronto, ON M4W 3K3
Tel 416-967-6000
Fax 416-967-9457
www.rachisholm.com
Line: Wholesales commodities such as
meat, dairy, and food ingredient raw
materials.
NAICS: 413110 413160
#Emp: 100-249 (Tor)
#TorLoc: 1
Own: Private Company
Key: Jeffrey Ryley, Mng Dir
Don Damiani, Cont

Rona Ontario Inc.

1170 Martin Grove Rd.
Toronto, ON M9W 4X1
Tel 416-241-8844
Fax 416-246-5261
www.rona.ca
AKA: Rona Cashway; Rona Home &
Garden; Rona Lansing
Line: Retails lumber, building materials
and related hardware to the home
improvement and construction
industry.
NAICS: 444130 444190
#Emp: 1000-4999 (Tor)
#TorLoc: 19
Own: Public Company
Par: Rona Inc. (CDA)
Key: Robert Dutton, Pres & CEO
Luc Rodier, VP Ops
Christian Prouly,
    Sr VP People & Culture

Roots Canada Ltd.

1400 Castlefield Ave.
Toronto, ON M6B 4C4
Tel 416-781-3574
Fax 416-781-3259
www.roots.com
NAICS: 448140
#Emp: 1000-4999 (Tor)
#TorLoc: 32
Own: Private Company
Key: Don Green, Co-Owner
Michael Budman, Co-Owner
Laura Clark, Dir of HR
Raymond Perkins,
    Dir of PR & Special Events
Robert Sarner,
    Dir of Commun & Pub Affairs

Ropak Canada Inc.

2240 Wyecroft Rd.
Oakville, ON L6L 6M1
Tel 905-827-9340
Fax 905-827-8841
www.ropakcorp.com
Line: Manufactures plastic containers and material handling products.
NAICS: 326198
#Emp: 100-249 (Tor)
#TorLoc: 1
Own: Private Company
Par: Ropak Corp. (US)
Key: Mark Gibson, Plant Mgr
Maggie Low, HR & Payroll Mgr
Elaine Sonoda, Dir of Sales

Rosedale Golf Club

1901 Mt. Pleasant Rd.
Toronto, ON M4N 2W3
Tel 416-485-9321
Fax 416-485-7087
www.rosedalegolf.org
NAICS: 713910
#Emp: 100-249 (Tor)
#TorLoc: 1
Own: Private Company
Key: Peter K. Oldfield, GM
Nico Barrett, Club House Mgr
Tracy Ott, HR
Bill Vining, Cont
Scott Dickie, Purch Agent

Rosedale Livery Ltd.

12-3687 Nashua Dr.
Mississauga, ON L4V 1R3
Tel 905-677-9444
Fax 905-677-7051
www.rosedalelivery.com
Line: Provides limousine services.
NAICS: 485320
#Emp: 75-99 (Tor)
#TorLoc: 1
Own: Private Company
Key: Peter Dinnick, Pres
Douglas McCutcheon, Owner
Warren Crossley, Fleet Mgr
Brian Turpin, CIO

Rosedale Transport Ltd.

6845 Invader Cres.
Mississauga, ON L5T 2B7
Tel 905-670-0057
Fax 905-670-7271
www.rosedalegroup.com
Line: Provides logistics and transportation services and warehousing.
NAICS: 484110 484121
#Emp: 250-499 (Tor)
#TorLoc: 1
Own: Private Company
Par: The Rosedale Group (CDA)
Key: Rolly Uloth, Pres
Ron Uloth, VP & GM
Rosana Preston, Dir of HR & Admin
Ron Picklyk, Dir of Fin
Ron Irvine, Dir of Sales

Rose E. Dee (International) Ltd.

1450 Castlefield Ave.
Toronto, ON M6M 1Y6
Tel 416-658-2222
Fax 416-658-2219
www.rose-e-dee.com
NAICS: 414130
#Emp: 100-249 (Tor)
#TorLoc: 1
Own: Private Company
Key: Steve Pippert, Pres
Irene Stepkowski, Cont

Rothmans, Benson & Hedges Inc.

1500 Don Mills Rd.
Toronto, ON M3B 3L1
Tel 416-449-5525
Fax 416-449-4486
www.pmi.com
Line: Manufactures tobacco products.
NAICS: 312220
#Emp: 100-249 (Tor)
#TorLoc: 2
Own: Private Company
Par: Philip Morris International (US)
Key: John R. Barnett, Pres & CEO
Warren Finlay, Dir of Ops
Faryl Hausman,
   VP Regulatory Affairs & HR
Michael E. Frater, VP Fin & Admin
Jean Roberge,
   Dir of Materials & Logistics
Stephen MacLachlan, Dir of MIS
Derek J. Guile, VP Sales & Mktg

Roto-Mill Services Ltd.

560 Riddell Rd.
Orangeville, ON L9W 5H3
Tel 519-941-7686
Fax 519-941-5272
www.roto-millservices.com
Line: Provides road reclamation and recycling construction services for municipal and provincial highways and airports.
NAICS: 231310
#Emp: 100-249 (Tor)
#TorLoc: 1
Own: Private Company
Key: Ted A.E. Arscott, Pres
Cameron Wood, HR Mgr
Roy Winegardner, Acctng Mgr
Chris Thompson,
   Mktg Product Dev Mgr

Rouge Valley Health System

2867 Ellesmere Rd.
Toronto, ON M1E 4B9
Tel 416-284-8131
Fax 416-281-7323
www.rougevalley.ca
Line: Operates full service community hospitals.
NAICS: 622111
#Emp: 1000-4999 (Tor)
#TorLoc: 3
Own: Not-for-profit
Key: Rik Ganderton, Pres & CEO
Naresh Mohan, Chief of Staff
Kathy Gooding, VP HR
John Aldis, VP Corp Services & CFO
Boris Tsinman, Joint Dir,
   Procurement & Supply Chain
Thodoros Topaloglou, Deputy CIO
David Brazeau, Dir of Community
   Relns & Pub Affairs

Roxul Inc.

105-420 Bronte St. South
Milton, ON L9T 0H9
Tel 905-878-8474
Fax 905-878-8077
www.roxul.com
Line: Manufactures mineral wool insulation and acoustics, water repellent and fire resistant products.
NAICS: 327990
#Emp: 100-249 (Tor)
#TorLoc: 1
Own: Private Company
Par: Rockwool International A/S (DEN)

Key: Trent Ogilvie, Pres
Bent Jorgensen, VP Ops
Kimberly Mathieson, Dir of HR
Gordon Brown, VP Fin
Chuck Quirback, Logistics & Purch Mgr
John Scott,
  Tech Services & Standards Mgr
Dennis Beamish, VP Sales
Michael McLaughlin, VP, Business Dev

Royal Botanical Gardens

680 Plains Rd. West
Burlington, ON L7T 4H4
Tel 905-527-1158
Fax 905-577-0375
www.rbg.ca
Line: Tends botanical gardens and
natural areas open to visitors.
NAICS: 712130
#Emp: 100-249 (Tor)
#TorLoc: 1
Own: Private Company
Key: Mark Runciman, CEO
Terry Caddo, Dir of Ops
Grace Poles, HR Mgr
Lynn Gallant, Account Mgr

Royal Canadian Mounted Police

A Div. of Government of Canada
130 Dufferin Ave.
P.O. Box 3240, Stn. B
London, ON N6A 4K3
Tel 519-640-7267
Fax 519-640-7255
www.rcmp-grc.gc.ca
AKA: RCMP
Line: Offers federal police services.
NAICS: 911230
#Emp: 250-499 (Tor)
#TorLoc: 2
Own: Government
Key: Norm Mazerolle, Acting
Commanding Officer

Royal Canadian Yacht Club

141 St. George St.
Toronto, ON M5R 2L8
Tel 416-967-7245
Fax 416-967-5710
www.rcyc.ca
AKA: RCYC
Line: Encourages members to become
proficient in the personal management,
maintenance, control and handling
of their yachts, navigation and in all
matters pertaining to seamanship;
promotes yacht architecture, building
and sailing in Canadian waters;
promotes excellence in competitive
sailing; promotes such other sports and
social activities as may be desirable in
the interests of the club members.

NAICS: 713940 813990
#Emp: 100-249 (Tor)
#TorLoc: 2
Own: Not-for-profit
Key: Brian Pope, GM
Verna James, Dir of HR
Mary Chan, Cont
Vanessa Kelly,
  Dir of Membership & Mktg

The Royal Conservatory of Music

273 Bloor St. West
Toronto, ON M5S 1W2
Tel 416-408-2824
Fax 416-408-3096
www.rcmusic.ca
AKA: RCM; The Royal Conservatory
Line: Provides music instruction,
pedagogical examinations, music
publishing and development of
learning through arts education and
the performing arts.
NAICS: 611610
#Emp: 250-499 (Tor)
#TorLoc: 2
Own: Not-for-profit
Key: Peter Simon, Pres & CEO
Tony Flynn, CAO
Patricia Agostini, HR Dir
John Kucherepa, Dir of Fin
Krista O'Donnell, Chief Dev Officer
Gerry Dimnik, CIO
Karen Leiter, VP Mktg & Commun

Royal Containers Ltd.

80 Midair Crt.
Brampton, ON L6T 5V1
Tel 905-789-8787
Fax 905-789-7518
www.royalcontainers.com
Line: Manufactures corrugated
packaging.
NAICS: 322211
#Emp: 100-249 (Tor)
#TorLoc: 1
Own: Private Company
Key: Ross Nelson, Pres
Derek Mitchell, Plant Mgr
Kim Nelson, GM
Linda Mason, Acctng Mgr
Bill Routledge, Sales Mgr

Royal Doulton Canada Ltd.

700-305 Milner Ave.
Toronto, ON M1H 3C4
Tel 416-431-4202
Fax 416-431-6512
www.royaldoulton.com
Line: Imports, markets and distributes
china gifts, dinnerware, glass, crystal
and accessories.
NAICS: 418990
#Emp: 100-249 (Tor)
#TorLoc: 4
Own: Private Company
Par: Royal Doulton plc (UK)
Key: Tom Volpe, VP
Dawn Beckingham, Nat'l Sales Mgr
Michael Pearl, VP Sales & Mktg

Royal Envelope Ltd.

111 Jacob Keffer Pkwy.
Concord, ON L4K 4V1
Tel 905-879-0000
Fax 905-879-0156
www.royalenvelope.com
AKA: Alliance Envelope Ltd.
Line: Manufactures and prints
envelopes.
NAICS: 322230
#Emp: 100-249 (Tor)
#TorLoc: 1
Own: Partnership
Key: Peter Bowles, Pres
Lou Tucci, VP
Sanjay Jeganathan, Cont

Royal Group, Inc.

30 Royal Group Cres.
Woodbridge, ON L4H 1X9
Tel 905-850-9700
Fax 905-264-9184
www.royalgrouptech.com
Line: Manufactures plastic products.
NAICS: 326198
#Emp: 1000-4999 (Tor)
#TorLoc: 31
Own: Public Company
Par: Georgia Gulf Corp. (US)
Key: Paul Carrico, CEO

Royal LePage Burloak Real Estate Services - Mainway

200-3060 Mainway
Burlington, ON L7M 1A3
Tel 905-335-3042
Fax 905-335-1659
www.royallepageburlington.com
Line: Operates a real estate agency.
NAICS: 531210
#Emp: 75-99 (Tor)
#TorLoc: 2
Own: Private Company
Key: David Landry, Broker & Owner

Royal LePage Connect Realty

335 Bayly St.
Ajax, ON L1S 6M2
Tel 905-427-6522
Fax 905-427-6524
www.royallepageconnect.com
Line: Operates a real estate firm.
NAICS: 531210
#Emp: 100-249 (Tor)
#TorLoc: 2
Own: Private Company
Key: Kira Cope, Pres

Royal LePage Kingsbury Realty

200-30 Eglinton Ave. West
Mississauga, ON L5R 3E7
Tel 905-568-2121
Fax 905-568-2588
www.kingsburyrealty.com
Line: Provides real estate services.
NAICS: 531210
#Emp: 100-249 (Tor)
#TorLoc: 1
Own: Private Company
Key: David A. Hume, Broker
R. Kelly Ticknor, Broker
Kathryn Hume, Admr
David Hume, Jr., Mktg & Tech Mgr

Royal LePage Realty Centre, Brokerage

2150 Hurontario St.
Mississauga, ON L5B 1M8
Tel 905-279-8300
Fax 905-279-5344
www.rlprc.ca
Line: Operates a real estate agency.
NAICS: 531210
#Emp: 100-249 (Tor)
#TorLoc: 1
Own: Private Company
Key: Filippo Sbrocchi,
  Owner & Broker of Record
Joseph Sbrocchi, GM

Royal LePage Signature Realty

201-8 Sampson Mews
Toronto, ON M3C 0H5
Tel 416-443-0300
Fax 416-443-8619
www.mytorontohome.com
Line: Operates a real estate sales and investment business.
NAICS: 531210
#Emp: 250-499 (Tor)
#TorLoc: 1
Own: Private Company
Key: Chris Slightham, Pres
Carol Collins, Office Mgr

Royal Ontario Museum

100 Queen's Park Cres.
Toronto, ON M5S 2C6
Tel 416-586-5549
Fax 416-586-5827
www.rom.on.ca
AKA: ROM
NAICS: 712111
#Emp: 250-499 (Tor)
#TorLoc: 1
Own: Government
Par: Government of Ontario
Key: Janet Carding, Dir & CEO
Glenn Dobbin,
  Deputy Dir of Ops & COO
Chris Koester,
  VP HR & Organizational Dev
Bill Graesser, VP Fin & CFO
Kelvin Browne,
  VP Mktg & Major Exhibitions
Julian Siggers,
  VP Programs & Content Commun

Royal Pipe Systems Ltd.

131 Regalcrest Crt.
Woodbridge, ON L4L 8P3
Tel 905-856-7550
Fax 905-856-4367
www.royalbuildinproducts.com
AKA: Royal Pipe Co.
Line: Manufactures plastic pipes and fittings.
NAICS: 326122
#Emp: 100-249 (Tor)
#TorLoc: 1
Own: Public Company
Par: Royal Group Technologies Ltd. (CDA)
Key: Paul Czachor, VP & GM
Mark Arcoutt, Exec VP
Brent Wetmore, VP Sales

Royal St. George's College

120 Howland Ave.
Toronto, ON M5R 3B5
Tel 416-533-9481
Fax 416-533-0028
www.rsgc.on.ca
Line: Operates a theological seminary college.
NAICS: 611310
#Emp: 75-99 (Tor)
#TorLoc: 1
Own: Private Company
Key: Stephen Beatty, Headmaster
Andrew Whiteley, Asst Headmaster,
  Dir of Fin & Ops

Royal & Sun Alliance Insurance Company of Canada

10 Wellington St. East
Toronto, ON M5E 1L5
Tel 416-366-7511
Fax 416-367-9869
www.rsagroup.ca
AKA: Royal & SunAlliance
Line: Sells property-casualty insurance products to Canadian business, industry and consumers.
NAICS: 524121
#Emp: 1000-4999 (Tor)
#TorLoc: 2
Own: Public Company
Par: The Royal & Sun Alliance Insurance Group plc (UK)
Key: Rowan Saunders, Pres & CEO
Mark Edgar, VP HR
Nick Creatura, CFO
Adrian Hall,
  Dir of Corp Mktg & Commun

The Royalton Hospitality Inc.

8201 Weston Rd.
Vaughan, ON L4L 1A6
Tel 905-851-2325
Fax 905-851-3208
www.theroyalton.ca
Line: Operates a banquet and convention centre.
NAICS: 722320
#Emp: 100-249 (Tor)
#TorLoc: 1
Own: Private Company
Key: Domenic Sili, Pres

Royal Windows & Doors

71 Royal Group Cres.
Woodbridge, ON L6H 1X9
Tel 905-851-6731
www.royalbuildingproducts.com
Line: Manufactures PVC extrusions.
NAICS: 326198
#Emp: 250-499 (Tor)
#TorLoc: 1
Own: Private Company
Par: Royal Group Technologies Ltd.
(CDA)
Key: Pino Consolmagno, Plant Mgr

Roy Foss Motors Ltd.

7200 Yonge St.
Thornhill, ON L4J 1V8
Tel 905-886-2000
Fax 905-886-1890
www.royfoss.com
Line: Sells and leases new and used
cars and trucks.
NAICS: 441110 441120
#Emp: 250-499 (Tor)
#TorLoc: 3
Own: Private Company
Key: Karen Foss-Ricci, Dealer Principal

Roynat Inc.

Scotia Plaza, 40 King St. West, 26th Fl.
Toronto, ON M5H 1H1
Tel 416-933-2730
Fax 416-933-2930
www.roynat.com
AKA: Roynat Capital
Line: Specializes in equity finance for
businesses.
NAICS: 523920
#Emp: 75-99 (Tor)
#TorLoc: 3
Own: Private Company
Key: Earl Lande, Pres & CEO
Stephanie D'Lima, Sr HR Mgr
Ian Tuttell, Sr VP Corp Support
    Services & Cont

Roytec Vinyl Co.

91 Royal Group Cres.
Woodbridge, ON L4H 1X9
Tel 905-851-7756
Fax 905-851-4441
www.royalbuildingproducts.com
AKA: Royal Building Products
Line: Manufactures vinyl siding.
NAICS: 326198
#Emp: 250-499 (Tor)
#TorLoc: 1
Own: Private Company
Par: Royal Group Technologies Ltd.
(CDA)
Key: Simon Bates, Pres
John Mckinnon, VP Ops
Guy Prentice, VP Fin

RPM Technologies Corp.

Air Canada Centre
900-50 Bay St.
Toronto, ON M5J 3A5
Tel 416-214-6232
Fax 416-214-4540
www.rpmtec.com
Line: Develops and markets wealth
management software for the financial
services sector.
NAICS: 511210
#Emp: 75-99 (Tor)
#TorLoc: 1
Own: Private Company
Par: Bayshore Capital (CDA)
Key: David Poppleton, Pres & CEO
Jeff Sherman, VP & Partner
Kim Aspden, HR Mgr
Jennifer O'Keefe, Cont
Karin Yorfido, VP Strategic Dev

RR Donelly Ltd.

180 Bond Ave.
Toronto, ON M3B 3P3
Tel 416-449-6400
Fax 416-449-1167
www.rrdonelly.com
Line: Provides financial, corporate and
commercial printing, with facilities
worldwide, linked by state-of-the-art
telecommunications and computer
networks.
NAICS: 323115 323114
#Emp: 100-249 (Tor)
#TorLoc: 3
Own: Private Company
Par: Bowne & Co., Inc. (US)
Key: Barry Scruton, Mng Dir
John Burke, GM

RSM Richter LLP

200 King St. West, 11th Fl.
Toronto, ON M5H 3T4
Tel 416-932-8000
Fax 416-932-6200
www.rsmrichter.com
Line: Provides accounting, business
advisory and consulting services.
NAICS: 541212 541611
#Emp: 100-249 (Tor)
#TorLoc: 1
Own: Private Company
Key: Bobby Kofman, Mng Partner
David Steinberg, Mng Partner
Lisa Fusina, Mgr of HR
Michael Ianni-Palarchio,
    Dir of Systems & Tech

RT Recycling Technology Inc.

801 Flint Rd.
Toronto, ON M3J 2J6
Tel 416-650-1498
Fax 416-650-0264
www.rtplastics.ca
Line: Operates an injection-moulding
business.
NAICS: 333220 333511
#Emp: 75-99 (Tor)
#TorLoc: 1
Own: Private Company
Par: Global Upholstery (CDA)
Key: Saul Feldberg, Pres

Rubbermaid Canada

2562 Stanfield Rd.
Mississauga, ON L4Y 1S5
Tel 905-279-1010
Fax 905-279-1054
www.rubbermaid.ca
Line: Manufactures, sells and services
rubber and plastic houseware
products.
NAICS: 326290 326198
#Emp: 250-499 (Tor)
#TorLoc: 5
Own: Public Company
Par: Newell Rubbermaid Co. (US)
Key: Patrick G. Bradley, Pres & GM

Rubie's Costume Company (Canada)

2710 14th Ave.
Markham, ON L3R 0J1
Tel 905-470-0300
Fax 905-470-0301
www.rubiescanada.com
Line: Wholesales Halloween costumes and accessories.
NAICS: 541490
#Emp: 75-99 (Tor)
#TorLoc: 1
Own: Private Company
Par: Rubie's Costume Company (US)
Key: Mike Maskery, Ops Mgr
Linda Franklin, HR Mgr

RuggedCom Inc.

1-300 Applewood Cres.
Concord, ON L4K 5C7
Tel 905-856-5288
Fax 905-856-1995
www.ruggedcom.com
NAICS: 334110
#Emp: 250-499 (Tor)
Own: Private Company
Key: Marzio Pozzuoli, Pres & CEO

Running Room

9750-47 Ave.
Edmonton, AB T6E 5P3
Tel 780-439-3099
Fax 780-439-6433
www.runningroom.com
NAICS: 448210
#Emp: 250-499 (Tor)
#TorLoc: 17
Own: Private Company
Key: John Stanton, Pres
Mike O'Dell, VP
Cathleen Monson, Cont
Kevin Higa, CFO
Ryan White, Dir of IT

Runnymede Healthcare Centre

625 Runnymede Rd.
Toronto, ON M6S 3A3
Tel 416-762-7316
Fax 416-762-3836
www.runnymedehc.ca
Line: Provides specialized complex continuing care.
NAICS: 622310
#Emp: 100-249 (Tor)
#TorLoc: 1
Own: Not-for-profit
Key: Connie Dejak, Pres & CEO
JoAnne Bunker, Purch Agent
Angela Copeland, Dir of IT

Russell Investments Canada Limited

First Canadian Pl.,
5900-100 King St. West
P.O. Box 476
Toronto, ON M5X 1E4
Tel 416-362-8411
Fax 416-362-4494
www.russell.com
Line: Offers asset management consulting advice, implementation management services and investment funds.
NAICS: 523930
#Emp: 100-249 (Tor)
#TorLoc: 1
Own: Private Company
Par: Russell Investments Ltd. (US)
Key: Irshaad Ahmad, Pres & Mng Dir
David Feather, CEO
David Steele, Mng Dir of Ops & CFO
Nicole Kilfor, HR Mgr
Keith Pangretitsch, Dir of Nat'l Sales
Susanne Desrochers,
    Dir of Mktg & Commun

Russel Metals Inc.

210-1900 Minnesota Crt.
Mississauga, ON L5N 3C9
Tel 905-819-7777
Fax 905-819-7364
www.russelmetals.com
Line: Provides metals processing and distribution.
NAICS: 332999
#Emp: 75-99 (Tor)
#TorLoc: 3
Own: Public Company
Key: Brian R. Hedges, Pres & CEO
Joe Mangialardi, GM, Ontario
Francine McMullen, Dir of HR
Marion E. Britton, VP & CFO
David Halcrow, VP Purch
Maureen Kelly, VP IT
Sherri Mooser, Asst Secy

R.V. Anderson Associates Ltd.

400-2001 Sheppard Ave. East
Toronto, ON M2J 4Z8
Tel 416-497-8600
Fax 416-497-0342
www.rvanderson.com
Line: Provides professional consulting engineering services in municipal and environmental fields to public and private sector clients.
NAICS: 541620 541330
#Emp: 100-249 (Tor)
#TorLoc: 1
Own: Private Company
Key: Kenneth A. Morrison, Pres
Reginald J. Andres, VP
Cindy Coish, Asst to Pres
Gary A. Farrell, Secy-Treas
Sebastian Lee, Computer Services

Ryan ULC

102-6775 Financial Dr.
Mississauga, ON L5N 0A4
Tel 905-846-3977
Fax 905-846-5997
www.ryanco.ca
Line: Provides sales tax consulting services.
NAICS: 541619
#Emp: 75-99 (Tor)
#TorLoc: 1
Own: Private Company
Par: Ryan Inc. (US)
Key: Garry Round, Mng Principal
Louis Galvao, VP Fin & Corp Services

Ryder Logistics & Transportation Solutions Worldwide

300-2233 Argentia Rd.
Mississauga, ON L5N 2X7
Tel 905-826-8777
Fax 905-826-0079
www.ryder.com
Line: Provides transportation logistics services.
NAICS: 488990
#Emp: 100-249 (Tor)
#TorLoc: 6
Own: Private Company
Key: Mike Howran,
    Group Logistics Mgr
Gregory T. Swienton, Chmn & CEO
Jeannine McIlmoyle, HR Mgr
Art A. Garcia, Exec VP & CFO

Ryder Truck Rental Canada Ltd.

300-2233 Argentia Rd.
Mississauga, ON L5N 2X7
Tel 905-826-8777
Fax 905-826-0079
www.ryder.com
AKA: Ryder Logistics; Ryder Canada Inc.
Line: Provides transportation logistics
solutions including truck leasing and
rental, warehousing and freight.
NAICS: 488519
#Emp: 1000-4999 (Tor)
#TorLoc: 15
Own: Private Company
Par: Ryder System Inc. (US)
Key: Chris Fairey, VP Business Dev
Robert Johnston, VP Ops,
    Fleet Management Solutions
Michael Cole, Sr Dir of HR
Sean Butler, VP
    Rental & Asset Management
Guy Toksoy, VP Ops,
    Supply Chain Solutions
Catherine Luzena, Mktg Mgr

Ryding-Regency Meat Packers Ltd.

70 Glen Scarlett Rd.
Toronto, ON M6N 1P4
Tel 416-767-3343
Fax 416-766-9167
www.rydingregency.com
NAICS: 413160
#Emp: 100-249 (Tor)
#TorLoc: 1
Own: Private Company
Key: Joe Petronaci, CEO
Stewart Manning, HR Mgr
Heera Bulkan, Cont
Lorenzo Gianasi,
    Maintenance & Purch Mgr

Ryerson Canada

161 The West Mall
Toronto, ON M9C 4V8
Tel 416-622-3100
Fax 416-622-8602
www.ryerson.com
Line: Distributes quality specialty metal
products including stainless steels,
aluminum, nickel alloys, tool and
machinery steels, fittings, valves and
fasteners.
NAICS: 332910 332999
#Emp: 100-249 (Tor)
#TorLoc: 2
Own: Private Company
Par: Ryerson Tull (US)

Key: Patrick Maher, GM
Premod Kanjirappallil, Dir of Ops
Nesha Brela, HR Dir
Jim Patskou, VP Fin

Ryerson University

350 Victoria St.
Toronto, ON M5B 2K3
Tel 416-979-5000
Fax 416-979-5292
www.ryerson.ca
Line: Operates a post-secondary
educational institution.
NAICS: 611310
#Emp: 1000-4999 (Tor)
#TorLoc: 1
Own: Government
Key: Sheldon Levy,
    Pres & Vice-Chancellor
Julia Hanigsberg, VP Admin & Fin
Larissa Allen, Exec Dir of HR
Janice S. Winton,
    Exec Dir of Financial Services
Stephen Hawkins, Dir of
    Computing & Commun Services
Adam B. Kahan, VP
    University Advancement

S.A. Armstrong Ltd.

23 Bertrand Ave.
Toronto, ON M1L 2P3
Tel 416-755-2291
Fax 416-759-9101
www.armstrongpumps.com
Line: Manufactures pumps, heat
transfer equipment, valves and related
fluid flow products.
NAICS: 333910 333416
#Emp: 100-249 (Tor)
#TorLoc: 1
Own: Private Company
Key: Charles A. Armstrong, Pres
James C. Armstrong, Exec VP
Allan Dias,
    HR Generalist & Payroll Specialist
Paul Novello, CFO
Dimitri Portolos, Dir of IT
Rob Clements, Ontario Sales Mgr
Brent Ross, Dir of Mktg

Saint Elizabeth Health Care

300-90 Allstate Pkwy.
Markham, ON L3R 6H3
Tel 905-940-9655
Fax 905-940-9934
www.saintelizabeth.com
Line: Serves the physical, emotional
and spiritual needs of individuals and
families in their homes and in the
community.
NAICS: 621390 623110
#Emp: 1000-4999 (Tor)
#TorLoc: 7
Own: Not-for-profit
Key: Shirlee Sharkey, Pres & CEO
Rheta Fanizza, Sr VP Ops
Nancy Hawkes, Sr VP HR
Peter Massel, Sr VP & CFO
Neil Barran, Sr VP
Ron Currie, VP Commun & Mktg

Salga Associates

161 Snidercroft Rd.
Concord, ON L4K 2J8
Tel 905-669-0999
Fax 905-669-0574
www.abcgroupinc.com
AKA: ABC Group
Line: Manufactures automotive
blow-moulded plastic parts.
NAICS: 336390
#Emp: 100-249 (Tor)
#TorLoc: 1
Own: Private Company
Par: ABC Group Inc. (CDA)
Key: Peter Tremmel, GM
Martin Komes, Plant Mgr

The Salvation Army Toronto Grace Health Centre

650 Church St.
Toronto, ON M4Y 2G5
Tel 416-925-2251
Fax 416-925-3211
www.torontograce.org
Line: Operates a complex continuing
care and palliative care hospital.
NAICS: 623110
#Emp: 250-499 (Tor)
#TorLoc: 1
Own: Not-for-profit
Key: Marilyn Rock, Pres & CEO
David Van Der Hout, Medical Dir
Vinnie Berman, Exec Dir of HR Ops
Fred Fotopoulos, CFO

Samaco Trading Limited

55E East Beaver Creek Rd.
Richmond Hill, ON L4B 1E8
Tel 905-731-3232
Fax 905-731-0872
www.samacotrading.com
Line: Distributes giftware, collectibles and garden products.
NAICS: 418990
#Emp: 75-99 (Tor)
#TorLoc: 1
Own: Private Company
Key: Andy Szandtner, Pres
Jasmin Drep, VP Ops
Suzanne Porcellato, VP Fin
Laurie Blaha, VP Product Dev
Scott McVerne, VP Sales

Sameday Worldwide

A Div. of Day & Ross Inc.
6975 Menkes Dr.
Mississauga, ON L5S 1Y2
Tel 905-676-3750
Fax 905-678-9274
www.sameday.ca
AKA: Sameday Right-O-Way
Line: Provides domestic, trans-border and international transportation service.
NAICS: 484110 484121 492110
#Emp: 250-499 (Tor)
#TorLoc: 1
Own: Private Company
Par: McCain Foods Ltd. (CDA)
Key: Eric de Maat, Pres
Kim Marquis, HR Coord
Steve Keeley, Dir of Fin & Admin

Samsung Electronics Canada Inc.

55 Standish Crt.
Mississauga, ON L5R 4B2
Tel 905-542-3535
Fax 905-819-4418
www.samsung.com
Line: Sells, markets, and distributes home electronic and information technology products.
NAICS: 334110
#Emp: 100-249 (Tor)
#TorLoc: 1
Own: Private Company
Par: Samsung Electronics Co. (KOREA)
Key: Benjamin Lee, Pres & CEO
Nick DiPonzio, Sr HR Mgr
Ronald Hulse, VP Sales & Mktg

Samtack Inc.

1100 Rodick Rd.
Markham, ON L3R 8C3
Tel 905-940-1880
Fax 905-940-0331
www.samtack.com
Line: Distributes personal computers, components, peripherals and multimedia products.
NAICS: 334110
#Emp: 75-99 (Tor)
#TorLoc: 1
Own: Private Company
Par: Pine Group (UK)
Key: Royson Ng, Pres
Robert Chin, VP Mktg & Commun

Samuel Lunenfeld Research Institute of Mount Sinai Hospital

600 University Ave.
Toronto, ON M5G 1X5
Tel 416-596-4200
Fax 416-586-8857
www.lunenfeld.ca
Line: Specializes in health research.
NAICS: 541710
#Emp: 500-999 (Tor)
#TorLoc: 1
Own: Association
Key: Stephen J. Lye, Associate Dir of Research
Jim Woodgett, Dir of Research
Mark Toone, Dir of Ops & Strategic Planning
Jamie Wickham, HR Mgr
Paul Kranjac, Dir of Fin & IT
Cindy Todoroff, Dir of Commun

Samuel Manu-Tech Inc.

1500-185 The West Mall
Toronto, ON M9C 5L5
Tel 416-626-2190
Fax 416-626-5969
www.samuelmanutech.com
Line: Produces a range of steel, plastic and related industrial products and services.
NAICS: 331210 416210
#Emp: 500-999 (Tor)
#TorLoc: 8
Own: Public Company
Par: Samuel, Son & Co., Limited. (CDA)
Key: John Morton, Pres
Mark C. Samuel, Vice Chmn
John Amodeo, Exec VP & CFO
Michael Evelyn, VP, Corp Cont & Secy

Samuel, Son & Co., Limited

2360 Dixie Rd.
Mississauga, ON L4Y 1Z7
Tel 905-279-5460
Fax 905-279-9658
www.samuel.com
Line: Operates steel service centres.
NAICS: 416210
#Emp: 250-499 (Tor)
#TorLoc: 7
Own: Private Company
Key: Ted Doyle, Pres, Flat Rolled Products Division
Wayne K. Bassett, Pres & CEO
Tom McGrogan, VP Ops, Ontario Flat Rolled Processing Group
Karen Fenton, Corp Mgr of HR

Samuel Strapping Systems

2370 Dixie Rd.
Mississauga, ON L4Y 1Z4
Tel 905-279-9580
Fax 905-279-9421
www.samuelstrapping.com
Line: Manufactures and distributes steel and plastic strapping, stretch film, packaging products, packaging machinery and tools.
NAICS: 333990 326114
#Emp: 100-249 (Tor)
#TorLoc: 3
Own: Public Company
Par: Samuel Manu-Tech Inc. (CDA)
Key: John Morton, Pres
Bruce Hannah, VP
Yvonne McCurbin, HR Mgr
Lou Sartor, VP Fin
Chris Batrynchuk, VP Sales & Mktg

Sandvik Canada Inc.

3-2550 Meadowvale Blvd.
Mississauga, ON L5N 8C2
Tel 905-826-8900
Fax 905-542-4394
www.sandvik.com
Line: Manufactures carbide-cutting tools.
NAICS: 333519
#Emp: 250-499 (Tor)
#TorLoc: 4
Own: Private Company
Par: Sandvik A.B (SWE)
Key: Dave Thompson, Pres & CFO
Ross Carpino, GM
Paul Figge, Dir of HR
Geoff Ireland, IT Mgr
Mike Hammond, Nat'l Sales Mgr
Randy Bossie, Mktg Mgr

Sandvik Mining and Construction Canada Inc.

4445 Fairview St.
Burlington, ON L7L 2A4
Tel 905-632-4940
Fax 905-333-3680
www.miningandcontruction.
   sandvik.com
Line: Manufactures trackless
underground mining equipment.
NAICS: 333130
#Emp: 100-249 (Tor)
#TorLoc: 1
Own: Private Company
Par: Sandvik AB (SWE)
Key: Matti Heinio, Pres
Gary McKinnon, Sr Mgr of Production
Michelle Bush, Dir of HR

Sanofi Pasteur Ltd.

1755 Steeles Ave. West
Toronto, ON M2R 3T4
Tel 416-667-2701
Fax 416-667-2950
www.sanofipasteur.com
Line: Conducts bio-technology research
and manufactures vaccines.
NAICS: 325410 621510
#Emp: 1000-4999 (Tor)
#TorLoc: 1
Own: Private Company
Key: Mark Lievonen, Pres
Julia O'Rawe, VP HR

Santa Maria Foods Corp.

10 Armthorpe Rd.
Brampton, ON L6T 5M4
Tel 905-790-1991
Fax 905-790-1627
www.santamariafoods.com
AKA: Mastro; San Daniele
Line: Processes and distributes meat.
NAICS: 311614 413160
#Emp: 250-499 (Tor)
Own: Private Company
Key: Eddie Zilli, Pres
Frederick Jacques, CEO
Andrew Linley, CFO
Ravinder Bhalwal, Cont

Sapa Extrusions

5675 Kennedy Rd.
Mississauga, ON L4Z 2H9
Tel 905-890-8821
Fax 905-890-8385
www.sapagroup.com
Line: Produces aluminum products.
NAICS: 331313
#Emp: 250-499 (Tor)
#TorLoc: 2
Own: Private Company
Par: Sapa Group (SWE)
Key: David McCallen, GM

SAP Canada Inc.

600-4120 Yonge St.
Toronto, ON M2P 2B8
Tel 416-229-0574
Fax 416-229-0575
www.sap.com
Line: Provides technology solutions to
businesses.
NAICS: 541510
#Emp: 250-499 (Tor)
#TorLoc: 2
Own: Public Company
Par: SAP AG (GER)
Key: Mark Aboud, Pres & Mng Dir
Maria Codipietro, Mng Dir, Labs
Tracey Arnish, VP HR
Arthur Gitajn, CFO
Bob Elliot, Nat'l VP Sales

Saputo Dairy Products Canada GP

279 Guelph St.
Georgetown, ON L7G 4B3
Tel 905-702-7200
Fax 905-702-7282
www.saputo.ca
AKA: Neilson Dairy; Saputo Cheese
Line: Manufactures and markets dairy
products.
NAICS: 311511 311515
#Emp: 1000-4999 (Tor)
#TorLoc: 3
Own: Private Company
Par: Saputo Cheese (CDA)
Key: Mike Cote, VP Logistics & Ops
Eric Morgenroth, Dir of Fin

Sardo Foods

99 Pillsworth Rd.
Bolton, ON L7E 4E4
Tel 905-951-9096
www.sardofoods.com
NAICS: 311420 311225
#Emp: 100-249 (Tor)
#TorLoc: 1
Own: Private Company
Key: Mario Sardo, Pres & CEO

Sarku Japan Restaurants Income Fund

7650 Birchmount Rd.
Markham, ON L3R 6B9
Tel 905-474-0710
Fax 905-474-1939
www.sarkujapan.com
Line: Operates Japanese quick service
restaurants.
NAICS: 722210
#Emp: 75-99 (Tor)
#TorLoc: 1
Own: Private Company
Key: James Chim, Pres & CEO

SAS Institute (Canada) Inc.

500-280 King St. East
Toronto, ON M5A 1K7
Tel 416-363-4424
Fax 416-363-5399
www.sas.com/canada
NAICS: 511210
#Emp: 100-249 (Tor)
#TorLoc: 1
Own: Private Company
Par: SAS Institute Inc. (US)
Key: Carl Farrell, Pres, Canada
   & SAS Americas Subsidiaries
E. Stuart Bowden, Sr VP Ops & Fin
Seta Kouyoumdjian, Sr Dir of HR
Steven Kelly, IS Mgr
Mario Ianniciello, VP Sales
Cameron Dow, VP Mktg

Satin Finish Hardwood Flooring Ltd.

8 Oak St.
Toronto, ON M9N 1R8
Tel 416-241-8631
Fax 416-241-8636
www.satinfinish.com
Line: Manufactures flooring.
NAICS: 321919
#Emp: 250-499 (Tor)
#TorLoc: 3
Own: Private Company
Key: Ivan Dalos, VP & Dir
Jo-Ann VanderDussen,
    Credit & Admin Mgr
David Zimmerman, Cont
Mahedi Manji, Comptr
Lou Novelli, VP Sales
John Giancani, VP Mktg & Product Dev

Satpanth Capital Inc.

100 Locke St.
Concord, ON L4K 5R4
Tel 905-660-3337
Fax 905-660-2259
www.kingkoil.ca
AKA: King Koil
Line: Manufactures mattresses and box springs.
NAICS: 337910
#Emp: 100-249 (Tor)
#TorLoc: 1
Own: Private Company
Key: Allan Erlick, Pres
Larry Lewis, GM
Nicole Hastings, Purch Mgr
Allan Snow, IT Mgr
Paul De Geer, VP Sales & Mktg

Savaria Concord Lifts Inc.

107 Alfred Kuehne Blvd.
Brampton, ON L6T 4K3
Tel 905-791-5555
Fax 905-791-2222
www.savariaconcord.com
Line: Manufactures elevators and lifts.
NAICS: 333920 232550
#Emp: 100-249 (Tor)
#TorLoc: 1
Own: Public Company
Key: Marcel Bourassa, Pres & CEO
Bruce Hayes, Dir of HR
Helene Bernier, VP Fin
Rob De Rooy, VP Customer Service

Sayers & Associates Ltd.

2240 Argentia Rd.
Mississauga, ON L5N 2X6
Tel 905-821-4500
Fax 905-821-0664
www.sayers.ca
Line: Provides plumbing, heating and sheet metal work.
NAICS: 232520
#Emp: 100-249 (Tor)
#TorLoc: 1
Own: Private Company
Par: Chriscot Holdings Ltd. (CDA)
Key: Scott Sayers, Pres
Diana Mota, HR Mgr
Marie McAlpine, Cont
Bruce Foley, Purch Mgr

Scarboro Golf & Country Club

321 Scarborough Golf Club Rd.
Toronto, ON M1J 3H2
Tel 416-266-4546
Fax 416-266-1259
www.scarborogolf.com
NAICS: 713910
#Emp: 100-249 (Tor)
#TorLoc: 1
Own: Private Company
Key: Maureen Barrey, Pres
Denis Matte, GM & COO
Karen Grant, Accounts Payable & HR

Scarborotown Chrysler Dodge Jeep Ltd.

4960 Sheppard Ave. East
Toronto, ON M1S 4A7
Tel 416-298-7600
Fax 416-298-9331
www.scarborotown.com
AKA: Quest Automotive Leasing
Line: Operates a car dealership.
NAICS: 441110 532111 532112
#Emp: 100-249 (Tor)
#TorLoc: 1
Own: Private Company
Key: Lance Hanson, Dealer Principal
Dina Macklin, Office Mgr
Edward Caldana, Cont

The Scarborough Hospital

3050 Lawrence Ave. East
Toronto, ON M1P 2V5
Tel 416-438-2911
Fax 416-431-8204
www.tsh.to
AKA: TSH
Line: Operates acute health care hospital and regional dialysis centre.
NAICS: 622111
#Emp: 1000-4999 (Tor)
#TorLoc: 2
Own: Not-for-profit
Key: John Wright, Pres & CEO
Emma Pavlov, VP
    HR & Organizational Dev
Ralph Anstey, VP & CFO
Cara Flemming, VP Performance & CIO

Scarborough Support Services

1045 McNicoll Ave.
Toronto, ON M1W 3W6
Tel 416-750-9885
Fax 416-750-1310
www.ssse.ca
Line: Offers support services to seniors and disabled adults.
NAICS: 624120
#Emp: 250-499 (Tor)
#TorLoc: 1
Own: Private Company
Key: Odette Maharaj, Exec Dir
Regina Kelly, Office Mgr
Sam Luu, Dir of Fin & Admin

Scarborough Town Centre Holdings Inc.

26-300 Borough Dr.
Toronto, ON M1P 4P5
Tel 416-296-5490
Fax 416-296-9949
www.scarboroughtowncentre.com
Line: Operates shopping centre.
NAICS: 531120
#Emp: 75-99 (Tor)
#TorLoc: 1
Own: Private Company
Par: Oxford Property Group (CDA)
Key: Steven Minielly, Head of Ops

Scarborough Toyota

1897 Eglinton Ave. East
Toronto, ON M1L 2L6
Tel 416-751-1530
Fax 416-752-0201
www.scarboroughtoyota.ca
AKA: 1216809 Ontario Ltd.
Line: Retails new and used automobiles.
NAICS: 441110 441120
#Emp: 100-249 (Tor)
#TorLoc: 1
Own: Private Company
Key: Gerry MacDonald, GM

S & C Electric Canada Ltd.

90 Belfield Rd.
Toronto, ON M9W 1G4
Tel 416-249-9171
Fax 416-249-6051
www.sandc.com
Line: Develops and manufactures switching and protection devices that assist in delivering electric power.
NAICS: 335315
#Emp: 250-499 (Tor)
#TorLoc: 1
Own: Private Company
Par: S & C Electric Co. (US)
Key: Grant S. Buchanan, Pres
Robert Arbuthnot, VP Manuf
Sandy Ferrera, Dir of HR
Bill H. Childerhose, Dir of Procurement
James McRobert,
    Dir of Engineering Services

Scepter Corporation

170 Midwest Rd.
Toronto, ON M1P 3A9
Tel 416-751-9445
Fax 416-751-4451
www.scepter.ca
Line: Designs and manufactures molded plastic products.
NAICS: 326198
#Emp: 250-499 (Tor)
#TorLoc: 1
Own: Private Company
Key: Robert Torokvei, Pres
Don Villers, Plant Mgr
Brian Moore, HR Mgr
Chris Luck, CFO
Liz Keen, Payroll & EDI Systems

Schaeffer & Associates Ltd.

6 Ronrose Dr.
Concord, ON L4K 4R3
Tel 905-738-6100
Fax 905-738-6875
www.schaeffers.com
AKA: Schaeffers Consulting Engineers
Line: Provides civil engineering services.
NAICS: 541330
#Emp: 100-249 (Tor)
#TorLoc: 1
Own: Private Company
Key: Al Steedman, Pres

Schenker of Canada Limited

3210 Airway Dr.
Mississauga, ON L4V 1Y6
Tel 905-676-0676
Fax 905-677-0582
www.schenker.ca
Line: Operates a global logistics company.
NAICS: 488519 541619
#Emp: 1000-4999 (Tor)
#TorLoc: 2
Own: Private Company
Key: Eric Dewey, Pres & CEO
Petra Kuester, Exec VP & CFO

Schindler Elevator Corp.

40 Cowdray Crt.
Toronto, ON M1S 1A1
Tel 416-332-8280
Fax 416-332-8276
www.us.schindler.com
Line: Sells, installs and services elevators, escalators and walkways.
NAICS: 232550
#Emp: 100-249 (Tor)
#TorLoc: 1
Own: Private Company
Par: Schindler Management Ltd. (SWITZ)
Key: Jack Elias, Pres
Tony Arcaro, VP Eastern Region
Tom Koch, VP Fin

Schneider Canada Inc.

19 Waterman Ave.
Toronto, ON M4B 1Y2
Tel 416-752-8020
Fax 416-752-6230
www.schneider-electric.ca
Line: Manufactures, sells, services and distributes automation and industrial control electrical equipment.
NAICS: 335315
#Emp: 500-999 (Tor)
#TorLoc: 4
Own: Private Company
Par: Schneider Electric SA (FR)
Key: Gary Abrams, Pres
Nicole Grosz, Dir of HR &
    Organizational Dev
John Whibbs, VP Industry Business

Scholastic Canada Ltd.

175 Hillmount Rd.
Markham, ON L6C 1Z7
Tel 905-887-7323
Fax 905-887-1131
www.scholastic.ca
AKA: Scholastic Book Fairs Canada Inc.
Line: Publishes and distributes children's books and educational material.
NAICS: 511130
#Emp: 500-999 (Tor)
#TorLoc: 4
Own: Private Company
Par: Scholastic Inc. (US)
Key: Linda Gosnell, Co-Pres
Iole Lucchese, Co-Pres
Christine Phillips,
    Dir of Warehouse Ops
Marlene Long, Dir of HR
Anne Browne, Dir of Fin
Judy Rose, Facilities Mgr
David Clarke, Dir of IT
Nancy Pearson, VP Book Group Mktg

Schwartz Levitsky Feldman LLP

1167 Caledonia Rd.
Toronto, ON M6A 2X1
Tel 416-785-5353
Fax 416-785-5663
www.slf.ca
AKA: HLB International
Line: Provides accounting and financial services.
NAICS: 541212
#Emp: 75-99 (Tor)
#TorLoc: 2
Own: Private Company
Key: Jeffrey Feldman, Partner

SciCan Ltd.

A Div. of Lux & Zwingenberger Limited
1440 Don Mills Rd.
Toronto, ON M3B 3P9
Tel 416-445-1600
Fax 416-445-2727
www.scican.com
Line: Manufactures autoclaves and distributes medical and dental equipment and supplies.
NAICS: 339110 417930
#Emp: 100-249 (Tor)
#TorLoc: 1
Own: Private Company
Key: Brian Douglas, Pres
Mark Vanvoorden, CEO
Kelly Makimoto, VP Ops
Donna McLean, CFO

SCI Group Inc.

600-180 Attwell Dr.
Toronto, ON M9W 6A9
Tel 416-401-3011
Fax 416-401-8811
www.group-sci.com
AKA: SCI Logistics Inc.; Progistix
Solutions; First Team Transport Inc.
Line: Provides outsourced logistics
services.
NAICS: 541619
#Emp: 500-999 (Tor)
#TorLoc: 12
Own: Private Company
Par: Canada Post Corp. (CDA)
Key: John Ferguson, Pres & CEO
Paul Ragan, Sr VP Ops
Ann Pompilio, CFO
Chris Galindo,
    VP Business Dev & Services

SCI Inc.

6591 Kitimat Rd.
Mississauga, ON L5N 3T4
Tel 905-858-8855
Fax 905-858-7808
www.flexoprint.com
AKA: Schiffenhaus Canada Inc.
Line: Specializes in printing.
NAICS: 323119
#Emp: 75-99 (Tor)
#TorLoc: 1
Own: Private Company
Par: Schiffenhaus Packaging Corp. (US)
Key: Alistair McLean, Pres
Terry Ray, Plant Mgr
Bob Cherrett, Fin & Admin Mgr

SCI Logistics Inc.

2450 Stanfield Rd.
Mississauga, ON L4Y 1S2
Tel 905-896-1920
Fax 905-897-2657
www.amglogistics.com
AKA: First Team Transport Inc.
Line: Provides logistics management
services including warehousing and
distribution strategy formulation,
systems and process development, and
operational partnerships.
NAICS: 541619
#Emp: 100-249 (Tor)
#TorLoc: 2
Own: Private Company
Par: SCI Logistics (CDA)
Key: Damian McMullen, GM
Monique Recce, HR Advisor

SCI Marketview Ltd.

7030 Woodbine Ave., 6th Fl.
Markham, ON L3R 6G2
Tel 905-479-1595
Fax 905-479-8264
www.scitorque.com
Line: Develops software focused
on retail process solutions for the
automotive industry.
NAICS: 541510
#Emp: 100-249 (Tor)
Own: Private Company
Key: Alan Bird, Pres & CEO
Christopher Moritz, COO
Desmond Reynolds, CFO

The Score Television Network Ltd.

435-370 King St. West
P.O. Box 10
Toronto, ON M5V 1J9
Tel 416-977-6787
Fax 416-977-0238
www.thescore.com
Line: Operates a sports television
network.
NAICS: 513210
#Emp: 100-249 (Tor)
#TorLoc: 1
Own: Public Company
Par: Score Media Inc. (CDA)
Key: Benjamin Levy, Exec VP & COO
John Levy, CEO
Sally Farrell, VP HR
Tom Hearne, CFO
Oliver Gayagoy, VP Broadcast & IT
Don Moen, Sr VP Sales
Sharon Lassman, Dir of Commun

Scotiabank - Wealth Management

40 King St. West, 13th Fl.
Toronto, ON M5H 1H1
Tel 416-933-3021
Fax 416-933-5599
www.scotiacassels.com
Line: Provides financial services.
NAICS: 523110
#Emp: 250-499 (Tor)
#TorLoc: 1
Own: Public Company
Par: Scotiabank (CDA)
Key: Cathy Welling, Mng Dir & Head
    of Scotia Private Client Group
Gregg Patterson, Reg VP Ontario,
    Investment Management Services

Scotia Capital Inc.

Scotia Plaza, 40 King St. West
P.O. Box 4085, Stn. A
Toronto, ON M5W 2X6
Tel 416-945-4564
Fax 416-863-7117
www.scotiacapital.com
Line: Provides investment banking and
wealth management services.
NAICS: 523110
#Emp: 1000-4999 (Tor)
#TorLoc: 18
Own: Private Company
Par: Scotiabank (CDA)
Key: Michael Durland,
    Co-Chmn & Co-CEO
Stephen D. McDonald,
    Co-Chmn & Co-CEO
Christopher J. Hodgson, Pres
Stephen Power, Mng Dir & Head of HR
Luc A. Vanneste, Exec VP & CFO
Kim B. McKenzie,
    Exec VP IT & Solutions

Scotia Life Insurance Company

400-100 Yonge St.
Toronto, ON M5H 1H1
Tel 416-866-7075
Fax 416-866-7773
www.scotiabank.com
Line: Provides life insurance.
NAICS: 524111 524210
#Emp: 75-99 (Tor)
#TorLoc: 1
Own: Private Company
Par: Scotiabank (CDA)
Key: Oscar Zimmerman, Pres & CEO
Alberta Cefis, Exec VP & Group GTB

The Scott Mission

502 Spadina Ave.
Toronto, ON M5S 2H1
Tel 416-923-8872
Fax 416-923-1067
www.scottmission.com
Line: Operates a Christian ministry for
the poor and needy of all ages.
NAICS: 624190
#Emp: 100-249 (Tor)
#TorLoc: 1
Own: Not-for-profit
Key: Peter Duraisami, Exec Dir
Lynwood Strickland, Dir of Ops
Sera Markovic-Rousalis, Dir of HR
Oliver Ng, Dir of Fin
Avril Henry, Dir of Commun

Scott-Woods Transport Inc.

140 Maloy St.
Maple, ON L6A 1R9
Tel 905-832-4224
Fax 905-832-9933
www.scottwoodstransport.com
Line: Provides specialized heavy haul services.
NAICS: 484121 484110
#Emp: 75-99 (Tor)
#TorLoc: 1
Own: Private Company
Key: Mark Alden, Pres
Dave Scott, Ops Mgr

S.D.R. Apparel Inc.

300 Applewood Cres.
Vaughan, ON L4K 4B4
Tel 905-625-7377
Fax 905-625-7399
www.sdrdistribution.com
AKA: SDR Distribution Services
Line: Manufactures children's clothing.
NAICS: 315239 315210
#Emp: 100-249 (Tor)
#TorLoc: 1
Own: Private Company
Key: Robert Resnick, Pres & CEO
Nasimul Hussain, VP Ops
Svetlana Voldman, Dir of Corp Fin

Seaboard/Harmac Transportation Group

55 Arrow Rd.
Toronto, ON M9M 2L4
Tel 416-642-0515
Fax 416-642-0935
www.harmactransport.com
Line: Operates a trucking company.
NAICS: 484231 484221
#Emp: 100-249 (Tor)
#TorLoc: 1
Own: Private Company
Key: Mark Shannon, Pres & COO
Todd Stauffer, VP Ops
Don Clarke, Dir of Fin
Joel Shannon, Dir of Purch & Fleet Ops
Jim Dibbin, VP Sales

Sealy Canada Ltd.

145 Milner Ave.
Toronto, ON M1S 3R1
Tel 416-699-7170
Fax 416-699-7107
www.sealy.ca
AKA: Sealy Posturepedic
Line: Manufactures line of mattresses and box springs.
NAICS: 337910
#Emp: 100-249 (Tor)
#TorLoc: 1
Own: Private Company
Par: Sealy Inc. (US)
Key: Kevin Sisson, COO
Danny Tosh, VP Ops
Rick Ryerson, HR Mgr
Monty Bagga, Corp Cont
Demetre Daratzikis, VP Sales
Simon Jervis, VP Mktg

Sears Canada Inc.

700-290 Yonge St.
Toronto, ON M5B 2C3
Tel 416-362-1711
Fax 416-941-4793
www.sears.ca
Line: Retails general merchandise and home-related services, with department and specialty stores nationwide.
NAICS: 452110 454110
#Emp: 5000-9999 (Tor)
#TorLoc: 36
Own: Public Company
Par: Sears Holdings (US)
Key: Calvin McDonald, Pres & CEO
Sharon Driscoll, Sr VP & CFO

Sears Liquidation Centre

253 Queen St. East
Brampton, ON L6W 2B8
Tel 905-796-1019
Fax 905-796-9447
www.sears.ca
Line: Operates a liquidation department store.
NAICS: 452999 452110
#Emp: 75-99 (Tor)
#TorLoc: 1
Own: Private Company
Par: Sears Canada Inc. (CDA)
Key: Steve Hale, Store Mgr

The Second City

99 Blue Jays Way
Toronto, ON M5B 9G9
Tel 416-343-0033
Fax 416-343-0034
www.secondcity.com
NAICS: 711111 711410
#Emp: 100-249 (Tor)
#TorLoc: 2
Own: Private Company
Key: Klaus Schuller, Exec Dir, Toronto
Andrew Alexander, Chmn & CEO
Erin Conway, GM, Toronto
Lou Carbone, CFO
Kevin Frank, Artistic Dir, Toronto

Securitas Canada Ltd.

500-265 Yorkland Blvd.
Toronto, ON M2J 1S5
Tel 416-774-2500
Fax 416-774-0545
www.securitas.ca
Line: Provides security guard, mobile patrol, alarm response, private investigation and consulting services.
NAICS: 561612
#Emp: 500-999 (Tor)
#TorLoc: 1
Own: Private Company
Par: Securitas AB (SWE)
Key: Dwayne Gulsby, Pres
Tracey Cook, VP, Greater Toronto
John Coletti, VP HR
Joseph Moutoussidis, Corp Cont
Rowan Hamilton, VP Sales

Security Management Services

1574 Queen St. East
Toronto, ON M4L 1G1
Tel 416-360-1902
Fax 416-360-1263
www.securitymanagementservices.com
Line: Provides security personnel for special events.
NAICS: 561611 561621
#Emp: 100-249 (Tor)
#TorLoc: 1
Own: Private Company
Key: Sean O'Brien, Pesident & Owner

Selba Industries Inc.

3231 Langstaff Rd.
Concord, ON L4K 4L2
Tel 905-660-1614
Fax 905-660-7075
www.selba.com
Line: Manufactures kitchen and
bathroom cabinets.
NAICS: 337110
#Emp: 75-99 (Tor)
#TorLoc: 3
Own: Private Company
Key: Marco Selvaggi, GM

Select Food Products Ltd.

120 Sunrise Ave.
Toronto, ON M4A 1B4
Tel 416-759-9316
Fax 416-759-9310
www.selectfoodproducts.com
Line: Manufactures sauces and
dressings for retail and foodservice
markets.
NAICS: 311940
#Emp: 100-249 (Tor)
#TorLoc: 2
Own: Private Company
Key: Paul Fredricks, Pres
Alex Polsinello, VP & Engineering Mgr
Paul MacIlwaine, HR
Lesa Warner, Dir of Sales

Semple Gooder Roofing Corporation

1365 Martin Grove Rd.
Toronto, ON M9W 4X7
Tel 416-743-5370
Fax 416-743-4257
www.semplegooder.com
Line: Offers roofing, siding and sheet
metal contracting services.
NAICS: 232330 232340
#Emp: 100-249 (Tor)
#TorLoc: 1
Own: Private Company
Key: Bill Gray, VP
Max Pearce, Cont & HR Mgr
Tina Rende, Purch Agent

Seneca College of Applied Arts & Technology

1750 Finch Ave. East
Toronto, ON M2J 2X5
Tel 416-491-5050
Fax 416-493-3958
www.senecac.on.ca
Line: Offers educational services.
NAICS: 611210
#Emp: 1000-4999 (Tor)
#TorLoc: 8
Own: Government
Key: David Agnew, Pres
Daniel Atlin,
   VP Strategy & College Affairs
Cindy Dundon Hazell, VP Academic
Robert DaCosta, Exec Dir of HR
Jeanette Dias D'Souza, VP Fin & Admin
Terry Wachna, Mgr of Purch Resources
Martha Lowrie, Dir of Mktg & Commun

SENES Consultants Limited

12-121 Granton Dr.
Richmond Hill, ON L4B 3N4
Tel 905-764-9380
Fax 905-764-9386
www.senes.ca
Line: Provides environmental
engineering, planning and health
consulting services specializing in
energy, nuclear and environmental
sciences.
NAICS: 541620
#Emp: 75-99 (Tor)
#TorLoc: 1
Own: Private Company
Key: Donald Gorber, Pres & Dir
Bruce Halbert, Treas

Senior Peoples Resources In North Toronto Inc.

140 Merton St., 2nd Fl.
Toronto, ON M4S 1A1
Tel 416-481-6411
Fax 416-481-9829
www.sprint-homecare.ca
Line: Provides home support services
to seniors including client intervention
and assistance, escort, transportation,
friendly visiting, respite care, home
help, congregate dining and meals-on-
wheels.
NAICS: 624120
#Emp: 100-249 (Tor)
Own: Private Company
Key: Jane Moore, Exec Dir

Seniors 4 Seniors

102-40 St. Clair Ave. West
Toronto, ON M4V 1M2
Tel 416-481-4579
Fax 416-481-3213
www.seniors4seniors.ca
AKA: 154644 Canada Inc.; Seniors for
Business
Line: Operates an employment agency
for people over the age of fifty and the
Seniors for Seniors division is a group
of seniors who provide care at home for
less mobile seniors.
NAICS: 813310
#Emp: 100-249 (Tor)
#TorLoc: 1
Own: Private Company
Key: Peter Cook, Founder & Pres
Jeannie McLoughlian, Acct & Admr

Sensient Flavors Canada Inc.

7200 West Credit Ave.
Mississauga, ON L5N 5N1
Tel 905-826-0801
Fax 905-826-0212
www.sensient-tech.com
Line: Manufactures food ingredients.
NAICS: 311930 311990
#Emp: 100-249 (Tor)
#TorLoc: 3
Own: Private Company
Par: Sensient Technologies
Corporation (US)
Key: David Rich, GM
Dave Gubekjian, Cont

Sentrex Communications Company

6400 Langstaff Rd.
Woodbridge, ON L4L 1A5
Tel 905-851-5243
Fax 905-851-9122
www.sentrexco.com
Line: Provides fiber optic cable
services.
NAICS: 232510
#Emp: 100-249 (Tor)
#TorLoc: 2
Own: Private Company
Key: Peter Nicoletti, Pres
Mary Fuda, Cont
Paul Furtado, Purch Mgr

Sentry Select Capital Corp.

2850-130 King St. West
P.O. Box 104
Toronto, ON M5X 1A4
Tel 416-364-8788
Fax 416-364-1197
www.sentryselect.com
Line: Provides investment management
services.
NAICS: 523120 523930
#Emp: 100-249 (Tor)
#TorLoc: 1
Own: Private Company
Key: Sandy McIntyre,
    Pres & Chief Investment Officer
John Driscoll, CEO
Philip Yuzpe, COO
Sheila Hansen, Dir of HR
Richard D'Archibio, CFO
Sean Driscoll, Exec VP
Brian McOstrich,
    VP Mktg & Investor Relns

Sephora

220 Yonge St.
Toronto-Eaton Centre
Toronto, ON M5B 2H1
Tel 416-595-7227
Fax 416-595-0723
www.sephora.com
NAICS: 446120
#Emp: 100-249 (Tor)
#TorLoc: 2
Own: Private Company
Key: Gary Taylor, Store Dir

The Sernas Group Inc.

41-110 Scotia Crt.
Whitby, ON L1N 8Y7
Tel 905-686-6402
Fax 905-432-7877
www.sernasgroup.com
Line: Specializes in consulting,
engineering and urban planning
services to private and public clients.
NAICS: 541330
#Emp: 100-249 (Tor)
#TorLoc: 3
Own: Private Company
Key: Reginald Webster, Pres
Jan Fontana, HR Mgr

Serta

2-40 Granite Ridge Rd.
Concord, ON L4K 5M8
Tel 905-761-1343
Fax 905-761-0876
www.serta.com
Line: Manufactures mattresses and
foundations.
NAICS: 337910
#Emp: 75-99 (Tor)
#TorLoc: 1
Own: Private Company
Key: Marsha Seow, Dir of Sales & Mktg

Servicemaster Contract Services

19 Ann St.
Mississauga, ON L5G 3E9
Tel 905-274-2327
Fax 905-274-6005
www.servicemaster.ca
Line: Provides janitorial cleaning.
NAICS: 561722
#Emp: 250-499 (Tor)
#TorLoc: 1
Own: Private Company
Key: Jeff Strong, Pres
Julie Strong, Office Mgr

Serv-U-Clean Ltd.

5-207 Edgeley Blvd.
Concord, ON L4K 4B5
Tel 905-660-0899
Fax 905-660-0550
www.serv-u-clean.com
Line: Provides commercial janitorial
services.
NAICS: 561722
#Emp: 100-249 (Tor)
#TorLoc: 1
Own: Private Company
Key: Rick Katz, Pres

Seton Canada

355 Apple Creek Blvd.
Markham, ON L3R 9X7
Tel 905-764-1122
Fax 905-764-3330
www.seton.ca
Line: Supplies safety, maintenance, and
industrial identification products.
NAICS: 326198
#Emp: 100-249 (Tor)
#TorLoc: 1
Own: Private Company
Par: Brady Corporation (US)
Key: Pascal Deman, VP & GM

Seven Continents Corporation

1-945 Wilson Ave.
Toronto, ON M3K 1E8
Tel 416-784-3717
Fax 416-784-3726
www.sevencontinents.com
Line: Manufactures store fixtures, bust
forms and mannequins.
NAICS: 339990
#Emp: 75-99 (Tor)
#TorLoc: 1
Own: Private Company
Par: Seven Continents (CDA)
Key: Ken Albright, Pres
Steve Singh, Plant Mgr
Carrie Lane, Cont
Ryan Beattie, IT Mgr

Seven Oaks

A Div. of The City of Toronto
9 Neilson Rd.
Toronto, ON M1E 5E1
Tel 416-392-3500
Fax 416-392-3579
www.toronto.ca/ltc/sevenoaks.htm
Line: Operates a home for the aged.
NAICS: 623310
#Emp: 100-249 (Tor)
#TorLoc: 1
Own: Government
Par: The City of Toronto
Key: Gail Campbell, Admr
Rosemary Steker, Asst Admr

SEW Eurodrive Company
of Canada Ltd.

210 Walker Dr.
Brampton, ON L6T 3W1
Tel 905-791-1553
Fax 905-791-2999
www.sew-eurodrive.ca
Line: Manufactures gear motors,
mechanical variable speed drives,
electronic AC frequency controls,
brake motors, gear reducers and
heads, motor controls, and motional
controllers.
NAICS: 333619
#Emp: 75-99 (Tor)
#TorLoc: 1
Own: Private Company
Par: SEW Eurodrive GmbH & Co. (GER)
Key: Larry Reynolds, Exec VP
Jim Plauntz, HR Mgr
Lyall Watson, Asst Sales Mgr

SF Partnership LLP

400-4950 Yonge St.
Toronto, ON M2N 6K1
Tel 416-250-1212
Fax 416-250-1225
www.sfgroup.ca
AKA: SF Valuations Inc; Kingston
Sorel; SF Partners Inc.
Line: Operates a full service accounting
firm.
NAICS: 541212
#Emp: 75-99 (Tor)
#TorLoc: 1
Own: Private Company
Key: Steven Goldberg, Mng Partner
Gady Wechsler, Cont
Jeffrey Mark, IS Dir

SGS Canada Inc.

6490 Vipond Dr.
Mississauga, ON L5T 1W8
Tel 905-364-3757
Fax 905-676-9519
www.ca.sgs.com
Line: Inspects, tests and verifies
expedited goods and provides quality
management system certification.
NAICS: 561990 541380
#Emp: 250-499 (Tor)
#TorLoc: 4
Own: Private Company
Par: SGS Geneva (SWITZ)
Key: Gerard O'Dell, Mng Dir
Chris Lowry, Dir of HR
Lynda Schultz, Cont
Greg Tompkins, Dir of IT

Shade-O-Matic

550 Oakdale Rd.
Toronto, ON M3N 1W6
Tel 416-742-1524
Fax 416-742-8477
www.shade-o-matic.com
Line: Manufactures vertical and
venetian blinds and window shades.
NAICS: 337920
#Emp: 250-499 (Tor)
#TorLoc: 1
Own: Private Company
Par: Hunter Douglas Canada Inc. (CDA)
Key: Angelo Bitondo, Pres
Graham Stanclik, HR Mgr
Angela DiIorio, Cont
Amir Moradi, VP Sales
Cathy Hupp, Dir of Mktg

Shadow Lake Outdoor Recreation Centre

15041 9th Line
Stouffville, ON L4A 7X3
Tel 905-640-6432
Fax 905-640-1339
www.shadowlakecentre.ca
Line: Operates a camp for the disabled.
NAICS: 624120
#Emp: 75-99 (Tor)
#TorLoc: 1
Own: Private Company
Par: Community Living Toronto (CDA)
Key: Gary Ouellette, Dir

Shaftesbury Films

100-163 Queen St. East
Toronto, ON M5A 1S1
Tel 416-363-1411
Fax 416-363-1428
www.shaftesbury.ca
Line: Operates a film company.
NAICS: 512110 512190
#Emp: 100-249 (Tor)
#TorLoc: 1
Own: Private Company
Key: Scott Garvie, Sr VP,
  Business & Legal Affairs
Christina Jennings, Chmn & CEO
Jan Peter Meyboom, VP Production
Gord Mcllquham, Sr VP Fin
Shane Kinnear, VP Sales & Mktg

Shah Trading Co. Ltd.

3451 McNicoll Ave.
Toronto, ON M1V 2V3
Tel 416-292-6927
Fax 416-292-7932
www.shahtrading.com
Line: Imports, manufactures and
distributes whole foods.
NAICS: 413190
#Emp: 100-249 (Tor)
#TorLoc: 1
Own: Private Company
Key: Kirit Shah, Pres

Sharpe Blackmore Inc.

300-473 Adelaide St. West
Toronto, ON M5V 1T1
Tel 416-920-6864
Fax 416-920-5043
www.sharpeblackmore.com
AKA: Sharpe Blackmore Euro RSCG
Inc.
Line: Operates an advertising agency.
NAICS: 541810
#Emp: 100-249 (Tor)
#TorLoc: 1
Own: Private Company
Key: Thomas G. Blackmore, Pres
Bill Sharpe, Chmn
Tom Olesinski, CFO

Sharp Electronics of Canada Ltd.

335 Britannia Rd. East
Mississauga, ON L4Z 1W9
Tel 905-890-2100
Fax 905-568-7144
www.sharp.ca
Line: Distributes consumer electronics
and telecommunications products.
NAICS: 414210 417320
#Emp: 100-249 (Tor)
#TorLoc: 1
Own: Public Company
Par: Sharp Corp. (JAPAN)
Key: Carmine Cinerari,
  Pres, Sharp Canada
Dan Merlini, VP, Business Solutions
  Divison
Bob Tucker, System VP, Corp Services

Shaw Broadcast Services

2055 Flavelle Blvd.
Mississauga, ON L5K 1Z8
Tel 905-403-2020
Fax 905-403-2022
www.shawbroadcast.com
AKA: Cancom; Star Choice
Line: Markets and delivers video and
audio services to consumers and cable
companies, and telecommunication
services via satellite to trucking
companies.
NAICS: 513340
#Emp: 250-499 (Tor)
#TorLoc: 3
Own: Private Company
Par: Shaw Communications Inc. (CDA)
Key: Peter Bissonnette, Pres
Don Fletcher, VP Tech Services
Gaston Dufour, GM Sales,
  Eastern Canada & US

Shaw Canada LP

2050 Derry Rd. West
Mississauga, ON L5N 0B9
Tel 905-816-7000
Fax 905-816-7010
www.shawgrp.com
Line: Provides full service engineering,
procurement and construction
management servicing to the power,
process and industrial sectors.
NAICS: 541330 231410
#Emp: 250-499 (Tor)
#TorLoc: 1
Own: Private Company
Par: The Shaw Group Inc. (US)
Key: Bob Lukas, Pres
Barbara D'Sylva, HR Mgr

ShawCor Ltd.

25 Bethridge Rd.
Toronto, ON M9W 1M7
Tel 416-743-7111
Fax 416-743-7199
www.shawcor.com
AKA: Bredero-Shaw
Line: Provides pipe-coating systems to
global energy service markets.
NAICS: 326198
#Emp: 250-499 (Tor)
#TorLoc: 1
Own: Public Company
Key: William P. Buckley, Pres & CEO
Fred Gallina, VP Ops
Gary Love, VP Fin & CFO
Larry Marshall, VP IT
Garry L. Graham, VP Corp Dev

ShawFlex

25 Bethridge Rd.
Toronto, ON M9W 1M7
Tel 416-743-7111
Fax 416-743-2565
www.shawflex.com
Line: Manufactures instrumentation,
controls and various types of low
voltage electrical cable.
NAICS: 335920 232510
#Emp: 75-99 (Tor)
#TorLoc: 1
Own: Public Company
Par: ShawCor Ltd. (CDA)
Key: Greg Passler, GM
Madjid Doreh, Cont
Tracy Walsh, Purch Mgr
Rob Kassies, Sales & Mktg Mgr

Shell Canada Ltd.

400-4th Ave. S.W.
P.O. Box 100, Stn. M.
Calgary, AB T2P 0J4
Tel 403-691-3111
Fax 403-691-4183
www.shell.ca
Line: Explores, develops, refines,
distributes and markets crude oil,
natural gas, and natural gas liquids.
NAICS: 324110 447190
#Emp: 500-999 (Tor)
#TorLoc: 1
Own: Public Company
Par: Shell Investments Ltd. (CDA)
Key: Lorraine Mitchelmore, Pres
John Abbott, Exec VP
Dwight van Kampen, Sr VP, Fin & Cont

Shell Lubricants Canada

1101 Blair Rd.
Burlington, ON L7M 1T3
Tel 905-335-5577
Fax 905-332-6406
www.shell.ca
Line: Sells, markets and distributes
automotive consumer products and
lubricants.
NAICS: 412110
#Emp: 75-99 (Tor)
#TorLoc: 1
Own: Private Company
Par: Shell Lubricants (US)
Key: Diane McFarlane, Pres

Shepell·fgi

700-895 Don Mills Rd.
Toronto, ON M3C 1W3
Tel 416-961-0023
Fax 416-961-4339
www.shepellfgi.com
Line: Provides behavioural health
services including employee assistance
programs, disability management
health care consulting, health
information service, trauma response
and wellness programs, and corporate
health practices.
NAICS: 624190 813310
#Emp: 250-499 (Tor)
#TorLoc: 10
Own: Private Company
Key: Stephen Liptrap, GM
Rita Fridella, Sr VP Ops
Michael Lin, VP IT
Neil King, Sr VP
　　Sales & Account Management

Shepherd Village Inc.

3760 Sheppard Ave. East
Toronto, ON M1T 3K9
Tel 416-609-5700
Fax 416-609-8329
www.shepherdvillage.org
AKA: Shepherd Gardens; Shepherd
Lodge; Shepherd Manor; Shepherd
Terrace
Line: Provides accommodation and
long-term care for seniors.
NAICS: 623310 813310
#Emp: 250-499 (Tor)
#TorLoc: 1
Own: Not-for-profit
Key: David S. Hillier, Pres & CEO
Brock Hall, VP Client Care Services
Marion Rourke, Mgr of HR
Farhad Sethna, VP Fin & Admin
Mario Gugliotta, Facilities Mgr
Alan Nummey, Mgr of IS

The Sheraton Gateway Hotel

Terminal 3
P.O. Box 3000
Toronto AMF, ON L5P 1C4
Tel 905-672-7000
Fax 905-672-7100
www.starwoodhotels.com
NAICS: 721111
#Emp: 250-499 (Tor)
#TorLoc: 1
Own: Public Company
Par: Starwood Hotels & Resorts
Worldwide Inc. (US)
Key: Jaumana Ghandar, GM
Anna Borssova, Dir of Fin
Eduardo Rafael, IT Mgr

Sheraton Parkway Toronto North Hotel & Suites

600 Hwy. 7 East
Richmond Hill, ON L4B 1B2
Tel 905-881-2121
Fax 905-881-7841
www.sheratonparkway.com
NAICS: 721111
#Emp: 250-499 (Tor)
#TorLoc: 1
Own: Private Company
Key: Suzanne Marshall, GM

Sheraton Toronto Airport Hotel & Conference Centre

801 Dixon Rd.
Toronto, ON M9W 1J5
Tel 416-675-6100
Fax 416-675-4022
www.sheraton.com
NAICS: 721111
#Emp: 100-249 (Tor)
#TorLoc: 2
Own: Private Company
Par: Larco Hospitality (CDA)·
Key: Dan Woodburn, GM
Leanne Simpson, Dir of HR
Natasha Melanson, Dir of Sales & Mktg

The Sheridan College Institute of Technology and Advanced Learning

1430 Trafalgar Rd.
Oakville, ON L6H 2L1
Tel 905-845-9430
Fax 905-815-4023
www.sheridaninstitute.ca
Line: Operates education and training college.
NAICS: 611210
#Emp: 1000-4999 (Tor)
#TorLoc: 3
Own: Government
Key: Jeff Zabudsky, Pres & CEO
Mary Preece, VP Academic
Cathi Berge, Dir of HR
Karam Daljit, VP Fin & Admin
Jim Greer, Purch
Ian Marley, VP IT & Student Services
Janine Gliener, Dir of Mktg & Commun

Sheridan Nurseries Limited

12302 10th Line, R.R. #4
Georgetown, ON L7G 4S7
Tel 416-798-7970
Fax 905-873-2478
www.sheridannurseries.com
Line: Operates nursery and garden centres.
NAICS: 444220
#Emp: 1000-4999 (Tor)
#TorLoc: 9
Own: Private Company
Key: Karl E. Stensson, Pres
William Stensson, CEO
Paul Smith, Product Mgr
Jim MacLeod, HR Mgr
Rick Friesen, Sr VP Fin
Pieter Joubert, VP Nursery Ops
Greg Kenny, IT & Commun Mgr
Manuel Sobrinho, VP Nursery Sales
Valerie Stensson, VP Mktg & Purch

Sheridan Villa

A Div. of Regional Municipality of Peel
2460 Truscott Dr.
Mississauga, ON L5J 3Z8
Tel 905-791-8668
Fax 905-823-7971
www.peelregion.ca
Line: Operates long-term care facility and adult day service.
NAICS: 623310
#Emp: 100-249 (Tor)
#TorLoc: 1
Own: Government
Key: Inga Mazuryk, Admr
Jason Thornton,
    Supr of Business Services

Sherson Group

100-1446 Don Mills Rd.
Toronto, ON M3B 3N6
Tel 416-449-9550
Fax 416-449-9555
www.sherson.com
AKA: Nine West; Madison; Shoe Studio
Line: Wholesales and retails footwear and accessories.
NAICS: 414120
#Emp: 250-499 (Tor)
Own: Private Company
Key: Stephen Applebaum, Pres & CEO
Patricia Csapo, Sr Mgr of HR
Linda O'Flaherty, Cont
Marlene Lavecchia, VP Retail Ops
Gina Lainas, VP Merchandise

Sherway Gardens

25 The West Mall
P.O. Box 101
Toronto, ON M9C 1B8
Tel 416-621-1070
Fax 416-620-7918
www.sherwaygardens.ca
Line: Operates shopping centres.
NAICS: 531120
#Emp: 75-99 (Tor)
Own: Private Company
Key: Andy Traynor, GM

Sherway Warehousing Inc.

325 Annagem Blvd.
Mississauga, ON L5T 3A7
Tel 905-364-3300
Fax 905-364-3301
www.sherwaywarehousing.com
AKA: Sherway Group
Line: Provides logistics solutions.

NAICS: 493110
#Emp: 100-249 (Tor)
#TorLoc: 5
Own: Private Company
Key: Kevin Leggett, Pres
Paul Rockett, CEO
Mark Rockett, VP

The Sherwin-Williams Company (Canada)

170 Brunel Rd.
Mississauga, ON L4Z 1T5
Tel 905-507-0166
Fax 905-507-4198
www.sherwin-williams.com
Line: Manufactures paint.
NAICS: 325510
#Emp: 100-249 (Tor)
#TorLoc: 12
Own: Public Company
Par: The Sherwin-Williams Co. (US)
Key: David Skinner, Dir of Sales & Ops
Mary Cole, Benefits Admr
Ernest Thibodeau, District Credit Mgr
Sal Bruno, Sales Mgr, Ontario
Ahan Bose, Mktg Mgr, Canada

Sherwood Electromotion Inc.

271 Hanlan Rd.
Woodbridge, ON L4L 3R7
Tel 905-851-6671
Fax 905-851-1638
www.sherwoodelectromotion.com
Line: Manufactures and repairs electric motors and other equipment.
NAICS: 335312
#Emp: 75-99 (Tor)
#TorLoc: 1
Own: Private Company
Key: George Gavrilidis, Pres
Joe Sabino, GM
Spiro Koumoulas, HR Mgr

Shibley Righton LLP

700-250 University Ave.
Toronto, ON M5H 3E5
Tel 416-214-5200
Fax 416-214-5400
www.shibleyrighton.com
Line: Operates a law firm.
NAICS: 541110
#Emp: 75-99 (Tor)
#TorLoc: 1
Own: Partnership
Key: Stacey Chandler,
Dir of HR & Admin

Shipway Stairs Ltd.

1820 Ironstone Dr.
Burlington, ON L7L 5V3
Tel 905-336-1296
Fax 905-336-8643
www.shipwaystairs.com
Line: Manufactures wood stairs and railings.
NAICS: 321919
#Emp: 100-249 (Tor)
#TorLoc: 2
Own: Private Company
Key: Larry Shipway, Co-Owner
Dale Shipway, Co-Owner
Craig Sharp, HR Mgr
Sandra Connell, Cont
Rob Cabral, Purch & Mktg Mgr
Bill Parchem, Contract Mgr

Shoppers Drug Mart/ Pharmaprix

243 Consumers Rd.
Toronto, ON M2J 4W8
Tel 416-493-1220
Fax 416-490-2700
www.shoppersdrugmart.ca
Line: Operates retail drug stores.
NAICS: 446110
#Emp: 10000+ (Tor)
#TorLoc: 261
Own: Public Company
Key: Jurgen Schreiber, Chmn & CEO

Shoppers HomeHealthCare

104 Bartley Dr.
Toronto, ON M4A 1C5
Tel 416-752-8885
Fax 416-752-5068
www.shoppershomehealthcare.ca
AKA: Therapy Supplies & Rental Ltd.
Line: Supplies hospital equipment.
NAICS: 417930
#Emp: 250-499 (Tor)
#TorLoc: 5
Own: Private Company
Par: Shoppers Drug Mart Inc. (CDA)
Key: Mike Dorman, VP Retail
Mike Morse, Ops Mgr

The Shopping Channel

A Div. of Rogers Broadcasting Ltd.
59 Ambassador Dr.
Mississauga, ON L5T 2P9
Tel 905-565-3500
Fax 905-362-7704
www.theshoppingchannel.ca
AKA: TSC
Line: Provides nationally broadcasted televised home shopping service.
NAICS: 513120 454390
#Emp: 500-999 (Tor)
#TorLoc: 3
Own: Private Company
Par: Rogers Communications Inc. (CDA)
Key: Ted Starkman, Exec VP & GM
Mike Mroczkowski, VP Ops
Claudia Livadas, Dir of HR
Lella Liuzzi, VP Merchandising
Ba Linh Le, VP Strategy Dev & Enterprise Transformation
Michael LeBlanc, VP Mktg

Shopsy's Downtown

96 Richmond St. West
The Sheraton Centre
Toronto, ON M5H 2A3
Tel 416-365-3354
Fax 416-365-7264
www.shopsys.ca
Line: Operates a full service restaurant/ deli/bar.
NAICS: 722210
#Emp: 75-99 (Tor)
#TorLoc: 3
Own: Private Company
Key: Gavin Quinn, Pres
Chao Tam, Mgr
Louise Quinn, CFO

Shorewood Packaging Corporation of Canada Ltd.

50-2220 Midland Ave.
Toronto, ON M1P 3E6
Tel 416-940-2400
Fax 416-940-2464
www.shorewoodpackaging.com
Line: Provides printing services for folding cartons for consumer packaging.
NAICS: 322212
#Emp: 250-499 (Tor)
#TorLoc: 2
Own: Private Company
Par: International Paper Co. (US)
Key: Grant Clark, GM
Terry O'Boyle, Ops Mgr
Natalie Chinaloy, HR Generalist
Kathy Salter, Logistics Mgr
Joseph Pang, Land Admr
Rob Hurst, VP Sales

Shouldice Hospital

7750 Bayview Ave.
Thornhill, ON L3T 4A3
Tel 905-889-1125
Fax 905-889-4216
www.shouldice.com
Line: Operates a hospital and walk in clinic.
NAICS: 622310
#Emp: 100-249 (Tor)
#TorLoc: 1
Own: Private Company
Key: Byrnes Shouldice, Pres & Chmn
John Hughes, CAO
Shirley MacLellan, Payroll
Paul Godard, Cont
Daryl Urquhart, Dir of Business Dev

Showa Canada Inc.

1 Showa Crt.
Schomberg, ON L0G 1T0
Tel 905-939-0575
Fax 905-939-0865
www.showa1.com
NAICS: 336390
#Emp: 250-499 (Tor)
#TorLoc: 1
Own: Private Company
Key: Brenda McKee, Pres
Rick Wolack, Fin Mgr

Shred-It

A Div. of Securit
2794 South Sheridan Way
Oakville, ON L6J 7T4
Tel 905-829-2222
Fax 905-829-9206
www.shredit.com
Line: Operates a mobile paper shredding and recycling company servicing the corporate business community.
NAICS: 561990
#Emp: 250-499 (Tor)
#TorLoc: 1
Own: Private Company
Key: Vince De Palma, Pres & CEO

Sibley & Associates Inc.

104-1122 International Blvd.
Burlington, ON L7L 6Z8
Tel 905-633-7800
Fax 905-633-7900
www.sibley.ca
Line: Operates a rehabilitation
management firm.
NAICS: 624310
#Emp: 100-249 (Tor)
#TorLoc: 5
Own: Private Company
Key: Steven Sibley, Pres & CEO
Gail Burnett, Dir of Exec Services

Sick Kids Foundation

525 University Ave.
14th Fl.
Toronto, ON M5G 2L3
Tel 416-813-6166
Fax 416-813-5024
www.sickkidsfoundation.com
Line: Operates a fundraising and
granting organization.
NAICS: 813210
#Emp: 100-249 (Tor)
#TorLoc: 1
Own: Not-for-profit
Key: Ted Garrard, Pres & CEO
Debbie Young, COO
Susan Lyon, HR Generalist
Patrick Manley, Dir of Fin
David Fisher, Dir of IT
Grant Stirling, VP Major Gifts
Rosalie McGovern, VP Direct Mktg
David Estok, VP Commun

Siemens Canada Limited

2185 Derry Rd. West
Mississauga, ON L5N 7A6
Tel 905-819-8000
Fax 905-819-5777
www.siemens.ca
Line: Designs and develops projects
in healthcare, information and
communications, energy and power,
industry, automation, transportation
and lighting.
NAICS: 335990
#Emp: 1000-4999 (Tor)
#TorLoc: 10
Own: Private Company
Par: Siemens AG (GER)
Key: Roland Aurich, Pres & CEO
Sean Walkinshaw, Sr VP HR
Manfred Doenz, Exec VP & CFO
Ann Adair, Dir of Corp Commun

Siemens Enterprise Communications Inc.

400-55 Commerce Valley Dr. West
Thornhill, ON L3T 7V9
Tel 905-695-7900
Fax 905-695-7912
www.enterprise-communications.
   siemens.com
AKA: SEN Canada
Line: Provides unified communication
voice, network and services solutions.
NAICS: 511210 541510
#Emp: 100-249 (Tor)
#TorLoc: 1
Own: Private Company
Par: Siemens Enterprise (GER)
Key: Scott McDonald,
   VP Contact Center
William Moore, VP Sales & Mktg

Siemens Healthcare Diagnostics

1200 Courtneypark Dr. East
Mississauga, ON L5T 1P2
Tel 905-564-7333
Fax 905-795-4499
www.diagnostics.siemens.com
AKA: Dade Behring Canada Inc.
Line: Offers products, systems and
services designed for labs.
NAICS: 334512
#Emp: 75-99 (Tor)
#TorLoc: 1
Own: Private Company
Par: Siemens Healthcare Diagnostics
(US)
Key: Gehane Youhan, HR Mgr

Siemens PLM Software

2550 Matheson Blvd. East
Mississauga, ON L4W 4Z1
Tel 905-212-4500
Fax 905-212-4502
www.plm.automation.siemens.com
Line: Provides product lifecycle
consulting services.
NAICS: 541619
#Emp: 75-99 (Tor)
#TorLoc: 1
Own: Public Company
Par: Siemens (GER)
Key: Phil Taylor, Pres

Sierra Systems Group Inc.

1910-150 York St.
Toronto, ON M5H 3S5
Tel 416-777-1212
Fax 416-777-0422
www.sierrasystems.com
Line: Provides management consulting
and systems integration services.
NAICS: 541611
#Emp: 100-249 (Tor)
#TorLoc: 1
Own: Private Company
Key: David Duff, Solutions Mgr

Sigma Global Solutions

1100-55 York St.
Toronto, ON M5J 1R7
Tel 416-362-8999
Fax 416-362-8131
www.sigmaglobal.ca
Line: Specializes in infrastructure
services, e-business, billing and
telecommunications systems solutions,
and application development.
NAICS: 541510
#Emp: 100-249 (Tor)
#TorLoc: 1
Own: Private Company
Par: Sigma Group (CDA)
Key: Andy Jasuja, CEO

Sigma Systems

1100-55 York St.
Toronto, ON M5J 1R7
Tel 416-943-9696
Fax 416-365-9227
www.sigma-systems.com
Line: Provides computer program
development services.
NAICS: 541510
#Emp: 100-249 (Tor)
#TorLoc: 1
Own: Private Company
Key: Tim Spencer, Pres & COO
Andy Jasuja, Chmn & CEO
Martin Kadey, VP Fin,
   Admin & Corp Secy
Brian Cappellani, CTO & VP Engineering
Jackie Berg, VP Worldwide Sales
Preston Gilmer, VP Product Mktg

Signature Aluminum Canada Inc.

1850 Clements Rd.
Pickering, ON L1W 3R8
Tel 905-427-6550
Fax 905-427-2239
www.signaturealuminumcanada.com
Line: Manufactures and sells aluminum ladders and extrusions used in the manufacturing of windows, auto parts and other goods.
NAICS: 332999
#Emp: 100-249 (Tor)
#TorLoc: 3
Own: Private Company
Key: Mark Blackmore, Dir of Ops
Dianne Grenaghan, HR Mgr
Don Cousins, Purch Mgr

Silcotech North America Inc.

54 Nixon Rd.
Bolton, ON L7E 1W2
Tel 905-857-9998
Fax 905-857-6004
www.silcotech.ca
Line: Operates a multinational silicone injection molding company.
NAICS: 333220
#Emp: 75-99 (Tor)
Own: Private Company
Key: Isolde Boettger, VP

Silex Innovations Inc.

6659 Ordan Dr.
Mississauga, ON L5T 1K6
Tel 905-612-4000
Fax 905-612-8999
www.silex.com
Line: Designs, manufactures and supplies noise control products for use in industrial applications.
NAICS: 334512
#Emp: 100-249 (Tor)
#TorLoc: 1
Own: Private Company
Key: Todd Stephens, Pres

Silliker Canada Co.

4-90 Gough Rd.
Markham, ON L3R 5V5
Tel 905-479-5255
Fax 905-479-4645
www.silliker.com
Line: Operates a food testing laboratory.
NAICS: 541380
#Emp: 75-99 (Tor)
#TorLoc: 2
Own: Private Company

Par: Silliker Inc. (US)
Key: Jocelyn Alfieri, Lab Dir
Patricia Taylor, Acctng & HR Mgr

Silverstein's Bakery Ltd.

195 McCaul St.
Toronto, ON M5T 1W6
Tel 416-598-3478
Fax 416-598-5459
Line: Manufactures artisan style specialty breads and rolls for hotels, restaurants, institutions and caterers.
NAICS: 311811 311814
#Emp: 100-249 (Tor)
#TorLoc: 1
Own: Private Company
Key: Harvey Silverstein, Pres
Jeff Silverstein, VP Sales & Mktg

Simcoe Manor Home for the Aged

5988 8th Line
P.O. Box 100
Beeton, ON L0G 1A0
Tel 905-729-2267
Fax 905-729-4350
www.simcoe.ca
Line: Operates a long term care facility and home for the aged.
NAICS: 623310
#Emp: 100-249 (Tor)
#TorLoc: 1
Own: Not-for-profit
Par: The County of Simcoe (CDA)
Key: Jane Sinclair, GM, Health & Cultural Services

Sim, Lowman, Ashton & McKay LLP

330 University Ave., 6th Fl.
Toronto, ON M5G 1R7
Tel 416-595-1155
Fax 416-595-1163
www.sim-mcburney.com
AKA: Sim & McBurney
Line: Provides patent and trademark legal services.
NAICS: 541110
#Emp: 100-249 (Tor)
#TorLoc: 1
Own: Private Company
Key: Kenneth McKay, Partner
Silvana Stojanovski, HR Mgr
Jeff Kolwich, IS Mgr

Simmons Canada Inc.

1-2550 Meadowvale Blvd.
Mississauga, ON L5N 8C2
Tel 905-817-9669
Fax 905-817-1514
www.simmonscanada.com
Line: Markets furniture products and manufactures mattresses and foundations.
NAICS: 337910 414390
#Emp: 100-249 (Tor)
#TorLoc: 1
Own: Public Company
Key: Paul Bognar, Pres

SimplexGrinnell

A Div. of Tyco International of Canada Ltd.
2400 Skymark Ave.
Mississauga, ON L4W 5K5
Tel 905-212-4400
Fax 905-212-4401
www.simplexgrinnell.com
Line: Designs, installs, services, and sells fire protection equipment including sprinklers, fire alarms, fire extinguishers and special systems.
NAICS: 333990 334290 339990
#Emp: 250-499 (Tor)
#TorLoc: 1
Own: Public Company
Par: Tyco International Ltd. (US)
Key: John Wrycraft, GM

Simplicious

A Div. of Job Skills
714-10 Milner Business Crt.
Toronto, ON M1B 3C6
Tel 416-412-1099
Fax 416-412-3218
www.jobskills.org
Line: Provides employability training services.
NAICS: 624310
#Emp: 75-99 (Tor)
#TorLoc: 11
Own: Not-for-profit
Key: Nella Iasci, Exec Dir

Sinclair-Cockburn Financial Group

910-3389 Steeles Ave. East
Toronto, ON M2H 3S8
Tel 416-494-7700
Fax 416-494-5343
www.scfg.ca
Line: Distributes insurance, deals mutual funds and brokers mortgages and real estate.
NAICS: 524210
#Emp: 75-99 (Tor)
#TorLoc: 1
Own: Private Company
Key: Jim Grieve, Pres
Jim Aston, Dir
Kelly Sinclair, Dir

Sinclair Technologies Inc.

85 Mary St.
Aurora, ON L4G 6X5
Tel 905-727-0165
Fax 905-727-0861
www.sinctech.com
Line: Manufactures and distributes antennas, combiners, receiver multicouplers, duplexers and cavity filters for the communications industry.
NAICS: 334220
#Emp: 100-249 (Tor)
#TorLoc: 1
Own: Private Company
Key: Calven Iwata, Pres
Martine Cardozo, Dir of Sales

Sing Tao Daily

417 Dundas St. West
Toronto, ON M5T 1G6
Tel 416-596-8140
Fax 416-599-6688
www.singtao.ca
Line: Publishes Chinese daily newspaper.
NAICS: 511110
#Emp: 100-249 (Tor)
#TorLoc: 2
Own: Private Company
Key: Carol Peddie, CEO
Peter Li, VP
Raphael Lai, Cont
Johnson Yuen, Dir of Mktg & Sales

SIR Corp.

200-5360 South Service Rd.
Burlington, ON L7L 5L1
Tel 905-681-2997
Fax 905-681-0394
www.sircorp.com
AKA: Al Frisco's; Alice Fazooli's!; Canyon Creek; Far Niente; Jack Astor's Bar & Grill; Loose Moose; Reds; Four/Petit Four
Line: Operates a system of privately owned restaurants and bars.
NAICS: 722210
#Emp: 1000-4999 (Tor)
#TorLoc: 32
Own: Private Company
Key: Bruce Elliot, Pres & COO
Peter Fowler, CEO
Karen Scanlan, VP HR
Jeff Good, CFO
George Kakaletris, VP Mktg

Sir Robert L. Borden Business & Technical Institute

200 Poplar Rd.
Toronto, ON M1E 1Z7
Tel 416-396-6810
Fax 416-396-6773
Line: Operates public high school.
NAICS: 611410
#Emp: 75-99 (Tor)
#TorLoc: 1
Own: Private Company
Par: Toronto District School Board (CDA)
Key: Anthony Hack, Principal
Robin Royten, Vice Principal
Duncan LeBlanc, Vice Principal
Karin Fussell, Vice Principal

Sisley Motors Limited

88 Steeles Ave. West
Thornhill, ON L4J 1A1
Tel 905-695-8888
Fax 905-695-8884
www.drivesisley.com
AKA: Sisley Honda; Sisley Hyundai
Line: Provides sales and service for new and used vehicles.
NAICS: 441110 441120
#Emp: 100-249 (Tor)
#TorLoc: 2
Own: Private Company
Key: Hugh Sisley, Pres
Pat Trotter, Cont

Sisters of St. Joseph Toronto

3377 Bayview Ave.
Toronto, ON M2M 3S4
Tel 416-222-1101
Fax 416-222-9816
www.csj-to.ca
Line: Operates a registered charity.
NAICS: 813110
#Emp: 100-249 (Tor)
#TorLoc: 1
Own: Religious
Key: Therese Meunire, Gen Superior
Gisela Cote, Dir of Commun

Skanna Systems Investigations

216-8130 Sheppard Ave.
Toronto, ON M1B 3W3
Tel 416-292-5353
Fax 416-292-3296
www.skanna.com
Line: Provides security guards and private investigators.
NAICS: 561612
#Emp: 100-249 (Tor)
#TorLoc: 1
Own: Private Company
Key: John Peters, Owner & Pres
Winston Bollers, Dir of Ops
Stacy Gray, Dir of HR
Simone Peters, Dir of Fin

SKF Canada Ltd.

40 Exec Crt.
Toronto, ON M1S 4N4
Tel 416-299-1220
Fax 416-292-0399
www.skf.ca
Line: Sells bearings and seals.
NAICS: 417230
#Emp: 75-99 (Tor)
#TorLoc: 1
Own: Private Company
Par: SKF AB (SWE)
Key: Joao Ricciarelli, Pres
Frank Bijnens, VP Quality & Ops
Joanne Neglia, HR Mgr

Skills for Change

791 St. Clair Ave. West
Toronto, ON M6C 1B8
Tel 416-658-3101
Fax 416-658-6292
www.skillsforchange.org
Line: Provides services to immigrants
and refugees to enter the Canadian
workplace, and provides assistance to
internationally-qualified professionals.
NAICS: 813920
#Emp: 75-99 (Tor)
#TorLoc: 3
Own: Association
Key: Cheryl May, Exec Dir
Bill Waicus, Mgr of Ops
Roland Rhooms,
    Program & Services Mgr
Manoj Paul, Acctng & Financial Mgr

Skor Food Group Inc.

10 Ronrose Dr.
Vaughan, ON L4K 4R3
Tel 905-660-1212
Fax 905-660-4848
www.skorfoodgroup.com
Line: Distributes dry and frozen foods.
NAICS: 413110
#Emp: 250-499 (Tor)
#TorLoc: 1
Own: Public Company
Key: Vince Capobianco, Pres & CEO
Bryan Knebel, CFO

Sleep Country Canada

1-140 Wendell Ave.
Toronto, ON M9N 3R2
Tel 416-242-4774
Fax 416-242-9644
www.sleepcountry.ca
Line: Retails mattresses.
NAICS: 442110
#Emp: 250-499 (Tor)
#TorLoc: 49
Own: Private Company
Key: Christine Magee, Pres
Stephen Gunn, Chmn & CEO
Sieg Will, VP Ops
Brett Abram, HR Dir
Vicki Jones, CFO & Secy
Eric Solomon, VP Merchandise & Mktg

S.L.H. Transport Inc.

9601 Hwy. 50
Vaughan, ON L4H 2B9
Tel 905-893-4318
Fax 905-893-5180
www.slh.ca
NAICS: 484110 484121
#Emp: 100-249 (Tor)
#TorLoc: 1
Own: Public Company
Par: Sears Canada Inc. (CDA)
Key: Sylvain Moffat, Reg Terminal Mgr
Surish Marajh, Vaughan Ops Mgr

Slidemaster

A Div. of Magna Seating Systems
564 Newpark Blvd.
Newmarket, ON L3Y 4X1
Tel 905-853-3604
Fax 905-853-3607
NAICS: 332999
#Emp: 100-249 (Tor)
#TorLoc: 1
Own: Private Company
Par: Magna International Inc. (CDA)
Key: Luciano Colozza, GM
Deana Hinscelwood, HR Coord

Slovenian Linden Foundation

52 Neilson Dr.
Toronto, ON M9C 1V7
Tel 416-621-3820
Fax 416-621-9773
www.domlipa.ca
AKA: Dom Lipa; Dom Lipa Nursing
Home
Line: Operates a nursing home.
NAICS: 623110
#Emp: 75-99 (Tor)
#TorLoc: 1
Own: Not-for-profit
Key: Theresa MacDermid, Admr

Smart Centres

100-700 Applewood Cres.
Vaughan, ON L4K 5X3
Tel 905-760-6200
Fax 905-760-6220
www.smartcentres.com
Line: Develops commercial real estate.
NAICS: 531310 231110
#Emp: 250-499 (Tor)
#TorLoc: 1
Own: Private Company
Key: Mitchell Goldhar, CEO
Peter Forde, COO
Fernando Vescio,
    Sr VP HR & Corp Services
Peter Nobre, Sr VP Leasing
Sandra Kaiser, VP Pub Affairs

Smart DM

A-324 Horner Ave.
Toronto, ON M8W 1Z3
Tel 416-461-9271
Fax 416-461-9201
www.smartdm.ca
AKA: The SMR Group
Line: Provides direct mail services
including data processing, laser, ink
jet, lettershop, and fulfillment.
NAICS: 541860 514210
#Emp: 100-249 (Tor)
#TorLoc: 1
Own: Private Company
Par: Cover-All Computer Services
Corp. (CDA)
Key: Michael Coverdale, Pres & CEO
David Dunnett, VP & GM
Martin Coe, VP Fin & Admin
John Leonard, VP Sales & Mktg

Smart Laser Grafix

106 East Dr.
Brampton, ON L6T 1C1
Tel 905-792-7887
Fax 905-793-7796
www.slgcp.ca
AKA: SLG Group; Smart Enterprises
Corp.
Line: Provides offset and laser printing
services.
NAICS: 323114
#Emp: 75-99 (Tor)
#TorLoc: 2
Own: Private Company
Key: Phil Hall, Pres
Maureen Roberts, VP
Karen Hall, Admr

SMC Pneumatics (Canada) Ltd.

2715 Bristol Circ.
Oakville, ON L6H 6X5
Tel 905-812-0400
Fax 905-812-8686
www.smcpneumatics.ca
Line: Manufactures and distributes
pneumatic products.
NAICS: 333990
#Emp: 100-249 (Tor)
#TorLoc: 1
Own: Public Company
Par: SMC Corporation (JAPAN)
Key: Robin Lane,
    Customer Service Supr
James Allen, IT Mgr

Smith & Andersen Consulting Engineering

500-4211 Yonge St.
Toronto, ON M2P 2A9
Tel 416-487-8151
Fax 416-487-9104
www.smithandandersen.com
Line: Provides design and contract administration for mechanical, electrical and communications building systems.
NAICS: 541330
#Emp: 100-249 (Tor)
#TorLoc: 1
Own: Private Company
Key: David Mewdell, Partner
Karol Goldman, Partner

Smith Detection

7030 Century Ave.
Mississauga, ON L5N 2V8
Tel 905-817-5990
Fax 905-817-5992
www.smithdetection.com
Line: Designs, markets and manufactures explosive narcotic and chemical warfare detection systems.
NAICS: 334512
#Emp: 250-499 (Tor)
#TorLoc: 1
Own: Private Company
Par: Smiths Group plc (US)
Key: Geoff Beyer, VP Ops
David Astles, Ops Mgr
John Richardson, Purch Mgr
Kevin Lee, IT Mgr
Paul Kennedy, Sales Mgr
John Screech, VP Product
    Management & Market Dev

Smith Induspac Toronto Ltd.

930A Brittania Rd. East
Mississauga, ON L4W 5M7
Tel 905-564-9037
Fax 905-564-8310
www.smithpackaging.com
AKA: Induspac
Line: Designs, packages and fabricates foam, corrugated boxes and packaging items.
NAICS: 322211 326140
#Emp: 75-99 (Tor)
#TorLoc: 1
Own: Private Company
Key: Paul Gaulin, Owner
Eric Laflamme, Pres
Scott Grills, GM, Toronto
Norm Hughes, Sales Mgr

SMTC Corporation

635 Hood Rd.
Markham, ON L3R 4N6
Tel 905-479-1810
Fax 905-479-1877
www.smtc.com
Line: Manufactures printed circuit boards, electronic assemblies and enclosure systems.
NAICS: 334410
#Emp: 250-499 (Tor)
#TorLoc: 1
Own: Public Company
Key: Alex Walker, Co-CEO
Claude Germain, Co-CEO
Don Simpson, Sr VP
    Engineering & Manuf
Betsy Smith, VP HR
Jane Todd, Sr VP Fin & CFO
Paul Blom, Sr VP, Supply Chain
Steven Hoffrogge, Sr VP, Business Dev

SMT Direct Marketing Inc.

1400-5255 Yonge St.
Toronto, ON M2N 6P4
Tel 416-485-6500
Fax 416-485-5635
www.smtdirect.com
Line: Offers marketing and advertising services.
NAICS: 454390
#Emp: 100-249 (Tor)
#TorLoc: 1
Own: Private Company
Key: Fez Fezi, Dir

Smucker Foods of Canada Co.

80 Whitehall Dr.
Markham, ON L3R 0P3
Tel 905-940-9600
Fax 905-940-5969
www.smuckersfoodservice.ca
Line: Processes and markets consumer grain-based foods, condiments and fruit spreads.
NAICS: 311420
#Emp: 100-249 (Tor)
#TorLoc: 1
Own: Private Company
Par: J.M. Smucker Company (US)
Key: Dave Lemmon, Mng Dir
Melody Crawford, Dir of HR
Steven Kouri, VP Sales & Trade Mktg

Smurfit-MBI

747 Appleby Line
Burlington, ON L7L 2Y6
Tel 905-634-5525
Fax 905-634-6985
www.smurfit-mbi.com
Line: Manufactures and sells corrugated paper products.
NAICS: 322211
#Emp: 250-499 (Tor)
#TorLoc: 5
Own: Public Company
Par: Smurfit-Stone Container Corp. (IRE/US)
Key: Craig Dunford,
    Dir of Sales, Canada
Jean Marc Thibodeau,
    Dir of HR, Canada

SNC-Lavalin Inc.

195 The West Mall
Toronto, ON M9C 5K7
Tel 416-252-5311
Fax 416-231-5356
www.snclavalin.com
Line: Provides consulting engineering and construction management services.
NAICS: 231410 541330
#Emp: 500-999 (Tor)
#TorLoc: 2
Own: Private Company
Par: SNC-Lavalin Inc. (CDA)
Key: Pierre Duhaime, Pres & CEO
Kevin Wallace, VP & GM
John Penny, VP HR

Soberman LLP

1100-2 St. Clair Ave. East
Toronto, ON M4T 2T5
Tel 416-964-7633
Fax 416-964-6454
www.soberman.com
AKA: BKR International
Line: Provides financial, audit, tax, business advisory, valuations and insolvency services.
NAICS: 541212 541215
#Emp: 100-249 (Tor)
#TorLoc: 1
Own: Private Company
Key: Jerry Cukier, Mng Partner
Susan Hodkinson, COO
Ravinder Sanghera, HR Mgr
Sean-Jacob Peters, IT Mgr
Heather MacDonald-Santiago,
    Mktg Mgr

Sobeys Ontario

1680 Tech Ave.
Mississauga, ON L4W 5S9
Tel 905-212-9511
Fax 905-671-5009
www.sobeys.com
AKA: Sobeys; IGA; Lumsden Brothers;
Price Chopper
Line: Distributes goods and services to
retail grocery stores.
NAICS: 445110
#Emp: 10000+ (Tor)
#TorLoc: 147
Own: Public Company
Par: Sobeys Inc. (CDA)
Key: David Jeffs, Pres, Ops,
  Sobeys Ontario
Bill McEwan, Pres & CEO
Glen Gonder, Sr VP Retail
David Hoad, VP HR
Francois Vimard, CFO
Dale MacDonald,
  Sr VP Nat'l Procurement
Clinton Keay, Sr VP & CIO
Andrew Walker, VP Commun

Society of Composers, Authors, and Music Publishers of Canada

41 Valleybrook Dr.
Toronto, ON M3B 2S6
Tel 416-445-8700
Fax 416-445-7108
www.socan.ca
AKA: SOCAN
Line: Facilitates the licensing of
public musical performances and the
distribution of royalties to composers
and music publishers.
NAICS: 813920 512230
#Emp: 250-499 (Tor)
#TorLoc: 1
Own: Association
Key: Eric Baptiste, CEO
Jeff King, COO
Randy Wark, VP HR
David Wood, CFO
Janice Scott, VP IT
Jennifer Brown, VP Licensing

Sodexo Canada Ltd.

3350 South Service Rd.
Burlington, ON L7N 3M6
Tel 905-632-8592
Fax 905-632-7114
www.sodexo.ca
Line: Provides comprehensive service
solutions.
NAICS: 561990
#Emp: 1000-4999 (Tor)
Own: Private Company
Key: Dean Johnson, Pres

Softchoice Corp.

200-173 Dufferin St.
Toronto, ON M6K 3H7
Tel 416-588-9000
Fax 416-588-9005
www.softchoice.com
Line: Assists businesses and
organizations to select, acquire, and
manage technology resources.
NAICS: 541510
#Emp: 250-499 (Tor)
#TorLoc: 2
Own: Public Company
Key: David MacDonald, Pres & CEO
Maria Odoardi, VP People
David Long, CFO
Kevin Wright, Sr VP & CIO
Nicole Wengle, VP Cdn Sales
Nick Foster, Sr VP Mktg
Eric Gardiner, Corp Commun

Soil Engineers Ltd.

100 Nugget Ave.
Toronto, ON M1S 3A7
Tel 416-754-8515
Fax 416-754-8516
www.soilengineersltd.com
Line: Provides engineering consulting
services.
NAICS: 541330
#Emp: 75-99 (Tor)
#TorLoc: 1
Own: Private Company
Key: Victor Chan, Chmn

Solarfective Products Limited

6 William Morgan Dr.
Toronto, ON M4H 1E5
Tel 416-421-3800
Fax 416-421-8424
www.solarfective.com
Line: Manufactures roller shades,
skylights and projection screens.
NAICS: 333310
#Emp: 75-99 (Tor)
#TorLoc: 1

Own: Private Company
Key: Anise Odeh, Pres

Solarsoft Business Systems

700-45 Vogell Rd.
Richmond Hill, ON L4B 3P6
Tel 905-224-2222
Fax 905-224-2221
www.solarsoft.com
Line: Manufactures software solutions
for manufacturers and distributors.
NAICS: 541510
#Emp: 75-99 (Tor)
#TorLoc: 1
Own: Private Company
Key: Rudy Joss, Chmn
Shawn McMorran, CEO
Paul Craven, COO
Peter Canley, VP Fin

Solidwear Enterprises Ltd.

75 Milner Ave.
Toronto, ON M1S 3P6
Tel 416-298-2667
Fax 416-298-7057
www.solidwear.com
Line: Manufactures garments.
NAICS: 313240
#Emp: 75-99 (Tor)
#TorLoc: 1
Own: Private Company
Key: Arthur Lee, Pres

Solo Canada

2121 Markham Rd.
Toronto, ON M1B 2W3
Tel 416-293-2877
Fax 416-332-3489
www.solocup.com
AKA: Solo Cup Canada
Line: Manufactures single use food
service products.
NAICS: 322299
#Emp: 250-499 (Tor)
#TorLoc: 2
Own: Private Company
Par: Solo Cup Company (US)
Key: Steven Schildt,
  VP Sales & Mktg & GM
Judith Tuazon, HR Mgr

Solutions

1400 Aimco Blvd.
Mississauga, ON L4W 1E1
Tel 905-282-9371
Fax 905-282-9362
www.solutions-stores.ca
Line: Operates a Canadian retailer
specializing in the storage and
organization of products for the home
and office.
NAICS: 442298
#Emp: 100-249 (Tor)
#TorLoc: 12
Own: Private Company
Key: Rick Walia, Pres
Batia Haber, Mktg Mgr

Solutions2Go Inc.

190 Statesman Dr.
Mississauga, ON L5S 1X7
Tel 905-564-1140
Fax 905-564-9114
www.solutions2go.ca
Line: Distributes video games and
accessories.
NAICS: 414210
#Emp: 75-99 (Tor)
Own: Private Company
Key: Gabrielle Chevalier, Pres & COO

Somerset Entertainment Ltd.

600-20 York Mills Rd.
Toronto, ON M2P 2C2
Tel 416-510-2800
Fax 416-510-8650
www.somersetent.com
Line: Produces and distributes music.
NAICS: 512230
#Emp: 75-99 (Tor)
#TorLoc: 2
Own: Public Company
Key: Andy Burgess, Pres

Sonnenberg Industries Ltd.

191 Finchdene Sq.
Toronto, ON M1X 1E3
Tel 416-297-1100
Fax 416-297-0427
AKA: Craftwood
Line: Manufactures high-end wood
office and custom furniture.
NAICS: 337213
#Emp: 100-249 (Tor)
#TorLoc: 1
Own: Private Company
Par: Tischler Holdings Inc. (CDA)
Key: Gary Sonnenberg, Pres
Andrea Sonnenberg, Cont
Peter Sawala, Sales Mgr

Sonoco Canada Corp.

7420A Bramalea Rd.
Mississauga, ON L5S 1W9
Tel 905-673-7373
Fax 905-673-8616
www.sonoco.com
Line: Provides packaging services and
manufactures consumer packaging,
engineered carriers and paper.
NAICS: 561910
#Emp: 75-99 (Tor)
Own: Private Company
Par: Sonoco (US)
Key: Linda Kerr, Office Admr
Ken McDonald, Plant Mgr

Sony of Canada Ltd.

115 Gordon Baker Rd.
Toronto, ON M2H 3R6
Tel 416-499-1414
Fax 416-497-1774
www.sony.ca
AKA: Sony Style
Line: Wholesales and retails consumer
electronics and professional products.
NAICS: 414210 443110
#Emp: 500-999 (Tor)
#TorLoc: 17
Own: Private Company
Par: Sony Corp. (JAPAN)
Key: Doug Wilson, Pres & COO
Howard Stringer, Chmn & CEO
Susan Bean, VP HR
Barry Hasler, CFO
Wayne Ground, CIO
Martin Huntington, Sr VP Consumer
    Products Group Sales & Retail
Ravi Nookala, Sr VP Mktg
Tony Smith, VP Mktg Commun

Soroc Technology Inc.

607 Chrislea Rd.
Vaughan, ON L4L 8A3
Tel 905-265-8000
Fax 905-265-8008
www.soroc.com
NAICS: 414210 417310
#Emp: 100-249 (Tor)
#TorLoc: 2
Own: Private Company
Key: Rudy Cheddie, Pres

Sota Glazing Inc.

443 Railside Dr.
Brampton, ON L7A 1E1
Tel 905-846-3177
Fax 905-846-3530
www.sotawall.com
Line: Designs, manufactures and offers
curtainwall installation services.
NAICS: 232390
#Emp: 100-249 (Tor)
#TorLoc: 3
Own: Private Company
Key: Juan Speck, Pres

The Source (Bell) Electronics Canada Inc.

279 Bayview Dr.
Barrie, ON L4M 4W5
Tel 705-728-2262
Fax 705-728-8312
www.thesource.ca
AKA: UpClose; THS Studio;
Battery Plus
Line: Sells consumer electronics and
computers.
NAICS: 443130 443110
#Emp: 1000-4999 (Tor)
Own: Private Company
Par: Circuit City Stores Inc. (US)
Key: Benoit Dube, Sr VP Sales & Ops
Bruce Dinan,
    Exec VP Merchandising & Mktg

Southern Graphic Systems

2 Dorchester Ave.
Toronto, ON M8Z 4W3
Tel 416-252-9331
Fax 416-252-3043
www.sgsintl.com
AKA: SGS
Line: Manufactures engraved cylinders
and flexographic prepress.
NAICS: 541430 541920
#Emp: 100-249 (Tor)
#TorLoc: 2
Own: Private Company
Key: Mark Spurgeon, Pres
Rick Degendorfer, Exec VP HR
Gray Gleed, Sales Mgr

Southlake Regional Health Centre

596 Davis Dr.
Newmarket, ON L3Y 2P9
Tel 905-895-4521
Fax 905-830-5972
www.southlakeregional.org
Line: Operates a regional hospital
including cardiac and cancer services.
NAICS: 622111
#Emp: 1000-4999 (Tor)
#TorLoc: 1
Own: Not-for-profit
Key: Louis Balogh, Pres & CEO
Gary Ryan, Interim COO
Anette Jones, Chief of Nursing & HR
Terry Kuula, Assoc VP Fin
Jim Talbot, Materials Dir
Diane Salois-Swallow,
    Dir of Info Resources
Tammy LaRue, PR Mgr

Southlake Residential Care Village

640 Grace St.
Newmarket, ON L3Y 2L1
Tel 905-895-7661
Fax 905-875-9806
www.southlakeregional.org
Line: Operates a nursing home.
NAICS: 623110
#Emp: 250-499 (Tor)
#TorLoc: 1
Own: Not-for-profit
Par: Southlake Regional Health Centre
(CDA)
Key: Anne Deelstra-McNamara,
    Exec Dir
Diana Reynolds, Office Mgr

Southwire Canada

5769 Main St.
Stouffville, ON L4A 2T1
Tel 905-640-4333
Fax 905-640-5607
www.southwire.com
Line: Manufactures electrical wire and
cable for general OEM's and electrical
wholesalers.
NAICS: 331420
#Emp: 100-249 (Tor)
#TorLoc: 2
Own: Private Company
Par: Southwire Company (US)
Key: Kevin Dancy, Plant Mgr
Mel Godfrey, Production Mgr
Joanne Peacock, HR Mgr
Dave Bolan, Cont
Alan James, Purch Mgr

Span International

100 Mcpherson St.
Markham, ON L3R 3V6
Tel 905-946-8972
Fax 905-946-8675
www.spanltd.com
AKA: UTI Markham
Line: Manufactures circuit boards,
cables and wires.
NAICS: 334410
#Emp: 250-499 (Tor)
#TorLoc: 5
Own: Public Company
Par: UTi Worldwide Company (US)
Key: Binny Jind, Pres & CEO
Tharma Kumar, VP & Dir of Manuf Ops
Jim Lancefield, VP & CFO
Patricia Croley, VP & Dir of Quality
Robert Rogut, VP & Dir of IT
Max Chipman,
    VP & Dir of Business Dev

Spec Furniture Inc.

165 City View Dr.
Toronto, ON M9W 5B1
Tel 416-246-5550
Fax 416-246-5549
www.specfurniture.com
Line: Manufactures furniture.
NAICS: 337127
#Emp: 100-249 (Tor)
#TorLoc: 1
Own: Private Company
Key: Donald Taylor, GM

Specialties Graphic Finishers Ltd.

946 Warden Ave.
Toronto, ON M1L 4C9
Tel 416-701-0111
Fax 416-701-1238
www.specialtiesgraphics.com
Line: Operates bindery finishing
company.
NAICS: 323120
#Emp: 100-249 (Tor)
#TorLoc: 1
Own: Private Company
Key: Norman Beange,
    Pres & Mktg Developer
Amelia Ferreira, Acctng Mgr
Natalie Roebuck,
    Computer Systems Mgr
James Beange, Commun Mgr

Specialty Care Inc.

110-400 Applewood Cres.
Vaughan, ON L4K 0B3
Tel 905-695-2930
www.specialty-care.com
Line: Operates a retirement home.
NAICS: 623310
#Emp: 1000-4999 (Tor)
#TorLoc: 4
Own: Private Company
Key: Lois Cormack, Pres
Paula Jourdain, CEO
Debbie Doherty, COO
Fiona Gardner, VP HR
Fern Ginsberg, CFO
Katie Head, Mktg & Commun Coord

Spectra Aluminum Products Inc.

95 Reagens Industrial Pkwy.
Bradford, ON L3Z 2A4
Tel 905-778-8093
Fax 905-778-8054
www.spectraaluminum.com
Line: Manufactures aluminum
extrusions as well as anodizing,
painting and polishing.
NAICS: 331317 332810
#Emp: 100-249 (Tor)
#TorLoc: 2
Own: Private Company
Par: The Spectra Group (CDA)
Key: David Hudson, CEO
Archie Proper, VP Ops
Robert Jong, VP Fin, IT & HR
Scott Chapman, Mktg & Sales Mgr

Spectrum Health Care

1200-2 Bloor St. East
Toronto, ON M4W 1A8
Tel 416-964-0322
Fax 416-964-3952
www.spectrumhealthcare.com
Line: Provides supplemental staffing
and home health care services.
NAICS: 621610
#Emp: 1000-4999 (Tor)
#TorLoc: 2
Own: Private Company
Key: Lori Lord, CEO
Patricia Sbrocchi, Sr Dir of Ops
Ann Tabuchi, Mgr of HR
George Swoboda, CFO

Spectrum Realty Services Inc.

9-8400 Jane St.
Vaughan, ON L4K 4L8
Tel 416-736-6500
Fax 416-736-9766
www.spectrumrealtyservices.com
Line: Operates a real estate agency.
NAICS: 531210 531310
#Emp: 100-249 (Tor)
#TorLoc: 1
Own: Private Company
Key: Marco Alberga, Pres

Spectrum Supply Chain Solutions

6099 McLaughlin Rd.
Mississauga, ON L5R 1B9
Tel 905-507-9862
Fax 905-507-9455
www.spectrumscm.ca
Line: Provides supply chain management.
NAICS: 488990
#Emp: 250-499 (Tor)
Own: Private Company
Key: Gord Crowther, Pres
Shane Edghill, VP Ops

Speedy Electric Contractors Ltd.

114A Caster Ave.
Woodbridge, ON L4L 5Y9
Tel 905-264-2344
Fax 905-264-1158
Line: Provides electrical services.
NAICS: 232510
#Emp: 100-249 (Tor)
#TorLoc: 1
Own: Private Company
Key: Albert Passero, Pres

Speedy Transport Group Inc.

265 Rutherford Rd. South
Brampton, ON L6W 1V9
Tel 905-455-8005
Fax 905-455-7190
www.speedy.ca
Line: Provides local and long distance trucking service for general commodities.
NAICS: 484110 484239
#Emp: 100-249 (Tor)
#TorLoc: 1
Own: Private Company
Key: Brian Comfort, CEO
Jared Martin, VP Ops
Jamie Temple, Sr HR Mgr
Funlola Smith, VP Fin & CFO
Bob Hall, CIO
Derek Comfort, VP Sales & Mktg

Spherion

601-419 King St. West
Oshawa Centre Executive Tower
Oshawa, ON L1J 2K5
Tel 905-579-2911
Fax 905-579-6050
www.spherion.ca
Line: Operates an employment agency.
NAICS: 561310
#Emp: 100-249 (Tor)
#TorLoc: 11
Own: Private Company
Par: Spherion Atlantic Enterprises LLC (US)
Key: Craig Brown, Pres & CEO
Carol Plummer, Area Mgr

Spin Master Ltd.

450 Front St. West
Toronto, ON M5V 1B6
Tel 416-364-6002
Fax 416-364-8005
www.spinmaster.com
Line: Manufactures toys and games.
NAICS: 339930
#Emp: 250-499 (Tor)
#TorLoc: 1
Own: Private Company
Key: Anton Rabie, Pres & Co-CEO
Ronnen Harary, Chmn & Co-CEO
Iain Kenedy, COO
Mike Bate, Exec VP HR
Mark Segal, CFO
Ben Varadi, Exec VP
William Cheung, VP IT
Chris Beardall, Exec VP Sales
Mark Sullivan, Exec VP Mktg
Harold Chizick, VP Commun

Sport Chek

636 Marcov Rd.
Mississauga, ON L5T 2R7
Tel 905-795-4700
Fax 905-795-4709
www.sportchek.ca
AKA: The Forzani Group
Line: Operates sporting goods retail stores.
NAICS: 451110 414470 448140
#Emp: 100-249 (Tor)
Own: Public Company
Par: The Forzani Group Ltd. (CDA)
Key: Thomas G. Quinn, Pres & COO

Sporting Life Inc.

2665 Yonge St.
Toronto, ON M4P 2J6
Tel 416-485-1611
Fax 416-485-7825
www.sportinglife.ca

AKA: Sporting Life Bikes
Line: Retails fashion and sporting goods.
NAICS: 451110 448140
#Emp: 500-999 (Tor)
#TorLoc: 4
Own: Private Company
Key: David Russell, Pres
Brian McGrath, Chmn
Jerry Rynda, GM
Rhonda Morris, HR Mgr
Howard Israelsohn, CFO
Patti Russell, Dir of Fashion
John Roe, Mktg Mgr

The Sports Network

9 Channel Nine Crt.
P.O. Box 9, Stn. O
Toronto, ON M1S 4B5
Tel 416-384-5000
Fax 416-384-3656
www.tsn.ca
AKA: TSN
Line: Operates sports television broadcasting company.
NAICS: 513120
#Emp: 250-499 (Tor)
#TorLoc: 2
Own: Private Company
Par: CTV Inc. (CDA)
Key: Stewart Johnson, Pres
Phil King, Pres of Sports & Exec VP Programing, CTV

Sport Swap Inc.

1440 Bayview Ave.
Toronto, ON M4G 3B3
Tel 416-481-7927
Fax 416-481-7090
www.sportswap.com
Line: Operates sporting goods store.
NAICS: 451110
#Emp: 75-99 (Tor)
#TorLoc: 1
Own: Private Company
Key: Alan Chow, Pres

Spring Air Sommer Corp.

53 Bakersfield St.
Toronto, ON M3J 1Z4
Tel 416-667-8871
Fax 888-567-7934
www.springair.com
Line: Manufactures mattresses.
NAICS: 337910
#Emp: 75-99 (Tor)
#TorLoc: 1
Own: Private Company
Key: Chris French, COO
Andre Lamy, VP Fin
Valerie Stranix, Chief Mktg Officer

Springco Inc.

25 Worcester Rd.
Toronto, ON M9W 1K9
Tel 416-675-9072
Fax 416-675-9074
www.hsspring.com
Line: Manufactures springs, spring clips, wire forms and cable end assemblies.
NAICS: 332611 332619
#Emp: 75-99 (Tor)
#TorLoc: 1
Own: Private Company
Par: Hasco LLC (US)
Key: Paul Cairoli, Pres & GM
Tom Featherstone, Plant Mgr
Harpit Dhillon, HR Mgr
Mary Breckinridge, Cont
Angie Yuzon, Purch Agent
Paul Young, VP Sales

Spring Knitwear Inc.

291 Progress Ave.
Toronto, ON M1P 2Z2
Tel 416-297-0292
Fax 416-297-7740
Line: Manufactures sportswear.
NAICS: 315299
#Emp: 75-99 (Tor)
Own: Private Company
Key: Yvonne Han, Pres

S & Q Plastic

A Div. of Uniglobe (Canada) Inc.
7890 Tranmere Dr.
Mississauga, ON L5S 1L9
Tel 905-678-1720
Fax 905-678-1711
www.sqplastic.com
Line: Manufactures film extrusions, and industrial bulk and retail bags.
NAICS: 326198
#Emp: 75-99 (Tor)
#TorLoc: 1
Own: Private Company
Key: Walia Singh, Pres

SS&C Technologies Canada Corp.

5255 Orbitor Dr.
Mississauga, ON L4W 5M6
Tel 905-629-8000
Fax 905-629-0022
www.ssctech.com
Line: Provides investment management systems, software consulting services and securities data.
NAICS: 541510
#Emp: 250-499 (Tor)

#TorLoc: 2
Own: Private Company
Key: Claude Johnson, VP
Stephen J. Ashbury, VP Fin

Stacey Electric Company Ltd.

B-179 Bartley Dr.
Toronto, ON M4A 1E6
Tel 416-752-6380
Fax 416-752-9740
www.staceyelectric.com
Line: Performs traffic signal and street light installation and maintenance.
NAICS: 232510
#Emp: 100-249 (Tor)
#TorLoc: 3
Own: Private Company
Key: Gary Bergeron, Pres
Todd Champion, Mgr

StackTeck Systems Ltd.

1 Paget Rd.
Brampton, ON L6T 5S2
Tel 416-749-0880
Fax 416-749-9669
www.stackteck.com
Line: Manufactures plastics injection moulds, hot runners and standard parts.
NAICS: 333511
#Emp: 100-249 (Tor)
#TorLoc: 1
Own: Private Company
Par: StackTeck Inc. (CDA)
Key: Randy Yakimishyn, Pres & CEO
Lou DiMaulo, VP Manuf
Gene Massa, HR Dir
Nelson Antunes, VP & Cont
Vince Travaglini, VP Engineering
Henry Rozema,
    VP Commercial Services
Paul Benson, CFO
Mike Gould, VP Business Dev

Stagevision Inc.

5610 McAdam Rd.
Mississauga, ON L4Z 1P1
Tel 905-890-8200
Fax 905-890-8316
www.stagevision.com
AKA: Stagevision Rentals Inc.
Line: Supplies audiovisual stage and events management services including equipment rental, customized set design and construction.
NAICS: 711321
#Emp: 75-99 (Tor)
#TorLoc: 1
Own: Private Company

Key: Roy Wasley, Pres
William Armstrong, VP & GM
Julian Joseph, CFO
Robert Doherty, Ops Mgr
Bryce Engleman, VP Sales
Stewart Hadden, VP Mktg

Stage West All-Suite Hotel & Theatre Restaurant

5400 Dixie Rd.
Mississauga, ON L4W 4T4
Tel 905-238-0159
Fax 905-238-9820
www.stagewest.com
NAICS: 721111
#Emp: 100-249 (Tor)
#TorLoc: 1
Own: Private Company
Par: Mayfield Suites Hotel (Mississauga) Ltd. (CDA)
Key: Muhammed Huq, GM
Andrea Tesolin, HR Coord
Cumar Nagalingam, Cont
Amanda Dailey, Dir of Hotel Sales
Laurie Wallace-Lynch, Mktg & PR

Stamptek

3-555 Petrolia Rd.
Bldg. 2
Toronto, ON M3J 2X8
Tel 416-663-5442
Fax 416-663-7680
Line: Manufactures metal products.
NAICS: 332118
#Emp: 100-249 (Tor)
#TorLoc: 1
Own: Private Company
Key: Arnold Klotz, Plant Mgr

Standard Auto Wreckers

1216 Sewells Rd.
Toronto, ON M1X 1S1
Tel 416-286-8686
Fax 416-286-8690
www.standardautowreckers.com
AKA: Goldy Metals Inc.
Line: Operates a car wrecking yard and sells auto parts.
NAICS: 418110
#Emp: 100-249 (Tor)
#TorLoc: 1
Own: Private Company
Key: Kenneth Gold, Pres
Steve Lucas, Ops Mgr
Jackie Grafe, Office Mgr

The Standard Life Assurance Co. of Canada

1245 Sherbrooke St. West
Montreal, PQ H3G 1G3
Tel 514-499-8855
Fax 514-499-8897
www.standardlife.ca
Line: Provides financial services and products.
NAICS: 524210
#Emp: 100-249 (Tor)
#TorLoc: 2
Own: Private Company
Key: Joseph Iannicelli, Pres & CEO
Sophie Fortin,
    Sr VP HR & Corp Services
Christian Martineau, Sr VP Fin & IT
Jean Guay, Sr VP Group Insurance

Standard Parking of Canada Ltd.

200-101 Duncan Mill Rd.
Toronto, ON M3B 1Z3
Tel 416-441-2227
Fax 416-441-0711
www.standardparking.com
Line: Provides parking management and development services.
NAICS: 812930
#Emp: 100-249 (Tor)
#TorLoc: 27
Own: Private Company
Par: Standard Parking Inc. (US)
Key: Mickey Narun, Pres & CEO
Kathleen Taylor, Sr VP Ops
Ellen Ashkenazi, HR Mgr

Standard & Poor's Credit Market Services

1100-130 King St. West
P.O. Box 486, First Canadian Pl.
Toronto, ON M5X 1E5
Tel 416-507-2500
Fax 416-507-2507
www.standardandpoors.com
Line: Provides credit rating analytical services.
NAICS: 523990 561450
#Emp: 75-99 (Tor)
#TorLoc: 1
Own: Public Company
Par: The McGraw-Hill Companies, Inc. (US)
Key: Thomas Connell, Mng Dir
Jan Haist, Admin Officer

Standex Electronics Canada

1130 Eighth Line
Oakville, ON L6H 2R4
Tel 905-844-6681
Fax 905-844-6895
www.standexelectronics.com
Line: Designs and manufactures transformers and inductors for the telecommunications, electronic and electrical industry.
NAICS: 334410 335311
#Emp: 75-99 (Tor)
#TorLoc: 1
Own: Public Company
Par: Standex International Corp. (US)
Key: Bob Stead, Ops Mgr
Cecilia Knights, Payroll & HR Mgr

St. Andrew's College

15800 Yonge St.
Aurora, ON L4G 3H7
Tel 905-727-3178
Fax 905-841-6911
www.sac.on.ca
Line: Operates independent boarding and day school for boys.
NAICS: 611110
#Emp: 100-249 (Tor)
#TorLoc: 1
Own: Not-for-profit
Key: Kevin McHenry, Headmaster
Beth McKay, Dir of Fin & Ops
Sherrill Knight, Dir of HR
Steve Rush, Dir of IT
Kim Sillcox, Dir of Commun

Stanley Black & Decker

1170 Invicta Dr.
Oakville, ON L6H 6G1
Tel 905-825-1981
Fax 905-825-2620
www.stanleytools.com
NAICS: 332510 332321
#Emp: 500-999 (Tor)
#TorLoc: 4
Own: Private Company
Par: Stanley Black & Decker Corp. (US)
Key: Jeff Crews, Pres
Rudy Daldin, Mgr of HR

Stanley Black & Decker Canada Inc.

125 Mural St.
Richmond Hill, ON L4B 1M4
Tel 905-886-9511
Fax 905-764-4627
www.blackanddecker.com
NAICS: 332510 333990
#Emp: 100-249 (Tor)
#TorLoc: 1
Own: Public Company
Par: The Black & Decker Corp. (US)
Key: Jeff Crews, Pres
Jennifer Le Donne, Dir of HR
Mark Carson, VP Fin
Joe Di Ilo, VP Sales

Stantec Architecture Ltd.

100-401 Wellington St. West
Toronto, ON M5V 1E7
Tel 416-596-6666
www.stantec.com
Line: Specializes in interior design for restaurants, offices and bars.
NAICS: 541410
#Emp: 250-499 (Tor)
#TorLoc: 3
Own: Private Company
Key: Colm Murphy, Principal
Tony Franceschini, Pres & CEO
Lloyd Hilgers, Principal
Michael Moxam, Principal

Stantec Consulting Ltd.

300-675 Cochrane Dr.
West Tower
Markham, ON L3R 0B8
Tel 905-944-7777
Fax 905-474-9889
www.stantec.com
Line: Provides professional services and technologies in planning, engineering, architecture, interior design, landscape architecture, surveying and geomatics, and project economics.
NAICS: 541330
#Emp: 250-499 (Tor)
#TorLoc: 4
Own: Public Company
Par: Stantec (CDA)
Key: Brad Frizzell, Principal
Bob Gomes, Pres & CEO
Brian Sirbovan, VP, GTA

Staples Advantage

550 Pendant Dr.
Mississauga, ON L5T 2W6
Tel 905-696-4444
Fax 905-696-4445
www.corporateexpress.ca
Line: Distributes office products,
supplies and services.
NAICS: 418210
#Emp: 500-999 (Tor)
#TorLoc: 1
Own: Public Company
Par: Staples Inc. (US)
Key: Mike Zahra, Pres, Canada
David Sobb, VP Supply Chain
Donna Pascal, VP HR
Brian Park, VP Fin
Luc Marotte, VP IT
Stan Dabic, VP Sales & Ops
Scott D'Cunla, Dir of Mktg & Commun

Staples Canada Inc.

6 Staples Ave.
Richmond Hill, ON L4B 4W3
Tel 905-737-1147
Fax 905-780-5607
www.staples.ca
AKA: Staples Business Depot; Bureau
en Gros; Staples
Line: Sells office equipment,
technology hardware, services and
supplies.
NAICS: 453210 417910 418210
#Emp: 1000-4999 (Tor)
#TorLoc: 37
Own: Private Company
Par: Staples Inc. (US)
Key: Steven E. Matyas, Pres
John Castiglione, VP Sales & Ops
Alan Ward, VP HR
Mary Sagat, CFO
Pete Gibel, VP Merchandising
Jeff Williams, VP IS
Lori Ross, VP Advertising & Mktg

Starcom Worldwide

175 Bloor St. East, 10th Fl.
North Tower
Toronto, ON M4W 3R9
Tel 416-927-3300
Fax 416-925-3202
www.starcomworldwide.com
Line: Operates an advertising agency.
NAICS: 541810
#Emp: 75-99 (Tor)
#TorLoc: 1
Own: Private Company
Par: Publicis Groupe (FRA)
Key: Lauren Richards, CEO

Starkey Labs Canada Co.

7310 Rapistan Crt.
Mississauga, ON L5N 6L8
Tel 905-542-7555
Fax 905-542-8644
www.starkeycanada.ca
Line: Manufactures custom hearing
aids.
NAICS: 334512
#Emp: 100-249 (Tor)
#TorLoc: 1
Own: Private Company
Par: Starkey Laboratories Inc. (US)
Key: Jerry Ruzicka, Pres
William Austin, Founder & CEO
Keith Gruggenberger, Sr VP Ops
Larry Miller, Sr VP HR
Scott Nelson, CFO
Jason Toone, Mng Dir

Star Plastics Inc.

1-1930 Drew Rd.
Mississauga, ON L5S 1J6
Tel 905-672-0298
Fax 905-672-0314
www.starplastics.ca
Line: Operates a custom injection
molding company.
NAICS: 326198
#Emp: 75-99 (Tor)
#TorLoc: 1
Own: Private Company
Key: Jas Dhami, Founder & Pres

Starplex Scientific Inc.

50 Steinway Blvd.
Toronto, ON M9W 6Y3
Tel 416-674-7474
Fax 416-674-6067
www.starplexscientific.com
Line: Manufactures hospital medical
supplies and pharmaceutical bottles.
NAICS: 334512
#Emp: 100-249 (Tor)
#TorLoc: 1
Own: Private Company
Par: Apotex Holdings Inc. (CDA)
Key: Fred Panini, Pres
Gary Deans, Dir of Ops
Ann McCarley, HR Mgr
Nalini Chandramohan, Cont
Bill Brydges, Dir of Starplex Sales
Paula Picavet, Dir of Mktg

Star Quality Office Furniture Manufacturing Ltd.

75 Westmore Dr.
Toronto, ON M9V 3Y6
Tel 416-741-8000
Fax 416-741-7900
www.starquality.ca
Line: Manufactures and imports
wooden office furniture.
NAICS: 337213
#Emp: 75-99 (Tor)
#TorLoc: 2
Own: Private Company
Key: Fred Mansoor, Pres
Ken Aviss, VP
Joe Lampert, VP Fin
Dan Beaudoin, Dir of Sales

Starr Culinary Delights Inc.

3-6845 Rexwood Rd.
Mississauga, ON L4V 1S5
Tel 905-612-1958
Fax 905-612-0162
www.starrculinary.com
Line: Operates a bakery.
NAICS: 311814
#Emp: 75-99 (Tor)
Own: Private Company
Par: Puratos (BELG)
Key: Kelly Perera, Pres

Starwood Canada Corp.

123 Queen St. West
Toronto, ON M5H 2M9
Tel 416-361-1000
Fax 416-947-4823
www.starwood.com
AKA: Sheraton Centre Hotel; Starwood
Hotels & Resorts Worldwide Inc.;
Westin Harbour Castle
Line: Provides hotel convention
services.
NAICS: 721111
#Emp: 5000-9999 (Tor)
#TorLoc: 4
Own: Private Company
Par: Starwood Hotels & Resorts
Worldwide, Inc. (US)
Key: Stephen Foster, Sr VP Ops
David Ogilvie, GM
Joanne Paquette, Dir of HR
Amnon Reshef, Dir of Fin
Blair Reid, Dir of IT
Cynthia Bond, Dir of PR

State Chemical Ltd.

1-1745 Meyerside Dr.
Mississauga, ON L5T 1C6
Tel 905-670-4669
Fax 905-670-0181
www.statechemical.com
Line: Manufactures specialty
maintenance and cleaning supplies.
NAICS: 325610
#Emp: 75-99 (Tor)
#TorLoc: 1
Own: Private Company
Par: State Industrial (US)
Key: Paul Chatterton, Cont

State Farm Mutual Automobile Insurance Co.

333 First Commerce Dr.
Aurora, ON L4G 8A4
Tel 905-750-4100
Fax 905-750-4717
www.statefarm.ca
Line: Provides life insurance, general
insurance and financial services.
NAICS: 524112
#Emp: 1000-4999 (Tor)
#TorLoc: 7
Own: Private Company
Par: State Farm Mutual Automobile
Insurance Companies (US)
Key: Barbara Bellissimo,
 Chief Agent & Sr VP
Lou Fiorino, Admin Services Mgr
Lauragaye Jackson, Mktg Mgr

The State Group

3206 Orlando Dr.
Mississauga, ON L4V 1R5
Tel 905-672-2772
Fax 905-672-1919
www.state.ca
Line: Assists customers with electrical,
mechanical and telecommunications
services for new and existing facilities.
NAICS: 232510 231320
#Emp: 250-499 (Tor)
#TorLoc: 1
Own: Private Company
Key: Mark Dumont, Pres
Dan Chomyshyn, Dir of Fin

State Street Trust Company Canada

1100-30 Adelaide St. East
Toronto, ON M5C 3G6
Tel 416-362-1100
Fax 416-956-2825
www.statestreet.ca
AKA: State Street Canada
Line: Provides asset servicing and asset
management services to institutional
investors.
NAICS: 523990
#Emp: 1000-4999 (Tor)
#TorLoc: 1
Own: Private Company
Par: State Street Corp. (US)
Key: Kevin Drynan, Pres & CEO
Ronald Robertson, Sr VP & Mng Dir
Angelo Pugliese, VP HR

Station Creek Golf Club

12657 Woodbine Ave.
Gormley, ON L0H 1G0
Tel 905-888-1219
Fax 905-888-0101
www.clublink.ca
NAICS: 713910
#Emp: 100-249 (Tor)
#TorLoc: 1
Own: Private Company
Par: ClubLink Corp. (CDA)
Key: Brad Sewards, Dir of Ops

Statistics Canada

25 St. Clair Ave. East, 5th Fl.
Toronto, ON M4T 1M4
Tel 416-973-6586
Fax 416-973-7475
www.statcan.gc.ca
Line: Operates a national statistical
agency that collects and disseminates
information on social and economic
life of the country.
NAICS: 911910 541910
#Emp: 100-249 (Tor)
#TorLoc: 1
Own: Government
Par: Government of Canada
Key: Gary Dillon, Dir

St. Clair O'Connor Community Inc.

2701 St.Clair Ave. East
Toronto, ON M4B 1M5
Tel 416-757-8757
Fax 416-751-7315
NAICS: 623110
#Emp: 75-99 (Tor)
#TorLoc: 1
Own: Private Company
Key: Susan Gallant, Exec Dir

Steam Whistle Brewing Co.

255 Bremner Blvd.
Toronto, ON M5V 3M9
Tel 416-362-2337
Fax 416-362-9916
www.steamwhistle.ca
Line: Manufactures beer.
NAICS: 312120
#Emp: 75-99 (Tor)
#TorLoc: 1
Own: Private Company
Key: Cameron Heaps,
 Pres & Co-Founder
Sergei Mikhniouk, Plant Mgr
Lorna Willner, HR Mgr
Adrian Joseph, CFO
Chris Johnston, Dir of Purch & Info
Richard Armstrong,
 Sales, Downtown Toronto
Jamie Humphries, Mktg Dir

Steel Art Signs Corp.

37 Esna Park Dr.
Markham, ON L3R 1C9
Tel 905-474-1678
Fax 905-474-0515
www.steelart.com
Line: Manufactures custom and
national illuminated signs.
NAICS: 339950
#Emp: 75-99 (Tor)
#TorLoc: 1
Own: Private Company
Key: Tom Hrivnak, Pres & CEO
Jorge DaSilva, GM
Tom Henderson, Cont

Steelcase Canada Limited

1 Steelcase Rd. West
Markham, ON L3R 0T3
Tel 905-475-6333
Fax 905-475-3450
www.steelcase.com
Line: Provides knowledge, products,
and services that integrate
architecture, furniture and technology.
NAICS: 337214
#Emp: 250-499 (Tor)
#TorLoc: 1
Own: Public Company
Par: Steelcase Inc. (US)
Key: James P. Hackett, Pres & CEO
Stacey Howard, Plant Mgr
Kelly Jarvis, Dir of HR
Scott Wilson, Team Leader, IT
Rory Plant, Reg Sales Dir
Gale Moutrey, Dir of Mktg

Stephenson's Rental Services Inc.

502-201 City Centre Dr.
Mississauga, ON L5B 2T4
Tel 905-507-3650
Fax 905-507-4024
www.stephensons.ca
Line: Rents and sells repair tools and
equipment.
NAICS: 532310
#Emp: 75-99 (Tor)
#TorLoc: 19
Own: Private Company
Key: William Swisher, Pres & CEO
Stirling McArthur, Dir of HR
Ian Bell, CFO

Steris Canada Inc.

6280 Northwest Dr.
Mississauga, ON L4V 1J7
Tel 905-677-0863
Fax 1-877-585-2279
www.steriscanada.com
Line: Develops, manufactures and
supplies infection prevention,
contamination prevention, microbial
reduction and surgical support
systems, products, services and
technologies.
NAICS: 325410
#Emp: 75-99 (Tor)
#TorLoc: 1
Own: Private Company
Key: Steve Timpano, VP
Deborah Michalowski,
   Customer Support Mgr

Sterling Tile & Carpet

1-505 Cityview Blvd.
Vaughan, ON L4H 0L8
Tel 416-630-4800
Fax 905-585-4801
www.sterlingflooring.ca
AKA: Sterling Flooring
Line: Sells and installs carpet, tiles
and hardwood to home builders and
residential retail homeowners.
NAICS: 232420 232430
#Emp: 100-249 (Tor)
#TorLoc: 1
Own: Private Company
Key: Mark Silver, Partner
Albert Silver, Partner
Julie Hoffman, Cont

The Stevens Company Ltd.

425 Railside Dr.
Brampton, ON L7A 0N8
Tel 905-791-8600
Fax 905-791-6143
www.stevens.ca
Line: Distributes medical and surgical
supplies.
NAICS: 334512
#Emp: 75-99 (Tor)
#TorLoc: 1
Own: Private Company
Key: Jeff Stevens, Pres
Helen Nasato, VP Ops & IS
Vince Pompilio, CFO
Sandy Peterson, Purch Dir
Bill Carson, VP Mktg & Sales

Stevenson Memorial Hospital

200 Fletcher Cres.
P.O. Box 4000
Alliston, ON L9R 1W7
Tel 705-435-6281
Fax 705-435-2327
www.smhosp.on.ca
NAICS: 622111
#Emp: 100-249 (Tor)
#TorLoc: 1
Own: Not-for-profit
Key: Gary Ryan, CEO
Karen Maisonneuve, HR Mgr
Kim Scales, Purch Clerk
Mike Bendell, Mgr, Environmental
   Services & Telecommunications
Ken Burns, Foundation Dir

St. George's Golf and Country Club

1668 Islington Ave.
Toronto, ON M9A 3M9
Tel 416-231-3393
Fax 416-231-6432
www.stgeorges.org
NAICS: 713910
#Emp: 100-249 (Tor)
#TorLoc: 1
Own: Not-for-profit
Key: Joseph Murphy, GM & COO
Patricia Mann, Clubhouse Mgr

St. Helens Meat Packers Ltd.

1 Glen Scarlett Rd.
Toronto, ON M6N 1P5
Tel 416-769-1788
Fax 416-769-0649
www.sthelensmeat.com
Line: Wholesales and exports fresh and
frozen meat.
NAICS: 413190
#Emp: 100-249 (Tor)
#TorLoc: 1
Own: Private Company
Key: Robert Bielak, Pres
Marsha Bielak, Chair
Marilyn Gold, VP
Sylvia Bielak, Secy-Treas

St. John's Rehabilitation Hospital

285 Cummer Ave.
Toronto, ON M2M 2G1
Tel 416-226-6780
Fax 416-226-6265
www.stjohnsrehab.com
Line: Provides short-term complex
rehabilitation services with specific
programs for those with orthopaedic,
amputee, neurological, trauma,
musculoskeletal and cardiac
diagnoses.
NAICS: 622111 622210
#Emp: 500-999 (Tor)
#TorLoc: 1
Own: Not-for-profit
Key: Malcolm Moffat, Pres & CEO
Gabrielle Bochynek, Dir of HR
Mary Lou Toop, VP Corp Services
Marcus Staviss,
   Dir of Strategic Commun

St. Joseph Pi Media

236 Lesmill Rd.
Toronto, ON M3B 2T5
Tel 416-449-9333
Fax 416-425-7831
www.stjosephcontent.com
AKA: Alchemy; DW+Partners;
Gottschalk+Ash
Line: Provides multi-channel
marketing services including strategy,
creative design, photography and
production.
NAICS: 541430
#Emp: 250-499 (Tor)
#TorLoc: 4
Own: Private Company
Par: St. Joseph Communications (CDA)
Key: Doug Templeton, Pres
Michael Cowman, VP Ops
Laura Russell, VP HR
Michael Chase, VP Mktg & Sales

St. Joseph Printing Ltd.

50 MacIntosh Blvd.
Vaughan, ON L4K 4P3
Tel 905-660-3111
Fax 905-660-6820
www.stjoseph.com
Line: Provides printing services from
creative process to finished products.
NAICS: 323115
#Emp: 250-499 (Tor)
#TorLoc: 1
Own: Private Company
Par: St. Joseph Corp. (CDA)
Key: John Gagliano, Pres
Tony Gagliano, CEO
Laura Russell, VP HR
Tim Zahavich, CFO
Martin Byrne, IT Mgr

St. Joseph's Health Centre

30 The Queensway
Toronto, ON M6R 1B5
Tel 416-530-6000
Fax 416-530-6034
www.stjoe.on.ca
Line: Operates community teaching
hospital.
NAICS: 622111
#Emp: 1000-4999 (Tor)
#TorLoc: 1
Own: Not-for-profit
Par: Catholic Health Corporation of
Ontario (CDA)

Key: Carolyn Baker, Pres & CEO
Tom Harmantas, Chief of Staff
Wendy Steele,
   Chief People Learning & Leadership
Dale McGregor,
   VP Corp Services & CFO
Andrew Brearton, Dir of IS

St. Lawrence Centre for the Arts

27 Front St. East
Toronto, ON M5E 1B4
Tel 416-366-1656
Fax 416-947-1387
www.stlc.com
Line: Operates a theatre and provides
facilities for corporate special events.
NAICS: 711311 531120
#Emp: 75-99 (Tor)
#TorLoc: 1
Own: Not-for-profit
Key: James Roe, GM
Ingrid Jones, HR Coord
Carol Henderson, Dir of Sales & Mktg

St Marys Cement Group

55 Industrial St.
Toronto, ON M4G 3W9
Tel 416-696-4411
Fax 416-696-4435
www.stmaryscement.com
AKA: St Marys CBM
Line: Manufactures ready mix concrete.
NAICS: 327330 327310
#Emp: 100-249 (Tor)
Own: Private Company
Par: St Marys Cement Inc. (CDA)
Key: Eric Madsen, CEO

St. Michael's Hospital

30 Bond St.
Toronto, ON M5B 1W8
Tel 416-360-4000
Fax 416-864-5870
www.stmichaelshospital.com
NAICS: 622111
#Emp: 1000-4999 (Tor)
#TorLoc: 15
Own: Not-for-profit
Par: Catholic Health Association of
Ontario (CDA)
Key: Robert J. Howard, Pres & CEO
Rob Fox, VP Planning
   & Chief Planning Officer
Sylvia Halliday, VP HR
Sarah Chow, Dir of Fin & CFO
Joan McLaughlin, Dir of Logistics &
   Support Services Admin
Anne Trafford, CIO
Sarah Baker, Dir of Corp Commun &
   Chief Commun Officer

STMicroelectronics

165 Commerce Valley Dr. West
Thornhill, ON L3T 7V8
Tel 905-889-5400
www.st.com
Line: Supplies digital image processors.
NAICS: 417320 334410
#Emp: 75-99 (Tor)
#TorLoc: 2
Own: Public Company
Par: STMicroelectronics (SWITZ)
Key: Harold Shaffer, Site Mgr

St. Mildred's-Lightbourn School

1080 Linbrook Rd.
Oakville, ON L6J 2L1
Tel 905-845-2386
Fax 905-845-4799
www.smls.on.ca
Line: Operates independent
kindergarten to university entrance
school for girls.
NAICS: 611110
#Emp: 75-99 (Tor)
#TorLoc: 1
Own: Not-for-profit
Key: Jane Wightman, Head of School
Leslie Boichuk, Dir of Fin & Admin

Stock Transportation Ltd.

14996 Yonge St.
Aurora, ON L4G 1M6
Tel 1-888-952-0878
www.stocktransportation.com
AKA: National Express Corporation
Line: Provides school bus
transportation.
NAICS: 485410
#Emp: 1000-4999 (Tor)
#TorLoc: 10
Own: Public Company
Par: National Express Group (UK)
Key: Kirk Flach, Sr VP Ops

StonCor Group

95 Sunray St.
Whitby, ON L1N 9C9
Tel 905-430-3333
Fax 905-430-3056
www.stoncor.ca
AKA: StonCor Canada
Line: Manufactures floors, coatings and
construction products.
NAICS: 325999
#Emp: 75-99 (Tor)
#TorLoc: 1
Own: Private Company
Key: Pirrette James, Office Mgr

Storefront Humber Inc.

2445 Lake Shore Blvd. West
Toronto, ON M8V 1C5
Tel 416-259-4207
Fax 416-259-4200
www.storefronthumber.ca
Line: Operates a non-profit charity that
provides home support for seniors and
the disabled.
NAICS: 623310
#Emp: 75-99 (Tor)
Own: Not-for-profit
Key: Mary Hansen, Exec Dir

St. Paul's L'Amoreaux Centre

3333 Finch Ave. East
Toronto, ON M1W 2R9
Tel 416-493-3333
Fax 416-493-3391
www.splc.ca
Line: Provides community support
services to seniors and seniors housing.
NAICS: 623310
#Emp: 100-249 (Tor)
Own: Not-for-profit
Key: Larry Burke, CEO
Roberta Wong, Dir of Client Care
Diane Duncan, Dir of HR
Louis Chan, Dir of Fin
Udo Rohmann,
    Dir of Facilities & Properties

Strataflex Canada Corp.

11 Dohme Ave.
Toronto, ON M4B 1Y7
Tel 416-752-2224
Fax 416-752-6719
www.strataflex.com
Line: Manufactures printed flexible
circuit boards.
NAICS: 335315
#Emp: 100-249 (Tor)
#TorLoc: 1
Own: Private Company
Par: Airborn Inc. (US)
Key: Michael Fielding, Pres
Tony Carnevale, Cont

The Strategic Coach Inc.

201-33 Fraser Ave.
Toronto, ON M6K 3J9
Tel 416-531-7399
Fax 416-531-1135
www.strategiccoach.com
NAICS: 541611
#Emp: 75-99 (Tor)
#TorLoc: 1
Own: Private Company
Key: Dan Sullivan, Pres
Babs Smith, CEO

Stress-Crete King Luminaire Ltd.

840 Walkers Line
P.O. Box 7
Burlington, ON L7R 3X9
Tel 905-632-9301
Fax 905-632-8116
www.stresscrete.com
AKA: Stress-Crete Ltd.
Line: Manufactures ornamental
streetlight fixtures, poles and related
metal products.
NAICS: 332329
#Emp: 100-249 (Tor)
#TorLoc: 1
Own: Private Company
Par: Stress-Crete Holdings Inc. (CDA)
Key: Greg Button, Pres
Michael Schwenger, CEO
Michael Schwenger Jr., VP & GM
Jacki Blythe, HR
Dianne Girard, CFO
Tom Moore, Purch & Inventory Mgr

Strongco Inc.

1640 Enterprise Rd.
Mississauga, ON L4W 4L4
Tel 905-670-5100
Fax 905-670-7869
www.strongco.com
NAICS: 417230
#Emp: 100-249 (Tor)
#TorLoc: 3
Own: Public Company
Key: Robert Dryburgh, Pres & CEO
Chris Forbes, VP HR
David Wood, VP Fin & CFO
Peter Duperrouzel, Mgr of IS
Anna Sgro, VP Sales & Mktg

Structform International Ltd.

84 Passmore Ave.
Toronto, ON M1V 4S9
Tel 416-291-7576
Fax 416-291-1267
www.structform.com
Line: Provides labour and materials
to form, place, and finish concrete for
large commercial and institutional
projects.
NAICS: 232230
#Emp: 250-499 (Tor)
#TorLoc: 1
Own: Private Company
Par: Structural Floor Finishing Ltd.
(CDA)
Key: Louis Bernardi, Pres
Edward Ziraldo, Founder & Dir
John Ienco, GM
    Structural Contracting Limited
Edward Paul Ziraldo, VP
    Structform, Central Corp

St. Stanislaus - St. Casimir's Polish Parishes Credit Union Ltd.

220 Roncesvalles Ave.
Toronto, ON M6R 2L7
Tel 416-537-2181
Fax 416-536-8525
www.polcu.com
Line: Offers a variety of banking
services.
NAICS: 522130
#Emp: 100-249 (Tor)
#TorLoc: 17
Own: Private Company
Key: Andrew Pitek, CEO
Shawn Mazurk, Branch & Corp
    Facilities Mgr
Tom Falfus, HR Mgr
Chris Dicuk, IT Mgr
Ted Best, Branding
    & Corp Commun Mgr

Stuart Budd & Sons Ltd.

2454 South Service Rd. West
Oakville, ON L6L 5M9
Tel 905-845-3577
Fax 905-825-9887
www.buddsbmw.com
AKA: Budd Brothers Holding Co.;
Budds Hamilton; Budds Imported Car
Collision Services
Line: Sells and leases new and used
luxury cars, parts and services.
NAICS: 441110
#Emp: 250-499 (Tor)
#TorLoc: 7
Own: Private Company
Key: Terrance Budd, VP
Darryl Budd, Pres
Rob Westroh, GM
Lori Garwood-Jones,
    Payroll & Benefits Mgr
Brent Bere, CFO

Student Transportation Canada

95 Forhan Ave.
Newmarket, ON L3Y 8X6
Tel 905-476-4396
Fax 905-853-5517
AKA: Simcoe Coach Lines Ltd.
Line: Provides school and non-school
charter trips, and home to school bus
transportation.
NAICS: 485510 485410
#Emp: 100-249 (Tor)
#TorLoc: 1
Own: Private Company
Par: Student Transportation of Canada
(CDA)
Key: Ted Wilson, Chmn

Subaru Canada Inc.

560 Suffolk Crt.
Mississauga, ON L5R 4J7
Tel 905-568-4959
Fax 905-568-8087
www.subaru.ca
Line: Imports and distributes vehicles
and automotive parts.
NAICS: 415110
#Emp: 100-249 (Tor)
#TorLoc: 1
Own: Private Company
Par: Fuji Heavy Industries Ltd. (JAPAN)
Key: Katsuhiro Yokoyama,
   Chmn, Pres & CEO
Gary Filippini, VP Admin, Corp
   Planning & Customer Loyalty
George Hamin, Dir of e-Business & IS
Don Durst, Sr VP Sales & Mktg
Ted Lalka, VP Mktg

Summer Fresh Salads

181 Sharer Rd.
Woodbridge, ON L4L 8Z3
Tel 905-856-8816
Fax 905-856-9298
www.summerfresh.com
Line: Manufactures all natural salad-
dips, appetizers and soups.
NAICS: 311940
#Emp: 250-499 (Tor)
#TorLoc: 1
Own: Private Company
Key: Susan Niczowski, Pres
Gilles Hamel, CFO
Lynn Sandell, VP Sales

Summit Food Service Distributors Inc.

A Div. of Colarbor Ltd.
6270 Kenway Dr.
Mississauga, ON L5T 2N3
Tel 905-795-2400
www.summitfoods.com
Line: Distributes national brand food
products.
NAICS: 413110
#Emp: 75-99 (Tor)
#TorLoc: 1
Own: Private Company
Key: Gary Englebrecht, Dir of Ops

Summit Ford Sales (1982) Ltd.

12 Carrier Dr.
Toronto, ON M9V 2C1
Tel 416-741-6221
Fax 416-741-2874
www.summitford.com
Line: Operates car dealership.
NAICS: 441110 441120
#Emp: 75-99 (Tor)
#TorLoc: 1
Own: Private Company
Key: Scott Vickers, Pres
Brian Vickers, VP
Diana Mocha, Cont

The Summit Golf & Country Club

11901 Yonge St.
Richmond Hill, ON L4E 3N9
Tel 905-884-8189
Fax 905-884-6398
www.summitgolfclub.on.ca
NAICS: 713910
#Emp: 75-99 (Tor)
#TorLoc: 1
Own: Private Company
Key: Tom Price, Dir of Golf
Richard Creally, GM

Summo Steel Corp.

1180 Burloak Dr.
Burlington, ON L7L 6B4
Tel 905-336-0014
Fax 905-336-0863
www.summosteel.com
Line: Manufactures and distributes
steel tubing and automotive parts.
NAICS: 331210
#Emp: 75-99 (Tor)
#TorLoc: 3
Own: Private Company
Key: Kevork Sevadjian, Pres
Demetra Mascherin, HR Admr
Manuel Santos, VP Fin

Sun Chemical Ltd.

10 West Dr.
Brampton, ON L6T 4Y4
Tel 905-796-2222
Fax 905-796-7716
www.sunchemical.com/canada/
NAICS: 325910
#Emp: 100-249 (Tor)
#TorLoc: 2
Own: Private Company
Par: Sun Chemical Corp. (US)

Key: Rod Staveley, Pres
David Giust, Dir of Ops
Greg Main, Dir of Admin Services
Tracey Thorn, Purch Mgr
Norm Anderson, VP Sales

Sungard

5225 Satellite Dr.
Mississauga, ON L4W 5P9
Tel 905-275-2299
Fax 905-275-6514
www.sungardinsurance.com
AKA: Sungard iWorks
Line: Provides insurance industry
software.
NAICS: 541510
#Emp: 75-99 (Tor)
#TorLoc: 1
Own: Private Company
Par: SunGard Insurance Systems (US)
Key: Greg Webber, Pres of Insurance

Sun Life Assurance Company of Canada

150 King St. West
Toronto, ON M5H 1J9
Tel 416-979-9966
Fax 416-585-9546
www.sunlife.ca
AKA: Sun Life Financial
Line: Provides individual and group life
and health insurance as well as wealth
management services.
NAICS: 524112
#Emp: 1000-4999 (Tor)
#TorLoc: 18
Own: Public Company
Par: Sun Life Financial Inc. (CDA)
Key: Dean Connor, Pres
Donald Stewart, CEO
K. Louise McLaren,
   Sr VP & Chief HR Officer
Colm Freyne, Exec VP & CFO
Greg Ausman,
   VP Shared Business Services
Mark Saunders, Exec VP & CIO
Mary De Paoli,
   Sr VP & Chief Mktg Officer
Frank Switzer, VP Corp Commun

Sun Media Corp.

333 King St. East
Toronto, ON M5A 3X5
Tel 416-947-2222
Fax 416-947-3119
www.sunmedia.ca
Line: Publishes newspapers.
NAICS: 511110
#Emp: 500-999 (Tor)
#TorLoc: 1
Own: Private Company
Par: Quebecor Inc. (CDA)
Key: Pierre Karl Peladeau,
   Pres & CEO, Quebecor
Chris Krygiel, VP HR

Sunnybrook Health Sciences Centre

2075 Bayview Ave.
Toronto, ON M4N 3M5
Tel 416-480-6100
Fax 416-480-5588
www.sunnybrook.ca
Line: Provides teaching, research, and acute medical and chronic care.
NAICS: 622111
#Emp: 5000-9999 (Tor)
#TorLoc: 3
Own: Not-for-profit
Key: Barry McLellan, Pres & CEO
Michael Young, Exec VP & CAO
Marilyn Reddick, VP HR
Alison Welch, VP & CFO
Sam Marafioti,
   VP Strategy & Dev & CIO
Susan VanDevelde Coke, Exec VP &
   Chief Health Professional
Keith Rose,
   Exec VP & Chief Medical Officer

Sunny Crunch Foods Ltd.

200 Shields Crt.
Markham, ON L3R 9T5
Tel 905-475-0422
Fax 905-475-9775
www.sunnycrunch.com
Line: Manufactures nutrition and energy bars, meal replacement bars and sports nutrition products.
NAICS: 311211 311230
#Emp: 100-249 (Tor)
#TorLoc: 1
Own: Private Company
Key: Willie Pelzer, Pres & CEO
Hitesh Vyas, VP New Business Dev
Richard Pelzer, VP Mktg

Sun Opta Food Distribution Group Inc.

2838 Bovaird Dr. West
Brampton, ON L7A 0H2
Tel 905-455-1990
Fax 905-455-2529
www.sunopta.com
AKA: SunOpta
Line: Distributes all types of food.
NAICS: 413190
#Emp: 100-249 (Tor)
#TorLoc: 3
Own: Public Company
Par: SunOpta Inc. (CDA)
Key: Steve Bromley, Pres & CEO
Jeremy Kendall, Chmn
Tony Tavares, COO
Eric Davis, CFO

Sun Pac Foods

10 Sun Pac Blvd.
Brampton, ON L6S 4R5
Tel 905-792-2700
Fax 905-792-8490
www.sunpac.ca
Line: Provides trucking and truck leasing services.
NAICS: 532120
#Emp: 100-249 (Tor)
#TorLoc: 1
Own: Public Company
Key: John Riddell, Pres
Albert Kuhner, VP Ops
Angela Papano, Payroll & Personnel
Vincent McEwan, VP Fin
Lisa Oneschuk, Dir of Mktg

Sun Rich Fresh Foods Inc.

1-35 Bramtree Crt.
Brampton, ON L6S 6G2
Tel 905-789-0200
Fax 905-789-1335
www.sun-rich.com
Line: Offers ready to serve cut fruit and fruit salad.
NAICS: 413150
#Emp: 250-499 (Tor)
Own: Private Company
Key: Cam Haygarth, VP Sales
Jeff Pitchford, Dir of Cdn Ops
Jill Ferenczi, HR Mgr

Sunrise Senior Living

38 Swansea Rd.
Markham, ON L3R 5K2
Tel 905-947-4566
Fax 905-947-8658
www.sunriseseniorliving.com
Line: Operates a retirement senior living care in a homelike environment offering memory impairment, incontinence management and medication administration services.
NAICS: 623310
#Emp: 75-99 (Tor)
Own: Private Company
Par: Sunrise Senior Living (CDA)
Key: Olga Sen, Exec Dir
Mark Ordan, CEO
Debbie Heller-Raphael,
   Dir of Community Relns
Marc Richards, CFO

Sunrise Senior Living, Inc.

1279 Burnhamthorpe Rd. East
Mississauga, ON L4Y 3V7
Tel 905-625-1344
Fax 905-625-4135
www.sunriseseniorliving.com
AKA: Sunrise of Mississauga
Line: Operates a retirement residence.
NAICS: 623310
#Emp: 75-99 (Tor)
#TorLoc: 2
Own: Not-for-profit
Key: Kelly Gillespie, Exec Dir

Sunshine Building Maintenance Inc.

2500 Industrial St.
Burlington, ON L7P 1A5
Tel 905-335-2020
Fax 905-335-6006
www.sunshineinc.ca
Line: Contracts janitorial and carpet cleaning services.
NAICS: 561722
#Emp: 100-249 (Tor)
#TorLoc: 1
Own: Private Company
Key: John Brouwers, Pres
Ted Brouwers, VP
Bob Pottruff, GM
Lisa Jones, HR Coord
Christine Adamczyk, Office Mgr
Nash Velinovic, Ops Mgr
Steve Debau, Sales Mgr

Sunsweet Fundraising Inc.

30 Rayette Rd.
Concord, ON L4K 2G3
Tel 905-669-6600
Fax 905-738-0443
www.sunsweetfundraising.com
Line: Supplies fundraising products to non-profit groups.
NAICS: 561490
#Emp: 100-249 (Tor)
#TorLoc: 1
Own: Private Company
Key: Howard Garr, Pres & CEO
Ian Dyment, Warehouse Mgr
Yola Lodovici, HR Mgr
Joanne Marchese, Cont
Aaron Garr, Ops Mgr
Tanya Dyment, Sales Mgr

Sun Valley Supermarket Inc.

468 Danforth Ave.
Toronto, ON M1K 1C6
Tel 416-264-2323
Fax 416-264-3360
www.sunvalleyfinefoods.com
AKA: Sun Valley Fine Foods
Line: Operates grocery stores.
NAICS: 445230
#Emp: 75-99 (Tor)
#TorLoc: 2
Own: Private Company
Key: Gerry Aravantinos, Pres

Sunview Doors Ltd.

500 Zenway Blvd.
Woodbridge, ON L4H 0S7
Tel 905-851-1006
Fax 905-851-9933
www.sunviewdoors.com
Line: Manufactures sliding and patio doors.
NAICS: 332321
#Emp: 100-249 (Tor)
#TorLoc: 2
Own: Private Company
Key: Tony Margiotta, Pres
Maurizio Fruci, HR Mgr

Sun Wah Trading Inc.

18 Canmotor Ave.
Toronto, ON M8Z 4E5
Tel 416-252-7757
Fax 416-255-5418
NAICS: 413110
#Emp: 75-99 (Tor)
#TorLoc: 1
Own: Private Company
Key: Ricky Luk, Pres
John Lee, Ops Mgr

Sunwing Travel Group

27 Fasken Dr.
Toronto, ON M9W 1K6
Tel 416-620-5999
Fax 416-620-4433
www.sunwing.ca
AKA: Red Seal Vacations; Sunwing Airlines; Sunwing Vacations; Signature Vacations; SellOffVacations.com; Sun Wing Tours
Line: Provides charter airline and tour operating services.
NAICS: 561520
#Emp: 500-999 (Tor)
Own: Private Company
Par: Sunwing Canada Inc. (CDA)
Key: Colin Hunter, Pres & CEO
Stephen Hunter, COO

Supercom of Canada Ltd.

4011 14th Ave.
Markham, ON L3R 0Z9
Tel 905-415-1166
Fax 905-415-1177
www.supercom.ca
Line: Wholesales computer components and peripherals.
NAICS: 417310
#Emp: 100-249 (Tor)
#TorLoc: 1
Own: Private Company
Key: Frank Luk, Pres
Sylvia Tam, HR Mgr
Brian Ho, Financial Cont
Terry Davies, Mktg Services Mgr

Superior Glove Works Ltd.

36 Vimy St.
Acton, ON L7J 1S1
Tel 519-853-1920
Fax 519-853-4496
www.superiorglove.com
NAICS: 315990
#Emp: 75-99 (Tor)
#TorLoc: 1
Own: Private Company
Key: Tony Geng, Pres & CEO
Joe Geng, VP
Deb Malady, Office Mgr
Frank MacDonald, Sales Mgr

Superior Pool Spa & Leisure Ltd.

24 Martin Ross Ave.
Toronto, ON M3J 2K8
Tel 416-665-0410
Fax 416-665-6877
www.superiorpool.com
Line: Provides swimming pool products and services.

NAICS: 232990 561799
#Emp: 100-249 (Tor)
#TorLoc: 1
Own: Private Company
Key: Steve Schechter, Pres

Super-Pufft Snacks Corp.

880 Gana Crt.
Mississauga, ON L5S 1N8
Tel 905-564-1180
Fax 905-564-9038
www.superpufft.com
Line: Manufactures potato chips, popcorn, canister chips and beverages.
NAICS: 311919
#Emp: 100-249 (Tor)
#TorLoc: 1
Own: Private Company
Key: Yahya Abbas, Pres & CEO

Super Shine Oakdale Janitorial Services Ltd.

28-4120 Ridgeway Dr.
Mississauga, ON L5L 5S5
Tel 905-607-8200
Fax 905-607-9892
www.supershine-oakdale.com
Line: Provides commercial, institutional and retail janitorial services.
NAICS: 561722
#Emp: 75-99 (Tor)
#TorLoc: 1
Own: Private Company
Key: Frank Novelli, Pres
John Dilworth, Cont

Superstyle Furniture Ltd.

123 Ashbridge Circ.
Woodbridge, ON L4L 3R5
Tel 905-850-6060
Fax 905-850-6061
www.superstylefurniture.com
Line: Manufactures upholstery.
NAICS: 337121
#Emp: 100-249 (Tor)
#TorLoc: 1
Own: Private Company
Key: Danny Colalillo, Pres
Anthony Colalillo, VP HR
Joan Fernandes, Acct

Supply Chain Management Inc.

6800 Maritz Dr.
Mississauga, ON L5W 1W2
Tel 905-670-9966
Fax 905-670-5826
www.scm3pl.com
AKA: SCM
NAICS: 493110
#Emp: 1000-4999 (Tor)
#TorLoc: 2
Own: Private Company
Par: Exel Logistics (US)
Key: Dan Gabbard, Pres
Troy Mascarenhas, Dir of Fin

Supremex Inc.

400 Humberline Dr.
Toronto, ON M9W 5T3
Tel 416-675-9370
Fax 416-675-1952
www.supremex.com
AKA: PNG Globe; Innova Envelope;
Regional Envelope Specialty Paper
Products
Line: Manufactures and markets a
broad range of stock and custom
envelopes and related products.
NAICS: 322230
#Emp: 250-499 (Tor)
#TorLoc: 3
Own: Public Company
Key: Gilles Cyr, Pres
Stewart Emerson,
   VP & GM, Central Region

Surex Community Services

311-40 Wynford Dr.
Toronto, ON M3C 1J5
Tel 416-469-4109
Fax 416-469-4184
www.surexcs.com
Line: Provides residential care and
programming to developmentally
handicapped adults.
NAICS: 624120
#Emp: 100-249 (Tor)
Own: Not-for-profit
Key: Colin Hamilton, Exec Dir
Wanda Lougheed, Program Dir
Lily Smith, HR Mgr
Paul Fung, Financial Cont

Surrey Place Centre

2 Surrey Pl.
Toronto, ON M5S 2C2
Tel 416-925-5141
Fax 416-923-8476
www.surreyplace.on.ca
Line: Operates a community-based
agency that provides specialized health
services and programs to help enhance
the quality of life for people with
developmental disabilities.
NAICS: 813310
#Emp: 250-499 (Tor)
#TorLoc: 5
Own: Not-for-profit
Key: John Flannery, CEO
Elspeth Bradley, VP Medical Affairs
Bruce Wilson, VP HR
Ken Chan, VP Fin & Admin

Sutton Group - Admiral Realty Inc.

12-1881 Steeles Ave. West
Toronto, ON M3H 5Y4
Tel 416-739-7200
Fax 416-739-9367
www.sutton.com/admiral
NAICS: 531210
#Emp: 250-499 (Tor)
#TorLoc: 1
Own: Private Company
Key: Murray Goldkind, Pres
Anna Stalierno, Admin

Sutton Group - Associates Realty Inc.

358 Davenport Rd.
Toronto, ON M5R 1K6
Tel 416-966-0300
Fax 416-966-0080
www.sutton.com/office/associates
NAICS: 531210
#Emp: 100-249 (Tor)
Own: Private Company
Key: Henry Balaban, Pres
Judy Colwill, Admr

Sutton Group Heritage Realty Inc.

300 Clements Rd. West
Ajax, ON L1S 3C6
Tel 905-619-9500
Fax 905-619-3334
www.suttonheritage.com
Line: Operates a real estate firm.
NAICS: 531210
#Emp: 100-249 (Tor)
#TorLoc: 3
Own: Private Company
Key: Rosalind Menary, Pres

Sutton Group Old Mill Realty Brokerage Inc.

4237 Dundas St. West
Toronto, ON M8X 1Y3
Tel 416-234-2424
Fax 416-234-2323
www.suttonoldmill.com
NAICS: 531310
#Emp: 75-99 (Tor)
#TorLoc: 1
Own: Private Company
Key: Ann Hannah,
   Broker of Record & Owner
Loic Danis, Supr

Sutton Group Quantum Realty Inc.

1673 Lakeshore Rd. West
Mississauga, ON L5J 1J4
Tel 905-822-5000
Fax 905-822-5617
www.suttonquantum.com
Line: Operates a real estate agency.
NAICS: 531210
#Emp: 75-99 (Tor)
#TorLoc: 2
Own: Private Company
Key: Tina Gardin,
Broker of Record & Owner

Sutton Group Realty Systems Inc.

2186 Bloor St. West
Toronto, ON M6S 1N3
Tel 905-896-3333
Fax 905-848-5327
www.suttonrealty.com
Line: Provides real estate and financial
services.
NAICS: 531210
#Emp: 100-249 (Tor)
#TorLoc: 2
Own: Private Company
Key: Marija Semen, Broker & Owner

Sutton Group - Summit Realty Inc.

27-1100 Burnhamthorpe Rd. West
Mississauga, ON L5C 4G4
Tel 905-897-9555
Fax 905-897-9610
www.suttongroupsummit.com
Line: Operates a real estate firm.
NAICS: 531210
#Emp: 100-249 (Tor)
#TorLoc: 1
Own: Private Company
Key: Brian Maguire,
Pres & Broker of Record

The Sutton Place Hotel Toronto

955 Bay St.
Toronto, ON M5S 2A2
Tel 416-924-9221
Fax 416-924-1778
www.toronto.suttonplace.com
NAICS: 721111
#Emp: 250-499 (Tor)
#TorLoc: 1
Own: Private Company
Par: The Sutton Place Grande Hotels
Group (CDA)
Key: Nick Vesely, GM
Christine Bartsiocas, Dir of HR
Robert Farolan, Purch Mgr
Christopher Ashby, Dir of Sales & Mktg

Suzuki Canada Inc.

100 East Beaver Creek Rd.
Richmond Hill, ON L4B 1J6
Tel 905-889-2600
Fax 905-764-1574
www.suzuki.ca
Line: Distributes automobiles,
motorcycles, ATVs, and marine related
parts and accessories.
NAICS: 415190 415290
#Emp: 100-249 (Tor)
#TorLoc: 1
Own: Private Company
Par: Suzuki Motor Corp. (JAPAN)
Key: Maruyama Seiichi, Pres
Cynthia Romano, HR Mgr

Swiftrans Services Ltd.

71 City View Dr.
Toronto, ON M9W 5A5
Tel 416-614-0999
Fax 416-614-0088
www.swiftrans.ca
NAICS: 561510
#Emp: 75-99 (Tor)
#TorLoc: 1
Own: Private Company
Key: Lorenzo Durso, Pres

Swiss Herbal Remedies Ltd.

35 Fulton Way
Richmond Hill, ON L4B 2N4
Tel 905-886-9500
Fax 905-886-5434
www.swissherbal.ca
Line: Distributes source vitamins,
minerals and herbal supplements.
NAICS: 414510
#Emp: 100-249 (Tor)
#TorLoc: 1
Own: Private Company
Key: John Ferris, Pres & CEO
Davinder Singh, Sr Mgr of Ops
Dorothy Artori,
    Sr HR & Customer Care Mgr
Lou Galvao, CFO
Jim Boyd, Dir of Nat'l Sales
Sheryl Willison, Dir of Mktg

Swissplas Ltd.

735 Intermodal Dr.
Brampton, ON L6T 5W2
Tel 905-789-9300
Fax 905-669-6445
www.swissplas.com
Line: Manufactures plastic bottles.
NAICS: 326160
#Emp: 75-99 (Tor)
#TorLoc: 1
Own: Private Company
Par: Monarch Plastics Ltd. (CDA)
Key: Hemang D. Mehta, Pres & CEO
Elroy DeXavier, VP Fin & Admin
Nadine Mortella, Mgr of Fin & Admin

Swissport Cargo Services, LP

6500 Silver Dart Dr., Core G
Mississauga, ON L5P 1A2
Tel 905-673-8153
Fax 905-676-8438
www.swissport.com
Line: Operates a cargo management
company.
NAICS: 488519
#Emp: 250-499 (Tor)
Own: Private Company
Par: Swissport International Ltd.
(SWITZ)
Key: Mike Stamcos, Station Mgr

Swiss Reinsurance Co. Canada

2200-150 King St. West
P.O. Box 50
Toronto, ON M5H 1J9
Tel 416-408-0272
Fax 416-408-4222
www.swissre.com
AKA: Swiss Re Life & Health Canada
Line: Operates reinsurance company.
NAICS: 524131 524133 524134
#Emp: 75-99 (Tor)
#TorLoc: 1
Own: Private Company
Key: Sharon Ludlow, Pres & CEO
Janet Podpora, VP HR
Jonathan Turner, CFO

SWI Systemware Inc.

1800-2300 Yonge St.
P.O. Box 2418
Toronto, ON M4P 1E4
Tel 416-932-4700
Fax 416-932-4710
www.swi.com
NAICS: 541510
#Emp: 75-99 (Tor)
#TorLoc: 1
Own: Private Company
Key: David Tremaine, CEO
Polly Lau, CFO

Sykes Assistance Services Corporation

A Div. of Sykes Enterprises, Inc.
248 Pall Mall St.
P.O. Box 5845
London, ON N6A 4T4
Tel 1-888-225-6824
www.sykesassistance.com
Line: Provides toll free telehealth
services such as symptom
management, compliance management
and health and wellness information.
NAICS: 624190
#Emp: 100-249 (Tor)
#TorLoc: 1
Own: Government
Key: Bruce Woods, Pres

Syl Apps Youth Centre

A Div. of Kinark Child & Family Services
475 Iroquois Shore Rd.
Oakville, ON L6H 1M3
Tel 905-844-4110
Fax 905-844-9197
www.kinark.on.ca
Line: Provides custody and detention programs to young people in conflict with the law and residential treatment to youth whose mental health issues require a secure setting.
NAICS: 624190
#Emp: 75-99 (Tor)
#TorLoc: 1
Own: Not-for-profit
Key: Carolyne Hooper, Dir of Youth
    Justice & Secure Treatment
Peter Moore, Exec Dir
Hank Vipari, Business Mgr

Symantec Corp.

3381 Steeles Ave. East, 4th Fl.
Toronto, ON M2H 3S7
Tel 416-774-0000
Fax 416-774-0001
www.symantec.ca
Line: Develops, markets, sells and supports software.
NAICS: 541510
#Emp: 75-99 (Tor)
#TorLoc: 1
Own: Private Company
Par: Symantec Corp. (US)
Key: Michael Murphy,
    VP, Enterprise Sales
Wendy Ducheck, Sr HR Mgr

Symcor Inc.

400-1 Robert Speck Pkwy.
Mississauga, ON L4Z 4E7
Tel 905-273-1000
Fax 905-273-1001
www.symcor.com
Line: Provides cheque processing, payment processing, statement production and document management services.
NAICS: 522329
#Emp: 1000-4999 (Tor)
#TorLoc: 6
Own: Private Company
Key: Meegan Hinds, Sr VP & GM
Murali Dorai, VP Ops
Cindy Gorelle, Sr VP HR
Norma Mayer, Sr VP Client Relns

Symtech Innovations Ltd.

2-3980 14th Ave.
Markham, ON L3R 0B1
Tel 905-940-8044
Fax 905-752-8900
www.symtech.com
AKA: Symtech Canada Ltd.
Line: Provides cable, electric and communications solutions.
NAICS: 232510
#Emp: 100-249 (Tor)
#TorLoc: 1
Own: Private Company
Key: Shawn Cohen, Pres
Denny Jackson, VP & GM

Synergex Corporation

1280 Courtneypark Dr. East
Mississauga, ON L5T 1N6
Tel 905-565-1212
Fax 905-670-9291
www.syx.ca
AKA: Synergex Retail Services
Line: Provides freight forwarding services.
NAICS: 488519
#Emp: 100-249 (Tor)
#TorLoc: 1
Own: Private Company
Key: David Aiello, Pres & CEO
Matt Reiter, VP
Nick Blasutto, CFO

SYNNEX Canada Ltd.

200 Ronson Dr.
Toronto, ON M9W 5Z9
Tel 416-240-7012
Fax 416-240-2605
www.synnex.ca
Line: Distributes computer hardware and software products.
NAICS: 541510 417310
#Emp: 250-499 (Tor)
#TorLoc: 1
Own: Private Company
Par: SYNNEX Corporation (US)
Key: Mitchell Martin, Pres
George Kelly, VP Ops
Dave Dukowsky, VP Retail Sales

Synovate Canada Ltd.

500-480 University Ave.
Toronto, ON M5G 2R4
Tel 416-964-6262
Fax 416-964-5882
www.synovate.com
Line: Operates a marketing research agency.
NAICS: 541910
#Emp: 75-99 (Tor)

#TorLoc: 1
Own: Private Company
Par: Aegis plc (UK)
Key: Sharon Paskowitz, Sr VP Canada
Rob Myers, Mng Dir

Sysco Milton, Inc.

2800 Peddie Rd.
Milton, ON L9T 6Y9
Tel 905-203-2166
Fax 905-568-2973
www.sysco.ca
AKA: Pronamic
Line: Supplies food.
NAICS: 722310
#Emp: 75-99 (Tor)
#TorLoc: 1
Own: Private Company
Par: Sysco Corporation (CDA)
Key: Rob Chapman, GM, Ops
Katie Wong, Sr HR Generalist
Harjot Kang, Cont

Sysco Toronto

7055 Kennedy Rd.
Mississauga, ON L5S 1Y7
Tel 905-670-8605
Fax 905-696-4707
www.sysco.ca
Line: Warehouses and distributes food and non-food products to restaurants, hotels and healthcare institutions.
NAICS: 413110
#Emp: 250-499 (Tor)
#TorLoc: 1
Own: Private Company
Par: SYSCO Food Services (CDA)
Key: Bart Dawdy, Pres & COO
Rod Stroud, CEO
Michelle Kerr, Dir of HR
Bob Horne, VP Fin & CFO
Geoff Teasdale, VP Merchandising
John MacKenzie, VP Sales
Ray Parkes, Dir of Supplier Dev

Systematix Inc.

301-41 Britain St.
Toronto, ON M5A 1R7
Tel 416-595-5331
Fax 416-595-1525
www.systematix.com
Line: Offers services that combine technologies with business management.
NAICS: 541510
#Emp: 500-999 (Tor)
Own: Private Company
Key: Norbert Rozko, Pres

T4G Limited

300-100 Broadview Ave.
Toronto, ON M4M 3H3
Tel 416-462-4200
Fax 416-462-9333
www.t4g.com
Line: Provides project-based
information technology services.
NAICS: 541510
#Emp: 100-249 (Tor)
#TorLoc: 1
Own: Private Company
Key: Geoff Flood, Pres
Michael Cottenden, Mng Partner & CIO
Faith Bisram, Dir of HR
Gary Morris, CFO
Shawn Crabtree, CTO
Darren Schisler, VP Commun

Tab Products of Canada, Co.

130 Sparks Ave.
Toronto, ON M2H 2S4
Tel 416-497-1585
Fax 416-497-2044
www.tab.com
Line: Assists companies to organize,
access and manage their information
through filing products and consulting
services.
NAICS: 337214 541510
#Emp: 75-99 (Tor)
#TorLoc: 1
Own: Private Company
Par: T. Acquisition Limited Partnership
(US)
Key: Arman Bourgoin, Pres
Randal Branden, Dir of IT
Henry Van Pypen, VP & GM, TTE Sales
Ross Nepeans, VP Global Mktg

T.A. Brannon Steel Ltd.

12 Tilbury Crt.
Brampton, ON L6T 3T4
Tel 905-453-4730
Fax 905-453-4483
www.brannonsteel.com
AKA: Brannon Steel
Line: Manufactures steel products from
steel plate.
NAICS: 332999
#Emp: 100-249 (Tor)
#TorLoc: 1
Own: Private Company
Key: Kirk Brannon, Pres
Allan Brannon, Chmn
Kevin Brannon, VP Ops
Ron Colasanti, Cont
David Brannon, Purch

Tacc Construction Ltd.

270 Chrislea Rd.
Woodbridge, ON L4L 8A8
Tel 905-856-8500
Fax 905-856-8508
www.tacc.com
NAICS: 231310 231390
#Emp: 250-499 (Tor)
#TorLoc: 1
Own: Private Company
Key: Silvio DeGasperis, Pres
Carlo Vatali, Cont & Fin Mgr

Tai Foong International Ltd.

2900 Markham Rd.
Toronto, ON M1X 1E6
Tel 416-299-7575
Fax 416-299-0143
www.taifoong.com
NAICS: 413140
#Emp: 100-249 (Tor)
#TorLoc: 1
Own: Private Company
Par: Tai Foong Investments Ltd. (CDA)
Key: David Lam, Pres
Willy Janz, Dir of Fin

Talmolder Inc.

325 Limestone Cres.
Toronto, ON M3J 2R1
Tel 416-736-1991
Fax 416-736-7942
www.talmolder.com
Line: Manufactures custom moulded
polyurethane products.
NAICS: 314990
#Emp: 75-99 (Tor)
#TorLoc: 1
Own: Private Company
Key: Hrindran Nithiananthan, Ops Mgr

Talon Systems Inc.

6200 Cantay Rd.
Mississauga, ON L5R 3Y9
Tel 905-501-9350
Fax 905-501-9355
Line: Manufactures household and
home office furniture.
NAICS: 337213 337214
#Emp: 100-249 (Tor)
#TorLoc: 1
Own: Private Company
Key: Derek Okada, Pres
Laurie Catsimbras, HR Mgr
Glenn Castelino, Cont
Neil Cleland, Production Mgr
Tony Marchitello, VP Sales

Tamarack Lumber Inc.

3269 North Service Rd.
Burlington, ON L7R 3Y3
Tel 905-335-4966
Fax 905-332-5611
www.tamaracklumber.ca
Line: Distributes lumber, doors,
windows and roof trusses to residential
builders.
NAICS: 416320
#Emp: 100-249 (Tor)
#TorLoc: 1
Own: Private Company
Par: Alpa Lumber Group (CDA)
Key: John Di Poce, Pres
Donald Corner, Secy-Treas

Tam Electrical Ltd.

456 Garyray Dr.
Toronto, ON M9L 1P7
Tel 416-743-6214
Fax 416-746-5719
www.tamelectric.ca
Line: Provides electrical contract
services.
NAICS: 232510
#Emp: 75-99 (Tor)
#TorLoc: 1
Own: Private Company
Key: Frank Talenti, Pres

Tam-Kal Limited

34 Cardico Dr.
P.O. Box 429
Gormley, ON L0H 1G0
Tel 905-888-9200
Fax 905-888-9202
www.tam-kal.com
Line: Operates a sheet metal
manufacturing and contracting
company specializing in HVAC
Systems.
NAICS: 332311
#Emp: 100-249 (Tor)
#TorLoc: 1
Own: Private Company
Key: Michael Tamburro, Pres
Lorraine Tamburro, Treas & Cont
Tony Vozza, Chief Estimator

Tank Truck Transport Inc.

11339 Albion Vaughan Line, R.R. #1
Kleinburg, ON L0J 1C0
Tel 905-893-3447
Fax 905-893-3430
www.ttttransport.com
AKA: Toll Leasing Ltd.
Line: Provides transportation services.
NAICS: 484110 484121
#Emp: 100-249 (Tor)
#TorLoc: 1
Own: Private Company
Key: John Lynde, Pres
Roxanna Tahzibi, Cont

Target Investigation & Security Ltd.

3-2900 Langstaff Rd.
Concord, ON L4K 4R9
Tel 905-760-9090
Fax 905-760-9191
www.targetprotection.com
Line: Provides security and detective services and systems.
NAICS: 561611 561612
#Emp: 500-999 (Tor)
#TorLoc: 1
Own: Private Company
Key: John Domonkos, Pres

Taro Pharmaceuticals

130 East Dr.
Brampton, ON L6T 1C1
Tel 905-791-8276
Fax 905-791-5008
www.taro.ca
NAICS: 325410
#Emp: 250-499 (Tor)
#TorLoc: 3
Own: Private Company
Key: Michael Buckley, GM

Tata Consultancy Services Canada Inc.

200-5750 Explorer Dr.
Mississauga, ON L4W 0A9
Tel 905-366-2800
Fax 905-366-2803
www.tcs.com
Line: Provides information technology consulting, services and business process outsourcing.
NAICS: 541510 541611
#Emp: 250-499 (Tor)
#TorLoc: 1
Own: Private Company

Par: Tata Consultancy Services Limited (INDIA)
Key: Akhilesh Tripathi,
  Country Mgr, Canada
Jayaraman Keerthi, Head of Ops
Keren Bandner, HR Mgr
Anish Mukherjee, Head of Fin
Douglas Long, Mktg Mgr

Taxi Canada Inc.

102-495 Wellington St. West
Toronto, ON M5V 1E9
Tel 416-979-7001
Fax 416-979-7626
www.taxi.ca
Line: Operates an advertising agency.
NAICS: 541810
#Emp: 100-249 (Tor)
#TorLoc: 2
Own: Private Company
Key: Rob Guenette, Pres
Ron Wilson, VP, COO & CFO
Joanne Arfo, Dir of HR & Commun

Taxi-Taxi

164 Bloor St. East
Oshawa, ON L1H 3M4
Tel 905-571-1234
Fax 905-725-4771
Line: Provides taxicab services.
NAICS: 485310
#Emp: 100-249 (Tor)
#TorLoc: 1
Own: Private Company
Key: Sue Wortman, Owner

Tayco Panelink Ltd.

630 Kipling Ave.
Toronto, ON M8Z 5G1
Tel 416-252-8000
Fax 416-252-4467
www.tayco.com
Line: Manufactures office furniture.
NAICS: 337214 337213
#Emp: 250-499 (Tor)
#TorLoc: 2
Own: Private Company
Key: Phil Philips, Pres & GM
Sunny Singh, Ops Mgr
Michael Diluaro, HR Mgr
Colin Clucas, Purch Mgr

The Taylor Group

255 Biscayne Cres.
Brampton, ON L6W 4R2
Tel 905-451-5800
Fax 905-451-1544
www.taylorinc.com
AKA: Taylor Manufacturing Industries Ltd.
Line: Provides design, manufacturing and site services for trade show exhibits, museums, and retail environments.
NAICS: 339990
#Emp: 100-249 (Tor)
#TorLoc: 1
Own: Private Company
Key: Dean Marks, Pres
Len Piccininni, VP Ops & CFO
Samantha Manteiga, Purch Mgr

Taylor Moving & Storage Ltd.

1200 Plains Rd. East
Burlington, ON L7S 1W6
Tel 905-632-8010
Fax 905-632-5083
www.ataylormoving.com
Line: Specializes in household moving and storage.
NAICS: 484210
#Emp: 75-99 (Tor)
#TorLoc: 1
Own: Private Company
Key: Chris Richards, Ops Mgr

TBWA Toronto

101-10 Lower Spadina Ave.
Toronto, ON M5V 2Z2
Tel 416-260-6600
Fax 416-260-8088
www.tbwa.com
Line: Operates advertising and communications firm.
NAICS: 541810
#Emp: 75-99 (Tor)
#TorLoc: 1
Own: Public Company
Par: Omnicom Group Inc. (US)
Key: Jay Bertram, Pres
Philip George, Mng Dir
Shanta Maula, Dir of Fin
Paul Halliday, MIS Dir

TD Asset Management Inc.

161 Bay St.,
Canada Trust Tower, 2nd Fl.
Toronto, ON M5J 2T2
Tel 416-982-8222
Fax 416-982-8728
www.tdassetmanagement.com
Line: Provides full range of investment
management products for retail and
institutional clients.
NAICS: 523920
#Emp: 250-499 (Tor)
Own: Private Company
Key: Barbara F. Palk,
 Pres, TD Asset Management
Reg Swamy, VP Wealth Management

TD Bank Financial Group

TD Centre, 55 King St. West, TD Tower
Toronto, ON M5K 1A2
Tel 416-982-8222
Fax 416-982-5671
www.td.com
AKA: The Toronto Dominion Bank; TD
Waterhouse Canada Inc.
Line: Serves businesses, financial
institutions, individuals and
governments in Canada, the U.S. and
other international financial capitals.
NAICS: 522111
#Emp: 10000+ (Tor)
#TorLoc: 280
Own: Public Company
Key: W. Edmund Clark, Pres & CEO
Ken Peaker, VP HR
Colleen Johnston, CFO
Matt Giliberto, VP Tech Solutions
Ted Currie, Group Head Mktg,
 Corp & People Strategies

TD Financing Services

101-25 Booth Ave.
P.O. Box 4086, Station A
Toronto, ON M4M 2M3
Tel 416-463-4422
Fax 416-463-5459
www.tdfinancingservices.com
Line: Finances car loans.
NAICS: 522291
#Emp: 250-499 (Tor)
#TorLoc: 1
Own: Private Company
Key: Erik De Witte, CEO
Sean O'Brien, VP Ops & Sales
Lesley Angus, Mgr of HR
David Ryde, VP Fin
Lise Dulong, IT Dir

TD Insurance Meloche Monnex

Valhalla Executive Centre
600-304 The East Mall
Toronto, ON M9B 6E2
Tel 800-268-8955
Fax 800-662-8024
www.melochemonnex.com
AKA: Meloche Monnex Financial
Services Inc.
Line: Markets group home and auto
insurance.
NAICS: 524123 524124
#Emp: 1000-4999 (Tor)
#TorLoc: 3
Own: Private Company
Par: TD Bank Financial Group (CDA)
Key: Jean Lachance, Chmn
Alain Thibault,
 Pres & CEO, TD Insurance

TDM Technical Services

3924 Chesswood Dr.
Toronto, ON M3T 2W6
Tel 416-777-0007
Fax 416-777-1117
www.tdm.ca
NAICS: 561310
#Emp: 100-249 (Tor)
#TorLoc: 1
Own: Private Company
Key: Mona Agius, VP
Ikis Walker, Dir of HR & Recruitment
Paul A. Bernard, VP Business Dev

TD Securities Inc.

66 Wellington St. West
P.O. Box 1, TD Centre
Toronto, ON M5K 1A2
Tel 416-982-8222
Fax 416-983-0615
www.tdsecurities.com
Line: Provides investment, corporate
and merchant banking services.
NAICS: 523110
#Emp: 1000-4999 (Tor)
#TorLoc: 1
Own: Private Company
Par: TD Bank Financial Group (CDA)
Key: Robert E. Dorrance,
 Chmn, Pres & CEO
Ajai Bambawale, COO
Helena Pagano, Sr VP HR
Mike French, CFO

Team Industrial Services

25 Bodrington Crt.
Markham, ON L6G 1B6
Tel 905-940-9334
Fax 905-940-1626
www.teamindustrial.com
Line: Performs industrial cleaning
services including water blasting,
janitorial, and chemical cleaning.
NAICS: 561722
#Emp: 250-499 (Tor)
#TorLoc: 3
Own: Private Company
Key: John Soullieri, Pres
Clint Griffin, CEO
Suresh Dhanjani, Cont

Team Industrial Services Inc.

389 Davis Rd.
Oakville, ON L6J 2X2
Tel 905-845-9542
Fax 905-845-9551
www.teamindustrialservices.com
Line: Operates a non destructive testing
laboratory and also provides services
to clients at plants and work-sites.
NAICS: 541380
#Emp: 75-99 (Tor)
#TorLoc: 2
Own: Private Company
Par: All Team (US)
Key: Tom Jackson, VP
David Brenzavich, CFO

Tech Data Canada Inc.

6911 Credit View Rd.
Mississauga, ON L5N 8G1
Tel 905-286-6800
Fax 905-286-6700
www.techdata.ca
Line: Warehouses, distributes and sells
computers and computer peripherals.
NAICS: 417310
#Emp: 250-499 (Tor)
#TorLoc: 1
Own: Private Company
Par: Tech Data Corp. (US)
Key: Rick Reid, Pres
Stefanie Bruno, Dir of HR
Howard Tuffnail, Sr VP Fin
David Gingerich, Dir of IS
Frank Haid, VP Sales
Greg Myers, VP Mktg

Technicolor

49 Ontario St.
Toronto, ON M5A 2V1
Tel 416-585-9995
Fax 416-364-1385
www.technicolor.com
AKA: Toybox; Alphacine; Command
Post; Thomson
Line: Provides audio and video post
and pre-production services as well as
laboratory services and visual effects.
NAICS: 512190
#Emp: 250-499 (Tor)
Own: Public Company
Par: Technicolor (US)
Key: Claude Gagnon, Pres & CEO
Louis Major, VP & GM

Tecsys Inc.

400-80 Tiverton Crt.
Markham, ON L3R 0G4
Tel 905-752-4550
Fax 905-752-6400
www.tecsys.com
Line: Provides e-business applications
for mid-market wholesalers,
distributors, and importers.
NAICS: 541510
#Emp: 75-99 (Tor)
#TorLoc: 1
Own: Private Company
Key: Tom Wilson, VP
Joanne Blair, Cont

Tectrol Inc.

39 Kodiak Cres.
Toronto, ON M3J 3E5
Tel 416-630-8108
Fax 416-638-0553
www.tectrol.com
Line: Manufactures power supplies,
DC-DC converters and switch mode
power supplies.
NAICS: 335990
#Emp: 500-999 (Tor)
#TorLoc: 1
Own: Private Company
Key: Richard H. Gelb, Pres

Teknion Corp.

1150 Flint Rd.
Toronto, ON M3J 2J5
Tel 416-661-3370
Fax 416-661-4586
www.teknion.com
Line: Manufactures wood and metal
office furniture.
NAICS: 337213 337214
#Emp: 1000-4999 (Tor)
#TorLoc: 4
Own: Private Company
Key: David Feldberg, Pres & CEO
Jeff Wilson, Sr VP Manuf
    & Supply Chain Management
Allan Bartolini, VP Corp HR & Dev
Scott Bond, CFO

Teknion Form

A Div. of TK Canada Ltd.
12-1400 Alness St.
Concord, ON L4K 2W6
Tel 905-669-2035
Fax 905-660-7323
www.teknionform.com
Line: Manufactures furniture.
NAICS: 337127
#Emp: 100-249 (Tor)
#TorLoc: 1
Own: Private Company
Par: Teknion Corporation (CDA)
Key: Ken Brown, GM

Telecom Computer Inc.

5245 Harvester Rd.
Burlington, ON L7L 5L4
Tel 905-333-9621
Fax 905-333-5590
www.telecomcomputer.com
Line: Distributes computers, computer
peripherals and pre-packaged software
and provides installation, networking,
configuration and repair services.
NAICS: 417310
#Emp: 75-99 (Tor)
#TorLoc: 1
Own: Private Company
Key: Phil Davidson, Pres
Jim Naysmith, GM
Irina Ilmokari, Cont
Jay Rymal, Purch Mgr
Wayne Anderson, Sales Mgr

Telecon Inc.

7-6685 Millcreek Dr.
Mississauga, ON L5N 5M5
Tel 905-821-3500
Fax 905-821-3688
www.telecon.ca
Line: Provides telecommunication
services.
NAICS: 513390
#Emp: 75-99 (Tor)
#TorLoc: 1
Own: Private Company
Par: Adecco SA (SWITZ)
Key: Paul Sikorski, GM,
Western Canada

Teleperformance Canada

200-300 The East Mall
Toronto, ON M9B 6B7
Tel 416-922-3519
Fax 416-922-7830
www.teleperformance.ca
Line: Provides customer relationship
management and contact centre
solutions.
NAICS: 561420 561430
#Emp: 500-999 (Tor)
#TorLoc: 1
Own: Private Company
Par: SR Teleperformance SA (FR)
Key: Charlotte Gummesson, Pres & CEO
Angela Calaiezzi, VP Ops

TELUS Business Solutions

25 York St.
Toronto, ON M5J 2V5
Tel 416-883-8783
Fax 416-364-6516
www.telus.com
AKA: TELUS Communications Inc.
Line: Provides data, Internet
Protocol (IP), voice and wireless
communications services.
NAICS: 513320 513390
#Emp: 1000-4999 (Tor)
#TorLoc: 6
Own: Public Company
Key: Joe Natale,
    Chief Commercial Officer
Darren Entwistle, Pres & CEO
Brent Dovziech,
    VP Business Enablement

TELUS Consumer Solutions

1600-200 Consilium Pl.
Toronto, ON M1H 3J3
Tel 416-279-9000
Fax 416-279-9001
www.telusmobility.com
Line: Operates wireless networks.
NAICS: 513310 513320
#Emp: 1000-4999 (Tor)
#TorLoc: 6
Own: Public Company
Par: TELUS Corp. (CDA)
Key: Darren Entwistle, Pres & CEO,
TELUS Corporation

TELUS Emergis Inc.

1000 Rue de Serigny
Bureau 600
Longueuil, PQ J4K 5B1
Tel 450-928-6000
Fax 450-928-6344
www.emergis.com
Line: Provides e-commerce and
networking services.
NAICS: 541510
#Emp: 100-249 (Tor)
#TorLoc: 4
Own: Public Company
Par: TELUS Corp. (CDA)
Key: Francois Cote, Pres & CEO
Carlos Carreiro, Exec VP, Service
    Delivery and Ops
Genevieve Marcoux, VP HR
Doug French, CFO

Telus Health & Financial Solutions

1000-5090 Explorer Dr.
Mississauga, ON L4W 4X6
Tel 905-602-8374
Fax 905-602-7343
www.telushealth.com
Line: Provides electronic transaction
processing services.
NAICS: 522329
#Emp: 500-999 (Tor)
#TorLoc: 3
Own: Public Company
Key: Paul Lepage, Sr VP

Tencorr Packaging Inc.

188 Cartwright Ave.
Toronto, ON M6A 1V6
Tel 416-787-1687
Fax 416-787-6821
www.tencorr.com
Line: Provides cargo box packaging
services.
NAICS: 322211
#Emp: 100-249 (Tor)
#TorLoc: 2
Own: Private Company
Key: Chris Bartlett, Pres
David Briggs, VP Manuf
Nicole Gaboury, VP Fin & Admin

Tendercare Nursing Homes Ltd.

1020 McNicoll Ave.
Toronto, ON M1W 2J6
Tel 416-499-3313
Fax 416-499-3379
www.tendercare.ca
AKA: Tendercare Living Centre;
McNicoll Manor; Moll Berczy Haus
Line: Operates long-term care facility
and retirement homes.
NAICS: 623310
#Emp: 250-499 (Tor)
Own: Private Company
Key: Francis Martis, Admr
Louise Chung, Office Coord

Tender Choice Foods Inc.

4480 Paletta Crt.
Burlington, ON L7L 5R2
Tel 905-632-3449
Fax 905-632-4081
NAICS: 413130 413160
#Emp: 250-499 (Tor)
#TorLoc: 1
Own: Private Company
Key: Paul Paletta, Pres

TeraGo Networks Inc.

500-55 Commerce Valley Dr. West
Thornhill, ON L3T 7V9
Tel 905-707-0788
Fax 905-707-6212
www.terago.ca
Line: Provides wireless broadband
services to businesses in Canada
including high speed internet, data
networking and internet redundancy.
NAICS: 513320
#Emp: 100-249 (Tor)
Own: Private Company

Key: Bryan Boyd, Pres & CEO
Kevin Hickey, VP Engineering & Ops
Tara Talbot, VP HR
Scott Browne, CFO
Allan Laudersmith, VP Sales
Michael Testa, VP Mktg

Teranet Inc.

700-123 Front St. West
Toronto, ON M5J 2M2
Tel 416-360-5263
Fax 416-360-1687
www.teranet.ca
Line: Provides computer consulting,
computer integrated systems design,
e-commerce solutions, information
retrieval, data entry, processing and
surveying services.
NAICS: 541510
#Emp: 500-999 (Tor)
#TorLoc: 5
Own: Public Company
Key: Jay Forbes, Pres & CEO
James MacQueen,
    Dir of Customer Relns
Julia Reed, Chief HR Officer
Greg Pope, CFO
Greg Kowal, CIO
Lawrence Franco,
    VP Value Added Solutions
Elgin Farewell,
    VP Electronic Search & Registration
Jody Warwaruk, Commun Leader

Terrazzo Mosaic & Tile Co. Ltd.

900 Keele St.
Toronto, ON M6N 3E7
Tel 416-653-6111
Fax 416-653-2594
www.tmtcoltd.com
Line: Manufactures, installs and
designs stone structures.
NAICS: 232420 232430
#Emp: 100-249 (Tor)
#TorLoc: 1
Own: Private Company
Key: Carlo Onorati, Pres
Enzo Costantino, Cont

T.E.S. Contract Services Inc.

500-40 Holly St.
Toronto, ON M4S 3C3
Tel 416-482-2420
Fax 416-482-9282
www.tes.net
AKA: The Employment Solution; Total
Employment Services; Temporary
Engineering Services
Line: Provides temporary, contract
and permanent staffing of engineers,
designers, technologists, technicians,
information systems and technology
personnel, and skilled labour
personnel.
NAICS: 561310 561320
#Emp: 1000-4999 (Tor)
#TorLoc: 3
Own: Private Company
Key: Frank A. Wilson, Pres
Christine Lusignan, VP Fin & Admin

Teskey Concrete & Construction Company Ltd.

20 Murray Rd.
Toronto, ON M3K 1T2
Tel 416-638-0340
Fax 416-638-4401
www.teskeyltd.ca
AKA: Teskey Concrete Co.
Line: Provides ready mix concrete
supply.
NAICS: 232110
#Emp: 100-249 (Tor)
#TorLoc: 1
Own: Private Company
Key: Mark Teskey, Pres
Roy Teskey, GM
Mark Remnant,
　Secy-Treas & Office Mgr

Tetra Pak Canada Inc.

1610 16th Ave.
Richmond Hill, ON L4B 4N6
Tel 905-780-6030
Fax 905-780-4903
www.tetrapak.ca
Line: Provide processing and packaging
solutions for food.
NAICS: 561910
#Emp: 75-99 (Tor)
#TorLoc: 1
Own: Private Company
Par: Tetra Pak (SWE)
Key: Santiago Fourcade, Mng Dir
Gwen Scott, Dir of HR
Douglas Kwon, Dir of Fin

Teva Canada Limited

30 Novopharm Crt.
Toronto, ON M1B 2K9
Tel 416-291-8876
Fax 416-335-4472
www.tevacanada.com
Line: Manufactures generic
pharmaceuticals.
NAICS: 325410
#Emp: 1000-4999 (Tor)
#TorLoc: 3
Own: Private Company
Par: Teva Pharmaceutical Industries
Ltd. (ISRAEL)
Key: Barry Fishman, Pres & CEO
Steve Liberty, Exec VP Ops
Sylvain Girard, VP HR
Domenic Della Pena, VP Fin & CFO
Tony Martins, VP Supply Chain
Doug Sommerville, VP Sales & Mktg

Thales Rail Signalling Solutions Inc.

1235 Ormont Dr.
Toronto, ON M9L 2W6
Tel 416-742-3900
Fax 416-742-1136
www.thalesgroup.com
Line: Provides engineering services.
NAICS: 541330
#Emp: 1000-4999 (Tor)
#TorLoc: 3
Own: Private Company
Key: Bruno Cohades, GM

TheMIGroup

6745 Financial Dr.
Mississauga, ON L5N 7J7
Tel 905-813-9600
Fax 905-814-6702
www.themigroup.com
Line: Operates a global relocation
management company.
NAICS: 561490
#Emp: 75-99 (Tor)
#TorLoc: 1
Own: Private Company
Key: Bryan C. Bennett, Chmn
Robert Johnson, VP, Client Relns
Darlene Hassall,
　VP & Dir of HR & Training
Marsha Mongeau, CFO
Colin Gordon, Dir of Quality Assurance
Joanne Hodge, CIO
Mark Bennett, Exec VP
Ida Caravolo, Dir of Mktg

Thermo Fisher Scientific Co.

112 Colonnade Rd.
Nepean, ON K2E 7L6
Tel 613-226-3273
Fax 613-226-7658
www.fishersci.ca
Line: Distributes and services
laboratory and safety systems.
NAICS: 417930
#Emp: 250-499 (Tor)
#TorLoc: 2
Own: Private Company
Par: Fisher Scientific International Inc.
(US)
Key: John Tourlas, Pres

Thistletown Regional Centre

51 Panorama Crt.
Toronto, ON M9V 4L8
Tel 416-326-0600
Fax 416-326-9078
Line: Operates treatment centre for
children and youth.
NAICS: 621494 624110
#Emp: 250-499 (Tor)
#TorLoc: 1
Own: Government
Par: Government of Ontario
Key: Mike Moosley, Admr

Thomas Cook North America

75 Eglinton Ave. East
Toronto, ON M4P 3A4
Tel 416-485-1700
Fax 416-485-1805
www.thomascook.com
AKA: Intair; Exotica; Boomerang;
FunSun Vacations; Holiday House;
Encore Cruise Escapes; MyTravel
Canada Inc.; Sunquest; Alba Tours;
The Holiday Network; Belair Travel;
Avion Travel; The Last Minute Club;
Wholesale Travel Group
Line: Sells travel package vacations,
flights, cruises and tours.
NAICS: 561510
#Emp: 1000-4999 (Tor)
#TorLoc: 8
Own: Public Company
Par: Thomas Cook Group plc (UK)
Key: Michael Friisdahl, CEO
Dean Moore, COO
Jill Wykes, VP HR
Dawn MacKelvie, CFO
Flemming Friisdahl, VP Sales

Thomson Carswell

2075 Kennedy Rd.
One Corporate Plaza
Toronto, ON M1T 3V4
Tel 416-609-8000
Fax 416-298-5094
www.carswell.com
Line: Produces legal, tax, and business legal compliance information in print and electronic formats for the legal, accounting, academic and business communities.
NAICS: 511120 511190
#Emp: 500-999 (Tor)
#TorLoc: 2
Own: Public Company
Par: The Thomson Corp. (CDA)
Key: Don Van Meer, Pres & CEO
Barb Conway, VP HR
Stewart Katz, CFO
Stephen Dyke, VP CIO
Lee Horigan, VP Mktg

Thomson-Gordon Group Ltd.

3225 Mainway Dr.
Burlington, ON L7M 1A6
Tel 905-335-1440
Fax 905-335-4033
www.thomson-gordongroup.com
AKA: Thordon Bearings Inc.
Line: Manufactures and sells marine bearings and air compressors.
NAICS: 333910
#Emp: 100-249 (Tor)
#TorLoc: 1
Own: Private Company
Par: Thomson-Gordon Group Inc. (CDA)
Key: Terry McGowan, Pres & COO
George (Sandy) Thomson, Chmn
Donna Mason, HR Mgr
Craig Carter,
    Dir of Mktg & Customer Service

Thomson Reuters

400-33 Bay St.
Toronto, ON M5H 2R2
Tel 416-941-8000
Fax 416-687-7744
www.thomsonreuters.com
Line: Provides the Canadian financial community and news media with a wide range of electronic information products.
NAICS: 514110
#Emp: 250-499 (Tor)
#TorLoc: 2
Own: Public Company
Par: Thomson Reuters (US)
Key: Mark Davidson, Mng Dir
Joe Grierson, Head of HR
Dave Hill, Dir of Sales

Thomson Rogers

3100-390 Bay St.
Toronto, ON M5H 1W2
Tel 416-868-3100
Fax 416-868-3134
www.thomsonrogers.com
AKA: Hathro Management Partnership
Line: Provides civil litigation services.
NAICS: 541110
#Emp: 100-249 (Tor)
#TorLoc: 1
Own: Private Company
Key: Alan A. Farrer, Mng Partner
Lina Ginevra, HR Mgr
George Haddad, Network Mgr
Joseph Pileggi, Dir of Client Services

Thomson Terminals Ltd.

55 City View Dr.
Toronto, ON M9W 5A5
Tel 416-240-0897
Fax 416-240-1292
www.thomsongroup.com
Line: Operates a logistics company specializing in warehousing, transportation and third party logistics.
NAICS: 493110 484110
#Emp: 500-999 (Tor)
#TorLoc: 1
Own: Private Company
Key: Sally Thomson, Co-Pres & CEO
James D. Thomson, Co-Pres & CEO
Al Russell, Mgr of Warehouse Ops
Moona Bedi, Corp Cont
Garry Wilks, Mgr of MIS

Thorncrest Sherway Inc.

1575 The Queensway
Toronto, ON M8Z 1T9
Tel 416-521-7000
Fax 416-521-7070
www.thorncrest.com
AKA: Thorncrest Ford Sales; Sherway Ford Truck Sales; Sterling Trucks of Toronto
Line: Retails motor vehicles (new & used) and heavy trucks.
NAICS: 532120 441110
#Emp: 100-249 (Tor)
#TorLoc: 1
Own: Private Company
Key: Delano Bedard, Pres
Rick Sinhuber, GM & CFO
Ray Messenger, Mktg Mgr

Thorncrete Construction Ltd.

381 Spinnaker Way
Vaughan, ON L4K 4N4
Tel 905-669-6510
Fax 416-667-9641
Line: Specializes in concrete construction.
NAICS: 232220
#Emp: 100-249 (Tor)
#TorLoc: 1
Own: Private Company
Key: John Ruscica, Pres

Thornhill Community Centre Library

7755 Bayview Ave.
Thornhill, ON L3T 4P1
Tel 905-513-7977
Fax 905-881-2935
www.markham.com/mpl
NAICS: 514121
#Emp: 75-99 (Tor)
#TorLoc: 6
Own: Private Company
Key: Margaret MacMillan, Mgr

Thornhill Golf & Country Club

7994 Yonge St.
Thornhill, ON L4J 1W3
Tel 905-881-3000
Fax 905-881-9870
www.thornhillgcc.com
NAICS: 713910
#Emp: 100-249 (Tor)
#TorLoc: 1
Own: Private Company
Key: Matthew Butko, GM
Warren Horowitz, Asst Clubhouse Mgr
Laura Horowitz, Membership Coord

Thornton View

186 Thornton Rd. South
Oshawa, ON L1J 5Y2
Tel 905-576-5181
Fax 905-576-0078
www.reveraliving.com
Line: Provides long-term care.
NAICS: 623110
#Emp: 100-249 (Tor)
#TorLoc: 1
Own: Private Company
Par: Revera Inc. (CDA)
Key: Heather Power, Admr
Marilyn Bowser, Office Mgr

ThoughtCorp Systems Inc.

1700-4950 Yonge St.
Toronto, ON M2N 6K1
Tel 416-591-4004
Fax 416-595-1551
www.thoughtcorp.com
Line: Operates a technology consulting company.
NAICS: 541510 541690
#Emp: 100-249 (Tor)
#TorLoc: 1
Own: Public Company
Key: David Bercovitch, Co-CEO
Kirk Robinson, Co-CEO
Valentina Hedow, HR Mgr
Dino Chronopoulos, Cont

Thunder Tool & Mfg. Ltd.

A Div. of Royal Laser Corp.
975 Martin Grove Rd.
Toronto, ON M9W 4V6
Tel 416-742-1936
Fax 416-742-6056
www.thundertool.com
Line: Manufactures medium sized stampings, dies, tools and other metalworking machinery.
NAICS: 333519 332118
#Emp: 75-99 (Tor)
#TorLoc: 1
Own: Public Company
Key: Louie Taonessa, GM

ThyssenKrupp Elevator Ltd.

1-410 Passmore Ave.
Toronto, ON M1V 5C3
Tel 416-291-2000
Fax 416-291-3671
www.thyssenkruppelevator.com
Line: Manufactures, installs, modernizes and maintains elevators and escalators.
NAICS: 232550
#Emp: 500-999 (Tor)
#TorLoc: 5
Own: Private Company
Par: Thyssen Aufzuege GmbH (GER)
Key: Kevin Lavallee, Pres & CEO
Joe Kerr, VP
Sal Najarali, VP Fin
Andrei Moffat, IT Mgr
Ian Ferrier, Construction
   Modernization Sales Mgr

ThyssenKrupp Materials

2821 Langstaff Rd.
Vaughan, ON L4K 5C6
Tel 905-669-9444
Fax 905-738-9033
www.tkmna.thyssenkrupp.com
Line: Distributes brass, copper and aluminum.
NAICS: 418990
#Emp: 100-249 (Tor)
Own: Public Company
Key: Andreas Heesch, Cont

TicketMaster Canada LP

3900-1 Blue Jays Way
Toronto, ON M5V 1J3
Tel 416-345-9200
Fax 416-341-8711
www.ticketmaster.ca
Line: Operates a computerized ticket distribution system.
NAICS: 561590
#Emp: 100-249 (Tor)
#TorLoc: 1
Own: Private Company
Par: Live Nation Entertainment (US)
Key: Tom Worrall, COO

TIC Travel Insurance Coordinators Ltd.

2100-250 Yonge St.
Toronto, ON M5B 2L7
Tel 416-340-1980
Fax 416-340-2707
www.travelinsurance.ca
AKA: Cooperators
Line: Operates a health and travel insurance company.
NAICS: 524210
#Emp: 100-249 (Tor)
#TorLoc: 2
Own: Private Company
Par: The Co-operators (CDA)
Key: David Hartman, Pres & CEO
John Webster, VP Client Services
Teresa Straatsma, Dir of HR &
   Organizational Dev
Sunder Mayuran, Fin Mgr
Gino Riola, VP Business Dev & Mktg

TIFF

TIFF Bell Lightbox
Reitman Square, 350 King St. West
Toronto, ON M5V 3X5
Tel 416-967-7371
Fax 416-967-9477
www.tiff.net
AKA: Toronto International Film Festival
Line: Promotes film exhibition, education and industry development.
NAICS: 711322 512130
#Emp: 100-249 (Tor)
#TorLoc: 1
Own: Not-for-profit
Key: Cameron Bailey,
   Co-Dir of Film Festival
Piers Handling, Dir & CEO
Michele Maheux, Exec Dir & COO
Allison Bain, VP HR & Planning
Bruce Hooui, CFO
Noah Cowan, Artistic Dir,
   TIFF Bell Lightbox
Maxine Bailey, VP Pub Affairs

TigerDirect.Ca Inc.

G-55 East Beaver Creek Rd.
Richmond Hill, ON L4B 1E5
Tel 905-482-3201
Fax 905-482-3129
www.tigerdirect.ca
Line: Distributes and retails computer supplies and accessories.
NAICS: 417310
#Emp: 100-249 (Tor)
#TorLoc: 7
Own: Private Company
Par: Systemax Inc. (US)
Key: Ludlow Williams, Dir of Cdn Ops

Tigertel Communications

2 Duncan Mill Rd.
Toronto, ON M3B 1Z4
Tel 416-445-3222
Fax 416-445-2325
www.tigertel.com
Line: Operates service bureau call centre providing inbound, outbound, and customer support work for client companies and organizations.
NAICS: 561420
#Emp: 100-249 (Tor)
#TorLoc: 2
Own: Public Company
Par: Tigertel Communications Inc. (CDA)
Key: Doug Swift, Pres
Ron Waine, VP Central Region
J. Sandy MacNaughton, CFO
Penny Livingstone, Dir of Corp Affairs

Tilley Endurables Inc.

900 Don Mills Rd.
Toronto, ON M3C 1V6
Tel 416-441-6141
Fax 416-444-3860
www.tilley.com
Line: Manufactures, retails and wholesales high quality travel, adventure and casual wear.
NAICS: 315229 315239
#Emp: 100-249 (Tor)
#TorLoc: 3
Own: Private Company
Key: Mary Coleen Shanahan, Pres & CEO
Alex Tilley, Chmn
Sandi Flaim, HR & Payroll Mgr
Thurstan Berkeley, CFO & Dir of US Ops
Adam Andrews, IT Mgr
David Kappele, Dir of North American Wholesale Sales
Kimberley Szucs, Mktg & Commun Mgr

Tilton Industries Inc.

120 Summerlea Rd.
Brampton, ON L6T 4X3
Tel 905-458-4555
Fax 905-458-9277
www.tiltonindustries.com
Line: Specializes in applications of sprayed enamel finishes and powder coatings.
NAICS: 325510
#Emp: 75-99 (Tor)
#TorLoc: 1
Own: Private Company
Key: Frank Colonna, GM
Jim Greenwood, Plant Mgr
Sally Smith, Cont
Sean Hiscock, Purch Agent

Timex Group Inc.

445 Hood Rd.
Markham, ON L3R 8H1
Tel 905-477-8463
Fax 905-477-8470
www.timex.ca
Line: Imports, markets and sells watches, straps and bands and clocks.
NAICS: 414410 448310
#Emp: 75-99 (Tor)
#TorLoc: 1
Own: Private Company
Par: Timex Corp. (US)
Key: Leo Fournier, Pres & COO
Lisa Weinreich, HR Mgr
Yves D'Amours, Dir of IS
Daniel Des Côtes, VP Sales
Paul Sine, VP Mktg

Tim Hortons Inc.

874 Sinclair Rd.
Oakville, ON L6K 2Y1
Tel 905-845-6511
Fax 905-845-0265
www.timhortons.com
Line: Franchises Tim Horton's coffee and baked goods chain.
NAICS: 722210
#Emp: 500-999 (Tor)
#TorLoc: 1
Own: Public Company
Key: Paul D. House, Interim Pres & CEO
Roland Walton, COO, Canada
Brigid Pelino, Sr VP HR
Cynthia Devine, CFO
John Hemeon, Exec VP Supply Chain
Bill Moir, Chief Brand & Mktg Officer
Nick Javor, Sr VP Corp Affairs

Timothy's Coffees of the World Inc.

400 Steeprock Dr.
Toronto, ON M3J 2X1
Tel 416-638-3333
Fax 416-638-7670
www.timothys.com
Line: Operates as master franchisor.
NAICS: 533110
#Emp: 100-249 (Tor)
#TorLoc: 106
Own: Private Company
Par: Green Mountain Coffee Roasters Inc. (US)
Key: Domenic Della Penna, Transition Leader
Gabrielle D'Alonzo, VP HR
Sunny Li, IT Mgr

Tippet-Richardson Ltd.

25 Metropolitan Rd.
Toronto, ON M1R 2T5
Tel 416-291-1200
Fax 416-291-2601
www.tippet-richardson.com
AKA: Tippet-Richardson/Allied
Line: Provides high quality residential and commercial moving services in the Toronto area.
NAICS: 484110 484121
#Emp: 100-249 (Tor)
#TorLoc: 3
Own: Private Company
Key: John Novak, Pres & CEO
Anita Fower, Branch Mgr
Candi Whiteman, HR Mgr
Altaz Lalji, VP Fin
Mike Zinger, IT Mgr
Martin Heal, Dir of Corp Services

Tip Top Bindery Ltd.

335 Passmore Ave.
Toronto, ON M1V 4B5
Tel 416-609-3281
Fax 416-609-3158
www.tiptopbindery.com
Line: Specializes in binding books.
NAICS: 323119
#Emp: 75-99 (Tor)
#TorLoc: 1
Own: Private Company
Key: Cal Johnson, Pres
Dean Johnson, Secy-Treas

Titan Cartage Ltd.

321 Orenda Rd.
Brampton, ON L6T 1G4
Tel 905-799-2675
Fax 905-792-0815
www.titancartage.com
Line: Offers local cartage, warehousing and distribution services as well as container and piggyback services.
NAICS: 484110 484121
#Emp: 75-99 (Tor)
#TorLoc: 1
Own: Private Company
Key: Ted Puccini, Partner
Jack Besser, Pres & CEO
Frank Gentile, VP
Bradley Codlin, Ops Mgr
Abbas Shirazi, Acctng Mgr

T.L.C. Health Services Ltd.

10 Thicket Rd.
Toronto, ON M9C 2T3
Tel 416-626-7023
Fax 416-626-7023
Line: Operates a health maintenance organization.
NAICS: 541690
#Emp: 250-499 (Tor)
Own: Private Company
Key: Nicki Bhanabhai, Pres

T. Lipson & Sons Ltd.

190 Norseman St.
Toronto, ON M8Z 2R4
Tel 416-236-3114
Fax 416-236-3100
www.lipsonshirtmakers.com
AKA: Lipson's Shirtmakers
Line: Manufactures men's dress shirts
and sportswear.
NAICS: 315226
#Emp: 75-99 (Tor)
#TorLoc: 1
Own: Private Company
Key: Jack Lipson, Pres
Jose Gabriel Maia, Cont
Jordan Lipson, IT Mgr
Lui Sguazzin, Sales Mgr

TMX Group Inc.

130 King St. West,
The Exchange Tower, 3rd Fl.
Toronto, ON M5X 1J2
Tel 416-947-4670
Fax 416-947-4662
www.tmx.com
AKA: Toronto Stock Exchange
Line: Owns and operates the Toronto
Stock Exchange and the TSX Venture
Exchange, serving the senior and
public venture equity markets.
NAICS: 523210
#Emp: 500-999 (Tor)
#TorLoc: 2
Own: Public Company
Key: Luc Bertrand,
  Deputy CEO, TMX Group
Thomas Kloet, CEO, TMX Group
Rik Parkhill, Exec VP & Pres, T
  SX Markets
Christine Ellison, VP HR
Michael Ptasznik, CFO
Brenda Hoffman, Sr VP & CIO

TMZ Employment Agency

203-2357 Finch Ave. West
Toronto, ON M9M 2W8
Tel 416-740-7892
Fax 416-740-0515
www.tmzemployment.com
Line: Operates an employment agency
offering temporary placement, full-
time and seasonal services.
NAICS: 561310
#Emp: 100-249 (Tor)
#TorLoc: 1
Own: Private Company
Key: Mike Williams, Mgr

TNS Canadian Facts

900-2 Bloor St. East
Toronto, ON M4W 3H8
Tel 416-924-5751
Fax 416-923-7085
www.tns.cf.com
Line: Operates a market research firm.
NAICS: 541910
#Emp: 100-249 (Tor)
#TorLoc: 1
Own: Public Company
Par: WPP (UK)
Key: Michael Ennameroto, Pres & CEO
Suzanne White, Dir & VP HR
Greg Fenton, CFO
Peter Chan, VP Statistical Services & IT

TNT Express (Canada) Inc.

3230 American Dr.
Mississauga, ON L4V 1B3
Tel 905-672-9753
Fax 905-676-6663
www.tnt.com
AKA: TNT International Express
Line: Provides international express
and mail services.
NAICS: 492110 481110
#Emp: 75-99 (Tor)
#TorLoc: 1
Own: Public Company
Par: TPG (NETH)
Key: Lynne Jerome, Reg Ops Mgr
Ben Robinson, Dir of Sales

TNT Foods International Inc.

10-17817 Leslie St. North
Newmarket, ON L3Y 3E3
Tel 905-841-8224
Fax 905-836-2251
www.tntfoods.com
Line: Provides a full line of fresh
poultry products.
NAICS: 311615
#Emp: 75-99 (Tor)
#TorLoc: 1
Own: Private Company
Key: Kristi Cachia Mussel, VP Ops
Ross Lysecki, GM
Mark Cachia, Sales & Mktg Mgr

Tobias House
Attendant Care Inc.

611-695 Coxwell Ave.
Toronto, ON M4C 5R6
Tel 416-690-3185
Fax 416-690-5487
www.tobiashouse.ca
Line: Provides attendant care services
for individuals living with physical
disabilities.

NAICS: 624120
#Emp: 100-249 (Tor)
#TorLoc: 3
Own: Not-for-profit
Key: Yona Frishman, Exec Dir
Peter Knaapen, Pres
Andrew Jardine, HR Mgr
Karen Shea, Acctng & Office Admr

Tony Stacey Centre

59 Lawson Rd.
Toronto, ON M1C 2J1
Tel 416-284-9235
Fax 416-284-7169
www.tonystaceycentre.ca
Line: Operates a home for the aged.
NAICS: 623310
#Emp: 100-249 (Tor)
#TorLoc: 1
Own: Private Company
Key: Catherine Hilge, Exec Dir
Stephanie Burgess, Bookeeper

Top Grade Molds Ltd.

929 Pantera Dr.
Mississauga, ON L4W 2R9
Tel 905-625-9865
Fax 905-625-5417
www.topgrademolds.com
Line: Manufactures and designs plastic
injection moulds.
NAICS: 333511
#Emp: 100-249 (Tor)
#TorLoc: 1
Own: Private Company
Key: Vince Ciccone, Pres
Joseph F. Slobodnik, Sr., CEO
Jerry Knezovic, VP Sales

Topper Linen Supply Ltd.

54 Junction Rd.
Toronto, ON M6N 1B6
Tel 416-763-4576
Fax 416-761-1047
www.topperlinen.com
Line: Offers uniform and linen rentals
and commercial laundry services.
NAICS: 812330
#Emp: 75-99 (Tor)
#TorLoc: 1
Own: Private Company
Key: Tim Topornicki, Pres
Bud Hoffman, Production Mgr
Robert Morley, VP

Torino Drywall Inc.

2-741 Rowntree Dairy Rd.
Woodbridge, ON L4L 5T9
Tel 905-851-6616
Fax 905-851-6619
Line: Provides residential and
commercial drywall sub-contracting
services.
NAICS: 232410
#Emp: 250-499 (Tor)
Own: Private Company
Key: Elem Rinomato, Pres
Elaine Brown, HR Mgr
Dino Catenacci, Cont

Torkin Manes LLP

1500-151 Yonge St.
Toronto, ON M5C 2W7
Tel 416-863-1188
Fax 416-863-0305
www.torkinmanes.com
NAICS: 541110
#Emp: 100-249 (Tor)
#TorLoc: 1
Own: Private Company
Key: Jeff Cohen, Mng Partner
Carol Paskin, Dir of Ops
Nazli Ghaforri, HR Mgr

Toro Aluminum

330 Applewood Cres.
Concord, ON L4K 4V2
Tel 905-738-5220
Fax 905-738-5481
www.toroaluminum.com
Line: Manufactures aluminum
windows and doors.
NAICS: 332999
#Emp: 500-999 (Tor)
#TorLoc: 10
Own: Private Company
Key: Gianfranco DiMarco, Pres
Sonya Borg, Group HR Mgr

Toromont Industries Ltd.

3131 Hwy. 7 West
P.O. Box 5511
Concord, ON L4K 1B7
Tel 416-667-5511
Fax 416-667-5555
www.toromont.com
AKA: Toromont & CAT; Battlefield
Equipment Rentals; CIMCO
Line: Distributes Caterpillar
equipment; designs, engineers,
fabricates, installs and services
refrigeration and gas compression
equipment; and rents construction
equipment.
NAICS: 417210 333416

#Emp: 1000-4999 (Tor)
#TorLoc: 8
Own: Public Company
Key: Robert M. Ogilvie, Chmn & CEO
Scott Medhurst, Pres, Toromont Cat
David Wetherald, VP HR & Legal
Paul Jewer, VP Fin & CFO
Mike Cuddy, VP & CIO
Peter Shanahan, VP Machine Sales,
    Toromont CAT
Rick Van Exan, VP Mktg,
    Toromont CAT

The Toronto Aged Men's and Women's Homes

55 Belmont St.
Toronto, ON M5R 1R1
Tel 416-964-9231
Fax 416-964-1448
www.belmonthouse.com
AKA: The Belmont House
Line: Operates a non-profit charitable
home for seniors.
NAICS: 623310
#Emp: 100-249 (Tor)
#TorLoc: 1
Own: Not-for-profit
Key: Maria Elias, CEO
Socrates Theophylactou, HR Mgr
Dennis Donovan, Dir of Fin & IT
Gail Walker, Dir
    of Retirement & Mktg Services

Toronto Airport Marriott

901 Dixon Rd.
Toronto, ON M9W 1J5
Tel 416-674-9400
Fax 416-674-8292
www.marriott.com/yyzot
AKA: Toronto Airport Marriott Hotel
Line: Operates a full service hotel.
NAICS: 721111
#Emp: 250-499 (Tor)
Own: Public Company
Par: Marriott International (US)
Key: Jeff Waters, GM
Sandy Prong, Dir of Ops
Meenu Puri, Dir of HR

Toronto Airways Ltd.

2833 16th Ave.
P.O. Box 100
Markham, ON L3R 0P8
Tel 905-477-8100
Fax 905-477-8053
www.torontoairways.com
AKA: Million Air; Canadian Flight
Academy
Line: Provides flight training services
and operates the Toronto Buttonville
municipal airport.

NAICS: 488119
#Emp: 100-249 (Tor)
#TorLoc: 1
Own: Private Company
Par: Armadale Company Ltd. (CDA)
Key: Derek Sifton, Pres
Heather Sifton, CEO
Dave Dayment, Airport Ops Mgr
David Ho, VP Fin & Ops
John Davis, Mgr of Business Dev
Frank Dennis, GM, FBO

Toronto and Region Conservation Authority

5 Shoreham Dr.
Toronto, ON M3N 1S4
Tel 416-661-6600
Fax 416-661-6898
www.trca.on.ca
Line: Operates regional conservation
authority.
NAICS: 911910
#Emp: 250-499 (Tor)
Own: Private Company
Key: Brian Denney, CAO
Catherine MacEwen, HR Mgr
James W. Dillane,
    Dir of Fin & Business Services

Toronto Blue Jays Baseball Club

3200-1 Blue Jays Way
Toronto, ON M5V 1J1
Tel 416-341-1000
Fax 416-341-1103
toronto.bluejays.mlb.com
AKA: Rogers Centre
Line: Operates a professional sports
club.
NAICS: 711211
#Emp: 250-499 (Tor)
#TorLoc: 1
Own: Private Company
Par: Rogers Communications Inc.
(CDA)
Key: Paul Beeston, Pres & CEO,
    Toronto Blue Jays & Rogers Centre
Alex Anthopoulos, Sr VP
    Baseball Ops & GM
Claudia Livadas, Dir of HR
Stephen Brooks, Sr VP Business Ops
Mike Maybee, Dir of IT
Anthony Partipilo, VP Mktg &
    Merchandising
Jay Stenhouse, VP Commun

Toronto Board of Trade

1 First Canadian Pl.
P.O. Box 60
Toronto, ON M5X 1C1
Tel 416-366-6811
Fax 416-366-4906
www.bot.com
AKA: World Trade Centre Toronto;
WTC Toronto
Line: Builds a better community
through business leadership
by providing business services,
advocating public policy positions,
participating in community
partnerships and facilitating economic
and business development.
NAICS: 813910
Own: Not-for-profit
Key: Carol Wilding, Pres & CEO
Mohamed Shafeek, VP Ops & Fin
Julie Johnstone, Dir of HR
Pankaj Bhargava, Cont
Callum Marshall, Dir of IT
Paul Gallucci,
    VP Sales & Member Services
Jacqueline Baptist,
    VP Mktg & Commun
Richard Joy, VP Policy & Gov't Relns
Jeffrey Veffer, Dir, Product Innovation

Toronto Catholic District School Board

80 Sheppard Ave. East
Toronto, ON M2N 6E8
Tel 416-222-8282
Fax 416-229-5345
www.tcdsb.org
AKA: TCDSB
Line: Provides Catholic education.
NAICS: 611110
#Emp: 5000-9999 (Tor)
#TorLoc: 234
Own: Government
Key: Ann Perron, Dir of Education
Ann Andrachuk, Chair
Gary Poole, Supt of HR
Sandra Pessione, CFO & Treas

Toronto Central Community Care Access Centre

305-250 Dundas St. West
Toronto, ON M5T 2Z5
Tel 416-506-9888
Fax 416-506-0124
www.torontoccac.com
AKA: Toronto Central CCAC
Line: Provides in-home health care and
placements in long-term care facilities
to clients in the community.

NAICS: 621494
#Emp: 250-499 (Tor)
#TorLoc: 1
Own: Not-for-profit
Key: Stacey Daub, CEO
Dipti Purbhoo, Sr Dir of Client Services
Dennis Fong, Sr Dir of HR &
    Organizational Dev
Bill Tottle, Sr Dir of Corp Services
Pamela Lugonzo,
    Sr Mgr of Commun & PR

Toronto Centre for the Arts

5040 Yonge St.
Toronto, ON M2N 6R8
Tel 416-733-9388
Fax 416-733-9478
www.tocentre.com
NAICS: 711311
#Emp: 100-249 (Tor)
#TorLoc: 1
Own: Private Company
Par: The City of Toronto
Key: Pim Schotanus, GM
Janette McDonald, Dir of Ops
Neil McGiveney, Dir of Fin & Admin
Doug Ottney, Box Office Mgr

Toronto Community Housing Corp.

931 Yonge St.
Toronto, ON M4W 2H2
Tel 416-981-5500
Fax 416-981-4260
www.torontohousing.ca
Line: Provides affordable rental
housing for seniors, families and adult
singles.
NAICS: 913910
#Emp: 1000-4999 (Tor)
#TorLoc: 1
Own: Municipal Crown Corp.
Key: Michelle Haney-Kileeg, GM
Len Koroneos, Interim CEO
Deborah Simon, COO
Mitzie Hunter, CAO

Toronto Community News

A Div. of Metroland Media Group Ltd.
100 Tempo Ave.
Toronto, ON M2H 2N8
Tel 416-493-4400
Fax 416-493-6190
www.insidetoronto.com
AKA: Scarborough Mirror; North York
Mirror; East York-Riverdale Mirror;
Beach-Riverdale Mirror; City Centre
Mirror; Annex Guardian; Etobicoke
Guardian; York Guardian; Bloor West
Villager

NAICS: 511110
#Emp: 250-499 (Tor)
#TorLoc: 3
Own: Private Company
Par: Torstar Corp. (CDA)
Key: Betty Carr, VP & Reg Publisher
Marg Middleton, GM
Kelly Atkinson, Reg HR Mgr
Bruce Espey, Dir of Admin
Tim Corcoran, Reg Dir of Advertising

Toronto Cricket Skating and Curling Club

141 Wilson Ave.
Toronto, ON M5M 3A3
Tel 416-487-4581
Fax 416-487-7595
www.torontocricketclub.com
Line: Operates private member athletic
club.
NAICS: 713940
#Emp: 100-249 (Tor)
#TorLoc: 1
Own: Not-for-profit
Key: Douglas Knights, GM
Terry Nolan, Asst GM
Kerrie Poleyko, HR Coord
Tilac DeSilva, Cont
David Disher, Membership & Mktg Mgr

Toronto District School Board

5050 Yonge St.
Toronto, ON M2N 5N8
Tel 416-397-3000
Fax 416-393-9969
www.tdsb.on.ca
NAICS: 611110
#Emp: 10000+ (Tor)
#TorLoc: 595
Own: Government
Par: The City of Toronto
Key: Penny Mustin, Associate Dir
Christopher Spence, Dir of Education
Sheila Penny, Exec Officer,
    Facility Services
Chuck Hay, Exec Officer,
    Employee Services
Don Higgins, Exec Supt,
    Business Services
Stuart Oakley, Mgr of Commun
Anji Husain,
    Dir of Commun & Pub Affairs

Toronto Don Valley Hotel & Suites

1250 Eglinton Ave. East
Toronto, ON M3C 1J3
Tel 416-449-4111
Fax 416-385-6700
www.torontodonvalleyhotel.com
NAICS: 721111
#Emp: 100-249 (Tor)
#TorLoc: 1
Own: Private Company
Par: Allied Hotel Properties Inc. (CDA)
Key: Kevin Porter, GM
Trevor Martins, Financial Cont

Toronto East General

825 Coxwell Ave.
Toronto, ON M4C 3E7
Tel 416-461-8272
Fax 416-469-6106
www.tegh.on.ca
Line: Operates a community teaching hospital.
NAICS: 622111
#Emp: 1000-4999 (Tor)
#TorLoc: 1
Own: Not-for-profit
Key: Rob Devitt, Pres & CEO
Ian Fraser, Chief of Staff
Marla Fryers, VP Programs
    & Chief Nursing Officer
Ralph Fernando, CFO
Betty Best, Dir of Materials
    & Food Services
Wolf Klassen, VP
    Clinical Support Services
Shelley Darling, Dir
    of Planning, Partnerships & PR

Toronto Emergency Medical Services

A Div. of Works & Emergency Services
4330 Dufferin St.
Toronto, ON M3H 5R9
Tel 416-392-2000
Fax 416-392-2115
www.city.toronto.on.ca/ems/
AKA: Toronto EMS
Line: Provides out-of-hospital emergency and non-emergency paramedic care and transportation.
NAICS: 621911
#Emp: 1000-4999 (Tor)
#TorLoc: 1
Own: Government
Par: The City of Toronto
Key: Paul Raftis, Chief
Gerrie Wright, Deputy Chief, Ops
John Lock,
    Deputy Chief, Operational Support
Alan Craig, Deputy Chief, Dir at Large

The Toronto French School

306 Lawrence Ave. East
Toronto, ON M4N 1T7
Tel 416-484-6533
Fax 416-488-3090
www.tfs.ca
Line: Operates independent bilingual school.
NAICS: 611110
#Emp: 100-249 (Tor)
#TorLoc: 1
Own: Private Company
Key: John Godfrey, Headmaster
Michael Burke, Exec Dir, Admin & HR
Kiran Little, CFO
Taline Malakian,
    Purch & Commun Coord
Matthew Connors, Mgr of IT
Suzanne Tobin, Mktg Dir

Toronto Hydro Corporation

14 Carlton St.
Toronto, ON M5B 1K5
Tel 416-542-3000
Fax 416-542-3429
www.torontohydro.com
AKA: Toronto Hydro Energy Services Inc.; Toronto Hydro Electric System Ltd.; Toronto Hydro Street Lighting Inc.
Line: Supplies electrical power within the City of Toronto.
NAICS: 221122
#Emp: 1000-4999 (Tor)
#TorLoc: 1
Own: Government
Par: The City of Toronto
Key: Anthony Haines, Pres & CEO
Ave Letbridge, VP Organizational
    Effectiveness & Environment,
    Health & Safety
Jean-Sebastian Couillard, CFO
Robert Wong, VP IT
Blair H. Peberdy, VP Mktg,
    Commun & Pub Affairs

Toronto Life Publishing Ltd.

320-111 Queen St. East
Toronto, ON M5C 1S2
Tel 416-364-3333
Fax 416-861-1169
www.torontolife.com
AKA: St. Joseph Media
Line: Publishes a magazine.
NAICS: 511120
#Emp: 100-249 (Tor)
#TorLoc: 1
Own: Private Company
Par: St. Joseph Corp. (CDA)

Key: Douglas Knight, Pres
Catheryn Kendall, HR Mgr
Karl Percy, VP Fin
Jean-Marc St.Pierre, Dir of IT

Toronto Marriott Bloor Yorkville

90 Bloor St. East
Toronto, ON M4W 1A7
Tel 416-961-8000
Fax 416-961-4635
www.marriott.com
Line: Operates full service hotel.
NAICS: 721111
#Emp: 250-499 (Tor)
#TorLoc: 1
Own: Private Company
Key: Andy Loges, GM
Nicole Aumell, HR Mgr
Debra Wilson, Dir of Sales

Toronto Marriott Downtown Eaton Centre

525 Bay St.
Toronto, ON M5G 2L2
Tel 416-597-9200
Fax 416-597-9211
www.marriott.com
Line: Operates a full service hotel.
NAICS: 721111
#Emp: 250-499 (Tor)
#TorLoc: 1
Own: Private Company
Key: George Camalier, GM
Nancy McTeague, Dir of HR
Jerry Chaboryk, Dir of Fin & Acctng

Toronto Montessori Schools

8569 Bayview Ave.
Richmond Hill, ON L4B 3M7
Tel 905-889-6882
Fax 905-886-6516
www.torontomontessori.ca
Line: Operates training institutes and schools.
NAICS: 611110
#Emp: 100-249 (Tor)
#TorLoc: 1
Own: Private Company
Key: Sheila Thomas,
    Head of TMS College
Kim Moir, Office Mgr
Erin Kenzie, HR Coord
Silvana Fazzari, Dir of Admissions
Ann Bianco-Harvey,
    Dir of Mktg & Commun

Toronto Parking Authority

33 Queen St. East
Toronto, ON M5C 1R5
Tel 416-393-7275
Fax 416-393-7352
www.greenp.com
Line: Constructs, maintains, operates and manages off- and on-street parking facilities within the City of Toronto.
NAICS: 812930
#Emp: 250-499 (Tor)
#TorLoc: 185
Own: Government
Par: The City of Toronto
Key: Gwyn Thomas, Pres
Barry Martin, Dir of HR
Gerard C. Daigle, VP Fin & Admin
Ian Maher, VP Strategic Planning & IT
Lorne Persiko,
    VP Real Estate Dev & Mktg

Toronto Police Service

A Div. of The City of Toronto
40 College St.
Toronto, ON M5G 2J3
Tel 416-808-2222
Fax 416-808-8002
www.torontopolice.on.ca
Line: Provides law and traffic enforcement services in the City of Toronto.
NAICS: 913130
#Emp: 5000-9999 (Tor)
#TorLoc: 52
Own: Government
Key: William Blair, Chief of Police
Tony Veneziano, CAO
Kim Derry, Deputy Chief
Aileen Ashman, Dir of HR
Angelo Cristofaro, Dir of Fin & Admin
Joseph Martino, Mgr of Purch Support
Celestino Giannotta, Dir of Computing
    & Telecommunications

Toronto Port Authority

60 Harbour St.
Toronto, ON M5J 1B7
Tel 416-863-2000
Fax 416-863-4830
www.torontoport.com
Line: Manages the marine infrastructure of Toronto's waterfront and provides support, distribution, storage and container services.
NAICS: 488310 488119
#Emp: 100-249 (Tor)
#TorLoc: 5
Own: Federal Crown Corp.

Key: Geoffrey Wilson, Pres & CEO
Ken Lundy, Dir of Infrastructure
Catherine Bui, HR Officer
Alan Paul, VP & CFO
Keith Dickson, IT Systems Mgr

Toronto Public Library

789 Yonge St.
Toronto, ON M4W 2G8
Tel 416-393-7000
Fax 416-395-5925
www.torontopubliclibrary.ca
Line: Operates public library branches, two research and reference libraries, and a large print collection complemented by Internet access and electronic databases.
NAICS: 514121
#Emp: 1000-4999 (Tor)
#TorLoc: 99
Own: Government
Par: The City of Toronto
Key: Jane Pyper, City Librarian
Vickery Bowles, Dir of Collections
    Management & City-Wide Services
Dan Keon, Dir of HR
Larry Hughsam, Dir of Fin & Treas
Ron Dyck, Dir of IT & Facilities
Linda Hazzan, Dir of Mktg & Commun

The Toronto Real Estate Board

1400 Don Mills Rd.
Toronto, ON M3B 3N1
Tel 416-443-8100
Fax 416-443-8134
www.torontorealestateboard.com
AKA: TREB
Line: Provides services and distributes information to aid members in the orderly, efficient, successful, and professional conduct of their business operations; and to promote the collective action of the members with respect to the preservation and extension of ownership, use and private development of real property.
NAICS: 813920
#Emp: 100-249 (Tor)
#TorLoc: 1
Own: Association
Key: Don Richardson, CEO
Hugh Foy, Dir of
    Commercial & Member Dev
Claudia Pugliese, HR Mgr
Dolores Bragagnolo, CFO
John DiMichele, CIO & Associate CEO

Toronto Rehabilitation Institute

550 University Ave.
Toronto, ON M5G 2A2
Tel 416-597-3422
Fax 416-597-1977
www.torontorehab.com
Line: Operates a teaching hospital of the University of Toronto specializing in adult rehabilitation and complex continuing care.
NAICS: 622310
#Emp: 1000-4999 (Tor)
#TorLoc: 5
Own: Not-for-profit
Key: Mark Rochon, Pres & CEO
Donna Marafioti,
    VP HR & Support Services
Stephen D'Arcy,
    VP Fin & Planning & CFO
Adele Wentzel, Dir of Info Managment
Jennifer Ferguson, VP Mktg & Commun

Toronto Star Newspapers Ltd.

1 Yonge St.
Toronto, ON M5E 1E6
Tel 416-367-2000
Fax 416-869-4762
www.thestar.ca
Line: Produces daily newspaper.
NAICS: 511110
#Emp: 1000-4999 (Tor)
#TorLoc: 2
Own: Public Company
Par: Torstar Corp. (CDA)
Key: John Cruickshank, Publisher
Michael Cook, Editor
Brian Daly, VP HR
Peter Bishop, VP & CFO
Sandy Muir, VP Advertising
Edward MacLeod,
    VP Consumer Mktg & Strategy
Ali Rahnema, Interim VP Digital Media

Toronto Symphony Orchestra

212 King St. West, 6th Fl.
Toronto, ON M5H 1K5
Tel 416-593-7769
Fax 416-977-2912
www.tso.ca
Line: Manages symphony orchestra.
NAICS: 711130
#Emp: 100-249 (Tor)
#TorLoc: 1
Own: Not-for-profit
Key: Andrew Shaw, Pres & CEO
Lisa Hamel,
    Dir of Business Admin & Fin
Matthew Jones, IT Mgr
Carey Suleiman, Sr Dir of Mktg
Lisa MacKay, VP Mktg & Business Dev

Toronto Terminals Railway Company Ltd.

1400-50 Bay St.
Toronto, ON M5J 3A5
Tel 416-864-3440
Fax 416-864-3487
www.ttrly.com
AKA: TTR
Line: Provides support operations for rail transportation.
NAICS: 488210
#Emp: 100-249 (Tor)
#TorLoc: 1
Own: Private Company
Par: CN/Canadian Pacific Railway Ltd. (CDA)
Key: Remi Landry, Dir of Ops
Kirk MacDonald, Admin Supr
Robert Willacy, Fin Mgr
George Huggins, Commun Mgr

Toronto Transit Commission

1900 Yonge St.
Toronto, ON M4S 1Z2
Tel 416-393-4000
Fax 416-485-9394
www.ttc.ca
AKA: TTC
Line: Provides public transportation services.
NAICS: 485110
#Emp: 10000+ (Tor)
#TorLoc: 25
Own: Municipal Crown Corp.
Par: The City of Toronto
Key: Gary Webster, Chief GM
Rick Cornacchia, GM of Ops
Scott Blakey, Exec Dir of HR
Vince Rodo,
   GM Exec Branch & Gen Secy
Allen Chocorlan, Deputy GM of Buses
John D. Cannon, CIO
Brad Ross, Dir of Commun

Toronto West Detention Centre

111 Disco Rd.
P.O. Box 4950
Toronto, ON M9W 5L6
Tel 416-675-1806
Fax 416-674-4186
Line: Operates detention centre.
NAICS: 913120
#Emp: 250-499 (Tor)
#TorLoc: 1
Own: Provincial Crown Corp.
Par: Ministry of Community Safety & Correctional Services
Key: Tony Valaitis, Superintendent
George Soljon, Business Admr

Torys LLP

TD Centre
3000-79 Wellington St. West
Toronto, ON M5K 1N2
Tel 416-865-0040
Fax 416-865-7380
www.torys.com
Line: Operates law firm.
NAICS: 541110
#Emp: 500-999 (Tor)
#TorLoc: 1
Own: Private Company
Key: Les M. Viner, Mng Partner
James M. Tory,
   Chair Emeritus, Counsel
Alan Pearson, COO
Cindy Bordin, Dir of HR
JoAnn Phillips, Dir of Financial
   Services & Records Managment
Patrick LaFlamme, Dir of IS
Stuart Wood, Chief Mktg Officer

Toshiba Business Solutions

191 McNabb St.
Markham, ON L3R 8H2
Tel 905-695-3658
Fax 905-695-3657
www.tbscanada.ca
Line: Distributes office equipment.
NAICS: 417910
#Emp: 100-249 (Tor)
#TorLoc: 1
Own: Private Company
Key: Dan Keogh, Mgr

Toshiba of Canada Ltd.

191 McNabb St.
Markham, ON L3R 8H2
Tel 905-470-3500
Fax 905-470-3509
www.toshiba.ca
Line: Wholesales notebook computers, photocopiers, fax machines, commercial phone systems, medical imaging equipment and consumer products.
NAICS: 417320 417310
#Emp: 250-499 (Tor)
#TorLoc: 1
Own: Private Company
Par: Toshiba Corp. (JAPAN)
Key: Kiyofumi Kakudo, Pres
Robert Assal, CFO

Total Credit Recovery Ltd.

225 Yorkland Blvd.
Toronto, ON M2J 4Y7
Tel 416-774-4000
Fax 416-774-4001
www.totalcrediting.com
Line: Operates a collection agency.

NAICS: 561490 541990
#Emp: 500-999 (Tor)
#TorLoc: 1
Own: Private Company
Key: George Krieser, Pres

Totalline Transport

100 Vaughan Valley Blvd.
Vaughan, ON L4H 3C5
Tel 905-851-9121
Fax 905-851-1640
www.totalline.com
Line: Offers a full range of logistics services comprising LTL & TL transportation and warehousing at terminals across Canada.
NAICS: 488519
#Emp: 100-249 (Tor)
#TorLoc: 1
Own: Private Company
Key: Uwe Petroschke, Pres
Alison Eacock, Dir of HR
Oltion Leka, Dir of Fin

Total Relocation Moving Systems

2-4090B Sladeview Cres.
Mississauga, ON L5L 5Y5
Tel 905-607-7990
Fax 905-607-7919
www.totalrelocation.ca/
AKA: North American Van Lines
Line: Provides international, long distance and local moving and storage services.
NAICS: 484210
#Emp: 100-249 (Tor)
#TorLoc: 2
Own: Private Company
Key: Richard Allen, GM

Tour East Holidays (Canada) Inc.

15 Kern Rd.
Toronto, ON M3B 1S9
Tel 416-929-0888
Fax 416-929-7210
www.toureast.com
Line: Operates a diversified and fully integrated travel company with a focus of marketing travel products and services between Canada and Asia.
NAICS: 561520
#Emp: 100-249 (Tor)
#TorLoc: 11
Own: Private Company
Key: Rita Tsang, Pres & CEO
Annie Tsu, Dir & Exec VP

Tourism Toronto

405-207 Queen's Quay West
P.O. Box 126
Toronto, ON M5J 1A7
Tel 416-203-2600
Fax 416-203-6753
www.torontotourism.com
Line: Promotes tourism in Toronto.
NAICS: 813910
#Emp: 75-99 (Tor)
#TorLoc: 1
Own: Association
Key: David Whitaker, Pres & CEO
Monique Holmes, HR Mgr
Mark Herron, VP Fin & Corp Services
Joel Peters, Sr VP & CMO
Andrew Weir, VP Commun

Towers Watson

1701-175 Bloor St. East, South Tower
Toronto, ON M4W 3T6
Tel 416-960-2700
Fax 416-960-2819
www.towerswatson.com
Line: Provides human resource consulting and financial risk management.
NAICS: 541611
#Emp: 250-499 (Tor)
#TorLoc: 2
Own: Private Company
Par: Towers Perrin Inc. (US)
Key: Kevin Aselstine, Mng Dir, Canada
Nancy Forsythe, Dir of HR, Canada
Keri Alletson, Management Consultant

Town & Country Motors (1989) Ltd.

8111 Kennedy Rd.
Markham, ON L3R 5M2
Tel 905-477-2212
Fax 905-477-2214
www.tcbmw.com
AKA: Town + Country BMW; Mini Markham
Line: Sells, leases and services new and pre-owned vehicles.
NAICS: 441110 441120
#Emp: 100-249 (Tor)
#TorLoc: 1
Own: Private Company
Key: Jim Cochrane, Owner & Pres
Andy Grillo, Fixed Ops Mgr
Cynthia Cochrane, Business Dev,
   PR & Quality Management Mgr
Kim Petrasso, Cont
Gilbert Paquette, Gen Sales Mgr

The Town of Ajax

65 Harwood Ave. South
Ajax, ON L1S 2H9
Tel 905-683-4550
Fax 905-686-8352
www.townofajax.com
AKA: Ajax
NAICS: 913910
#Emp: 250-499 (Tor)
Own: Government
Key: Brian J. Skinner, CAO
Steve Parish, Mayor
John Fleck, Dir of HR
Rob Ford, Dir of Fin & Treas

The Town of Aurora

100 John West Way.
P.O. Box 1000
Aurora, ON L4G 6J1
Tel 905-727-1375
Fax 905-726-4738
www.aurora.ca
AKA: Aurora
NAICS: 913910
#Emp: 100-249 (Tor)
Own: Government
Key: Geoffrey Dawe, Mayor
Neil Garbe, CAO
Dan Levesque, HR Mgr
Kathie Bishop, Purch Coord
Karen Bates-Denney, MIS Coord
Jason Ballantyne,
   Mgr of Corp Commun

The Town of Georgina

26557 Civic Centre Rd.
Keswick, ON L4P 3G1
Tel 905-476-4301
Fax 905-476-8100
www.georgina.ca
AKA: Georgina
NAICS: 913910
#Emp: 100-249 (Tor)
Own: Government
Key: Robert Grossi, Mayor
Susan Plamondon, CAO
Robert Magloughlen, Dir of
   Engineering & Public Works
Claire Marsden, HR Mgr
Rebecca Mathewson, Dir of Admin
   Services & Town Treas
Brian Jordan, Mgr of Purch
Shawn Condé, IT Mgr

The Town of Halton Hills

1 Halton Hills Dr.
Halton Hills, ON L7G 5G2
Tel 905-873-2600
www.haltonhills.ca
AKA: Halton Hills
NAICS: 913910

#Emp: 100-249 (Tor)
#TorLoc: 1
Own: Government
Key: Richard Bonnette, Mayor
Dennis Perlin, CAO
Jacqueline Kerr, HR Mgr
Edward DeSousa, Dir of Corp Affairs
Simone Gourlay, Purch Mgr
Murray Colquhoun, IS Mgr
John Linhardt, Dir of Planning

The Town of Milton

150 Mary St.
Milton, ON L9T 6Z5
Tel 905-878-7252
Fax 905-878-6995
www.milton.ca
AKA: Milton
NAICS: 913910
#Emp: 250-499 (Tor)
#TorLoc: 1
Own: Government
Key: Gordon Krantz, Mayor
Mario Belvedere, CAO
Paul Cripps,
   Dir of Engineering Services
Marilyn Lehmke, Sr Mgr of HR
Linda Leeds, Dir of Corp Services
Leslie Williamson, Purch Mgr
Pam Ross, Sr Mgr of IT
Andrew Siltala, Sr Mgr of Econ Dev

The Town of Newmarket

395 Mulock Dr.
P.O. Box 328
Newmarket, ON L3Y 4X7
Tel 905-895-5193
Fax 905-953-5135
www.newmarket.ca
AKA: Newmarket
Line: Provides municipal services to the Town of Newmarket and fire services to both Newmarket and Aurora.
NAICS: 913910
#Emp: 500-999 (Tor)
#TorLoc: 15
Own: Government
Key: Tony Van Bynen, Mayor
Robert N. Shelton, CAO
Brian Jones,
   Dir of Public Works Services
K. Lynn Georgeff, HR Mgr
Robert K. Dixon,
   Comr of Corp & Financial Services
Robert M. Prentice,
   Comr of Community Services
Wanda Bennett, Corp Commun Mgr

Town of Richmond Hill/ Municipal Operations Centre

1200 Elgin Mills Rd. East
Richmond Hill, ON L4C 4Y5
Tel 905-884-8013
Fax 905-884-0395
www.richmondhill.ca
Line: Provides maintenance services to roads, sewers and parks.
NAICS: 913910
#Emp: 100-249 (Tor)
#TorLoc: 1
Own: Government
Par: Town of Richmond Hill
Key: John Armstrong, Dir

The Town of Whitby

575 Rossland Rd. East
Whitby, ON L1N 2M8
Tel 905-668-5803
Fax 905-686-7005
www.whitby.ca
AKA: Whitby
NAICS: 913910
#Emp: 500-999 (Tor)
#TorLoc: 1
Own: Government
Key: Pat Perkins, Mayor
Robert Petrie, CAO
Suzanne Beale, Dir of Public Works
Janice Stubbs, Acting HR Mgr
Ken Nix, Dir of Corp Services
Gary Cudmore, IS Mgr
Peter LeBel, Dir of Community
  & Mktg Services

The Town of Whitchurch-Stouffville

37 Sandiford Dr., 4th Fl.
Stouffville, ON L4A 7X5
Tel 905-640-1900
Fax 905-640-7957
www.townofws.com
AKA: Whitchurch-Stouffville
NAICS: 913910
#Emp: 250-499 (Tor)
#TorLoc: 1
Own: Government
Key: Wayne Emmerson, Mayor
David Cash, CAO
Paul Whitehouse, Dir of Public Works
Gary Sumner, HR Services
Marc Pourvahidi, Dir of Fin & Treas

Township of King

2075 King Rd.
King City, ON L7B 1A1
Tel 905-833-5321
Fax 905-833-2300
www.township.king.on.ca
NAICS: 913910
#Emp: 75-99 (Tor)
#TorLoc: 1
Own: Government
Key: Steve Pellegrini, Mayor
Scott Somerville, CAO
Robert Flindall, Dir of Ops,
  Public Works
Marilyn Loan, Mgr of HR
Barbara Harris, Mgr of IT

Town Shoes Ltd.

44 Kodiak Cres.
Toronto, ON M3J 3G5
Tel 416-638-5011
Fax 416-638-3847
www.townshoes.com
AKA: Shoe Company
Line: Retails shoes.
NAICS: 448210
#Emp: 500-999 (Tor)
#TorLoc: 14
Own: Private Company
Key: Alan Simpson, CEO
Peter Gerhardt, CFO

Toyota Canada Inc.

One Toyota Pl.
Toronto, ON M1H 1H9
Tel 416-438-6320
Fax 416-431-1867
www.toyota.ca
Line: Distributes Toyota and Lexus vehicles, industrial equipment and related parts through franchised dealers across Canada.
NAICS: 415190
#Emp: 500-999 (Tor)
#TorLoc: 2
Own: Private Company
Par: Toyota Motor Corp./Mitsui & Co. Ltd. (JAPAN)
Key: Yoichi Tomihara, Pres & CEO
Cyril Dimitris, Secy, Dir & Officer
Hao Tien, Dir & CIO
Anthony Wearing, Mng Dir & Officer
Stephen Beatty, Mng Dir & Officer

Toyota Credit Canada Inc.

200-80 Micro Crt.
Markham, ON L3R 9Z5
Tel 905-513-8200
Fax 905-513-9776
www.toyota.ca

AKA: Toyota Financial Services; TCCI
Line: Provides financial services.
NAICS: 532112
#Emp: 100-249 (Tor)
#TorLoc: 1
Own: Private Company
Key: Larry Baldesarra, Pres
Anne-Marie Leger, HR Mgr

Toys R Us (Canada) Ltd.

2777 Langstaff Rd.
Concord, ON L4K 4M5
Tel 905-660-2000
Fax 905-660-2022
www.toysrus.ca
Line: Retails children's toys, electronics, furnishings, baby products and children's apparel.
NAICS: 451120
#Emp: 1000-4999 (Tor)
#TorLoc: 16
Own: Private Company
Par: Toys R Us, Inc. (US)
Key: Kevin Macnab, Pres
Gary Blew, VP Sales & Ops
Mary Hewton, VP HR

Trader Corporation

110-405 The West Mall
Toronto, ON M9C 5J1
Tel 416-784-5200
www.tradercorporation.com
Line: Publishes classified and display advertising in magazine format and operates related Internet websites.
NAICS: 541840
#Emp: 1000-4999 (Tor)
#TorLoc: 1
Own: Public Company
Par: Yellow Media Inc (CDA)
Key: Doug A. Clarke, Pres
Marc P. Tellier, Pres & CEO
Jamie Blundell, VP Ops
Josee Dubuc, Chief Talent Officer
Christian M. Paupe, Exec VP & CFO
Mark O'Brien, VP Sales

Trade World Realty Inc. Brokerage

D1-4394 Steeles Ave. East, P.O. Box 33
Markham, ON L3R 9V9
Tel 416-491-3228
Fax 416-491-0288
www.tradeworldrealty.com
Line: Operates a commercial and residential real estate agency.
NAICS: 531210
#Emp: 100-249 (Tor)
#TorLoc: 3
Own: Private Company
Key: Tung Chee Chan, Owner

Tradition Fine Foods Ltd.

663 Warden Ave.
Toronto, ON M1L 3Z5
Tel 416-444-4777
Fax 416-444-7084
www.tradition.ca
Line: Produces frozen bakery products including muffins, croissants, cookies and cakes.
NAICS: 311410
#Emp: 75-99 (Tor)
#TorLoc: 1
Own: Private Company
Key: Peter Glowczewski, Pres
Thomas Glowczewski, VP
Csilla Tefoglou, Purch & Planning Mgr
Catherine Glowczewski, VP

Traffic Tech Inc.

200-5580 Explorer Dr.
Mississauga, ON L4W 4Y1
Tel 905-629-1876
Fax 905-629-1990
www.traffictech.com
Line: Operates global logistics company.
NAICS: 488519
#Emp: 75-99 (Tor)
#TorLoc: 1
Own: Private Company
Key: Brad Jones, Exec VP

Trancontinental Interactive

37 Front St. East
Toronto, ON M5E 1B3
Tel 416-360-7339
Fax 416-640-6168
www.totembrandstories.com
Line: Operates a marketing communications agency.
NAICS: 511190
#Emp: 100-249 (Tor)
#TorLoc: 1
Own: Private Company
Key: Eric Schneider, Pres & CEO
Maria Deotto, Sr VP Ops
Theresa O'Connell, VP HR & Admin
Brian Jackson, VP Fin
Loretta George, Office Mgr
David Maw, Dir of IS
Joseph Barbieri,
    VP Mktg & Business Dev

Trane Ontario/ Trane Canada ULC

4051 Gordon Baker Rd.
Toronto, ON M1W 2P3
Tel 416-499-3600
Fax 416-499-3615
www.trane.com
AKA: Trane Canada; Trane Toronto; Trane Central Ontario
Line: Distributes, sells and services heating, ventilating, refrigerating, air conditioning and controls equipment for commercial, industrial and institutional markets.
NAICS: 416120 232520
#Emp: 100-249 (Tor)
#TorLoc: 2
Own: Private Company
Par: Ingersoll Rand (IRE)
Key: Phil Owens, Area Mgr
Paul Davignon, Ops Mgr
Joey Walters, HR Dir
Andrew Kolbin, Cont
Jim Dunn, MIS Mgr
Jim Boyce, Sales Mgr
Melissa Sudama, Mktg Coord

Trans4 Logistics

101-5425 Dixie Rd.
Mississauga, ON L4W 1E6
Tel 905-212-9001
Fax 905-212-1548
www.trans4.com
Line: Provides transportation services.
NAICS: 484110
#Emp: 75-99 (Tor)
#TorLoc: 1
Own: Public Company
Par: TransForce Inc. (CDA)
Key: Brenda Everitt, VP
Jim Houston, Pres
Robert Cristant,
    Logistics, Pricing & Ops Mgr
Paul Guillemette, Cont

Transamerica Life Canada

5000 Yonge St.
Toronto, ON M2N 7J8
Tel 416-883-5003
Fax 416-883-5520
www.transamerica.ca
AKA: Aegon Canada Inc.
Line: Offers and operates life insurance and annuity product development, sales and distribution.
NAICS: 524111
#Emp: 500-999 (Tor)
#TorLoc: 3
Own: Private Company

Par: Aegon NV (NETH)
Key: Scott Sinclair, COO
Douglas Brooks, Pres & CEO
Ethne Freedman, Sr VP Client Services
    & Customer Experience
Sheilagh MacDonald, Sr VP HR
Robin Fitzgerald, Exec VP Fin & CFO
Sandra McPherson, Mgr of
    Procurement Services
James Betton, VP IT & CIO
Doug Paul, Exec VP,
    Sales & Chief Mktg Officer
Ray McKenzie, Sr VP
    Mktg & Dist Management
Glenn Daniels, Sr VP,
    Gen Counsel & Corp Secy

Transat A.T.

191 The West Mall, 8th Fl.
Toronto, ON M9C 5K8
Tel 416-620-8050
Fax 416-620-9267
www.transat.com
Line: Operates tour company.
NAICS: 561520 561510
#Emp: 250-499 (Tor)
#TorLoc: 1
Own: Private Company
Key: Denise Heffron,
    VP Nat'l Sales & Commun
Jean-Marc Eustache, CEO
Nelson Gentiletti, COO
Stewart Juelich, Dir of HR

Transcontinental Digital Services GP Inc.

6688 Kitimat Rd.
Mississauga, ON L5N 1P8
Tel 905-826-4664
Fax 905-826-7222
www.transcontinental.com
Line: Performs digital and pre-press services.
NAICS: 541920 323115
#Emp: 100-249 (Tor)
#TorLoc: 6
Own: Private Company
Par: Transcontinental Printing Inc. (CDA)
Key: Francois Olivier, Pres & CEO
Kevin Kelly, GM
Gina Deprisco,
    HR Advisor & Office Mgr

Transcontinental Media

100-25 Sheppard Ave. West
Toronto, ON M2N 6S7
Tel 416-733-7600
www.transcontinental-media.com
Line: Publishes magazines and newspapers.
NAICS: 511120
#Emp: 100-249 (Tor)
#TorLoc: 1
Own: Public Company
Par: Transcontinental Inc. (CDA)
Key: Natalie Lariviere, Pres
Marc N. Ouellette,
    Sr VP, Local Solutions Group
Lyne Pothier, VP HR
Haig Poutchigian, VP Fin
Pierre Marcoux, Sr VP, Business &
    Consumer Solutions Group
Reneault Poliquin, Sr VP Sales & Mktg
Bruno Leclaire, Sr VP, New Media &
    Digital Solutions Group

Transcontinental PLM Inc.

210 Duffield Dr.
Markham, ON L6G 1C9
Tel 416-848-8500
Fax 416-848-8501
www.plmgroup.com
AKA: PLM Group
Line: Provides web printing services.
NAICS: 323115
#Emp: 250-499 (Tor)
Own: Public Company
Par: Transcontinental Inc. (CDA)
Key: Marcel Courville, VP
Jackie Roberts, Payroll & Benefits Admr
Louis de Bellefeuille, Dir of Sales

Transcontinental Printing Inc.

138 East Dr.
Brampton, ON L6T 1C1
Tel 905-458-4777
Fax 905-458-6957
www.transcontinental-printing.com
Line: Provides printing services.
NAICS: 323113 323119
#Emp: 250-499 (Tor)
#TorLoc: 2
Own: Private Company
Key: Mike McInnes, GM,
    Ontario Retail Group
Angie Bartella, Mgr of HR
Volly Sekhon, Cont
Joe Silvestro, Dir of Sales,
    Ontario Retail Group

TransGlobe Property Management Services

223-5955 Airport Rd.
Mississauga, ON L4V 1R9
Tel 905-672-1100
Fax 905-293-9444
www.gotransglobe.com
NAICS: 531310
#Emp: 500-999 (Tor)
#TorLoc: 10
Own: Private Company
Key: Kelly Hanczyk, CEO
Daniel Drimmer, Chmn
Michael Bolahood, COO
Barry Kadoch, CFO
Simone Webb, Dir of Mktg

Trans-Ontario Express

3555 McNicoll Ave.
Toronto, ON M1V 5M9
Tel 416-298-1060
Fax 416-298-9443
www.trans-ontario.com
Line: Provides courier, trucking and transportation services.
NAICS: 488990
#Emp: 75-99 (Tor)
#TorLoc: 1
Own: Private Company
Key: Jim Kawli, Pres
Bill Kawli, VP Ops
Richard Kawli, VP Sales

TransportAction Lease Systems Inc.

51 Constellation Crt.
Toronto, ON M9W 1K4
Tel 416-674-5100
Fax 416-674-5151
www.tlsi.ca
NAICS: 532112 532120
#Emp: 100-249 (Tor)
#TorLoc: 1
Own: Private Company
Key: James Neate, CEO
Henry Mulder, Sr VP Fin
Doug Corbett, Dir of IT
Paul Turner, Sr VP Sales

Transport CFQI

5425 Dixie Rd.
Mississauga, ON L4W 1E6
Tel 905-238-5477
Fax 905-238-1087
www.epicexpress.com
AKA: Epic Express; Canadian Freightways
Line: Provides freight pick-up and delivery services, regionally, nationally and internationally.
NAICS: 484110 484121

#Emp: 100-249 (Tor)
#TorLoc: 1
Own: Private Company
Par: CF Managing Movement (CDA)
Key: Darshan Kailly, Pres & CEO
Tavis Valentine, VP Sales

Trans Power Utility Contractors Inc.

585 Applewood Cres.
Concord, ON L4K 5V7
Tel 905-660-9575
Fax 905-660-9577
www.transpower.ca
AKA: Trans Power
Line: Provides underground utility services.
NAICS: 231390
#Emp: 100-249 (Tor)
Own: Private Company
Key: Simone De Gasperis, VP
Frank Mongillo, Pres & CEO
Tony Sanginesi, GM
Eirdley Low, Cont

TransX Ltd.

7225 Transmark Crt.
Mississauga, ON L5S 1Z5
Tel 905-362-3600
Fax 905-362-3616
www.transx.com
AKA: TransX Group of Companies
Line: Provides integrated transportation solutions throughout North America.
NAICS: 484110 484121
#Emp: 100-249 (Tor)
#TorLoc: 1
Own: Private Company
Key: Joe Trigiani,
    Dir of Eastern Terminal
Rick Johnson, Terminal Mgr
Rick Drinkwater, Dir of LTL Sales,
    Eastern Canada

Trapeze Software Group Inc.

5800 Explorer Dr., 5th Fl.
Mississauga, ON L4W 5K9
Tel 905-629-8727
Fax 905-238-8408
www.trapezegroup.com
Line: Delivers innovative software and services to public transit, demand response and school transportation organizations.
NAICS: 541619
#Emp: 100-249 (Tor)
#TorLoc: 1
Own: Private Company
Par: Constellation Software Inc. (CDA)
Key: John Hines, Pres
Fran Fendelet, VP Business Dev

Travel Cuts

A Div. of Merit Travel Grp
200-111 Peter St.
Toronto, ON M5V 2H1
Tel 416-364-3775
Fax 416-364-9918
www.travelcuts.com
AKA: Canadian Universities Travel
Service Ltd.; Senate Travel; The
Adventure Travel Company; Student
Work Abroad Program; Voyages
Campus
Line: Operates a retail and wholesale
travel agency.
NAICS: 561510
#Emp: 100-249 (Tor)
#TorLoc: 20
Own: Private Company
Par: Canadian Federation of Students
(CDA)
Key: Michael Merrithew,
  Pres & Co-Owner
Louise De-Granderpre, Co-Owner
Leslie Gora, Dir of Ops
Lillian Ingram-Watts, Dir of HR
George Erinobou, Cont

Travelers Guarantee Company of Canada

300-20 Queen St. West, P.O. Box 6
Toronto, ON M5H 3R3
Tel 416-360-8183
Fax 416-360-8267
www.travelersguarantee.com
Line: Operates a property and casualty
insurance company.
NAICS: 524121
#Emp: 100-249 (Tor)
Own: Private Company
Key: George Petropoulos, Pres & CEO
Robert Burns, Sr VP, Underwriting
Desmond Sue-Chan, VP Fin

Travelers Insurance

300-20 Queen St. West
Toronto, ON M5H 3R3
Tel 416-366-8183
Fax 416-366-8267
www.travelers.com
AKA: St. Paul Travelers; Travelers
Line: Provides commercial insurance
through broker base.
NAICS: 524210
#Emp: 250-499 (Tor)
#TorLoc: 2
Own: Private Company
Par: The Travelers Indemnity Company
(US)
Key: George Petropoulos, Pres
Barry Normet, Reg VP
Robyn Layng, Asst VP HR
Joe Hannigan, Mgr of BusInsurance

Travelers Transportation Services Ltd.

195 Heart Lake Rd. South
Brampton, ON L6W 3N6
Tel 905-457-8789
Fax 905-457-8084
www.travelers.ca
Line: Operates a trucking company.
NAICS: 484122
#Emp: 250-499 (Tor)
#TorLoc: 1
Own: Private Company
Key: Jim Hicks, Pres & CEO
Dennis Balzer, VP Fin

Travelex Canada Ltd.

Scotia Bank Plaza
100 Yonge St., 15th Fl.
Toronto, ON M5C 2W1
Tel 416-359-3700
Fax 416-981-2252
www.travelexamericas.com
AKA: Travelex America Inc.; Travelex
Currency Services Inc.
Line: Provides foreign exchange
services.
NAICS: 523130
#Emp: 100-249 (Tor)
#TorLoc: 1
Own: Private Company
Par: Travelex Currency Services (UK)
Key: Judy Adams, VP Fin
Kevin Agnew, Dir of IT

Travelodge Hotel Toronto Airport

925 Dixon Rd.
Toronto, ON M9W 1J8
Tel 416-674-2222
Fax 416-674-5757
www.travelodgedixon.com
NAICS: 721111
#Emp: 75-99 (Tor)
#TorLoc: 1
Own: Private Company
Par: Royal Host (CDA)
Key: Kevin Kluts, GM
D.J Marco, Ops Mgr
Akif Srajeldin, Acctng Mgr
Eric Proskurnicki, Dir of Sales

Trebor Personnel Inc.

203-1090 Dundas St. East
Mississauga, ON L4Y 2B8
Tel 905-566-0922
Fax 905-566-0925
www.tpipersonnel.com
AKA: TPI Staffing Inc.; TPI
Line: Supplies temporary, contract and
full-time personnel to companies.

NAICS: 561310
#Emp: 500-999 (Tor)
#TorLoc: 6
Own: Private Company
Key: Bob Bryce, Pres
Brenda Bryce, VP
Karen Towers, Office Mgr

Tree of Life Canada ULC

6030 Freemont Blvd.
Mississauga, ON L5R 3X4
Tel 905-507-6161
Fax 905-507-2727
www.kehe.com
Line: Distributes specialty and natural
foods.
NAICS: 413190
#Emp: 100-249 (Tor)
#TorLoc: 1
Own: Public Company
Par: KeHE Distributors (US)
Key: Jamie Moody,
  Region Pres, Canada
Barry Sheldrick, VP Ops & IT
Helen Morrison, VP HR
Gordon Walker, VP Fin
Chris Powell, VP Sales
Helen Pike, VP Mktg

Tre Mari Bakery Ltd.

1311 St. Clair Ave. West
Toronto, ON M6E 1C2
Tel 416-654-8960
Fax 416-654-6681
www.tremaribakery.ca
NAICS: 311814
#Emp: 75-99 (Tor)
#TorLoc: 1
Own: Private Company
Key: Frank Deleo, Pres & GM

Tremco Canada Division

220 Wicksteed Ave.
Toronto, ON M4H 1G7
Tel 416-421-3300
Fax 416-467-2448
www.tremcosealants.com
AKA: Tremco Global Sealants Division
Line: Manufactures specialty
chemicals.
NAICS: 325510 325520
#Emp: 250-499 (Tor)
#TorLoc: 1
Own: Private Company
Par: RPM International Inc. (US)
Key: David Haigh, VP Ops
Bosville Salmon, Dir of HR
Gail Mitchell, Fin Mgr
Greg Roberts, IT Mgr

Trench Ltd.

71 Maybrook Dr.
Toronto, ON M1V 4B6
Tel 416-298-8108
Fax 416-298-2209
www.trenchgroup.com
NAICS: 335311
#Emp: 500-999 (Tor)
#TorLoc: 4
Own: Private Company
Key: Diane Thiel, CFO
Caroline East, HR Mgr
Dave Caverly, VP Mktg

Trentway-Wagar Inc.

791 Webber Ave.
P.O. Box 4017
Peterborough, ON K9J 7B1
Tel 705-748-6411
Fax 705-748-2452
www.coachcanada.com
AKA: Coach Canada
Line: Provides scheduled, school
bus, transit operations and airport
transportation services.
NAICS: 485410 485210
#Emp: 500-999 (Tor)
#TorLoc: 2
Own: Private Company
Par: Stagecoach Group (US)
Key: Don Carmichael, Pres
John Crowley, VP Safety & Ops
Deborah Nayler, VP HR
Byron Thompson, Reg Cont
Dave Pettapiece, Network Specialist
Susan Adlam, VP Sales & Mktg

Tribute Communities

1-1815 Ironstone Manor
Pickering, ON L1W 3W9
Tel 905-839-3500
Fax 905-839-3757
www.tributecommunities.com
Line: Operates a home building
company.
NAICS: 231110 531210
#Emp: 100-249 (Tor)
#TorLoc: 1
Own: Private Company
Par: Tribute Development Ltd. (CDA)
Key: Al Libfeld, Pres
David Speigel, VP Ops
Raymond Jankelow, CFO

Tri-Con Concrete Finishing Co. Ltd.

100-835 Supertest Rd.
Toronto, ON M3J 2M9
Tel 416-736-7700
Fax 416-736-6686
www.triconconcrete.com
Line: Installs patterned concrete in
commercial and residential areas.
NAICS: 232220
#Emp: 100-249 (Tor)
#TorLoc: 1
Own: Private Company
Key: Frank Guida, Pres

Tricrest Professional Services

27-5200 Dixie Rd.
Mississauga, ON L4W 1E4
Tel 1-866-877-9192
Fax 905-290-8359
www.tricrest.ca
Line: Provides telecom, professional
and enterprise network services.
NAICS: 541611
#Emp: 100-249 (Tor)
#TorLoc: 1
Own: Private Company
Key: Rob May, Pres & CEO
Frank Palmieri, VP Sales
   & Business Development
Kash Krishan, Corp Cont

Tridel Corp.

200-4800 Dufferin St.
Toronto, ON M3H 5S9
Tel 416-661-9290
Fax 416-661-4461
www.tridel.com
Line: Operates a home construction
company.
NAICS: 231110 231210
#Emp: 500-999 (Tor)
Own: Private Company
Key: Angelo DelZotto, Chmn
Dino Carmel, COO
Julia Kelly-Horowitz, Payroll Mgr
Ted Maulucci, CIO
James Ritchie, Sr VP

Tri-Ed Ltd.

A-F 3688 Nashua Dr.
Mississauga, ON L4V 1M5
Tel 905-677-8664
Fax 905-677-0698
www.tri-ed.com
Line: Distributes security equipment.
NAICS: 416110
#Emp: 75-99 (Tor)
#TorLoc: 2
Own: Private Company
Par: Tri-Ed Ltd. (US)
Key: Adriana Richards, Branch Mgr
Paul Swan, Dir of Mktg

Trillium Health Centre

100 Queensway West
Mississauga, ON L5B 1B8
Tel 905-848-7100
Fax 905-848-5598
www.trilliumhealthcentre.org
Line: Operates full service community
hospital with territory and regional
programs.
NAICS: 622111
#Emp: 1000-4999 (Tor)
#TorLoc: 2
Own: Not-for-profit
Key: Janet Davidson, Pres & CEO
Patti Cochrane,
   VP Patient Services & Quality
Morag McLean, VP People Services &
   Organizational Effectiveness
May Chang,
   VP Decision Support & CFO

Trillium Security Services Inc.

226-1550 Enterprise Rd.
Mississauga, ON L4W 4P4
Tel 416-621-3404
Fax 905-795-2256
www.trilliumsecurityservices.com
Line: Provides security services
for trade and consumer shows and
conventions.
NAICS: 561612
#Emp: 75-99 (Tor)
#TorLoc: 1
Own: Private Company
Key: Lee Miller, Owner

Trilogy Long Term Care

340 McCowan Rd.
Toronto, ON M1J 3P4
Tel 416-443-1074
Fax 416-386-0464
www.chartwellreit.ca
Line: Operates a nursing home.
NAICS: 623110
#Emp: 100-249 (Tor)
#TorLoc: 1
Own: Private Company
Par: Chartwell Seniors Housing REIT
(CDA)
Key: Marva Griffiths, Admr

Trimac Transportation Limited Partnership

200-5063 North Service Rd.
Burlington, ON L7L 5H6
Tel 905-315-1100
Fax 905-315-1143
www.trimac.com
Line: Provides liquid and dry bulk material transportation services.
NAICS: 488990
#Emp: 100-249 (Tor)
#TorLoc: 1
Own: Partnership
Key: Glenn Sherman, Sr VP
Jeffery J. McCaig, Pres & CEO
Willie Hamel, Division VP
Edward V. Malysa, CFO & COO
Alan Potts, Dir
    of Nat'l Accounts, Petroleum
David Gatti, VP Mktg & Business Dev

Trimark Sportswear Group Inc.

8688 Woodbine Ave.
Markham, ON L3R 8B9
Tel 905-475-1712
Fax 905-475-9389
www.trimarksportswear.com
AKA: Trimark Sportswear
Line: Distributes sportswear.
NAICS: 414110
#Emp: 100-249 (Tor)
#TorLoc: 1
Own: Private Company
Key: Stuart Campbell, Pres
Derrick Milne, CEO
Jim Doris, Dir Logistics & Ops
Justin Rieder,
    Commun & Creative Service Mgr

Trimen Food Service Equipment Inc.

1240 Ormont Dr.
Toronto, ON M9L 2V4
Tel 416-744-3313
Fax 416-744-3377
www.trimen.com
Line: Manufactures and wholesales stainless steel restaurant equipment.
NAICS: 332210 417920
#Emp: 100-249 (Tor)
#TorLoc: 1
Own: Private Company
Key: Paul Cesario, Pres
Grace Giuliano, Cont

Trimont Manufacturing Inc.

115 Milner Ave.
Toronto, ON M1S 4L7
Tel 416-640-2045
Fax 416-847-3935
Line: Manufactures automotive parts and seat covers.
NAICS: 336360
#Emp: 75-99 (Tor)
#TorLoc: 2
Own: Private Company
Key: Steven Li, Pres

triOS College Business Technology Healthcare

103-6755 Mississauga Rd.
Mississauga, ON L5N 7Y2
Tel 905-814-7212
Fax 905-813-8250
www.trios.com
Line: Operates an education and technology solutions organization.
NAICS: 541510 611420
#Emp: 100-249 (Tor)
Own: Private Company
Par: Trios Corporation (CDA)
Key: Stuart Bentley, Pres
Frank Gerencser, CEO
Janet Popovic, Reg Dir of Admissions
Debbie Jane, Exec Asst HR
Jason Johnston, Mktg Mgr

Tripar Transportation Inc.

2180 Buckingham Rd.
Oakville, ON L6H 6H1
Tel 905-829-8500
Fax 905-829-8513
www.contrans.ca
Line: Operates a trucking company.
NAICS: 484121 484110
#Emp: 75-99 (Tor)
#TorLoc: 1
Own: Private Company
Key: Don Burditt, GM
Patrick Pelton, Cont

Triple M Metal

471 Intermodal Dr.
Brampton, ON L6T 5G4
Tel 905-793-7083
Fax 905-793-7285
www.triplemmetal.com
Line: Collects and sells scrap metal, truck and crane parts.
NAICS: 418110
#Emp: 250-499 (Tor)
#TorLoc: 3

Own: Private Company
Par: 1335192 Ontario Ltd. (CDA)
Key: Joe Caruso, Pres
Mike Giampaolo, Chmn & CEO
Oscar Moniz, COO
Larry Rose, VP HR
Lionel Prasad, CFO

Triple Seal Ltd.

1-250 Brockport Rd.
Toronto, ON M9W 5S1
Tel 416-798-2345
Fax 416-798-9242
www.tripleseal.ca
Line: Distributes glass products.
NAICS: 444190
#Emp: 100-249 (Tor)
#TorLoc: 1
Own: Private Company
Key: Steve Morren, Pres
Louis Papaconstantinos, VP

Triplewell Enterprises Ltd.

9-3440 Pharmacy Ave.
Toronto, ON M1W 2P8
Tel 416-498-5637
Fax 416-498-6034
Line: Manufactures and wholesales sewing products.
NAICS: 414130
#Emp: 250-499 (Tor)
#TorLoc: 2
Own: Private Company
Key: Lincoln Wong, Pres & CEO
Henry Tang, VP Ops
Jenny Qiu, HR Mgr
Finy Auwyang, Acctng Mgr
James Wong, Mktg Mgr

Tri R Foods Ltd.

5246 Timberlea Blvd.
Mississauga, ON L4W 2S5
Tel 905-361-5604
Fax 905-238-9720
www.trirfoods.com
Line: Produces processed poultry products.
NAICS: 311615
#Emp: 75-99 (Tor)
#TorLoc: 1
Own: Private Company
Key: Karen Vanstone, Pres

Trisan Construction

205-17250 Hwy. 27
P.O. Box 502
Schomberg, ON L0G 1T0
Tel 416-410-3839
Fax 905-939-4082
www.trisanconstruction.com
Line: Performs road and sewer
construction.
NAICS: 231310 231320
#Emp: 100-249 (Tor)
Own: Private Company
Key: Angelo Santorelli, Pres

Trophy Foods Inc.

71 Admiral Blvd.
Mississauga, ON L5T 2T1
Tel 905-670-8050
Fax 905-670-4256
www.trophyfoods.com
Line: Processes and packages edible
nuts, confectionary and snack foods.
NAICS: 311911 311919
#Emp: 100-249 (Tor)
#TorLoc: 1
Own: Private Company
Key: Brian Paul, Pres & COO
Brenda McMurtry, HR Mgr
Gino Truant, VP Fin
Joseph Milando, Dir of Sales

Trott Transit Ltd.

15 James St.
Mississauga, ON L5M 1R4
Tel 905-826-6629
Fax 905-819-1157
www.trott.ca
Line: Provides school bus services and
charter bus trips.
NAICS: 485410 485510
#Emp: 100-249 (Tor)
#TorLoc: 1
Own: Private Company
Key: Raymond Trott, Pres
Ursula Trott-Hiller, Secy-Treas

T & R Sargent Farms Ltd.

61 Garden Lane
Milton, ON L9T 2P7
Tel 905-878-4401
Fax 905-878-8998
www.sargentfarms.ca
Line: Retails, wholesales and processes
poultry.
NAICS: 413130 311615
#Emp: 100-249 (Tor)
#TorLoc: 1
Own: Private Company

Key: Tom Sargent, Pres
Robert Giguere, CEO
Bob Sargent, VP
Mike McLaughlin, HR Mgr
Kristy Sargent, Fin Mgr
Tahir Qureshi, Sales Mgr

True Davidson Acres Home for the Aged

A Div. of The City of Toronto
200 Dawes Rd.
Toronto, ON M4C 5M8
Tel 416-397-0400
Fax 416-397-0401
www.toronto.ca/ltc/truedavidson.htm
Line: Provides medical and nursing
care for elderly persons.
NAICS: 623110 623310
#Emp: 100-249 (Tor)
#TorLoc: 2
Own: Government
Key: Nelson Rebeiro, Admr
George Sirioboulos, Dir of Care
Sophia Kyriazis, Sr Clerk
Greg O'Grady,
    Mgr of Program & Services

True North Hockey Canada Inc.

304-4920 Dundas St. West
Toronto, ON M9A 1B7
Tel 416-231-8642
Fax 416-231-3501
www.truenorthhockey.com
NAICS: 713990
#Emp: 250-499 (Tor)
#TorLoc: 3
Own: Private Company
Key: Steve Edgar, Pres

Trulite Industries Ltd.

1820 Courtneypark Dr. East
Mississauga, ON L5T 1W1
Tel 905-670-7040
Fax 905-670-7041
www.trulite.com
Line: Fabricates flat glass, tempers
glass and distributes glass products.
NAICS: 327214
#Emp: 75-99 (Tor)
#TorLoc: 2
Own: Private Company
Key: Ian Marshall, GM
Gavan Durkin, Ops Mgr

Trusted Retail Solutions

9 West Dr.
Brampton, ON L6T 4T2
Tel 416-247-4257
Fax 905-291-0757
www.trustedretail.com
Line: Provides third party logistics.
NAICS: 488519
#Emp: 100-249 (Tor)
#TorLoc: 1
Own: Private Company
Par: Metro Canada Logistics Inc. (CDA)
Key: David Sloman, GM

Trustwell Realty Inc.

3622 Victoria Park Ave.
Toronto, ON M2H 3B2
Tel 416-498-9995
Fax 416-498-0037
www.trustwellrealtyinc.com
Line: Operates real estate and property
management company.
NAICS: 531210
#Emp: 100-249 (Tor)
#TorLoc: 2
Own: Private Company
Key: Peter Wong, Broker of Record
Bertram Mak, Broker

TSM Ltd.

201A-5145 Steeles Ave. West
Toronto, ON M9L 1R5
Tel 416-740-8560
Fax 416-740-1816
www.tuffcontrol.ca
AKA: Total Security Management
Line: Provides retail security services.
NAICS: 561612
#Emp: 100-249 (Tor)
Own: Private Company
Par: TSM Inc. (US)
Key: Debi Bellis, VP

TS Tech Canada Inc.

17855 Leslie St.
Newmarket, ON L3Y 3E3
Tel 905-953-0098
Fax 905-953-0104
www.tstna.com
Line: Assembles automotive seating
and interior components.
NAICS: 336390
#Emp: 250-499 (Tor)
#TorLoc: 1
Own: Private Company
Par: TS Tech Holding Co. (US)
Key: Randy Walsh, Plant Mgr
Don Briggs, Mgr of Associate Services

TST Overland Express

A Div. of TST Solutions Inc.
5200 Maingate Dr.
Mississauga, ON L4W 1G5
Tel 905-625-7500
Fax 905-212-6354
www.tstoverland.com
NAICS: 484110 484121
#Emp: 1000-4999 (Tor)
#TorLoc: 1
Own: Private Company
Par: TransForce Inc. (CDA)
Key: Rob O'Reilly, Pres

TST Truckload Express Inc.

A Div. of TST Solutions Inc.
B-5425 Dixie Rd.
Mississauga, ON L4W 1E6
Tel 905-602-5962
Fax 905-602-7559
www.tsttruckloadexpress.com
AKA: TST Load Brokerage Services
Line: Provides road transportation for general commodities.
NAICS: 484110
#Emp: 75-99 (Tor)
#TorLoc: 1
Own: Public Company
Par: TransForce Inc. (CDA)
Key: Tom Philips, VP & GM
Robert Yarnell, Dir of Ops

Tsubaki of Canada Ltd.

1630 Drew Rd.
Mississauga, ON L5S 1J6
Tel 905-676-0400
Fax 905-676-0904
www.tsubaki.ca
Line: Manufactures sprockets, chains and drives.
NAICS: 333619
#Emp: 100-249 (Tor)
#TorLoc: 1
Own: Private Company
Par: Tsubakimoto Chain Co. (JAPAN)
Key: Sam Udea, Pres
Robert Mitchell, Ops Mgr
Fernando Andrade, VP Fin
Jos Sueters, VP Sales
Tim Morrison, Mktg Mgr

TTR Transport Inc.

219 Wentworth St. East
Oshawa, ON L1H 3V7
Tel 905-725-5544
Fax 905-725-9411
www.ttrtransport.com
Line: Provides local and long distance trucking services.

NAICS: 484110 484121
#Emp: 100-249 (Tor)
#TorLoc: 1
Own: Private Company
Key: Steven Chandler, Pres
Karen Howell, Secy-Treas

Tube-Fab Ltd.

6845 Davand Dr.
Mississauga, ON L5T 1L4
Tel 905-565-0223
Fax 905-565-0065
www.tube-fab.com
Line: Supplies machined and tubular components and assemblies.
NAICS: 332999
#Emp: 75-99 (Tor)
#TorLoc: 1
Own: Private Company
Par: Tube-Fab Ltd. (CDA)
Key: Eric Foley, VP Ops

Tubular Steel Inc.

285 Raleigh Ave.
Toronto, ON M1K 1A5
Tel 416-261-2089
Fax 416-261-9517
www.tubularsteel.ca
Line: Manufactures welded steel tubes.
NAICS: 331210
#Emp: 100-249 (Tor)
#TorLoc: 2
Own: Private Company
Key: Robert D. McKinnon, Pres
Tony Da Silva, VP Ops

Tucker's Marketplace

5975 Mavis Rd.
Mississauga, ON L5R 3T7
Tel 905-502-8555
Fax 905-502-1361
www.tuckersmarketplace.ca
AKA: Newgen Restaurant Services Inc.
NAICS: 722110
#Emp: 75-99 (Tor)
#TorLoc: 4
Own: Private Company
Key: Kevin Chong, GM

Tucker's Marketplace Restaurant

880 Warden Ave.
Toronto, ON M1L 4R1
Tel 416-759-5688
Fax 416-759-0440
www.tuckersmarketplace.ca
AKA: Champs Food Systems Ltd.
NAICS: 722110
#Emp: 75-99 (Tor)
#TorLoc: 4

Own: Private Company
Key: Mike Coulliard, GM

Tucows Inc.

96 Mowat Ave.
Toronto, ON M6K 3M1
Tel 416-535-0123
Fax 416-531-5584
www.tucowsinc.com
Line: Provides software libraries and wholesale Internet services.
NAICS: 417310
#Emp: 100-249 (Tor)
#TorLoc: 1
Own: Public Company
Key: Elliot Noss, Pres & CEO
Carla Goertz, VP HR
Michael Cooperman, CFO
Dave Woroch, VP Sales
Ken Schafer,
    VP Mktg & Product Management

Turf Care Products Canada Limited

200 Pony Dr.
Newmarket, ON L3Y 7B6
Tel 905-836-0988
Fax 905-836-6442
www.turfcare.ca
AKA: Turf Care
Line: Distributes turf maintenance equipment.
NAICS: 417110
#Emp: 75-99 (Tor)
#TorLoc: 3
Own: Private Company
Key: Ronald Craig, Pres
John Jarman, VP Fin

Turning Point Youth Services

95 Wellesley St. East
Toronto, ON M4Y 2X9
Tel 416-925-9250
Fax 416-925-9926
www.turningpoint.ca
Line: Offers a range of mental health and support services to individuals, youth and families.
NAICS: 624190
#Emp: 100-249 (Tor)
#TorLoc: 1
Own: Not-for-profit
Key: Colin Dart, Exec Dir
Jeanetta Hoffman, Dir of Ops

Turtle Island Recycling Company Inc.

242 Cherry St.
P.O. Box 6762, Stn. A
Toronto, ON M5A 3L2
Tel 416-406-2040
Fax 416-406-2044
www.turtleislandrecycling.com
NAICS: 562920
#Emp: 250-499 (Tor)
#TorLoc: 1
Own: Private Company
Key: John Ferreira, Pres
Louis Anagnostakos,
   Chief Innovative Officer
Kelly Ng, Cont

Tuxedo Royale

185 Konrad Cres.
Markham, ON L3R 8T9
Tel 905-474-0304
Fax 905-474-1697
www.tuxedoroyale.com
Line: Provides formal wear rentals and sales.
NAICS: 532220
#Emp: 100-249 (Tor)
#TorLoc: 13
Own: Private Company
Key: Ivan Zichy, Pres
Kevin Slaney, VP

TVO

P.O. Box 200 Stn. Q
Toronto, ON M4T 2T1
Tel 416-484-2600
Fax 416-484-2633
www.tvo.org
AKA: Ontario Educational
Communications Authority; TFO; TV
Ontario
NAICS: 513120
#Emp: 250-499 (Tor)
#TorLoc: 1
Own: Provincial Crown Corp.
Par: Government of Ontario
Key: Lisa de Wilde, CEO
Clara Arnold, Dir of HR
Rob Crocker, Dir of Fin & Admin

Tyco Electronics Canada ULC

20 Esna Park Dr.
Markham, ON L3R 1E1
Tel 905-475-6222
Fax 905-474-5519
www.tycoelectronics.com
Line: Manufactures electronic and electrical connectors.
NAICS: 335930 335990
#Emp: 100-249 (Tor)
#TorLoc: 1
Own: Public Company
Par: TE Connectivity (US)
Key: Kevin Irons, Cont
Dean McCreadie,
   Mgr of Materials & Logistics
Anaheet Sethna, HR Mgr
Kevin Earle, Cdn Quality Dir
Barbara Meloff, Customer Service Mgr

Tycos Tool & Die Inc.

A Div. of Exteriors & Interiors Inc.
2000 Langstaff Rd.
Concord, ON L4K 3B5
Tel 905-669-2350
Fax 905-669-1048
www.tycostool.com
Line: Manufactures plastic injection moulds.
NAICS: 333511
#Emp: 100-249 (Tor)
#TorLoc: 1
Own: Private Company
Par: Magna International Inc. (CDA)
Key: Pat Radice, GM
Keith Johnston, Production Mgr
Sarah Booth, HR, Health & Safety Mgr
Jutta Cornish, Cont
Neil Yan, Systems Admr
Ron Nesselberger, Asst GM

Tyndale University College & Seminary

25 Ballyconnor Crt.
Toronto, ON M2M 4B3
Tel 416-226-6380
Fax 416-226-6746
www.tyndale.ca
AKA: Tyndale; Tyndale University;
Tyndale Seminary
Line: Operates a university and seminary.
NAICS: 611310
#Emp: 100-249 (Tor)
#TorLoc: 1
Own: Not-for-profit
Key: Gary Nelson, Pres & CEO
Randy Henderson, Sr VP Fin & COO
Nancy Dodsworth, Dir of HR
Sandra Eng, Cont
Phil Kay,
   Dir of Admissions & Financial Aid
Lina van der Wel,
   Dir of Mktg & Commun

Tyndall Nursing Home Ltd.

1060 Eglinton Ave. East
Mississauga, ON L4W 1K3
Tel 905-624-1511
Fax 905-629-9346
www.tyndallestates.net
Line: Operates a nursing home.
NAICS: 623110
#Emp: 100-249 (Tor)
#TorLoc: 1
Own: Private Company
Key: Denham Jolly, Owner & Admr

UBS Bank (Canada)

800-154 University Ave.
Toronto, ON M5H 3Z4
Tel 416-343-1800
Fax 416-343-1900
www.ubs.com/canada
AKA: UBS Wealth Management
Line: Provides wealth management services.
NAICS: 522112
#Emp: 100-249 (Tor)
#TorLoc: 1
Own: Private Company
Par: UBS AG (SWITZ)
Key: Grant Rasmussen, CEO
Kelly McMillan, Exec Dir of HR

UCC Group Inc.

262 Galaxy Blvd.
Toronto, ON M9W 5R8
Tel 416-675-7455
Fax 416-675-7445
www.uccgroup.com
Line: Operates a construction company.
NAICS: 232220
#Emp: 100-249 (Tor)
#TorLoc: 1
Own: Private Company
Key: Pat Dipaolo, Pres

UFCW Canada - Locals 175 & 633

2200 Argentia Rd.
Mississauga, ON L5N 2K7
Tel 905-821-8329
Fax 905-821-7144
www.ufcw175.com
AKA: United Food & Commercial
Workers Union of Canada
Line: Operates a local union.
NAICS: 813930
#Emp: 75-99 (Tor)
#TorLoc: 1
Own: Association
Key: Shawn Haggerty, Pres, Local 175
Dan Bondy, Pres, Local 633
Teresa Magee, Secy Treas

UJA Federation of Greater Toronto

4600 Bathurst St.
Toronto, ON M2R 3V2
Tel 416-635-2883
Fax 416-631-5701
www.jewishtoronto.com
AKA: United Jewish Welfare Fund;
Jewish Foundation of Greater Toronto
Line: Operates charitable organization
that provides social services.
NAICS: 624190
#Emp: 100-249 (Tor)
#TorLoc: 1
Own: Not-for-profit
Key: Ted Sokolsky, Pres & CEO
Ron Eilath, CFO
Helen Finder-Guttman, Dir of HR
Les Horenfeldt, VP Fin & Admin
Bruce Gilbert, IT Mgr

Ukrainian Canadian Care Centre

60 Richview Rd.
Toronto, ON M9A 5E4
Tel 416-243-7653
Fax 416-243-7452
www.stdemetrius.ca
Line: Operates long-term care facility.
NAICS: 623310
#Emp: 100-249 (Tor)
#TorLoc: 1
Own: Private Company
Key: Sandy Lomaszewycz, Exec Dir
Deborah Kroeger, Dir of Ops
Blanca Allende, HR Coord

Ultra-Fit Manufacturing Inc.

1840 Courtney Park Dr.
Mississauga, ON L5T 1W1
Tel 905-795-0344
Fax 905-795-0346
www.ultrafit.net
AKA: UFM
Line: Manufactures automotive exhaust
parts and offers tube bending and
custom pipe fabrication.
NAICS: 336390
#Emp: 75-99 (Tor)
#TorLoc: 1
Own: Private Company
Key: Don Hockin, Pres

Ultra-Form Manufacturing Company Ltd.

73 Baywood Rd.
Toronto, ON M9V 3Y8
Tel 416-749-9323
Fax 416-749-7555
www.ultra-form.com
Line: Manufactures precision screw
machine products for the automotive
industry.
NAICS: 333519
#Emp: 75-99 (Tor)
#TorLoc: 1
Own: Private Company
Key: Mo Shahid, CEO
Farooq Shahid, GM
Parag Shah, CFO

Umbra Ltd.

40 Emblem Crt.
Toronto, ON M1S 1B1
Tel 416-299-0088
Fax 416-299-6168
www.umbra.com
Line: Picture frames, trash cans,
kitchen accessories, gifts and furniture.
NAICS: 314120 414390
#Emp: 100-249 (Tor)
#TorLoc: 1
Own: Private Company
Key: Les Mandelbaum, Pres & CEO
Howard Rosenberg, VP Fin
Paula Burtt, VP Sales

Umicore Autocat Canada Corp.

4261 Mainway Dr.
P.O. Box 5097
Burlington, ON L7R 3Y8
Tel 905-336-3424
Fax 905-319-4183
www.umicore.com
Line: Produces automotive emission
catalysts.
NAICS: 336390
#Emp: 100-249 (Tor)
#TorLoc: 1
Own: Public Company
Par: Umicore (BELG)
Key: William Powell, Plant Mgr
Shirley Dodman, HR Mgr
Tim Weegar, Cont

Underwriters Laboratories of Canada

7 Underwriters Rd.
Toronto, ON M1R 3B4
Tel 416-757-3611
Fax 416-757-9540
www.ulc.ca
AKA: ULC; UL of Canada
Line: Engages in testing, product
certification, standard writing and
quality registration in the electrical
fire protection, burglary protection,
environmental and life safety fields.
NAICS: 541380
#Emp: 100-249 (Tor)
#TorLoc: 1
Own: Not-for-profit
Key: Martin Oughton, Pres & GM
Rose Marie Thompson, HR Mgr
John Arrabito, VP Fin & Treas

Unicco Facility Services Canada Co.

107-411 Richmond St. East
Toronto, ON M5A 3S5
Tel 416-369-0040
Fax 416-369-9156
www.unicco.com
Line: Provides janitorial and
mechanical maintenance services.
NAICS: 561722
#Emp: 1000-4999 (Tor)
Own: Private Company
Par: Unicco Service Company (US)
Key: Earl Bannister, VP
Joe De Sousa, Dir of Ops
Allan Boucher, Dir of HR

Unifirst Canada Ltd.

2190 Winston Park Dr.
Oakville, ON L6H 5W1
Tel 905-829-5960
Fax 905-829-5957
www.unifirst.ca
Line: Provides uniform, corporate
clothing and facility services to
businesses.
NAICS: 812330
#Emp: 100-249 (Tor)
#TorLoc: 3
Own: Private Company
Par: UniFirst Corp. (US)
Key: Michael Szymanski, VP Cdn Ops
Tim Sullivan, GM Ops
Patricia Janicki, HR & Admin Mgr
Steve Hufton, Systems Mgr

Unilever Canada Inc.

1500-160 Bloor St. East
Toronto, ON M4W 3R2
Tel 416-964-1857
Fax 416-964-8831
www.unilever.ca
AKA: U L Canada Inc.
Line: Manufactures and sells consumer products including foods, and home and personal care products.
NAICS: 311225 325610 311990
#Emp: 1000-4999 (Tor)
#TorLoc: 7
Own: Private Company
Par: Unilever plc (UK)
Key: Christopher Luxon, Pres & CEO
Eric Tiziani, Nat'l Fin Dir
John Coyne,
  VP Gen Counsel & Corp Secy

Unilock Ltd.

610-401 The West Mall
Toronto, ON M9C 5J5
Tel 416-646-5182
Fax 416-646-5181
www.unilock.com
Line: Manufactures and sells interlocking paving stones and retaining walls.
NAICS: 324121
#Emp: 100-249 (Tor)
#TorLoc: 5
Own: Private Company
Key: Edward Bryant, Pres
Scott Swierad, Exec VP & COO
Don Fasken, Cont
Brent Turner, IT Mgr
Mike McIntyre, GM, Ontario
Ray Rodenburgh, Dir of Mktg

Uni-Motion Gear

245 Edward St.
Aurora, ON L4G 3M7
Tel 905-713-0746
Fax 905-713-2614
www.magnapowertrain.com
Line: Manufactures flex plates for the automotive industry.
NAICS: 336350
#Emp: 250-499 (Tor)
#TorLoc: 1
Own: Private Company
Par: Magna Powertrain Inc. (US)
Key: Anh Dang, Cont
Kathryn Ryan, HR Mgr

Unionville Home Society

4300 Hwy. 7 East
Unionville, ON L3R 1L8
Tel 905-477-2822
Fax 905-477-6080
www.uhs.on.ca
AKA: Union Villa; Heritage Village; Heritage Centre; Wyndham Gardens
Line: Provides long-term care facility, housing and programs to seniors.
NAICS: 623310
#Emp: 100-249 (Tor)
#TorLoc: 1
Own: Not-for-profit
Key: Deborah Cooper-Berger,
  Pres & CEO
Juanita Goodhen, Dir of LTC Ops
Cecilia Ho, Dir of Fin
Marion Menezes, Privacy Officer

Unionville Letter Carrier Depot

A Div. of Canada Post
3930 14th Ave.
Markham, ON L3R 0A8
Tel 905-474-1705
Fax 905-479-6616
www.canadapost.com
Line: Provides mailing services.
NAICS: 491110
#Emp: 100-249 (Tor)
Own: Government
Key: Katie Nicholson, Mgr

Unique Restoration Ltd.

1220 Matheson Blvd. East
Mississauga, ON L4W 1R2
Tel 905-629-9100
Fax 905-629-0300
www.uniquerestoration.ca
Line: Provides restoration services.
NAICS: 231220
#Emp: 100-249 (Tor)
#TorLoc: 1
Own: Private Company
Key: John Kennedy, Pres
Steve Leblanc, Secy-Treas

Unique Store Fixtures Ltd.

554 Millway Ave.
Vaughan, ON L4K 3V5
Tel 905-738-6588
Fax 905-738-6674
www.uniquestorefixtures.com
Line: Manufactures wood, metal and glass showcases and counters.
NAICS: 337215
#Emp: 75-99 (Tor)
#TorLoc: 1
Own: Private Company
Key: Ferruccio Corrente, Pres

Unis Lumin Inc.

105-1175 North Service Rd. West
Oakville, ON L6M 2W1
Tel 905-847-6800
Fax 905-847-6584
www.unislumin.com
Line: Provides technology based business solutions.
NAICS: 541510
#Emp: 100-249 (Tor)
#TorLoc: 1
Own: Private Company
Key: John Breakey, CEO
Mauro Lollo, VP & CTO

Unisync Group Ltd.

5-1660 Tech Ave.
Mississauga, ON L4W 5S7
Tel 905-274-2681
Fax 905-361-1514
www.unisyncgroup.com
AKA: York Uniforms LTd.; Hammill; ShowroomOne
Line: Designs, sells and distributes uniforms.
NAICS: 414110
#Emp: 100-249 (Tor)
#TorLoc: 2
Own: Private Company
Key: Carmin Garafalo, Pres
Craig Chambers, Dir of HR

Unisys Canada Inc.

2001 Sheppard Ave. East
Toronto, ON M2J 4Z7
Tel 416-495-0515
Fax 416-495-4495
www.unisys.ca
Line: Provides computer sales and service, systems integration, networking services and deskside support.
NAICS: 417310 541510
#Emp: 250-499 (Tor)
#TorLoc: 3
Own: Private Company
Par: Unisys Corp. (US)
Key: Tim Feick, VP Ops & GM
Bruce Markowitz, HR Consultant
Mary Joynt, Treas

The United Church of Canada

300-3250 Bloor St. West
Toronto, ON M8X 2Y4
Tel 416-231-5931
Fax 416-231-3103
www.united-church.ca
Line: Operates religious organization.
NAICS: 813110
#Emp: 500-999 (Tor)

#TorLoc: 1
Own: Religious
Key: Mardi Tindal, Moderator
Nora Sanders, Gen Secy
William Kennedy, Exec Officer of Fin

United Driver Services Inc.

203A-170 Brockport Dr.
Toronto, ON M9W 5C8
Tel 416-675-2141
Fax 416-675-9643
www.uds.ca
Line: Provides temporary truck drivers.
NAICS: 561310
#Emp: 75-99 (Tor)
#TorLoc: 1
Own: Private Company
Key: Paul Donelle, GM
Justin Olds, Ops Mgr
Sheri Donatucci, Payroll & Admin

United Parcel Service Canada Ltd.

400-6285 Northam Dr.
Mississauga, ON L4V 1X5
Tel 905-676-6055
Fax 905-676-6035
www.ups.com/canada
AKA: UPS Supply Chain Solutions
Line: Provides package delivery and
supply chain services.
NAICS: 492110
#Emp: 1000-4999 (Tor)
#TorLoc: 4
Own: Public Company
Par: UPS Inc. (US)
Key: Mike Tierney, Pres, UPS Canada
Scott Childress, Cont

United Rentals of Canada Inc.

75 Commissioners St.
Toronto, ON M5A 1A6
Tel 416-461-9887
Fax 416-461-8224
www.ur.com
Line: Offers equipment rentals, sales
and service.
NAICS: 532310
#Emp: 75-99 (Tor)
#TorLoc: 4
Own: Public Company
Key: Mark Pigot, District Mgr

United Van Lines (Canada) Ltd.

7229 Pacific Circ.
Mississauga, ON L5T 1S9
Tel 905-564-6400
Fax 905-564-0253
www.uvl.com
Line: Provides household goods moving
services through member companies.
NAICS: 484210
#Emp: 75-99 (Tor)
Own: Private Company
Key: Anne Martin, Pres
Marc Gosselin, VP Ops
Anne Yashar, HR Specialist
Dan Lawrence, VP Fin
Brad Lawrence,
    Purch & Property Management
Angelo Fantegrossi, VP IT
Lisa Hulet, VP Mktg

United Way of Greater Toronto

26 Wellington St. East, 2nd Fl.
Toronto, ON M5E 1W9
Tel 416-777-2001
Fax 416-777-0962
www.unitedwaytoronto.com
Line: Operates an incorporated non-
profit charity focused on improving the
long-term health of the community.
NAICS: 813310
#Emp: 100-249 (Tor)
#TorLoc: 1
Own: Not-for-profit
Key: Susan McIsaac, Pres & CEO
Amy Tong, COO
Rahima Mamdani,
    Dir of HR & Organizational Dev
Michael Herrera, VP Fin
Louise Bellingham, VP Mktg

Unity Life of Canada

3-1660 Tech Ave.
Mississauga, ON L4W 5S8
Tel 905-219-8000
Fax 905-219-8102
www.unitylife.ca
Line: Operates an insurance company.
NAICS: 524111
#Emp: 100-249 (Tor)
#TorLoc: 2
Own: Private Company
Par: Foresters Company (CDA)
Key: Tony Poole, Pres & CEO
Nancy Manning, VP

Univar Canada Ltd.

64 Arrow Rd.
Toronto, ON M9M 2L9
Tel 416-740-5300
Fax 416-740-2227
www.univarcanada.com
Line: Distributes chemicals.
NAICS: 418410
#Emp: 100-249 (Tor)
#TorLoc: 3
Own: Private Company
Key: John J. Zillmer, Pres & CEO
Chris Halberg, Ontario GM
Joan Wood,
    HR Mgr, Eastern Canada Region
Wendy Howorth, Purch Mgr
Jamie Canfield, Gen Sales Mgr

Universal Drum Reconditioning Co.

2460 Royal Windsor Dr.
Mississauga, ON L5J 1K7
Tel 905-822-3280
Fax 905-822-1248
Line: Services and sells reconditioned
drums.
NAICS: 811310
#Emp: 100-249 (Tor)
#TorLoc: 2
Own: Private Company
Key: Angelo Petrucci, Pres & GM
Ed Noy, Financial Cont
Tony Petrucci, Purch Mgr

Universal Music

1-2450 Victoria Park Ave.
Toronto, ON M2J 5H3
Tel 416-718-4000
Fax 416-718-4212
www.umusic.ca
Line: Develops, manufactures, markets
and distributes recorded music.
NAICS: 512230
#Emp: 100-249 (Tor)
#TorLoc: 1
Own: Private Company
Key: Randy Lennox, Pres & CEO
Joel Pye, VP Ops
Voula Vagdatis, Dir of HR
Gordon Lee Chan, VP IT
Jeremy Summers, VP Mktg
Tyson Parker, VP Corp Commun,
    Artist & Media Relns

Universal Studios Canada Inc.

2450 Victoria Park Ave.
Toronto, ON M2J 4A2
Tel 416-491-3000
Fax 416-491-2307
www.universalpictures.ca
AKA: NBC Universal Canada
Line: Distributes motion picture films, television products, and DVDs.
NAICS: 512110 512190
#Emp: 100-249 (Tor)
#TorLoc: 1
Own: Private Company
Par: Universal Studios Inc. (US)
Key: Ron Suter, Pres
Francis Sirugo, HR Mgr

Universal Workers Union Local 183

1263 Wilson Ave.
Toronto, ON M3M 3G3
Tel 416-241-1183
Fax 416-241-9845
www.liunalocal183.ca
Line: Operates a labour union.
NAICS: 813930
#Emp: 100-249 (Tor)
#TorLoc: 1
Own: Private Company
Par: Laborers International Union of North America (US)
Key: Walter Kent, Cont

University Health Network

190 Elizabeth St.
Toronto, ON M5G 2C4
Tel 416-340-3078
Fax 416-340-3849
www.uhn.ca
Line: Operates acute care teaching hospitals.
NAICS: 622111
#Emp: 5000-9999 (Tor)
#TorLoc: 3
Own: Not-for-profit
Key: Robert S. Bell, Pres & CEO
Emma Pavlov, Sr VP HR,
    Organizational Dev & Laboratory
    Medicine Program
Justine Jackson, Sr VP Fin & CFO
Lydia Lee, VP & CIO
Gillian Howard, VP
    Pub Affairs & Commun

University of Ontario Institute of Technology

2000 Simcoe St. North
Oshawa, ON L1H 7L7
Tel 905-721-8668
Fax 905-721-3178
www.uoit.ca
AKA: UOIT
Line: Operates a post secondary educational institution.
NAICS: 611310
#Emp: 250-499 (Tor)
#TorLoc: 1
Own: Public Company
Key: Ronald Bordessa,
    Pres & Vice-Chancellor
Richard Marceau,
    Provost & VP Academic
Murray Lapp, Dir of HR
Tom Austin, VP Fin & Ops
Steve Zucker, VP IT
Donna McFarlane, VP Commun &
    Mktg

University of Toronto

27 King's College Circ.
Toronto, ON M5S 1A1
Tel 416-978-2011
www.utoronto.ca
Line: Offers post secondary education.
NAICS: 611310
#Emp: 10000+ (Tor)
#TorLoc: 3
Own: Government
Key: David Naylor, Pres
Cathy Riggall, VP Business Affairs
Angela Hildyard, VP HR & Equity
Sheila Brown, CFO
Stephen Whittaker,
    Dir of Procurement Service
Robert Steiner,
    Asst VP Strategic Commun

University of Toronto at Scarborough

1265 Military Trail
Toronto, ON M1C 1A4
Tel 416-287-8872
Fax 416-287-7013
www.utsc.utoronto.ca
NAICS: 611310
#Emp: 500-999 (Tor)
#TorLoc: 1
Own: Government
Par: Government of Ontario
Key: Franco Vaccarino, Principal
Rick Halpern, Dean & Vice-Principal
Kim McLean, CAO
Kim Richard, Dir of HR

University of Toronto Institute for Aerospace Studies

4925 Dufferin St.
Toronto, ON M3H 5T6
Tel 416-667-7700
Fax 416-667-7799
www.utias.utoronto.ca
AKA: UTIAS
Line: Operates research institute.
NAICS: 813910
#Emp: 100-249 (Tor)
#TorLoc: 1
Own: Association
Key: David W. Zingg, Professor & Dir
J. DaCosta, HR & Payroll

University of Toronto Mississauga

3359 Mississauga Rd. North
Mississauga, ON L5L 1C6
Tel 905-828-3935
Fax 905-828-5472
www.utm.utoronto.ca
AKA: Erindale College
NAICS: 611310
#Emp: 500-999 (Tor)
#TorLoc: 1
Own: Government
Key: Ian Orchard, VP & Principal
Paul Donoghue, CAO
Lynda J. Collins, Dir of HR
Christine Capewell,
    Dir of Business Services
Joe Lim, CIO
Mark Overton, Dean of Student Affairs
Andrew Stelmacovich,
    Exec Dir of Advancement

University of Toronto Press Inc.

700-10 St. Mary St.
Toronto, ON M4Y 2W8
Tel 416-978-2239
Fax 416-978-4738
www.utppublishing.com
AKA: UTP
Line: Publishes, prints, and distributes scholarly materials.
NAICS: 511130
#Emp: 100-249 (Tor)
#TorLoc: 12
Own: Not-for-profit
Par: University of Toronto Inc. (CDA)
Key: John Yates, Pres, Publisher & CEO
Kathryn Bennett, Sr VP Admin
Shawn O'Grady, VP Fin
Hamish Cameron, VP Management IS

University Plumbing & Heating Ltd.

3655 Keele St.
Toronto, ON M3J 1M8
Tel 416-630-6010
Fax 416-635-9274
AKA: Zentil Group
Line: Provides plumbing, heating, air conditioning and fire protection contracting services.
NAICS: 232520
#Emp: 100-249 (Tor)
#TorLoc: 1
Own: Private Company
Key: Mario Fattore, Pres
James Fair, Cont

University Settlement

23 Grange Rd.
Toronto, ON M5T 1C3
Tel 416-598-3444
Fax 416-598-4401
www.universitysettlement.ca
Line: Provides social, educational and recreational services for clients from different ethno-specific communities.
NAICS: 624190 813310
#Emp: 100-249 (Tor)
#TorLoc: 4
Own: Not-for-profit
Key: Debra Shime, Exec Dir
Lucy Poon, Sr Dir of Fin & Admin

U-Pak Disposals Ltd.

15 Tidemore Ave.
Toronto, ON M9W 7E9
Tel 416-747-7447
Fax 416-747-0878
www.upak.net
Line: Provides recycling and garbage disposal services.
NAICS: 562210
#Emp: 100-249 (Tor)
#TorLoc: 1
Own: Private Company
Key: Tim O'Conner Jr., GM
Don Sisti, Ops Mgr
Mary Molony, Cont

Uplands Golf & Ski Club

46 Uplands Ave.
Thornhill, ON L4J 1K2
Tel 905-889-3291
Fax 905-889-6559
www.uplandsgolfandski.com
AKA: Uplands Golf Club; Uplands Ski Centre
NAICS: 713910 713920
#Emp: 100-249 (Tor)
#TorLoc: 1
Own: Private Company
Par: Smirnov Golf Management Ltd. (CDA)
Key: Ben Smirnov, Owner & Operator
Scott Smirnov, GM
Julian Carver, CFO

Upper Canada Child Care Centres of Ontario

2-2900 John St.
Markham, ON L3R 5G3
Tel 905-946-1113
Fax 905-946-1116
www.uppercanadachildcare.com
Line: Operates a non-profit government licensed organization operating over 50 locations throughout North York, York Region and Simcoe County.
NAICS: 624410
#Emp: 500-999 (Tor)
#TorLoc: 53
Own: Private Company
Key: Josie Harlow, Exec Dir
Roger Charlesworth, GM
Marcia Kemper, HR Mgr
Jim McGowan, Dir of Fin
Shelley McTavish, Dir of Purch
Shirley Black, Asst Exec Dir of Ops
Sari Connell, Advertising Coord

Upper Canada College

200 Lonsdale Rd.
Toronto, ON M4V 1W6
Tel 416-488-1125
Fax 416-484-8611
www.ucc.on.ca
AKA: UCC
Line: Operates an independent school for boys.
NAICS: 611110
#Emp: 250-499 (Tor)
#TorLoc: 2
Own: Not-for-profit
Key: Jim Power, Principal
Donald Kawasoe,
    Head of Preparatory & Upper School
Deborah Douma, Exec Dir
    of People & Organization Dev
Patti MacNicol, CAO
Andrea Aster, Assoc Dir
    of Mktg & Commun

Upper Canada Forest Products Ltd.

7088 Financial Dr.
Mississauga, ON L5N 7H5
Tel 905-814-8000
Fax 905-814-8788
www.ucfp.com
Line: Distributes specialty forest products.
NAICS: 416320
#Emp: 75-99 (Tor)
#TorLoc: 1
Own: Private Company
Par: USC (CDA)
Key: Mark Mah, VP
Mark Warne, Division Mgr

Upper Crust Ltd.

55 Canarctic Dr.
Toronto, ON M3J 2N7
Tel 416-661-7744
Fax 416-661-3574
www.uppercrustltd.com
Line: Manufactures frozen dough and bread products.
NAICS: 311814
#Emp: 100-249 (Tor)
#TorLoc: 1
Own: Private Company
Key: David Gelbloom, Pres
Mahendra Bungaroo, VP Fin

UPS Supply Chain Solutions Canada

4156 Mainway
Burlington, ON L7L 0A7
Tel 905-315-5500
Fax 905 315-8919
www.ups-scs.ca
Line: Consults in materials management, cost control and provides customized logistics solutions to health care, high tech, consumer products, and financial sectors.
NAICS: 541619 493110
#Emp: 1000-4999 (Tor)
#TorLoc: 13
Own: Private Company
Par: UPS Supply Chain Solutions (US)
Key: Brad Mitchell, Mng Dir

Urbacon Ltd.

750 Lakeshore Blvd. East
Toronto, ON M4M 3M3
Tel 416-865-9405
Fax 416-865-9429
www.urbacon.net
Line: Operates a full service
construction management, project
management and general contracting
firm with expertise in commercial
interiors, renovations, structural
modifications, new building
construction and custom homes.
NAICS: 231410
#Emp: 100-249 (Tor)
#TorLoc: 1
Own: Private Company
Key: Marco Mancini, Pres & CEO
Antonio Mancini, Partner
Nicole Fairman,
    Admin & Personnel Mgr
David Bailey, Cont
Nancy Gee, Dir of Corp Dev

Urban Edge Shading Inc.

155 Shields Crt.
Markham, ON L3R 9T5
Tel 905-470-6901
Fax 905-470-6906
www.urbanedgeshading.com
Line: Manufactures and supplies
manual and motorized window
treatment systems.
NAICS: 337920
#Emp: 75-99 (Tor)
#TorLoc: 1
Own: Private Company
Key: Hans Munger, Pres & GM
Reynaldo Cayetano, HR & Fin Mgr

Urban Electrical Contractors

790 Creditstone Rd.
Concord, ON L4K 4P4
Tel 905-669-0280
Fax 905-669-0836
www.urbanelectrical.ca
Line: Provides electrical contracting
services.
NAICS: 232510
#Emp: 75-99 (Tor)
#TorLoc: 1
Own: Private Company
Key: Phil Bartuccio, Pres

Urban Mechanical Contracting Ltd.

254 Attwell Dr.
Toronto, ON M9W 5B2
Tel 416-240-8830
Fax 416-240-8846
NAICS: 232520
#Emp: 100-249 (Tor)
Own: Private Company
Key: Edward Winter, Pres & CEO
Andrew Basso, VP
Alan Lipszye, VP Fin

URS Canada Inc.

75 Commerce Valley Dr. East
Markham, ON L3T 7N9
Tel 905-882-4401
Fax 905-882-4399
www.urscorp.com
Line: Provides a comprehensive range
of professional planning, design,
systems engineering and technical
assistance, program and construction
management, and operations and
maintenance services.
NAICS: 541330 541310
#Emp: 100-249 (Tor)
#TorLoc: 1
Own: Private Company
Par: URS Corp. (US)
Key: Murray D. Thompson, VP
Paul Hudspith, VP
Judy Miller, HR Mgr
Bob Eddington, Reg Cont
Susan Sherman, VP

USC Education Savings Plans Inc.

1000-50 Burnhamthorpe Rd. West
Mississauga, ON L5B 4A5
Tel 905-270-8777
Fax 800-668-5007
www.usc.ca
Line: Administers, distributes and sells
education savings plans.
NAICS: 523990
#Emp: 100-249 (Tor)
#TorLoc: 1
Own: Private Company
Par: International Scholarship
Foundation (CDA)
Key: R. George Hopkinson, Pres & CEO
Patricia Ballantyne,
    VP Customer Experience
Sarah Toth, HR Generalist
Steve Rotz, CFO

UTI Canada

8590 Airport Rd.
Brampton, ON L6T 5A3
Tel 905-789-6211
Fax 905-789-6621
www.go2uti.com
Line: Provides integrated logistics
services.
NAICS: 541510 541619
#Emp: 250-499 (Tor)
#TorLoc: 4
Own: Public Company
Key: Greg Stamkos, Sr VP
Tisha Bruno, VP HR & Admin
Carlo Lepore, VP Client Solutions

UTi Canada Inc.

6956 Columbus Rd.
Mississauga, ON L5T 2G1
Tel 289-562-3000
Fax 289-562-5650
www.go2uti.com
Line: Operates a logistics company.
NAICS: 488519
#Emp: 75-99 (Tor)
#TorLoc: 1
Own: Public Company
Key: Chris Penley, Pres
Judy Carvajal, CFO

Util Capital Tool & Design

270 Spinnaker Way
Concord, ON L4K 4W1
Tel 905-760-8088
Fax 905-660-5142
www.ctdonline.com
AKA: All-Metal Brake Shoe Co.
Line: Manufactures new unlined drum
brake shoes and disc brakes.
NAICS: 336340
#Emp: 250-499 (Tor)
#TorLoc: 1
Own: Private Company
Par: Util Industries (ITALY)
Key: Francesco Rangoni, Chair & CEO
Kevin Bull, Dir of Ops
Jack Van Den Boogaart,
    VP Sales & Mktg

Vac-Aero International Inc.

1371 Speers Rd.
Oakville, ON L6L 2X5
Tel 905-827-4171
Fax 905-827-7489
www.vacaero.com
Line: Manufactures heat treating
furnaces and provides heat treating
services.
NAICS: 336410
#Emp: 75-99 (Tor)

#TorLoc: 2
Own: Private Company
Key: Scott Rush, Pres
Greg Salai, VP Fin
Jean Herrington, Purch Mgr

Valeant Pharmaceuticals

7150 Mississauga Rd.
Mississauga, ON L5N 8M5
Tel 905-286-3000
Fax 905-286-3150
www.valeant.com
Line: Engages in the formulation,
clinical testing, registration,
manufacture, sale and promotion of
pharmaceutical products.
NAICS: 325410
#Emp: 250-499 (Tor)
#TorLoc: 3
Own: Public Company
Key: Rajiv De Silva, Pres & COO
J. Michael Pearson, Chmn & CEO
Philip W. Loberg, Exec VP & CFO

Vale Inco Limited

1600-200 Bay St.
Royal Bank Plaza, South Tower
Toronto, ON M5J 2K2
Tel 416-361-7511
Fax 416-361-7781
www.valeinco.com
Line: Operates a mining and metals
company.
NAICS: 212233 212299
#Emp: 250-499 (Tor)
#TorLoc: 2
Own: Private Company
Par: CVRD (BRZ)
Key: Tito Martins, Pres & CEO
Jennifer Hopper, Exec VP HR
Jennifer Maki, Exec VP & CFO
Roberto Moretzsohn, Exec VP Mktg
Mark Travers, Exec VP Corp Affairs

Valle Foam Industries (1995) Inc.

4 West Dr.
Brampton, ON L6T 2H7
Tel 905-453-8054
Fax 905-453-6348
www.vallefoam.com
Line: Manufactures flexible foam
carpet underlay and other fine comfort
products for furniture and bedding
including a new bio-foam product.
NAICS: 326150
#Emp: 250-499 (Tor)
#TorLoc: 5
Own: Private Company
Par: Domfoam International (CDA)
Key: Tony Vallecoccia, Pres & GM
Dale McNeill, VP Ops

Valspar Inc.

7655 Tranmere Dr.
Mississauga, ON L5S 1L4
Tel 905-671-8333
Fax 905-671-0254
www.valsparglobal.com
AKA: Plastikote
Line: Manufactures paints and related
products.
NAICS: 325510
#Emp: 100-249 (Tor)
#TorLoc: 1
Own: Private Company
Par: Valspar Corp. (US)
Key: Matt Carlson, Dist Mgr
William L. Mansfield, Chmn & CEO

Van Der Graaf Inc.

2 Van der Graaf Crt.
Brampton, ON L6T 5R6
Tel 905-793-8100
Fax 905-793-8129
www.vandergraaf.com
Line: Manufactures power transmission
equipment for the conveyor belt
industry.
NAICS: 333619
#Emp: 100-249 (Tor)
#TorLoc: 1
Own: Private Company
Key: Alexander Kanaris, Pres

Vandermeer Nursery Ltd.

588 Lakeridge Rd. South
Ajax, ON L1Z 1X3
Tel 905-427-2525
Fax 905-427-2955
www.vandermeernursery.com
Line: Operates a garden and nursery
centre.
NAICS: 444220
#Emp: 100-249 (Tor)
#TorLoc: 1
Own: Private Company
Key: John Vandermeer, Pres
Pradeep Suriar, GM
MaryAnn Vandermeer, Acctng
Jane Vandermeer, Purch

Van Houtte Coffee Services

1870 Courtney Park Dr. East
Mississauga, ON L5T 1W1
Tel 905-298-0101
Fax 905-298-2202
www.vanhoutte.com
AKA: Red Carpet Food Systems Inc.
Line: Manufactures coffee equipment
and provides coffee services to offices.
NAICS: 417920 413190

#Emp: 75-99 (Tor)
#TorLoc: 1
Own: Public Company
Par: Van Houtte Inc. (CDA)
Key: Tim Weichel, VP Central Region
Jason Sweet, Dir of Ops
Ian Emery, Sales Mgr

Van Rob Inc.

200 Vandorf Sideroad
Aurora, ON L4G 0A2
Tel 905-727-8585
Fax 905-727-2689
www.van-rob.com
NAICS: 336370 336390
#Emp: 500-999 (Tor)
#TorLoc: 4
Own: Private Company
Key: Peter van Schaik, CEO
Dorian Munk, VP Ops
Paul Dilworth, VP HR
Matthew Posno, VP Fin
Stuart Greidanus, VP Sales

Variety Children's Charity

3701 Danforth Ave.
Toronto, ON M1N 2G2
Tel 416-699-7167
Fax 416-367-0028
www.varietyontario.ca
AKA: Variety Village
NAICS: 713990
#Emp: 100-249 (Tor)
#TorLoc: 1
Own: Private Company
Key: John Willson, Pres & CEO
Susan Sanderson, Dir of HR
Carolyn Smith-Green, CFO
Stephanie Widenoja,
    Mgr of IT & Telecommunications
Lynda Elmy, Dir of Commun

Vaughan Fire and Rescue Service

A Div. of The City of Vaughan
2800 Rutherford Rd.
Vaughan, ON L4K 2N9
Tel 905-832-8506
Fax 905-832-8593
www.vaughan.ca
NAICS: 913140
#Emp: 100-249 (Tor)
#TorLoc: 1
Own: Government
Key: Gregory Senay, Fire Chief
Larry Bentley, Deputy Fire Chief, Ops

Vaughan Paving Ltd.

220 Basaltic Rd.
Concord, ON L4K 1G6
Tel 905-669-9579
Fax 905-669-3931
AKA: Maple Crete Inc.; Direct
Underground
Line: Operates a road construction
company.
NAICS: 231310
#Emp: 75-99 (Tor)
#TorLoc: 1
Own: Private Company
Key: Lorenzo Antonini, Pres
Angie Didomizio,
    Payroll & Personnel Mgr

Vaughan Public Libraries

A Div. of The City of Vaughan
900 Clark Ave. West
Thornhill, ON L4J 8C1
Tel 905-653-7323
Fax 905-709-1330
www.vaughanpl.info
NAICS: 514121
#Emp: 100-249 (Tor)
#TorLoc: 7
Own: Private Company
Key: Margie Singleton, CEO
Marilyn Guy, Dir of Ops
Sandy Vander Werff,
    Dir of Fin & Facilities
Terri Watman, Dir of Service Delivery
Aleksandra Dowiat Vine,
    Dir of Planning & Commun

Vegfresh Inc.

1290 Ormont Dr.
Toronto, ON M9L 2V4
Tel 416-667-0518
Fax 416-667-0523
www.vegfreshinc.com
AKA: NuWay Potato; Pro Pac Foods
Line: Produces fruits and vegetables.
NAICS: 311420
#Emp: 100-249 (Tor)
#TorLoc: 1
Own: Private Company
Key: Mike Sangiorgio, Pres
Predrag Ostojic, GM
Nelson Ardon, Cont
Joe Montalbano, Sales & Mktg Mgr

Velcro Canada Inc.

114 East Dr.
Brampton, ON L6T 1C1
Tel 905-791-1630
Fax 905-791-5329
www.velcro.ca
Line: Produces and markets Velcro
brand fastening system.
NAICS: 313220
#Emp: 100-249 (Tor)
#TorLoc: 1
Own: Private Company
Par: Velcro Industries NV (US)
Key: Peter Buchanan, Plant Mgr
Heather Kelly, HR Mgr
Garth Jones, Cont

Venture Steel

60 Disco Rd.
Toronto, ON M9W 1L8
Tel 416-798-9396
Fax 416-798-9832
www.venturesteel.com
Line: Operates a steel service centre
with custom coil slitting.
NAICS: 331221
#Emp: 100-249 (Tor)
#TorLoc: 2
Own: Public Company
Par: Royal Laser Corp. (CDA)
Key: Beric Sykes, Pres
Sabrina Delfino, HR Mgr
Diana Spina, Purch Mgr
Tom McCracken, VP Sales & Purch
Rob DeBoer, Dir of Sales

Verdi Alliance

91 Parr Blvd.
Bolton, ON L7E 4E3
Tel 416-749-5030
Fax 416-744-5030
www.verdialliance.com
Line: Operates a construction company
specializing in concrete forming.
NAICS: 232210 231220
#Emp: 250-499 (Tor)
#TorLoc: 1
Own: Private Company
Key: Danny Verrilli, Partner
Anna Sassi, Payroll
Lynn Coke, Cont

Veri-Cheque Ltd.

500-8500 Leslie St.
Thornhill, ON L3T 7M8
Tel 905-709-0927
Fax 905-709-0952
www.vericheque.com
Line: Provides financial management
services.

NAICS: 522329
#Emp: 75-99 (Tor)
#TorLoc: 1
Own: Private Company
Key: Ronald Renwick, Pres

Veridian Corp.

55 Taunton Rd. East
Ajax, ON L1T 3V3
Tel 905-427-9870
Fax 905-619-0210
www.veridian.on.ca
AKA: Veridian Connections; Veridian
Energy
Line: Distributes electric power and
provides services including billing for
utility clients, central water heaters
and fibre optic communicators.
NAICS: 221122
#Emp: 100-249 (Tor)
#TorLoc: 5
Own: Government
Key: Michael Angemeer, Pres & CEO

Verizon Business

60 Adelaide St. East
Toronto, ON M5C 3E4
Tel 416-368-6621
Fax 416-368-1350
www.verizonbusiness.com
Line: Provides Internet services.
NAICS: 514191
#Emp: 100-249 (Tor)
#TorLoc: 1
Own: Public Company
Par: Verizon Communications Inc. (US)
Key: Douglas Churchill, VP Gen Sales
Catherine Laframboise, VP HR
Margaret Jodha, Cont

Vermont Square Nursing Home

914 Bathurst St.
Toronto, ON M5R 3G5
Tel 416-533-9473
Fax 416-538-2685
www.vermontsquare.ca
Line: Operates long-term care facility.
NAICS: 623110
#Emp: 100-249 (Tor)
#TorLoc: 1
Own: Private Company
Key: Christine Marajh, Admr
Laura Morgan, Admin Nursing Asst
Thelma Owens, Bookkeeper

Versacold Group - Walker Facility

107 Walker Dr.
Brampton, ON L6T 5K5
Tel 905-793-2653
Fax 905-793-4918
www.versacold.com
Line: Distributes fresh and frozen food products.
NAICS: 413190
#Emp: 100-249 (Tor)
Own: Public Company
Key: Robert Bascom,
VP Ops, Eastern Region
Donald Williams, Ops Mgr
Beverley Dunn, HR Admr

Versacold - Vaughan Facility

316 Aviva Park Dr.
Woodbridge, ON L4L 9C7
Tel 905-850-9334
Fax 905-850-6224
www.atlascold.com
Line: Operates refrigerated warehousing facilities.
NAICS: 493120
#Emp: 500-999 (Tor)
Own: Public Company
Par: Avion Group (ICE)
Key: Robert Bascom,
VP Ops, Eastern Canada
Henry Van Oudenaren, GM
Jason Dillman, HR Mgr
Brian Ware, Business Dev Mgr

Versa Fittings & Manufacturing Inc.

290 Courtneypark Dr. East
Mississauga, ON L5T 2S5
Tel 905-564-2600
Fax 905-564-2619
www.versafittings.com
Line: Manufactures and wholesales custom screw machine products as well as plumbing and heating connections.
NAICS: 332999 416120
#Emp: 75-99 (Tor)
#TorLoc: 1
Own: Private Company
Key: Kelly Burton, Pres & CEO

Versent Corporation ULC

3269 American Dr.
Mississauga, ON L4V 1V4
Tel 905-678-7272
Fax 905-678-9898
www.versent.com
AKA: Laser Quest; Threshold Financial Technologies Inc.
Line: Owns and operates Laser Quest and provides outsourced ABM and post transaction switching and turnkey ABM solutions to financial institutions and corporate retailers.
NAICS: 522329 713990
#Emp: 100-249 (Tor)
#TorLoc: 5
Own: Private Company
Key: Matthew McIver,
Pres, Threshold Financial Technologies Inc.
F. Gregory Thompson, Pres & CEO
David James, Pres, Laser Quest
Theresa Stairs, Dir of HR
Clinton Wolff, VP Fin
Tracy Boyd, VP Mktg

Veterinary Emergency Clinic and Referral Centre

117-920 Yonge St.
Toronto, ON M4W 3C7
Tel 416-920-2002
Fax 416-920-6185
www.vectoronto.com
Line: Operates veterinary clinic.
NAICS: 541940
#Emp: 75-99 (Tor)
#TorLoc: 2
Own: Private Company
Key: Heather Dales, Office Mgr

Via Rail Canada Inc.

C-50 Drummond St.
Toronto, ON M8V 4B5
Tel 416-253-2473
Fax 416-253-2401
www.viarail.ca
Line: Provides inter-city passenger rail service.
NAICS: 482114
#Emp: 500-999 (Tor)
#TorLoc: 5
Own: Federal Crown Corp.
Par: Government of Canada
Key: Marc Laliberte,
Pres & CEO, Montreal
Bernard A. LeBlanc, Dir of Ops, Central
Catherine Kaloutsky,
Sr Officer, Pub Affairs

Vibro Acoustics

727 Tapscott Rd.
Toronto, ON M1X 1A2
Tel 416-291-7371
Fax 416-291-8049
www.vibro-acoustics.com
AKA: BVA Systems Ltd.; D.W. Murray & Associates Ltd.
Line: Manufactures noise control equipment for mechanical systems.
NAICS: 335315 334512
#Emp: 100-249 (Tor)
#TorLoc: 1
Own: Private Company
Key: Brian Guenther, Pres

Viceroy Rubber & Plastics Ltd.

707 Arrow Rd.
Toronto, ON M9M 2L4
Tel 416-762-1111
Fax 416-762-0889
www.viceroyrubber.com
AKA: Viceroy Reliable Group; Allied Viceroy Group
Line: Manufactures moulded rubber and plastic products.
NAICS: 326290 326198
#Emp: 75-99 (Tor)
#TorLoc: 1
Own: Private Company
Par: Allied Group of Companies (CDA)
Key: Ronald Bruhm, Pres
Todd Bruhm, GM
Renate Messer, Payroll & HR Mgr

Victaulic Custom Casting Company

123 Newkirk Rd.
Richmond Hill, ON L4C 3G5
Tel 905-884-9091
Fax 905-884-2669
www.victauliccastings.com
Line: Manufactures non-ferrous sand castings including brass, bronze, copper, and aluminum.
NAICS: 331523
#Emp: 250-499 (Tor)
#TorLoc: 2
Own: Private Company
Par: Victaulic Company of America Inc. (US)
Key: Tim Meadows, VP & GM
Julia Buceiarelli, HR Mgr
Rosalyn Hobden,
Payroll & Benefits Admr

Victoria University

73 Queen's Park Cres.
Toronto, ON M5S 1K7
Tel 416-585-4521
Fax 416-585-4580
www.vicu.utoronto.ca
Line: Provides educational services.
NAICS: 611310
#Emp: 250-499 (Tor)
Own: Government
Key: Paul Gooch, Pres
Ray DeSouza, Bursar & CAO
Helen Zias, HR Mgr
Anthony Lennie, Dir of Fin

VICWEST

1296 South Service Rd. West
Oakville, ON L6L 5T7
Tel 905-825-2252
Fax 905-825-2272
www.vicwest.com
Line: Manufactures and distributes steel roofing and cladding products for the Canadian industrial, commercial, recreational, and agricultural markets.
NAICS: 416210
#Emp: 75-99 (Tor)
#TorLoc: 1
Own: Public Company
Key: Colin Osbourne, Pres & CEO
Emile Mabro, VP & GM,
   Vicwest Business Unit
Gwen Hughes, VP HR
John Slattery, Exec VP Fin & CFO
Tim Armstrong, VP IT
Greg Zimmer, GM, Central Region
Scott Ringler, Nat'l Mktg Dir
Darren Occleston, Dir of Procurement

Vienna Meat Products Ltd.

170 Nugget Ave.
Toronto, ON M1S 3A7
Tel 416-297-1062
Fax 416-297-0836
www.sofinafoods.com
Line: Manufactures prepared meat products.
NAICS: 311614
#Emp: 100-249 (Tor)
#TorLoc: 1
Own: Private Company
Par: Sofina Foods (CDA)
Key: Michael Latifi, Pres & Owner

Villa Colombo Homes for the Aged Inc.

40 Playfair Ave.
Toronto, ON M6B 2P9
Tel 416-789-2113
Fax 416-789-5986
www.villacharities.com
AKA: Villa Colombo Services for Seniors
Line: Operates long-term care facility.
NAICS: 623310
#Emp: 500-999 (Tor)
#TorLoc: 1
Own: Not-for-profit
Par: Villa Charities Inc. (CDA)
Key: Fernando A. Scopa, CEO
Stephanie Polsinelli, Commun Coord

Villa Forum

175 Forum Dr.
Mississauga, ON L4Z 4E5
Tel 905-501-1443
Fax 905-501-0094
www.micbaforumitalia.com
Line: Operates a long term care facility.
NAICS: 623110
#Emp: 100-249 (Tor)
#TorLoc: 1
Own: Not-for-profit
Par: Chartwell Seniors Housing REIT (CDA)
Key: Celia Lisi,
Dir of Care & Acting Admr

Village Manor (TO) Ltd.

14 Madison Ave.
Toronto, ON M5R 2S1
Tel 416-927-1722
Fax 416-963-4325
www.madisonavenuepub.com
AKA: Madison Avenue Pub; Paupers Pub; Madison Manor Boutique Hotel; Casa Isabel Resort
NAICS: 722110
#Emp: 100-249 (Tor)
#TorLoc: 2
Own: Private Company
Key: Isabel Manore, Pres
David Manore, CEO
Chris Haslett, Dir of Opperations

Village Masonry Construction Inc.

270 Toryork Dr.
Toronto, ON M9L 1Y1
Tel 416-231-7291
Fax 416-231-6504
Line: Provides masonry contracting.
NAICS: 232310
#Emp: 75-99 (Tor)
#TorLoc: 1
Own: Private Company
Key: Tiberio Mascarin, Pres
Emilio Manarin, Site Supt
Laura Benti, Cont

The Village of Erin Meadows

2930 Erin Centre Blvd.
Mississauga, ON L5M 7M4
Tel 905-569-7155
Fax 905-569-8617
www.oakwoodretirement.com
Line: Operates a long term care home for seniors.
NAICS: 623310
#Emp: 75-99 (Tor)

#TorLoc: 1
Own: Private Company
Par: Oakwood Retirement Residences (CDA)
Key: Denis Zafirovski, Dir of Care

The Village of Taunton Mills

3800 Brock St. North
Whitby, ON L1R 3A5
Tel 905-666-3156
Fax 905-666-9601
www.oakwoodretirement.com
Line: Operates a general long term care facility.
NAICS: 624120
#Emp: 100-249 (Tor)
#TorLoc: 1
Own: Private Company
Key: Rose Lamb, GM

Vinci Parking Services

700-69 Yonge St.
Toronto, ON M5E 1K3
Tel 416-506-1000
Fax 416-506-1488
www.vincipark.ca
NAICS: 812930
#Emp: 100-249 (Tor)
#TorLoc: 2
Own: Private Company
Key: Adamo Donatucci, GM
Corey Greenberg, VP Mktg

Vincor Canada

441 Courtneypark Dr. East
Mississauga, ON L5T 2V3
Tel 905-564-6900
Fax 905-564-6909
www.vincorinternational.com
Line: Produces and markets wine, wine kits, ciders and coolers.
NAICS: 312130
#Emp: 1000-4999 (Tor)
#TorLoc: 1
Own: Private Company
Par: Constellation Brands Inc. (US)
Key: Eric Morham, Pres & CEO
Martin Vander Merwe, Sr VP Ops
Melina Param, Sr VP HR
Don Dychuck, CFO

Vinnie Zucchini's Corp.

9100 Jane St., Bldg. G
Vaughan, ON L4K 0A4
Tel 905-761-1361
Fax 416-686-0010
www.vinniezucchini.com
Line: Operates a restaurant.
NAICS: 722110
#Emp: 75-99 (Tor)
#TorLoc: 1
Own: Private Company
Key: Michael Gitto, GM

Vintage Flooring

409 Evans Ave.
Toronto, ON M8Z 1K8
Tel 416-252-4182
Fax 416-252-3487
www.vintageflooring.com
Line: Manufactures hardwood flooring.
NAICS: 321919
#Emp: 75-99 (Tor)
#TorLoc: 1
Own: Public Company
Par: Tembec Industries Inc. (CDA)
Key: Kenton Martin, GM

Vinyl Window Designs Ltd.

300 Chrislea Rd.
Vaughan, ON L4L 8A8
Tel 905-850-3222
Fax 905-850-9940
www.vinylwindowdesigns.com
AKA: Performance Windows & Doors
Inc.; Majestic Windows; Aluminum
Window Designs Ltd.; Performance
Shutters Inc.; The Vinyl Company
Line: Cuts glass and profiles to make
various sizes of vinyl windows.
NAICS: 326198 326130
#Emp: 100-249 (Tor)
#TorLoc: 1
Own: Private Company
Key: Philip Spatafora, Pres
Lino D'Uva, VP
Diane Biggs, HR Mgr
Lorenzo Raponi, Cont
Tony Camileri, Materials Mgr
Phil Lewin, VP Mktg

Vipond Inc.

6380 Vipond Dr.
Mississauga, ON L5T 1A1
Tel 905-564-7060
Fax 905-564-7070
www.vipond.ca
Line: Installs fire protection and
suppression systems.
NAICS: 232530 334512
#Emp: 100-249 (Tor)

#TorLoc: 1
Own: Private Company
Par: API Group (US)
Key: Bernie Beliveau, VP Ops
Grant Neal, VP Admin
Paul Donnelly, Cont
Jackie Ruiters, Purch Mgr

VISA Canada Corporation

3710-40 King St. West
Toronto, ON M5H 3Y2
Tel 416-367-8472
Fax 416-860-8891
www.visa.ca
Line: Provides marketing and
payment system services to financial
institutions.
NAICS: 522210
#Emp: 75-99 (Tor)
#TorLoc: 1
Own: Private Company
Par: Visa Inc. (US)
Key: Tim Wilson, Head of Visa Canada
Fanda Chiang, HR Mgr
Brenda Woods, Head of Mktg

Vision 2000 Travel Group Inc.

201-1200 Sheppard Ave. East
Toronto, ON M2K 2S5
Tel 416-487-5385
Fax 416-225-7334
www.vision2000.ca
AKA: Luxurycruise.com; Conference
World Tours; Skyventure Travel;
Holidayoutlet.ca
Line: Provides a full range of business,
vacation, meeting and incentive travel
services.
NAICS: 561510
#Emp: 100-249 (Tor)
#TorLoc: 3
Own: Private Company
Key: Brian Robertson, Pres & COO
Arend Roos, CEO
Darlene Roos, VP Fin & Admin
Ian Race, VP Sales & Client Services

Visioneering Corp.

35 Oak St.
Toronto, ON M9N 1A1
Tel 416-245-7991
Fax 416-245-4778
www.viscor.com
NAICS: 335120
#Emp: 100-249 (Tor)
#TorLoc: 1
Own: Private Company
Key: Bill Wiener, Pres
Emily Abrenica, Office Mgr
Steven Gosal, Cont
Doug Wilson, Nat'l Sales Mgr

Vistek Ltd.

496 Queen St. East
Toronto, ON M5A 4G8
Tel 416-365-1777
Fax 416-365-7776
www.vistek.ca
Line: Provides imaging equipment.
NAICS: 414430
#Emp: 100-249 (Tor)
#TorLoc: 2
Own: Private Company
Key: Ronald Silverstein, Pres
Kevin Parker, VP
Sandy MacDonald, HR Mgr

Vita Community Living Services of Toronto Inc.

4301 Weston Rd.
Toronto, ON M9L 2Y3
Tel 416-749-6234
Fax 416-749-1456
www.vitacls.org
AKA: Villa Charities Inc.
Line: Provides life skill and vocational
training, supported employment
recreational programs, and
residential programs for persons with
developmental and other co-existing
disabilities.
NAICS: 624120 624310
#Emp: 250-499 (Tor)
#TorLoc: 22
Own: Not-for-profit
Par: Villa Charities Inc. (CDA)
Key: Manuela Dalla-Nora, Exec Dir
Dunia Monaghan,
    Dir of Support Services
Silvana Rosa, HR Dir
Donna Escott, Program Dir

VitaFoam Products Canada Ltd.

150 Toro Rd.
Toronto, ON M3J 2A9
Tel 416-630-6633
Fax 416-630-9921
www.vitafoam.ca
NAICS: 326150
#Emp: 100-249 (Tor)
#TorLoc: 1
Own: Private Company
Key: Peter Farah, Pres & COO
Kevin Day, Cont
Mollify Selva, Purch

VitalAire Canada Inc.

6-6990 Creditview Rd.
Mississauga, ON L5N 8R9
Tel 905-855-0440
Fax 905-855-0742
www.vitalaire.ca
AKA: GH Medical
Line: Provides respiratory home care
services and sells respiratory clinical
products, medical gases and medical
gas systems.
NAICS: 621610 446199
#Emp: 100-249 (Tor)
#TorLoc: 2
Own: Private Company
Par: Air Liquide (FRA)
Key: Franck Virey, Pres & CEO
Matthieu Giard, VP Industrial Ops
Joan Whitman, Dir of HR
Carlos Gallardo, VP Fin
Nick Dimovski, Dir of Supply Chain
Dan Blumenthal, Dir of IT
John Hunter, VP Homecare
   Mktg Sales & Business Dev

Vitran Corporation Inc.

701-185 The West Mall
Toronto, ON M9C 5L5
Tel 416-596-7664
Fax 416-596-8039
www.vitran.com
Line: Provides transportation and
logistics services.
NAICS: 484110 484121
#Emp: 250-499 (Tor)
#TorLoc: 6
Own: Public Company
Key: Rick E. Gaetz, Pres & CEO
Sean Washchuk, VP Fin & CFO

Vitran Express Canada

1201 Creditstone Rd.
Concord, ON L4K 0C2
Tel 416-798-4965
Fax 416-798-4753
www.vitran.com
AKA: Vitran Express; Vitran
Distribution
Line: Provides freight forwarding
services.
NAICS: 488519
#Emp: 250-499 (Tor)
#TorLoc: 1
Own: Private Company
Par: Vitran Corporation Inc. (CDA)
Key: Tony Trichilo, Pres
Raymond Vigneault, VP Eastern Region
Heidi Saccucci, HR Mgr
Kelvin Kwan, VP Fin
Nelson Lau, MIS Mgr

Viva Magnetics (Canada) Ltd.

1663 Neilson Rd.
Toronto, ON M1X 1T1
Tel 416-321-0622
Fax 416-321-6030
www.viva.com.hk
NAICS: 333310
#Emp: 500-999 (Tor)
#TorLoc: 2
Own: Private Company
Key: May Chan, CEO
Willy Thian, Dir of Manuf
Loletta Chu, HR Sr Mgr
Carlos Chan, CFO
Darryl Laing, Dir of Mktg

Voith Hydro Inc.

2185 North Sheridan Way
Mississauga, ON L5K 1A4
Tel 905-855-0242
Fax 905-855-0249
www.voithhydro.com
Line: Manufactures hydroelectric
generators and motor coils.
NAICS: 335312
#Emp: 100-249 (Tor)
#TorLoc: 1
Own: Private Company
Par: Voith AG (GER)
Key: Bill Malus, Dir of Ops

Volkswagen Group Canada

777 Bayly St. West
Ajax, ON L1S 7G7
Tel 905-428-6700
Fax 905-428-5898
www.vw.ca
NAICS: 415190 415290
#Emp: 100-249 (Tor)
#TorLoc: 1
Own: Private Company
Par: Volkswagen AG (GER)
Key: John White, Pres & CEO,
   Exec VP Ops
Shelley Burden, HR Consultant

Volt Human Resources

100-10 Kelfield St.
Toronto, ON M9W 5A2
Tel 416-306-3390
Fax 416-306-1449
www.volt.com
AKA: VHRI
Line: Operates an employment agency.
NAICS: 541612
#Emp: 75-99 (Tor)
#TorLoc: 1
Own: Private Company
Key: Ed Coleman, VP

VON Toronto York Branch

301-2150 Islington Ave.
Toronto, ON M9P 3V4
Tel 866-817-8589
Fax 647-788-3176
www.von.ca
AKA: Victorian Order of Nurses
Line: Operates a not-for-profit
charitable organization dedicated
to the provision of health and social
related services.
NAICS: 621610 621390
#Emp: 100-249 (Tor)
#TorLoc: 1
Own: Not-for-profit
Par: VON Canada (CDA)
Key: Anne Zielinski, Exec Dir
Judith Shamian, Pres & CEO
John Gallinger, COO
Richard McConnell,
   VP People & Organization
Sandy Finnigan, VP Fin

Voortman Cookies Ltd.

4475 North Service Rd.
Burlington, ON L7R 4L4
Tel 905-335-9500
Fax 905-332-5499
www.voortman.com
Line: Manufactures, sells, and
transports baked goods.
NAICS: 311821
#Emp: 250-499 (Tor)
#TorLoc: 1
Own: Private Company
Key: Garry Postma, Pres
Harry Voortman, Chmn & CEO

Voxdata Call Centre Inc.

706-4141 Yonge St.
Toronto, ON M2P 1N6
Tel 416-224-8482
Fax 416-226-1530
www.voxdata.com
Line: Operates a call centre.
NAICS: 561420
#Emp: 250-499 (Tor)
Own: Private Company
Key: Nadia DeSantis, Dir of Customer
Contact Centre

VSI Inc.

31-18 Regan Rd.
Brampton, ON L7A 1C2
Tel 905-840-4085
Fax 905-840-3371
www.vistasecurity.com
AKA: Vista Security & Investigations
NAICS: 561611
#Emp: 100-249 (Tor)
#TorLoc: 1
Own: Private Company
Key: Domenic Todaro, Pres
Rob McKnight, Mng Partner
Janice McKnight, Office Mgr
Len Todaro, Sales Mgr

VWR International, Ltd.

2360 Argentia Rd.
Mississauga, ON L5N 5Z7
Tel 905-813-7377
Fax 905-821-3460
www.vwrcanlab.com
Line: Wholesales laboratory equipment
and supplies.
NAICS: 417930
#Emp: 100-249 (Tor)
#TorLoc: 1
Own: Private Company
Par: VWR International Inc. (US)
Key: Steve Harsh, VP & GM
Greg Blakely, Dir of Ops & Fin

Wainbee Ltd.

5789 Coopers Ave.
Mississauga, ON L4Z 3S6
Tel 905-568-1700
Fax 905-568-0083
www.wainbee.com
Line: Distributes industrial equipment
including pneumatics, hydraulics
and motion control and production
equipment.
NAICS: 417230
#Emp: 75-99 (Tor)
#TorLoc: 1
Own: Private Company
Par: Wainbee Holdings Inc. (CDA)
Key: Ronald Rodger, Pres

Wajax Income Fund

3280 Wharton Way
Mississauga, ON L4X 2C5
Tel 905-212-3300
Fax 905-624-6020
www.wajax.com
Line: Sells, and provides after-sales
parts and service support, for mobile
equipment, industrial components and
diesel engines.
NAICS: 417990 417210
#Emp: 250-499 (Tor)
#TorLoc: 7
Own: Public Company
Par: Wajax Income Fund (CDA)
Key: Neil D. Manning, Pres & CEO
John Hamilton, Sr VP Fin & CFO

Walker Information Canada

300-1 Eglinton Ave. East
Toronto, ON M4P 3A1
Tel 416-391-1844
Fax 416-391-3290
www.walkerinfo.ca
Line: Conducts stakeholder research
and measurement in customer
satisfaction and loyalty, employee
commitment, corporate reputation and
business ethics.
NAICS: 541910
#Emp: 100-249 (Tor)
#TorLoc: 1
Own: Private Company
Par: Walker Information, Inc. (US)
Key: Stacey Leid-Redhead, Mng Dir
Yvonne Towell, Dir of Payroll,
    Acctng & Benefits
Geoff Fage, Land Admr

Wallace & Carey Inc.

2226 South Service Rd. West
Oakville, ON L6L 5N1
Tel 905-825-9640
Fax 905-825-9709
www.wacl.com
Line: Distributes grocery, confection,
health and beauty, sundry, tobacco,
frozen, cooler, and automotive
products.
NAICS: 413110
#Emp: 100-249 (Tor)
#TorLoc: 1
Own: Private Company
Key: Peter Predko, Dir of Sales & Ops
Deanie Jones, Staffing Admr
Joanne Smith, Customer Service Mgr

Wal-Mart Canada Corp.

1940 Argentia Rd.
Mississauga, ON L5N 1P9
Tel 905-821-2111
Fax 905-821-6828
www.walmartcanada.ca
NAICS: 452110
#Emp: 5000-9999 (Tor)
Own: Public Company
Par: Wal-Mart Stores Inc. (US)
Key: David Cheesewright, Pres & CEO
Jim Thompson, COO
Bob Hakeem, Sr VP People Division
Sean Clarke, VP & CFO

Gale Blank, VP & CIO
Jeff Lobb, Sr VP Mktg
Andrew Pelletier,
    VP Corp Affairs & Sustainability

Wardrop Engineering Inc.

6835A Century Ave.
Mississauga, ON L5N 2L2
Tel 905-369-3000
Fax 905-369-3200
www.wardrop.com
AKA: Wardrop Technologies
Line: Provides engineering consulting
services.
NAICS: 541330
#Emp: 100-249 (Tor)
#TorLoc: 3
Own: Private Company
Key: Brent Thompson,
    Sr VP Minning & Minerals
Shayne Smith, Pres
Hany Michael, Sr VP Energy
James Popel, VP HR
Robert Sumsion, VP Corp Fin

Warner Bros. Entertainment Canada Inc.

1503-5000 Yonge St.
Toronto, ON M2N 6P1
Tel 416-250-8384
www.warnerbroscanada.com
AKA: Warner Home Video; Warner
Bros. Int'l Television Distribution
Line: Operates a film video and motion
picture distribution company.
NAICS: 512110
#Emp: 100-249 (Tor)
#TorLoc: 1
Own: Private Company
Par: Warner Bros. Entertainment Inc.
(US)
Key: Mickie Steinmann, VP & GM (TV)
Rocca Morra Hodge, Dir of HR
John Grant, VP Mktg, Home Video

Warren Gibson Ltd.

206 Church St. South
Alliston, ON L9R 1T9
Tel 705-435-4342
Fax 705-435-9863
www.warrengibson.com
AKA: Gibson Transport
Line: Provides transportation services.
NAICS: 484110 484121
#Emp: 250-499 (Tor)
Own: Private Company
Key: Brian J. Gibson, Pres
Marilyn Lawrence, HR Mgr
Tom Ioannou, IS Mgr
Michael Gibson, VP

Warren Industries Ltd.

401 Spinnaker Way
Concord, ON L4K 4N4
Tel 905-669-1260
Fax 905-669-1707
Line: Manufactures automotive parts.
NAICS: 332118
#Emp: 100-249 (Tor)
#TorLoc: 2
Own: Private Company
Key: David Freedman, Pres
Perry Alampay, Cont

Warren Protective Services Ltd.

500-5799 Yonge St.
Toronto, ON M2M 3V3
Tel 416-222-7144
www.wpsl.ca
NAICS: 561612
#Emp: 100-249 (Tor)
#TorLoc: 1
Own: Private Company
Key: Laurie Morris, Pres & CEO
Paul D. Pittman, Ops Mgr
Jeremy S. Goldberg, VP

WASTECO

A Div. of Southern Sanitation Inc.
161 Bridgeland Ave.
Toronto, ON M6A 1Z1
Tel 416-787-5000
Fax 416-781-7797
www.wastecogroup.com
AKA: Columbus Recycling Centre;
Orenda Recycling Centre
Line: Provides waste removal and
recycling services.
NAICS: 562210 562110
#Emp: 100-249 (Tor)
#TorLoc: 4
Own: Private Company
Key: Stephen G. Caudwell, Pres
Carl Lorusso, VP
Linga Easwaran, Cont

Waste Management of Canada

117 Wentworth Crt.
Brampton, ON L6T 5L4
Tel 905-595-3360
Fax 905-791-9595
www.wmcanada.com
AKA: Waste Management
Line: Provides waste management
services.
NAICS: 562210
#Emp: 250-499 (Tor)
#TorLoc: 11
Own: Private Company
Par: Waste Management Inc. (US)
Key: Cal Bricker, VP Pub Affairs
Jasmine Dyer-Thomas, HR Coord

Waterford Building Maintenance Inc.

7-800 Denison St.
Markham, ON L3R 5M9
Tel 905-470-7766
Fax 905-470-7075
www.waterfordservices.com
Line: Provides cleaning services.
NAICS: 561722
#Emp: 250-499 (Tor)
#TorLoc: 1
Own: Private Company
Key: Kenneth Crystal, Pres
Joe De Melo, Dir of Ops
William H. Wagner,
    Mgr of Sales & Quality Control

The Waterside Inn

15 Stavebank Rd. South
Mississauga, ON L5G 2T2
Tel 905-891-7770
Fax 905-891-5333
www.watersideinn.ca
NAICS: 721111
#Emp: 75-99 (Tor)
#TorLoc: 1
Own: Private Company
Key: Ralph Schwengers, GM

The Watson Group Ltd.

10-95 West Beaver Creek Rd.
Richmond Hill, ON L4B 1H2
Tel 905-889-9119
Fax 905-889-8976
Line: Provides heating and air
conditioning, and fireplace services.
NAICS: 232520
#Emp: 75-99 (Tor)
#TorLoc: 1
Own: Private Company
Key: John Watson, Pres
Paul Watson, VP
Patricia Peterson, Office Mgr
Jeff Fata, Sales Mgr

Watt International Inc.

300 Bayview Ave.
Toronto, ON M5A 3R7
Tel 416-364-9384
Fax 416-364-1098
www.wattinternational.com
AKA: Watt Retail; Watt Gilchrist
North America
Line: Provides strategic design
consulting and graphic design
preproduction.
NAICS: 541430
#Emp: 100-249 (Tor)
#TorLoc: 2

Own: Public Company
Par: Envoy Communications Group
Inc. (CDA)
Key: Patrick Rodmell, Pres & CEO
Donna Davis-Young, VP HR
Mike Grace, Exec VP Fin & Ops

Watts Water Technologies (Canada) Inc.

5435 North Service Rd.
Burlington, ON L7L 5H7
Tel 905-332-4090
Fax 905-332-7068
www.wattscanada.ca
Line: Manufactures valve products for
residential, commercial, industrial and
municipal markets.
NAICS: 332910
#Emp: 100-249 (Tor)
#TorLoc: 1
Own: Public Company
Par: Watts Industries Inc. (US)
Key: Dan Bowes, VP Fin & GM
George Darnowski, VP Ops
Michelle Vontrella, HR Mgr
Meredith McNiff, MIS Mgr
Charles Mann, VP Sales & Mktg

The Wawanesa Mutual Insurance Co.

100-4110 Yonge St.
Toronto, ON M2P 2B7
Tel 416-250-9292
Fax 416-228-7828
www.wawanesa.com
NAICS: 524112 524129
#Emp: 100-249 (Tor)
#TorLoc: 1
Own: Private Company
Key: Kenneth E. McCrea, Pres & CEO
G. N. Bass, VP, Gen Counsel & Secy
Tracy L. Nelson, VP HR
Cam Loeppky, VP IS
Chris Luby, VP Mktg & Business Dev

Wayne Gretzky's

A Div. of Lettuce Serview
Group of Companies
99 Blue Jays Way
Toronto, ON M5V 9G9
Tel 416-348-0099
Fax 416-341-2337
www.gretzkys.com
Line: Operates a licensed restaurant.
NAICS: 722110
#Emp: 75-99 (Tor)
#TorLoc: 1
Own: Private Company
Key: Adrienne Barnhardt, GM

Webcom Inc.

3480 Pharmacy Ave.
Toronto, ON M1W 2S7
Tel 416-496-1000
Fax 416-496-1537
www.webcomlink.com
Line: Prints books, catalogues,
directories and provides creative
services for layout, design and Internet.
NAICS: 323114 323115 323120
#Emp: 100-249 (Tor)
#TorLoc: 1
Own: Private Company
Key: Mike Collinge, Pres & CEO
Gabe Preczner, Dir of Ops
Vidhu Rajasingham, HR Mgr
Neno Vukosa, Dir of Fin
Cris Vortisch, Dir of Sales
Mike Dingee, Mgr of Application Dev

Web Offset Publications Ltd.

1800 Ironstone Manor
Pickering, ON L1W 3J9
Tel 905-831-3000
Fax 905-831-3266
www.ironstonemedia.com
AKA: Ironstone Media
NAICS: 323119 323120
#Emp: 100-249 (Tor)
#TorLoc: 1
Own: Private Company
Par: Ironstone Media (US)
Key: John Pizale, Pres
John Bacopulos, Chmn
Trudy Hunter, VP Ops
Karen Hume, HR & Payroll Mgr
Dave Nicholls,
    Mgr of Data Systems & Purch
Daniel Glazerman, VP Sales & Mktg

We Care Home Health Services - Toronto

602-151 Bloor St. West
Toronto, ON M5S 1S4
Tel 416-922-7601
Fax 416-922-6280
www.wecare.ca
Line: Provides home care services.
NAICS: 621610
#Emp: 100-249 (Tor)
#TorLoc: 6
Own: Private Company
Par: We Care Home Health Services
(CDA)
Key: John Schram, Pres & CEO
Larry Smith, VP Franchising & Ops
Barbara Toccacelli,
    Dir of HR & Commun
Graham Neil, CFO
Brian Lyons, Dir of IT

Wedlock Paper Converters Ltd.

2327 Stanfield Rd.
Mississauga, ON L4Y 1R6
Tel 905-277-9461
Fax 905-272-1108
www.wedlockpaper.com
Line: Produces paper bags.
NAICS: 322220
#Emp: 100-249 (Tor)
#TorLoc: 1
Own: Private Company
Key: Sean Wedlock, Pres & GM
Frank Lascelles, HR Dir
Tony Scopazzi, Cont

Weed Man Canada

11 Grand Marshall Dr.
Toronto, ON M1B 5N6
Tel 416-269-8333
Fax 416-269-5746
www.weed-man.com
AKA: Turf Operations Scarborough Inc.
NAICS: 541320
#Emp: 75-99 (Tor)
#TorLoc: 1
Own: Private Company
Key: Roger Mongeon, Pres

Weight Watchers Canada Ltd.

200-2295 Bristol Circ.
Oakville, ON L6H 6P8
Tel 905-491-2100
www.weightwatchers.ca
Line: Provides weight control services.
NAICS: 812190
#Emp: 250-499 (Tor)
Own: Private Company
Par: Weight Watchers International
(US)
Key: Marguerite Neri,
    Dir of Business Dev
Paul Schiffner, GM
Natasha Rambaran, HR Mgr

Weir Canada Inc.

2360 Millrace Crt.
Mississauga, ON L5N 1W2
Tel 905-812-7100
Fax 905-812-0069
www.weirservicesamericas.com
AKA: Peacock Inc.
Line: Sells, distributes and services
instrumentation, process control
equipment, and industrial products.
NAICS: 416110 417990
#Emp: 100-249 (Tor)
#TorLoc: 2
Own: Private Company
Par: Weir Group plc (SCOT)
Key: Ruth Silveira, Cont
Gilles Kegle, Dir of IT

WeirFoulds LLP

130 King St. West
Exchange Tower, #1600, P.O. Box 480
Toronto, ON M5X 1J5
Tel 416-365-1110
Fax 416-365-1876
www.weirfoulds.com
NAICS: 541110
#Emp: 100-249 (Tor)
#TorLoc: 1
Own: Private Company
Key: Lisa Borsook, Partner
Scott Du Bois, COO
Karen Gerhardt, HR Mgr
John Pitman, CFO
Murray Herbert, Facilities & IT Mgr
Kathy Chan, Mktg Mgr

Welded Tube of Canada

111 Rayette Rd.
Concord, ON L4K 2E9
Tel 905-669-1111
Fax 905-738-4070
www.weldedtube.com
Line: Manufactures welded steel
tubing.
NAICS: 331210
#Emp: 250-499 (Tor)
#TorLoc: 3
Own: Private Company
Key: Barry Sonshine, Exec VP
Barbara Waterman, Payroll & HR Coord
Joe Alexandre, CFO
Rob Bennett, IT Mgr

Wells Fargo Financial Corporation Canada

55 Standish Crt.
Mississauga, ON L5R 4J4
Tel 905-755-7000
www.wellsfargofinancial.ca
AKA: Trans Canada Retail Services
Line: Provides finance, insurance and
real estate services.
NAICS: 522299
#Emp: 1000-4999 (Tor)
Own: Private Company
Key: Rick Valade, Pres

Wells Gordon Limited

720 Mount Pleasant Rd.
Toronto, ON M4S 2N4
Tel 416-487-3392
Fax 416-482-0469
www.britonhouse.com
Line: Operates a home for the aged.
NAICS: 623310
#Emp: 100-249 (Tor)
#TorLoc: 1
Own: Private Company
Key: Russell B. Wells, Pres

Wellspring Pharmaceutical Canada Corp.

400 Iroquois Shore Rd.
Oakville, ON L6H 1M5
Tel 905-337-4500
Fax 905-337-3539
www.wellspringpharm.com
Line: Manufactures pharmaceutical products.
NAICS: 325410
#Emp: 100-249 (Tor)
#TorLoc: 1
Own: Private Company
Par: Wellspring Pharmaceutical Corp. (US)
Key: Bonnie Feeney, Pres & COO
Robert Vukovich, Chmn & CEO
Joe Salmon, Dir of Ops
Vladimir Spenar,
    Associate Dir of Business Dev

Wendy's Restaurants of Canada Inc.

240 Wyecroft Rd.
Oakville, ON L6K 2G7
Tel 905-849-7685
Fax 905-849-5545
www.wendys.ca
Line: Operates quick service restaurant chain.
NAICS: 722210
#Emp: 1000-4999 (Tor)
#TorLoc: 46
Own: Public Company
Par: Wendy's International Inc. (US)
Key: Ron Baugh, Sr VP
Paul Hilder, Divisional VP Ops
Mark White, VP Fin & Dev
Lorraine Green, VP Supply Chain
    Management & Dist
Lisa Deletroz, Dir of Mktg

The WenLeigh Long-Term Care Residence

2065 Leanne Blvd.
Mississauga, ON L5K 2L6
Tel 905-822-4663
Fax 905-822-8290
www.chartwellreit.ca
Line: Operates a long-term care centre for seniors.
NAICS: 623310
#Emp: 75-99 (Tor)
#TorLoc: 1
Own: Private Company
Par: Chartwell Reit (CDA)
Key: Lorianne Ledwez, Admr

Werek Enterprises Inc.

3-200 Riviera Dr.
Markham, ON L3R 5M1
Tel 905-479-3131
Fax 905-479-7025
www.emswerek.com
AKA: Executive Maintenance Services Inc.
Line: Provides residential and commercial cleaning services.
NAICS: 561722
#Emp: 250-499 (Tor)
Own: Private Company
Key: Zeev Werek, Pres
Monia Campoli, Office Mgr

Wertex Hosiery Inc.

1191 Bathurst St.
Toronto, ON M5R 3H4
Tel 416-537-2137
Fax 416-537-0437
Line: Manufactures ladies', men's and children's hosiery and body wear, including pantyhose, tights, trouser socks, knee-highs, dress and sport socks.
NAICS: 315110
#Emp: 100-249 (Tor)
#TorLoc: 1
Own: Private Company
Key: Ernest Werner, Pres
Andre Tarka, GM

Wesbell Group of Companies

50 Devon Rd.
Brampton, ON L6T 5B5
Tel 905-595-8000
Fax 905-595-7986
www.wesbell.com
Line: Offers inventory control, commercial moving and telecommunication equipment repair, test and installation services.
NAICS: 541619 232510

#Emp: 250-499 (Tor)
#TorLoc: 1
Own: Private Company
Key: Paul Mazze, Pres & CEO
Nick Mazze, COO & Chief Legal Officer
Armando Ty, CFO

Wesburn Manor

400 The West Mall
Toronto, ON M9C 5S1
Tel 416-394-3600
Fax 416-394-3606
www.toronto.ca/ltc/wesburn.htm
Line: Operates a general long-term health care facility.
NAICS: 623110
#Emp: 100-249 (Tor)
#TorLoc: 1
Own: Private Company
Key: Elaine Russell, Home Admr

Wescam

649 North Service Rd. West
Burlington, ON L7P 5B9
Tel 905-633-4000
Fax 905-633-4100
www.wescam.com
Line: Captures stabilized; high-magnification images from fixed-wing, rotary-wing, UAV and aerostat platforms.
NAICS: 334310
#Emp: 500-999 (Tor)
#TorLoc: 2
Own: Public Company
Par: L-3 Communications Corp. (US)
Key: John Dehne, Pres & CEO
Alan Bignell, VP & GM, Ops
Roman Turchyn, VP HR
Larry Spanier, VP Fin
Mike Parsons, Dir of Procurement
Daniel Smith, Dir of IT
Paul Jennison, VP Government
    Sales & Business Dev
Sara McDonald,
    Mktg & Commun Specialist

Wesco Distribution Canada LP

475 Hood Rd.
Markham, ON L3R 0S8
Tel 905-475-7400
Fax 905-475-0293
www.wesco.ca
Line: Distributes electrical products.
NAICS: 416110
#Emp: 100-249 (Tor)
#TorLoc: 2

Own: Public Company
Par: Wesco Distribution Inc. (US)
Key: Harald Henze, Group VP & GM
Elissa Gould, HR Mgr
Robert Budgeon, Group Cont
Dan Drazilov, Dir of Supplier Relns

West-ADS Employment Services Inc.

311-5425 Dixie Rd.
Mississauga, ON L4W 1E6
Tel 905-564-3077
Fax 905-624-3358
www.ads-employment.com
AKA: ADS Employment Services
Line: Provides employment services
for drivers, managers, dispatchers, and
warehouse and clerical workers.
NAICS: 561310
#Emp: 100-249 (Tor)
#TorLoc: 1
Own: Private Company
Key: Joe Buscema, Pres
Tim Vance, Ops Mgr

Westburne Ruddy Electric

A Div. of Rexel Canada Electrical Inc.
600 Thornton Rd. South
Oshawa, ON L1J 6W7
Tel 905-576-7100
Fax 905-728-5939
www.westburnedirect.ca
NAICS: 416110
#Emp: 250-499 (Tor)
#TorLoc: 14
Own: Public Company
Key: Ken McCallum, GM
Jason Bowen, District Mgr

Westbury National Show Systems Ltd.

772 Warden Ave.
Toronto, ON M1L 4T7
Tel 416-752-1371
Fax 416-752-1382
www.westbury.com
Line: Operates a full-service
entertainment technology company
that supplies production, design and
installation services.
NAICS: 532490
#Emp: 100-249 (Tor)
#TorLoc: 1
Own: Private Company
Key: David Bennett, Pres
Robert Sandolowich, VP
Kelvin Fosberry, HR
Frank Gerstein, VP

Westdale Construction Co. Ltd.

440 Adelaide St. West
Toronto, ON M5V 1S7
Tel 416-703-1877
Fax 416-504-9216
www.westdaleproperties.com
NAICS: 231220
#Emp: 75-99 (Tor)
#TorLoc: 1
Own: Private Company
Key: Peter Lebedewski, GM
Ronald Kimel, Pres
Glenda Lee, Ops Mgr
Miguel Vieira, HR Mgr

Western Assurance Co.

1000-2225 Erin Mills Pkwy.
Mississauga, ON L5K 2S9
Tel 905-403-3318
Fax 905-403-3319
www.rsagroup.ca
NAICS: 524210
#Emp: 100-249 (Tor)
#TorLoc: 2
Own: Not-for-profit
Key: Dave Pickard, Reg VP

Western Toronto International Trucks Inc.

7450 Torbram Rd.
Mississauga, ON L4T 1G9
Tel 905-671-7600
Fax 416-946-1299
www.wtitrucks.ca
AKA: Western Toronto Idealease
Line: Sells and leases international
brand trucks and provides truck parts
and service.
NAICS: 532490 415290 811111
#Emp: 100-249 (Tor)
#TorLoc: 1
Own: Private Company
Key: John Werkhoven,
Dir of Parts & Service
Patricia Behenna, HR Mgr
Fred Hildebrand,
VP Truck Sales & Leasing

Westin Bristol Place Toronto Airport

950 Dixon Rd.
Toronto, ON M9W 5N4
Tel 416-675-9444
Fax 416-675-2053
www.westinbristolplace.com
Line: Provides hospitality services.
NAICS: 721111
#Emp: 100-249 (Tor)
#TorLoc: 1
Own: Private Company
Key: Yari Khan, GM

The Westin Harbour Castle

1 Harbour Sq.
Toronto, ON M5J 1A6
Tel 416-869-1600
Fax 416-869-0863
www.westin.com
AKA: Blue Tree Hotels LP
Line: Operates accommodation,
restaurants, banquet, meeting and
convention facilities.
NAICS: 721111
#Emp: 500-999 (Tor)
#TorLoc: 1
Own: Private Company
Par: Starwood Hotels & Resorts
Worldwide, Inc. (US)
Key: Rekhah Khote, GM
Joshua Karam, Dir of HR
Mike Flint, Dir of Fin

Westjet Airlines Ltd.

22 Aerial Pl. N.E.
Calgary, AB T2E 3J1
Tel 403-444-2600
Fax 403-444-2301
www.westjet.com
NAICS: 481110
#Emp: 100-249 (Tor)
#TorLoc: 1
Own: Private Company
Key: Gregg Saretsky, Pres & CEO
Ferio Pugliese,
Exec VP People & Culture
Bob Cummings, Exec VP Mktg & Sales

Westmont Hospitality Group

700-5090 Explorer Dr.
Mississauga, ON L4W 4T9
Tel 905-629-3400
Fax 905-624-7805
www.whg.com
AKA: Innvest Reit Hotels
Line: Provides management services
for the hotel industry.
NAICS: 541611
#Emp: 100-249 (Tor)
#TorLoc: 1
Own: Private Company
Key: Kenny Gibson, CEO

Weston Fine Foods Inc.

8020 Bathurst St.
Vaughan, ON L4J 0B8
Tel 905-886-6130
Fax 905-886-6121
www.westonproduce.ca
Line: Operates a supermarket.
NAICS: 445110
#Emp: 100-249 (Tor)
#TorLoc: 2
Own: Private Company
Key: Antonio Fuda, Pres
Terry Samaroo,
    Grocery Buyer & Store Mgr

Weston Foods Inc.

1425 The Queensway
Toronto, ON M8Z 1T3
Tel 416-252-7323
Fax 416-252-5553
www.weston.ca
AKA: Weston Bakeries; Ready Bake;
Neilson Dairy
Line: Manufactures bread and other
bakery and dairy products.
NAICS: 311814
#Emp: 1000-4999 (Tor)
#TorLoc: 7
Own: Public Company
Par: George Weston Ltd. (CDA)
Key: Ralph A. Robinson, Pres
Maria Liang, VP Nat'l Ops
Rolondo Sardellitti, VP Fin & CFO
Lorena M. Ferino, VP IT & Systems
Sumit Luthra, VP Mktg

Weston Forest Products

7600 Torbram Rd.
Mississauga, ON L4T 3L8
Tel 905-677-0179
Fax 905-677-1639
www.westonforestgroup.com
AKA: Weston Premium Woods; Weston
Wood Solutions; Neos Forest Inc.
Line: Wholesales, distributes and
remanufactures forest products.
NAICS: 416320
#Emp: 100-249 (Tor)
#TorLoc: 3
Own: Private Company
Key: Rick Ekstein, Pres
Doug Kong, CFO

The Weston Golf and Country Club Ltd.

50 St. Phillips Rd.
Toronto, ON M9P 2N6
Tel 416-241-5254
Fax 416-241-0239
www.westongolfcc.com
Line: Operates a golf and curling club.
NAICS: 713910
#Emp: 100-249 (Tor)
#TorLoc: 1
Own: Private Company
Key: Peter Holt, GM
Carlo Huiskamp, Member Service Mgr
Elaine Lancaster, Mgr of Fin & Admin

West Park Healthcare Centre

82 Buttonwood Ave.
Toronto, ON M6M 2J5
Tel 416-243-3600
Fax 416-243-8947
www.westpark.org
Line: Provides a continuing care, long-
term care and rehabilitation hospital.
NAICS: 622310
#Emp: 500-999 (Tor)
#TorLoc: 1
Own: Not-for-profit
Key: Anne Marie Malek, Pres & CEO
Jay Cooper, VP, Corp & Support
    Services & CFO
Liliana Catapano, Dir of HR
Nancy Martin-Ronson, CIO

West Scarborough Neighbourhood Community Centre

313 Pharmacy Ave.
Toronto, ON M1L 3E7
Tel 416-755-9215
Fax 416-755-7521
www.wsncc.on.ca
AKA: West Scarborough Boys & Girls
Club
Line: Provides recreation, employment
training, daycare, early years and
seniors services, after school programs,
and day camps.
NAICS: 624190 624110
#Emp: 100-249 (Tor)
#TorLoc: 7
Own: Not-for-profit
Key: Cynthia duMont, Exec Dir
Jolanta Styla, Program Mgr
Mary Kernohan,
    Accounts & Payroll Admr
Nadine Pendelton,
    Dir of Acctng Services

West Star Printing Ltd.

10 North Queen St.
Toronto, ON M8Z 2C4
Tel 416-201-0881
Fax 416-201-8885
www.west-star.com
Line: Operates a full-service printing
agency.
NAICS: 323114
#Emp: 75-99 (Tor)
#TorLoc: 1
Own: Private Company
Key: Gulam-Abibas Jaffer, Pres

The Wexford Residence Inc.

1860 Lawrence Ave. East
Toronto, ON M1R 5B1
Tel 416-752-8877
Fax 416-752-8414
www.thewexford.org
Line: Provides long term care and
operates seniors' apartments.
NAICS: 623310
#Emp: 100-249 (Tor)
#TorLoc: 1
Own: Not-for-profit
Key: Sandy Bassett, Exec Dir
Esther Spencer, Dir of Care
Shantha Joseph, Dir of Fin
Roger Hickling, Environmental Mgr

WHB Identification Solutions Inc.

50 Vogell Rd.
Richmond Hill, ON L4B 3K6
Tel 905-764-1717
Fax 905-764-5557
www.bradycanada.ca
AKA: Teklynx; Brady Canada; Seton
Canada
Line: Distributes workplace safety,
security, property management and
material handling products.
NAICS: 561990 339950
#Emp: 75-99 (Tor)
#TorLoc: 1
Own: Private Company
Par: Brady Corp. (US)
Key: Pascal Deman, GM
Rabia Goolsarran, HR Mgr

Wheelabrator Canada Inc.

1219 Corporate Dr.
Burlington, ON L7L 5V5
Tel 905-319-7930
Fax 905-319-7757
www.wheelabratorgroup.com
Line: Manufactures blast cleaning
machines and dust collectors.
NAICS: 333310

#Emp: 100-249 (Tor)
#TorLoc: 1
Own: Private Company
Par: Norican Group (DEN)
Key: Doug Lofranco, VP & GM
Jim Oake, IT Mgr

The Wheels Group

1-5090 Orbitor Dr.
Mississauga, ON L4W 5B5
Tel 905-602-2700
Fax 905-602-2799
www.wheelsgroup.com
AKA: Wheels International Freight
Systems.; Wheels Clipper
Line: Offers road, rail, ocean and air
transportation.
NAICS: 488519
#Emp: 100-249 (Tor)
Own: Private Company
Key: Doug Tozer, Pres & CEO
Peter Jamieson, COO
Tracey Okolisan, HR Mgr
Laurie Fox, VP Fin
Bob Maro, VP IT
Barry Murphy, Nat'l Sales Mgr

Whirlpool Canada LP

6750 Century Ave.
Mississauga, ON L5N 0B7
Tel 905-821-6400
Fax 905-821-7871
www.whirlpoolcanada.ca
Line: Manufactures, markets and sells
major home appliances and portable
appliances.
NAICS: 335223 811210
#Emp: 250-499 (Tor)
#TorLoc: 3
Own: Private Company
Par: Whirlpool Corp. (US)
Key: Karim Lalani, VP & GM
Tom Allen, Dir of Fin
Gary Power, VP Mktg

Whitby Fire and Emergency Services

A Div. of The Town of Whitby
111 McKinney Dr.
Whitby, ON L1R 3M2
Tel 905-668-3312
Fax 905-430-8956
www.whitby.ca
NAICS: 913140
#Emp: 100-249 (Tor)
#TorLoc: 7
Own: Government
Key: Michael Gerrard, Fire Chief

WhiteHat Inc.

5500 North Service Rd.
Millennium Tower, 9th Fl.
Burlington, ON L7L 6W6
Tel 905-332-6677
Fax 905-332-6673
www.whitehatinc.com
Line: Operates an information
technology security provider.
NAICS: 541510
#Emp: 75-99 (Tor)
#TorLoc: 1
Own: Private Company
Key: Rick Lambrick, Pres

Whiteoak Ford Lincoln Sales Limited

3285 Mavis Rd.
Mississauga, ON L5C 1T7
Tel 905-270-8210
www.whiteoakford.com
Line: Operates an automotive
dealership.
NAICS: 441110
#Emp: 75-99 (Tor)
Own: Private Company
Key: Ron Loveys, Pres
David McQuilkin, VP Dealer
Ann Harris, Cont
James Larmour, Parts Mgr
Ben Cliff, Gen Sales Mgr
Michael Loveys, Sales Mgr

Wholesale Travel Group

75 Eglinton Ave. East
Toronto, ON M4P 3A4
Tel 416-366-0062
Fax 416-441-9754
www.wholesaletravel.com
Line: Operates travel agency.
NAICS: 561510
#Emp: 75-99 (Tor)
#TorLoc: 1
Own: Private Company
Key: Michelle Loveridge, Dir
John Kirk, VP Retail Sales

W.H. Stuart & Associates

16 Main St.
Unionville, ON L3R 2E4
Tel 905-305-0880
Fax 905-305-0878
www.whstuart.com
Line: Provides investment services.
NAICS: 541611
#Emp: 250-499 (Tor)
#TorLoc: 1
Own: Private Company

Key: Howard Stuart, Pres & CEO
Dino DeRusa,
    Chief Compliance Officer
Michael McBurney, Sr VP Sales & Mktg

Wikoff Corp.

475 Bowes Rd.
Concord, ON L4K 1J5
Tel 905-669-1311
Fax 905-669-6299
www.wikoff.com
Line: Manufactures printing inks.
NAICS: 325910
#Emp: 500-999 (Tor)
#TorLoc: 2
Own: Private Company
Key: Martin Hambrock, VP
David Cartwright, Nat'l Sales Mgr

Wild Water Kingdom Ltd.

7855 Finch Ave. West
Brampton, ON L6T 0B2
Tel 905-794-0565
Fax 905-794-1071
www.wildwaterkingdom.com
Line: Operates amusement park.
NAICS: 713110
#Emp: 250-499 (Tor)
#TorLoc: 1
Own: Private Company
Par: ESC Group of Companies (CDA)
Key: Edward Sui Chong, Pres & Owner
Heidi Drake, Ops Mgr
Alex Sui Chong, Acctng Mgr

William Ashley Ltd.

55 Bloor St. West
Manulife Centre
Toronto, ON M4W 3V1
Tel 416-964-2900
Fax 416-960-9348
www.williamashley.com
Line: Retails china, crystal, silver and
giftware.
NAICS: 442298
#Emp: 100-249 (Tor)
#TorLoc: 2
Own: Private Company
Key: Dean Stark, GM
Jackie Chiesa, GM,
    William Ashley China

William F. White International Inc.

800 Islington Ave.
Toronto, ON M8Z 6A1
Tel 416-239-5050
Fax 416-207-2777
www.whites.com
Line: Supplies motion picture,
television, and theatrical equipment.
NAICS: 512190
#Emp: 100-249 (Tor)
#TorLoc: 1
Own: Private Company
Par: Comweb Group Inc. (CDA)
Key: Paul A. Bronfman, Chmn & CEO
Dan St. Amour, VP & GM
Helen Rector, HR Mgr
Munir Noorbhai, Exec VP & CFO
Trica Martin, Purch Agent
Mano Del Carmen, IT Mgr
Lowell Schrieder,
    Dir of Mktg & Commun

William L. Rutherford Limited

3350 Airway Dr.
Mississauga, ON L4V 1T3
Tel 905-673-2222
Fax 905-673-2656
www.rutherfordglobal.com
AKA: Rutherford Terminals Ltd.;
Rutherford International Freight;
Rutherford Global Logistics;
Montgomery International U.S.
Brokerage; Buffalo Forwarding &
Warehousing Group
Line: Provides importers and exporters
the complexity of international trade
through their Customs, Freight and
Warehousing services.
NAICS: 488519
#Emp: 100-249 (Tor)
#TorLoc: 5
Own: Private Company
Key: Romas Krilavicius, Pres
Perry L. Spice, VP

William M. Dunne Associates Ltd.

300-10 Director Crt.
Woodbridge, ON L4L 7E8
Tel 905-856-5240
Fax 905-856-5241
Line: Sells and markets consumer
products.
NAICS: 414520 413110
#Emp: 75-99 (Tor)
#TorLoc: 1
Own: Private Company

Key: Robert Brema, Pres
Steven Hillion, Mgr of Ops & IS
Rita Lappano,
    Mgr of Employee Benefits
Mike Crosby, Exec VP Fin & Commun
Brent Falvo, VP Sales
Sue Voussield, Customer Service Mgr

William Osler Health System

2100 Bovaird Dr. East
Brampton, ON L6R 3J7
Tel 905-494-2120
Fax 905-494-6872
www.williamoslerhc.on.ca
Line: Provides community hospital care
including paediatrics.
NAICS: 622111
#Emp: 1000-4999 (Tor)
#TorLoc: 3
Own: Not-for-profit
Key: Ian Smith, Chief of Staff
Matt Anderson, Supr
Elizabeth Buller, Sr VP Patient Services
Lori Diduch,
    VP HR & Organizational Dev
David McCaig, VP Fin & CFO
Joanne Flewwelling, VP Strategic Info
    & Performance Systems
Dawne Barbieri,
    VP & Chief Nursing Exec
Ian Marshall, VP & Gen Counsel

The Williams Brothers Corp.

777 Tapscott Rd.
Toronto, ON M1X 1A2
Tel 416-299-7767
Fax 416-299-8039
www.williams-brothers.com
Line: Manufactures metal access doors.
NAICS: 332321
#Emp: 75-99 (Tor)
#TorLoc: 1
Own: Private Company
Key: Bill Williams, Pres
Kimberly Sheppard, CEO

Williams Telecommunications Corp.

5610 Kennedy Rd.
Mississauga, ON L4Z 2A9
Tel 905-712-4242
Fax 905-712-1754
www.williamsglobal.com
Line: Distributes telecommunications
parts and offers installation and
maintenance services.
NAICS: 513390
#Emp: 75-99 (Tor)
#TorLoc: 1
Own: Private Company

Key: Jim Williams, Pres & CEO
Clive Huzinga, VP Ops
Marg Newton, Mktg Mgr

Willis Canada Inc.

1200-145 King St. West
Toronto, ON M5H 1J8
Tel 416-368-9641
Fax 416-869-1649
www.willis.com
Line: Operates an insurance company,
specializing in insurance brokerage,
loss prevention services, and risk
management.
NAICS: 524210 524124
#Emp: 100-249 (Tor)
#TorLoc: 1
Own: Private Company
Par: Willis Group (UK)
Key: Rick Hynes, Pres & CEO
Sarah Flint, VP Ops
Eric Brooks, VP & Dir of Fin
Daniel Beaudry,
    Exec VP Reg Mktg Officer

Willows Estate Nursing Home

13837 Yonge St.
Aurora, ON L4G 3G8
Tel 905-727-0128
Fax 905-841-0454
www.omni-way.com
Line: Provides nursing home services.
NAICS: 623110
#Emp: 75-99 (Tor)
#TorLoc: 1
Own: Private Company
Par: Omni Health Care (CDA)
Key: Patrick McCarthy, Pres & CEO
Candace Chartier, COO
April Dowdall, Dir of HR
Glen Boyd, CFO

Willson International

201-2345 Argentia Rd.
Mississauga, ON L5N 8K4
Tel 905-363-1133
Fax 905-363-1178
www.willsonintl.com
Line: Operates a logistics company.
NAICS: 488990
#Emp: 75-99 (Tor)
#TorLoc: 1
Own: Private Company
Key: Peter Willson, Pres & CEO
Debbie Chan, Dir of Fin
Jack Langelaan, VP Sales
Angela Collins,
    VP Client Relns & Transitions

Wilson's Truck Lines Ltd.

111 The West Mall
Toronto, ON M9C 1C1
Tel 416-621-9020
Fax 416-621-0784
www.wilsonstrucklines.com
Line: Operates a local trucking
business.
NAICS: 484110
#Emp: 250-499 (Tor)
#TorLoc: 1
Own: Private Company
Key: Marc Mousseau, Pres
James D. Wilson, Owner
Grey Biles, Dir of Ops
Claude Beland, Cont
Dave Saunders, Dir of IT

Windmill Mushroom Farms

9760 Heron Rd.
Ashburn, ON L0B 1A0
Tel 905-655-3373
Fax 905-655-8435
www.windmillfarms.ca
AKA: Greenwood Mushroom Farm
NAICS: 111411
#Emp: 100-249 (Tor)
#TorLoc: 1
Own: Private Company
Key: Clay Taylor, Mng Partner
Amedeo Guzzo-Foliaro,
    Dir of Sales & Mktg

Window City Mfrs Inc.

5690 Steeles Ave. West
Vaughan, ON L4L 9T4
Tel 905-265-9975
Fax 905-265-9976
www.windowcity.net
Line: Manufactures vinyl patio door
and window extrusions.
NAICS: 326198 332321
#Emp: 100-249 (Tor)
#TorLoc: 1
Own: Private Company
Key: Jeff Sadr, Pres

The Windsor Arms Hotel

18 St. Thomas St.
Toronto, ON M5S 3E7
Tel 416-971-9666
Fax 416-921-9121
www.windsorarmshotel.com
NAICS: 721111
#Emp: 75-99 (Tor)
#TorLoc: 1
Own: Private Company
Key: George Friedmann, Pres

Wing's Food Products Ltd.

50 Torlake Cres.
Toronto, ON M8Z 1B8
Tel 416-259-2662
Fax 416-259-3414
www.wings.ca
AKA: Wing Hing Lung Ltd.
Line: Manufacturer of sauces, syrups,
salad dressings, condiments, cookies,
noodles, and wraps.
NAICS: 311990 311410
#Emp: 100-249 (Tor)
#TorLoc: 2
Own: Private Company
Key: Neal Lee, Pres
Peter Lee, Chmn
Sherri Solway, Dir of Sales

Winners Merchants International

6715 Airport Rd.
Mississauga, ON L4V 1Y2
Tel 905-405-8000
Fax 905-405-7687
www.winners.ca
AKA: HomeSense; Winners;
WINNERS'n more
Line: Operates as an off-price apparel
and home fashion retailer.
NAICS: 448150 442298 448140
#Emp: 5000-9999 (Tor)
#TorLoc: 53
Own: Private Company
Par: TJX Companies Inc. (US)
Key: Bob Cataldo, Pres

Winroc

A Div. of Superior Plus LP
3-1121 Walkers Line
Burlington, ON L7N 2G4
Tel 905-335-5012
Fax 905-335-5083
www.winroc.com
Line: Distributes residential insulation,
drywall, basement wrap, drainage
wrap, metal building insulation, and
related products.
NAICS: 416390
#Emp: 75-99 (Tor)
#TorLoc: 1
Own: Private Company
Key: Dan Derochers, GM

Wirecomm Systems Inc.

10-3687 Nashua Dr.
Mississauga, ON L4V 1V5
Tel 905-405-8018
Fax 905-405-8024
www.wirecomm.ca
Line: Provides telecommunication
services.
NAICS: 541510
#Emp: 100-249 (Tor)
#TorLoc: 1
Own: Public Company
Par: 180 Connect Inc. (US)
Key: Domenic Sorbara, Pres
Danny Herrera, Toronto Area Mgr

W Network Inc.

Corus Quay, 25 Dockside Dr.
Toronto, ON M5A 0B5
Tel 416-408-3343
Fax 416-479-7005
www.wnetwork.com
Line: Operates a television
broadcasting station.
NAICS: 513210
#Emp: 100-249 (Tor)
#TorLoc: 1
Own: Private Company
Par: Corus Entertainment (CDA)
Key: Gerry Mackrell, VP Sales
Marilyn Orecchio,
    VP Women's Television Sales

Wolfedale Electric Ltd.

415 Ambassador Dr.
Mississauga, ON L5T 2J3
Tel 905-564-8999
Fax 905-564-5677
www.dialonewolfedale.com
AKA: Dial One Wolfedale Electric
Line: Provides electrical contracting
services.
NAICS: 232510
#Emp: 100-249 (Tor)
#TorLoc: 1
Own: Private Company
Key: Jackie Strachan, GM
Jim Graham, Ops Mgr
Allyson Rea, HR Mgr
Mark Benson, Cont
Catherine Chamberlain, Purch Agent

Woodbine Centre and Fantasy Fair

500 Rexdale Blvd.
Toronto, ON M9W 6K5
Tel 416-674-5200
Fax 416-675-1543
www.woodbinecentre.ca
Line: Operates shopping centre and indoor amusement park.
NAICS: 531120
#Emp: 100-249 (Tor)
#TorLoc: 1
Own: Private Company
Par: 2058790 Ontario Limited (CDA)
Key: Peter McCallion, GM
Jeff Quinn, Ops Supr
Christopher Couch, Mktg Coord

Woodbine Entertainment Group

555 Rexdale Blvd.
P.O. Box 156
Toronto, ON M9W 5L2
Tel 416-675-7223
Fax 416-213-2126
www.woodbineentertainment.com
AKA: Turf Lounge; Greenwood Teletheatre; Mohawk Raceway; Woodbine Racetrack; WEGZ Stadium Bar; Champions
Line: Offers horse racing and facilities for the public and those engaged in the industry.
NAICS: 711213 713990
#Emp: 1000-4999 (Tor)
Own: Not-for-profit
Key: Nick Eaves, Pres & CEO
David Willmot, Chmn
Eddie Stutz, Sr VP Ops
Debra Carey, VP HR
Stephen Mitchell, Exec VP & CFO
Jane Holmes, VP Corp Affairs
Andrew McDonald,
    VP Mktg & Commun
Glenn Crouter,
    VP Media Relns & Sponsorship

Woodbine Tool & Die Manufacturing Ltd.

190 Royalcrest Crt.
Markham, ON L3R 9X6
Tel 905-475-5223
Fax 905-475-3443
www.wtd.ca
Line: Designs and manufactures tools and dies and produces stampings and welded assemblies.
NAICS: 332118 333519
#Emp: 100-249 (Tor)
#TorLoc: 2

Own: Private Company
Key: Tibor Urbanek, Pres & CEO
Gunter Riegel, VP Manuf
Dorothy Adams, Office Mgr
Dan Radulescu, Purch Agent
Max Popov, Sales Mgr

Woodbridge Foam Corp.

4240 Sherwoodtowne Blvd.
Mississauga, ON L4Z 2G6
Tel 905-896-3626
Fax 905-896-9262
www.woodbridgegroup.com
AKA: The Woodbridge Group
Line: Manufactures polyurethane flexible foam.
NAICS: 326150
#Emp: 250-499 (Tor)
#TorLoc: 4
Own: Private Company
Key: Robert Magee, Chmn & CEO
Paul McKay, VP HR & Health,
    Safety & Environment
Richard Jocsak, CFO
Joe Plati, Dir of Worldwide Purch
Martin Mazza, Sr VP
    Global Sales & Mktg

Woodchester Nissan

2560 Motorway Blvd.
Mississauga, ON L5L 1X3
Tel 905-828-7001
Fax 905-828-1847
www.woodchester.ca
AKA: Woodchester Infiniti Nissan
Line: Operates an automotive dealership.
NAICS: 441110
#Emp: 75-99 (Tor)
#TorLoc: 1
Own: Private Company
Par: Woodchester Autogroup (CDA)
Key: John Shoeck, Business Mgr
Michael England, Sales Mgr

Woodgreen Community Services

100-815 Danforth Ave.
Toronto, ON M4J 1L2
Tel 416-645-6000
www.woodgreen.org
Line: Provides programs and services to the East Toronto community including children's services, support programs for seniors and persons with disabilities, employment and training programs, immigrant services, neighbourhood programs and non-profit housing.
NAICS: 624190 624110 624120
#Emp: 500-999 (Tor)

#TorLoc: 18
Own: Not-for-profit
Key: Brian Smith, Pres
Anne Babcock, VP Planning & Ops
Aviva Attas, Dir of HR
Larry Whatmore,
    Dir of Fin & Business Dev
Mehran Mehrdadi, Dir of IS

WoodGreen Red Door Family Shelter

21 Carlaw Ave.
Toronto, ON M4M 2R6
Tel 416-915-5671
Fax 416-915-5698
www.reddoorshelter.ca
AKA: Red Door Family Shelter
Line: Operates an emergency family shelter serving and supporting families in crises, abused women and their children and newcomers to Canada.
NAICS: 624190
#Emp: 75-99 (Tor)
#TorLoc: 2
Own: Not-for-profit
Key: Bernnitta Hawkins, Exec Dir
Marija Petrovic, HR Coord

The Woodhaven

380 Church St.
Markham, ON L6B 1E1
Tel 905-472-3320
Fax 905-472-1347
www.chartwellreit.ca
Line: Provides general long-term care services and nursing home facilities.
NAICS: 623110
#Emp: 100-249 (Tor)
Own: Private Company
Par: Chartwell Seniors Housing REIT (CDA)
Key: Michelle Stroud, Admr
Cortney Kay, Business Mgr

Woodlore International Inc.

160 Delta Park Blvd.
Brampton, ON L6T 5T6
Tel 905-791-9555
Fax 905-791-2228
www.woodlore.ca
Line: Manufactures office furniture.
NAICS: 337213
#Emp: 100-249 (Tor)
#TorLoc: 1
Own: Private Company
Key: Peter Loerke, Pres & CEO
Maria Benson, HR Mgr
Leo Fleury, IT Mgr
Debbie Young, VP Sales & Mktg

Workplace Safety and Insurance Board

200 Front St. West
Toronto, ON M5V 3J1
Tel 416-344-1000
Fax 416-344-4684
www.wsib.on.ca
Line: Provides prevention and disability benefits; monitors the quality of healthcare; and assists in the early and safe return to work for workers who are injured on the job.
NAICS: 912210
#Emp: 1000-4999 (Tor)
#TorLoc: 1
Own: Government
Par: Government of Ontario
Key: David Marshall, Pres
John Slinger, COO

Workplace Safety & Prevention Services

500-5110 Creekbank Rd.
Mississauga, ON L4W 0A1
Tel 905-614-4272
Fax 905-614-1414
www.wsps.ca
AKA: IAPA
Line: Contributes to the continuous improvement of member firms' workplace-related health and safety by providing client-focused, quality, educational programs, products and services.
NAICS: 813930
#Emp: 100-249 (Tor)
#TorLoc: 5
Own: Association
Key: Elizabeth Mills, Pres & CEO
Jim Armstrong, Chief, Client Services
Dominic Chung, Mgr of IS

World Travel Protection Canada Inc.

400 University Ave., 15th Fl.
Toronto, ON M5J 1S7
Tel 416-977-3565
Fax 416-205-4676
www.wtp.ca
Line: Offers emergency travel assistance and health support programs to banks, insurers, pharmaceutical and health companies.
NAICS: 524210
#Emp: 75-99 (Tor)
#TorLoc: 1
Own: Private Company
Par: Zurich Financial Services (SWITZ)

Key: Ron Mayer, Pres & CMO
Arnie DeFias, Dir of Platform Ops
Wendy Shibata, Cont
David McLean, VP Sales & Mktg

World Vision Canada

1 World Dr.
Mississauga, ON L5T 2Y4
Tel 905-565-6100
Fax 905-696-2163
www.worldvision.ca
Line: Operates a Christian humanitarian organization involved in worldwide emergency relief and sustainable community development.
NAICS: 813310
#Emp: 500-999 (Tor)
#TorLoc: 1
Own: Not-for-profit
Par: World Vision International (US)
Key: Dave Toycen, Pres & CEO
Dirk Booy, Exec VP
Charlie Guy, VP People & Culture
Charlie Fluit, VP Corp Services & CFO
Chantal Tomlinson, CIO
Kathryn Goddard,
    VP Donor Engagement
Peter Ward,
    Sr VP Supporter Engagement

Worldwide Food Distribution

130 Fernstaff Crt.
Vaughan, ON L4K 3L8
Tel 905-669-8002
Fax 905-669-4530
www.worldwidefoods.com
AKA: Worldwide Foods
Line: Distributes non-perishable food.
NAICS: 413190
#Emp: 100-249 (Tor)
#TorLoc: 1
Own: Private Company
Key: Marshall Usher, Pres
Joel Usher, GM

WorleyParsons

2645 Skymark Ave.
Mississauga, ON L4W 4H2
Tel 905-614-1778
Fax 905-614-0188
www.worleyparsons.com
Line: Provides professional services to the energy, resource and complex process industries.
NAICS: 541690 541330
#Emp: 100-249 (Tor)
#TorLoc: 2
Own: Public Company
Par: WorleyParsons (AUS)
Key: Cameron Harris,
VP, Process & Tech

WorleyParsons Canada

8133 Warden Ave.
Markham, ON L6G 1B3
Tel 905-940-4774
Fax 905-940-4778
www.worleyparsons.com
Line: Provides multidiscipline engineering services for industrial plants and facilities including petroleum, petrochemical, chemical and manufacturing industries.
NAICS: 541330
#Emp: 250-499 (Tor)
#TorLoc: 1
Own: Private Company
Par: Colt Engineering Corp. (CDA)
Key: Andrew Bain, Divisional Cont
Grace Davidian, HR Mgr
Andrew Bain, Divisional Cont
Mark Palfi, Dir of IT

W. Ralston (Canada) Inc.

135 East Dr.
Brampton, ON L6T 1B5
Tel 905-791-3980
Fax 905-791-0587
www.cttgroup.com
Line: Manufactures polythene blown film serving the retail and industrial sectors.
NAICS: 326198
#Emp: 75-99 (Tor)
#TorLoc: 1
Own: Private Company
Key: Leonard Cohen, Pres
Howard Cohen, VP
Paul Cohen, VP Mktg

Wrigley Canada

1123 Leslie St.
Toronto, ON M3C 2K1
Tel 416-449-8600
Fax 416-449-1774
www.wrigley.com
Line: Manufactures and markets confection products including cough and cold remedies.
NAICS: 311340
#Emp: 500-999 (Tor)
#TorLoc: 2
Own: Private Company
Par: William Wrigley Jr. Company Ltd. (US)
Key: Angie Gross, GM
Doug Wittenberg, VP Manuf
Janis Hazlewood, VP HR
Chris Coughlin, VP Fin

WSI Internet Consulting & Education

600-5580 Explorer Dr.
Mississauga, ON L4W 4Y1
Tel 905-678-7588
Fax 905-678-7242
www.wsiconsultants.com
Line: Provides Internet consulting services.
NAICS: 541510
#Emp: 75-99 (Tor)
#TorLoc: 1
Own: Private Company
Key: Ron McArthur, Pres
Maribel Guiste, VP Ops

Wunderman

800-60 Bloor St. West
Toronto, ON M4W 3B8
Tel 416-921-9050
Fax 416-961-0971
www.wunderman.com
Line: Offers direct marketing, e-marketing, sales promotion, creative communications and direct media services.
NAICS: 454110
#Emp: 100-249 (Tor)
#TorLoc: 1
Own: Public Company
Key: Mark Russell, Pres
Trish Wheaton, Chmn
Jennifer Issely, Sr HR Business Mgr

Wurth Canada Ltd.

6330 Tomken Rd.
Mississauga, ON L5T 1N2
Tel 905-564-6225
Fax 905-564-6227
www.wurthcanada.com
AKA: Zebra; Mepla; Alfit; ORSY
Line: Distributes hardware and chemicals to the automotive, industrial, maintenance and wood industries.
NAICS: 418410
#Emp: 100-249 (Tor)
#TorLoc: 1
Own: Private Company
Par: Wurth KG (GER)
Key: Ernest Sweeney, Pres & CEO
Heather Furlotte, HR Mgr
Steve Revell, Fin Mgr
Tracey Kipin, Purch Mgr
Richard Kipin, IT Mgr

WW Hotels Ltd.

55 Hallcrown Pl.
Toronto, ON M2J 4R1
Tel 416-493-7000
Fax 416-493-0681
www.radisson.com/torontoca_east
AKA: Radisson Hotel Toronto East
NAICS: 721111
#Emp: 75-99 (Tor)
#TorLoc: 1
Own: Private Company
Par: Westmont Hospitality Group (CDA)
Key: Chad Hope, GM

Wyeth Consumer Healthcare Inc.

5975 Whittle Rd.
Mississauga, ON L4Z 3M6
Tel 905-507-7000
Fax 905-507-7119
www.wyethconsumer.ca
Line: Markets and sells non-prescription pharmaceuticals.
NAICS: 325410
#Emp: 100-249 (Tor)
#TorLoc: 1
Own: Public Company
Par: Pfizer (US)
Key: Suneet Varma, Pres
James Thibault, VP Fin
James Bruce, VP Mktg

Wyndance Golf Club

450 Durham Rd., R.R. #21
Uxbridge, ON L9P 1R4
Tel 905-649-8545
Fax 905-649-6400
www.clublink.ca
NAICS: 713910
#Emp: 100-249 (Tor)
#TorLoc: 1
Own: Private Company
Par: ClubLink Corp. (CDA)
Key: Jamie Al-Jbouri, Dir of Ops

The Wynfield

451 Woodmount Dr.
Oshawa, ON L1G 8E3
Tel 905-571-0065
Fax 905-579-4902
www.chartwellreit.ca
Line: Offers long term residential care.
NAICS: 623310
#Emp: 100-249 (Tor)
Own: Private Company
Par: Chartwell Seniors Housing REIT (CDA)
Key: W. Brent Binions, Pres & CEO
Katherine Jackson, Admr
Vlad Volodarski, CFO

Wynford

1125 Leslie St.
Toronto, ON M3C 2J6
Tel 416-443-9696
Fax 416-443-9702
www.wynfordmotivates.com
Line: Operates internal marketing company and travel agency.
NAICS: 561510
#Emp: 75-99 (Tor)
#TorLoc: 1
Own: Private Company
Key: Bernie Koth, Co-Pres
Keith Arthur, Chmn
Debi Niven, Co-Pres

Xerox Canada Inc.

5650 Yonge St.
Toronto, ON M2M 4G7
Tel 416-229-3769
Fax 416-229-6826
www.xerox.ca
AKA: The Document Company
Line: Provides equipment, supplies and services that facilitate the creation, reproduction, distribution and storage of documents.
NAICS: 333310 334110
#Emp: 1000-4999 (Tor)
#TorLoc: 8
Own: Public Company
Par: Xerox Corp. (US)
Key: Mandy Shapansky, Pres & CEO
Martine Normand, VP HR
Diane Smalley, VP Fin
James Doherty, VP Sales,
    Central Region
Steve Connor, VP Mktg

Xerox Research Centre of Canada

2660 Speakman Dr.
Mississauga, ON L5K 2L1
Tel 905-823-7091
Fax 905-822-7022
www.xerox.com
Line: Operates materials research centre enabling the flow of imaging and consumable materials from research concepts to supplies solutions.
NAICS: 541710
#Emp: 100-249 (Tor)
#TorLoc: 1
Own: Public Company
Par: Xerox Corp. (US)
Key: Hadi K. Mahabadi, VP

Xstrata Canada Corporation

First Canadian Pl.
6900-100 King St. West
Toronto, ON M5X 1E3
Tel 416-775-1500
Fax 416-775-1744
www.xstrata.com
AKA: Xstrata Nickel
Line: Produces zinc, nickel, copper,
primary and fabricated aluminum,
lead, silver, sulphuric acid, and cobalt;
recycles secondary copper, nickel and
precious metals.
NAICS: 212233 212299
#Emp: 100-249 (Tor)
#TorLoc: 2
Own: Public Company
Par: Xstrata Plc (SWITZ)
Key: Ian Pearce, CEO
Lee Nehring, VP HR
Rebecca Ng, Cont
Dominique Dionne, VP Commun

XTL Transport Inc.

75 Rexdale Blvd.
Toronto, ON M9W 1P1
Tel 416-742-0610
Fax 416-742-2983
www.xtl.com
Line: Provides distribution and logistics
services.
NAICS: 484239 493110
#Emp: 250-499 (Tor)
#TorLoc: 1
Own: Private Company
Key: Serge Gagnon, Pres
Jean Martincourt, VP Ops
Lorraine Gard, VP Safety
Marcel Francoeur, VP Fin
Doug Kimmerly, VP MIS
Luc Francoeur, VP Sales & Mktg

xwave, A Division of Bell Aliant Regional Communications LP

120-1550 Enterprise Rd.
Mississauga, ON L4W 4P4
Tel 905-670-1225
Fax 905-670-1344
www.xwave.com
Line: Provides end-to-end solutions
from systems integration through to
product fulfillment.
NAICS: 541510
#Emp: 100-249 (Tor)
#TorLoc: 1
Own: Private Company
Par: Bell Canada (CDA)

Key: Anthony Wright, VP
Paul Khawaja, VP, ATS
Nadeem Ahmed, Mng Dir, Healthcare
Andrew Parlee, Mktg & Planning Dir
Karen Ewing-Wilson, Mktg Dir

Yale Industrial Trucks Ontario Ltd.

340 Hanlan Rd.
Woodbridge, ON L4L 3P6
Tel 905-851-6620
Fax 905-851-6866
www.yaleforklifts.com
Line: Wholesales and distributes
industrial machinery and equipment.
NAICS: 417210
#Emp: 75-99 (Tor)
#TorLoc: 1
Own: Private Company
Key: Alan McFayden, Pres
Peter Johnson, Cont

Yamaha Canada Music Ltd.

135 Milner Ave.
Toronto, ON M1S 3R1
Tel 416-298-1311
Fax 416-292-0732
www.yamaha.ca
Line: Imports and distributes musical
instruments, audio electronics, and
computer-related products.
NAICS: 414210 339990
#Emp: 75-99 (Tor)
#TorLoc: 1
Own: Private Company
Par: Yamaha Corp. (JAPAN)
Key: Ken Hiraoka, Pres
Robert Barg, Corp VP

Yamaha Motor Canada Ltd.

480 Gordon Baker Rd.
Toronto, ON M2H 3B4
Tel 416-498-1911
Fax 416-491-3122
www.yamaha-motor.ca
Line: Distributes motorcycles,
snowmobiles, A.T.V., outboards, water
vehicles, outdoor power equipment,
parts and accessories.
NAICS: 415190 415290
#Emp: 100-249 (Tor)
#TorLoc: 1
Own: Private Company
Par: Yamaha Motor Company Ltd.
(JAPAN)

Key: Hank Sujita, Pres
Christine Stewart,
    Nat'l Mgr, Fin & Logistics
Jim Chiu, Nat'l IT Mgr
Peter Smallman-Tew, VP Sales & Mktg
Tim Kennedy, Nat'l Mktg Mgr
Peter Hastings, VP Corp Services

Yardi Systems Inc.

510-5925 Airport Rd.
Mississauga, ON L4V 1W1
Tel 905-671-0315
Fax 905-362-0939
www.yardi.com
Line: Designs and manufactures asset
and property management software.
NAICS: 541510
#Emp: 75-99 (Tor)
#TorLoc: 1
Own: Private Company
Par: Yardi Systems Inc. (US)
Key: Peter Altobelli, VP, Cdn Ops
Robert Podlesnik,
    Dir of Professional Services Group

Yee Hong Centre for Geriatric Care

2311 McNicoll Ave.
Toronto, ON M1V 5L3
Tel 416-231-6333
Fax 416-321-6313
www.yeehong.com
Line: Operates a long term care
community services housing.
NAICS: 624120
#Emp: 500-999 (Tor)
Own: Private Company
Key: Nerissa Fung, Exec Dir
Florence Wong, CEO
Julie Tang, Dir of HR
Peter Chung, CFO

Yellow Pages Group

325 Milner Ave.
Toronto, ON M1B 5S8
Tel 416-412-5000
Fax 416-412-5427
www.yellowpages.ca
Line: Publishes directories.
NAICS: 511140
#Emp: 250-499 (Tor)
#TorLoc: 1
Own: Private Company
Key: Lorne Richmond, VP Ops
Catherine Caplice, Dir of Mktg

YMCA of Greater Toronto

42 Charles St. East
Toronto, ON M4Y 1T4
Tel 416-928-9622
Fax 416-928-2030
www.ymcatoronto.org
Line: Promotes opportunities for
personal growth and service to others.
NAICS: 713940 624410
#Emp: 1000-4999 (Tor)
#TorLoc: 250
Own: Not-for-profit
Key: Medhat Mahdy, Pres & CEO
Steve Boone, Exec VP Ops
Karen Hume, Interim VP HR
Wendy Richardson, CFO
Ann Edmonds, VP IT
Laura Graham Prentice, VP Commun

YM Inc. Sales

50 Dufflaw Rd.
Toronto, ON M6A 2W1
Tel 416-789-1071
Fax 416-789-6969
www.stitchesonline.com
AKA: Stitches; Sirens; Urban Planet
Line: Retails Clothing.
NAICS: 448150 448140
#Emp: 500-999 (Tor)
Own: Private Company
Key: Michael Gold, Pres

York Catholic District School Board

320 Bloomington Rd. West
Aurora, ON L4G 3G8
Tel 905-713-1211
Fax 905-713-1272
www.ycdsb.ca
NAICS: 611110
#Emp: 5000-9999 (Tor)
#TorLoc: 81
Own: Government
Key: Susan La Rosa, Dir of Education
Lynda Coulter, Supt of HR

York Central Hospital

10 Trench St.
Richmond Hill, ON L4C 4Z3
Tel 905-883-1212
Fax 905-883-2455
www.yorkcentral.on.ca
Line: Operates a large community
hospital offering emergency, medicine,
surgery, mental health, chronic
kidney disease, woman and child, and
continuing care services.
NAICS: 622111
#Emp: 1000-4999 (Tor)
#TorLoc: 5

Own: Not-for-profit
Key: Altaf Stationwala, Pres & CEO
Beth Snyder, VP, Patient Care Services
Richard Tam, CFO
Diane Salois-Swallow,
   CIO & Chief Privacy Officer
Bill Leacey, CEO,
   York Central Hospital Foundation
Melina Cormier,
   Chief of Commun & Pub Affairs

The Yorkdale Rainforest Restaurant Inc.

3401 Dufferin St.
Toronto, ON M6A 2T9
Tel 416-780-4080
Fax 416-780-4081
www.rainforestcafe.com
NAICS: 722110
#Emp: 100-249 (Tor)
#TorLoc: 1
Own: Private Company
Par: Landrys (US)
Key: George Chami, GM
John Bennett, Asst GM

Yorkdale Shopping Centre Holdings Inc.

500-1 Yorkdale Rd.
Toronto, ON M6A 3A1
Tel 416-256-5066
Fax 416-256-5064
www.yorkdale.com
Line: Specializes in property
management.
NAICS: 531120
#Emp: 100-249 (Tor)
#TorLoc: 1
Own: Private Company
Par: Oxford Properties Group (CDA)
Key: Anthony Casalanguida,
   GM, Oxford Properties Group
John Giddings, Dir of Retail
Robert Horst, Property Mgr
Claire Santamaria, Dir of Mktg

York Downs Golf & Country Club

4134 16th Ave.
Markham, ON L3R 0P1
Tel 905-477-3105
Fax 905-477-0989
www.yorkdowns.com
NAICS: 713910
#Emp: 100-249 (Tor)
#TorLoc: 1
Own: Not-for-profit

Key: Leonardo De La Fuente, GM
Manuel Fernandes,
   Golf Course Superintendent
Ian Crebbin, Golf Professional
Kevin Mann, Cont

York International Ltd.

2-2323 Winston Park Dr.
Oakville, ON L6H 6R7
Tel 905-829-1411
Fax 905-829-5194
www.york.com
AKA: York; Coleman; Luxaire; Airpro;
York Unitary Products Group
Line: Distributes, sells and services
residential, commercial and industrial
heating and air conditioning.
NAICS: 416120
#Emp: 100-249 (Tor)
#TorLoc: 1
Own: Private Company
Par: Johnson Control Inc. (US)
Key: Rick Little, Branch Mgr
Dawn Redel, HR Mgr
Tony D'Alesio, Reg Service Sales Mgr

York Marble Tile & Terrazzo Inc.

2 Sheffield St.
Toronto, ON M6M 3E7
Tel 416-235-0161
Fax 416-235-1247
www.yorkmarble.com
Line: Specializes in the fabrication
and installation of architectural stone,
interior stone, terrazzo and tile.
NAICS: 232420
#Emp: 100-249 (Tor)
#TorLoc: 1
Own: Private Company
Key: Glen Pestrin, Pres
Tony Paluzzi, Cont

York Regional Police

A Div. of Regional Municipality of York
17250 Yonge St.
Newmarket, ON L3Y 4W5
Tel 905-895-1221
Fax 905-895-4149
www.yrp.ca
NAICS: 913130
#Emp: 1000-4999 (Tor)
#TorLoc: 7
Own: Government
Key: Eric Jolliffe, Chief of Police
Bruce Herridge, Deputy Chief, Ops
Gilda Sutton,
   Mgr of Human Resource Services
Mark Holland,
   Mgr of Financial Services
Ron Huber, Mgr of IT
Kathleen Griffin, Mgr of Corp Commun

York Region District School Board

60 Wellington St. West
P.O. Box 40
Aurora, ON L4G 3H2
Tel 905-727-3141
Fax 905-727-1931
www.yrdsb.edu.on.ca
NAICS: 611110
#Emp: 5000-9999 (Tor)
#TorLoc: 150
Own: Government
Key: Ken Thurston, Dir of Education
Chris Tulley, Coordinating Supt of
   Education & HR Services

York Region Media Group

A Div. of Metroland Media Group Ltd.
580 Steven Crt., Bldg. B
P.O. Box 236
Newmarket, ON L3Y 4X1
Tel 905-853-8888
Fax 905-853-5379
www.yorkregion.com
AKA: Markham Economist; Newmarket
Era Banner; Richmond Hill Liberal;
Stouffville Tribune; Vaughan Citizen
NAICS: 511110
#Emp: 250-499 (Tor)
#TorLoc: 7
Own: Private Company
Par: Torstar Corp. (CDA)
Key: Ian Proudfoot, Publisher
Debra Kelly, Editor-in-Chief
Rob Lazurko, Business Mgr
Dawna Andrews,
   Advertising & Mktg Mgr

York Support Services Network

25 Millard Ave,
Newmarket, ON L3Y 7R6
Tel 905-898-6455
Fax 905-898-1171
www.yssn.ca
Line: Provides case management
services to adults and children with
developmental disabilities or serious
mental illnesses and provides crisis
support.
NAICS: 624110 624120
#Emp: 100-249 (Tor)
#TorLoc: 5
Own: Not-for-profit
Key: Marie Lauzier, Exec Dir
Sandy McClymont, Fin & Ops Mgr
Maureen Smith, HR Coord

York University

4700 Keele St.
Toronto, ON M3J 1P3
Tel 416-736-5200
Fax 416-736-5641
www.yorku.ca
Line: Offers full and part-time graduate
and undergraduate degree programs.
NAICS: 611310
#Emp: 10000+ (Tor)
#TorLoc: 3
Own: Government
Key: Mamdouh Shoukri,
   Pres & Vice-Chancellor
Gary Brewer, VP Fin & Admin
Helen Huang,
   Asst VP HR & Employee Relns
Renata Faverin, Dir of Procurement
   Services & Fin
Bob Gagne, CIO
Alex Bilyk, Dir of Media Relns

Yorkville Sound Ltd.

A Div. of Long & McQuade Ltd.
550 Granite Crt.
Pickering, ON L1W 3Y8
Tel 905-837-8481
Fax 905-839-5776
www.yorkville.com
Line: Manufactures and distributes
professional audio equipment.
NAICS: 334310 417320
#Emp: 250-499 (Tor)
#TorLoc: 1
Own: Private Company
Key: Steven Long, Pres
Jack E. Long, Chmn

Young Rosedale Charitable Foundation

877 Yonge St.
Toronto, ON M4W 3M2
Tel 416-923-8887
Fax 416-923-1343
www.fellowshiptowers.com
AKA: Fellowship Towers
Line: Operates a retirement residence.
NAICS: 531111
#Emp: 75-99 (Tor)
#TorLoc: 1
Own: Private Company
Key: Pam McGowan, Cont
Joyce Thomson, Admr

Young & Rubicam Ltd.

60 Bloor St. West, 7th Fl.
Toronto, ON M4W 1J2
Tel 416-961-5111
Fax 416-961-7890
www.yr.com
AKA: Y&R
Line: Operates an advertising agency.
NAICS: 541810
#Emp: 100-249 (Tor)
#TorLoc: 1
Own: Public Company
Par: WPP Group plc (UK)
Key: Chris Jordon, Pres & CEO
Susan Murray, Exec VP & CMO
Diane Graves, HR Mgr
Carl McMurray, CFO
Bharat Puri, IT Dir

Young & Wright / IBI Architects

230 Richmond St. West, 5th Fl.
Toronto, ON M5V 1V6
Tel 416-928-1496
Fax 416-596-0644
www.ibigroup.com
AKA: Robbie/Young & Wright
Architects Inc.
Line: Operates an architectural firm.
NAICS: 541310
#Emp: 100-249 (Tor)
#TorLoc: 1
Own: Private Company
Key: Richard Young, Exec Dir
Jamie Wright, Exec Dir
Drummond Hassan, Exec Dir
Catherine Low, Fin Mgr
Neil Munro, Exec Dir

Youthdale Treatment Centres Ltd.

227 Victoria St.
Toronto, ON M5B 1T8
Tel 416-368-4896
Fax 416-368-3192
www.youthdale.ca
Line: Provides comprehensive,
integrated mental health services to
troubled children and their families.
NAICS: 624110
#Emp: 100-249 (Tor)
Own: Not-for-profit
Key: Dan Hagler, CEO
Thomas Macdonald, Chair
Paul Allen, Clinical Dir

YRC Reimer

6130 Netherhart Rd.
Mississauga, ON L5T 1B7
Tel 905-670-9366
Fax 905-670-4525
www.yrc.com
AKA: Fast as Flite
Line: Provides transportation services within North America.
NAICS: 488990 484110 484121
#Emp: 250-499 (Tor)
#TorLoc: 1
Own: Private Company
Par: Roadway Express Inc. (US)
Key: Clayton Gording, Pres
Paul Hildebrand, Dir
Kurt Brandes, VP Sales
Frank Washburn, VP
    Mktg Exhibit & Customer Services
Andrew Milne, Service Centre Mgr

YWCA of Toronto

Bongard House
80 Woodlawn Ave. East
Toronto, ON M4T 1C1
Tel 416-961-8100
Fax 416-961-7739
www.ywcatoronto.org
AKA: YWCA of Greater Toronto; Young Women's Christian Association of Greater Toronto
Line: Operates multi-service women's organization that assists women with economic independence, emotional well-being, community belonging and leadership.
NAICS: 624310 624110
#Emp: 250-499 (Tor)
#TorLoc: 12
Own: Not-for-profit
Key: Kristin Blakely-Kozman, Pres
Heather M. McGregor, CEO
Joan White, Dir of Housing Dev
Jeannette Manguiat, Dir of HR & Admin
Lois Fine, Dir of Fin & IT
Marilda Tselepis, Dir of Employment
Sally Palmateer,
    Dir of Girls & Family Programs
Mary-Ann Kerr, Dir of Philanthropy
Sarah Blackstock,
    Dir of Advocacy & Commun

Zara Canada

1550-1200 McGill College St.
Montreal, PQ H3B 4G7
Tel 514-868-1516
Fax 514-868-1522
www.zara.com
Line: Retails men's, women's and children's clothing.
NAICS: 448140
#Emp: 100-249 (Tor)
#TorLoc: 4
Own: Private Company
Par: Inditex (SPAIN)
Key: David Pastrana, Pres
Emma Redondo, Dir of HR
Alexis Drouault, Dir of Fin & Admin

Zeidler Partnership Architects

200-315 Queen St. West
Toronto, ON M5V 2X2
Tel 416-596-8300
Fax 416-596-1408
www.zeidlerpartnership.com
AKA: ZRV Holding Ltd.
Line: Operates architectural firm that provides interior design, master planning, project management as well as architectural services.
NAICS: 541330
#Emp: 75-99 (Tor)
#TorLoc: 1
Own: Partnership
Key: Alan Munn, Sr Partner
Agnes Cheung, Cont
Ian Fairlie, Dir of IT
Don Vetere, Dir of Business Dev

Zenith Optimedia Canada Inc.

200-111 Queen St. East
Toronto, ON M5C 1S2
Tel 416-925-9988
Fax 416-975-8208
www.zenithoptimedia.com
Line: Operates an advertising agency.
NAICS: 541810
#Emp: 100-249 (Tor)
#TorLoc: 1
Own: Private Company
Key: Sunni Boot, Pres & CEO, Toronto
Steve King, CEO, Worldwide

Zip Signs Ltd.

5040 North Service Rd.
Burlington, ON L7L 5R5
Tel 905-332-8332
Fax 905-332-9994
www.zipsigns.com
Line: Designs and manufactures signage.
NAICS: 339950
#Emp: 75-99 (Tor)
#TorLoc: 1
Own: Private Company
Key: Fred Bennink, Pres & CEO

Zodiac Swim School Limited

160 Steeprock Dr.
Toronto, ON M3J 2T4
Tel 416-789-1989
Fax 416-789-5525
www.zodiacswim.on.ca
Line: Offers swim lessons for infants to adults.
NAICS: 721213
#Emp: 100-249 (Tor)
#TorLoc: 2
Own: Private Company
Key: Rick Howard, Dir
Ellen Howard, Dir
Gilbert Dias, Cont

Zurich North America Canada

400 University Ave.
Toronto, ON M5G 1S7
Tel 416-586-3000
Fax 416-586-2525
www.zurichcanada.com
AKA: Peopleplus Insurance Co.
Line: Sells property, casualty, aircraft, automobile and liability insurance.
NAICS: 524112
#Emp: 500-999 (Tor)
#TorLoc: 1
Own: Private Company
Par: Zurich Financial Services (SWITZ)
Key: Alister Campbell, Pres & CEO
Darren Joslin, VP Tech & Ops
Sandra Walsh, VP HR
Nigel Ayers, Sr VP & CFO

Zylog Systems (Canada) Ltd.

2000-2 Sheppard Ave. East
Toronto, ON M2N 5Y7
Tel 416-225-9900
Fax 416-225-9104
www.zylog.ca
Line: Operates an information technology and engineering staffing and recruiting firm.
NAICS: 541510
#Emp: 100-249 (Tor)
#TorLoc: 1
Own: Public Company
Par: Zylog Systems Ltd. (CDA)
Key: John Mahramn, CEO
Siva Cherla, VP Corp Cont
Helen Trinh, HR Mgr
Sri Hari, CFO

CONTACT 11
TORONTO 12

Part 2

Affiliated Names Index

100 Huntley St.
See: Crossroads Christian
Communications Inc.

102.1 The Edge
See: CFNY FM 102.1

1216809 Ontario Ltd.
See: Scarborough Toyota

1263528 Ontario Ltd.
See: The Guvernment

1313256 Ontario Inc.
See: FactoryDirect.ca

154644 Canada Inc.
See: Seniors 4 Seniors

1548383 Ontario Inc.
See: Radisson Admiral Hotel

1733379 Ontario Ltd.
See: The Alliance Group Inc.

3499481 Canada Inc.
See: PJ's Pet Centres Ltd.

410385 Ontario Ltd.
See: Maple Drywall

488491 Ontario Inc.
See: Avalon Retirement Centre

582958 Ontario Ltd.
See: The Grenadier Retirement
Residence

733907 Ontario Ltd.
See: European Quality Meats

A&P
See: Metro Ontario Inc.

AAL
See: The Administrative
Assistants Ltd.

ABC Group
See: Salga Associates

Access Personnel
See: Access Care Inc.

Accounting Advantage
See: AppleOne Employment
Services Ltd.

Acrylic Fabricators Ltd.
See: AFL Display Group

ACTRA
See: Alliance of Canadian Cinema,
Television & Radio Artists

**Addison-Wesley Longman
Publishers Ltd.**
See: Pearson Education Canada Inc.

Adelaide Club
See: Cambridge Group of Clubs

Adminserv
See: Livingston International Inc.

ADS Employment Services
See: West-ADS Employment
Services Inc.

ADSK Canada Inc.
See: Autodesk Canada

ADT Advanced Integration
See: Intercon Security Ltd.

Advanced Micro Devices
See: AMD

**Advantage Group
Advantage Labour Resources
Advantage Services Personnel**
See: Advantage Personnel Ltd.

The Adventure Travel Company
See: Travel Cuts

AECL
See: Atomic Energy of Canada Ltd.

Aegon Canada Inc.
See: Transamerica Life Canada

Affiliated Computer Services, Inc.
See: Buck Consultants Limited

AFGD Glass
See: AGC Flat Glass
North America Ltd.

AGITT
See: AGI Traffic Technology

AGO
See: Art Gallery of Ontario

AIIM Inc.
See: Avant Imaging & Information
Management Inc.

Air Canada Centre
See: Maple Leaf Sports
& Entertainment Ltd.

Air Miles Reward Program
See: Loyalty One Inc.

Airpro
See: York International Ltd.

Ajax
See: The Town of Ajax

Ajax-Pickering News Advertiser
See: Durham Region Media Group

**Ajilon Communications
Ajilon Consulting**
See: Modis

Al Frisco's
See: SIR Corp.

Alba Tours
See: Thomas Cook North America

Alchemy
See: St. Joseph Pi Media

Alfield Industries
See: Martinrea International Inc.

Alfit
See: Wurth Canada Ltd.

Alice Fazooli's!
See: SIR Corp.

All-Metal Brake Shoe Co.
See: Util Capital Tool & Design

Alliance Envelope Ltd.
See: Royal Envelope Ltd.

Alliance Fitness Corp.
See: Goodlife Fitness

Allied Credit
See: General Motors Acceptance
Corporation of Canada Ltd.

Allied Viceroy Group
See: Viceroy Rubber & Plastics Ltd.

Alphacine
See: Technicolor

Aluminum Window Designs Ltd.
See: Vinyl Window Designs Ltd.

Amalgamet Canada
See: National Concrete Accessories

American Essentials
See: McGregor Industries Inc.

American Express Canada
See: Amex Canada Inc.

Anglican Church of Canada
See: The General Synod
of the Anglican Church of Canada

Anglican Diocese of Toronto
See: Incorporated Synod
of the Diocese of Toronto

Annex Guardian
See: Toronto Community News

Aon Canada Inc.
See: Combined Insurance Company
of America

Aon Risk Services
See: Aon Reed Stenhouse Inc.

Aramis
See: Estee Lauder Cosmetics Ltd.

**Architects + Research
+ Knowledge Inc.**
See: Petroff Partnership Architects

ASL Group Ltd.
See: All Stick Label Ltd.

Assa Abloy Door Group Inc.
See: Baron Metal Industries Inc.

Athletic Knit
See: Bernard Athletic Knit

Auberge du Pommier
See: Oliver & Bonacini Restaurants

Audi Uptown
See: Downtown Fine Cars Inc.

Audience Response Systems
See: Frischkorn Associates Inc.

The Audit Group
See: PRG Schultz Canada Corp.

Aunt Irene's Outlet Store
See: Future Bakery Ltd.

Aurora
  See: The Town of Aurora

Aurora Filters
  See: All-Weld Company Ltd.

Avion Travel
  See: Thomas Cook North America

Azimuth 3 Enterprises
  See: AZ3 Enterprises Inc.

B-Line
  See: Cooper Industries (Canada) Inc.

B.W. Law Limited Partnership
  See: Beard Winter LLP

B2 Retail Solutions
  See: Glenn A. Davis & Associates Ltd.

BA Roofing Co.
  See: Bothwell-Accurate Co.
  (2006) Limited

Baby Gap
  See: Gap Inc. Canada

Bacchanalia Foods
  See: The Kitchen Table Inc.

The Baker's Counter
  See: Open Window Health Bread
  Bakery Limited

Bakery Deluxe Company
  See: Fiera Foods Inc.

Banana Republic Canada
  See: Gap Inc. Canada

Bangkok Garden Restaurant
  See: Brydson Group Ltd.

Bank of Montreal
  See: BMO Financial Group

The Barn Markets
  See: Metro Ontario Inc.

Batise Investments Ltd.
  See: H & R Developments

Battery Plus
  See: The Source (Bell) Electronics
  Canada Inc.

Battlefield Equipment Rentals
  See: Toromont Industries Ltd.

The Bay
  See: Hudson's Bay Company

The Bay Area Learning Centre
  See: Centre for Skills Development
  & Training

BCPV
  See: Black Creek Pioneer Village

BD Canada
  See: Becton Dickinson Canada Inc.

BDC
  See: Business Development Bank
  of Canada

Beach-Riverdale Mirror
  See: Toronto Community News

Beauport Wallcoverings
  See: Blue Mountain
  Wallcovering Inc.

Beauticians Beauty Supply
  See: Beauty Systems Group
  (Canada) Inc.

Becker's Milk
  See: Mac's Convenience Stores Inc.

The Beer Store
  See: Brewers' Retail Inc.

Belair Direct
  See: Belair Insurance Company Inc.

Belair Travel
  See: Thomas Cook North America

The Belmont House
  See: The Toronto Aged Men's and
  Women's Homes

Belpak Foods
  See: Janes Family Foods Ltd.

Bengard Manufacturing
  See: Loxcreen Canada Ltd.

Best Kosher Haimishe Farfel
  See: Open Window Health Bread
  Bakery Limited

Bethany West
  See: Bethany Lodge

BFG Canada
  See: PL Foods Ltd.

Bienvenue
  See: Hachette Distribution Services
  Retail North America

Biff's Bistro
  See: Oliver & Bonacini Restaurants

Big Daddy's Crab Shack & Oyster Bar
  See: 1561716 Ontario Ltd.

BilingualOne
  See: AppleOne Employment
  Services Ltd.

Birks Jewellers
  See: Birks & Mayors Inc.

BKR International
  See: Soberman LLP

Black's Cameras
  See: Black Photo Corporation

BLJC
  See: Brookfield LePage
  Johnson Controls

Bloor West Villager
  See: Toronto Community News

Blue Tree Hotels LP
  See: The Westin Harbour Castle

Blumont Capital
  See: Integrated Asset
  Management Corp.

BM2 Remediation
  See: Quantum Murray LP

The Book Company
  See: Indigo Books & Music, Inc.

Boomerang
  See: Thomas Cook North America

Bosch
  See: Robert Bosch Inc.

Bounty
  See: Mars Canada Inc.

Brady Canada
  See: WHB Identification
  Solutions Inc.

Brafasco
  See: HD Supply Canada

Brampton Guardian
  See: North Peel Media Group

Brannon Steel
  See: T.A. Brannon Steel Ltd.

Bredero-Shaw
  See: ShawCor Ltd.

The Briars Resort
  See: Briars Estates Ltd.

Bristol Aerospace
  See: Magellan Aerospace Corp.

Britches
  See: Grafton-Fraser Inc.

Broadcast News Ltd.
  See: The Canadian Press

Brock
  See: The Corporation of the
  Township of Brock

Brookfield Properties
  See: BPO Properties Ltd.

Brooks Athletic Shoes
  See: RMP Athletic Locker Ltd.

BTW Services Inc.
BTW Trucking Inc.
  See: Behind the Wheel
  Transportation Services Inc.

Budd Brothers Holding Co.
Budds Hamilton
Budds Imported Car Collision Services
  See: Stuart Budd & Sons Ltd.

**Buffalo Forwarding
& Warehousing Group**
  See: William L. Rutherford Limited

Bureau en Gros
  See: Staples Canada Inc.

Burlington
  See: The City of Burlington

Burlington Post
  See: Halton Region Media Group

Bussmann
See: Cooper Industries (Canada) Inc.

BVA Systems Ltd.
See: Vibro Acoustics

C W Henderson
See: CWH Distribution Services Inc.

CA Ontario
See: Institute of Chartered
Accountants of Ontario

CableTalk Systems Inc.
See: BMP Metals Inc.

Calea's Pharmacy
See: Calea Ltd.

Caledon
See: The Corporation of the
Town of Caledon

Caledon Enterprise
See: North Peel Media Group

Cambridge Club
See: Cambridge Group of Clubs

CAMH
See: Centre for Addiction
and Mental Health

Can-Sling/DBI
See: Capital Safety - Canada

Canada Millwrights Ltd.
See: All-Weld Company Ltd.

Canadian Automobile Association
See: CAA South Central Ontario

Canadian Erectors Ltd.
See: Canerector Inc.

Canadian Flight Academy
See: Toronto Airways Ltd.

Canadian Freightways
See: Transport CFQI

Canadian Home Income Plan Corp.
See: HomEquity Bank

Canadian Litigation Counsel
See: McCague Borlack LLP

Canadian Mass Media Inc.
See: Metro News

Canadian National Exhibition
See: The Board of Governors
of Exhibition Place

Canadian National Railway Co.
See: CN

Canadian Scene
See: Hachette Distribution Services
Retail North America

Canadian Tire
See: Grandview Sales
& Distribution Ltd.
See: K.W. Mann Inc.

Canadian Universities

Travel Service Ltd.
See: Travel Cuts

Cancom
See: Shaw Broadcast Services

CANDU
See: Atomic Energy of Canada Ltd.

Canoe
See: Oliver & Bonacini Restaurants

Canon Theatre
See: Mirvish Productions

Canyon Creek
See: SIR Corp.

CAPREIT
See: Canadian Apartment Properties
Real Estate Investment Trust

Casa Isabel Resort
See: Village Manor (TO) Ltd.

Casa Verde Health Centre
See: Paragon Health Care
(Ontario) Inc.

Casey's
See: Prime Restaurants
of Canada Inc.

Cash & Carry
See: Loblaw Companies Limited

CAST
See: Children's Aid Society
of Toronto

Casual Concepts
See: Reflections Furniture
Industries Ltd.

CAW Canada
CAW-TCA Canada
See: Canadian Auto Workers Union

CBC
See: Canadian Broadcasting Corp.

CBRE
See: CB Richard Ellis Limited

CCAS
See: The Catholic Children's Aid
Society of Toronto

CCS
See: Catholic Cross-Cultural Services

CCT Logistics
See: 1149318 Ontario Inc.

CDS
See: Canadian Depository for
Securities Ltd.

Cedar Brook
See: Fernie House

CEL
See: Crossey Engineering Ltd.

Central CCAC
See: Central - Community Care
Access Centre

The Central Group
See: Central Graphics & Container
Group Ltd.

Centreville Amusement Park
See: Beasley Amusements

CET
See: Centre for Education & Training

Champions
See: Woodbine Entertainment Group

Champs Food Systems Ltd.
See: Tucker's Marketplace
Restaurant

Chartered Accountants of Canada
See: Canadian Institute of Chartered
Accountants

Chester Village
See: Broadview Foundation

Chicopee Manufacturing
See: Magellan Aerospace Corp.

CHIP
See: HomEquity Bank

CHS
See: Canadian Hearing Society

CHSI
See: Infrastructure Health & Safety
Association of Ontario

Chubb Security
See: CSG Security Inc.

CIBC
See: Canadian Imperial Bank
of Commerce

CICA
See: Canadian Institute
of Chartered Accountants

CICS
See: Centre for Information
and Community Services

CIHI
See: Canadian Institute
for Health Information

CILQ-FM
See: Q107 FM

CIM Ltd.
See: Consumer Impact
Marketing Ltd.

CIMCO
See: Toromont Industries Ltd.

CISCO Industrial Supply
See: Acklands-Grainger Inc.

City Centre Mirror
See: Toronto Community News

The City of Pickering
See: The Corporation of
The City of Pickering

CLAPW
See: Community Living Ajax, Pickering & Whitby

Clarington
See: The Municipality of Clarington

Clarington This Week
See: Durham Region Media Group

Classic Books
See: Indigo Books & Music, Inc.

CLEO
See: Comark Services Inc.

Clinique
See: Estee Lauder Cosmetics Ltd.

CLOC
See: Community Living Oshawa / Clarington

Closing the Gap Healthcare Group
See: Rehab Express Inc.
See: Respiron Care-Plus Inc.

CMCC
See: Canadian Memorial Chiropractic College

CMHC
See: Canada Mortgage and Housing Corp.

CMI
See: Pi Media / St Joseph's Content

CN Tower Ltd.
See: Canada Lands Company Ltd.

CNA Canada
See: Continental Casualty Company

CNIB
See: The Canadian National Institute for the Blind / Ontario Div.

Coach Canada
See: Trentway-Wagar Inc.

Coast Paper
See: PaperlinX Canada Limited

Coleman
See: Jarden Consumer Solutions

Coleman
See: York International Ltd.

Coles, The Book People
See: Indigo Books & Music, Inc.

Colour Your World
See: AkzoNobel

Columbus Recycling Centre
See: WASTECO

Command Post
See: Technicolor

Community Care Services
See: ProHome Health Services

Computer Associates Canada Co.
See: CA Canada

Computer Logistics
See: Bigtech Inc.

Computer Trust Company of Canada
See: Computershare Canada

Conference World Tours
See: Vision 2000 Travel Group Inc.

Continental Penn Services
See: All-Weld Company Ltd.

Conway Central Express
See: Con-way Freight Canada

Cooperators
See: TIC Travel Insurance Coordinators Ltd.

Corus Radio Toronto
See: Q107 FM

Coseco Insurance Co.
See: HB Group Insurance Management Ltd.

CosmoProf
See: Beauty Systems Group (Canada) Inc.

Cotton Country
See: Dorothea Knitting Mills Ltd.

Country Fresh Packaging
See: Dominion Citrus Income Fund

Coverall
See: Postlinx
See: Robson Enterprises Inc.

Coza
See: Cara Operations Limited

CP Images
See: The Canadian Press

CPL
See: Contract Pharmaceuticals Limited Canada

CPSO
See: College of Physicians and Surgeons of Ontario

Craftwood
See: Sonnenberg Industries Ltd.

Credit Bureau of Canada Collections
See: Collectcents Inc.

CREIT Management LP
See: Canadian Real Estate Investment Trust

CSA
See: Canadian Standards Association

CSDCSO
See: Conseil Scolaire de District du Centre-Sud-Ouest

CSTC Inc.
See: C.S.T. Consultants Inc.

Curtiss-Wright Flow Control Company
See: Indal Technologies Inc.

D'Arcy McGee's
See: Prime Restaurants of Canada Inc.

D+H Ltd.
See: Davis + Henderson

D.W. Murray & Associates Ltd.
See: Vibro Acoustics

Dade Behring Canada Inc.
See: Siemens Healthcare Diagnostics

David Brown Union Pumps
See: Clyde Union

Davis Bridgemark
See: Glenn A. Davis & Associates Ltd.

DBA Metal Koting
See: Metal Koting - Continuous Colour Coat Limited

DCC
See: Dominion Colour Corp.

DCFS Canada Corp.
See: Daimler Trucks Financial Ltd.

The Debiasi Group
See: DBG

Debro Chemical

Debro Steel
See: National Concrete Accessories

Decorr Display & Design
See: The Hughes Group

Deep Foundation Group Management
See: Deep Foundations Contractors Inc.

Delfour
See: Accellos Canada Inc.

Delta Chelsea

Denta Bone
See: Mars Canada Inc.

Dependable IT
See: Cancable Inc.

Design Plastics Int.
See: The Hughes Group

DGI
See: The Dominion Group Inc.

Dial One Wolfedale Electric
See: Wolfedale Electric Ltd.

Digital V6
See: Concord Idea Corp.

Direct Protect
See: HB Group Insurance Management Ltd.

Direct Underground
See: Vaughan Paving Ltd.

Distributions Alimentaires Le Marquis
See: Johnvince Foods

Diverse Business & Personnel Corporation
See: DBPC Group of Companies

DMB & B
See: Bensimon Byrne

The Document Company
See: Xerox Canada Inc.

Dofino & Buko
See: Arla Foods, Inc.

Dollar Rent-A-Car
See: Dollar Thrifty Automotive Group Canada Inc.

Dom Lipa
Dom Lipa Nursing Home
See: Slovenian Linden Foundation

Don Park Fire Protection Systems
See: Don Park LP

Donbarton
See: Fernie House

Dorasort
See: Metex Heat Treating Ltd.

Dorvict Home & Health Care Services
See: Dorvict Resource & Consulting Centre Inc.

Downsview Kitchens
See: Downsview Woodworking Ltd.

Downtown Infiniti
Downtown Porsche
See: Downtown Fine Cars Inc.

Draftworldwide Canada Inc.
See: Fuel Advertising Inc.

Drummond Metal Products
See: Loxcreen Canada Ltd.

DSC
See: Digital Security Controls Ltd.

Ducartor Holdings Ltd.
See: Beard Winter LLP

Dun & Bradstreet Canada
See: D & B Canada

Dura-Trim Products
See: Loxcreen Canada Ltd.

Durham
See: Regional Municipality of Durham

DW+Partners
See: Pi Media / St Joseph's Content
See: St. Joseph Pi Media

DWPV Management Limited
DWPV Services Limited Partnership
See: Davies Ward Phillips & Vineberg LLP

Dynamic Mutual Funds
See: Dundee Wealth

East Side Mario's
See: Prime Restaurants of Canada Inc.

East York-Riverdale Mirror
See: Toronto Community News

The Economical Insurance Group
See: Economical Mutual Insurance Co.

eCustoms
See: Management Systems Resources Inc.

ECWalkers
See: Grosnor Industries Inc.

Ed Mirvish Enterprises Ltd.
See: Mirvish Productions

Eleventh Floor Apparel Ltd.
See: Lundstrom

Elmcrest College
elmspa
Elmwood Spa
See: Brydson Group Ltd.

Elvidge Paper Box Inc.
See: Ellis Packaging Ltd.

The Employment Solution
See: T.E.S. Contract Services Inc.

Encore Cruise Escapes
See: Thomas Cook North America

Enerscan Controls
See: Jay Electric Ltd.

EOH - Meta Foundation
See: Meta Centre for the Developmentally Disabled

Epic Express
See: Transport CFQI

Erin Advocate
See: North Peel Media Group

Erindale College
See: University of Toronto Mississauga

Esplanade Bier Market
See: Prime Restaurants of Canada Inc.

Etobicoke Guardian
See: Toronto Community News

Eva's Phoenix
Eva's Place
Eva's Satellite
See: Eva's Initiatives

EVault Canada Inc.
See: i365

Exchanger Industries
See: National Concrete Accessories

Executive Maintenance Services Inc.
See: Werek Enterprises Inc.

Exhibition Place
See: The Board of Governors of Exhibition Place

Exotica
See: Thomas Cook North America

Extendicare
See: The McCall Centre for Continuing Care

Family Fitness
See: Goodlife Fitness

Far Niente
See: SIR Corp.

Farber CFO Resources
Farber Financial Group
See: A. Farber & Partners Inc.

Fast as Flite
See: YRC Reimer

FCI Custom Manufacturing
See: Flying Colours International

Federation Insurance
See: Economical Mutual Insurance Co.

FEDEX
See: Federal Express Canada Ltd.

Fellowship Towers
See: Young Rosedale Charitable Foundation

Fenco
See: Fenwick Automotive Products Ltd.

Fernbrook Homes
See: Oxville Homes Ltd.

Fields
See: Hudson's Bay Company

Fionn MacCool's Irish Pub
See: Prime Restaurants of Canada Inc.

First Alert
See: Jarden Consumer Solutions

First Team Transport Inc.
See: SCI Logistics Inc.

Flamborough Review
See: Halton Region Media Group

Fleet Industries
See: Magellan Aerospace Corp.

Fletcher Davis
See: Davis Group of Companies Corp.

Flexillume
See: Cooper Industries (Canada) Inc.

Focus Promotion Products
See: Davis Group of Companies Corp.

Food Basics
See: Metro Ontario Inc.

Food Depot
See: The Kitchen Table Inc.

Foote, Cone & Belding Canada Ltd.
See: Draft FCB Canada

Formula Honda
See: Pauldonlam Investments Inc.

Fortinos Supermarkets
See: Loblaw Companies Limited

The Forzani Group
See: Sport Chek

Four/Petit Four
See: SIR Corp.

Four Seasons Hotels & Resorts
See: Four Seasons Hotels Limited

Four Star Group
See: Four Star Plating Industries Ltd.

Freightlogix
See: Accellos Canada Inc.

Fresh Start
See: Cross Toronto Community
Development Corp.

Freshmart
See: Loblaw Companies Limited

Frigidaire
See: Electrolux Home Products

Front Page
See: Hachette Distribution Services
Retail North America

FTG Aerospace Division
See: Firan Technology Group
- Aerospace Division

FunSun Vacations
See: Thomas Cook North America

G.E. Shnier Co.
See: Gesco Industries Inc.

Gap Kids
See: Gap Inc. Canada

GDI
See: Omni Facility Services
Canada Limited

GE Canada
See: General Electric Canada

George Richards
See: Grafton-Fraser Inc.

**Georgeson Shareholder
Communications Inc.**
See: Computershare Canada

**Georgetown Independent
& Free Press**
See: North Peel Media Group

Georgina
See: The Town of Georgina

GH Medical
See: VitalAire Canada Inc.

Gibson Transport
See: Warren Gibson Ltd.

Gilmour
See: Robert Bosch Inc.

Glen Cedars Golf Club
See: Deer Creek Golf
& Banquet Facility

Glidden Paint
See: AkzoNobel

Global Group
See: Allwood Products Limited

Global Upholstery
See: Global File Inc.

Globalive Communications
See: Canopco

Glopak
See: Hood Packaging Corporation

GO Packaging
See: Gerrard-Oval Strapping

Goldy Metals Inc.
See: Standard Auto Wreckers

Goodmans LLP
See: Goodlaw Services Limited
Partnership

Gopher Express Delivery Ltd.
See: Atripco Delivery Service

Gormley Automotive Centre
See: Don Valley North
Automotive Inc.

Gottschalk+Ash
See: St. Joseph Pi Media

Grafton & Co.
See: Grafton-Fraser Inc.

Grand Toronto Venture Corp.
See: Park Hyatt Toronto

**The Great Canadian Book Co.
The Great Canadian Newsstand Co.**
See: Hachette Distribution Services
Retail North America

Greatway Imports Ltd.
See: Indeka Imports Ltd.

Greenwood Mushroom Farm
See: Windmill Mushroom Farms

Greenwood Teletheatre
See: Woodbine Entertainment Group

Griffiths McBurney & Partners
See: GMP Securities LP

Group 4 Securicor (Canada) Ltd.
See: G4S Cash Solutions
(Canada) Ltd.

Groupe Robert
See: Robert Transport

GTAA
See: Greater Toronto Airports
Authority

H.W. & Associates
See: Hoodex Industries Ltd.

Halo
See: Cooper Industries (Canada) Inc.

Halton
See: Regional Municipality of Halton

Halton Hills
See: The Town of Halton Hills

Halton Public School Board
See: Halton District School Board

Hammill
See: Unisync Group Ltd.

Hard Rock Cafe Toronto
See: HRC Canada Inc.

Hardwall Construction
See: Hardrock Forming Co.

Harley Owners Group of Canada
See: Deeley Harley Davidson Canada

Harvey's
See: Cara Operations Limited

Hatch Mott MacDonald
See: Hatch Ltd.

Hathro Management Partnership
See: Thomson Rogers

HBC
See: Hudson's Bay Company

HDS Retail North America
See: Hachette Distribution Services
Retail North America

Head Shots
See: Henry's

Headwater Technology Solutions Inc.
See: Accellos Canada Inc.

Health Bread
See: Open Window Health Bread
Bakery Limited

Heinz
See: H.J. Heinz Company
of Canada Ltd.

Helyar & Associates
See: Altus Group Ltd.

Heritage General Insurance Co.
See: Canadian Premier Life
Insurance Co.

Heritage Centre

Heritage Village
See: Unionville Home Society

Highbourne Lifecare Center
See: Lifecare Operations

HLB International
See: Schwartz Levitsky Feldman LLP

Hogg Robinson Group
See: HRG North America

Hok Architects Corporation
See: Hok Canada, Inc.

Holiday House
The Holiday Network
　See: Thomas Cook North America

Holidayoutlet.ca
　See: Vision 2000 Travel Group Inc.

Home Outfitters
　See: Hudson's Bay Company

HomeSense
　See: Winners Merchants
　International

Honest Ed's
　See: Mirvish Productions

The Hospitality Group
　See: Marcus Evans

HPPDL
　See: BDI World Class World Wide

HSFO
　See: Heart and Stroke Foundation
　of Ontario

Hughes Containers
　See: The Hughes Group

Hunt Brothers
　See: Hurley Group

The Huron Group of Companies
　See: Huron Services Group Ltd.

Hyatt Hotels & Resorts
　See: Park Hyatt Toronto

IAPA
　See: Workplace Safety
　& Prevention Services

IBC
　See: Insurance Bureau of Canada

ICAO
　See: Institute of Chartered
　Accountants of Ontario

ICD
　See: Innovative Cooling Dynamics

ICES
　See: Institute for Clinical
　Evaluative Sciences

ICP
　See: International Custom
　Products Inc.

IFDS Canada
　See: International Financial Data
　Services (Canada) Ltd.

IGA
　See: Sobeys Ontario

IGI
　See: The International Group, Inc.

IHG Intercontinental Hotels Group
　See: Holiday Inn Toronto
　International Airport

IIROC
　See: Investment Industry Regulatory
　Organization of Canada

IKO
　See: IG Machine & Fibres Ltd.

iLORi
　See: Luxottica Retail

IMG Inc.
　See: Interior Manufacturing
　Group Inc.

Imperial Life Financial
　See: Desjardins Financial Security
　Life Assurance Company - Toronto

IMS
　See: Inquiry Management
　Systems Ltd.

Impulse
Inclination
　See: Hachette Distribution Services
　Retail North America

Independent & Free Press
　See: North Peel Media Group

The Independent Order of Foresters
　See: Foresters

Induspac
　See: Smith Induspac Toronto Ltd.

Industrial Motion
　See: BDI World Class World Wide

Innocon Inc.
　See: Lafarge Canada Inc.

Innova Envelope
　See: Supremex Inc.

Innvest Reit Hotels
　See: Westmont Hospitality Group

**Institute of Naturopathic Education
& Research**
　See: The Canadian College
　of Naturopathic Medicine

Intair
　See: Thomas Cook North America

Integrated Managed Futures
Integrated Partners
　See: Integrated Asset
　Management Corp.

Interbase Consultants Ltd.
　See: IBI Group

**International Championship
Management Ltd.**
　See: Marcus Evans

International Fasteners Ltd.
　See: Interfast Inc.

**International Logistics & Stone
Distribution**
　See: Maple Group

International Waxes
　See: The International Group, Inc.

Investors Syndicate
　See: Investors Group Inc.

IRMC - Intellirisk
　See: iQor Canada Inc.

Ironstone Media
　See: Web Offset Publications Ltd.

Island Road Rosebank
　See: Fernie House

ITC Inc.
　See: Clarke Inc.

ITL Circuits
　See: Integrated Technology Ltd.

IVHS
　See: Kapsch TrafficCom

Jack Astor's Bar & Grill
　See: SIR Corp.

Jack Fraser
　See: Grafton-Fraser Inc.

Jaguar Beauty Supplies Ltd.
　See: Beauty Systems Group
　(Canada) Inc.

Jewish Foundation of Greater Toronto
　See: UJA Federation of Greater
　Toronto

JKIL
　See: Robert Bosch Inc.

Johnston Equipment
　See: G.N. Johnston Equipment
　Company Ltd.

Jones New York
　See: Jones Apparel Group
　Canada Ltd.

Jump Café & Bar
　See: Oliver & Bonacini Restaurants

JVS Toronto
　See: Jewish Vocational Service of
　Greater Toronto

K-Tek Electro-Services Ltd.
　See: K-Line Maintenance
　& Construction Ltd.

KEBOC
　See: Korea Exchange Bank of Canada

Kelsey's
　See: Cara Operations Limited

Kendrew Distribution Services
　See: Atripco Delivery Service

Kengrove Tree & Topsoil
　See: Cornerstone Landscaping Ltd.

Kenscott
　See: BDI World Class World Wide

Kensington Cancer Screening Clinic
Kensington Eye Institute
 See: Kensington Health Centre

Kester Electric Supply Limited
 See: Paul Wolf Lighting & Electric
 Supply Ltd.

Kewl Sports
 See: Accolade Group Inc.

KFC
 See: Priszm Income Fund

Kimit Transportation Logistics
 See: Atripco Delivery Service

King Edward Hotel
 See: Le Méridien King Edward

King Koil
 See: Satpanth Capital Inc.

Kingston Sorel
 See: SF Partnership LLP

Kingsway Financial Services
 See: Jevco Insurance Company

Kirlin Leasing
 See: Atripco Delivery Service

KIT Inc.
 See: Priszm Income Fund

Klein Farber Corporate Finance
 See: A. Farber & Partners Inc.

KN Air
KN Customs
KN Lead Logistics
KN Logistics
KN Sea
KN VIA
 See: Kuehne & Nagel Ltd.

KOG
 See: Knights On Guard
 Protective Services

Kroehler Furniture Inc.
 See: Distinctive Designs
 Furniture Inc.

Kronis Rotsztain Margles Cappel
Barristers & Solicitors
 See: KRMC Barristers & Solicitors

L'Optique Centennial Lteé
 See: Centennial Optical Limited

L&T
 See: Hudson's Bay Company

Laidlaw Education Services
 See: First Canada/Greyhound

Lamplighter
 See: Hachette Distribution Services
 Retail North America

Laser Quest
 See: Versent Corporation ULC

The Last Minute Club
 See: The Last Minute Experts Inc.
 See: Thomas Cook North America

Laurentian Financial Services
 See: Desjardins Financial Security
 Life Assurance Company - Toronto

Law Pro
 See: Lawyers Professional
 Indemnity Co.

LCBO
 See: Liquor Control Board of Ontario

Legacy Pork
 See: Quality Meat Packers Ltd.

LensCrafters
 See: Luxottica Retail

Levelwear
 See: Accolade Group Inc.

Lexis Nexis
 See: Reed Construction Data

Lexus of Richmond Hill
 See: Don Valley North
 Automotive Inc.

Librairie Smith
 See: Indigo Books & Music, Inc.

Lingerie & Company
 See: Boutique La Vie en Rose Inc.

Lipson's Shirtmakers
 See: T. Lipson & Sons Ltd.

Loeb
 See: Metro Ontario Inc.

Lonestar Cafe
Lonestar Texas Grill
 See: 1561716 Ontario Ltd.

Loose Moose
 See: SIR Corp.

Lumark
Lumiere
 See: Cooper Industries (Canada) Inc.

Lumsden Brothers
 See: Sobeys Ontario

Luxaire
 See: York International Ltd.

Luxurycruise.com
 See: Vision 2000 Travel Group Inc.

M·A·C
 See: Estee Lauder Cosmetics Ltd.

M-C Dairy Ltd.
 See: Future Bakery Ltd.

M.R.A. Abatement Services
 See: Quantum Murray LP

Madison
 See: Sherson Group

Madison Avenue Pub
Madison Manor Boutique Hotel
 See: Village Manor (TO) Ltd.

Mag Monde
Maison de la Presse
 See: Hachette Distribution Services
 Retail North America

Majestic Windows
 See: Vinyl Window Designs Ltd.

Mann Equitest
 See: Maxxam Analytics

Manor Foundation
 See: Nisbet Lodge

The Manufacturers Life Insurance Co.
 See: Manulife Financial

Maple Crete Inc.
 See: Vaughan Paving Ltd.

Marel Contractors
 See: Muzzo Brothers Group Inc.

Mark IV Industries Ltd.
 See: Kapsch TrafficCom

Markham
 See: The Corporation of the
 Town of Markham

Markham Economist
 See: York Region Media Group

Markham Woodbine Management Ltd.
 See: Holiday Inn Hotel & Suites
 Toronto - Markham

Markville Toyota
 See: Don Valley North
 Automotive Inc.

Marrow Bone
 See: Mars Canada Inc.

Martin Building Maintenance
Martin Services
 See: Hurley Group

Massey Hall
 See: The Corporation of Massey Hall
 and Roy Thomson Hall

Mastro
 See: Santa Maria Foods Corp.

Matsu Manufacturing
 See: Matcor Automotive

Matthews Equipment Limited
 See: Hertz Canada Ltd.

MCA
 See: Merchandising Consultants
 Associates

MCC
MCCI
 See: Mobile Climate Control Inc.

McClintock Manor
 See: Nisbet Lodge

McGraw-Edison
 See: Cooper Industries (Canada) Inc.

McNairn Packaging
 See: J.H. McNairn Ltd.

McNicoll Manor
See: Tendercare Nursing Homes Ltd.

MCSCS
See: Ministry of Community Safety and Correctional Services

MDA
See: MacDonald Dettwiler & Associates Inc.

MDS Analytical Technologies
MDS Nordion
MDS Pharma Services
See: Nordion Inc.

MEC
See: Mountain Equipment Cooperative

Medi-inn
See: Grosnor Industries Inc.

Medialogix
See: Metro News

Meloche Monnex Financial Services Inc.
See: TD Insurance Meloche Monnex

Mendelssohn Trade Shows
See: Livingston International Inc.

Mepla
See: Wurth Canada Ltd.

Metalux
See: Cooper Industries (Canada) Inc.

Metro Capital Group
See: MetCap Living Management Inc.

MHS
See: Multi-Health Systems Inc.

Mighty Digital Direct & Design
See: Bensimon Byrne

Milestone's
See: Cara Operations Limited

The Miller Group
See: Miller Paving Ltd.

Million Air
See: Toronto Airways Ltd.

Milton
See: The Town of Milton

Milton Canadian Champion
See: Halton Region Media Group

Minacs Worldwide Inc.
See: Aditya Birla Minacs

Mini Markham
See: Town & Country Motors (1989) Ltd.

The Missisquoi Insurance Company
See: Economical Mutual Insurance Co.

Mississauga
See: The Corporation of the City of Mississauga

Mississauga Fire Department
See: Mississauga Fire and Emergency Services

MJ Manufacturing
See: Martinrea International Inc.

MLSQ
See: Maple Leaf Sports & Entertainment Ltd.

MMOD Industries
See: Davis Group of Companies Corp.

Mohawk Raceway
See: Woodbine Entertainment Group

Moll Berczy Haus
See: Tendercare Nursing Homes Ltd.

Montana's
See: Cara Operations Limited

Montgomery International U.S. Brokerage
See: William L. Rutherford Limited

Mothercraft
See: Canadian Mothercraft Society

Motor Express Terminals (MET)
See: Meyers Transport Ltd.

The Movie Network
See: Astral Television Networks

Mr. Big & Tall
See: Grafton-Fraser Inc.

Mr. Coffee
See: Jarden Consumer Solutions

Mr. Greenjeans
See: The Kalen Group

MRS
See: Multiple Retirement Services Inc.

MTC
See: Manufacturing and Technology Centre

MTCC
See: Metro Toronto Convention Centre Corporation

The Multi-Media Partners
See: CFA Communications Ltd.

Multitube Division
See: Multichair Inc.

Mumby & Associates Ltd.
See: Dynamic Paint Products Inc.

Muscle Mag International
See: Robert Kennedy Publishing

MWV Packaging Systems LP
See: MeadWestvaco Packaging Systems LP

MyTravel Canada Inc.
See: Thomas Cook North America

N.L. Technologies
See: Levitt-Safety Ltd.

Narcourt
See: Reed Construction Data

National Express Corporation
See: Stock Transportation Ltd.

National Trade Centre
See: The Board of Governors of Exhibition Place

NBC Universal Canada
See: Universal Studios Canada Inc.

NBCN Clearing Inc.
See: National Bank Financial Inc.

NCN
See: Nor-Don Collection Network Inc.

NDI Inc.
See: Northern Digital Inc.

Nebs Deluxe Co.
See: All Trade Computer Forms Inc.

Neilson Dairy
See: Saputo Dairy Products Canada GP

Neilson Dairy
See: Weston Foods Inc.

Neo-Ray
See: Cooper Industries (Canada) Inc.

Neos Forest Inc.
See: Weston Forest Products

New Image
See: First Lady Coiffures

New Tecumseth
See: The Corporation of the Town of New Tecumseth

Newgen Restaurant Services Inc.
See: Tucker's Marketplace

Newmarco Foods Ltd.
See: East Side Mario's

Newmarket
See: The Town of Newmarket

Newmarket Era Banner
See: York Region Media Group

Newroads National Leasing
See: The Newroads Automotive Group

Niagara This Week
See: Halton Region Media Group

Nicklen Logistics
See: Johnvince Foods

Nine West
See: Sherson Group

NIS
See: National Instore Services Corp.

NLS
See: National Logistics Services

No Frills
See: Loblaw Companies Limited

Norcan
See: BDI World Class World Wide

North American Van Lines
See: Total Relocation
Moving Systems

North Screen Studios
See: NS Studios

North York Mirror
See: Toronto Community News

Nouvelles Télé-Radio
See: The Canadian Press

Nova Pack
See: The Hughes Group

Novaflex Group
See: Flexmaster Canada Limited

Now Magazine
See: Now Communications Inc.

NPI NexCycle Plastics
See: NexCycle Plastics Inc.

NuWay Potato
See: Vegfresh Inc.

O.P.P.
See: Ontario Provincial Police

Oakville
See: The Corporation of the
Town of Oakville

Oakville Beaver
See: Halton Region Media Group

OCAD
See: Ontario College of Art & Design

OCWA
See: Ontario Clean Water Agency

OHA
See: Ontario Hospital Association

The Old Mill Inn and Spa
The Old Mill Lark Hospitality Inc.
The Old Mill Restaurant
See: Lark Hospitality Inc.

Old Navy Canada
See: Gap Inc. Canada

The Old Spaghetti Factory
See: Esplanade Restaurants Ltd.

Olney Wallcoverings
See: Blue Mountain
Wallcovering Inc.

OMA
See: Ontario Medical Association

OMERS
See: Ontario Municipal Employees
Retirement System

Omni Television
See: Rogers Media Television

ONA
See: Ontario Nurses' Association

One Connect Services
See: Canopco

**The Ontario Community Centre
for the Deaf**
See: Bob Rumball Centre for the
Deaf

**Ontario Educational
Communications Authority**
See: TVO

**Ontario Federation of Food
Co-operatives and Clubs Inc.**
See: Ontario Natural Food Co-Op

Ontario News Service
See: Metro News

OPG
See: Ontario Power Generation Inc.

OPLS
See: On Premise Laundry
Systems Inc.

OPSEU
See: Ontario Public Service
Employees Union

Optiance
See: Cooper Industries (Canada) Inc.

Orangeville
See: The Corporation of the
Town of Orangeville

Orangeville Banner
See: North Peel Media Group

OREA Real Estate College
See: Ontario Real Estate Association

Orenda Aerospace Corp.
See: Magellan Aerospace Corp.

Orenda Recycling Centre
See: WASTECO

Orkin Canada
See: PCO Services Corp.

ORMI
See: Organic Resource
Management Inc.

ORSY
See: Wurth Canada Ltd.

OSC
See: Ontario Securities Commission

Oshawa
See: The City of Oshawa

Oshawa This Week
See: Durham Region Media Group

Osowski Company
See: Livingston International Inc.

OSSTF
See: Ontario Secondary School
Teachers Federation

OTPP
See: Ontario Teachers'
Pension Plan Board

Owens Illinois Canada Corp.
See: O-I Canada Corp.

P&H Milling Group
See: Dover Industries Ltd.

P.W. Transportation
See: Pacific Western

Paddy Flaherty's
See: Prime Restaurants
of Canada Inc.

Pafco Insurance
See: Allstate Insurance Company
of Canada

PaperlinX Canada
See: Coast Paper

Parkhurst
See: Dorothea Knitting Mills Ltd.

Participation House
See: Cerebral Palsy Parent Council
of Toronto

Partners In Learning
See: CFA Communications Ltd.

Pat & Mario's
See: Prime Restaurants
of Canada Inc.

Paulmac's Pet Food
See: Pet Valu Canada Inc.

Paupers Pub
See: Village Manor (TO) Ltd.

PBN
See: BDI World Class World Wide

Peacock Inc.
See: Weir Canada Inc.

Pearle Vision
See: Luxottica Retail

Pedigree
See: Mars Canada Inc.

Peel
See: Regional Municipality of Peel

Peel CCAC
See: Community Care Access Centre
- Central West

Pembridge Insurance Co.
See: Allstate Insurance Company
of Canada

Penguin Canada
See: Pearson Education Canada Inc.

PEO
See: Professional Engineers Ontario

Region of York
See: The Regional Municipality of York

Regional Envelope Specialty Paper Products
See: Supremex Inc.

Rehabilitation Foundation for the Disabled
See: Ontario March of Dimes

Relay
See: Hachette Distribution Services Retail North America

Rembrandt Charms
See: Nuco Jewellery Products Inc.

Revera Inc.
See: Cedarbrook Lodge Ltd.

Rexall
See: Katz Group Canada Ltd.

Richmond Hill
See: The Corporation of the Town of Richmond Hill

Richmond Hill Liberal
See: York Region Media Group

Rigo Products
See: Richards Packaging Inc.

Roadfast
See: Quik X Transportation Inc.

Robbie/Young & Wright Architects Inc.
See: Young & Wright / IBI Architects

Robertson House
See: Canadian Mothercraft Society

Rocamora Triangle
See: Desco Plumbing and Heating Supply Inc.

Roche Canada
See: Hoffmann-LaRoche Ltd.

Rogers Centre
See: Toronto Blue Jays Baseball Club

Roll-O-Vert
See: PaperlinX Canada Limited

ROM
See: Royal Ontario Museum

Rosenborg
See: Arla Foods, Inc.

Roy Thomson Hall
See: The Corporation of Massey Hall and Roy Thomson Hall

Royal Alexandra Theatre
See: Mirvish Productions

Royal Bank of Canada
See: RBC Financial Group

Royal Building Products
See: Roytec Vinyl Co.

RR Donnelley
See: Moore Canada Corp.

Rutherford Global Logistics
Rutherford International Freight
Rutherford Terminals Ltd.
See: William L. Rutherford Limited

The Safety Roof Anchor Co.
See: Pro-Bel Enterprises

The Salvation Army
See: The Governing Council of the Salvation Army in Canada

SampleWorks
See: Grosnor Industries Inc.

San Daniele
See: Santa Maria Foods Corp.

Scarborough Mirror
See: Toronto Community News

Schiffenhaus Canada Inc.
See: SCI Inc.

SCM
See: Supply Chain Management Inc.

Scotiabank
See: Bank of Nova Scotia

Scotland Yard
See: Esplanade Restaurants Ltd.

SDS
See: Critical Control Solutions

Sealy Posturepedic
See: Sealy Canada Ltd.

Sears Optical
See: Luxottica Retail

Select Overhead Door Service Inc.
See: Richards Wilcox Door Systems Limited

SellOffVacations.com
See: Sunwing Travel Group

SEN Canada
See: Siemens Enterprise Communications Inc.

Senate Travel
See: Travel Cuts

Seniors for Business
See: Seniors 4 Seniors

Seton Canada
See: WHB Identification Solutions Inc.

SGS
See: Southern Graphic Systems

Shepherd Gardens
See: Shepherd Village Inc.

Shepherd Lodge
Shepherd Manor
Shepherd Terrace
See: Shepherd Village Inc.

Sheraton Centre Hotel
See: Starwood Canada Corp.

Sherway Ford Truck Sales
See: Thorncrest Sherway Inc.

Shoe Company
See: Town Shoes Ltd.

Shoe Studio
See: Sherson Group

Showflex Inc.
See: James Moto Enterprises Inc.

ShowroomOne
See: Unisync Group Ltd.

Showtech Power & Lighting
See: GES Canada Exposition Services Ltd.

SickKids
See: The Hospital for Sick Children

Signature Vacations
See: Sunwing Travel Group

Silk and Satin
See: La Senza Inc.

Simcoe Coach Lines Ltd.
See: Student Transportation Canada

Sirens
See: YM Inc. Sales

Six Point Canadian Tire
See: Paul K. Brennan Holdings Inc.

Skyventure Travel
See: Vision 2000 Travel Group Inc.

Slainte
See: Prime Restaurants of Canada Inc.

SLG Group
Smart Enterprises Corp.
See: Smart Laser Grafix

Smarter Business Gifts
See: Myron

SmithBooks
See: Indigo Books & Music, Inc.

The SMR Group
See: Smart DM

Snickers
See: Mars Canada Inc.

SOCAN
See: Society of Composers, Authors, and Music Publishers of Canada

Solo Cup Canada
See: Solo Canada

The Solution People
See: Core Logistics International Inc.

Sony Style
See: Sony of Canada Ltd.

South Asian Focus
See: North Peel Media Group

South St. Burger Co.
See: New York Fries/ South St. Burger Co.

Space Aid
See: M. & P. Tool Products Inc.

Spicers
See: PaperlinX Canada Limited

Spray-Pak Industries
See: K-G Packaging Inc.

St. Joseph Media
See: Toronto Life Publishing Ltd.

St. Paul Travelers
See: Travelers Insurance

Star Case Canada Inc.
See: A.C.I. Accessory Concepts Inc.

Star Choice
See: Shaw Broadcast Services

Sterling Flooring
See: Sterling Tile & Carpet

Sterling Trucks of Toronto
See: Thorncrest Sherway Inc.

steven b.
See: Dorothea Knitting Mills Ltd.

Stitches
See: YM Inc. Sales

Stoneworx Marble & Granite
See: Maple Group

Store Fixtures & Wilson Display
See: J.A. Wilson Display

Stouffville Tribune
See: York Region Media Group

Student Work Abroad Program
See: Travel Cuts

Studies 4 U
See: Kendle Early Stage

The Suit Exchange
See: Grafton-Fraser Inc.

Sun Life Financial
See: Sun Life Assurance Company of Canada

Sun Opta Inc.
See: Purity Life Health Products - A Sunopta Company

Sunbeam-Oster
See: Jarden Consumer Solutions

Sunglass Hut
See: Luxottica Retail

Sunquest
See: Thomas Cook North America

Suntech Heat Treating
See: Metex Heat Treating Ltd.

SureLites
See: Cooper Industries (Canada) Inc.

Sweet Expressions Foods Inc.
See: Regal Confections

Swiss Chalet
See: Cara Operations Limited

Swissotel Hotels & Resorts
See: Fairmont Hotels & Resorts Inc.

Syspro Proven Systems Ltd.
See: MicroAge

T.I.C.C. Ltd.
See: International Centre

Taco Bell
See: Priszm Income Fund

TCCI
See: Toyota Credit Canada Inc.

TCDSB
See: Toronto Catholic District School Board

TCH International
See: Alliance One Ltd.

Teamboard
See: Egan & Teamboard

Teklynx
See: WHB Identification Solutions Inc.

TEKsystems Canada Inc.
See: Aerotek Canada

Temporary Engineering Services
See: T.E.S. Contract Services Inc.

TFO
See: TVO

Therapy Supplies & Rental Ltd.
See: Shoppers HomeHealthCare

Thomson
See: Technicolor

Thordon Bearings Inc.
See: Thomson-Gordon Group Ltd.

Thorncrest Ford Sales
See: Thorncrest Sherway Inc.

Threshold Financial Technologies Inc.
See: Versent Corporation ULC

Thrifty Car Rental
See: Dollar Thrifty Automotive Group Canada Inc.

THS Studio
See: The Source (Bell) Electronics Canada Inc.

TicketKing
See: Mirvish Productions

Tidefall
See: Fernie House

Timberland
Tip Top Tailors
See: Grafton-Fraser Inc.

Tir Nan Og
See: Prime Restaurants of Canada Inc.

Toll Leasing Ltd.
See: Tank Truck Transport Inc.

Tony Roma's (Famous for Ribs)
See: Esplanade Restaurants Ltd.

Toronto
See: The City of Toronto

Toronto Athletic Club
See: Cambridge Group of Clubs

The Toronto Dominion Bank
See: TD Bank Financial Group

Toronto EMS
See: Toronto Emergency Medical Services

Toronto FC
See: Maple Leaf Sports & Entertainment Ltd.

Toronto International Film Festival
See: TIFF

Toronto Maple Leafs Hockey Club
Toronto Marlies
Toronto Raptors Basketball Club Inc.
See: Maple Leaf Sports & Entertainment Ltd.

Toronto Pearson
See: Greater Toronto Airports Authority

Toronto Stock Exchange
See: TMX Group Inc.

Toronto Zoo
See: Board of Management of the Toronto Zoo

Total Employment Services
See: T.E.S. Contract Services Inc.

Total Security Management
See: TSM Ltd.

Township of Brock
See: The Corporation of the Township of Brock

Toybox
See: Technicolor

Toyota Financial Services
See: Toyota Credit Canada Inc.

TPH
See: The Printing House Ltd.

TPI
TPI Staffing Inc.
See: Trebor Personnel Inc.

Trans Canada Retail Services
See: Wells Fargo Financial Corporation Canada

Transit Shop
See: Hachette Distribution Services Retail North America

Tre Stelle
See: Arla Foods, Inc.

TREB
See: The Toronto Real Estate Board

TRO Air
See: Quik X Transportation Inc.

Truth Hardware
See: Atlas Bearings Inc.

TSC
See: The Shopping Channel

TSH
See: The Scarborough Hospital

TSN
See: The Sports Network

TTC
See: Toronto Transit Commission

TTR
See: Toronto Terminals Railway
Company Ltd.

Turf Lounge
See: Woodbine Entertainment Group

Turf Operations Scarborough Inc.
See: Weed Man Canada

TV Ontario
See: TVO

Twyn Rivers
See: Fernie House

U L Canada Inc.
See: Unilever Canada Inc.

U-Nova Hose
U-Nova Plastics
See: Flexmaster Canada Limited

UCC
See: Upper Canada College

UCS
See: Hachette Distribution Services
Retail North America

UFM
See: Ultra-Fit Manufacturing Inc.

UL of Canada
ULC
See: Underwriters Laboratories
of Canada

Ultra Food & Drug
See: Metro Ontario Inc.

The Uniform People
See: Cintas Canada Ltd.

Union Villa
See: Unionville Home Society

**United Food & Commercial Workers
Union of Canada**
See: UFCW Canada
- Locals 175 & 633

United Jewish Welfare Fund
See: UJA Federation of Greater
Toronto

Universal Showcase Ltd.
See: IDX Toronto

UOIT
See: University of Ontario
Institute of Technology

UpClose
See: The Source (Bell) Electronics
Canada Inc.

UPS Supply Chain Solutions
See: United Parcel Service
Canada Ltd.

Urban Planet
See: YM Inc. Sales

UTI Markham
See: Span International

UTIAS
See: University of Toronto Institute
for Aerospace Studies

UTP
See: University of Toronto Press Inc.

Uxbridge Cottage Hospital
See: Markham Stouffville Hospital
Corporation

Uxbridge Times Journal
See: Durham Region Media Group

Valumart
See: Loblaw Companies Limited

Variety Village
See: Variety Children's Charity

Vaughan
See: The City of Vaughan

Vaughan Citizen
See: York Region Media Group

VHRI
See: Volt Human Resources

Victorian Order of Nurses
See: VON Toronto York Branch

Villa Charities Inc.
See: Columbus Centre of Toronto
See: Vita Community Living Services
of Toronto Inc.

Vintages
See: Liquor Control Board of Ontario

Vista Security & Investigations
See: VSI Inc.

Volvo Trucks Toronto
See: Performance Equipment
Limited

Voyages Campus
See: Travel Cuts

**Walter Carsen Centre for the
National Ballet of Canada**
See: The National Ballet of Canada

Warren Paving
See: Lafarge Canada Inc.

Waste Recycling Inc.
See: Metro Waste Paper
Recovery Inc.

Waterloo Insurance
See: Economical Mutual
Insurance Co.

The Weather Network
See: Pelmorex Media Inc.

Weedeater
See: Electrolux Home Products

WEGZ Stadium Bar
See: Woodbine Entertainment Group

Wellesley Central Place
See: The Drs. Paul & John Rekai
Centre

Westin Harbour Castle
See: Starwood Canada Corp.

Westmont Hopitality Group
See: Prince Spa & Resort Operations
Toronto Ltd.

Weston Bakeries
See: Weston Foods Inc.

Weston Premium Woods
Weston Wood Solutions
See: Weston Forest Products

Westward
See: Acklands-Grainger Inc.

Wheels Clipper
Wheels International Freight Systems.
See: The Wheels Group

Whiskas
See: Mars Canada Inc.

Whitby
See: The Town of Whitby

Whitby This Week
See: Durham Region Media Group

Whitchurch-Stouffville
See: The Town of Whitchurch-
Stouffville

Wholesale Travel Group
See: Thomas Cook North America

Wilkinson Steel
See: National Concrete Accessories

The Willowdale Club Fitness Institute
See: Fitness Institute

Wing Hing Lung Ltd.
See: Wing's Food Products Ltd.

Woodbine Racetrack
See: Woodbine Entertainment Group

The Woodbridge Group
See: Woodbridge Foam Corp.

World's Biggest Bookstore
See: Indigo Books & Music, Inc.

**World Trade Centre Toronto
WTC Toronto**
  See: Toronto Board of Trade

Wound Care Direct
  See: Derma Sciences Canada Inc.

Wyndham Gardens
  See: Unionville Home Society

Xpress
  See: Hachette Distribution Services
  Retail North America

Y&R
  See: Young & Rubicam Ltd.

York
  See: York International Ltd.

York Guardian
  See: Toronto Community News

York Region
  See: The Regional Municipality
  of York

York Uniforms LTd.
  See: Unisync Group Ltd.

York Unitary Products Group
  See: York International Ltd.

**Young Women's Christian Association
of Greater Toronto**
  See: YWCA of Toronto

Your Independent Grocer
  See: Loblaw Companies Limited

YTV Television
  See: Corus Entertainment Inc.

Z-Flex
  See: Flexmaster Canada Limited

Zebra
  See: Wurth Canada Ltd.

Zehrs
  See: Loblaw Companies Limited

Zellers
  See: Hudson's Bay Company

Zenith Insurance Co.
  See: Lombard Canada Ltd.

Zentil Group
  See: University Plumbing
  & Heating Ltd.

ZRV Holding Ltd.
  See: Zeidler Partnership Architects

CONTACT 11
TORONTO 12

Part 3

North American Industry
Classification System (NAICS)
Index

NAICS INDEX SUMMARY TABLE

KEYWORD INDEX TO NAICS INDEX

Use our keyword index to navigate the following Main NAICS Index section.

C

G

H

I

R

U/V

W/X/Y/Z

MAIN NAICS INDEX

AGRICULTURE 11

111330
Non-Citrus Fruit and Tree Nut Farming

Andrews' Scenic Acres

111411
Mushroom Production

Windmill Mushroom Farms

111421
Nursery and Tree Production

Brookdale Treeland Nurseries Ltd.

111422
Floriculture Production

Ontario Flower Growers Co-op

MINING 21

211113
Conventional Oil and Gas Extraction

Pacific Rubiales Energy Corp.

212220
Gold and Silver Ore Mining

Barrick Gold Corp.
Kinross Gold Corp.

212233
Copper-Zinc Ore Mining

Lundin Mining Corp.
Vale Inco Limited
Xstrata Canada Corporation

212299
All Other Metal Ore Mining

Lundin Mining Corp.
Vale Inco Limited
Xstrata Canada Corporation

212314
Granite Mining and Quarrying

Nelson Aggregate Co.

213119
Other Support Activities for Mining

Hudbay Minerals Inc.
Iamgold Corp.

UTILITIES 22

221111
Hydro-Electric Power Generation

Algonquin Power Corporation Inc.
Burlington Hydro Inc.

221113
Nuclear Electric Power Generation

Ontario Power Generation Inc./
    Pickering Nuclear

221121
Electric Bulk Power Transmission and Control

Independent Electricity System
    Operator
Just Energy

221122
Electric Power Distribution

Brookfield Power
Enersource Corp.
Hydro One Brampton Networks Inc.
Ontario Power Generation Inc.
Oshawa PUC Networks Inc.
PowerStream Inc.
Toronto Hydro Corporation
Veridian Corp.

221210
Natural Gas Distribution

Direct Energy Marketing Ltd.
Enbridge Gas Distribution Inc.

221310
Water Supply and Irrigation Systems

Ontario Clean Water Agency

221330
Steam and Air-Conditioning Supply

Enwave Energy Corporation

CONSTRUCTION 23

231110
Land Subdivision and Land Development

Gottardo Construction
Kaneff Group of Companies
Menkes Developments Ltd.
Monarch Corporation
Orlando Corp.
Smart Centres
Tribute Communities
Tridel Corp.

231210
Residential Building Construction

Aspen Ridge Homes Ltd.
Bird Construction Company
The Daniels Group Inc.
Di Crete Construction Ltd.
EllisDon Corporation
Greenpark Homes
Monarch Corporation
Oxville Homes Ltd.
Tridel Corp.

231220
Non-Residential Building Construction

The Atlas Corp.
Bird Construction Company
Carwell Construction Ltd.
Eastern Construction Company Ltd.
EllisDon Corporation
Maple Reinders Constructors Ltd.
Maxim Group General Contracting Ltd.
Monarch Corporation
Orlando Corp.
Quantum Murray LP
Unique Restoration Ltd.
Verdi Alliance
Westdale Construction Co. Ltd.

231310
Highway- Street and Bridge Construction

Aecon Group Inc.
Bot Construction Ltd.
Carillion Canada Inc.
Coco Paving Inc.
Dagmar Construction Ltd.
D. Crupi & Sons Ltd.
Di Crete Construction Ltd.
Dufferin Construction Co.
Ferma Construction Company Inc.
Gazzola Paving Ltd.
Graham Bros. Construction Limited
Kenaidan Contracting Ltd.
K.J. Beamish Construction Co., Limited
Miller Paving Ltd.
MSO Construction Ltd.
Pilen Construction of Canada Ltd.
Roto-Mill Services Ltd.
Tacc Construction Ltd.
Trisan Construction
Vaughan Paving Ltd.

231320
Water and Sewer Construction

Aecon Group Inc.
CDC Contracting
Clearway Construction Inc.
Con-Drain Company (1983) Ltd.
Con-Elco Ltd.
Dagmar Construction Ltd.
Dom-Meridian Construction Ltd.
Dranco Construction Ltd.
Fer-Pal Construction Ltd.
Graham Bros. Construction Limited
Kenaidan Contracting Ltd.
Memme Excavation Company Ltd.
The State Group
Trisan Construction

231330
Oil and Gas Pipelines and Related Industrial Complexes Construction

ECS Engineering & Construction Ltd.
Link-Line Group of Companies
Robert B. Somerville Company Ltd.

231390
Other Engineering Construction

Aecon Group Inc.
AZ3 Enterprises Inc.
Carillion Canada Inc.
Con-Elco Ltd.
Hard-Co Construction Ltd.
Oakville Hydro Corp.
Tacc Construction Ltd.
Trans Power Utility Contractors Inc.

231410
Construction Management

Belrock Construction Ltd.
Bird Construction Company
Bondfield Construction Company Ltd.
Dufferin Construction Co.
Hatch Ltd.
PCL Constructors Canada Inc.
Shaw Canada LP
SNC-Lavalin Inc.
Urbacon Ltd.

232110
Site Preparation Work

Biggs & Narciso
    Construction Service Inc.
Boart Longyear Canada
Deep Foundations Contractors Inc.
Donald Construction Ltd.
Greenspoon Specialty Contracting Ltd.
Quantum Murray LP
Teskey Concrete & Construction
    Company Ltd.

232210
Forming Work

Delgant Construction Ltd.
Halton Forming Ltd.
Lee Rocca Forming Ltd.
Verdi Alliance

232220
Concrete Pouring and Finishing Work

Brennan Paving & Construction Ltd.
Camp Forming Ltd.
C.I.P. Group Ltd.
Concord Concrete & Drain Ltd.
Delgant Construction Ltd.
Donald Construction Ltd.
Hardrock Forming Co.
KPM Industries
Thorncrete Construction Ltd.
Tri-Con Concrete Finishing Co. Ltd.
UCC Group Inc.

232230
Structural Steel and Precast Concrete Erection Work

Canerector Inc.
Etobicoke Ironworks Ltd.
Global Precast Inc.
Structform International Ltd.

232250
Framing and Rough Carpentry Work

Lisi Mechanical Contractors Ltd.

232290
Other Building Structure Work

ConCreate USL Ltd.
Delso Restoration Ltd.

232310
Masonry Work

Lido Wall Systems Inc.
Maple Group
Medi Group Masonry Ltd.
Village Masonry Construction Inc.

232330
Roofing and Related Work

Atlas-Apex Roofing Inc.
Bothwell-Accurate Co. (2006) Limited
Chouinard Bros. Roofing
Flynn Canada Ltd.
Lifestyle Sunrooms Inc.
Semple Gooder Roofing Corporation

232340
Metallic and Other Siding Work

Alumicor Ltd.
Flynn Canada Ltd.
Kawneer Company Canada Ltd.
Semple Gooder Roofing Corporation

232390
Other Building Exterior Finishing Work

Sota Glazing Inc.

232410
Drywall and Plaster Work

4 Star Drywall Ltd.
CGC Inc.
Decoustics Ltd.
Downsview Drywall Contracting
Four Seasons Drywall Ltd.
Lido Wall Systems Inc.
Maple Drywall
Muzzo Brothers Group Inc.
Oakdale Drywall & Acoustics Ltd.
RF Porter Plastering Ltd.
Torino Drywall Inc.

232420
Terrazzo and Tile Work

Premier Contractors Ltd.
Sterling Tile & Carpet
Terrazzo Mosaic & Tile Co. Ltd.
York Marble Tile & Terrazzo Inc.

232430
Carpet and Resilient Flooring Work

Sterling Tile & Carpet
Terrazzo Mosaic & Tile Co. Ltd.

232440
Insulation Work

Crossby Dewar Inc.
Custom Insulation Systems
Icynene Inc.

232450
Building Painting and Paperhanging Work

Ace Painting & Decorating Co. Inc.

232460
Finish Carpentry and Wood Flooring Work

AYA Kitchens and Baths, Ltd.
Cortina Kitchens Inc.

232490
Other Building Interior Finishing Work

CGC Inc.

232510
Electrical Work

Ainsworth Inc.
Ampere Limited
Applewood Air Conditioning Ltd.
Black & McDonald Ltd.
Cable Control Systems Inc.
Comstock Canada Ltd.
CSG Security Inc.
Galmar Electrical Contracting Inc.
Garda World Security
Guild Electric Ltd.
Industrial Electrical Contractors Ltd.
Jay Electric Ltd.
K-Line Maintenance
    & Construction Ltd.
Naylor Group Inc.
Nortown Electrical Contractors Ltd.
Ontario Electrical Construction
    Company Ltd.
Ontario Power Contracting Ltd.
The Plan Group
Powerline Plus Ltd.
Sentrex Communications Company
ShawFlex
Speedy Electric Contractors Ltd.
Stacey Electric Company Ltd.
The State Group
Symtech Innovations Ltd.
Tam Electrical Ltd.
Urban Electrical Contractors
Wesbell Group of Companies
Wolfedale Electric Ltd.

232520
Plumbing- Heating and Air-Conditioning Installation

Adelt Mechanical Works Ltd.
Ainsworth Inc.
Applewood Air Conditioning Ltd.
Black & McDonald Ltd.
Brenmar Heating
    & Air Conditioning Ltd.
Comstock Canada Ltd.
Geo. A. Kelson Company Limited
Halton Indoor Climate Systems, Ltd.
Johnson Controls LP
Leader Plumbing & Heating Inc.
Mapleridge Mechanical
    Contracting Ltd.
MDF Mechanical Ltd.
Modern Niagara Toronto Inc.
Naylor Group Inc.
Primo Mechanical Inc.
Reliance Comfort Limited Partnership
Riva Plumbing Ltd.
Sayers & Associates Ltd.
Trane Ontario/Trane Canada ULC
University Plumbing & Heating Ltd.
Urban Mechanical Contracting Ltd.
The Watson Group Ltd.

232530
Automatic Sprinkler System Installation

General Sprinklers Inc.
Vipond Inc.

232540
Commercial Refrigeration Installation

Cimco Refrigeration

232550
Elevator and Escalator Installation

EHC Global Inc.
Fujitec Canada Inc.
KONE Inc.
Otis Canada Inc.
Savaria Concord Lifts Inc.
Schindler Elevator Corp.
ThyssenKrupp Elevator Ltd.

232590
Other Building Equipment Installation

Broan-Nutone Canada Inc.
Matcom Industrial Installations Inc.

232910
Fencing and Interlocking Stone Contracting

Roma Fence Ltd.

232920
Residential and Commercial Paving Contracting

Duron Ontario Ltd.
Miller Paving Ltd.
Pave-Tar Construction Ltd.

232990
All Other Special Trade Contracting

AGI Traffic Technology
Aquicon Construction Co. Ltd.
Gib-San Pools Ltd.
Kafko Pool Products
Pool People Ltd.
Superior Pool Spa & Leisure Ltd.

MANUFACTURING   31 - 33

311111
Dog and Cat Food Manufacturing

Mars Canada Inc.
Menu Foods Ltd.
Pet Valu Canada Inc.

311119
Other Animal Food Manufacturing

Mars Canada Inc.

311211
Flour Milling

Dover Industries Ltd.
Sunny Crunch Foods Ltd.

311225
Fat and Oil Refining and Blending

Bunge Canada
Hubbert Processing & Sales Ltd.
Sardo Foods
Unilever Canada Inc.

311230
Breakfast Cereal Manufacturing

General Mills Canada Corp.
Kellogg Canada Inc.
Sunny Crunch Foods Ltd.

311310
Sugar Manufacturing

Redpath Sugar Ltd.

311330
Confectionery Manufacturing from Purchased Chocolate

Hershey Canada Inc.
Imperial Flavours Inc.
Laura Secord
Nestlé Canada Inc.

311340
Non-Chocolate Confectionery Manufacturing

Ce De Candy Company Ltd.
Concord Confections
Hershey Canada Inc.
Oak Leaf Confections Co.
Wrigley Canada

311410
Frozen Food Manufacturing

apetito Canada Ltd.
Chudleigh's Ltd.
Molinaro's Fine Italian Foods Ltd.
Morrison Lamothe Inc.
Plats du Chef
Tradition Fine Foods Ltd.
Wing's Food Products Ltd.

311420
Fruit and Vegetable Canning- Pickling and Drying

Campbell Company of Canada
Gerber Canada Inc.
H.J. Heinz Company of Canada Ltd.
Lassonde Industries Inc.
Marsan Foods Ltd.

Reinhart Foods Ltd.
Sardo Foods
Smucker Foods of Canada Co.
Vegfresh Inc.

311511
Fluid Milk Manufacturing

Liberté Natural Foods Inc.
Parmalat Canada Inc.
Saputo Dairy Products Canada GP

311515
Butter- Cheese- and Dry and Condensed Dairy Products Manufacturing

Arla Foods, Inc.
Grande Cheese Company Ltd.
Janes Family Foods Ltd.
Kraft Canada Inc.
Parmalat Canada Inc.
Saputo Dairy Products Canada GP

311611
Animal (except Poultry) Slaughtering

Belmont Meat Products Ltd.
Kretschmar Inc.
Maple Leaf Foods Inc.
Quality Meat Packers Ltd.

311614
Rendering and Meat Processing from Carcasses

G. Brandt Meat Packers Ltd.
Macgregor's Meat & Seafood Ltd.
Maple Lodge Farms Ltd.
Santa Maria Foods Corp.
Vienna Meat Products Ltd.

311615
Poultry Processing

Belmont Meat Products Ltd.
Erie Meat Products Ltd.
Golden Cut Poultry Ltd.
King Cole Ducks Ltd.
Macgregor's Meat & Seafood Ltd.
Maple Leaf Foods Inc.
Maple Lodge Farms Ltd.
Olymel
Pinty's Delicious Foods Inc.
Puddy Brothers Ltd.
TNT Foods International Inc.
Tri R Foods Ltd.
T & R Sargent Farms Ltd.

311710
Seafood Product Preparation and Packaging

Janes Family Foods Ltd.
Macgregor's Meat & Seafood Ltd.

311811
Retail Bakeries

Silverstein's Bakery Ltd.

311814
Commercial Bakeries and Frozen Bakery Product Manufacturing

Ace Bakery Ltd.
Backerhaus Veit Ltd.
Canada Bread Company Limited
Del's Pastry Ltd.
Dimpflmeier Bakery Ltd.
Dufflet Pastries
Fiera Foods Inc.
Furlani's Food Corp.
Future Bakery Ltd.
Imperial Flavours Inc.
Italian Home Bakery Ltd.
King's Pastry
Maple Leaf Foods Inc.
Maple Leaf Frozen Bakery
    - Canada Bread
Nino D'Aversa Bakery Ltd.
Open Window Health Bread
    Bakery Limited
Plats du Chef
Silverstein's Bakery Ltd.
Starr Culinary Delights Inc.
Tre Mari Bakery Ltd.
Upper Crust Ltd.
Weston Foods Inc.

311821
Cookie and Cracker Manufacturing

Commercial Bakeries Corp.
Dover Industries Ltd.
Nafta Foods & Packaging Ltd.
Nino D'Aversa Bakery Ltd.
PL Foods Ltd.
Voortman Cookies Ltd.

311822
Flour Mixes and Dough Manufacturing from Purchased Flour

Benevito Foods Inc.
English Bay Batter (Toronto) Inc.

311823
Dry Pasta Manufacturing

Italpasta Ltd.
Molinaro's Fine Italian Foods Ltd.

311830
Tortilla Manufacturing

Pepes Mexican Foods

311911
Roasted Nut and Peanut Butter Manufacturing

Trophy Foods Inc.

311919
Other Snack Food Manufacturing

Olde York Potato Chips
Super-Pufft Snacks Corp.
Trophy Foods Inc.

311920
Coffee and Tea Manufacturing

Club Coffee
Mother Parker's Tea & Coffee Inc.
Nestlé Canada Inc.

311930
Flavouring Syrup and Concentrate Manufacturing

D'Angelo Brands Ltd.
Dawn Food Products Canada Ltd.
Pepsico Beverages Canada
Sensient Flavors Canada Inc.

311940
Seasoning and Dressing Manufacturing

Dawn Food Products Canada Ltd.
Griffith Laboratories Ltd.
H.J. Heinz Company of Canada Ltd.
Marsan Foods Ltd.
Reinhart Foods Ltd.
Select Food Products Ltd.
Summer Fresh Salads

311990
All Other Food Manufacturing

Burnbrae Farms Mississauga
Culinary Destinations
Dr. Oetker Canada Ltd.
Gay Lea Foods
General Mills Canada Corp.
Griffith Laboratories Ltd.
Marsan Foods Ltd.
Nealanders International Inc.
Newly Weds Foods Co.
Olymel
Reckitt Benckiser (Canada) Inc.
Sensient Flavors Canada Inc.
Unilever Canada Inc.
Wing's Food Products Ltd.

312110
Soft Drink and Ice Manufacturing

Arctic Glacier Inc.
Coca-Cola Bottling Company
Cott Beverages Canada
D'Angelo Brands Ltd.
Pepsico Beverages Canada

312120
Breweries

Labatt Breweries of Canada
Magnotta Winery Corporation
Molson Canada
Steam Whistle Brewing Co.

312130
Wineries

Andrews' Scenic Acres
Colio Estates Wines Inc.
Diageo Canada Inc.
Magnotta Winery Corporation
Vincor Canada

312140
Distilleries

Bacardi Canada Inc.
Diageo Canada Inc.

312220
Tobacco Product Manufacturing

JTI-Macdonald Corp.
Rothmans, Benson & Hedges Inc.

313210
Broad-Woven Fabric Mills

Apparel Trimmings Inc.
Covertech Fabricating Inc.
Elte

313220
Narrow Fabric Mills and Schiffli Machine Embroidery

Velcro Canada Inc.

313230
Nonwoven Fabric Mills

Brand Felt of Canada
Fybon Industries Ltd.

313240
Knit Fabric Mills

Solidwear Enterprises Ltd.

313310
Textile and Fabric Finishing

Accolade Group Inc.
Ajax Textile Processing Company Ltd.

314110
Carpet and Rug Mills

Elte
Korhani of Canada Inc.
National Carpet Mills Ltd.

314120
Curtain and Linen Mills

Antex Design Inc.
Hollander Canada Home Fashions
    Limited
Umbra Ltd.

314910
Textile Bag and Canvas Mills

Flying Colours International
International Custom Products Inc.

314990
All Other Textile Product Mills

Flying Colours International
Fybon Industries Ltd.
International Custom Products Inc.
Jem Pak GK Inc.
Talmolder Inc.

315110
Hosiery and Sock Mills

Gertex Hosiery Inc.
McGregor Industries Inc.
Phantom Industries Inc.
Wertex Hosiery Inc.

315190
Other Clothing Knitting Mills

Dorothea Knitting Mills Ltd.
Regency Apparel Company Ltd.

315210
Cut and Sew Clothing Contracting

Picadilly Fashions
S.D.R. Apparel Inc.

315222
Men's and Boys' Cut and Sew Suit- Coat and Overcoat Manufacturing

Ash City

315226
Men's and Boys' Cut and Sew Shirt Manufacturing

RJ McCarthy Ltd.
T. Lipson & Sons Ltd.

315229
Other Men's and Boys' Cut and Sew Clothing Manufacturing

Apparel Resource Group Inc.
Bernard Athletic Knit
Canada Goose
Duvet Comfort Inc.
Jaytex of Canada Ltd.
Tilley Endurables Inc.

315233
Women's and Girls' Cut and Sew Dress Manufacturing

Anewtex Inc.
Lundstrom

315234
Women's and Girls' Cut and Sew Suit- Coat- Tailored Jacket and Skirt Manufacturing

RJ McCarthy Ltd.

315239
Other Women's and Girls' Cut and Sew Clothing Manufacturing

Apparel Resource Group Inc.
Canada Goose
Duvet Comfort Inc.
Picadilly Fashions
S.D.R. Apparel Inc.
Tilley Endurables Inc.

315292
Fur and Leather Clothing Manufacturing

Danier Leather Inc.
James Moto Enterprises Inc.

315299
All Other Cut and Sew Clothing Manufacturing

Bernard Athletic Knit
Gruven International Inc.
Outdoor Outfits Ltd.
Spring Knitwear Inc.

315990
Clothing Accessories and Other Clothing Manufacturing

H.A. Sheldon Canada Ltd.
Ranka Enterprises Ltd.
Superior Glove Works Ltd.

316210
Footwear Manufacturing

The Orthotic Group Inc.

321211
Hardwood Veneer and Plywood Mills

Executive Woodwork Ltd.

321215
Structural Wood Product Manufacturing

Alpa Roof Trusses Inc.
Lake Scugog Lumber Company Ltd.

321911
Wood Window and Door Manufacturing

Brown Window Corp.
Decora Window & Door Systems
Kingstar Products Inc.
Masonite International Corporation
Newmar Window Manufacturing Inc.

321919
Other Millwork

Brenlo Ltd.
Central Fairbank Lumber
Ell-Rod Holdings Inc.
Satin Finish Hardwood Flooring Ltd.
Shipway Stairs Ltd.
Vintage Flooring

321999
All Other Miscellaneous Wood Product Manufacturing

Norbord Inc.

322121
Paper (except Newsprint) Mills

Atlantic Packaging Products Ltd.
Domtar Inc.
Irving Tissue
Kruger Products Limited

322122
Newsprint Mills

Atlantic Packaging Products Ltd.
Kruger Inc.

322130
Paperboard Mills

Bellwyck Packaging Solutions
Cascades Boxboard Group Inc.
Gerrity Corrugated Paper Products Ltd.

322211 Corrugated and Solid Fibre Box Manufacturing

Central Graphics &
    Container Group Ltd.
Coyle Corrugated Containers Inc.
Domtar Inc.
The Hughes Group
Norampac/Lithotech
Packaging Technologies Inc.
Propak Ltd.
Royal Containers Ltd.
Smith Induspac Toronto Ltd.
Smurfit-MBI
Tencorr Packaging Inc.

322212
Folding Paperboard Box Manufacturing

Bellwyck Packaging Solutions
Cascades Boxboard Group Inc.
MeadWestvaco Packaging Systems LP
Shorewood Packaging
    Corporation of Canada Ltd.

322219
Other Paperboard Container Manufacturing

CKF Inc.

322220
Paper Bag and Coated and Treated Paper Manufacturing

A1 Label
Acorn Packaging
Atlantic Packaging Products Ltd.
Atlas Paper Bag Co. Ltd.
Esselte Canada Inc.
FPC Flexible Packaging Corp.
Gerrard-Oval Strapping
Hood Packaging Corporation
J.H. McNairn Ltd.
Kruger Inc.
Labelad
Multipak Ltd.
Multiple Pakfold Business Forms
Packall Packaging Inc.
Peel Plastic Products Ltd.
Wedlock Paper Converters Ltd.

322230
Stationery Product Manufacturing

All Stick Label Ltd.
Esselte Canada Inc.
Royal Envelope Ltd.
Supremex Inc.

322291
Sanitary Paper Product Manufacturing

Irving Tissue

322299
All Other Converted Paper Product Manufacturing

CKF Inc.
Ellis Packaging Ltd.
Fraser Papers Inc.
Solo Canada

323113
Commercial Screen Printing

Accolade Group Inc.
Middleton Graphics Group Inc.
Quadgraphics Inc.
Transcontinental Printing Inc.

323114
Quick Printing

Cenveo, McLaren Morris and Todd
The Printing House Ltd.
RR Donelly Ltd.
Smart Laser Grafix
Webcom Inc.
West Star Printing Ltd.

323115
Digital Printing

Astley Gilbert Limited
Avant Imaging & Information
    Management Inc.
CBS Outdoor Canada
C.J. Graphics Inc.
Eclipse Colour and Imaging Corp.
Ernest Green & Son Ltd.
The Printing House Ltd.
RR Donelly Ltd.
St. Joseph Printing Ltd.
Transcontinental Digital
    Services GP Inc.
Transcontinental PLM Inc.
Webcom Inc.

323116
Manifold Business Forms Printing

All Trade Computer Forms Inc.
The DATA Group of Companies
Davis + Henderson
Moore Canada Corp.
Multiple Pakfold Business Forms

323119
Other Printing

ACCO Brands Canada Inc.
All Stick Label Ltd.
Astley Gilbert Limited
Bemis Flexible Packaging
Carlton Cards Ltd.
Continental Press Ltd.
The DATA Group of Companies
Davis Group of Companies Corp.
Eastend Bindery Limited
Hallmark Canada
Intria Items Inc.
Marwick Manufacturing Inc.
Metro Label Co. Ltd.
Metroland Media Group Ltd.
Reprodux Copy Centres Ltd.
SCI Inc.
Tip Top Bindery Ltd.
Transcontinental Printing Inc.
Web Offset Publications Ltd.

323120
Support Activities for Printing

Annan & Bird Lithographers
GBC Canada
Prodigy Graphics Group Inc.
Reliable Bookbinders Ltd.
Reprodux Copy Centres Ltd.
Specialties Graphic Finishers Ltd.
Webcom Inc.
Web Offset Publications Ltd.

324110
Petroleum Refineries

Imperial Oil Limited
Koch-Glitsch Canada LP
Petro-Canada
Petro-Canada Lubricants Centre
Shell Canada Ltd.

324121
Asphalt Paving Mixture and Block Manufacturing

Coco Paving Inc.
Duron Ontario Ltd.
Fermar Paving Ltd.
McAsphalt Industries Ltd.
Unilock Ltd.

324122
Asphalt Shingle and Coating Material Manufacturing

IG Machine & Fibres Ltd.
IKO Industries Ltd.

325120
Industrial Gas Manufacturing

Hydrogenics Corp.
Linde Canada Ltd.

325130
Synthetic Dye and Pigment Manufacturing

Dominion Colour Corp.

325181
Alkali and Chlorine Manufacturing

Diversey Inc.

325189
All Other Basic Inorganic Chemical Manufacturing

ERCO Worldwide LP

325190
Other Basic Organic Chemical Manufacturing

Dominion Colour Corp.

325210
Resin and Synthetic Rubber Manufacturing

Hymopack Ltd.
Ingenia Polymers Corp.
The International Group, Inc.
National Rubber Technologies Corp.
Owens Corning Canada Inc.

325220
Artificial and Synthetic Fibres and Filaments Manufacturing

BASF Canada

325313
Chemical Fertilizer (except Potash) Manufacturing

Plant Products Company Ltd.

325320
Pesticide and Other Agricultural Chemical Manufacturing

Dalton Chemical Laboratories Inc.
Plant Products Company Ltd.

325410
Pharmaceutical and Medicine Manufacturing

Apotex Inc.
AstraZeneca Canada Inc.
Baxter Corp.
Bayer Inc.
bioMérieux
Boehringer Ingelheim (Canada) Ltd.
Canadian Custom Packaging Co.
Cobalt Pharmaceuticals Inc.
Contract Pharmaceuticals
   Limited Canada
Dalton Chemical Laboratories Inc.
Eli Lilly Canada Inc.
EMD Serono Canada Inc.
GlaxoSmithKline Inc.
Hoffmann-LaRoche Ltd.
Janssen Inc.
Mylan Inc.
Nordion Inc.
Novo Nordisk Canada Inc.
Nucro-Technics
Nycomed Canada Inc.
Patheon Inc.
Pharma Medica Research Inc.
Purdue Pharma
Sanofi Pasteur Ltd.
Steris Canada Inc.
Taro Pharmaceuticals
Teva Canada Limited
Valeant Pharmaceuticals
Wellspring Pharmaceutical
   Canada Corp.
Wyeth Consumer Healthcare Inc.

325510
Paint and Coating Manufacturing

BASF Canada
Benjamin Moore & Co.
Coatings 85 Ltd.
Protech Chemicals Ltd.
The Sherwin-Williams Company
   (Canada)
Tilton Industries Inc.
Tremco Canada Division
Valspar Inc.

325520
Adhesive Manufacturing

3M Canada Co.
Chembond
Deco Labels & Tags
Henkel Canada Corporation
Tremco Canada Division

325610
Soap and Cleaning Compound Manufacturing

Colgate-Palmolive Canada Inc.
Diversey Inc.
Ecolab Co.
Hunter Amenities International Ltd.
Jem Pak GK Inc.
KIK Investment Holdings LP
Korex Canada
Procter & Gamble Inc.
Reckitt Benckiser (Canada) Inc.
State Chemical Ltd.
Unilever Canada Inc.

325620
Toilet Preparation Manufacturing

Belvedere International Inc.
Body Blue 2006 Inc.
Cosmetica Laboratories Inc.
Crystal Claire Cosmetics Inc.
Estee Lauder Cosmetics Ltd.
Kao Brands Canada Inc.
M·A·C Cosmetics

325910
Printing Ink Manufacturing

Hostmann-Steinberg Ltd.
Sun Chemical Ltd.
Wikoff Corp.

325999
All Other Miscellaneous Chemical Product Manufacturing

Assured Packaging Inc.
BASF Canada
Chemtura Corp.
Clariant (Canada) Inc.
Colgate-Palmolive Canada Inc.
E.I duPont Canada Company
GlaxoSmithKline Inc.
Imperial Oil Limited
K-G Packaging Inc.
KIK Investment Holdings LP
Nalco Canada Co.
Recochem Inc.
StonCor Group

326111
Unsupported Plastic Bag Manufacturing

Alte-Rego Corp.
Belle-Pak Packaging Inc.
Direct Plastics Ltd.

326114
Unsupported Plastic Film and Sheet Manufacturing

AEP Canada Inc.
Alros Products Ltd.
Alte-Rego Corp.
Berry Plastics
Exopack Performance Films Inc.
Polytainers Inc.
Samuel Strapping Systems

326122
Plastic Pipe and Pipe Fitting Manufacturing

Corma Inc.
IPEX Management Inc.
Royal Pipe Systems Ltd.

326130
Laminated Plastic Plate- Sheet and Shape Manufacturing

Doellken-Woodtape Ltd.
Vinyl Window Designs Ltd.

326140
Polystyrene Foam Product Manufacturing

FPC Flexible Packaging Corp.
Icynene Inc.
Industrial Thermo Polymers Ltd.
Kristofoam Industries Inc.
Smith Induspac Toronto Ltd.

326150
Urethane and Other Foam Product (except Polystyrene) Manufacturing

Carpenter Canada Co.
Cousins-Currie
Valle Foam Industries (1995) Inc.
VitaFoam Products Canada Ltd.
Woodbridge Foam Corp.

326160
Plastic Bottle Manufacturing

Easy Plastic Containers Ltd.
Graham Packaging Canada Ltd.
Matrix Packaging of Canada ULC
Swissplas Ltd.

326191
Plastic Plumbing Fixture Manufacturing

Hydropool Industries
Mirolin Industries Corp.

326193
Motor Vehicle Plastic Parts Manufacturing

ABC Group Exterior Systems
MSB Plastics Manufacturing Ltd.

326198
All Other Plastic Product Manufacturing

ABC Group Exterior Systems
Amhil Enterprises Ltd.
Axiom Group Inc.
Bericap North America Inc.
Blue Mountain Wallcovering Inc.
Compact Mould Ltd.
E. Hofmann Plastics Canada Inc.
El-En Packaging Company Ltd.
Exopack Concord
Fabricated Plastics Ltd.
Genpak LP
Giesecke & Devrient Systems
    Canada, Inc.
Grosnor Industries Inc.
Integrated Plastics Inc.
Kubik Inc.
Monarch Plastics Ltd.
Multy Home LP
Nemato Corp.
NexCycle Plastics Inc.
Norex Ltd.
Novelis Foil Products
Oran Industries Ltd.
Orbis Canada Ltd.
Par-Pak Ltd.
Pine Valley Packaging Ltd.
Plastic Packaging & Components Inc.
Plastipak Industries Inc.
Polytainers Inc.
Ray Plastics Ltd.
Revere Industries, LLC
Richards Packaging Inc.
Ropak Canada Inc.

Royal Group, Inc.
Royal Windows & Doors
Roytec Vinyl Co.
Rubbermaid Canada
Scepter Corporation
Seton Canada
ShawCor Ltd.
S & Q Plastic
Star Plastics Inc.
Viceroy Rubber & Plastics Ltd.
Vinyl Window Designs Ltd.
Window City Mfrs Inc.
W. Ralston (Canada) Inc.

326210
Tire Manufacturing

Dynamic Tire Corp.
Goodyear Canada Inc.

326220
Rubber and Plastic Hose and Belting Manufacturing

Flexmaster Canada Limited

326290
Other Rubber Product Manufacturing

Hamilton Kent Inc.
Rubbermaid Canada
Viceroy Rubber & Plastics Ltd.

327120
Clay Building Material and Refractory Manufacturing

Hanson Brick Ltd.
IG Machine & Fibres Ltd.
Olympia Tile International Inc.
RHI Canada Inc.

327214
Glass Manufacturing

AGC Flat Glass North America Ltd.
O-I Canada Corp.
PPG Canada Inc.
Richards Packaging Inc.
Trulite Industries Ltd.

327310
Cement Manufacturing

Holcim (Canada) Inc.
Innocon Inc.
Lafarge Canada Inc.
St Marys Cement Group

327320
Ready-Mix Concrete Manufacturing

Innocon Inc.

327330
Concrete Pipe- Brick and Block Manufacturing

Brampton Brick Limited
Hanson Pressure Pipes
    (Stouffville Pressure Facility)
St Marys Cement Group

327390
Other Concrete Product Manufacturing

ARMTEC
Brooklin Concrete Products
Innocon Inc.
James Dick Construction Ltd.

327420
Gypsum Product Manufacturing

CertainTeed Gypsum Canada Inc.
Formglas Inc.

327910
Abrasive Product Manufacturing

3M Canada Co.

327990
All Other Non-Metallic Mineral Product Manufacturing

Inline Fiberglass Ltd.
Owens Corning Canada Inc.
Roxul Inc.

331110
Iron and Steel Mills and Ferro-Alloy Manufacturing

C & T Reinforcing Steel Co. (1987)
    Limited
Gilbert Steel Ltd.
Johnson Matthey Limited

331210
Iron and Steel Pipes and Tubes Manufacturing from Purchased Steel

Associated Tube Industries
Multichair Inc.
Samuel Manu-Tech Inc.
Summo Steel Corp.
Tubular Steel Inc.
Welded Tube of Canada

331221
Cold-Rolled Steel Shape Manufacturing

Laurel Steel
Venture Steel

331222
Steel Wire Drawing

Falcon Fasteners Registered

331313
Primary Production of Alumina and Aluminum

Rochester Aluminum Smelting
    Canada Ltd.
Sapa Extrusions

331317
Aluminum Rolling- Drawing- Extruding and Alloying

Aleris Specifications Alloy Products
    Canada Company
Almag Aluminum Inc.
Extrudex Aluminum
Indalco Alloys
Spectra Aluminum Products Inc.

331420
Copper Rolling- Drawing- Extruding and Alloying

Nexans Canada Inc.
Southwire Canada

331490
Non-Ferrous Metal (except Copper and Aluminum) Rolling- Drawing- Extruding and Alloying

Roll Form Group

331523
Non-Ferrous Die-Casting Foundries

Victaulic Custom Casting Company

331529
Non-Ferrous Foundries (except Die-Casting)

Alcoa Howmet Georgetown Casting

332113
Forging

Crosby Canada

332118
Stamping

ABM Tool & Die Co. Ltd.
Clover Tool Manufacturing Ltd.
Commercial Spring & Tool Company Ltd.
Crown Metal Packaging Canada LP
F & K Manufacturing Company Ltd.
F & P Manufacturing Inc.
Karmax Heavy Stamping
Kobay Enstel Limited
Massiv Die Form
MetriCan Mfg. Co. Inc.
M. & P. Tool Products Inc.
MTD Metro Tool & Die Ltd.
Stamptek
Thunder Tool & Mfg. Ltd.
Warren Industries Ltd.
Woodbine Tool & Die
    Manufacturing Ltd.

332210
Cutlery and Hand Tool Manufacturing

Clover Tool Manufacturing Ltd.
Exacta Precision Products Ltd.
Trimen Food Service Equipment Inc.

332311
Prefabricated Metal Building and Component Manufacturing

Tam-Kal Limited

332319
Other Plate Work and Fabricated Structural Product Manufacturing

Canam
General Switchgear & Controls Ltd./
    Markham Electric Division
Novaquest Metal Finishing Inc.

332321
Metal Window and Door Manufacturing

Allan Windows Technologies
Aluminart Products Ltd.
Baron Metal Industries Inc.
Casa Bella Windows Inc.
Clearview Industries Ltd.
Decora Window & Door Systems
Fleming Door Products
Kingstar Products Inc.
Oldcastle Glass Engineered Products
Ostaco 2000 Windoors Inc.
Pollard Windows Inc.
Renin Corp.
Richards-Wilcox Canada
Stanley Black & Decker
Sunview Doors Ltd.
The Williams Brothers Corp.
Window City Mfrs Inc.

332329
Other Ornamental and Architectural Metal Products Manufacturing

Bothwell-Accurate Co. (2006) Limited
Etobicoke Ironworks Ltd.
Fisher & Ludlow
Jeld-Wen Windows & Doors
Kawneer Company Canada Ltd.
Nailor Industries Inc.
Pro-Bel Enterprises
Qualified Metal Fabricators Ltd.
Stress-Crete King Luminaire Ltd.

332410
Power Boiler and Heat Exchanger Manufacturing

Atomic Energy of Canada Ltd.

332420
Metal Tank (Heavy Gauge) Manufacturing

All-Weld Company Ltd.

332431
Metal Can Manufacturing

Crown Metal Packaging Canada LP

332510
Hardware Manufacturing

Atlas Bearings Inc.
Flex-N-Gate Seeburn
Haremar Plastic Manufacturing Ltd.
National Concrete Accessories
Renin Corp.
Stanley Black & Decker
Stanley Black & Decker Canada Inc.

332611
Spring (Heavy Gauge) Manufacturing

Springco Inc.

332619
Other Fabricated Wire Product Manufacturing

Commercial Spring
   & Tool Company Ltd.
Globe Spring
Springco Inc.

332710
Machine Shops

CFN Precision Ltd.

332720
Turned Product and Screw-Nut and Bolt Manufacturing

Flex-N-Gate Seeburn
H. Paulin & Company Ltd.
Leland Industries Inc.
RB & W Corporation of Canada

332810
Coating- Engraving- Heat Treating and Allied Activities

Catelectric Inc.
Dependable Anodizing Ltd.
Durapaint Industries Ltd.
Four Star Plating Industries Ltd.
Metal Koting - Continuous
   Colour Coat Limited
Metex Heat Treating Ltd.
PPG Canada Inc.
Spectra Aluminum Products Inc.

332910
Metal Valve Manufacturing

Cello Products Inc.
C/S Construction Specialties Company
Dahl Brothers (Canada) Ltd.
Grohe Canada Inc.
Moen Inc.
Mueller Canada
Oetiker Ltd.

Ryerson Canada
Watts Water Technologies
   (Canada) Inc.

332991
Ball and Roller Bearing Manufacturing

NSK Canada Inc.
NTN Bearing Corporation
   of Canada Ltd.

332999
All Other Miscellaneous Fabricated Metal Product Manufacturing

ABS Machining Inc.
American-Standard
Bailey Metal Products Ltd.
BMP Metals Inc.
Flexmaster Canada Limited
Flex-N-Gate Seeburn
Hydropool Industries
Lite Products Inc.
Loxcreen Canada Ltd.
Moen Inc.
Nelson Industrial Inc.
Russel Metals Inc.
Ryerson Canada
Signature Aluminum Canada Inc.
Slidemaster
T.A. Brannon Steel Ltd.
Toro Aluminum
Tube-Fab Ltd.
Versa Fittings & Manufacturing Inc.

333110
Agricultural Implement Manufacturing

Reversomatic Manufacturing

333120
Construction Machinery Manufacturing

Hilti (Canada) Corp.
Lovat Inc.

333130
Mining and Oil and Gas Field Machinery Manufacturing

Sandvik Mining and Construction
   Canada Inc.

333220
Rubber and Plastics Industry Machinery Manufacturing

Gracious Living Corporation
Husky Injection Molding Systems Ltd.
Macro Engineering & Technology Inc.
Plastic Moulders Limited
Proco Machinery Inc.
RT Recycling Technology Inc.
Silcotech North America Inc.

333291
Paper Industry Machinery Manufacturing

Langen Packaging Inc.

333299
All Other Industrial Machinery Manufacturing

Castool Tooling Systems
Cleveland Range Ltd.
Eco-Tec Inc.

333310
Commercial and Service Industry Machinery Manufacturing

Allied Systems (Canada) Company
Atlantis Systems International Inc.
Blue Giant Equipment Corp.
Brampton Engineering Inc.
Bunn-O-Matic Corporation
   of Canada Ltd.
Cashcode Company Inc.
Certified Laboratories
Cleveland Range Ltd.
Crown Food Service Equipment Ltd.
Eco-Tec Inc.
Garland Commercial Ranges Ltd.
Longford International Ltd.
Mailing Innovations
Pentax Canada Inc.
Polyair Canada Ltd.
Solarfective Products Limited
Viva Magnetics (Canada) Ltd.
Wheelabrator Canada Inc.
Xerox Canada Inc.

333413
Industrial and Commercial Fan and Blower and Air Purification Equipment Manufacturing

Garland Commercial Ranges Ltd.

333416
Heating Equipment and Commercial Refrigeration Equipment Manufacturing

Canadian Springs
Carmichael Engineering Ltd.
CCI Thermal Technologies Inc.
Cimco Refrigeration
Drive Products
Engineered Air
Mersen Canada
Mobile Climate Control Inc.
S.A. Armstrong Ltd.
Toromont Industries Ltd.

333511
Industrial Mould Manufacturing

Husky Injection Molding Systems Ltd.
Plastic Moulders Limited
RT Recycling Technology Inc.
StackTeck Systems Ltd.
Top Grade Molds Ltd.
Tycos Tool & Die Inc.

333519
Other Metalworking Machinery Manufacturing

A. Berger Precision Ltd.
Cana-Datum Moulds Ltd.
Exco Technologies Ltd.
Graff Concrete
J.M. Die Limited
MetriCan Mfg. Co. Inc.
MSP
MTD Metro Tool & Die Ltd.
Pure Metal Galvanizing
Sandvik Canada Inc.
Thunder Tool & Mfg. Ltd.
Ultra-Form Manufacturing
    Company Ltd.
Woodbine Tool
    & Die Manufacturing Ltd.

333611
Turbine and Turbine Generator Set Unit Manufacturing

General Electric Canada

333619
Other Engine and Power Transmission Equipment Manufacturing

Harper Power Products
Litens Automotive Partnership
Pullmatic Manufacturing
SEW Eurodrive Company
    of Canada Ltd.
Tsubaki of Canada Ltd.
Van Der Graaf Inc.

333910
Pump and Compressor Manufacturing

Clyde Union
CPC Pumps International Inc.
Innovative Cooling Dynamics
Presvac Systems (Burlington) Ltd.
S.A. Armstrong Ltd.
Thomson-Gordon Group Ltd.

333920
Material Handling Equipment Manufacturing

Del Equipment Limited
Savaria Concord Lifts Inc.

333990
All Other General-Purpose Machinery Manufacturing

ABB Inc.
ABS Machining Inc.
B.C. Instruments
Bosch Rexroth Canada Corp.
Deacro Industries Ltd.
Festo Inc.
Hibar Systems Ltd.
Howard Marten Company Ltd.
ITW Construction Products
Kinecor
Makita Canada Inc.
Mold-Masters (2007) Limited
Oetiker Ltd.
Parker Hannifin
Powerlasers Ltd.
Samuel Strapping Systems
SimplexGrinnell
SMC Pneumatics (Canada) Ltd.
Stanley Black & Decker Canada Inc.

334110
Computer and Peripheral Equipment Manufacturing

AMD
Amphenol Canada Corp.
Apple Canada Inc.
Autoliv Electronics Canada Inc.
AxiSource Inc.
Canon Canada Inc.
Concord Idea Corp.
Delphax Technologies
Epson Canada Ltd.
Evertz Microsystems Ltd.
Hewlett-Packard (Canada) Co.
IBM Canada Ltd.
Lexmark Canada Inc.
Logitech Remote Controls
Luxell Technologies Inc.
MDG Computers Canada Inc.
Nortel Networks Corp.
Oracle Canada ULC
Panasonic Canada Inc.
Pentax Canada Inc.
RuggedCom Inc.
Samsung Electronics Canada Inc.
Samtack Inc.
Xerox Canada Inc.

334220
Radio and Television Broadcasting and Wireless Communications Equipment Manufacturing

ASC Signal Corp.
Bell Mobility
CPI Canada Inc.
Gennum Corp.
Harris Corporation
Larcan Inc.
Lotek Wireless Inc.
Nanowave Inc.
Sinclair Technologies Inc.

334290
Other Communications Equipment Manufacturing

CSG Security Inc.
SimplexGrinnell

334310
Audio and Video Equipment Manufacturing

Paradigm Electronics Inc.
Wescam
Yorkville Sound Ltd.

334410
Semiconductor and Other Electronic Component Manufacturing

Adeptron Technologies Corp.
CELESTICA Inc.
Cisco Systems Canada Co.
Communications Repair
    Logistics Company
Creation Technologies LP
Crest Circuit Inc.
DDi
EPM Global Services Inc.
Firan Technology Group
    - Aerospace Division
Flextronics
Hamsar Diversco Inc.
Ilsco of Canada Company
Integrated Technology Ltd.
Kapsch TrafficCom
Milplex Circuit (Canada) Inc.
Nortel Networks Corp.
ON Semiconductor
Paradigm Electronics Inc.
SMTC Corporation
Span International
Standex Electronics Canada
STMicroelectronics

334511
Navigational and Guidance Instruments Manufacturing

Applanix Corp.
Citiguard Security Services Inc.
Escort Manufacturing Corporation

334512
Measuring, Medical and Controlling Devices Manufacturing

Aastra Technologies Limited
Alcohol Countermeasure Systems
Applanix Corp.
Beltone Electronics of Canada Ltd.
Benlan Inc.
Classic Fire Protection Inc.
CTS of Canada Company
DCL International Inc.

George Kelk Corp.
KCI Medical Canada, Inc.
L-3 Communications Electronic
    Systems
Lakeside Process Controls Ltd.
Medtronic of Canada Ltd.
Nailor Industries Inc.
Neopost Canada Limited
Northern Digital Inc.
Novadaq Technologies Inc.
Optech Inc.
Ortho-Clinical Diagnostics
Oticon Canada
Phonak Canada Ltd.
Siemens Healthcare Diagnostics
Silex Innovations Inc.
Smith Detection
Starkey Labs Canada Co.
Starplex Scientific Inc.
The Stevens Company Ltd.
Vibro Acoustics
Vipond Inc.

334515
Instrument Manufacturing for Measuring and Testing Electricity and Electrical Signals

Iris Power LP

334610
Manufacturing and Reproducing Magnetic and Optical Media

Cinram International Inc.
Duplium
EMI Music Canada
Iron Mountain Canada Corp.

335110
Electric Lamp Bulb and Parts Manufacturing

Levitt-Safety Ltd.
Osram Sylvania Ltd.

335120
Lighting Fixture Manufacturing

Beta-Calco Inc.
Cooper Industries (Canada) Inc.
Esmond Manufacturing
Osram Sylvania Ltd.
Visioneering Corp.

335210
Small Electrical Appliance Manufacturing

Air King Ltd.
Hobart Food Equipment Group
    Canada Inc.

335223
Major Kitchen Appliance Manufacturing

Whirlpool Canada LP

335311
Power- Distribution and Specialty Transformers Manufacturing

Allanson International Inc.
Atomic Energy of Canada Ltd.
Cogent Power Inc.
Moloney Electric Inc.
Standex Electronics Canada
Trench Ltd.

335312
Motor and Generator Manufacturing

Emerson Electric Canada Ltd.
General Electric Canada
Sherwood Electromotion Inc.
Voith Hydro Inc.

335315
Switchgear and Switchboard, and Relay and Industrial Control Apparatus Manufacturing

Bosch Rexroth Canada Corp.
Eaton Electrical Group
Etratech Inc.
Ferraz Shawmut Canada Inc.
Firan Technology Group
    - Aerospace Division
General Switchgear & Controls Ltd./
    Markham Electric Division
S & C Electric Canada Ltd.
Schneider Canada Inc.
Strataflex Canada Corp.
Vibro Acoustics

335920
Communication and Energy Wire and Cable Manufacturing

CTI Industries
ShawFlex

335930
Wiring Device Manufacturing

Hubbell Canada LP
K-Line Maintenance
    & Construction Ltd.
Lincoln Electric Company of Canada
Tyco Electronics Canada ULC

335990
All Other Electrical Equipment and Component Manufacturing

Circa Metals
Hubbell Canada LP
Levitt-Safety Ltd.
Lincoln Electric Company of Canada
Siemens Canada Limited
Tectrol Inc.
Tyco Electronics Canada ULC

336110
Automobile and Light-Duty Motor Vehicle Manufacturing

Chrysler Canada Inc.
Ford Motor Company of Canada,
    Limited
General Motors of Canada Ltd.
Honda Canada Inc.

336120
Heavy-Duty Truck Manufacturing

Daimler Buses North America
Harper Ontario Truck Centres

336211
Motor Vehicle Body Manufacturing

Cosma International Inc.
Daimler Buses North America
Del Equipment Limited
Dependable Truck & Tank Repairs Ltd.
Morgan Commercial Babcock Inc.
Multivans Inc.

336310
Motor Vehicle Gasoline Engine and Engine Parts Manufacturing

Canadian Starter Drives Inc.
Magna International Inc.

336320
Motor Vehicle Electrical and Electronic Equipment Manufacturing

Advanced Product Technologies
ArcelorMittal Tubular Products
    Canada Inc.
Dixie Electric Ltd.
Magna International Inc.
RCP Inc.

336330
Motor Vehicle Steering and Suspension Components (except Spring) Manufacturing

Fenwick Automotive Products Ltd.
General Kinetics Engineering Corp.

336340
Motor Vehicle Brake System Manufacturing

Accucut Profile & Grinding Ltd.
Fenwick Automotive Products Ltd.
OE Quality Friction Inc.
Replex Automotive Corp.
Util Capital Tool & Design

336350
Motor Vehicle Transmission and Power Train Parts Manufacturing

Drive Products
Gates Canada Inc.
Litens Automotive Partnership
Magna International Inc.
Martinrea International Inc.
Mascot Truck Parts Ltd.
Uni-Motion Gear

336360
Motor Vehicle Seating and Interior Trim Manufacturing

IAC Automotive Components
    Alberta Ltd.
Trimont Manufacturing Inc.

336370
Motor Vehicle Metal Stamping

ABM Tool & Die Co. Ltd.
Advanced Metal Stamping Corp.
A.G. Simpson Automotive Inc.
Cosma International Inc.
DBG
Magna Exteriors & Interiors Corp.
Maple Stamping
Matcor Automotive
Nucap Industries Inc.
Rollstamp Manufacturing
Van Rob Inc.

336390
Other Motor Vehicle Parts Manufacturing

ABC Group
A. Berger Precision Ltd.
Active Exhaust Corporation
Anton Manufacturing
Automodular Corporation
Benteler Automotive Canada Corp.
Burlington Technologies Inc.
Carbone of America
Co-Ex-Tec
Cooper-Standard Automotive
    Canada Ltd.
Dortec Industries
Eurospec Tooling Inc.
Gates Canada Inc.
General Motors of Canada Ltd.
Goodyear Canada Inc.
Greeley Containment & Rework Inc.
H.L. Blachford Ltd.
Jitsu Manufacturing Inc.
Magna Closures Inc.
Magna Exteriors & Interiors Corp.
Magna Powertrain Inc.
Mancor Canada Inc.
Martinrea International Inc.
Matcor Automotive
Motor Specialty Manufacturers
Mytox Manufacturing
Polybrite
Salga Associates

Showa Canada Inc.
TS Tech Canada Inc.
Ultra-Fit Manufacturing Inc.
Umicore Autocat Canada Corp.
Van Rob Inc.

336410
Aerospace Product and Parts Manufacturing

Atlantis Systems International Inc.
Bombardier Aerospace
Comtek Advanced Structures Ltd.
Cyclone Manufacturing Inc.
Donlee Precision
Field Aviation Company Inc.
General Electric Canada
Goodrich Aerospace Canada Ltd.
Honeywell
Indal Technologies Inc.
MacDonald Dettwiler & Associates Inc.
Magellan Aerospace Corp.
Messier-Bugatti-Dowty
Noranco Inc. - Woodbine Division
Noranco Manufacturing Ltd.
Northstar Aerospace (Canada) Inc.
Pratt & Whitney Canada Corp.
Vac-Aero International Inc.

336510
Railroad Rolling Stock Manufacturing

Bombardier Transportation
Procor Ltd.

337110
Wood Kitchen Cabinet and Counter Top Manufacturing

Cartier Kitchens Inc.
Downsview Woodworking Ltd.
Frendel Kitchens Limited
Irpinia Kitchens
Normac Kitchens Ltd.
Raywal Ltd.
Selba Industries Inc.

337121
Upholstered Household Furniture Manufacturing

Barrymore Furniture Co.
Campio Furniture Ltd.
Decor-Rest Furniture Ltd.
Distinctive Designs Furniture Inc.
Global Upholstery Company Inc.
Superstyle Furniture Ltd.

337123
Other Wood Household Furniture Manufacturing

Allwood Products Limited
Neff Kitchen Manufacturing Ltd.

337126
Household Furniture (except Wood and Upholstered) Manufacturing

Jetco Manufacturing Ltd.
Reflections Furniture Industries Ltd.

337127
Institutional Furniture Manufacturing

College Woodwork
Fleetwood Fine Furniture LP
Global Upholstery Company Inc.
Keilhauer
Spec Furniture Inc.
Teknion Form

337213
Wood Office Furniture- including Custom Architectural Woodwork- Manufacturing

College Woodwork
D & E Wood Industries Ltd.
Egan & Teamboard
Herman Miller Canada Inc.
IOF Business Furniture
    Manufacturing Inc.
Knoll North America Corp.
Nienkamper Furniture
    & Accessories Inc.
Olon Industries Inc.
Purewood Inc.
Sonnenberg Industries Ltd.
Star Quality Office Furniture
    Manufacturing Ltd.
Talon Systems Inc.
Tayco Panelink Ltd.
Teknion Corp.
Woodlore International Inc.

337214
Office Furniture (except Wood) Manufacturing

Allseating Corporation
Canadian Business Machines Ltd.
Egan & Teamboard
Fileco Inc.
Global Contract Inc.
Global File Inc.
Herman Miller Canada Inc.
Inscape Corp.
Interior Manufacturing Group Inc.
Lyreco (Canada) Inc.
Nienkamper Furniture
    & Accessories Inc.
Nightingale Corporation
Profile Industries Ltd.
Steelcase Canada Limited
Tab Products of Canada, Co.
Talon Systems Inc.
Tayco Panelink Ltd.
Teknion Corp.

337215
Showcase- Partition- Shelving and Locker Manufacturing

Array Canada Inc.
Canadian Business Machines Ltd.
Concord Metal Manufacturing
D & E Wood Industries Ltd.
Econo-Rack Storage Equipment Ltd.
Hadrian Manufacturing Inc.
IDX Toronto
Interior Manufacturing Group Inc.
J.A. Wilson Display
Kubik Inc.
Nelson Industrial Inc.
North America Steel Equipment Company Ltd.
NS Studios
Protagon Display Inc.
Provincial Store Fixtures Ltd.
Unique Store Fixtures Ltd.

337910
Mattress Manufacturing

Kingsdown Owen & Co. Ltd.
Satpanth Capital Inc.
Sealy Canada Ltd.
Serta
Simmons Canada Inc.
Spring Air Sommer Corp.

337920
Blind and Shade Manufacturing

Antamex International Inc.
Elite Window Fashions
Hunter Douglas Canada Limited Partnership
Levolor Kirsch Window Fashions
Shade-O-Matic
Urban Edge Shading Inc.

339110
Medical Equipment and Supplies Manufacturing

AB SCIEX
Amico Corp.
Bard Canada Inc.
Calea Ltd.
Capital Safety - Canada
Carl Zeiss Canada Ltd.
Ciba Vision Canada Inc.
CiF Lab Casework Solutions
Dentsply Canada Inc.
Derma Sciences Canada Inc.
Excel Tech Ltd.
Hill-Rom Canada
Innova Medical Ophthalmics Inc.
Johnson & Johnson Medical Products
Medtronic of Canada Ltd.
The Orthotic Group Inc.
Patterson Dental Canada Inc.
Rapid Aid Ltd.
SciCan Ltd.

339910
Jewellery and Silverware Manufacturing

Corona Jewellery Company
Libman Manufacturing Ltd.
Nuco Jewellery Products Inc.

339920
Sporting and Athletic Goods Manufacturing

Flite Hockey Inc.
H.S.T. Synthetics Ltd.
Latham Splash Canada
Nike Canada Corp.

339930
Doll- Toy and Game Manufacturing

Ganz
Gerber Canada Inc.
Mattel Canada Inc.
Spin Master Ltd.

339940
Office Supplies (except Paper) Manufacturing

BIC Inc.

339950
Sign Manufacturing

Harding Display Corp.
Pattison Sign Group
Provincial Sign Systems
Steel Art Signs Corp.
WHB Identification Solutions Inc.
Zip Signs Ltd.

339990
All Other Miscellaneous Manufacturing

BIC Inc.
Jacobs & Thompson Inc.
J.J. Home Products Inc.
Premier Candle Corp.
Roma Moulding Inc.
Seven Continents Corporation
SimplexGrinnell
The Taylor Group
Yamaha Canada Music Ltd.

WHOLESALE TRADE 41

411130
Nursery Stock and Plant Wholesaler-Distributors

John G. Hofland Ltd.

412110
Petroleum Product Wholesaler-Distributors

Consolidated Aviation Fuelling of Toronto ULC
Shell Lubricants Canada

413110
General-Line Food Wholesaler-Distributors

ConAgra Foods Canada Inc.
General Mills Canada Corp.
Johnvince Foods
Ontario Natural Food Co-Op
Ronald A. Chisholm Ltd.
Skor Food Group Inc.
Summit Food Service Distributors Inc.
Sun Wah Trading Inc.
Sysco Toronto
Wallace & Carey Inc.
William M. Dunne Associates Ltd.

413120
Dairy and Milk Products Wholesaler-Distributors

Liberté Natural Foods Inc.
Saputo Dairy Products Canada GP

413130
Poultry and Egg Wholesaler-Distributors

Burnbrae Farms Mississauga
Cargill Foods Toronto
Planway Poultry Inc.
Tender Choice Foods Inc.
T & R Sargent Farms Ltd.

413140
Fish and Seafood Product Wholesaler-Distributors

Allseas Fisheries Inc.
Charlie's Meat & Seafood Supply Ltd.
Export Packers Company Limited
Tai Foong International Ltd.

413150
Fresh Fruit and Vegetable Wholesaler-Distributors

A.J. Lanzarotta Wholesale Fruit & Vegetables Ltd.
Dominion Citrus Income Fund
F G Lister & Company Ltd.
Freshline Foods Ltd.
Fresh Taste Produce Ltd.
Gambles Ontario Produce Inc.
Longo Brothers Fruit Markets Inc.
Morris Brown & Sons Company Ltd.
Pride Pak Canada Ltd.
Rite Pak Produce Co. Ltd.
Sun Rich Fresh Foods Inc.

413160
Red Meat and Meat Product
Wholesaler-Distributors

The Butcher Shoppe
Cardinal Meat Specialists Ltd.
Cargill Foods Toronto
Charlie's Meat & Seafood Supply Ltd.
European Quality Meats
Maple Leaf Consumer Foods
Ronald A. Chisholm Ltd.
Ryding-Regency Meat Packers Ltd.
Santa Maria Foods Corp.
Tender Choice Foods Inc.

413190
Other Specialty-Line Food
Wholesaler-Distributors

Ace Bakery Ltd.
Allseas Fisheries Inc.
Bento Nouveau Ltd.
Export Packers Company Limited
Give & Go Prepared Foods Ltd.
Johnvince Foods
Karrys Bros., Limited
Linsey Foods Ltd.
New Zealand Lamb Company Ltd.
Purity Life Health Products
  - A Sunopta Company
Shah Trading Co. Ltd.
St. Helens Meat Packers Ltd.
Sun Opta Food Distribution Group Inc.
Tree of Life Canada ULC
Van Houtte Coffee Services
Versacold Group - Walker Facility
Worldwide Food Distribution

414110
Clothing and Clothing Accessories
Wholesaler-Distributors

Canadian Clothing International Inc.
Caulfeild Apparel Group Ltd.
Debco Bag Distributors Ltd.
Griffen Manimpex Ltd.
Jaytex of Canada Ltd.
Jones Apparel Group Canada Ltd.
Levi Strauss & Co. (Canada) Inc.
NIH Enterprises Inc.
Nygard International Ltd.
PYA Importer Ltd.
RMP Athletic Locker Ltd.
Trimark Sportswear Group Inc.
Unisync Group Ltd.

414120
Footwear Wholesaler-Distributors

Indeka Imports Ltd.
RMP Athletic Locker Ltd.
Sherson Group

414130
Piece Goods- Notions and Other Dry
Goods Wholesaler-Distributors

Fabricland Distributors Inc.
Rose E. Dee (International) Ltd.
Triplewell Enterprises Ltd.

414210
Home Entertainment Equipment
Wholesaler-Distributors

E1 Entertainment
Panasonic Canada Inc.
Sharp Electronics of Canada Ltd.
Solutions2Go Inc.
Sony of Canada Ltd.
Soroc Technology Inc.
Yamaha Canada Music Ltd.

414220
Household Appliance
Wholesaler-Distributors

Coinamatic Canada Inc.
Electrolux Home Products
Jarden Consumer Solutions
LG Electronics Canada Inc.
Panasonic Canada Inc.
Philips Electronics Ltd.

414310
China- Glassware- Crockery and Pottery
Wholesaler-Distributors

Browne & Co. Ltd.

414320
Floor Covering Wholesaler-Distributors

Gesco Industries Inc.

414390
Other Home Furnishings
Wholesaler-Distributors

Dynamic Paint Products Inc.
Encore Sales Ltd.
Larson-Juhl Ltd.
Simmons Canada Inc.
Umbra Ltd.

414410
Jewellery and Watch
Wholesaler-Distributors

Harry Winston Diamond Corporation
Timex Group Inc.

414420
Book- Periodical and Newspaper
Wholesaler-Distributors

Metro News
Pearson Canada

414430
Photographic Equipment and Supplies
Wholesaler-Distributors

Canon Canada Inc.
Fujifilm Canada Inc.
Kodak Canada Inc.
Nikon Canada Inc.
Vistek Ltd.

414440
Sound Recording Wholesalers

Anderson Merchandisers-Canada Inc.

414470
Amusement and Sporting Goods
Wholesaler-Distributors

adidas Canada Limited
Amer Sports Canada Inc.
Bauer Hockey Corp.
Nike Canada Corp.
Sport Chek

414510
Pharmaceuticals and Pharmacy Supplies
Wholesaler-Distributors

Alcon Canada Inc.
EMD Serono Canada Inc.
Hoffmann-LaRoche Ltd.
Kohl & Frisch Ltd.
McKesson Canada
Swiss Herbal Remedies Ltd.

414520
Toiletries- Cosmetics and Sundries
Wholesaler-Distributors

Apollo Health & Beauty Care
Beauty Systems Group (Canada) Inc.
Belvedere International Inc.
First Lady Coiffures
Janssen Inc.
Mary Kay Cosmetics Ltd.
William M. Dunne Associates Ltd.

415110
New and Used Automobile and Light-Duty
Truck Wholesaler-Distributors

ADESA Canada
BMW Canada Inc.
Hyundai Auto Canada Corp.
Nissan Canada Inc.
Subaru Canada Inc.

415190
Recreational and Other Motor Vehicles
Wholesaler-Distributors

Deeley Harley Davidson Canada
Honda Canada Inc.
Mazda Canada Inc.
Mercedes-Benz Canada Inc.
Suzuki Canada Inc.
Toyota Canada Inc.
Volkswagen Group Canada
Yamaha Motor Canada Ltd.

415210
Tire Wholesaler-Distributors

Bridgestone/Firestone (Canada) Inc.

415290
Other New Motor Vehicle Parts and
Accessories Wholesaler-Distributors

Carquest Canada Ltd.
C&S Auto Parts Limited
Federal Mogul Canada Ltd.
Ford Motor Company of Canada,
    Limited
Grote Industries
IIyundai Auto Canada Corp.
Motorcade Industries Ltd.
Multimatic Inc.
NAPA Auto Parts
Nissan Canada Inc.
Robert Bosch Inc.
Suzuki Canada Inc.
Volkswagen Group Canada
Western Toronto International
    Trucks Inc.
Yamaha Motor Canada Ltd.

416110
Electrical Wiring and Construction Supplies
Wholesaler-Distributors

Anixter Canada Inc.
Eurofase Inc.
Gerrie Electric Wholesale Ltd.
Nedco Ontario
Paul Wolf Lighting
    & Electric Supply Ltd.
Tri-Ed Ltd.
Weir Canada Inc.
Wesco Distribution Canada LP
Westburne Ruddy Electric

416120
Plumbing- Heating and
Air-Conditioning Equipment and Supplies
Wholesaler-Distributors

Carrier Canada
Crane Supply
Desco Plumbing and Heating
    Supply Inc.
EMCO Corporation
Fairview Fittings & Manufacturing
    Limited

HTS Engineering Ltd.
Noble Trade Inc.
Trane Ontario/Trane Canada ULC
Versa Fittings & Manufacturing Inc.
York International Ltd.

416210
Metal Service Centres

Alumicor Ltd.
Antalex Inc.
ASA Alloys
Bailey Metal Products Ltd.
Concord Steel Centre Ltd.
Don Park LP
Galvcast Manufacturing Inc.
Gatsteel Industries Inc.
Gerdau Ameristeel
Maksteel
Marmon/Keystone Canada Inc.
Premetalco Inc.
Samuel Manu-Tech Inc.
Samuel, Son & Co., Limited
VICWEST

416310
General-Line Building Supplies
Wholesaler-Distributors

Broadleaf Logistics Company
KP Building Products

416320
Lumber, Plywood and Millwork
Wholesaler-Distributors

Alpa Lumber Inc.
Central Fairbank Lumber
Cutler Forest Products Inc.
Goodfellow Inc.
Nicholson & Cates Ltd.
Richards Wilcox Door Systems Limited
Roma Fence Ltd.
Tamarack Lumber Inc.
Upper Canada Forest Products Ltd.
Weston Forest Products

416330
Hardware Wholesaler-Distributors

Centura (Toronto) Ltd.
Encore Sales Ltd.
HD Supply Canada
Interfast Inc.
The Mibro Group
Olympia Tile International Inc.
Robert Bosch Inc.

416340
Paint- Glass and Wallpaper
Wholesaler-Distributors

AkzoNobel
Jems Coating Ltd.

416390
Other Specialty-Line Building Supplies
Wholesaler-Distributors

Architectural Precast Systems Inc.
FM Windows & Doors
Gentek Building Products Ltd.
Georgia-Pacific Canada, Inc.
James Dick Construction Ltd.
Paramount Pallet Inc.
Winroc

417110
Farm- Lawn and Garden Machinery and
Equipment Wholesaler-Distributors

Electrolux Home Products
Turf Care Products Canada Limited

417210
Construction and Forestry
Machinery, Equipment and Supplies
Wholesaler-Distributors

Canadian Industrial Distributors Inc.
HD Supply Canada
Kubota Canada Ltd.
Nortrax
PERI Performance Systems
Toromont Industries Ltd.
Wajax Income Fund
Yale Industrial Trucks Ontario Ltd.

417230
Industrial Machinery- Equipment and
Supplies Wholesaler-Distributors

Acklands-Grainger Inc.
Air Liquide Canada Inc.
BDI World Class World Wide
Canadian Bearings Ltd.
Emerson Electric Canada Ltd.
Glasvan Trailers Inc.
G.N. Johnston Equipment
    Company Ltd.
Haremar Plastic Manufacturing Ltd.
Heidelberg Canada Graphic
    Equipment Limited
Hobart Food Equipment Group
    Canada Inc.
J.H. Ryder Machinery Ltd.
John Brooks Company Ltd.
Kinecor
Liftow Ltd.
L.V. Lomas Ltd.
NSK Canada Inc.
Peterbilt Ontario Truck Centres
SKF Canada Ltd.
Strongco Inc.
Wainbee Ltd.

417310

Computer- Computer Peripheral and Pre-Packaged Software Wholesaler-Distributors

The Administrative Assistants Ltd.
Ahearn and Soper Inc.
Apple Canada Inc.
AxiSource Inc.
CDW
Compugen Inc.
Dell Canada Inc.
Dell Financial Services Canada Ltd.
Delphax Technologies
Hewlett-Packard (Canada) Co.
Ingram Micro
MDG Computers Canada Inc.
Motorola Canada Ltd.
Soroc Technology Inc.
Supercom of Canada Ltd.
SYNNEX Canada Ltd.
Tech Data Canada Inc.
Telecom Computer Inc.
TigerDirect.Ca Inc.
Toshiba of Canada Ltd.
Tucows Inc.
Unisys Canada Inc.

417320

Electronic Components- Navigational and Communications Equipment and Supplies Wholesaler-Distributors

Anixter Canada Inc.
Baka Communications Inc.
Electro Sonic Inc.
Ericsson Canada Inc.
Gentec International Ltd.
Harris Corporation
LG Electronics Canada Inc.
Mircom Technologies Ltd.
Motorola Canada Ltd.
Philips Electronics Ltd.
Rexel Canada Electrical Inc.
Sharp Electronics of Canada Ltd.
STMicroelectronics
Toshiba of Canada Ltd.
Yorkville Sound Ltd.

417320

Electronic Components, Navigational and Communications Equipment and Supplies Wholesaler-Distributors

Hamsar Diversco Inc.
Lenbrook Industries Ltd.

417910

Office and Store Machinery and Equipment Wholesaler-Distributors

Konica Minolta Business Solutions (Canada) Ltd.
Lyreco (Canada) Inc.
Pitney Bowes Canada Ltd.
POI Business Interiors Inc.
QBD Modular Systems Inc.
Staples Canada Inc.
Toshiba Business Solutions

417920

Service Establishment Machinery, Equipment and Supplies Wholesaler-Distributors

Collega International Inc.
On Premise Laundry Systems Inc.
Trimen Food Service Equipment Inc.
Van Houtte Coffee Services

417930

Professional Machinery- Equipment and Supplies Wholesaler-Distributors

Abbott Laboratories Ltd./ Diagnostic Division
Alcon Canada Inc.
Baylis Medical Company Inc.
Becton Dickinson Canada Inc.
Calea Ltd.
Cardinal Health Canada
Centennial Optical Limited
Curry's Art Store Ltd.
Fujifilm Canada Inc.
Medical Mart Supplies Ltd.
Optech Inc.
Phonak Canada Ltd.
SciCan Ltd.
Shoppers HomeHealthCare
Thermo Fisher Scientific Co.
VWR International, Ltd.

417990

All Other Machinery- Equipment and Supplies Wholesaler-Distributors

Harper Power Products
Wajax Income Fund
Weir Canada Inc.

418110

Recyclable Metal Wholesaler-Distributors

Standard Auto Wreckers
Triple M Metal

418120

Recyclable Paper and Paperboard Wholesaler-Distributors

Corpap Inc.

418210

Stationery and Office Supplies Wholesaler-Distributors

Aviva
Coast Paper
Hilroy
Myron
Newell Rubbermaid Canada
Staples Advantage
Staples Canada Inc.

418220

Other Paper and Disposable Plastic Product Wholesaler-Distributors

Canada Fibers Ltd.
Georgia-Pacific Canada/ Consumer Products, Inc.
Kimberly-Clark Inc.
Kruger Products Limited
Metro Paper Industries Inc.
Norampac Inc.
PaperlinX Canada Limited
Progress Packaging Ltd.

418410

Chemical (except Agricultural) and Allied Product Wholesaler-Distributors

Ashland Canada Corp.
Brenntag Canada Inc.
Canada Colors & Chemicals Ltd.
Clariant (Canada) Inc.
L.V. Lomas Ltd.
Praxair Canada Inc.
Univar Canada Ltd.
Wurth Canada Ltd.

418990

All Other Wholesaler-Distributors

A.C.I. Accessory Concepts Inc.
Comda Calendar
CTG Brands
East Penn Power Battery Sales Ltd.
Enesco Canada Corp.
First Lady Coiffures
Giftcraft Ltd.
Group of Goldline
Myron
Royal Doulton Canada Ltd.
Samaco Trading Limited
ThyssenKrupp Materials

419130

Food- Beverage and Tobacco Agents and Brokers

Crossmark Canada Inc.

419170

Machinery, Equipment and Supplies Agents and Brokers

4 Office Automation Ltd.

419190
Other Wholesale Agents and Brokers

Christie Lites Ltd.

RETAIL TRADE   44 - 45

441110
New Car Dealers

Acura of North Toronto
Addison Chevrolet
Addison Chevrolet Buick GMC
Agincourt Autohaus Inc.
Agincourt Chrysler Inc.
Agincourt Infiniti Nissan Ltd.
Applewood Chevrolet Cadillac
BMW Autohaus
Courtesy Chevrolet
Dean Myers Chevrolet Corvette
Discovery Ford Sales Limited
Don Valley North Automotive Inc.
Donway Ford Sales Ltd.
Downsview Chrysler
    Plymouth (1964) Ltd.
Downtown Fine Cars Inc.
Erin Dodge Chrysler Ltd.
Erin Park Automotive Partnership
Erinwood Ford Sales Ltd.
Frost Pontiac Buick Cadillac Ltd.
Gateway Chevrolet Inc.
Highland Chevrolet Cadillac Ltd.
Hogan Chevrolet Limited
Ideal Honda
Ken Shaw Lexus Toyota
Kia Canada Inc.
Marvin Starr Motors Ltd.
Meadowvale Ford Sales
    and Services Ltd.
Mills Pontiac Buick GMC Ltd.
Mississauga Honda
The Newroads Automotive Group
Oak-Land Ford Lincoln Sales Ltd.
Old Mill Pontiac Buick Cadillac Ltd.
Ontario Chrysler Jeep Dodge Inc.
Ontario Motor Sales Ltd.
Parkway Automotive Sales Ltd.
Pauldonlam Investments Inc.
Performance Equipment Limited
Pine Tree Ford Lincoln
Pine View Hyundai Ltd.
Plaza Pontiac Buick Ltd.
Queensway Volkswagen Inc.
Raceway Plymouth Chrysler Ltd.
Ready Honda
Roadsport Honda
Roy Foss Motors Ltd.
Scarborotown Chrysler
    Dodge Jeep Ltd.
Scarborough Toyota
Sisley Motors Limited
Stuart Budd & Sons Ltd.
Summit Ford Sales (1982) Ltd.
Thorncrest Sherway Inc.
Town & Country Motors (1989) Ltd.
Whiteoak Ford Lincoln Sales Limited
Woodchester Nissan

441120
Used Car Dealers

Acura of North Toronto
Addison Chevrolet
Addison Chevrolet Buick GMC
Agincourt Autohaus Inc.
Agincourt Chrysler Inc.
Agincourt Infiniti Nissan Ltd.
Applewood Chevrolet Cadillac
Courtesy Chevrolet
Discovery Ford Sales Limited
Don Valley North Automotive Inc.
Donway Ford Sales Ltd.
Downsview Chrysler
    Plymouth (1964) Ltd.
Downtown Fine Cars Inc.
Erin Dodge Chrysler Ltd.
Erin Park Automotive Partnership
Erinwood Ford Sales Ltd.
Frost Pontiac Buick Cadillac Ltd.
Gateway Chevrolet Inc.
Highland Chevrolet Cadillac Ltd.
Hogan Chevrolet Limited
Ken Shaw Lexus Toyota
Kia Canada Inc.
Marvin Starr Motors Ltd.
Meadowvale Ford Sales
    and Services Ltd.
Mills Pontiac Buick GMC Ltd.
The Newroads Automotive Group
Oak-Land Ford Lincoln Sales Ltd.
Old Mill Pontiac Buick Cadillac Ltd.
Ontario Chrysler Jeep Dodge Inc.
Ontario Motor Sales Ltd.
Parkway Automotive Sales Ltd.
Pauldonlam Investments Inc.
Pine Tree Ford Lincoln
Plaza Pontiac Buick Ltd.
Queensway Volkswagen Inc.
Raceway Plymouth Chrysler Ltd.
Roadsport Honda
Roy Foss Motors Ltd.
Scarborough Toyota
Sisley Motors Limited
Summit Ford Sales (1982) Ltd.
Town & Country Motors (1989) Ltd.

441310
Automotive Parts and Accessories Stores

NAPA Auto Parts
Paul K. Brennan Holdings Inc.

441320
Tire Dealers

Kal Tire Ontario

442110
Furniture Stores

Art Shoppe Limited
De Boer's Furniture Ltd.
IKEA Canada Ltd.
Leon's Furniture Ltd.
Sleep Country Canada

442210
Floor Covering Stores

Gesco Industries Inc.

442292
Print and Picture Frame Stores

Images 2000 Inc.

442298
All Other Home Furnishings Stores

AkzoNobel
Hudson's Bay Company
IKEA Canada Ltd.
Pier 1 Imports
Solutions
William Ashley Ltd.
Winners Merchants International

443110
Appliance- Television and Other Electronics Stores

Arrow North American Electronics
    Components
Best Buy Canada
The Brick Warehouse Corp.
Sony of Canada Ltd.
The Source (Bell) Electronics
    Canada Inc.

443120
Computer and Software Stores

CDI Computer Dealers Inc.
FactoryDirect.ca

443130
Camera and Photographic Supplies Stores

Black Photo Corporation
Henry's
The Source (Bell) Electronics
    Canada Inc.

444110
Home Centres

Lowe's Canada

444130
Hardware Stores

Canadian Tire Corporation Ltd.
Grandview Sales & Distribution Ltd.
Home Depot Canada
K.W. Mann Inc.
Rona Ontario Inc.

444190
Other Building Material Dealers

Acan Windows Systems Inc.
Home Depot Canada
Pollard Windows Inc.
Rona Ontario Inc.
Triple Seal Ltd.

444220
Nursery and Garden Centres

Humber Nurseries Limited
Plant World Ltd.
Sheridan Nurseries Limited
Vandermeer Nursery Ltd.

445110
Supermarkets and Other Grocery (except Convenience) Stores

Big Carrot Natural Food Market
Concord Food Centre Ltd.
Frank's Food Basics
The Garden Basket Food Markets Inc.
Highland Farms Inc.
The Kitchen Table Inc.
Loblaw Companies Limited
Longo Brothers Fruit Markets Inc.
Marc's No Frills
Metro Ontario Inc.
Michael-Angelo's Market Place Inc.
Pusateri's Ltd.
Sobeys Ontario
Weston Fine Foods Inc.

445120
Convenience Stores

Mac's Convenience Stores Inc.

445230
Fruit and Vegetable Markets

Sun Valley Supermarket Inc.

445291
Baked Goods Stores

Open Window Health Bread
    Bakery Limited

445292
Confectionery and Nut Stores

Hachette Distribution Services Retail
    North America
Regal Confections

445299
All Other Specialty Food Stores

Bulk Barn Foods Limited
Laura Secord

445310
Beer- Wine and Liquor Stores

Brewers' Retail Inc.
Liquor Control Board of Ontario

446110
Pharmacies and Drug Stores

Katz Group Canada Ltd.
Medical Pharmacies Group Inc.
Shoppers Drug Mart/Pharmaprix

446120
Cosmetics- Beauty Supplies and Perfume Stores

M·A·C Cosmetics
Sephora

446130
Optical Goods Stores

Hakim Optical Laboratory Ltd.
Luxottica Retail

446191
Food (Health) Supplement Stores

Big Carrot Natural Food Market

446199
All Other Health and Personal Care Stores

VitalAire Canada Inc.

447110
Gasoline Stations with Convenience Stores

Petro-Canada

447190
Other Gasoline Stations

Husky Truck Stop
Imperial Oil Limited
Shell Canada Ltd.

448110
Men's Clothing Stores

Grafton-Fraser Inc.
Harry Rosen Inc.
International Clothiers Inc.
Moores the Suit People, Inc.

448120
Women's Clothing Stores

Boutique La Vie en Rose Inc.
Comark Services Inc.
Cotton Ginny Inc.
La Senza Inc.
Olsen Fashion Canada Inc.

448140
Family Clothing Stores

Club Monaco Corp.
Danier Leather Inc.
Eddie Bauer Inc.
Gap Inc. Canada
H & M Hennes & Mauritz Inc.
Holt Renfrew & Company Ltd.
Le Chateau Inc.
Mountain Equipment Cooperative
National Sports
Roots Canada Ltd.
Sport Chek
Sporting Life Inc.
Winners Merchants International
YM Inc. Sales
Zara Canada

448150
Clothing Accessories Stores

Club Monaco Corp.
Danier Leather Inc.
Eddie Bauer Inc.
Grafton-Fraser Inc.
International Clothiers Inc.
Le Chateau Inc.
Moores the Suit People, Inc.
Winners Merchants International
YM Inc. Sales

448199
All Other Clothing Stores

The John Forsyth Shirt Co. Ltd.

448210
Shoe Stores

Athletes World
New Balance Toronto
Running Room
Town Shoes Ltd.

448310
Jewellery Stores

Birks & Mayors Inc.
Timex Group Inc.

451110
Sporting Goods Stores

Flite Hockey Inc.
Golf Town Canada Inc.
Mountain Equipment Cooperative
National Sports
Sport Chek
Sporting Life Inc.
Sport Swap Inc.

451120
Hobby- Toy and Game Stores

Toys R Us (Canada) Ltd.

451130
Sewing- Needlework and Piece Goods Stores

Fabricland Distributors Inc.
H.A. Kidd and Company Limited

451140
Musical Instrument and Supplies Stores

Long & McQuade Musical Instruments
Merriam School of Music

451210
Book Stores and News Dealers

Hachette Distribution Services Retail
    North America
Indigo Books & Music, Inc.

451220
Pre-Recorded Tape- Compact Disc and Record Stores

HMV Canada Inc.

452110
Department Stores

Hudson's Bay Company
Mirvish Productions
Sears Canada Inc.
Sears Liquidation Centre
Wal-Mart Canada Corp.

452910
Warehouse Clubs and Superstores

Costco Wholesale - Ajax

452999
All Other Miscellaneous General Merchandise Stores

The Bargain! Shop Holdings Inc.
Sears Liquidation Centre

453110
Florists

Aldershot Greenhouses

453210
Office Supplies and Stationery Stores

Grand & Toy Ltd.
Hilroy
Konica Minolta Business Solutions (Canada) Ltd.
Office Depot
Staples Canada Inc.

453220
Gift, Novelty and Souvenir Stores

Mister Keys Ltd.
Nuance Global Traders (Canada) Inc.

453310
Used Merchandise Stores

Afcan Interlink Ltd.
DYN Exports Inc.
Five Star Rags Inc.
Fripes Export Ltd.
Goodwill Toronto
Griffen Manimpex Ltd.
Ontex Clothing Inc.

453910
Pet and Pet Supplies Stores

Pet Valu Canada Inc.
PJ's Pet Centres Ltd.

453999
All Other Miscellaneous Store Retailers (except Beer and Wine-Making Supplies Stores)

Brita Canada Corp.
Hachette Distribution Services Retail North America
Party Packagers

454110
Electronic Shopping and Mail-Order Houses

Cornerstone Group of Companies Limited
Sears Canada Inc.
Wunderman

454210
Vending Machine Operators

Canada Catering Company Ltd.
Escar Entertainment Ltd.
Imperial Coffee Services Inc.

454390
Other Direct Selling Establishments

The Shopping Channel
SMT Direct Marketing Inc.

TRANSPORTATION & WAREHOUSING   48 - 49

481110
Scheduled Air Transportation

Air Canada
Air Canada Jazz
Air Georgian Ltd.
American Airlines, Inc.
Porter Airlines Inc.
TNT Express (Canada) Inc.
Westjet Airlines Ltd.

481214
Non-Scheduled Chartered Air Transportation

Air Transat A.T. Inc.
Chartright Air Group

482112
Short-Haul Freight Rail Transportation

Canadian Pacific Railway

482113
Mainline Freight Rail Transportation

Canadian Pacific Railway
CN

482114
Passenger Rail Transportation

Via Rail Canada Inc.

484110
General Freight Trucking- Local

Active Transport Inc.
Armbro Transport Inc.
Beacon Transit Lines Inc.
Buckley Cartage Ltd.
Bulk Transfer Systems Inc.
Canada Cartage System Ltd.
Cavalier Transportation Services Inc.
Consolidated Fastfrate Inc.
CWH Distribution Services Inc.
Day & Ross Inc.
Don Anderson Haulage Ltd.
D & W Forwarders Inc.
Erb Transport Ltd.
FedEx Freight Canada
J.D. Smith and Sons Limited
Melburn/Musket Group
Midnight Express & Cartage Ltd.
MIQ Logistics
MSM Transportation Inc.
Muirs Cartage Ltd.
Pinnacle Transport Ltd.
Rosedale Transport Ltd.
Sameday Worldwide
Scott-Woods Transport Inc.
S.L.H. Transport Inc.
Speedy Transport Group Inc.
Tank Truck Transport Inc.
Thomson Terminals Ltd.
Tippet-Richardson Ltd.
Titan Cartage Ltd.
Trans4 Logistics
Transport CFQI
TransX Ltd.
Tripar Transportation Inc.
TST Overland Express
TST Truckload Express Inc.
TTR Transport Inc.
Vitran Corporation Inc.
Warren Gibson Ltd.
Wilson's Truck Lines Ltd.
YRC Reimer

484121
General Freight Trucking- Long Distance-Truck-Load

Active Transport Inc.
Armbro Transport Inc.
Beacon Transit Lines Inc.
Bison Transport Inc.
Canada Cartage System Ltd.
Canamex Trucking System Inc.
Caravan Logistics Inc.
Cavalier Transportation Services Inc.
Consolidated Fastfrate Inc.
CWH Distribution Services Inc.
Day & Ross Inc.
D & W Forwarders Inc.
Erb Transport Ltd.
FedEx Freight Canada
Forbes Hewlett Transport Inc.
J.D. Smith and Sons Limited
Maritime Ontario Freight Lines Ltd.
Midland Transport Ltd.
Midnight Express & Cartage Ltd.
MIQ Logistics
MSM Transportation Inc.
Muirs Cartage Ltd.
Rosedale Transport Ltd.
Sameday Worldwide
Scott-Woods Transport Inc.
S.L.H. Transport Inc.
Tank Truck Transport Inc.
Tippet-Richardson Ltd.
Titan Cartage Ltd.
Transport CFQI
TransX Ltd.
Tripar Transportation Inc.
TST Overland Express
TTR Transport Inc.
Vitran Corporation Inc.
Warren Gibson Ltd.
YRC Reimer

484122
General Freight Trucking- Long Distance-Less Than Truck-Load

Travelers Transportation Services Ltd.

484210
Used Household and Office Goods Moving

Atlas Van Lines (Canada) Ltd.
Mackie Moving Systems Corp.
Taylor Moving & Storage Ltd.
Total Relocation Moving Systems
United Van Lines (Canada) Ltd.

484221
Bulk Liquids Trucking- Local

Liquid Cargo Lines Ltd.
Seaboard/Harmac
    Transportation Group

484222
Dry Bulk Materials Trucking- Local

Peter Hodge Transport Ltd.

484229
Other Specialized Freight (except Used Goods) Trucking- Local

AMJ Campbell Van Lines
APPS Transport Group
Armbro Transport Inc.
ASL Distribution Services Ltd.
Chester Cartage & Movers Ltd.
Gordon Food Service
Highland Transport
John Grant Haulage Ltd.
Meyers Transport Ltd.
Nesel Fast Freight Inc.
Reefer Sales and Service
Roff Logistics Inc.

484231
Bulk Liquids Trucking- Long Distance

Seaboard/Harmac
    Transportation Group

484232
Dry Bulk Materials Trucking- Long Distance

Peter Hodge Transport Ltd.

484239
Other Specialized Freight (except Used Goods) Trucking- Long Distance

AMJ Campbell Van Lines
APPS Transport Group
ASL Distribution Services Ltd.
Auto Warehousing Co. Canada
Chester Cartage & Movers Ltd.
Clarke Inc.
Highland Transport
Itwal Ltd.
John Grant Haulage Ltd.
Meyers Transport Ltd.
Quik X Transportation Inc.
Speedy Transport Group Inc.
XTL Transport Inc.

485110
Urban Transit Systems

Brampton Transit
Durham Region Transit
Metrolinx
Mississauga Transit
Toronto Transit Commission

485210
Interurban and Rural Bus Transportation

Can-Ar Coach Service
Greyhound Canada
    Transportation Corp.
Metrolinx
Trentway-Wagar Inc.

485310
Taxi Service

ABlackCab
Beck Taxi Ltd.
Burlington Taxi Inc.
City Taxi
Maple Leaf Taxi-Cab Ltd.
Taxi-Taxi

485320
Limousine Service

Rosedale Livery Ltd.

485410
School and Employee Bus Transportation

Attridge Transportation Inc.
First Canada/Greyhound
McCluskey Transportation
    Services Ltd.
Parkview Transit
Stock Transportation Ltd.
Student Transportation Canada
Trentway-Wagar Inc.
Trott Transit Ltd.

485510
Charter Bus Industry

Greyhound Canada
    Transportation Corp.
Student Transportation Canada
Trott Transit Ltd.

485990
Other Transit and Ground Passenger Transportation

Durham Region Transit
Pacific Western

487210
Scenic and Sightseeing Transportation- Water

Mariposa Cruise Line Ltd.

488119
Other Airport Operations

Greater Toronto Airports Authority
Penauille Servisair
Toronto Airways Ltd.
Toronto Port Authority

488190
Other Support Activities
for Air Transportation

NAV Canada

488210
Support Activities for Rail Transportation

Toronto Terminals Railway
    Company Ltd.

488310
Port and Harbour Operations

Toronto Port Authority

488410
Motor Vehicle Towing

A Towing Service Ltd.
Abram's Towing Services Ltd.
Lyons Auto Body Ltd.

488490
Other Support Activities
for Road Transportation

407 ETR
Motor Express Toronto

488519
Other Freight Transportation Arrangement

Agility
All-Connect Logistical Services Inc.
Apex Motor Express Ltd.
Behind the Wheel Transportation
    Services Inc.
Bestway Cartage Ltd.
Bruce R. Smith Ltd.
CEVA Logistics
CHEP Canada Inc.
Consolidated Fastfrate Inc.
Con-way Freight Canada
Core Logistics International Inc.
DGN Marketing Services Ltd.
DHL Global Forwarding (Canada) Inc.
Expeditors Canada Inc.
FedEx Trade Networks Transport &
    Brokerage (Canada) Inc.
G.A. Foss Transport Ltd.
Kingsway Transport
Kintetsu World Express (Canada) Inc.
Livingston International Inc.
Maersk Canada Inc.
Manitoulin Transport Inc.
National Fast Freight
Nippon Express Canada Ltd.
Panalpina Inc.
Purolator Courier Ltd.
Ryder Truck Rental Canada Ltd.
Schenker of Canada Limited
Swissport Cargo Services, LP
Synergex Corporation

Totalline Transport
Traffic Tech Inc.
Trusted Retail Solutions
UTi Canada Inc.
Vitran Express Canada
The Wheels Group
William L. Rutherford Limited

488990
Other Support Activities for
Transportation

1149318 Ontario Inc.
Atripco Delivery Service
ATS Andlauer Transportation
    Services LP
Ryder Logistics & Transportation
    Solutions Worldwide
Spectrum Supply Chain Solutions
Trans-Ontario Express
Trimac Transportation Limited
    Partnership
Willson International
YRC Reimer

491110
Postal Service

Canada Post Corp./Central Region
Unionville Letter Carrier Depot

492110
Couriers

A & B Courier
Apple Express Courier Ltd.
Atripco Delivery Service
ATS Andlauer Transportation
    Services LP
Blizzard Courier Service Ltd.
CANPAR Transport Ltd.
Cardinal Couriers Ltd.
Datarush Courier
Day & Ross Inc.
DHL Express (Canada), Ltd.
Dicom Express
Dynamex Canada Limited
Federal Express Canada Ltd.
FedEx Ground Package System Ltd.
ICS Courier
The Messengers International
Purolator Courier Ltd.
QRC Logistics Ltd.
Quest Courier Services (1996) Ltd.
Quick Messenger Services Ontario Ltd.
Sameday Worldwide
TNT Express (Canada) Inc.
United Parcel Service Canada Ltd.

492210
Local Messengers and Local Delivery

A-Way Express Courier Service

493110
General Warehousing and Storage

Accuristix
ASL Distribution Services Ltd.
Cavalier Transportation Services Inc.
DGN Marketing Services Ltd.
Exel Logistics Canada Inc.
Georgetown Terminal Warehouses Ltd.
J.D. Smith and Sons Limited
Kuehne & Nagel Ltd.
Matrix Logistics Services Ltd.
Metro Canada Logistics Inc.
National Logistics Services
QRC Logistics Ltd.
Sherway Warehousing Inc.
Supply Chain Management Inc.
Thomson Terminals Ltd.
UPS Supply Chain Solutions Canada
XTL Transport Inc.

493120
Refrigerated Warehousing and Storage

Conestoga Cold Storage
Confederation Freezers
Robert Transport
Versacold - Vaughan Facility

493190
Other Warehousing and Storage

Auto Warehousing Co. Canada
Chester Cartage & Movers Ltd.
Dominion Warehousing & Distribution
    Services Ltd.
Graphic Transportation Services
Mackie Moving Systems Corp.

INFORMATION & CULTURAL
INDUSTRIES 51

511110
Newspaper Publishers

Durham Region Media Group
The Globe & Mail Newspaper
Halton Region Media Group
Metroland Media Group Ltd.
Ming Pao Newspapers (Canada) Ltd.
Mississauga Business Times
The Mississauga News
National Post
North Peel Media Group
Now Communications Inc.
Postmedia Network Inc.
Sing Tao Daily
Sun Media Corp.
Toronto Community News
Toronto Star Newspapers Ltd.
York Region Media Group

511120
Periodical Publishers

Brunico Communication Ltd.
Business Information Group
Canada Law Book Inc.
CCH Canadian Ltd.
House & Home Media
Now Communications Inc.
Robert Kennedy Publishing
Rogers Publishing
Thomson Carswell
Toronto Life Publishing Ltd.
Transcontinental Media

511130
Book Publishers

Canada Law Book Inc.
Firefly Books Ltd.
Harlequin Enterprises Ltd.
HarperCollins Canada Ltd.
John Wiley & Sons Canada Ltd.
McGraw-Hill Ryerson Ltd.
Nelson Education Ltd.
Pearson Education Canada Inc.
Random House of Canada Ltd.
Scholastic Canada Ltd.
University of Toronto Press Inc.

511140
Database and Directory Publishers

Cornerstone Group of Companies
  Limited
D & B Canada
ICOM Information
  & Communications Inc.
LexisNexis Canada Inc.
McGraw-Hill Ryerson Ltd.
Postlinx
Yellow Pages Group

511190
Other Publishers

Canadian Posters International Inc.
LexisNexis Canada Inc.
Multimedia Nova Corporation
Thomson Carswell
Trancontinental Interactive

511210
Software Publishers

Algorithmics Inc.
CA Canada
Certicom Corp.
Computer Methods International Corp.
CPAS Systems Inc.
Gary Jonas Computing Ltd.
KOEI Canada Inc.
Longview Solutions Inc.
McGraw-Hill Ryerson Ltd.
MicroAge
Microsoft Canada Co.

Multi-Health Systems Inc.
Open Solutions Canada
Open Text Communications
  Solutions Group
RedKnee Inc.
RPM Technologies Corp.
SAS Institute (Canada) Inc.
Siemens Enterprise
  Communications Inc.

512110
Motion Picture and Video Production

Mijo Corp.
Radke Films
Shaftesbury Films
Universal Studios Canada Inc.
Warner Bros. Entertainment
  Canada Inc.

512130
Motion Picture and Video Exhibition

Cineplex Entertainment LP
IMAX Corporation
Ontario Place Corp.
TIFF

512190
**Post-Production and Other Motion Picture
and Video Industries**

Arc Productions Animation z
  & Visual Effects
Deluxe Laboratories
Shaftesbury Films
Technicolor
Universal Studios Canada Inc.
William F. White International Inc.

512210
Record Production

EMI Music Canada

512220
Integrated Record Production-Distribution

EMI Music Canada

512230
Music Publishers

Society of Composers, Authors, and
  Music Publishers of Canada
Somerset Entertainment Ltd.
Universal Music

513110
Radio Broadcasting

88.5 FM The Jewel
Astral Media Radio
Canadian Broadcasting Corp.
CFNY FM 102.1
Q107 FM
Rogers Media Inc.

513120
Television Broadcasting

BNN - Business News Network
Canadian Broadcasting Corp.
The Comedy Network
Corus Entertainment Inc.
CTV Inc.
Pelmorex Media Inc.
Postmedia Network Inc.
Rogers Media Inc.
Rogers Media Television
Rogers Sportsnet Inc.
The Shopping Channel
The Sports Network
TVO

513210
Pay and Specialty Television

Astral Television Networks
Rogers Communications Inc.
The Score Television Network Ltd.
W Network Inc.

513220
Cable and Other Program Distribution

Astral Television Networks
Cogeco Cable Canada Inc.
Fairchild Television Ltd.
Rogers Communications Inc.
Rogers Media Television

513310
Wired Telecommunications Carriers

Bell Canada
Connex See Service
TELUS Consumer Solutions

513320
**Wireless Telecommunications Carriers
(except Satellite)**

Bell Canada
National Wireless
Primus Telecommunications
  Canada Inc.
Rogers Communications Inc.
TELUS Business Solutions
TELUS Consumer Solutions
TeraGo Networks Inc.

513330
Telecommunications Resellers

Canopco
MTS Allstream Inc.
Paging Network of Canada Inc.
Phonetime Inc.
Prestige Telecom Ltd.
Primus Telecommunications
  Canada Inc.

513340
Satellite Telecommunications

Aastra Technologies Limited
Bell Mobility
MTS Allstream Inc.
Shaw Broadcast Services

513390
Other Telecommunications

Bell Conferencing Inc.
Bell Sympatico
Capital C Communications Inc.
MTS Allstream Inc.
Telecon Inc.
TELUS Business Solutions
Williams Telecommunications Corp.

514110
News Syndicates

The Canadian Press
CNW Group
Thomson Reuters

514121
Libraries

Brampton Public Library
Burlington Public Library
Markham Public Library Board
Mississauga Library System
Oakville Public Library
Oshawa Public Library/
  McLaughlin Branch
Richmond Hill Public Library
Thornhill Community Centre Library
Toronto Public Library
Vaughan Public Libraries

514191
On-Line Information Services

AOL Canada Inc.
Bell Sympatico
Canoe Inc.
Capital Safety - Canada
Cogeco Cable Canada Inc.
Q9 Networks Inc.
Verizon Business

514199
All Other Information Services

Recall

514210
Data Processing Services

ADP Canada Co.
AJD Data Services Inc.
Burman & Fellows Group Inc.
CDS Global Inc.
Critical Control Solutions
DST Output Inc.
Inquiry Management Systems Ltd.
Kubra
Recall
Reed Construction Data
Rogers Shared Operations
Smart DM

FINANCE & INSURANCE   52

521110
Monetary Authorities - Central Bank

Bank of Canada

522111
Personal and Commercial Banking Industry

Alterna Savings & Credit Union Ltd.
Bank of Nova Scotia
BMO Financial Group
Canadian Imperial Bank of Commerce
Credit Suisse Securities (Canada), Inc.
HSBC Bank Canada
ICICI Bank Canada
ING Bank of Canada
Korea Exchange Bank of Canada
Presidents Choice Financial
RBC Financial Group
TD Bank Financial Group

522112
Corporate and Institutional Banking Industry

B2B Trust
Bank of America National Association/
  Canada Branch
Bank of Nova Scotia
BMO Financial Group
Business Development Bank of Canada
Canadian Imperial Bank of Commerce
CIT Group Inc.
Citi Cards Canada
Credit Suisse Securities (Canada), Inc.
Deutsche Bank AG/ Canada Branch
ICICI Bank Canada
Laurentian Bank of Canada
RBC Financial Group
UBS Bank (Canada)

522130
Local Credit Unions

Alterna Savings & Credit Union Ltd.
Buduchnist Credit Union Ltd.
Central 1 Credit Union
DUCA Financial Services Credit
  Union Ltd.
Meridian Credit Union
St. Stanislaus - St. Casimir's Polish
  Parishes Credit Union Ltd.

522190
Other Depository Credit Intermediation

GE Commercial Distribution
  Finance Canada
Ontario Financing Authority

522210
Credit Card Issuing

Amex Canada Inc.
Capital One Services (Canada), Inc.
VISA Canada Corporation

522220
Sales Financing

Daimler Trucks Financial Ltd.
General Motors Acceptance
  Corporation of Canada Ltd.

522291
Consumer Lending

Honda Canada Finance Inc.
TD Financing Services

522299
All Other Non-Depository Credit Intermediation

GE Capital
Home Trust Co.
Innovation Institute of Ontario
John Deere Credit Inc.
JP Morgan Chase Bank, N.A.
Wells Fargo Financial
  Corporation Canada

522310
Mortgage and Non-mortgage Loan Brokers

Canada Mortgage and Housing Corp.
MCAP Commercial Limited
  Partnership
Northwood Mortgage Ltd.

522329
Other Financial Transactions Processing and Clearing House Activities

International Financial Data Services (Canada) Ltd.
Moneris Solutions Corp.
Symcor Inc.
Telus Health & Financial Solutions
Veri-Cheque Ltd.
Versent Corporation ULC

523110
Investment Banking and Securities Dealing

BMO Harris Private Banking
BMO Nesbitt Burns Inc.
Canaccord Capital Corp.
CIBC World Markets Inc.
Investors Group Inc.
JP Morgan Chase Bank, N.A.
Macquarie Capital Markets Canada Ltd.
Macquarie Private Wealth
Merrill Lynch Canada Inc.
Raymond James Ltd.
RBC Dominion Securities Inc.
Scotiabank - Wealth Management
Scotia Capital Inc.
TD Securities Inc.

523120
Securities Brokerage

BMO Guardian Group of Funds Ltd.
CI Fund Management Inc.
Cormark Securities Inc.
D.C. Security Inc.
Desjardins Securities
Dundee Corporation
Edward Jones
GMP Securities LP
HSBC Securities (Canada) Inc.
Investors Group Inc.
Jones, Gable & Company Limited
Mackie Research Capital Corporation
National Bank Financial Inc.
Raymond James Ltd.
RBC Dominion Securities Inc.
Sentry Select Capital Corp.

523130
Commodity Contracts Dealing

Infinium Capital Corp.
Travelex Canada Ltd.

523210
Securities and Commodity Exchanges

TMX Group Inc.

523910
Miscellaneous Intermediation

HomEquity Bank

523920
Portfolio Management

AGF Management Ltd.
CIBC Global Asset Management
Dundee Wealth
Franklin Templeton Investments Corp.
Guardian Capital Group Ltd.
Healthcare of Ontario Pension Plan
Invesco Trimark
Mackenzie Financial Corp.
McLean Budden Ltd.
Morguard Investments Ltd.
Multiple Retirement Services Inc.
Ontario Pension Board
Ontario Teachers' Pension Plan Board
RBC Global Asset Management
Roynat Inc.
TD Asset Management Inc.

523930
Investment Advice

Citco (Canada) Inc.
Investment Planning Counsel Inc.
Morningstar Research Inc.
Primerica Financial Services (Canada) Ltd.
Russell Investments Canada Limited
Sentry Select Capital Corp.

523990
All Other Financial Investment Activities

Canadian Depository for Securities Ltd.
CIBC Mellon
Computershare Canada
Heritage Education Funds Inc.
Integrated Asset Management Corp.
Ontario Securities Commission
Standard & Poor's Credit Market Services
State Street Trust Company Canada
USC Education Savings Plans Inc.

524111
Direct Individual Life- Health and Medical Insurance Carriers

Combined Insurance Company of America
Co-operators General Insurance Company
Desjardins Financial Security Life Assurance Company - Toronto
Foresters
Industrial Alliance Insurance & Financial Services Inc.
London Life Insurance Co.
Scotia Life Insurance Company
Transamerica Life Canada
Unity Life of Canada

524112
Direct Group Life- Health and Medical Insurance Carriers

The Canada Life Assurance Co.
Combined Insurance Company of America
Desjardins Financial Security Life Assurance Company
Desjardins Financial Security Life Assurance Company - Toronto
Industrial Alliance Insurance & Financial Services Inc.
London Life Insurance Co.
Manulife Financial
State Farm Mutual Automobile Insurance Co.
Sun Life Assurance Company of Canada
The Wawanesa Mutual Insurance Co.
Zurich North America Canada

524121
Direct General Property and Casualty Insurance Carriers

Allstate Insurance Company of Canada
Aviva Canada Inc.
AXA Insurance (Canada)
Chartis Insurance Company of Canada
Chubb Insurance Company of Canada
The Dominion of Canada General Insurance Co.
Economical Mutual Insurance Co.
Liberty International Underwriters Canada
Lombard Canada Ltd.
Royal & Sun Alliance Insurance Company of Canada
Travelers Guarantee Company of Canada

524123
Direct- Public- Automobile Insurance Carriers

Allstate Insurance Company of Canada
TD Insurance Meloche Monnex

524124
Direct Property Insurance Carriers

GCAN Insurance Co.
TD Insurance Meloche Monnex
Willis Canada Inc.

524129

**Other Direct Insurance
(except Life- Health and Medical) Carriers**

The Boiler Inspection & Insurance
  Company of Canada
Continental Casualty Company
Co-operators General Insurance
  Company
The CUMIS Group Ltd.
First Canadian Title
GCAN Insurance Co.
HB Group Insurance Management Ltd.
Pethealth Inc.
The Wawanesa Mutual Insurance Co.

524131

Life Reinsurance Carriers

Swiss Reinsurance Co. Canada

524132

Accident and Sickness Reinsurance Carriers

ACE INA Insurance

524133

Automobile Reinsurance Carriers

Swiss Reinsurance Co. Canada

524134

Property Reinsurance Carriers

Swiss Reinsurance Co. Canada

524139

General and Other Reinsurance Carriers

AON Benfield Canada ULC
Munich Reinsurance Company
  of Canada

524210

Insurance Agencies and Brokerages

Aon Reed Stenhouse Inc.
Baird MacGregor Insurance Brokers LP
Belair Insurance Company Inc.
CAA South Central Ontario
Canada Loyal Financial
Canadian Premier Life Insurance Co.
The CG&B Group Inc.
Continental Casualty Company
The Co-Operators Group Ltd.
Cornerstone Insurance Brokers Inc.
Desjardins General Insurance Group
Echelon General Insurance Co.
Great West Life Assurance Co.
Grey Power Insurance Brokers Inc.
HUB International Ontario Limited
Hunter Keilty Muntz & Beatty Ltd.

The Insurers Financial Group
Intact Financial Corporation
Jevco Insurance Company
Johnson Inc.
Lawyers Professional Indemnity Co.
Marsh Canada Limited
Munich Life Management Corp Ltd.
RBC Insurance Holdings Inc.
Rocca Dickson Andreis Inc.
Scotia Life Insurance Company
Sinclair-Cockburn Financial Group
The Standard Life Assurance Co.
  of Canada
TIC Travel Insurance Coordinators Ltd.
Travelers Insurance
Western Assurance Co.
Willis Canada Inc.
World Travel Protection Canada Inc.

524291

Claims Adjusters

CGI Adjusters Inc.
Crawford & Company (Canada) Inc.
Cunningham Lindsey Canada Ltd.
ESI Canada

524299

All Other Insurance Related Activities

Assurant Solutions
Hooper-Holmes Canada Limited
Insurance Bureau of Canada

526112

Non-Trusteed Pension Funds

Ontario Municipal Employees
  Retirement System

526910

Open-End Investment Funds

AGF Management Ltd.
Fidelity Investments Canada ULC
Guardian Capital Group Ltd.
Invesco Trimark
Just Energy Group Inc.

526920

Mortgage Investment Funds

Canadian Apartment Properties Real
  Estate Investment Trust
Canadian Real Estate Investment Trust
First National Financial Corp.

526989

**All Other Miscellaneous Funds and
Financial Vehicles**

Fidelity Investments Canada ULC
Fundserv Inc.

REAL ESTATE & RENTAL & LEASING 53

531111

**Lessors of Residential Buildings and
Dwellings (except Social Housing Projects)**

The Grenadier Retirement Residence
H & R Property Management Ltd.
Realstar Management
Young Rosedale Charitable Foundation

531112

Lessors of Social Housing Projects

Fred Victor Centre
Homes First Society

531120

**Lessors of Non-Residential Buildings
(except Mini-Warehouses)**

The Board of Governors
  of Exhibition Place
The Cadillac Fairview Corp. Limited
Centrecorp Management Services Ltd.
The Corporation of Massey Hall and
  Roy Thomson Hall
Dundee Realty Management Corp.
First Capital Realty Inc.
Kingbridge Centre
Lark Hospitality Inc.
Metro Toronto Convention Centre
  Corporation
Oakville Place
Paradise Banquet & Convention Centre
Premier Operating Corp. Ltd.
Riviera Parque
Scarborough Town Centre
  Holdings Inc.
Sherway Gardens
St. Lawrence Centre for the Arts
Woodbine Centre and Fantasy Fair
Yorkdale Shopping Centre
  Holdings Inc.

531210
Offices of Real Estate Agents and Brokers

Bosley Real Estate Ltd., Brokerage
Brookfield LePage Johnson Controls
CB Richard Ellis Limited
Century 21 Heritage Group Ltd.
Century 21 King's Quay Real Estate
    Inc., Brokerage
Century 21 Landstars Realty Inc.
Century 21 Leading Edge Realty Inc.
Century 21 Percy Fulton Ltd.
Chestnut Park Real Estate Ltd.
Coldwell Banker Terrequity Realty
Cushman & Wakefield Ltd.
Forest Hill Real Estate Inc. Brokerage
Harvey Kalles, Real Estate Ltd.
HomeLife Bayview Realty Inc.
HomeLife Cholkan Realty Corp.
HomeLife Cimerman Real Estate Ltd.
HomeLife Gold Pacific Realty Inc.
HomeLife Gold Trade Realty Ltd.
HomeLife Metro Realty Inc.
HomeLife Miracle Realty Ltd.
HomeLife New World Realty Inc.
HomeLife Response Realty Inc.
HomeLife United Realty Inc.
HomeLife Vision Realty Inc.
Intercity Realty Inc. Brokerage
iPro Realty Inc.
Living Realty Inc.
Medallion Properties Inc.
Norman Hill Realty Inc.
Prudential Sadie Moranis Realty
    Brokerage
Re/Max 2000 Realty Inc., Brokerage
Re/Max Aboutowne Realty Corp.
Re/Max Condos Plus Corp., Brokerage
Re/Max Crossroads Realty Inc.,
    Brokerage
Re/Max Excellence Realty Inc.
Re/Max Executive Realty Inc.
Re/Max First Realty Ltd.
Re/Max Garden City Realty Inc.
Re/Max Hallmark Realty Ltd.
Re/Max Performance Realty Inc.,
    Brokerage
Re/Max Professionals Inc.
Re/Max Realtron Realty Inc., Brokerage
Re/Max Realty Enterprises Inc.
Re/Max Realty One Inc., Brokerage
Re/Max Realty Services Inc.
Re/Max Realty Specialists Inc.
Re/Max Rouge River Realty Inc.
Re/Max Ultimate Realty Inc.
Re/Max West Realty Inc.
Royal LePage Burloak Real Estate
    Services - Mainway
Royal LePage Connect Realty
Royal LePage Kingsbury Realty
Royal LePage Realty Centre., Brokerage
Royal LePage Signature Realty

Spectrum Realty Services Inc.
Sutton Group - Admiral Realty Inc.
Sutton Group - Associates Realty Inc.
Sutton Group Heritage Realty Inc.
Sutton Group Quantum Realty Inc.
Sutton Group Realty Systems Inc.
Sutton Group - Summit Realty Inc.
Trade World Realty Inc. Brokerage
Tribute Communities
Trustwell Realty Inc.

531310
Real Estate Property Managers

Asbury Building Services Inc.
Bentall Kennedy LP
BPO Properties Ltd.
Del Property Management Inc.
DTZ Barnicke
FirstService Corp.
Greenwin Property Management Inc.
H & R Developments
H & R Property Management Ltd.
Ivanhoe Cambridge
Kaneff Group of Companies
MetCap Living Management Inc.
Minto Communities Toronto Inc.
Morguard Investments Ltd.
Ontario Realty Corporation
Oxford Properties Group Inc.
PMA Brethour Real Estate
    Corporation Inc.
Redcliff Realty Management Inc.
RioCan Real Estate Investment Trust
RioCan Yonge Eglinton Centre
Smart Centres
Spectrum Realty Services Inc.
Sutton Group Old Mill Realty
    Brokerage Inc.
TransGlobe Property Management
    Services

531390
Other Activities Related to Real Estate

Colliers Macaulay Nicolls Inc.
First Gulf Corp.
FirstService Corp.

532111
Passenger Car Rental

ARI Financial Services Inc.
Avis Budget Group Inc.
Dollar Thrifty Automotive Group
    Canada Inc.
GE Capital Fleet Services
Hertz Canada Ltd.
Scarborotown Chrysler Dodge
    Jeep Ltd.

532112
Passenger Car Leasing

ARI Financial Services Inc.
Chrysler Financial
Colombo Chrysler Dodge Ltd.
Dollar Thrifty Automotive Group
    Canada Inc.
Enterprise Holdings
General Motors Financial
    of Canada Ltd.
Scarborotown Chrysler Dodge
    Jeep Ltd.
Toyota Credit Canada Inc.
TransportAction Lease Systems Inc.

532120
Truck- Utility Trailer and RV (Recreational Vehicle) Rental and Leasing

Chrysler Financial
General Motors Financial
    of Canada Ltd.
Penske Truck Leasing
Sun Pac Foods
Thorncrest Sherway Inc.
TransportAction Lease Systems Inc.

532210
Consumer Electronics and Appliance Rental

Coinamatic Canada Inc.

532220
Formal Wear and Costume Rental

Freeman Formalwear Limited
Moores the Suit People, Inc.
Tuxedo Royale

532230
Video Tape and Disc Rental

Blockbuster Canada Co.

532290
Other Consumer Goods Rental

Chair-Man Mills Inc.

532310
General Rental Centres

Stephenson's Rental Services Inc.
United Rentals of Canada Inc.

532410
Construction- Transportation- Mining- and Forestry Machinery and Equipment Rental and Leasin

All Canada Crane Rental Corp.

532490

Other Commercial and Industrial Machinery and Equipment Rental and Leasing

Aluma Systems Canada Inc.
Frischkorn Associates Inc.
Hewitt Material Handling, Inc.
Imperial Coffee Services Inc.
On Premise Laundry Systems Inc.
Ontario Laser Rentals Ltd.
Westbury National Show Systems Ltd.
Western Toronto International
   Trucks Inc.

533110

Lessors of Non-Financial Intangible Assets (Except Copyrighted Works)

Coffee Time Donuts Inc.
Mandarin Restaurant Franchise Corp.
New York Fries/South St. Burger Co.
Timothy's Coffees of the World Inc.

PROFESSIONAL, SCIENTIFIC & TECHNICAL SERVICES 54

541110

Offices of Lawyers

Aird & Berlis LLP
Baker & McKenzie LLP
Beard Winter LLP
Bennett Jones LLP
Bereskin & Parr
Blake, Cassels & Graydon LLP
Blaney McMurtry LLP
Borden Ladner Gervais LLP
Bratty & Partners Barristers and
   Solicitors
Cassels Brock & Blackwell LLP
Cavalluzzo Hayes Shilton McIntyre &
   Cornish LLP
Davies Ward Phillips & Vineberg LLP
Devry Smith & Frank LLP
Dickinson Wright LLP
Dutton Brock LLP
Egan LLP
Fasken Martineau DuMoulin LLP
Fogler, Rubinoff LLP
Fraser Milner Casgrain LLP
Gardiner Roberts LLP
Goodlaw Services Limited Partnership
Gowling Lafleur Henderson LLP
Heenan Blaikie LLP
Hicks Morley Hamilton Stewart
   Storie LLP
Koskie Minsky
KRMC Barristers & Solicitors
Legal Aid Ontario
Lenczner Slaght Royce Smith
   Griffin LLP
Lerners LLP
McCague Borlack LLP
McCarthy Tetrault
McMillan

Miller Thomson LLP
Minden Gross LLP
Ogilvy Renault
Osler Hoskin & Harcourt, LLP
Pallett Valo LLP
Shibley Righton LLP
Sim, Lowman, Ashton & McKay LLP
Thomson Rogers
Torkin Manes LLP
Torys LLP
WeirFoulds LLP

541190

Other Legal Services

The Law Society of Upper Canada

541212

Offices of Accountants

BDO Canada LLP
Deloitte & Touche LLP
Ernst & Young LLP
Grant Thornton LLP
KPMG LLP
Meyers Norris Penny LLP
PricewaterhouseCoopers LLP
RSM Richter LLP
Schwartz Levitsky Feldman LLP
SF Partnership LLP
Soberman LLP

541213

Tax Preparation Services

H & R Block Canada Inc.

541215

Bookkeeping- Payroll and Related Services

KPMG LLP
NRT Technology Corp.
Soberman LLP

541310

Architectural Services

Adamson Associates Architects
AECOM Canada Ltd.
B + H Architects
Diamond and Schmitt Architects Inc.
Hok Canada, Inc.
Kuwabara Payne McKenna Blumberg
   Architects
Page + Steele Architects
Parkin Architects Ltd.
Petroff Partnership Architects
URS Canada Inc.
Young & Wright / IBI Architects

541320

Landscape Architectural Services

Aldershot Landscape Contractors Ltd.
MMM Group Limited
Weed Man Canada

541330

Engineering Services

Acuren Group Inc.
Aecom
AECOM Canada Ltd.
AMEC Americas Ltd.
AMEC Earth & Environmental Ltd.
ASECO Integrated Systems Ltd.
CH2M HILL Canada Limited
Cisco Systems Canada Co.
Coffey Geotechnics Inc.
Construction Control Inc.
Crossey Engineering Ltd.
Delcan Corp.
ECS Engineering & Construction Ltd.
EXP.
Golder Associates Ltd.
Halcrow Yolles
Halsall Associates Ltd.
Hatch Ltd.
H.H. Angus & Associates Ltd.
Hidi Rae Consulting Engineers Inc.
Hydro One Networks Inc.
IBI Group
J.D. Barnes Ltd.
LKM
McCormick Rankin Corp.
MCW Consultants Ltd.
The Mitchell Partnership Inc.
MMM Group Limited
Morrison Hershfield Ltd.
Mulvey & Banani International Inc.
NORR Ltd.
Page + Steele Architects
Peto MacCallum Ltd.
Pinchin Environmental Ltd.
Promation Engineering Ltd.
Roan International Inc.
R.V. Anderson Associates Ltd.
Schaeffer & Associates Ltd.
The Sernas Group Inc.
Shaw Canada LP
Smith & Andersen Consulting
   Engineering
SNC-Lavalin Inc.
Soil Engineers Ltd.
Stantec Consulting Ltd.
Thales Rail Signalling Solutions Inc.
URS Canada Inc.
Wardrop Engineering Inc.
WorleyParsons
WorleyParsons Canada
Zeidler Partnership Architects

541340

Drafting Services

Roan International Inc.

541360

Geophysical Surveying and Mapping Services

Fugro Airborne Surveys Corp.
Pacific Rubiales Energy Corp.

541370

Surveying and Mapping (except Geophysical) Services

J.D. Barnes Ltd.

541380

Testing Laboratories

AGAT Laboratories Ltd.
Exova
Kendle Early Stage
Maxxam Analytics
SGS Canada Inc.
Silliker Canada Co.
Team Industrial Services Inc.
Underwriters Laboratories of Canada

541410

Interior Design Services

B + H Architects
Diamond and Schmitt Architects Inc.
POI Business Interiors Inc.
Stantec Architecture Ltd.

541430

Graphic Design Services

Autodesk Canada
Entire Imaging Solutions Inc.
Glenn A. Davis & Associates Ltd.
Perennial Design Inc.
Southern Graphic Systems
St. Joseph Pi Media
Watt International Inc.

541490

Other Specialized Design Services

Autodesk Canada
Forrec Ltd.
Rubie's Costume Company (Canada)

541510

Computer Systems Design and Related Services

Accellos Canada Inc.
ACI Worldwide (Canada) Inc.
Adastra Corporation
ADP Dealer Services Ontario
Agfa Canada
AMD
Amdocs Canada
Angus Consulting Management Ltd.
Autodesk Canada
Avanade Canada Inc.
AXYZ Automation Inc.
Bevertec CST Inc.
Bigtech Inc.
CA Canada
Camilion Solutions Inc.
Cancable Inc.
Capgemini Canada Inc.
Catech Systems Ltd.
CCSI CompuCom
CGI Group Inc.

Compugen Inc.
Computer Methods International Corp.
Compuware Corp.
ConceptWave Software Inc.
Constellation Software Inc.
Cryptologic Inc.
Cyberplex Inc.
D-Link Canada Inc.
DMTI Spatial Inc.
Dundas Data Visualization
Dyadem International Ltd.
Dynamic Details Canada Inc.
EMC Corporation of Canada
ESRI Canada Limited
First Data
FlexITy Solutions Inc.
Fujitsu Consulting (Canada) Inc.
Genesis Worldwide Inc.
Gensys Telecommunications
    Laboratories Inc.
GenX Inc.
GeoSoft Inc.
Giesecke & Devrient Systems
    Canada, Inc.
Guardall
Hostopia.com Inc.
i365
IBM Canada Ltd.
Infor Global Solutions
Information Builders (Canada) Inc.
Infusion Development Corp.
Ingenico Canada Ltd.
Innovapost
Intec Billing Canada Ltd.
Intelliware Development Inc.
Invensys Systems Canada Inc.
Iron Mountain Canada Corp.
Management Systems Resources Inc.
Merge Healthcare
Metafore Limited Partnership
Microsoft Canada Co.
Modis
Momentum Advanced Solutions
Moneris Solutions Corp.
M.R.S. Company Ltd.
Navantis Inc.
NCR Canada Ltd.
Novator Systems Ltd.
Omron Canada Inc.
OnX Enterprise Solutions Inc.
Oracle Canada ULC
Oracle Corporation Canada Inc.
Perle Systems Ltd.
Platform Computing Corp.
PointClickCare
Pro Pharm Ltd.
Prophix Software Inc.
Psion Teklogix Inc.
Q & I Computer Systems Inc.
Qualicom Innovations Inc.
RCM Technologies Canada Corp.
Redline Communications
ReserveAmerica
Rockwell Automation Canada Ltd.
SAP Canada Inc.
SCI Marketview Ltd.

Siemens Enterprise
    Communications Inc.
Sigma Global Solutions
Sigma Systems
Softchoice Corp.
Solarsoft Business Systems
SS&C Technologies Canada Corp.
Sungard
SWI Systemware Inc.
Symantec Corp.
SYNNEX Canada Ltd.
Systematix Inc.
T4G Limited
Tab Products of Canada, Co.
Tata Consultancy Services Canada Inc.
Tecsys Inc.
TELUS Emergis Inc.
Teranet Inc.
ThoughtCorp Systems Inc.
triOS College Business
    Technology Healthcare
Unis Lumin Inc.
Unisys Canada Inc.
UTI Canada
WhiteHat Inc.
Wirecomm Systems Inc.
WSI Internet Consulting & Education
xwave, A Division of Bell Aliant
    Regional Communications LP
Yardi Systems Inc.
Zylog Systems (Canada) LOTD.

541611

Administrative Management and General Management Consulting Services

Accenture Inc.
Altus Group Ltd.
Assante Wealth Management
BDO Canada LLP
The Boston Consulting Group of
    Canada Ltd.
Buck Consultants Limited
Cash Money Financial Services Inc.
CFA Communications Ltd.
CGI Group Inc.
C.S.T. Consultants Inc.
DealerTrack Canada Inc.
Deloitte & Touche LLP
Ernst & Young LLP
FNF Canada
Gemma Communications LP
GenX Inc.
Grant Thornton LLP
Homestarts Inc.
Huron Services Group Ltd.
Ideaca Knowledge Services Inc.
Inforica Inc.
Kenna
The Logit Group Inc.
Loyalty One Inc.
Management Systems Resources Inc.
Manion Wilkins & Associates Ltd.
Marcus Evans
Maritz Canada Inc.
Maxium Financial Services Inc.

Mayhew & Associates
Munich Life Management Corp Ltd.
National Instore Services Corp.
Odyssey Financial Technologies
PHH Arval
Pitney Bowes Business Insights
PricewaterhouseCoopers LLP
RSM Richter LLP
Sierra Systems Group Inc.
The Strategic Coach Inc.
Tata Consultancy Services Canada Inc.
Towers Watson
Tricrest Professional Services
Westmont Hospitality Group
W.H. Stuart & Associates

541612
Human Resource and Executive Search Consulting Services

The Alliance Group Inc.
Aon Hewitt
Ceridian Canada Ltd.
Drakkar Human Resources Ontario Inc.
Eckler Ltd.
Hay Group Ltd.
Knightsbridge Human Capital
 Management Inc.
Mercer (Canada) Limited
Morneau Sobeco
Procom Consultants Group Ltd.
Volt Human Resources

541613
Marketing Consulting Services

Klick Communications Inc.

541619
Other Management Consulting Services

Acosta Canada
Acrobat Research Ltd.
Aditya Birla Minacs
Advantage Sales & Marketing
Carlson Marketing Group Canada Ltd.
Consumer Impact Marketing Ltd.
Core Logistics International Inc.
Delcan Corp.
Digital Cement Inc.
Environics Research Group Ltd.
Exchange Solutions Inc.
FireFox Marketing Services
Genivar Ontario Inc.
i3 Canada
Keane Canada Inc.
Kinectrics Inc.
Match Marketing Group
McKinsey & Company
Pareto Corporation
PRG Schultz Canada Corp.
Ryan ULC
Schenker of Canada Limited
SCI Group Inc.
SCI Logistics Inc.

Siemens PLM Software
Trapeze Software Group Inc.
UPS Supply Chain Solutions Canada
UTI Canada
Wesbell Group of Companies

541620
Environmental Consulting Services

AMEC Earth & Environmental Ltd.
Peto MacCallum Ltd.
Pinchin Environmental Ltd.
R.V. Anderson Associates Ltd.
SENES Consultants Limited

541690
Other Scientific and Technical Consulting Services

Aim Health Group
Ameresco Canada Inc.
Carecor Health Services Ltd.
Centre for Skills Development &
 Training
Golder Associates Ltd.
McKesson Specialty
The Medcan Clinic
Medisys Health Group Inc.
ThoughtCorp Systems Inc.
T.L.C. Health Services Ltd.
WorleyParsons

541710
Research and Development in the Physical- Engineering and Life Sciences

i3 Canada
Idexx Reference Laboratories Ltd.
Institute for Clinical Evaluative
 Sciences
Institute for Work & Health
Luminex Molecular Diagnostics Inc.
Medisys Health Group Inc.
Piramal Healthcare Torcan (Toronto)
 Canada Ltd.
Samuel Lunenfeld Research Institute of
 Mount Sinai Hospital
Xerox Research Centre of Canada

541720
Research and Development in the Social Sciences and Humanities

Multi-Health Systems Inc.

541810
Advertising Agencies

Arnold Worldwide
BBDO Canada Inc.
Bensimon Byrne
Cossette Communication Group
The Cundari Group
DDB Canada
Draft FCB Canada
Fuel Advertising Inc.

Grey Group Canada
J. Walter Thompson Company Ltd.
Leo Burnett Company Ltd.
MacLaren McCann
MediaCom Canada
mediaedge:cia
Mindshare Canada
Ogilvy & Mather (Canada) Ltd.
OMD Canada
Padulo Integrated Inc.
PHD Canada
Publicis Inc.
Sharpe Blackmore Inc.
Starcom Worldwide
Taxi Canada Inc.
TBWA Toronto
Young & Rubicam Ltd.
Zenith Optimedia Canada Inc.

541820
Public Relations Services

Hill & Knowlton Canada Inc.
NATIONAL Public Relations Inc.

541840
Media Representatives

Trader Corporation

541850
Display Advertising

AFL Display Group
Astral Media Outdoor
CBS Outdoor Canada
Pattison Outdoor Advertising

541860
Direct Mail Advertising

ActionPak
D & B Canada
Mailmarketing Corp.
Postlinx
Reliable Bookbinders Ltd.
Smart DM

541870
Advertising Material Distribution Services

ActionPak
Postlinx

541899
All Other Services Related to Advertising

Add Ink
News Marketing Canada

541910
Marketing Research and
Public Opinion Polling

BBM Canada
Cision Canada Inc.
Environics Research Group Ltd.
ICOM Information &
    Communications Inc.
Ipsos Reid Corp.
The Linkage Group Inc.
MDC Partners Inc.
News Marketing Canada
The Nielsen Company
Opinion Search Inc.
Pollara Inc.
Statistics Canada
Synovate Canada Ltd.
TNS Canadian Facts
Walker Information Canada

541920
Photographic Services

Pi Media / St Joseph's Content
Southern Graphic Systems
Transcontinental Digital
    Services GP Inc.

541940
Veterinary Services

Veterinary Emergency Clinic and
    Referral Centre

541990
All Other Professional, Scientific and
Technical Services

A. Farber & Partners Inc.
Municipal Property Assessment Corp.
Total Credit Recovery Ltd.

551113
Holding Companies

Onex Corp.

ADMINISTRATIVE & SUPPORT,
WASTE MANAGEMENT &
REMEDIATION SERVICES   56

561110
Office Administrative Services

Citigroup Fund Services Inc.
G4S Cash Solutions (Canada) Ltd.

561310
Employment Placement Agencies

1st Choice Staffing Ltd.
Adecco Employment Services Limited
Advantage Personnel Ltd.
Affordable Personnel Services Inc.
The Alliance Group Inc.
Comcare Health Services
Commissionaires Great Lakes

DBPC Group of Companies
Drakkar Human Resources Ontario Inc.
The Employment Solution
Excel Employment Tempro Inc.
Global Driver Services Inc.
Ian Martin Group
J & L Personnel Inc.
Kee Management Solutions Inc.
Keith Bagg Staffing Resources Inc.
Kelly Services (Canada) Ltd.
Labour Ready, Inc.
Manpower Services Canada Limited
Mosaic Sales Solutions Canada
    Operating Co.
M S Employment Consultants Ltd.
OfficeTeam
The People Bank
Quantum Management Services Ltd.
Randstad Technologies
Ready Staffing Solutions Inc.
Robert Half Canada Inc.
Spherion
TDM Technical Services
T.E.S. Contract Services Inc.
TMZ Employment Agency
Trebor Personnel Inc.
United Driver Services Inc.
West-ADS Employment Services Inc.

561320
Temporary Help Services

Aerotek Canada
AppleOne Employment Services Ltd.
Global Human Resource Centre
In Transit Personnel Inc.
Kelly Services (Canada) Ltd.
Manpower Services Canada Limited
Pivotal HR Solutions
T.E.S. Contract Services Inc.

561410
Document Preparation Services

Ricoh Canada Inc.

561420
Telephone Call Centres

Answer Plus Inc.
Genworth Financial Mortgage
    Insurance Company Canada
Innovative Vision Marketing Inc.
Miratel Solutions Inc.
Optima Communications
    International Inc.
Teleperformance Canada
Tigertel Communications
Voxdata Call Centre Inc.

561430
Business Service Centres

The FSA Group
Miratel Solutions Inc.
Teleperformance Canada

561440
Collection Agencies

Alliance One Ltd.
Allied International Credit Corp.
Canada Bonded Attorney & Legal
    Directory Ltd.
CBV Collection Services Ltd.
Collectcents Inc.
Collectcorp Inc.
D & A Collection Corp.
iQor Canada Inc.
Nor-Don Collection Network Inc.

561450
Credit Bureaus

Equifax Canada Inc.
Standard & Poor's Credit Market
    Services

561490
Other Business Support Services

Electronic Imaging Systems Corp.
Masterfile Corp.
Merchandising Consultants Associates
O.C. Tanner Recognition Company Ltd.
Sunsweet Fundraising Inc.
TheMIGroup
Total Credit Recovery Ltd.

561510
Travel Agencies

Air Canada Vacations Inc.
Carlson Wagonlit Travel
CWT Concierge
G.A.P Adventures Inc.
Goway Travel Ltd.
HRG North America
itravel 2000
The Last Minute Experts Inc.
Merit Travel Group Inc.
Swiftrans Services Ltd.
Thomas Cook North America
Transat A.T.
Travel Cuts
Vision 2000 Travel Group Inc.
Wholesale Travel Group
Wynford

561520
Tour Operators

Jonview Canada Inc.
Sunwing Travel Group
Tour East Holidays (Canada) Inc.
Transat A.T.

561590
Other Travel Arrangement
and Reservation Services

CAA South Central Ontario
TicketMaster Canada LP

561611
Investigation Services

Intelligarde International Inc.
Investigation Services Ltd.
The Investigators Group Inc.
Northwest Protection Services Ltd.
Reilly's Security Services
Security Management Services
Target Investigation & Security Ltd.
VSI Inc.

561612
Security Guard and Patrol Services

Blue Star Investigations & Security Inc.
Citiguard Security Services Inc.
G4S Security Services (Canada) Ltd.
Knights On Guard Protective Services
Magnum Protective Services Ltd.
Nexus Protective Services Ltd.
Northwest Protection Services Ltd.
Paragon Protection Ltd.
Patrolman Security Services Inc.
Philips Lifeline
Primary Response Inc.
Reilly's Security Services
Securitas Canada Ltd.
Skanna Systems Investigations
Target Investigation & Security Ltd.
Trillium Security Services Inc.
TSM Ltd.
Warren Protective Services Ltd.

561613
Armoured Car Services

Brink's Canada Ltd.

561621
Security Systems Services
(except Locksmiths)

ADT Security Services Canada Inc.
AlarmForce Industries Inc.
Counterforce Inc.
CSG Security Inc.
Diebold Company of Canada Ltd.
Digital Security Controls Ltd.
Garda World Security
Intercon Security Ltd.
LaBrash Security Services Ltd.
Metro Protective Services
Paragon Protection Ltd.
Security Management Services

561710
Exterminating and Pest Control Services

Abell Pest Control Inc.
PCO Services Corp.

561721
Window Cleaning Services

Omni Facility Services Canada Limited

561722
Janitorial Services
(except Window Cleaning)

Amphora Maintenance Systems
Andorra Building Maintenance Ltd.
Apollo 8 Maintenance Services Inc.
ARAMARK Canada Ltd.
Bass Building Maintenance Ltd.
Bee-Clean
Columbia Building Maintenance
    Co. Ltd.
Corvin Building Maintenance Ltd.
Cross Toronto Community
    Development Corp.
Hallmark Housekeeping Services Inc.
Hoodex Industries Ltd.
Hurley Group.
Impact Cleaning Services Ltd.
J&A Cleaning Solutions Ltd.
Magic Maintenance Inc.
Nova Services Group Inc.
Omni Facility Services Canada Limited
Quinterra Property Maintenance Inc.
Robson Enterprises Inc.
Servicemaster Contract Services
Serv-U-Clean Ltd.
Sunshine Building Maintenance Inc.
Super Shine Oakdale Janitorial
    Services Ltd.
Team Industrial Services
Unicco Facility Services Canada Co.
Waterford Building Maintenance Inc.
Werek Enterprises Inc.

561730
Landscaping Services

Clintar - Franchise Support Office
Cornerstone Landscaping Ltd.
Greenlawn Ltd.
International Landscaping Inc.

561740
Carpet and Upholstery Cleaning Services

Nova Services Group Inc.

561791
Duct and Chimney Cleaning Services

Burke's Restoration Inc.

561799
All Other Services to Buildings and
Dwellings

PGC
Superior Pool Spa & Leisure Ltd.

561910
Packaging and Labelling Services

A1 Label
Bemis Flexible Packaging
CCL Label
Conros Corporation
Contract Pharmaceuticals Limited
    Canada
The Dominion Group Inc.
Econ-O-Pac Ltd.
Ellis Packaging Ltd.
Green Grove Foods Corp.
Ivers-Lee Inc.
Multipak Ltd.
Norpak Custom Packaging
Packaging Technologies Inc.
Peel Plastic Products Ltd.
Rex Pak Ltd.
Sonoco Canada Corp.
Tetra Pak Canada Inc.

561920
Convention and Trade Show Organizers

GES Canada Exposition Services Ltd.
International Centre
Metro Toronto Convention Centre
    Corporation

561990
All Other Support Services

Canadian Food Inspection Agency
SGS Canada Inc.
Shred-It
Sodexo Canada Ltd.
WIIB Identification Solutions Inc.

562110
Waste Collection

WASTECO

562210
Waste Treatment and Disposal

BFI Canada Inc.
Miller Waste Systems
Organic Resource Management Inc.
U-Pak Disposals Ltd.
WASTECO
Waste Management of Canada

562920
Material Recovery Facilities

Metro Waste Paper Recovery Inc.
Turtle Island Recycling Company Inc.

EDUCATIONAL SERVICES 61

611110
Elementary and Secondary Schools

Appleby College
Bayview Glen
The Bishop Strachan School
Branksome Hall
Conseil Scolaire de District du Centre-
Sud-Ouest
The Country Day School
Crescent School
The Dufferin-Peel Catholic District
School Board
Durham Catholic District School Board
Durham District School Board
Halton Catholic District School Board
Halton District School Board
Havergal College
Holy Trinity School
Peel District School Board
Pickering College
St. Andrew's College
St. Mildred's-Lightbourn School
Toronto Catholic District School Board
Toronto District School Board
The Toronto French School
Toronto Montessori Schools
Upper Canada College
York Catholic District School Board
York Region District School Board

611210
Community Colleges and C.E.G.E.P.s

Academy of Design
Centennial College
Durham College
George Brown College of Applied Arts
and Technology
Humber Institute of Technology &
Advanced Learning
Ontario College of Art & Design
Seneca College of Applied Arts &
Technology
The Sheridan College Institute of
Technology and Advanced Learning

611310
Universities

Ontario College of Art & Design
Osgoode Hall Law School
Royal St. George's College
Ryerson University
Tyndale University College & Seminary
University of Ontario Institute of
Technology
University of Toronto
University of Toronto at Scarborough
University of Toronto Mississauga
Victoria University
York University

611410
Business and Secretarial Schools

CSI Global Education Inc.
Everest College
Sir Robert L. Borden Business &
Technical Institute

611420
Computer Training

Global Knowledge
triOS College Business Technology
Healthcare

611430
Professional and Management
Development Training

Global Knowledge

611510
Technical and Trade Schools

FlightSafety Canada Ltd.

611519
Other Technical and Trade Schools

The Michener Institute for Applied
Health Sciences

611610
Fine Arts Schools

Merriam School of Music
The National Ballet School
Randolph Academy
for the Performing Arts
The Royal Conservatory of Music

611690
All Other Schools and Instruction

The Canadian College of Naturopathic
Medicine
Canadian Memorial Chiropractic
College
Centre for Education & Training
Forest Hill Tutoring
The Princeton Review Canada

611710
Educational Support Services

The Learning Enrichment Foundation

HEALTH CARE &
SOCIAL ASSISTANCE 62

621110
Offices of Physicians

The Drs. Paul & John Rekai Centre
The Etobicoke Medical Centre
Oshawa Clinic

621340
Offices of Physical, Occupational, and
Speech Therapists and Audiologists

Rehab Express Inc.

621390
Offices of All Other Health Practitioners

Access Care Inc.
Bayshore Home Health
Carecor Health Services Ltd.
College of Nurses of Ontario
College of Physicians and
Surgeons of Ontario
First Health Care Services Inc.
Integracare Inc.
Ontario Medical Association
Ontario Nurses' Association
Regional Nursing Services
Saint Elizabeth Health Care
VON Toronto York Branch

621420
Out-Patient Mental Health
and Substance Abuse Centres

Centre for Addiction
and Mental Health
The Hincks-Dellcrest Centre

621494
Community Health Centres

Albany Medical Clinic
Elliott Family Care Limited
Kensington Health Centre
Ontario Shores Centre for Mental
Health Sciences
Thistletown Regional Centre
Toronto Central Community Care
Access Centre

621499
All Other Out-Patient Care Centres

Bob Rumball Centre for the Deaf

621510
Medical and Diagnostic Laboratories

Alpha Laboratories Inc.
Bramalea Medical Centre X-Ray &
Ultrasound
Cetero Research
CML Healthcare Inc.
Gamma-Dynacare Medical
Laboratories
Kendle Early Stage
KMH Cardiology & Diagnostic Centres
Nordion Inc.
Sanofi Pasteur Ltd.

621610
Home Health Care Services

Can-Care Health Services Inc.
CBI Home Health
Central - Community Care Access
    Centre
Circle of Home Care Services (Toronto)
Dorvict Resource
    & Consulting Centre Inc.
Ontario Nursing Services
Personal Attendant Care Inc.
Preferred Health Care Services
ProHome Health Services
Respiron Care-Plus Inc.
Spectrum Health Care
VitalAire Canada Inc.
VON Toronto York Branch
We Care Home Health Services -
    Toronto

621911
Ambulance
(except Air Ambulance) Services

Toronto Emergency Medical Services

621990
All Other Ambulatory Health Care Services

Canadian Blood Services

622111
General (except Paediatric) Hospitals

The Credit Valley Hospital
Halton Healthcare Services
    - Oakville Site
Humber River Regional Hospital
Joseph Brant Memorial Hospital
Markham Stouffville Hospital
    Corporation
Mount Sinai Hospital
North York General Hospital
Rouge Valley Health System
The Scarborough Hospital
Southlake Regional Health Centre
Stevenson Memorial Hospital
St. John's Rehabilitation Hospital
St. Joseph's Health Centre
St. Michael's Hospital
Sunnybrook Health Sciences Centre
Toronto East General
Trillium Health Centre
University Health Network
William Osler Health System
York Central Hospital

622112
Paediatric Hospitals

Holland Bloorview Kids Rehab
The Hospital for Sick Children

622210
Psychiatric and Substance Abuse Hospitals

Bellwood Health Services Inc.
Centre for Addiction
    and Mental Health
Ontario Shores Centre for Mental
    Health Sciences
Peel Children's Centre
St. John's Rehabilitation Hospital

622310
Specialty (except Psychiatric and
Substance Abuse) Hospitals

Bridgepoint Health
Holland Bloorview Kids Rehab
Lakeridge Health Corp.
Runnymede Healthcare Centre
Shouldice Hospital
Toronto Rehabilitation Institute
West Park Healthcare Centre

623110
Nursing Care Facilities

Aurora Resthaven
Avalon Retirement Centre
Ballycliffe Lodge
Bloomington Cove
Cedarvale Terrace Nursing Home
Chartwell Seniors Housing REIT
Cooksville Care Centre
Craiglee Nursing Home Ltd.
The Drs. Paul & John Rekai Centre
Elm Grove Living Centre Inc.
Erin Mills Retirement Nursing Home
Extendicare (Canada) Inc.
Fairview Nursing Home Ltd.
Forest Hill Place
Harold & Grace Baker Centre
Hellenic Care for Seniors (Toronto) Inc.
Humber Valley Terrace
King Nursing Home Ltd.
Kristus Darzs Latvian Home
Leisureworld Caregiving Centre,
    Cheltenham
Leisureworld Caregiving Centre,
    Rockcliffe
Leisureworld Caregiving Centre,
    Streetsville
Leisureworld Senior Care LP
Lifecare Operations
Main Street Terrace
Malton Village Long Term Care Centre
Maple Health Centre
Mariann Home
Markhaven Inc.
The McCall Centre
    for Continuing Care
Mon Sheong Home for the Aged
Newmarket Health Centre
The O'Neill Centre
Paragon Health Care (Ontario) Inc.
Peel Manor Long Term Care Facility

Revera Inc.
Saint Elizabeth Health Care
The Salvation Army Toronto Grace
    Health Centre
Slovenian Linden Foundation
Southlake Residential Care Village
St. Clair O'Connor Community Inc.
Thornton View
Trilogy Long Term Care
True Davidson Acres Home
    for the Aged
Tyndall Nursing Home Ltd.
Vermont Square Nursing Home
Villa Forum
Wesburn Manor
Willows Estate Nursing Home
The Woodhaven

623210
Residential Developmental Handicap
Facilities

Community Living Oakville
Erinoak Kids

623310
Community Care Facilities for the Elderly

Allendale
Avalon Retirement Centre
Baycrest Geriatric Health System
Bendale Acres
Bethany Lodge
Broadview Foundation
Castleview-Wychwood Towers
Cawthra Gardens Long Term Care
    Community
Cedarbrook Lodge Ltd.
Cedarvale Terrace Nursing Home
Central East - Community Care
    Access Centre
Christie Gardens Apartments
    and Care Inc.
Community Care Access Centre -
    Central West
Community Care - East York
Copernicus Lodge
Cummer Lodge
Fudger House
Heritage Nursing Homes Inc.
Hillsdale Estates
Holland Christian Homes Inc.
Ina Grafton Gage Home
Kennedy Lodge Nursing Home Inc.
Lakeshore Lodge
Leisureworld Caregiving Centre -
    Tullamore
Leisureworld Chelsey Park
    Mississauga
Leisureworld Senior Care LP
Malton Village Long Term Care Centre
North Park Nursing Home Ltd.
Parkview Home Long Term Care
Providence Healthcare

Revera Inc.
Riverglen Haven Nursing Home-
  Sutton
Seven Oaks
Shepherd Village Inc.
Sheridan Villa
Simcoe Manor Home for the Aged
Specialty Care Inc.
Storefront Humber Inc.
St. Paul's L'Amoreaux Centre
Sunrise Senior Living
Sunrise Senior Living, Inc.
Tendercare Nursing Homes Ltd.
Tony Stacey Centre
The Toronto Aged Men's and Women's
  Homes
True Davidson Acres Home for the Aged
Ukrainian Canadian Care Centre
Unionville Home Society
Villa Colombo Homes for the Aged Inc.
The Village of Erin Meadows
Wells Gordon Limited
The WenLeigh Long-Term Care
  Residence
The Wexford Residence Inc.
The Wynfield

623992
Homes for Emotionally Disturbed Children

Fernie House

623999
All Other Residential Care Facilities

Lifemark Health
Montage Support Services
Nisbet Lodge

624110
Child and Youth Services

Canadian Mothercraft Society
The Catholic Children's Aid Society
  of Toronto
Children's Aid Society of Toronto
Covenant House Toronto
Eva's Initiatives
Thistletown Regional Centre
West Scarborough Neighbourhood
  Community Centre
Woodgreen Community Services
York Support Services Network
Youthdale Treatment Centres Ltd.
YWCA of Toronto

624120
Services for the Elderly and Persons with Disabilities

Bayshore Home Health
Brampton Caledon Community Living
Central - Community Care Access
  Centre
Central East - Community Care
  Access Centre
Central West Specialized Development
  Service
CHATS - Community Home Assistance
  To Seniors
Community Care Access Centre -
  Central West
Community Care - East York
Community Living Ajax, Pickering &
  Whitby
Community Living Association for
  South Simcoe
Community Living Burlington
Community Living Mississauga
Community Living - Newmarket/
  Aurora District
Community Living Oshawa/Clarington
Community Living Toronto
Neighbourhood Link Support Services
Reena
Scarborough Support Services
Senior Peoples Resources In North
  Toronto Inc.
Shadow Lake Outdoor Recreation
  Centre
Surex Community Services
Tobias House Attendant Care Inc.
The Village of Taunton Mills
Vita Community Living Services of
  Toronto Inc.
Woodgreen Community Services
Yee Hong Centre for Geriatric Care
York Support Services Network

624190
Other Individual and Family Services

Associated Youth Services of Peel
Brown Community Centre
Canadian Hearing Society
The Catholic Children's Aid Society of
  Toronto
Catholic Cross-Cultural Services
Community Living Georgina
COSTI
Garnet A. Williams Community Centre
Goodwill Toronto
Kids Help Phone
PACE Independent Living
Polycultural Immigrant Community
  Services
The Scott Mission
Shepell·fgi
Sykes Assistance Services Corporation
Syl Apps Youth Centre
Turning Point Youth Services
UJA Federation of Greater Toronto

University Settlement
West Scarborough Neighbourhood
  Community Centre
Woodgreen Community Services
WoodGreen Red Door Family Shelter

624230
Emergency and Other Relief Services

The Canadian Red Cross/Ontario Zone

624310
Vocational Rehabilitation Services

Brampton Caledon Community Living
The Canadian National Institute for the
  Blind/Ontario Div.
Community Living Ajax, Pickering &
  Whitby
Community Living Association for
  South Simcoe
Community Living Burlington
Community Living Mississauga
Community Living - Newmarket/
  Aurora District
Community Living Oshawa/Clarington
Community Living Toronto
COSTI
COTA Health
Jewish Vocational Service of Greater
  Toronto
Lifemark Health
Sibley & Associates Inc.
Simplicious
Vita Community Living Services of
  Toronto Inc.
YWCA of Toronto

624410
Child Day-Care Services

Aisling Discoveries Child and
  Family Centre
Centre for Early Learning-West Hill
Family Day Care Services
Kids and Company Ltd.
Nyad Community Inc.
Upper Canada Child Care Centres
  of Ontario
YMCA of Greater Toronto

ARTS, ENTERTAINMENT & RECREATION   71

711111
Theatre (except Musical) Companies

Medieval Times Dinner & Tournament
  Toronto Inc.
The Second City

711112
Musical Theatre and Opera Companies

Canadian Opera Company

711120
Dance Companies

The National Ballet of Canada

711130
Musical Groups and Artists

Canadian Opera Company
Toronto Symphony Orchestra

711190
Other Performing Arts Companies

Farco Enterprises Ltd.

711211
Sports Teams and Clubs

Toronto Blue Jays Baseball Club

711213
Horse Race Tracks

Woodbine Entertainment Group

711311
**Live Theatres and Other Performing Arts
Presenters with Facilities**

Atlantis Pavilions
The Corporation of Massey Hall and
    Roy Thomson Hall
The Elgin & Winter Garden
    Theatre Centre
Harbourfront Centre
St. Lawrence Centre for the Arts
Toronto Centre for the Arts

711319
**Sports Stadiums and Other Presenters
with Facilities**

Hershey Centre
Maple Leaf Sports
    & Entertainment Ltd.
Powerade Centre
The Rogers Centre

711321
**Performing Arts Promoters (Presenters)
without Facilities**

The National Ballet of Canada
Stagevision Inc.

711322
Festivals without Facilities

TIFF

711410
**Agents and Managers for Artists- Athletes-
Entertainers and Other Public Figures**

The Second City

712111
**Non-Commercial Art Museums and
Galleries**

Art Gallery of Ontario
Hockey Hall of Fame
McMichael Canadian Art Collection
Royal Ontario Museum

712119
**Museums
(except Art Museums and Galleries)**

Black Creek Pioneer Village
Ontario Science Centre

712130
Zoos and Botanical Gardens

Board of Management
    of the Toronto Zoo
Royal Botanical Gardens

712190
Other Heritage Institutions

Credit Valley Conservation

713110
Amusement and Theme Parks

Beasley Amusements
The Board of Governors
    of Exhibition Place
Canada's Wonderland Company
Ontario Place Corp.
Wild Water Kingdom Ltd.

713120
Amusement Arcades

Escar Entertainment Ltd.
Playdium Corp.

713210
Casinos (except Casino Hotels)

Ontario Lottery and Gaming Corp.

713291
Lotteries

Ontario Lottery and Gaming Corp.

713910
Golf Courses and Country Clubs

Angus Glen Golf Club
Bayview Golf & Country Club
Blue Springs Golf Club
The Boulevard Club
Burlington Golf & Country Club
Caledon Woods Golf Club
Cardinal Golf Club
ClubLink Corp.
Copper Creek Golf Club

The Country Club
Credit Valley Golf and Country Club
Deer Creek Golf & Banquet Facility
Devil's Pulpit Golf Association
DiamondBack Golf Club
Donalda Club
Eagle Ridge Golf Club
Emerald Hills Golf Club
Glen Abbey Golf Club
Glencairn Golf Club
Glenway Country Club (1994) Ltd.
Granite Club
Greystone Golf Club
Islington Golf Club Ltd.
King Valley Golf Club
Maple Downs Golf & Country Club Ltd.
Markland Wood Golf Club
Mississauga Golf & Country Club
    Limited
The National Golf Club of Canada
Nobleton Lakes Golf Course Ltd.
The Oakdale Golf & Country Club Ltd.
Richmond Hill Country Club
Rolling Hills Golf Club
Rosedale Golf Club
Scarboro Golf & Country Club
Station Creek Golf Club
St. George's Golf and Country Club
The Summit Golf & Country Club
Thornhill Golf & Country Club
Uplands Golf & Ski Club
The Weston Golf and Country Club Ltd.
Wyndance Golf Club
York Downs Golf & Country Club

713920
Skiing Facilities

Caledon Ski Club Limited
Uplands Golf & Ski Club

713940
Fitness and Recreational Sports Centres

The Badminton & Racquet Club of
    Toronto
Cambridge Group of Clubs
Canlan Ice Sports Corp.
Cedar Springs Health,
    Racquet & Sports Club
Club Markham
Columbus Centre of Toronto
Etobicoke Olympium
Extreme Fitness, Inc.
Fitness Institute
Glenway Country Club (1994) Ltd.
Goodlife Fitness
Granite Club
Mayfair Racquet & Fitness Clubs
Royal Canadian Yacht Club
Toronto Cricket Skating
    and Curling Club
YMCA of Greater Toronto

713990
All Other Amusement and Recreation Industries

Canada Lands Company Ltd.
True North Hockey Canada Inc.
Variety Children's Charity
Versent Corporation ULC
Woodbine Entertainment Group

ACCOMMODATION & FOOD SERVICES   72

721111
Hotels

Best Western Primrose Hotel
Bradgate Arms Retirement Residence
Cambridge Suites Hotel Toronto
Courtyard By Marriott Downtown Toronto
Crowne Plaza - Toronto Airport
Delta Hotels Limited
Delta Markham
Delta Meadowvale Hotel and Conference Centre
Delta Toronto Airport West
Delta Toronto East
Doubletree by Hilton - Toronto Airport
Fairmont Hotels & Resorts Inc.
The Fairmont Royal York
Four Points By Sheraton Mississauga - Meadowvale
Four Points by Sheraton Toronto Airport
Four Seasons Hotels Limited
Hilton Garden Inn Toronto City Centre
The Hilton Suites Toronto/ Markham Conference Centre & Spa
Hilton Toronto
Hilton Toronto Airport Hotel & Suites
Holiday Inn Burlington
Holiday Inn Hotel & Suites Toronto - Markham
Holiday Inn Oakville @ Bronte
Holiday Inn Oshawa
Holiday Inn Toronto Airport East
Holiday Inn Toronto Airport West
Holiday Inn Toronto Downtown Centre
Holiday Inn Toronto International Airport
Holiday Inn - Toronto Yorkdale
Hyatt Regency Toronto
InterContinental Toronto Centre
InterContinental Toronto-Yorkville
Le Méridien King Edward
Metropolitan Hotel Toronto
Montecassino Hospitality Group Inc.
Nottawasaga Inn
Novotel Hotel North York
Novotel Mississauga
Novotel Toronto Centre
Park Hyatt Toronto
Prince Spa & Resort Operations Toronto Ltd.

Quality Suites Toronto Airport
Radisson Admiral Hotel
Renaissance Toronto Hotel Downtown
The Sheraton Gateway Hotel
Sheraton Parkway Toronto North Hotel & Suites
Sheraton Toronto Airport Hotel & Conference Centre
Stage West All-Suite Hotel & Theatre Restaurant
Starwood Canada Corp.
The Sutton Place Hotel Toronto
Toronto Airport Marriott
Toronto Don Valley Hotel & Suites
Toronto Marriott Bloor Yorkville
Toronto Marriott Downtown Eaton Centre
Travelodge Hotel Toronto Airport
The Waterside Inn
Westin Bristol Place Toronto Airport
The Westin Harbour Castle
The Windsor Arms Hotel
WW Hotels Ltd.

721113
Resorts

Briars Estates Ltd.
Caledon Ski Club Limited
Fairmont Hotels & Resorts Inc.
Hockley Valley Resort Ltd.

721213
Recreational (except Hunting and Fishing) and Vacation Camps

Zodiac Swim School Limited

722110
Full-Service Restaurants

1561716 Ontario Ltd.
Boston Pizza International Inc.
Canada Lands Company Ltd.
Dave and Busters
Delta Markham
Druxy's Inc.
East Side Mario's
Ellas Restaurant (Scarborough) Ltd.
Esplanade Restaurants Ltd.
The Fish House
Frankie Tomatto's Ltd.
The Guvernment
Hot House Cafe
HRC Canada Inc.
Husky Truck Stop
Il Fornello Restaurants Ltd.
J.F. & L. Restaurants Ltd.
Joe Badali's Piazza On Front Inc.
The Kalen Group
Keg Restaurants Ltd.
Le Méridien King Edward
Mandarin Restaurant Franchise Corp.
Medieval Times Dinner & Tournament Toronto Inc.
Mirvish Productions
Nottawasaga Inn

Oliver & Bonacini Restaurants
Pinnacle Caterers
Pizza Pizza Ltd.
Prime Restaurants of Canada Inc.
Tucker's Marketplace
Tucker's Marketplace Restaurant
Village Manor (TO) Ltd.
Vinnie Zucchini's Corp.
Wayne Gretzky's
The Yorkdale Rainforest Restaurant Inc.

722210
Limited-Service Eating Places

ARAMARK Canada Ltd.
Beatty Foods Ltd.
Bento Nouveau Ltd.
Burger King Restaurants of Canada Inc.
Canada Catering Company Ltd.
Cara Operations Limited
Coffee Time Donuts Inc.
Compass Group Canada Ltd.
Dana Hospitality Inc.
Dove Foods Limited
Druxy's Inc.
Esplanade Restaurants Ltd.
Future Bakery Ltd.
HMSHost
Lick's Concepts Inc.
McDonald's Restaurants of Canada Limited
New York Fries/South St. Burger Co.
Ontario Place Corp.
Pizza Nova Restaurants Ltd.
Pizza Pizza Ltd.
Priszm Income Fund
Richtree Market Restaurants Inc.
Sarku Japan Restaurants Income Fund
Shopsy's Downtown
SIR Corp.
Tim Hortons Inc.
Wendy's Restaurants of Canada Inc.

722310
Food Service Contractors

ARAMARK Canada Ltd.
HMSHost
Sysco Milton, Inc.

722320
Caterers

byPeterandPauls.com
Canada Catering Company Ltd.
Cara Operations Limited
Centerplate
CLS Catering Services Ltd.
Da Vinci Banquet Hall & Restaurant
The Estates of Sunnybrook
Le Parc Dining & Banquet Ltd.
Montecassino Hospitality Group Inc.
Paradise Banquet & Convention Centre
Premiere Ballroom & Convention Centre
The Royalton Hospitality Inc.

OTHER SERVICES (EXCEPT PUBLIC ADMINISTRATION) 81

811111
General Automotive Repair

Kenworth Toronto Ltd.
Western Toronto International
Trucks Inc.

811121
Automotive Body, Paint and Interior Repair and Maintenance

Atlantic Collision Group
Butcher Engineering Enterprises Ltd.
MTB Truck & Bus Collision
The Newroads Automotive Group

811210
Electronic and Precision Equipment Repair and Maintenance

Agilent Technologies Canada Inc.
DecisionOne Corp.
Digi Canada Inc.
LaserNetworks
Manufacturing and Technology Centre
Whirlpool Canada LP

811310
Commercial and Industrial Machinery and Equipment (except Automotive and Electronic) Repair

Nortrax
Universal Drum Reconditioning Co.

811420
Reupholstery and Furniture Repair

Lyreco (Canada) Inc.

812116
Unisex Hair Salons

Donato Salon & Spa
Premier Salon Canada Inc.

812190
Other Personal Care Services

Bernstein Health & Diet Clinics
Brydson Group Ltd.
Donato Salon & Spa
Weight Watchers Canada Ltd.

812210
Funeral Homes

Arbor Memorial Services Inc.

812220
Cemeteries and Crematoria

Arbor Memorial Services Inc.
Mount Pleasant Group of Cemeteries

812320
Dry Cleaning and Laundry Services (except Coin-Operated)

Booth Centennial Healthcare
Linen Services Inc.
K-Bro Linen Systems (Ontario) Ltd.

812330
Linen and Uniform Supply

Canadian Linen and Uniform
Service Inc.
Cintas Canada Ltd.
Faster Linen Service Ltd.
G & K Services Canada Inc.
K-Bro Linen Systems (Ontario) Ltd.
Topper Linen Supply Ltd.
Unifirst Canada Ltd.

812921
Photo Finishing Laboratories (except One-Hour)

Black Photo Corporation

812930
Parking Lots and Garages

Canpark Services Ltd.
Car Park Management Services Ltd.
Imperial Parking Canada Corp.
Park 'N Fly
Standard Parking of Canada Ltd.
Toronto Parking Authority
Vinci Parking Services

813110
Religious Organizations

Archdiocese of Toronto
Beth Tzedec Congregation Inc.
Crossroads Christian
Communications Inc.
The General Synod of the Anglican
Church of Canada
The Governing Council of the Salvation
Army in Canada
Holy Blossom Temple
Incorporated Synod of the
Diocese of Toronto
Sisters of St. Joseph Toronto
The United Church of Canada

813210
Grant-Making and Giving Services

Ontario Trillium Foundation
Sick Kids Foundation

813310
Social Advocacy Organizations

Canadian Blood Services
Canadian Cancer Society Ontario Div.
Canadian Diabetes Association
Canadian Hearing Society
Canadian Institute for Health
Information
The Canadian National Institute
for the Blind/Ontario Div.
Canadian Standards Association
Cancer Care Ontario
Cerebral Palsy Parent
Council of Toronto
Children's Aid Society of York Region
Dixon Hall
Durham Children's Aid Society
Electrical Safety Authority
Heart and Stroke Foundation of Ontario
Meta Centre for the
Developmentally Disabled
MukiBaum Treatment Centres
Multiple Sclerosis Society of Canada
Ontario Federation for Cerebral Palsy
Ontario Hospital Association
Ontario March of Dimes
Seniors 4 Seniors
Shepell·fgi
Shepherd Village Inc.
Surrey Place Centre
United Way of Greater Toronto
University Settlement
World Vision Canada

813410
Civic and Social Organizations

Caledon Community Services
Carefirst Seniors & Community
Services Association
Centre for Information and Community
Services
Heart and Stroke Foundation of Ontario
Oakville Family YMCA
Ontario Lung Association
Plan International Canada Inc.

813910
Business Associations

Central 1 Credit Union
Certified General Accountants of
Ontario
GS1 Canada
Infrastructure Health & Safety
Association of Ontario
Insurance Bureau of Canada
Investment Industry Regulatory
Organization of Canada
Ontario Hospital Association
Toronto Board of Trade
Tourism Toronto
University of Toronto Institute
for Aerospace Studies

813920
Professional Organizations

Canadian Institute of Chartered
Accountants
The Canadian Mental Health
Association - Toronto Branch
Certified General Accountants
of Ontario
The College of Family Physicians
of Canada
College of Nurses of Ontario
College of Physicians and Surgeons
of Ontario
Elementary Teachers' Federation
of Ontario
Institute of Chartered Accountants
of Ontario
The Law Society of Upper Canada
Mutual Fund Dealers Association
of Canada
The National Club
Ontario College of Teachers
Ontario Medical Association
Ontario Nurses' Association
Ontario Real Estate Association
Ontario Secondary School Teachers
Federation
Professional Engineers Ontario
Skills for Change
Society of Composers, Authors, and
Music Publishers of Canada
The Toronto Real Estate Board

813930
Labour Organizations

Alliance of Canadian Cinema,
Television & Radio Artists
Canadian Auto Workers Union
Elementary Teachers' Federation
of Ontario
Ontario Public Service
Employees Union
Ontario Secondary School
Teachers Federation
Ontario Teachers' Pension Plan Board
UFCW Canada - Locals 175 & 633
Universal Workers Union Local 183
Workplace Safety & Prevention
Services

813990
Other Membership Organizations

Royal Canadian Yacht Club

PUBLIC ADMINISTRATION   91

911230
Federal Police Services

Royal Canadian Mounted Police

911390
Other Federal Labour, Employment and Immigration Services

Industry Canada-Ontario Region

911910
Other Federal Government Public Administration

Canada Centre for Inland Waters
Canada Mortgage and Housing Corp.
Public Works & Government
Services Canada
Statistics Canada
Toronto and Region Conservation
Authority

912120
Provincial Correctional Services

Ministry of Community Safety and
Correctional Services

912130
Provincial Police Services

Ontario Provincial Police

912150
Provincial Regulatory Services

Financial Services Commission
of Ontario

912210
Provincial Labour and Employment Services

Workplace Safety and Insurance Board

912910
Other Provincial and Territorial Public Administration

Alcohol & Gaming Commission of
Ontario
Cancer Care Ontario
Ontario Energy Board

913120
Municipal Correctional Services

Toronto West Detention Centre

913130
Municipal Police Services

Durham Regional Police Service
Halton Regional Police Service
Peel Regional Police
Toronto Police Service
York Regional Police

913140
Municipal Fire-Fighting Services

Burlington Fire Department
Markham Fire & Emergency Services
Mississauga Fire and Emergency
Services
Oakville Fire Department
Oshawa Fire Services
Richmond Hill Fire Department
Vaughan Fire and Rescue Service
Whitby Fire and Emergency Services

913910
Other Local- Municipal and Regional Public Administration

The City of Brampton
The City of Burlington
The City of Oshawa
The City of Toronto
The City of Vaughan
The Corporation of the
City of Mississauga
The Corporation of The
City of Pickering
The Corporation of the
Town of Caledon
The Corporation of the
Town of Markham
The Corporation of the
Town of New Tecumseth
The Corporation of the
Town of Oakville
The Corporation of the
Town of Orangeville
The Corporation of the
Town of Richmond Hill
The Corporation of the
Township of Brock
The Municipality of Clarington
Regional Municipality of Durham
Regional Municipality of Halton
Regional Municipality of Peel
The Regional Municipality of York
Toronto Community Housing Corp.
The Town of Ajax
The Town of Aurora
The Town of Georgina
The Town of Halton Hills
The Town of Milton
The Town of Newmarket
Town of Richmond Hill/
Municipal Operations Centre
The Town of Whitby
The Town of Whitchurch-Stouffville
Township of King

CONTACT 11
TORONTO 12

Part 4

Postal Code Index

G6V 6R2	Desjardins Financial Security Life Assurance Company	
H1V 1A6	Boutique La Vie en Rose Inc.	
H3A 1G1	Cascades Boxboard Group Inc.	
H3A 1L6	Domtar Inc.	
H3A 3K3	Laurentian Bank of Canada	
H3B 2M9	CN	
H3B 4G7	Zara Canada	
H3B 4Y7	Bell Canada	
H3G 1G3	The Standard Life Assurance Co. of Canada	
H3S 1G5	Kruger Inc.	
H4P 2P5	Le Chateau Inc.	
H4S 2E6	Air Transat A.T. Inc.	
H4Y 1H4	Air Canada	
J4K 5B1	TELUS Emergis Inc.	
K1P 5L6	NAV Canada	
K2E 7L6	Thermo Fisher Scientific Co.	
K2K 1X8	Nordion Inc.	
K8N 4Z5	Meyers Transport Ltd.	
K9J 7B1	Trentway-Wagar Inc.	
L0B 1A0	Windmill Mushroom Farms	
L0B 1M0	Ell-Rod Holdings Inc.	
L0E 1E0	The Corporation of the Township of Brock	
L0E 1L0	Briars Estates Ltd.	
L0E 1R0	Community Living Georgina Riverglen Haven Nursing Home-Sutton	
L0G 1A0	Simcoe Manor Home for the Aged	
L0G 1J0	Cardinal Golf Club	
L0G 1M0	AGC Flat Glass North America Ltd.	
L0G 1N0	Nobleton Lakes Golf Course Ltd.	
L0G 1T0	B.C. Instruments Brookdale Treeland Nurseries Ltd. Showa Canada Inc. Trisan Construction	
L0G 1W0	Flex-N-Gate Seeburn F & P Manufacturing Inc.	
L0H 1G0	Deep Foundations Contractors Inc. Don Anderson Haulage Ltd. Station Creek Golf Club Tam-Kal Limited	
L0J 1C0	Bulk Transfer Systems Inc. Copper Creek Golf Club McMichael Canadian Art Collection Tank Truck Transport Inc.	
L0P 1B0	Goodfellow Inc.	
L0P 1E0	International Landscaping Inc.	
L1C 1A4	Greeley Containment & Rework Inc.	
L1C 3A6	The Municipality of Clarington	
L1G 1B5	Mills Pontiac Buick GMC Ltd.	

L1G 5T9	Hillsdale Estates
L1G 8E3	The Wynfield
L1H 1B9	Oshawa Clinic
L1H 1N2	Oshawa Public Library/ McLaughlin Branch
L1H 3M4	Taxi-Taxi
L1H 3V7	TTR Transport Inc.
L1H 3Y1	Community Living Oshawa / Clarington
L1H 3Z7	The City of Oshawa
L1H 7K4	Durham Children's Aid Society Durham College
L1H 7K6	Holiday Inn Oshawa
L1H 7L5	Durham Region Media Group
L1H 7L7	University of Ontario Institute of Technology
L1H 7L8	Ontario Motor Sales Ltd.
L1H 7M7	Oshawa PUC Networks Inc.
L1H 7N1	Auto Warehousing Co. Canada
L1H 8P7	General Motors of Canada Ltd.
L1J 2K5	Spherion
L1J 5Y2	Thornton View
L1J 5Y7	Mackie Moving Systems Corp.
L1J 6W7	Westburne Ruddy Electric
L1J 6Z7	EHC Global Inc.
L1J 7B1	Oshawa Fire Services
L1J 7C4	Durham Catholic District School Board
L1J 8R2	Lakeridge Health Corp.
L1K 2H5	College Woodwork
L1M 1B5	Brooklin Concrete Products
L1N 0B8	Durham Regional Police Service
L1N 0T9	Manufacturing and Technology Centre
L1N 1C4	J.H. McNairn Ltd.
L1N 2B9	North America Steel Equipment Company Ltd.
L1N 2K8	Personal Attendant Care Inc.
L1N 2M8	The Town of Whitby
L1N 5S2	ASC Signal Corp.
L1N 5S6	Exopack Performance Films Inc.
L1N 5S9	Ontario Shores Centre for Mental Health Sciences
L1N 5T1	Gerdau Ameristeel
L1N 6A3	Durham Region Transit Regional Municipality of Durham
L1N 6K9	BMW Canada Inc.
L1N 7B7	Makita Canada Inc.
L1N 7H8	Central East - Community Care Access Centre
L1N 7L4	Nemato Corp.
L1N 8Y3	Pro-Bel Enterprises
L1N 8Y7	The Sernas Group Inc.
L1N 9B6	McGraw-Hill Ryerson Ltd.
L1N 9C9	StonCor Group

L1R 2K6	Durham District School Board
L1R 2W8	Hard-Co Construction Ltd.
L1R 3A5	The Village of Taunton Mills
L1R 3M2	Whitby Fire and Emergency Services
L1S 1M7	Community Living Ajax, Pickering & Whitby
L1S 1R7	MeadWestvaco Packaging Systems LP
L1S 1R9	Ballycliffe Lodge
L1S 1S3	Lifestyle Sunrooms Inc.
L1S 2E3	Ashland Canada Corp. Latham Splash Canada
L1S 2G8	Messier-Bugatti-Dowty
L1S 2H5	Ajax Textile Processing Company Ltd.
L1S 2H9	The Town of Ajax
L1S 3C6	Sutton Group Heritage Realty Inc.
L1S 6M2	Royal LePage Connect Realty
L1S 7G7	Volkswagen Group Canada
L1T 3V3	Veridian Corp.
L1V 1B4	Re/Max First Realty Ltd.
L1V 1E7	Phonetime Inc.
L1V 2R5	Ontario Power Generation Inc./ Pickering Nuclear
L1V 3P2	Municipal Property Assessment Corp.
L1V 6K7	The Corporation of The City of Pickering
L1W 1Z7	Mapleridge Mechanical Contracting Ltd.
L1W 1Z8	Hubbell Canada LP
L1W 2Y5	Howard Marten Company Ltd.
L1W 3C1	RCM Technologies Canada Corp.
L1W 3J9	Web Offset Publications Ltd.
L1W 3K1	Lenbrook Industries Ltd.
L1W 3P1	Knights On Guard Protective Services
L1W 3R4	Provincial Sign Systems
L1W 3R8	Noranco Manufacturing Ltd. Signature Aluminum Canada Inc.
L1W 3T9	Eco-Tec Inc. Nelson Industrial Inc.
L1W 3V7	Crossby Dewar Inc.
L1W 3W8	Purdue Pharma
L1W 3W9	Tribute Communities
L1W 3X6	Medical Pharmacies Group Inc.
L1W 3Y1	Ellis Packaging Ltd.
L1W 3Y8	Yorkville Sound Ltd.
L1W 4B2	Long & McQuade Musical Instruments
L1Z 0B1	Automodular Corporation
L1Z 1E5	Costco Wholesale - Ajax
L1Z 1L9	East Penn Power Battery Sales Ltd.
L1Z 1T7	Deer Creek Golf & Banquet Facility

L1Z 1X3	Vandermeer Nursery Ltd.
L3P 2G4	Markhaven Inc.
L3P 3A7	Markham Public Library Board
L3P 3M1	Cerebral Palsy Parent Council of Toronto
L3P 7P3	Markham Stouffville Hospital Corporation
L3R 0A3	Delta Markham
L3R 0A8	Unionville Letter Carrier Depot
L3R 0A9	HomeLife Gold Trade Realty Ltd.
L3R 0B1	Symtech Innovations Ltd.
L3R 0B8	Ceridian Canada Ltd.
	Stantec Consulting Ltd.
L3R 0E1	Perle Systems Ltd.
L3R 0E8	Leisureworld Senior Care LP
	Redline Communications
L3R 0G4	Canadian Premier Life Insurance Co.
	Tecsys Inc.
L3R 0G7	Premier Salon Canada Inc.
L3R 0H8	FireFox Marketing Services
L3R 0H9	DST Output Inc.
	Highland Transport
L3R 0J1	Amer Sports Canada Inc.
	Rubie's Costume Company (Canada)
L3R 0J3	Linsey Foods Ltd.
L3R 0J7	PMA Brethour Real Estate Corporation Inc.
L3R 0P1	York Downs Golf & Country Club
L3R 0P3	Smucker Foods of Canada Co.
L3R 0P8	Toronto Airways Ltd.
L3R 0S8	Wesco Distribution Canada LP
L3R 0S9	Critical Control Solutions
L3R 0T3	Steelcase Canada Limited
L3R 0T5	Johnson & Johnson Medical Products
	Ortho-Clinical Diagnostics
L3R 0T9	Pier 1 Imports
L3R 0X3	Combined Insurance Company of America
L3R 0Y6	Emerson Electric Canada Ltd.
L3R 0Z7	Nexans Canada Inc.
L3R 0Z9	Supercom of Canada Ltd.
L3R 1A3	Frankie Tomatto's Ltd.
	Holiday Inn Hotel & Suites Toronto - Markham
L3R 1A5	Corpap Inc.
L3R 1A7	Associated Tube Industries
L3R 1B5	Middleton Graphics Group Inc.
L3R 1B6	J.F. & L. Restaurants Ltd.
L3R 1C3	Dependable Anodizing Ltd.
L3R 1C4	Integrated Technology Ltd.
L3R 1C9	Rogers Shared Operations
	Steel Art Signs Corp.

L3R 1E1	Tyco Electronics Canada ULC
L3R 1E3	Browne & Co. Ltd.
	Clintar - Franchise Support Office
L3R 1E8	Mayfair Racquet & Fitness Clubs
L3R 1G9	Don Valley North Automotive Inc.
L3R 1L8	Unionville Home Society
L3R 2C2	Bethany Lodge
L3R 2E4	W.H. Stuart & Associates
L3R 2M7	Ranka Enterprises Ltd.
L3R 2N2	The Garden Basket Food Markets Inc.
	Northwood Mortgage Ltd.
L3R 2N8	Miller Waste Systems
L3R 2W1	The Fish House
L3R 2W5	Crest Circuit Inc.
L3R 2Z3	Chouinard Bros. Roofing
L3R 2Z5	Norex Ltd.
L3R 3B1	Advantage Sales & Marketing
L3R 3J9	Adeptron Technologies Corp.
	Neopost Canada Limited
L3R 3L3	Pet Valu Canada Inc.
L3R 3T7	Platform Computing Corp.
L3R 3V6	Span International
L3R 3Y1	Biggs & Narciso Construction Service Inc.
L3R 4B6	Black Photo Corporation
L3R 4B8	The Nielsen Company
L3R 4B9	Connex See Service
L3R 4C1	M·A·C Cosmetics
L3R 4E6	Brookfield LePage Johnson Controls
L3R 4G5	Gensys Telecommunications Laboratories Inc.
L3R 4H8	Amex Canada Inc.
L3R 4N6	SMTC Corporation
L3R 4Z6	Concord Idea Corp.
L3R 5B4	Reinhart Foods Ltd.
L3R 5C2	Autoliv Electronics Canada Inc.
L3R 5E5	Multimatic Inc.
L3R 5G2	Apple Canada Inc.
L3R 5G3	Upper Canada Child Care Centres of Ontario
L3R 5H6	Exco Technologies Ltd.
L3R 5K2	Sunrise Senior Living
L3R 5K3	Genivar Ontario Inc.
L3R 5K4	The FSA Group
L3R 5L7	Oracle Canada ULC
L3R 5M1	Werek Enterprises Inc.
L3R 5M2	Town & Country Motors (1989) Ltd.
L3R 5M9	Waterford Building Maintenance Inc.
L3R 5P8	Allstate Insurance Company of Canada
L3R 5R7	Centrecorp Management Services Ltd.

L3R 5V2	Idexx Reference Laboratories Ltd.
L3R 5V4	Johnson Controls LP
L3R 5V5	Silliker Canada Co.
L3R 5V7	Pro Pharm Ltd.
L3R 5X9	Belle-Pak Packaging Inc.
L3R 5Y6	Lyreco (Canada) Inc.
L3R 5Z6	AJD Data Services Inc.
L3R 5Z8	CDS Global Inc.
L3R 6A7	POI Business Interiors Inc.
L3R 6B3	J.D. Barnes Ltd.
L3R 6B9	Sarku Japan Restaurants Income Fund
L3R 6G2	First Health Care Services Inc.
	Living Realty Inc.
	SCI Marketview Ltd.
L3R 6G3	Epson Canada Ltd.
L3R 6H2	Hyundai Auto Canada Corp.
L3R 6H3	Golf Town Canada Inc.
	Saint Elizabeth Health Care
L3R 8B8	The Linkage Group Inc.
L3R 8B9	Trimark Sportswear Group Inc.
L3R 8C3	Samtack Inc.
L3R 8E1	Intec Billing Canada Ltd.
L3R 8E3	Labelad
	Pullmatic Manufacturing
L3R 8H1	Timex Group Inc.
L3R 8H2	Toshiba Business Solutions
	Toshiba of Canada Ltd.
L3R 8H3	Electro Sonic Inc.
L3R 8H8	Petroff Partnership Architects
L3R 8N4	Davis Group of Companies Corp.
L3R 8T7	Re/Max Realtron Realty Inc., Brokerage
L3R 8T8	RF Porter Plastering Ltd.
L3R 8T9	Four Seasons Drywall Ltd.
	Tuxedo Royale
L3R 9R6	Athletes World
	National Sports
L3R 9R8	Miller Paving Ltd.
L3R 9R9	Delcan Corp.
	DMTI Spatial Inc.
L3R 9T3	G4S Security Services (Canada) Ltd.
L3R 9T5	Sunny Crunch Foods Ltd.
	Urban Edge Shading Inc.
L3R 9V1	Ontario Nursing Services
L3R 9V9	Trade World Realty Inc. Brokerage
L3R 9W2	Extendicare (Canada) Inc.
L3R 9W3	The Corporation of the Town of Markham
	Markham Fire & Emergency Services
L3R 9X1	Longview Solutions Inc.
L3R 9X6	EPM Global Services Inc.
	Gentec International Ltd.
	Woodbine Tool & Die Manufacturing Ltd.
L3R 9X7	Seton Canada

L3R 9Y3	Catech Systems Ltd.
L3R 9Z3	Reed Construction Data
L3R 9Z5	Toyota Credit Canada Inc.
L3R 9Z6	Century 21 King's Quay Real Estate Inc., Brokerage
	The Co-Operators Group Ltd.
L3R 9Z7	IBM Canada Ltd.
L3S 3J1	Grote Industries
	ITW Construction Products
L3S 3K1	Dagmar Construction Ltd.
L3S 4K4	Kubota Canada Ltd.
L3S 4M4	Bigtech Inc.
L3T 0A1	MMM Group Limited
L3T 1N8	Normac Kitchens Ltd.
L3T 2C7	Extreme Fitness, Inc.
L3T 3X1	Bayview Golf & Country Club
L3T 4A3	Shouldice Hospital
L3T 4P1	Thornhill Community Centre Library
L3T 6K8	Raywal Ltd.
L3T 7M8	Adastra Corporation
	Veri-Cheque Ltd.
L3T 7N5	Duplium
L3T 7N9	URS Canada Inc.
L3T 7P6	Nike Canada Corp.
L3T 7P9	CAA South Central Ontario
L3T 7T1	HomeLife Bayview Realty Inc.
L3T 7T2	Momentum Advanced Solutions
	OnX Enterprise Solutions Inc.
L3T 7T4	Mayhew & Associates
L3T 7V8	STMicroelectronics
L3T 7V9	Siemens Enterprise Communications Inc.
	TeraGo Networks Inc.
L3T 7W3	AECOM Canada Ltd.
L3T 7W4	Accellos Canada Inc.
L3T 7W8	Camilion Solutions Inc.
	LexisNexis Canada Inc.
L3T 7X6	AMD
L3T 7X8	Kids and Company Ltd.
L3T 7Z3	CGI Adjusters Inc.
L3V 7V3	Ontario Provincial Police
L3X 1B8	Glenway Country Club (1994) Ltd.
L3X 1V6	Allied International Credit Corp.
L3Y 1J6	Newmarket Health Centre
L3Y 2A7	Community Living - Newmarket/Aurora District
L3Y 2L1	Southlake Residential Care Village
L3Y 2P9	Southlake Regional Health Centre
L3Y 3E3	TNT Foods International Inc.
	TS Tech Canada Inc.
L3Y 3J2	A & B Courier
L3Y 4W5	York Regional Police

L3Y 4X1	Architectural Precast Systems Inc.
	Slidemaster
	York Region Media Group
L3Y 4X2	Pickering College
L3Y 4X7	Dortec Industries
	Magna Closures Inc.
	The Town of Newmarket
L3Y 5H6	Century 21 Heritage Group Ltd.
L3Y 5L8	East Side Mario's
L3Y 6Z1	The Regional Municipality of York
L3Y 7B2	Ce De Candy Company Ltd.
	Eurospec Tooling Inc.
L3Y 7B4	Pearson Canada
L3Y 7B5	Lotek Wireless Inc.
L3Y 7B6	Dove Foods Limited
	Turf Care Products Canada Limited
L3Y 7B8	Geo. A. Kelson Company Limited
L3Y 7R6	York Support Services Network
L3Y 8C6	Burke's Restoration Inc.
L3Y 8T3	Flextronics
L3Y 8V1	The Newroads Automotive Group
L3Y 8X6	Student Transportation Canada
L3Y 9A1	Children's Aid Society of York Region
L3Y 9C8	Engineered Air
L3Z 2A4	Parkview Transit
	Spectra Aluminum Products Inc.
L42 1S1	Jevco Insurance Company
L4A 0G8	Parkview Home Long Term Care
L4A 2T1	Southwire Canada
L4A 7X3	Bloomington Cove
	Hanson Pressure Pipes (Stouffville Pressure Facility)
	Shadow Lake Outdoor Recreation Centre
L4A 7X5	Emerald Hills Golf Club
	K-Line Maintenance & Construction Ltd.
	Rolling Hills Golf Club
	The Town of Whitchurch-Stouffville
L4B 0B4	Ash City
L4B 1A3	Fujitec Canada Inc.
L4B 1A8	Hibar Systems Ltd.
L4B 1B2	Sheraton Parkway Toronto North Hotel & Suites
L4B 1B3	Fairchild Television Ltd.
L4B 1B4	Group of Goldline
L4B 1B7	Flexmaster Canada Limited
L4B 1E5	TigerDirect.Ca Inc.
L4B 1E7	Acklands-Grainger Inc.
L4B 1E8	Samaco Trading Limited
L4B 1H1	Anderson Merchandisers-Canada Inc.
	Firefly Books Ltd.

L4B 1H2	The Watson Group Ltd.
L4B 1H9	DecisionOne Corp.
L4B 1J5	Regional Nursing Services
L4B 1J6	Suzuki Canada Inc.
L4B 1JA	Keane Canada Inc.
L4B 1L8	Eurofase Inc.
L4B 1M4	Stanley Black & Decker Canada Inc.
L4B 2N4	Amico Corp.
	Swiss Herbal Remedies Ltd.
L4B 3B3	Applanix Corp.
L4B 3K5	Mazda Canada Inc.
L4B 3K6	Maxium Financial Services Inc.
	WHB Identification Solutions Inc.
L4B 3K7	Riva Plumbing Ltd.
L4B 3M7	Toronto Montessori Schools
L4B 3N2	Century 21 Landstars Realty Inc.
L4B 3N4	SENES Consultants Limited
L4B 3P4	The Corporation of the Town of Richmond Hill
L4B 3P6	FlexITy Solutions Inc.
	Gary Jonas Computing Ltd.
	Solarsoft Business Systems
L4B 3S5	Johnson Inc.
L4B 3Y2	Bulk Barn Foods Limited
L4B 4A3	Premiere Ballroom & Convention Centre
L4B 4C6	Levi Strauss & Co. (Canada) Inc.
L4B 4J3	Lexmark Canada Inc.
L4B 4N4	Compuware Corp.
	The Insurers Financial Group
L4B 4N6	Tetra Pak Canada Inc.
L4B 4N8	Open Text Communications Solutions Group
L4B 4T8	Preferred Health Care Services
L4B 4W3	Staples Canada Inc.
L4C 0H4	Richmond Hill Country Club
L4C 0H5	Richmond Hill Public Library
L4C 1A8	Polybrite
L4C 1V1	Mariann Home
L4C 3G3	Innocon Inc.
L4C 3G5	Victaulic Custom Casting Company
L4C 3G7	Irpinia Kitchens
L4C 3T8	Re/Max Executive Realty Inc.
L4C 4Y5	Town of Richmond Hill/ Municipal Operations Centre
L4C 4Z3	York Central Hospital
L4C 8H2	Cousins-Currie
L4E 1A2	DiamondBack Golf Club
L4E 1A8	Maxim Group General Contracting Ltd.
L4E 1K3	Maple Group
L4E 3N9	The Summit Golf & Country Club

L4F 1M4	Richmond Hill Fire Department
L4G 0A2	Van Rob Inc.
L4G 1G3	Axiom Group Inc.
L4G 1M6	Stock Transportation Ltd.
L4G 1P4	Highland Chevrolet Cadillac Ltd.
L4G 2N9	CHATS - Community Home Assistance To Seniors
L4G 2R9	Aurora Resthaven
L4G 3G8	Willows Estate Nursing Home
	York Catholic District School Board
L4G 3H2	York Region District School Board
L4G 3H3	King Cole Ducks Ltd.
L4G 3H4	Piramal Healthcare Torcan (Toronto) Canada Ltd.
L4G 3H7	St. Andrew's College
L4G 3M7	Uni-Motion Gear
L4G 3T9	Bunn-O-Matic Corporation of Canada Ltd.
L4G 3V8	Genpak LP
L4G 4C4	Avant Imaging & Information Management Inc.
L4G 6J1	The Town of Aurora
L4G 6J9	Quadgraphics Inc.
L4G 6X5	Sinclair Technologies Inc.
L4G 7K1	Magna International Inc.
L4G 8A4	State Farm Mutual Automobile Insurance Co.
L4H 0A5	Kingsdown Owen & Co. Ltd.
L4H 0A9	PowerStream Inc.
L4H 0L8	Sterling Tile & Carpet
L4H 0P5	Campio Furniture Ltd.
L4H 0S7	Sunview Doors Ltd.
L4H 1A7	Econo-Rack Storage Equipment Ltd.
L4H 1J1	407 ETR
L4H 1X9	Decoustics Ltd.
	Royal Group, Inc.
	Roytec Vinyl Co.
L4H 2B9	S.L.H. Transport Inc.
L4H 2G4	Consolidated Fastfrate Inc.
L4H 3C5	Totalline Transport
L4H 3G9	Jeld-Wen Windows & Doors
L4H 3H1	Morris Brown & Sons Company Ltd.
L4H 3H9	PGC
L4J 0B8	Weston Fine Foods Inc.
L4J 1A1	Sisley Motors Limited
L4J 1K2	Uplands Golf & Ski Club
L4J 1V7	Acura of North Toronto
L4J 1V8	Roy Foss Motors Ltd.
L4J 1W3	Thornhill Golf & Country Club
L4J 3N1	Concord Food Centre Ltd.
L4J 4E5	Garnet A. Williams Community Centre
L4J 6X6	BMW Autohaus
L4J 7L2	Farco Enterprises Ltd.

L4J 8C1	Vaughan Public Libraries
L4J 8G6	Reena
L4K 0A4	Vinnie Zucchini's Corp.
L4K 0A6	Mobile Climate Control Inc.
L4K 0A7	Downsview Drywall Contracting
L4K 0B3	Specialty Care Inc.
L4K 0B6	Carillion Canada Inc.
L4K 0B8	Cara Operations Limited
L4K 0C2	Vitran Express Canada
L4K 0C3	BFI Canada Inc.
L4K 1A1	Central Fairbank Lumber
L4K 1A7	Noble Trade Inc.
L4K 1B2	Clarke Inc.
L4K 1B7	Toromont Industries Ltd.
L4K 1G6	J.D. Smith and Sons Limited
	Vaughan Paving Ltd.
L4K 1J1	Clearway Construction Inc.
L4K 1J5	Wikoff Corp.
L4K 1J9	Ostaco 2000 Windoors Inc.
L4K 1K1	Ontario Power Contracting Ltd.
L4K 1K2	Lido Wall Systems Inc.
L4K 1K5	DCL International Inc.
L4K 1K8	Con-Elco Ltd.
L4K 1L3	AFL Display Group
	Decora Window & Door Systems
L4K 1M8	Aluma Systems Canada Inc.
L4K 1N3	Di Crete Construction Ltd.
L4K 1N8	National Fast Freight
L4K 1P6	Gerrity Corrugated Paper Products Ltd.
	Muirs Cartage Ltd.
L4K 1R9	Rochester Aluminum Smelting Canada Ltd.
L4K 1W7	Oxville Homes Ltd.
L4K 1W8	Riviera Parque
L4K 1X2	Paradise Banquet & Convention Centre
L4K 1X6	Easy Plastic Containers Ltd.
L4K 1Y2	Bratty & Partners Barristers and Solicitors
L4K 1Y8	K-G Packaging Inc.
L4K 1Z1	Cleveland Range Ltd.
	Clover Tool Manufacturing Ltd.
L4K 1Z9	Korhani of Canada Inc.
L4K 2A3	Crown Metal Packaging Canada LP
L4K 2A5	AkzoNobel
L4K 2B9	Plats du Chef
L4K 2C7	Kristofoam Industries Inc.
L4K 2E9	Welded Tube of Canada
L4K 2G3	Sunsweet Fundraising Inc.
L4K 2G9	Arla Foods, Inc.
L4K 2H2	Le Parc Dining & Banquet Ltd.
L4K 2J8	Fileco Inc.
	Salga Associates
L4K 2K1	Rollstamp Manufacturing
L4K 2L7	Affordable Personnel Services Inc.
L4K 2L8	Maple Leaf Frozen Bakery - Canada Bread

L4K 2N6	IDX Toronto
L4K 2N9	Vaughan Fire and Rescue Service
L4K 2R5	Kohl & Frisch Ltd.
L4K 2R8	Federal Mogul Canada Ltd.
L4K 2T2	Concord Metal Manufacturing
L4K 2T3	CDC Contracting
L4K 2V3	Mister Keys Ltd.
L4K 2W6	Teknion Form
L4K 2X3	Co-Ex-Tec
L4K 2Z3	Corma Inc.
L4K 3A8	G.A. Foss Transport Ltd.
L4K 3B5	Tycos Tool & Die Inc.
L4K 3C4	Belrock Construction Ltd.
L4K 3E4	De Boer's Furniture Ltd.
L4K 3E6	Allwood Products Limited
L4K 3L8	Worldwide Food Distribution
L4K 3M3	The Atlas Corp.
	Carwell Construction Ltd.
L4K 3N7	Encore Sales Ltd.
L4K 3P1	Jem Pak GK Inc.
L4K 3S4	Magic Maintenance Inc.
L4K 3S6	CiF Lab Casework Solutions
	Concord Concrete & Drain Ltd.
L4K 3S8	Prodigy Graphics Group Inc.
L4K 3V5	Unique Store Fixtures Ltd.
L4K 3V8	Hewitt Material Handling, Inc.
L4K 3X2	Continental Press Ltd.
L4K 3Z3	Kenworth Toronto Ltd.
L4K 3Z9	Allan Windows Technologies
	Bailey Metal Products Ltd.
	Can-Ar Coach Service
L4K 4A5	Hardrock Forming Co.
L4K 4B4	Jones Apparel Group Canada Ltd.
	S.D.R. Apparel Inc.
L4K 4B5	Serv-U-Clean Ltd.
L4K 4E1	ECS Engineering & Construction Ltd.
L4K 4G7	Lafarge Canada Inc.
L4K 4H3	Oakdale Drywall & Acoustics Ltd.
L4K 4J3	FactoryDirect.ca
L4K 4J5	Magna Exteriors & Interiors Corp.
L4K 4K1	Elite Window Fashions
L4K 4K2	Debco Bag Distributors Ltd.
L4K 4L2	Digital Security Controls Ltd.
	Selba Industries Inc.
L4K 4L8	Spectrum Realty Services Inc.
L4K 4M5	Toys R Us (Canada) Ltd.
L4K 4M9	Custom Insulation Systems
L4K 4N4	Thorncrete Construction Ltd.
	Warren Industries Ltd.

L4K 4N7	Metro Canada Logistics Inc.	L4K 5W1	Antamex International Inc.	L4L 7Z6	Primo Mechanical Inc.
L4K 4N9	Aastra Technologies Limited		Circa Metals	L4L 8A3	Soroc Technology Inc.
	Brown Window Corp.		El-En Packaging Company Ltd.	L4L 8A8	Tacc Construction Ltd.
L4K 4P3	St. Joseph Printing Ltd.		Haremar Plastic		Vinyl Window Designs Ltd.
L4K 4P4	Urban Electrical Contractors		Manufacturing Ltd.	L4L 8K8	Organic Resource Management Inc.
L4K 4P8	CFN Precision Ltd.	L4K 5W3	Mircom Technologies Ltd.	L4L 8L4	Grande Cheese Company Ltd.
L4K 4R1	Con-Drain Company (1983) Ltd.	L4K 5W6	Accucut Profile & Grinding Ltd.	L4L 8L6	Cortina Kitchens Inc.
L4K 4R3	Schaeffer & Associates Ltd.	L4K 5X3	Smart Centres	L4L 8N4	Extrudex Aluminum
	Skor Food Group Inc.	L4K 5X6	Holcim (Canada) Inc.	L4L 8N6	Decor-Rest Furniture Ltd.
L4K 4R5	KIK Investment Holdings LP	L4K 5Z8	Optech Inc.		Magnotta Winery Corporation
L4K 4R8	Digi Canada Inc.	L4L 0B9	Coast Paper	L4L 8P3	Royal Pipe Systems Ltd.
	Kinecor		HD Supply Canada	L4L 8P4	Antalex Inc.
L4K 4R9	4 Star Drywall Ltd.		PaperlinX Canada Limited	L4L 8P6	Roma Moulding Inc.
	Target Investigation & Security Ltd.	L4L 1A5	Sentrex Communications Company	L4L 8R1	Colombo Chrysler Dodge Ltd.
L4K 4S3	Cashcode Company Inc.	L4L 1A6	Kristus Darzs Latvian Home	L4L 8Z3	Summer Fresh Salads
L4K 4S6	Greenpark Homes		Pine View Hyundai Ltd.	L4L 8Z7	All Stick Label Ltd.
L4K 4T8	Muzzo Brothers Group Inc.		The Royalton Hospitality Inc.		Link-Line Group of Companies
L4K 4V1	Royal Envelope Ltd.	L4L 1T8	Graphic Transportation Services	L4L 9C1	Eddie Bauer Inc.
L4K 4V2	Toro Aluminum	L4L 2B9	The Country Club		Mytox Manufacturing
L4K 4V8	AB SCIEX	L4L 2S6	Re/Max Excellence Realty Inc.	L4L 9C7	Martinrea International Inc.
L4K 4W1	Executive Woodwork Ltd.				Versacold - Vaughan Facility
	Exopack Concord	L4L 2W2	The National Golf Club of Canada	L4L 9C8	Cornerstone Insurance Brokers Inc.
	Util Capital Tool & Design	L4L 3A2	Da Vinci Banquet Hall & Restaurant	L4L 9E7	Intercity Realty Inc. Brokerage
L4K 4W3	Jems Coating Ltd.	L4L 3P6	Carpenter Canada Co.		
L4K 4W8	Bondfield Construction Company Ltd.		Egan & Teamboard Merchandising Consultants Associates	L4L 9J3	Gracious Living Corporation
	Dixie Electric Ltd.			L4L 9J7	Acosta Canada
	IAC Automotive Components Alberta Ltd.		Motor Specialty Manufacturers		Rocca Dickson Andreis Inc.
L4K 4X1	Deeley Harley Davidson Canada		Yale Industrial Trucks Ontario Ltd.	L4L 9T4	Window City Mfrs Inc.
L4K 4X9	Multy Home LP	L4L 3R5	Baron Metal Industries Inc.	L4L 9T5	Pine Tree Ford Lincoln
L4K 4Y6	Packaging Technologies Inc.		Concord Steel Centre Ltd.	L4L 9T7	Maple Drywall
L4K 4Y7	Powerlasers Ltd.		Fleming Door Products	L4M 4W5	The Source (Bell) Electronics Canada Inc.
L4K 4Y9	Anton Manufacturing		Superstyle Furniture Ltd.	L4N 1R9	Air Canada Jazz
L4K 4Z2	RCP Inc.	L4L 3R7	Sherwood Electromotion Inc.	L4N 8Z9	Mueller Canada
L4K 4Z6	Kingstar Products Inc.	L4L 3T2	Ganz	L4P 3G1	The Town of Georgina
L4K 5A6	Concord Confections	L4L 4A3	Dentsply Canada Inc.	L4S 0B8	Compugen Inc.
L4K 5B2	adidas Canada Limited		Oran Industries Ltd.	L4S 1L4	Holy Trinity School
L4K 5C2	Advanced Product Technologies	L4L 4S5	MicroAge	L4T 0A7	HomeLife United Realty Inc.
L4K 5C3	Dave and Busters	L4L 5T7	Litens Automotive Partnership	L4T 1A9	Magellan Aerospace Corp.
L4K 5C5	Aspen Ridge Homes Ltd.		Noranco Inc. - Woodbine Division	L4T 1G6	Downsview Woodworking Ltd.
L4K 5C6	ThyssenKrupp Materials			L4T 1G7	All Canada Crane Rental Corp.
L4K 5C7	RuggedCom Inc.	L4L 5T9	Torino Drywall Inc.		
L4K 5M8	Apollo Health & Beauty Care	L4L 5V3	Reversomatic Manufacturing	L4T 1G9	Aleris Specifications Alloy Products Canada Company
	Serta	L4L 5V4	Compact Mould Ltd.		Western Toronto International Trucks Inc.
L4K 5N9	byPeterandPauls.com		Construction Control Inc.		
L4K 5P1	Maple Stamping	L4L 5V5	Leader Plumbing & Heating Inc.	L4T 1T2	Iris Power LP
L4K 5P2	Nova Services Group Inc.	L4L 5Y9	Speedy Electric Contractors Ltd.	L4T 3C8	Ferma Construction Company Inc.
L4K 5R4	Satpanth Capital Inc.			L4T 3L8	Imperial Flavours Inc.
L4K 5R6	Priszm Income Fund	L4L 7E8	William M. Dunne Associates Ltd.		Weston Forest Products
L4K 5R8	Cardinal Health Canada	L4L 7Z4	Backerhaus Veit Ltd.	L4T 4A8	Maksteel
L4K 5R9	Gottardo Construction			L4T 4G6	Alpa Lumber Inc.
L4K 5V1	CTG Brands				Casa Bella Windows Inc.
L4K 5V5	FM Windows & Doors				Newmar Window Manufacturing Inc.
L4K 5V6	Matcom Industrial Installations Inc.			L4T 4H1	McKesson Canada
L4K 5V7	Trans Power Utility Contractors Inc.				

L4T 4M1	Malton Village Long Term Care Centre
L4V 1B3	TNT Express (Canada) Inc.
L4V 1B4	Liftow Ltd.
L4V 1B5	Cenveo, McLaren Morris and Todd
L4V 1C5	Core Logistics International Inc.
L4V 1C7	Janes Family Foods Ltd.
L4V 1C8	Park 'N Fly
L4V 1E3	Orlando Corp.
L4V 1E4	Four Points by Sheraton Toronto Airport
L4V 1E8	International Centre
L4V 1G5	Dollar Thrifty Automotive Group Canada Inc.
L4V 1H3	Patterson Dental Canada Inc.
L4V 1H6	Cott Beverages Canada
L4V 1J2	Kintetsu World Express (Canada) Inc.
L4V 1J7	Steris Canada Inc.
L4V 1K2	Flynn Canada Ltd.
L4V 1K8	Multipak Ltd.
L4V 1K9	Cardinal Meat Specialists Ltd.
L4V 1L5	Booth Centennial Healthcare Linen Services Inc.
L4V 1L8	Dynamex Canada Limited
L4V 1L9	The Bargain! Shop Holdings Inc.
L4V 1M5	Tri-Ed Ltd.
L4V 1N1	Hilton Toronto Airport Hotel & Suites
L4V 1N2	The John Forsyth Shirt Co. Ltd.
L4V 1N3	G & K Services Canada Inc.
L4V 1P6	Marwick Manufacturing Inc.
L4V 1R3	Longo Brothers Fruit Markets Inc.
	Rosedale Livery Ltd.
L4V 1R5	The State Group
L4V 1R8	Merge Healthcare
L4V 1R9	Nortel Networks Corp.
	TransGlobe Property Management Services
L4V 1S5	Starr Culinary Delights Inc.
L4V 1T1	Hostopia.com Inc.
	Penauille Servisair
L4V 1T3	William L. Rutherford Limited
L4V 1T8	Mailing Innovations
L4V 1V4	Versent Corporation ULC
L4V 1V5	Wirecomm Systems Inc.
L4V 1W1	Nuance Global Traders (Canada) Inc.
	Yardi Systems Inc.
L4V 1W5	Bevertec CST Inc.
	CA Canada
	ConAgra Foods Canada Inc.
	ConceptWave Software Inc.
L4V 1X5	United Parcel Service Canada Ltd.
L4V 1Y2	Winners Merchants International
L4V 1Y6	Schenker of Canada Limited
L4W 0A1	Infrastructure Health & Safety Association of Ontario
	Workplace Safety & Prevention Services
L4W 0A2	Hill-Rom Canada
L4W 0A5	Daimler Trucks Financial Ltd.
L4W 0A7	Paging Network of Canada Inc.
L4W 0A9	Tata Consultancy Services Canada Inc.
L4W 0B1	Hershey Canada Inc.
L4W 0B3	Carlton Cards Ltd.
	Masonite International Corporation
L4W 0C2	J & L Personnel Inc.
L4W 0H5	Echelon General Insurance Co.
L4W 1B3	Glasvan Trailers Inc.
L4W 1B9	Bass Building Maintenance Ltd.
	Cutler Forest Products Inc.
L4W 1C1	Nikon Canada Inc.
L4W 1C4	Manitoulin Transport Inc.
	Memme Excavation Company Ltd.
	Motor Express Toronto
L4W 1C5	Frendel Kitchens Limited
L4W 1E1	Solutions
L4W 1E3	Ready Staffing Solutions Inc.
L4W 1E4	Tricrest Professional Services
L4W 1E6	Con-way Freight Canada
	Trans4 Logistics
	Transport CFQI
	TST Truckload Express Inc.
	West-ADS Employment Services Inc.
L4W 1G4	National Carpet Mills Ltd.
L4W 1G5	TST Overland Express
L4W 1G6	Replex Automotive Corp.
L4W 1G7	RB & W Corporation of Canada
L4W 1H8	J.A. Wilson Display
L4W 1J2	Gilbert Steel Ltd.
L4W 1K3	Tyndall Nursing Home Ltd.
L4W 1K7	Peterbilt Ontario Truck Centres
L4W 1N2	Cetero Research
L4W 1P2	Burnbrae Farms Mississauga
L4W 1R2	Unique Restoration Ltd.
L4W 1R7	Duron Ontario Ltd.
L4W 1S2	Canada Post Corp./ Central Region
L4W 1S5	Nortrax
L4W 1T7	Drive Products
L4W 1T9	Buckley Cartage Ltd.
L4W 1V1	Furlani's Food Corp.
L4W 1X4	Garland Commercial Ranges Ltd.
L4W 2A7	Ontario Chrysler Jeep Dodge Inc.
L4W 2B1	Loxcreen Canada Ltd.
L4W 2L2	Delta Toronto Airport West
L4W 2M2	Kafko Pool Products
L4W 2M7	Addison Chevrolet
L4W 2P1	Kapsch TrafficCom
L4W 2R9	J.M. Die Limited
	Top Grade Molds Ltd.
L4W 2S1	ABlackCab
L4W 2S5	Delphax Technologies
	Olsen Fashion Canada Inc.
	Richards-Wilcox Canada
	Tri R Foods Ltd.
L4W 2S6	Recall
L4W 2T1	Kingsway Transport
L4W 2T3	Panasonic Canada Inc.
L4W 2T7	Central Graphics & Container Group Ltd.
L4W 2X4	MTD Metro Tool & Die Ltd.
L4W 2X5	Ecolab Co.
L4W 3C3	Erb Transport Ltd.
L4W 3R7	Halton Indoor Climate Systems, Ltd.
	Proco Machinery Inc.
L4W 3W5	Bison Transport Inc.
L4W 3W6	D'Angelo Brands Ltd.
L4W 4C3	Marc's No Frills
L4W 4H1	CSG Security Inc.
	Guardall
L4W 4H2	WorleyParsons
L4W 4J4	Office Depot
L4W 4L4	Penske Truck Leasing
	Strongco Inc.
L4W 4L5	Novadaq Technologies Inc.
L4W 4N3	Ideal Honda
L4W 4P1	Hoodex Industries Ltd.
L4W 4P4	Metafore Limited Partnership
	Trillium Security Services Inc.
	xwave, A Division of Bell Aliant Regional Communications LP
L4W 4P7	Random House of Canada Ltd.
L4W 4T4	Stage West All-Suite Hotel & Theatre Restaurant
L4W 4T5	Canadian Springs
L4W 4T9	Westmont Hospitality Group
L4W 4V9	Air Canada Vacations Inc.
	DealerTrack Canada Inc.
	Laura Secord
	Mosaic Sales Solutions Canada Operating Co.
L4W 4X3	Counterforce Inc.
L4W 4X5	Cotton Ginny Inc.
L4W 4X6	Telus Health & Financial Solutions
L4W 4X7	Central 1 Credit Union
L4W 4Y1	Traffic Tech Inc.
	WSI Internet Consulting & Education

L4W 4Y3	Calea Ltd.	
	FedEx Ground Package	
	System Ltd.	
L4W 4Y6	Ernest Green & Son Ltd.	
	Logitech Remote Controls	
L4W 4Y9	RedKnee Inc.	
L4W 4Z1	Siemens PLM Software	
L4W 4Z5	Nissan Canada Inc.	
L4W 5A1	Cash Money Financial	
	Services Inc.	
L4W 5A4	The College of Family	
	Physicians of Canada	
	First Data	
L4W 5B1	Kubra	
L4W 5B3	Greenlawn Ltd.	
L4W 5B4	Gay Lea Foods	
L4W 5B5	The Wheels Group	
L4W 5C7	Pitney Bowes Canada Ltd.	
L4W 5E1	First Lady Coiffures	
L4W 5E3	Ericsson Canada Inc.	
L4W 5G1	Hewlett-Packard	
	(Canada) Co.	
L4W 5G4	Festo Inc.	
L4W 5G7	Lakeside Process	
	Controls Ltd.	
L4W 5G9	itravel 2000	
L4W 5H1	Maersk Canada Inc.	
L4W 5J2	Apple Express Courier Ltd.	
L4W 5J4	Citigroup Fund	
	Services Inc.	
L4W 5J7	Pepsico Beverages Canada	
L4W 5J8	ADT Security Services	
	Canada Inc.	
L4W 5K2	Carlson Marketing Group	
	Canada Ltd.	
L4W 5K4	Odyssey Financial	
	Technologies	
L4W 5K5	SimplexGrinnell	
L4W 5K6	Federal Express Canada Ltd.	
L4W 5K9	Trapeze Software	
	Group Inc.	
L4W 5L1	Certicom Corp.	
	Ricoh Canada Inc.	
L4W 5L2	Brewers' Retail Inc.	
L4W 5L6	Investment Planning	
	Counsel Inc.	
	Novo Nordisk Canada Inc.	
L4W 5M1	Avanade Canada Inc.	
L4W 5M3	Compass Group Canada Ltd.	
	Hurley Group	
L4W 5M6	Inforica Inc.	
	SS&C Technologies	
	Canada Corp.	
L4W 5M7	Premier Candle Corp.	
	Smith Induspac	
	Toronto Ltd.	
L4W 5M8	Innovapost	
L4W 5N2	Bell Conferencing Inc.	
	Bell Mobility	
L4W 5N4	CEVA Logistics	
L4W 5N6	Canadian Standards	
	Association	
L4W 5N7	Chrysler Financial	
L4W 5P6	General Mills Canada Corp.	

L4W 5P9	Sungard	
L4W 5S1	Kellogg Canada Inc.	
L4W 5S4	Baylis Medical	
	Company Inc.	
L4W 5S7	Unisync Group Ltd.	
L4W 5S8	Unity Life of Canada	
L4W 5S9	Reckitt Benckiser	
	(Canada) Inc.	
	Sobeys Ontario	
L4X 1K1	G. Brandt Meat Packers Ltd.	
L4X 1M4	ABS Machining Inc.	
L4X 2A8	Brand Felt of Canada	
L4X 2C1	Erie Meat Products Ltd.	
L4X 2C5	Wajax Income Fund	
L4X 2G1	Carmichael	
	Engineering Ltd.	
L4X 2Z6	AYA Kitchens and	
	Baths, Ltd.	
L4X 3A5	Kubik Inc.	
L4Y 1M4	AstraZeneca Canada Inc.	
L4Y 1R6	Freshline Foods Ltd.	
	Kal Tire Ontario	
	Wedlock Paper	
	Converters Ltd.	
L4Y 1S2	SCI Logistics Inc.	
L4Y 1S4	Mother Parker's Tea &	
	Coffee Inc.	
L4Y 1S5	Rubbermaid Canada	
L4Y 1Y6	Colio Estates Wines Inc.	
L4Y 1Z4	Samuel Strapping Systems	
L4Y 1Z6	Roll Form Group	
L4Y 1Z7	Samuel, Son & Co., Limited	
L4Y 1Z9	Nightingale Corporation	
L4Y 2B8	Trebor Personnel Inc.	
L4Y 3V7	Sunrise Senior Living, Inc.	
L4Y 3Y3	Molinaro's Fine Italian	
	Foods Ltd.	
L4Y 4C5	Glenn A. Davis	
	& Associates Ltd.	
L4Z 0A2	JTI-Macdonald Corp.	
L4Z 1N4	NSK Canada Inc.	
L4Z 1N9	AGAT Laboratories Ltd.	
L4Z 1P1	Stagevision Inc.	
L4Z 1P5	Plastic Packaging &	
	Components Inc.	
L4Z 1R1	Commercial Spring & Tool	
	Company Ltd.	
L4Z 1R2	Pool People Ltd.	
L4Z 1S2	HomeLife Response	
	Realty Inc.	
L4Z 1T5	The Sherwin-Williams	
	Company (Canada)	
L4Z 1W7	Amhil Enterprises Ltd.	
L4Z 1W9	Sharp Electronics	
	of Canada Ltd.	
L4Z 1X1	Associated Youth Services	
	of Peel	
L4Z 1X2	Pave-Tar Construction Ltd.	
L4Z 1X3	D & A Collection Corp.	
L4Z 1X9	Antex Design Inc.	
L4Z 1Y3	Larson-Juhl Ltd.	
L4Z 2A9	Williams	
	Telecommunications Corp.	
L4Z 2C2	Cardinal Couriers Ltd.	

L4Z 2E5	Macro Engineering &	
	Technology Inc.	
L4Z 2E7	Oldcastle Glass Engineered	
	Products	
L4Z 2G1	Holiday Inn Toronto	
	Airport West	
L4Z 2G6	Woodbridge Foam Corp.	
L4Z 2H5	Konica Minolta Business	
	Solutions (Canada) Ltd.	
L4Z 2H9	Sapa Extrusions	
L4Z 3G1	Acrobat Research Ltd.	
L4Z 3K3	Centre for Education &	
	Training	
L4Z 3K7	AMEC Earth &	
	Environmental Ltd.	
	ProHome Health Services	
L4Z 3M3	Brink's Canada Ltd.	
L4Z 3M6	Wyeth Consumer	
	Healthcare Inc.	
L4Z 3S6	Wainbee Ltd.	
L4Z 3Y4	Baxter Corp.	
L4Z 3Z9	Desjardins General	
	Insurance Group	
L4Z 4B6	Hershey Centre	
L4Z 4B8	Allseating Corporation	
	Regal Confections	
L4Z 4E5	Villa Forum	
L4Z 4E7	Symcor Inc.	
L4Z 4G3	LG Electronics Canada Inc.	
L4Z 4J3	Matrix Packaging	
	of Canada ULC	
L5A 1W9	Ready Honda	
L5A 2Y9	RBC Insurance	
	Holdings Inc.	
L5A 3V3	Frischkorn Associates Inc.	
L5A 3X6	Acorn Packaging	
L5A 4A8	Curry's Art Store Ltd.	
L5A 4G1	PCL Constructors	
	Canada Inc.	
	Respiron Care-Plus Inc.	
L5A 4N8	Cawthra Gardens Long	
	Term Care Community	
L5B 1B5	Cooksville Care Centre	
L5B 1B8	Trillium Health Centre	
L5B 1K7	Mississauga Fire and	
	Emergency Services	
L5B 1M2	Boston Pizza	
	International Inc.	
	The Employment Solution	
	Praxair Canada Inc.	
L5B 1M3	Morguard Investments Ltd.	
L5B 1M8	Leisureworld Chelsey Park	
	Mississauga	
	Royal LePage Realty	
	Centre, Brokerage	
L5B 1P3	Novotel Mississauga	
L5B 2C9	Donato Salon & Spa	
L5B 2N5	Quantum Management	
	Services Ltd.	
L5B 2T4	Stephenson's Rental	
	Services Inc.	
L5B 2V2	EllisDon Corporation	
L5B 3C1	The Corporation of the City	
	of Mississauga	

L5B 3C2	ADESA Canada
	Cunningham Lindsey
	Canada Ltd.
	Re/Max Realty One Inc.,
	Brokerage
L5B 3C3	Edward Jones
	Kenna
	Pallett Valo LLP
L5B 3J1	Aerotek Canada
	CGC Inc.
	Prophix Software Inc.
L5B 3Y3	Mississauga Library System
L5B 3Y5	Kimberly-Clark Inc.
L5B 3Y7	Labour Ready, Inc.
L5B 4A5	USC Education Savings
	Plans Inc.
L5B 4C1	Playdium Corp.
L5C 1T7	Whiteoak Ford Lincoln
	Sales Limited
L5C 1T8	Graham Packaging
	Canada Ltd.
L5C 1W1	Metroland Media
	Group Ltd.
L5C 1Y7	Credit Valley Golf and
	Country Club
L5C 2S4	Lyons Auto Body Ltd.
L5C 2V1	Applewood Air
	Conditioning Ltd.
L5C 2V5	Provincial Store
	Fixtures Ltd.
L5C 2V8	Indal Technologies Inc.
L5C 3A9	Mississauga Business Times
	The Mississauga News
L5C 3B1	Mississauga Transit
L5C 3K1	Enersource Corp.
L5C 4E9	Re/Max Performance Realty
	Inc., Brokerage
L5C 4G4	Sutton Group - Summit
	Realty Inc.
L5C 4P4	ARI Financial Services Inc.
L5C 4R3	Canadian Pacific Railway
	GE Commercial Distribution
	Finance Canada
L5C 4R9	CANPAR Transport Ltd.
	ICS Courier
L5E 1E4	A.J. Lanzarotta Wholesale
	Fruit & Vegetables Ltd.
	Ilsco of Canada Company
	Interior Manufacturing
	Group Inc.
L5E 1E9	Grohe Canada Inc.
L5E 1H2	Richards Wilcox Door
	Systems.Limited
L5E 2C2	C/S Construction Specialties
	Company
L5G 2T2	The Waterside Inn
L5G 3E9	Servicemaster Contract
	Services
L5H 2K4	Mississaugua Golf &
	Country Club Limited
L5J 1J4	Re/Max Realty
	Enterprises Inc.
	Sutton Group Quantum
	Realty Inc.

L5J 1J9	John Grant Haulage Ltd.
L5J 1K2	Petro-Canada Lubricants
	Centre
L5J 1K4	CertainTeed Gypsum
	Canada Inc.
L5J 1K5	H.L. Blachford Ltd.
	Melburn/Musket Group
L5J 1K7	Universal Drum
	Reconditioning Co.
L5J 2M4	Dahl Brothers (Canada) Ltd.
L5J 2M7	Boart Longyear Canada
L5J 2Y4	Liquid Cargo Lines Ltd.
L5J 3Z8	Sheridan Villa
L5J 4C7	IPEX Management Inc.
L5J 4T8	Daimler Buses North
	America
L5K 1A4	Voith Hydro Inc.
L5K 1A8	Petro-Canada
L5K 1B1	IMAX Corporation
L5K 1B2	Atomic Energy
	of Canada Ltd.
L5K 1B3	Exova
L5K 1Z8	Shaw Broadcast Services
L5K 2K7	Erin Mills Retirement
	Nursing Home
L5K 2L1	Xerox Research Centre of
	Canada
L5K 2L3	KMH Cardiology &
	Diagnostic Centres
L5K 2L6	The WenLeigh Long-Term
	Care Residence
L5K 2N6	EMD Serono Canada Inc.
L5K 2P8	McCormick Rankin Corp.
L5K 2R7	Hatch Ltd.
L5K 2S9	Western Assurance Co.
L5L 0A2	Flite Hockey Inc.
L5L 1C6	University of Toronto
	Mississauga
L5L 1V4	Erinwood Ford Sales Ltd.
L5L 1X3	Mississauga Honda
	Woodchester Nissan
L5L 2M4	Erin Dodge Chrysler Ltd.
L5L 2M5	Erinoak Kids
L5L 2R4	Applewood Chevrolet
	Cadillac
L5L 3P9	Michael-Angelo's Market
	Place Inc.
L5L 3R2	Erin Park Automotive
	Partnership
L5L 3S6	Honeywell
L5L 4L4	Brenmar Heating & Air
	Conditioning Ltd.
L5L 4M1	Bayshore Home Health
	Roan International Inc.
L5L 5R3	PJ's Pet Centres Ltd.
L5L 5S5	Super Shine Oakdale
	Janitorial Services Ltd.
L5L 5Y5	Total Relocation Moving
	Systems
L5L 5Z3	Rapid Aid Ltd.
L5L 5Z7	Escort Manufacturing
	Corporation
L5M 1R4	Trott Transit Ltd.
L5M 1X9	Leisureworld Caregiving
	Centre, Streetsville

L5M 1Y1	The Alliance Group Inc.
L5M 1Y9	CTS of Canada Company
L5M 2H3	E.I duPont Canada
	Company
L5M 2N1	The Credit Valley Hospital
L5M 7M4	The Village of Erin
	Meadows
L5N 0A4	Ryan ULC
L5N 0A6	Oticon Canada
L5N 0A8	Maple Leaf Consumer Foods
L5N 0A9	Creation Technologies LP
L5N 0B3	Becton Dickinson
	Canada Inc.
L5N 0B7	D & B Canada
	Whirlpool Canada LP
L5N 0B9	Shaw Canada LP
L5N 1A6	Homestarts Inc.
L5N 1B1	Menu Foods Ltd.
L5N 1P8	Transcontinental Digital
	Services GP Inc.
L5N 1P9	Wal-Mart Canada Corp.
L5N 1R1	Robert Bosch Inc.
L5N 1V2	Magna Powertrain Inc.
L5N 1V8	Luxottica Retail
L5N 1W2	Weir Canada Inc.
L5N 2B8	Cobalt Pharmaceuticals Inc.
L5N 2E2	NCR Canada Ltd.
L5N 2K7	UFCW Canada
	- Locals 175 & 633
L5N 2L2	Wardrop Engineering Inc.
L5N 2L3	Delta Meadowvale Hotel
	and Conference Centre
L5N 2L7	Icynene Inc.
L5N 2L8	Diebold Company
	of Canada Ltd.
	Maxxam Analytics
L5N 2M2	Quinterra Property
	Maintenance Inc.
L5N 2M6	Ciba Vision Canada Inc.
L5N 2R7	Primerica Financial
	Services (Canada) Ltd.
L5N 2V8	Smith Detection
L5N 2X6	Sayers & Associates Ltd.
L5N 2X7	Crossmark Canada Inc.
	Gerber Canada Inc.
	PHH Arval
	Ryder Logistics &
	Transportation Solutions
	Worldwide
	Ryder Truck Rental
	Canada Ltd.
L5N 3C9	Russel Metals Inc.
L5N 3E7	Aim Health Group
L5N 3K6	Meadowvale Ford Sales and
	Services Ltd.
L5N 3R3	Abbott Laboratories Ltd./
	Diagnostic Division
L5N 3S7	Pentax Canada Inc.
L5N 3T4	SCI Inc.
L5N 4G8	Four Points By Sheraton
	Mississauga - Meadowvale
L5N 4J9	Re/Max Realty
	Specialists Inc.

L5N 5M4	Agilent Technologies Canada Inc.	
	Comark Services Inc.	
L5N 5M5	Telecon Inc.	
L5N 5M8	Benjamin Moore & Co.	
L5N 5N1	Sensient Flavors Canada Inc.	
L5N 5P9	GE Capital	
	GE Capital Fleet Services	
	General Electric Canada	
L5N 5R5	Kruger Products Limited	
L5N 5R8	Community Living Mississauga	
L5N 5S1	Cyclone Manufacturing Inc.	
L5N 5S2	D-Link Canada Inc.	
	Fugro Airborne Surveys Corp.	
L5N 5V4	Maple Reinders Constructors Ltd.	
L5N 5Z1	Addison Chevrolet Buick GMC	
L5N 5Z7	Communications Repair Logistics Company	
	Golder Associates Ltd.	
	VWR International, Ltd.	
L5N 6C5	Adelt Mechanical Works Ltd.	
L5N 6L4	GlaxoSmithKline Inc.	
L5N 6L6	Contract Pharmaceuticals Limited Canada	
L5N 6L7	Hoffmann-LaRoche Ltd.	
L5N 6L8	Starkey Labs Canada Co.	
L5N 6R4	Credit Valley Conservation	
L5N 6R8	Luxell Technologies Inc.	
L5N 6S2	Hilti (Canada) Corp.	
	National Instore Services Corp.	
L5N 6Y2	Mary Kay Cosmetics Ltd.	
L5N 7A6	Siemens Canada Limited	
L5N 7E6	Conestoga Cold Storage	
L5N 7H5	Dynamic Paint Products Inc.	
	Upper Canada Forest Products Ltd.	
L5N 7J6	KONE Inc.	
	Pride Pak Canada Ltd.	
L5N 7J7	TheMIGroup	
L5N 7J9	Psion Teklogix Inc.	
L5N 7K5	John Brooks Company Ltd.	
L5N 7K9	Patheon Inc.	
L5N 7P2	Henkel Canada Corporation	
L5N 7W5	Pinchin Environmental Ltd.	
L5N 7Y1	CCSI CompuCom	
L5N 7Y2	triOS College Business Technology Healthcare	
L5N 8B3	Bauer Hockey Corp.	
	MIQ Logistics	
L5N 8C2	Sandvik Canada Inc.	
	Simmons Canada Inc.	
L5N 8C6	CHEP Canada Inc.	
L5N 8C7	Alcon Canada Inc.	
L5N 8E2	Nealanders International Inc.	
L5N 8E9	PointClickCare	
L5N 8G1	Tech Data Canada Inc.	
L5N 8K4	Beauty Systems Group (Canada) Inc.	
	Willson International	
L5N 8L9	Microsoft Canada Co.	
L5N 8M5	Valeant Pharmaceuticals	
L5N 8M6	ReserveAmerica	
L5N 8R9	VitalAire Canada Inc.	
L5P 1A2	CLS Catering Services Ltd.	
	Consolidated Aviation Fuelling of Toronto ULC	
	Swissport Cargo Services, LP	
L5P 1B2	Greater Toronto Airports Authority	
L5P 1B6	American Airlines, Inc.	
L5P 1C4	The Sheraton Gateway Hotel	
L5R 0A2	Linde Canada Ltd.	
L5R 0B7	Pharma Medica Research Inc.	
L5R 0K1	Kuehne & Nagel Ltd.	
L5R 1B8	Cooper Industries (Canada) Inc.	
L5R 1B9	Spectrum Supply Chain Solutions	
L5R 1C5	The Dufferin-Peel Catholic District School Board	
L5R 1C6	Peel District School Board	
L5R 3E7	Royal LePage Kingsbury Realty	
L5R 3E9	The Canadian Red Cross/ Ontario Zone	
	HB Group Insurance Management Ltd.	
	Intria Items Inc.	
L5R 3G3	Belvedere International Inc.	
	Coinamatic Canada Inc.	
	Nedco Ontario	
	On Premise Laundry Systems Inc.	
	Rexel Canada Electrical Inc.	
L5R 3G5	Bridgestone/Firestone (Canada) Inc.	
	ESI Canada	
L5R 3K5	GES Canada Exposition Services Ltd.	
	Ontario Natural Food Co-op	
L5R 3K6	Prime Restaurants of Canada Inc.	
L5R 3L5	Electrical Safety Authority	
L5R 3L8	King's Pastry	
L5R 3L9	Medical Mart Supplies Ltd.	
L5R 3M1	Robert Kennedy Publishing	
L5R 3M3	American-Standard	
L5R 3P4	Oracle Corporation Canada Inc.	
L5R 3R2	G.N. Johnston Equipment Company Ltd.	
L5R 3T7	Tucker's Marketplace	
L5R 3T8	Purolator Courier Ltd.	
L5R 3W2	Mattel Canada Inc.	
L5R 3X4	Tree of Life Canada ULC	
L5R 3Y5	Anixter Canada Inc.	
L5R 3Y9	Talon Systems Inc.	
L5R 3Z9	Esselte Canada Inc.	
L5R 4A1	Expeditors Canada Inc.	
	Ingram Micro	
L5R 4B2	Revera Inc.	
	Samsung Electronics Canada Inc.	
L5R 4B5	PCO Services Corp.	
L5R 4E2	Panalpina Inc.	
L5R 4E6	RMP Athletic Locker Ltd.	
L5R 4G4	Fujifilm Canada Inc.	
L5R 4H1	AMJ Campbell Van Lines	
	BASF Canada	
	Chartwell Seniors Housing REIT	
L5R 4J3	John Wiley & Sons Canada Ltd.	
L5R 4J4	Wells Fargo Financial Corporation Canada	
L5R 4J5	Kia Canada Inc.	
L5R 4J7	Subaru Canada Inc.	
L5S 1A7	Five Star Rags Inc.	
L5S 1B2	Air Georgian Ltd.	
	Chartright Air Group	
	Field Aviation Company Inc.	
L5S 1B8	Body Blue 2006 Inc.	
L5S 1C4	Hilroy	
L5S 1E5	Dr. Oetker Canada Ltd.	
L5S 1J5	Canam	
L5S 1J6	Star Plastics Inc.	
	Tsubaki of Canada Ltd.	
L5S 1L4	Valspar Inc.	
L5S 1L6	Delso Restoration Ltd.	
L5S 1L8	Canada Cartage System Ltd.	
L5S 1L9	1149318 Ontario Inc.	
	S & Q Plastic	
L5S 1N8	Super-Pufft Snacks Corp.	
L5S 1N9	Indalco Alloys	
L5S 1R1	Kenaidan Contracting Ltd.	
L5S 1R6	Advantage Personnel Ltd.	
L5S 1S4	Osram Sylvania Ltd.	
L5S 1S5	Canadian Bearings Ltd.	
L5S 1S6	Enesco Canada Corp.	
L5S 1V5	Multiple Pakfold Business Forms	
L5S 1W9	Sonoco Canada Corp.	
L5S 1X7	Arctic Glacier Inc.	
	Solutions2Go Inc.	
L5S 1Y2	Sameday Worldwide	
L5S 1Y7	Sysco Toronto	
L5S 1Y8	Carrier Canada	
L5S 1Y9	Capital Safety - Canada	
L5S 1Z5	TransX Ltd.	
L5S 2A2	Robert Transport	
L5S 2A5	The Dominion Group Inc.	
L5T 0A6	The Brick Warehouse Corp.	
L5T 1A1	National Logistics Services	
	Vipond Inc.	
L5T 1A6	Armbro Transport Inc.	
L5T 1A7	Novaquest Metal Finishing Inc.	
L5T 1B7	YRC Reimer	
L5T 1B8	D & E Wood Industries Ltd.	
L5T 1B9	DGN Marketing Services Ltd.	

L5T 1C6	State Chemical Ltd.
L5T 1C8	IOF Business Furniture Manufacturing Inc.
L5T 1C9	Pivotal HR Solutions
L5T 1H9	Annan & Bird Lithographers
	Broan-Nutone Canada Inc.
L5T 1J3	Pratt & Whitney Canada Corp.
L5T 1J5	Jitsu Manufacturing Inc.
	Multichair Inc.
L5T 1J6	Dom-Meridian Construction Ltd.
	Prestige Telecom Ltd.
L5T 1J9	Bestway Cartage Ltd.
L5T 1K2	BDI World Class World Wide
L5T 1K5	Aviva
L5T 1K6	FedEx Trade Networks Transport & Brokerage (Canada) Inc.
	Pacific Western
	Silex Innovations Inc.
L5T 1L4	Tube-Fab Ltd.
L5T 1L5	Coatings 85 Ltd.
L5T 1N2	Wurth Canada Ltd.
L5T 1N6	Canada Bonded Attorney & Legal Directory Ltd.
	Syncrgex Corporation
L5T 1N7	Atlantic Collision Group
L5T 1P2	Siemens Healthcare Diagnostics
L5T 1P3	Drakkar Human Resources Ontario Inc.
L5T 1P7	Canon Canada Inc.
L5T 1R2	Global Driver Services Inc.
L5T 1R8	bioMérieux
L5T 1S8	OE Quality Friction Inc.
L5T 1S9	United Van Lines (Canada) Ltd.
L5T 1T9	Ontario Flower Growers Co-op
L5T 1V6	John G. Hofland Ltd.
L5T 1W1	Trulite Industries Ltd.
	Ultra-Fit Manufacturing Inc.
	Van Houtte Coffee Services
L5T 1W8	SGS Canada Inc.
L5T 1X2	Lite Products Inc.
L5T 1Y9	Mersen Canada
L5T 1Z2	Langen Packaging Inc.
L5T 2A8	Harper Ontario Truck Centres
L5T 2B7	Rosedale Transport Ltd.
L5T 2C1	Puddy Brothers Ltd.
L5T 2E1	In Transit Personnel Inc.
L5T 2E6	Just Energy
L5T 2G1	Green Grove Foods Corp.
	UTi Canada Inc.
L5T 2G8	English Bay Batter (Toronto) Inc.
L5T 2H6	Innovative Cooling Dynamics
L5T 2J2	Larcan Inc.
L5T 2J3	Wolfedale Electric Ltd.
L5T 2K4	Behind the Wheel Transportation Services Inc.

L5T 2L3	Heidelberg Canada Graphic Equipment Limited
L5T 2L6	Arrow North American Electronics Components
	Hydropool Industries
L5T 2L9	Kee Management Solutions Inc.
L5T 2M7	Richards Packaging Inc.
L5T 2M9	1st Choice Staffing Ltd.
L5T 2N1	Mascot Truck Parts Ltd.
L5T 2N3	Summit Food Service Distributors Inc.
L5T 2N5	Collectcents Inc.
L5T 2N6	Agility
	Hydrogenics Corp.
L5T 2P4	Midnight Express & Cartage Ltd.
L5T 2P9	The Shopping Channel
L5T 2R6	Matrix Logistics Services Ltd.
L5T 2R7	Sport Chek
L5T 2R8	Deacro Industries Ltd.
L5T 2R9	Newly Weds Foods Co.
L5T 2S3	Performance Equipment Limited
L5T 2S5	Karrys Bros., Limited
	Versa Fittings & Manufacturing Inc.
L5T 2S6	Bruce R. Smith Ltd.
L5T 2S9	Reefer Sales and Service
L5T 2T1	Trophy Foods Inc.
L5T 2T2	Quik X Transportation Inc.
L5T 2V1	Paradigm Electronics Inc.
L5T 2V3	Vincor Canada
L5T 2V4	Assured Packaging Inc.
L5T 2V5	J.H. Ryder Machinery Ltd.
L5T 2V6	H.S.T. Synthetics Ltd.
L5T 2V7	DHL Global Forwarding (Canada) Inc.
L5T 2W1	All Trade Computer Forms Inc.
L5T 2W4	Husky Truck Stop
L5T 2W5	4 Office Automation Ltd.
L5T 2W6	Staples Advantage
L5T 2X1	Moore Canada Corp.
L5T 2X3	Nippon Express Canada Ltd.
L5T 2X5	Cintas Canada Ltd.
L5T 2X8	DBG
L5T 2X9	FNF Canada
L5T 2Y4	World Vision Canada
L5T 2Y6	Peel Children's Centre
L5T 3A7	Sherway Warehousing Inc.
L5V 3E4	Electrolux Home Products
L5W 0B3	CML Healthcare Inc.
	Kao Brands Canada Inc.
	Phonak Canada Ltd.
	PRG Schultz Canada Corp.
L5W 0E3	KCI Medical Canada, Inc.
L5W 1L8	Maritz Canada Inc.
L5W 1W2	Supply Chain Management Inc.
L5W 1Y4	NTN Bearing Corporation of Canada Ltd.
L6A 0K6	Genesis Worldwide Inc.

L6A 1A2	Maple Downs Golf & Country Club Ltd.
L6A 1R3	Global Precast Inc.
L6A 1R9	Scott-Woods Transport Inc.
L6A 1S6	Canada's Wonderland Company
L6A 1T1	The City of Vaughan
L6A 1T3	Fabricated Plastics Ltd.
L6A 2L1	Maple Health Centre
L6A 3Y9	Alpa Roof Trusses Inc.
L6B 1E1	The Woodhaven
L6C 0C1	Giesecke & Devrient Systems Canada, Inc.
L6C 0C6	The Orthotic Group Inc.
L6C 0H9	Honda Canada Inc.
L6C 1N9	Angus Glen Golf Club
L6C 1T6	General Switchgear & Controls Ltd./ Markham Electric Division
L6C 1Z7	Scholastic Canada Ltd.
L6C 2S3	Philips Electronics Ltd.
L6C 3G1	Norman Hill Realty Inc.
L6G 1A5	Club Markham
	The Hilton Suites Toronto/ Markham Conference Centre & Spa
L6G 1B2	Brennan Paving & Construction Ltd.
	CDI Computer Dealers Inc.
L6G 1B3	Motorola Canada Ltd.
	WorleyParsons Canada
L6G 1B6	Team Industrial Services
L6G 1C3	The CG&B Group Inc.
L6G 1C9	Transcontinental PLM Inc.
L6H 0G5	HUB International Ontario Limited
L6H 0H3	The Corporation of the Town of Oakville
L6H 1A5	Naylor Group Inc.
L6H 1M3	Syl Apps Youth Centre
L6H 1M5	Wellspring Pharmaceutical Canada Corp.
L6H 1X9	Royal Windows & Doors
L6H 2L1	The Sheridan College Institute of Technology and Advanced Learning
L6H 2R4	Standex Electronics Canada
L6H 3H6	Oakville Place
L6H 5R2	Huron Services Group Ltd.
L6H 5R3	Indeka Imports Ltd.
L6H 5R5	CCI Thermal Technologies Inc.
L6H 5R7	Genworth Financial Mortgage Insurance Company Canada
L6H 5S1	Excel Tech Ltd.
L6H 5S7	Moen Inc.
L6H 5T4	Benlan Inc.
L6H 5T5	Levitt-Safety Ltd.
L6H 5W1	Unifirst Canada Ltd.
L6H 5W8	Canada Loyal Financial
L6H 6G1	Stanley Black & Decker

L6H 6G4	Accuristix
	MDG Computers
	Canada Inc.
L6H 6H1	Tripar Transportation Inc.
L6H 6J4	Promation Engineering Ltd.
L6H 6M7	ASL Distribution
	Services Ltd.
L6H 6P1	Diversey Inc.
L6H 6P6	PPG Canada Inc.
L6H 6P8	i365
	Merriam School of Music
	Weight Watchers
	Canada Ltd.
L6H 6R1	Cable Control Systems Inc.
L6H 6R7	York International Ltd.
L6H 6X5	Bard Canada Inc.
	LaserNetworks
	SMC Pneumatics
	(Canada) Ltd.
L6H 6X7	AMEC Americas Ltd.
L6H 6Z8	National Wireless
L6H 7H7	Algonquin Power
	Corporation Inc.
L6H 7W1	Pelmorex Media Inc.
L6J 2L1	St. Mildred's-Lightbourn
	School
L6J 2X2	Team Industrial
	Services Inc.
L6J 2Z4	Oakville Public Library
L6J 3J2	Oak-Land Ford Lincoln
	Sales Ltd.
L6J 3J3	Levolor Kirsch Window
	Fashions
	Newell Rubbermaid Canada
L6J 3L7	Halton Healthcare Services
	- Oakville Site
L6J 4Z3	Glen Abbey Golf Club
L6J 5A6	Oakville Fire Department
L6J 5E1	Procor Ltd.
L6J 5E3	Oakville Hydro Corp.
L6J 5E4	Ford Motor Company of
	Canada, Limited
L6J 5M7	Atlas Van Lines
	(Canada) Ltd.
L6J 7L5	Dana Hospitality Inc.
L6J 7T4	Shred-It
L6J 7Y5	First Canadian Title
L6J 7Z2	A.C.I. Accessory
	Concepts Inc.
L6K 1C9	Re/Max Aboutowne
	Realty Corp.
L6K 1K7	Oakville Family YMCA
L6K 1L8	Central West Specialized
	Development Service
L6K 2G7	Wendy's Restaurants of
	Canada Inc.
L6K 2H2	Community Living Oakville
L6K 2Y1	Tim Hortons Inc.
L6K 3C7	Frank's Food Basics
L6K 3P1	Appleby College
L6K 3S4	Halton Region Media Group
L6K 3V3	Open Solutions Canada
L6K 3V7	Pethealth Inc.

L6K 3W4	1561716 Ontario Ltd.
	Lee Rocca Forming Ltd.
L6K 3W6	Ian Martin Group
L6K 3W7	Dufferin Construction Co.
L6L 2X4	Bot Construction Ltd.
L6L 2X5	Vac-Aero International Inc.
L6L 2X8	Acuren Group Inc.
L6L 2X9	Mancor Canada Inc.
L6L 5B3	ASECO Integrated
	Systems Ltd.
L6L 5L7	All-Connect Logistical
	Services Inc.
	Pattison Outdoor
	Advertising
L6L 5M9	Stuart Budd & Sons Ltd.
L6L 5N1	Advanced Metal
	Stamping Corp.
	Bunge Canada
	Wallace & Carey Inc.
L6L 5T7	VICWEST
L6L 5V6	Metrican Mfg. Co. Inc.
L6L 5Y7	Goodrich Aerospace
	Canada Ltd.
L6L 6M1	Caravan Logistics Inc.
	Ropak Canada Inc.
L6L 6P8	Holiday Inn Oakville @
	Bronte
L6M 2W1	Unis Lumin Inc.
L6M 3L1	Halton Regional
	Police Service
	Regional Municipality
	of Halton
L6M 4X8	Nycomed Canada Inc.
L6P 0X4	Pilen Construction of
	Canada Ltd.
L6R 3J7	William Osler Health
	System
L6S 4J3	MacDonald Dettwiler &
	Associates Inc.
L6S 4L5	Apex Motor Express Ltd.
L6S 4R5	Sun Pac Foods
L6S 5P2	Air King Ltd.
L6S 5X6	Revere Industries, LLC
L6S 5X7	Chembond
L6S 5Z6	Canadian Industrial
	Distributors Inc.
L6S 6B7	ACCO Brands Canada Inc.
	GBC Canada
L6S 6E1	Broadleaf Logistics
	Company
L6S 6G2	Sun Rich Fresh Foods Inc.
L6S 6G4	Maritime Ontario Freight
	Lines Ltd.
L6S 6H2	The DATA Group of
	Companies
L6S 6H3	Benteler Automotive
	Canada Corp.
L6S 6K7	Canamex Trucking
	System Inc.
L6T 0A5	Humber Nurseries Limited
L6T 0B2	Wild Water Kingdom Ltd.
L6T 1A1	Bacardi Canada Inc.
L6T 1A5	Matcor Automotive
L6T 1A6	Air Liquide Canada Inc.
L6T 1A7	MDF Mechanical Ltd.

L6T 1A9	Almag Aluminum Inc.
L6T 1B5	Neff Kitchen
	Manufacturing Ltd.
	W. Ralston (Canada) Inc.
L6T 1B6	Hubbert Processing
	& Sales Ltd.
L6T 1C1	General Kinetics
	Engineering Corp.
	Smart Laser Grafix
	Taro Pharmaceuticals
	Transcontinental
	Printing Inc.
	Velcro Canada Inc.
L6T 1E5	Par-Pak Ltd.
L6T 1E6	Certified Laboratories
L6T 1E9	Doellken-Woodtape Ltd.
L6T 1G1	Olymel
	Plant Products
	Company Ltd.
L6T 1G4	Acan Windows Systems Inc.
	Titan Cartage Ltd.
L6T 2H4	Beacon Transit Lines Inc.
L6T 2H7	Valle Foam Industries
	(1995) Inc.
L6T 2J5	O-I Canada Corp.
L6T 2J6	iPro Realty Inc.
L6T 3T4	T.A. Brannon Steel Ltd.
L6T 3T6	Norpak Custom Packaging
L6T 3T7	APPS Transport Group
L6T 3V1	Atlas Bearings Inc.
	Brampton Engineering Inc.
L6T 3V6	Confederation Freezers
L6T 3W1	SEW Eurodrive Company of
	Canada Ltd.
L6T 3X7	Hostmann-Steinberg Ltd.
	Packall Packaging Inc.
L6T 3Y3	apetito Canada Ltd.
L6T 3Y4	BMP Metals Inc.
	Cartier Kitchens Inc.
	Morgan Commercial
	Babcock Inc.
L6T 3Z8	Roma Fence Ltd.
L6T 4A7	Gateway Chevrolet Inc.
L6T 4B9	Regional Municipality
	of Peel
L6T 4G6	Brampton Transit
L6T 4G9	Monarch Plastics Ltd.
L6T 4H6	ABM Tool & Die Co. Ltd.
	J.J. Home Products Inc.
	Renin Corp.
L6T 4J5	Aecom
L6T 4K3	Savaria Concord Lifts Inc.
L6T 4M2	Metex Heat Treating Ltd.
	NexCycle Plastics Inc.
L6T 4P6	Iron Mountain Canada
	Corp.
L6T 4S5	Bramalea Medical Centre
	X-Ray & Ultrasound
L6T 4T2	Trusted Retail Solutions
L6T 4T5	European Quality Meats
L6T 4V2	Aluminart Products Ltd.
	L.V. Lomas Ltd.
L6T 4X3	Tilton Industries Inc.
L6T 4Y4	Sun Chemical Ltd.
L6T 4Y5	Massiv Die Form

L6T 4Y6	Allied Systems (Canada) Company
L6T 5A3	Giftcraft Ltd.
	UTI Canada
L6T 5A9	Italpasta Ltd.
L6T 5B5	Wesbell Group of Companies
L6T 5E6	Atlantis Systems International Inc.
L6T 5E7	Liberté Natural Foods Inc.
L6T 5G4	Triple M Metal
L6T 5G7	Jay Electric Ltd.
L6T 5J4	QRC Logistics Ltd.
L6T 5K5	Export Packers Company Limited
	Versacold Group - Walker Facility
L6T 5L4	Waste Management of Canada
L6T 5M1	Brita Canada Corp.
L6T 5M3	Gamma-Dynacare Medical Laboratories
L6T 5M4	Santa Maria Foods Corp.
L6T 5M8	Aquicon Construction Co. Ltd.
	AZ3 Enterprises Inc.
	Dynamic Tire Corp.
L6T 5N4	Midland Transport Ltd.
L6T 5R3	Cosma International Inc.
L6T 5R6	Van Der Graaf Inc.
L6T 5R8	Olde York Potato Chips
L6T 5S2	StackTeck Systems Ltd.
L6T 5S6	ABB Inc.
	DHL Express (Canada), Ltd.
L6T 5S8	Gesco Industries Inc.
L6T 5T6	Woodlore International Inc.
L6T 5V1	Afcan Interlink Ltd.
	Royal Containers Ltd.
L6T 5V2	E1 Entertainment
L6T 5W2	Nafta Foods & Packaging Ltd.
	Swissplas Ltd.
L6V 1C2	Frost Pontiac Buick Cadillac Ltd.
L6V 3W6	Peel Regional Police
L6V 4M8	EXP.
L6W 1L4	Greenspoon Specialty Contracting Ltd.
L6W 1T4	Graham Bros. Construction Limited
L6W 1V7	D & W Forwarders Inc.
	IG Machine & Fibres Ltd.
L6W 1V9	Speedy Transport Group Inc.
L6W 1W2	Butcher Engineering Enterprises Ltd.
L6W 2B8	Sears Liquidation Centre
L6W 3G3	Leisureworld Caregiving Centre-Tullamore
L6W 3H7	Ivers-Lee Inc.
L6W 3J3	Peel Plastic Products Ltd.
L6W 3J4	ARMTEC
L6W 3J9	Graff Concrete
L6W 3K2	Blue Giant Equipment Corp.

L6W 3K3	Crosby Canada
L6W 3K6	QBD Modular Systems Inc.
L6W 3K8	Purewood Inc.
L6W 3L2	Forbes Hewlett Transport Inc.
L6W 3L6	Brampton Public Library
L6W 3M8	Johnson Matthey Limited
L6W 3N6	Travelers Transportation Services Ltd.
L6W 3R1	Re/Max Realty Services Inc.
L6W 3R3	Dependable Truck & Tank Repairs Ltd.
L6W 4P2	Roff Logistics Inc.
L6W 4P3	Community Care Access Centre - Central West
L6W 4R2	The Taylor Group
L6W 4S1	Dicom Express
L6W 4T2	Powerade Centre
L6W 4T7	Hunter Douglas Canada Limited Partnership
L6W 4T9	Mandarin Restaurant Franchise Corp.
L6X 1A9	Georgia-Pacific Canada/ Consumer Products, Inc.
L6X 1H3	Brampton Caledon Community Living
L6X 1N9	Peel Manor Long Term Care Facility
L6X 2M3	ArcelorMittal Tubular Products Canada Inc.
L6Y 0A2	Maple Lodge Farms Ltd.
L6Y 0M1	Jarden Consumer Solutions
L6Y 0R3	Medtronic of Canada Ltd.
L6Y 4M3	North Peel Media Group
L6Y 4R2	The City of Brampton
L6Y 5A7	Holland Christian Homes Inc.
L6Y 5G8	Kaneff Group of Companies
L6Y 5S5	Loblaw Companies Limited
L6Z 1Y5	Beatty Foods Ltd.
L7A 0H2	Sun Opta Food Distribution Group Inc.
L7A 0N8	The Stevens Company Ltd.
L7A 1A4	Industrial Thermo Polymers Ltd.
L7A 1A7	A. Berger Precision Ltd.
L7A 1A8	Exel Logistics Canada Inc.
L7A 1B3	M. & P. Tool Products Inc.
L7A 1C2	VSI Inc.
L7A 1E1	Sota Glazing Inc.
L7A 1E8	Hydro One Brampton Networks Inc.
L7A 1E9	Brampton Brick Limited
L7A 1K9	Day & Ross Inc.
L7A 1L1	Itwal Ltd.
L7B 1A1	Township of King
L7B 1A3	Kingbridge Centre
L7B 1B2	K.J. Beamish Construction Co., Limited
L7B 1K5	ClubLink Corp.
	The Country Day School
	King Valley Golf Club
	Robert B. Somerville Company Ltd.

L7C 1J6	The Corporation of the Town of Caledon
L7C 2E9	Cornerstone Landscaping Ltd.
L7E 1E8	Caledon Community Services
L7E 1G6	Nesel Fast Freight Inc.
L7E 1H3	Delgant Construction Ltd.
L7E 1K1	PERI Performance Systems
L7E 1K4	MSM Transportation Inc.
L7E 1W2	Silcotech North America Inc.
L7E 2J3	ConCreate USL Ltd.
L7E 3E5	Caledon Woods Golf Club
L7E 4E3	Verdi Alliance
L7E 4E4	Sardo Foods
L7E 4G3	Premier Contractors Ltd.
L7E 5S4	Mars Canada Inc.
L7E 5S5	Husky Injection Molding Systems Ltd.
L7E 5T1	Cavalier Transportation Services Inc.
	King Nursing Home Ltd.
L7E 5T2	Multivans Inc.
L7E 5T4	James Dick Construction Ltd.
L7G 2J4	CPI Canada Inc.
L7G 4B3	Saputo Dairy Products Canada GP
L7G 4B5	Cooper-Standard Automotive Canada Ltd.
L7G 4J6	Alcoa Howmet Georgetown Casting
L7G 4R9	Georgetown Terminal Warehouses Ltd.
	Olon Industries Inc.
L7G 4S3	PL Foods Ltd.
L7G 4S7	Eagle Ridge Golf Club
	Sheridan Nurseries Limited
L7G 4X5	Mold-Masters (2007) Limited
L7G 5G2	The Town of Halton Hills
L7J 0A1	C.I.P. Group Ltd.
L7J 1S1	Superior Glove Works Ltd.
L7J 2L7	Blue Springs Golf Club
L7J 2M4	KP Building Products
L7J 2X2	Galvcast Manufacturing Inc.
L7J 2X3	Purity Life Health Products - A Sunopta Company
L7K 0E9	Caledon Ski Club Limited
L7K 3L3	Devil's Pulpit Golf Association
L7L 0A7	UPS Supply Chain Solutions Canada
L7L 0E6	The Administrative Assistants Ltd.
L7L 2A4	RHI Canada Inc.
	Sandvik Mining and Construction Canada Inc.
L7L 2Y6	Smurfit-MBI
L7L 4X4	Propak Ltd.
L7L 4X5	Gerrie Electric Wholesale Ltd.
L7L 4X7	Otis Canada Inc.

L7L 4X9	Marmon/Keystone Canada Inc.	
L7L 4Y8	O.C. Tanner Recognition Company Ltd.	
L7L 5H4	Boehringer Ingelheim (Canada) Ltd.	
L7L 5H6	Pinty's Delicious Foods Inc.	
	Trimac Transportation Limited Partnership	
L7L 5H7	Watts Water Technologies (Canada) Inc.	
L7L 5J7	Attridge Transportation Inc.	
L7L 5L1	AXYZ Automation Inc.	
	SIR Corp.	
L7L 5L4	Telecom Computer Inc.	
L7L 5L5	Presvac Systems (Burlington) Ltd.	
L7L 5M4	Gennum Corp.	
L7L 5N9	Clyde Union	
L7L 5P5	ON Semiconductor	
L7L 5R2	Tender Choice Foods Inc.	
L7L 5R5	Zip Signs Ltd.	
L7L 5S3	Hadrian Manufacturing Inc.	
L7L 5V3	Shipway Stairs Ltd.	
L7L 5V5	Gentek Building Products Ltd.	
	Hunter Amenities International Ltd.	
	Wheelabrator Canada Inc.	
L7L 5Y2	Comtek Advanced Structures Ltd.	
L7L 5Z1	CPC Pumps International Inc.	
	Eaton Electrical Group	
L7L 5Z4	John Deere Credit Inc.	
L7L 5Z9	Evertz Microsystems Ltd.	
L7L 6A9	Gerrard-Oval Strapping	
L7L 6B4	Summo Steel Corp.	
L7L 6B8	i3 Canada	
L7L 6C5	Bericap North America Inc.	
L7L 6M2	Hamsar Diversco Inc.	
L7L 6W1	First Canada/Greyhound Greyhound Canada Transportation Corp.	
L7L 6W6	WhiteHat Inc.	
L7L 6Z8	Sibley & Associates Inc.	
L7M 1A1	Community Living Burlington	
L7M 1A3	Nicholson & Cates Ltd.	
	Royal LePage Burloak Real Estate Services - Mainway	
L7M 1A6	Burlington Technologies Inc.	
	Thomson-Gordon Group Ltd.	
L7M 1A8	Bosch Rexroth Canada Corp.	
L7M 1S8	Burlington Taxi Inc.	
L7M 1T3	Shell Lubricants Canada	
L7M 1T4	Comstock Canada Ltd.	
L7N 2G4	Winroc	
L7N 3E9	Holiday Inn Burlington	
L7N 3J6	Cedar Springs Health, Racquet & Sports Club	

L7N 3M6	Sodexo Canada Ltd.
L7N 3N4	Centre for Skills Development & Training
L7N 3W7	Cogent Power Inc.
	Eclipse Colour and Imaging Corp.
L7O 5Y7	Invensys Systems Canada Inc.
L7P 1A5	Sunshine Building Maintenance Inc.
L7P 5B9	Wescam
L7R 1J4	Burlington Public Library
L7R 2E3	Cancable Inc.
L7R 2J5	Discovery Ford Sales Limited
L7R 2Y2	Halton Catholic District School Board
L7R 3V7	Nalco Canada Co.
L7R 3X5	Aldershot Landscape Contractors Ltd.
L7R 3X9	Stress-Crete King Luminaire Ltd.
L7R 3Y2	Hanson Brick Ltd.
L7R 3Y3	Pollard Windows Inc.
	Tamarack Lumber Inc.
L7R 3Y5	KPM Industries
L7R 3Y8	Fisher & Ludlow
	Laurel Steel
	Umicore Autocat Canada Corp.
L7R 3Z2	Halton District School Board
L7R 3Z6	The City of Burlington
L7R 3Z7	Burlington Hydro Inc.
L7R 4A1	Hood Packaging Corporation
L7R 4A6	Canada Centre for Inland Waters
L7R 4C2	The CUMIS Group Ltd.
L7R 4C8	CIT Group Inc.
L7R 4E2	Re/Max Garden City Realty Inc.
L7R 4L4	Voortman Cookies Ltd.
L7R 4L8	Nelson Aggregate Co.
L7R 4M2	Crossroads Christian Communications Inc.
L7R 4S6	Cogeco Cable Canada Inc.
L7S 1W6	Taylor Moving & Storage Ltd.
L7S 1W7	Joseph Brant Memorial Hospital
L7S 1Y3	Burlington Fire Department
L7T 1W9	Burlington Golf & Country Club
L7T 2M7	Aldershot Greenhouses
L7T 4A8	Etratech Inc.
L7T 4H4	Royal Botanical Gardens
L7T 4K1	IKEA Canada Ltd.
L9G 4V5	Gates Canada Inc.
L9L 1G3	Lake Scugog Lumber Company Ltd.
L9N 1H2	Inscape Corp.
L9P 1C6	Koch-Glitsch Canada LP

L9P 1R1	Castool Tooling Systems
	Pine Valley Packaging Ltd.
L9P 1R4	Wyndance Golf Club
L9R 1A1	The Corporation of the Town of New Tecumseth
L9R 1A4	Nottawasaga Inn
L9R 1E9	Community Living Association for South Simcoe
L9R 1T9	Warren Gibson Ltd.
L9R 1W7	Oetiker Ltd.
	Stevenson Memorial Hospital
L9T 0H9	Roxul Inc.
L9T 0K3	Canadian Business Machines Ltd.
L9T 0L9	Chudleigh's Ltd.
L9T 2M4	Allendale
L9T 2P7	T & R Sargent Farms Ltd.
L9T 2X7	Glencairn Golf Club
	Greystone Golf Club
L9T 2X9	Andrews' Scenic Acres
L9T 3G9	Parker Hannifin
L9T 3H5	Northstar Aerospace (Canada) Inc.
	Peter Hodge Transport Ltd.
L9T 3J2	Halton Forming Ltd.
L9T 3N7	Active Transport Inc.
L9T 4Z7	Karmax Heavy Stamping
L9T 5C4	MTB Truck & Bus Collision
L9T 5G4	Gordon Food Service
L9T 5G7	Recochem Inc.
L9T 6Y9	Sysco Milton, Inc.
L9T 6Z5	The Town of Milton
L9W 1K1	The Corporation of the Town of Orangeville
L9W 2Y8	Hockley Valley Resort Ltd.
L9W 3R1	E. Hofmann Plastics Canada Inc.
L9W 3Y3	Avalon Retirement Centre
L9W 3Z9	Direct Plastics Ltd.
L9W 5H3	Roto-Mill Services Ltd.
L9Z 1R9	Katz Group Canada Ltd.
M1B 1G8	Re/Max Rouge River Realty Inc.
M1B 1T1	Coyle Corrugated Containers Inc.
M1B 2K9	Teva Canada Limited
M1B 2T9	CTI Industries
M1B 2W3	Chester Cartage & Movers Ltd.
	Cinram International Inc.
	Solo Canada
M1B 2W4	Pauldonlam Investments Inc.
M1B 3C6	Simplicious
M1B 3V4	Mac's Convenience Stores Inc.
M1B 3W3	Skanna Systems Investigations
M1B 4Z9	Century 21 Leading Edge Realty Inc.
M1B 5K2	DDi
	Dynamic Details Canada Inc.

M1B 5K7   Board of Management
of the Toronto Zoo
M1B 5M8   HarperCollins Canada Ltd.
M1B 5N1   Aisling Discoveries Child
and Family Centre
Nor-Don Collection
Network Inc.
M1B 5N6   Weed Man Canada
M1B 5P8   Norampac/Lithotech
M1B 5R4   McAsphalt Industries Ltd.
M1B 5S1   Canadian Clothing
International Inc.
M1B 5S8   Yellow Pages Group
M1B 5V3   Rex Pak Ltd.
M1B 5V8   Omron Canada Inc.
M1B 5X6   Amphenol Canada Corp.
M1B 6A6   Myron
M1B 6J1   Metro Label Co. Ltd.
M1C 1A4   University of Toronto at
Scarborough
M1C 2J1   Tony Stacey Centre
M1C 2P5   Fernie House
M1E 1Z7   Sir Robert L. Borden
Business & Technical
Institute
M1E 2K3   Chemtura Corp.
M1E 2K4   AEP Canada Inc.
M1E 2R4   Centre for Early Learning-
West Hill
M1E 2S2   Quest Courier Services
(1996) Ltd.
M1E 4B9   Rouge Valley Health System
M1E 5E1   Seven Oaks
M1H 1H2   NS Studios
M1H 1H9   Toyota Canada Inc.
M1H 2W4   Nucro-Technics
M1H 2W9   A.G. Simpson
Automotive Inc.
M1H 2Z7   Burman & Fellows
Group Inc.
M1H 3A1   Cedarbrook Lodge Ltd.
M1H 3C4   Royal Doulton Canada Ltd.
M1H 3J3   TELUS Consumer Solutions
M1J 2H1   Marvin Starr Motors Ltd.
M1J 3H2   Scarboro Golf
& Country Club
M1J 3P4   Trilogy Long Term Care
M1K 1A5   Tubular Steel Inc.
M1K 1C6   Sun Valley Supermarket Inc.
M1K 5E3   Enbridge Gas
Distribution Inc.
M1K 5E9   Centennial College
M1K 5G4   Nelson Education Ltd.
M1L 0E2   Ina Grafton Gage Home
M1L 1E3   Broadview Foundation
M1L 1W1   Providence Healthcare
M1L 2H6   Oak Leaf Confections Co.
M1L 2L6   Scarborough Toyota
M1L 2L7   FPC Flexible
Packaging Corp.
M1L 2M5   Cosmetica Laboratories Inc.
M1L 2N1   Donway Ford Sales Ltd.
M1L 2P3   S.A. Armstrong Ltd.

M1L 3E7   West Scarborough
Neighbourhood
Community Centre
M1L 3J8   Griffith Laboratories Ltd.
M1L 3W5   Ellas Restaurant
(Scarborough) Ltd.
M1L 3Z5   Tradition Fine Foods Ltd.
M1L 4C3   Global Human Resource
Centre
M1L 4C9   Specialties Graphic
Finishers Ltd.
M1L 4J2   Metro Paper Industries Inc.
M1L 4N1   Metro News
M1L 4N3   H. Paulin & Company Ltd.
M1L 4R1   Tucker's Marketplace
Restaurant
M1L 4S6   The Mibro Group
M1L 4S8   Aviva Canada Inc.
M1L 4T7   Westbury National Show
Systems Ltd.
M1L 4W2   Marsan Foods Ltd.
M1M 1P2   Nyad Community Inc.
M1M 3T9   Bento Nouveau Ltd.
Charlie's Meat & Seafood
Supply Ltd.
M1N 2E8   Eli Lilly Canada Inc.
M1N 2G2   Variety Children's Charity
M1N 2M7   Craiglee Nursing Home Ltd.
M1P 2E3   Keilhauer
M1P 2E8   Innova Medical
Ophthalmics Inc.
M1P 2H7   Eastend Bindery Limited
M1P 2J5   Active Exhaust Corporation
M1P 2P2   Esmond Manufacturing
Falcon Fasteners Registered
M1P 2T8   Bendale Acres
M1P 2V5   The Scarborough Hospital
M1P 2V7   Leisureworld Caregiving
Centre, Rockcliffe
M1P 2W8   Roadsport Honda
M1P 2X1   Kawneer Company
Canada Ltd.
M1P 2Y6   Array Canada Inc.
M1P 2Y7   Coffee Time Donuts Inc.
M1P 2Y9   Atlantic Packaging
Products Ltd.
M1P 2Z2   Spring Knitwear Inc.
M1P 3A9   Econ-O-Pac Ltd.
Fripes Export Ltd.
Scepter Corporation
M1P 3E6   H.A. Sheldon Canada Ltd.
Shorewood Packaging
Corporation of
Canada Ltd.
M1P 3G9   Citiguard Security
Services Inc.
M1P 4P5   Scarborough Town Centre
Holdings Inc.
M1P 4R1   Pizza Nova Restaurants Ltd.
M1P 4S7   Nuco Jewellery
Products Inc.
M1P 4V6   Kennedy Lodge Nursing
Home Inc.
M1P 4X4   Catholic Cross-Cultural
Services

M1P 4Y5   Guild Electric Ltd.
M1P 5E3   Postlinx
M1R 2T5   ICOM Information &
Communications Inc.
Tippet-Richardson Ltd.
M1R 3B4   Underwriters Laboratories
of Canada
M1R 3C7   International Custom
Products Inc.
M1R 4E8   Pattison Sign Group
M1R 4G2   Reliable Bookbinders Ltd.
M1R 5B1   The Wexford Residence
Inc.
M1S 1A1   Agincourt Chrysler Inc.
Schindler Elevator Corp.
M1S 1A8   Longford International Ltd.
M1S 1B1   Umbra Ltd.
M1S 2A8   The International
Group, Inc.
M1S 3A4   M S Employment
Consultants Ltd.
M1S 3A7   Soil Engineers Ltd.
Vienna Meat Products Ltd.
M1S 3B1   C&S Auto Parts Limited
M1S 3C8   Integrated Plastics Inc.
M1S 3H7   Duvet Comfort Inc.
M1S 3J1   Electronic Imaging
Systems Corp.
Ming Pao Newspapers
(Canada) Ltd.
M1S 3L1   Innovative Vision
Marketing Inc.
M1S 3L9   Apparel Trimmings Inc.
M1S 3M7   Catelectric Inc.
NIH Enterprises Inc.
M1S 3P6   Solidwear Enterprises Ltd.
M1S 3P8   Apparel Resource
Group Inc.
M1S 3R1   Sealy Canada Ltd.
Yamaha Canada Music Ltd.
M1S 3S4   Derma Sciences Canada
Inc.
M1S 3S9   Leland Industries Inc.
M1S 3Y3   AxiSource Inc.
M1S 3Y6   The Investigators Group
Inc.
M1S 4A7   Scarborotown Chrysler
Dodge Jeep Ltd.
M1S 4B5   CTV Inc.
The Sports Network
M1S 4L4   Agincourt Infiniti Nissan
Ltd.
M1S 4L7   Trimont Manufacturing Inc.
M1S 4L9   Hogan Chevrolet Limited
M1S 4M6   Regency Apparel
Company Ltd.
M1S 4N4   SKF Canada Ltd.
M1S 4Z4   HomeLife Metro Realty Inc.
M1S 5A2   Morrison Lamothe Inc.
M1S 5G5   Centre for Information and
Community Services
M1S 5N3   Ontario Electrical
Construction Company Ltd.
M1S 5R3   NRT Technology Corp.

M1T 3G2	Delta Toronto East
M1T 3J5	Robson Enterprises Inc.
M1T 3K4	Agincourt Autohaus Inc.
M1T 3K9	Shepherd Village Inc.
M1T 3V4	Canada Law Book Inc.
	Thomson Carswell
M1V 1S8	Century 21 Percy
	Fulton Ltd.
M1V 1Z5	Owens Corning Canada Inc.
M1V 2V1	Atlas Paper Bag Co. Ltd.
M1V 2V3	Shah Trading Co. Ltd.
M1V 2W3	ActionPak
	Kobay Enstel Limited
M1V 3V5	Grandview Sales &
	Distribution Ltd.
M1V 4A9	Pinnacle Transport Ltd.
M1V 4B5	Tip Top Bindery Ltd.
M1V 4B6	Milplex Circuit
	(Canada) Inc.
	Trench Ltd.
M1V 4S9	C & T Reinforcing Steel Co.
	(1987) Limited
	D. Crupi & Sons Ltd.
	Structform
	International Ltd.
M1V 4T1	All-Weld Company Ltd.
M1V 4Y1	Exacta Precision
	Products Ltd.
M1V 5A5	Harding Display Corp.
M1V 5C3	ThyssenKrupp Elevator
	Ltd.
M1V 5J7	Ontex Clothing Inc.
M1V 5L3	Yee Hong Centre for
	Geriatric Care
M1V 5M9	Trans-Ontario Express
M1V 5P2	Powerline Plus Ltd.
M1W 2J6	Bellwood Health
	Services Inc.
	Tendercare Nursing
	Homes Ltd.
M1W 2P3	Trane Ontario/Trane
	Canada ULC
M1W 2P8	Triplewell Enterprises Ltd.
M1W 2R9	St. Paul's L'Amoreaux
	Centre
M1W 2S7	Webcom Inc.
M1W 3K4	Nucap Industries Inc.
M1W 3W6	Hooper-Holmes
	Canada Limited
	Re/Max Crossroads Realty
	Inc., Brokerage
	Scarborough
	Support Services
M1W 3Y3	Carefirst Seniors
	& Community Services
	Association
	HomeLife Gold Pacific
	Realty Inc.
M1W 3Z4	First Gulf Corp.
M1X 1A2	Protagon Display Inc.
	Vibro Acoustics
	The Williams
	Brothers Corp.

M1X 1B6	Gruven International Inc.
M1X 1B9	Durapaint Industries Ltd.
	Nienkamper Furniture &
	Accessories Inc.
M1X 1E3	Sonnenberg Industries Ltd.
M1X 1E6	AGI Traffic Technology
	Tai Foong International Ltd.
M1X 1S1	Standard Auto Wreckers
M1X 1T1	Viva Magnetics
	(Canada) Ltd.
M1X IA5	Firan Technology Group -
	Aerospace Division
M2H 2N5	Canlan Ice Sports Corp.
M2H 2N8	Toronto Community News
M2H 2S4	Tab Products of Canada, Co.
M2H 3B2	Trustwell Realty Inc.
M2H 3B4	Hobart Food Equipment
	Group Canada Inc.
	Yamaha Motor Canada Ltd.
M2H 3H9	Canadian Auto Workers
	Union
M2H 3J1	Canadian Memorial
	Chiropractic College
M2H 3M5	Family Day Care Services
M2H 3M6	Multi-Health Systems Inc.
M2H 3N5	Dell Canada Inc.
	Dell Financial Services
	Canada Ltd.
	Dyadem International Ltd.
M2H 3P7	Honda Canada Finance Inc.
M2H 3P8	Grey Power Insurance
	Brokers Inc.
M2H 3R1	ING Bank of Canada
M2H 3R6	Sony of Canada Ltd.
M2H 3S7	Symantec Corp.
M2H 3S8	Qualicom Innovations Inc.
	Sinclair-Cockburn
	Financial Group
M2H 4H2	Mailmarketing Corp.
M2J 1R4	Comcare Health Services
	iQor Canada Inc.
M2J 1S5	The Mitchell
	Partnership Inc.
	Securitas Canada Ltd.
M2J 1T1	Morrison Hershfield Ltd.
M2J 1T5	Rehab Express Inc.
M2J 2X5	Seneca College of Applied
	Arts & Technology
M2J 4A2	Universal Studios
	Canada Inc.
M2J 4G8	Coldwell Banker
	Terrequity Realty
	HomeLife New World
	Realty Inc.
M2J 4P8	Reliance Comfort Limited
	Partnership
M2J 4R1	WW Hotels Ltd.
M2J 4T1	Re/Max Hallmark
	Realty Ltd.
M2J 4V6	DBPC Group of Companies
	Primary Response Inc.
M2J 4W8	Shoppers Drug Mart/
	Pharmaprix
M2J 4Y1	Crossey Engineering Ltd.
M2J 4Y7	Total Credit Recovery Ltd.

M2J 4Z2	Dominion Colour Corp.
M2J 4Z7	Unisys Canada Inc.
M2J 4Z8	General Motors
	Financial of Canada Ltd.
	R.V. Anderson
	Associates Ltd.
M2J 5A9	Monarch Corporation
M2J 5B4	Great West Life
	Assurance Co.
	Heritage Education
	Funds Inc.
M2J 5B5	Fitness Institute
M2J 5B6	CH2M HILL Canada Limited
M2J 5C1	Ingenia Polymers Corp.
M2J 5C2	C.S.T. Consultants Inc.
	Direct Energy
	Marketing Ltd.
	Pareto Corporation
M2J 5E2	Hallmark Canada
M2J 5G2	Eastern Construction
	Company Ltd.
M2J 5H3	Universal Music
M2K 1E1	North York General Hospital
M2K 1E2	The Canadian College of
	Naturopathic Medicine
M2K 1E3	ADP Dealer Services
	Ontario
	Escar Entertainment Ltd.
	Paragon Protection Ltd.
M2K 2R8	A. Farber & Partners Inc.
M2K 2S3	Alliance One Ltd.
M2K 2S5	Vision 2000 Travel
	Group Inc.
M2L 1A2	Bob Rumball Centre
	for the Deaf
	Crescent School
M2L 1E4	Granite Club
M2M 2E8	Cummer Lodge
M2M 2G1	St. John's Rehabilitation
	Hospital
M2M 3S4	Sisters of St. Joseph Toronto
M2M 3V3	Warren Protective
	Services Ltd.
M2M 4B3	Tyndale University College
	& Seminary
M2M 4G3	Equifax Canada Inc.
M2M 4G7	Xerox Canada Inc.
M2M 4H5	Ontario Teachers' Pension
	Plan Board
M2M 4K2	AXA Insurance (Canada)
M2N 0A7	Franklin Templeton
	Investments Corp.
M2N 4Y2	Reprodux Copy Centres Ltd.
M2N 5N8	Toronto District School
	Board
M2N 5P9	DUCA Financial Services
	Credit Union Ltd.
M2N 5W9	Can-Care Health
	Services Inc.
	Central - Community Care
	Access Centre
	HMSHost
M2N 5Y7	Zylog Systems (Canada) Ltd.

M2N 6A6	Public Works & Government Services Canada
M2N 6E8	Toronto Catholic District School Board
M2N 6K1	Korea Exchange Bank of Canada
	Manpower Services Canada Limited
	SF Partnership LLP
	ThoughtCorp Systems Inc.
M2N 6K9	Intercon Security Ltd.
	Professional Engineers Ontario
M2N 6L3	Novotel Hotel North York
M2N 6L7	Capital One Services (Canada), Inc.
M2N 6L9	Financial Services Commission of Ontario
	Lowe's Canada
M2N 6N5	Canerector Inc.
	CBV Collection Services Ltd.
M2N 6P1	Warner Bros. Entertainment Canada Inc.
M2N 6P4	SMT Direct Marketing Inc.
M2N 6P6	CBI Home Health
M2N 6R8	Toronto Centre for the Arts
M2N 6S6	KRMC Barristers & Solicitors
M2N 6S7	Transcontinental Media
M2N 6S8	Nestlé Canada Inc.
M2N 6X1	CCH Canadian Ltd.
M2N 6X3	Ameresco Canada Inc.
M2N 6X7	Invesco Trimark
M2N 6Z1	Canada Mortgage and Housing Corp.
M2N 7A3	Eckler Ltd.
M2N 7C7	Assurant Solutions
M2N 7E4	Menkes Developments Ltd.
M2N 7J8	Transamerica Life Canada
M2N 7K5	H.J. Heinz Company of Canada Ltd.
M2P 1N6	Voxdata Call Centre Inc.
M2P 2A9	Smith & Andersen Consulting Engineering
M2P 2B7	Canadian Institute for Health Information
	The Wawanesa Mutual Insurance Co.
M2P 2B8	Ontario Lottery and Gaming Corp.
	SAP Canada Inc.
M2P 2C2	Somerset Entertainment Ltd.
M2P 2E9	Ideaca Knowledge Services Inc.
M2R 1Y8	Leisureworld Caregiving Centre, Cheltenham
M2R 3T4	Sanofi Pasteur Ltd.
M2R 3V2	UJA Federation of Greater Toronto
M3A 2P8	Kretschmar Inc.
M3A 2Z7	Donalda Club
M3A 3R4	Chair-Man Mills Inc.

M3B 1S9	Bernstein Health & Diet Clinics
	Tour East Holidays (Canada) Inc.
M3B 1V7	Harris Corporation
M3B 1Z2	Ontario Real Estate Association
M3B 1Z3	Standard Parking of Canada Ltd.
M3B 1Z4	Tigertel Communications
M3B 1Z6	Aditya Birla Minacs
M3B 2M3	Blizzard Courier Service Ltd.
	HomeLife Vision Realty Inc.
M3B 2R7	Garda World Security
M3B 2S6	Carl Zeiss Canada Ltd.
	Society of Composers, Authors, and Music Publishers of Canada
M3B 2S7	Greenwin Property Management Inc.
	Parkin Architects Ltd.
M3B 2T3	Prudential Sadie Moranis Realty Brokerage
M3B 2T5	Collega International Inc.
	George Kelk Corp.
	St. Joseph Pi Media
M3B 2V1	LKM
M3B 2W7	Alpha Laboratories Inc.
	Premier Operating Corp. Ltd.
M3B 2X7	National Post
M3B 3A8	Don Park LP
M3B 3H2	Prince Spa & Resort Operations Toronto Ltd.
M3B 3H9	Bayview Glen
M3B 3K9	Harlequin Enterprises Ltd.
M3B 3L1	GS1 Canada
	Rothmans, Benson & Hedges Inc.
M3B 3L6	Kraft Canada Inc.
M3B 3L7	BBM Canada
M3B 3N1	The Toronto Real Estate Board
M3B 3N6	Sherson Group
M3B 3P3	RR Donelly Ltd.
M3B 3P8	Ontario Public Service Employees Union
M3B 3P9	SciCan Ltd.
M3B 3R5	Postmedia Network Inc.
M3C 0H5	Royal LePage Signature Realty
M3C 1H7	CELESTICA Inc.
M3C 1H9	Druxy's Inc.
M3C 1J3	Toronto Don Valley Hotel & Suites
M3C 1J5	Surex Community Services
M3C 1L9	Janssen Inc.
M3C 1M1	Grand & Toy Ltd.
M3C 1T3	Ontario Science Centre
M3C 1T9	Foresters
M3C 1V6	Tilley Endurables Inc.
M3C 1W3	Colgate-Palmolive Canada Inc.
	Morneau Sobeco Shepell·fgi

M3C 2J6	Angus Consulting Management Ltd.
	H.H. Angus & Associates Ltd.
	Wynford
M3C 2J9	CFA Communications Ltd.
M3C 2K1	Wrigley Canada
M3C 2K8	Four Seasons Hotels Limited
M3C 2T8	Pearson Education Canada Inc.
M3C 3E5	Cision Canada Inc.
	G4S Cash Solutions (Canada) Ltd.
	ICICI Bank Canada
M3C 3E9	Devry Smith & Frank LLP
	Philips Lifeline
M3C 3G8	CPAS Systems Inc.
	Dundas Data Visualization
	Infor Global Solutions
M3C 3L4	McDonald's Restaurants of Canada Limited
M3C 3N6	McKesson Specialty
M3C 3N7	Masterfile Corp.
M3C 3R8	ESRI Canada Limited
M3C 4H9	Home Depot Canada
M3C 4J2	Business Information Group
M3H 2V2	Management Systems Resources Inc.
M3H 3N2	Nortown Electrical Contractors Ltd.
M3H 5R9	Toronto Emergency Medical Services
M3H 5S7	Highland Farms Inc.
M3H 5S9	Del Property Management Inc.
	Tridel Corp.
M3H 5T6	University of Toronto Institute for Aerospace Studies
M3H 5Y4	Sutton Group - Admiral Realty Inc.
M3H 5Y9	Circle of Home Care Services (Toronto)
M3J 1M7	Paragon Health Care (Ontario) Inc.
M3J 1M8	University Plumbing & Heating Ltd.
M3J 1P3	Osgoode Hall Law School
	York University
M3J 1Y8	Beta-Calco Inc.
M3J 1Y9	Omni Facility Services Canada Limited
M3J 1Z4	Spring Air Sommer Corp.
M3J 1Z9	Abram's Towing Services Ltd.
M3J 2A3	Alros Products Ltd.
M3J 2A4	Nino D'Aversa Bakery Ltd.
M3J 2A9	VitaFoam Products Canada Ltd.
M3J 2B1	Progress Packaging Ltd.
M3J 2B5	Party Packagers
M3J 2B7	The Plan Group
M3J 2B9	Globe Spring
M3J 2C5	Formglas Inc.

M3J 2C6	Meta Centre for the Developmentally Disabled
M3J 2E2	Canadian Food Inspection Agency
M3J 2E8	Open Window Health Bread Bakery Limited
M3J 2H2	Blue Star Investigations & Security Inc.
M3J 2J5	Teknion Corp.
M3J 2J6	RT Recycling Technology Inc.
M3J 2J7	Global File Inc.
M3J 2K3	Ampere Limited
M3J 2K8	Superior Pool Spa & Leisure Ltd.
M3J 2L6	Columbia Building Maintenance Co. Ltd.
M3J 2M4	Beltone Electronics of Canada Ltd.
M3J 2M6	Global Upholstery Company Inc.
M3J 2M9	Tri-Con Concrete Finishing Co. Ltd.
M3J 2N2	The Hughes Group
M3J 2N7	Upper Crust Ltd.
M3J 2P1	Miratel Solutions Inc.
M3J 2P3	Black Creek Pioneer Village
M3J 2P4	Libman Manufacturing Ltd.
M3J 2R1	Talmolder Inc.
M3J 2S3	Dalton Chemical Laboratories Inc.
M3J 2T4	Zodiac Swim School Limited
M3J 2W4	Montecassino Hospitality Group Inc.
M3J 2W6	Dorvict Resource & Consulting Centre Inc.
M3J 2X1	Timothy's Coffees of the World Inc.
M3J 2X8	Global Contract Inc. Stamptek
M3J 2Z6	Johnvince Foods
M3J 3A7	Caulfeild Apparel Group Ltd.
M3J 3C6	Downsview Chrysler Plymouth (1964) Ltd.
M3J 3E5	Tectrol Inc.
M3J 3G5	Imperial Coffee Services Inc. Town Shoes Ltd.
M3J 3J9	Canadian Custom Packaging Co.
M3J 3K1	Computer Methods International Corp.
M3K 1E8	Griffen Manimpex Ltd. Picadilly Fashions Seven Continents Corporation
M3K 1G2	Coco Paving Inc.
M3K 1G4	FedEx Freight Canada
M3K 1N4	H & R Developments H & R Property Management Ltd.
M3K 1T2	Teskey Concrete & Construction Company Ltd.
M3K 1Y5	Bombardier Aerospace
M3K 2A5	FlightSafety Canada Ltd.
M3K 2C1	DYN Exports Inc.
M3L 1G5	Commercial Bakeries Corp. Ingenico Canada Ltd.
M3M 1A8	The Oakdale Golf & Country Club Ltd.
M3M 3G3	Universal Workers Union Local 183
M3N 1S4	Toronto and Region Conservation Authority
M3N 1V9	Crown Food Service Equipment Ltd.
M3N 1W2	BIC Inc.
M3N 1W6	Shade-O-Matic
M3N 1W7	Metro Protective Services
M3N 1W8	HTS Engineering Ltd.
M3N 1X6	Centennial Optical Limited
M3T 2W6	TDM Technical Services
M4A 1B4	Select Food Products Ltd.
M4A 1C5	Shoppers HomeHealthCare
M4A 1E6	A Towing Service Ltd. Stacey Electric Company Ltd.
M4A 1J6	Parkway Automotive Sales Ltd.
M4A 1X3	Conros Corporation
M4A 1X4	Ainsworth Inc.
M4A 2K7	Astley Gilbert Limited Bellwyck Packaging Solutions
M4A 2P2	Mulvey & Banani International Inc.
M4A 2P3	Ontario Secondary School Teachers Federation
M4A 2S6	Beck Taxi Ltd.
M4A 2T7	Freeman Formalwear Limited
M4B 1M5	St. Clair O'Connor Community Inc.
M4B 1Y2	Schneider Canada Inc.
M4B 1Y7	Strataflex Canada Corp.
M4B 3H2	Allanson International Inc.
M4B 3H3	A1 Label
M4B 3H6	Ace Painting & Decorating Co. Inc.
M4B 3P2	H.A. Kidd and Company Limited
M4B 3P4	Access Care Inc.
M4C 1K3	A-Way Express Courier Service
M4C 1K4	HomeLife Cimerman Real Estate Ltd.
M4C 1N2	Neighbourhood Link Support Services
M4C 3E7	Toronto East General
M4C 5M8	True Davidson Acres Home for the Aged
M4C 5R6	Tobias House Attendant Care Inc.
M4C 5T2	Community Care - East York
M4E 0A2	Mindshare Canada
M4E 2V6	Main Street Terrace
M4E 3A8	Elliott Family Care Limited
M4G 1C7	Integracare Inc.
M4G 1G2	Canada Catering Company Ltd.
M4G 1R8	Holland Bloorview Kids Rehab
M4G 2B9	Lincoln Electric Company of Canada
M4G 2G6	Dorothea Knitting Mills Ltd.
M4G 3B3	Sport Swap Inc.
M4G 3C1	Re/Max Ultimate Realty Inc.
M4G 3E8	The Canadian National Institute for the Blind/ Ontario Div.
M4G 3V6	Del Equipment Limited
M4G 3W9	St Marys Cement Group
M4G 4C9	Mercedes-Benz Canada Inc.
M4G 4H7	Davis + Henderson
M4H 1A4	Crystal Claire Cosmetics Inc. Ontario March of Dimes
M4H 1B6	Add Ink
M4H 1B8	Coca-Cola Bottling Company
M4H 1E5	Solarfective Products Limited
M4H 1G7	Tremco Canada Division
M4H 1G8	Lundstrom
M4H 1H2	Bee-Clean Corvin Building Maintenance Ltd.
M4H 1P1	Mount Pleasant Group of Cemeteries
M4H 1P4	The Governing Council of the Salvation Army in Canada
M4J 1L2	Amphora Maintenance Systems Woodgreen Community Services
M4J 1N4	Apollo 8 Maintenance Services Inc.
M4J 5B5	Maple Leaf Taxi-Cab Ltd.
M4K 1N8	Big Carrot Natural Food Market
M4K 2P8	Albany Medical Clinic
M4K 3S7	Nisbet Lodge
M4L 1G1	Security Management Services
M4L 1J4	Lick's Concepts Inc.
M4M 1G4	Mijo Corp.
M4M 1H8	Baird MacGregor Insurance Brokers LP
M4M 1L6	Heritage Nursing Homes Inc.
M4M 2B5	Bridgepoint Health
M4M 2M3	TD Financing Services
M4M 2R6	WoodGreen Red Door Family Shelter
M4M 2T4	Accolade Group Inc.
M4M 3H3	T4G Limited
M4M 3M3	Urbacon Ltd.
M4N 1T7	The Toronto French School
M4N 2W3	Rosedale Golf Club

M4N 3M5	The Estates of Sunnybrook Institute for Clinical Evaluative Sciences
	Sunnybrook Health Sciences Centre
M4N 3M7	Goway Travel Ltd.
M4P 1A4	Everest College
M4P 1E4	Halsall Associates Ltd.
	Heart and Stroke Foundation of Ontario
	Ontario Energy Board
	RioCan Real Estate Investment Trust
	SWI Systemware Inc.
M4P 1G8	LaBrash Security Services Ltd.
M4P 1K5	Canpark Services Ltd.
M4P 1K8	Certified General Accountants of Ontario
M4P 2C9	Procom Consultants Group Ltd.
M4P 2E5	Opinion Search Inc.
M4P 2E7	Oliver & Bonacini Restaurants
M4P 2J6	Sporting Life Inc.
M4P 2V8	Canadian Tire Corporation Ltd.
M4P 3A1	Lifemark Health
	Walker Information Canada
M4P 3A4	The Last Minute Experts Inc.
	Thomas Cook North America Wholesale Travel Group
M4P 3C2	Draft FCB Canada
M4R 1K8	Cornerstone Group of Companies Limited
	RioCan Yonge Eglinton Centre
M4S 1A1	Senior Peoples Resources In North Toronto Inc.
M4S 1A9	Bosley Real Estate Ltd., Brokerage
M4S 1Y5	Cryptologic Inc.
M4S 1Z2	Toronto Transit Commission
M4S 2A7	Art Shoppe Limited
M4S 2B5	Minto Communities Toronto Inc.
M4S 2N4	Wells Gordon Limited
M4S 3C3	T.E.S. Contract Services Inc.
M4T 1C1	YWCA of Toronto
M4T 1M4	Statistics Canada
M4T 1W1	New York Fries/South St. Burger Co.
M4T 1W2	Archdiocese of Toronto
M4T 1X3	Chestnut Park Real Estate Ltd.
	Jonview Canada Inc.
M4T 1Z6	New Balance Toronto
M4T 2T1	TVO
M4T 2T5	Soberman LLP
M4T 2Y9	Cineplex Entertainment LP
M4V 1K6	The Badminton & Racquet Club of Toronto

M4V 1K7	Padulo Integrated Inc.
M4V 1K9	HomEquity Bank
M4V 1L5	Astral Media Outdoor
M4V 1L6	Astral Media Radio
M4V 1M2	Seniors 4 Seniors
M4V 1N6	Medisys Health Group Inc.
	Page + Steele Architects
M4V 1N7	Desjardins Financial Security Life Assurance Company - Toronto
M4V 1T3	Canadian Mothercraft Society
M4V 1W6	Upper Canada College
M4V 1X2	The Bishop Strachan School
M4V 2G6	Bradgate Arms Retirement Residence
M4V 2G7	The Kalen Group
M4V 2J1	Brown Community Centre
M4V 2Y7	AOL Canada Inc.
	Canadian Cancer Society Ontario Division
M4V 3A2	Maple Leaf Foods Inc.
M4V 3B5	Plan International Canada Inc.
M4W 1A7	Toronto Marriott Bloor Yorkville
M4W 1A8	Black & McDonald Ltd.
	Citco (Canada) Inc.
	Knightsbridge Human Capital Management Inc.
	Meyers Norris Penny LLP
	Spectrum Health Care
M4W 1B3	Institute of Chartered Accountants of Ontario
M4W 1B9	Ipsos Reid Corp.
M4W 1E5	Manulife Financial
M4W 1G9	Rogers Communications Inc.
	Rogers Publishing
M4W 1J2	Young & Rubicam Ltd.
M4W 1N4	Branksome Hall
M4W 2G8	Toronto Public Library
M4W 2H2	K.W. Mann Inc.
	Toronto Community Housing Corp.
M4W 3B8	Gap Inc. Canada
	Holt Renfrew & Company Ltd.
	Randstad Technologies
	Wunderman
M4W 3C7	Veterinary Emergency Clinic and Referral Centre
M4W 3E2	Global Knowledge
M4W 3H1	Environics Research Group Ltd.
M4W 3H8	TNS Canadian Facts
M4W 3K3	Ronald A. Chisholm Ltd.
M4W 3L4	Goodwill Toronto
M4W 3M2	Young Rosedale Charitable Foundation
M4W 3P7	Hill & Knowlton Canada Inc.
	J. Walter Thompson Company Ltd.
M4W 3R2	Unilever Canada Inc.

M4W 3R6	BBDO Canada Inc.
M4W 3R8	Canada Colors & Chemicals Ltd.
	Canadian Real Estate Investment Trust
	Multiple Sclerosis Society of Canada
	NORR Ltd.
M4W 3R9	Klick Communications Inc.
	Leo Burnett Company Ltd.
	Starcom Worldwide
M4W 3S7	mediaedge:cia
M4W 3T4	DDB Canada
M4W 3T6	Towers Watson
M4W 3V1	William Ashley Ltd.
M4W 3Y7	Amdocs Canada
M4X 1K6	Fudger House
M4Y 1C6	The Catholic Children's Aid Society of Toronto
M4Y 1N1	Car Park Management Services Ltd.
	Children's Aid Society of Toronto
M4Y 1P1	Il Fornello Restaurants Ltd.
M4Y 1S2	Ontario Trillium Foundation
M4Y 1T4	YMCA of Greater Toronto
M4Y 1X7	Courtyard By Marriott Downtown Toronto
M4Y 2G1	Alliance of Canadian Cinema, Television & Radio Artists
M4Y 2G5	The Salvation Army Toronto Grace Health Centre
M4Y 2G6	The National Ballet School
M4Y 2H4	The Hincks-Dellcrest Centre
M4Y 2H9	Pizza Pizza Ltd.
M4Y 2W8	University of Toronto Press Inc.
M4Y 2X9	Turning Point Youth Services
M4Y 3A1	Rogers Sportsnet Inc.
M4Y 3B7	Rogers Media Inc.
M4Y 3G2	The General Synod of the Anglican Church of Canada
M5A 0B5	CFNY FM 102.1
	Corus Entertainment Inc.
	Q107 FM
	W Network Inc.
M5A 1A2	Intelligarde International Inc.
M5A 1A4	McGregor Industries Inc.
M5A 1A6	United Rentals of Canada Inc.
M5A 1B4	Imperial Parking Canada Corp.
M5A 1E1	Infinium Capital Corp.
M5A 1E8	Canadian Opera Company
M5A 1G1	Downtown Fine Cars Inc.
M5A 1J7	Autodesk Canada
M5A 1K7	SAS Institute (Canada) Inc.
M5A 1K8	Capital C Communications Inc.

M5A 1P4	Arc Productions Animation & Visual Effects
	MetCap Living Management Inc.
M5A 1R4	The Messengers International
M5A 1R7	Systematix Inc.
M5A 1S1	Fred Victor Centre
	Shaftesbury Films
M5A 2N4	Radke Films
M5A 2S3	The Drs. Paul & John Rekai Centre
M5A 2V1	Technicolor
M5A 3J7	Dixon Hall
M5A 3L2	Turtle Island Recycling Company Inc.
M5A 3R7	Watt International Inc.
M5A 3S1	Cimco Refrigeration
M5A 3S5	Unicco Facility Services Canada Co.
M5A 3X5	Canoe Inc.
	Sun Media Corp.
M5A 3Y5	The Guvernment
M5A 4G8	Vistek Ltd.
M5A 4L3	Ontario Lung Association
M5A 4R6	Hilton Garden Inn Toronto City Centre
M5B 1K5	Toronto Hydro Corporation
M5B 1L2	Magnum Protective Services Ltd.
M5B 1M4	The Elgin & Winter Garden Theatre Centre
M5B 1N8	HRC Canada Inc.
M5B 1T8	Youthdale Treatment Centres Ltd.
M5B 1W8	St. Michael's Hospital
M5B 1Y7	Now Communications Inc.
M5B 2C3	Sears Canada Inc.
M5B 2E7	Carecor Health Services Ltd.
	Collectcorp Inc.
M5B 2E9	Holiday Inn Toronto Downtown Centre
M5B 2G3	Best Western Primrose Hotel
M5B 2H1	The People Bank
	Sephora
M5B 2K3	Ryerson University
M5B 2K6	Homes First Society
M5B 2L7	The Boiler Inspection & Insurance Company of Canada
	CGI Group Inc.
	Continental Casualty Company
	Lawyers Professional Indemnity Co.
	TIC Travel Insurance Coordinators Ltd.
M5B 2M8	BMO Guardian Group of Funds Ltd.
M5B 2P3	Covenant House Toronto
M5B 9G9	The Second City
M5C 1E9	Le Méridien King Edward

M5C 1H6	Datarush Courier
M5C 1L8	Incorporated Synod of the Diocese of Toronto
M5C 1N2	Cambridge Suites Hotel Toronto
M5C 1R5	Toronto Parking Authority
M5C 1S2	Publicis Inc.
	Toronto Life Publishing Ltd.
	Zenith Optimedia Canada Inc.
M5C 1T6	Jones, Gable & Company Limited
M5C 2C5	BDO Canada LLP
	Exchange Solutions Inc.
M5C 2G1	Commissionaires Great Lakes
M5C 2G5	Henry's
M5C 2L9	The Canadian Press
M5C 2T6	Constellation Software Inc.
M5C 2V9	Chubb Insurance Company of Canada
	Dundee Wealth
	Hudbay Minerals Inc.
M5C 2W1	Travelex Canada Ltd.
M5C 2W4	Morningstar Research Inc.
	Norbord Inc.
M5C 2W7	Industry Canada - Ontario Region
	Marcus Evans
	Torkin Manes LLP
M5C 2Z2	Colliers Macaulay Nicolls Inc.
M5C 3B2	Healthcare of Ontario Pension Plan
M5C 3E4	Verizon Business
M5C 3G5	Blaney McMurtry LLP
M5C 3G6	State Street Trust Company Canada
M5C 3G7	Assante Wealth Management
	CI Fund Management Inc.
	Deloitte & Touche LLP
M5C 3G9	International Financial Data Services (Canada) Ltd.
M5C 3H1	Dundee Realty Management Corp.
M5E 1A3	Redpath Sugar Ltd.
M5E 1A4	Liquor Control Board of Ontario
M5E 1A6	Esplanade Restaurants Ltd.
M5E 1A7	Nexus Protective Services Ltd.
M5E 1B3	Trancontinental Interactive
M5E 1B4	St. Lawrence Centre for the Arts
M5E 1E5	Hidi Rae Consulting Engineers Inc.
	Ontario Clean Water Agency
M5E 1E6	Toronto Star Newspapers Ltd.
M5E 1G4	Altus Group Ltd.
M5E 1G6	Canopco
M5E 1K3	Vinci Parking Services
M5E 1L5	Royal & Sun Alliance Insurance Company of Canada

M5E 1S2	Novator Systems Ltd.
	Pitney Bowes Business Insights
M5E 1S9	Cushman & Wakefield Ltd.
M5E 1T3	Hot House Cafe
M5E 1W1	Canadian Apartment Properties Real Estate Investment Trust
M5E 1W2	Novotel Toronto Centre
M5E 1W9	United Way of Greater Toronto
M5E 1X6	Ogilvy & Mather (Canada) Ltd.
M5E 1X8	Hockey Hall of Fame
M5G 0A1	Intact Financial Corporation
M5G 0A2	Belair Insurance Company Inc.
M5G 1G7	Brydson Group Ltd.
M5G 1L7	Innovation Institute of Ontario
M5G 1R3	Metropolitan Hotel Toronto
M5G 1R7	Sim, Lowman, Ashton & McKay LLP
M5G 1R8	The Canada Life Assurance Co.
M5G 1S7	Zurich North America Canada
M5G 1V2	Elementary Teachers' Federation of Ontario
M5G 1X5	Mount Sinai Hospital
	Samuel Lunenfeld Research Institute of Mount Sinai Hospital
M5G 1X6	Ontario Power Generation Inc.
M5G 1X8	The Hospital for Sick Children
M5G 1Y7	Industrial Alliance Insurance & Financial Services Inc.
M5G 1Y8	Kids Help Phone
	Luminex Molecular Diagnostics Inc.
M5G 1Z1	MediaCom Canada
M5G 1Z3	H & M Hennes & Mauritz Inc.
	Ontario Financing Authority
M5G 1Z8	Investigation Services Ltd.
M5G 2A2	Toronto Rehabilitation Institute
M5G 2C3	Best Buy Canada
M5G 2C4	University Health Network
M5G 2C8	Insurance Bureau of Canada
	Meridian Credit Union
M5G 2E2	College of Physicians and Surgeons of Ontario
M5G 2E3	Hunter Keilty Muntz & Beatty Ltd.
M5G 2E9	Institute for Work & Health
M5G 2H1	Legal Aid Ontario

M5G 2H4	B + H Architects
M5G 2J3	Toronto Police Service
M5G 2L1	Loyalty One Inc.
M5G 2L2	Toronto Marriott Downtown Eaton Centre
M5G 2L3	Sick Kids Foundation
M5G 2L5	Ontario Realty Corporation
M5G 2L7	Cancer Care Ontario
M5G 2L9	Dutton Brock LLP
M5G 2M1	Canadian Blood Services
M5G 2N4	Multiple Retirement Services Inc.
M5G 2N6	Alcohol & Gaming Commission of Ontario
M5G 2N7	Fidelity Investments Canada ULC
M5G 2P5	Hydro One Networks Inc.
M5G 2R4	Synovate Canada Ltd.
M5G 2R5	Canadian Diabetes Association
M5H 1H1	Bank of Nova Scotia Roynat Inc. Scotiabank - Wealth Management Scotia Life Insurance Company
M5H 1J8	Accenture Inc. CB Richard Ellis Limited Desjardins Securities GMP Securities LP Home Trust Co. McLean Budden Ltd. Willis Canada Inc.
M5H 1J9	AON Benfield Canada ULC Bank of Canada Lundin Mining Corp. Sun Life Assurance Company of Canada Swiss Reinsurance Co. Canada
M5H 1K5	Toronto Symphony Orchestra
M5H 1P9	Lombard Canada Ltd.
M5H 1S4	Quick Messenger Services Ontario Ltd.
M5H 1T1	EMC Corporation of Canada
M5H 1W2	Thomson Rogers
M5H 1X9	KOEI Canada Inc.
M5H 1Z5	OMD Canada
M5H 2A3	Shopsy's Downtown
M5H 2C9	Canadian Depository for Securities Ltd. Keith Bagg Staffing Resources Inc.
M5H 2K4	Beard Winter LLP
M5H 2L2	Hilton Toronto
M5H 2M9	Starwood Canada Corp.
M5H 2N2	The City of Toronto
M5H 2N6	The Law Society of Upper Canada
M5H 2R1	The National Club
M5H 2R2	Pacific Rubiales Energy Corp. Thomson Reuters

M5H 2S5	KPMG LLP
M5H 2S7	Goodlaw Services Limited Partnership
M5H 2T4	Heenan Blaikie LLP
M5H 2T6	Fasken Martineau DuMoulin LLP
M5H 2Y2	Munich Life Management Corp Ltd. Munich Reinsurance Company of Canada
M5H 2Y4	DTZ Barnicke Hudson's Bay Company Iamgold Corp.
M5H 3B7	Fujitsu Consulting (Canada) Inc.
M5H 3B9	The Dominion of Canada General Insurance Co.
M5H 3C2	Cassels Brock & Blackwell LLP
M5H 3C6	Capgemini Canada Inc.
M5H 3E5	Shibley Righton LLP
M5H 3K6	Cambridge Group of Clubs
M5H 3M7	Enwave Energy Corporation GCAN Insurance Co.
M5H 3P5	B2B Trust Lenczner Slaght Royce Smith Griffin LLP Lerners LLP
M5H 3R3	The Daniels Group Inc. Koskie Minsky Travelers Guarantee Company of Canada Travelers Insurance
M5H 3R4	The Cadillac Fairview Corp. Limited
M5H 3S1	Miller Thomson LLP
M5H 3S5	Information Builders (Canada) Inc. The Medcan Clinic Sierra Systems Group Inc.
M5H 3S8	Ontario Securities Commission
M5H 3T4	MCAP Commercial Limited Partnership RSM Richter LLP
M5H 3T9	Business Development Bank of Canada Investment Industry Regulatory Organization of Canada Mutual Fund Dealers Association of Canada
M5H 3X6	Ontario Pension Board
M5H 3X7	Hay Group Ltd.
M5H 3Y2	Bereskin & Parr Gardiner Roberts LLP VISA Canada Corporation
M5H 3Y4	Borden Ladner Gervais LLP
M5H 3Z4	UBS Bank (Canada)
M5H 4A6	CIBC Mellon
M5H 4A9	Dundee Corporation
M5H 4G2	Minden Gross LLP
M5J 1A6	The Westin Harbour Castle

M5J 1A7	Bell Sympatico GeoSoft Inc. Halcrow Yolles Labatt Breweries of Canada Mariposa Cruise Line Ltd. Tourism Toronto
M5J 1B7	Toronto Port Authority
M5J 1E3	The Fairmont Royal York
M5J 1H8	Chartis Insurance Company of Canada
M5J 1R7	Sigma Global Solutions Sigma Systems
M5J 1S7	World Travel Protection Canada Inc.
M5J 1S9	HSBC Bank Canada HSBC Securities (Canada) Inc.
M5J 1T1	Redcliff Realty Management Inc.
M5J 1V6	First National Financial Corp.
M5J 2G4	Re/Max Condos Plus Corp., Brokerage
M5J 2G8	Harbourfront Centre
M5J 2H5	The Corporation of Massey Hall and Roy Thomson Hall
M5J 2H7	Bentall Kennedy LP
M5J 2J2	Cormark Securities Inc. JP Morgan Chase Bank, N.A. Oxford Properties Group Inc.
M5J 2J5	RBC Financial Group
M5J 2K2	Vale Inco Limited
M5J 2L2	Maple Leaf Sports & Entertainment Ltd.
M5J 2L6	Joe Badali's Piazza On Front Inc. MCW Consultants Ltd.
M5J 2L7	Optima Communications International Inc.
M5J 2M2	Crawford & Company (Canada) Inc. Teranet Inc.
M5J 2M3	Citi Cards Canada
M5J 2M4	Integrated Asset Management Corp.
M5J 2N5	Radisson Admiral Hotel
M5J 2N8	CNW Group
M5J 2N9	Aon Reed Stenhouse Inc.
M5J 2P1	Kelly Services (Canada) Ltd. Ontario Municipal Employees Retirement System
M5J 2P9	Grant Thornton LLP
M5J 2R2	Ivanhoe Cambridge
M5J 2R8	Adecco Employment Services Limited Modis
M5J 2S1	Barrick Gold Corp. Canaccord Capital Corp. Onex Corp.
M5J 2S3	MacLaren McCann
M5J 2S4	Marsh Canada Limited
M5J 2S5	Mercer (Canada) Limited

M5J 2S8	CIBC World Markets Inc.	M5M 3X4	Pusateri's Ltd.	M5T 1G6	Sing Tao Daily
M5J 2T2	TD Asset Management Inc.	M5M 4B2	Harvey Kalles,	M5T 1J7	Mon Sheong Home
M5J 2T3	Astral Television Networks		Real Estate Ltd.		for the Aged
	Baker & McKenzie LLP	M5N 2H9	Havergal College	M5T 1V4	The Michener Institute for
	The Boston Consulting	M5N 3A5	Forest Hill Place		Applied Health Sciences
	Group of Canada Ltd.	M5P 2W3	Forest Hill Real Estate Inc.	M5T 1W1	Ontario College
	BPO Properties Ltd.		Brokerage		of Art & Design
	Brookfield Power	M5P 2X9	Cedarvale Terrace	M5T 1W6	Silverstein's Bakery Ltd.
	Cisco Systems Canada Co.		Nursing Home	M5T 2C6	Algorithmics Inc.
	Fraser Papers Inc.	M5P 3K3	Beth Tzedec	M5T 2C7	Eva's Initiatives
	Liberty International		Congregation Inc.	M5T 2S6	Cavalluzzo Hayes Shilton
	Underwriters Canada	M5P 3K9	Holy Blossom Temple		McIntyre & Cornish LLP
	Macquarie Capital Markets	M5P 3M6	Forest Hill Tutoring	M5T 2T9	George Brown College
	Canada Ltd.	M5R 1K6	Sutton Group		of Applied Arts and
	Macquarie Private Wealth		- Associates Realty Inc.		Technology
	McMillan	M5R 1R1	The Toronto Aged Men's	M5T 2Z5	Toronto Central Community
	OfficeTeam		and Women's Homes		Care Access Centre
	Robert Half Canada Inc.	M5R 2A9	Cyberplex Inc.	M5V 1A1	Porter Airlines Inc.
M5J 2T9	Aird & Berlis LLP		Pollara Inc.	M5V 1A3	Rogers Media Television
M5J 2V5	ACE INA Insurance		The Princeton Review	M5V 1B6	Anewtex Inc.
	Kinross Gold Corp.		Canada		Spin Master Ltd.
	TELUS Business Solutions	M5R 2E3	MDC Partners Inc.	M5V 1C2	Nygard International Ltd.
M5J 2V7	The Kitchen Table Inc.	M5R 2E5	Hakim Optical	M5V 1E3	Bensimon Byrne
M5J 2V8	Merrill Lynch Canada Inc.		Laboratory Ltd.		Herman Miller Canada Inc.
M5J 2W3	Metrolinx	M5R 2E8	Park Hyatt Toronto	M5V 1E7	Adamson Associates
M5J 2W7	RBC Dominion Securities	M5R 2L8	Royal Canadian Yacht Club		Architects
	Inc.	M5R 2S1	Village Manor (TO) Ltd.		Stantec Architecture Ltd.
M5J 2X2	Pinnacle Caterers	M5R 2S7	Community Living Toronto	M5V 1E9	Taxi Canada Inc.
M5J 2Y1	Computershare Canada	M5R 2V3	Canadian Hearing Society	M5V 1J1	The Rogers Centre
M5J 2Z4	Ogilvy Renault	M5R 3B5	Royal St. George's College		Toronto Blue Jays
M5J 2Z9	Fogler, Rubinoff LLP	M5R 3G5	Vermont Square Nursing		Baseball Club
M5J 3A5	RPM Technologies Corp.		Home	M5V 1J2	Kuwabara Payne McKenna
	Toronto Terminals Railway	M5R 3H4	Wertex Hosiery Inc.		Blumberg Architects
	Company Ltd.	M5R 3H8	The Printing House Ltd.		Mirvish Productions
M5K 0A1	Fraser Milner Casgrain LLP	M5R 3P1	College of Nurses of Ontario	M5V 1J3	TicketMaster Canada LP
M5K 1A2	TD Bank Financial Group	M5S 0A1	Ontario College of Teachers	M5V 1J4	Renaissance Toronto Hotel
	TD Securities Inc.	M5S 1A1	University of Toronto		Downtown
M5K 1B7	Fairmont Hotels	M5S 1K7	Victoria University	M5V 1J9	Hachette Distribution
	& Resorts Inc.	M5S 1K9	McKinsey & Company		Services Retail North
M5K 1E6	McCarthy Tetrault	M5S 1M2	Harry Rosen Inc.		America
M5K 1E9	AGF Management Ltd.		Realstar Management		HRG North America
M5K 1G8	PricewaterhouseCoopers	M5S 1N5	Estee Lauder Cosmetics Ltd.		Hyatt Regency Toronto
	LLP	M5S 1P7	Club Monaco Corp.		The Score Television
M5K 1H1	Dickinson Wright LLP	M5S 1S4	We Care Home Health		Network Ltd.
M5K 1H6	Egan LLP		Services - Toronto	M5V 1K2	Mountain Equipment
M5K 1J3	Delta Hotels Limited	M5S 1T8	InterContinental Toronto		Cooperative
	Q9 Networks Inc.		- Yorkville	M5V 1K4	Presidents Choice Financial
M5K 1J7	Ernst & Young LLP	M5S 1W2	The Royal Conservatory	M5V 1L7	Cossette Communication
M5K 1K8	Hicks Morley Hamilton		of Music		Group
	Stewart Storie LLP	M5S 1X8	Academy of Design	M5V 1L8	Indigo Books & Music, Inc.
M5K 1N2	Torys LLP	M5S 2A2	The Sutton Place Hotel	M5V 1P8	James Moto Enterprises Inc.
M5L 1A2	Canadian Imperial Bank of		Toronto	M5V 1R7	Diamond and Schmitt
	Commerce	M5S 2B1	GenX Inc.		Architects Inc.
M5L 1A9	Blake, Cassels & Graydon	M5S 2B4	FirstService Corp.	M5V 1R9	Brunico Communication
	LLP	M5S 2C2	Surrey Place Centre		Ltd.
M5L 1E8	Guardian Capital Group Ltd.	M5S 2C6	Royal Ontario Museum	M5V 1S7	Westdale Construction
M5L 1E9	Deutsche Bank AG/	M5S 2H1	The Scott Mission		Co. Ltd.
	Canada Branch	M5S 2L9	Kensington Health Centre	M5V 1T1	Arnold Worldwide
M5L 1G2	Mackie Research Capital	M5S 2R4	Randolph Academy for the		Sharpe Blackmore Inc.
	Corporation		Performing Arts	M5V 1V6	IBI Group
M5M 2Y4	Richtree Market	M5S 3A2	Ontario Nurses' Association		Young & Wright /
	Restaurants Inc.	M5S 3C1	Ontario Medical Association		IBI Architects
M5M 3A3	Toronto Cricket Skating and	M5S 3E7	The Windsor Arms Hotel	M5V 1X6	Outdoor Outfits Ltd.
	Curling Club	M5T 1C3	University Settlement	M5V 2B9	The Cundari Group
		M5T 1G4	Art Gallery of Ontario		

M5V 2H1	Merit Travel Group Inc.
	Travel Cuts
M5V 2H5	G.A.P Adventures Inc.
M5V 2H8	Grey Group Canada
M5V 2J6	PHD Canada
M5V 2L1	Infusion Development Corp.
M5V 2R5	Quality Meat Packers Ltd.
M5V 2S9	The Globe & Mail
	Newspaper
M5V 2T3	Hok Canada, Inc.
	Kendle Early Stage
M5V 2T6	Canada Lands Company
	Ltd.
M5V 2W6	Metro Toronto Convention
	Centre Corporation
M5V 2X2	Zeidler Partnership
	Architects
M5V 2X3	InterContinental Toronto
	Centre
M5V 2Z2	TBWA Toronto
M5V 2Z4	House & Home Media
M5V 2Z5	BNN - Business
	News Network
	The Comedy Network
M5V 3B5	NATIONAL Public
	Relations Inc.
M5V 3C7	ACI Worldwide
	(Canada) Inc.
	CSI Global Education Inc.
M5V 3G2	MTS Allstream Inc.
M5V 3H1	Buck Consultants Limited
M5V 3H2	Canadian Institute of
	Chartered Accountants
M5V 3J1	Workplace Safety and
	Insurance Board
M5V 3K1	Mackenzie Financial Corp.
M5V 3K4	The National Ballet of
	Canada
M5V 3L1	Ontario Hospital
	Association
M5V 3L2	Bank of America National
	Association/ Canada Branch
M5V 3M2	Aon Hewitt
M5V 3M9	Steam Whistle Brewing Co.
M5V 3X5	TIFF
M5V 9G9	Wayne Gretzky's
M5W 1A6	Metro Ontario Inc.
M5W 1C5	Procter & Gamble Inc.
M5W 1E6	Canadian Broadcasting
	Corp.
M5W 1P9	RBC Global Asset
	Management
M5W 2X6	Scotia Capital Inc.
M5W 4E5	Independent Electricity
	System Operator
M5W 4T9	Harry Winston Diamond
	Corporation
M5X 1A1	BMO Financial Group
M5X 1A4	Bennett Jones LLP
	News Marketing Canada
	Sentry Select Capital Corp.

M5X 1B1	CIBC Global Asset
	Management
	Davies Ward Phillips &
	Vineberg LLP
M5X 1B8	Osler Hoskin & Harcourt,
	LLP
M5X 1C1	Toronto Board of Trade
M5X 1C7	McCague Borlack LLP
M5X 1C9	Credit Suisse Securities
	(Canada), Inc.
M5X 1E1	Just Energy Group Inc.
M5X 1E3	Xstrata Canada Corporation
M5X 1E4	Russell Investments Canada
	Limited
M5X 1E5	Fundserv Inc.
	Standard & Poor's
	Credit Market Services
M5X 1G5	Gowling Lafleur Henderson
	LLP
M5X 1H3	BMO Harris Private Banking
	BMO Nesbitt Burns Inc.
M5X 1J2	TMX Group Inc.
M5X 1J5	WeirFoulds LLP
M5X 1J9	National Bank Financial Inc.
M5X 1K7	Birks & Mayors Inc.
M6A 1C3	Columbus Centre of Toronto
M6A 1J6	MukiBaum Treatment
	Centres
M6A 1M4	International Clothiers Inc.
M6A 1V5	Peto MacCallum Ltd.
M6A 1V6	Tencorr Packaging Inc.
M6A 1Z1	WASTECO
M6A 2E1	Baycrest Geriatric Health
	System
M6A 2T1	Dean Myers Chevrolet
	Corvette
M6A 2T9	The Yorkdale Rainforest
	Restaurant Inc.
M6A 2V1	Holiday Inn
	- Toronto Yorkdale
	Plaza Pontiac Buick Ltd.
M6A 2V2	Grafton-Fraser Inc.
M6A 2V6	Centura (Toronto) Ltd.
	PYA Importer Ltd.
M6A 2W1	YM Inc. Sales
M6A 2W5	Barrymore Furniture Co.
	Canadian Posters
	International Inc.
	Fenwick Automotive
	Products Ltd.
	Reilly's Security Services
M6A 2X1	Schwartz Levitsky
	Feldman LLP
M6A 3A1	IKO Industries Ltd.
	Yorkdale Shopping Centre
	Holdings Inc.
M6A 3B4	The Canadian Mental
	Health Association
	Toronto Branch
	Gemma Communications LP
M6A 3B6	Medallion Properties Inc.
	PACE Independent Living
M6B 1G7	Canada Goose
M6B 1P8	Multimedia Nova
	Corporation

M6B 1S9	Jaytex of Canada Ltd.
M6B 1V9	Jewish Vocational Service
	of Greater Toronto
M6B 2P9	Villa Colombo Homes for
	the Aged Inc.
M6B 3S7	COTA Health
M6B 3X7	Hollander Canada Home
	Fashions Limited
M6B 4A8	Olympia Tile
	International Inc.
M6B 4C4	Roots Canada Ltd.
M6B 4C5	Fybon Industries Ltd.
M6C 1B8	Skills for Change
M6E 1C2	Tre Mari Bakery Ltd.
M6E 2J7	Northwest Protection
	Services Ltd.
M6E 2X1	Montage Support Services
M6E 3P2	COSTI
M6E 5A2	Elte
M6G 3B1	The O'Neill Centre
M6G 3C3	Castleview-Wychwood
	Towers
M6G 3Z4	Christie Gardens
	Apartments and Care Inc.
M6G 3Z7	Hellenic Care for Seniors
	(Toronto) Inc.
M6J 1G1	Cross Toronto Community
	Development Corp.
M6J 1H4	Centre for Addiction and
	Mental Health
M6J 1S8	Fairview Nursing Home Ltd.
M6K 1X4	EMI Music Canada
M6K 2J2	Elm Grove Living Centre Inc.
M6K 3B9	Atlantis Pavilions
	Ontario Place Corp.
M6K 3C2	The Boulevard Club
M6K 3C3	The Board of Governors
	of Exhibition Place
	Centerplate
	Medieval Times Dinner &
	Tournament Toronto Inc.
M6K 3H7	Softchoice Corp.
M6K 3J1	Forrec Ltd.
	Fuel Advertising Inc.
M6K 3J9	The Strategic Coach Inc.
M6K 3L7	Digital Cement Inc.
M6K 3M1	Tucows Inc.
M6K 3S3	First Capital Realty Inc.
M6L 1C5	Ontario Federation for
	Cerebral Palsy
M6L 1W9	North Park Nursing
	Home Ltd.
M6L 2K5	Conseil Scolaire de District
	du Centre-Sud-Ouest
M6M 1Y6	Fabricland Distributors Inc.
	Rose E. Dee
	(International) Ltd.
M6M 2J5	West Park Healthcare
	Centre
M6M 2J7	Harold & Grace Baker
	Centre
M6M 2P5	Comda Calendar
	Gertex Hosiery Inc.
M6M 2V6	Ace Bakery Ltd.

M6M 3E7 York Marble Tile & Terrazzo Inc.

M6M 3G2 Pi Media / St Joseph's Content

M6M 4L8 The Learning Enrichment Foundation

M6M 4Y4 Irving Tissue

M6M 5G1 J&A Cleaning Solutions Ltd. Motorcade Industries Ltd.

M6N 1B6 Topper Linen Supply Ltd.

M6N 1K8 Ken Shaw Lexus Toyota

M6N 1M2 Danier Leather Inc.

M6N 1P4 Ryding-Regency Meat Packers Ltd.

M6N 1P5 St. Helens Meat Packers Ltd.

M6N 2J1 Paul Wolf Lighting & Electric Supply Ltd.

M6N 3E7 Terrazzo Mosaic & Tile Co. Ltd.

M6N 3T4 Bothwell-Accurate Co. (2006) Limited

M6N 4J6 Bernard Athletic Knit

M6N 4Z3 Phantom Industries Inc.

M6N 4Z5 Old Mill Pontiac Buick Cadillac Ltd.

M6N 5B3 National Rubber Technologies Corp.

M6P 4E5 Intelliware Development Inc.

M6P 4G4 Navantis Inc.

M6R 1B5 St. Joseph's Health Centre

M6R 2B7 Flying Colours International

M6R 2L7 St. Stanislaus - St. Casimir's Polish Parishes Credit Union Ltd.

M6R 3A7 Copernicus Lodge

M6S 1M7 The Grenadier Retirement Residence

M6S 1N3 Sutton Group Realty Systems Inc.

M6S 1N9 Buduchnist Credit Union Ltd.

M6S 3A3 Runnymede Healthcare Centre

M6S 3N9 Corona Jewellery Company

M6S 4W8 Arbor Memorial Services Inc.

M7A 1Y6 Ministry of Community Safety and Correctional Services

M8V 1C5 Storefront Humber Inc.

M8V 1V1 Q & I Computer Systems Inc.

M8V 1Y7 Images 2000 Inc.

M8V 2B8 Campbell Company of Canada

M8V 2C7 Berry Plastics

M8V 3X5 Lakeshore Lodge

M8V 4B5 Via Rail Canada Inc.

M8W 1T3 Blue Mountain Wallcovering Inc.

M8W 1Z3 Canada Fibers Ltd. Smart DM

M8W 1Z6 CBS Outdoor Canada Quantum Murray LP

M8W 2T5 Norampac Inc.

M8W 2T7 Carbone of America

M8W 2T8 Harper Power Products

M8W 3R9 Christie Lites Ltd.

M8W 4W3 Nanowave Inc.

M8W 4X7 F G Lister & Company Ltd.

M8X 1G2 Polycultural Immigrant Community Services

M8X 1G5 Lark Hospitality Inc.

M8X 1Y3 Sutton Group Old Mill Realty Brokerage Inc.

M8X 2X2 Moneris Solutions Corp.

M8X 2X5 General Motors Acceptance Corporation of Canada Ltd.

M8X 2X9 ADP Canada Co.

M8X 2Y4 The United Church of Canada

M8Y 1H8 Fresh Taste Produce Ltd. Gambles Ontario Produce Inc. Rite Pak Produce Co. Ltd.

M8Y 3H9 C.J. Graphics Inc.

M8Z 1A4 Bombardier Transportation

M8Z 1B4 Faster Linen Service Ltd.

M8Z 1B8 Wing's Food Products Ltd.

M8Z 1J5 Novelis Foil Products

M8Z 1K2 Asbury Building Services Inc.

M8Z 1K5 Deluxe Laboratories RJ McCarthy Ltd.

M8Z 1K8 Vintage Flooring

M8Z 1S4 Queensway Volkswagen Inc.

M8Z 1T3 Weston Foods Inc.

M8Z 1T8 Courtesy Chevrolet

M8Z 1T9 Thorncrest Sherway Inc.

M8Z 2C4 West Star Printing Ltd.

M8Z 2C9 Fleetwood Fine Furniture LP

M8Z 2E2 Future Bakery Ltd.

M8Z 2G6 Brenntag Canada Inc. Culinary Destinations

M8Z 2J8 Korex Canada

M8Z 2R4 Dufflet Pastries T. Lipson & Sons Ltd.

M8Z 2R5 Polytainers Inc.

M8Z 2S6 Mylan Inc.

M8Z 2T4 Dimpflmeier Bakery Ltd.

M8Z 2T7 Beasley Amusements

M8Z 2Z4 Andorra Building Maintenance Ltd.

M8Z 3A7 Del's Pastry Ltd.

M8Z 4E5 Answer Plus Inc. Atripco Delivery Service Planway Poultry Inc. Sun Wah Trading Inc.

M8Z 4W3 Southern Graphic Systems

M8Z 4X6 Inquiry Management Systems Ltd.

M8Z 5B5 HomeLife Cholkan Realty Corp.

M8Z 5E1 Goodyear Canada Inc.

M8Z 5G1 Tayco Panelink Ltd.

M8Z 5K1 Metro Waste Paper Recovery Inc. Mirolin Industries Corp.

M8Z 5K7 The Butcher Shoppe

M8Z 5L2 Canadian Linen and Uniform Service Inc.

M8Z 5L6 Hymopack Ltd.

M8Z 5S7 Cana-Datum Moulds Ltd.

M8Z 5W8 ARAMARK Canada Ltd.

M8Z 5Y3 Ferraz Shawmut Canada Inc.

M8Z 5Y4 Plastic Moulders Limited

M8Z 5Z8 Allseas Fisheries Inc.

M8Z 6A1 William F. White International Inc.

M8Z 6A3 Impact Cleaning Services Ltd.

M8Z 6C4 Kinectrics Inc.

M9A 1B7 True North Hockey Canada Inc.

M9A 3M9 St. George's Golf and Country Club

M9A 4M2 Plant World Ltd.

M9A 5B8 Islington Golf Club Ltd.

M9A 5E4 Ukrainian Canadian Care Centre

M9B 0A5 Manion Wilkins & Associates Ltd.

M9B 1B1 Paul K. Brennan Holdings Inc.

M9B 1B3 88.5 FM The Jewel

M9B 1C1 Benevito Foods Inc.

M9B 3S3 New Zealand Lamb Company Ltd.

M9B 3S4 K-Bro Linen Systems (Ontario) Ltd.

M9B 3Z9 The Etobicoke Medical Centre Lifecare Operations

M9B 4B1 Baka Communications Inc.

M9B 6B6 Dawn Food Products Canada Ltd.

M9B 6B7 Teleperformance Canada

M9B 6C7 ERCO Worldwide LP

M9B 6E2 TD Insurance Meloche Monnex

M9B 6G8 Re/Max Professionals Inc.

M9B 6H7 Canada Bread Company Limited

M9B 6H8 The Logit Group Inc.

M9B 6K5 Primus Telecommunications Canada Inc.

M9C 1A4 The McCall Centre for Continuing Care

M9C 1B4 Perennial Design Inc.

M9C 1B7 AppleOne Employment Services Ltd.

M9C 1B8 Sherway Gardens

M9C 1C1 Wilson's Truck Lines Ltd.

M9C 1R1 Markland Wood Golf Club

M9C 1V7 Slovenian Linden Foundation

M9C 2T3 T.L.C. Health Services Ltd.

M9C 3T3   Etobicoke Olympium
M9C 4V8   Ryerson Canada
M9C 4Z4   Keg Restaurants Ltd.
M9C 5J1   Parmalat Canada Inc.
         Trader Corporation
M9C 5J4   Burger King Restaurants of
         Canada Inc.
M9C 5J5   Blockbuster Canada Co.
         Unilock Ltd.
M9C 5K5   M.R.S. Company Ltd.
M9C 5K6   Bird Construction Company
         HMV Canada Inc.
         La Senza Inc.
M9C 5K7   Livingston International Inc.
         SNC-Lavalin Inc.
M9C 5K8   Consumer Impact
         Marketing Ltd.
         Transat A.T.
M9C 5L5   Samuel Manu-Tech Inc.
         Vitran Corporation Inc.
M9C 5P8   Diageo Canada Inc.
M9C 5R9   Clariant (Canada) Inc.
M9C 5S1   Wesburn Manor
M9L 1L5   Donlee Precision
M9L 1M1   Clearview Industries Ltd.
M9L 1M6   Fer-Pal Construction Ltd.
M9L 1P2   Macgregor's Meat
         & Seafood Ltd.
M9L 1P7   Tam Electrical Ltd.
M9L 1P9   Classic Fire Protection Inc.
M9L 1R2   AlarmForce Industries Inc.
M9L 1R5   TSM Ltd.
M9L 1T9   Apotex Inc.
M9L 1V2   Belmont Meat Products Ltd.
M9L 1X3   Protech Chemicals Ltd.
M9L 1X5   Four Star Plating
         Industries Ltd.
M9L 1X6   Nailor Industries Inc.
M9L 1Y1   Village Masonry
         Construction Inc.
M9L 1Y8   Gib-San Pools Ltd.
M9L 1Z4   Jetco Manufacturing Ltd.
M9L 1Z9   Canadian Starter Drives Inc.
M9L 2A6   MSP
M9L 2A9   Modern Niagara Toronto
         Inc.
M9L 2B1   Industrial Electrical
         Contractors Ltd.
M9L 2R3   Jacobs & Thompson Inc.
M9L 2R8   Leon's Furniture Ltd.
M9L 2S7   F & K Manufacturing
         Company Ltd.
M9L 2T2   Profile Industries Ltd.
M9L 2V4   Trimen Food Service
         Equipment Inc.
         Vegfresh Inc.
M9L 2W6   Thales Rail Signalling
         Solutions Inc.
M9L 2X6   ABC Group
M9L 2Y3   Vita Community Living
         Services of Toronto Inc.
M9M 1A2   Re/Max 2000 Realty Inc.,
         Brokerage

M9M 2H2   Distinctive Designs
         Furniture Inc.
         Reflections Furniture
         Industries Ltd.
M9M 2L4   Seaboard/Harmac
         Transportation Group
         Viceroy Rubber
         & Plastics Ltd.
M9M 2L9   Univar Canada Ltd.
M9M 2M1   Bemis Flexible Packaging
M9M 2M6   Camp Forming Ltd.
         Etobicoke Ironworks Ltd.
M9M 2W8   TMZ Employment Agency
M9M 2X5   Fiera Foods Inc.
M9M 2Y7   Knoll North America Corp.
M9M 2Z2   General Sprinklers Inc.
M9N 1A1   Visioneering Corp.
M9N 1N8   Humber River Regional
         Hospital
M9N 1R8   Satin Finish Hardwood
         Flooring Ltd.
M9N 3R2   Sleep Country Canada
M9P 2N6   The Weston Golf and
         Country Club Ltd.
M9P 3V4   VON Toronto York Branch
M9R 0A1   Kodak Canada Inc.
M9V 2C1   Summit Ford Sales
         (1982) Ltd.
M9V 3Y6   Orbis Canada Ltd.
         Ray Plastics Ltd.
         Star Quality Office
         Furniture Manufacturing
         Ltd.
M9V 3Y8   Ultra-Form Manufacturing
         Company Ltd.
M9V 4B7   Moloney Electric Inc.
M9V 4L8   Thistletown Regional
         Centre
M9V 5B5   Humber Valley Terrace
M9V 5C6   HomeLife Miracle Realty Ltd.
M9V 5E2   City Taxi
         Excel Employment
         Tempro Inc.
M9W 0A3   ATS Andlauer
         Transportation Services LP
M9W 0B5   Patrolman Security
         Services Inc.
M9W 1A4   Coffey Geotechnics Inc.
M9W 1E1   Deco Labels & Tags
M9W 1E4   CCL Label
M9W 1G1   National Concrete
         Accessories
         Premetalco Inc.
M9W 1G4   S & C Electric Canada Ltd.
M9W 1G6   Bayer Inc.
M9W 1G8   Agfa Canada
M9W 1H9   Crane Supply
M9W 1J1   Holiday Inn Toronto
         Airport East
M9W 1J3   Doubletree by Hilton
         - Toronto Airport
M9W 1J5   Sheraton Toronto Airport
         Hotel & Conference Centre
         Toronto Airport Marriott
M9W 1J8   Travelodge Hotel Toronto
         Airport

M9W 1J9   Holiday Inn Toronto
         International Airport
M9W 1K1   Inline Fiberglass Ltd.
M9W 1K4   Entire Imaging
         Solutions Inc.
         TransportAction Lease
         Systems Inc.
M9W 1K6   Sunwing Travel Group
M9W 1K9   Carquest Canada Ltd.
         Springco Inc.
M9W 1L1   Interfast Inc.
M9W 1L4   Lassonde Industries Inc.
M9W 1L8   Venture Steel
M9W 1M2   Atlas-Apex Roofing Inc.
         MSB Plastics
         Manufacturing Ltd.
M9W 1M4   Lisi Mechanical
         Contractors Ltd.
M9W 1M7   ShawCor Ltd.
         ShawFlex
M9W 1N5   MSO Construction Ltd.
M9W 1N7   Re/Max West Realty Inc.
M9W 1P1   XTL Transport Inc.
M9W 1P6   Raceway Plymouth
         Chrysler Ltd.
M9W 1R2   Plastipak Industries Inc.
M9W 1R5   Polyair Canada Ltd.
M9W 1R9   Grosnor Industries Inc.
M9W 2Z3   Hallmark Housekeeping
         Services Inc.
M9W 2Z4   Alumicor Ltd.
         Brenlo Ltd.
M9W 3A8   Golden Cut Poultry Ltd.
M9W 4V6   Thunder Tool & Mfg. Ltd.
M9W 4X1   Rona Ontario Inc.
M9W 4X2   CWH Distribution
         Services Inc.
M9W 4X3   Paramount Pallet Inc.
M9W 4X7   Semple Gooder Roofing
         Corporation
M9W 4Y1   Metal Koting - Continuous
         Colour Coat Limited
M9W 5A2   Volt Human Resources
M9W 5A3   Dominion Citrus Income
         Fund
M9W 5A5   Swiftrans Services Ltd.
         Thomson Terminals Ltd.
M9W 5A7   L-3 Communications
         Electronic Systems
M9W 5B1   Spec Furniture Inc.
M9W 5B2   Enterprise Holdings
         Urban Mechanical
         Contracting Ltd.
M9W 5B4   Abell Pest Control Inc.
M9W 5B9   Italian Home Bakery Ltd.
M9W 5C2   Gatsteel Industries Inc.
         Pure Metal Galvanizing
M9W 5C4   Fairview Fittings &
         Manufacturing Limited
M9W 5C8   United Driver Services Inc.
M9W 5E4   Molson Canada
M9W 5E6   Hamilton Kent Inc.
M9W 5E7   Moores the Suit People, Inc.
M9W 5G1   Quality Suites Toronto
         Airport

M9W 5G6	Match Marketing Group
M9W 5G7	Lovat Inc.
M9W 5H2	Gazzola Paving Ltd.
M9W 5H4	Alte-Rego Corp.
M9W 5L2	Woodbine Entertainment Group
M9W 5L6	Toronto West Detention Centre
M9W 5L7	Humber Institute of Technology & Advanced Learning
M9W 5N1	Medi Group Masonry Ltd.
M9W 5N4	Westin Bristol Place Toronto Airport
M9W 5N7	Desco Plumbing and Heating Supply Inc.
M9W 5R1	Pepes Mexican Foods
M9W 5R3	McCluskey Transportation Services Ltd.
M9W 5R8	UCC Group Inc.
M9W 5S1	ABC Group Exterior Systems Triple Seal Ltd.
M9W 5S6	Ahearn and Soper Inc.
M9W 5S8	Fermar Paving Ltd.
M9W 5T2	Dominion Warehousing & Distribution Services Ltd.
M9W 5T3	Supremex Inc.
M9W 5T6	Covertech Fabricating Inc.
M9W 5V9	Club Coffee
M9W 5X3	Donald Construction Ltd.
M9W 5Y5	Alterna Savings & Credit Union Ltd.
M9W 5Y6	Give & Go Prepared Foods Ltd.
M9W 5Z7	Hertz Canada Ltd.
M9W 5Z9	SYNNEX Canada Ltd.
M9W 6A9	SCI Group Inc.
M9W 6H5	Crowne Plaza - Toronto Airport
M9W 6H6	ASA Alloys Ontario Laser Rentals Ltd. Qualified Metal Fabricators Ltd.
M9W 6J2	Alcohol Countermeasure Systems
M9W 6J9	Dranco Construction Ltd.
M9W 6K5	Woodbine Centre and Fantasy Fair
M9W 6L2	Carlson Wagonlit Travel CKF Inc. CWT Concierge
M9W 6R2	D.C. Security Inc.
M9W 6S9	Galmar Electrical Contracting Inc.
M9W 6Y2	Cargill Foods Toronto
M9W 6Y3	Starplex Scientific Inc.
M9W 6Z9	Avis Budget Group Inc.
M9W 7E9	U-Pak Disposals Ltd.
M9W 7K6	Aecon Group Inc. CDW
N1H 6P8	Co-operators General Insurance Company
N1R 5S9	Cello Products Inc.
N1R 5X1	Rockwell Automation Canada Ltd.
N2J 4S4	Economical Mutual Insurance Co.
N2V 1C5	Northern Digital Inc.
N3E 0A1	Dover Industries Ltd.
N3E 1A5	NAPA Auto Parts
N3W 1M2	Georgia-Pacific Canada, Inc.
N5V 4M9	3M Canada Co.
N5W 3A7	EMCO Corporation
N6A 1C9	Goodlife Fitness
N6A 4K1	London Life Insurance Co.
N6A 4K3	Royal Canadian Mounted Police
N6A 4T4	Sykes Assistance Services Corporation
N9A 4H6	Chrysler Canada Inc.
R3C 3B6	Investors Group Inc.
T2E 3J1	Westjet Airlines Ltd.
T2P 0J4	Shell Canada Ltd.
T2P 3M9	Imperial Oil Limited
T2X 1P1	H & R Block Canada Inc.
T6E 5P3	Running Room
V6C 3L2	Raymond James Ltd.